EXPERIENCING LAW SERIES

EXPERIENCING CRIMINAL LAW

■

Gabriel J. Chin

Professor of Law
UC Davis School of Law

Wesley M. Oliver

Professor of Law and
Associate Dean for Faculty Research and Scholarship
Duquesne University School of Law

WEST
ACADEMIC
PUBLISHING

© 2015 LEG, Inc. d/b/a West Academic
444 Cedar Street, Suite 700
St. Paul, MN 55101
1-877-888-1330

Printed in the United States of America
ISBN: 978-0-314-28693-2

Acknowledgment

The authors gratefully acknowledge the substantial research assistance of Micah Youngdale. His technological savvy saved us countless hours of frustration, his legal acumen and research skills led to the inclusion of interesting cases neither of us had discovered, and his dedication to this project allowed us to complete this fairly comprehensive work within the ambitious timetable we projected.

Table of Contents

Table of Cases

The principal cases are in bold type. Cases cited or discussed in the text are in roman type. References are to pages. Cases cited in principal cases and within other quoted materials are not included.

EXPERIENCING CRIMINAL LAW

CHAPTER ONE

The Nature of Criminal Law

A. Introduction

CRIMINAL LAW is different than other subjects you will study in the first year of law school. For several reasons, the law "on the books" does not always, in fact often does not, match the law on the street or in the courts. This section addresses some of the important characteristics of the criminal justice system.

1. The Adversary System

In many fields of law, property and contracts, for example, the law is generally used in a nonadversarial context. Of the millions of daily transactions involving the sale of cars and groceries, gasoline and electricity, restaurant meals and condominiums, only a tiny fraction result in litigation. The law is involved—every sale of a six pack involves a seller who expects to own the purchase price and a buyer who expects to own the beer—but the transactions are nonadversarial. Should litigation arise, the parties in civil cases may well share some basic agreement about background legal principles; after all, many businesses who are defendants today may be plaintiffs tomorrow in other cases. There is enduring value, at least to repeat players in civil cases, of having clear law. Therefore, even in the context of a lawsuit, parties might agree, for example, that the state's Uniform Commercial Code was validly adopted, or that a particular standard form deed complies with the state's property statute.

By contrast, criminal law is used virtually exclusively in the context of litigation. It is not used by ordinary people for everyday dealings. Virtually no defendant voluntarily agrees to participate in a prosecution; they would refuse the transaction if they could. Therefore, defendants will always, if they can, take the position that a statute does not apply. Criminal law, therefore, develops primarily in the crucible of litigation.

The roles of the parties in criminal litigation are different than they are in civil cases. Criminal cases are prosecuted by public officials, not private parties. A civil plaintiff injured in a car accident, for instance, has every reason to try to obtain every bit of money he can out of the law suit, employing whatever legal theories are necessary to achieve this goal. Certainly civil cases settle, but civil plaintiffs enter into negotiations with the threat of seeking every possible theory of recovery available and once civil cases go to trial every reasonably possible theory of recovery will be advanced. Rational actors seek to maximize their own wealth.

With the rise of public prosecutors in the mid-nineteenth century, injured parties were no longer responsible for the conduct of criminal prosecutions. As the criminal justice system punishes offenders rather than compensates victims, one could even imagine that victims would not always seek the maximum possible punishment—their outrage that leads them to seek *some* criminal punishment may not have always led them to seek the maximum amount of punishment.

The incentives for public prosecutors are even more complicated. Their constitutional role requires them to seek justice, not maximize punishments. As the Supreme Court explained:

> The United States Attorney is the representative not of an ordinary party to a controversy, but of a sovereignty whose obligation to govern impartially is as compelling as its obligation to govern at all; and whose interest, therefore, in a criminal prosecution is not that it shall win a case, but that justice shall be done. As such, he is in a peculiar and very definite sense the servant of the law, the twofold aim of which is that guilt shall not escape or innocence suffer. He may prosecute with earnestness and vigor-indeed, he should do so. But, while he may strike hard blows, he is not at liberty to strike foul ones. It is as much his duty to refrain from improper methods calculated to produce a wrongful conviction as it is to use every legitimate means to bring about a just one.

Berger v. United States, 295 U.S. 78, 88 (1935).

Thus, prosecutors in principle are not to be rewarded or evaluated simply based on the amount of jail-time they are able to obtain; indeed, a motto inscribed over the door to the Attorney General's office stated "the United States wins its case whenever justice is done for one of its citizens in the courts." Yet, being "tough on crime" is a politically popular stance when seeking election as a district attorney, or to a higher office, such as a judgeship, mayoral office, or governorship. The desire of victims, or the officers who investigated the matter, can further serve to put pressure on prosecutors to seek greater penalties, though sometimes victims can temper prosecutors, for example in capital cases where surviving family members oppose the death penalty.

The justices have also addressed the special role of defense attorneys in the adversary system:

> Law enforcement officers have the obligation to convict the guilty and to make sure they do not convict the innocent. They must be dedicated to making the criminal trial a procedure for the ascertainment of the true facts surrounding the commission of the crime. To this extent, our so-called adversary system is not adversary at all; nor should it be. But defense counsel has no comparable obligation to ascertain or present the truth. Our system assigns him a different mission. He must be and is interested in preventing the conviction of the innocent, but, absent a voluntary plea of guilty, we also insist that he defend his client whether he is innocent or guilty. The State has the obligation to present the evidence. Defense counsel need present nothing, even if he knows what the truth is. He need not furnish any witnesses to the police, or reveal any confidences of his client, or furnish any other information to help the prosecution's case. If he can confuse a witness, even a truthful one, or make him appear at a disadvantage, unsure or indecisive, that will be his normal course. Our interest in not convicting the innocent permits counsel to put the State to its proof, to put the State's case in the worst possible light, regardless of what he thinks or knows to be the truth. Undoubtedly there are some limits which defense counsel must observe but more often than not, defense counsel will cross-examine a prosecution witness, and impeach him if he can, even if he thinks the witness is telling the truth, just as he will attempt to destroy a witness who he thinks is lying. In this respect, as part of our modified adversary system and as part of the duty imposed on the most honorable defense counsel, we countenance or require conduct which in many instances has little, if any, relation to the search for truth.

United States v. Wade, 388 U.S. 218, 256-58, 87 S. Ct. 1926, 1947-48, 18 L. Ed. 2d 1149 (1967) (White J., dissenting). The duty of counsel Justice White describes may go beyond the responsibilities of counsel in civil cases. Counsel in civil cases are generally required to, for example, admit undisputed facts, while in criminal cases counsel need admit nothing. Federal Rule of Civil Procedure 11(b) requires pleadings to have evidentiary support, and be warranted by existing law, or a nonfrivolous argument for extending, modifying or reversing existing law, and provides for sanctions if attorneys fail to comply. However, as the U.S. Court of Appeals for the First Circuit noted, there is no counterpart to Rule 11(b) in the criminal context. That is unlikely to be mere happenstance: "because of the significant liberty deprivation often at stake in a criminal prosecution, courts generally tolerate arguments on behalf of criminal defendants that would likely be met with sanctions if advanced in a civil proceeding." *In re Becraft*, 885 F.2d 547, 550 (9th Cir.1989) (per curiam). As the Seventh Circuit perspicaciously observed, "novel arguments that may keep people out of jail ought not to be discouraged by the threat of [fines]." *Wisconsin v. Glick*, 782 F.2d 670, 673 (7th Cir.1986).

United States v. Figueroa-Arenas, 292 F.3d 276, 281 n.5 (1st Cir. 2002).

Indeed, "[i]n searching for the strongest arguments available, the [defense] attorney must be zealous and must resolve all doubts and ambiguous legal questions in favor of his or her client." *McCoy v. Court of Appeals of Wisconsin, Dist. 1*, 486 U.S. 429, 444, 108 S. Ct. 1895, 1905, 100 L. Ed. 2d 440 (1988). "'While serving as an advocate, a lawyer should resolve in favor of his client doubts as to the bounds of the law.' This duty of zealous representation is a duty owed by a lawyer both to his client and to the adversary system of justice." *Stuart v. State*, 360 So. 2d 406, 413 n.* (Fla. 1978) (quoting Florida Ethical Consideration 7-3 and citing Ethical Consideration 7-19).

It is important to understand that in an important way, the lawyers run the system. "The very premise of our adversary system of criminal justice is that partisan advocacy on both sides of a case will best promote the ultimate objective that the guilty be convicted and the innocent go free." *United States v. Cronic*, 466 U.S. 648, 655, 104 S. Ct. 2039, 2045, 80 L. Ed. 2d 657 (1984) (quoting *Herring v. New York*, 422 U.S. 853, 862, 95 S.Ct. 2550, 2555, 45 L.Ed.2d 593 (1975)). Frequently, if the lawyers do not make legal arguments or raise facts, those issues will not be considered by the court. Thus, in *Greenlaw v. United States,* 554 U.S. 237 (2008), the Court held that a court of appeal could not correct sua sponte an illegally low sentence imposed on a defendant, in spite of the clarity of the error, because the prosecution had not appealed. Similarly, there are many cases where defendants have been convicted in violation of the Constitution but were executed nonetheless because their lawyers failed to raise the claims in a procedurally correct way. *See, e.g.,* Del Dickson, *State Court Defiance and the Limits of Supreme Court Authority: Williams v. Georgia Revisited*, 103 Yale L.J. 1423 (1994).

By the same token, if lawyers agree to something not authorized by law, the court may accept it. For example several courts have held that the parties may agree to guilty pleas to non-existent crimes, and the resulting convictions are valid. *Spencer v. State*, 942 P.2d 646 (Kan. App. 1997); *People v. Mayo,* 908 N.Y.S.2d 353 (App. Div. 2010).

2. Discretion About Whether (and Which) Charges to Bring

Another critical aspect of the system is prosecutorial discretion. Legislatures understand that when they enact criminal laws that prosecutors do not fully enforce the laws in every case in which they could; just because a crime occurs does not mean an arrest or prosecution will or should follow. This is a feature of the system, not a bug. As one of the drafters of the Model Penal Code explained:

> The paradoxical fact is that arrest, conviction, and punishment of every criminal would be a catastrophe. Hardly one of us would escape, for we have all at one time or another committed acts that the law regards as serious offenses. Kinsey has tabulated our extensive sexual misdeeds. The Bureau of Internal Revenue is the great archive of our false swearing and cheating. The highway death statistics inadequately record our predilection for manslaughter. 100% law enforcement would not leave enough people at large to build and man the prisons in which the rest of us would reside. Somehow we manage to conduct a fairly orderly, stable society although arrests are made in a small percentage of the offenses committed, and convictions lag very far behind arrests.

Louis B. Schwartz, *On Current Proposal to Legalize Wire Tapping*, 103 U. Pa. L. Rev. 157 (1954). "As a rule of thumb, 25%–50% of all cases referred to prosecutors are declined for prosecution." Erik Luna, *Prosecutorial Decriminalization*, 102 J. Crim. L. & Criminology 785, 795 (2012). That is, in a substantial share of the cases in which law enforcement agencies believe charges should be brought, prosecutors disagree.

Some of this is a matter of lack of evidence; a prosecutor might be willing to bring charges but finds the evidence lacking. In other cases, lesser charges are brought instead of more serious ones. For example, broad theories of conspiracy liability would allow small-time drug dealers to be prosecuted for homicides occurring in the smuggling of the drugs into the country, but such cases are almost never brought. Former Philadelphia District Attorney Ed Rendell reported that he would charge college students with disorderly conduct when they sold their college roommates small amounts of marijuana, even though Pennsylvania law at the time defined this crime as drug distribution in a school zone, punishable by a mandatory minimum of two years in the state penitentiary. In other cases, the evidence might be satisfactory, but a conviction for some reason would be unjust.

Legislatures write statutes in ways that define any particular act under a variety of statutes, each of which provides very different degrees of punishment. Prosecutors are therefore given the opportunity to charge a crime—

the elements of which are satisfied by the defendant's conduct—but which provide for a punishment in excess of what the prosecutor would find reasonable for the crime. They are thus able to put pressure on defendants to accept pleas. Except in cases in which there is a realistic chance that the defendant is innocence (which happens less often than you might think), the real case turns on the negotiation between the prosecutor and the defense lawyer to determine which of the many possible charges the defendant will enter a plea to.

Legislatures provide many different crimes that could be used punish any given unlawful conduct, but generally provide little guidance on how to select among those offenses. Equitable considerations about the defendant's past, the circumstances of his offense, his remorse, and potential for rehabilitation can thus all play a role in what charge a prosecutor chooses to bring and what plea the prosecutor is willing to accept. Utilitarian considerations can also affect what plea the prosecution will accept. These include the amount of time, expense, and difficulty involved in trying the case, the chance that the defendant may actually prevail before a jury, and cooperation the defendant is willing to offer in solving other crimes or testifying against other defendants.

3. Plea Bargaining

It is essential to understand plea bargaining to understand this system you are about to study. The vast majority of convictions are obtained as a result of guilty pleas, not trials; the percentage of state cases resolved by plea bargaining is in the mid-90s; in the federal system it is higher. This means that an important part of the criminal justice system is informal, administrative, and inquisitorial, in that prosecutors function both as advocates for the state and, effectively, as judges who evaluate the merits of the defendant's claims and make plea offers in light of their evaluation. Prosecutors have an extraordinary adjudicative role in our criminal justice system; their discretion is surpassingly important. This means that defense counsel normally must make factual and legal arguments to prosecutors as well as courts in order to represent their clients effectively; given the number of cases not prosecuted or disposed of on favorable terms, defense counsel must understand this as an opportunity.

To understand a criminal case is therefore to understand several things: (1) what *can* the prosecutor charge, or, put another way, what are the elements of the potentially available offenses; (2) what *should* a reasonable, or typical, prosecutor charge based on the circumstances; (3) what kind of plea agreement should a reasonable prosecutor be willing to accept given the unique circumstances of this case, and (4) what can the defense do to increase the prosecutor's cost or decrease the benefit, and thereby induce a better offer? As the cases in this book show, trials do regularly occur. These appellate cases are important for understanding the first of these three considerations. As you read these cases, however, be sensitive to an issue we will raise as we consider specific examples throughout the book—what other than the statutory elements of the crime bear on how a defendant should be punished? In some cases, after you have learned the various statutes, and how courts have interpreted them, you will be asked to negotiate an outcome with a partner. At other times you will be asked what other types of information you would like to know about the case, if you were a district attorney, to decide how to bring a charge—or what else you would like to know if you were about to try to negotiate a settlement with the district attorney.

4. Criminal Law Is Statutory

The most fundamental problem in criminal law is determining the elements of a particular offense and identifying what facts are necessary and sufficient to prove a given crime. The answer to this question involves reading statutes, because criminal law is for the most part set forth in statutes, often called a jurisdiction's "Penal Code" or "Criminal Code." Thus, the answer to the question "What *can* prosecutors charge?" is given by the criminal codes of the fifty states, the District of Columbia, and the United States.

Because criminal law is statutory, one might reasonably assume that the elements of an offense would be easy to determine: simply read the statute and identify the facts it requires; the same technique should identify the elements of defenses and sentencing enhancement provisions. It is true that familiarity with the entire criminal code is essential for criminal practitioners. However, because of the eclectic origins of criminal statutes in many jurisdictions, simply reading the criminal code is insufficient to identify what it means. Based on traditions and principles of criminal law, elements are often read-in even if they do not appear in black and white in the text of a statute. In addition, criminal statutes are almost always ambiguous to some degree.

States draw upon a number of sources in developing the language for their statutes. Before American independence, English and colonial American judges developed and refined common law definitions of crimes which many states use.[1] These rules were reduced to statutes in some jurisdictions early in the American Republic and these rules continue to form the basis of many criminal statutes. Nationally recognized reform proposals then came from a number of sources.

---

[1] Common law offenses have dramatically diminished but are not completely gone. Several states, including Florida, Idaho, Michigan, Mississippi, and Rhode Island punish offenses which were crimes at common law, that is, in the colonial period, even though the conduct violates no statute now on the books in the state. See, e.g., Mich. Comp. Laws Ann. § 750.505 ("Any person who shall commit any indictable offense at the common law, for the punishment of which no provision is expressly made by any statute of this state, shall be guilty of a felony"); R.I. Gen. Laws Ann. § 11-1-1 ("Every act and omission which is an offense at common law, and for which no punishment is prescribed by the general laws, may be prosecuted and punished as an offense at common law").

Thomas Jefferson's *Notes on the State of Virginia,* for instance, recommended creating degrees of homicide. Early in the nineteenth century, Edward Livingston of Louisiana proposed the first comprehensive code of criminal law and procedure in the United States. While it was rejected by the Louisiana Legislature, it was largely adopted by the New York Legislature under the leadership of David Dudley Field, the leader of what is known to legal historians as the codification movement of the nineteenth century. The definitions of crimes from Livingston's Code, that made their way into the New York Criminal Code, continue to exist in the Empire State and elsewhere. Finally, an influential reform known as the Model Penal Code was proposed by the American Law Institute in 1962. While no state has fully adopted the Model Penal Code, many states have adopted some of its provisions. Finally, as crime is a hot topic politically, with the public often calling for changes after specific incidents occur, a hodgepodge of unique rules has developed in state legislatures.

While there are variations among the states in every branch of the law, nevertheless it may be meaningful to speak of American contract law, or American tort law. The American Law Institute, through its Restatements of the Law project, has established national principles in torts, property and contracts which are widely relied upon by courts and legislatures. The Uniform Law Commission, formerly known as the National Conference of Commissioners on Uniform State Laws, has a specific purpose of developing national laws to be adopted by the states. Versions of laws such as the Uniform Commercial Code, the Uniform Partnership Act, and the Uniform Trade Secrets Act are in force in most of the United States. States often adopt the recommended language recommended by the Uniform Law Commission: "In applying and construing this uniform act, consideration shall be given to the need to promote uniformity of the law with respect to its subject matter among states that enact it." Cal. Corp. Code § 17713.01.

By contrast, it is not meaningful to speak of American criminal law. No major organization has proposed a Uniform Penal Code, intended to be the virtually identical in every state; there is no Restatement of Criminal Law intended to be applied by the states. There are considerable state differences in what is criminalized and in the language used to define particular offenses, even in states which adopted parts of the Model Penal Code. It is true that one group of jurisdictions have codes based primarily on the common law (including the United States, California, and Virginia), and others have codes based on the Model Penal Code (including Illinois, New York, and Texas). It is also true that Model Penal Code states are more similar to each other than they are to common law states, and vice versa. But they are not particularly similar. Therefore, for many crimes discussed, we will provide you with various definitions used in different states as well as judicial interpretations of these statutes.

5. The Means of Defining Criminal Law

Like all statutes, criminal statutes are defined by courts and there are surprisingly few types of situations in which courts have an opportunity to interpret the meaning of a criminal statute.

(a) ***Challenges to the Indictment or Information.*** Prosecutors begin a case with an indictment or information. This is the document that announces the crime the prosecution believes the defendant has committed and describes the facts the defendant is believed to have committed that violates the law allegedly violated. An information is produced solely by the prosecutor, while the indictment is, at least in theory, the product of the grand jury, a body of citizens assembled to determine whether there is adequate evidence to proceed with a crime. Either an information or indictment must be supported by probable cause that the alleged crime has occurred. Some jurisdictions require that the grand jury return an indictment, but a grand jury finding is not required by the Constitution. Courts sometimes, though certainly not often, conclude that the indictment or information fails to identify a crime, or fails to give a defendant notice of the acts he is accused of committing.

(b) ***Challenges to the Admissibility of Evidence.*** Depending on what a statute requires the state to demonstrate to establish liability, or what the statute permits the defendant to raise by way of a defense, certain types of evidence will be relevant or irrelevant. In deciding the admissibility of evidence, courts are thus frequently required to interpret what statutes mean.

(c) ***Jury Instructions.*** After the prosecution and defense have presented their cases and concluded their arguments, the trial judge instructs the jury on the law, essentially telling the jurors what they must find to convict the defendant. In crafting these jury instructions (though judges frequently refer to books of pattern instructions) and deciding which instructions to give, judges must interpret what the statutes mean.

(d) ***Challenges to the Sufficiency of the Evidence.*** At the close of the prosecution's case, the defense will typically ask a judge to find that the prosecution has failed to meet its burden in demonstrating that the defendant had committed the alleged crimes. Often this claim will be renewed at the close of the defense's case.

Throughout this book, you will be asked to draft indictments, write motions opposing or supporting the admission of evidence (documents known as "Motions in Limine"), draft jury instructions, and draft arguments for judgments of acquittal, as well as oppositions to those arguments. You will be asked to produce the sort of documents courts rely upon in determining the meaning of criminal statutes.

While these typical means of judicially interpreting statutes obviously occur at the trial level, we study how appellate courts have interpreted what the trial courts have done. Often trial court rulings on these issues are done orally and even when they are in writing, trial courts have several issues to deal with and therefore typically do not spend as much time writing down the reasons for their decisions as appellate courts. Finally, the written orders of trial courts are not as readily accessible in printed volumes and computer data bases, making appellate courts' work in defining criminal statutes the preferable source of our study.

As in many areas of law, understanding how statutes are interpreted is essential to understanding the statutes. The meaning of a law is a conclusion reached after litigation, not a natural or obvious fact. Different jurisdictions often take differing views in large and small ways when construing virtually identical statutes, and state supreme courts have often unanimously reversed or overruled unanimous decisions of intermediate appellate courts on questions of statutory interpretation, or overruled their own earlier decisions. Therefore, you should construe a statute against your client only if you have clear avenues of victory on other grounds, or after exhausting every reasonable argument you can marshal to make the court come out your way.

Notwithstanding state-by-state variation, there are some common features of criminal statutes. Most statutes require some sort of voluntary act, unless the defendant has failed to take an action that the law requires him to take, such as report an accident. This requirement is referred to by the Latin term *actus reus*.

Most criminal statutes also require that the defendant demonstrate some level of mental culpability—that the crime occurred because of some fault by the defendant, that the crime was not merely an accident. There are rare exceptions to this requirement, but this requirement is known as the *mens rea* element of the crime. The *mens rea* term can apply to either conduct or results, or both. An arson statute, for instance, that requires the defendant to intentionally create a fire that destroys property may require that the defendant intentionally engage in conduct, i.e., start the fire, or cause a result, i.e., intentionally destroy property.

Often criminal statutes define a number of acts (or omissions), circumstances, or results, and legislatures are unclear in defining which *mens rea* terms apply to each of these acts, circumstances or results. Consider the arson example. Some states require the defendant to intentionally start the fire to be guilty of arson, but do not require the defendant to have any culpability for the resulting destruction. Others require that the defendant intend to destroy the property. Consider why this distinction matters. In some jurisdictions, if a defendant intentionally starts a fire—say by lighting a candle in his girlfriend's living room—he is guilty of arson if, while he goes to the restroom, her cat knocks over the candle. *See Copeland v. State*, 2 P.3d 1283, 1290-91 (Colo. 2000) (Martinez, dissenting) (observing that under the majority's interpretation of Colorado's fourth-degree arson statute, "any person starting a fire in her fireplace, without perceiving a risk of danger to person or property, would nonetheless be criminally liable for a class four felony if the fire endangered any person"). In other jurisdictions, he is liable for arson only if he desires the destruction of her apartment by fire. In the first type of jurisdiction, a prosecutor is very unlikely to bring charges for arson, but notice how much discretion the potential to bring such a charge gives a prosecutor if something else about the defendant's conduct that evening was questionable. Assume the girlfriend in the first type of jurisdiction also raised a very questionable date-rape charge. In the second type of jurisdiction, a district attorney would have little choice but to charge nothing. In the first type of jurisdiction, a district attorney could threaten an arson prosecution and reach a settlement with the defendant for some sort of crime, if he believes in his victim even though he knew the date-rape count would not be successful. Prosecutorial discretion overlaps with the substantive elements of crimes.

The prosecution must address *actus reus* and *mens rea* elements of all crimes. (As discussed, for some crimes, the act is an omission, and some crimes are defined as strict liability offenses, which require no *mens rea*, but these elements must be addressed.) Some crimes, including many familiar crimes require a certain result. Homicide requires that a death have occurred. (Many familiar crimes, such as drug possession, require no result.) For crimes requiring results, the defendant must have caused that result. Causation is a difficult concept in philosophy as well as in law. It is a concept that you will also encounter in tort law. At this stage, it is sufficient to understand that causation requires that the defendant's actions were not so remote and unforeseeable from the result that holding him responsible seems unfair. In tort law, this is known as proximate cause, to be contrasted with the concept of cause-in-fact, which essentially means that without the defendant's action, the result would not have occurred. Cause-in-fact covers a lot of ground as a person leaving for the office on time is *a* cause in fact of an accident involving his car on an interstate three miles away for had he been early or late, his car would not have been at the point of the accident for the collision to occur. So you can see why cause-in-fact is a requirement for liability but not a sufficient condition.

We begin with an introduction to the four general concepts that commonly appear in criminal statutes.

B. The Elements of Crimes

1. Actus Reus

In order to be guilty of a crime, a defendant must normally engage in some sort of an act, unless his omission is criminalized by law. It is a crime, for instance, to leave the scene of an accident without reporting the accident. It is also a crime to fail to feed and clothe your children. Aside from fairly unusual circumstances where the law has imposed an affirmative duty to act, there must be an *act*, an *actus reus*.

Rare are the cases in which defendants deny that they committed a voluntary act. The requirement of voluntariness, that is most often satisfied by the prosecution, is not reducible to any single description. Professor Michael S. Moore has stated:

> [I]f there is an act requirement Anglo-American law, it is not *an* act requirement; rather, there are several, because there are several concepts at work. As George Fletcher asks, 'An act as opposed to what?' Sometimes the concept of a human act is contrasted with an 'omission'; sometimes with a status or condition; sometimes with acting involuntarily as in the case of hypnotism and sleepwalking.[2]

A defendant, that is, must do *something* and it must be *voluntary*. A defendant may, that is, not be punished for being addicted to heroin, though he may be punished for acquiring, possessing, or even using heroin.

There are several rationales for the *actus reus* requirement. Defendants must have an ability to avoid committing the proscribed conduct and society must be certain that the defendant has in fact engaged in something contrary to law. If the defendant's actions are not voluntary, he could not have avoided running afoul of the law. If the defendant is punishable for his evil intent, without some manifestation of that evil, then we legitimately worry whether the defendant actually had an evil intent, and whether he was going to act upon it. (This latter concern will also play an important role in how far an attempt or conspiracy must go before it may be punished.)

---

2 Michael S. Moore, *Act and Crime: The Philosophy of Action and Its Implications for Criminal Law* 6 (1994).

The *Gastello* case raises the question of whether a defendant has voluntarily brought controlled substances into a jail when he is arrested and brought there. As you read this case—and every other case—make sure you identify:

1) what part or language of the statute is at issue;

2) what the parties argue it means and how the position of each would help;

3) what evidence or legal principles are invoked to support a particular outcome; and

4) what are the elements of the offense as determined by the court.

People v. Gastello

Court of Appeal, Fifth District, California
57 Cal. Rptr. 3d 293 (2007)

WISEMAN, J.

Defendant Tommy Gastello was convicted of bringing drugs into a jail. His case presents one question: Is an accused guilty of bringing drugs into jail if he or she entered the jail only due to being arrested and brought there in custody? The answer has to be no. Before defendant went out and encountered the police, he intentionally put the drugs in his pocket and was guilty of simple possession, but, as we explain in the published part of this opinion, he did not engage in the voluntary act (actus reus) necessary for the crime of *bringing them into the jail.* He was driven to the jail in custody, in a police car, in handcuffs. In the unpublished part of the opinion, we address the question of whether he had the criminal intent (mens rea) necessary for the crime.

The conviction of bringing drugs into a jail is reversed. The case is remanded to the trial court for resentencing on the remaining charges, which include simple possession of methamphetamine.

FACTUAL AND PROCEDURAL HISTORIES
Officer Jennifer Machado of the Hanford Police Department was on patrol in her car at about 11:00 o'clock on Thanksgiving night, 2005, when she saw defendant and his adult son, Johnny, riding bicycles. The Gastellos were riding from defendant's house to his brother-in-law's house. Machado stopped them because defendant's bicycle had no light. Johnny's bicycle had one.

Two more officers arrived to assist with this traffic stop. One officer separated Johnny from defendant and began questioning Johnny. Officer Machado had begun questioning defendant, asking for his name and date of birth so that she could carry out a warrant check, when she noticed that he was "fidgety, agitated." He was angry about the stop—Machado admitted that, "to be honest, . . . a cite for that Vehicle Code violation is not very common"—and the officer thought "he was trying to hide something." She suspected he was intoxicated and confirmed her suspicion by comparing his pupils with dots printed on a card prepared for that purpose and by observing how his pupils responded when she shined her flashlight in his eyes. She further suspected that defendant had drugs in his possession when he spontaneously volunteered that the pants he was wearing did not belong to him.

Machado arrested defendant on suspicion of being under the influence of a controlled substance. She did not read him his Miranda rights. When she asked if he had used drugs recently, he said he had smoked marijuana laced with "ice" the day before. "Ice" is a form of methamphetamine. She searched him but found no drugs.

* * *

Defendant was handcuffed and placed in Machado's car and she drove him to the Kings County Jail. On the way, Machado told defendant that it was a felony to bring drugs or weapons into the jail. She asked if he understood and he said yes.

Inside, defendant was booked. He was instructed to take everything out of his pockets and remove all of his clothing except for a t-shirt, pants, and underpants. As he obeyed, he recommended that Machado not look at the items he was removing too closely, as he had fleas. Machado searched them anyway and found in defendant's sweatshirt a small plastic bag containing a crystalline substance. Defendant accused Machado of planting it. Chemical testing showed that the substance was a usable quantity of methamphetamine.

A blood test was taken. Defendant's blood was found to contain potentially toxic levels of methamphetamine and morphine. Morphine is a metabolite of heroin. A technician testified that the levels were "quite high, very consistent with someone who is, what we would call, 'speed balling [,]' . . . [i.e.,] [m]ixing . . . a central nervous system stimulant with a central nervous system depressant."

The district attorney filed an information charging defendant with. . . bringing a controlled substance into a jail (Pen.Code, § 4573).

The court imposed an aggregate prison sentence of seven years. This consisted of a six-year doubled middle term for count two and a one-year enhancement for count two. The court also imposed a concurrent four-year doubled middle term for count one and a concurrent one-year term for count three.

DISCUSSION

The offense of bringing drugs into a jail is defined in Penal Code section 4573:

> "Except when otherwise authorized . . . any person who, knowingly brings or sends into, or knowingly assists in bringing into, or sending into, any state prison . . . or into any county . . . jail . . . any controlled substance . . . is guilty of a felony. . . ."

Defendant argues that there was insufficient evidence to prove the crime. "When an appellant asserts there is insufficient evidence to support the judgment, our review is circumscribed. [Citation.] We review the whole record most favorably to the judgment to determine whether there is substantial evidence—that is, evidence that is reasonable, credible, and of solid value—from which a reasonable trier of fact could have made the requisite finding under the governing standard of proof." (*In re Jerry M.* (1997) 59 Cal.App.4th 289, 298, 69 Cal.Rptr.2d 148.) The case presents the questions of whether there was insufficient evidence to prove either the required actus reus or the required mens rea here.

I. Actus reus

An accused must do a guilty act (actus reus), or omit to do a required act, to be guilty of a crime. A statutory expression in California of this fundamental concept is in Penal Code section 20, which provides: "In every crime or public offense there must exist a union, or joint operation of act and intent, or criminal negligence." (*See also* Pen.Code, § 15 [definition of crime includes act, law forbidding or commanding it, and prescribed punishment]; *People v. Crutcher* (1968) 262 Cal.App.2d 750, 754, 68 Cal.Rptr. 904 [some act, committed or omitted in violation of law forbidding or commanding it, is necessary for there to be crime].) We are dealing here with a crime requiring an affirmative act (bringing drugs into a jail), not a crime of omission (e.g., failing to file a tax return). As a result, the first question we must answer is whether defendant did an affirmative act.

We conclude he did not. From the time of his detention during the traffic stop to the time when the drugs were discovered, defendant did nothing that can be regarded as the affirmative act of bringing something into a jail. He was detained, questioned, arrested, handcuffed, transported to the jail grounds and led into the jail building. He *omitted* to confess to having the drugs, but that is not an affirmative act. Defendant *did* nothing but submit to the lawful authority of the police. In sum, defendant did not bring drugs into the jail. The facts can best be described by the statement that defendant *was brought* to the jail while *not confessing* that he had drugs on his person. This statement describes passivity and omission, not the doing of an act. He *possessed* the drugs, of course, and that is an affirmative act for purposes of the crime of simple possession. Defendant does not challenge his conviction of simple possession. The conviction he does contest requires a different act, "bringing" or "sending." (Pen.Code, § 4573.)

This case is even stronger for the defendant than *Martin v. State* (1944) 31 Ala.App. 334, 17 So.2d 427. *Martin* is a criminal-law classic on the subject of actus reus and is a favorite of casebooks and law review articles. Martin was arrested in his house. Police officers then took him out onto the street. There, he "manifested a drunken condition by using loud and profane language. . . ." (*Martin v. State, supra,* 17 So.2d at p. 427.) He was convicted of public drunkenness. The Alabama Court of Appeals reversed. "Under the plain terms of this statute, a voluntary appearance [in a public place] is presupposed. The rule has been declared, and we think it sound, that an accusation of drunkenness in a designated public place cannot be established by proof that the accused, while in an intoxicated condition, was involuntarily and forcibly carried to that place by the arresting officer." (*Ibid.*) Some other often-cited cases reach a similar result. (*People v. Newton* (1973) 72 Misc.2d 646, 340 N.Y.S.2d 77, 79–80 [no actus reus to support conviction under New York law of possessing unlicensed firearm where defendant was on flight—scheduled to fly from Bahamas to Luxembourg with no stops in United States—that made unscheduled landing in New York]; *People v. Shaughnessy* (1971) 66 Misc.2d 19, 319 N.Y.S.2d 626, 628 [no actus reus to support conviction of trespassing where defendant was passenger in car that entered property and therefore lacked control over entry].)

Martin at least did the affirmative act of yelling profanities after bring arrested and brought into the street. Here defendant did nothing at all after police officers took custody of him; he omitted to confess to having drugs and submitted to being taken to prison. For these reasons, the evidence did not support the essential element of actus reus. The prosecution did not present sufficient evidence to prove the crime.

Notes and Questions

1. The California Supreme Court rejected the Court of Appeal's reasoning in *People v. Low,* 232 P.3d 635, 643–45 (Cal. 2010):

   [The] defendant argues that an arrestee does not "bring [ ]" a controlled substance into jail under section 4573 simply because the drug is in his possession when he is brought into the facility in custody for another crime. However, this narrow interpretation of the term defies common usage.

As defendant suggests, the verb "to bring" certainly means "to take or carry along" an object as the actor moves in a self-directed fashion from one place to another. (Webster's 3d New Internat. Dict. (2002) p. 278; see 2 Oxford English Dict. (2d ed. 1989) p. 554 ["carrying or bearing in one's hand"].) But it also contemplates scenarios in which a person or object is "cause[d] to come along" because someone or something is "leading, conducting, or propelling" such movement. (2 Oxford English Dict., *supra*, p. 554; accord, Webster's 3d New Internat. Dict., *supra*, p. 278; *see People v. Waid* (1954) 127 Cal.App.2d 614, 617–618, 274 P.2d 217 (*Waid*) [using latter definition to conclude that accused "brings" drugs into prison under § 4573.5 by mailing them there].) Either way, when defendant walked into the jail carrying methamphetamine in the band of his sock, he was "bring[ing]" the substance into the facility under section 4573, even though such movement was caused by his earlier arrest and directed by the arresting officer.

* * *

To the extent we now conclude that the act prohibited by section 4573 can occur when someone is brought into jail in custody for another crime, this interpretation is consistent with cases deciding what it means to "bring [ ]" contraband into a penal setting in violation of similar statutory prohibitions. (*E.g., People v. Ross* (2008) 162 Cal.App.4th 1184, 1187–1189, 76 Cal. Rptr.3d 477 (*Ross*) [holding that defendant who carried knife in her undergarments, and who denied having it when arrested and booked for assault, violated § 4574(a) despite her claim that she did not voluntarily enter jail or commit affirmative act of bringing weapon inside]; *People v. James* (1969) 1 Cal.App.3d 645, 650, 81 Cal.Rptr. 845 (*James*) [similar conclusion under same statute as to defendant who kept pistol hidden in his waistband during booking search, and who later gave it to another jail inmate].) The critical factors are the lack of any compulsion to bring contraband inside, and the rejection of a clear opportunity to avoid doing so by voluntarily relinquishing the forbidden object or substance before entering the premises. (*Ross, supra*, 162 Cal.App.4th at p. 1191, 76 Cal.Rptr.3d 477 [defendant "had no choice whether to go to jail, but she was afforded the choice not to violate section 4574"]; *James, supra*, 1 Cal.App.3d at p. 650, 81 Cal.Rptr. 845 [defendant "knowingly possessed a firearm while in jail, after he had ample time to surrender it," such that his "choice about going to jail is irrelevant"].) We agree that such volitional conduct falls within the parameters of section 4573.

For the most part, defendant ignores the foregoing principles and authorities. He focuses instead on out-of-state case law, mainly, and in particular, a 1944 Alabama decision, *Martin v. State* (1944) 31 Ala.App. 334, 17 So.2d 427 (*Martin*). This reliance is misplaced.

According to the opinion in *Martin*, which is quite terse, police officers arrived at the defendant's home, found that he was intoxicated, and placed him under arrest. The arresting officers then took the defendant from his home and brought him onto a public highway. There, while still intoxicated, the defendant spoke loudly and used profanity. He was ultimately charged and convicted under a state law prohibiting anyone from "'appear[ing]'" in a public place and "'manifest[ing]'" a drunken condition through either boisterous or indecent conduct or loud and profane language. (*Martin, supra*, 17 So.2d at p. 427.)

The Alabama Court of Appeals reversed. Relying on a commonsense meaning of the statute, the court determined that "a voluntary appearance [while drunk in a public place] is presupposed." Guilt could not be established, the court said, where the intoxicated person "was involuntarily and forcibly carried to that place by the arresting officer." (*Martin, supra*, 17 So.2d at p. 427.) In other words, it appears every part of the alleged criminal transaction was deemed involuntary on appeal. By taking the defendant from the private confines of his own home, knowing he was intoxicated and already under arrest, and placing him in a public place where the terms of the statute under which he was later charged could be violated, police officers effectively compelled, and arguably manufactured, commission of the crime.

Such is not the case here. After being stopped by Detective Jones, defendant was arrested by Officer Wahl for driving a stolen vehicle. No evidence shows that either officer knew or suspected that defendant had any illegal drugs in his possession. In fact, the patdown search that Wahl conducted incident to the arrest at the scene revealed no contraband. Wahl then took defendant to the local county jail, as any arresting officer presumably would be obligated to do. Before entering the facility, the officer gave defendant ample opportunity to avoid violating section 4573. In particular, Wahl advised defendant that it was illegal to bring drugs into the jail, asked whether he had any drugs in his clothes or on his person, and warned that he would be searched inside. Despite this warning, methamphetamine was found in defendant's sock during the booking process.

Thus, unlike in *Martin, supra*, 31 Ala.App. 334, 17 So.2d 427, nothing supports defendant's suggestion that he was forced to bring drugs into jail, that commission of the act was engineered by the police, or that he had no choice but to violate section 4573. Defendant entered jail in the possession of methamphetamine that he had previously secreted on his person. Hence, he committed the act that section 4573 proscribes.

2. The *Low* decision finds a distinction between taking drugs into a jail and the arrest of the defendant in the *Martin* case that the court in *Gastello* did not find. Which opinion do you find more compelling? The California Supreme Court regards the defendant's opportunity to relinquish the drugs as a key fact in supporting the conviction. Did the defendant have a true chose between relinquishing the drugs and entering the jail with them? Should it matter that he was between a rock and a hard place?

3. There is a split on this question in the states; many jurisdictions agree with the California Court of Appeals, while others agree with the California Supreme Court. *See Herron v. Commonwealth*, 688 S.E.2d 901, 905 (Va. App. 2010) (recognizing variety of opinions). Both the decision of the intermediate court of appeals and the state supreme court rely on different interpretations of the text of the statute to determine whether the defendant committing the crime of bringing drugs into a correctional facility. Each opinion turns on what the word "bring" means, in this case, the operative word in the statute. The debate between the two courts seems, however, to be about more than how the word "bring" ought to be linguistically interpreted in this context. The differing interpretations of the word "bring" ultimately determine whether a defendant will punished for the crime of bring the drugs into the facility—in addition to the crime of possessing the drugs themselves. Once we realize that the defendant will be punished for the possession regardless of how this statute is interpreted (because he will either surrender the drugs when he enters the facility, or they will find them on him), what policy supports additionally punishing him for failing to surrender them before entering? What policy supports not punishing him for failing to surrender them before entering?

---

2. Mens Rea

Generally, the prosecution must demonstrate that the defendant acted with some sort of culpable mental state, often referred to by the Latin term *mens rea*. Even young children understand this. Parents have all heard their children raise the defense, "I didn't mean to." The children raising this defense typically mean something broader. They typically mean several things, "I didn't intend to commit this act, and I was exercising an appropriate level of caution to ensure that this act did not occur." A parent may find carelessness problematic as well, depending on the circumstance. The same is true in criminal law. Only some crimes require that defendants intend to engage in certain conduct, or cause a certain result, to be guilty. A defendant does not have to intend to operate a car in an unsafe manner to be guilty of reckless driving—in fact, it would be meaningless to define such a crime in terms of a defendant's intent.

It is common, even for courts (as you will see in *Staples*), however, to describe there being an "intent" requirement to crimes. In reality there is a requirement of some form of culpability, which can be anywhere on a scale from the desire to engage in the prohibited conduct (or cause the prohibited result) to being careless in avoiding the prohibited conduct (or result). The Model Penal Code, the culpability definitions of which have been adopted by a number of states, provides for four different types of culpability: purpose (often called intent), knowledge, recklessness, and negligence. Other states, before and after the proposal of the Model Code, have used a variety of terms creating roughly the same categories. Prior to the Model Penal Code, states tended to create crimes of three types: specific intent, malice, and general intent. Specific intent crimes require the defendant to desire a particular result, much like crimes using the MPC's terminology require intent. Malice crimes require the defendant to take an extraordinary and unreasonable risk. General intent crimes merely require that the defendant intend to engage in conduct that turns out to be dangerous, whether or not he realizes the danger. Following the Model Penal Code, state laws are a hodgepodge of *mens rea* terms.

As you will discover, each of these terms are best understood in context. The type of proof the prosecution will require to show that a defendant knowingly took a life is very different than the type of proof the prosecution will need to show that the defendant knowingly possessed drugs. In subsequent chapters, we will consider the most prosecuted crimes and identify variations in how they are defined.

Each of these levels of culpability will be described in the context of the various crimes we will be discussing in subsequent chapters, but for now it is important to recognize that some form of culpability is generally required for a defendant to be guilty of a crime. Under special circumstances, however, courts find that the legislature has eliminated a *mens rea* requirement and created a strict liability offense. On rare occasions, courts find that strict liability crimes are inconsistent with constitutional limits on punishment, but those sorts of decisions are extremely rare.

Legislatures are almost never clear in omitting *mens rea* terms. Legislatures with some frequency do, however, write statutes without any *mens rea* term. Many state legislatures have provided that unless the statute's intent to omit the term is clear, that the prosecution must demonstrate that the defendant committed the acts in a manner that was at least reckless. *But see* Darryl K. Brown, *Criminal Law Reform and the Persistence of Strict Liability*, 62 Duke L. J. 285 (2012) (concluding that even in states with such presumptions, courts frequently find strict liability in the absence of a mental element). In states without such a legislative presumption, courts have created common law rules that imply a requirement of at least recklessness on their own. The work of courts is, as you will see, to determine how clear the legislature was in creating a strict liability when facing a statute that merely omits any *mens rea* term. Defendants sometimes—with little success—argue that either the federal or state constitution requires there to be a *mens rea* term in the statute. Most often, this is a question of statutory interpretation.

The *Thompson* case is probably the most thorough of any case in the country in laying out the factors that a court ought to consider in deciding whether a legislature intended, by its omission of a *mens rea* term, to create a strict liability offense.

Thompson v. State

Court of Appeals of Texas, Houston
44 S.W.3d 171 (2001)

FROST, Justice.

Appellant, Amanda Sylvia Thompson, entered a plea of guilty to the misdemeanor offense of violating a City of Houston ordinance requiring an "entertainer" employed by sexually oriented enterprises to conspicuously display a permit upon her person. *See* HOUSTON, TEX., CODE § 28–256(a) (2000). The trial court accepted her plea, found her guilty, assessed punishment at two days' confinement in the Harris County Jail, and imposed a fine of $100. In eight points of error, she alleges the trial court erred in entering judgment because the county court at law lacked jurisdiction over the case and because the information was fundamentally defective. We reverse and order the information dismissed.

BACKGROUND AND PROCEDURAL HISTORY

The State charged appellant with violating chapter 28 of the Code of Ordinances of the City of Houston. The information stated, in relevant part:

> AMANDA SYLVIA THOMPSON . . . did then and there unlawfully while an entertainer in a sexually oriented enterprise, namely, TROPHY CLUB, an adult cabaret . . ., and having a duty, pursuant to Section 28–25(a) of the Code of Ordinances of the City of Houston, while acting as an entertainer on the premises of the aforesaid sexually oriented enterprise, to conspicuously display upon his [sic] person at all times his [sic] personal card . . . pursuant to Section 28–254 of the Code of Ordinances of the City of Houston, did fail to conspicuously display upon his [sic] person at all times his [sic] personal card while acting as an entertainer on the premises of TROPHY CLUB.

* * *

Appellant timely filed a motion to quash the information complaining that the State failed to allege a culpable mental state in the information. At the hearing, appellant argued that by not quashing the information based on the omission of a culpable mental state and by not requiring the State to amend, the trial court was effectively holding that the charged offense was one of strict liability. The trial court specifically found that section 28–254 of the ordinance did not require a culpable mental state because the ordinance did not contain one. Therefore, the trial court reasoned, the information was not fundamentally defective in omitting a culpable mental state.

Appellant now argues that, although the ordinance does not specifically prescribe a culpable mental state, the Texas Penal Code mandates a culpable mental state as an element of the offense. Section 6.02 of the Texas Penal Code provides:

> (a) Except as provided in Subsection (b), . . . a person does not commit an offense unless he intentionally, knowingly, recklessly, or with criminal negligence engages in conduct as the definition of the offense requires.

> (b) *If the definition of an offense does not prescribe a culpable mental state, a culpable mental state is nevertheless required unless the definition plainly dispenses with any mental element.*

(c) If the definition of an offense does not prescribe a culpable mental state, but one is nevertheless required under Subsection (b), . . . intent, knowledge, or recklessness suffices to establish criminal responsibility.

TEX.PEN.CODE ANN. § 6.02 (Vernon 1994) (emphasis added).

If an offense does not contain a culpable mental state element, the offense is one of strict liability. *Aguirre v. State,* 978 S.W.2d 605, 607 (Tex.App.—El Paso 1998), *aff'd,* 22 S.W.3d 463 (Tex.Crim.App.1999). Strict criminal liability is based upon the principle that "a person who commits an act in violation of the law may be held criminally liable even though he might be innocent of any criminal intent." *Vaughan & Sons, Inc. v. State,* 737 S.W.2d 805, 818 (Tex.Crim.App.1987) (Teague, J., dissenting). In charging the accused with a strict liability offense, culpability is irrelevant and, thus, need not be alleged in the charging instrument. *See id.* If the individual commits the act, she is, *ipso facto,* held strictly criminally liable. *Id; Honeycutt v. State,* 627 S.W.2d 417, 421 n. 4 (Tex.Crim.App.1981).

In *Aguirre v. State,* the Texas Court of Criminal Appeals set out guidelines for determining whether a statute plainly dispenses with a culpable mental state as an element of a charged offense. 22 S.W.3d 463, 470–77 (Tex.Crim. App.1999). In making this determination, a court must first consider whether the statute affirmatively states that the conduct is a crime though done without fault. *Id.* at 471. If so, the statute dispenses with a mental state requirement, and the offense is one of strict liability. *Id.* However, a statute's mere omission of a mental state cannot be construed to plainly dispense with one. *Id.* Instead, "the silence of a statute about whether a culpable mental state is an element of the offense leaves a presumption that one is." *Ex parte Weise,* 23 S.W.3d 449, 452 (Tex.App.—Houston [1st Dist.] 2000, pet. ref'd, pet. granted) (citations omitted).

The ordinance at issue provides that "[e]ach manager or entertainer shall conspicuously display his personal card upon his person at all times while acting as an entertainer or manager of or in an enterprise." § 28–256. Section 28–256 does not provide an affirmative statement that its violation is a strict liability offense; rather, this ordinance is silent as to mental state. Thus, in determining whether a culpable mental state is a required element of an offense under this ordinance, we begin with the presumption that culpability is required. *See Aguirre,* 22 S.W.3d at 472.

Next, we determine whether the ordinance manifests an intent to dispense with a culpability requirement by examining other attributes of the ordinance in light of a non-exhaustive list of suggested factors articulated in *Aguirre. See id.* at 470–77.

(1) Language of the Statute.

If any section of the statute prescribes a mental state while another section omits a mental state, we presume the legislature intended to dispense with a mental element in that section. *Id.* at 473. In this case, the "Division" regulating sexually oriented businesses is silent as to mental state. Thus, we do not presume the drafters of the ordinance intended to dispense with a culpable mental state as an element of an offense under section 28–256.

(2) Nature of the Offense: *Malum Prohibitum* or *Malum in Se.*

Criminal offenses are characterized as either *malum in se,* meaning "inherently evil" or *malum prohibitum,* meaning "prohibited evil." *Aguirre,* 22 S.W.3d at 473; *Tovar v. State,* 978 S.W.2d 584, 591 (Tex.Crim.App.1998). These distinctions are deeply rooted in American and English jurisprudence. *Malum in se* offenses traditionally include acts that are inherently immoral, such as murder, arson, or rape. BLACK'S LAW DICTIONARY 971 (7th ed.1999). A *mala prohibitum* offense is defined as: "[a]n act that is a crime merely because it is prohibited by statute, although the act itself is not necessarily immoral." *Id.* at 971. Examples of *mala prohibita* offenses include speeding, illegal dumping of trash, and possession of a firearm while under a domestic restraining order. *State v. Houdaille Indus.,* 632 S.W.2d 723, 728 (Tex.1982); *Ex parte Weise,* 23 S.W.3d at 453; *United States v. Emerson,* 46 F.Supp.2d 598, 612 (N.D.Tex.1999).

Offenses requiring a culpability element are normally considered *malum in se* while strict liability offenses are generally considered *malum prohibitum.* *See, e.g., Ex parte Weise,* 23 S.W.3d at 452. Although regulatory violations are often characterized as *malum prohibitum* offenses, the Texas Court of Criminal Appeals has analogized offenses under ordinances regulating sexually oriented businesses as being akin to public nudity, an offense common law classified as a *malum in se. Aguirre,* 22 S.W.3d at 477; *Ex parte Weise,* 23 S.W.3d 449, 452 ("strict liability offenses must be *malum prohibitum.* The opposite is not necessarily true, as illustrated by many regulatory crimes, such as drug violations. Although illegal dumping is *malum prohibitum,* that classification neither requires nor precludes strict liability."). This classification indicates that "entertaining," as that term is defined in the ordinance, without properly displaying a permit, is similarly a *malum in se* offense. *See Aguirre,* 22 S.W.3d at 477 (presuming that the offense of conducting a public nudity business within a thousand feet of a residence, church, school, etc. was *malum in se*). This characterization favors interpreting an offense under ordinance 28–256 as requiring a culpable mental state. *See id.* at 475–77.

(3) Subject of the Statute.

The court in *Aguirre* stated that the most important factor "in the more recent cases," for determining whether a statute manifests an intent to dispense with a mental element, is the subject of the statute. *Id.* at 473. Although strict criminal liability statutes are generally looked upon with disfavor, "'public welfare offenses,' which offenses represent society's attempts to regulate nuisances that might affect or be detrimental to the general health, safety, and welfare of the citizenry" are a noteworthy exception. *Vaughan & Sons, Inc. v. State*, 737 S.W.3d 805, 818 (Tex.Crim.App.1987) (Teague, J., dissenting). Strict liability is traditionally associated with the protection of public health, safety, or welfare. *Aguirre*, 22 S.W.3d at 473. The Court of Criminal Appeals has upheld statutes imposing strict liability for a number of offenses affecting public health and safety, including driving while intoxicated, speeding, driving with a suspended license, air and water pollution.

The State urges that the City enacted the ordinance in response to a "public emergency" and concomitant need to protect the public's health, safety, and welfare. However, like the ordinance in *Aguirre*, section 28–256 is not in the class of public-safety statutes generally found to impose strict liability. *See Aguirre*, 22 S.W.3d at 475 n. 47; *Aguirre*, 978 S.W.2d at 608 (listing public-safety strict liability offenses as including speeding, driving while intoxicated, air pollution, water pollution, and sale of adulterated meat); *Ex parte Weise*, 23 S.W.3d at 455 (finding that an illegal dumping statute required a culpable mental state of at least "recklessly" despite fact it was clearly intended to protect public health, safety, and welfare). In addition, the importance of any public health, safety, and welfare features of this ordinance diminishes considering the relatively low level of harm to the public expected to flow from the act of "entertaining" without conspicuously displaying the requisite permit. *See Ex parte Weise*, 23 S.W.3d at 455.

(4) Gravity of Expected Harm to the Public.

Generally, the more serious the consequences to the public, the more likely the legislature meant to impose liability without regard to fault, and vice versa. *Aguirre*, 22 S.W.3d at 471 n. 27 (citing 1 WAYNE R. LAFAVE & AUSTIN W. SCOTT, JR., SUBSTANTIVE CRIMINAL LAW 343 n. 10 (2d ed.1986)).

Although the State argues that the ordinance is intended to protect the public from disease-spreading conduct, the State does not explain how a failure to conspicuously display a permit impacts the potential for spread of disease. The permit application process has no screening mechanism for disease. Moreover, permits issued to entertainers under the auspices of Chapter 28 do not disclose the existence of any diseases. *See* § 28–254. Given these facts, it seems unlikely that the mere display of a permit while "entertaining," no matter how conspicuous, would operate to protect public health by discouraging disease-spreading casual sexual acts. Thus, there appears to be no direct impact on the public health from an entertainer's failure to conspicuously display a permit.

Moreover, unlike the ordinance at issue here, each of the statutes underlying the aforementioned strict liability offenses protects unwitting and unwilling members of the public from the noxious and harmful behavior of others, in situations in which it would be difficult for members of the public to protect themselves, e.g. drunk and unsafe driving, hazardous pollutants, contaminated food, etc. In contrast, the patron of a sexually oriented entertainment enterprise who engages in the "disease-spreading conduct" thought by the State to be the target of this ordinance, presumably does so willingly and with full knowledge of the inherent risks of contracting sexually transmitted disease.

Given the lack of nexus between the conspicuous display of the permit and any direct impact on public health, we must conclude the harm to the public from an entertainer's failure to conspicuously display the requisite permit is not great. This finding further supports an interpretation that this ordinance requires a culpable mental state.

(5) Severity of Punishment.

Strict liability is generally associated with civil violations that incur only a fine. *Aguirre*, 22 S.W.3d at 472; *Ex parte Weise*, 23 S.W.3d at 452. Conversely, if the offense is punishable by confinement, the presumption against strict liability strengthens. *Ex parte Weise*, 23 S.W.3d at 452.

The greater the possible punishment, the more likely fault is required. *Aguirre*, 22 S.W.3d at 475–76 (citing 1 WAYNE R. LAFAVE & AUSTIN W. SCOTT, JR., SUBSTANTIVE CRIMINAL LAW 342 (2d ed.1986)); *Ex parte Weise*, 23 S.W.3d at 454. A violation of section 28–256 is punishable by fine and/ or jail time for up to a year. Although the adult businesses ordinance in *Aguirre* carried only a fine, the Court of Criminal Appeals found it to require a culpable mental state. *Aguirre*, 22 S.W.3d at 475–76. Therefore, we find possible confinement up to a year, for violation of the ordinance at issue here, is strong indicia that a culpable mental state is required. *Id.; Ex parte Weise*, 23 S.W.3d at 454 (finding the seriousness of possible punishment "to be a particularly weighty factor that militates against strict liability.").

(6) Legislative History.

The Texas legislature has found that "the unrestricted operation of certain sexually oriented businesses may be detrimental to the public health, safety, and welfare by contributing to the decline of residential and business neighborhoods and the growth of criminal activity." Tex. Local Gov't Code Ann. § 243.001(a) (Vernon 1999). As noted, Houston's sexually oriented business ordinances were enacted pursuant to this enabling legislation, presumably to address public health, safety, and welfare concerns. However, the State fails to point to any legislative history or other authority which supports its contention that the drafters of the ordinance intended to make an entertainer's failure to conspicuously display the requisite permit a strict liability offense.

(7) Difficulty in Proving Mental State.

The greater the difficulty in proving mental state, the more likely legislators intended to make the offense strict liability to ensure more effective law enforcement. *Aguirre*, 22 S.W.3d at 476. In light of the ordinance's stringent demand that each manager or entertainer "conspicuously display" the permit at all times, prosecutors would seemingly encounter relatively little difficulty in proving that an entertainer was aware that the requisite permit was not conspicuously displayed. To display a permit conspicuously, it must be striking and obvious to the eye so as to attract attention. This means the permit must be openly and prominently displayed, noticeable, and readily apparent to others. Common sense dictates that one who is not conspicuously displaying the requisite permit would be aware of its absence or lack of prominence. Indeed, if a permit is required to be displayed conspicuously so that it will easily attract the attention of others, its presence or absence would be all the more apparent to the one charged with the duty to display it. Under these circumstances, a prosecutor likely would encounter minimal difficulty in proving that one who entertained without conspicuously displaying her permit did so "recklessly, knowingly, or intentionally." *See* Tex. Pen.Code Ann. § 6.02 (Vernon 1994). This lack of difficulty in establishing a culpable mental state weighs in favor of requiring one. *See Aguirre*, 22 S.W.3d at 476–77.

(8) Defendant's Opportunity to Ascertain the "True Facts."

The very reasons that make proof of a culpable mental state a relatively simple task also enable an entertainer to quite easily ascertain the "true facts" as to whether she is conspicuously displaying the requisite permit on her person. *Cf. Aguirre*, 22 S.W.3d at 476–77 (finding that defendant *would* have difficulty in determining whether the place in which she was conducting business was within a prohibited range from one of the specified properties). As previously noted, if one is not displaying the permit in a manner that would draw attention, that fact would almost certainly be apparent to the entertainer. The entertainer's ability to easily ascertain the "true facts" favors the imposition of strict liability. *See id.* at 476 and n.52 ("'The defendant's opportunity to ascertain the true facts is yet another factor which may be important in determining whether the legislature really meant to impose liability on one who was without fault because he lacked knowledge of these facts.'") (quoting 1 WAYNE R. LAFAVE & AUSTIN W. SCOTT, JR., SUBSTANTIVE CRIMINAL LAW 342 (2d ed.1986)).

(9) Number of Prosecutions Expected.

The fewer the expected prosecutions for commission of an offense, the more likely the legislature meant to require prosecuting officials to delve into the issue of fault. *Id.* at 475–76, 476 n. 51. It is difficult to accurately predict the number of prosecutions reasonably expected under Chapter 28 of this ordinance, and the State has provided no guidance with respect to this factor.[7] Nothing in the record now before us relates to the matter. Consequently, like other courts confronted with a lack of data on this issue, we find the expected number of prosecutions for violations of the ordinance is a neutral factor in our analysis. *See Ex parte Weise*, 23 S.W.3d at 455.

Having considered the relevant attributes of section 28–256 in light of the guiding rules and principles articulated by the Court of Criminal Appeals, we find the ordinance does not manifest an intent to dispense with a culpable mental state sufficient to rebut the presumption that one is required under Texas Penal Code sections 1.03 and 6.02. Thus, we conclude that a culpable mental state is an essential element of the offense. Because the information failed to allege a culpable mental state, it contained a defect of substance. This error, alone, provides sufficient basis to find the trial court erred in denying appellant's motion to quash the information. *Sanchez v. State*, 32 S.W.3d 687, 698 (Tex.App.—San Antonio 2000, pet. filed). Accordingly, we find the trial court abused its discretion in denying appellant's motion to quash. We now must determine if the trial court's error was harmless.

* * *

The judgment of the trial court is reversed and the case remanded with instructions to dismiss the information.

Notes and Questions

1. The court observes that if one section of a statute contains a requirement of a mental state, while another section does not, this creates a presumption that the legislature did not intend a mental state in the provision of the statute in which it was omitted. This makes some sense, of course. The legislature clearly thought about mental elements when it drafted the statute and decided not to include one. What, though, does that conclude about the legislature that con-

---

7 The State is in the best position to know the frequency with which violations of this ordinance occur or to evaluate how imputing a culpability requirement may affect the number of prosecutions.

tained no mental elements anywhere in the statute? Isn't the court essentially saying that in such a case we can't be sure that the legislature *thought* about whether it ought to include a mental element in the crime? Most members of legislatures are lawyers and took a class like the one you're taking now. Is it not a bit odd to require proof that the legislature thought about something as elemental as whether a crime ought to include a mental state requirement?

2. Why would a court assume that a legislature would have meant to include (if it thought about it) a mental state requirement for a *malum in se* crime but not a *malum prohibitum* crime? Certainly *malum prohibitum* crimes tend to be punished less severely than *malum in se* crimes, and one would expect a legislature to require a culpable mental state for crimes carrying severe punishment, but the court addresses the severity of punishment in another portion of the opinion. Is there something about a conviction for a *malum in se* crime, regardless of the punishment, that is different than a conviction for a *malum prohibitum* crime?

3. The third and fourth factors considered by the court overlap to a large degree. Typically strict liability crimes involve relatively small acts that can produce widespread harm. Mislabeling drugs is a paradigm example of a strict liability offense. *See* Kenneth W. Simmons, *When Is Strict Liability Just?*, 87 J. Crim. L. & Criminology 1075, 1136 n.193 (1997). A manufacturer may accidentally have allowed a drug to leave his factory with an incorrect label, but the harm from this error would be widespread. In such a case, the legislature would want to design its statute to encourage manufacturers to take care, especially in light of the fact that the penalties for less-than-serious misdeeds tend to carry less-than-severe penalties. Strict liability is believed to encourage a greater degree of caution than crimes requiring proof of a mental state.

4. Considering legislative history to inform a statute's meaning is controversial in every setting. Legislatures do not vote on the legislative history and those who vote for a bill may do so for reasons other than the reasons offered by supporters who commented in the process of drafting, conference, public hearings, and floor debate.

5. What do you make of consideration of the number of prosecutions expected to determine what the legislature meant when it wrote a statute without a *mens rea* term? Certainly proving mental state is burdensome in a prosecution, but does it make sense that blameless crime is somehow more acceptable because there will be more defendants rather than less? In criminal procedure, often

questions of judicial economy are raised. It is interesting that a factor in defining the law requires proof of culpability is how burdensome it would be for the state to include greater protections.

———————————

The two cases that follow, *Staples and Dean*, do not address all of the factors in *Thompson* to determine whether Congress intended the require a mental state for criminal offenses involving weapon possession. *Staples* involves the question of whether the defendant was required to know that the weapon he possessed was in fact an automatic weapon. *Dean* involved the question of whether a defendant, whose weapon discharged during a robbery, had to have at least handled his weapon in a reckless manner which caused it to discharge. Neither the statute prohibiting possession of automatic weapons, nor the statute forbidding the discharge of weapons during a crime, included a *mens rea* term—and neither statute expressly stated that the offense was one of strict liability. The Court reach opposite conclusions in the two cases, with many of the justices that found a *mens rea* term in *Staples* finding the offense in *Dean* to be strict liability. As you read the cases, first try to apply the factors from the *Thompson* decision to these facts. Then try to figure out how the same Court—with admittedly some personnel changes—could arrive at different conclusions on these two cases.

Staples v. United States

Supreme Court of the United States
511 U.S. 600 (1994)

Justice THOMAS delivered the opinion of the Court.

The National Firearms Act makes it unlawful for any person to possess a machine gun that is not properly registered with the Federal Government. Petitioner contends that, to convict him under the Act, the Government should have been required to prove beyond a reasonable doubt that he knew the weapon he possessed had the characteristics that brought it within the statutory definition of a machine gun. We agree and accordingly reverse the judgment of the Court of Appeals.

I

The National Firearms Act (Act), 26 U.S.C. §§ 5801–5872, imposes strict registration requirements on statutorily defined "firearms." The Act includes within the term "firearm" a machine gun, § 5845(a)(6), and further defines a machine gun as "any weapon which shoots, . . . or can be readily restored to shoot, automatically more than one shot, without manual reloading, by a single function of the trigger," § 5845(b). Thus, any fully automatic weapon is a "firearm" within the meaning of the Act. Under the Act, all firearms must be registered in the National Firearms Registration and Transfer Record maintained by the Secretary of the Treasury. § 5841. Section 5861(d) makes it a crime, punishable by up to 10 years in prison, see § 5871, for any person to possess a firearm that is not properly registered.

Upon executing a search warrant at petitioner's home, local police and agents of the Bureau of Alcohol, Tobacco and Firearms (BATF) recovered, among other things, an AR–15 rifle. The AR–15 is the civilian version of the military's M–16 rifle, and is, unless modified, a semiautomatic weapon. The M–16, in contrast, is a selective fire rifle that allows the operator, by rotating a selector switch, to choose semiautomatic or automatic fire. Many M–16 parts are interchangeable with those in the AR–15 and can be used to convert the AR–15 into an automatic weapon. No doubt to inhibit such conversions, the AR–15 is manufactured with a metal stop on its receiver that will prevent an M–16 selector switch, if installed, from rotating to the fully automatic position. The metal stop on petitioner's rifle, however, had been filed away, and the rifle had been assembled with an M–16 selector switch and several other M–16 internal parts, including a hammer, disconnector, and trigger. Suspecting that the AR–15 had been modified to be capable of fully automatic fire, BATF agents seized the weapon. Petitioner subsequently was indicted for unlawful possession of an unregistered machine gun in violation of § 5861(d).

At trial, BATF agents testified that when the AR–15 was tested, it fired more than one shot with a single pull of the trigger. It was undisputed that the weapon was not registered as required by § 5861(d). Petitioner testified that the rifle had never fired automatically when it was in his possession. He insisted that the AR–15 had operated only semiautomatically, and even then imperfectly, often requiring manual ejection of the spent casing and chambering of the next round. According to petitioner, his alleged ignorance of any automatic firing capability should have shielded him from criminal liability for his failure to register the weapon. He requested the District Court to instruct the jury that, to establish a violation of § 5861(d), the Government must prove beyond a reasonable doubt that the defendant "knew that the gun would fire fully automatically." 1 App. to Brief for Appellant in No. 91–5033 (CA10), p. 42.

The District Court rejected petitioner's proposed instruction and instead charged the jury as follows:

> "The Government need not prove the defendant knows he's dealing with a weapon possessing every last characteristic [which subjects it] to the regulation. It would be enough to prove he knows that he is dealing with a dangerous device of a type as would alert one to the likelihood of regulation." Tr. 465.

Petitioner was convicted and sentenced to five years' probation and a $5,000 fine. The Court of Appeals affirmed. . . .We granted certiorari to resolve a conflict in the Courts of Appeals concerning the *mens rea* required under § 5861(d).

II

A

Whether or not § 5861(d) requires proof that a defendant knew of the characteristics of his weapon that made it a "firearm" under the Act is a question of statutory construction. . . .

The language of the statute . . . provides little explicit guidance in this case. Section 5861(d) is silent concerning the *mens rea* required for a violation. It states simply that "[i]t shall be unlawful for any person . . . to receive or possess a firearm which is not registered to him in the National Firearms Registration and Transfer Record." 26 U.S.C. § 5861(d). Nevertheless, silence on this point by itself does not necessarily suggest that Congress intended to dispense with a conventional *mens rea* element, which would require that the defendant know the facts that make his conduct illegal. See *Balint, supra*, at 251, 42 S.Ct., at 302 (stating that traditionally, *"scienter"* was a necessary element in every crime). . . . On the contrary, we must construe the statute in light of the background rules of the common law, in which the requirement of some *mens rea* for a crime is firmly embedded. As we have observed, "[t]he existence of a mens rea is the rule of, rather than the exception to, the principles of Anglo–American criminal jurisprudence." *Id.*, at 436, 98 S.Ct., at 2873 (internal quotation marks omitted). See also *Morissette v. United States*, 342 U.S. 246, 250, 72 S.Ct. 240, 243, 96 L.Ed. 288 (1952) ("The contention that an injury can amount to a crime only when inflicted by intention is no provincial or transient notion. It is as universal and persistent in mature systems of law as belief in freedom of the human will and a consequent ability and duty of the normal individual to choose between good and evil").

There can be no doubt that this established concept has influenced our interpretation of criminal statutes. Indeed, we have noted that the common-law rule requiring *mens rea* has been "followed in regard to statutory crimes even where the statutory definition did not in terms include it." *Balint, supra*, at

251–252, 42 S.Ct., at 302. Relying on the strength of the traditional rule, we have stated that offenses that require no *mens rea* generally are disfavored, *Liparota, supra*, at 426, 105 S.Ct., at 2088, and have suggested that some indication of congressional intent, express or implied, is required to dispense with *mens rea* as an element of a crime.

According to the Government, however, the nature and purpose of the Act suggest that the presumption favoring *mens rea* does not apply to this case. The Government argues that Congress intended the Act to regulate and restrict the circulation of dangerous weapons. Consequently, in the Government's view, this case fits in a line of precedent concerning what we have termed "public welfare" or "regulatory" offenses, in which we have understood Congress to impose a form of strict criminal liability through statutes that do not require the defendant to know the facts that make his conduct illegal. In construing such statutes, we have inferred from silence that Congress did not intend to require proof of *mens rea* to establish an offense.

For example, in *Balint*, we concluded that the Narcotic Act of 1914, which was intended in part to minimize the spread of addictive drugs by criminalizing undocumented sales of certain narcotics, required proof only that the defendant knew that he was selling drugs, not that he knew the specific items he had sold were "narcotics" within the ambit of the statute. See *Balint, supra*, at 254, 42 S.Ct., at 303. . . .

Such public welfare offenses have been created by Congress, and recognized by this Court, in "limited circumstances." *United States Gypsum, supra*, 438 U.S., at 437, 98 S.Ct., at 2873. Typically, our cases recognizing such offenses involve statutes that regulate potentially harmful or injurious items. Cf. *United States v. International Minerals & Chemical Corp.*, 402 U.S. 558, 564–565, 91 S.Ct. 1697, 1701–1702, 29 L.Ed.2d 178 (1971) (characterizing *Balint* and similar cases as involving statutes regulating "dangerous or deleterious devices or products or obnoxious waste materials"). In such situations, we have reasoned that as long as a defendant knows that he is dealing with a dangerous device of a character that places him "in responsible relation to a public danger," *Dotterweich, supra*, at 281, 64 S.Ct., at 136, he should be alerted to the probability of strict regulation, and we have assumed that in such cases Congress intended to place the burden on the defendant to "ascertain at his peril whether [his conduct] comes within the inhibition of the statute." *Balint, supra*, 258 U.S., at 254, 42 S.Ct., at 303. Thus, we essentially have relied on the nature of the statute and the particular character of the items regulated to determine whether congressional silence concerning the mental element of the offense should be interpreted as dispensing with conventional *mens rea* requirements. See generally *Morissette, supra*, at 252–260, 72 S.Ct., at 244–248.[3]

B

The Government argues that § 5861(d) defines precisely the sort of regulatory offense described in *Balint*. In this view, all guns, whether or not they are statutory "firearms," are dangerous devices that put gun owners on notice that they must determine at their hazard whether their weapons come within the scope of the Act. On this understanding, the District Court's instruction in this case was correct, because a conviction can rest simply on proof that a defendant knew he possessed a "firearm" in the ordinary sense of the term.

The Government seeks support for its position from our decision in *United States v. Freed*, 401 U.S. 601, 91 S.Ct. 1112, 28 L.Ed.2d 356 (1971), which involved a prosecution for possession of unregistered grenades under § 5861(d).[4] The defendant knew that the items in his possession were grenades, and we concluded that § 5861(d) did not require the Government to prove the defendant also knew that the grenades were unregistered. *Id.*, at 609, 91 S.Ct., at 1118. To be sure, in deciding that *mens rea* was not required with respect to that element of the offense, we suggested that the Act "is a regulatory measure in the interest of the public safety, which may well be premised on the theory that one would hardly be surprised to learn that possession of hand grenades is not an innocent act." *Ibid.* Grenades, we explained, "are highly dangerous offensive weapons, no less dangerous than the narcotics involved in *United States v. Balint*." *Ibid.* But that reasoning provides little support for dispensing with *mens rea* in this case.

[I]n our view, [not] all guns can be compared to hand grenades. [T]here is a long tradition of widespread lawful gun ownership by private individuals in this country. Such a tradition did not apply to the possession of hand grenades in *Freed* or to the selling of dangerous drugs that we considered in *Balint*. In fact, in *Freed* we construed § 5861(d) under the assumption that "one would hardly be surprised to learn that possession of hand grenades is not an innocent act." *Freed, supra*, at 609, 91 S.Ct., at 1118. Here, the Government essentially suggests that we should interpret the section under the altogether different assumption that

---

3 By interpreting such public welfare offenses to require at least that the defendant know that he is dealing with some dangerous or deleterious substance, we have avoided construing criminal statutes to impose a rigorous form of strict liability. . . . While use of the term "strict liability" is really a misnomer, we have interpreted statutes defining public welfare offenses to eliminate the requirement of *mens rea;* that is, the requirement of a "guilty mind" with respect to an element of a crime. Under such statutes we have not required that the defendant know the facts that make his conduct fit the definition of the offense. Generally speaking, such knowledge is necessary to establish *mens rea*, as is reflected in the maxim *ignorantia facti excusat.*

4 A grenade is a "firearm" under the Act. 26 U.S.C. §§ 5845(a)(8), 5845(f)(1)(B).

"one would hardly be surprised to learn that owning a gun is not an innocent act." That proposition is simply not supported by common experience. Guns in general are not "deleterious devices or products or obnoxious waste materials," *International Minerals, supra*, at 565, 91 S.Ct., at 1701, that put their owners on notice that they stand "in responsible relation to a public danger," *Dotterweich*, 320 U.S., at 281, 64 S.Ct., at 136.

The Government protests that guns, unlike food stamps, but like grenades and narcotics, are potentially harmful devices. Under this view, it seems that *Liparota's* concern for criminalizing ostensibly innocuous conduct is inapplicable whenever an item is sufficiently dangerous—that is, dangerousness alone should alert an individual to probable regulation and justify treating a statute that regulates the dangerous device as dispensing with *mens rea*. But that an item is "dangerous," in some general sense, does not necessarily suggest, as the Government seems to assume, that it is not also entirely innocent. Even dangerous items can, in some cases, be so commonplace and generally available that we would not consider them to alert individuals to the likelihood of strict regulation. As suggested above, despite their potential for harm, guns generally can be owned in perfect innocence. Of course, we might surely classify certain categories of guns—no doubt including the machineguns, sawed-off shotguns, and artillery pieces that Congress has subjected to regulation—as items the ownership of which would have the same quasi-suspect character we attributed to owning hand grenades in *Freed*. But precisely because guns falling outside those categories traditionally have been widely accepted as lawful possessions, their destructive potential, while perhaps even greater than that of some items we would classify along with narcotics and hand grenades, cannot be said to put gun owners sufficiently on notice of the likelihood of regulation to justify interpreting § 5861(d) as not requiring proof of knowledge of a weapon's characteristics.

* * *

On a slightly different tack, the Government suggests that guns are subject to an array of regulations at the federal, state, and local levels that put gun owners on notice that they must determine the characteristics of their weapons and comply with all legal requirements. But regulation in itself is not sufficient to place gun ownership in the category of the sale of narcotics in *Balint*. [D]espite the overlay of legal restrictions on gun ownership, we question whether regulations on guns are sufficiently intrusive that they impinge upon the common experience that owning a gun is usually licit and blameless conduct. Roughly 50 percent of American homes contain at least one firearm of some sort, and in the vast majority of States, buying a shotgun or rifle is a simple transaction that would not alert a person to regulation any more than would buying a car.

If we were to accept as a general rule the Government's suggestion that dangerous and regulated items place their owners under an obligation to inquire at their peril into compliance with regulations, we would undoubtedly reach some untoward results. Automobiles, for example, might also be termed "dangerous" devices and are highly regulated at both the state and federal levels. Congress might see fit to criminalize the violation of certain regulations concerning automobiles, and thus might make it a crime to operate a vehicle without a properly functioning emission control system. But we probably would hesitate to conclude on the basis of silence that Congress intended a prison term to apply to a car owner whose vehicle's emissions levels, wholly unbeknownst to him, began to exceed legal limits between regular inspection dates.

Here, there can be little doubt that, as in *Liparota*, the Government's construction of the statute potentially would impose criminal sanctions on a class of persons whose mental state—ignorance of the characteristics of weapons in their possession—makes their actions entirely innocent. The Government does not dispute the contention that virtually any semiautomatic weapon may be converted, either by internal modification or, in some cases, simply by wear and tear, into a machine gun within the meaning of the Act. Cf. *United States v. Anderson*, 885 F.2d 1248, 1251, 1253–1254 (CA5 1989) (en banc). Such a gun may give no externally visible indication that it is fully automatic. *See United States v. Herbert*, 698 F.2d 981, 986 (CA9), cert. denied, 464 U.S. 821, 104 S.Ct. 87, 78 L.Ed.2d 95 (1983). But in the Government's view, any person who has purchased what he believes to be a semiautomatic rifle or handgun, or who simply has inherited a gun from a relative and left it untouched in an attic or basement, can be subject to imprisonment, despite absolute ignorance of the gun's firing capabilities, if the gun turns out to be an automatic.

* * *

C

The potentially harsh penalty attached to violation of § 5861(d)—up to 10 years' imprisonment—confirms our reading of the Act. Historically, the penalty imposed under a statute has been a significant consideration in determining whether the statute should be construed as dispensing with mens rea. Certainly, the cases that first defined the concept of the public welfare offense almost uniformly involved statutes that provided for only light penalties such as fines or short jail sentences, not imprisonment in the state penitentiary. *See, e.g., Commonwealth v. Raymond*, 97 Mass. 567 (1867) (fine of up to $200 or six months in jail, or both);

Commonwealth v. Farren, 91 Mass. 489 (1864) (fine); *People v. Snowburger*, 113 Mich. 86, 71 N.W. 497 (1897) (fine of up to $500 or incarceration in county jail).

III

In short, we conclude that the background rule of the common law favoring *mens rea* should govern interpretation of § 5861(d) in this case. Silence does not suggest that Congress dispensed with *mens rea* for the element of § 5861(d) at issue here. Thus, to obtain a conviction, the Government should have been required to prove that petitioner knew of the features of his AR–15 that brought it within the scope of the Act.

Justice STEVENS, with whom Justice BLACKMUN joins, dissenting.

To avoid a slight possibility of injustice to unsophisticated owners of machineguns and sawed-off shotguns, the Court has substituted its views of sound policy for the judgment Congress made when it enacted the National Firearms Act (or Act). Because the Court's addition to the text of 26 U.S.C. § 5861(d) is foreclosed by both the statute and our precedent, I respectfully dissent.

The Court is preoccupied with guns that "generally can be owned in perfect innocence." *Ante*, at 1800. This case, however, involves a semiautomatic weapon that was readily convertible into a machine gun—a weapon that the jury found to be "'a dangerous device of a type as would alert one to the likelihood of regulation.'" *Ante*, at 1796. These are not guns "of some sort" that can be found in almost "50 percent of American homes." *Ante*, at 1801.[1] They are particularly dangerous—indeed, a substantial percentage of the unregistered machineguns now in circulation are converted semiautomatic weapons.[2]

[E]ven assuming that the Court is correct that the mere possession of an ordinary rifle or pistol does not entail sufficient danger to alert one to the possibility of regulation, that conclusion does not resolve this case. Petitioner knowingly possessed a semiautomatic weapon that was readily convertible into a machine gun. The "'character and nature'" of such a weapon is sufficiently hazardous to place the possessor on notice of the possibility of regulation. . . .

---

1   Indeed, only about 15 percent of all the guns in the United States are semiautomatic. See National Rifle Association, Fact Sheet, Semi–Automatic Firearms 1 (Feb. 1, 1994). Although it is not known how many of those weapons are readily convertible into machineguns, it is obviously a lesser share of the total.

2   See U.S. Dept. of Justice, Attorney General's Task Force on Violent Crime: Final Report 29, 32 (Aug. 17, 1981) (stating that over an 18–month period over 20 percent of the machineguns seized or purchased by the Bureau of Alcohol, Tobacco and Firearms had been converted from semiautomatic weapons by "simple tool work or the addition of readily available parts") (citing U.S. Dept. of Treasury, Bureau of Alcohol, Tobacco and Firearms, Firearms Case Summary (Washington: U.S. Govt. Printing Office 1981)).

No significant difference exists between imposing upon the possessor a duty to determine whether such a weapon is registered, *Freed*, 401 U.S., at 607–610, 91 S.Ct., at 1117–1119, and imposing a duty to determine whether that weapon has been converted into a machine gun.

* * *

The enforcement of public welfare offenses always entails some possibility of injustice. Congress nevertheless has repeatedly decided that an overriding public interest in health or safety may outweigh that risk when a person is dealing with products that are sufficiently dangerous or deleterious to make it reasonable to presume that he either knows, or should know, whether those products conform to special regulatory requirements. The dangerous character of the product is reasonably presumed to provide sufficient notice of the probability of regulation to justify strict enforcement against those who are merely guilty of negligent, rather than willful, misconduct.

* * *

V

This case presents no dispute about the dangerous character of machine-guns and sawed-off shotguns. Anyone in possession of such a weapon is "standing in responsible relation to a public danger." See *Dotterweich*, 320 U.S., at 281, 64 S.Ct. at 136–137 (citation omitted). In the National Firearms Act, Congress determined that the serious threat to health and safety posed by the private ownership of such firearms warranted the imposition of a duty on the owners of dangerous weapons to determine whether their possession is lawful. Semiautomatic weapons that are readily convertible into machineguns are sufficiently dangerous to alert persons who knowingly possess them to the probability of stringent public regulation. The jury's finding that petitioner knowingly possessed "a dangerous device of a type as would alert one to the likelihood of regulation" adequately supports the conviction.

Accordingly, I would affirm the judgment of the Court of Appeals.

Notes and Questions

1. How exactly would the prosecution go about proving that Staples was aware that his weapon had been altered to allow it to fire multiple shots with a single pull of a trigger? Recall that in *Thompson* concluded that the prosecution's "difficulty in proving mental state" was a factor suggesting that the legislature had intended a strict liability crime.

2. The Court in *Thompson* also concluded that "the defendant's opportunity to ascertain the true facts is yet another factor which may be important in determining whether the legislature really meant to impose liability on one who was without fault because he lacked knowledge of the facts." The nude dancer in *Thompson* was certainly very able to know whether she was wearing the required permit.

3. Justice Stevens noted that when the National Firearms Act was adopted in 1934, the statute covered "a relatively narrow category of weapons such as submachine-guns and sawed-off shotgun—weapons characteristically used only by professional gangsters like Al Capone, Pretty Boy Floyd, and their henchmen." Semi-automatic weapons are now frequently owned by law abiding weapons enthusiasts. *See* Markus Boser, *Go Ahead, State, Make Them Pay: An Analysis of Washington D.C.'s Assault Weapons Manufacturing Strict Liability Act*, 25 Colum. J.L. & Soc. Probs. 313, 320 n.46 (1992) ("Many of the semi-automatics now being sold are easily convertible into fully automatic weapons that, until recently, have not been seen since their complete ban in 1934."). Whether or not that fact was true in 1934, does that fact undermine or support Justice Stevens argument?

4. Obviously your view of who has the better argument in this debate between Thomas and Stevens turns on whether you find hand grenades and semi-automatic weapons to be analogous items. Do automatic weapons pose the same sort of risk to large numbers of people as misbranded drugs? Your view on whether the Court in *Staples* was considering a public welfare offense, in no small measure, likely turns on your view of the power of the government to place limitations on the type of weapons individuals are allowed to possess.

5. Justice Stevens appears to be quite deferential to Congress, criticizing the majority for "substitut[ing] its view of sound policy for the judgment of Congress." (Less sophisticated, or more political types offer describe this same criticism as "legislating from the bench.") As you read the *Dean* case, consider what causes his deference to Congress to wane.

Dean v. United States

Supreme Court of the United States
556 U.S. 568 (2009)

Chief Justice ROBERTS delivered the opinion of the Court.

Accidents happen. Sometimes they happen to individuals committing crimes with loaded guns. The question here is whether extra punishment Congress imposed for the discharge of a gun during certain crimes applies when the gun goes off accidentally.

I

TITLE 18 U.S.C. § 924(C)(1)(A) criminalizes using or carrying a firearm during and in relation to any violent or drug trafficking crime, or possessing a firearm in furtherance of such a crime. An individual convicted of that offense receives a 5–year mandatory minimum sentence, in addition to the punishment for the underlying crime. § 924(c)(1)(A)(i). The mandatory minimum increases to 7 years "if the firearm is brandished" and to 10 years "if the firearm if the firearm is discharged."

In this case, a masked man entered a bank, waved a gun, and yelled at every-one to get down. He then walked behind the teller counter and started removing money from the teller stations. He grabbed bills with his left hand, holding the gun in his right. At one point, he reached over a teller to remove money from her drawer. As he was collecting the money, the gun discharged, leaving a bullet hole in the partition between two stations. The robber cursed and dashed out of the bank. Witnesses later testified that he seemed surprised that the gun had gone off. No one was hurt.

Police arrested Christopher Michael Dean and Ricardo Curtis Lopez for the crime. Both defendants were charged with conspiracy to commit a robbery affecting interstate commerce, in violation of 18 U.S.C. § 1951(a), and aiding and abetting each other in using, carrying, possessing, and discharging a firearm during an armed robbery, in violation of § 924(c)(1)(A)(iii) and § 2. At trial, Dean admitted that he had committed the robbery, *id.*, at 76–81, and a jury found him guilty on both the robbery and firearm counts. The District Court sentenced Dean to a mandatory minimum term of 10 years in prison on the firearm count, because the firearm "discharged" during the robbery. § 924(c)(1)(A)(iii); App. 136.

Dean appealed, contending that the discharge was accidental, and that the sentencing enhancement in § 924(c)(1)(A)(iii) requires proof that the defendant intended to discharge the firearm. . . .

II

SECTION 924(C)(1)(A) provides:

"[A]ny person who, during and in relation to any crime of violence or drug trafficking crime . . . uses or carries a firearm, or who, in furtherance of any such crime, possesses a firearm, shall, in addition to the punishment provided for such crime of violence or drug trafficking crime—

"(i) be sentenced to a term of imprisonment of not less than 5 years;

"(ii) if the firearm is brandished, be sentenced to a term of imprisonment of not less than 7 years; and

"(iii) if the firearm is discharged, be sentenced to a term of imprisonment of not less than 10 years."

The principal paragraph defines a complete offense and the subsections "explain how defendants are to 'be sentenced.'" *Harris v. United States*, 536 U.S. 545, 552, 122 S.Ct. 2406, 153 L.Ed.2d 524 (2002). Subsection (i) "sets a catchall minimum" sentence of not less than five years. *Id.*, at 552–553, 122 S.Ct. 2406. Subsections (ii) and (iii) increase the minimum penalty if the firearm "is brandished" or "is discharged." See *id.*, at 553, 122 S.Ct. 2406. The parties disagree over whether § 924(c)(1)(A)(iii) contains a requirement that the defendant intend to discharge the firearm. We hold that it does not.

A

"We start, as always, with the language of the statute." *Williams v. Taylor*, 529 U.S. 420, 431, 120 S.Ct. 1479, 146 L.Ed.2d 435 (2000). The text of subsection (iii) provides that a defendant shall be sentenced to a minimum of 10 years "if the firearm is discharged." It does not require that the discharge be done knowingly or intentionally, or otherwise contain words of limitation. As we explained in *Bates v. United States*, 522 U.S. 23, 118 S.Ct. 285, 139 L.Ed.2d 215 (1997), in declining to infer an "'intent to defraud'" requirement into a statute, "we ordinarily resist reading words or elements into a statute that do not appear on its face." *Id.*, at 29, 118 S.Ct. 285.

Congress's use of the passive voice further indicates that subsection (iii) does not require proof of intent. The passive voice focuses on an event that occurs without respect to a specific actor, and therefore without respect to any actor's intent or culpability. Cf. *Watson v. United States*, 552 U.S. 74, ––––, 128 S.Ct. 579, 584, 169 L.Ed.2d 472 (2007) (use of passive voice in statutory phrase "to be used" in 18 U.S.C. § 924(d)(1) reflects "agnosticism . . . about who does

the using"). It is whether something happened—not how or why it happened—
that matters.

The structure of the statute also suggests that subsection (iii) is not limited
to the intentional discharge of a firearm. Subsection (ii) provides a 7–year mandatory minimum sentence if the firearm "is brandished." Congress expressly
included an intent requirement for that provision, by defining "brandish" to
mean "to display all or part of the firearm, or otherwise make the presence of the
firearm known to another person, *in order to intimidate* that person." § 924(c)
(4) (emphasis added). The defendant must have intended to brandish the firearm,
because the brandishing must have been done for a specific purpose. Congress
did not, however, separately define "discharge" to include an intent requirement. "[W]here Congress includes particular language in one section of a statute but omits it in another section of the same Act, it is generally presumed that
Congress acts intentionally and purposely in the disparate inclusion or exclusion." *Russello v. United States*, 464 U.S. 16, 23, 104 S.Ct. 296, 78 L.Ed.2d 17 (1983)
(internal quotation marks omitted).

Dean argues that the statute is not silent on the question presented.
Congress, he contends, included an intent element in the opening paragraph of
§ 924(c)(1)(A), and that element extends to the sentencing enhancements. Section
924(c)(1)(A) criminalizes using or carrying a firearm "during and in relation
to" any violent or drug trafficking crime. In *Smith v. United States*, 508 U.S. 223,
113 S.Ct. 2050, 124 L.Ed.2d 138 (1993), we stated that the phrase "in relation to"
means "that the firearm must have some purpose or effect with respect to the
drug trafficking crime; its presence or involvement cannot be the result of accident or coincidence." *Id.*, at 238, 113 S.Ct. 2050. Dean argues that the adverbial
phrase thus necessarily embodies an intent requirement, and that the phrase
modifies all the verbs in the statute—not only use, carry, and possess, but also
brandish and discharge. Such a reading requires that a perpetrator knowingly
discharge the firearm for the enhancement to apply. If the discharge is accidental,
Dean argues, it is not "in relation to" the underlying crime.

The most natural reading of the statute, however, is that "in relation
to" modifies only the nearby verbs "uses" and "carries." The next verb—
"possesses"—is modified by its own adverbial clause, "in furtherance of." The
last two verbs—"is brandished" and "is discharged"—appear in separate subsections and are in a different voice than the verbs in the principal paragraph.
There is no basis for reading "in relation to" to extend all the way down to
modify "is discharged." The better reading of the statute is that the adverbial
phrases in the opening paragraph—"in relation to" and "in furtherance of"—
modify their respective nearby verbs, and that neither phrase extends to the
sentencing factors.

But, Dean argues, such a reading will lead to absurd results. The discharge provision on its face contains no temporal or causal limitations. In the absence of an intent requirement, the enhancement would apply "regardless of when the actions occur, or by whom or for what reason they are taken." *Brief for Petitioner 11–12.* It would, for example, apply if the gun used during the crime were discharged "weeks (or years) before or after the crime." *Reply Brief for Petitioner 11.*

We do not agree that implying an intent requirement is necessary to address such concerns. As the Government recognizes, sentencing factors such as the one here "often involve . . . special features of the manner in which a basic crime was carried out." Brief for United States 29 (quoting *Harris*, 536 U.S., at 553, 122 S.Ct. 2406; internal quotation marks omitted). The basic crime here is using or carrying a firearm during and in relation to a violent or drug trafficking crime, or possessing a firearm in furtherance of any such crime. Fanciful hypotheticals testing whether the discharge was a "special featur[e]" of how the "basic crime was carried out," *Harris*, 536 U.S., at 553, 122 S.Ct. 2406 (internal quotation marks omitted), are best addressed in those terms, not by contorting and stretching the statutory language to imply an intent requirement.

B

Dean further argues that even if the statute is viewed as silent on the intent question, that silence compels a ruling in his favor. There is, he notes, a presumption that criminal prohibitions include a requirement that the Government prove the defendant intended the conduct made criminal. In light of this presumption, we have "on a number of occasions read a state-of-mind component into an offense even when the statutory definition did not in terms so provide." *United States v. United States Gypsum Co.*, 438 U.S. 422, 437, 98 S.Ct. 2864, 57 L.Ed.2d 854 (1978). "[S]ome indication of congressional intent, express or implied, is required to dispense with *mens rea* as an element of a crime." *Staples v. United States*, 511 U.S. 600, 606, 114 S.Ct. 1793, 128 L.Ed.2d 608 (1994).

Dean argues that the presumption is especially strong in this case, given the structure and purpose of the statute. In his view, the three subsections are intended to provide harsher penalties for increasingly culpable conduct: a 5–year minimum for using, carrying, or possessing a firearm; a 7–year minimum for brandishing a firearm; and a 10–year minimum for discharging a firearm. Incorporating an intent requirement into the discharge provision is necessary to give effect to that progression, because an accidental discharge is less culpable than intentional brandishment. See *Brown*, 449 F.3d, at 156.

It is unusual to impose criminal punishment for the consequences of purely accidental conduct. But it is not unusual to punish individuals for the unintended consequences of their *unlawful* acts. See 2 W. LaFave, Substantive Criminal Law § 14.4, pp. 436–437 (2d ed.2003). The felony-murder rule is a familiar example: If a defendant commits an unintended homicide while committing another felony, the defendant can be convicted of murder. *See* 18 U.S.C. § 1111. The Sentencing Guidelines reflect the same principle. *See* United States Sentencing Commission, Guidelines Manual § 2A2.2(b)(3) (Nov.2008) (USSG) (increasing offense level for aggravated assault according to the seriousness of the injury); § 2D2.3 (increasing offense level for operating or directing the operation of a common carrier under the influence of alcohol or drugs if death or serious bodily injury results).

Blackstone expressed the idea in the following terms:

> "[I]f any accidental mischief happens to follow from the performance of a *lawful* act, the party stands excused from all guilt: but if a man be doing any thing *unlawful*, and a consequence ensues which he did not foresee or intend, as the death of a man or the like, his want of foresight shall be no excuse; for, being guilty of one offence, in doing antecedently what is in itself unlawful, he is criminally guilty of whatever consequence may follow the first misbehaviour." 4 W. Blackstone, Commentaries on the Laws of England 26–27 (1769).

Here the defendant is already guilty of unlawful conduct twice over: a violent or drug trafficking offense and the use, carrying, or possession of a firearm in the course of that offense. That unlawful conduct was not an accident. See *Smith*, 508 U.S., at 238, 113 S.Ct. 2050.

The fact that the actual discharge of a gun covered under § 924(c)(1)(A)(iii) may be accidental does not mean that the defendant is blameless. The sentencing enhancement in subsection (iii) accounts for the risk of harm resulting from the manner in which the crime is carried out, for which the defendant is responsible. See *Harris, supra*, at 553, 122 S.Ct. 2406. An individual who brings a loaded weapon to commit a crime runs the risk that the gun will discharge accidentally. A gunshot in such circumstances—whether accidental or intended—increases the risk that others will be injured, that people will panic, or that violence (with its own danger to those nearby) will be used in response. Those criminals wishing to avoid the penalty for an inadvertent discharge can lock or unload the firearm, handle it with care during the underlying violent or drug trafficking crime, leave the gun at home, or—best yet—avoid committing the felony in the first place.

* * *

SECTION 924(C)(1)(A)(III) requires no separate proof of intent. The 10–year mandatory minimum applies if a gun is discharged in the course of a violent or drug trafficking crime, whether on purpose or by accident. The judgment of the Court of Appeals for the Eleventh Circuit is affirmed.

It is so ordered.

Justice STEVENS, dissenting.

Accidents happen, but they seldom give rise to criminal liability. Indeed, if they cause no harm they seldom give rise to any liability. The Court today nevertheless holds that petitioner is subject to a mandatory additional sentence—a species of criminal liability—for an accident that caused no harm.

* * *

Consistent with the common-law tradition, the requirement of *mens rea* has long been the rule of our criminal jurisprudence. *See United States v. United States Gypsum Co.*, 438 U.S. 422, 98 S.Ct. 2864, 57 L.Ed.2d 854 (1978). The concept of crime as a "concurrence of an evil-meaning mind with an evil-doing hand . . . took deep and early root in American soil." *Morissette v. United States*, 342 U.S. 246, 251–252, 72 S.Ct. 240, 96 L.Ed. 288 (1952). Legislating against that backdrop, States often omitted intent elements when codifying the criminal law, and "courts assumed that the omission did not signify disapproval of the principle but merely recognized that intent was so inherent in the idea of the offense that it required no statutory affirmation." *Id.*, at 252, 72 S.Ct. 240. Similarly, absent a clear statement by Congress that it intended to create a strict-liability offense, a *mens rea* requirement has generally been presumed in federal statutes. See *id.*, at 273, 72 S.Ct. 240; *Staples v. United States*, 511 U.S. 600, 605–606, 114 S.Ct. 1793, 128 L.Ed.2d 608 (1994). With only a few narrowly delineated exceptions for such crimes as statutory rape and public welfare offenses, the presumption remains the rule today. See *Morissette*, 342 U.S., at 251–254, and n. 8, 72 S.Ct. 240; *see also* Staples, 511 U.S., at 606–607, 114 S.Ct. 1793 (discussing *United States v. Balint*, 258 U.S. 250, 42 S.Ct. 301, 66 L.Ed. 604 (1922)).

Although mandatory minimum sentencing provisions are of too recent genesis to have any common-law pedigree, *see Harris v. United States*, 536 U.S. 545, 579, 581, n. 5, 122 S.Ct. 2406, 153 L.Ed.2d 524 (2002) (THOMAS, J., dissenting), there is no sensible reason for treating them differently from offense elements for purposes of the presumption of *mens rea*. Sentencing provisions of this type have substantially the same effect on a defendant's liberty as aggravated offense provisions. . . .

As the foregoing shows, mandatory minimum sentencing provisions are in effect no different from aggravated offense provisions. The common-law tradition of requiring proof of *mens rea* to establish criminal culpability should thus apply equally to such sentencing factors. Absent a clear indication that Congress intended to create a strict liability enhancement, courts should presume that a provision that mandates enhanced criminal penalties requires proof of intent. . . . Accordingly, I would apply the presumption in this case and avoid the strange result of imposing a substantially harsher penalty for an act caused not by an "evil-meaning mind" but by a clumsy hand.

* * *

Notes and Questions

1. Is there not at least as good an argument for finding the aggravating act of discharging a weapon to be a strict liability offense as there was for finding the possession charge in *Staples* to be a strict liability offense? How can Justice Stevens' willingness to allow possession to be a strict liability offense be reconciled with his insistence that Dean must bear some culpability for the weapon's discharge to be liable for that act?

2. The majority opinions in *Staples* and *Dean* can be reconciled by looking at the posture of the two cases. In the *Staples* case, the question was whether the defendant was guilty of *something*. In the *Dean* case, the question was *how guilty* is the defendant. As the majority recognizes, in a number of areas of criminal law, a lesser quantum of proof is required to convict a defendant of a crime once it has been demonstrated that he has committed *some* sort of wrong. Under the felony murder doctrine, if a death occurs while a defendant is committing a felony, then he is responsible for that death—and in most jurisdictions, he is liable to the same penalty as if he had intentionally taken the life. Under a particularly controversial theory of conspiracy liability, all the members of a conspiracy are liable for the acts of their co-conspirators that further the objectives of the conspiracy. Once you agree with others to commit an unlawful act, the government is not required to prove that you intended, or took inadequate precaution to prevent an act that was not part of the agreement, but merely *furthers* the ends of the conspiracy. The old phrase "in for a penny, in for a pound" aptly describes this state of the law. Chief Justice Roberts seems to explain that this is simply the way the world works, once Dean crossed the threshold of criminality, he is liable for whatever bad acts follow, regardless of his degree of fault in bringing about those events.

3. There is something morally random about punishing a defendant differently because his bad act led to, or did not lead to, a harmful consequence. If the weapon had not discharged accidentally, then this enhancement would not have applied. Does this moral randomness not also extend, to a greater extent in fact, to a differential in punishment that turns on whether or not one's co-conspirators commit crimes beyond the original agreement—or whether one dies during a felony under circumstances that would otherwise be inadequate for a homicide prosecution? And does additional punishment for an accidental discharge of a gun not also look like an example of punishment on the basis of luck, or bad luck? David Lewis' article that follows takes a stab at justifying, while also criticizing criminal law's "in for a penny, in for a pound" principle.

---

3. Results

Some offenses require that some bad consequence flow from the defendant's action or, in some cases, omission. Often a crime that requires a result is punished as a lesser crime when that result does not occur. Vehicular homicide, for instance, occurs when an intoxicated driver kills during the operation of a motor vehicle. If he injures no one, the driver may still be punished for driving under the influence. A person who intends to kill and achieves his goal is guilty of first-degree murder, if his effort came sufficiently close to completion, his crime is attempted murder. If through very dangerous conduct, not carried out for the purpose of taking a life a defendant kills, his crime in most jurisdictions will either be second-degree murder or involuntary manslaughter. If this same conduct does not take anyone's life, in most jurisdictions he could be charged with reckless endangerment.

As you might guess, these lesser crimes tend to carry less severe punishments. The following article by David Lewis challenges the legitimacy of this differential in punishment and offers a rather creative justification. As you engage in the study of criminal law this semester, consider the aspects of a defendant's punishment are driven by chance and consider whether you are satisfied by this, or other, justifications for punishment that are not related to the defendant's culpability.

DAVID LEWIS

The Punishment that Leaves Something to Chance

16 Philosophy and Public Affairs 53 (1989)

I.

We are accustomed to punish criminal attempts much more severely if they succeed than if they fail. We are also accustomed to wonder why. It is hard to find any rationale for our leniency toward the unsuccessful. Leniency toward aborted attempts, or mere preparation, might be easier to understand. (And whether easy or hard, it is not my present topic.) But what sense can we make of leniency toward a completed attempt—one that puts a victim at risk of harm, and fails only by luck to do actual harm?

Dee takes a shot at his enemy, and so does Dum. They both want to kill; they both try, and we may suppose they try equally hard. Both act out of malice, without any shred of justification or excuse. Both give us reason to fear that they might be ready to kill in the future. The only difference is that Dee hits and Dum misses. So Dee has killed, he is guilty of murder, and we put him to death. Dum has not killed, he is guilty only of attempted murder, and he gets a short prison sentence.

Why? Dee and Dum were equally wicked in their desires. They were equally uninhibited in pursuing their wicked desires. Insofar as the wicked deserve to be punished, they deserve it equally. Their conduct was equally dangerous: they inflicted equal risks of death on their respective victims. Insofar as those who act dangerously deserve to be punished, again they deserve it equally. Maybe Dee's act was worse than Dum's act, just because of Dee's success; but it is not the act that suffers punishment, it is the agent. Likewise, if we want to express our abhorrence of wickedness or of dangerous conduct, either exemplar of what we abhor is fit to star in the drama of crime and punishment. Further, Dee and Dum have equally engaged in conduct we want to prevent by deterrence. For we prevent successful attempts by preventing attempts generally. We cannot deter success separately from deterring attempts, since attempters make no separate choice about whether to succeed. Further, Dee and Dum have equally shown us that we might all be safer if we defended ourselves against them; and one function of punishment (at any rate if it is death, imprisonment, or transportation) is to get dangerous criminals off the streets before they do more harm. So how does their different luck in hitting or missing make any difference to considerations of desert, expression, deterrence, or defense? How can it be just, on any credible theory of just punishment, to punish them differently?

Here is one rationale for our peculiar practice. If the gods see innocent blood shed, they will be angry; if they are angry, none of us will be safe until they are propitiated; and to propitiate the gods, we must shed guilty blood. Whereas if by luck no innocent blood is shed, the gods will not be angered just by the sight of unsuccessful wickedness, so there will be no need of propitiation. This rationale would make sense, if its premises were true. And if we put "the public" or "the victim's kin" for "the gods" throughout it still makes sense; and that way, maybe the premises are true, at least sometimes and to some extent. But this rationale does nothing at all to defend our practice as just. If our practice is unjust, then the ways of the gods (or the public, or the kin) are unjust, although if the powers that be want to see injustice done, it might be prudent to ignore justice and do their bidding.

A purely conservative rationale is open to the same complaint. Maybe it is a good idea to stay with the practice we have learned how to operate, lest a reform cause unexpected problems. Maybe it is good for people to see the law go on working as they are accustomed to expect it to. Maybe a reform would convey unintended and disruptive messages: as it might be, that we have decid-ed to take murder less seriously than we used to. These considerations may be excellent reasons why it is prudent to leave well enough alone, and condone whatever injustice there may be in our present practice. They do nothing at all to defend our practice as just. Another rationale concerns the deterrence of sec-ond attempts. If at first you don't succeed, and if success would bring no extra punishment, then you have nothing left to lose if you try, try again. "If exactly the same penalty is prescribed for successes as for attempts, there will be every reason to make sure that one is successful." It cannot hurt to have some deter-rence left after deterrence has failed. Maybe the experience of having tried once will make the criminal more deterrable than he was at first. But why is this any reason for punishing successful attempts more severely? It might as well just be a reason for punishing two attempts more severely than one, which we could do regardless of success. If each separate attempt is punished, and if one share of punishment is not so bad that a second share would be no worse, then we have some deterrence against second attempts.

Another rationale sees punishment purely as a deterrent, and assumes that we will have deterrence enough if we make sure that crime never pays. If so, there is no justification for any more penal harm than it takes to offset the gains from a crime. Then a failed attempt needs no punishment: there are no gains to be offset, so even if unpunished it still doesn't pay. I reply that in the first place, this system of minimum deterrence seems likely to dissuade only the most calculating of criminals. In the second place, punishment is not just a deterrent. I myself might not insist on retribution per se, but certainly the expressive and defensive functions of punishment are not to be lightly forsaken.

* * *

Finally, another rationale invokes the difference between wholehearted and halfhearted attempts. Both are bad, but wholehearted attempts are worse. A wholehearted attempt involves more careful planning, more precautions against failure, more effort, more persistence, and perhaps repeated tries. *Ceteris paribus*, a wholehearted attempt evinces more wickedness—stronger wicked desires, or less inhibition about pursuing them. *Ceteris paribus*, a wholehearted attempt is more dangerous. It is more likely to succeed; it subjects the victim, knowingly and wrongfully, to a greater risk. Therefore it is more urgently in need of prevention by deterrence. *Ceteris paribus*, the perpetrator of a wholehearted attempt is more of a proven danger to us all, so it is more urgent to get him off the streets. So from every standpoint—desert, expression, deterrence, defense—it makes good sense to punish attempts more severely when they are wholehearted. Now, since wholehearted attempts are more likely to succeed, success is some evidence that the attempt was wholehearted. Punishing success, then, is a rough and ready way of punishing wholeheartedness.

I grant that it is just to punish wholehearted attempts more severely or better, since "heartedness" admits of degrees, to proportion the punishment to the heartedness of the attempt. And I grant that in so doing we may take the probability of success—in other words, the risk inflicted on the victim—as our measure of heartedness. That means not proportioning the punishment simply to the offender's wickedness, because two equally wicked attempters may not be equally likely to succeed. One may be more dangerous than the other because he has the advantage in skill or resources or information or opportunity. Then if we proportion punishment to heartedness measured by risk, we may punish one attempter more severely not because he was more wicked, but because his conduct was more dangerous. From a purely retributive standpoint, wickedness might seem the more appropriate measure; but from the expressive standpoint, we may prefer to dramatize our abhorrence not of wickedness per se but of dangerous wickedness; and from the standpoint of deterrence or defense, clearly it is dangerous conduct that matters.

So far, so good; but I protest that it is unjust to punish success as a rough and ready way of punishing wholeheartedness. It's just too rough and ready. Success is some evidence of wholeheartedness, sure enough. But it is very unreliable evidence: the wholehearted attempt may very well be thwarted, the half- or quarter-hearted attempt may succeed. And we can have other evidence that bears as much or more on whether the attempt was wholehearted. If what we really want is to punish wholeheartedness, we have no business heeding only one unreliable fragment of the total evidence, and then treating that fragment as if it were conclusive. Suppose we had reason—good reason—to think that on average the old tend to be more wholehearted than the young in their criminal attempts. Suppose even that we could infer wholeheartedness from age somewhat more reliably than we can infer it from success. Then if we punished attempters more severely in proportion to their age, that would be another rough and ready way of punishing wholeheartedness. *Ex hypothesi*, it would be less rough and ready than what we do in punishing success. It would still fall far short of our standards of justice.

II.

In what follows, I shall propose a new rationale. *I do not say that it works.* I do say that the new rationale works better than the old ones. It makes at least a prima facie case that our peculiar practice is just, and I do not see any decisive rebuttal. All the same, I think that the prima facie case is probably not good enough, and probably there is no adequate justification for punishing attempts more severely when they succeed.

Our present practice amounts to a disguised form of *penal lottery*—a punishment that leaves something to chance. Seen thus, it does in some sense punish all attempts alike, regardless of success. It is no less just, and no more just, than an undisguised penal lottery would be. Probably any penal lottery is seriously unjust, but it is none too easy to explain why.

By a penal lottery, I mean a system of punishment in which the convicted criminal is subjected to a risk of punitive harm. If he wins the lottery, he escapes the harm. If he loses, he does not. A pure penal lottery is one in which the winners suffer no harm at all; an impure penal lottery is one in which winners and losers alike suffer some harm, but the losers suffer more harm. It is a mixture: part of the punishment is certain harm, part is the penal lottery.

An overt penal lottery is one in which the punishment is announced explicitly as a risk—there might be ways of dramatizing the fact, such as a drawing of straws on the steps of the gallows. A covert penal lottery is one in which the punishment is not announced as a risk, but it is common knowledge that it brings risk with it. (A covert lottery must presumably be impure.)

A historical example of an overt penal lottery is the decimation of a regiment as punishment for mutiny. Each soldier is punished for his part in the mutiny by a one-in-ten risk of being put to death. It is a fairly pure penal lottery, but not entirely pure: the terror of waiting to see who must die is part of the punishment, and this part falls with certainty on all the mutineers alike.

Covert and impure penal lotteries are commonplace in our own time. If one drawback of prison is that it is a place where one is exposed to capricious violence, or to a serious risk of catching AIDS, then a prison sentence is in part a penal lottery. If the gulag is noted for its abysmal standards of occupational health and safety, then a sentence of forced labor is in part a penal lottery.

III.

What do we think, and what should we think, of penal lotteries? Specifically, what should we think of a penal lottery, with death for the losers, as the punishment for all attempts at murder, regardless of success? Successful or not, the essence of the crime is to subject the victim, knowingly and wrongfully, to a serious risk of death. The proposed punishment is to be subjected to a like risk of death.

We need a standard of comparison. Our present system of leniency toward the unsuccessful is too problematic to make a good standard, so let us instead compare the penal lottery with a hypothetical reformed system. How does the lottery compare with a system that punishes all attempts regardless of success, by the certain harm of a moderate prison term? A moderate term, because if we punished successful and unsuccessful attempts alike, we would presumably set the punishment somewhere between our present severe punishment of the one and our lenient punishment of the other. (Let the prison be a safe one, so that in the comparison case we have no trace of a penal lottery.) Both for the lottery and for the comparison case, I shall assume that we punish regardless of success. In the one case, success per se makes no difference to the odds; in the other case, no difference to the time in prison. This is not to say that every convicted criminal gets the very same sentence. Other factors might still make a difference. In particular, heartedness (measured by the risk inflicted) could make a difference, and success could make a difference to the extent that it is part of our evidence about heartedness.

Now, how do the two alternatives compare?

The penal lottery may have some practical advantages. It gets the case over and done with quickly. It is not a crime school. A prison costs a lot more than a gallows plus a supply of long and short straws.

(Likewise a prison with adequate protection against random brutality by guards and fellow inmates costs more than a prison without. So it seems that we have already been attracted by the economy of a system that has at least some covert admixture of lottery.)

Like a prison term (or fines, or flogging) and unlike the death penalty simpliciter, the penal lottery can be graduated as finely as we like. When we take the crime to be worse, we provide fewer long straws to go with the fatal short straws.

In particular, that is how we can provide a more severe punishment for the more wholehearted attempt that subjected the victim to a greater risk.

From the standpoint of dramatizing our abhorrence of wicked and dangerous conduct, a penal lottery seems at least as good as a prison sentence. Making the punishment fit the crime, Mikado-fashion, is poetic justice. The point we want to dramatize, both to the criminal and to the public, is that what we think of the crime is just like what the criminal thinks of his punishment. If it's a risk for a risk, how can anybody miss the point?

From the standpoint of deterrence, there is no doubt that we are sometimes well deterred by the prospect of risk. It happens every time we wait to cross the street. It is an empirical question how effective a deterrent the penal lottery might be. Compared with the alternative punishment of a certain harm, such as a moderate prison term, the lottery might give us more deterrence for a given amount of penal harm, or it might give us less. Whether it gives us more or less might depend a lot on the details of how the two systems operate. If the lottery gave us more, that would make it preferable from the standpoint of deterrence.

(We often hear about evidence that certainty is more deterring than severity. But to the extent that this evidence pertains only to the uncertainty of getting caught, getting convicted, and serving the full sentence, it is scarcely relevant. The criminal might think of escaping punishment as a game of skill—his skill, or perhaps his lawyer's. For all we know, a risk of losing a game of chance might be much more deterring than an equal risk of losing a game of skill.)

From the standpoint of defense, the penal lottery gets some dangerous criminals off the streets forever, while others go free at once. Moderate prison terms would let all go free after a longer time, some of them perhaps reformed and some of them hardened and embittered. It is another empirical question which alternative is the more effective system of defense. Again, the answer may depend greatly on the details of the two systems, and on much else that we cannot easily find out.

IV.

So far we have abundant uncertainties, but no clear-cut case against the penal lottery. If anything, the balance may be tipping in its favor. So let us turn finally to the standpoint of desert. Here it is a bit hard to know what to make of the penal lottery. If the court has done its job correctly, then all who are sentenced to face the same lottery, with the same odds, are equally guilty of equally grave crimes. They deserve equal treatment. Do they get it? Yes and no.

Yes. We treat them alike because we subject them all to the very same penal lottery, with the very same odds. And when the lots are drawn, we treat them alike again, because we follow the same predetermined contingency plan—death for losers, freedom for winners—for all of them alike.

No. Some of them are put to death, some are set free, and what could be more unequal than that?

Yes. Their fates are unequal, of course. But that is not our doing. They are treated unequally by Fortune, not by us.

No. But it is we who hand them over to the inequity of Fortune. We are Fortune's accomplices.

Yes. Everyone is exposed to the inequity of Fortune, in ever so many ways. However nice it may be to undo some of these inequities, we do not ordinarily think of this as part of what is required for equal treatment.

No. It's one thing not to go out of our way to undo the inequities of Fortune; it's another thing to go out of our way to increase them. This question would have to be reconsidered if something other than death were the maximum penalty, and so the penalty for losers of the lottery. It would remain an empirical question, and probably a difficult one, which is the more effective system of defense.

Yes. We do that too, and think it not at all contrary to equal treatment. When we hire astronauts, or soldiers or sailors or firemen or police, we knowingly subject these people to more of the inequities of Fortune than are found in ordinary life.

No. But the astronauts are volunteers . . .

Yes. And so are the criminals, when they commit the crimes for which they know they must face the lottery. The soldiers, however, sometimes are not.

No. Start over. We agreed that the winners and losers deserve equal punishment. That is because they are equally guilty. Then they deserve to suffer equally. But they do not.

Yes. They do not suffer equally; but if they deserve to, that is not our affair. We seldom think that equal punishment means making sure of equal suffering. Does the cheerful man get a longer prison sentence than the equally guilty morose man, to make sure of equal suffering? If one convict gets lung cancer in prison, do we see to it that the rest who are equally guilty suffer equally? When we punish equally, what we equalize is not the suffering itself. What we equalize is our contribution to expected suffering.

No. This all seems like grim sophistry. Surely, equal treatment has to mean more than just treating people so that some common description of what we are doing will apply to them all alike.

Yes. True. But we have made up our minds already, in other connections, that lotteries count as equal treatment, or near enough. When we have an indivisible benefit or burden to hand out (or even one that is divisible at a significant cost) we are very well content to resort to a lottery. We are satisfied that all who have equal chances are getting equal treatment—and not in some queer philosophers' sense, but in the sense that matters to justice.

It seems to me that "Yes" is winning this argument, but that truth and justice are still somehow on the side of "No." The next move, dear reader, is up to you. I shall leave it unsettled whether a penal lottery would be just. I shall move on to my second task, which is to show that our present practice amounts to a covert penal lottery. If the penal lottery is just, so is our present practice. If not, not.

V.

To show that they do not matter, I shall introduce the differences between an overt penal lottery and our present practice one at a time, by running through a sequence of cases. I claim that at no step is there any significant difference of justice between one case and the next. Such differences as there are will be practical advantages only, and will come out much in favor of our present practice.

Case 1 is the overt penal lottery as we have imagined it already, with one added stipulation, as follows. We will proportion the punishment to the heartedness of the attempt, as measured by the risk of death the criminal knowingly and wrongfully inflicted on the victim. We will do this by sentencing the criminal to a risk equal to the one he inflicted on the victim. If the criminal subjected his victim to an 80 percent risk of death, he shall draw his straw from a bundle of eight short and two long; whereas if he halfheartedly subjected the victim to a mere 40 percent risk, he shall draw from four short and six long; and in this way his punishment shall fit his crime. Therefore the court's task is not limited to ascertaining whether the defendant did knowingly and wrongfully subject the victim to a risk of death; also the court must ascertain how much of a risk it was.

Case 2 is like Case 1, except that we skip the dramatic ceremony on the steps of the gallows and draw straws ahead of time. In fact, we have the drawing even before the trial. It is not the defendant himself who draws, but the Public Drawer. The Drawer is sworn to secrecy; he reveals the outcome only when and if the defendant has been found guilty and sentenced to the lottery. If the defendant is acquitted and the drawing turns out to have been idle, no harm done. Since it is not known ahead of time whether the sentence will be eight and two, four and six, or what, the Drawer must make not one but many drawings ahead of time. He reveals the one, if any, that turns out to be called for.

Case 3 is like Case 2, except without the secrecy. The Drawer announces at once whether the defendant will win or lose in case he is found guilty and sentenced. (Or rather, whether he will win or lose if he is sentenced to eight and two, whether he will win or lose if he is sentenced to four and six, and so on.) This means that the suspense in the courtroom is higher on some occasions than others. But that need not matter, provided that the court can stick conscientiously to the task of ascertaining whether the defendant did knowingly and wrongfully subject the victim to risk, and if so how much risk. It is by declaring that a criminal deserves the lottery that the court expresses society's abhorrence of the crime. So the court's task is still worth doing, even when it is a foregone conclusion that the defendant will win the lottery if sentenced (as might happen if he had won all the alternative draws). But the trial may seem idle, and the expression of abhorrence may fall flat, when it is known all along that, come what may, the defendant will never face the lottery and lose.

Case 4 is like Case 3, except that we make the penal lottery less pure. Losers of the penal lottery get death, as before; winners get a short prison sentence. Therefore it is certain that every criminal who is sentenced to the lottery will suffer at least some penal harm. Thus we make sure that the trial and the sentence will be taken seriously even when it is a foregone conclusion that the defendant, if sentenced, will win the lottery.

Case 1 also was significantly impure. If the draw is held at the last minute, on the very steps of the gallows, then every criminal who is sentenced to face the lottery must spend a period of time—days? weeks? years?—in fear and trembling, and imprisoned, waiting to learn whether he will win or lose. This period of terror is a certain harm that falls on winners and losers alike. Case 2 very nearly eliminates the impurity, since there is no reason why the Drawer should not reveal the outcome very soon after the criminal is sentenced. Case 3 eliminates it entirely. (In every case, a defendant must spend a period in fear as he waits to learn whether he will be convicted. But this harm cannot count as penal, because it falls equally on the guilty and the innocent, on those who will be convicted and those who will be acquitted.) Case 4 restores impurity, to whatever extent we see fit, but in a different form.

Case 5 is like Case 4, except that the straws are replaced by a different chance device for determining the outcome of the lottery. The Public Drawer conducts an exact reenactment of the crime. If the victim in the reenactment dies, then the criminal loses the lottery. If it is a good reenactment, the risk to the original victim equals the risk to the new victim in the reenactment, which in turn equals the risk that the criminal will lose the lottery; and so, as desired, we punish a risk by an equal risk.

If the outcome of the lottery is to be settled before the trial, as in Cases 2, 3, and 4, then it will be necessary for the Drawer to conduct not just one but several reenactments. He will entertain all reasonable alternative hypotheses about exactly how the crime might have happened—exactly what the defendant might have done by way of knowingly and wrongfully inflicting risk on the victim. He will conduct one reenactment for each hypothesis. The court's task changes. If the court finds the defendant guilty of knowingly and wrongfully inflicting a risk of death, it is no longer required also to measure the amount of risk. Nobody need ever figure out whether it was 80 percent, 40 percent, or what. Instead, the court is required to ascertain which hypothesis about exactly how the crime happened is correct. Thereby the court chooses which of all the hypothetical reenactments is the one that determines whether the criminal wins or loses his lottery. If the court finds that the criminal took careful aim, then the chosen reenactment will be one in which the criminal's stand-in also took careful aim, whereas if the court finds that the criminal halfheartedly fired in the victim's general direction, the chosen reenactment will be one in which the stand-in did likewise. So the criminal will be more likely to lose his lottery in the first case than in the second.

The drawbacks of a lottery by reenactment are plain to see. Soon we shall find the remedy. But first, let us look at the advantages of a lottery by reenactment over a lottery by drawing straws. We have already noted that with straws, the court had to measure how much risk the criminal inflicted, whereas with reenactments, the court has only to ascertain exactly how the crime happened. Both tasks look well-nigh impossible. But the second must be easier, because the first task consists of the second plus more besides. The only way for the court to measure the risk would be to ascertain just what happened, and then find out just how much risk results from such happenings.

Another advantage of reenactments over straws appears when we try to be more careful about what we mean by "amount of risk." Is it (1) an "objective chance"? Or is it (2) a reasonable degree of belief for a hypothetical observer who knows the situation in as much minute detail as feasible instruments could permit? Or is it (3) a reasonable degree of belief for someone who knows just as much about the details of the situation as the criminal did? Or is it (4) the criminal's actual degree of belief, however unreasonable that might have been? It would be nice not to have to decide. But if we want to match the criminal's risk in a lottery by straws to the victim's risk, then we must decide. Not so for a lottery by reenactment. If the reenactment is perfect, we automatically match the amount of risk in all four senses. Even if the reenactment is imperfect, at least we can assure ourselves of match in senses (3) and (4). It may or may not be feasible to get assured match in senses (1) and (2), depending on the details of what happened. (If it turns out that the criminal left a bomb hooked up to a quantum randomizer, it will be comparatively easy. If he committed his crime in a more commonplace way, it will be much harder.) But whenever it is hard to get assured match in senses (1) and (2), it will be harder still to measure the risk and get assured match in a lottery by straws. So however the crime happened, and whatever sense of match we want, we do at least as well by reenactment as by straws, and sometimes we do better.

Case 6 is like Case 5, except that enactment replaces reenactment. We use the original crime, so to speak, as its own perfect reenactment. If the criminal is sentenced to face the lottery, then if his victim dies, he loses his lottery and he dies too, whereas if the victim lives, the criminal wins, and he gets only the short prison sentence. It does not matter when the lottery takes place, provided only that it is not settled so soon that the criminal may know its outcome before he decides whether to commit his crime.

The advantages are many: we need no Drawer to do the work; we need not find volunteers to be the stand-in victims in all the hypothetical reenactments; the "reenactment" is automatically perfect, matching the risk in all four senses; we spare the court the difficult task of ascertaining exactly how the crime happened. If we want to give a risk for a risk, and if we want to match risks in any but a very approximate and uncertain fashion, the lottery by enactment is not only the easy way, it is the only remotely feasible way.

The drawback is confusion. When a criminal is sentenced to face the lottery by straws, nobody will think him more guilty or more wicked just because his straw is short. And when a criminal is sentenced to face the lottery by reenactment, nobody will think him more guilty just because the stand-in victim dies. But if he is sentenced to the lottery by enactment, then one and the same event plays a double role: if his victim dies, that death is at once the main harm done by his crime and also the way of losing his lottery. If we are not careful, we are apt to misunderstand. We may think that the successful attempter suffers a worse fate because he is more guilty when he does a worse harm, rather than because he loses his lottery. But it is not so: his success is irrelevant to his guilt, his wicked-ness, his desert, and his sentence to face the lottery—exactly as the shortness of his straw would have been, had he been sentenced to the lottery by straws.

VI.

I submit that our present practice is exactly Case 6: punishment for attempts regardless of success, a penal lottery by enactment, impurity to help us take the affair seriously even when the lottery is won, and the inevitable confusion. We may not understand our practice as a penal lottery—confused as we are, we have trouble understanding it at all—but, so understood, it does make a good deal of sense. It is another question whether it is really just. Most likely it isn't, but I don't understand why not.

Notes and Questions

1. The criminal justice system is certainly hard-wired to punish acts causing harms more severely than the same acts when they do not cause harm. Think back to Justice Stevens' opinion in *Dean*. Stevens criticized the majority for imposing "a species of criminal liability . . . for an accident *that caused no harm.*" In a number of areas, in addition to those identified by Chief Justice Roberts, in the criminal justice system is willing to consider the harm a defendant caused. In capital cases, for instance, the prosecution is permitted to introduce evidence on how the victim's death affected the victim's family. *See Payne v. Tennessee*, 501 U.S. 808 (1991).

2. Lewis starts with an assumption that punishment based on harm caused is unjust if done to satisfy society's desire for greater punishment for harm caused. Do you accept his premise?

---

4. Causation

When a harmful result is required as an element of a crime, the harmful result must have been caused by the defendant's conduct. Just as the Lewis article raised an excellent question about the legitimacy of punishing a defendant differently because his criminal act produced a harmful result, the *Rose* case raises a similar and very difficult question. Should the defendant's punishment be different merely because his criminal conduct, which certainly *could* have produced the harmful result, happened not to have caused the result?

State v. Rose

Supreme Court of Rhode Island
311 A.2d 281 (1973)

ROBERTS, Chief Justice.

These are two indictments, one (No. 70-573) charging the defendant, Henry Rose, with leaving the scene of an accident, death resulting, in violation of G.L.1956 (1968 Reenactment) § 31-26-1[1] and the other (No. 70-572) charging the defendant with manslaughter. The defendant was tried on both indictments to a jury in the Superior Court, and a verdict of guilty was returned in each case. Thereafter the defendant's motions for a new trial were denied, and he is now prosecuting a bill of exceptions in each case in this court.

These indictments followed the death of David J. McEnery, who was struck by defendant's motor vehicle at the intersection of Broad and Summer Streets in Providence at about 6:30 p.m. on April 1, 1970. According to the testimony of a bus driver, he had been operating his vehicle north on Broad Street and had stopped at a traffic light at the intersection of Summer Street. While the bus was standing there, he observed a pedestrian starting to cross Broad Street, and as the pedestrian reached the middle of the southbound lane he was struck by a 'dirty, white station wagon' that was proceeding southerly on Broad Street. The pedestrian's body was thrown up on the hood of the car. The bus driver further testified that the station wagon stopped momentarily, the body of the pedestrian rolled off the hood, and the car immediately drove off along Broad Street in a southerly direction. The bus operator testified that he had alighted from his bus, intending to attempt to assist the victim, but was unable to locate the body.

Subsequently, it appears from the testimony of a police officer, about 6:40 p.m. the police located a white station wagon on Haskins Street, a distance of some 610 feet from the scene of the accident. The police further testified that a

---

1   General Laws 1956 (1968 Reenactment) § 31-26-1 reads, in part, as follows: 'Duty to stop in accidents resulting in personal injury. (a) The driver of any vehicle knowingly involved in an accident resulting in injury to or death of any person shall immediately stop such vehicle at the scene of such accident or as close thereto as possible but shall then forthwith return to and in every event shall remain at the scene of the accident until he has fulfilled the requirements of § 31-26-3. Every such stop shall be made without obstructing traffic more than is necessary. * * *'

body later identified as that of David J. McEnery was wedged beneath the vehicle when it was found and that the vehicle had been registered to defendant.

Testifying on behalf of the state was a Robert Buckley, who stated that he had worked with defendant and that about 5 p.m. on the day of the accident he had gone to a place located in Central Falls that he identified as The Palms where he met defendant about 5:15 p.m. Buckley further testified that about 7 p.m. that evening defendant phoned him, told him that he had been involved in an accident, and asked Buckley to help him look for his car. According to Buckley, he picked up defendant's girl friend, identified as Pat, and went to the vicinity of the accident and drove around for some time but was unable to locate the car.

Buckley testified that later he picked up defendant, who asked him to take him to a cafe in Central Falls known as The Well, where he would attempt to establish an alibi. After arriving at The Well, defendant asked Buckley to take him to the Central Falls police station, where defendant reported that his car had been stolen from in front of The Well sometime between 5:30 p.m. and 9 p.m. on that day. Buckley later drove defendant to Pat's home, and while there defendant answered a telephone call. After the telephone call had been completed, defendant told Buckley that 'a guy had been killed.' According to Buckley, defendant was denying it on the 'phone' during the conversation.

We turn, first, to defendant's contention that the trial court erred in denying his motion for a directed verdict of acquittal in each case. . . .

* * *

The defendant is contending that if the evidence is susceptible of a finding that McEnery was killed upon impact, he was not alive at the time he was being dragged under defendant's vehicle and defendant could not be found guilty of manslaughter. An examination of the testimony of the only medical witness makes it clear that, in his opinion, death could have resulted immediately upon impact by reason of a massive fracture of the skull. The medical witness also testified that death could have resulted a few minutes after the impact but conceded that he was not sure when it did occur.

We are inclined to agree with defendant's contention in this respect. Obviously, the evidence is such that death could have occurred after defendant had driven away with McEnery's body lodged under his car and, therefore, be consistent with guilt. On the other hand, the medical testimony is equally consistent with a finding that McEnery could have died instantly upon impact and, therefore, be consistent with a reasonable conclusion other than the guilt of defendant. It is clear, then, that, the testimony of the medical examiner lacking any reasonable medical certainty as to the time of the death of McEnery, we are unable to conclude that on such evidence defendant was guilty of manslaughter beyond a reasonable doubt. Therefore, we conclude, with respect to Indictment No. 70-572, that it was error to deny defendant's motion for a directed verdict of acquittal. *See State v. Dancyger*, supra.

We are unable, however, to reach the same conclusion concerning the denial of the motion for a directed verdict of acquittal with respect to Indictment No. 70-573, in which defendant was charged with leaving the scene of an accident. The testimony adduced through the bus driver clearly establishes that at the time McEnery was struck his body was thrown up on the hood of the car and that while the car was standing still the body rolled off the hood and thereupon defendant drove off in a southerly direction. Later, the police found defendant's station wagon on a side street some 610 feet from the point of impact with McEnery's body wedged under the front of the car. The circumstances here are clearly consistent with a hypothesis of guilt, but it is clear that they are not consistent with any other reasonable hypothesis. We conclude, therefore, with respect to Indictment No. 70-573, that the trial court did not err in denying the motion for a directed verdict.

Because we conclude that the trial court erred in denying defendant's motion for a directed verdict of acquittal in the case charging him with manslaughter, it is unnecessary for us to consider his contentions of error concerning his motion for a new trial in that case.

Notes and Questions

1. Notice that this homicide case turns on the prosecutor's ability to prove that the victim had a pulse after he initially collided with the defendant's car. Even if the victim would have ultimately died, if being dragged under the defendant's car hastened his death, then the defendant is guilty of homicide. Otherwise, under the facts of this case, the defendant is guilty of nothing, though the facts leave an inference that the defendant was probably intoxicated at the time of the initial impact, a fact that the prosecution appeared to be unable to prove. Regardless, defendant dragged a man he knew he had struck with car for a distance of 610 feet beneath his car. Does it make sense for a substantial amount of punishment to turn on whether there was a pulse—or more precisely whether the prosecution can prove that the victim had a pulse—immediately after the impact?

2. Henry Rose is a lousy human being. He had utter indifference to the life of David Mcenery but may have killed him on impact without any culpability for this act. Draft a statute that would punish Rose's reprehensible conduct regardless of when death occurred.

---

5. Crimes Not (Yet) Involving Harm or Forbidden Conduct

Some offenses do not involve results; they punish only conduct. Drug possession is such a crime. Other offenses punish efforts to achieve prohibited results or engage in unlawful conduct. These crimes punish attempts and agreements to achieve unlawful goals as well as requests that others commit crimes. These crimes—attempt, conspiracy, and solicitation—apply to efforts to achieve any crime, with sentences varying depending on the crime the defendant sought to achieve. Other crimes have similar characteristics, punishing specific acts that come close to achieving harm. Burglary and possession of drugs with the intent to distribute are examples. Each is punished for the efforts the defendant took toward achieving a dangerous and forbidden end. Professor Ira Robbins' *Double Inchoate Crimes*, an excerpt of which is provided below, describes these crimes. Examples of each of these theories of liability will be provided in context as various types of crimes are described. Robbins' article, however, provides a nice introduction to various type of liability for crimes not involving harm.

IRA P. ROBBINS

Double Inchoate Crimes

26 Harvard Journal on Legislation 1 (1989)

Inchoate—or anticipatory or relational—crimes allow the judicial system to impose criminal liability on conduct designed to culminate in the commission of a substantive offense. The inchoate offenses of attempt and solicitation, for example, provide the legal basis for courts to punish the actor who has performed every act necessary to effect his criminal design, but has failed to achieve the prohibited result due to an intervening fortuity. More importantly, however, attempt and other inchoate offenses allow law-enforcement officials to prevent the consummation of substantive offenses by permitting intervention once an individual's actions, though not criminal in themselves, have sufficiently manifested an intent to commit a criminal act.

Like a completed offense, an inchoate offense requires both a mens rea and an actus reus. Unlike the actus reus in a completed offense, however, the proscribed act in an anticipatory crime is not prohibited because of its harmful effect, but because it demonstrates a firm purpose on the part of an individual to act in furtherance of a criminal intent. The mens rea for inchoate crimes, therefore, is the specific intent to commit a particular completed offense, or target or object crime. A central premise of Anglo-American criminal jurisprudence is that a court may not punish a bad intent that is not accompanied by a bad act. Nevertheless, inchoate crimes focus on the mens rea and render ancillary the actus reus to realize the predictive and preventive purposes of the criminal law.

The three main formulations of inchoate liability are attempt, conspiracy, and solicitation. The treatment of these concepts as substantive offenses, distinct from the completed offenses that are their objects, is of comparatively late origin. Each of the three had its beginning in the authority of common-law courts to create offenses. Despite the independent origins and development of the three offenses, conspiracy and solicitation can be viewed as early stages of an attempt to commit a completed offense. Further, specific substantive crimes such as assault and burglary have inchoate aspects and can therefore be viewed as crimes in the nature of attempt.

A. Attempt

Although the law of attempt has roots in the early English law, its formulation as a general substantive offense is a relatively recent development. Generally, the elements of attempt are: (1) the intent to commit the completed crime; (2) the performance of some step, usually a substantial one, toward its commission; and (3) the failure to consummate the substantive crime. Many American jurisdictions now make specific provisions for the punishment of attempts to commit certain offenses, and almost all cover the rest of the field with a general attempt statute. With few exceptions, these general statutes cover attempts to commit any felony or misdemeanor.

Among modern American jurisdictions, some statutes provide that failure is an element of the offense. Further, the rule of merger operates only to the extent that a defendant cannot be convicted of both a completed offense and an attempt to commit it. All jurisdictions treat attempt as a lesser included offense of the completed crime. Moreover, many jurisdictions have held that a defendant may be convicted of the attempt if the state proves the completed crime, and several states so provide by statute.

The distinction in attempt law between attempt and preparation reflects the notion that the act on which liability is based must sufficiently manifest criminal intent. The standards developed by courts and criminal-law experts to determine the sufficiency of an act for attempt liability reflect the developing rationales that are unique to anticipatory crimes. The principal purpose behind punishing an attempt, unlike that of a completed crime, is not deterrence. The threat posed by the sanction for an attempt is unlikely to deter a person willing to risk the penalty for the object crime. Instead, the primary function of the crime of attempt is to provide a basis for law-enforcement officers to intervene before an individual can commit a completed offense. A secondary function is to punish those who have carried out their criminal scheme but have failed to effect the harmful result due to the intervention of external physical circumstances, including on-the-spot prevention.

The first case to distinguish attempt and preparation, *Regina v. Eagleton* [,169 Eng. Rep 826 (Crim. App. 1855)] introduced a 'last proximate act' standard for determining the actus reus of attempt. Under this approach, an actor is not liable for attempt unless he has done all that he intends to do to accomplish the target crime. For example, a would-be murderer commits the last proximate act when he shoots at his intended victim. Courts since *Eagleton* uniformly have rejected the last-proximate-act standard in favor of standards that give police a margin of safety by allowing them to intervene after an actor's criminal intent becomes sufficiently apparent.

The two basic standards developed since *Eagleton* reflect different rationales behind criminalizing attempt. The first, a 'proximity' standard, focuses on the *dangerousness of the actor's conduct* and emphasizes what steps remain for him to take to complete the object crime. The second, and more recent development, an 'equivocality' standard, focuses on the *dangerousness of the actor himself* and emphasizes what the actor has already done in imputing criminal intent to his actions.

The Model Penal Code has incorporated the equivocality standard in its definition of an attempt as 'an act or omission constituting a *substantial step* in a course of conduct planned to culminate in commission of the crime.' The Code goes on to define certain preparatory acts as substantial steps that may be 'strongly corroborative of an actor's criminal purpose.' Because it does not consider proximity to the actus reus of the object crime, the Model Penal Code's approach effectively draws the line between attempt and preparation further back in the continuum of preparatory acts leading to culmination of the object offense. The Code's subjective approach also comes closer to punishing evil intent alone, but seeks to mitigate this criticism by defining substantial step—the actus reus—in terms of acts that constitute necessary elements of specific offenses. The acts from which the Code allows factfinders to infer wrongful intent and a resolute purpose to realize that intent, however, include acts not necessarily unlawful in themselves.

B. Crimes in the Nature of Attempt

Prosecution for the substantive crime of attempt is just one means by which the criminal law can reach conduct that merely tends toward the commission of a completed offense. Several other substantive crimes also have major inchoate elements. These include assault and burglary, which originally dealt with the most common forms of attempt prior to recognition of attempt as a discrete substantive offense, and the category of offenses prohibiting possession of materials that the actor would be likely to use to commit a crime.

1. Assault

At common law, a criminal assault was defined as an attempt, combined with present ability, to commit a battery. Any criminal assault was a misdemeanor. Because the law of assault crystallized before the law of attempt, the element of present ability requires an act with closer proximity to the completed act—the causing of bodily injury contemplated by battery—than does an attempt. Nevertheless, many courts and commentators have contended that, because assault is itself an attempt to commit a battery, the crime of attempted assault cannot exist.

Currently, a few American jurisdictions define assault as an attempt to commit a battery or to produce bodily harm, while several more add to this definition the requirement that the actor have a present ability to commit the battery. A majority of states have weakened the inchoate aspect of assault by defining it in the alternative as an unlawful act that places another in reasonable apprehension of an immediate battery. This adjunctive definition not only broadens the concept of criminal assault to include aspects of assault's definition in tort, but also treats assault as a substantive offense with a different mental element than battery—an intent to put another in apprehension of a battery, rather than an intent to commit a battery. In addition, an increasing number of states, following the Model Penal Code, have entirely eliminated the inchoate aspect of assault by redefining assault to constitute the completed offense of battery.

All of the states retaining the traditional definitions of assault have expanded the concept statutorily by codifying so-called 'aggravated assaults' as distinct felony offenses. The aggravating circumstance that justifies the more serious punishment usually includes a grievous intent in the mind of the assailant, such as in assault with intent to kill, or suggests a dangerous means of perpetration, such as in assault with a deadly weapon. Some states have also enacted general aggravated-assault statutes that penalize an assault to commit any felony not otherwise provided for by statute. Consequently, an assault with intent to commit a particular crime is the same as an attempt to commit that crime, except that the former requires a greater degree of proximity.

2. Burglary

At common law, burglary was defined as the breaking and entering into the dwelling house of another at night with the intent to commit a felony therein. The common law classified burglary, with arson, as a crime against habitation rather than as a crime against property. The distinction reflected the greater likelihood of violence incident to burglary, and justified treating the offense as a felony. Likewise, the importance the common-law courts accorded the security of the home and the increased chance of violence to the dwelling's inhabitants, as well as the undeveloped state of attempt law, justified imposing liability on an actor before he completed the intended felony.

Burglary at common law was but a form of attempt, in which the required elements merely constituted a step taken toward the commission of some other offense. Statutory revision of the elements of burglary, however, has resulted in an offense even more similar to attempt. Burglary is no longer limited to dwellings, but in most jurisdictions embraces any structure, including uninhabited buildings, tents, boats, cars, and even motorcycles. Most jurisdictions have abolished the requirements of breaking and of committing the offense under cover of the night. Also, most jurisdictions have diluted the specific intent requirement by expanding the scope of the object offense to include all crimes, rather than only felonies. The modern law of burglary thus aims to protect not only persons in their dwellings, but also people and property within any structure.

Burglary is distinguished from attempt in that it is not subject to the rule of merger. An actor who makes an unprivileged entry into a structure and commits a crime therein is criminally liable for both the completed offense and the burglary. Thus, the crime of burglary allows punishment for the offense committed and also for the attempt to commit it in a particular manner—by making an unprivileged entry. Compounded liability is imposed to punish both aspects of intent in burglary: (1) the intent to make an unlawful entry; and (2) the added mental element of intent to commit another offense within the violated structure.

3. Constituent-Element Crimes

Many modern criminal codes include offenses defined in terms of conduct in itself arguably harmless, but still penalized because it very likely constitutes a step towards the harm punished by a completed offense. These crimes include the possessory offenses—such as possession of burglars' tools, possession of a forged instrument with intent to issue or use it, possession of narcotics with intent to distribute them, possession of an instrument adapted for the use of narcotics by subcutaneous injection, possession of a weapon with intent to use it against another unlawfully, and possession of explosives with intent to use them in committing an offense.

The rationale behind punishing these offenses is that it is improbable that an individual would possess such materials unless he intended to use them to commit a specific crime. To a large extent, the law imputes an intent to commit a completed crime to the mere act of possession. For example, most statutes penalizing possession of narcotics with intent to distribute erect a legal presumption that the added mental element exists if the defendant was holding a certain controlled substance or more than a specified quantity of the controlled substance. Also, in some jurisdictions, the possession of a controlled firearm such as a sawed-off shotgun or an automatic weapon raises a presumption that the possessor intended to use if for an unlawful purpose.

In addition to possessory crimes, some jurisdictions punish conduct that constitutes only part of the conduct required by a specific completed offense. These substantive offenses are defined in terms of using certain items for a particular purpose, offering to perform an illegal act, attracting an intended victim, or being in a certain place for a bad purpose. This category of offenses shares with the Model Penal Code's definition of attempt the underlying purpose of punishing an actor for those acts that he has already committed, rather than the proximity of his acts to a completed offense. As with the Code's definition of attempt, 'these statutes reach conduct that is merely preparatory' as measured by traditional proximity standards and, therefore, 'is not encompassed within most jurisdictions' general law of attempts.'

C. Conspiracy

The modern concept of conspiracy as a separate substantive crime originated in the seventeenth-century English courts. The common law defined conspiracy as a combination of two or more persons to perform an unlawful act or a lawful act by unlawful means. Like burglary, the mental element of conspiracy has a dual aspect: (1) an intent to agree to commit an offense; and (2) the added mental element of an intent to commit a specific target crime. Also as with burglary, the common law does not generally merge the conspiracy into the target offense if both are successfully completed. Rather, both the common and statutory law of conspiracy allow the compounding of penalties for conspiracy and its realized object offense. Statutory revision of the offense produced a hierarchy of penalties comparable in relative magnitude to the object crimes. Although some statutes require only the act of agreement, most jurisdictions require an overt act in furtherance of the conspiracy. The common law and many modern statutes require the agreement of two or more parties to constitute the actus reus of conspiracy.

The Model Penal Code and many jurisdictions, however, have adopted the notion of *unilateral* conspiracy. This concept limits the defense of impossibility to agree by holding liable any party who believes he has consummated an agreement, even though the other party is incapable of committing the crime, immune to prosecution for it, or only pretending to go along with the importuning party's scheme.

Like burglary, the purpose behind the substantive offense of conspiracy is twofold: (1) preventing a completed offense; and (2) punishing a special danger. While burglary focuses on the violence incident to breach of the dwelling, conspiracy focuses on the additional dangers inherent in group activity. In theory, once an individual reaches an agreement with one or more persons to perform an unlawful act, it becomes more likely that the individual will feel a greater commitment to carry out his original intent, providing a heightened group danger.

As an inchoate crime, conspiracy allows law-enforcement officials to intervene at a stage far earlier than attempt does. To obtain an attempt conviction, the prosecutor must prove that the actor performed an act beyond mere preparation or took a substantial step toward committing a completed crime. To obtain a conspiracy conviction, however, the prosecutor need only prove that the conspirators agreed to undertake a criminal scheme or, at most, that they took an overt step in pursuance of the conspiracy. Even an insignificant act may suffice.

D. Solicitation

Solicitation, or incitement, is the act of trying to persuade another to commit a crime that the solicitor desires and intends to have committed. The mens rea of solicitation is a specific intent to have someone commit a completed crime. As in common-law conspiracy, disclosure of the criminal scheme to another party constitutes a part of the actus reus of solicitation. But, while the actus reus of a conspiracy is an agreement with another to commit a specific completed offense, the actus reus of a solicitation includes an attempt to persuade another to commit a specific offense. A necessary element of solicitation is the solicitant's rejection of the solicitor's request. Thus, solicitation can be viewed as an attempt to conspire.

The view that the judicial system should punish one who unsuccessfully solicits another by reason of the solicitation itself is a recent development in criminal jurisprudence. Viewed solely as an inchoate offense, solicitation appears to impose criminal liability on an act that presents no significant social danger, and approaches punishing evil intent alone. Penalties for solicitation allow the judiciary to punish conduct far back on the continuum of acts leading to a completed crime—conduct that constitutes 'mere preparation' by attempt standards.

The rationale for the substantive offense of solicitation is that, like conspiracy, it treats the special hazards posed by potential concerted criminal activity. As with conspiracy, the special-danger rationale modifies the standards of attempt to place liability at a far earlier stage than in an attempt. The act of revealing the criminal scheme to another extends beyond mere preparation because the act is so unequivocal as to make evident the solicitor's criminal intent.

Solicitation developed as a common-law notion, but American jurisdictions increasingly have defined the offense statutorily. Unlike the common law, which generally and vaguely described the object crimes that solicitation covered as those that breached the public peace, current state statutes define the offense's coverage to restrict judicial discretion. Most states impose penalties for soliciting the commission of any crime, but some states and the federal government apply solicitation only to felonies. Others specifically enumerate the particular object felonies subject to solicitation charges.

The Model Penal Code's solicitation provisions broaden the scope of solicitation statutes to reach more behavior, in three ways. First, the Code imposes liability for the solicitation of any crime. Second, the Code incorporates the double inchoate offense of attempt to solicit by making the solicitor's failure to communicate the criminal scheme immaterial as long as he acted on his intent to effect such communication. Third, the Code defines the actus reus of solicitation as acting 'with the purpose of promoting or facilitating' the commission of a crime. This language incorporates the crime of facilitation into the solicitation provision. Facilitation, viewed as both a lower level of complicity and as an inchoate crime, punishes the individual who knowingly provides assistance to another who intends to commit a crime.

The Code's solicitation provisions appear to have influenced some states to penalize solicitation as harshly or almost as harshly as the completed object crime. The common-law courts traditionally treated solicitation as a less serious offense than the object crime or an attempt to commit it. Most states with solicitation statutes continue this pattern by providing penalties either less stringent than those for attempt or one grade lower than the range of sanctions for the object crime. Several states, however, following the Model Penal Code, have enacted penalties for solicitation that correspond to the most serious offense solicited.

---

6. Liability for the Crimes of Others

One final type of liability needs to be addressed in this introduction to the elements of crimes. A defendant can become liable for the crimes of another when he agrees, assists, encourages, or entices another to commit the crime. This type of liability is different from conspiracy, which was discussed in the previous section. Conspiracy is an agreement to commit a crime and is punished separately (and most often less severely) than the crime itself. One who aids, assists or encourages another to commit a crime, in the eyes of the law, is no different from the person who commits the crime.

There is no uniform standard on the *mens rea* required to be liable under a complicity theory. The difference is not just a matter of judicial interpretation, though courts facing similar statutory language have certainly arrived at differing standards. Some states require that the defendant intend a result to be guilty of complicity. A number of others require only intent for crimes requiring intent, but permit complicity liability whenever the aiding defendant shares the culpability of the principal actor.

Perhaps even more significantly, if A encourages B to commit a crime, A is liable not only for the crime he encouraged B to commit, but also in many jurisdictions for all the crimes B commits that are the "natural and probable consequences" of the crime A encouraged. This doctrine holding a defendant responsible for the natural and probable consequences of the acts he encourages has been sharply criticized, but remains in the majority of jurisdictions. The *Carson* case offers the majority rule on the doctrine of natural and probable consequences while the *Sharma* case offers the minority view. Given the significance of the doctrine of natural and probable consequences, it is interesting that the question of whether a state embraces the doctrine is largely left to courts—and as you will see, courts have very different views about the whether the doctrine should exist.

State v. Carson

Supreme Court of Tennessee
950 S.W.2d 951 (1997)

ANDERSON, Justice.

The issue presented by this appeal is whether the defendant, who assisted his co-defendants in committing an aggravated robbery, was criminally responsible under Tenn.Code Ann. § 39–11–402(2) for additional offenses committed by them.

The defendant, who planned the store robbery, furnished guns and inside information to his co-defendants but waited in the car outside the store, was convicted of aggravated robbery, aggravated assault, and felony reckless endangerment.[1] The Court of Criminal Appeals affirmed the convictions, finding that the defendant was criminally responsible for the acts of his co-defendants.

---

1   The defendant, a Range III persistent offender, was sentenced to 30 years for the aggravated robbery, 15 years for each of the aggravated assaults, and 6 years for the reckless endangerment. The sentences for aggravated assault are to run concurrently; the sentences for the remaining offenses are to run consecutively, for an effective term of 51 years in the Department of Correction.

After reviewing the applicable law and the evidence, we conclude that the defendant was criminally responsible for the acts of his co-defendants under Tenn.Code Ann. § 39–11–402(2) because, in our view, the common law rule (that a defendant who aids and abets a co-defendant in the commission of a criminal act is liable not only for that crime but also for any other crime committed by the co-defendant as a natural and probable consequence of the crime originally aided and abetted) is applicable under the statute. We therefore affirm the judgment of the Court of Criminal Appeals.

BACKGROUND

The defendant, Jubal Carson, and two co-defendants, Aaron Gary and Alton Stover, met to discuss robbing "Jim and Dave's TV Repair" store in Knoxville, Tennessee. Carson, who had been in the store before, described the layout of the store to the co-defendants and told them that a large sum of money could be found in a drawer in a back room. Carson gave a handgun to each of the co-defendants and the three men drove to the scene. While Carson waited in the car, Gary and Stover entered the store under the pretense of having repairs made to a portable stereo system.

Once inside the store, the co-defendants held two employees, James Adams and Dave McGaha, at gunpoint and forced them into a room in the rear of the building. Both employees were searched and $130 was taken from Adams. Adams and McGaha were ordered onto a couch while Gary and Stover searched the room. After binding Adams and McGaha with telephone cord, Gary and Stover closed the office door, told the victims not to attempt to free themselves, and then fired three shots through the office door, narrowly missing them. As they left the store, Gary and Stover were confronted by police officers. To their surprise, neither the car, nor the defendant Carson, was in the parking lot. Gary and Stover fled from the scene on foot, exchanging gunfire with officers. All three men were later found and arrested.

The lightning quick police response to the robbery was apparent later. Carson and his co-defendants did not realize that "Jim and Dave's TV Repair" store was an undercover sting operation run by the Knoxville Police Department. Unbeknownst to them, the co-defendants' actions were monitored by police officers and recorded on video tape located in the store.

The defendant Carson was charged, along with his co-defendants Gary and Stover. The co-defendants pled guilty and testified at trial against the defendant.[2] Carson did not testify; however, he made a statement to police admitting that he drove the co-defendants to the scene but denying that he knew a robbery would

---

2 Gary pled guilty to attempted first-degree murder and was sentenced to 23 years. Stover pled guilty to aggravated kidnapping and was sentenced to 21 years.

occur. He said he believed the co-defendants were going to the store to sell the guns and that he was across the street from the store at a Hardee's restaurant when he heard shots being fired.

The jury found the defendant Carson guilty of aggravated robbery, aggravated assault against Adams, aggravated assault against McGaha, and felony reckless endangerment.[3] The Court of Criminal Appeals affirmed.

The defendant argues on appeal that the evidence was insufficient to sustain the convictions because he lacked the culpable mental state for the offenses committed by Gary and Stover. The State insists that the defendant was criminally responsible for the aggravated robbery, as well as the additional offenses, because they were a natural and probable consequence of the robbery.

We granted this appeal to determine the scope of criminal responsibility for the acts of another under Tenn.Code Ann. §§ 39–11–401 and –402.

CRIMINAL RESPONSIBILITY

As part of the Criminal Sentencing Reform Act of 1989, the Legislature determined that "a person is criminally responsible as a party to an offense if the offense is committed . . . by the conduct of another for which the person is criminally responsible," and that a person is criminally responsible for an offense committed by another if "acting with intent to promote or assist the commission of the offense, or to benefit in the proceeds or results of the offense, the person solicits, directs, aids, or attempts to aid another person to commit the offense. . . ." Tenn.Code Ann. §§ 39–11–401 and –402(2)(1991).

The Sentencing Commission comments to Tenn.Code Ann. § 39–11–401 explain that the statute

> is a restatement of the principles of Tennessee common law which provide equal criminal liability for principals, accessories before the fact, and aiders and abettors. The revised code does not utilize these terms; instead, it provides that any person may be charged as a party if he or she is criminally responsible for the perpetration of the offense. (Emphasis added).

Similarly, the Commission comments to Tenn.Code Ann. § 39–11–402(2) indicate that this portion of the statute sets forth the conduct of defendants formerly known as accessories before the fact and aiders and abettors.

The Criminal Sentencing Reform Act of 1989 also provides that the foregoing statutes "be construed according to the fair import of their terms, including reference to judicial decisions and common law interpretations, to promote justice, and effect the objectives of the criminal code." *See* Tenn.Code Ann. § 39–11–

---

3 The jury also convicted the defendant of aggravated kidnapping, which the trial court set aside post-trial under *State v. Anthony*, 817 S.W.2d 299 (Tenn.1991).

104. The Sentencing Commission comments to the statute explain the legislative intent as follows:

> The commission intends the language of the sections themselves to be an authoritative statement of the law. Since some of the terms utilized have been clearly defined by judicial decisions, those decisions and common law interpretations should be consulted where necessary. . . . The comments in this code are intended to explain its provisions and to aid in their interpretation.

Accordingly, it is evident that Tenn.Code Ann. § 39–11–402(2), which states that one may be criminally responsible if he or she "solicits, directs, aids or attempts to aid another person to commit [an] offense," is derived from common law. An aider and abettor, for instance (sometimes referred to as a principal in the second degree), was one who advised, counseled, procured, or encouraged the principal to commit the offense and was present at the scene of the crime. *Flippen v. State*, 211 Tenn. 507, 365 S.W.2d 895 (1963). The common law requirement that the defendant be present at the scene included "constructive" presence, which

> does not require a strict, actual, immediate presence, such a presence as would make him an eye or ear witness of what occurs, for if the abettor, at the time of the commission of the crime, were assenting to it, and in a situation where he might render some aid to the perpetrator, ready to give it if necessary, according to an appointment or agreement with him for that purpose, he would, in the judgment of the law, be present and aiding in the commission of the crime. . . .

Cavert v. State, 158 Tenn. 531, 14 S.W.2d 735, 738 (1929).

Criminal responsibility for another under Tenn.Code Ann. § 39–11–402(2) also requires that a defendant act with a culpable mental state, specifically, the "intent to promote or assist the commission of the offense or to benefit in the proceeds or results of the offense." A person acts with intent as to the nature or result of conduct when it is that person's conscious objective or desire to engage in the conduct or cause the result. Tenn.Code Ann. § 39–11–302(a)(1991); *see also State v. Maxey*, 898 S.W.2d 756, 757 (Tenn.Crim.App.1994). This statutory language is also similar to common law:

> In order to aid and abet another to commit a crime, it is necessary that [the] accused in some sort associate himself with the venture, act with knowledge that an offense is to be committed, and share in the criminal intent of the principal in the first degree; the same criminal intent must exist in the minds of both.

See Jenkins v. State, 509 S.W.2d 240, 245 (Tenn.Crim.App.1974). In other words, under common law, a defendant "must knowingly, voluntarily, and with common intent unite with the principal offenders in the commission of the crime." *State v. Foster*, 755 S.W.2d 846, 848 (Tenn.Crim.App.1988).

Although not specifically addressed in the statute, the scope of criminal responsibility for accessories before the fact and aiders and abettors under the common law was addressed by this Court in *Key v. State*, 563 S.W.2d 184, 186 (Tenn.1978). The *Key* court stated the general common law rule as follows:

> The common purpose need not be to commit the particular crime which is committed; if two persons join in a purpose to commit a crime, each of them, if actually or constructively present, is not only guilty as a principal, if the other commits that particular crime, *but he is also guilty of any other crime committed by the other in pursuance of the common purpose, or as a natural or probable consequence thereof.* (Emphasis added).

This common law principle was illustrated in the later Tennessee case of *State v. Grooms*, 653 S.W.2d 271 (Tenn.Crim.App.1983). The female defendant and two armed co-defendants carried out the robbery of a pharmacy by forcing employees and customers into a back room, where they bound and robbed them. During the robbery, two additional customers entered the store who were shot by a co-defendant. As the defendant and co-defendants fled the scene, one of the co-defendants fired shots at the pursuing officers. The defendant was convicted of armed robbery, assault, and assault with intent to murder. In affirming the convictions, the Court of Criminal Appeals said:

> The crimes of which defendant says that she had no intent, were all committed as a part of the common purpose of committing these robberies at the drugstore and effecting an escape. Although she may not have had the particular intent to commit some of these offenses, *they were natural and probable consequences of the common purposes of robbery with firearms. Id.,* at 275 (emphasis added).

The "natural and probable consequence" rule has been widely accepted and applied by other jurisdictions.[4] It is based on the recognition that "aiders and

---

4   *See e.g., United States v. Andrews,* 75 F.3d 552, 556 (9th Cir.), *cert. denied,* 517 U.S. 1239, 116 S.Ct. 1890, 135 L.Ed.2d 183 (1996); *United States v. Powell,* 929 F.2d 724, 726 (D.C.Cir.1991); *Roy v. United States,* 652 A.2d 1098, 1105 (D.C.App.1995); *State v. Trackwell,* 235 Neb. 845, 458 N.W.2d 181, 184 (1990); *Sheppard v. State,* 312 Md. 118, 538 A.2d 773, 774 (1988); *State v. Linscott,* 520 A.2d 1067, 1069 (Me.1987); *State v. Marchesano,* 162 Ariz. 308, 783 P.2d 247, 253 (App.1989); *Karlos v. State,* 476 N.E.2d 819, 822 (Ind.1985); *State v. Ivy,* 119 Wis.2d 591, 350 N.W.2d 622, 628 (1984); *People v. Kessler,* 57 Ill.2d 493, 315 N.E.2d 29, 32, *cert. denied,* 419 U.S. 1054, 95 S.Ct. 635, 42 L.Ed.2d 650 (1974).

abettors should be responsible for the criminal harms they have naturally, probably and foreseeably put in motion."

The California Supreme Court has expressed it this way: "[A] person who aids and abets a confederate in the commission of a criminal act is liable not only for that crime (the target crime), but also for any other offense (nontarget crime) committed by the confederate as a 'natural and probable consequence' of the crime originally aided and abetted." The rule frequently has been applied to offenses that are a natural and probable consequence of a planned armed robbery. *People v. Prettyman*, 14 Cal.4th 248, 58 Cal.Rptr.2d 827, 827, 832, 835, 926 P.2d 1013, 1015, 1019, 1021 (1996); *see also State v. Grooms*, 653 S.W.2d at 275; *State v. Marchesano*, 783 P.2d at 253; *Sheppard v. State*, 538 A.2d at 775.[5] A "'natural and probable consequence' in the 'ordinary course of things' presupposes an outcome within a reasonably predictable range." *Roy v. United States*, 652 A.2d 1098, 1105 (D.C.App.1995).

We recognize, as have other courts, that the common law rule has been subject to criticism by some commentators, primarily for being too broad. See LaFave & Scott, *Substantive Criminal Law*, § 6.8(b), p. 158 (1987 & Supp.1996); Mod. Pen.Code § 2.06 (1985). It continues, however, to be applied by the majority of courts under a variety of statutes governing criminal responsibility, and a number have observed that the doctrine is an established rule of American jurisprudence. Moreover, we note that many states have codified the common law rule.[6] In our view, the rule continues to be a viable principle underlying criminal responsibility.

As we have frequently observed, the Legislature is presumed to know the existing state of the law when it enacts a statute. *Owens v. State*, 908 S.W.2d 923, 926 (Tenn.1995). Moreover, the Legislature has said that statutes must "be construed according to the fair import of their terms, including reference to judicial decisions and common law interpretations. . . ." Tenn.Code Ann. § 39–11–104.

In our view, the Sentencing Commission comments to Tenn.Code Ann. §§ 39–11–401 and –402 clearly indicate the legislative intent that the statutory provisions embrace the common law principles governing aiders and abettors and accessories before the fact. The statutory predecessors to these provisions likewise embraced the common law definitions. *See* Tenn.Code Ann. § 39–1–301 (1982)("any person who shall feloniously move, incite, counsel, hire, command,

---

5   The principle also has been applied to accomplices under the felony murder doctrine: "A defendant who is a willing and active participant in a robbery becomes accountable for all of the consequences flowing from the robbery and may be convicted of first-degree murder where a co-perpetrator of the felony is the actual killer." *State v. Middlebrooks*, 840 S.W.2d 317, 336 (Tenn.1992); *Dupes v. State*, 209 Tenn. 506, 512, 354 S.W.2d 453, 456 (1962).

6   *See* Iowa Code Ann. § 703.2; Kan. Stat. Ann. § 21–3205(2); Me.Rev.Stat. Ann. tit. 17–A, § 57; Minn.Stat. Ann. § 609.05; Wis. Stat. Ann. § 939.05.

or procure any other person to commit a felony is an accessory before the fact."); Tenn.Code Ann. § 39–1–303 (1982)("all persons present, aiding and abetting, or ready and consenting to aid and abet, in any criminal offense, shall be deemed principal offenders and punished as such."). Accordingly, we conclude that the natural and probable consequence rule, which derives from the common law and has been applied in our case law, as well as in the case law of a majority of jurisdictions, is applicable under Tenn.Code Ann. §§ 39–11–401 and –402.

Applying the foregoing principles to the present case, we have determined that the evidence was sufficient for the jury to find that the defendant aided and assisted in the offense of aggravated robbery, which requires evidence of an intentional theft from the person of another by violence and by placing the victims in fear with the use of a deadly weapon. Tenn.Code Ann. §§ 39–13–401(a) and –402(a)(1). The defendant planned the robbery, described the layout of the store, supplied weapons, and accompanied the co-defendants to the scene, where he was to wait in the car. The co-defendants entered the store, held the victims at gunpoint, and took money. Accordingly, there was sufficient evidence from which the jury could find that the defendant solicited and aided in the offense with the intent to promote and benefit from its commission.

Likewise, we conclude that the evidence was sufficient to find that the defendant was criminally responsible for the aggravated assaults committed against the victims inside the store and the reckless endangerment committed when the co-defendants fled from the scene.[7] The defendant initiated the robbery, supplied weapons, and was present at or near the scene of the offense. The aggravated assaults and the reckless endangerment were committed by the co-defendants with the weapons supplied by the defendant and in furtherance of the robbery. The offenses were the natural and probable consequence of the robbery that was initiated, directed, and aided by the defendant. Accordingly, we conclude that the evidence was sufficient to sustain these convictions under Tenn.Code Ann. § 39–11–402(2).

CONCLUSION

We conclude that the natural and probable consequence rule which derives from the common law is applicable under Tenn.Code Ann. §§ 39–11–401 and –402, and that the evidence was sufficient to find that the defendant, having direct-

---

7   The aggravated assault against Adams required an intentional or knowing act causing the victim to reasonably fear imminent bodily injury, as well as the use or display of a deadly weapon. Tenn.Code Ann. §§ 39–13–101(a)(2) & –102(a)(1)(B). The aggravated assault against McGaha required an intentional, knowing or reckless act causing bodily injury to the victim, as well as the use or display of a deadly weapon. Tenn.Code Ann. §§ 39–13–101(a)(1) & –102(a)(1)(B). The felony reckless endangerment required reckless conduct that placed another person in imminent danger of death or serious bodily injury, and the use of a deadly weapon. Tenn.Code Ann. § 39–13–103(a) & (b).

ed and aided in the aggravated robbery with the intent to promote or benefit from its commission, was criminally responsible for all of the offenses committed by his co-defendants, to wit: aggravated assault and felony reckless endangerment.

Accordingly, the judgment of the Court of Criminal Appeals is affirmed. The costs of this appeal are taxed to the defendant-appellant, Jubal Carson. BIRCH, C.J., and DROWOTA, REID and HOLDER, JJ., concur.

As you will discover in *Sharma*, the Nevada Legislature has not identified the *mens rea* required for complicity, leading to a variety of opinions on the mental state required for this type of liability. The Nevada Supreme Court in *Sharma* rejected the doctrine of natural and probable consequences.

Sharma v. State

Supreme Court of Nevada
56 P.3d 868 (2002)

PER CURIAM.

The State prosecuted appellant Sonu Sharma for the attempted murder of Amit Ranadey under two alternate theories of criminal liability: (1) that he directly attempted to kill Ranadey by shooting him in the back, and (2) that he aided and abetted another person's attempt to kill Ranadey. Sharma was convicted, pursuant to a jury verdict, of attempted murder with the use of a deadly weapon. On appeal, he contends that the district court failed to properly instruct the jury on the essential elements of aiding and abetting attempted murder. We agree, and we issue this opinion to clarify Nevada law respecting the requisite mens rea or state of mind for aiding and abetting a specific intent crime.

THE FACTS

On November 18, 1998, Amit Ranadey was shot in the back. Testimony at trial established that Rajesh Vig, Anthony Barela, Arthur Richardson, and appellant Sharma were present at the time of the shooting. After an investigation, the State charged all four men with the attempted murder of Ranadey with the use of a deadly weapon. The cases were severed for trial, and the State tried Sharma first.

The day after the shooting, police detectives approached Sharma at work. They explained that Ranadey had been shot and asked Sharma to speak with them. Sharma agreed and accompanied them to the police station. At first, Sharma denied knowing anything about the shooting. He claimed that he and Vig spent the evening together at a restaurant, walking around the mall, and visiting with Vig's family.

After further interrogation, however, Sharma told a different story. He explained that Ranadey and Barela sold marijuana together, but when Barela began working with someone else and no longer included Ranadey in the transactions, Ranadey asked Vig to help him attack Barela. Vig then recruited Sharma to assist because he owned a vehicle. Although they originally planned to beat Barela with baseball bats, the plan changed when they subsequently included Richardson. Richardson owned a gun and wanted to use it instead of the bats. Sharma claimed that he was surprised when Richardson shot Ranadey instead of Barela.

Later, Sharma related another version of the shooting. He admitted that although the original plan was to attack Barela, the plan changed when Vig warned Barela what was going to happen. Barela decided to let the plan proceed and to attack Ranadey instead. Sharma also admitted to the police that when Richardson joined the plan, the group intended to kill Ranadey.

At trial, Ranadey testified that, as far as he knew, Vig, Richardson, and Sharma intended to help him attack Barela. He had no idea that the plan had changed. Although he did not know who actually shot him, he remembered that Sharma had told him it was Richardson. Ranadey, however, suspected that Sharma had a gun and may have shot him because of the way Sharma was holding his hand in his jacket. But Ranadey also remembered seeing Richardson with a gun in his hand after the shooting.

Sharma testified in his own defense at trial. In contrast to some of his prior statements to police, he denied that the group planned to attack Ranadey. Rather, he repeatedly testified that Ranadey wanted to have a fistfight with Barela. Sharma also claimed that he did not think anyone intended to kill Barela. Although Sharma admitted that he knew Richardson owned a gun, he maintained that there was never a plan to use it. When asked about his inconsistent statements to the police, Sharma claimed he did not understand most of the interview because he does not speak English well, and the detective was "putting words in [his] mouth."

The jury found Sharma guilty of attempted murder with the use of a deadly weapon. The district court sentenced him to serve two consecutive terms of forty-eight months to one hundred and twenty months in the Nevada State Prison. This appeal followed.

On June 14, 2001, following oral argument in this appeal, this court issued an order directing the parties to file supplemental briefs. The order specifically requested the parties to address two concerns raised by the court during oral argument: (1) whether the jury was correctly instructed on the "mens rea" or "intent" required to convict an accused of aiding and abetting an attempted murder, and (2) whether the jury was correctly instructed that it must find that acts were in fact committed that tended, but failed to complete the crime of murder. Supplemental briefing is now complete, and this appeal is fully at issue and ready for decision.

DISCUSSION

Before we can determine whether the jury was properly instructed respecting the element of intent involved in aiding and abetting attempted murder, we must first determine what the intent requirements actually are under Nevada law. Unfortunately, this court's case law has inconsistently defined these requirements with respect to specific intent crimes.[1] Accordingly, we begin our analysis with a discussion of the existing law in this state.

The Elements of Attempted Murder

An "attempt" under Nevada law is an act done with the intent to commit a crime, and tending, but failing to accomplish it.[2] Murder is the unlawful killing of a human being with malice aforethought, either express or implied.[3] In *Keys v. State*,[4] however, we clarified that attempted murder can only be committed with express malice. *Keys* held that implied malice alone is insufficient to support a conviction for attempted murder.

An attempt, by nature, is a failure to accomplish what one *intended* to do. Attempt means to try; it means an effort to bring about a desired result. Thus one cannot *attempt* to be negligent or *attempt* to have the general malignant recklessness contemplated by . . . "implied malice."[5]

Therefore, *Keys* held, "[a]ttempted murder is the performance of an act or acts which tend, but fail, to kill a human being, when such acts are done with express malice, namely, with the deliberate intention unlawfully to kill."[6]

---

1   *Compare Tanksley v. State*, 113 Nev. 844, 944 P.2d 240 (1997) (holding that a conviction for an attempt to obtain money by false pretenses could not stand where the jury was not instructed that the accused had to have either the intent to obtain money by false pretenses, or the intent to aid and abet in the obtaining of money by false pretenses), *with Mitchell v. State*, 114 Nev. 1417, 971 P.2d 813 (1998) (holding that a conviction for attempted murder will stand even if the accused did not have the specific intent to kill, provided that the attempted murder was the natural and probable consequence of the aider and abettor's target crime).

2   NRS 193.330(1).

3   NRS 200.010.

4   104 Nev. 736, 766 P.2d 270 (1988).

5   *Id.* at 740, 766 P.2d at 273.

6   *Id.*

Aider and Abettor Liability

Nevada law does not distinguish between an aider or abettor to a crime and an actual perpetrator of a crime; both are equally culpable. Under NRS 195.020, every person concerned in the commission of a crime, whether he directly commits the act constituting the offense or aids or abets in its commission is guilty as a principal. Although NRS 195.020 also provides that a lack of criminal intent by the person directly committing the crime shall not be a defense to an aider or abettor, the statute does not specify what mental state is required to be convicted as an aider or abettor. Perhaps for that reason, this court has over time defined that mental state inconsistently. Thus, Nevada law is vulnerable to the general criticism that "[c]onsiderable confusion exists as to what the accomplice's mental state must be in order to hold him accountable for an offense committed by another."[7]

In one line of cases, for example, this court has required the State to show that the defendant knowingly and intentionally aided another to commit the charged crime.[8] In *Tanksley v. State*, a case representative of this line of cases, this court held that a defendant could not be convicted of attempting to obtain money by false pretenses without a finding that she either intended to obtain the money by false pretenses, or intended to aid or abet in the obtaining of money by false pretenses.[9] *Tanksley* stressed that "[a]n attempt crime is a specific intent crime; thus, the act constituting [the] attempt must be done with the intent to commit that crime."[10]

In *Mitchell v. State*, however, this court rejected the "assertion that one may never be convicted of attempted murder as an aider and abettor in the absence of a specific intent to kill." Instead, this court adopted and approved the "natural and probable consequences doctrine," concluding that "a conviction for attempted murder will lie even if the defendant did not have the specific intent to kill provided the attempted murder was the natural and probable

---

7   *See* Wayne R. LaFave & Austin W. Scott, Jr., *Criminal Law* § 6.7(b), at 579 (2d ed.1986).

8   *See, e.g., Labastida v. State*, 115 Nev. 298, 303, 986 P.2d 443, 446 (1999) (approving of jury instructions that required a finding that the accomplice knowingly and intentionally aided in the acts that resulted in the charged crime); *Evans v. State*, 113 Nev. 885, 944 P.2d 253 (1997) (implicitly holding that the accomplice must assist with the intent that the other person commit the charged crime); *Ewish v. State*, 111 Nev. 1365, 904 P.2d 1038 (1995) (recognizing that an accomplice can be convicted of a lesser related crime if he did not harbor the specific intent required to be convicted of his cohort's crime); *Hooper v. State*, 95 Nev. 924, 604 P.2d 115 (1979) (approving of an instruction that required the jury to find that the accomplice acted knowingly, voluntarily, and with a common intent to commit the crime).

9   113 Nev. 844, 849–50, 944 P.2d 240, 243 (1997).

10   *Id.* at 849, 944 P.2d at 243 (citing NRS 193.330; *Curry v. State*, 106 Nev. 317, 319, 792 P.2d 396, 397 (1990)).

consequence of the aider and abettor's target crime."[11] *Mitchell* directed the trial courts to use a specific model instruction incorporating the natural and probable consequences doctrine in all future cases involving charges of aiding and abetting attempted murder.[12]

This court again applied the natural and probable consequences doctrine to a specific intent crime in *Garner v. State*.[13] In addressing Garner's challenge to his kidnapping conviction, this court held that "when a person enters into a common plan or scheme but does not intend a particular crime committed by the principal, the person is liable for the crime if 'in the ordinary course of things [the crime] was the natural or probable consequence of such common plan or scheme.'"[14]

This doctrine has been harshly criticized by "[m]ost commentators . . . as both 'incongruous and unjust' because it imposes accomplice liability solely upon proof of foreseeability or negligence when typically a higher degree of mens rea is required of the principal."[15] It permits criminal "liability to be predicated upon negligence even when the crime involved requires a different state of mind."[16] Having reevaluated the wisdom of the doctrine, we have concluded that its general application in Nevada to specific intent crimes is unsound precisely for that reason: it permits conviction without proof that the accused possessed the state of mind required by the statutory definition of the crime.

To be convicted of an attempt to commit a crime in Nevada, the State must show, among other things, that the accused committed an act with the intent to commit that crime.[17] Under the natural and probable consequences doctrine, however, an accused may be convicted upon a far different showing, *i.e.*, that the charged crime, although not intended, was nonetheless foreseeable. As the Supreme Court of New Mexico observed in rejecting the doctrine for similar

---

11   114 Nev. 1417, 1426–27, 971 P.2d 813, 819–20 (1998).

12   *Id.* at 1427 n. 3, 971 P.2d at 820 n. 3; *see also People v. Prettyman*, 14 Cal.4th 248, 58 Cal.Rptr.2d 827, 926 P.2d 1013, 1018 n. 3 (1996). Notably, the jury in the instant case was not instructed in accordance with the model instruction set forth in *Mitchell*.

13   116 Nev. 770, 6 P.3d 1013 (2000).

14   *Id.* at 782, 6 P.3d at 1021 (quoting *State v. Cushing, Et Al.*, 61 Nev. 132, 148, 120 P.2d 208, 216 (1941)).

15   Audrey Rogers, *Accomplice Liability for Unintentional Crimes: Remaining Within the Constraints of Intent*, 31 Loy. L.A. L.Rev. 1351, 1361 & n. 33 (1998) (citing LaFave & Scott, *supra* note 7, at 590; Joshua Dressler, *Reassessing the Theoretical Underpinnings of Accomplice Liability: New Solutions to an Old Problem*, 37 Hastings L.J. 91, 97–98 (1985); Sanford H. Kadish, *Complicity, Cause and Blame: A Study in the Interpretation of Doctrine*, 73 Cal. L.Rev. 323, 351–52 (1985)).

16   LaFave & Scott, *supra* note 7, at 590.

17   NRS 193.330(1).

reasons, the doctrine thus "allows a defendant to be convicted for crimes the defendant may have been able to foresee but never intended."[18]

This court has repeatedly emphasized that, under Nevada law, "'[t]here is no such criminal offense as an attempt to achieve an unintended result.'"[19] We have also reasoned that "[a]n attempt, by nature, is a failure to accomplish what one *intended* to do."[20] Because the natural and probable consequences doctrine permits a defendant to be convicted of a specific intent crime where he or she did not possess the statutory intent required for the offense, we hereby disavow and abandon the doctrine. It is not only "inconsistent with more fundamental principles of our system of criminal law,"[21] but is also inconsistent with those Nevada statutes that require proof of a specific intent to commit the crime alleged.

We observe as well that the doctrine may potentially undermine certain legislative sentencing determinations. By assigning a larger statutory sentence to attempted murder than to battery, the legislature arguably has determined that certain acts accompanied by the intent to kill are more serious than acts involving the willful use of force without such intent.[22] Application of the doctrine, however, could negate such legislative determinations.

Accordingly, we reaffirm *Tanksley* and hold that in order for a person to be held accountable for the specific intent crime of another under an aiding or abetting theory of principal liability, the aider or abettor must have knowingly aided the other person with the intent that the other person commit the charged crime. To the extent that *Garner* and *Mitchell* conflict with this holding and endorse the natural and probable consequences doctrine, they are hereby disapproved and overruled.

---

18   *State v. Carrasco*, 124 N.M. 64, 946 P.2d 1075, 1079–80 (1997).

19   *Keys*, 104 Nev. at 740, 766 P.2d at 273 (quoting *Ramos v. State*, 95 Nev. 251, 253, 592 P.2d 950, 951 (1979) (quoting *People v. Viser*, 62 Ill.2d 568, 343 N.E.2d 903, 910 (1975))).

20   *Keys*, 104 Nev. at 740, 766 P.2d at 273.

21   LaFave & Scott, *supra* note 7, at 590.

22   *Compare* NRS 200.481, *with* NRS 193.165, NRS 193.330, *and* NRS 200.030.

e

PRACTICE EXERCISE

The Nevada Supreme Court observed the trial court in *Sharma* inadequately instructed the jury on aiding and abetting attempted murder. The trial court instructed:

The elements of ATTEMPTED MURDER which the State must prove beyond a reasonable doubt in this case are that on or about the 18th day of November, 1998, the defendant did:

> 1) in Washoe County, State of Nevada;
>
> 2) willfully, unlawfully, with premeditation, deliberation, and malice aforethought;
>
> 3) directly attempt to kill AMIT RANADEY;
>
> 4) or aid, abet, counsel or encourage another person or persons to attempt to do so.

Identify the problem with this version of the instruction and rewrite the instruction to be consistent with the conclusion of the Nevada Supreme Court.

Notes and Questions

1. The United States Supreme Court has weighed in with its own criticism of the doctrine of natural and probable consequences. In *Rosemond v. United States*, 134 S.Ct. 1240, 1248-54 (2014), the Supreme Court held that a defendant had to know that his confederate in a drug deal was armed—and know at a point when he still had an opportunity to withdraw from the deal. The Court claimed that it was not addressing the doctrine of natural and probable consequences, which it acknowledged had been heavily criticized, as the issue had not been raised by in litigation. The logical consequence of the Court's decision is, however, inconsistent with the doctrine. *See e.g.*, Wesley M. Oliver, *Limiting the Criminal Law's "In for a Penny, In for a Pound" Doctrine*, 103 Geo. L. J. Online 8, 16 (2014). The District of Columbia Court of Appeals reached a similar decision in *Perry v. United States*, 36 A.3d 799 (D.C. 2011).

2. Some states reject the doctrine of natural and probable consequences entirely. Interestingly, a few states reject the doctrine of natural and probable consequences *except* when applying the felony murder doctrine. *See, e.g., Commonwealth v. Hanright*, 994 N.E.2d 363 (Mass. 2013); *People v. Kessler*, 296 N.E.2d 631 (Ill. 1973). This distinction makes sense only as a matter of legislative intent—not as a matter of consistency. The doctrine of natural and probable consequences is most often a judicially created doctrine while the felony murder doctrine (which we will study in considerably more depth in the next chapter) is created by the legislature.

3. There is a very important limitation to the *Sharma* decision. *Sharma* requires the defendant to specifically intend either the conduct or results of a *specific intent crime*; in other words a crime requiring a defendant to desire a particular result. But a number of crimes do not require a specific result and *Sharma* does not require intent for complicity liability for such crimes. The Nevada Supreme Court approved the following instruction in a second-degree murder case, which as you will learn more about in our next chapter, often does not require the defendant to desire the victim's death, only that he take an extraordinarily high and unreasonable risk of his death. In Nevada, implied malice in a homicide case means that the defendant took such a risk, but did not necessarily desire his victim's death; express malice means that the defendant desired the death. This is the common law formulation of *mens rea* in homicide cases. When implied malice is the basis of the charge, the Nevada Supreme Court concluded that *Sharma* does not require the aider and abettor to intend the death as you will see in the instruction the court approved:

> Under a theory of aiding and abetting for Murder in the Second Degree, the State has the burden to prove beyond a reasonable doubt that the defendant(s) did intend to commit or aid in the commission of a battery upon the victim with implied malice.

> To find defendant(s) guilty of Murder in the Second Degree under a theory of aiding and abetting, the State must prove beyond a reasonable doubt that the defendant(s) intended to commit a battery upon the victim and aided, abetted, counseled, or encouraged another defendant with malignant recklessness of another's life and safety or in disregard of social duty.

> *Schunueringer v. State*, 2014 WL 819462 (Nev. 2014).

4. There has been a very interesting criticism of requiring intent for complicity liability in all cases. Specifically, it has been suggested that the *mens rea* ought to focus on the type of harm that will result from the defendant's encouragement or assistance. In *People v. Lauria*, 251 Cal. App.2d 471, 481, 59 Cal. Rptr. 628, 634 (1967), the California Court of Appeal observed that while mere knowledge of a principal's intent should be insufficient for assistance to become complicity, the same could not be true for more dangerous crimes. The proprietor of an answer service with a known prostitute as a customer would not be liable under this reasoning, but providing gasoline to a terrorist knowing that it will be used to make a Molotov cocktail should, according the court in *Lauria,* be sufficient for liability. Judge Richard Posner adopted a similar view in *United States v. Fountain*, 768 F.2d 790 (7th Cir. 1985), finding that an inmate, who provided a homemade knife to another inmate, liable for first-degree murder when he knew that the weapon would be used to stab a guard, but did not necessarily intend the guard's death. This is an interesting theory of liability—if the defendant had stabbed the guard without desiring his death, he could not be liable for first-degree murder, but by aiding someone he knows to have a murderous intent, he becomes liable for the other's murderous intent.

5. You may be wondering when a defendant would aid or abet a crime but not agree with another to commit the crime. Very often those who are guilty of conspiracy to commit a crime are also guilty of aiding and abetting the crime (and therefore liable for the commission of the crime itself). These are illegal plans, not corporate charters. Agreements to commit crimes are inferred from circumstances as those committing crimes do not draft their agreements and file them with the Secretary of State. The proof demonstrating an agreement is often the same proof that demonstrates assistance. It is possible to have one without the other—as when one mails an anonymous donation to a terrorist group—but very often, if one form of liability can be demonstrated, so can the other. This begs the question of why criminal law creates two types of liability with different penalties. We will return to the legal significance of this fact later in this chapter in *Batchelder v. United States*. But for now, begin to consider why this might be the case.

6. Conspiracy liability can be just as far reaching as complicity liability. A defendant in many jurisdictions is liable for any act of his co-conspirators in furtherance of the conspiracy. *See Pinkerton v. United States*, 328 U.S. 640 (1946). Just as the doctrine of natural and probable consequences is frequently challenged, so this theory of liability, most frequently known as the *Pinkerton*

Doctrine. This discussion from the *Bolden v. State*, 124 P.2d 191, 197-99 (Nev. 2005) nicely lays out the doctrine and its criticisms:

> Nearly 60 years ago in *Pinkerton v. United States*, the United States Supreme Court defined coconspirator liability in terms of reasonable fore-seeability and reaffirmed the concept that a conspiracy and the completion of the substantive offense are two distinct criminal acts. The Court con-cluded:
>
>> The criminal intent to do the act is established by the formation of the conspiracy. Each conspirator instigated the commission of the crime. The unlawful agreement contemplated precisely what was done. It was formed for the purpose. The act done was in execution of the enter-prise. The rule which holds responsible one who counsels, procures, or commands another to commit a crime is founded on the same prin-ciple. That principle is recognized in the law of conspiracy when the overt act of one partner in crime is attributable to all. . . . If [the overt act] can be supplied by the act of one conspirator, we fail to see why the same or other acts in furtherance of the conspiracy are likewise not attributable to the others for the purpose of holding them responsible for the substantive offense.
>>
>> A different case would arise if the substantive offense committed by one of the conspirators was not in fact done in furtherance of the con-spiracy, did not fall within the scope of the unlawful project, or was merely a part of the ramifications of the plan which could not be rea-sonably foreseen as a necessary or natural consequence of the unlaw-ful agreement.
>
> *Pinkerton* applies to federal criminal proceedings and thus federal courts have employed the rule.[26] The individual states, however, are not obligated to follow *Pinkerton*. The Nevada Legislature has not adopted the *Pinkerton* rule, but a number of states have addressed the issue by judicial decision. Several states have embraced the rule and permit defendants to be held liable for the criminal acts of a coconspirator so long as the crime was foreseeable and committed in furtherance of the conspiracy[27] Nonetheless,

---

26 *See, e.g., U.S. v. Silvestri*, 409 F.3d 1311 (11th Cir.2005); *U.S. v. Si*, 343 F.3d 1116 (9th Cir.2003); *U.S. v. Curtis*, 324 F.3d 501 (7th Cir.2003); *U.S. v. Newsome*, 322 F.3d 328 (4th Cir.2003); *U.S. v. Wade*, 318 F.3d 698 (6th Cir.2003); *U.S. v. Navarrete–Barron*, 192 F.3d 786 (8th Cir.1999).

27 *See Matthews v. State*, 56 Ark.App. 141, 940 S.W.2d 498 (1997); *State v. Walton*, 227 Conn. 32, 630 A.2d 990

the *Pinkerton* rule has garnered significant disfavor. Concerns respecting the ramifications of the rule arose shortly after the opinion was issued:

> In the final analysis the *Pinkerton* decision extends the wide limits of the conspiracy doctrine to the breaking-point and opens the door to possible new abuses by over-zealous public prosecutors. While membership in a conspiracy may well be evidence for the jury's consideration in holding others than the direct actor guilty, it should not be sufficient, in the absence of some further showing of knowledge, acquiescence, aid or assistance, to convict one conspirator for another's criminal act. [28]

Others have criticized the rule as well. "Under the better view, one is not an accomplice to a crime merely because that crime was committed in furtherance of a conspiracy of which he is a member, or because that crime was a natural and probable consequence of another offense as to which he is an accomplice." [29] The drafters of the Model Penal Code have similarly rejected the *Pinkerton* view, commenting that the "law would lose all sense of just proportion" if by virtue of his crime of conspiracy a defendant was "held accountable for thousands of additional offenses of which he was completely unaware and which he did not influence at all." [30]

The Washington Supreme Court has rejected *Pinkerton* as an inaccurate reflection of state law. [31] A Washington criminal statute provides liability for criminal conspiracy but is silent respecting vicarious liability for coconspirators. The Washington court concluded that vicarious liability of coconspirators, if any, must be based on a state accomplice liability statute, which requires knowledge of the crime charged. [32] Therefore, the court held that liability based on foreseeability alone is incompatible with its state law.

(1993); *State v. Tyler*, 251 Kan. 616, 840 P.2d 413 (1992); *Martinez v. State*, 413 So.2d 429 (Fla.Dist.Ct.App.1982); *Everritt v. State*, 277 Ga. 457, 588 S.E.2d 691, 693 (2003); *State v. Harnois*, 853 A.2d 1249 (R.I.2004); *Barnes v. State*, 56 S.W.3d 221 (Tex.App.2001).

28 Note, *Vicarious Liability for Criminal Offenses of Co-conspirators*, 56 Yale L.J. 371, 378 (1947).

29 Wayne R. LaFave & Austin W. Scott, Jr., *Criminal Law* § 6.8, at 587 (2d ed.1986).

30 Model Penal Code § 2.06 cmt. 6(a), at 307 (1985).

31 *State v. Stein*, 144 Wash.2d 236, 27 P.3d 184, 187–89 (2001).

32 *Id.* at 188–89.

The Arizona Supreme Court has also rejected the *Pinkerton* rule, holding that conspiratorial liability does not extend to separate criminal acts of coconspirators when a particular coconspirator is not an accomplice or principal to those crimes, even though he may be guilty of conspiracy.[33] That court noted that its holding "simply prevents a conspirator, who is not also an accomplice, from being held liable for a potentially limitless number of criminal acts which, though later determined to be 'foreseeable,' are at the time of their commission totally beyond the conspirator's knowledge and control."[34]

New York has similarly considered and rejected the *Pinkerton* view, as explained in *People v. McGee:*

> In rejecting the notion that one's status as a conspirator standing alone is sufficient to support a conviction for a substantive offense committed by a coconspirator, it is noted that the Legislature has defined the conduct that will render a person criminally responsible for the act of another. Conspicuously absent from section 20.00 of the Penal Law is reference to one who conspires to commit an offense. That omission cannot be supplied by construction. Conduct that will support a conviction for conspiracy will not perforce give rise to accessorial liability. True, a conspirator's conduct in many instances will suffice to establish liability as an accomplice, but the concepts are, in reality, analytically distinct. To permit mere guilt of conspiracy to establish the defendant's guilt of the substantive crime without any evidence of further action on the part of the defendant, would be to expand the basis of accomplice liability beyond the legislative design.

> The crime of conspiracy is an offense separate from the crime that is the object of the conspiracy. Once an illicit agreement is shown, the overt act of any conspirator may be attributed to other conspirators to establish the offense of conspiracy and that act may be the object crime. But the overt act itself is not the crime in a conspiracy prosecution; it is merely an element of the crime that has as its basis the agreement. It is not offensive to permit a conviction of conspiracy to stand on the overt act committed by another, for the act merely provides corroboration of the existence of the agreement and indicates that the agreement has

---

33 *See Evanchyk v. Stewart*, 202 Ariz. 476, 47 P.3d 1114, 1118 (2002); *State ex rel. Woods v. Cohen*, 173 Ariz. 497, 844 P.2d 1147, 1148–51 (1992).

34 *Cohen*, 844 P.2d at 1151.

reached a point where it poses a sufficient threat to society to impose sanctions. But it is repugnant to our system of jurisprudence, where guilt is generally personal to the defendant, to impose punishment, not for the socially harmful agreement to which the defendant is a party, but for substantive offenses in which he did not participate.[35]

The doctrine of natural and probable consequences is not the only way that complicity liability can be given an extraordinarily broad reach. A number of courts conclude that an aider or abettor is liable for results when he shares the principal's mental state.

Commonwealth v. Roebuck

Supreme Court of Pennsylvania
32 A.3d 613 (2011)

Justice SAYLOR.

In this appeal, we consider whether it is possible, as a matter of law, to be convicted as an accomplice to third-degree murder.

The complete factual background is somewhat cumbersome. For present purposes, it is enough to say the Commonwealth presented evidence that the victim was lured to an apartment complex, where he was ambushed, shot, and mortally wounded. Appellant participated, with others, in orchestrating the events, but he did not shoot the victim.

For his role, Appellant was charged with, among other offenses, murder of the third degree. *See* 18 Pa.C.S. § 2502(c). As he did not physically perpetrate the homicide, the Commonwealth relied upon accomplice theory, which is codified in Section 306 of the Crimes Code along with other complicity-based account- ability principles. *See id.* § 306 (entitled "Liability for conduct of another; com- plicity" and establishing the terms of legal accountability for the conduct of another). The matter proceeded to a bench trial, and a verdict of guilt ensued.

On appeal, Appellant argued that there is no rational legal theory to support accomplice liability for third-degree murder. He rested his position on the fol- lowing syllogism: accomplice liability attaches only where the defendant *intends* to facilitate or promote an underlying offense; third-degree murder is an *unin-*

------

35 *People v. McGee*, 49 N.Y.2d 48, 424 N.Y.S.2d 157, 399 N.E.2d 1177, 1181–82 (1979) (citations omitted).

tentional killing committed with malice; therefore, to adjudge a criminal defendant guilty of third-degree murder as an accomplice would be to accept that the accused *intended* to aid an *unintentional* act, which is a logical impossibility.

* * *

Presently, Appellant maintains that accomplice liability for third-degree murder is a legal anomaly in view of his impossibility syllogism. In passing, Appellant observes that Section 306 of the Pennsylvania Crimes Code was derived from the Model Penal Code. *See* MODEL PENAL CODE § 2.06 (1962) (the "MPC" or the "Code").

I. THE MODEL PENAL CODE

A. The Code Generally

In addressing the terms of the Model Penal Code, it is important to bear in mind that the Code employs an elements approach to substantive criminal law, which recognizes that a single offense definition may require different culpable mental states for each objective offense element. . . . The MPC further narrows *mens rea* analysis by pruning from the lexicon a plethora of common-law culpability terms, leaving four core terms. *See id.* § 2.02(1) (indicating, subject to one express exception, that "a person is not guilty of an offense unless he acted purposely, knowingly, recklessly or negligently, as the law may require").

Conceptually, the MPC also recognizes three objective categories of offense elements—conduct, attendant circumstances, and result. *See* MODEL PENAL CODE § 2.02, cmt. 1, at 229. The Code frequently distinguishes among these offense-element categories in its various prescriptions regarding which of the four levels of culpability must be established for any given offense element. *See generally id.* at 229–30 ("The question of which level of culpability suffices to establish liability must be addressed separately with respect to each material element, and will be resolved either by the particular definition of the offense or the general provisions of [Section 2.02].").

* * *

The Model Penal Code has had its share of detractors, and, certainly, it does not provide perfect formulations. For example, as relevant to Appellant's arguments, the Code has been criticized for failing to provide an adequate description and overlay relating the four levels of culpability (purposeful, knowing, reckless, negligent) to the objective element categories (conduct, attendant circumstances, result) in the context of particular offense elements. *See, e.g.,* Robinson & Grall, *Element Analysis*, 35 STAN. L. REV. at 706–07. Such criticism has been leveled in the accomplice-liability setting. *See, e.g., id.* at 739

("The greatest flaw in the Model Penal Code provision [directed to accomplice liability], and those provisions modeled after it, is their failure to specify all of the culpability requirements of the substantive offense that the accomplice must satisfy."). We bear these observations in mind in proceeding to address the Code's treatment of complicity theory.

B. MPC Treatment of Accomplice Liability

The legal accountability of accomplices for the conduct of others is treated in 2.06 of the Code. *See* MODEL PENAL CODE § 2.06(2)(c) ("A person is legally accountable for the conduct of another person when . . . he is an accomplice of such other person in the commission of the offense."). Two material passages follow, developing the meaning of the term "accomplice" and the requisite *mens rea*, as relevant to the present case:

> (3) A person is an accomplice of another person in the commission of an offense if . . . with the purpose of promoting or facilitating the commission of the offense, he . . . aids or agrees or attempts to aid such other person in planning or committing it[.]

> (4) When causing a particular result is an element of an offense, an accomplice in the conduct causing such result is an accomplice in the commission of that offense if he acts with the kind of culpability, if any, with respect to that result that is sufficient for the commission of the offense.

Id. § 2.06(3), (4).

Section 206(4) thus prescribes that an accomplice may be held legally accountable where he is an "accomplice in the conduct"—or, in other words, aids another in planning or committing the conduct with the purpose of promoting or facilitating it—and acts with recklessness (*i.e.*, the "kind of culpability . . . sufficient for the commission of" a reckless-result offense).[11]

* * *

To the extent any aspect of this accountability scheme is unclear, ample clarification is provided in the explanatory note and commentary. As a threshold matter, the commentary explains that the term "commission of the offense," as used in Section 2.06(3), focuses on the *conduct*, not the result. *See id.* § 2.06, cmt. 6(b), at 310 ("Subsection 3(a) requires that the actor have the purpose of promot-

---

11 Under the MPC, where the result element requires a higher level of culpability, this extends to accomplices as well. For example, within the context of the Pennsylvania Crimes Code, first-degree murder requires of a principal the specific intent to kill; thus, specific intent is also required to support accomplice liability to first-degree murder. See, e.g., *Commonwealth v. Markman*, 591 Pa. 249, 269 n. 8, 916 A.2d 586, 597 n. 8 (2007); *accord State v. Garnica*, 209 Ariz. 96, 98 P.3d 207, 213–14 (Ariz.Ct.App.2004) (making the same point under Arizona law).

ing or facilitating the commission of the offense, i.e., that *he have as his conscious objective the bringing about of conduct that that the Code has declared to be criminal[.]*" (emphasis added)).[12] This diffuses any impression that an accomplice must always intend results essential to the completed crime. *See Wheeler*, 772 P.2d at 103 (explaining that the "'intent to promote or facilitate the commission of the offense' . . . does not include an intent that death occur even though the underlying crime . . . has death as an essential element" (citation and quotation marks omitted)). The commentary then points to the fourth subsection as supplying the essential culpability requirement, as follows:

> One who solicits an end, or aids or agrees to aid in its achievement, is an accomplice in whatever means may be employed, insofar as they constitute or commit an offense fairly envisaged in the purposes of the association. But *when a wholly different crime has been committed, thus involving conduct not within the conscious objectives of the accomplice, he is not liable for it unless the case falls within the specific terms of Subsection (4).* MODEL PENAL CODE § 2.06, cmt. 6(b), at 311 (emphasis added). According to the commentary, the purport of the fourth subsection is to hold the accomplice accountable for contributing to the conduct to the degree his culpability equals what is required to support liability of a principal actor.[13]

> The most common situation in which Subsection (4) will become relevant is where unanticipated results occur from conduct for which the actor is responsible under Subsection (3). *His liability for unanticipated occurrences rests upon two factors: his complicity in the conduct that causes the result, and his culpability towards the result to the degree required by law, that makes the result criminal.* Accomplice liability in this event is thus assimilated to the liability of the principal actor[.] . . . *This formulation combines the policy that accomplices are equally accountable within the range of their complicity with the policies underlying those crimes defined according to the*

---

12 *Accord Riley v. State*, 60 P.3d 204, 213–14 (Alaska Ct.App.2002) (discussing the relevant commentary); *State v. Nelson*, 214 Ariz. 196, 150 P.3d 769, 772 (Ariz.Ct.App.2007) ("[F]or accomplice liability to exist, [the Code-based governing statute] only requires proof of intent to promote or facilitate the *conduct* of another, not proof of intent to promote or facilitate the unintended result of the conduct."); *People v. Wheeler*, 772 P.2d 101, 103 (Colo.1989) (*en banc*) ("The 'intent to promote or facilitate the commission of the offense' of which the complicity statute speaks is the intent to promote or facilitate the act or conduct of the principal.").

13 The full text of the relevant passage is as follows:

> *Result Elements.* Subsection (4) makes it clear that complicity in conduct causing a particular criminal result entails accountability for that result so long as the accomplice is personally culpable with respect to the result to the extent demanded by the definition of the crime. Thus, if the accomplice recklessly endangers life by rendering assistance to another, he can be convicted of manslaughter if a death results, even though the principal actor's liability is at a different level. In effect, therefore, *the homicidal act is attributed to both participants, with the liability of each measured by his own degree of culpability toward the result.*

results. It is thus a desirable extension of accomplice liability beyond the principles stated in Subsection (3).

MODEL PENAL CODE § 2.06, cmt. 7, at 321–22 (emphasis added); *accord id.* § 2.06, Explanatory Note; *Garnica*, 98 P.3d at 212 ("Section 2.06(4) of the Model Penal Code was intended to make clear that an accomplice must nonetheless meet the required mental state for the offense under the statute."); *Riley*, 60 P.3d at 221 ("The Model Penal Code was written to impose accomplice liability for crimes involving unintended injury or death if the accomplice intentionally promotes or facilitates the *conduct* that produces the injury or death, even though the accomplice did not intend this result. Among the states that have complicity statutes based on the Model Penal Code, most courts have interpreted their statutes this way." (emphasis in original)).

* * *

For the above reasons, at least under the regime of the Model Penal Code, holding an accomplice criminally liable for a result requiring a mental state of recklessness is not theoretically impossible, as Appellant asserts. To the contrary, it is precisely the norm. *Accord Riley*, 60 P.3d at 221 ("With respect to offenses that require proof of a particular result, the government must prove that the accomplice acted with the culpable mental state that applies to that result, as specified in the underlying statute.").[15]

II. THE PENNSYLVANIA CRIMES CODE

As Appellant indicates (albeit lacking the above elaboration), Section 306 of the Pennsylvania Crimes Code derives from the Model Penal Code. See 18 Pa.C.S. § 306, cmt. Furthermore, the provisions of the Crimes Code establishing legal accountability for accomplice conduct are materially identical to the corresponding terms of Section 206 of the MPC in all relevant respects. *Compare id.* § 306(c), (d), *with* MODEL PENAL CODE § 206(3), (4).

* * *

---

15 *See Riley*, 60 P.3d at 211 ("The rule at common law is that when a person purposely assists or encourages another person to engage in conduct that is dangerous to human life or safety, and unintended injury or death results, it does not matter which person actually caused the injury or death by their personal conduct.") (citing, *inter alia*, ROLLIN M. PERKINS & RONALD N. BOYCE, CRIMINAL LAW 739–40 (3d ed.1982)). The Model Penal Code tempered the common law—which held accomplices automatically accountable for any and all objectively foreseeable consequences of a joint unlawful endeavor—by basing accountability on conduct and the level of the accomplice's personal, culpable mental state. *See id.* at 220–21.

III. ATTEMPT AND CONSPIRACY

We turn now to Appellant's citations to judicial decisions involving attempt and conspiracy. In this regard, we appreciate that many of these hold that persons cannot attempt or conspire to commit offenses that require unintended results. It is beyond the scope of this opinion for this Court to address whether such decisions are consistent with Pennsylvania statutory law. Here, we observe only that these lines of cases are materially distinguishable, given that the culpability requirements are different. *See, e.g., Palmer*, 964 P.2d at 528 ("[C]onspiracy, attempt, and complicity are distinct legal principles with different requirements for mental culpability.").

To commit the crime of criminal attempt, a person must act with "intent to commit a specific crime." 18 Pa.C.S. § 901(a) (emphasis added). Therefore, in the attempt setting, the *mens rea* level of "intentionally" attaches to the result (for example, a homicide).[20] This is materially different from the accomplice scenario—in which the required culpability derives from the mental state required for liability of a principal and may be of a lesser degree. See supra part I.

The conspiracy decisions of other courts referenced by Appellant likewise accept that conspiracy encompassed the intent to cause a particular result, cast in terms of the "object."[21] Again, this focus on result serves as the material distinction from the accomplice scenario, where the focus is on the underlying conduct. *See supra* parts I and II.

* * *

This point was cogently made by the Connecticut Supreme Court in [*State v.*] *Foster* [522 A.2d 277 (1987)]. There, the appellant had argued that accomplice to criminally negligent homicide was not a cognizable offense under Connecticut law, because, like attempt or conspiracy liability, such a crime would require finding that the defendant intended to aid an unintended result—a logical impossibility. The *Foster* court disagreed, reasoning, in relevant part, as follows:

---

20 This point is made clearer from the Crimes Code's provisions establishing the general requirements of culpability. *See* 18 Pa.C.S. § 302. For offense elements involving the nature of the actor's conduct or a result thereof, the statute prescribes that a person acts intentionally with respect to a material element of an offense when "it is his conscious object . . . to cause such a *result.*" *Id.* § 302(b)(1)(i) (emphasis added); *see, e.g., Commonwealth v. Hall*, 574 Pa. 233, 240, 830 A.2d 537, 541 (2003) (explaining that, to be guilty of criminal attempt, a defendant's conscious objective must be to cause the result necessary to the substantive crime).

21 *See generally* 15A C.J.S. *Conspiracy* § 112 (2011) ("A conspiracy is a specific intent crime, requiring the intent to agree or conspire and the intent to commit the offense which is object of the conspiracy." (footnote omitted)); WAYNE R. LAFAVE, 2 SUBST. CRIM. L. § 12.2(c)(2) (2d ed.2010) ("[I]t may generally be said that the mental state required [for conspiracy] is an intent to achieve a particular result which is criminal or which though noncriminal is nonetheless covered by the law of conspiracy." (footnotes omitted)).

[T]o be guilty of attempt, a defendant's conscious objective must be to cause the result which would constitute the substantive crime. A person cannot attempt to commit a crime which requires that an unintended result occur, such as involuntary manslaughter, because it is logically impossible for one to intend to bring about an unintended result. Similarly, to be guilty of conspiracy, the defendant, upon entering an agreement, must intend that his conduct achieve the requisite criminal result. When the substantive crime requires an unintended result, a person cannot conspire to commit that crime because it is logically impossible to agree to achieve a specific result unintentionally.

Contrary to the [appellant's] assertions, and unlike attempt or conspiratorial liability, accessorial liability does not require that a defendant act with the conscious objective to cause the result described by a statute.

* * *

[The accomplice statute] merely requires that a defendant have the *mental state required for the commission of a crime* while intentionally aiding another.

Foster, 522 A.2d at 282–83 (citations and footnotes omitted; emphasis in original).

Consistent with the Model Penal Code, the Pennsylvania Crimes Code, and the weight of the authorities, the court thus held that a defendant may be held liable for a criminally negligent act under complicity theory "if he has the requisite culpable mental state for the commission of the substantive offense, and he intentionally aids another in the crime." *Id.* at 284.

* * *

Notes and Questions

1. Roebuck argued that the government should be required to show his intent to kill to convict him. He argued by that if the state was required to show intent to show he was part of a conspiracy to kill, then it ought to be required to show his intent to kill to show he is guilty under a theory of complicity. Isn't there considerable intuitive appeal to this claim? Both conspiracy and complicity involve interacting with others. Conspiracy is punished less severely than the crime itself. One who is guilty of a crime under a theory of

complicity is punished just as if he had committed the crime with his own hands. Why, then, is a theory of group criminal conduct *harder* to prove when it carries less punishment?

2. The drafters of the Model Penal Code wanted to make it easier to prove conspiracy and attempt so that crimes could be more easily prevented and make the amount of punishment turn more on the defendant's actions than the harmful result he caused. Complicity liability is relevant, of course, only if the crime is completed and is punished more severely than conspiracy or attempt. And the same proof that demonstrates a conspiracy, in almost all cases, demonstrates complicity. Does it make sense that the drafters of the Model Penal Code would have required a different and more demanding *mens rea* standard for the lesser crimes of attempt and conspiracy than for complicity liability?

3. Think back to the *Lauria* and *Fountain* decisions in the notes after *Sharma*. Under these decisions, assisting someone known to be committing a crime that requires intent makes the aider or abettor liable for the crime requiring intent, even though the aider or abettor did not have intent. Notice that under the Model Penal Code formulation, an aider or abettor is liable only for a crime containing the mental state he possessed. If he provided gasoline to someone knowing that person was going to make a Molotov cocktail, but not desiring the cocktail to be made or used, he could not, under the MPC, be complicitous in the murders that followed.

4. Imagine you jump into a cab in New York City and tell the driver to "step on it." You tell him that you have an interview at a midtown law firm at 11:00. It's now 10:30. You really should have flown in the night before. You say, "There's a $50 tip in it for you if you get me there by 11:00." Darting through traffic and taking every stop light at least orange, he strikes and kills a pedestrian. Are you criminally liable for the death? How would it matter if your jurisdiction had a statutory scheme identical to Pennsylvania's except that your jurisdiction did not adopt MPC § 206(4).

———————

C. The Inevitable Exercise of Prosecutorial and Police Discretion

Once we have decided that certain acts should be criminal, we have only begun to assess who actually will—or indeed *should*—be punished for violating these laws. Part of the problem is practical. With limited resources, police and prosecutors must figure out which cases to investigate and how limited jail space will be filled. All speeders can't be stopped. Cold cases must eventually be abandoned. Triage must occur.

But there's a more fundamental problem. Legislatures cannot draft laws with such precision that everyone who is technically guilty of violating criminal laws should be punished for violating them. There are times when an individual has committed all the elements of a crime, yet prosecutors, for reasons relating to the uniqueness of the facts of the case, conclude that the defendant should not be punished. Alan Dershowitz has said "the law is a blunderbuss, not a scalpel." The law, that is, cannot define all the special circumstances that explain why an occasional jaywalker should be punished; or the special circumstances explaining why a rare person who took another's life with premeditation should not be punished as one of society's worst offenders. Factors that defy codification require human actors to decide whether the criminal law ought to be invoked to punish and, if so, how much.

As the following cases demonstrate, courts generally engage in little or no oversight of how police and prosecutors exercise this essential discretion. The first two cases look at the power of police and prosecutors to decide which offenders to charge—and how severely to pursue them. The third case in this section examines the prosecutor's discretion in the context of plea bargaining. Plea bargaining is often viewed as largesse by the prosecutor, but as you will see plea bargains highlight the power of power of prosecutors to seek sentences far in excess of those they may find just.

1. Broad Discretion in Charging Decisions

The criminal justice process begins with an arrest or an indictment. An arrest can occur with or without a warrant. For most warrantless arrests—and indeed for many arrests conducted with a warrant—a police officer decided to make the arrest. An indictment—obtained when a prosecutor goes to the grand jury and asks them to find that there was probable cause to believe the defendant committed a crime—follows an arrest, but can occur without an arrest. An arrest would then follow an indictment.

The upshot for our purposes is that the process of prosecution can be initiated by either the police or the prosecutor. As the cases below describe, the power of each to decide which violators to pursue prosecutions against is virtually limitless. So long as the officer or the prosecutor has probable cause (a term you will learn more about in criminal procedure) to believe the defendant is guilty of a crime, the charge will not be questioned even if most, or nearly all, prosecutors would forego such a prosecution.

Oyler and *Batchelder* are the Supreme Court's two primary cases dealing with the broad power of prosecutors to bring charges. Both were unanimous decisions. As you read them consider what you find problematic about the regime they create.

Oyler v. Boles

Supreme Court of the United States
368 U.S. 448 (1962)

Mr. Justice CLARK delivered the opinion of the Court.

The petitioners in these consolidated cases are serving life sentences imposed under West Virginia's habitual criminal statute. This Act provides for a mandatory life sentence upon the third conviction 'of a crime punishable by confinement in a penitentiary.' The increased penalty is to be invoked by an information filed by the prosecuting attorney 'immediately upon conviction and before sentence.' Alleging that this Act had been applied . . . to only a minority of those subject to its provisions, in violation respectively of the Due Process and Equal Protection Clauses of the Fourteenth Amendment, the petitioners filed separate petitions for writs of habeas corpus in the Supreme Court of Appeals of West Virginia. Both of their petitions were denied without opinion. . . . Finding the cases representative of the many recidivist cases that have been docketed in this Court the past few Terms, we granted certiorari. 365 U.S. 810, 81 S.Ct. 701, 5 L.Ed.2d 690. We now affirm the judgment in each case.

William Oyler, the petitioner in No. 56, was convicted of murder in the second degree on February 5, 1953, which offense carried a penalty of from 5 to 18 years' imprisonment. Sentence was deferred, and on February 11 his motion for a new trial was overruled. On that same date the Prosecuting Attorney requested and was granted leave to file an information in writing alleging that Oyler was the same person who had suffered three prior convictions in Pennsylvania which were punishable by confinement in a penitentiary. After being cautioned as to the effect of such information, Oyler, accompanied by his counsel, acknowledged in open court that he was the person named in the information. The court then determined that the defendant had thrice been convicted of crimes punishable by confinement in a penitentiary and sentenced him to life imprisonment. . . . He . . . attacked his sentence on the equal protection ground previously set forth.

In 1957 Paul Crabtree, the petitioner in No. 57, pleaded guilty to forging a $35 check, which offense carried a penalty of from 2 to 10 years' imprisonment. Sentence was deferred, and a week later the Prosecuting Attorney informed the court that Crabtree had suffered two previous felony convictions, one in the State of Washington and one in West Virginia. The trial judge, after cautioning Crabtree of the effect of the information and his rights under it, inquired if he was in fact the accused person. Crabtree, who had been represented by counsel throughout, admitted in open court that he was such person. Upon this admission and the accused's further statement that he had nothing more to say, the court proceeded to sentence him to life imprisonment. Like Oyler, he also raised the equal protection ground.

* * *

II.

Petitioners . . . claim they were denied the equal protection of law guaranteed by the Fourteenth Amendment. In his petition for a writ of habeas corpus to the Supreme Court of Appeals of West Virginia, Oyler stated:

> Petitioner was discriminated against as an Habitual Criminal in that from January, 1940, to June, 1955, there were six men sentenced in the Taylor County Circuit Court who were subject to prosecution as Habitual offenders, Petitioner was the only man thus sentenced during this period. It is a matter of record that the five men who were not prosecuted as Habitual Criminals during this period, all had three or more felony convictions and sentences as adults, and Petitioner's former convictions were a result of Juvenile Court actions.

> #5. The Petitioner was discriminated against by selective use of a mandatory State Statute, in that 904 men who were known offenders throughout the State of West Virginia were not sentenced as required by the mandatory Statutes, Chapter 61, Article 11, Sections 18 and 19 of the Code. Equal Protection and Equal Justice was (sic) denied.

Statistical data based on prison records were appended to the petition to support the latter allegation. Crabtree in his petition included similar statistical support and alleged:

'The said Statute are (sic) administered and applied in such a manner as to be in violation of Equal Protection and Equal Justice therefor in conflict with the Fourteenth Amendment to the Constitution of the United States.'

Thus petitioners' contention is that the habitual criminal statute imposes a mandatory duty on the prosecuting authorities to seek the severer penalty against all persons coming within the statutory standards but that it is done only in a minority of cases.[10] This, petitioners argue, denies equal protection to those persons against whom the heavier penalty is enforced. We note that it is not stated whether the failure to proceed against other three-time offenders was due to lack of knowledge of the prior offenses on the part of the prosecutors or was the result of a deliberate policy of proceeding only in a certain class of cases or against specific persons. The statistics merely show that according to penitentiary records a high percentage of those subject to the law have not been proceeded against. There is no indication that these records of previous convictions, which may not have been compiled until after the three-time offenders had reached the penitentiary, were available to the prosecutors.[11] Hence the allegations set out no more than a failure to prosecute others because of a lack of knowledge of their prior offenses. This does not deny equal protection due petitioners under the Fourteenth Amendment. *See Sanders v. Waters*, 199 F.2d 317 (C.A. 10th Cir. 1952); *Oregon v. Hicks*. 213 Or. 619, 325 P.2d 794 (1958).

Moreover, the conscious exercise of some selectivity in enforcement is not in itself a federal constitutional violation. Even though the statistics in this case might imply a policy of selective enforcement, it was not stated that the selection was deliberately based upon an unjustifiable standard such as race, religion, or other arbitrary classification. Therefore grounds supporting a finding of a denial of equal protection were not alleged. *Oregon v. Hicks*, supra; cf. *Snowden v. Hughes*, 321 U.S. 1, 64 S.Ct. 397, 88 L.Ed. 497 (1944); *Yick Wo v. Hopkins*, 118 U.S. 356, 6 S.Ct. 1064, 30 L.Ed. 220 (1886) (by implication).

＊ ＊ ＊

Affirmed.

---

10   The denial of relief by West Virginia's highest court may have involved the determination that the statute, like its counterpart § 6260, infra, note 11, is not mandatory. Such an interpretation would be binding upon this Court. However, we need not inquire into this point.

11   After prisoners are confined in the penitentiary, the warden is granted discretion as to the invocation of the severer penalty. W.Va.Code, 1961, § 6260. Thus the failure to invoke the penalty in the cases cited by petitioners may reflect the exercise of such discretion.

Notes and Questions

1. Think back to David Lewis' article on moral luck. The third-strike enhancement, of course, is not the function of chance but the unstated and unreviewable decision of a prosecutor. Is this better than blind luck? Do we have any way of knowing the answer to that last question?

2. Prosecutors are typically elected by county-wide votes and, within any given state, would come from locations with very different political dynamics. Perhaps more importantly, people are elected to prosecutors with very different agendas and, once there, have very different management styles. Some will give individual line prosecutors enormous authority to decide how to charge and plead cases, others will create very hierarchical offices with strict policies on how certain types of cases should be handled. One should not expect consistency in how prosecutors charge or settle cases—the system is all but engineered to create inconsistency. Would Paul Crabtree, who at the time of *Oyler* was decided was serving life in a West Virginia penitentiary for forging a $35.00 check, have been any worse off if life sentences for third-time offenders were decided by the drawing of straws?

Batchelder takes a look at a different angle of the question in *Oyler*. Again, the Court is considering the question of the type of oversight it may exercise over prosecutorial charging decisions.

Batchelder v. United States

Supreme Court of the United States
442 U.S. 114 (1979)

Mr. Justice MARSHALL delivered the opinion of the Court.

At issue in this case are two overlapping provisions of the Omnibus Crime Control and Safe Streets Act of 1968 (Omnibus Act). Both prohibit convicted felons from receiving firearms, but each authorizes different maximum penalties. We must determine whether a defendant convicted of the offense carrying the greater penalty may be sentenced only under the more lenient provision when his conduct violates both statutes.

I

Respondent, a previously convicted felon, was found guilty of receiving a firearm that had traveled in interstate commerce, in violation of 18 U.S.C. § 922(h).[2] The District Court sentenced him under 18 U.S.C. § 924(a) to five years' imprisonment, the maximum term authorized for violation of § 922(h).[3]

The Court of Appeals affirmed the conviction but, by a divided vote, remanded for resentencing. 581 F.2d 626 (CA7 1978). The majority recognized that respondent had been indicted and convicted under § 922(h) and that § 924(a) permits five years' imprisonment for such violations. 581 F.2d, at 629. However, noting that the substantive elements of § 922(h) and 18 U.S.C.App. § 1202(a) are identical as applied to a convicted felon who unlawfully receives a firearm, the court interpreted the Omnibus Act to allow no more than the 2-year maximum sentence provided by § 1202(a). 581 F.2d, at 629.[4] In so holding, the Court of Appeals relied on three principles of statutory construction. Because, in its view, the "arguably contradict[ory]" penalty provisions for similar conduct and the "inconclusive" legislative history raised doubt whether Congress had intended the two penalty provisions to coexist, the court first applied the doctrine that ambiguities in criminal legislation are to be resolved in favor of the defendant. Id. at 630. Second, the court determined that since § 1202(a) was "Congress' last word on the issue of penalty," it may have implicitly repealed the punishment provisions of § 924(a). 581 F.2d, at 630. Acknowledging that the "first two principles cannot be applied to these facts without some difficulty," the majority also invoked the maxim that a court should, if possible, interpret a statute to avoid constitutional questions. Id., at 630–631. Here, the court reasoned, the "prosecutor's power to select one of

---

2   In pertinent part, 18 U.S.C. § 922(h) provides: "It shall be unlawful for any person—"(1) who is under indictment for, or who has been convicted in any court of, a crime punishable by imprisonment for a term exceeding one year; "(2) who is a fugitive from justice; "(3) who is an unlawful user of or addicted to marihuana or any depressant or stimulant drug . . . or narcotic drug . . .; or "(4) who has been adjudicated as a mental defective or who has been committed to any mental institution;"to receive any firearm or ammunition which has been shipped or transported in interstate or foreign commerce."

3   Title 18 U.S.C. § 924(a) provides in relevant part: "Whoever violates any provision of this chapter . . . shall be fined not more than $5,000, or imprisoned not more than five years, or both, and shall become eligible for parole as the Board of Parole shall determine."

4   Section 1202(a) states: "Any person who—"(1) has been convicted by a court of the United States or of a State or any political subdivision thereof of a felony, or "(2) has been discharged from the Armed Forces under dishonorable conditions, or "(3) has been adjudged by a court of the United States or of a State or any political subdivision thereof of being mentally incompetent, or "(4) having been a citizen of the United States has renounced his citizenship, or "(5) being an alien is illegally or unlawfully in the United States,"and who receives, possesses, or transports in commerce or affecting commerce, after the date of enactment of this Act, any firearm shall be fined not more than $10,000 or imprisoned for not more than two years, or both." 18 U.S.C.App. § 1202(a).

two statutes that are identical except for their penalty provisions" implicated "important constitutional protections." Id., at 631.

The dissent found no basis in the Omnibus Act or its legislative history for engrafting the penalty provisions of § 1202(a) onto §§ 922(h) and 924(a). 581 F.2d, at 638–639. Relying on "the long line of cases . . . which hold that where an act may violate more than one criminal statute, the government may elect to prosecute under either, even if [the] defendant risks the harsher penalty, so long as the prosecutor does not discriminate against any class of defendants," the dissent further concluded that the statutory scheme was constitutional. *Id.*, at 637.

We granted certiorari, 439 U.S. 1066, 99 S.Ct. 830, 59 L.Ed.2d 30 (1979), and now reverse the judgment vacating respondent's 5-year prison sentence.

II

. . . [W]e find nothing in the language, structure, or legislative history of the Omnibus Act to suggest that because of this overlap, a defendant convicted under § 922(h) may be imprisoned for no more than the maximum term specified in § 1202(a). As we read the Act, each substantive statute, in conjunction with its own sentencing provision, operates independently of the other.

* * *

In construing § 1202(a) to override the penalties authorized by § 924(a), the Court of Appeals relied, we believe erroneously, on three principles of statutory interpretation. First, the court invoked the well-established doctrine that ambiguities in criminal statutes must be resolved in favor of lenity. Although this principle of construction applies to sentencing as well as substantive provisions, see *Simpson v. United States*, 435 U.S. 6, 14–15, 98 S.Ct. 909, 913–914, 55 L.Ed.2d 70 (1978), in the instant case there is no ambiguity to resolve. Respondent unquestionably violated § 922(h), and § 924(a) unquestionably permits five years' imprisonment for such a violation. That § 1202(a) provides different penalties for essentially the same conduct is no justification for taking liberties with unequivocal statutory language. See *Barrett v. United States*, 423 U.S. 212, 217, 96 S.Ct. 498, 501, 46 L.Ed.2d 450 (1976). By its express terms, § 1202(a) limits its penalty scheme exclusively to convictions obtained under that provision. Where as here, "Congress has conveyed its purpose clearly, . . . we decline to manufacture ambiguity where none exists." *United States v. Culbert, supra*, 435 U.S., at 379, 98 S.Ct., at 1117.

Nor can § 1202(a) be interpreted as implicitly repealing § 924(a) whenever a defendant's conduct might violate both Titles. For it is "not enough to show that the two statutes produce differing results when applied to the same factual situation." *Radzanower v. Touche Ross & Co.*, 426 U.S. 148, 155, 96 S.Ct. 1989, 1993, 48 L.Ed.2d 540 (1976). Rather, the legislative intent to repeal must be manifest in the "'positive repugnancy between the provisions.'" *United States v. Borden Co.*, 308 U.S. 188, 199, 60 S.Ct. 182, 188, 84 L.Ed. 181 (1939). In this case, however, the penalty provisions are fully capable of coexisting because they apply to convictions under different statutes.

Finally, the maxim that statutes should be construed to avoid constitutional questions offers no assistance here. This "'cardinal principle' of statutory construction . . . is appropriate only when [an alternative interpretation] is 'fairly possible'" from the language of the statute. *Swain v. Pressley*, 430 U.S. 372, 378 n.11 (1977) * * *. We simply are unable to discern any basis in the Omnibus Act for reading the term "five" in § 924(a) to mean "two."

III

In resolving the statutory question, the majority below expressed "serious doubts about the constitutionality of two statutes that provide different penalties for identical conduct." 581 F.2d, at 633–634 (footnote omitted). Specifically, the court suggested that the statutes might (1) be void for vagueness, (2) implicate "due process and equal protection interest[s] in avoiding excessive prosecutorial discretion and in obtaining equal justice," and (3) constitute an impermissible delegation of congressional authority. *Id.*, at 631–633. We find no constitutional infirmities.

A

It is a fundamental tenet of due process that "[n]o one may be required at peril of life, liberty or property to speculate as to the meaning of penal statutes." *Lanzetta v. New Jersey*, 306 U.S. 451, 453, 59 S.Ct. 618, 619, 83 L.Ed. 888 (1939). A criminal statute is therefore invalid if it "fails to give a person of ordinary intelligence fair notice that his contemplated conduct is forbidden." *United States v. Harriss*, 347 U.S. 612, 617, 74 S.Ct. 808, 812, 98 L.Ed. 989 (1954). * * * So too, vague sentencing provisions may post constitutional questions if they do not state with sufficient clarity the consequences of violating a given criminal statute. See *United States v. Evans*, 333 U.S. 483, 68 S.Ct. 634, 92 L.Ed. 823 (1948); *United States v. Brown*, 333 U.S. 18, 68 S.Ct. 376, 92 L.Ed. 442 (1948); *cf. Giaccio v. Pennsylvania*, 382 U.S. 399, 86 S.Ct. 518, 15 L.Ed.2d 447 (1966).

The provisions in issue here, however, unambiguously specify the activity proscribed and the penalties available upon conviction. See *supra*, at 2201–2202. That this particular conduct may violate both Titles does not detract from the notice afforded by each. Although the statutes create uncertainty as to which crime may be charged and therefore what penalties may be imposed, they do so to no greater extent than would a single statute authorizing various alternative punishments. So long as overlapping criminal provisions clearly define the conduct prohibited and the punishment authorized, the notice requirements of the Due Process Clause are satisfied.

B

This Court has long recognized that when an act violates more than one criminal statute, the Government may prosecutes under either so long as it does not discriminate against any class of defendants. See *United States v. Beacon Brass Co.*, 344 U.S. 43, 45–46, 73 S.Ct. 77, 79, 97 L.Ed. 61 (1952) * * *. Whether to prosecute and what charge to file or bring before a grand jury are decisions that generally rest in the prosecutor's discretion. See *Confiscation Cases*, 7 Wall. 454, 19 L.Ed. 196 (1869); *United States v. Nixon*, 418 U.S. 683, 693, 94 S.Ct. 3090, 3100, 41 L.Ed.2d 1039 (1974); *Bordenkircher v. Hayes*, 434 U.S. 357, 364, 98 S.Ct. 663, 668, 54 L.Ed.2d 604 (1978).

The Court of Appeals acknowledged this "settled rule" allowing prosecutorial choice. 581 F.2d, at 632. Nevertheless, relying on the dissenting opinion in *Berra v. United States*, 351 U.S. 131, 76 S.Ct. 685, 100 L.Ed. 1013 (1956),[8] the court distinguished overlapping statutes with identical standards of proof from provisions that vary in some particular. 581 F.2d, at 632–633. In the court's view, when two statutes prohibit "exactly the same conduct," the prosecutor's "selection of which of two penalties to apply" would be "unfettered." *Id.*, at 633, and n.11. Because such prosecutorial discretion could produce "unequal justice," the court expressed doubt that this form of legislative redundancy was constitutional. *Id.*, at 631. We find this analysis factually and legally unsound.

Contrary to the Court of Appeals' assertions, a prosecutor's discretion to choose between §§ 922(h) and 1202(a) is not "unfettered." Selectivity in the enforcement of criminal laws is, of course, subject to constitutional constraints.[9] And a decision to proceed under § 922(h) does not empower the Government to predetermine ultimate criminal sanctions. Rather, it merely enables the sentencing judge to impose a longer prison sentence than § 1202(a) would permit and precludes him from imposing the greater fine authorized by § 1202(a). More

---

8 *Berra* involved two tax evasion statutes, which the Court interpreted as proscribing identical conduct. The defendant, who was charged and convicted under the felony provision, argued that the jury should have been instructed on the misdemeanor offense as well. The Court rejected this contention and refused to consider whether the defendant's sentence was invalid because in excess of the maximum authorized by the misdemeanor statute. The dissent urged that permitting the prosecutor to control whether a particular act would be punished as a misdemeanor or a felony raised "serious constitutional questions." 351 U.S., at 139–140, 76 S.Ct., at 691.

9 The Equal Protection Clause prohibits selective enforcement "based upon an unjustifiable standard such as race, religion, or other arbitrary classification." *Oyler v. Boles*, 368 U.S. 448, 456, 82 S.Ct. 501, 506, 7 L.Ed.2d 446 (1962). Respondent does not allege that his prosecution was motivated by improper considerations.

importantly, there is no appreciable difference between the discretion a prosecutor exercises when deciding whether to charge under one of two statutes with different elements and the discretion he exercises when choosing one of two statutes with identical elements. In the former situation, once he determines that the proof will support conviction under either statute, his decision is indistinguishable from the one he faces in the latter context. The prosecutor may be influenced by the penalties available upon conviction, but this fact, standing alone, does not give rise to a violation of the Equal Protection or Due Process Clause. *Cf. Rosenberg v. United States, supra*, 346 U.S., at 294, 73 S.Ct., at 1163 (Clark, J., concurring); *Oyler v. Boles, supra*, 368 U.S., at 456, 82 S.Ct., at 505. Just as a defendant has no constitutional right to elect which of two applicable federal statutes shall be the basis of his indictment and prosecution neither is he entitled to choose the penalty scheme under which he will be sentenced. *See* U.S.Const., Art. II, §§ 2, 3; 28 U.S.C. §§ 515, 516; *United States v. Nixon, supra*, 418 U.S., at 694, 94 S.Ct., at 3100.

Approaching the problem of prosecutorial discretion from a slightly different perspective, the Court of Appeals postulated that the statutes might impermissibly delegate to the Executive Branch the Legislature's responsibility to fix criminal penalties. *See United States v. Hudson*, 7 Cranch 32, 34, 3 L.Ed. 259 (1812); *United States v. Grimaud*, 220 U.S. 506, 516–517, 519, 31 S.Ct. 480, 482–483, 484, 55 L.Ed. 563 (1911); *United States v. Evans*, 333 U.S., at 486, 68 S.Ct., at 636. We do not agree. The provisions at issue plainly demarcate the range of penalties that prosecutors and judges may seek and impose. In light of that specificity, the power that Congress has delegated to those officials is no broader than the authority they routinely exercise in enforcing the criminal laws. Having informed the courts, prosecutors, and defendants of the permissible punishment alternatives available under each Title, Congress has fulfilled its duty. *See United States v. Evans, supra*, at 486, 492, 495, 68 S.Ct., at 636, 639, 640.

Accordingly, the judgment of the Court of Appeals is
Reversed.

Notes and Questions

1. Are you satisfied, as Justice Thurgood Marshall apparently is, that so long as a prosecutor does not make his decision on the basis of an illegitimate factor, such as race or religion, that there is no reason to be concerned about whether the prosecutor chooses to seek a two- or five-year penalty for the same offense? Could the government legitimately prosecute everyone who committed a crime on, say, a Tuesday and let everyone else go?

2. Both *Oyler* and *Batchelder* observe that laws may not be enforced on the basis of race, religion, or other impermissible grounds. Practically, however, this is not a very substantial limitation. To prevail on a claim that a prosecution is based on race, gender, or religious ground is very difficult to demonstrate. In *Armstrong v. United States*, 517 U.S. 456 (1996), the Supreme Court denied an African American defendant limited discovery to prove his claim that crack cocaine prosecutions in his federal jurisdiction were racially motivated. His case was far from frivolous. He demonstrated that the state criminal justice system had prosecuted white crack cocaine offenders and that all of the crack cocaine defendants in the federal court had been African American. *See* Melissa L. Jampol, *Goodbye to the Defense of Selective Prosecution*, 87 J. Crim. L. & Criminology 932 (1997).

3. The fact that there are few judicially enforceable restrains on prosecutorial discretion does not mean that there are no principles whatsoever. Consider the following.

U.S. Attorney's Manual
U.S. Department of Justice

§ 9-27.220 *Grounds for Commencing or Declining Prosecution*

A. The attorney for the government should commence or recommend Federal prosecution if he/she believes that the person's conduct constitutes a Federal offense and that the admissible evidence will probably be sufficient to obtain and sustain a conviction, unless, in his/her judgment, prosecution should be declined because:

1. No substantial Federal interest would be served by prosecution;

2. The person is subject to effective prosecution in another jurisdiction; or

3. There exists an adequate non-criminal alternative to prosecution.

B. Comment. * * *

Merely because the attorney for the government believes that a person's conduct constitutes a Federal offense and that the admissible evidence will be sufficient to obtain and sustain a conviction, does not mean that he/she necessarily should initiate or recommend prosecution: USAM 9-27.220 notes three situations in which the prosecutor may property decline to take action nonetheless: when no substantial Federal interest would be served by prosecution; when the person is subject to effective prosecution in another jurisdiction; and when there exists an adequate non-criminal alternative to prosecution. It is left to the judgment of the attorney for the government whether such a situation exists. In exercising that judgment, the attorney for the government should consult USAM 9-27.230, 9-27.240, or 9-27.250, as appropriate.

§ 9-27.230 Initiating and Declining Charges—Substantial Federal Interest

A. In determining whether prosecution should be declined because no substantial Federal interest would be served by prosecution, the attorney for the government should weigh all relevant considerations, including:

1. Federal law enforcement priorities;

2. The nature and seriousness of the offense;

3. The deterrent effect of prosecution;

4. The person's culpability in connection with the offense;

5. The person's history with respect to criminal activity;

6. The person's willingness to cooperate in the investigation or prosecution of others; and

7. The probable sentence or other consequences if the person is convicted.

B. Comment. USAM 9-27.230 lists factors that may be relevant in determining whether prosecution should be declined because no substantial Federal interest would be served by prosecution in a case in which the person is believed to have committed a Federal offense and the admissible evidence is expected to be sufficient to obtain and sustain a conviction. The list of relevant considerations is not intended to be all-inclusive. Obviously, not all of the factors will be applicable to every case, and in any particular case one factor may deserve more weight than it might in another case.

1. *Federal Law Enforcement Priorities.* Federal law enforcement resources and Federal judicial resources are not sufficient to permit prosecution of every alleged offense over which Federal jurisdiction exists. Accordingly, in the interest of allocating its limited resources so as to achieve an effective nationwide law enforcement program, from time to time the Department establishes national investigative and prosecutorial priorities. * * *

2. *Nature and Seriousness of Offense.* It is important that limited Federal resources not be wasted in prosecuting inconsequential cases or cases in which the violation is only technical. Thus, in determining whether a substantial Federal interest exists that requires prosecution, the attorney for the government should consider the nature and seriousness of the offense involved. A number of factors may be relevant. One factor that is obviously of primary importance is the actual or potential impact of the offense on the community and on the victim.

   The impact of an offense on the community in which it is committed can be measured in several ways: in terms of economic harm done to community interests; in terms of physical danger to the citizens or damage to public property; and in terms of erosion of the inhabitants' peace of mind and sense of security. In assessing the seriousness of the offense in these terms, the prosecutor may properly weigh such questions as whether the violation is technical or relatively inconsequential in nature and what the public attitude is toward prosecution under the circumstances of the case. The public may be indifferent, or even opposed, to enforcement of the controlling statute whether on substantive grounds, or because of a history of nonenforcement, or because the offense involves essentially a minor matter of private concern and the victim is not interested in having it pursued. On the other hand, the nature and circumstances of the offense, the identity of the offender or the victim, or the attendant publicity, may be such as to create strong public sentiment in favor of prosecution. While public interest, or lack thereof, deserves the prosecutor's careful attention, it should not be used to justify a decision to prosecute, or to take other action, that cannot be supported on other grounds. Public and professional responsibility sometimes will require the choosing of a particularly unpopular course.

   Economic, physical, and psychological considerations are also important in assessing the impact of the offense on the victim. In this connection, it is appropriate for the prosecutor to take into account such matters as the victim's age or health, and whether full or partial restitution has been made. Care should be taken in weighing the matter of restitution, however, to ensure against contributing to an impression that an offender can escape prosecution merely by returning the spoils of his/her crime.

3. *Deterrent Effect of Prosecution.* Deterrence of criminal conduct, whether it be criminal activity generally or a specific type of criminal conduct, is one of the primary goals of the criminal law. This purpose should be kept in mind, particularly when deciding whether a prosecution is warranted for an offense that appears to be relatively minor; some offenses, although seemingly not of great importance by themselves, if commonly committed would have a substantial cumulative impact on the community.

4. *The Person's Culpability.* Although the prosecutor has sufficient evidence of guilt, it is nevertheless appropriate for him/her to give consideration to the degree of the person's culpability in connection with the offenses, both in the abstract and in comparison with any others involved in the offense. If for example, the person was a relatively minor participant in a criminal enterprise conducted by others, or his/her motive was worthy, and no other circumstances require prosecution, the prosecutor might reasonably conclude that some course other than prosecution would be appropriate.

5. *The Person's Criminal History.* If a person is known to have a prior conviction or is reasonably believed to have engaged in criminal activity at an earlier time, this should, be considered in determining whether to initiate or recommend Federal prosecution. In this connection particular attention should be given to the nature of the person's prior criminal involvement, when it occurred, its relationship if any to the present offense, and whether he/she previously avoided prosecution as a result of an agreement not to prosecute in return for cooperation or as a result of an order compelling his/her testimony. By the same token, a person's lack of prior criminal involvement or his/her previous cooperation with the law enforcement officials should be given due consideration in appropriate cases.

6. *The Person's Willingness to Cooperate.* A person's willingness to cooperate in the investigation or prosecution of others is another appropriate consideration in the determination whether a Federal prosecution

should be undertaken. Generally speaking, a willingness to cooperate should not by itself relieve a person of criminal liability. There may be some cases, however, in which the value of a person's cooperation clearly outweighs the Federal interest in prosecuting him/her. * * *

7. *The Person's Personal Circumstances.* In some cases, the personal circumstances of an accused may be relevant in determining whether to prosecute or to take other action. Some circumstances peculiar to the accused, such as extreme youth, advanced age, or mental or physical impairment, may suggest that prosecution is not the most appropriate response to his/her offense; other circumstances, such as the fact that the accused occupied a position of trust or responsibility which he/she violated in committing the offense, might weigh in favor of prosecution.

8. *The Probable Sentence.* In assessing the strength of the Federal interest in prosecution, the attorney for the government should consider the sentence, or other consequence, that is likely to be imposed if prosecution is successful, and whether such a sentence or other consequence would justify the time and effort of prosecution. If the offender is already subject to a substantial sentence, or is already incarcerated, as a result of a conviction for another offense, the prosecutor should weigh the likelihood that another conviction will result in a meaningful addition to his/her sentence, might otherwise have a deterrent effect, or is necessary to ensure that the offender's record accurately reflects the extent of his/her criminal conduct. For example, it might be desirable to commence a bail-jumping prosecution against a person who already has been convicted of another offense so that law enforcement personnel and judicial officers who encounter him/her in the future will be aware of the risk of releasing him/her on bail. On the other hand, if the person is on probation or parole as a result of an earlier conviction, the prosecutor should consider whether the public interest might better be served by instituting a proceeding for violation of probation or revocation of parole, than by commencing a new prosecution. The prosecutor should also be alert to the desirability of instituting prosecution to prevent the running of the statute of limitations and to preserve the availability of a basis for an adequate sentence if there appears to be a chance that an offender's prior conviction may be reversed on appeal or collateral attack. Finally, if a person previously has been prosecuted in another jurisdiction for the same offense or a closely related offense, the attorney for the government should consult existing departmental policy statements on the subject of "successive prosecution" or "dual prosecution," depending on whether

the earlier prosecution w as Federal or nonfederal. See USAM 9-2.031 (Petite Policy).

Just as there are factors that are appropriate to consider in determining whether a substantial Federal interest would be served by prosecution in a particular case, there are considerations that deserve no weight and should not influence the decision. These include the time and resources expended in Federal investigation of the case. No amount of investigative effort warrants commencing a Federal prosecution that is not fully justified on other grounds.

§ 9-27.250 Non-Criminal Alternatives to Prosecution

A. In determining whether prosecution should be declined because there exists an adequate, non-criminal alternative to prosecution, the attorney for the government should consider all relevant factors, including:

1. The sanctions available under the alternative means of disposition;

2. The likelihood that an effective sanction will be imposed; and

3. The effect of non-criminal disposition on Federal law enforcement interests.

B. Comment. When a person has committed a Federal offense, it is important that the law respond promptly, fairly, and effectively. This does not mean, however, that a criminal prosecution must be initiated. In recognition of the fact that resort to the criminal process is not necessarily the only appropriate response to serious forms of antisocial activity, Congress and state legislatures have provided civil and administrative remedies for many types of conduct that may also be subject to criminal sanction. Examples of such non-criminal approaches include civil tax proceedings; civil actions under the securities, customs, antitrust, or other regulatory laws; and reference of complaints to licensing authorities or to professional organizations such as bar associations. Another potentially useful alternative to prosecution in some cases is pretrial diversion. See USAM 9-22.000.

Attorneys for the government should familiarize themselves with these alternatives and should consider pursuing them if they are available in a particular case. Although on some occasions they should be pursued in addition to the criminal law procedures, on other occasions they can be expected to provide an effective substitute for criminal prosecution. In weighing the adequacy of such an alternative in a particular case, the prosecutor should consider the nature and severity of the sanctions that could be imposed, the likelihood that an adequate sanction would in fact be imposed, and the effect of such a non-criminal disposition on Federal law enforcement interests. * * *

§ 9-27.260 Initiating and Declining Charges—Impermissible Considerations

A. In determining whether to commence or recommend prosecution or take other action against a person, the attorney for the government should not be influenced by:

1. The person's race, religion, sex, national origin, or political association, activities or beliefs;

2. The attorney's own personal feelings concerning the person, the person's associates, or the victim; or

3. The possible effect of the decision on the attorney's own professional or personal circumstances.

4. The National District Attorneys' Association publishes the National Prosecution Standards which also offer thoughtful guidance on the exercise of prosecutorial discretion. *See* NDAA, National Prosecution Standards 4-1.3, 4-1.4 (3d ed. 2009).

PRACTICE EXERCISE

Mitchel Amfree grew up in a rural area in the State of Eastern Washington, as the oldest of seven children. He learned the value of hard work from his father and mother, Russian immigrants, who fled the oppressive Stalinist regime in Russia in the 1930's. His parents worked hard to provide for him and their six other children, barely making ends meet as potato farmers, but being scrupulously honest people, never missed a payment on their farm, nor renegotiated their output contracts when the market rate for potatoes fluctuated in their favor.

Mitchel worked on the farm, maintained equipment, performed back-breaking labor in the sweltering summers and bleak winters, and helped make a better life for his family. He felt a sense of responsibility as the oldest child to ensure that his siblings did not have to work as he did, but could instead go to school and make an even better life for themselves.

One day, Mitchel was instructed to cut a check as a down-payment for the fertilizer ordered for the upcoming season. As the new bookkeeper for the farm (despite his lack of formal education), Mitchel knew there were insufficient funds, because of a terrible drought that destroyed most of the prior season's crop. Mitchel wrote a check using a fake account number, in order to buy some time to acquire the necessary funds. Besides, he knew the fertilizer seller utilized illegal credit methods when he sold to buyers, and thought "fair is fair." The new prosecuting attorney, rearing to fight injustice, decided to prosecute Mitchel to the fullest extent of the law. The WadWalla Court of Eastern Washington sentenced Mitchel to 20 years in prison, an intermediate sentence. Because of Mitchel's good behavior in prison, he was paroled after 3.5 years.

Shamed and unwilling to bear the scorn of the farming community in Eastern Washington, Mitchel traveled to North Virginia, where he performed odd jobs and worked as a farm-hand, until his reputation as a hard worker, "just down on his luck," earned him a spot as a bookkeeper for a small farm. Mitchel never "grafted" crops as a "bonus" as other seasonal farmhands were known to do. When the farm's creditor called for payment on the farm, Mitchel showed him a falsified, "rough" sketch of accounts, to keep the farm going until next pay period, and offered payment on those accounts. It worked. The creditor deferred payment two months. But North Virginia prosecuted Mitchel, found him guilty, and sentenced him to 1-5 years in prison.

Upon release, having no place to work and bitterly angry at his loyal attempts to first protect his family and then his employer, Mitchel became homeless, wandering the backwoods in North Virginia, living off the land and contemplating what do to with his life. He decided to return home to Eastern Washington and seek forgiveness from his family. The Bluehound bus ride cost only $35. Mitchel didn't hesitate to draw up a forged check for the amount. "I just need to get out of here," he thought, "Or I'll never amount to anything." Besides, half the passengers had bribed the driver to pick them up just outside of town. But when the account was found to be falsified, Bluehound stopped the bus at a federal law enforcement office in West Dakota where federal agents arrested Mitchel.

You are a Mitchel's defense counsel. Using the Federal Handbook factors as a guide, outline a plea letter to the federal prosecutor with the aim of avoiding a prosecution or obtaining a minimal charge. Assume: (1) the federal government sometimes hands cases over to states for prosecution, but prefers to avoid dual-prosecutions (federal and state); (2) North Virginia has a habitual offender statute that imposes a minimum life sentence for a third felony, pooling felonies committed anywhere in the United States; and (3) the federal prosecutor will try to retain negotiating power by threatening to hand the case over to North Virginia for prosecution.

Consider: (a) what extra facts would you try to find out which may be helpful in your letter to the prosecutor? (b) Is there a double jeopardy bar for concurrent federal and state prosecutions? (c) As a matter of policy, should the mens rea element for Mitchel's mental state be: (1) knowledge of the falsification; (2) knowledge of illegality; (3) or knowledge and desire to cause harm?

D. De Minimis Statutes

There are very rare pockets of the law that give judges the ability to review prosecutorial charging decisions. Only about ten jurisdictions have statutes that allow judges to dismiss minor charges in the interests of justice and where they exist, they are rarely used. The *Smith* case is an example of one of the rare applications of a *de minimis* statute to stop a prosecution. The significance of these statutes and the *Smith* decision should not be overstated. In jurisdictions with *de minimis* statutes, however, there is a limited vehicle for judges to check the charging power of prosecutors.

In the Smith case, though, the judge is exercising the type of discretion typically exercised by a prosecutor. This case therefore provides some insight into on how prosecutors do—and perhaps should—look at cases.

State v. Smith

Superior Court of New Jersey
480 A.2d 236 (1984)

LENOX, A.J.S.C.

Defendant contends the charge that he stole three pieces of bubble gum has been blown out of proportion. "Truly trivial cases are rarely prosecuted." *State v. Hegyi*, 185 *N.J.Super.* 229, 233, 447 A.2d 1369 (Law Div.1982). The issue of whether this case is an exception is a sticky one which invites analysis.

Defendant is charged with shoplifting (*N.J.S.A.* 2C:20–11) by "concealing merchandise of three (3) pieces of bazooka bubble gum valued at $.15 with the intention of depriving the merchant of the full retail value (thereof). He has moved before the assignment judge for a dismissal of the prosecution under *N.J.S.A.* 2C:2–11(b), entitled "De minimis infractions," which reads:

> The assignment judge may dismiss a prosecution if, having regard to the nature of the conduct charged to constitute an offense and the nature of the attendant circumstances, it finds that the defendant's conduct:
>
> > b. Did not actually cause or threaten the harm or evil sought to be prevented by the law defining the offense or did so only to an extent too trivial to warrant the condemnation of conviction. . . .

Defendant is enrolled as a full-time student at Trenton State College where he is pursuing a degree in electrical engineering. On March 8, 1984, he entered a "7–11" grocery store. He first selected three pieces of bubble gum and slipped them into his pocket. After selecting his other purchases he went to the register at the checkout counter where he was apprehended by the store manager. The police were summoned and he was arrested and charged on the complaint which was signed by the manager. The record is unclear as to whether he was accused by the manager before paying for his purchases. He had not yet left the store premises.

In his certification in support of the motion defendant further contends that he placed the bubble gum in his pocket "for convenience," as he was carrying a large AM–FM portable radio weighing 10 pounds and intended to purchase other items. The offense charged under *N.J.S.A.* 2C:20–11(b)(2) is complete upon concealment of the merchandise purposely with the proscribed intention. Since defendant's allegation in this regard is contrary to the charge in the complaint it must be disregarded. This motion is to be decided on the basis of the State's contention regarding the commission of the offense and uncontroverted facts of record. A defendant's innocence may not be adjudicated by motion filed pursuant to the statute. *State v. Brown,* 188 *N.J.Super.* 656, 671, 458 A.2d 165 (Law Div.1983); *but see State v. Hegyi, supra,* and *State v. Evans,* 193 *N.J.Super.* 560, 475 A.2d 97 (Law Div.1984) to the contrary.

Defendant acknowledges the other sections of the statute (that the conduct was within a customary license or tolerance, or that it presents other extenuations not envisaged by the Legislature) are inapplicable. He further concedes that he has no recourse under the other criterion of section (b) as the conduct charged did "actually cause or threaten the harm or evil sought to be prevented by the law defining the offense." His sole contention is that it "did so only to an extent too trivial to warrant the condemnation of conviction." In short, he asserts that his conduct was *de minimis* within the meaning of the statute.[1]

---

1   The term *de minimis* appears in the headnote but not in the statute. *See State v. Brown,* supra, for an analysis of why contrary to ordinary principles of statutory interpretation the headnote of this statute is appropriate for

The Legislature has committed the resolution of this question to the discretion of the assignment judge. *State v. Brown, supra* at 672–674, 458 A.2d 165. The intention of the Legislature to do so is highlighted by the use of the word "may" rather than "shall" in the statute. This is a change from the language of the Model Penal Code on which the statute was based. However, this "discretion is not an arbitrary or personal (one) to be exercised according to the whim or caprice of the individual judge." *McFeely v. Pension Comm'rs of Hoboken,* 1 *N.J.* 212, 215, 62 A.2d 686 (1948), nor may it be arbitrary, vague or fanciful. *State v. Standard Oil,* 5 *N.J.* 281, 308, 74 A.2d 565 (1950), aff'd 341 *U.S.* 428, 71 *S.Ct.* 822, 95 *L.Ed.* 1078 (1950). Judicial discretion means sound discretion guided by established principles of law, *Beronio v. Pension Comm. of Hoboken,* 130 *N.J.L.* 620, 623, 33 A.2d 855 (E. & A.1943), which the court has a duty to follow. *State v. Hunter,* 4 *N.J.Super.* 531, 536, 68 A.2d 274 (App.Div.1949), on remand 12 *N.J.Super.* 128, 79 A.2d 80 (App.Div.1951).

While "sympathetic considerations play no part in a determination under" the *de minimis* statute, *State v. Brown, supra* 188 *N.J.Super.* at 670, 458 A.2d 165, an objective consideration of surrounding circumstances is authorized. "Judicial discretion . . . takes into account . . . the particular circumstances of the case before the court." *Higgins v. Polk,* 14 *N.J.* 490, 493, 103 A.2d 1 (1954). Defendant has no prior history of arrest or conviction. Were the contrary true that fact would militate against dismissal of the complaint. His certification evidences the serious consequences to him which a conviction would entail. Upon graduation from college he will seek a career in the electronics field. Defense contractors for the Federal government are major employers of graduate engineers. Security clearance is often a requisite to employment and a record of conviction in this case could cause career problems for him for years to come. He is an industrious young man. He engages in part-time employment while attending classes and full-time employment in the summer to assist in the payment of his educational costs. And he has suffered substantial detriment in his personal life from the notoriety given his arrest. Not only have there been local newspaper articles and even an editorial regarding his case, but the story was distributed widely by the Associated Press. While these are considerations tangential to the "defendant's conduct" on which the statute focuses they take on special significance in a close case such as this. "The exercise of judicial discretion implies conscientious judgment. . .," *In re Koretzky,* 8 *N.J.* 506, 535, 86 A.2d 238 (1951), and requires that each fact in the surrounding circumstances receive the consideration to which it is entitled.

---

consideration in ascertaining legislative intent.

In *State v. Park*, 55 *Hawaii* 610, 525 *P.2d* 586 (Sup.Ct.1974), in discussing factors to be considered on a motion under an almost identical *de minimis* statute, the court stated:

> We think that before the code's § 236 can be properly applied in a criminal case, all of the relevant facts bearing upon the defendant's conduct and the nature of the attendant circumstances regarding the commission of the offense should be shown to the judge. *See People v. Davis*, 55 Misc.2d 656, 286 N.Y.S.2d 396 (1967). Such a disclosure would then enable the judge to consider all of the facts on this issue, so that he can intelligently exercise a sound discretion, consistent with the public interest, whether to grant the dismissal of a criminal case, based upon the standards set forth in the Hawaii Penal Code § 236. [55 Hawaii at 616, 525 P.2d at 591]

This case involved an indictment against primary election candidates for failure to file, within the statutory time period, mandated statements of expenses incurred. While indicating that the factors recited were not exclusive, the court found appropriate for consideration: the background, experience and character of the defendant which may indicate whether he knew or ought to have known of the illegality; the knowledge of the defendant of the consequences to be incurred upon violation of the statute; the circumstances concerning the offense; the resulting harm or evil, if any, caused or threatened by the infraction; the probable impact of the violation upon the community; the seriousness of the infraction in terms of punishment, bearing in mind that punishment can be suspended; mitigating circumstances as to the offender; possible improper motives of the complainant or prosecutor; and any other data which may reveal the nature and degree of the culpability in the offense committed by the defendant.

N.J.S.A. 2C:2–11(b) directs that in making his determination the assignment judge shall have "regard to the nature of the conduct charged to constitute an offense *and the nature of the attendant circumstances.*" Emphasis supplied. Defendant's conduct was not intended to be the sole criterion. Motions to dismiss a prosecution based upon identical unlawful conduct by two different individuals, when considered in the light of the attendant circumstances might justify the granting of one and denial of the other. Every surrounding fact is entitled to consideration, not for its sympathetic import, but for such legitimate influence it may have in honoring the legislative intent. While there is nothing "trivial" in the retail theft of a minor item by a professional shoplifter, there may be in an aberrative "isolated excursion beyond the pale of the law," *State v. Ivan*, 33 *N.J.* 197, 202, 162 *A.2d* 881 (1960), by an otherwise reputable and law-abiding citizen.

The State has argued that to dismiss the prosecution of this defendant will grant a license to other students to shoplift with impunity. This is not a realistic likelihood in this case. The consequences which have already attended the arrest of this defendant are more punitive than those which would follow conviction. The prospect of the public humiliation suffered by this student is certainly a forceful deterrent to the youths in his academic community. Those to whom the deterrent effect of a judgment of conviction would be directed have been instructed at defendant's expense. They have learned that a trivial violation has visited upon a fellow student the condemnation of arrest and charge if not conviction, shame before his family, friends and peers, local and national newspaper publicity, damage to his reputation, and legal expenses countless times greater than the insignificant items he is charged with having taken unlawfully. To say that in the face of these consequences a statutory dismissal of the complaint found to be in conformity with the legislative intent would invite others to shoplift is sophistry. The conviction if imposed would be anticlimatic, and the minor penalty which might be imposed would pale in significance to that already endured.

It is true that a legitimate goal of a criminal prosecution has long been the deterrence to the commission of similar unlawful acts by others. Redmount, "Some Basic Considerations Regarding Penal Policy," 49 *Journal of Criminal Law, Criminology and Police Science* 426 (1959); *N.J.S.A.* 2C:44–1(a)(9). Deterrence is, however, but a factor for consideration in any case. It cannot itself justify making a sacrificial lamb of the most minor of offenders. This is especially so when there are others available for prosecution whose offenses are not trivial. Were there evidence that shoplifting of small items of merchandise by students or other youths was an epidemic problem in the store where this event occurred or in the general area, it would be a significant countervailing factor for consideration on this motion. However, the State produced no affidavit, certification or other evidence in opposition to that filed by defendant. Arguments by the State unsupported in the record are improper. *R.* 1:6–6; *Smithey v. Johnson Motor Lines*, 140 *N.J.Super.* 202, 206, 356 A.2d 10 (App.Div.1976).

Counsel have joined issue on whether the Legislature intended to authorize the dismissal of a prosecution of this nature. The role of the court in construing any statute is to give effect to the legislative purpose. *State v. Carter*, 64 *N.J.* 382, 390, 316 A.2d 449 (1974). The goal against which the section of the statute is to be tested is found in the recommendation of the Criminal Law Revision Commission to the Legislature in the final report issued October, 1971. The Commission commented:

> In criminal law enforcement, many agencies exercise discretion as to the appropriateness of prosecution in a particular case. The police constantly must make decisions as to whether to arrest or, after arrest, whether to pro-

ceed with the case. Thereafter, both the prosecutor and the Grand Jury are charged with the obligation of determining both the sufficiency of the evidence to proceed and the appropriateness of doing so. Further, at least as to the Municipal Courts, experience has shown that judges will, on occasion, enter a finding of not guilty even in the face of proven guilt because, under the circumstances, a conviction is considered to be inappropriate.

The drafters of the MPC summarize all of this as a "kind of unarticulated authority to mitigate the general provisions of the criminal law to prevent absurd applications." In order to bring this exercise of discretion to the surface and to be sure that it is exercised uniformly throughout the judicial system, this Section of the Code has been included.

Countless filed complaints charging offenses of greater magnitude than that involving this defendant are routinely dismissed by prosecutors under the authority of *R.* 3:25–1. Thus, the Legislature has indicated by its enactment that the exercise of similar discretion by assignment judges comports with, rather than offends, its statutory definition of unlawful conduct under the Code of Criminal Justice.

Further evidence of the legislative purpose is found in a later portion of the same commentary.

Subsection b is the situation where the conduct literally comes within the Section as drafted but only to an extent which is too trivial to warrant the condemnation of a conviction. Attributing common sense to the Legislature, it would not have intended the prosecution of every single instance even though there is a technical violation of the statute. [*The New Jersey Penal Code, Final Report of the New Jersey Criminal Law Revision Commission*, vol. II, *Commentary* at 74].

Having commissioned a study of the proposed legislation and enacted this section into law it is reasonable to assume that the lawmakers found a need for it in the extant prosecution of trivial offenses. A prosecution for "stealing a penny dropped in the street," an example suggested in *State v. Hegyi, supra* 185 *N.J.Super.* at 233, 447 A.2d 1369, is not of a nature likely to ever occur nor to have motivated the Legislature to enact the law. Furthermore, such a prosecution would invoke the prior section of the statute (*N.J.S.A.* 2C:2–11(a)) authorizing a dismissal when the conduct is "within a customary license or tolerance." A statute is to be interpreted to give effect to each section. *Peper v. Princeton Univ. Bd. of Trustees*, 77 *N.J.* 55, 68, 389 A.2d 465 (1978). Section (b) was intended to abort prosecutions of more serious import. Viewed from that perspective it is difficult to envision a prosecution more acceptable to the Legislature for the invocation of the discretion granted the assignment judge than one for the theft of three pieces of bubble gum. In the milieu of bubble gum pilferage the only cases more trivial are those involving two pieces or one. It is difficult to conclude the lawmakers would have intended the dividing line to be drawn at three. It would seem the larceny of a single piece of bubble gum would fall within the statutory intendment of a trivial offense. Does then the theft of three pieces remove the actor's conduct from the scope of discretionary protection afforded? In a case involving substantially different conduct and attending circumstances perhaps it would; in this case it does not.

The exercise of the discretion granted to the assignment judge is "controlled by the will of the law-making body," *Beronio v. Pension Comm. of Hoboken, supra* 130 *N.J.L.* at 623, 33 *A.2d* 855. The Legislature has by its enactment indicated its intention that trivial matters should be dismissed when the "condemnation of conviction" is not warranted. The use of the word condemnation is significant. It means reprobation or censure. The Legislature in recognition of the serious consequences which may attend a conviction has granted this dismissal option to avoid an injustice in a case of technical but trivial guilt. The goal of a judge in exercising judicial discretion is a just result. *Kavanaugh v. Quigley, 63 N.J.Super.* 153, 158, 164 *A.2d* 179 (App.Div.1960). He is to "use the authority reposed in him when the essential requisites for its exercise exist and the justice of the course is apparent." *Cortese v. Cortese*, 10 *N.J.Super.* 152, 158, 76 *A.2d* 717 (App.Div.1950). This is such a case.

Motion granted.

Notes and Questions

1. How do you explain the court's decision in this case? Is the court doing anything more than second-guessing the prosecutor's decision to bring this charge?

2. Do you agree with the decision, however it was made, not to prosecute this defendant? If so, do you understand why this is a fundamentally different question than whether a *court* should make this decision?

E. Plea Bargaining

Perhaps the most important procedure in the criminal justice system is one that is almost entirely unregulated. Well over ninety percent of all criminal cases in state and federal courts are resolved through guilty pleas. As you will see, legislatures have given prosecutors extraordinary discretion to seek very substantial penalties for relatively minor conduct. Consider Paul Hayes's dilemma in the case below. The prosecution brought a charge against the defendant, passing a forged check, a crime that could also carry a life sentence under the Habitual Criminal Act because this was his third offense. Unless Hayes took a five year sentence, at hard labor, the prosecutor would seek the life sentence. A world that allows a prosecutor to present a defendant with a choice of life, or whatever lesser offer the prosecutor makes, has made the prosecutor by far the most important actor in the system.

Prosecutors and police are required to have probable cause before they can arrest, or obtain an indictment, against a defendant. There is no restriction on the gap that can exist between the punishment a prosecutor can seek and the sentence that he is willing to settle for in a plea. At first glance, this seems unproblematic as the lack of restriction appears to be an unlimited license to be generous. Viewed in a different light, however, this lack of limitation on largesse means that there is no limit on the gap between a sentence that the prosecutor deems fair and the sentence he can threaten if the "fair" offer is refused. This places great pressure on defendants to accept the "fair" offer, rendering the prosecutor jury and sentencing judge in a large number of cases.

Brady v. United States

Supreme Court of the United States
397 U.S. 742 (1970)

Mr. Justice WHITE delivered the opinion of the Court.

In 1959, petitioner was charged with kidnaping in violation of 18 U.S.C. § 1201(a).[1] Since the indictment charged that the victim of the kidnaping was not

---

1   'Whoever knowingly transports in interstate or foreign commerce, any person who has been unlawfully seized, confined, inveigled, decoyed, kidnaped, abducted, or carried away and held for ransom or reward or otherwise, except, in the case of a minor, by a parent thereof, shall be punished (1) by death if the kidnaped person has not been liberated unharmed, and if the verdict of the jury shall so recommend, or (2) by imprisonment for any

liberated unharmed, petitioner faced a maximum penalty of death if the verdict of the jury should so recommend. Petitioner, represented by competent counsel throughout, first elected to plead not guilty. Apparently because the trial judge was unwilling to try the case without a jury, petitioner made no serious attempt to reduce the possibility of a death penalty by waiving a jury trial. Upon learning that his codefendant, who had confessed to the authorities, would plead guilty and be available to testify against him, petitioner changed his plea to guilty. His plea was accepted after the trial judge twice questioned him as to the voluntariness of his plea. Petitioner was sentenced to 50 years' imprisonment, later reduced to 30.

In 1967, petitioner sought relief under 28 U.S.C. § 2255, claiming that his plea of guilty was not voluntarily given because § 1201(a) operated to coerce his plea. . . .

* * *

I

In *United States v. Jackson*, supra, the defendants were indicted under § 1201(a). The District Court dismissed the § 1201(a) count of the indictment, holding the statute unconstitutional because it permitted imposition of the death sentence only upon a jury's recommendation and thereby made the risk of death the price of a jury trial. This Court held the statute valid, except for the death penalty provision; with respect to the latter, the Court agreed with the trial court 'that the death penalty provision * * * imposes an impermissible burden upon the exercise of a constitutional right * * *.' 390 U.S., at 572, 88 S.Ct., at 1211. The problem was to determine 'whether the Constitution permits the establishment of such a death penalty, applicable only to those defendants who assert the right to contest their guilt before a jury.' 390 U.S., at 581, 88 S.Ct., at 1216. The inevitable effect of the provision was said to be to discourage assertion of the Fifth Amendment right not to plead guilty and to deter exercise of the Sixth Amendment right to demand a jury trial. Because the legitimate goal of limiting the death penalty to cases in which a jury recommends it could be achieved without penalizing those defendants who plead not guilty and elect a jury trial, the death penalty provision 'needlessly penalize(d) the assertion of a constitutional right,' 390 U.S., at 583, 88 S.Ct., at 1217, and was therefore unconstitutional.

Since the 'inevitable effect' of the death penalty provision of § 1201(a) was said by the Court to be the needless encouragement of pleas of guilty and waivers of jury trial, Brady contends that Jackson requires the invalidation of every

term of years or for life, if the death penalty is not imposed.'

plea of guilty entered under that section, at least when the fear of death is shown to have been a factor in the plea. Petitioner, however, has read far too much into the Jackson opinion.

The Court made it clear in Jackson that it was not holding § 1201(a) inherently coercive of guilty pleas: 'the fact that the Federal Kidnaping Act tends to discourage defendants from insisting upon their innocence and demanding trial by jury hardly implies that every defendant who enters a guilty plea to a charge under the Act does so involuntarily.' 390 U.S., at 583, 88 S.Ct., at 1217. . . .

That a guilty plea is a grave and solemn act to be accepted only with care and discernment has long been recognized. Central to the plea and the foundation for entering judgment against the defendant is the defendant's admission in open court that he committed the acts charged in the indictment. He thus stands as a witness against himself and he is shielded by the Fifth Amendment from being compelled to do so—hence the minimum requirement that his plea be the voluntary expression of his own choice. But the plea is more than an admission of past conduct; it is the defendant's consent that judgment of conviction may be entered without a trial—a waiver of his right to trial before a jury or a judge. Waivers of constitutional rights not only must be voluntary but must be knowing, intelligent acts done with sufficient awareness of the relevant circumstances and likely consequences. On neither score was Brady's plea of guilty invalid.

II

* * *

The voluntariness of Brady's plea can be determined only by considering all of the relevant circumstances surrounding it. *Cf. Haynes v. Washington*, 373 U.S. 503, 513, 83 S.Ct. 1336, 1343, 10 L.Ed.2d 513 (1963); *Leyra v. Denno*, 347 U.S. 556, 558, 74 S.Ct. 716, 717, 98 L.Ed. 948 (1954). One of these circumstances was the possibility of a heavier sentence following a guilty verdict after a trial. It may be that Brady, faced with a strong case against him and recognizing that his chances for acquittal were slight, preferred to plead guilty and thus limit the penalty to life imprisonment rather than to elect a jury trial which could result in a death penalty.[7] But even if we assume that Brady would not have pleaded guilty except for the death penalty provision of § 1201(a), this assumption merely identifies the penalty provision as a 'but for' cause of his plea. That the statute caused the plea in this sense does not necessarily prove that the plea was coerced and invalid as an involuntary act.

---

7   Such a possibility seems to have been rejected by the District Court in the § 2255 proceedings. That court found that 'the plea of guilty was made by the petitioner by reason of other matters and not by reason of the statute * * *.'

The State to some degree encourages pleas of guilty at every important step in the criminal process. For some people, their breach of a State's law is alone sufficient reason for surrendering themselves and accepting punishment. For others, apprehension and charge, both threatening acts by the Government, jar them into admitting their guilt. In still other cases, the post-indictment accumulation of evidence may convince the defendant and his counsel that a trial is not worth the agony and expense to the defendant and his family. All these pleas of guilty are valid in spite of the State's responsibility for some of the factors motivating the pleas; the pleas are no more improperly compelled than is the decision by a defendant at the close of the State's evidence at trial that he must take the stand or face certain conviction.

Of course, the agents of the State may not produce a plea by actual or threatened physical harm or by mental coercion overbearing the will of the defendant. But nothing of the sort is claimed in this case; nor is there evidence that Brady was so gripped by fear of the death penalty or hope of leniency that he did not or could not, with the help of counsel, rationally weigh the advantages of going to trial against the advantages of pleading guilty. Brady's claim is of a different sort: that it violates the Fifth Amendment to influence or encourage a guilty plea by opportunity or promise of leniency and that a guilty plea is coerced and invalid if influenced by the fear of a possibly higher penalty for the crime charged if a conviction is obtained after the State is put to its proof.

Insofar as the voluntariness of his plea is concerned, there is little to differentiate Brady from (1) the defendant, in a jurisdiction where the judge and jury have the same range of sentencing power, who pleads guilty because his lawyer advises him that the judge will very probably be more lenient than the jury; (2) the defendant, in a jurisdiction where the judge alone has sentencing power, who is advised by counsel that the judge is normally more lenient with defendants who plead guilty than with those who go to trial; (3) the defendant who is permitted by prosecutor and judge to plead guilty to a lesser offense included in the offense charged; and (4) the defendant who pleads guilty to certain counts with the understanding that other charges will be dropped. In each of these situations,[8] as in Brady's case, the defendant might never plead guilty absent the possibility or certainty that the plea will result in a lesser penalty than the sentence that could be imposed after a trial and a verdict of guilty. We decline to hold, however, that a guilty plea is compelled and invalid under the Fifth Amendment whenever motivated by the defendant's desire to accept the certain-

---

8   We here make no reference to the situation where the prosecutor or judge, or both, deliberately employ their charging and sentencing powers to induce a particular defendant to tender a plea of guilty. In Brady's case there is no claim that the prosecutor threatened prosecution on a charge not justified by the evidence or that the trial judge threatened Brady with a harsher sentence if convicted after trial in order to induce him to plead guilty.

ty or probability of a lesser penalty rather than face a wider range of possibilities extending from acquittal to conviction and a higher penalty authorized by law for the crime charged.

The issue we deal with is inherent in the criminal law and its administration because guilty pleas are not constitutionally forbidden, because the criminal law characteristically extends to judge or jury a range of choice in setting the sentence in individual cases, and because both the State and the defendant often find it advantageous to preclude the possibility of the maximum penalty authorized by law. For a defendant who sees slight possibility of acquittal, the advantages of pleading guilty and limiting the probable penalty are obvious—his exposure is reduced, the correctional processes can begin immediately, and the practical burdens of a trial are eliminated. For the State there are also advantages—the more promptly imposed punishment after an admission of guilt may more effectively attain the objectives of punishment; and with the avoidance of trial, scarce judicial and prosecutorial resources are conserved for those cases in which there is a substantial issue of the defendant's guilt or in which there is substantial doubt that the State can sustain its burden of proof. It is this mutuality of advantage that perhaps explains the fact that at present well over three-fourths of the criminal convictions in this country rest on pleas of guilty, a great many of them no doubt motivated at least in part by the hope or assurance of a lesser penalty than might be imposed if there were a guilty verdict after a trial to judge or jury.

Of course, that the prevalence of guilty pleas is explainable does not necessarily validate those pleas or the system which produces them. But we cannot hold that it is unconstitutional for the State to extend a benefit to a defendant who in turn extends a substantial benefit to the State and who demonstrates by his plea that he is ready and willing to admit his crime and to enter the correctional system in a frame of mind that affords hope for success in rehabilitation over a shorter period of time than might otherwise be necessary.

A contrary holding would require the States and Federal Government to forbid guilty pleas altogether, to provide a single invariable penalty for each crime defined by the statutes, or to place the sentencing function in a separate authority having no knowledge of the manner in which the conviction in each case was obtained. In any event, it would be necessary to forbid prosecutors and judges to accept guilty pleas to selected counts, to lesser included offenses, or to reduced charges. The Fifth Amendment does not reach so far.

Bram v. United States, 168 U.S. 532, 18 S.Ct. 183, 42 L.Ed. 568 (1897), held that the admissibility of a confession depended upon whether it was compelled within the meaning of the Fifth Amendment. To be admissible, a confession must be "free and voluntary: that is, must not be extracted by any sort of threats or violence, nor obtained by any direct or implied promises, however slight, nor by the exertion of any improper influence." 168 U.S., at 542–543, 18 S.Ct., at 187. More recently, *Malloy v. Hogan*, 378 U.S. 1, 84 S.Ct. 1489, 12 L.Ed.2d 653 (1964), carried forward the Bram definition of compulsion in the course of holding applicable to the States the Fifth Amendment privilege against compelled self-incrimination.

Bram is not inconsistent with our holding that Brady's plea was not compelled even though the law promised him a lesser maximum penalty if he did not go to trial. Bram dealt with a confession given by a defendant in custody, alone and unrepresented by counsel. In such circumstances, even a mild promise of leniency was deemed sufficient to bar the confession, not because the promise was an illegal act as such, but because defendants at such times are too sensitive to inducement and the possible impact on them too great to ignore and too difficult to assess. But Bram and its progeny did not hold that the possibly coercive impact of a promise of leniency could not be dissipated by the presence and advice of counsel, any more than *Miranda v. Arizona*, 384 U.S. 436, 86 S.Ct. 1602, 16 L.Ed.2d 694 (1966), held that the possibly coercive atmosphere of the police station could not be counteracted by the presence of counsel or other safeguards.[12]

Brady's situation bears no resemblance to Bram's. Brady first pleaded not guilty; prior to changing his plea to guilty he was subjected to no threats or promises in face-to-face encounters with the authorities. He had competent counsel and full opportunity to assess the advantages and disadvantages of a trial as compared with those attending a plea of guilty; there was no hazard of an impulsive and improvident response to a seeming but unreal advantage. His plea of guilty was entered in open court and before a judge obviously sensitive to the requirements of the law with respect to guilty pleas. Brady's plea, unlike Bram's confession, was voluntary.

* * *

III

The record before us . . . supports the conclusion that Brady's plea was intelligently made. He was advised by competent counsel, he was made aware of the nature of the charge against him, and there was nothing to indicate that he was incompetent or otherwise not in control of his mental faculties; once his confederate had pleaded guilty and became available to testify, he chose to plead guilty, perhaps to ensure that he would face no more than life imprisonment or a term

---

12 'The presence of counsel, in all the cases before us today, would be the adequate protective device necessary to make the process of police interrogation conform to the dictates of the privilege (against compelled self-incrimination). His presence would insure that statements made in the government-established atmosphere are not the product of compulsion.' *Miranda v. Arizona*, 384 U.S. 436, 466, 86 S.Ct. 1602, 1623 (1966).

of years. Brady was aware of precisely what he was doing when he admitted that he had kidnaped the victim and had not released her unharmed.

It is true that Brady's counsel advised him that § 1201(a) empowered the jury to impose the death penalty and that nine years later in *United States v. Jackson, supra,* the Court held that the jury had no such power as long as the judge could impose only a lesser penalty if trial was to the court or there was a plea of guilty. But these facts do not require us to set aside Brady's conviction.

Often the decision to plead guilty is heavily influenced by the defendant's appraisal of the prosecution's case against him and by the apparent likelihood of securing leniency should a guilty plea be offered and accepted. Considerations like these frequently present imponderable questions for which there are no certain answers; judgments may be made that in the light of later events seem improvident, although they were perfectly sensible at the time. The rule that a plea must be intelligently made to be valid does not require that a plea be vulnerable to later attack if the defendant did not correctly assess every relevant factor entering into his decision. A defendant is not entitled to withdraw his plea merely because he discovers long after the plea has been accepted that his calculus misapprehended the quality of the State's case or the likely penalties attached to alternative courses of action. More particularly, absent misrepresentation or other impermissible conduct by state agents, *cf. Von Moltke v. Gillies,* 332 U.S. 708, 68 S.Ct. 316, 92 L.Ed. 309 (1948), a voluntary plea of guilty intelligently made in the light of the then applicable law does not become vulnerable because later judicial decisions indicate that the plea rested on a faulty premise. A plea of guilty triggered by the expectations of a competently counseled defendant that the State will have a strong case against him is not subject to later attack because the defendant's lawyer correctly advised him with respect to the then existing law as to possible penalties but later pronouncements of the courts, as in this case, hold that the maximum penalty for the crime in question was less than was reasonably assumed at the time the plea was entered.

The fact that Brady did not anticipate *United States v. Jackson, supra,* does not impugn the truth or reliability of his plea. We find no requirement in the Constitution that a defendant must be permitted to disown his solemn admissions in open court that he committed the act with which he is charged simply because it later develops that the State would have had a weaker case than the defendant had thought or that the maximum penalty then assumed applicable has been held inapplicable in subsequent judicial decisions.

This is not to say that guilty plea convictions hold no hazards for the innocent or that the methods of taking guilty pleas presently employed in this country are necessarily valid in all respects. This mode of conviction is no more foolproof than full trials to the court or to the jury. Accordingly, we take great precautions against unsound results, and we should continue to do so, whether conviction is by plea or by trial. We would have serious doubts about this case if the encouragement of guilty pleas by offers of leniency substantially increased the likelihood that defendants, advised by competent counsel, would falsely condemn themselves. But our view is to the contrary and is based on our expectations that courts will satisfy themselves that pleas of guilty are voluntarily and intelligently made by competent defendants with adequate advice of counsel and that there is nothing to question the accuracy and reliability of the defendants' admissions that they committed the crimes with which they are charged. In the case before us, nothing in the record impeaches Brady's plea or suggests that his admissions in open court were anything but the truth.

Although Brady's plea of guilty may well have been motivated in part by a desire to avoid a possible death penalty, we are convinced that his plea was voluntarily and intelligently made and we have no reason to doubt that his solemn admission of guilt was truthful.

Affirmed.

Notes and Questions

1. You should have been struck, as Brady himself was, with the difference between the way Brady and Jackson were treated. The entire scheme under which Brady was threatened with a death sentence was unconstitutional. Jackson filed a pre-trial motion and had the potential of the death penalty removed from his case, permitting him to either have a jury trial without risking a possible death sentence, or enter into plea negotiations with the prosecutor without the threat of the death penalty looming in the background. Brady pled guilty avoiding the threat of the death penalty. Does it not seem troubling that Brady was motivated to plea to avoid a penalty that the Supreme Court held in *Jackson* to be unconstitutional?

2. Notice the unique deference that *Brady* gives prosecutors. The Court in *Brady* holds that his plea is valid even if it is motivated by the desire to avoid the death penalty, but a *statute* which requires a jury recommendation of death for this penalty to be imposed is an unconstitutional tax on a defendant's right to a jury trial. *Congress*, under *Jackson*, may not decide to categorically incentivize guilty pleas (or even *just bench trials*) in kidnapping cases by removing the possibility of death for those who do not seek jury trial. But a *prosecutor*, after *Brady*, may constitutionally offer an individual defendant a sentence of less than death for a capital crime. Does this unique deference

to prosecutors seem justified? Is there something less fair about offering *all* defendants a chance to trade their jury trial rights to eliminate the risk of death than allowing individual prosecutors to make such offers to defendants of their choosing? An argument can certainly be made that prosecutors are the most powerful government actors in our constitutional scheme. Professor Rachel Barkow has argued that prosecutors are not only given unique deference when compared to the legislative branch, she argues that prosecutorial decisions are given more deference than the decisions of other agents in the executive branch. *See* Rachel E. Barkow, *Institutional Design and the Policing of Prosecutors: Lessons from Administrative Law*, 61 Stan. L. Rev. 869 (2009).

3. The trial judge in *Brady*'s case played a substantial role in this case. The case notes that the judge was unwilling to allow the defendant to proceed with a bench trial. Take another look at the statute. Defendants under the federal kidnapping statute could avoid the death penalty *either* by pleading guilty, which Brady did, or by having a bench trial. Apparently the federal district judge had to agree to let the defendant proceed in this manner. Trial judges have a very limited ability to reject plea offers to charges less than those alleged in the indictment—only in extraordinary cases when they believe prosecutors are being unreasonably lenient may they reject pleas to charges less serious than those in the indictment. *See United States v. Ammidown*, 497 F.2d 615 (D.C. Cir. 1973). The Court does not address the extraordinary role the trial judge played in this case.

———————

The last few cases we have looked at would typically be categorized as criminal procedure, not criminal *law* cases. But the procedure creates the law, especially in the case of *Bordenkircher v. Hayes*. As you read this case, the Court's conclusion may seem inescapable, particularly when you look at the only alternative proposed by the dissent. The case, however, has quite a latent significance. The late William J. Stuntz who taught at Harvard Law School, a mentor to so many who have chosen to study criminal law and procedure, regarded this case to be one of the most important cases the Supreme Court decided. In a paper he never published, he wrote, "*Bordenkircher* mattered a lot, more so than many cases whose names are better known. More than two million men and women make their beds in prisons and jails in America today. Many thousands of them (no one knows *how* many) live where they live because of what happened to Paul

Hayes, and what the Supreme Court had to say about it."[1] As you read the case, try to figure out why Stuntz thought the case was so profound.

Bordenkircher v. Hayes

Supreme Court of the United States
434 U.S. 357 (1978)

Mr. Justice STEWART delivered the opinion of the Court.

The question in this case is whether the Due Process Clause of the Fourteenth Amendment is violated when a state prosecutor carries out a threat made during plea negotiations to reindict the accused on more serious charges if he does not plead guilty to the offense with which he was originally charged.

I

The respondent, Paul Lewis Hayes, was indicted by a Fayette County, Ky., grand jury on a charge of uttering a forged instrument in the amount of $88.30, an offense then punishable by a term of 2 to 10 years in prison. Ky.Rev.Stat. § 434.130 (1973) (repealed 1975). After arraignment, Hayes, his retained counsel, and the Commonwealth's Attorney met in the presence of the Clerk of the Court to discuss a possible plea agreement. During these conferences the prosecutor offered to recommend a sentence of five years in prison if Hayes would plead guilty to the indictment. He also said that if Hayes did not plead guilty and "save[d] the court the inconvenience and necessity of a trial," he would return to the grand jury to seek an indictment under the Kentucky Habitual Criminal Act,[1] then Ky.Rev.Stat. § 431.190 (1973) (repealed 1975), which would subject Hayes to a mandatory sentence of life imprisonment by reason of his two prior felony convictions.[2] Hayes chose not to plead guilty, and the prosecutor did

---

1   William J. Stuntz, Bordenkircher v. Hayes: *The Rise of Plea Bargaining and the Decline of the Rule of Law*, available at: http://papers.ssrn.com/sol3/papers.cfm?abstract-id=854284.

1   While cross-examining Hayes during the subsequent trial proceedings the prosecutor described the plea offer in the following language: "Isn't it a fact that I told you at that time [the initial bargaining session] if you did not intend to plead guilty to five years for this charge and . . . save the court the inconvenience and necessity of a trial and taking up this time that I intended to return to the grand jury and ask them to indict you based upon these prior felony convictions?" Tr. 194.

2   At the time of Hayes' trial the statute provided that "[a]ny person convicted a . . . third time of felony . . . shall be confined in the penitentiary during his life." Ky.Rev.Stat. § 431.190 (1973) (repealed 1975). That statute has been replaced by Ky.Rev.Stat. § 532.080 (Supp. 1977) under which Hayes would have been sentenced to, at most, an indeterminate term of 10 to 20 years. § 532.080(6)(b). In addition, under the new statute a previous con-

obtain an indictment charging him under the Habitual Criminal Act. It is not disputed that the recidivist charge was fully justified by the evidence, that the prosecutor was in possession of this evidence at the time of the original indictment, and that Hayes' refusal to plead guilty to the original charge was what led to his indictment under the habitual criminal statute.

A jury found Hayes guilty on the principal charge of uttering a forged instrument and, in a separate proceeding, further found that he had twice before been convicted of felonies. As required by the habitual offender statute, he was sentenced to a life term in the penitentiary. The Kentucky Court of Appeals rejected Hayes' constitutional objections to the enhanced sentence, holding in an unpublished opinion that imprisonment for life with the possibility of parole was constitutionally permissible in light of the previous felonies of which Hayes had been convicted,[3] and that the prosecutor's decision to indict him as a habitual offender was a legitimate use of available leverage in the plea-bargaining process.

On Hayes' petition for a federal writ of habeas corpus, the United States District Court for the Eastern District of Kentucky agreed that there had been no constitutional violation in the sentence or the indictment procedure, and denied the writ [and the Court of Appeals reversed.]

II

It may be helpful to clarify at the outset the nature of the issue in this case. While the prosecutor did not actually obtain the recidivist indictment until after the plea conferences had ended, his intention to do so was clearly expressed at the outset of the plea negotiations. Hayes was thus fully informed of the true terms of the offer when he made his decision to plead not guilty. This is not a situation, therefore, where the prosecutor without notice brought an additional and more serious charge after plea negotiations relating only to the original indictment had ended with the defendant's insistence on pleading not guilty. As a practical matter, in short, this case would be no different if the grand jury had indicted Hayes as a recidivist from the outset, and the prosecutor had offered to drop that charge as part of the plea bargain.

The Court of Appeals nonetheless drew a distinction between "concessions relating to prosecution under an existing indictment," and threats to bring more

---

viction is a basis for enhanced sentencing only if a prison term of one year or more was imposed, the sentence or probation was completed within five years of the present offense, and the offender was over the age of 18 when the offense was committed. At least one of Hayes' prior convictions did not meet these conditions. See n. 3, *infra*.

3 According to his own testimony, Hayes had pleaded guilty in 1961, when he was 17 years old, to a charge of detaining a female, a lesser included offense of rape, and as a result had served five years in the state reformatory. In 1970 he had been convicted of robbery and sentenced to five years' imprisonment, but had been released on probation immediately.

severe charges not contained in the original indictment-a line it thought neces-sary in order to establish a prophylactic rule to guard against the evil of prosecu-torial vindictiveness.[6] Quite apart from this chronological distinction, however, the Court of Appeals found that the prosecutor had acted vindictively in the present case since he had conceded that the indictment was influenced by his desire to induce a guilty plea.[7] The ultimate conclusion of the Court of Appeals thus seems to have been that a prosecutor acts vindictively and in violation of due process of law whenever his charging decision is influenced by what he hopes to gain in the course of plea bargaining negotiations.

III

We have recently had occasion to observe: "[W]hatever might be the situ-ation in an ideal world, the fact is that the guilty plea and the often concomi-tant plea bargain are important components of this country's criminal justice system. Properly administered, they can benefit all concerned." *Blackledge v. Allison*, 431 U.S. 63, 71, 97 S.Ct. 1621, 1627, 52 L.Ed.2d 136. The open acknowl-edgment of this previously clandestine practice has led this Court to rec-ognize the importance of counsel during plea negotiations, *Brady v. United States*, 397 U.S. 742, 758, 90 S.Ct. 1463, 1474, 25 L.Ed.2d 747, the need for a public record indicating that a plea was knowingly and voluntarily made, *Boykin v. Alabama*, 395 U.S. 238, 242, 89 S.Ct. 1709, 1711, 23 L.Ed.2d 274, and the requirement that a prosecutor's plea-bargaining promise must be kept, *Santobello v. New York*, 404 U.S. 257, 262, 92 S.Ct. 495, 498, 30 L.Ed.2d 427. The decision of the Court of Appeals in the present case, however, did not deal with considerations such as these, but held that the substance of the plea offer itself violated the limitations imposed by the Due Process Clause of the Fourteenth Amendment. Cf. *Brady v. United States, supra*, 397 U.S., at 751 n. 8, 90 S.Ct., at 1470. For the reasons that follow, we have concluded that the Court of Appeals was mistaken in so ruling.

---

6 "Although a prosecutor may in the course of plea negotiations offer a defendant concessions relating to prosecution under an existing indictment . . . he may not threaten a defendant with the consequence that more severe charges may be brought if he insists on going to trial. When a prosecutor obtains an indictment less severe than the facts known to him at the time might permit, he makes a discretionary determination that the interests of the state are served by not seeking more serious charges. . . . Accordingly, if after plea negotiations fail, he then procures an indictment charging a more serious crime, a strong inference is created that the only reason for the more serious charges is vindictiveness. Under these circumstances, the prosecutor should be required to justify his action." 547 F.2d, at 44-45.

7 "In this case, a vindictive motive need not be inferred. The prosecutor has admitted it." *Id.*, at 45.

IV

This Court held in *North Carolina v. Pearce*, 395 U.S. 711, 725, 89 S.Ct. 2072, 2080, 23 L.Ed.2d 656, that the Due Process Clause of the Fourteenth Amendment "requires that vindictiveness against a defendant for having successfully attacked his first conviction must play no part in the sentence he receives after a new trial." The same principle was later applied to prohibit a prosecutor from reindicting a convicted misdemeanant on a felony charge after the defendant had invoked an appellate remedy, since in this situation there was also a "realistic likelihood of 'vindictiveness.'" *Blackledge v. Perry*, 417 U.S., at 27, 94 S.Ct., at 2102.

In those cases the Court was dealing with the State's unilateral imposition of a penalty upon a defendant who had chosen to exercise a legal right to attack his original conviction-a situation "very different from the give-and-take negotiation common in plea bargaining between the prosecution and defense, which arguably possess relatively equal bargaining power." *Parker v. North Carolina*, 397 U.S. 790, 809, 90 S.Ct. 1458, 1474, 1479, 25 L.Ed.2d 785 (opinion of Brennan, J.). The Court has emphasized that the due process violation in cases such as *Pearce* and *Perry* lay not in the possibility that a defendant might be deterred from the exercise of a legal right, *see Colten v. Kentucky*, 407 U.S. 104, 92 S.Ct. 1953, 32 L.Ed.2d 584; *Chaffin v. Stynchcombe*, 412 U.S. 17, 93 S.Ct. 1977, 36 L.Ed.2d 714, but rather in the danger that the State might be retaliating against the accused for lawfully attacking his conviction. *See Blackledge v. Perry, supra*, 417 U.S., at 26-28, 94 S.Ct., at 2101-02.

To punish a person because he has done what the law plainly allows him to do is a due process violation of the most basic sort, *see North Carolina v. Pearce, supra*, 395 U.S., at 738, 89 S.Ct., at 2082 (opinion of Black, J.), and for an agent of the State to pursue a course of action whose objective is to penalize a person's reliance on his legal rights is "patently unconstitutional." *Chaffin v. Stynchcombe, supra*, 412 U.S., at 32-33, n. 20, 93 S.Ct., at 1986. See *United States v. Jackson*, 390 U.S. 570, 88 S.Ct. 1209, 20 L.Ed.2d 138. But in the "give-and-take" of plea bargaining, there is no such element of punishment or retaliation so long as the accused is free to accept or reject the prosecution's offer.

Plea bargaining flows from "the mutuality of advantage" to defendants and prosecutors, each with his own reasons for wanting to avoid trial. *Brady v. United States, supra*, 397 U.S., at 752, 90 S.Ct., at 1471. Defendants advised by competent counsel and protected by other procedural safeguards are presumptively capable of intelligent choice in response to prosecutorial persuasion, and unlikely to be driven to false self-condemnation. 397 U.S., at 758, 90 S.Ct., at 1474. Indeed, acceptance of the basic legitimacy of plea bargaining necessarily implies rejection of any notion that a guilty plea is involuntary in a constitutional sense simply because it is the end result of the bargaining process. By hypothesis, the plea may have been induced by promises of a recommendation of a lenient sentence or a reduction of charges, and thus by fear of the possibility of a greater penalty upon conviction after a trial. See ABA Project on Standards for Criminal Justice, Pleas of Guilty § 3.1 (App. Draft 1968); Note, Plea Bargaining and the Transformation of the Criminal Process, 90 Harv.L.Rev. 564 (1977). *Cf. Brady v. United States, supra,* at 751, 90 S.Ct., at 1470; *North Carolina v. Alford,* 400 U.S. 25, 91 S.Ct. 160, 27 L.Ed.2d 162.

While confronting a defendant with the risk of more severe punishment clearly may have a "discouraging effect on the defendant's assertion of his trial rights, the imposition of these difficult choices [is] an inevitable"-and permissible-"attribute of any legitimate system which tolerates and encourages the negotiation of pleas." *Chaffin v. Stynchcombe, supra,* 412 U.S., at 31, 93 S.Ct., at 1985. It follows that, by tolerating and encouraging the negotiation of pleas, this Court has necessarily accepted as constitutionally legitimate the simple reality that the prosecutor's interest at the bargaining table is to persuade the defendant to forgo his right to plead not guilty.

It is not disputed here that Hayes was properly chargeable under the recidivist statute, since he had in fact been convicted of two previous felonies. In our system, so long as the prosecutor has probable cause to believe that the accused committed an offense defined by statute, the decision whether or not to prosecute, and what charge to file or bring before a grand jury, generally rests entirely in his discretion.[8] Within the limits set by the legislature's constitutionally valid definition of chargeable offenses, "the conscious exercise of some selectivity in enforcement is not in itself a federal constitutional violation" so long as "the selection was [not] deliberately based upon an unjustifiable standard such as race, religion, or other arbitrary classification." *Oyler v. Boles,* 368 U.S. 448, 456, 82 S.Ct. 501, 506, 7 L.Ed.2d 446. To hold that the prosecutor's desire to induce a guilty plea is an "unjustifiable standard," which, like race or religion, may play no part in his charging decision, would contradict the very premises that underlie the concept of plea bargaining itself. Moreover, a rigid constitutional rule that would prohibit a prosecutor from acting forthrightly in his dealings with the defense could only invite unhealthy subterfuge that would drive the practice of plea bargaining back into the shadows from which it has so recently emerged. *See Blackledge v. Allison,* 431 U.S., at 76, 97 S.Ct., at 1630.

---

8   This case does not involve the constitutional implications of a prosecutor's offer during plea bargaining of adverse or lenient treatment for some person other than the accused, see ALI Model Code of Pre-Arraignment Procedure, Commentary to § 350.3, pp. 614-615 (1975), which might pose a greater danger of inducing a false guilty plea by skewing the assessment of the risks a defendant must consider. *Cf. Brady v. United States,* 397 U.S. 742, 758, 90 S.Ct. 1463, 1474, 25 L.Ed.2d 747.

There is no doubt that the breadth of discretion that our country's legal system vests in prosecuting attorneys carries with it the potential for both individual and institutional abuse.[9] And broad though that discretion may be, there are undoubtedly constitutional limits upon its exercise. We hold only that the course of conduct engaged in by the prosecutor in this case, which no more than openly presented the defendant with the unpleasant alternatives of forgoing trial or facing charges on which he was plainly subject to prosecution, did not violate the Due Process Clause of the Fourteenth Amendment.

Accordingly, the judgment of the Court of Appeals is

Reversed.

Notes and Questions

1. Go back and look at footnote 8 of the *Brady* opinion. The Court expressed no opinion about a situation in which the prosecutor or judge "deliberately employ[ed] their charging and sentencing powers to induce a particular defendant to tender a plea of guilty." What exactly would this mean—and why would the prosecutor's, or the judge's, intent matter? While the Court had decided a number of cases dealing with prosecutorial vindictiveness between *Brady* and *Bordenkircher* that weakened a legal claim that Paul Hayes would have had on the grounds of vindictiveness, if any case involved an effort to deliberately use the prosecutor's charging power to extract a guilty plea, it would have been this one. In the post-conviction proceedings in *Bordenkircher v. Hayes*, the prosecutor examining Paul Hayes asked him: "[I]sn't it a fact that I told you at that time if you did not intend to save the court the inconvenience and necessity of a trial and taking up this time that I intended to return to the grand jury and ask them to indict you [under the three-strikes law]?" Even if the prosecutor's threat did not violate the constitution, notice how fundamentally this decision transfers power to prosecutors. They can now threaten life sentences when they are satisfied with five-year sentences and be fairly sure they will be able to obtain them except in the case of the heartiest, or foolish, defendants like Paul Hayes, or perhaps in the cases of the innocent.

2. Go back and take another look at the contrast the *Brady* Court drew between uncounseled police interrogations and plea bargains in exchange for leniency.

---

9 This potential has led to many recommendations that the prosecutor's discretion should be controlled by means of either internal or external guidelines. See ALI Model Code of Pre-Arraignment Procedure for Criminal Justice §§ 350.3(2)-(3) (1975); ABA Project on Standards for Criminal Justice, The Prosecution Function §§ 2.5, 3.9 (App. Draft 1971); Abrahms, *Internal Policy: Guiding the Exercise of Prosecutorial Discretion,* 19 UCLA L.Rev. 1 (1971).

The advice of counsel demonstrated to Justice White that the plea was not induced by a threat or promise as it would have been if a promise had been made in an uncounseled jailhouse interrogation. In essence, counsel aided Brady in deciding whether he was wiser to plead guilty and take the death penalty off the table while still facing a very substantial potential jail sentence, up to fifty years, for most defendants a life sentence. Is the value of counsel's advice different in *Bordenkircher* where the gap between five years and life is considerably broader? Or, to put it another way, would defense counsel recommend settling on a much weaker prosecution case in *Bordenkircher* than it would in *Brady*? Was Paul Hayes given an offer he couldn't refuse? Consider the case of Chinese scientist Wen Ho Lee, who was indicted for multiple espionage counts which would have carried roughly a thousand years of prison time, and who was held in solitary confinement pending trial. As the prosecution's case collapsed, he was offered, and accepted, a plea to a minor felony and a sentence of time served. Does defense counsel's advice in either *Bordenkircher v. Hayes*, or in Wen Ho Lee's case, do anything to mitigate the very coercive nature of the plea?

3. Let's return to Stuntz's argument. He observed that at the same time the Supreme Court was recognizing the power of prosecutors to threaten a substantially greater sentence than he offered in a plea bargain, legislatures were increasingly creating mandatory minimums for recidivists, those possessing weapons, and those possessing certain quantities of drugs. These new laws, Stuntz argued, gave prosecutors more leverage over defendants in negotiations, the rate of plea bargaining *and* the average sentence increased at the same time. *See* William J. Stuntz, *The Collapse of the American Criminal Justice System* 258-60 (2011). As he describes, "We are supposed to have a system of checks and balances: legislatures write the laws, police and prosecutors enforce them, and judges interpret them. [But] power is increasingly concentrated in the hands of police and prosecutors. Especially prosecutors." Stuntz, *Rule of Law*, at 33-34. This scheme, he contended, has produced the highest incarceration rate this country have ever known and one of the highest incarceration rates in the world with minimal strain on prosecution budgets.

F. Jury Discretion and Nullification

Ultimately, juries have a check on the power of prosecutors to decide which crimes to prosecute. Juries are always permitted to return a verdict of not guilty even when there is overwhelming evidence of the defendant's guilt. Jury nullification can occur for any number of reasons. Many thought the verdict in the O.J. Simpson murder case was an act of jury nullification, but in that case because of the missteps and arguably illegal conduct of the Los Angeles Police Department.

Jury nullification can take another—and arguably more legitimate—form: correcting for prosecutorial over-charging. Over-charging in this context means that while the defendant has committed all the elements of the offense, the facts of the case evokes sympathy from reasonable people. Jury nullification can produce an acquittal or a conviction on a lesser charge.

The jury's power to always render a verdict of not guilty on any or all counts of an indictment effectively gives a jury the power to second-guess the prosecutor's decision to seek a criminal sanction in the first place. A number of limits, however, have been placed on this power in modern times. Though jury nullification has a long history that predates the American Republic, there is necessarily a great tension between a jury's duty to follow the law and its absolute power to act contrary to it. In stark contrast to prosecutorial and police discretion, which has steadily increased over the last half century, there have been substantial efforts to constrain the power of juries to do anything other than render a verdict finding a defendant guilty of the crimes established by the facts.

1. Instructing the Jury on Its Power to Nullify

As you will discover in the *Kryzske* case, juries are never instructed about their right to render verdicts contrary to the evidence, but what should a trial judge tell a jury when it inquires about this unqualified right a jury possesses? Is the majority's rule in this case consistent with the jury's right to return a verdict of not guilty even in the face of overwhelming evidence? Would the logical extension of the dissent's argument require juries to always be instructed on their right to nullify the law by rendering a not guilty verdict regardless of the evidence?

United States v. Krzyske

United States Court of Appeals for the Sixth Circuit
836 F.2d 1013 (1998)

WELLFORD, Circuit Judge.

Defendant-appellant Kevin Elwood Krzyske was indicted on April 16, 1985, and charged with ten tax-related counts: five counts of tax evasion for the years 1978 through 1982, 26 U.S.C. § 7201 (counts 1-5); four counts of failure to file tax returns for the years 1979 through 1982, 26 U.S.C. § 7203 (counts 6-9); and one count of filing a false withholding exemption certificate in 1982, 26 U.S.C. § 7205 (count 10). He was arraigned on April 17, 1985.

Jury deliberations commenced on June 25, 1985, and on June 26, 1985, Krzyske was acquitted on count 5 of tax evasion for 1982 and on count 10 of filing a false withholding exemption certificate in 1982. On June 27, 1985, Krzyske was convicted on counts 8 and 9 of failure to file tax returns for 1981 and 1982. The jury completed its deliberations on June 28, 1985, by acquitting on counts 2, 3, and 4 of tax evasion for 1979, 1980, and 1981 but convicting Krzyske on one count of tax evasion for 1978 and on counts 6 and 7 for failure to file tax returns for 1979 and 1980.

Trial Judge Joiner sentenced Krzyske to five years imprisonment on the count 1 felony conviction, and one year each on the misdemeanor convictions, counts 6 through 9. The sentences imposed on counts 6 through 9 were to run consecutive to one another and concurrent with the custody sentences imposed on count 1. Krzyske was also fined a total of $20,000.

* * *

[H]e claims he was entitled to a jury instruction concerning the doctrine of jury nullification of a conviction. For the reasons set out below, we affirm the district court...

* * *

The trial court denied defendant's request to instruct the jury on his asserted doctrine of jury nullification. The court also denied the government's motion to prohibit the use of this term during the proceedings and, as a result, Krzyske mentioned the doctrine of jury nullification in his closing argument. During its deliberation the jury asked the court what the doctrine stood for. The court responded, "There is no such thing as valid jury nullification. Your obligation is to follow the instructions of the Court as to the law given to you. You would violate your oath and the law if you willfully brought in a verdict contrary to the law given you in this case." Defendant objected and claims it was error for the court to so instruct the jury.

Krzyske defines jury nullification as a jury's power to return a verdict of not guilty despite law and facts indicating guilt under the indictment. Krzyske acknowledges at the same time that no federal court has yet specifically permitted a jury nullification instruction and that few courts have even permitted arguments to the jury on the topic urging this "doctrine." He claims that this case is unique because the court specifically told the jury that there is no such thing as valid jury nullification.

We recently addressed the question of jury nullification in *United States v. Avery*, 717 F.2d 1020 (6th Cir.1983), *cert. denied,* 466 U.S. 905, 104 S.Ct. 1683, 80 L.Ed.2d 157 (1984), in the following terms:

> Defendant's final contention is that the district court committed reversible error when it refused to instruct the jury that it had the power to acquit the defendant even though he was guilty of the charged offense. The instruction itself reads that "a jury is entitled to acquit the defendant because it has no sympathy for the government's position."

> This argument is completely without merit. Although jurors may indeed have the power to ignore the law, their duty is to apply the law as interpreted by the court and they should be so instructed.

Id. at 1027 (citations omitted). A jury's "right" to reach any verdict it wishes does not, however, infringe on the duty of the court to instruct the jury only as to the correct law applicable to the particular case.

The right of a jury, as a buffer between the accused and the state, to reach a verdict despite what may seem clear law must be kept distinct from the court's duty to uphold the law and to apply it impartially. This has been recognized by the Supreme Court in *Horning v. District of Columbia*, 254 U.S. 135, 138, 41 S.Ct. 53, 54, 65 L.Ed. 185 (1920), where Justice Holmes stated, "[T]he jury has the power to bring in a verdict in the teeth of both law and facts. But the judge always has the right and duty to tell them what the law is upon this or that state of facts. . . ." This directive has been recognized by this court in *United States v. Burkhart*, 501 F.2d 993, 996-97 (6th Cir.1974), where we approved a district court's instruction that the jury consider only the facts and law before them. In light of *Horning, Avery,* and *Burkhart*, we are compelled to approve the district court's refusal to discuss jury nullification with the jury. To have given an instruction on nullification would have undermined the impartial determination of justice based on law.

Thus, we find no merit in the defendant's objection concerning the court's instructions to the jury.

MERRITT, Circuit Judge, dissenting.

I disagree with the Court's disposition of this case. I would reverse the case and remand it for a new trial. It is clear to me that the District Court erred in responding to the jury's specific question concerning "jury nullification" raised after several hours of jury deliberation. The jury returned to the courtroom concerned about the issue of "jury nullification." The jury wanted to know to what extent it had the right to acquit the defendant because it disagreed with the government's prosecution. It wanted to know what was meant by the idea of "jury nullification." The Court responded by telling the jury that it had no power to engage in jury nullification and that was the end of the matter. It told the jury in effect that it had no general authority to veto the prosecution. This is simply error. The Court should have explained the jury's function in our system. Our Court has made it clear in the past that the jury does have veto power and the jury should have been so instructed. For example, in *United States v. Wilson*, 629 F.2d 439, 443 (6th Cir.1980), in an opinion which I wrote for a unanimous panel we stated:

> In criminal cases, a jury is entitled to acquit the defendant because it has no sympathy for the government's position. It has a general veto power, and this power should not be attenuated by requiring the jury to answer in writing a detailed list of questions or explain its reasons. The jury's veto power was settled in *Throckmorton's* case in 1544 according to Professor Plucknett:
>
> In Crompton's treatise on the jurisdiction of courts (1594) we read:
>> "Note that the London jury which acquitted Sir Nicholas Throckmorton, Knight, about the first year of Queen Mary, of high treason, was called into the Star Chamber in October, 1544 (sic), forasmuch as the matter was held to have been sufficiently proved against him; and eight of them were there fined in great sums, at least five hundred pounds each, and remanded back to prison to dwell there until further order were taken for their punishment. The other four were released, because they submitted and confessed that they had offended in not considering the truth of the matter."

* * *

Throckmorton's prominent share in Wyatt's rebellion put his guilt beyond the slightest question, but he was a protestant hero to the Londoners, and the jury's verdict was purely political. From now onwards the jury enters on a new phase of its history, and for the next three centuries it will exercise its power of veto on the use of the criminal law against political offenders who have succeeded in obtaining popular sympathy. Plucknett, A Concise History of The Common Law 133-34 (5th ed. 1956).

The District Court gave short shrift to this legal tradition and made no effort to explain to the jury its historical role as the protector of the rights of the accused in a criminal case. Our Court unfortunately has done no better.

I would reverse the case and remand it for a new trial with instructions that the Court advise the jury, if requested, concerning the jury's "general veto power," in accordance with the *Wilson* case and the historical prerogatives of the jury to return a general verdict of not guilty.

ON REHEARING

MERRITT, Circuit Judge, dissenting. For the reasons stated in my panel dissent, I would grant en banc rehearing on the "jury nullification" issue. The law is settled that the jury has the power to decide against the law and the facts. The jury specifically asked about its power to do so, and was told by the District Court that it had no such power. The least that the jury should have been told was "the jury has the power to bring in a verdict in the teeth of both law and facts . . . the technical right, if it can be called so, to decide against the law and the facts . . . ." *Horning v. District of Columbia*, 254 U.S. 135, 138-39 41 S.Ct. 53, 54, 65 L.Ed. 185 (1920). These were the words of Justice Holmes speaking for the Court. The Supreme Court has never taken these words back or indicated that they do not properly state the law. The District Court and our Court are simply refusing to apply these words because they do not agree with them. It is not our prerogative to overrule the Supreme Court.

Notes and Questions

1. Did the trial court in this case not effectively tell the jury that it had no right to nullification?

2. Would it make sense to tell juries that they always had the right to return a verdict of "not guilty," regardless of the strength of the evidence? A group of citizens posted billboards in a Metro stop in the District of Columbia near the courthouse alerting passersby of their right to jury nullification. *See* Keith L. Alexander, *Billboard Advocating Jury Nullification Concerns Local Prosecutors*, Washington Post, Oct. 29, 2013. In 2012, New Hampshire passed a law permitting defense lawyers to inform juries about their right to nullification. *See* N.H.

Rev. Stat. § 519:23-a. What concerns do you have about giving juries the power to decide whether prosecutors have brought the appropriate charges in a particular case?

---

2. Limiting the Defense's Arguments

How far may a lawyer's argument go in advocating a verdict contrary to the law? As you will discover in *Craigimire*, a trial court has substantial discretion to prevent a lawyer from arguing for an acquittal for reasons other than the sufficiency of the evidence to satisfy the elements of the crime.

Craigimire v. State

Court of Criminal Appeals of Tennessee at Knoxville
1999 WL 508445

NORMA McGEE OGLE, Judge.

[The defendant was convicted of being an habitual criminal, which requires evidence of multiple convictions. The defendant's lawyer attempted to argue that the jury should find the defendant not guilty even though the defendant had been convicted the requisite number of times. The trial judge prevented portions of his argument.]

* * *

The petitioner further argues that, in the second habitual criminal proceeding, the actions of the trial court and the prosecutor during closing arguments denied the petitioner a closing argument, prejudiced the jury, and shifted the burden of proof to the petitioner, thereby denying the petitioner the effective assistance of counsel, due process, and a fair trial. Again, the petitioner failed to raise this issue on direct appeal and now alleges that his appellate counsel's omission constituted ineffective assistance. In order to evaluate the prejudicial impact of appellate counsel's performance, we will address the merits of this issue. *Henley*, 960 S.W.2d at 580.

The petitioner specifically contends that the trial court erroneously precluded his attorney from making the following arguments in closing:

Ladies and gentlemen, you looked at the records that were entered. Everyone of these offenses occurred in 1981. The record is silent on any offenses on him other than this receiving stolen property that he was convicted on in November of 1987.

* * *

Ladies and gentlemen, there are lots of things that you can use to look at in this matter-the records that have been entered here-and you can use your own sense of freedom, justice, and fair play in this. Ladies and gentlemen, I ask you: Is it fair for a person to be sentenced to serve a life sentence? He asserts that, because he was precluded from making the above arguments, "the court and state deprived [the petitioner] of *any* meaningful closing argument. . . ." In connection with his claim that he was denied a closing argument, the petitioner also contends that the prosecutor's objection to his closing argument constituted prosecutorial misconduct. Moreover, the petitioner contends that, in light of the limitations placed upon his closing argument, the State's rebuttal argument was improper. Finally, the petitioner argues that the conduct of the prosecutor and the trial court shifted the burden of proof to the petitioner, denying him due process of law.

Following the post-conviction hearing, the post-conviction court made the following findings of fact and conclusions of law:

The gravamen of [the petitioner's] complaint in this prosecution for habitual offender status was that his lawyer was not allowed to argue that it was unfair to sentence this individual to prison for life for a relatively minor felony offense; that is, receiving stolen property.

The record, of course, establishes that he had the requisite number of previous convictions to place him in the status of being an habitual offender, and under the law in effect at the time, he was eligible to be considered an habitual offender.

His lawyer had successfully, on two prior occasions, argued to a jury that this was the only offense that he had had in a number of years; that it was a relatively minor offense, and that they should not send Mr. Craigimire to prison for the rest of his life for this offense of receiving stolen property.

Those trials ended in a mistrial. He was retried then in 198[9] before Judge Nichols. At the urging of [the prosecutor], the Court admonished [defense counsel] not to make, basically, a jury-nullification argument.

During the course of [defense counsel's argument] . . . objections were made by the State and, apparently, sustained by the Court, although we do not have the benefit of the bench conference that took place. We do not have that on record. But I think everybody would agree that the Court admonished him and threatened even to hold him in contempt, if he continued in that argument.

The argument, essentially, was that it just was not fair to send this man to prison for the rest of his life for committing what would amount to, basically, a class-E felony. For what its worth, my personal opinion is that he probably shouldn't get life in prison for committing a class-E felony. But that was not the law in effect at the time.

It is clear to me, in reviewing the cases, that it is not appropriate to argue jury nullification to the jury. . . . I would not allow him to argue that they were allowed to disregard the law, but I think I would have allowed him to argue that this was a relatively minor offense. But, in essence, he got to do that during his closing argument, although it was very brief.

In conclusion, I am of the opinion that there was not denial of due process. There was no denial of effective assistance of counsel in this case.

These findings of fact are conclusive on appeal unless this court finds that the evidence preponderates against the findings of the post-conviction court. *Alley v. State*, 958 S.W.2d 138, 147 (Tenn.Crim.App.), *perm. to appeal denied*, (Tenn.1997).

i. Denial of Closing Argument

As noted earlier, the petitioner contends that the trial court effectively denied him a closing argument by sustaining the State's objections during his attorney's presentation. In *Herring v. New York*, 422 U.S. 853, 858, 95 S.Ct. 2550, 2553, 45 L.Ed.2d 593 (1975), the United States Supreme Court held that the right to the assistance of counsel includes the right of counsel for the defense to make a closing summation to the jury. *See also Patty v. Bordenkircher*, 603 F.2d 587, 589 (6th Cir.1979) (the trial court's refusal to permit defense counsel in an habitual criminal trial to make a final argument constituted a denial of the right to counsel). A trial court's refusal to permit closing argument is reversible error per se.

See, e.g., United States v. Davis, 993 F.2d 62, 64 (5th Cir.1993) ("[g]iven the difficulty of determining the prejudicial impact of the failure to afford summation, the denial of a request for it is reversible error per se); *Patty*, 603 F.2d at 589 (the rule announced in *Herring* is a per se rule, precluding harmless error analysis); *United States v. Bowden*, 579 F.Supp. 337, 343 (M.D.Tenn.1982), *affirmed*, 723 F.2d 911 (1983) ("it would have been reversible error per se to have denied [the defendant] an opportunity to make any closing argument at all").

However, the Court in *Herring*, 422 U.S. at 862, 95 S.Ct. at 2555, also observed:

> This is not to say that closing arguments in a criminal case must be uncontrolled or even unrestrained. The presiding judge must be and is given great latitude in controlling the duration and limiting the scope of closing summations. He may limit counsel to a reasonable time and may terminate argument when continuation would be repetitive or redundant. He may ensure that argument does not stray unduly from the mark, or otherwise impede the fair and orderly conduct of the trial. In all these respects he must be given broad discretion.

See also State v. Nesbit, 978 S.W.2d 872, 900 (Tenn.1998), *cert. denied*, 526 U.S. 1052, 119 S.Ct. 1359, 143 L.Ed.2d 520, 1999 WL 181566 (U.S.1999) (trial courts are accorded wide discretion in controlling closing arguments). Thus, in *Bowden*, 579 F.Supp. at 343-344, the federal district court denied the defendant's motion for new trial, concluding that the court had properly forbidden defense counsel from "arguing the law" during closing argument. The court observed:

> "Because it is the court's function and duty to instruct the jury on the controlling law [it is] the better practice . . ., of course, . . . that any arguments of this type be limited solely toward demonstrating how the evidence, or reasonable inferences therefrom, conform to the law. . . ."

Id. at 344 (citation omitted).

It is apparent from the record in this case that the trial court similarly limited defense counsel to arguing how the evidence or reasonable inferences therefrom conformed to the law. It is equally apparent in this case that there was no question that the petitioner possessed the requisite number of prior convictions to establish his status as an habitual criminal and that the State otherwise adduced sufficient proof at trial to support all the elements of the charged offense. Accordingly, as noted by the post-conviction court, the petitioner's real complaint is that, because he was in fact guilty of being an habitual offender, he was left with nothing to argue in closing except jury nullification, which argument the trial court prohibited.

ii. Jury Nullification

In other words, despite the petitioner's protestations, we agree with the post-conviction court that the excluded argument constituted an attempt by defense counsel to prompt jury nullification. As noted earlier, the State was required to establish beyond a reasonable doubt that the petitioner had been convicted of a triggering offense; the habitual criminal charge was contained in a separate count of the indictment; and the petitioner had previously been convicted of three felonies, as prescribed by statute. Tenn.Code. Ann. § 39-1-801 to -803 (Repealed November 1, 1989). Therefore, the defense attorney's references to the number of intervening years between the prior convictions and the triggering offense and the absence of additional offenses during those intervening years were not relevant to any issue at the habitual criminal trial other than the possibility of nullification. Rather, defense counsel was clearly attempting to argue that the petitioner had not committed a crime in several years and that, therefore, the jurors should exercise compassion notwithstanding the harsh mandates of the habitual criminal statutes.[7] Similarly, defense counsel's query to the jury concerning the fairness of imposing a life sentence was, in the context of this case and in light of defense counsel's failure to point to any deficiency in the proof, an invitation to the jury to exercise its de facto power of nullification.

A trial court not only has the discretion to control closing argument but a duty to prevent improper argument. Arguments by counsel must be based upon the evidence introduced at trial. *State v. Tate*, No. 02C01-9605-CR-00164, 1997 WL 746441, at *10 (Tenn.Crim.App.1997). Moreover, confusing or irrelevant arguments should not be permitted. *Id.* On the basis of these guidelines and the following discussion, we conclude that the trial court correctly prohibited defense counsel from arguing jury nullification. To the extent that defense counsel's argument was further limited by the evidence adduced at trial, this limitation was certainly no fault of the trial court.

A defendant does not possess a constitutional right, whether pursuant to the due process provisions of the state and federal constitutions or embodied in those documents' guarantees of a right to a trial by an impartial jury, to place the issue of jury nullification before a jury in a criminal trial. Thus, Tennessee

---

7   Following the petitioner's habitual criminal trial, the trial court observed that he had sustained the prosecutor's objection to defense counsel's statement concerning the silence of the record on offenses committed during the intervening years, because the statement was misleading. The trial court noted that, at the time of his habitual criminal trial, the petitioner was being prosecuted for offenses committed during the intervening years, including grand larceny, possession of a controlled substance, and burglary. We conclude that the trial court's limitation of closing argument on this basis was not unduly restrictive. As noted subsequently, the petitioner *was* permitted to argue briefly that the prior convictions occurred in 1981 and the triggering offense occurred in 1987. Furthermore, the absence of intervening criminal conduct was only relevant to the possibility of jury nullification.

courts have upheld refusals by trial courts, in response to defendants' requests, to inform juries that they may disregard the applicable law in reaching a verdict. *See, e.g., State v. Taylor*, 771 S.W.2d 387, 397 (Tenn.1989); *Janow v. State*, 567 S.W.2d 483, 485 (Tenn.Crim.App.1978). Moreover, in *State v. West*, No. 182, 1988 WL 13559, at *1 (Tenn.Crim.App. at Knoxville, February 22, 1988), a case arising under the habitual criminal statutes, this court additionally rejected the propriety of evidence and argument by a defendant concerning jury nullification:

> [D]efendants sought to have the jury determine that they were not deserving of a life sentence even though the record clearly shows they were habitual criminals as defined by statute. In effect the defendants wanted to convince the jury by irrelevant evidence, instruction, and argument to ignore relevant facts, law, and evidence and to return a not guilty verdict in this phase of the trial. This is not proper. . . .

Again, in *State v. Shropshire,* 874 S.W.2d 634, 639 (Tenn.Crim.App.1993), this court noted that "a trial court cannot be held in error for prohibiting a defendant from advising a jury not to follow the law as the trial court instructs it."

This issue is often articulated in terms of a limitation upon juries' rights notwithstanding their de facto power of nullification. In *Wright v. State*, 217 Tenn. 85, 394 S.W.2d 883 (Tenn.1965), another case arising under the habitual criminal statutes, five jurors filed affidavits following the defendant's conviction stating that they felt the defendant's prior convictions were not serious enough to make the defendant an habitual criminal. *Id.* at 884. They explained that they had voted to convict the defendant, because, as they understood the charge of the court, if the defendant had been convicted of crimes as defined in the habitual criminal statutes, there was nothing else for them to do. *Id.* at 885. The Supreme Court responded, "As a matter of fact they didn't have the *right* to disregard what the legislature had defined as making an habitual offender." *Id.* at 885 (emphasis added). Just as the jury's de facto power of nullification is not a "right" of the jury, the power confers no constitutional rights upon defendants.

Tennessee case law is consistent with the early United States Supreme Court case of *Sparf v. United States,* 156 U.S. 51, 15 S.Ct. 273, 39 L.Ed. 343 (1895). In that case, Justice Harlan stated:

> [U]pon principle, where the matter is not controlled by express constitutional or statutory provisions, it cannot be regarded as the right of counsel to dispute before the jury the law as declared by the Court. . . .[8] We must hold firmly

---

8   The state constitutions of Indiana and Maryland provide that jurors are judges of law and fact. Therefore, trial courts in those states instruct jurors on the "prerogative" of nullification and presumably defense counsel argues accordingly. *People v. Douglas,* 178 Misc.2d 918, 680 N.Y.S.2d 145, 150 n. 1 (N.Y.App.Div.1998).

to the doctrine that in the courts of the United States it is the duty of juries in criminal cases to take the law from the court, and apply that law to the facts as they find them to be from the evidence.

* * *

Under any other system, the courts, although established in order to declare the law, would for every practical purpose be eliminated from our system of government as instrumentalities devised for the protection equally of society and of individuals in their essential rights. When that occurs our government will cease to be a government of laws, and become a government of men. Liberty regulated by law is the underlying principle of our institutions.

Id. at 102-103, 293 (footnote added).

Other jurisdictions have applied this principle in addressing the question of whether a defendant possesses a constitutional right to propose nullification to a jury during closing argument. Thus, in *Medley v. Commonwealth*, 704 S.W.2d 190, 191 (Ky.1985), a Kentucky court held that, in a prosecution under Kentucky's persistent felon statute, a defendant did not have the right to argue in closing that the jury could disregard the law if it believed that the minimum penalty was too severe. In *United States v. Brown*, 548 F.2d 204, 210 (7th Cir.1977), the Seventh Circuit Court of Appeals held that the trial court properly precluded defense counsel from addressing in closing argument the historical role of the jury as the conscience of the community. The court observed that allowing this argument in the context of that case "would have been an invitation to the jury to disregard the instructions of the court; as such it was clearly improper." *Id.* In *United States v. Sepulveda*, 15 F.3d 1161, 1190 (1st Cir.1993), the First Circuit Court of Appeals observed:

[W]hile jurors may choose to flex their muscles, ignoring both law and evidence in a gadarene rush to acquit a criminal defendant, neither the court nor counsel should encourage jurors to exercise this power. . . . A trial judge, therefore, may block defense attorneys' attempts to serenade a jury with the siren song of nullification.

. . . To the extent that appellants, during closing argument, managed to mention nullification, they received more than was their due.

See also People v. Moore, 171 Ill.2d 74, 215 Ill.Dec. 75, 662 N.E.2d 1215, 1231 (Ill.1996)(a defendant has no right to argue nullification to the jury); *State v.*

Bjerkaas, 163 Wis.2d 949, 472 N.W.2d 615, 620 (Wis.Ct.App.1991) (a defendant has no right to encourage jury nullification during closing argument).

In any case, as noted by the post-conviction court, the petitioner was effectively permitted to argue nullification, albeit briefly. Defense counsel argued the following without objection:

> Ladies and Gentlemen, you are the sole triers of the facts and circumstances of this case. You have to go back there and deliberate, and make up your minds whether Mr. Craigmire is to receive a life sentence for receiving stolen property, or whether he is to be allowed to be sentenced by Judge Nichols. Sentence between three and ten years in the State pentitentiary.

* * *

> Ladies and gentlemen, all these things happened in 1981. Then he is convicted of receiving stolen property in 1987. Ladies and Gentlemen, three to ten years in the State Penitentiary is enough for anyone to serve for a receiving stolen property. Thus, contrary to the petitioner's argument, he received "more than was [his] due." We conclude that the trial court's limitations upon the petitioner's closing argument did not deprive the petitioner of the effective assistance of counsel, due process, or a fair trial by an impartial jury.

Notes and Questions

1. The role of juries in determining whether a defendant goes to prison—and if so, for how long—is the subject of considerable debate beyond jury nullification issues. Tennessee, where *Craigimire* was decided, first attempted to change from jury to judge sentencing in 1982, a law which underwent amendments in 1989 but failed to change the scheme.[1] Tennessee then amended the law in 1994, requiring the judge to instruct the jury on the meaning of the sentence for the offense charged and any lesser included offenses.[2] The 1994 amendment also required the judge to notify the jury of the earliest possible release date for the minimum sentence.[3] Finally, the Tennessee Legislature invalidated the jury

---

1   PAULA R. VOSS & W. MARK WARD, TENNESSEE CRIMINAL TRIAL PRACTICE § 28:2 (2013).

2   1994 Tenn. Pub. Acts ch. 847.

3   *Id.*

sentencing scheme in May, 1998.[4] Interestingly, the Tennessee Supreme Court's *State v. King* decision found the jury sentencing scheme valid two months later in July, 1998.[5] Since the Tennessee Criminal Sentencing Reform Act of 1989, Tennessee has officially described the purpose of its sentencing laws to assure fair and consistent treatment of defendants, eliminate unjustified disparity in sentencing, and provide predictability for criminal sanctions.[6]

2. Other states expressly give juries sentencing power. Virginia and Texas permit juries to determine the sentence once they have convicted the defendant. In Virginia, the jury issues the sentence in non-capital cases, unless the case is tried without a jury.[7] The judge has authority to modify or suspend the sentence, and must record a written explanation of any modification.[8] In Texas, the judge is presumed to issue the sentence, unless (1) the crime warrants a punishment of community supervision and the defendant files a motion for community supervision before trial, or (2) the defendant files a motion for the jury to determine the sentence before commencement of voir dire.[9] If the defendant is found guilty, the defendant may change his choice before sentencing with the consent of the prosecution.[10] (Can you see why the defendant's attorney would try to change his/her choice?) If the defendant is found guilty of a capital offense where the state does not seek the death penalty, the judge will issue the sentence.[11] If the state seeks the death penalty, as is true in every state, the jury will issue the sentence.[12] The right to a jury sentence is not a Texas constitutional right, and at least one court has overturned a jury's sentence on the issue of community supervision.[13]

---

4   1998 Tenn. Pub. Acts ch. 1041 (codified as amended in Tenn. Code § 40-35-201); *see* Voss & Ward, *supra* note 1.

5   *State v. King*, 973 S.W.2d 586, 589 (Tenn. 1998).

6   Tenn. Code Ann. § 40-35-102 (West 2013).

7   Va. Code Ann. § 19.2-295(A) (West 2013). See generally Ronald J. Bacigal, Virginia Practice Series— Criminal Procedure §§ 19:1, 19:5 (West 2013) (discussing Virginia's sentencing scheme).

8   *Id.* § 19.2-295(B); § 19.2-303.

9   Tex. Code Crim. Proc. Ann. art. 37.07(2)(b) (West 2013). *See generally* Thomas J. Czelusta et al., *Assessment by Jury, in* 26 Texas Jurisprudence 3d, § 194 (2014) (discussing Texas' sentencing scheme).

10 *Id.*

11 Tex. Code Crim. Proc. Ann. art. 37.071(1) (West 2013).

12 *Id.* art. 37.071(2)(a)(1).

13 *Ivey v. State*, 277 S.W.3d 43, 52 (Tex. Crim. App. 2009).

3. Limits on the Power of Juries to Acquit

Evans v. Michigan

Supreme Court of the United States
133 S.Ct. 1069 (2013)

Justice SOTOMAYOR delivered the opinion of the Court.

When the State of Michigan rested its case at petitioner Lamar Evans' arson trial, the court entered a directed verdict of acquittal, based upon its view that the State had not provided sufficient evidence of a particular element of the offense. It turns out that the unproven "element" was not actually a required element at all. We must decide whether an erroneous acquittal such as this nevertheless constitutes an acquittal for double jeopardy purposes, which would mean that Evans could not be retried. This Court has previously held that a judicial acquittal premised upon a "misconstruction" of a criminal statute is an "acquittal on the merits . . . [that] bars retrial." *Arizona v. Rumsey*, 467 U.S. 203, 211, 104 S.Ct. 2305, 81 L.Ed.2d 164 (1984). Seeing no meaningful constitutional distinction between a trial court's "misconstruction" of a statute and its erroneous addition of a statutory element, we hold that a midtrial acquittal in these circumstances is an acquittal for double jeopardy purposes as well.

I

The State charged Evans with burning "other real property," a violation of Mich. Comp. Laws § 750.73 (1981). The State's evidence at trial suggested that Evans had burned down an unoccupied house. At the close of the State's case, however, Evans moved for a directed verdict of acquittal. He pointed the court to the applicable Michigan Criminal Jury Instructions, which listed as the "Fourth" element of the offense "that the building was not a dwelling house." 3 Mich. Crim. Jury Instr. § 31.3, p. 31–7 (2d ed., Supp. 2006/2007). And the commentary to the Instructions emphasized, "an essential element is that the structure burned is *not* a dwelling house." *Id.*, at 31–8. Evans argued that Mich. Comp. Laws § 750.72 criminalizes common-law arson, which requires that the structure burned be a dwelling, while the provision under which he was charged, § 750.73, covers all other real property.[1] Persuaded, the trial court granted the motion. 491 Mich. 1,

---

1   Mich. Comp. Laws § 750.72 (1981), "Burning dwelling house," provides: "Any person who wilfully or maliciously burns any dwelling house, either occupied or unoccupied, or the contents thereof, whether owned by himself or another, or any building within the curtilage of such dwelling house, or the contents thereof, shall be guilty of a felony, punishable by imprisonment in the state prison not more than 20 years."

8, 810 N.W.2d 535, 539 (2012). The court explained that the "'testimony [of the homeowner] was this was a dwelling house,'" so the nondwelling requirement of § 750.73 was not met. *Ibid.*

On the State's appeal, the Michigan Court of Appeals reversed and remanded. 288 Mich.App. 410, 794 N.W.2d 848 (2010). Evans had conceded, and the court held, that under controlling precedent, burning "other real property" is a lesser included offense under Michigan law, and disproving the greater offense is not required. *Id.*, at 416, 794 N.W.2d, at 852 (citing *People v. Antonelli*, 66 Mich.App. 138, 140, 238 N.W.2d 551, 552 (1975) (on rehearing).[2] The court thus explained it was "undisputed that the trial court misperceived the elements of the offense with which [Evans] was charged and erred by directing a verdict." 288 Mich.App., at 416, 794 N.W.2d, at 852. But the court rejected Evans argument that the Double Jeopardy Clause barred retrial. *Id.*, at 421–422, 794 N.W.2d, at 856.

In a divided decision, the Supreme Court of Michigan affirmed. It held that "when a trial court grants a defendant's motion for a directed verdict on the basis of an error of law that did not resolve any factual element of the charged offense, the trial court's ruling does not constitute an acquittal for the purposes of double jeopardy and retrial is therefore not barred." 491 Mich., at 4, 810 N.W.2d, at 536–537.

We granted certiorari to resolve the disagreement among state and federal courts on the question whether retrial is barred when a trial court grants an acquittal because the prosecution had failed to prove an "element" of the offense that, in actuality, it did not have to prove. 567 U.S. ––––, 132 S.Ct. 2753, 183 L.Ed.2d 614 (2012). We now reverse.

II

A

In answering this question, we do not write on a clean slate. Quite the opposite. It has been half a century since we first recognized that the Double Jeopardy Clause bars retrial following a court-decreed acquittal, even if the acquittal is "based upon an egregiously erroneous foundation." *Fong Foo v. United States*, 369 U.S. 141, 143, 82 S.Ct. 671, 7 L.Ed.2d 629 (1962) (*per curiam*). A mistaken acquit-

---

And § 750.73, "Burning of other real property," provides: "Any person who wilfully or maliciously burns any building or other real property, or the contents thereof, other than those specified in the next preceding section of this chapter, the property of himself or another, shall be guilty of a felony, punishable by imprisonment in the state prison for not more than 10 years."

2   In other words, the pattern jury instructions were incorrect. The State later revised them. See 288 Mich.App. 410, 416, n. 3, 794 N.W.2d 848, 852, n. 3 (2010).

tal is an acquittal nonetheless, and we have long held that "[a] verdict of acquittal
. . . could not be reviewed, on error or otherwise, without putting [a defendant]
twice in jeopardy, and thereby violating the Constitution." *United States v. Ball*,
163 U.S. 662, 671, 16 S.Ct. 1192, 41 L.Ed. 300 (1896).

Our cases have applied *Fong Foo's* principle broadly. An acquittal is unreviewable whether a judge directs a jury to return a verdict of acquittal, *e.g.*, *Fong
Foo*, 369 U.S., at 143, 82 S.Ct. 671, or forgoes that formality by entering a judgment of acquittal herself. *See Smith v. Massachusetts*, 543 U.S. 462, 467–468, 125
S.Ct. 1129, 160 L.Ed.2d 914 (2005) (collecting cases). And an acquittal precludes
retrial even if it is premised upon an erroneous decision to exclude evidence,
Sanabria v. United States, 437 U.S. 54, 68–69, 78, 98 S.Ct. 2170, 57 L.Ed.2d 43
(1978); a mistaken understanding of what evidence would suffice to sustain a
conviction, *Smith*, 543 U.S., at 473, 125 S.Ct. 1129; or a "misconstruction of the
statute" defining the requirements to convict, *Rumsey*, 467 U.S., at 203, 211, 104
S.Ct. 2305; cf. *Smalis v. Pennsylvania*, 476 U.S. 140, 144–145, n. 7, 106 S.Ct. 1745,
90 L.Ed.2d 116 (1986). In all these circumstances, "the fact that the acquittal may
result from erroneous evidentiary rulings or erroneous interpretations of governing legal principles affects the accuracy of that determination, but it does not
alter its essential character." *United States v. Scott*, 437 U.S. 82, 98, 98 S.Ct. 2187,
57 L.Ed.2d 65 (1978) (internal quotation marks and citation omitted).

Most relevant here, our cases have defined an acquittal to encompass any
ruling that the prosecution's proof is insufficient to establish criminal liability
for an offense. See *ibid.*, and n. 11; *Burks v. United States*, 437 U.S. 1, 10, 98 S.Ct.
2141, 57 L.Ed.2d 1 (1978); *United States v. Martin Linen Supply Co.*, 430 U.S. 564,
571, 97 S.Ct. 1349, 51 L.Ed.2d 642 (1977). Thus an "acquittal" includes "a ruling by the court that the evidence is insufficient to convict," a "factual finding
[that] necessarily establish[es] the criminal defendant's lack of criminal culpability," and any other "rulin[g] which relate[s] to the ultimate question of guilt or
innocence." *Scott*, 437 U.S., at 91, 98, and n. 11, 98 S.Ct. 2187 (internal quotation
marks omitted). These sorts of substantive rulings stand apart from procedural
rulings that may also terminate a case midtrial, which we generally refer to as
dismissals or mistrials. Procedural dismissals include rulings on questions that
"are unrelated to factual guilt or innocence," but "which serve other purposes,"
including "a legal judgment that a defendant, although criminally culpable, may
not be punished" because of some problem like an error with the indictment. *Id.*,
at 98, and n. 11, 98 S.Ct. 2187.

Both procedural dismissals and substantive rulings result in an early end
to trial, but we explained in *Scott* that the double jeopardy consequences of
each differ. "[T]he law attaches particular significance to an acquittal," so a
merits-related ruling concludes proceedings absolutely. *Id.*, at 91, 98 S.Ct. 2187.

This is because "[t]o permit a second trial after an acquittal, however mistaken the acquittal may have been, would present an unacceptably high risk that the Government, with its vastly superior resources, might wear down the defendant so that 'even though innocent he may be found guilty,'" *ibid.* (quoting *Green v. United States*, 355 U.S. 184, 188, 78 S.Ct. 221, 2 L.Ed.2d 199 (1957)). And retrial following an acquittal would upset a defendant's expectation of repose, for it would subject him to additional "embarrassment, expense and ordeal" while "compelling him to live in a continuing state of anxiety and insecurity." *Id.*, at 187, 78 S.Ct. 221. In contrast, a "termination of the proceedings against [a defendant] on a basis unrelated to factual guilt or innocence of the offense of which he is accused," 437 U.S., at 98–99, 98 S.Ct. 2187, *i.e.*, some procedural ground, does not pose the same concerns, because no expectation of finality attaches to a properly granted mistrial.

Here, "it is plain that the [trial court] . . . evaluated the [State's] evidence and determined that it was legally insufficient to sustain a conviction." *Martin Linen*, 430 U.S., at 572, 97 S.Ct. 1349. The trial court granted Evans' motion under a rule that requires the court to "direct a verdict of acquittal on any charged offense as to which the evidence is insufficient to support conviction." Mich. Rule Crim. Proc. 6.419(A) (2012). And the court's oral ruling leaves no doubt that it made its determination on the basis of "'[t]he testimony'" that the State had presented. 491 Mich., at 8, 810 N.W.2d, at 539. This ruling was not a dismissal on a procedural ground "unrelated to factual guilt or innocence," like the question of "preindictment delay" in *Scott*, but rather a determination that the State had failed to prove its case. 437 U.S., at 98, 99, 98 S.Ct. 2187. Under our precedents, then, Evans was acquitted.

There is no question the trial court's ruling was wrong; it was predicated upon a clear misunderstanding of what facts the State needed to prove under State law. But that is of no moment. *Martin Linen, Sanabria, Rumsey, Smalis*, and *Smith* all instruct that an acquittal due to insufficient evidence precludes retrial, whether the court's evaluation of the evidence was "correct or not," *Martin Linen*, 430 U.S., at 571, 97 S.Ct. 1349, and regardless of whether the court's decision flowed from an incorrect antecedent ruling of law. Here Evans' acquittal was the product of an "erroneous interpretatio[n] of governing legal principles," but as in our other cases, that error affects only "the accuracy of [the] determination" to acquit, not "its essential character." *Scott*, 437 U.S., at 98, 98 S.Ct. 2187 (internal quotation marks omitted).

B

The court below saw things differently. It identified a "constitutionally meaningful difference" between this case and our previous decisions. Those cases, the court found, "involve[d] evidentiary errors regarding the proof needed to establish a factual element of the . . . crimes at issue," but still ultimately involved "a resolution regarding the sufficiency of the factual elements of the charged offense." 491 Mich., at 14–15, 810 N.W.2d, at 542–543. When a court mistakenly "identifie[s] an extraneous element and dismisse[s] the case solely on that basis," however, it has "not resolve[d] or even address[ed] any factual element necessary to establish" the offense. *Id.*, at 15, 20, 810 N.W.2d, at 543, 546. As a result, the court below reasoned, the case terminates "based on an error of law unrelated to [the] defendant's guilt or innocence on the elements of the charged offense," and thus falls outside the definition of an acquittal. *Id.*, at 21, 810 N.W.2d, at 546.

We fail to perceive the difference. This case, like our previous ones, involves an antecedent legal error that led to an acquittal because the State failed to prove some fact it was not actually required to prove. Consider *Rumsey*. There the trial court, sitting as sentencer in a capital case involving a murder committed during a robbery, mistakenly held that Arizona's statutory aggravating factor describing killings for pecuniary gain was limited to murders for hire. Accordingly, it found the State had failed to prove the killing was for pecuniary gain and sentenced the defendant to life imprisonment. After the State successfully appealed and obtained a death sentence on remand, we held that retrial on the penalty phase question was a double jeopardy violation.[4]

The only relevant difference between that situation and this one is that in *Rumsey* the trial court's error was called a "misinterpretation" and a "misconstruction of the statute," 467 U.S., at 207, 211, 104 S.Ct. 2305, whereas here the error has been designated the "erroneous addition of [an] extraneous element to the charged offense." 491 Mich., at 3–4, 810 N.W.2d, at 536. But we have emphasized that labels do not control our analysis in this context; rather, the substance of a court's decision does. See *Smalis*, 476 U.S., at 144, n. 5, 106 S.Ct. 1745; *Scott*, 437 U.S., at 96–97, 98 S.Ct. 2187; *Martin Linen*, 430 U.S., at 571, 97 S.Ct. 1349. The error in *Rumsey* could just as easily have been characterized as the erroneous addition of an element of the statutory aggravating circumstance: that the homicide be a murder-for-hire. Conversely, the error here could be viewed as a misinterpretation of the statute's phrase "building

---

4   Under *Bullington v. Missouri*, 451 U.S. 430, 101 S.Ct. 1852, 68 L.Ed.2d 270 (1981), a capital defendant is "acquitted" of the death penalty if, at the end of a separate sentencing proceeding, the factfinder concludes that the prosecution has failed to prove required additional facts to support a sentence of death. Thus in *Rumsey*, the trial court's initial "judgment, based on findings sufficient to establish legal entitlement to the life sentence, amounts to an acquittal on the merits and, as such, bars any retrial of the appropriateness of the death penalty." 467 U.S., at 211, 104 S.Ct. 2305.

or other real property" to exclude dwellings.[5] This is far too fine a distinction to be meaningful, and we reject the notion that a defendant's constitutional rights would turn on the happenstance of how an appellate court chooses to describe a trial court's error.

Echoing the Michigan Supreme Court, the State and the United States, as well as the dissent, emphasize *Martin Linen*'s description of an acquittal as the "resolution, correct or not, of some or all of the factual *elements* of the *offense* charged." 430 U.S., at 571, 97 S.Ct. 1349 (emphasis added); see Brief for Respondent 11–17; see Brief for United States as *Amicus Curiae* 11–15 (herein-after U.S. Brief); see *post*, at 1084–1086. They observe that the Double Jeopardy Clause protects against being twice placed in jeopardy for the same "offence," U.S. Const., Amdt. 5, cl. 2, and they note that an offense comprises constituent parts called elements, which are facts that must be proved to sustain a conviction. *See, e.g., United States v. Dixon*, 509 U.S. 688, 696–697, 113 S.Ct. 2849, 125 L.Ed.2d 556 (1993). Consequently, they argue, only if an actual element of the offense is resolved can it be said that there has been an acquittal of the offense, because "'innocence of the charged offense' cannot turn on something that is concededly not an element of the offense." U.S. Brief 15. Because Evans' trial ended without resolution of even one actual element, they conclude, there was no acquittal.

This argument reads *Martin Linen* too narrowly, and it is inconsistent with our decisions since then. Our focus in *Martin Linen* was on the significance of a judicial acquittal under Fed. Rule Crim. Proc. 29. The District Court in that case had "evaluated the Government's evidence and determined that it was legally insufficient to sustain a conviction." 430 U.S., at 572, 97 S.Ct. 1349. That determination of nonculpability was enough to make the acquittal akin to a jury verdict; our holding did not depend upon defining the "elements" of the offense. As we have explained, *supra*, at 1084–1085, *Scott* confirms that the relevant distinction is between judicial determinations that go to "the criminal defendant's lack of criminal culpability," and those that hold "that a defendant, although criminally

---

5   Indeed, it is possible that this is what the trial court thought it was doing, not articulating an additional element. The statute criminalizes burning "any building or other real property, . . . other than those specified in" the previous section, which criminalizes the burning of a dwelling house. Mich. Comp. Laws § 750.73. In light of the statute's phrasing, the trial court interpreted "building or other real property" to be exclusive of the type of property described in § 750.72, although the Michigan courts have explained that the term is actually meant to be inclusive. So the trial court decision could be viewed as having given the statutory "building" element an unduly narrow construction (by limiting it to nondwellings), just as the trial court in *Rumsey* gave the pecuniary-gain provision an unduly narrow construction (by limiting it to contract killings). Nevertheless, we accept the parties' and the Michigan courts' alternative characterization of the trial court's error as the "addition" of an extraneous element. Our observation simply underscores how malleable the distinction adopted by the Michigan Supreme Court, and defended by the State and the United States, can be. And it belies the dissent's suggestion, post, at 1087 (opinion of ALITO, J.), that drawing this distinction is "quite easy" here, and that the basis for the trial court's ruling could not be subject to "real dispute."

culpable, may not be punished because of a supposed" procedural error. 437 U.S., at 98, 98 S.Ct. 2187. Culpability (*i.e.*, the "ultimate question of guilt or innocence") is the touchstone, not whether any particular elements were resolved or whether the determination of nonculpability was legally correct. *Id.*, at 98, n. 11, 98 S.Ct. 2187 (internal quotation marks omitted).

Perhaps most inconsistent with the State's and United States' argument is *Burks*. There we held that when a defendant raises insanity as a defense, and a court decides the "Government ha[s] failed to come forward with sufficient proof of [the defendant's] capacity to be responsible for criminal acts," the defendant has been acquitted because the court decided that "criminal culpability ha[s] not been established." 437 U.S., at 10, 98 S.Ct. 2141. Lack of insanity was not an "element" of Burks' offense, bank robbery by use of a dangerous weapon. See 18 U.S.C. § 2113(d) (1976 ed.). Rather, insanity was an affirmative defense to criminal liability. Our conclusion thus depended upon equating a judicial acquittal with an order finding insufficient evidence of culpability, not insufficient evidence of any particular element of the offense.[6]

In the end, this case follows those that have come before it. The trial court's judgment of acquittal resolved the question of Evans' guilt or innocence as a matter of the sufficiency of the evidence, not on unrelated procedural grounds. That judgment, "however erroneous" it was, precludes reprosecution on this charge, and so should have barred the State's appeal as well. *Sanabria*, 437 U.S., at 69, 98 S.Ct. 2170.

III

A

The State, supported by the United States, offers three other reasons why the distinction drawn by the court below should be maintained. None persuades us.

To start, the State argues that unless an actual element of the offense is resolved by the trial court, the only way to know whether the court's ruling was an "acquittal" is to rely upon the label used by the court, which would wrongly allow the form of the trial court's action to control. Brief for Respondent 17–18, 21–22. We disagree. Our decision turns not on the form of the trial court's action, but rather whether it "serve[s]" substantive "purposes" or procedural ones. *Scott*, 437 U.S., at 98, n. 11, 98 S.Ct. 2187. If a trial court were to announce, midtrial,

---

6   To account for *Burks*, the United States posits that, "[a]s used in [its] brief, the 'elements' of an offense encompass legally recognized defenses that would negate culpability." U.S. Brief 11, n. 3. So too would the dissent hold that, "as used in this opinion, the 'elements' of an offense include legally recognized affirmative defenses that would negate culpability." Post, at 1085, n. 2. Rather than adopt a novel definition of the word "element" to mean "elements and affirmative defenses," and then promptly limit that novel definition to these circumstances, we prefer to read *Burks* for what it says, which is that the issue is whether the bottom-line question of "criminal culpability" was resolved. 437 U.S., at 10, 98 S.Ct. 2141.

"The defendant shall be acquitted because he was prejudiced by preindictment delay," the Double Jeopardy Clause would pose no barrier to reprosecution, notwithstanding the "acquittal" label. Cf. *Scott*, 437 U.S. 82, 98 S.Ct. 2187, 57 L.Ed.2d 65. Here we know the trial court acquitted Evans, not because it incanted the word "acquit" (which it did not), but because it acted on its view that the prosecution had failed to prove its case.

Next, the State and the United States fear that if the grounds for an acquittal are untethered from the actual elements of the offense, a trial court could issue an unreviewable order finding insufficient evidence to convict for any reason at all, such as that the prosecution failed to prove "that the structure burned [was] blue." Brief for Respondent 16–17; U.S. Brief 15. If the concern is that there is no limit to the magnitude of the error that could yield an acquittal, the response is that we have long held as much. See *supra*, at 1074–1075. If the concern is instead that our holding will make it easier for courts to insulate from review acquittals that are granted as a form of nullification, see Brief for Respondent 30, n. 58, we reject the premise. We presume here, as in other contexts, that courts exercise their duties in good faith. Cf. *Harrington v. Richter*, 562 U.S. ––––, ––––, 131 S.Ct. 770, 786–787, 178 L.Ed.2d 624 (2011).

Finally, the State suggests that because Evans induced the trial court's error, he should not be heard to complain when that error is corrected and the State wishes to retry him. Brief for Respondent 32–33; cf. *id.*, at 1075–1077, 131 S.Ct., at 782–785. But we have recognized that "most [judgments of acquittal] result from defense motions," so "[t]o hold that a defendant waives his double jeopardy protection whenever a trial court error in his favor on a midtrial motion leads to an acquittal would undercut the adversary assumption on which our system of criminal justice rests, and would vitiate one of the fundamental rights established by the Fifth Amendment." *Sanabria*, 437 U.S., at 78, 98 S.Ct. 2170 (citation omitted).[7] It is true that when a defendant persuades the court to declare a mistrial, jeopardy continues and retrial is generally allowed. See *United States v. Dinitz*, 424 U.S. 600, 96 S.Ct. 1075, 47 L.Ed.2d 267 (1976). But in such circumstances the defendant consents to a disposition that contemplates reprosecution, whereas when a defendant moves for acquittal he does not. See *Sanabria*, 437 U.S., at 75, 98 S.Ct. 2170.

The United States makes a related argument. It contends that Evans could have asked the court to resolve whether nondwelling status is an element of the offense before jeopardy attached, so having elected to wait until trial was under-

---

7   The dissent says that "defense counsel fooled the judge," *post*, at 1084, but surely that charge is not fair. Nothing suggests counsel exceeded the permissible bounds of zealous advocacy on behalf of his client. Counsel presented a colorable legal argument, and marshaled persuasive authority: Michigan's own criminal jury instructions, which, at the time, supported his position. See *supra*, at 1073, 1074, n. 2.

way to raise the point, he cannot now claim a double jeopardy violation. U.S. Brief 22–25. The Government relies upon *Lee v. United States*, 432 U.S. 23, 97 S.Ct. 2141, 53 L.Ed.2d 80 (1977), in which the District Court dismissed an indictment midtrial because it had failed to allege the required intent element of the offense. We held that retrial on a corrected indictment was not barred, because the dismissal was akin to a mistrial, not an acquittal. This was clear because the District Court had separately denied the defendant's motion for judgment of acquittal, explaining that the defendant "'has been proven [guilty] beyond any reasonable doubt in the world,'" while acknowledging that the error in the indictment required dismissal. *Id.*, at 26–27, 97 S.Ct. 2141. Because the defendant "invited the court to interrupt the proceedings before formalizing a finding on the merits" by raising the indictment issue so late, we held the principles governing a defendant's consent to mistrial should apply. *Id.*, at 28, 97 S.Ct. 2141 (citing *Dinitz*, 424 U.S. 600, 96 S.Ct. 1075, 47 L.Ed.2d 267).

The Government suggests the situation here is "functionally similar," because "identifying the elements of an offense is a necessary step in determining the sufficiency of a charging document." U.S. Brief 23. But we cannot ignore the fact that what the trial court actually did here was rule on the sufficiency of the State's proof, not the sufficiency of the information filed against him. *Lee* demonstrates that the two need not rise or fall together. And even if the Government is correct that Evans could have challenged the charging document on the same legal theory he used to challenge the sufficiency of the evidence, it matters that he made only the latter motion, a motion that necessarily may not be made until trial is underway. Evans cannot be penalized for requesting from the court a ruling on the merits of the State's case, as the Michigan Rules entitled him to do; whether he could have also brought a distinct procedural objection earlier on is beside the point.

B

In the alternative, the State and the United States ask us to reconsider our past decisions. Brief for Respondent 34–56 (suggesting overruling our cases since at least *Fong Foo*); U.S. Brief 27–32 (suggesting overruling *Smith*, *Rumsey*, and *Smalis*).[8] We declined to revisit our cases when the United States made a similar request in *Smalis*, 476 U.S., at 144, 106 S.Ct. 1745; *see* Brief for United States as

---

8   The dissent's true gripe may be with these cases as well, rather than our result here, which, we have explained, follows inevitably from them. *See post*, at 1084 (noting "how far [our cases] have departed from the common-law principles that applied at the time of the founding"); compare *post*, at 1087 ("Permitting retrial in these egregious cases is especially appropriate"), with *Fong Foo v. United States*, 369 U.S. 141, 143, 82 S.Ct. 671, 7 L.Ed.2d 629 (1962) (*per curiam*) (according finality to even those acquittals "based upon an egregiously erroneous foundation").

Amicus Curiae in *Smalis v. Pennsylvania*, O.T. 1985, No. 85–227, pp. 19–25. And we decline to do so here.

First, we have no reason to believe the existing rules have become so "unworkable" as to justify overruling precedent. *Payne v. Tennessee*, 501 U.S. 808, 827, 111 S.Ct. 2597, 115 L.Ed.2d 720 (1991). The distinction drawn in *Scott* has stood the test of time, and we expect courts will continue to have little "difficulty in distinguishing between those rulings which relate to the ultimate question of guilt or innocence and those which serve other purposes." 437 U.S., at 98, n. 11, 98 S.Ct. 2187 (internal quotation marks omitted). See, *e.g., United States v. Dionisio*, 503 F.3d 78, 83–88 (C.A.2 2007) (collecting cases); 6 W. LaFave, J. Israel, N. King, & O. Kerr, Criminal Procedure § 25.3(a), p. 629 (3d ed. 2007) (same).

Second, the logic of these cases still holds. There is no question that a jury verdict of acquittal precludes retrial, and thus bars appeal of any legal error that may have led to that acquittal. See *Ball*, 163 U.S., at 671, 16 S.Ct. 1192. So, had the trial court here instructed the jury that it must find the burned structure was not a dwelling in order to convict, the jury would have acquitted Evans accordingly; "'[a] jury is presumed to follow its instructions.'" *Blueford v. Arkansas*, 566 U.S. ––––, ––––, 132 S.Ct. 2044, 2051, 182 L.Ed.2d 937 (2012) (quoting *Weeks v. Angelone*, 528 U.S. 225, 234, 120 S.Ct. 727, 145 L.Ed.2d 727 (2000)). And that would have been the end of the matter. From that premise, *Fong Foo*'s holding follows: If a trial court instead exercises its discretion to direct a jury to return a verdict of acquittal, jeopardy also terminates notwithstanding any legal error, because there too it is the jury that returns an acquittal. And from there, *Martin Linen*'s conclusion is unavoidable: It should make no difference whether the court employs the formality of directing the jury to return an acquittal or whether the court enters an acquittal itself. *Sanabria, Rumsey, Smalis*, and *Smith* merely apply *Fong Foo* and *Martin Linen* in tandem: If a trial court makes an antecedent legal error (as in *Fong Foo*), and then grants a judgment of acquittal rather than directing the jury to acquit (as in *Martin Linen*), the result is an acquittal all the same.

In other words, there is no way for antecedent legal errors to be reviewable in the context of judicial acquittals unless those errors are also reviewable when they give rise to jury acquittals (contrary to the settled understanding that a jury verdict of acquittal is unreviewable), or unless we distinguish between juries that acquit pursuant to their instructions and judicial acquittals (notwithstanding that this is a purely formal distinction). Neither option has become more attractive with time. We therefore reiterate: "any contention that the Double Jeopardy Clause must itself . . . leave open a way of correcting legal errors is at odds with the well-established rule that the bar will attach to a preverdict acquittal that is patently wrong in law." *Smith*, 543 U.S., at 473, 125 S.Ct. 1129.

Finally, the State and the United States object that this rule denies the prosecution a full and fair opportunity to present its evidence to the jury, while the defendant reaps a "windfall" from the trial court's unreviewable error. Brief for Respondent 6; U.S. Brief 31–32. But sovereigns are hardly powerless to prevent this sort of situation, as we observed in *Smith*, 543 U.S., at 474, 125 S.Ct. 1129. Nothing obligates a jurisdiction to afford its trial courts the power to grant a midtrial acquittal, and at least two States disallow the practice. *See* Nev.Rev.Stat. § 175.381(1) (2011); *State v. Parfait*, 96,1814 (La.App. 1 Cir. 05/09/97), 693 So.2d 1232, 1242. Many jurisdictions, including the federal system, allow or encourage their courts to defer consideration of a motion to acquit until after the jury returns a verdict, which mitigates double jeopardy concerns.[9] See Fed. Rule Crim. Proc. 29(b). And for cases such as this, in which a trial court's interpretation of the relevant criminal statute is likely to prove dispositive, we see no reason why jurisdictions could not provide for mandatory continuances or expedited interlocutory appeals if they wished to prevent misguided acquittals from being entered.[10] But having chosen to vest its courts with the power to grant midtrial acquittals, the State must bear the corresponding risk that some acquittals will be granted in error.

We hold that Evans' trial ended in an acquittal when the trial court ruled the State had failed to produce sufficient evidence of his guilt. The Double Jeopardy Clause thus bars retrial for his offense and should have barred the State's appeal. The judgment of the Supreme Court of Michigan is

Reversed.

Justice ALITO, dissenting.

The Court holds that the Double Jeopardy Clause bars petitioner's retrial for arson because his attorney managed to convince a judge to terminate petitioner's first trial prior to verdict on the specious ground that the offense with which he was charged contains an imaginary "element" that the prosecution could not prove. The Court's decision makes no sense. It is not consistent with the original meaning of the Double Jeopardy Clause; it does not serve the purposes of the prohibition against double jeopardy; and contrary to the Court's reasoning, the trial judge's ruling was not an "acquittal," which our cases have

---

9   If a court grants a motion to acquit after the jury has convicted, there is no double jeopardy barrier to an appeal by the government from the court's acquittal, because reversal would result in reinstatement of the jury verdict of guilt, not a new trial. *United States v. Wilson*, 420 U.S. 332, 95 S.Ct. 1013, 43 L.Ed.2d 232 (1975).

10   Here, the prosecutor twice asked the court for a recess to review the Michigan statutes and to discuss the question with her supervisor. 491 Mich., at 7, 810 N.W.2d, at 538–539. If the trial court's refusal was ill-advised, that is a matter for state procedure to address, but it does not bear on the double jeopardy consequences of the acquittal that followed. * * *

"consistently" defined as a decision that "'actually represents a resolution, correct or not, of some or all of the factual *elements of the offense charged.*'" *E.g., Smith v. Massachusetts*, 543 U.S. 462, 468, 125 S.Ct. 1129, 160 L.Ed.2d 914 (2005) (quoting *United States v. Martin Linen Supply Co.*, 430 U.S. 564, 571, 97 S.Ct. 1349, 51 L.Ed.2d 642 (1977); emphasis added). For no good reason, the Court deprives the State of Michigan of its right to have one fair opportunity to convict petitioner, and I therefore respectfully dissent.

I

After Detroit police officers heard an explosion at a burning house, they observed petitioner running away from the building with a gasoline can. The officers pursued and ultimately apprehended petitioner, who admitted that he had burned down the house. No one was living in the house at the time of the fire.

If the house in question had been a "dwelling house," petitioner could have been charged under Mich. Comp. Laws § 750.72 (1981) for burning a dwelling, an offense punishable by imprisonment for up to 20 years. But petitioner was instead charged with "[b]urning other real property" in violation of Mich. Comp. Laws § 750.73. This offense, which carries a maximum penalty of 10 years' imprisonment, applies to "[a]ny person who wilfully or maliciously burns any building or other real property . . . other than those specified in [§ 750.72]." This crime is a lesser included offense of the crime of burning a dwelling house. The "necessary elements to prove either offense are the same, except to prove the greater [offense] it must be shown that the building is a dwelling." 491 Mich. 1, 19–20, 810 N.W.2d 535, 545–546 (2012) (internal quotation marks omitted). To prove the lesser offense, however, "'it is not necessary to prove that the building is *not* a dwelling.'" *Id.*, at 20, 810 N.W.2d, at 546 (emphasis added).

At the close of the prosecution's case, petitioner's attorney moved for a directed verdict on the ground that (1) the prosecution was required to prove, as an "element" of the charged offense, that "the building was *not* a dwelling" and (2) "the prosecution had failed to prove that the burned building was not a dwelling house." *Id.*, at 5, 810 N.W.2d, at 537. The prosecutor responded by arguing that nothing in the charged offense requires proof that the building was not a dwelling, and the prosecutor requested "a moment" to "pull the statute" and "consult with [her] supervisors." *Id.*, at 5–7, 810 N.W.2d, at 537–539. The trial judge denied the prosecutor's requests and erroneously concluded that the prosecution was required to prove that the burned building was not a dwelling. After determining that the State had not proved this nonexistent "element," the trial judge granted petitioner's motion for a directed verdict and entered an order that it labeled an "[a]cquittal." App. to Pet. for Cert. 72.

The trial judge's ruling was plainly wrong, and on appeal, defense counsel did not even attempt to defend its correctness, conceding that the judge had "wrongly added an extraneous element to the statute" under which his client was charged. 491 Mich., at 3, 810 N.W.2d, at 536; *see also* 288 Mich.App. 410, 416, and n. 2, 794 N.W.2d 848, 852, and n. 2 (2010). The Michigan Court of Appeals agreed with this concession and went on to hold that the trial judge's ruling did not constitute an "acquittal" for double jeopardy purposes because the ruling did not represent "a resolution in the defendant's favor . . . of a factual element necessary for a criminal conviction." *Id.*, at 421–422, 794 N.W.2d, at 856 (internal quotation marks omitted). The Michigan Supreme Court affirmed, holding that when, as here, a trial judge erroneously adds an extra "element" to a charged offense and subsequently determines that the prosecution did not prove that extra "element," the trial judge's decision is not based on the defendant's guilt or innocence of the elements of the charged offense. 491 Mich., at 3–4, 19–21, 810 N.W.2d, at 536–537, 545–546. Accordingly, the Michigan Supreme Court concluded that the judge's ruling in this case "does not constitute an acquittal for the purposes of double jeopardy and retrial is . . . not barred." *Id.*, at 4, 810 N.W.2d, at 537.

II

This Court now reverses the decision of the State Supreme Court, but the Court's holding is supported by neither the original understanding of the prohibition against double jeopardy nor any of the reasons for that prohibition.

A

The prohibition against double jeopardy "had its origin in the three common-law pleas of *autrefois acquit, autrefois convict,* and pardon," which "prevented the retrial of a person who had previously been acquitted, convicted, or pardoned for the same offense." *United States v. Scott,* 437 U.S. 82, 87, 98 S.Ct. 2187, 57 L.Ed.2d 65 (1978); *see Crist v. Bretz,* 437 U.S. 28, 33, 98 S.Ct. 2156, 57 L.Ed.2d 24 (1978). As the Court has previously explained, "the common-law protection against double jeopardy historically applied only to charges on which a *jury* had rendered a *verdict.*" *Smith,* 543 U.S., at 466, 125 S.Ct. 1129 (emphasis added).[1] As a result, the original understanding of the Clause, which is "hardly a

---

1   See also *Crist,* 437 U.S., at 33, 98 S.Ct. 2156 ("The Fifth Amendment guarantee against double jeopardy derived from English common law, which followed . . . the relatively simple rule that a defendant has been put in jeopardy only when there has been a conviction or an acquittal—after a complete trial. . . . And it is clear that in the early years of our national history the constitutional guarantee against double jeopardy was considered to be equally limited in scope"); 3 J. Story, Commentaries on the Constitution of the United States § 1781, p. 659 (1833) ("The meaning of [the Double Jeopardy Clause] is, that a party shall not be tried a second time for the same offence, after he has once been convicted, or acquitted of the offence charged, *by the verdict of a jury,* and judgment has passed thereon for or against him. *But it does not mean, that he shall not be tried for the offence a second time, if the jury have been discharged without giving any verdict. . . .*" (emphasis added)); 2 M. Hale, Pleas of the

matter of dispute," *Scott, supra*, at 87, 98 S.Ct. 2187, does not compel the Court's conclusion that a defendant is acquitted for double jeopardy purposes whenever a *judge* issues a *preverdict* ruling that the prosecution has failed to prove a non-existent "element" of the charged offense.

Although our decisions have expanded double jeopardy protection beyond its common-law origins, see, *e.g.*, *Smith, supra*, at 466–467, 125 S.Ct. 1129 (acknowledging the Court's expansion of "the common-law protection against double jeopardy"); *Crist, supra*, at 33–34, 98 S.Ct. 2156, I nonetheless count it significant that the result the Court reaches today finds no support in the relevant common-law analogues that "lie at the core of the area protected by the Double Jeopardy Clause," see *Scott*, 437 U.S., at 96, 98 S.Ct. 2187. And given how far we have departed from the common-law principles that applied at the time of the founding, we should at least ensure that our decisions in this area serve the underlying *purposes* of the constitutional prohibition against double jeopardy. See *id.*, at 95–96, 100–101, 98 S.Ct. 2187. Yet today's decision fails to advance the purposes of the Double Jeopardy Clause.

B

The Double Jeopardy Clause is largely based on "the deeply ingrained principle that the State with all its resources and power should not be allowed to make repeated attempts to convict an individual for an alleged offense, thereby subjecting him to embarrassment, expense and ordeal and compelling him to live in a continuing state of anxiety and insecurity, as well as enhancing the possibility that even though innocent he may be found guilty." *Yeager v. United States*, 557 U.S. 110, 117–118, 129 S.Ct. 2360, 174 L.Ed.2d 78 (2009) (internal quotation marks omitted); *see also Blueford v. Arkansas*, 566 U.S. ––––, ––––, 132 S.Ct. 2044, 2050, 182 L.Ed.2d 937 (2012); *Martin Linen*, 430 U.S., at 569, 97 S.Ct. 1349. Allowing retrial in the circumstances of the present case would not result in any such abuse. The prosecution would not be afforded a second opportunity to persuade the factfinder that its evidence satisfies the actual elements of the offense. Instead, because the trial judge's ruling in the first trial was not based on an actual element of the charged offense, retrial would simply give the prosecution one fair opportunity to prove its case.

Allowing retrial in this case would not permit prosecutors "to make repeated attempts to convict an individual for an alleged offense," *Yeager, supra*, at 117, 129 S.Ct. 2360. It was *petitioner*, not the prosecutor, who sought to terminate the trial prior to verdict. Thus, contrary to the Court's unexplained suggestion, see ante, at 1084–1085, "[t]his case hardly presents the specter of 'an

---

Crown 246 (1778) ("It must be an acquittal upon trial either by verdict or battle").

all-powerful state relentlessly pursuing a defendant who had either been found not guilty or who had at least insisted on having the issue of guilt submitted to the first trier of fact.'" *Sattazahn v. Pennsylvania*, 537 U.S. 101, 114–115, 123 S.Ct. 732, 154 L.Ed.2d 588 (2003) (quoting *Scott, supra*, at 96, 98 S.Ct. 2187). On the contrary, this is a case in which defense counsel fooled the judge into committing an error that provided his client with an undeserved benefit, the termination of a trial that the defense obviously did not want to run to completion. The Double Jeopardy Clause does not require that the defense receive an even greater benefit, the protection provided by an acquittal. As this Court has repeatedly emphasized in double jeopardy cases, a State has an interest in receiving "one complete opportunity to convict those who have violated its laws," *Sattazahn, supra*, at 115, 123 S.Ct. 732 (internal quotation marks omitted); *Scott, supra*, at 100, 98 S.Ct. 2187, but today's decision deprives the State of Michigan of this valuable right.

C

The Court's decision also flies in the face of our established understanding of the meaning of an acquittal for double jeopardy purposes. The Double Jeopardy Clause provides that no person shall "be subject for the same *offence* to be twice put in jeopardy of life or limb." U.S. Const., Amdt. 5 (emphasis added). Thus, "[d]ouble-jeopardy analysis focuses on the individual 'offence' charged." *Smith*, 543 U.S., at 469, n. 3, 125 S.Ct. 1129. And to determine what constitutes "the individual 'offence' charged," *ibid.*, the Court homes in on the elements of the offense. *See United States v. Dixon*, 509 U.S. 688, 696, 113 S.Ct. 2849, 125 L.Ed.2d 556 (1993) ("In both the multiple punishment and multiple prosecution contexts, this Court has concluded that where the two offenses for which the defendant is punished or tried cannot survive the 'same-elements' test, the double jeopardy bar applies"). Consistent with the constitutional text's focus on the "offence"—and thus the elements—with which a defendant is charged, the Court's "double-jeopardy cases have consistently" defined an acquittal as a decision that "'actually represents a resolution, correct or not, of some or all of the factual elements of the offense charged.'" *Smith, supra*, at 468, 125 S.Ct. 1129 (quoting *Martin Linen, supra*, at 571, 97 S.Ct. 1349); *see also Scott, supra*, at 97, 98 S.Ct. 2187 ("[A] defendant is acquitted only when the ruling of the judge, whatever its label, actually represents a resolution in the defendant's favor, correct or not, of some or all of the factual elements of the offense charged" (internal quotation marks and brackets omitted).

Today, the Court effectively abandons the well-established definition of an acquittal. Indeed, in the face of our repeated holdings that an acquittal for double jeopardy purposes requires a "resolution, correct or not, of some or all of the factual elements of the offense charged," *Smith, supra,* at 468, 125 S.Ct. 1129; *Martin Linen, supra,* at 571, 97 S.Ct. 1349; *see also Scott, supra,* at 97, 98 S.Ct. 2187, the Court now declares that "the touchstone [is] *not* whether any particular elements were resolved," *ante,* at 1077 (emphasis added). Instead, the Court proclaims that the dispositive question is whether a midtrial termination represented a "procedural dismissa[l]" or a "substantive rulin[g]," *ante,* at 1075. This reformulation of double jeopardy law is not faithful to our precedents—or to the Double Jeopardy Clause itself. The key question is not whether a ruling is "procedural" or "substantive" (whatever those terms mean in this context), but whether a ruling relates to the defendant's factual guilt or innocence with respect to the "offence," see U.S. Const., Amdt. 5—and thus the elements—with which he is charged. See *Scott, supra,* at 87, 97–99, and n. 11, 98 S.Ct. 2187.

When a judge evaluates the evidence and determines that the prosecution has not proved facts that are legally sufficient to satisfy the actual elements of the charged offense, the ruling, however labeled, represents an acquittal because it is founded on the defendant's factual innocence. See *Martin Linen,* 430 U.S., at 572, 97 S.Ct. 1349. But when a judge manufactures an additional "element" of an offense and then holds that there is insufficient evidence to prove that extra "element," the judge has not resolved the defendant's "factual guilt or innocence" as to any of the actual elements of the offense.[2] Thus, the ruling, no matter what the judge calls it, does not acquit the defendant of the offense with which he is charged. No acquittal occurs when a criminal trial is terminated "on a basis unrelated to factual guilt or innocence of the offense of which [a defendant] is accused." *Scott,* 437 U.S., at 87, 94–95, 98–99, 98 S.Ct. 2187. "[I]n a case such as this the defendant, by deliberately choosing to seek termination of the proceedings against him on a basis unrelated to factual guilt or innocence of the offense of which he is accused, suffers no injury cognizable under the Double Jeopardy Clause if the Government is permitted to appeal from such a ruling of the trial court in favor of the defendant." *Id.,* at 98–99, 98 S.Ct. 2187 (reasoning that, in such a case, the defendant was "neither acquitted nor convicted, because he himself successfully undertook to persuade the trial court not to submit the issue of guilt or innocence to the jury which had been empaneled to try him").

---

2   Because culpability for an offense can be negated by proof of an affirmative defense, the Court has held that a ruling that the prosecution did not submit sufficient evidence to rebut an affirmative defense constitutes an acquittal for double jeopardy purposes. *See Burks v. United States,* 437 U.S. 1, 10–11, 98 S.Ct. 2141, 57 L.Ed.2d 1 (1978); *Scott,* 437 U.S., at 97–98, 98 S.Ct. 2187. Thus, as used in this opinion, the "elements" of an offense include legally recognized affirmative defenses that would negate culpability.

III

Contrary to the Court's opinion, its decision in this case is not supported by prior precedent. In all three of the principal cases on which the Court relies— *Smalis v. Pennsylvania*, 476 U.S. 140, 106 S.Ct. 1745, 90 L.Ed.2d 116 (1986); *Smith*, 543 U.S. 462, 125 S.Ct. 1129, 160 L.Ed.2d 914; and *Arizona v. Rumsey*, 467 U.S. 203, 104 S.Ct. 2305, 81 L.Ed.2d 164 (1984)—trial judges ruled that the prosecution had failed to introduce sufficient evidence to prove one or more of the *actual* elements of the offenses in question. In none of these cases (and in none of our other double jeopardy cases) did a trial judge terminate a prosecution before verdict based on an element of the judge's own creation.

The first two cases, *Smalis* and *Smith*, involved garden variety preverdict acquittals, *i.e.*, rulings based on the ground that the prosecution had failed to introduce sufficient evidence to prove one or more of the *actual* elements of an offense. (Using conventional modern terminology, Rule 29(a) of the Federal Rules of Criminal Procedure explicitly labels such rulings "acquittal[s].")

In *Smalis*, the judge, at the close of the prosecution's case in chief, granted a demurrer with respect to certain charges on the ground that the evidence regarding those charges was "legally insufficient to support a conviction." 476 U.S., at 141, 106 S.Ct. 1745. The State Supreme Court held that this ruling was not an acquittal for double jeopardy purposes because it was based on a legal determination (i.e., that the evidence was not sufficient) rather than a factual finding, but we rejected that distinction. *Id.*, at 143–144, 106 S.Ct. 1745. *See also Sanabria v. United States*, 437 U.S. 54, 71–72, 98 S.Ct. 2170, 57 L.Ed.2d 43 (1978).

Smith involved a similar situation. There, one of the elements of a firearms offense with which the defendant was charged required proof that the gun "had a barrel 'less than 16 inches' in length," 543 U.S., at 464, 125 S.Ct. 1129, and the trial judge dismissed this charge before verdict on the ground that the prosecution had not introduced sufficient evidence to establish this undisputed element, *id.*, at 464–465, 125 S.Ct. 1129. Before the remaining charges were submitted to the jury, however, the judge reversed this ruling and allowed the charge to go to the jury. *Id.*, at 465, 125 S.Ct. 1129. We held, however, that the judge's prior ruling constituted an acquittal and therefore barred the defendant's conviction for this offense. *Id.*, at 467–469, 125 S.Ct. 1129. Thus, both *Smalis* and *Smith* involved rulings that were very different from the one at issue here. In both of those earlier cases, the trial judges held that the evidence was insufficient to prove undisputed elements of the offenses in question. In neither case did the judge invent a new element.

The final case, *Rumsey*, differs from *Smalis* and *Smith* in only one particular. Like *Smalis* and *Smith*, *Rumsey* involved a ruling that the prosecution's evidence was insufficient to prove an element, but in *Rumsey* the ruling was predicated on a misconstruction of an element. In that case, after the defendant was found guilty of first-degree murder, the "trial judge, with no jury, . . . conducted a separate sentencing hearing" at which he determined that no aggravating circumstances were present. 467 U.S., at 205, 104 S.Ct. 2305. In particular, the judge found that the prosecution had not proved that the murder had been committed "'as consideration for the receipt, or in expectation of the receipt, of anything of pecuniary value.'" *Id.*, at 205–206, 104 S.Ct. 2305 (quoting Ariz.Rev.Stat. Ann. § 13–703(F)(5) (Supp.1983–1984)). The judge reached this conclusion because, in his (incorrect) view, that aggravating circumstance was limited to contract killings. 467 U.S., at 205–206, 104 S.Ct. 2305. Holding that the judge's ruling constituted an acquittal on the merits of the question whether a death sentence was appropriate, we noted that the ruling rested on "a misconstruction of the statute defining the pecuniary gain aggravating circumstance." *Id.*, at 211, 104 S.Ct. 2305. Accordingly, the ruling was based on a determination that there was insufficient evidence to prove a real element; it was not based on the judicial invention of an extra "element." And for that reason, it does not support the nonsensical result that the Court reaches today.

The Court may feel compelled to reach that result because it thinks that it would be unworkable to draw a distinction between a preverdict termination based on the trial judge's misconstruction of an element of an offense and a preverdict termination based on the judge's perception that a statute contains an "element" that is actually nonexistent. This practical concern is overblown. There may be cases in which this determination presents problems, but surely there are many cases in which the determination is quite easy. The present case is a perfect example, for here there is no real dispute that the trial judge's ruling was based on a nonexistent statutory "element." As noted, defense counsel conceded on appeal that the judge had "wrongly added an extraneous element to the statute" under which his client was charged. 491 Mich., at 3, 810 N.W.2d, at 536.

Another good example is provided by *State v. Korsen*, 138 Idaho 706, 69 P.3d 126 (2003), where a Magistrate erroneously concluded that the offense of criminal trespass under Idaho law requires a showing that the defendant did something to justify the property owner's request for the defendant to leave the premises. *Id.*, at 710, 716–717, 69 P.3d, at 130, 136–137. There is no question that the Magistrate in *Korsen* "effectively created an additional statutory element" before concluding that the prosecution had presented insufficient evidence as to this purported "element." See *ibid.* (holding that double jeopardy did not bar a retrial because the Magistrate's "finding did not actually determine in [defendant's] favor any of the essential elements of the crime of trespass").

Cases in which it can be said that a trial judge did not simply misinterpret a real element of an offense but instead invented an entirely new and nonexistent "element" are cases in which the judge's error is particularly egregious. Permitting retrial in these egregious cases is especially appropriate.

* * *

I would hold that double jeopardy protection is not triggered by a judge's erroneous preverdict ruling that creates an "element" out of thin air and then holds that the element is not satisfied. I therefore respectfully dissent.

Notes and Questions

1. *Evans* demonstrates the importance of understanding the elements of the offense. The prosecution rightly construed the relationship between the statutes, as the Michigan Court of Appeals later ruled, but because the defense counsel convinced the trial court that "[other than] a dwelling house" was not proved by the prosecution as an element of the offense, the trial court acquitted Evans. The United States Supreme Court then upheld the acquittal because, erroneously or not, an acquittal on the elements resolves the case in favor of the defendant. Double jeopardy bars retrial. Therefore, Evans' acquittal resolved, however erroneously, the elements of the charged offense in his favor.

2. Further, note the importance of effective advocacy in *Evans*, where the prosecution's correct understanding of the law was overcome by the defense counsel's ability to convince the trial court that "[other than] a dwelling house" is an element that must be proved. As you study criminal law, you should take a perspective that each facet of a case is a "battle ground" for your client. Each stage of a case, pretrial, trial, and post-trial, provides an opportunity for each side to tip the scales in favor of one's client. In *Evans*, defense counsel effectively barred what appeared to be a difficult case to defend, because Evans appeared to have burnt a dwelling house. Perhaps defense counsel knew of this discrepancy, and strategically proceeded to trial knowing that this ambiguity in the jury instructions could provide an opportunity to obtain an acquittal from the trial judge before the prosecution could effectively rebut: "at the close of the State's case." If this was the defense counsel's strategy, it worked.

3. Note the unreliability of the pattern jury instructions. The trial court relied on the "commentary to the Instructions" emphasizing "[other than] a dwelling house" as an element that must be proved, but these notes were ultimately

deemed faulty, or at least the trial court's interpretation of them, by the Court of Appeals. How can that be? Committees of judges and lawyers, as part of the state bar or appointed by the judiciary, compile these pattern jury instructions for ease of reference. But as you can see, these instructions lay out the elements of the offense and must be evaluated by each side before proceeding, because the judiciary must ultimately interpret and apply the statutes, not the jury instruction drafters or commentators.

4. Lastly, note the ambiguity in the statutes: "other than those specified in the next preceding section of this chapter" (§ 750.73) is an odd way of conveying the idea "including those listed above," referring to § 750.72 and "dwelling house." Legislatures sometimes hastily draft criminal statutes and leave it to the judiciary to interpret ambiguities in statutes. These ambiguities provide a prime opportunity for effective advocacy, as *Evans* demonstrates.

CHAPTER TWO

Jurisdiction

CRIMINAL laws are enacted by the federal government, states, counties and cities, as well as Indian tribes. The states have inherent police power to enact criminal statutes with regard to any matter, except as restricted by the state or federal constitutions. Congress, by contrast, is a legislature of limited powers; it can enact criminal laws only to the extent that they are a necessary and proper exercise of an enumerated power in the Constitution, such as its authority to regulate interstate and foreign commerce and commerce with Indian tribes, and its authority over federal enclaves and activities, like Washington, D.C., military bases, post offices and federally insured banks. Criminal jurisdiction can potentially be based on authority over the person, the conduct, or over the territory where the crime occurred. Jurisdiction also requires authority over the subject matter.

A. Jurisdiction over the Person

When interpreting laws, there is a presumption that "legislation of Congress, unless a contrary intent appears, is meant to apply only within the territorial jurisdiction of the United States." *Morrison v. Nat'l Australia Bank Ltd.*, 561 U.S. 247, 130 S. Ct. 2869, 2877, 177 L. Ed. 2d 535 (2010) (quoting *EEOC v. Arabian American Oil Co.*, 499 U.S. 244, 248, 111 S.Ct. 1227, 113 L.Ed.2d 274 (1991)). States, including Florida, from which the following case originated, often follows this rule as to its statutes. *Jackson Lumber Co. v. Walton Cnty.*, 116 So. 771, 786 (Fla. 1928). However, this is only a presumption which can be overcome in particular cases; that is, sometimes the legislature intends its law to apply beyond its borders. Yet, there must be some limit to extraterritorial authority; it would clearly be unconstitutional for Kentucky, say, to set a national speed limit, or for Connecticut to make it a crime to sell alcohol in Missouri. *Skiriotes v. Florida* and *United States v. Frank* address the circumstances when the Constitution permits jurisdictions to regulate conduct occurring outside of their territory.

Skiriotes v. Florida

Supreme Court of the United States
313 U.S. 69 (1941)

Mr. Chief Justice HUGHES delivered the opinion of the Court.

Appellant, Lambiris Skiriotes, was convicted in the county court of Pinellas County, Florida, of the use on March 8, 1938, of diving equipment in the taking of sponges from the Gulf of Mexico off the coast of Florida in violation of a state statute. Compiled General Laws of Florida (1927), Section 8087. The conviction was affirmed by the Supreme Court of Florida (197 So. 736) and the case comes here on appeal.

The case was tried without a jury and the facts were stipulated. The statute, the text of which is set forth in the margin,[1] forbids the use of diving suits, helmets or other apparatus used by deep sea divers, for the purpose of taking commercial sponges from the Gulf of Mexico, or the Straits of Florida or other waters within the territorial limits of that State.

The charge was that appellant was using the forbidden apparatus 'at a point approximately two marine leagues from mean low tide on the West shore line of the State of Florida and within the territorial limits of the County of Pinellas'. The state court held that the western boundary of Florida was fixed by the state constitution of 1885 at three marine leagues (nine nautical miles) from the shore; that this was the same boundary which had been defined by the state constitution of 1868 to which the Act of Congress had referred in admitting the State of Florida to representation in Congress. Act of June 25, 1868, 15 Stat. 73. The

---

1   The statute, originally Section 4 of Chapter 7389 of the Laws of Florida of 1917, carried forward as Section 5846 of the Revised General Statutes of Florida and as Section 8087 of the Compiled General Laws of 1927, is as follows:

'It shall be unlawful for any person, persons, firm or corporation to maintain and use for the purpose of catching or taking commercial sponges from the Gulf of Mexico, or the Straits of Florida or other waters within the territorial limits of the State of Florida, diving suits, helmets or other apparatus used by deep sea divers.

'Anyone violating any of the provisions of this section shall be fined in the sum not exceeding five hundred dollars or by imprisonment not exceeding one year, or by both such fine and imprisonment.' *See Lipscomb v. Gialourakis*, 101 Fla. 1130, 133 So. 104.

state court sustained the right of the State to fix its marine boundary with the approval of Congress, and concluded that the statute was valid in its application to appellant's conduct.

By motions to quash the information and in arrest of judgment, appellant contended that the constitution of Florida fixing the boundary of the State and the statute under which he was prosecuted violated the Constitution and treaties of the United States; that the criminal jurisdiction of the courts of Florida could not extend beyond the international boundaries of the United States and hence could not extend 'to a greater distance than one marine league from mean low tide' on the mainland of the State and adjacent islands included within its territory.

In support of this contention appellant invoked several provisions of the Constitution of the United States, to wit, Article I, Section 10, Clauses 1 and 3, Article II, Section 2, Clause 2, Article VI, and the Fourteenth Amendment. Appellant also relied upon numerous treaties of the United States, including the Treaty with Spain of February 22, 1919, and the treaties with several countries, signed between 1924 and 1930, inclusive, for the prevention of smuggling of intoxicating liquors. There were also introduced in evidence diplomatic correspondence and extracts from statements of our Secretaries of State with respect to the limits of the territorial waters of the United States. These contentions were presented to the highest court of the State and were overruled.

The first point of inquiry is with respect to the status of appellant. The stipulation of facts states that appellant 'is by trade and occupation a deep-sea diver engaged in sponge fishery, his resident address being at Tarpon Springs, Pinellas County, Florida', and that he 'has been engaged in this business for the past several years'. Appellant has not asserted or attempted to show that he is not a citizen of the United States, or that he is a citizen of any State other than Florida, or that he is a national of any foreign country. It is also significant that in his brief in this Court, replying to the State's argument that as a citizen of Florida he is not in a position to question the boundaries of the State as defined by its constitution, appellant has not challenged the statement as to his citizenship, while he does contest the legal consequences which the State insists flow from that fact.

It further appears that upon appellant's arrest for violation of the statute, he sued out a writ of habeas corpus in the District Court of the United States and was released, but this decision was reversed by the Circuit Court of Appeals. *Cunningham, Sheriff, v. Skiriotes,* 5 Cir., 101 F.2d 635. That court thought that the question of the statute's validity should be determined in orderly procedure by the state court subject to appropriate review by this Court, but the court expressed doubt as to the right of the appellant to raise the question, saying: 'Skiriotes states he is a citizen of the United States resident in Florida, and therefore is a citizen of Florida. His boat, from which his diving operations were conducted, we may assume was a Florida vessel, carrying Florida law with her, but of course as modified by superior federal law'. *Id.*, 101 F.2d pages 636, 637.

In the light of appellant's statements to the federal court, judicially recited, and upon the present record showing his long residence in Florida and the absence of a claim of any other domicile or of any foreign allegiance, we are justified in assuming that he is a citizen of the United States and of Florida. Certainly appellant has not shown himself entitled to any greater rights than those which a citizen of Florida possesses.

In these circumstances, no question of international law, or of the extent of the authority of the United States in its international relations, is presented. International law is a part of our law and as such is the law of all States of the Union (*The Paquete Habana*, 175 U.S. 677, 700, 20 S.Ct. 290, 44 L.Ed. 320), but it is a part of our law for the application of its own principles, and these are concerned with international rights and duties and not with domestic rights and duties. * * *

For the same reason, none of the treaties which appellant cites are applicable to his case. He is not in a position to invoke the rights of other governments or of the nationals of other countries. If a statute similar to the one in question had been enacted by the Congress for the protection of the sponge fishery off the coasts of the United States there would appear to be no ground upon which appellant could challenge its validity.

The question then is whether such an enactment, as applied to those who are subject to the jurisdiction of Florida, is beyond the competency of that State. We have not been referred to any legislation of Congress with which the state statute conflicts. By the Act of August 15, 1914, 38 Stat. 692, 16 U.S.C., Sec. 781, 16 U.S.C.A. § 781, Congress has prohibited 'any citizen of the United States, or person owing duty of obedience to the laws of the United States' from taking 'in the waters of the Gulf of Mexico or the Straits of Florida outside of state territorial limits' any commercial sponges which are less than a given size, or to possess such sponges or offer them for sale. But that Act is limited to the particular matter of size and does not deal with the divers' apparatus which is the particular subject of the Florida statute. According to familiar principles, Congress having occupied but a limited field, the authority of the State to protect its interests by additional or supplementary legislation otherwise valid is not impaired. *Reid v. Colorado*, 187 U.S. 137, 147, 150, 23 S.Ct. 92, 96, 97, 47 L.Ed. 108; *Savage v. Jones*, 225 U.S. 501, 533, 32 S.Ct. 715, 725, 56 L.Ed. 1182; *Mintz v. Baldwin*, 289 U.S. 346, 350, 53 S.Ct. 611, 613, 77 L.Ed. 1245; *Kelly v. Washington*, 302 U.S. 1, 10, 58 S.Ct. 87, 92, 82 L.Ed. 3. It is also clear that Florida has an interest in the proper maintenance of the sponge fishery and that the statute so far as applied to conduct within the territorial waters of Florida, in the absence of conflicting federal legislation, is within the police power of the State. *Manchester v. Massachusetts*, 139 U.S. 240, 266, 11 S.Ct. 559, 565, 35 L.Ed. 159. * * * Nor is there any repugnance in the provisions of the statute to the equal protection clause of the Fourteenth Amendment. The statute applies equally to all persons within the jurisdiction of the State.

Appellant's attack thus centers in the contention that the State has transcended its power simply because the statute has been applied to his operations inimical to its interests outside the territorial waters of Florida. The State denies this, pointing to its boundaries as defined by the state constitution of 1868, which the State insists had the approval of Congress and in which there has been acquiescence over a long period. *See Lipscomb v. Gialourakis*, 101 Fla. 1130, 1134, 1135, 133 So. 104; *Pope v. Blanton*, D.C., 10 F.Supp. 18, 22. Appellant argues that Congress by the Act of June 25, 1868, to which the state court refers, did not specifically accept or approve any boundaries as set up in the state constitution but merely admitted Florida and the other States mentioned to representation in Congress. And, further, that if Congress can be regarded as having approved the boundaries defined by the state constitution, these have been changed by the treaties with foreign countries relating to the smuggling of intoxicating liquors, in which the principle of the three-mile limit was declared.

But putting aside the treaties, which appellant has no standing to invoke, we do not find it necessary to resolve the contentions as to the interpretation and effect of the Act of Congress of 1868. Even if it were assumed that the locus of the offense was outside the territorial waters of Florida, it would not follow that the State could not prohibit its own citizens from the use of the described divers' equipment at that place. No question as to the authority of the United States over these waters, or over the sponge fishery, is here involved. No right of a citizen of any other State is here asserted. The question is solely between appellant and his own State. The present case thus differs from that of *Manchester v. Massachusetts*, supra, for there the regulation by Massachusetts of the menhaden fisheries in Buzzards Bay was sought to be enforced as against citizens of Rhode Island (*Id.*, page 242 of 139 U.S., page 559 of 11 S.Ct., 35 L.Ed. 159) and it was in that relation that the question whether Buzzards Bay could be included within the territorial limits of Massachusetts was presented and was decided in favor of that Commonwealth. The question as to the extent of the authority of a State over its own citizens on the high seas was not involved.

If the United States may control the conduct of its citizens upon the high seas, we see no reason why the State of Florida may not likewise govern the conduct of its citizens upon the high seas with respect to matters in which the State has a legitimate interest and where there is no conflict with acts of Congress. Save for the powers committed by the Constitution to the Union, the State of

Florida has retained the status of a sovereign. Florida was admitted to the Union 'on equal footing with the original States, in all respects whatsoever'. And the power given to Congress by Section 3 of Article IV of the Constitution to admit new States relates only to such States as are equal to each other 'in power, dignity, and authority, each competent to exert that residuum of sovereignty not delegated to the United States by the Constitution itself'. *Coyle v. Smith*, 221 U.S. 559, 567, 31 S.Ct. 688, 690, 55 L.Ed. 853.

There is nothing novel in the doctrine that a State may exercise its authority over its citizens on the high seas. That doctrine was expounded in the case of *The Hamilton (Old Dominion S.S. Co. v. Gilmore)*, 207 U.S. 398, 28 S.Ct. 133, 52 L.Ed. 264. There, a statute of Delaware giving damages for death was held to be a valid exercise of the power of the State, extending to the case of a citizen of that State wrongfully killed on the high seas in a vessel belonging to a Delaware corporation by the negligence of another vessel also belonging to a Delaware corporation. If it be said that the case was one of vessels and for the recognition of the formula that a vessel at sea is regarded as part of the territory of the State, that principle would also be applicable here. There is no suggestion that appellant did not conduct his operations by means of Florida boats. That he did so conduct them was assumed by the Circuit Court of Appeals in dealing with appellant's arrest in *Cunningham, Sheriff, v. Skiriotes*, supra, and that reasonable inference has not in any way been rebutted here.

But the principle recognized in *The Hamilton*, supra, was not limited by the conception of vessels as floating territory. There was recognition of the broader principle of the power of a sovereign State to govern the conduct of its citizens on the high seas. The court observed that 'apart from the subordination of the State of Delaware to the Constitution of the United States' there was no doubt of its power to make its statute applicable to the case at bar. And the basic reason was, as the court put it, that when so applied 'the statute governs the reciprocal liabilities of two corporations, existing only by virtue of the laws of Delaware, and permanently within its jurisdiction, for the consequences of conduct set in motion by them there, operating outside the territory of the state, it is true, but within no other territorial jurisdiction'. If confined to corporations, 'the state would have power to enforce its law to the extent of their property in every case'. But the court went on to say that 'the same authority would exist as to citizens domiciled within the state, even when personally on the high seas, and not only could be enforced by the state in case of their return, which their domicil by its very meaning promised, but, in proper cases, would be recognized in other jurisdictions by the courts of other states'. That is, 'the bare fact of the parties being outside the territory, in a place belonging to no other sovereign, would not limit the authority of the state, as accepted by civilized theory'. *The Hamilton*, supra, 207 U.S. page 403, 28 S.Ct. page 134, 52 L.Ed. 264. When its action does not conflict with federal legislation, the sovereign authority of the State over the conduct of its citizens upon the high seas is analogous to the sovereign authority of the United States over its citizens in like circumstances.

We are not unmindful of the fact that the statutory prohibition refers to the 'Gulf of Mexico, or the Straits of Florida or other waters within the territorial limits of the State of Florida'. But we are dealing with the question of the validity of the statute as applied to appellant from the standpoint of state power. The State has applied it to appellant at the place of his operations and if the State had power to prohibit the described conduct of its citizen at that place we are not concerned from the standpoint of the Federal Constitution with the ruling of the state court as to the extent of territorial waters. The question before us must be considered in the light of the total power the State possesses (*Del Castillo v. McConnico*, 168 U.S. 674, 684, 18 S.Ct. 229, 233, 42 L.Ed. 622; *Hebert v. Louisiana*, 272 U.S. 312, 316, 47 S.Ct. 103, 104, 71 L.Ed. 270, 48 A.L.R. 1102; *United Gas Co. v. Texas*, 303 U.S. 123, 142, 58 S.Ct. 483, 492, 82 L.Ed. 702), and so considered we find no ground for holding that the action of the State with respect to appellant transcended the limits of that power.

The judgment of the Supreme Court of Florida is affirmed.
Affirmed.

Notes and Questions

1. Did the act take place in Florida or outside of Florida? If the crime took place on the high seas, and the statute by its terms applies only in Florida, how could the defendant be convicted?

2. If Skiriotes had been from Georgia, how would the Court have ruled?

3. Given the different grounds used by the Florida and U.S. supreme courts, is there an argument that the case should have been remanded rather than affirmed?

United States v. Frank

United States District Court, S.D. Florida
486 F.Supp.2d 1353 (2007)

ORDER ON CONSTITUTIONALITY OF 18 U.S.C. § 2423(C)

JORDAN, District Judge.

A grand jury charged Kent Frank, an American citizen, with violating 18 U.S.C. § 2423(c) on five occasions. According to Counts 1–5 of the indictment, Mr. Frank traveled from the United States to Cambodia from September of 2003 to January of 2004 and engaged in "illicit sexual conduct" in that country with various females under the age of 18. This order addresses Mr. Frank's motion to dismiss Counts 1–5.

Entitled "Engaging in illicit sexual conduct in foreign places," § 2423(c) was enacted by Congress in April of 2003. It provides as follows:

> Any United States citizen or alien admitted for permanent residence who travels in foreign commerce, and engages in any illicit sexual conduct with another person shall be fined under this title or imprisoned not more than 30 years, or both.

As it pertains to this case, the term "illicit sexual conduct" means "any commercial sex act (as defined in [18 U.S.C. §] 1591) with a person under 18 years of age." *See* § 2423(f)(2). In turn, § 1591(c)(1) defines "commercial sex act" as "any sex act, on account of which anything of value is given to or received by any person." There is a built-in affirmative defense for cases involving a "commercial sex act." Under § 2423(g), a defendant may establish, by a preponderance of the evidence, that he "reasonably believed that the person with whom [he] engaged in the commercial sex act had attained the age of 18 years."

Mr. Frank argues principally that Congress, in enacting § 2423(c), exceeded its powers under the Foreign Commerce Clause, U.S. Const. Art. I, § 8, cl. 3. He also presents other challenges, including the assertion that § 2423(c) violates international law because it fails to recognize that the age of consent in Cambodia is 15, and the contention that the extra-territorial application of § 2423(c) violates the Due Process Clause of the Fifth Amendment.

In an earlier order, issued prior to trial, I denied Mr. Frank's motion to dismiss Counts 1–5. This order sets out the bases for that ruling. I conclude that, insofar as it criminalizes commercial sex (i.e., prostitution) with minors, § 2423(c) is constitutional under the Necessary and Proper Clause, U.S. Const. Art. VI, § 8, cl. 18, and that all of Mr. Frank's other challenges lack merit.

I

A statute's constitutionality presents a question of law. *See United States v. Evans*, 476 F.3d 1176, 1178 (11th Cir.2007). In ruling on the motion to dismiss, however, I cannot consider any facts alleged by Mr. Frank. Nor can I decide contested issues of fact. Instead, I am limited to the allegations contained in the indictment. *See United States v. Sharpe*, 438 F.3d 1257, 1263 (11th Cir.2006).

A

Mr. Frank contends that Congress exceeded its powers under the Foreign Commerce Clause, U.S. Const. Art. I, § 8, cl. 3. Last year, a panel of the Ninth Circuit, over a strong dissent, rejected this argument. *See United States v. Clark*, 435 F.3d 1100, 1116 (9th Cir.2006). I need not decide whether § 2423(c) is a constitutional exercise by Congress of its Foreign Commerce Clause powers. Even if the dissent in *Clark* is correct, *see* 435 F.3d at 1117–21(Ferguson, J., dissenting), Congress had the authority to enact § 2423(c) under the Necessary and Proper Clause to implement a treaty which the Senate had ratified. *See generally* J. High, *The Basis for Jurisdiction Over U.S. Sex Tourists: An Examination of the Case Against Michael Lewis Clark*, 11 U.C. Davis J. of Int'l Law & Pol. 343, 361–62 (Spring 2005); Note, *Ninth Circuit Holds that Congress Can Regulate Sex Crimes Committed by U.S. Citizens Abroad*, 119 Harv. L.Rev. 2612, 1618 (June 2006).

The treaty power does not "extend[ ] so far as to authorize what the [C]onstitution forbids, or a change in the character of the government, or in that of the states, or a cession of any portion of the territory of the latter, without its consent. But, with these exceptions, it is not perceived that there is any limit to the questions which can be adjusted touching any matter which is properly the subject of negotiation with a foreign country." *Geofroy v. Riggs*, 133 U.S. 258, 267, 10 S.Ct. 295, 33 L.Ed. 642 (1890) (citations omitted). If a "treaty is valid[,] there can be no dispute about the validity of the [implementing] statute under Article I, [§] 8, as a necessary and proper means to execute the powers of the government." *Missouri v. Holland*, 252 U.S. 416, 432, 40 S.Ct. 382, 64 L.Ed. 641 (1920). Here is the way the Supreme Court summarized the treaty power just a couple of years ago: "The treaty power does not literally authorize Congress to act legislatively, for it is an Article II power authorizing the President, not Congress, 'to make Treaties.' U.S. Const. Art. II, § 2, cl. 2. But, as Justice Holmes pointed out [in *Holland*], treaties made pursuant to that power can authorize Congress to deal with 'matters' with which otherwise 'Congress could not deal.'" *United States v. Lara*, 541 U.S. 193, 200, 124 S.Ct. 1628, 158 L.Ed.2d 420 (2004) (citation omitted). *See also United States v. Ferreira*, 275 F.3d 1020, 1027–28 (11th Cir.2001) (because "Congress' authority under the Necessary and Proper Clause extends beyond those powers specifically enumerated in Article I, [§] 8, [it] may enact laws necessary to effectuate the treaty power, enumerated in Article II of the Constitution") (citation and internal quotation marks omitted).

B

In July of 2000, President Clinton signed the Optional Protocol to the United Nations Convention on the Rights of the Child on the Sale of Children, Child Prostitution, and Child Pornography (the "Optional Protocol"), S. Treaty Doc. No. 106–37, 39 L.L.M. 1285, 2000 WL 333666017. The Senate ratified the Optional Protocol in 2002, and it entered into force in January of 2003. Cambodia ratified the Optional Protocol in May of 2002.

The Preamble to the Optional Protocol states that the countries involved are "[d]eeply concerned at the widespread and continuing practice of sex tourism, to which children are especially vulnerable, as it directly promotes the sale of children, child prostitution, and child pornography." In relevant part, the Optional Protocol provides as follows:

> Article 1: State parties shall prohibit the sale of children, child prostitution, and child pornography as provided by the present Protocol.

> Article 2(b): Child prostitution means the use of a child in sexual activities for remuneration or any other form of consideration.

> Article 3(1): Each state party shall ensure that, as a minimum, the following acts and activities are fully covered under its criminal or penal law, whether these offenses are committed domestically or transnationally or on an individual or organized basis: . . . (1)(b): Offering, obtaining, procuring, or providing a child for child prostitution, as defined in Article 2; . . . (3) Each state party shall make these offenses punishable by appropriate penalties that take into account their grave nature; (4) Subject to these provisions of its national law, each state party shall take measures, where appropriate, to establish the liability of legal persons for offenses established in paragraph 1 of the present Article.

> Article 3(4): Subject to the provisions of its national law, each state party shall take measures, where appropriate, to establish the liability of legal persons for offenses established in paragraph 1 of this Article. Subject to the legal principles of the state party, this liability of legal persons may be criminal, civil, or administrative.

> Article 4(2): Each state party may take such measures as may be necessary to establish its jurisdiction over the offenses referred to in Article 3, para-

graph 1, in the following cases: (a) when the alleged offender is a national of the state or a person who has habitual residence in its territory. . . .

One of the statutes that Congress enacted to implement the Optional Protocol was § 2423(c), part of the Prosecutorial Remedies and Other Tools to End the Exploitation of Children Act of 2003 (the "PROTECT Act"), Pub.L. 108–21, 117 Stat. 650 (2003). The provision that became § 2423(c) was first proposed as part of the Sex Tourism Prohibition Improvement Act of 2002, and the House of Representatives relied at that time on Article I, § 8 of the Constitution as the authority for enactment. *See* H.R.Rep. No. 525 at 5, 107th Cong., 2nd Sess., 2002 WL 1376220, *5 (June 24, 2002). The 2002 provision was incorporated verbatim into the PROTECT Act in 2003, but, as the Ninth Circuit noted in *Clark*, 435 F.3d at 1104, the legislative history of the PROTECT Act does not contain any reference to the constitutional authority for enactment of § 2423(c). *See generally* H.R.Rep. No. 108–66 at 51, 108th Cong., 1st Sess., reprinted in 2003 U.S.C.C.A.N. 683, 686 (April 9, 2003).

C

Mr. Frank does not contend that the Optional Protocol was beyond the treaty power granted to the President by the Constitution. Nor could he. First, nothing in the Optional Protocol—insofar as it relates to commercial sex with minors—is prohibited by the Constitution or the Bill of Rights. Second, child sex tourism is undoubtedly a significant problem and is, by its very nature, a global concern. Not only are American citizens going abroad to have sex with child prostitutes, there is the possibility that foreigners will come to the United States for the same purpose. *See, e.g.,* H.R.Rep. No. 525 at 2, 2002 WL 1376220, at *2 ("According to the National Center for Missing and Exploited Children, child sex tourism is a major component of the worldwide exploitation of children and is increasing. There are more than 100 web sites devoted to promoting teenage commercial sex in Asia alone."); N. Svensson, *Extraterritorial Accountability: An Assessment of the Effectiveness of Child Sex Tourism Laws*, 28 Loy. L.A. Int'l & Comp. L.Rev. 641, 642–44 (2006) (citing statistics, and noting that "child sex tourism is an extremely lucrative industry, sustained by the increasing demands of foreigners from wealthy nations"); D. Edelson, *The Prosecution of Persons Who Sexually Exploit Children in Countries Other than Their Own: A Model for Amending Existing Legislation*, 25 Fordham Int'l L.J. 483, 484–93 (2001) (providing studies and statistics showing that "child sex tourism is a global problem," and summarizing legislative efforts by some countries to punish their own citizens for extra-territorial conduct). President Clinton therefore could reasonably have believed, as he said in his letter of transmittal to the Senate, that child sex tourism requires an international solution like the one contained in the Optional Protocol, including extra-territorial criminal prosecution by countries of their own citizens for engaging in commercial sex with minors abroad. *See* Letter of Transmittal from President Clinton to the United States Senate, 2000 WL 33366017 (July 13, 2000). As in *Holland*, "a national interest of very nearly the first magnitude is involved," and "can be protected only by national action in concert with that of another power." 252 U.S. at 434, 40 S.Ct. 382.

The next questions are whether, under rational basis review, Congress could enact § 2423(c) under the Necessary and Proper Clause to implement the Optional Protocol and, if so, whether the statute—insofar as commercial sex with minors is concerned—reasonably implements the Optional Protocol. *See, e.g., United States v. Yian*, 905 F.Supp. 160, 163 (S.D.N.Y.1995) (in determining whether legislation is properly enacted to implement a treaty, rational basis review applies). The answer to both questions is yes. First, § 2423(c) bears a rational relationship to the Optional Protocol in general, and to Articles 2(b) and 3(1)(b)—which deal with child prostitution—in particular. The statute is therefore necessary and proper under the framework of *M'Culloch v. Maryland*, 17 U.S. (4 Wheat.) 316, 421, 4 L.Ed. 579 (1819), and its progeny. *Cf. Ferreira*, 275 F.3d at 1027–28 (holding that Hostage Taking Act, 18 U.S.C. § 1203, was valid under the Necessary and Proper Clause to implement the Hostage Taking Convention entered into by the United States). Second, § 2423(c) reasonably implements the Optional Protocol. Articles 3(4) and 4(2) require that countries take appropriate measures to establish the liability of individuals for offenses such as paying a child for sex. Extra-territorial criminal liability is one of the options allowed by the Optional Protocol, and § 2423(c) has extra-territorial application. *See United States v. Strevell*, 2006 WL 1697529, *3 (11th Cir.2006) (holding that § 2423(c) applies to conduct of American citizens abroad: "Congress realized the potential effects of domestic harm that come with foreign sex trafficking. Congress purposefully passed this statute in order to stop United States citizens from traveling abroad in order to engage in commercial sex act with minors.").

Moreover, defining a minor as a person under the age of 18, *see* § 2423(f)(2), is also congruent with the Optional Protocol. The task of a court is to give specific meaning to a term in a treaty "consistent with the shared expectations of the contracting parties." *El Al Israel Airlines. Ltd. v. Tseng*, 525 U.S. 155, 167, 119 S.Ct. 662, 142 L.Ed.2d 576 (1999) (citation and internal quotation marks omitted). Although the Optional Protocol does not define the words "child" or "children," the Article by Article analysis provided by the United Nations to accompany the Optional Protocol explains that "[d]uring the negotiations the term 'child' was understood to mean anyone under the age of 18[.]" *See* United Nations Article by Article Analysis of Optional Protocol, Summary of Article I, 2000 WL 33366017. This analysis—a form of legislative history—indicates that the shared expectation of the countries involved in drafting and ratifying the Optional Protocol was that those under 18 would be considered "children." *See, e.g., Eastern Airlines, Inc. v. Floyd*, 499 U.S. 530, 542–46, 111 S.Ct. 1489, 113 L.Ed.2d 569 (1991) (reviewing, among other things, treaty's negotiating and drafting history to determine meaning of disputed treaty term); *In re Commissioner's Subpoenas*, 325 F.3d 1287, 1296–1304 (11th Cir.2003) (consulting extraneous sources to figure out meaning of ambiguous term in treaty). To the extent more is needed, a treaty generally is to be construed liberally to effectuate its purpose, *see United States v. Stuart*, 489 U.S. 353, 368, 109 S.Ct. 1183, 103 L.Ed.2d 388 (1989), and defining a "child" as a person below the age of 18 is consistent with the protection of the young and defenseless. *Cf. United States v. Bach*, 400 F.3d 622, 628–29 (8th Cir.2005) (regulating child pornography "by defining a minor as an individual under eighteen is rationally related to the government's legitimate interest in enforcing child pornography laws"). It is also not inconsistent with the common understanding of the words "child" or "children." *See, e.g.*, Black's Law Dictionary 254 (8th ed.2004) (defining "child" as a "person under the age of majority").

II

Mr. Frank attacks § 2423(c) on other grounds. But, as explained below, all of those challenges fail too.

First, Mr. Frank asserts that the exercise of extra-territorial jurisdiction violates precepts of international law. That assertion, however, is foreclosed by binding precedent. Congress has the power to control (and punish) the conduct of American citizens abroad. *See, e.g., Blackmer v. United States*, 284 U.S. 421, 437, 52 S.Ct. 252, 76 L.Ed. 375 (1932); *United States v. Plummer*, 221 F.3d 1298, 1304 (11th Cir.2000); *United States v. Mitchell*, 553 F.2d 996, 1001 (5th Cir.1977). International law, moreover, generally allows a country to exert extra-territorial jurisdiction over its own citizens, as long as the exercise of such jurisdiction is not unreasonable. *See Plummer*, 221 F.3d at 1307; Restatement (Third) of Foreign Relations §§ 402(2), 403(1)-(2) (1987). Finally, "public international law is controlling only 'where there is no treaty and no controlling executive or legislative act or judicial decision [.]'" *Garcia–Mir v. Meese*, 788 F.2d 1446, 1453 (11th Cir.1986) (quoting *The Paquete Habana*, 175 U.S. 677, 700, 20 S.Ct. 290, 44 L.Ed. 320 (1900)). Here there is a treaty—the Optional Protocol—ratified by both the United States and Cambodia.

Second, Mr. Frank argues that § 2423(c) is unconstitutional because it fails to recognize the domestic law of Cambodia, which provides that the age of consent is 15.[5] I disagree that the statute infringes on the sovereignty of Cambodia.

---

5   It is not at all clear—at least not to me—that the age of consent for prostitution in Cambodia is 15. The parties have only provided me with selected provisions of Cambodian penal law, and I have not read any provision

As an initial matter, § 2423(c) does not regulate the conduct of Cambodian nationals (or, for that matter, the nationals of any countries other than the United States). In addition, as noted earlier, Cambodia ratified the Optional Protocol in May of 2002. Thus, Cambodia, notwithstanding its own domestic laws on consent, and because of a concern over the impact of child sex tourism, decided as a nation that it would sign an international agreement requiring countries to enact legislation to forbid commercial sex with those under the age of 18 by their own nationals. If Cambodia does not believe that the Optional Protocol infringes on its sovereignty—and it obviously does not—it will not be offended by laws enacted by the United States to implement the Optional Protocol, which regulate the conduct of American citizens abroad.

Third, Mr. Frank contends that § 2423(c), as applied to his conduct in Cambodia, violates the substantive component of the Due Process Clause of the Fifth Amendment. Unfortunately for Mr. Frank, under substantive due process jurisprudence, the applicable standard is whether the legislation is "rationally related to a lawful government purpose." *Plummer*, 221 F.3d at 1309. Here, the prevention of child prostitution (domestically and/or internationally) is certainly a legitimate government goal, and given the international aspects of child sex tourism, the application of § 2423(c) to the conduct of American citizens abroad is rationally related to achievement of that goal.

Fourth, Mr. Frank, citing to cases like *United States v. X–Citement Video, Inc.*, 513 U.S. 64, 69–70, 115 S.Ct. 464, 130 L.Ed.2d 372 (1994), says without much explanation that § 2423(c) is constitutionally deficient because it does not require scienter for the sexual act itself. According to Mr. Frank, in order for the statute to survive, it must be interpreted to require that he knowingly engaged in sex. This argument, insofar as it seeks dismissal, is misplaced. Engaging in sex generally, and commercial sex in particular, is not a passive activity, and there has been no claim in this case by Mr. Frank that he engaged in sex unknowingly or involuntarily. More to the point, § 2423(g) allows for a "reasonable belief" defense when the charge under § 2423(c) involves a commercial sex act. The jury was

---

which expressly sets the age of consent at 15. The provisions I have read, as discussed below, deal instead with "debauchery" offenses.

Article 7 of the Cambodian Law on Suppression of the Kidnapping, Trafficking, and Exploitation of Human Persons ("Law on Suppression") [D.E. 147, Ex. 2] provides that any person who "opens a place for committing a debauchery [sic] or obscene acts" shall be punished by a term of imprisonment ranging from one to five years. Article 8 provides that any person who "commits debauchery acts [sic] onto a minor person of below 15 years old, even if there is consent from the concerned minor person or if [sic] upon buying such minor from somebody else or the head of the prostitutes," shall be punished by a term of imprisonment ranging from 10 to 20 years.

The term "debauchery" is not defined in the Law on Suppression, and the parties have not provided any evidence as to what it means in Cambodia. Contemporary English dictionaries define "debauchery" as "excessive indulgence in sensual pleasures; immorality; licentiousness." 1 Shorter Oxford English Dictionary 611 (5th ed.2002).

instructed on this defense at trial [D.E. 231 at 10–11], and understood (from the evidence presented and the arguments of counsel) that one of the critical issues at trial was whether Mr. Frank knew that the females were under the age of 18 when he had sex with them. By allowing a "reasonable belief" defense, Congress made it clear that a defendant's subjective knowledge (or reasonable belief) as to age is a relevant matter for the jury to consider. In short, § 2423(c) is not a strict liability offense, as Mr. Frank suggests.

III

Mr. Frank's motion to dismiss Counts 1–5, which charge violations of § 2423(c), is denied.

Notes and Questions

1. How, precisely, does the United States have jurisdiction to regulate conduct in foreign lands? The Supreme Court is now considering the question of jurisdiction based on treaties. *See Bond v. United States*, No. 12-158, http://www.scotusblog.com/case-files/cases/bond-v-united-states-2/

2. *Do states have criminal jurisdiction over their citizens in other states?*

3. States now have very different criminal laws in a number of areas, including the use of drugs (recreational use of marijuana is lawful in Colorado and Washington) and abortion. States might want to control the conduct of their citizens outside of the territory of the state itself. *See* C. Steven Bradford, *What happens if Roe is overruled? Extraterritorial Regulation of Abortion by the States*, 35 Ariz. L. Rev. 87 (1993).

4. Based on the cases you have read, would the following statute be constitutional?

Missouri Revised Statutes

Unlawful use, possession or sale of marijuana. No citizen of Missouri shall, anywhere in the world, use, possess or sell marijuana when such conduct would be unlawful had it taken place in Missouri.

Unlawful possession of marijuana metabolite.

1. For the purposes of this section, a metabolite means any chemical compound found in blood, urine or saliva produced when the human body processes or reacts to the inhalation or other consumption of marijuana in any form, and which are not normally present in blood, urine or saliva other than because of the inhalation or other consumption of marijuana.

2. Any person in this state whose blood, urine or saliva reveals the presence of metabolites of marijuana is guilty of a Class E Felony. It is not a defense to a charge under this section that the marijuana was used or consumed out of the state of Missouri.

B. Jurisdiction Over Territory

In general, states have authority over conduct taking place within that state, regardless of the citizenship or status of the people involved. For example, the states have criminal jurisdiction over federal officers acting in the state. However, federal officers may have a defense of immunity under the Supremacy Clause (U.S. Const., Art IV, § 1 ("This Constitution, and the laws of the United States which shall be made in Pursuance thereof, shall be the supreme Law of the Land; and the Judges in every state shall be bound thereby, any thing in the Constitution or Laws of any State to the Contrary notwithstanding") if they acted reasonably. *See, e.g., New York v. Tanella*, 281 F. Supp. 2d 606 (E.D.N.Y. 2003). In addition, federal officers charged in state court may remove the case to federal court if they raise a federal defense. 28 U.S.C. § 1442.

States also have criminal jurisdiction over non-citizens. They have jurisdiction over foreign diplomats, but under federal law, some diplomats have a defense of immunity. *See, e.g., Traore v. State*, 431 A.2d 96 (Md. 1981) (reversing conviction and dismissing case).

However, territory within the state may be under the exclusive jurisdiction of the federal government. *State v. Ingram* outlines the difficulty in determining whether a particular piece of territory is under state or federal authority.

State v. Ingram

Superior Court of New Jersey, Law Division, Criminal Part, Gloucester County
226 N.J. Super. 680, 545 A.2d 268 (1988)

HOLSTON, J.S.C.

In Counts # 4 and # 8 of Indictment SGJ-113-83-3, the State alleges the unlawful abandonment and/or disposal of hazardous waste at the U.S. Army Corps of Engineers site in Oldmans Township, N.J. by the defendant, Albert Ingram, contrary to N.J.S.A. 2C:17-2 and N.J.S.A. 13:1E-9(g)(2) respectively.

Defendant moved to dismiss these counts at the end of the State's case on the basis of lack of jurisdiction in the Superior Court of New Jersey to hear and try these counts. It was the defendant's contention that abandonment of hazardous waste on property owned by the U.S. Army Corps of Engineers would have to be heard by the United States District Court for the District of New Jersey based on a federal indictment alleging a violation of federal law.[1]

Defendant also moved for dismissal of these counts on the alternate ground that the State had failed to prove an essential element of the offense, namely, that the illegal abandonment or disposal of hazardous waste had occurred within the territorial jurisdiction of the State since the land in question is a Federal facility. The defendant contends that N.J.S.A. 2C:1-3 makes territorial jurisdiction an essential element of any crime alleged under 2C:1-1 et seq. of our statutes, citing *State v. Schumann*, 218 N.J. Super. 501, 528 A.2d 68 (App.Div.1987). *See also State in Interest of G.W.*, 206 N.J. Super. 50, 501 A.2d 1012 (App.Div.1985).

* * *

Generally, territorial jurisdiction is not specifically required to be proved as an element of an offense until it is placed in issue. *State v. Schumann*. Therefore, the Court at the conclusion of the State's case, since the defendant had not placed territorial jurisdiction in issue until the State had rested, permitted the State to

---

1   Defendant, Albert Ingram, has, himself, filed a pro se motion similarly attacking the jurisdiction of the State. While not addressing the Federal/State dichotomy, he instead alleges that the United States Coast Guard has exclusive jurisdiction over the site, not the EPA. As authority, he cites 33 C.F.R. § 126. For purposes of this opinion, it is irrelevant which of the multitude of Federal government agencies has jurisdiction over the disposal site since the result would remain the same. However, in the interest of covering all the bases, it is noted that the referenced section vests the Coast Guard with jurisdiction over "waterfront facilities." A designated "waterfront facility" means a waterfront facility designated for the handling and storage of and for vessel loading and discharging of various hazardous materials. 33 C.F.R. § 126.05. Such is not the case at bar and, hence, the regulation has no effect.

reopen its case for the sole purpose of proving the territorial jurisdiction of the offenses in Counts # 4 and # 8.

* * *

The State, after being given three days to produce evidence evidencing territorial jurisdiction, conceded that for purposes of the motion to dismiss Counts # 4 and # 8 that the land on which the hazardous waste was allegedly abandoned and/or disposed was federally owned land. The defendant did not dispute the State's contention.

The State cited 42 U.S.C.A. § 6961 (a section of the Federal Solid Waste Disposal Act) as establishing in clear and unambiguous language the waiver of sovereign immunity by the United States and thus, vesting in the State of New Jersey the authority to regulate the disposal of hazardous waste within the State. Absent such a waiver, the jurisdiction of the United States over lands purchased for forts, magazines, arsenals, dockyards and other needful buildings is exclusive. *Surplus Trading Co. v. Cook*, 281 U.S. 647, 50 S.Ct. 455, 74 L.Ed. 1091 (1930).

Section 6001 of the Solid Waste Disposal Act, in relevant part, reads:

> Each department, agency and instrumentality of the executive, legislative and judicial branches of the Federal Government (1) having jurisdiction over any solid waste management facility or disposal site, or (2) engaged in any activity resulting, or which may result, in the disposal or management of solid waste or hazardous waste shall be subject to and comply with all Federal, State, interstate and local requirements, both substantive and procedural (including any requirement for permits or reporting or any provisions for injunctive relief and such sanctions as may be imposed by a court to enforce such relief), respecting control and abatement of solid waste or hazardous waste disposal in the same manner and, to the same extent, as any person is subject to such requirements, including the payment of reasonable service charges. * * *.

This Court concluded in an oral ruling, giving all inferences to the State from the evidence, that the State had put forward sufficient evidence which, if believed, would establish territorial jurisdiction beyond a reasonable doubt and, therefore, denied defendant's motion to dismiss. *State v. Reyes*, 50 N.J. 454, 458-459, 236 A.2d 385 (1967).

Counts # 4 and # 8 were, thus, submitted to the jury. The jury returned a verdict of guilty on all counts of the indictment, including Counts # 4 and # 8.

At the time the Court made its ruling on March 7, 1988, it reserved to itself the right to further research the issue and to more specifically outline its findings of fact and conclusions of law in a written opinion. Because of the belief that the analysis to follow will constitute a significant and non-duplicative contribution to an analysis of the territorial jurisdiction of State criminal laws on federally owned lands, this opinion is being written.

For the reasons hereinafter expressed, the ruling of this Court heretofore made in its opinion from the bench is hereby reversed and indictment Counts # 4 and # 8 are dismissed with prejudice as a result of the failure of the State to prove beyond a reasonable doubt territorial jurisdiction as an essential element of each count. *State v. Reyes.*

The court's holding in *State v. Schumann*, 218 N.J. Super. 501, 528 A.2d 68 (App. Div. 1987) is instructive in framing the issue presented. As stated by Judge Landau:

> ... jurisdiction when placed in issue, is an element of an offense which must be proved beyond a reasonable doubt. Consistent with constitutional mandate, N.J.S.A. 2C:1-13(a) provides: No person may be convicted of an offense unless each element of such offense is proved beyond a reasonable doubt. In the absence of such proof, the innocence of defendant is assumed. Under N.J.S.A. 2C:1-14(h), element of an offense means (1) such conduct or (2) such attendant circumstances or (3) such a result of conduct as ... (e) establishes jurisdiction or venue.... [at 506-507, 528 A.2d 68].

The jurisdiction referred to in the criminal code definition of the elements of an offense is territorial jurisdiction, defined in N.J.S.A. 2C:1-3. *State in Interest of G.W.*, 206 N.J. Super. 50, 501 A.2d 1012 (App.Div.1985). This requirement or element of an offense is applicable to all offenses defined by other statutes enacted in New Jersey. N.J.S.A. 2C:1-5(b). It thus applies to offenses prescribed by both N.J.S.A. 2C:17-2 and N.J.S.A. 13:1E-9(g)(2).

Generally, evidence establishing territorial jurisdiction is supplied by showing the sites of the alleged offense. In this case, such evidence was offered through the testimony of Bruce Comfort, Supervisor, Bureau of Emergency Response, New Jersey Department of Environmental Protection. Comfort testified that drums allegedly owned by defendant were found abandoned ¼ of a mile down a dirt road off of Route # 130 in Oldsmans Township, N.J. This land is owned by the U.S. Army Corps of Engineers.

As previously mentioned, the State concedes the ownership by the Federal government but argues that 42 U.S.C.A. § 6961 acts as a waiver of sovereign immunity and vests the State of New Jersey with the authority to regulate the disposal of hazardous waste within the State, including land owned by the United States. Initially, the Court was in agreement that this section provided New Jersey with jurisdiction and, therefore, ruled that sufficient evidence had been presented to establish territorial jurisdiction.

However, further research has proven to the contrary. The section cited by the State does provide in clear and unambiguous terms for a waiver of sovereign immunity for acts by the Federal government, its agencies and officers but in no way acts as a blanket relinquishment of jurisdiction by the Federal government over its own land. *People of the State of California v. Walters*, 751 F.2d 977 (9th Cir.1984) (waiver of sovereign immunity does not extend to criminal sanctions); *Meyer v. U.S. Coast Guard*, 644 F. Supp. 221 (E.D.N.C.1986) (§ 6961 waiver does not allow for the imposition of civil penalties). Dicta in *Walters* suggests that the same result might not apply if a Federal agency or officer was the defendant as opposed to the United States itself.

The act does contemplate the cession of jurisdiction to the states after the State has had a Solid Waste Program approved by the Administrator of the Environmental Protection Agency. 42 U.S.C.A. § 6926. * * *

The sole purpose of this section appears to be to shift the regulation and enforcement of solid waste to the states. * * *

While the procedure set forth in section 6926 has been followed in New Jersey, the EPA only authorized New Jersey's program partially in 1983 and fully in February 1985. 48 Fed.Reg. 4661 (1983); 50 Fed. Reg. 5260 (1985). All of the acts alleged in the indictment occurred between March 25 and August 27, 1982, when the Federal government continued to exercise exclusive jurisdiction.

Coming full circle, the question returns to what is the impact of the land being owned by the Federal government.

Art. I, § 8, cl. 17 of the United States Constitution establishes exclusive jurisdiction in the Federal government over all places purchased by the consent of the legislature of the state in which the same shall be for the erection of forts, magazines, arsenals, dockyards and other needful buildings. "Other needful buildings" embraces whatever structures are necessary for performance of the function of the Federal government. *Silas Mason Co. v. Tax Commissioner of the State of Washington*, 302 U.S. 186, 58 S.Ct. 233, 82 L.Ed.2d 187 (1937). Exclusive jurisdiction in the Federal government applies to the entire tract not simply to those portions actually used for the legally reserved purpose. *Benson v. United States*, 146 U.S. 325, 13 S.Ct. 60, 36 L.Ed. 991 (1982); *Black Hills Power & Light Co. v. Weinberger*, 808 F.2d 665 (8th Cir.1987).

While the language of clause 17 has been construed to allow for the acquisition of land by the United States through condemnation as well as purchase, *Paul v. United States*, 371 U.S. 245, 83 S.Ct. 426, 9 L.Ed.2d 292 (1963); *Humble Pipe Line Co. v. Waggoner*, 376 U.S. 369, 84 S.Ct. 857, 11 L.Ed.2d 782 (1964) the consent of the state legislature is still required. *State v. Allard*, 313 A.2d 439 (Me. Sup.Ct.1973).

N.J.S.A. 52:30-1 states that:

> The consent of this state is hereby given, pursuant to the provisions of article one, section eight, paragraph seventeen, of the Constitution of the United States, to the acquisition by the United States, by purchase, condemnation or otherwise, of any land within this state, for the erection of dockyards, custom houses, courthouses, post offices or other needful buildings.

Similarly, N.J.S.A. 52:30-2 provides that:

> Exclusive jurisdiction in and over any land so acquired by the United States is hereby ceded to the United States for all purposes except the service of process issued out of any of the courts of this state in any civil or criminal proceeding.

Such jurisdiction shall not vest until the United States shall have actually acquired ownership of said lands and shall continue only so long as the United States shall retain ownership of said lands.

Clearly, New Jersey has manifested its consent to the purchase of land by the Federal government and to the cession of all jurisdiction over such land. Notwithstanding the language of the statute, such is not the case. The cession of exclusive jurisdiction to the Federal government has been interpreted to apply only to those cases involving crimes committed within the Federal enclave, *State v. Morris*, 76 N.J.L. 222, 224, 68 A.2d 1103 (Sup.Ct.1908); *State in Interest of D.B.S.*, 137 N.J.Super. 371, 374, 237 A.2d 640 (App.Div.1975) and to foreclose state statutes which would conflict with Federal laws. *Freeholders of Burlington County v. McCorkle*, 98 N.J.Super. 451 (Law Div.1968); *In re: Salem Transportation Co. of N.J.*, 55 N.J. 559, 264 A.2d 47 (1970) (citing *Howard v. Commissioners of Louisville*, 344 U.S. 624, 73 S.Ct. 465, 97 L.Ed. 617 (1953)).

In any case, the cession of exclusive jurisdiction to the Federal government by the State cannot take place unless and until the United States has accepted jurisdiction over lands acquired. 40 U.S.C.A. § 255. This section reads in pertinent part:

> Notwithstanding any other provision of law, the obtaining of exclusive jurisdiction in the United States over lands or interest therein which have been or shall hereafter be acquired by it shall not be required; but the head or other authorized officer of any department or independent establishment or agency of the Government may, in such cases and at such times as he may deem desirable, accept or secure from the State in which any lands or interests therein under his immediate jurisdiction, custody, or control are situated, consent to or cession of such jurisdiction, exclusive or partial, not theretofore obtained, over any such lands or interest as

he may deem desirable and indicate acceptance of such jurisdiction on behalf of the United States by filing a notice of such acceptance with the Governor of such State or in such other manner as may be prescribed by the laws of the State where such lands are situated. Unless and until the United States has accepted jurisdiction over lands hereafter to be acquired as aforesaid, it shall be conclusively presumed that no such jurisdiction has been accepted.

The perfection of acceptance of exclusive jurisdiction by the Federal government can only be accomplished by the "head or other authorized officer of any department or independent establishment or agency of the government" filing a notice of such acceptance with the Governor of the State. Absent such an acceptance, it shall be conclusively presumed that no Federal jurisdiction has been accepted.

The necessity of showing acceptance of exclusive jurisdiction is not required if the transfer took place prior to the enactment of 40 U.S.C.A. § 255 in 1940. *United States v. Johnson*, 426 F.2d 1112 (7th Cir.1970); *Markham v. United States*, 215 F.2d 56 (4th Cir.1954). Instead, a presumption exists that there has been acceptance of exclusive Federal jurisdiction if any benefit was conferred on the Federal government by the transfer, i.e., that the Federal government has used the land for any Federal purpose. *Fort Leavenworth R.R. v. Lowe*, 114 U.S. 525, 5 S.Ct. 995, 29 L.Ed. 264 (1885).

Independent research, which is not meant to be exhaustive, reveals that the parcel in question was purchased from numerous land owners over a period of years. The earliest transfer occurred in 1911 while the last was in 1966. The total site encompasses well over 1200 acres. The Chief Operations Officer responsible for the site, Tom Schina, indicates that the site was originally used as a storage arsenal for materials which were brought up the Delaware River. Later, the site was converted to a prisoner of war camp during World War II. Finally, in 1959-60, the site was converted to a disposal site for the mud and silt dredged from the navigation channel of the Delaware River.

Based on the foregoing, to succeed on its case, the State would have had to proffer some evidence which would have established that the alleged abandonment or disposal took place on land acquired by the Federal government after 1940 and that the United States had not filed an acceptance of exclusive jurisdiction. The State has not proffered such evidence. The testimony, including all reasonable inferences, establishes the abandonment or disposal on the property but does not establish the location with any specificity. The unique character of land ownership requires that there be proof of when the specific section of land on which the abandoned barrels containing hazardous waste found on the federal lands owned by the U.S. Army Corps of Engineers was acquired by the United States and if acquired post 1940, that there had not been a federal acceptance of jurisdiction, pursuant to 40 U.S.C.A. § 255, thereby allowing enforcement of the State's criminal laws.

Therefore, based upon the findings of fact and conclusion of law set forth above, defendant's motion to dismiss Counts # 4 and # 8 is granted. Defendant's motion challenging the Court's jurisdiction to entertain those Counts is moot.

Notes and Questions

1. Why, specifically, was the defendant not guilty if the state could not prove "when the specific section of land on which the abandoned barrels containing hazardous waste found on the federal lands owned by the U.S. Army Corps of Engineers was acquired by the United States and if acquired post 1940, that there had not been a federal acceptance of jurisdiction, pursuant to 40 U.S.C.A. § 255"? What element of the offense did that go to? Why was the federal waiver of sovereign immunity insufficient?

2. If the events had taken place in 1987, what result?

3. For a case suggesting that defense counsel was ineffective under the Sixth Amendment for failing to investigate a potentially meritorious claim of lack of territorial jurisdiction, *see Waggy v. State*, 935 So.2d 571 (Fla. Dist. Ct. App. 2006).

4. The Assimilative Crimes Act, 18 U.S.C. § 13, makes violation of state law in places subject to federal jurisdiction a federal crime prosecutable in federal court. Ironically, then, perhaps the same violation of New Jersey law could have been prosecuted in federal court by federal prosecutors.

5. By statute, Congress has granted states authority over some federal facilities. *See, e.g.,* 8 U.S.C. § 1358 (local jurisdiction over breaches of the peace (i.e., violence) in immigration facilities).

The problem in *Ingram* was that it was not clear which jurisdiction the crime occurred. *State v. Miller* deals with the problem of crimes which take place in more than one jurisdiction.

State v. Miller

Court of Appeals of Arizona
157 Ariz. 129, 755 P.2d 434 (1988)

KLEINSCHMIDT, Judge.

Allen Miller was indicted on one count of theft in violation of A.R.S. § 13–1802. Prior to trial, his motion to dismiss the prosecution for lack of jurisdiction was granted. The state appealed pursuant to A.R.S. § 13–4032(1). We affirm the dismissal.

Jerry Farmer and Julie Hart stole eleven diamond rings from a J.C. Penney store in Flagstaff, Arizona. They traveled to Durango, Colorado, with the rings in their possession. In Durango, Farmer and Hart met Allen Miller, the defendant in this case. Farmer and Hart did not know Miller prior to their meeting in Durango.

Farmer told Miller about the rings, and Miller agreed to help dispose of them in Las Vegas, Nevada. Miller and his new companions traveled to Las Vegas and sold some of the rings. They did not re-enter Arizona. Miller was given two of the rings in payment. He was subsequently arrested in Utah and extradited to Arizona.

The issue on appeal is whether the trial court erred in dismissing the charge of theft against Miller. The state asserts that Arizona has jurisdiction to prosecute Miller under A.R.S. § 13–108. That statute, in pertinent part, reads as follows:

A. This state has jurisdiction over an offense that a person commits by his own conduct or the conduct of another for which such person is legally accountable if:

1. Conduct constituting any element of the offense or a result of such conduct occurs within this state; or

2. The conduct outside this state constitutes an attempt or conspiracy to commit an offense within this state and an act in furtherance of the attempt or conspiracy occurs within this state; or

* * *

4. The offense consists of an omission to perform a duty imposed by the law of this state regardless of the location of the defendant at the time of the offense[.]

* * *

Based on this statute the state asserts four theories that it claims give Arizona courts jurisdiction over Miller. They are:

(1) that Miller's conduct produced a "result" in Arizona;

(2) that Miller failed to perform a duty required under Arizona law;

(3) that Miller was an accomplice to a crime committed in Arizona; and

(4) that Miller was a conspirator to a crime committed in Arizona.

Because these theories raise questions about the extent of Arizona's power to punish conduct that occurs outside the state, they are governed by principles of international law. Although the theories are intertwined, we will discuss each of them separately.

International Law Applies

We look to international law to determine whether the state may assert jurisdiction based upon a statute that attempts to punish extraterritorial conduct. In *Skiriotes v. Florida*, 313 U.S. 69, 61 S.Ct. 924, 85 L.Ed. 1193 (1941), reh'g denied 313 U.S. 599, 61 S.Ct. 1093, 85 L.Ed. 1552, the Supreme Court, in upholding a state's jurisdiction over the extraterritorial acts of one of its own residents, observed that international law "is a part of our law and as such is the law of all States of the Union." *Id.* at 72–73, 61 S.Ct. at 927, 85 L.Ed. at 1198.

The Supreme Court has also recognized that international law applies to the states of the United States in their relations with one another except as modified by the federal constitution. *Kansas v. Colorado*, 185 U.S. 125, 146, 22 S.Ct. 552, 560, 46 L.Ed. 838, 846 (1902); *see also Sinclair Pipe Line Co. v. State Comm'n of Revenue and Taxation*, 184 Kan. 713, 718, 339 P.2d 341, 346 (1959).

The parameters of A.R.S. § 13–108, Arizona's jurisdictional statute, are discussed in the Arizona Criminal Code Commission Commentary (1975):

The primary constitutional question for jurisdictional statutes involves the power of a state to legislate other than on a strict territorial basis. The following excerpt from the Michigan Revised Criminal Code (proposed), commentary to § 140 summarizes the law:

Unless the state constitution contains a provision limiting the power of the legislature to enact legislation with extraterritorial application, the Tenth Amendment to the United States Constitution and United States Supreme Court cases like *Skiriotes v. Florida*, 61 S.Ct. 924, 313 U.S. 69, 85 L.Ed. 1193 (1941), and *Strasheim [sic] v. Daily*, 31 S.Ct. 558, 221 U.S. 280, 55 L.Ed. 735 (1911), appear clearly to permit a state to exercise any basis of legislative jurisdiction recognized in international law unless (1) the actual application of state legislation conflicts with the paramount power of the federal government to regulate and conduct foreign relations, (2) the legislation covers an area that the Congress has preempted under one of the powers delegated to it, or (3) there is an impermissible conflict with the legislative policies of the other state or states in which the defendant's actual conduct took place.

Id. at 20 (emphasis added). Thus, the Code Commission recognized that the principles of international law circumscribe the state's criminal jurisdiction.

International Law Applied—The Result Theory

The state argues that, when out-of-state criminal conduct "results" in deprivation of personal property to an Arizona citizen, Arizona courts are vested with jurisdiction by virtue of A.R.S. § 13–108(A)(1). The state cites no case that has stretched jurisdiction to reach an offender, like Miller, who was not a resident, who never entered the state, and who had nothing to do with the theft until the initial taking of the victim's property was complete. The case we find most closely in point, *United States v. Columba–Colella*, 604 F.2d 356 (5th Cir.1979), is squarely contrary to the state's position.

In *Columba–Colella*, the defendant was a British citizen and resident of Mexico who had no apparent contact with the United States. He lived in a Mexican border town where he took possession of a car that he knew had been stolen in the United States. The defendant was convicted of receiving a stolen vehicle in foreign commerce, in violation of 18 U.S.C. § 2313. The United States Court of Appeals for the Fifth Circuit ruled that the courts of the United States had no jurisdiction over the offense because the defendant's knowledge that the car had been stolen in the United States and transported into Mexico arose after those acts were completed. When the defendant first learned those facts he was in Mexico, where all his contacts with the person who stole the car took place. The court concluded that the defendant's act of receiving and attempting to sell the stolen car was "no constituent element" of the principal thief's crime, "and [was] not made so by the coincidence that the property subject to their agreement belonged to a citizen of the jurisdiction in which the theft occurred." *Id.* at 359. The defendant's crime was "legally unrelated" to the prior theft. *Id.*

The *Columba–Colella* court suggested that, when criminal conduct has taken place wholly within a jurisdiction, its character must be determined by the law of the place where the act was done:

It is difficult to distinguish the present case from one in which the defendant had attempted not to fence a stolen car but instead to pick the pockets of American tourists in Acapulco. No one would argue either that Congress would be competent to prohibit such conduct or that the courts of the United States would have jurisdiction to enforce such a prohibition were the offender in their control.

Id. at 360.

Recognizing the limitations on the power of Congress to punish crimes committed wholly outside the United States, the *Columba–Colella* court said, "We find that because the defendant's act in this case is beyond its competence to prescribe, Congress did not intend to assert jurisdiction here under 18 U.S.C. § 2313." Id. (emphasis added).

The result reached in *Columba–Colella* is consistent with international law as it is expressed in the *Restatement (Second) of the Law, Foreign Relations Law of the United States* (1965), in the tentative drafts of the *proposed Restatement (Third) of the Law, Foreign Relations Law of the United States*, and in the Model Penal Code (1985). While we recognize that neither the Restatements nor the Model Penal Code control the reach of specific state legislation, they are indicative of what authorities in the field believe as to how far a state may extend its criminal jurisdiction.

The Restatement (Second) of the Law of Foreign Relations of the United States § 30(2) reads as follows:

§ 30. Jurisdiction to Prescribe with Respect to Nationals

. . . .

(2) A state does not have jurisdiction to prescribe a rule of law attaching legal consequences to conduct of an alien outside its territory merely on the ground that the conduct affects one of its nationals.

Comment (e) to § 30 explains that subsection (2)

rejects the so-called 'passive personality' principle under which a number of [nations] assert that they may prescribe rules governing the criminal conduct of aliens outside their territory if the victims of the crime are their nationals.

Thus, something more than an effect on one of its citizens is usually required for a country or state to assert jurisdiction over a person whose criminal act committed in another country or state affects one of its citizen's interest. Section 402 of the proposed *Restatement (Revised) of the Law, Foreign Relations Law of the United States*, however, does expand jurisdiction to allow a state to reach those whose crimes have a substantial effect within the state:

Subject to § 403, a state has jurisdiction to prescribe law with respect to

. . . .

(c) conduct outside its territory which has or is intended to have substantial effect within its territory[.]

Restatement (Revised) of the Law, Foreign Relations Law of the United States, § 402(1)(c) (Tent.Draft No. 6, 1985) (emphasis added). The state's "result" theory and the Restatement's reference to "substantial effect" are directly related. Both address the same concept. The difference, as the state defines "result," is one of degree. The "result" of activity outside Arizona's jurisdiction must, at a minimum, however, have a "substantial effect" within Arizona.

As a guide to what constitutes a "substantial" in-state effect we look to *Strassheim v. Daily,* 221 U.S. 280, 31 S.Ct. 558, 55 L.Ed. 735 (1911), an early case dealing with the exercise of extraterritorial jurisdiction. The Arizona Criminal Code Commission cited Strassheim as a basis for the exercise of extraterritorial jurisdiction. Arizona Criminal Code Commission Commentary at 20.

In *Strassheim,* a defendant named Daily had been indicted in Michigan for bribery and false pretenses. He had committed the offenses while in Illinois as part of a scheme to sell the State of Michigan used machinery that he said was new. In finding that Daily was subject to the jurisdiction of Michigan, Justice Holmes said:

If a jury should believe the evidence, and find that Daily did the acts that led Armstrong to betray his trust, deceived the board of control, and induced by fraud the payment by the state, the usage of the civilized world would warrant Michigan in punishing him, although he never had set foot in the state until after the fraud was complete. Acts done outside a jurisdiction, but intended to produce and producing detrimental effects within it, justify a state in punishing the cause of the harm as if he had been present at the effect, if the state should succeed in getting him within its power.

Id. at 284, 31 S.Ct. at 560, 55 L.Ed. at 738.

Many cases in addition to *Strassheim* discuss the extraterritorial reach of state criminal jurisdiction. They all involve more substantial contact than occurred here. *See, e.g., State v. Winckler,* 260 N.W.2d 356 (S.D.1977) (firing shots from outside a state's jurisdiction at individuals within the state without hitting them constitutes assault within the state); and *Hanks v. State,* 13 Tex.App. 289 (1882) (forging a certificate of land transfer for land within the state is within the jurisdiction of the state even though the forger never comes within the boundaries of the state.) What cases like *Strassheim, Winckler,* and *Hanks* share in common is criminal activity occurring outside a state's jurisdiction that does or is intended to do future direct harm within the state. Miller is not subject to the jurisdiction of the Arizona courts under a "result" theory because he is not an Arizona resident, all of his conduct occurred outside Arizona, and the conduct had, at most, only an insubstantial and indirect effect in Arizona. The "result"— the harm to the Arizona victim—had already occurred before Miller had any connection with the stolen property.

Finally, under § 1.03(1)(a) of the Model Penal Code, which we mentioned above as a third authority that is consistent with the rationale of *Columba-Colella*, Arizona would not have jurisdiction to punish Miller. Section 1.03(1) (a) reads:

> (1) . . . [A] person may be convicted under the law of this State of an offense committed by his own conduct or the conduct of another for which he is legally accountable if:

> (a) either the conduct is an element of the offense or the result that is such an element occurs within this State . . . (Emphasis added.)

Our statute, A.R.S. § 13–108(A)(1), mirrors the Model Penal Code language, *see* Model Penal Code § 1.03 n. 12, except that Arizona attempts to maximize the reach of its criminal jurisdiction by omitting the restriction that the result occurring within the state must be an element of the offense. This language in the Model Penal Code appears to equate with the Restatement's requirement that the criminal conduct have a substantial effect within the state. While we do not need to decide whether jurisdiction must be predicated on an element of the crime having occurred within the state, an effect more substantial than a continuing deprivation of property is required. Arizona must conform to international law in its exercise of extraterritorial jurisdiction.

Failure to Perform a Duty

The state argues that A.R.S. § 13–1802(A)(4) imposes a duty on Miller to return the stolen property and that since he failed to do so, A.R.S. § 13–108(A) (4) extends jurisdiction to him because he has omitted the performance of "a duty imposed by the law of this state regardless of the location of the defendant at the time of the offense." Id. Section 13–108(A)(4) may, in some circumstances, reach persons outside the state who have failed to perform a duty imposed by Arizona law. The Arizona Criminal Code Commission Commentary suggests, as an example, a failure to pay child support ordered by an Arizona court. Arizona Criminal Code Commission Commentary at 21. There are, however, two problems with the state's argument, either of which is fatal to it.

Under A.R.S. § 13–1802(A)(4), a person commits theft if he knowingly misappropriates lost, mislaid or misdelivered property when the true owner could be notified. Those are not the facts of this case. While nothing in the indictment specifies which subsection of A.R.S. § 13–1802 Miller was charged under, Miller's offense is found under subsection (5) of the statute, which defines theft as the control of property of another knowing that it was stolen. The property here was not lost, mislaid or misdelivered so the duty to return it is simply not an element of Miller's offense.

The second problem with the state's "failure to perform a duty" argument is that it is subject to the same analysis as is the state's "result" theory and thus succumbs to the rationale of *Columba–Colella*. We add that if the state were correct, i.e., if Miller had an ongoing duty to return the property such as would support Arizona's exercise of jurisdiction, then any and every state to which a theft victim might journey would have jurisdiction over a defendant who received personal property stolen from that victim. Criminal jurisdiction must rest on something more concrete, less transitory, and less provocative of interstate conflict and confusion than this.

Accomplice Theory

The state also suggests that the Arizona courts have jurisdiction over Miller under an accomplice theory, the basis for which is found in A.R.S. § 13–108(A)(1). The state argues as follows. The language of the theft statutes, A.R.S. §§ 13–1801 and 13–1802, is broad enough to criminalize the conduct of all knowing participants in the chain of a fencing operation. When Miller exercised control of the stolen rings, as well as aided in the sale of them, he became an accomplice to Farmer and Hart's theft. Further, since Farmer and Hart's conduct within Arizona was a violation of A.R.S. §§ 13–1801 and 13–1802 and was within the jurisdiction of the Arizona courts, Miller, as an accomplice, is liable for the principals' criminal acts. Therefore, the state's argument concludes, A.R.S. § 13–108(A)(1) confers jurisdiction over Miller as an accomplice. We disagree.

An accomplice is one who knowingly and with criminal intent participates, associates, or concurs with another in the commission of a crime. *State v. McNair*, 141 Ariz. 475, 480, 687 P.2d 1230, 1235 (1984). By receiving and selling the stolen rings Miller did not participate, associate or concur in the commission of Farmer and Hart's theft, because all of Miller's relevant conduct occurred after the theft that Farmer and Hart had committed was complete and after Farmer and Hart had left Arizona. Instead, Miller committed what would be a separate offense under Arizona law, if it had been committed in Arizona, and is not liable as an accomplice for the earlier theft. *State v. Sims*, 99 Ariz. 302, 308–09, 409 P.2d 17, 21–22 (1966) cert. denied 384 U.S. 980, 86 S.Ct. 1880, 16 L.Ed.2d 691. In addition, the accomplice theory, like the "failure to perform a duty" theory, is intertwined with the "result" theory, and does not survive the *Columba–Colella* analysis.

Conspiracy Theory

The state's final argument is that the existence of a conspiracy gives Arizona courts jurisdiction over Miller under A.R.S. § 13–108(A)(2). However, the completion of a substantive crime that is the only purpose of a conspiracy signals the end of the conspiracy. *State v. Yslas*, 139 Ariz. 60, 64, 676 P.2d 1118, 1122 (1984). What Miller did is different from those situations "where conspirators make specific pre-planned efforts of escape, payment, concealment, or conversion of the fruits of the crime." *Id.* While Miller may be guilty of a conspiracy to commit theft (receiving stolen property) under subsection (5) of A.R.S. § 13–1802(A), it cannot be said that his agreement to possess and sell the jewelry was pre-planned as a part of a crime to be committed in Arizona. The result would be different if Miller's "intent [had] anticipated and embraced" Farmer and Hart's theft in Arizona. *Columba–Colella*, 604 F.2d at 359.

The judgment of the trial court is affirmed.

SHELLEY, P.J., and GRANT, J., concur.

Notes and Questions

Could Colorado have prosecuted the defendant for receiving stolen property? Colo. Rev. Stat. Ann. § 18-4-404 ("Every person who obtains control over any stolen thing of value, knowing the thing of value to have been stolen by another, may be tried, convicted, and punished whether or not the principal is charged, tried, or convicted.") *See also* Cal. Penal Code § 497 ("Every person who, in another state or country steals or embezzles the property of another, or receives such property knowing it to have been stolen or embezzled, and brings the same into this state, may be convicted and punished in the same manner as if such larceny, or embezzlement, or receiving, had been committed in this state.") Does the presumption against extraterritorial application of laws apply to either of these statutes?

C. Jurisdiction in Indian Country

State v. Winckler

Supreme Court of South Dakota
260 N.W.2d 356 (1977)

WINANS, Justice.

Sometime during the night of May 1, and the early morning hours of May 2, 1975, the Coast-to-Coast store in Wagner, South Dakota was burglarized. Several weapons, including rifles and shotguns, were taken from the store, along with some ammunition. At approximately 3:00 a. m. on May 2, the seven defendants, who were armed, broke into the Yankton Sioux Tribe Pork Plant (hereinafter Pork Plant); they occupied the Pork Plant until 8:30 p. m. that same evening when the seven finally surrendered to authorities.

The authorities had surrounded the Pork Plant at approximately 7:00 a. m. on May 2. During the day several shots, coming from the Pork Plant, were fired at them. After the surrender, the weapons taken from the Coast-to-Coast store were found in the Pork Plant; no other persons were found on the premises.

Defendants were charged with burglary in violation of SDCL 22-32-9, grand larceny in violation of SDCL 22-37-1, and three counts of assault with a danger-ous weapon, without intent to kill, in violation of SDCL 22-18-11. The assault charges were dismissed by the trial court prior to trial for want of jurisdiction. Defendants were tried conjointly on the burglary and larceny charges and a jury found them guilty of both charges. Defendants appeal from the judgment of con-viction. The state appeals from the order dismissing the three counts of assault with a dangerous weapon. We deal with the state's appeal first.

A state's sovereignty over its own territory is plenary and yields only in matters that fall within the constitutional scope of exclusive federal jurisdic-tion. *State v. Smith*, 26 Or.App. 49, 552 P.2d 261 (1976). It is well established that crimes committed by Indian people within Indian Country are matters of exclusive federal jurisdiction and state courts therefore have no power over those crimes.* *Application of DeMarrias*, 77 S.D. 294, 91 N.W.2d 480 (1958).[1] *See also*

---

*   [Ed. Note: This is not correct in certain states which have been granted jurisdiction by federal statute. *See* note, Casebook, 42.]

1   SDCL 23-9-4 provides:

"Exclusive jurisdiction and authority to arrest, prosecute, convict, and punish all persons who shall commit any act in violation of the penal laws of the United States upon any Indian reservation within this state

United States v. Kagama, 118 U.S. 375, 6 S.Ct. 1109, 30 L.Ed. 228 (1886); *White v. Schneckloth*, 56 Wash.2d 173, 351 P.2d 919 (1960). While this court has ruled that the Yankton Indian Reservation was disestablished, *State v. Williamson*, 87 S.D. 512, 211 N.W.2d 182 (1973), trust land is still Indian Country as defined by 18 U.S.C. § 1151.[2] *DeCoteau v. District County Court*, 87 S.D. 555, 211 N.W.2d 843 (1973), *affirmed* 420 U.S. 425, 95 S.Ct. 1082, 43 L.Ed.2d 300 (1975). It is undisputed that the seven defendants are Indian people; it is also admitted that the Pork Plant is on trust land. Because the alleged shooting originated from trust land, the trial court concluded that any alleged assault occurred in Indian Country and jurisdiction properly lay with the federal government.

However, the fact that an offense originated outside the state's jurisdiction does not necessarily deprive the state of jurisdiction. A state can exercise jurisdiction to punish any criminal offense committed in whole or in part within that state.[3] *People v. Kirby*, 42 Mich.App. 97, 201 N.W.2d 355 (1972). State jurisdiction properly lies when acts done outside its jurisdiction are intended to produce and do produce a detrimental effect within that jurisdiction. *Commonwealth v. Bighum*, 452 Pa. 554, 307 A.2d 255 (1973). The law holds that a crime is committed where the criminal act takes effect. *Simpson v. State*, 92 Ga. 41, 17 S.E. 984 (1893). And this holds true even though the accused is never actually present within the state's jurisdiction. *State v. Brundage*, 53 S.D. 257, 220 N.W. 473 (1928). One who puts in force an agency for the commission of a crime is deemed to have accompanied the agency to the point where it takes effect. The state is then justified in punishing the cause of the harm as if he were in fact present at the effect should it ever succeed in getting him within its power. *Strassheim v. Daily*, 221 U.S. 280, 31 S.Ct. 558, 55 L.Ed. 735 (1911); *Rivard v. United States*, 375 F.2d 882 (5th Cir. 1967); *People v. Anonymous*, 52 Misc.2d 772, 276 N.Y.S.2d 717 (1965); *Simpson v. State*,

---

shall be given and relinquished to the United States and the officers and courts thereof, whenever such jurisdiction shall be assumed by the United States."

2   Indian Country includes Indian allotments or trust land:

"Except as otherwise provided in sections 1154 and 1156 of this title, the term "Indian country", as used in this chapter, means (a) all land within the limits of any Indian reservation under the jurisdiction of the United States government, notwithstanding the issuance of any patent, and, including rights-of-way running through the reservation, (b) all dependent Indian communities within the borders of the United States whether within the original or subsequently acquired territory thereof, and whether within or without the limits of a state, and (c) all Indian allotments, the Indian titles to which have not been extinguished, including rights-of-way running through the same. June 25, 1948, c. 645, 62 Stat. 757; May 24, 1949, c. 139, § 25, 63 Stat. 94."

3   SDCL 23-9-12:

"All persons who commit, in whole or in part, any crime within this state are liable to punishment under the laws of this state."

supra. Admittedly the doctrine of constructive presence is a legal fiction, but it is a fiction necessary to the practical administration of criminal justice.

"(T)here may be a constructive presence in a State, distinct from a personal presence, by which a crime may be consummated. And if it may be consummated it may be punished by an exercise of jurisdiction; that is, a person committing it may be brought to trial and condemnation. And this must be so if we would fit the laws and their administration to the acts of men and not be led away by mere 'bookish theorick.'" *Hyde v. United States*, 225 U.S. 347, 362-63, 32 S.Ct. 793, 800, 56 L.Ed. 1114 (1912).

South Dakota deals with this problem by statute. SDCL 23-9-10 provides: "When the commission of a public offense commenced without this state is consummated within its boundaries, the defendant is liable to punishment therefor in this state, and though he were out of the state at the time of the commission of the offense charged, if he consummated it in this state through the intervention of an innocent or guilty agent or by any other means proceeding directly from himself; and in such case the jurisdiction is in the county in which the offense is consummated."

The question facing us is whether the crime alleged assault with a dangerous weapon, without intent to kill is consummated within the jurisdiction of the state. If the crime is consummated when the trigger is pulled, jurisdiction properly lies with the federal government under 18 U.S.C. § 1153 (assault with a dangerous weapon). However, if the assault continues beyond the act of firing the weapon, the state may properly exercise jurisdiction.

Defendants were charged in the information as follows: "(Defendants) did commit the public offense of Assault With A Dangerous Weapon Without Intent To Kill (SDCL 22-18-11) in that they * * * committed an assault * * * by shooting * * * with a firearm with intent to injure * * *, but without intent to kill * * *." Simple assault is an essential criminal element in this allegation. *See State v. Grimes*, S.D., 237 N.W.2d 900 (1976); *People v. Odell*, 1 Dak. 197, 46 N.W. 601 (1875). Assault is defined as "any willful and unlawful attempt or offer, with force or violence, to do a corporal hurt to another." SDCL 22-18-1. Breaking down this definition, we see that an assault may be committed by one of two methods. It may either be an attempt to commit a battery or an offer to commit a battery.

As an offer to commit a battery the assault is completed when the object of the offer is put in fear of the immediate bodily injury under circumstances which would produce fear in the mind of an ordinary man. *State v. Mier*, 74 S.D. 515, 55 N.W.2d 74 (1952); *State v. Wiley*, 52 S.D. 110, 216 N.W. 866 (1927). Fear of immediate bodily injury need not be shown in instances where the assault consists of an attempted battery. All that is required under the latter definition is some overt act toward commission of the battery. 1 Wharton's Criminal Law and Procedure, § 332, at 678 (1957). *But see State v. Archer*, 22 S.D. 137, 115 N.W. 1075 (1908). We need not decide which definition of assault should apply under these facts, however, because we find that the state would have jurisdiction in either instance.

Viewing the alleged assault as an attempted battery, we find that the crime would be consummated in state jurisdiction. That is the place where the object of the attempted battery is found. In this vein we find the reasoning of the court in *Simpson v. State*, 92 Ga. 41, 17 S.E. 984 (1893) to be persuasive. There the accused was convicted of shooting at another. At the time of the shooting, the accused was standing in South Carolina and the prosecutor was in a boat situated in waters under the jurisdiction of Georgia. The court held that Georgia had jurisdiction over the offense. "The law deems that a crime is committed in the place where the criminal act takes effect. * * * (W)here one puts in force an agency for the commission of crime, he, in legal contemplation, accompanies the same to the point where it becomes effectual." 17 S.E. at 985. The court concluded that the crime became effectual where the intended victim was located, the place where the bullets hit. The crime is complete when the criminal agent, the bullets, cease to move. That the bullet failed to achieve the desired effect is of no consequence; it nevertheless had an effect in state jurisdiction.

Viewing the alleged assault as an offer to commit a battery, it may not be denied that any fear of bodily harm necessarily occurred in state jurisdiction. That is where the intended victim experienced apprehension because the bullets were landing around him. The crime is consummated where the intended victim is put in fear of immediate bodily harm. *State v. Mier*, supra.

The defendants are charged with placing in force a criminal agency and are deemed to accompany that agency to the point where it becomes effectual. *Simpson v. State*, supra. Under either definition, the assault alleged in the information was consummated in state jurisdiction. Therefore, we hold that the State of South Dakota could properly exercise jurisdiction over the alleged violation of SDCL 22-18-11. The order of the trial court dismissing the three counts of assault with a dangerous weapon, without intent to kill, is accordingly reversed and this portion of the matter is remanded for further proceedings not inconsistent with this opinion.

We turn now to the questions raised by the defendants on appeal from their conviction of burglary and grand larceny. It is urged on behalf of four of the defendants that the circuit court had no jurisdiction to try them for these offenses. They argue that their only guilt can be as aiders and abettors. Because these defendants never left trust land, they contend that jurisdiction over the aiding and abetting in the state crimes properly lies with the federal government.

* * *

Assuming that defendants' contention that they are guilty only as aiders and abettors is supported by the evidence, an assumption that the state disputes, we find that the circuit had jurisdiction even though they never physically left Indian Country.

> "Only a constructive presence is necessary to sustain a charge against a defendant as an aider or abettor * * * in the commission of a criminal offense. * * * The law is well settled to this effect everywhere. One may be entirely out of the jurisdiction of the court, in another state, in person, and still be constructively present in the jurisdiction where the criminal transaction takes place." *Watson v. State*, 158 Tenn. 212, 12 S.W.2d 375, 377 (1928).

Accord State v. Brundage, supra; SDCL 23-9-10. *See also Ex Parte Morgan*, 86 Cal.App.2d 217, 194 P.2d 800 (1948); *Newton v. People*, 96 Colo. 246, 41 P.2d 300 (1935); *State v. Owen*, 119 Or. 15, 244 P. 516 (1926).

One who aids and abets is guilty as a principal. *State v. Bonrud*, S.D., 246 N.W.2d 790 (1976). He is deemed to accompany the principal to the place where the criminal offense occurred. *State v. Brundage*, supra; *Watson v. State*, supra; SDCL 23-9-10. Here, although four defendants never physically left Indian Country, the law holds they were constructively present at the scene of the crime. Therefore, the circuit court had jurisdiction to try them for the offenses alleged in the information.

* * *

We find no reason to disturb the convictions in this case. The judgments of conviction are affirmed; the order dismissing the three counts of assault with a dangerous weapon, without intent to kill, for lack of jurisdiction is reversed and the matter remanded for further action on those charges.

All the Justices concur.

WINANS, Retired Justice, sitting for ZASTROW, J., disqualified.

Notes and Questions

1. Why were the defendants not charged with assault with intent to kill? If they were, would the state have had jurisdiction to try them?

2. How can the conviction of Winckler and the acquittal of Miller be reconciled?

3. Note South Dakota's definition of assault. If D attempts to strike V on the head with a club, misses, and V never knows about it, has A committed an assault? What does the statute mean by a "offer" to commit a battery?

United States v. Chrestopher Patrick Cruz

United States Court of Appeals for the Ninth Circuit
554 F.3d 840 (2009)

REINHARDT, Circuit Judge:

At first glance, there appears to be something odd about a court of law in a diverse nation such as ours deciding whether a specific individual is or is not "an Indian."[1] Yet, given the long and complex relationship between the government of the United States and the sovereign tribal nations within its borders, the criminal jurisdiction of the federal government often turns on precisely this question-whether a particular individual "counts" as an Indian-and it is this question that we address once again today.

As our court has noted before, the law governing "[t]he exercise of criminal jurisdiction over Indians and Indian country [encompasses] a 'complex patchwork of federal, state, and tribal law,' which is better explained by history than by logic." *United States v. Bruce*, 394 F.3d 1215, 1218 (9th Cir.2005) (quoting *Duro v. Reina*, 495 U.S. 676, 680 n. 1, 110 S.Ct. 2053, 109 L.Ed.2d 693 (1990)). From that history, and from various cases we have decided over the years, our circuit has distilled a specific test for determining whether an individual can be prosecuted by the federal government under 18 U.S.C. § 1153, a statute governing the conduct of Indians in Indian Country. We announced that test in *United States v. Bruce*, 394 F.3d 1215 (9th Cir.2005), a case that both parties agree controls our analysis today. Because the evidence adduced during Christopher Cruz's trial does not satisfy any of the four factors outlined in the second prong of the *Bruce* test, we hold that, even when viewed in the light most favorable to the government, his conviction cannot stand. The district court's failure to grant Cruz's motion for judgment of acquittal was plain error, and accordingly we reverse.

I.

Cruz was born in 1987 to Roger Cruz and Clara Clarice Bird. His father is Hispanic and his mother is 29/64 Blackfeet Indian and 32/64 Blood Indian. The

---

[1]   Although some prefer the term "Native American" or "American Indian," we use the term "Indian" throughout this opinion as that is the term employed in the statutes at issue in this appeal.

Blackfeet are a federally recognized tribe based in northern Montana; the Blood Indians are a Canadian tribe. Given his parents' heritage, Cruz is $^{29}/_{128}$ Blackfeet Indian and $^{32}/_{128}$ Blood Indian.

For a period of three or four years during his childhood, Cruz lived in the town of Browning, Montana on the Blackfeet Reservation. Between the age of seven and eight, he moved off the reservation and spent the next ten years living first with his father in Great Falls, Montana and subsequently with his uncle in Delano, California. Neither Great Falls nor Delano is located on an Indian reservation or otherwise located in Indian country.[2] In 2005, Cruz returned to Montana, living for a period of time in the town of Cut Bank, which is located just outside the boundaries of the Blackfeet Reservation. Shortly before the incident underlying this case, Cruz moved back to Browning, where he rented a room at the Town Motel.

On December 21, 2006, Cruz and a group of friends spent a part of the evening drinking in his room at the Town Motel. While standing outside the motel talking on a cordless phone to his girlfriend, Cruz was approached by Eudelma White Grass, who had been drinking in a neighboring room and was heavily intoxicated. An altercation took place in which White Grass was severely injured.

Cruz was arrested and charged with "[a]ssault resulting in serious bodily injury," 18 U.S.C. § 113(a)(6), which is a federal offense when committed by an Indian on an Indian reservation, 18 U.S.C. § 1153. He pled not guilty and went to trial, where his Indian status was a contested issue. At the close of the government's case-in-chief, Cruz moved for judgment of acquittal, contending that the government failed to establish his Indian status by proof beyond a reasonable doubt.[3] The district court denied the motion. Cruz subsequently took the stand in his own defense and was ultimately convicted. He now appeals, arguing that there was insufficient evidence that he is an Indian under § 1153 and that the district court committed reversible error when instructing the jury as to how to determine his Indian status.

II.

* * *

---

2   "[T]he term 'Indian country' . . . means (a) all land within the limits of any Indian reservation under the jurisdiction of the United States Government . . . (b) all dependent Indian communities within the borders of the United States whether within the original or subsequently acquired territory thereof . . . and (c) all Indian allotments, the Indian titles to which have not been extinguished, including rights-of-way running through the same." 18 U.S.C. § 1151.

3   As Cruz's Indian status is the central issue on appeal, we discuss the evidence introduced regarding this question in the text below.

III.

A "defendant's Indian status is an essential element of a § 1153 offense which the government must allege in the indictment and prove beyond a reasonable doubt." *Bruce*, 394 F.3d at 1229. We recently established the test for determining an individual's Indian status under 18 U.S.C. § 1152 in *United States v. Bruce*, 394 F.3d 1215 (9th Cir.2005), and the same test applies to the determination of Indian status under § 1152's companion statute, 18 U.S.C. § 1153. The *Bruce* test requires that the Government prove two things: that the defendant has a sufficient "degree of Indian blood," and has "tribal or federal government recognition as an Indian." *Id.* at 1223, 1224 (quoting *United States v. Keys*, 103 F.3d 758, 761 (9th Cir.1996)).

Cruz concedes that he meets the first prong of the test since his blood quotient is twenty-two percent Blackfeet. Only the second prong, therefore, is at issue here. In *Bruce* we outlined four factors that govern the second prong; those four factors are, "in declining order of importance, evidence of the following: 1) tribal enrollment; 2) government recognition formally and informally through receipt of assistance reserved only to Indians; 3) enjoyment of the benefits of tribal affiliation; and 4) social recognition as an Indian through residence on a reservation and participation in Indian social life." *Id.* at 1224 (quoting *United States v. Lawrence*, 51 F.3d 150, 152 (8th Cir.1995)); *accord United States v. Ramirez*, 537 F.3d 1075, 1082 (9th Cir.2008). * * *

Taken in the light most favorable to the government, the record reveals the following facts related to Cruz's Indian status:

1. Cruz is not an enrolled member of the Blackfeet Tribe of Indians or any other tribe.

2. Cruz has "descendant" status in the Blackfeet Tribe as the son of an enrolled member (his mother), which entitles him to use Indian Health Services, to receive some educational grants, and to fish and hunt on the reservation.

3. Cruz has never taken advantage of any of the benefits or services to which he is entitled as a descendant.

4. Cruz lived on the Blackfeet Reservation from the time he was four years old until he was seven or eight. He rented a room in a motel on the reservation shortly before the time of the offense.

5. As a descendant, Cruz was subject to the criminal jurisdiction of the tribal court[7] and was at one time prosecuted in tribal court.

---

7   The parties have not cited to us any Blackfeet ordinances or codes establishing this point. As we explain infra pp. 849-50 & note 15, the fact that charges were brought against Cruz in tribal court does not necessarily mean the tribal court had jurisdiction over him. Our own reading of the Blackfeet code suggests that per-

6. Cruz attended a public school on the reservation that is open to non-Indians and worked as a firefighter for the federal Bureau of Indian Affairs, a job that is also open to non-Indians.

7. Cruz has never participated in Indian religious ceremonies or dance festivals, has never voted in a Blackfeet tribal election, and does not have a tribal identification card.

Analyzing this evidence, it is clear that Cruz does not satisfy any of the four *Bruce* factors. As to the first and most important factor, it is undisputed that Cruz is not an enrolled member of the Blackfeet Tribe or any other tribe. In fact, Cruz is not even eligible to become an enrolled member of the Blackfeet Tribe, as he has less than one quarter Blackfeet blood, which is the minimum amount necessary for enrollment. * * * See BLACKFEET CONST. art. II, amd. III, § 1(c). Our dissenting colleague would hold that the government has "plainly" met its burden under *Bruce* because it has established that Cruz has "'descendant' status" and has therefore been "recognized" by "the tribal authorities." Dissenting Op. at 851-52. The government, however, has expressly waived any argument that Cruz satisfies the first *Bruce* factor, and does not contend that his descendant status, in and of itself, is a factor we should consider in performing the *Bruce* analysis.[9] Rather, the government's argument is that "descendant status" is relevant only insofar as it renders someone "eligible to receive certain assistance reserved for Native Americans," language that directly tracks the second *Bruce* factor, except for substituting "eligible to receive" for actually receives. However, as we explain below, mere eligibility for benefits is of no consequence under *Bruce*. Given *Bruce's* clear admonition that "tribal enrollment," and therefore a fortiori descendant status, "is not dispositive of Indian status," 394 F.3d at 1224-25, we reject the dissent's argument that mere descendant status with the concomitant eligibility to receive benefits is effectively sufficient to demonstrate "tribal recognition." To do otherwise would elevate tribal status to a "dispositive"

---

haps the tribe's criminal jurisdiction is limited to enrolled members of the Blackfeet Tribe and other tribes. Cf. BLACKFEET CODE § 1.1 ("The Blackfeet Tribal Court has jurisdiction over all persons of Indian descent, who are members of the Blackfeet Tribe of Montana and over all other American Indians unless its authority is restricted by an Order of the Secretary of the Interior.") (emphasis added). It is undisputed that Cruz is not an enrolled member of the Blackfeet Tribe or a member of any other American Indian tribe. However, because the Director of Tribal Enrollment testified that Cruz was subject to the tribe's criminal jurisdiction by virtue of his descendant status, and because Cruz did not contest this point below or on appeal, we assume for purposes of our analysis that Cruz was subject to the tribal court's jurisdiction.

9   This concession reflects a sensible understanding of the law. If, for example, a tribal authority declared that anyone with an ancestor who was a member of the tribe, no matter how distant, counts as a "descendant," we would be hard pressed to consider such an individual subject to prosecution under § 1153, even though "tribal authorities [would clearly] recognize [such a person] as an Indian" under our dissenting colleague's formulation. Dissenting Op. at 852 (emphasis omitted).

determinant of Indian status, as *Bruce* explicitly forbids. Furthermore, given the government's explicit waiver of the argument, to hold as the dissent suggests would violate our longstanding general rule that we will not decide questions not raised by the parties before us. *See, e.g., Kimes v. Stone*, 84 F.3d 1121, 1126 (9th Cir.1996); *cf. United States v. Ziegler*, 497 F.3d 890, 901 (9th Cir.2007) (Kozinski, J., dissenting from denial of rehearing en banc) ("We apply [the waiver] rule with some vigor against criminal defendants; we should be no less vigorous in applying it against the government." (internal citation omitted)).

Nor is there any evidence that Cruz satisfies the second most important factor, "government recognition . . . through receipt of assistance reserved only to Indians." *Bruce*, 394 F.3d at 1224 (emphasis added). To the contrary, the only evidence in the record demonstrates that the opposite is true: Cruz testified that he had never "received . . . any benefits from the Blackfeet Tribe," and the government did not present any evidence to the contrary. Nor did Cruz enjoy any benefits of tribal affiliation, as required by *Bruce*'s third most important factor. There is no evidence that he hunted or fished on the reservation, nor has it been suggested that his employment with the BIA was related to or contingent upon his tribal heritage.[11] The only evidence supporting any of the *Bruce* factors is that, for less than a quarter of his short life, Cruz lived on the Blackfeet Reservation. But even this only partially supports the government's position under the fourth *Bruce* factor, which also requires a showing of "participation in Indian social life." *Id.* Testimony both from Cruz and from a government witness indicated that Cruz does not practice Indian religion, has never "in any way participated in Native religious ceremonies," does not participate in Indian cultural festivals or dance competitions, has never voted in a Blackfeet election, and does not carry a tribal identification card. The government did not present any evidence suggesting that Cruz participated in any way in Indian social life.

In sum, the evidence in this case, when taken in the light most favorable to the government, demonstrates that Cruz satisfies at best only a small part of the least important of the four *Bruce* factors. He does not satisfy any of the factors in full, and there is not even a scintilla of evidence suggesting that he satisfies a single one of the three most important factors. Were we to hold that evidence satisfying merely a portion of the least important *Bruce* factor is, in itself, sufficient to support a § 1153 conviction, we would be ignoring *Bruce*'s mandate in various respects, including its requirement that the factors be considered "in

---

11 Employment with the BIA is open to non-Indians. While it is true that the BIA is permitted to give preference to Indians when making hiring decisions, *see* 25 U.S.C. §§ 472, 472a; *Morton v. Mancari*, 417 U.S. 535, 94 S.Ct. 2474, 41 L.Ed.2d 290 (1974); 25 C.F.R. § 5.1, there is no indication in the trial record that Cruz ever received any preferential treatment on the basis of his ancestry. In fact, Cruz would not have been eligible for preferential treatment under the Indian Preference Laws, as he is not a member of a recognized tribe and has less than "one-half or more Indian blood of tribes indigenous to the United States." 25 C.F.R. § 5.1.

declining order of importance." Id. The first three factors could not realistically be deemed more important than the fourth if a partial satisfaction of the fourth could outweigh the complete failure to satisfy any of the first three.

The government does not dispute our assessment of the record. Rather, in light of the near total lack of evidence that could satisfy the *Bruce* test as it is written, it urges us to expand *Bruce* by holding that mere "eligibility for . . . assistance" reserved to Indians is sufficient under the second *Bruce* factor.[14] But this is not what *Bruce* says. *Bruce* says that the second factor requires a showing of "receipt of assistance reserved only to Indians." *Id.* (emphasis added). We are not empowered to ignore such clear language in our circuit's precedent, *see Miller v. Gammie*, 335 F.3d 889, 899 (9th Cir.2003) (en banc), especially when construing a statute that creates a "carefully limited intrusion of federal power into the otherwise exclusive jurisdiction of the Indian tribes," *Bruce*, 394 F.3d at 1220 (emphasis added) (quoting *United States v. Antelope*, 430 U.S. 641, 642-43 n. 1, 97 S.Ct. 1395, 51 L.Ed.2d 701 (1977)).

Even were we free to follow the government's recommended course, we would not. The four factors that constitute the second *Bruce* prong are designed to "probe[ ] whether the Native American has a sufficient non-racial link to a formerly sovereign people." *Bruce*, 394 F.3d at 1224 (quoting *St. Cloud v. United States*, 702 F.Supp. 1456, 1461 (D.S.D.1988)). *Bruce* intentionally requires more than a simple blood test to determine whether someone is legally deemed an Indian. Given that many descendants of Indians are eligible for tribal benefits based exclusively on their blood heritage, the government's argument would effectively render the second *Bruce* factor a de facto nullity, and in most, if not all, cases would transform the entire *Bruce* analysis into a "blood" test. *Cf. id.* at 1223. For similar reasons, we cannot accept our dissenting colleague's argument that the sole test under *Bruce's* second prong "is whether the tribal authorities recognize [someone] as an Indian, not whether he considers himself one." Dissenting op. at 852 (second emphasis added). Under *Bruce*, the extent to which an individual considers himself an Indian-whether by deciding, for example, to "reside[ ] on a reservation," to "participat[e] in Indian social life," or to "recei[ve] assistance reserved only to Indians," *Bruce*, 394 F.3d at 1224—is most certainly relevant in determining his Indian status. The dissent simply ignores the fact that *Bruce* clearly requires an analysis from the perspective of both the tribe and the individual.

The government and our dissenting colleague also argue that the fact that Cruz was prosecuted by the Blackfeet tribal court demonstrates that he is an

---

14   As indicated above, the record demonstrates that descendants of enrolled Blackfeet members are entitled to use Indian Health Services, are eligible for certain scholarships, and are permitted to hunt and fish on the reservation. The government does not dispute that Cruz never took advantage of any of these benefits.

Indian because a "tribe has no jurisdiction to punish anyone but an Indian." *Id.* at 1227; *see* Dissenting Op. at 852. This argument is meritless for multiple reasons. First and foremost, the record in this case is incredibly thin with respect to Cruz's contact with the tribal justice system: all we know is that he has "been prosecuted." There is no evidence regarding the nature of that prosecution, to what stage, if any, it proceeded, and certainly the record does not indicate whether Cruz was ever determined for purposes of that prosecution to be an Indian. Finally, the record does not suggest that the prosecution resulted in a conviction. Based on the evidence contained in the trial record, which is all that we may consider, Cruz's case may well have been dismissed for lack of jurisdiction after a finding that he is not an Indian.

Furthermore, while the government makes much of the fact that the court in *Bruce* considered the exercise of tribal jurisdiction over the defendant throughout her entire lifetime relevant, it fails to recognize the significantly different posture of that case. *Bruce* addressed a prosecution under § 1152. However, under § 1152, the question of Indian status is an affirmative defense. *Id.* at 1222-23 (citing *United States v. Hester*, 719 F.2d 1041, 1043 (9th Cir.1983)). Generally, "the defendant must prove the elements of [an] affirmative defense by a preponderance of the evidence," unless some other standard is set by statute. *United States v. Beasley*, 346 F.3d 930, 935 (9th Cir.2003); *see also United States v. Dominguez-Mestas*, 929 F.2d 1379, 1383 (9th Cir.1991); cf. 18 U.S.C. § 17 (affirmative defense of insanity requires clear and convincing evidence). By contrast, under § 1153 Indian status is "an essential element of [the] offense which the government must . . . prove beyond a reasonable doubt" in every case. *Bruce*, 394 F.3d at 1229 (emphasis added). All that *Bruce* held was that "[t]he assumption and exercise of a tribe's criminal jurisdiction . . . bolster[ed] the argument that *Bruce* met her burden of producing sufficient evidence" for an affirmative defense. *Id.* at 1227. The court explicitly "caution[ed] that *Bruce* was only required to meet a production burden," which it later described as a "mere" burden of production. *Id.* (emphasis added). The burden here, by contrast, is on the government to prove Cruz's Indian status beyond a reasonable doubt. In this context, a showing that a tribal court on one occasion may have exercised jurisdiction over a defendant is of little if any consequence in satisfying the status element in a § 1153 prosecution.

Because the evidence viewed in the light most favorable to the government does not demonstrate that Cruz is an Indian or that he meets any of the *Bruce* factors, no rational trier of fact could have found that the government proved the statutory element of § 1153 beyond a reasonable doubt. Accordingly, the district court's denial of the motion for judgment of acquittal was error. * * * We reverse the decision below and instruct the district court to grant the motion for judgment of acquittal.

IV.

For the reasons stated above, the decision below is REVERSED and the judgment of conviction VACATED. The district court is instructed to grant the motion for judgment of acquittal.

KOZINSKI, Chief Judge, dissenting:

Because defendant has the requisite amount of Indian blood, the only question is whether he has "tribal or government recognition as an Indian." *United States v. Bruce*, 394 F.3d 1215, 1223 (9th Cir.2005) (quoting *United States v. Broncheau*, 597 F.2d 1260, 1263 (9th Cir.1979) for the "generally accepted test," derived from *United States v. Rogers*, 45 U.S. (4 How.) 567, 573, 11 L.Ed. 1105 (1846)). He plainly does. The record discloses that the Blackfeet tribal authorities have accorded Cruz "descendant" status, which entitles him to many of the benefits of tribal membership, including medical treatment at any Indian Health Service facility in the United States, certain educational grants, housing assistance and hunting and fishing privileges on the reservation.

That Cruz may not have taken advantage of these benefits doesn't matter because the test is whether the tribal authorities recognize him as an Indian, not whether he considers himself one. That they do is confirmed by the fact that, when he was charged with an earlier crime on the reservation, the tribal police took him before the tribal court rather than turning him over to state or federal authorities. How that case was finally resolved is irrelevant; what matters is that the tribal authorities protected him from a state or federal prosecution by treating him as one of their own. Finally, Cruz was living on the reservation when he was arrested, another piece of evidence supporting the jury's verdict.

The majority manages to work its way around all of this evidence by taking a stray comment in *Bruce* to the effect that certain factors have been considered in "declining order of importance" and turning it into a four-part balancing test. But *Bruce* was not announcing a rule of law; it was merely reporting what it thought other courts had done: "[C]ourts have considered, in declining order of importance, evidence of [four factors]." 394 F.3d at 1224. *Bruce* did not adopt this as any sort of standard, nor did it have any cause to do so, as nothing in *Bruce* turned on the relative weight of the factors. The majority strains hard to make this part of *Bruce's* holding, but a fair reading of the opinion discloses that it's not even dicta because it's descriptive rather than prescriptive. We recognized this the last time we applied the test by omitting any reference to the declining order of importance. *See United States v. Ramirez*, 537 F.3d 1075, 1082 (9th Cir.2008).

Bruce borrowed the "declining order of importance" language from *United States v. Lawrence*, 51 F.3d 150, 152 (8th Cir.1995), and *Lawrence* itself was quoting the observation of a district judge in an earlier case, *St. Cloud v. United States*, 702 F.Supp. 1456, 1461-62 (D.S.D. 1988). The district judge in *St. Cloud* did not cite most of the cases he relied on, so it's hard to tell whether his observation is correct, but he did offer a note of caution that my colleagues overlook: "These factors do not establish a precise formula for determining who is an Indian. Rather, they merely guide the analysis of whether a person is recognized as an Indian." Id. at 1461.

This is the opposite of what my colleagues do today: They turn the four factors into a rigid multi-part balancing test, with the various prongs reinforcing or offsetting each other, depending on how they are analyzed. This is not what the judge in *St. Cloud* had in mind, and certainly nothing like what *Bruce* adopted as the law of our circuit. It is an invention of the majority in our case, designed to take power away from juries and district judges and give it to appellate judges. Nothing in the law, dating back to the Supreme Court's opinion in *Rogers*, justifies this fine mincing of the evidence. The question we must answer is whether there is enough evidence from which a rational jury could have concluded beyond a reasonable doubt that Cruz was recognized as an Indian. Clearly there was, and that's the end of our task.

The majority misreads *Bruce* and misrepresents my position: "Given *Bruce's* clear admonition that 'tribal enrollment,' and therefore a fortiori descendant status, 'is not dispositive of Indian status,' we reject the dissent's argument that mere descendant status with the concomitant eligibility to receive benefits is effectively sufficient to demonstrate 'tribal recognition.'" Maj. op. at 847 (quoting *Bruce*, 394 F.3d at 1224-25). *Bruce* certainly doesn't hold that tribal enrollment is insufficient to support a finding of Indian status. *Bruce* holds the converse: that the absence of tribal enrollment does not preclude finding that defendant is an Indian-which was the question presented here. To suggest, as does the majority, that an individual who is enrolled as a member of a tribe might not be an Indian after all is not only preposterous, it's unnecessary, as no one claims that Cruz was enrolled.

Nor do I maintain, as the majority makes believe, that Cruz's descendant status is enough to make him an Indian. Whether or not it is, there are additional facts here: Cruz's residence on the reservation and the fact that he was previously arrested and brought before the tribal court. The latter is a fact that the *Bruce* majority held to be highly significant. *Bruce* did not consider the disposition of prior tribal court cases relevant and we are not free to disregard the arrest and prosecution by tribal authorities on this spurious basis.

* * *

Not satisfied with merely reversing the verdict, the majority goes a bridge too far by converting its novel four-part test into a jury instruction. This is wholly unnecessary, as Cruz cannot be tried again for violating 18 U.S.C. § 1153 because of double jeopardy. It is also wrong. We don't instruct juries as to how to weigh the evidence; that is their function, not ours. Yet the majority now requires jurors to assign relative weight to various pieces of evidence presented to them. I am aware of no such instruction anywhere else in our jurisprudence and the majority points to none. It is a bold step into uncharted territory and, in my judgment, an unwise one.

* * *

The majority engages in vigorous verbal calisthenics to reach a wholly counter-intuitive-and-wrong-result. Along the way, it mucks up several already complex areas of the law and does grave injury to our plain error standard of review. I hasten to run in the other direction.

Notes and Questions

1. There are two questions when it comes to criminal jurisdiction in Indian Country. The first is which jurisdiction's law applies. The second is which jurisdiction has authority to prosecute.

   The general criminal laws of the United States apply in Indian Country in the same way they do in other parts of the United States. So if a person allegedly made a false statement to a federal officer in violation of 18 U.S.C. § 1001, that charge could be prosecuted in federal court regardless of whether it took place on a reservation.

   Geographical criminal jurisdiction over crimes in Indian country is shared among the federal, state and tribal governments, depending on the identity of the offender and victim. In Indian County in all states, if a non-Indian commits a crime against a non-Indian, or commits a victimless crime, the state has exclusive criminal jurisdiction. In a prosecution, the state would apply its own criminal laws, not those of the federal government or of the tribe. Similarly, if an Indian committed a crime in Indian Country, the tribal court has at least concurrent jurisdiction, and it would apply its own laws. Under the Constitution, tribal courts do not have criminal jurisdiction over non-Indians. *Oliphant v. Squamish Indian Tribe*, 435 U.S. 191 (1978).

Beyond that, the rules are complex. Generally, though, under 18 U.S.C. § 1162(a), often called Public Law 280, California, Nebraska and Wisconsin, and Alaska, Minnesota and Oregon with certain exceptions, have jurisdiction over crimes committed by or against Indians in Indian Country which is exclusive of federal jurisdiction. Other states, such as Florida, Idaho and Washington, which opted in to an earlier version of Public Law 280, have jurisdiction concurrent with the federal courts, as do certain states, including Iowa, Kansas and New York, which were granted criminal jurisdiction in Indian Country by specific statute. When prosecuting, they apply state law.

Where Congress has not granted exclusive criminal jurisdiction to the states, federal courts have jurisdiction over certain serious crimes committed by Indians under the Major Crimes Act, 18 U.S.C. § 1153, or against Indians, under the General Crimes Act, 18 U.S.C. § 1152. Under these statutes, the prosecutions in federal court are generally based on state criminal law, although some specific federal statutes apply. Tribal courts have concurrent jurisdiction over Indian defendants, and they apply tribal law.

2. Who has the better of the argument about the importance of the fact that Cruz was taken before the tribal court on an earlier occasion? What could the prosecution have done to strengthen their case on this point?

D. Jurisdiction over the Subject Matter

1. The Limits of State Jurisdiction/Exclusive Federal Jurisdiction

People v. Hassan

California Court of Appeal, Second District, Division 2
168 Cal.App.4th 1306 (2008)

BOREN, P.J.

Ahmed Ali Hassan * * * appeals from the judgment entered upon his convictions in a court trial of offering a false or forged instrument for recording (Pen. Code, § 115, subd. (a), count 1)[2] and offering false evidence (§ 132, count 2). The

---

2   All further statutory references are to the Penal Code unless otherwise indicated.

trial court sentenced him to the middle term of two years on count 1, staying execution of sentence and placing him on three years' probation on condition he serve one year in county jail. On count 2, it suspended imposition of sentence and placed him on three years' probation. Appellant contends that there is insufficient evidence * * * (2) he violated section 132.

We reverse the conviction of count 2 * * *.

FACTUAL BACKGROUND

The Prosecution's Evidence

On October 4, 2002, appellant and codefendant, Ana Beatriz Sequen Deleon (Deleon), went to the offices of Candice Espinoza (Espinoza), a commissioned notary authorized to certify a "confidential marriage,"[4] and Baldomero Aguilera (Aguilera), a minister authorized by a church to solemnize the marriage. After Aguilera solemnized the marriage, appellant and Deleon signed a "License and Certificate of Confidential Marriage" (License) in his presence. Aguilera had reviewed it with them, read the affidavit to them, and explained that a confidential marriage required the parties to be "living together as husband and wife." Espinoza signed and notarized the License and mailed it to the county recorder for recording. A copy given to the parties stated that a certified copy could be obtained from the county recorder.

Teresa Wieland (Wieland), a special agent with Immigration and Customs Enforcement (I.C.E.), investigated cases of marriage fraud that is, marriage entered for the purpose of obtaining a green card for a new spouse. She investigated a petition against appellant filed by Deleon. Wieland suspected marriage fraud because of the difference in the parties' ages, religious affiliation and cultural background. She examined a photocopy of appellant's Egyptian passport and "P–1" visa, which is granted to a person who is an athlete or entertainer. The visa was valid between March 12, 1998, and April 5, 1998.

On January 28, 2005, at approximately 5:30 a.m., Wieland and F.B.I. Special Agent, Craig Moringiello (Moringiello), went to 3911 Lugo Avenue in Lynwood (Lugo residence) to conduct a home inspection to determine if appellant and Deleon were living together as husband and wife. After waiting outside for an hour and seeing no one enter or exit, they knocked on the door and went inside. Appellant was not there, but Deleon and members of her family were.

---

4   A confidential marriage is described in Family Code section 500, as follows: "When an unmarried man and an unmarried woman not minors, have been living together as husband and wife, they may be married pursuant to this chapter by a person authorized to solemnize a marriage under Chapter 1 (commencing with Section 400) of Part 3, without the necessity of first obtaining health certificates." (Italics added.) Family Code section 511 provides that a recorded confidential marriage certification is not open to the public for inspection.

Wieland observed family photographs, but none of appellant, and a crucifix in Deleon's bedroom, but no other religious symbols. It appeared that only one person had slept in Deleon's bed, as one part was unmade and the other part was "perfectly spread."

Deleon was allowed to make a call while Wieland was in the house. Appellant arrived while Wieland was still there. She interviewed him, asking about his "P–1" visa status. After initially claiming he was a drummer, Wieland testified that he admitted to her that he was not and that his visa was fraudulently obtained so he could enter the United States. Wieland asked him for his "departure documents." He gave her his "I–94" document, which indicated that he entered the United States on April 29, 1999, at Los Angeles International Airport, as an "F–1" status (student), contradicting the information on his passport and visa. Wieland then asked if appellant had a form "I–20," which would confirm enrollment in school. Appellant said it had been taken by immigration, and Wieland saw a copy of it in his immigration file. Appellant said he procured these documents to illegally obtain a Social Security card.

Appellant also gave Wieland a "marriage contract," written in Arabic and dated October 4, 2000, which stated that "the marriage took place at Omar Ibn al Khattab Mosque." He explained that before they could have sex, he had to be married in his religion. He said they had sex at his apartment after they were married at the mosque.

Based on this inspection, Wieland believed appellant's marriage to Deleon was fraudulent. She did not believe he was living in the Lugo residence at that time. Therefore, on March 30, 2005, before 7:00 a.m., she, Moringiello, Los Angeles Police Detective Oakley Fungaroli, and a joint task force returned to the Lugo residence with a search warrant. Wieland waited outside and, this time, saw appellant leave. She then entered the residence and saw that both sides of the bed had been slept in.

Anselmo Hernandez (Anselmo), whose wife, Luz, was Deleon's friend for 25 years, signed a letter, dated October 4, 2002, stating that appellant and Deleon had been living together at the Lugo residence since October 4, 2002, and not before. Deleon's mother, Consuelo, had lived at the Lugo residence with Deleon for 16 years and stated that appellant had not lived with Deleon before the confidential marriage and had never been married in the Muslim faith.

Dafer Dakhil (Dakhil), a director of the Omar Ibn Al Khattab Foundation Mosque in downtown Los Angeles, testified that the Arabic marriage contract was not issued by his mosque. He was unaware of any other mosque in Los Angeles with the name Omar Ibn Al Khattab and found no marriage records at his mosque relating to appellant and Deleon.

The Defense's Evidence

Appellant testified on his own behalf that on October 4, 2000, he went to "Omar Ibn Al Khattab Mosque" in Downey, where he and Deleon signed a marriage contract. Afterwards, they went to his apartment in Lakewood and had sex. Appellant did not move in with Deleon after the mosque marriage.

On October 4, 2002, appellant and Deleon signed the License and were married in what appellant referred to as an "American Marriage." Before that ceremony, he thought he and Deleon were living together as husband and wife, though they did not live in the same house. He introduced her as his wife and believed they were married before God. After the confidential marriage, he moved in with Deleon at the Lugo residence, opened a bank account with her, obtained insurance on his life for her benefit, and paid utility bills.

Appellant claimed he had left for work on January 28, 2005, at approximately 5:15 a.m., before Wieland arrived, and made his part of the bed before leaving. His clothes were in the closet, and a Koran was in the bedroom.

Appellant testified that he obtained a "P–1" visa in Egypt because he worked there as a drummer with a singing and music group for three or four years. He claimed he told Wieland he had an entertainment visa and was a drummer in Egypt. Appellant applied to Long Beach City College to take an English course and intended to return to school, but could not do so because he was working too much.

Deleon testified that on October 4, 2000, she had an Islamic marriage. After the ceremony, she had sex with appellant for the first time at his apartment. But she had given a written statement that she had never been in appellant's apartment. On October 4, 2002, she had a confidential civil marriage, and began living with appellant afterwards. She was unaware that she and appellant were required to be living together in order to have a confidential marriage, and Aguilera (the minister) did not explain it. She nonetheless believed that they were living together after October 4, 2000, but in different houses. She denied that their marriage was a sham.

Rebuttal

Denise Kinsella, the manager of the international student program at Long Beach State College, testified. She prepared "I–20" documents for students to use to apply for an F–1 student visa to enter the United States. She testified that appellant's "I–20" was not produced by her school, as item No. 6 was not checked, there were at least five discrepancies on it, including the class dates, and there were several typographical errors, spelling errors and other inaccuracies. Also, the signature of Roger Schultz on the "I–20" was not genuine; at that time he was not signing the "I–20's," his title on the form was also incorrect, and records at the college did not indicate that a student named "Abdel Azim," as written on the "I–20," had attended.

On January 28, 2005, when Wieland asked Deleon about the marriage at the mosque, Deleon said she had a blessing at a mosque on the day of the civil ceremony. She also said that they first had sex on her wedding day, and she had never been to appellant's apartment.

DISCUSSION

I. Appellant was properly convicted of violating section 115 (count 1)

* * *

II. Appellant was improperly convicted of offering false evidence.

A. *Introduction*

Count 2 charged appellant with violating section 132, which states: "Every person who upon any trial, proceeding, inquiry, or investigation whatever, authorized or permitted by law, offers in evidence, as genuine or true, any book, paper, document, record, or other instrument in writing, knowing the same to have been forged or fraudulently altered or ante-dated, is guilty of a felony." (Italics added.) Appellant's conviction was based upon his giving a false "marriage contract," and "I–94" and "I–20" forms to Wieland and the I.C.E. in connection with the I.C.E. investigation into whether his marriage to Deleon was fraudulent.

B. *Contention*

Appellant contends that his conviction of offering false evidence is unsupported by the evidence and contrary to law. He argues that there is no evidence that his marriage contract was forged, fraudulently altered or antedated because he had entered an Islamic marriage. With respect to the "I–94" and "I –20" forms, while he does not contend that they are authentic, he claims that there was no evidence he knew they were forged or fraudulently altered. Appellant further contends that in any event, providing these documents to federal immigration investigators is not a "trial, proceeding, inquiry, or investigation whatever" because it is unclear whether those terms apply to state or local proceedings or whether they also apply to federal proceedings. We agree with appellant's contention that section 132 is inapplicable to the federal proceeding here. We therefore need not consider his first contention.

C. *Federal Investigation*

Nearly a century and a half ago, our Supreme Court considered an analogous situation in *People v. Kelly* (1869) 38 Cal. 145 (*Kelly*). There, the defendant was convicted in state court of perjury for making a false oath before the Register of the United States Land Office in his application to make proof of settlement and cultivation of a tract of land. (*Id.* at p. 148.) The federal statute making the defendant's conduct a crime stated in part: "'[I]n all cases where any oath, affirmation or affidavit shall be made, or taken before any Register or Receiver . . . of any local Land Office in the United States . . . and such oaths, affirmations or affidavits are made, used or filed in any of said local Land Offices . . . and any person or persons shall, taking such oath, affirmation or affidavit, knowingly, wilfully or corruptly swear or affirm falsely, the same shall be deemed and taken to be perjury, and the person or persons guilty thereof shall, upon conviction, be liable to the punishment prescribed for that offense by the laws of the United States.'" (*Id.* at p. 149.) The California statute under which the defendant was indicted read in part: "'Every person having taken a lawful oath or made affirmation in any judicial proceeding, or in any other matter where by law an oath or affirmation is required, who shall swear or affirm wilfully, corruptly and falsely in a matter material to the issue or point in question . . . shall be deemed guilty of perjury . . . and upon conviction thereof shall be punished by imprisonment in the State Prison for any term not less than one nor more than fourteen years.'" (Ibid.)

The Supreme Court held that while defendant's conduct was clearly an offense against the federal law, it was unclear whether the California statute referred only to judicial proceedings and oaths required by California. (*Kelly*, supra, 38 Cal. at p. 150.) The Court stated: "State tribunals have no power to punish crimes against the laws of the United States, as such [,] " although the state could punish as an offense against the state any act that was an offense against the laws of both the state and the federal government. (Ibid.) In determining that the perjury conviction was not cognizable in the state court, the Court concluded: "'In those cases the acts done and charged as violations of the laws of both Governments, are not done in the course of the administration of the laws of either Government; but the matters from which the charge now before us arises are alleged to have occurred under and in the course of the execution of the laws of the United States. Those laws required certain things to be done. Congress had the right to prescribe how they should be done, to regulate the duties of all persons who acted under the law, and to prescribe penalties for the violation of such duties. In such case, if acts are done which, if transacted under the laws of this State, would have constituted offenses under the provisions of our Criminal Code, yet, being done in pursuance of the laws of another Government (having the sole power to regulate the whole proceeding), authorizing the act to be done, prescribing the mode, imposing the duty, and affixing the penalty for the violation of it, the acts cannot be regarded as having been done under the sanction of the laws of this State, so as to subject the parties to punishment under those laws.'" (*Kelly*, at pp. 150–151.)

In short, the Court resolved the ambiguity in the state statute by holding that the state had no authority to enforce the federal criminal law by extending the words "judicial proceeding" to encompass the federal proceeding involving the United States Land Office. (*See also Thomas v. Loney* (1890) 134 U.S. 372, 375, 10 S.Ct. 584, 33 L.Ed. 949 [courts of a state have no jurisdiction of a complaint for perjury in a contested election case involving a seat in the Congress of the United States, although the false swearing was before a notary public of the state, the Court holding that the "'power of punishing a witness for testifying falsely in a judicial proceeding belongs peculiarly to the government in whose tribunals that proceeding is had'"].)

Analogously here, as in *Kelly*, we are concerned with false documents provided in connection with a federal immigration investigation. Several federal laws potentially criminalize the presentation of false or fraudulent documents in connection with that investigation. (See, i.e., 8 U.S.C. § 1324c [providing penalties for document fraud]; 18 U.S.C. § 1546 [fraud and misuse of visas, permits and other documents].) As in *Kelly*, it is unclear whether the language "trial, proceeding, inquiry, or investigation whatever" in section 132 refers only to state or local proceedings or whether it also applies to federal proceedings. The ambiguity is resolved by limiting section 132 to its manifest purpose to protect the integrity of state and not federal proceedings. That avoids a construction in which the federal criminal law is simply enforced by the state law. Because the documents appellant provided I.C.E. were produced pursuant to the laws of the United States which was the sole source of authorization for the I.C.E. investigation, the integrity of the federal proceeding is protected by the federal law.

DISPOSITION

The judgment of conviction of section 132 is reversed and the judgment is otherwise affirmed. On remand the trial court is directed to dismiss count 2. We concur: ASHMANN–GERST and DOI TODD, JJ.

People v. Cohen

New York Supreme Court, Appellate Division, First Department
773 N.Y.S.2d 371 (2004)

TOM, J.P.

This appeal arises from the perjury convictions of an inter-related group of persons who, while under oath before the National Association of Securities Dealers (NASD), falsely denied that one of the defendants, Stanley Cohen, supervised a retail sales operation of a stock brokerage firm, Renaissance Securities Financial Corporation (Renaissance), despite a 1973 SEC order barring him for life from associating with any broker-dealer in a proprietary or supervisory capacity.

* * *

At the criminal trial resulting in the instant conviction, Stanley Cohen contended, and still maintains, that an oath was never administered in connection with his participation and hence perjury had not occurred. We reject the contention, as did the trial court.
* * * The evidence otherwise was also legally sufficient and the verdict was not against the weight of the evidence.

* * *

Defendants moved before trial to dismiss the perjury counts, and after trial sought dismissal pursuant to CPL 330.30. In two thoughtful and comprehensive decisions, the trial court rejected defendants' challenges to the perjury prosecution, reasoning with which we agree. The trial court did dismiss several fraud-related charges and a conspiracy charge on various theories.

We turn, first, to jurisdiction. Defendants direct us to *Thomas v. Loney*, 134 U.S. 372, 10 S.Ct. 584, 33 L.Ed. 949, an 1890 Supreme Court perjury ruling that defendants construe to be binding precedent for the proposition that an oath given in a proceeding involving federal law cannot be the basis for a state perjury conviction. However, that is not quite the proposition asserted in *Loney*, nor are the peculiar circumstances undergirding *Loney* remotely analogous to either the present factual or legal contexts. The *Loney* prosecution was predicated on a state perjury charge arising from the defendant's deposition conducted before a state notary public involving a contested congressional election. The Supreme Court noted that despite the trappings of state authority conferred by the fact of a state licensed notary, the oath was required to be administered only by virtue of federal, and not state, law. The entire point of the deposition concerned a congressional matter, with Congress acting in its constitutionally conferred quasi-judicial capacity to adjudge the election of its members. The deponent's state had no interest in the matter, and its laws did not require that the oath be administered. Insofar as an oath had to be administered in connection with the taking of deposition testimony, though, the services of a person authorized to do so were required. The notary was state licensed, a happenstance that did not convert enforcement regarding a federally required oath into a state matter that could give rise to a state perjury charge. Hence, *Loney* does not apply.

Defendants also argue that this case involved a federal investigation by a federal entity from which exclusive federal jurisdiction flows. Preliminarily, the NASD is a private entity incorporated under the laws of Delaware (*Jones v. Securities & Exchange Commission*, 115 F.3d 1173, 1183 [4th Cir.1997], cert. denied 523 U.S. 1072, 118 S.Ct. 1512, 140 L.Ed.2d 666). Unlike *Loney*, where the proceeding was before an exclusively federal entity and the oath was authorized solely by federal law, the NASD is not an exclusively federal tribunal, nor was it acting solely pursuant to federal law when it investigated defendant's actions. Rather, NASD is a self-regulatory body that protects both federal and state interests in policing the securities industry. The State of New York therefore has jurisdiction to prosecute the crime of perjury committed within the State of New York, though before the NASD. By way of comparison we note that Justice Fried dismissed state perjury charges in an unrelated case involving perjury before the SEC, an undisputed federal agency, which violated the federal perjury statute, and which thus exclusively vested jurisdiction in federal court (*People v. D.H. Blair & Co.*, 2002 WL 766119, 2002 N.Y. Misc. LEXIS 317), factors against which the present case stands in contrast.

Spehler also argues, though, that the NASD acts as a federal tribunal in that it enforces federal securities laws, and that basic tenets of federalism require dismissal. The NASD has consistently been recognized by federal courts to be a private non-governmental entity (*see D.L. Cromwell Investments, Inc. v. NASD Regulation, Inc.*, 279 F.3d 155, 162 (and cites therein) [2d Cir.2002], cert. denied 537 U.S. 1028, 123 S.Ct. 580, 154 L.Ed.2d 442) which self-regulates among its constituent members, albeit subject to oversight by the SEC pursuant to the Maloney Act (15 USC § 78o–3, et seq.), in a cooperative arrangement (*see Jones v. Securities & Exchange Commission*, supra at 1182–1183 [4th Cir.1997], cert. denied 523 U.S. 1072, 118 S.Ct. 1512, 140 L.Ed.2d 666; *Austin Municipal Securities, Inc. v. NASD*, 757 F.2d 676–680 [5th Cir.1985]) so as to avoid governmental regulatory overreach. We agree with the trial court that just as there is no legal basis to construe the NASD to be a federal agency, there is no de facto basis to construe that the NASD enjoys some measure of federal sovereignty by virtue of SEC oversight and the NASD's necessary reference to federal laws. Hence, as the trial court put it, "[w]hile Congress certainly provided for comprehensive Federal regulation of the securities industry, and charged [self-regulatory organizations] with the duty of self-regulation, the fact that the NASD is subject to extensive oversight by the SEC, and ultimately Federal court review, does not metamorphose the NASD into an organ of the Federal government" (187 Misc.2d 117, 122, 718 N.Y.S.2d 147; *see also Perpetual Securities, Inc. v. Tang*, 290 F.3d 132, 137–138 [2d Cir.2002]).

Further, it has long been clear that the mere fact of intrusive governmental regulation that circumscribes a private entity's scope of operations does not by virtue of that regulation convert the private entity into a state actor (*Jackson v. Metropolitan Edison*, 419 U.S. 345, 95 S.Ct. 449, 42 L.Ed.2d 477 [intrusive regulation does not make a utility's private action, such as terminating a customer's service, state action]). Pursuant to the Maloney Act, Congress, without surrendering the SEC's regulatory and enforcement powers, nevertheless allowed the securities industry to regulate itself. This alternate, privatized, means of self-regulation was intended in part to relieve federal regulatory authorities from the burden of exclusively controlling the manner and methods of securities trading while still ensuring accommodation with the goals of the Securities Exchange Act. Yet self-regulating organizations such as the NASD are not mere alter egos of the SEC; the NASD need not exclusively reference the federal statute or the SEC regulations in its actions, but may also formulate ethical standards binding on constituent members that exceed federal law (Austin Municipal Securities, supra at 680; *Merrill Lynch v. NASD*, 616 F.2d 1363, 1367 [5th Cir.1980]; *Jones v. Securities & Exchange Commission, supra* at 1182; *see also* Norman S. Poser, "Reply to Lowenfels," 64 Cornell L. Rev. 402, 403 [1979]). In that sense, the NASD not only performs the salutary service of ensuring that members comply with the letter of federal law, but also pursues the self-interest of preventing fraudulent and manipulative practices so as to protect members, investors and the public interest (*United States v. NASD*, 422 U.S. 694, 700, n. 6, 95 S.Ct. 2427, 45 L.Ed.2d 486 [1975]; *Jones v. Securities & Exchange Commission, supra* at 1182).

* * *

Thus, we reject the claim that the NASD is the functional equivalent of a federal entity. Moreover, as also previously noted, the NASD interfaces with state securities regulators, too, thus acting with reference to state securities laws. Hence, this substantial NASD involvement with the several states, and in the present case with New York law, further undermines any characterization of the NASD as being the creature and expression of federal sovereignty.

Defendants' claim that state jurisdiction runs afoul of the principles of federalism is equally unavailing. It has long been recognized that, in order to sustain a claim that the state's jurisdiction has been preempted by federal law, the defendant must show a clear and unambiguous intent of Congress to do so: "There can be no presumption that state authority is excluded from the mere fact that congress has legislated" (*People v. Welch*, 141 N.Y. 266, 273, 36 N.E. 328). Thus, the existence of a federal perjury statute does not preclude a state prosecution for perjury involving the same act (*see People v. Materon*, 107 A.D.2d 408, 411, 487 N.Y.S.2d 334 [2d Dept.1985]). Indeed, *Loney* recognized that state and federal authorities, in many instances, have concurrent jurisdiction to prosecute the same act, and its ruling was limited to those instances where the oath was "authorized to be administered by the laws of the United States, and by those laws only" (134 U.S. at 374, 10 S.Ct. 584). Here as noted, the NASD simultaneously enforces both federal and state securities laws, and there is no inherent conflict between federal and state laws governing the securities industry. Thus, we can dispose of this novel theory of federalism as urged by defendants.

On appeal, though, defendants also advance an additional, nuanced, theory that New York is without power to enforce perjury committed before the NASD insofar as the NASD's power to enforce New York's broker registration requirements is conferred by the federal Maloney Act (15 USC § 78f, § 78k and § 78s). Returning again to *Loney*, defendants urge that it compels the conclusion that the jurisdictional issue is governed by the source of the authority pursuant to which the oath is administered rather than just the particular forum in which the oath is administered, so that even if we were to find that the NASD is not a federal entity, the NASD's power delegated under federal laws to require an oath creates exclusively federal jurisdiction pertaining to perjury committed in an NASD proceeding. Again, though, *Loney* is easily distinguishable, defendants' application of *Loney* to these facts is unduly elastic and the argument is ultimately sophistic. It must be recalled that whatever the ultimate authority allowing the NASD to take testimony under oath, the NASD does not serve exclusively federal interests, but also references state law, most notably enjoying delegated authority to enforce New York's broker registration requirements (13 NYCRR § 10.1, et seq.) and serves the interests of its constituent members. Thus, the power delegated to the NASD to enforce compliance with state securities regulations is substantive and not merely procedural. Indeed, in conducting the on-the-record hearings pursuant to NASD Rule 8210, the NASD was investigating Stanley Cohen's failure to register and his role at Renaissance in general (leading to charges of securities fraud in violation of New York's Martin Act).

* * *

Judgments, Supreme Court, New York County (Bernard Fried, J.), rendered February 5, 2002, and judgment, same court and Justice, rendered January 25, 2002, affirmed.

All concur.

---

2. The Limits of Federal Jurisdiction/Exclusive State Jurisdiction

United States v. Wang

United States Court of Appeals, Sixth Circuit
222 F.3d 234 (2000)

BATCHELDER, Circuit Judge.

Min Nan Wang appeals his convictions of robbery affecting interstate commerce in violation of 18 U.S.C. § 1951 and of using and carrying a firearm in relation to a crime of violence (robbery) in violation of 18 U.S.C. § 924(c)(1). For the reasons that follow, we reverse these convictions.

I

Paul and Patricia Tsai are the owners of the China Star Restaurant in Cookeville, Tennessee. The China Star purchases meat and seafood from out-of-state suppliers approximately twice per month. On September 11, 1995, Mrs. Tsai closed the restaurant at approximately 9:00 p.m. and drove to her home in Algood, Tennessee, followed by Mr. Tsai in a separate car. She took with her $1200 from the cash register, $900 of which she intended to deposit in the restaurant's bank account the next morning. Mrs. Tsai drove into the garage of her home and then entered the house, placing the money from the restaurant on the dining room floor. She then went to her bedroom, where, unbeknownst to her, Wang, who had broken into the house sometime earlier, was lurking. Wang grabbed Mrs. Tsai from behind and told her in Chinese to be quiet. When Mrs. Tsai resisted, Wang hit her on the head with a hard object, handcuffed her and put something over her face, telling her to shut up or he would kill her. He then pulled her into the bathroom, deposited her in the bathtub, and secured her to a railing on the wall next to the bathtub. Mrs. Tsai recognized Wang's voice because he had once worked as a cook in her restaurant.

As Mr. Tsai parked his car in the garage he heard his wife screaming. When he entered the house, Wang's accomplice attacked him from the side, hitting him in the head with a hard object. The accomplice took him to the bedroom closet, handcuffed him to the clothes rail and threatened to kill him unless Tsai told him where the money in the house was. The assailant showed him a gun, loaded it in front of him, and pointed it at his head.

By this time, Wang had placed tape on Mrs. Tsai's mouth. He told her repeatedly, "Your money or your life." Wang and his accomplice left their victims on several occasions to confer in a dialect that neither of the Tsais could understand. Each time Wang returned from meeting with his accomplice, he would demand money from Mrs. Tsai. Mrs. Tsai eventually told Wang about $3000 she had earlier withdrawn from her personal account and left in an envelope on her dining room table. Before the pair left the house, Wang's accomplice moved Mr. Tsai from the bedroom closet to the utility room. The robbers drove away in the Tsais' Toyota Corolla automobile.

Wang was later arrested in Chamblee, Georgia, pursuant to a Putnam County, Tennessee, warrant for especially aggravated robbery, especially aggravated kidnapping, and especially aggravated burglary. On August 21, 1996, a federal grand jury returned a four-count indictment charging Wang with robbery affecting interstate commerce in violation of 18 U.S.C. § 1951 (Count I); using and carrying a firearm in relation to a crime of violence in violation of 18 U.S.C. § 924(c)(1) (Count II); carjacking in violation of 18 U.S.C. § 2119 (Count III); and transporting a stolen motor vehicle in interstate commerce, in violation of 18 U.S.C. § 2312 (Count IV). Wang was also charged with aiding and abetting under 18 U.S.C. § 2 as to all four counts.

The case was tried without a jury. The district court granted Wang's motion for judgment of acquittal on Count III of the indictment and found Wang guilty of the remaining counts. The court sentenced Wang to twenty-four months on Counts I and IV, the robbery and the interstate transportation of stolen motor vehicle counts, followed by five years on Count II for the violation of 18 U.S.C. § 924(c). In handing down this sentence, the district court departed downward ten levels from a total offense level of 26, finding that Wang had been subjected to abuse and threats by individuals who had smuggled him into the United States, that he had been shabbily treated by the United States criminal justice system, and that his offense conduct was aberrational.

Wang timely appealed. He challenges only his convictions with respect to Counts I and II.

II

Wang first assails his conviction for robbery affecting interstate commerce in violation of 18 U.S.C. § 1951. That statute, the Hobbs Act, provides in relevant part:

> Whoever in any way or degree obstructs, delays, or affects commerce or the movement of any article or commodity in commerce, by robbery or extortion or attempts or conspires so to do, or commits or threatens physical violence to any person or property in furtherance of a plan or purpose to do anything in violation of this section shall be fined under this title or imprisoned not more than twenty years, or both.

18 U.S.C. § 1951(a). Wang maintains that, in light of *United States v. Lopez*, 514 U.S. 549, 115 S.Ct. 1624, 131 L.Ed.2d 626 (1995), insufficient evidence existed to support a finding that his robbery affected interstate commerce. The district court expressed a certain level of discomfort with its conclusions in this regard, noting:

> This Court finds that there is no effect on interstate commerce beyond an absolute de minimis effect of $1,200. There is no proof that Dr. and Mrs. Tsai closed the restaurant, that they were unable to order any further goods from out of state. There is no evidence of an [e]ffect upon interstate commerce.

Nevertheless, the court decided that precedent from this circuit compelled a finding of guilt with respect to Count I. We review the sufficiency of the evidence supporting Wang's conviction by determining "whether after reviewing the evidence in the light most favorable to the prosecution, any rational trier of fact could have found the essential elements of the crime beyond a reasonable doubt." *United States v. Brown*, 959 F.2d 63, 67 (6th Cir.1992) (quoting *Jackson v. Virginia*, 443 U.S. 307, 319, 99 S.Ct. 2781, 61 L.Ed.2d 560 (1979)).

Historically, we have erected a rather low threshold for determining whether robbery directed at a business establishment will give rise to federal criminal jurisdiction under § 1951. To support a conviction under the Hobbs Act, we have required the government to demonstrate nothing more than a de minimis effect on interstate commerce. *See United States v. Harding*, 563 F.2d 299, 302 (6th Cir.1977). "There is no requirement that there be an actual effect on interstate commerce—only a realistic probability that [an offense] will have an effect on interstate commerce." *United States v. Peete*, 919 F.2d 1168, 1174 (6th Cir.1990) (emphasis omitted). Thus, for example, we have upheld a Hobbs Act conviction where the defendant attempted to steal between $7,000 and $8,000 from a tavern that purchased goods from local distributors who in turn purchased goods from outside the state. *See Brown*, 959 F.2d at 65. Had the heist been successful, we noted, there was a "realistic probability that the depletion of the bar's assets would have affected the amount of its purchases of beer having moved through interstate commerce." *Id.* at 68.

The jurisprudential landscape has not much changed in the wake of *Lopez*, the landmark case that struck down the Gun–Free School Zones Act of 1990, 18 U.S.C. § 922(q), as an invalid exercise of Congress's power under the Commerce Clause. *See Lopez*, 514 U.S. at 551, 115 S.Ct. 1624. Facial constitutional challenges to the Hobbs Act followed close on the heels of *Lopez*. In turning away the first of these in *United States v. Valenzeno*, we remarked in dicta that "[i]f *Lopez* indicates that the Commerce Clause gives Congress less power than was previously thought to be the case, the proper remedy would be to give the statute a narrower interpretation, or to require a more substantial jurisdictional nexus, not to hold facially invalid an Act of Congress." *Valenzeno*, 123 F.3d 365, 368 (6th Cir.1997). Ultimately, however, "[w]e join[ed] our sister circuits and [held] that the de minimis standard for the interstate commerce effects of individual Hobbs Act violations survived *Lopez*." *United States v. Smith*, 182 F.3d 452, 456 (6th Cir.1999).

The *Lopez* Court had recognized that the commerce power includes regulation of activities that are connected with a commercial transaction which, viewed in the aggregate, substantially affects interstate commerce. *Lopez*, 514 U.S. at 561, 115 S.Ct. 1624. On this basis, we decided that *Lopez* did not require realignment of the Hobbs Act's jurisdictional nexus because individual instances arising under the statute could, through repetition, have a substantial effect on interstate commerce. *See Smith*, 182 F.3d at 456. So in *United States v. Smith*, we upheld the Hobbs Act conviction of a defendant who robbed various Michigan "party stores" of sums in the low four figures, saying, "By proving that the stores Smith robbed did substantial business in beer, wine, and tobacco products, and that virtually none of such products originate in Michigan, the government met its burden." *Id.*

Even as broadly phrased as our precedents are, however, they do not compel the result that the district court reluctantly reached in this case. As with "the overwhelming majority of cases involving the statute," *United States v. Quigley*, 53 F.3d 909, 910 (8th Cir.1995), our precedents have involved robberies in which the victims were businesses engaged in interstate commerce. But where, as here, the criminal act is directed at a private citizen, the connection to interstate commerce is much more attenuated. *See id.* ("Actions normally have a lesser effect on interstate commerce when directed at individuals rather than businesses."). This case presents our first opportunity to address the showing that the government must make to demonstrate that the robbery of an individual had a "realistic probability" of affecting interstate commerce. *Cf. United States v. Taylor*, 176 F.3d 331, 339 (6th Cir.1999) (rejecting a blanket constitutional challenge to the Hobbs Act as applied to robberies of private citizens, or burglaries of a private residences). We hold that the required showing is of a different order than in cases in which the victim is a business entity.

Those Courts of Appeals that have considered this question—even in the pre-*Lopez* era—have recognized that a robbery of a private citizen that causes only a speculative indirect effect on a business engaged in interstate commerce will not satisfy the jurisdictional requirement of the Hobbs Act. The Fifth Circuit, for example, refused to apply the Act to the robbery of an automobile and a cellular telephone from a computer company executive, even though the crime might have prevented the victim from attending business meetings or making business calls. *United States v. Collins*, 40 F.3d 95, 100 (5th Cir.1994) (holding that "[c]riminal acts directed toward individuals may violate section 1951(a) only if: (1) the acts deplete the assets of an individual who is directly and customarily engaged in interstate commerce; (2) if the acts cause or create the likelihood that the individual will deplete the assets of an entity engaged in interstate commerce; or (3) if the number of individuals victimized or the sum at stake is so large that there will be some 'cumulative effect on interstate commerce'" (footnotes omitted)). Another court held that a robbery of two individuals who were en route to a liquor store to make a purchase had no effect or realistic potential effect on interstate commerce. *Quigley*, 53 F.3d at 910–11 (following *Collins*). Similar concerns were voiced in cases involving extortion directed at private citizens. *See, e.g., United States v. Mattson*, 671 F.2d 1020, 1024–25 (7th Cir.1982) (holding that extortion directed against an individual does not affect interstate commerce where the payoff does not deplete the assets of an entity engaged in interstate commerce and no other connection with interstate commerce exists); *see also United States v. DeParias*, 805 F.2d 1447, 1451 (11th Cir.1986) (citing *Mattson* for this proposition), *overruled on other grounds by United States v. Kaplan*, 171 F.3d 1351, 1357 (11th Cir.1999).

The conclusions of our sister circuits are bolstered by *Lopez*. The Hobbs Act's de minimis standard survives *Lopez* by virtue of the aggregation principle. But the *Lopez* Court declined to apply the aggregation principle in conjunction with long chains of causal inference that would have been necessary to arrive at a substantial effect on interstate commerce. Thus, when the United States argued that gun possession in school zones would, in the aggregate, result in violent crime which would result in costs which would affect the national economy through the mechanism of insurance, the Court responded: "To uphold the Government's contentions here, we would have to pile inference upon inference in a manner that would bid fair to convert congressional authority under the Commerce Clause to a general police power of the sort retained by the States." *Lopez*, 514 U.S. at 567, 115 S.Ct. 1624; *see also A.L.A. Schecter Poultry Corp. v. United States*, 295 U.S. 495, 554, 55 S.Ct. 837, 79 L.Ed. 1570 (1935) (Cardozo, J., concurring) ("There is a view of causation that would obliterate the distinction between what is national and what is local in the activities of commerce. . . . Activities local in their immediacy do not become interstate and national because of distant repercussions."). Just this sort of "butterfly effect" theory of causation would be required to find liability in the great majority of Hobbs Act cases in which the victim is a private citizen.[1] See James Gleick, Chaos: Making a New Science 8 (1987) (discussing the parable of the flapping of a butterfly's wings that creates a minor air current in China, that adds to the accumulative effect in global wind systems, that ends with a hurricane in the Caribbean). Per *Lopez*, a small sum stolen from a private individual does not, through aggregation, affect interstate commerce merely because the individual happens to be an employee of a national company, or happens to be on his way to a store, or happens to be carrying proceeds from a restaurant.

This is not to say that criminal acts directed at private citizens will never create jurisdiction under the Hobbs Act. The federal courts have acknowledged, for example, that victimization of a large number of individuals, or victimization of a single individual for a very large sum, can have the potential directly to affect interstate commerce. *See, e.g., United States v. Farrell*, 877 F.2d 870, 875–76 (11th Cir.1989) (holding that extortion demand of $1,540,000 "would have affected interstate commerce to a legally cognizable degree"). But when the Government seeks to satisfy the Act's jurisdictional nexus by showing a connection between an individual victim and a business engaged in interstate commerce, that connection must be a substantial one—not one that is fortuitous or speculative. We have suggested that the Government might make such a showing by demonstrating that the defendant knew of or was motivated by the individual victim's connection to interstate commerce. *See United States v. Mills*, 204 F.3d 669, 670 (6th Cir.2000) (holding that solicitation of bribes from individuals gave rise to federal jurisdiction under the Hobbs Act because the defendants "had actual knowledge that the bribe money would be obtained through loans made in interstate commerce"). Other avenues of proof will no doubt present themselves. We would anticipate, however, that the "overwhelming majority" of Hobbs Act cases brought before the federal courts will continue to be ones in which the victims are businesses directly engaged in interstate commerce.

---

1   This might also be viewed as the "dog, dog bite pig" theory of causation. *See The Little Old Woman and Her Pig*, in The Tall Book of Nursery Tales 92 (1972). The little old woman had been stymied in her attempt to get home because her recalcitrant pig refused to cross a stile. So the old woman gave water to a haymaker for a wisp of hay to give to a cow for some milk to induce a cat to begin to kill a rat that began to gnaw a rope that began to hang a butcher who began to kill an ox who began to drink some water that began to quench a fire that began to burn a stick that began to beat the dog who began to bite the pig who jumped over the stile in a fright. Id. at 97. While this sequence of events got the little old woman home that night, such a causal chain will not suffice to put Mr. Wang in federal court.

In the present case, application of these principles dictates reversal of Wang's conviction with respect to Count I. Wang robbed private citizens in a private residence of approximately $4,200, a mere $1,200 of which belonged to a restaurant doing business in interstate commerce. The Government made no showing of a substantial connection between the robbery and the restaurant's business, and the district court held that "[t]here is no evidence of an [e]ffect on interstate commerce." In the absence of such a showing, there is no realistic probability that the aggregate of such crimes would substantially affect interstate commerce. Indeed, upholding federal jurisdiction over Wang's offense would, in essence, acknowledge a general federal police power with respect to the crimes of robbery and extortion. The Supreme Court, however, has this Term reminded us that:

> The Constitution requires a distinction between what is truly national and what is truly local. In recognizing this fact we preserve one of the few principles that has been consistent since the Clause was adopted. The regulation and punishment of intrastate violence that is not directed at the instrumentalities, channels, or goods involved in interstate commerce has always been the province of the States. Indeed, we can think of no better example of the police power, which the Founders denied the National Government and reposed in the States, than the suppression of violent crime and vindication of its victims.

United States v. Morrison, 529 U.S. 598, ––––, 120 S.Ct. 1740, 1754, 146 L.Ed.2d 658 (2000) (citations omitted). Due regard for this admonition requires that Wang's case be heard in state court. We therefore reverse his Hobbs Act conviction.

III

Wang next challenges his conviction for using a firearm in relation to a crime of violence in violation of 18 U.S.C. § 924(c)(1). The district court held Wang liable for his accomplice's possession of a gun during the robbery under the doctrine of *Pinkerton v. United States*, 328 U.S. 640, 66 S.Ct. 1180, 90 L.Ed. 1489 (1946), and, in the alternative, under an aiding and abetting theory. Wang maintains that a *Pinkerton* theory is inapplicable because he was not charged with conspiracy, and that the government did not prove (as it must on an aiding and abetting theory) that he knew "to a practical certainty" that his accomplice was carrying a gun. *See United States v. Morrow*, 977 F.2d 222, 231 (6th Cir.1992) (en banc).

We need not resolve these thorny questions. Section 924(c)(1) provides for a term of imprisonment for "any person who, during and in relation to any crime of violence . . . for which the person may be prosecuted in a court of the United States, uses or carries a firearm . . . ." (emphasis supplied). This circuit has held that this language requires that "the defendant have committed a violent crime for which he may be prosecuted in federal court." *Smith*, 182 F.3d at 457 (emphasis omitted). And in *Smith*, we cited with approval the holding of the Fifth Circuit in Collins that a § 924(c) conviction cannot stand when the trial court had no jurisdiction over the predicate crime. *See Collins*, 40 F.3d at 101 ("Section 924(c)(1) requires that the underlying offense be a federal crime and, as the robbery [ ] conviction for violation of section 1951(a) is now voided, the conviction for unlawful use of a firearm during that robbery also must be reversed."). Because Wang's robbery did not have even a de minimis effect on interstate commerce, the crime could not properly have been prosecuted in federal court. Accordingly, Wang's § 924(c) conviction must also be reversed.

DENISE PAGE HOOD, District Judge, concurring. [omitted]

Notes and Questions

1. If the defendant had stolen a case of beer from a 7-11 by force would the court have upheld the conviction under the Hobbs Act?

2. Can a state prosecute a person for counterfeiting U.S. Currency? Passing counterfeit U.S. currency? *See Fox v. Ohio*, 46 U.S. 410 (1847). Robbing a federally insured bank at gunpoint?

3. In *Arizona v. United States*, 132 S. Ct. 2492 (2012), the Court held that Arizona's laws criminalizing various actions by unauthorized migrants, including working or seeking work, or failing to carry immigration documents, were preempted because they were within the exclusive authority of Congress. The Court so held even though some of this conduct had been criminalized by Congress. The Ninth Circuit recently invalidated another Arizona law making it a crime to transport unauthorized migrants. *Valle Del Sol Incorporated v. Whiting*, 732 F.3d 1006 (9th Cir. 2013). The laws which were invalidated were part of SB1070, an Arizona statute designed to drive out unauthorized migrants. *See generally* Gabriel J. Chin & Marc L. Miller, *The Unconstitutionality of State Regulation of Immigration Through Criminal Law*, 61 Duke L.J. 251 (2011); Gabriel J. Chin, Carissa Byrne Hessick, Toni M. Massaro & Marc L. Miller, *A Legal Labyrinth: Issues Raised by Arizona Senate Bill 1070*, 25 Geo. Immigr. L. J. 47 (2010).

C

PRACTICE EXERCISE

Alexis is a citizen of Oregon. Bancroft is a non-Native American citizen of Idaho who lives on the Nez Perce Indian Reservation in Idaho. Both are avid motorcycle riders. They met three years ago at the "Northern Lights" ride in Alaska, where they became good friends. Alexis maintains citizenship in Oregon, and has moved to Washington, where she operates a prosperous credit union, which issues debit cards to its biker-based clientele, who often "swipe" them as "credit." Bancroft lost his job in Moscow, Idaho.

Bancroft phoned Alexis to discuss his troubles, and she recommended he join her friend Clyde's Alaskan shipping vessel for the summer. Bancroft gratefully consented, inwardly wondering how he was going to support himself until fishing season. When Alexis' friend Captain Clyde asked Bancroft if Bancroft had a criminal past, Bancroft lied and told him he had none. Clyde accepted Bancroft as a crewman. Then, Bancroft convinced Alexis to "lend" him $1500 from the credit union to keep him afloat. Alexis stole the funds from the credit union's overhead using some fishy bookkeeping.

Before hopping on his motorcycle for the long ride to Alaska, Bancroft stole his roommate's credit union debit card to fund his trip to Alaska. He stopped at the Bad-to-the-Bone Biker Bar in in Moscow, maxed out the debit card (as credit), and made it through Washington using only his "borrowed" cash. While riding the Seattle ferry across the water to Victoria, Canada, he tossed the debit card into the Puget Sound to conceal any trace of the debit card. The ferry captain saw Bancroft discard the card, and yelled at him, "That will cost you!"

Bancroft hurried off the ferry in Victoria, Canada, fired up his motorcycle, and sped off toward Alaska. Because he was scared of being detained and missing the start of the salmon season, Bancroft rushed off the boat and accidentally hit a pedestrian at the intersection near the ferry drop-off, but failed to stop. Finally, he reached port in Homer, Alaska, using only his cash reserves. Alas, the captain of the ferry reported Bancroft to Canadian officials, who caught him at season's end, on his return en route to Washington.

Each of the following jurisdictions has filed a criminal indictment against Bancroft for any illegal actions before and during his trip: Alaska, Idaho, Oregon, Washington, and the United States. Each of these jurisdictions then filed an indictment against Alexis.

Both Alexis and Bancroft have hired you. Try to dismiss the indictment for lack of jurisdiction. For each jurisdiction: (1) list the type of jurisdictional issue based on the cases read; (2) the law based on the cases read; and (3) the facts which support your position.

Consider: is there a good argument, according to the U.S. Attorney's Manual in Chapter 1, that neither Alexis nor Bancroft should be prosecuted for all their crimes in all jurisdictions? Also, is there a double jeopardy bar?

CHAPTER THREE

Constitutional Limitations on Criminalization and Conviction

THE U.S. CONSTITUTION, applicable to all state and federal prosecutions, limits legislative power to convict. State constitutions also impose limits, sometimes going beyond the restrictions imposed by federal law. This chapter deals with two broad categories of constitutional restrictions. The first goes to requirements for criminalization; what kind of law (if any) must be on the books before it can be the basis for prosecution and conviction? This problem is addressed by the *ex post facto* clause, and the due process restriction on conviction based on unforeseeable judicial interpretation. Other constitutional provisions, such as, for example, the First and Second Amendments, also limit the power of the states and the United States to criminalize conduct; it is unconstitutional, for example, for the government to convict someone for a crime that consisted of speech or religious exercise protected by the First Amendment.

Another set of state and federal constitutional restrictions regulates the nature and quality of evidence which is necessary for conviction. This includes the requirements of proof beyond a reasonable doubt, and the limits on legislative substitutes for evidence, such as evidentiary presumptions.

A. *Ex Post Facto*

1. Introduction

In general, prosecution and conviction require a preexisting law covering the conduct at issue. MPC § 2.04(3)(a). However, rules of evidence and other aspects of the law sometimes change. There is no constitutional problem with applying new rules to conduct occurring after enactment. The *ex post facto* clauses of the U.S. Constitution, and their state constitutional and statutory analogues, sometimes restrict their applicability to conduct which took place before the law was passed.

Carmell v. Texas

Supreme Court of the United States
529 U.S. 513 (2000)

Justice STEVENS delivered the opinion of the Court.

An amendment to a Texas statute that went into effect on September 1, 1993, authorized conviction of certain sexual offenses on the victim's testimony alone. The previous statute required the victim's testimony plus other corroborating evidence to convict the offender. The question presented is whether that amendment may be applied in a trial for offenses committed before the amendment's effective date without violating the constitutional prohibition against state "*ex post facto*" laws.

I

In 1996, a Texas grand jury returned a 15–count indictment charging petitioner with various sexual offenses against his stepdaughter. The alleged conduct took place over more than four years, from February 1991 to March 1995, when the victim was 12 to 16 years old. The conduct ceased after the victim told her mother what had happened. Petitioner was convicted on all 15 counts. The two most serious counts charged him with aggravated sexual assault, and petitioner was sentenced to life imprisonment on those two counts. For each of the other 13 offenses (5 counts of sexual assault and 8 counts of indecency with a child), petitioner received concurrent sentences of 20 years.

Until September 1, 1993, the following statute was in effect in Texas:

"A conviction under Chapter 21, Section 22.011, or Section 22.021, Penal Code, is supportable on the uncorroborated testimony of the victim of the sexual offense if the victim informed any person, other than the defendant, of the alleged offense within six months after the date on which the offense is alleged to have occurred. The requirement that the victim inform another person of an alleged offense does not apply if the victim was younger than 14 years of age at the time of the alleged offense." Tex. Code Crim. Proc. Ann., Art. 38.07 (Vernon 1983).

We emphasize three features of this law that are critical to petitioner's case.

The first is the so-called "outcry or corroboration" requirement. Under that provision, a victim's testimony can support a conviction for the specified offenses only if (1) that testimony is corroborated by other evidence, or (2) the victim informed another person of the offense within six months of its occurrence (an "outcry"). The second feature is the "child victim" provision, which is an exception to the outcry or corroboration requirement. According to this provision, if the victim was under 14 years old at the time of the alleged offense, the outcry or corroboration requirement does not apply and the victim's testimony alone can support a conviction—even without any corroborating evidence or outcry. The third feature is that Article 38.07 establishes a sufficiency of the evidence rule respecting the minimum quantum of evidence necessary to sustain a conviction. If the statute's requirements are not met (for example, by introducing only the uncorroborated testimony of a 15-year-old victim who did not make a timely outcry), a defendant cannot be convicted, and the court must enter a judgment of acquittal. See *Leday v. State*, 983 S.W.2d 713, 725 (Tex.Crim.App.1998); *Scoggan v. State*, 799 S.W.2d 679, 683 (Tex.Crim.App.1990). Conversely, if the requirements are satisfied, a conviction, in the words of the statute, "is supportable," and the case may be submitted to the jury and a conviction sustained. See *Vickery v. State*, 566 S.W.2d 624, 626–627 (Tex.Crim.App.1978); *see also Burnham v. State*, 821 S.W.2d 1, 3 (Tex.App.1991).

Texas amended Article 38.07, effective September 1, 1993. The amendment extended the child victim exception to victims under 18 years old.[3] For four of petitioner's counts, that amendment was critical. The "outcry or corroboration" requirement was not satisfied for those convictions; they rested solely on the victim's testimony. Accordingly, the verdicts on those four counts stand or fall depending on whether the child victim exception applies. Under the old law, the exception would *not* apply, because the victim was more than 14 years old at

---

3 The new statute read in full:

"A conviction under Chapter 21, Section 22.011, or Section 22.021, Penal Code, is supportable on the uncorroborated testimony of the victim of the sexual offense if the victim informed any person, other than the defendant, of the alleged offense within one year after the date on which the offense is alleged to have occurred. The requirement that the victim inform another person of an alleged offense does not apply if the victim was younger than 18 years of age at the time of the alleged offense." Tex.Code Crim. Proc. Ann., Art. 38.07, as amended by Act of May 29, 1993, 73d Leg., Reg. Sess., ch. 900, § 12.01, 1993 Tex. Gen. Laws 3765, 3766, and Act of May 10, 1993, 73d Leg., Reg. Sess., ch. 200, § 1, 1993 Tex. Gen. Laws 387, 388.

the time of the alleged offenses. Under the new law, the exception would apply, because the victim was under 18 years old at that time. In short, the validity of four of petitioner's convictions depends on whether the old or new law applies to his case, which, in turn, depends on whether the *Ex Post Facto* Clause prohibits the application of the new version of Article 38.07 to his case.

As mentioned, only 4 of petitioner's 15 total convictions are implicated by the amendment to Article 38.07; the other 11 counts—including the 2 convictions for which petitioner received life sentences—are uncontested. Six counts are uncontested because they were committed when the victim was under 14 years old, so his convictions stand even under the old law; the other five uncontested counts were committed after the new Texas law went into effect, so there could be no *ex post facto* claim as to those convictions. See *Weaver v. Graham*, 450 U.S. 24, 31, 101 S.Ct. 960, 67 L.Ed.2d 17 (1981) ("The critical question [for an *ex post facto* violation] is whether the law changes the legal consequences of acts completed before its effective date"). What are at stake, then, are the four convictions on counts 7 through 10 for offenses committed between June 1992 and July 1993 when the victim was 14 or 15 years old and the new Texas law was not in effect.

Petitioner appealed his four convictions to the Court of Appeals for the Second District of Texas in Fort Worth. See 963 S.W.2d 833 (1998). Petitioner argued that under the pre–1993 version of Article 38.07, which was the law in effect at the time of his alleged conduct, those convictions could not stand, because they were based *solely* on the victim's testimony, and the victim was not under 14 years old at the time of the offenses, nor had she made a timely outcry.

The Court of Appeals rejected petitioner's argument. Under the 1993 amendment to Article 38.07, the court observed, petitioner could be convicted on the victim's testimony alone because she was under 18 years old at the time of the offenses. The court held that applying this amendment retrospectively to petitioner's case did not violate the *Ex Post Facto* Clause:

> "The statute as amended does not increase the punishment nor change the elements of the offense that the State must prove. It merely 'removes existing restrictions upon the competency of certain classes of persons as witnesses' and is, thus, a rule of procedure. *Hopt v. Utah*, 110 U.S. 574, 590, 4 S.Ct. 202, 28 L.Ed. 262 (1884)." *Id.*, at 836.

The Texas Court of Criminal Appeals denied discretionary review. Because the question whether the retrospective application of a statute repealing a corroboration requirement has given rise to conflicting decisions, we granted petitioner's *pro se* petition for certiorari, 527 U.S. 1002, 119 S.Ct. 2336, 144 L.Ed.2d 234 (1999), and appointed counsel, *id.*, at 1051.

II

To prohibit legislative Acts "contrary to the first principles of the social compact and to every principle of sound legislation,"[6] the Framers included provisions they considered to be "perhaps greater securities to liberty and republicanism than any [the Constitution] contains."[7] The provisions declare:

> "No State shall . . . pass any Bill of Attainder, *ex post facto* Law, or Law impairing the Obligation of Contracts . . . ." U.S. Const., Art. I, § 10.[48]

The proscription against *ex post facto* laws "necessarily requires some explanation; for, naked and without explanation, it is unintelligible, and means nothing." *Calder v. Bull*, 3 Dall. 386, 390, 1 L.Ed. 648 (1798) (Chase, J.). In *Calder v. Bull*, Justice Chase stated that the necessary explanation is derived from English common law well known to the Framers: "The expressions 'ex post facto laws,' are technical, they had been in use long before the Revolution, and had acquired an appropriate meaning, by Legislators, Lawyers, and Authors." *Id.*, at 391; *see also id.*, at 389 ("The prohibition . . . very probably arose from the knowledge, that the Parliament of Great Britain claimed and exercised a power to pass such laws . . ."); *id.*, at 396 (Paterson, J.). Specifically, the phrase "*ex post facto*" referred only to certain types of criminal laws. Justice Chase cataloged those types as follows:

> "I will state what laws I consider *ex post facto* laws, within the words and the intent of the prohibition. 1st. Every law that makes an action done before the passing of the law, and which was innocent when done, criminal; and punishes such action. 2d. Every law that aggravates a crime, or makes it greater than it was, when committed. 3d. Every law that changes the punishment, and inflicts a greater punishment, than the law annexed to the crime, when committed. 4th. Every law that alters the legal rules of evidence, and receives less, or different, testimony, than the law required at the time of the commission of the offence, in order to convict the offender." *Id.*, at 390 (emphasis in original).[9]

---

6   The Federalist No. 44, p. 282 (C. Rossiter ed. 1961) (J. Madison).

7   *Id.*, No. 84, at 511 (A.Hamilton).

8   Article I, § 9, cl. 3, has a similar prohibition applicable to Congress: "No Bill of Attainder or *ex post facto* Law shall be passed."

9   Elsewhere in his opinion, Justice Chase described his taxonomy of *ex post facto* laws as follows:

> "Sometimes [*ex post facto* laws] respected the crime, by declaring acts to be treason, which were not treason, when committed; at other times, they violated the rules of evidence (to supply a deficiency of legal proof) by admitting one witness, when the existing law required two; by receiving evidence without oath; or the oath of the wife against the husband; or other testimony, which the courts of justice would not admit; at other times they inflicted punishments, where the party was not, by law, liable to any punishment; and in

It is the fourth category that is at issue in petitioner's case.

The common-law understanding explained by Justice Chase drew heavily upon the authoritative exposition of one of the great scholars of the common law, Richard Wooddeson. See *id.*, at 391 (noting reliance on Wooddeson's treatise). Wooddeson's classification divided *ex post facto* laws into three general categories: those respecting the crimes themselves; those respecting the legal rules of evidence; and those affecting punishment (which he further subdivided into laws creating a punishment and those making an existing punishment more severe). See 2 R. Wooddeson, A Systematical View of the Laws of England 625–640 (1792) (Lecture 41) (hereinafter Wooddeson). Those three categories (the last of which was further subdivided) correlate precisely to *Calder*'s four categories. Justice Chase also used language in describing the categories that corresponds directly to Wooddeson's phrasing. Finally, in four footnotes in Justice Chase's opinion, he listed examples of various Acts of Parliament illustrating each of the four categories. See 3 Dall., at 389, 1 L.Ed. 648, nn. *, †, ‡, t. Each of these examples is exactly the same as the ones Wooddeson himself used in his treatise. See 2 Wooddeson 629 (case of the Earl of Strafford); *id.*, at 634 (case of Sir John Fenwick); *id.*, at 638 (banishments of Lord Clarendon and of Bishop Atterbury); *id.*, at 639 (Coventry Act).

Calder's four categories, which embraced Wooddeson's formulation, were, in turn, soon embraced by contemporary scholars. Joseph Story, for example, in writing on the *Ex post facto* Clause, stated:

> "The general interpretation has been, and is, . . . that the prohibition reaches every law, whereby an act is declared a crime, and made punishable as such, when it was not a crime, when done; or whereby the act, if a crime, is aggravated in enormity, or punishment; or whereby different, or less evidence, is required to convict an offender, than was required, when the act was committed." 3 Commentaries on the Constitution of the United States § 1339, p. 212 (1833).

James Kent concurred in this understanding of the Clause:

> "[T]he words *ex post facto* laws were technical expressions, and meant every law that made an act done before the passing of the law, and which was innocent when done, criminal; or which aggravated a crime, and made it greater than it was when committed; or which changed the punishment, and inflicted a greater punishment than the law annexed to the crime when committed; or which altered the legal rules of evidence, and received

---

other cases, they inflicted greater punishment, than the law annexed to the offence." 3 Dall., at 389 (emphasis deleted).

less or different testimony than the law required at the time of the commission of the offence, in order to convict the offender." 1 Commentaries on American Law 408 (3d ed. 1836) (Lecture 19).

This Court, moreover, has repeatedly endorsed this understanding, including, in particular, the fourth category (sometimes quoting Chase's words verbatim, sometimes simply paraphrasing). See Lynce v. Mathis, 519 U.S. 433, 441, n. 13, 117 S.Ct. 891, 137 L.Ed.2d 63 (1997); * * *

III

As mentioned earlier, Justice Chase and Wooddeson both cited several examples of *ex post facto* laws, and, in particular, cited the case of Sir John Fenwick as an example of the fourth category. To better understand the type of law that falls within that category, then, we turn to Fenwick's case for preliminary guidance.

Those who remained loyal to James II after he was deposed by King William III in the Revolution of 1688 thought their opportunity for restoration had arrived in 1695, following the death of Queen Mary. 9 T. Macaulay, History of England 31 (1899) (hereinafter Macaulay). Sir John Fenwick, along with other Jacobite plotters including George Porter and Cardell Goodman, began concocting their scheme in the spring of that year, and over the next several months the original circle of conspirators expanded in number. *Id.*, at 32, 47–48, 109–110. Before the conspirators could carry out their machinations, however, three members of the group disclosed the plot to William. *Id.*, at 122–125. One by one, the participants were arrested, tried, and convicted of treason. *Id.*, at 127–142. Fenwick, though, remained in hiding while the rest of the cabal was brought to justice. During that time, the trials of his accomplices revealed that there were only two witnesses among them who could prove Fenwick's guilt, Porter and Goodman. *Id.*, at 170–171. As luck would have it, an act of Parliament proclaimed that two witnesses were necessary to convict a person of high treason. See An Act for Regulateing of Tryals in Cases of Treason and Misprision of Treason, 7 & 8 Will. III, ch. 3, § 2 (1695– 696), in 7 Statutes of the Realm 6 (reprint 1963). Thus, Fenwick knew that if he could induce either Porter or Goodman to abscond, the case against him would vanish. 9 Macaulay 171.

Fenwick first tried his hand with Porter. Fenwick sent his agent to attempt a bribe, which Porter initially accepted in exchange for leaving for France. But then Porter simply pocketed the bribe, turned in Fenwick's agent (who was promptly tried, convicted, and pilloried), and proceeded to testify against Fenwick (along with Goodman) before a grand jury. *Id.*, at 171–173. When the grand jury returned an indictment for high treason, Fenwick attempted to flee the country himself, but was apprehended and brought before the Lord Justices in London. Sensing an impending conviction, Fenwick threw himself on the mercy of the court and offered to disclose all he knew of the Jacobite plotting, aware all the while that the judges would soon leave the city for their circuits, and a delay would thus buy him a few weeks time. *Id.*, at 173–174.

Fenwick was granted time to write up his confession, but rather than betray true Jacobites, he concocted a confession calculated to accuse those loyal to William, hoping to introduce embarrassment and perhaps a measure of instability to the current regime. *Id.*, at 175–178. William, however, at once perceived Fenwick's design and rejected the confession, along with any expectation of mercy. *Id.*, at 178–180, 194. Though his contrived ploy for leniency was unsuccessful in that respect, it proved successful in another: during the delay, Fenwick's wife had succeeded in bribing Goodman, the other witness against him, to leave the country. *Id.*, at 194–195.

Without a second witness, Fenwick could not be convicted of high treason under the statute mentioned earlier. For all his plotting, however, Fenwick was not to escape. After Goodman's absence was discovered, the House of Commons met and introduced a bill of attainder against Fenwick to correct the situation produced by the combination of bribery and the two-witness law. *Id.*, at 198–199. A lengthy debate ensued, during which the Members repeatedly discussed whether the two-witness rule should apply. Ultimately, the bill passed by a close vote of 189 to 156, *id.*, at 210, notwithstanding the objections of Members who (foreshadowing *Calder*'s fourth category) complained that Fenwick was being attainted "upon less Evidence" than would be required under the two-witness law, and despite the repeated importuning against the passing of an *ex post facto* law. The bill then was taken up and passed by the House of Lords, and the King gave his assent. *Id.*, at 214–225; *see also An Act to Attaint Sir John Fenwick Baronet of High Treason*, 8 Will. III, ch. 4 (1696). On January 28, 1697, Sir John Fenwick was beheaded. 9 Macaulay 226–227.

IV

Article 38.07 is unquestionably a law "that alters the legal rules of evidence, and receives less, or different, testimony, than the law required at the time of the commission of the offence, in order to convict the offender." Under the law in effect at the time the acts were committed, the prosecution's case was legally insufficient and petitioner was entitled to a judgment of acquittal, unless the State could produce both the victim's testimony and corroborative evidence. The amended law, however, changed the quantum of evidence necessary to sustain a conviction; under the new law, petitioner could be (and was) convicted on the victim's testimony alone, without any corroborating evidence. Under any commonsense understanding of *Calder*'s fourth category, Article 38.07 plainly fits. Requiring only the victim's testimony to convict, rather than the victim's testimony plus other corroborating evidence is surely "less testimony required to convict" in any straightforward sense of those words.

Indeed, the circumstances of petitioner's case parallel those of Fenwick's case 300 years earlier. Just as the relevant law in Fenwick's case required more than one witness' testimony to support a conviction (namely, the testimony of a second witness), Texas' old version of Article 38.07 required more than the victim's testimony alone to sustain a conviction (namely, other corroborating evidence).[20] And just like Fenwick's bill of attainder, which permitted the House of Commons to convict him with less evidence than was otherwise required, Texas' retrospective application of the amendment to Article 38.07 permitted petitioner to be convicted with less than the previously required quantum of evidence. It is true, of course, as the Texas Court of Appeals observed, that "[t]he statute as amended does not increase the punishment nor change the elements of the offense that the State must prove." 963 S.W.2d, at 836. But that observation simply demonstrates that the amendment does not fit within *Calder*'s first and third categories. Likewise, the dissent's remark that "Article 38.07 does not establish an element of the offense," post, at 1646, only reveals that the law does not come within *Calder*'s first category. The fact that the amendment authorizes a conviction on less evidence than previously required, however, brings it squarely within the fourth category.

V

The fourth category, so understood, resonates harmoniously with one of the principal interests that the *Ex post facto* Clause was designed to serve, fundamental justice.

Justice Chase viewed all *ex post facto* laws as "manifestly unjust and oppressive." *Calder*, 3 Dall., at 391. Likewise, Blackstone condemned them as "cruel and unjust," 1 Commentaries on the Laws of England 46 (1765), as did every state constitution with a similar clause, see n. 25, infra. As Justice Washington explained in characterizing "[t]he injustice and tyranny" of *ex post facto* laws:

> "Why did the authors of the constitution turn their attention to this subject, which, at the first blush, would appear to be peculiarly fit to be left to the discretion of those who have the police and good government of the

---

20   Texas argues that the corroborative evidence required by Article 38.07 "need not be more or different from the victim's testimony; it may be entirely cumulative of the victim's testimony." Brief for Respondent 19; *see also* post, at 1647, n. 6 (dissenting opinion). The trouble with that argument is that the same was true in Fenwick's case. The relevant statute there required the "Testimony of Two lawfull Witnesses either both of them to the same Overt act or one of them to one and another of them to another Overt act of the same Treason." See n. 15, *supra* (emphasis added).

State under their management and control? The only answer to be given is, because laws of this character are oppressive, unjust, and tyrannical; and, as such, are condemned by the universal sentence of civilized man." *Ogden v. Saunders*, 12 Wheat. 213, 266, 6 L.Ed. 606 (1827).

In short, the *Ex post facto* Clause was designed as "an additional bulwark in favour of the personal security of the subject," *Calder*, 3 Dall., at 390 (Chase, J.), to protect against "the favorite and most formidable instruments of tyranny," The Federalist No. 84, p. 512 (C. Rossiter ed. 1961) (A. Hamilton), that were "often used to effect the most detestable purposes," *Calder*, 3 Dall., at 396 (Paterson, J.).

Calder's fourth category addresses this concern precisely. A law reducing the quantum of evidence required to convict an offender is as grossly unfair as, say, retrospectively eliminating an element of the offense, increasing the punishment for an existing offense, or lowering the burden of proof (see infra, at 1636–1639). In each of these instances, the government subverts the presumption of innocence by reducing the number of elements it must prove to overcome that presumption; by threatening such severe punishment so as to induce a plea to a lesser offense or a lower sentence; or by making it easier to meet the threshold for overcoming the presumption. Reducing the quantum of evidence necessary to meet the burden of proof is simply another way of achieving the same end. All of these legislative changes, in a sense, are mirror images of one another. In each instance, the government refuses, after the fact, to play by its own rules, altering them in a way that is advantageous only to the State, to facilitate an easier conviction. There is plainly a fundamental fairness interest, even apart from any claim of reliance or notice, in having the government abide by the rules of law it establishes to govern the circumstances under which it can deprive a person of his or her liberty or life.[23]

Indeed, Fenwick's case is itself an illustration of this principle. Fenwick could claim no credible reliance interest in the two-witness statute, as he could not possibly have known that only two of his fellow conspirators would be able to testify as to his guilt, nor that he would be successful in bribing one of them to leave the country. Nevertheless, Parliament had enacted the two-witness law,

---

23 We do not mean to say that every rule that has an effect on whether a defendant can be convicted implicates the *Ex post facto* Clause. Ordinary rules of evidence, for example, do not violate the Clause. See infra, at 1638–1640. Rules of that nature are ordinarily evenhanded, in the sense that they may benefit either the State or the defendant in any given case. More crucially, such rules, by simply permitting evidence to be admitted at trial, do not at all subvert the presumption of innocence, because they do not concern whether the admissible evidence is sufficient to overcome the presumption. Therefore, to the extent one may consider changes to such laws as "unfair" or "unjust," they do not implicate the same kind of unfairness implicated by changes in rules setting forth a sufficiency of the evidence standard. Moreover, while the principle of unfairness helps explain and shape the Clause's scope, it is not a doctrine unto itself, invalidating laws under the *Ex post facto* Clause by its own force. Cf. W.S. *Kirkpatrick & Co. v. Environmental Tectonics Corp., Int'l*, 493 U.S. 400, 409, 110 S.Ct. 701, 107 L.Ed.2d 816 (1990).

and there was a profound unfairness in Parliament's retrospectively altering the very rules it had established, simply because those rules prevented the conviction of the traitor—notwithstanding the fact that Fenwick could not truly claim to be "innocent." (At least one historian has concluded that his guilt was clearly established, see 9 Macaulay 203–204, and the debate in the House of Commons bears out that conclusion, see, e.g., Proceedings 219, 230, 246, 265, 289.) Moreover, the pertinent rule altered in Fenwick's case went directly to the general issue of guilt, lowering the minimum quantum of evidence required to obtain a conviction. The Framers, quite clearly, viewed such maneuvers as grossly unfair, and adopted the *Ex Post Facto* Clause accordingly.[24]

VI

The United States as amicus asks us to revisit the accuracy of the fourth category as an original matter. None of its reasons for abandoning the category is persuasive.

* * *

VIII

Texas argues (following the holding of the Texas Court of Appeals) that the present case is controlled by *Hopt v. Territory of Utah*, 110 U.S. 574, 4 S.Ct. 202, 28 L.Ed. 262 (1884), and *Thompson v. Missouri*, 171 U.S. 380, 18 S.Ct. 922, 43 L.Ed. 204 (1898). In *Hopt*, the defendant was convicted of murder. At trial, the prosecution introduced the testimony of a convicted felon that tended to inculpate the defendant. *Hopt* objected to the competency of the witness on the basis of a law in place at the time of the alleged murder, which stated: "'[T]he rules for determining the competency of witnesses in civil actions are applicable also to criminal actions . . . .'" The relevant civil rules, in turn, specified that "'all persons, without exception, . . . may be witnesses in any action or proceeding,'" but "'persons against whom judgment has been rendered upon a conviction for felony . . . shall not be witnesses.'" 110 U.S., at 587–588, 4 S.Ct. 202. After the date

---

24 Fenwick's case also illustrates how such *ex post facto* laws can operate similarly to retrospective increases in punishment by adding to the coercive pressure to accept a plea bargain. When Fenwick was first brought before the Lord Justices, he was given an opportunity to make a confession to the King. Though he squandered the opportunity by authoring a plain contrivance, Fenwick could have reasonably assumed that a sincere confession would have been rewarded with leniency—the functional equivalent of a plea bargain. See 9 Macaulay 125. When the bill of attainder was taken up by the House of Commons, there is evidence that this was done to pressure Fenwick into making the honest confession he had failed to make before. See, *e.g.*, Proceedings 197 ("'Tis a Matter of Blood, 'tis true, but I do not aim at this Gentleman's Life in it . . . all I Propose by it, is to get his Confession"); *id.*, at 235 ("[W]e do not aim at Sir *John Fenwick's* Blood, (God forbid we should) but at his Confession"); *id.*, at 255 ("Why, give me leave to say to you, 'tis a new way not known in *England*, that you will Hang a Man unless he will Confess or give Evidence . . ."). And before the House of Lords, Fenwick was explicitly threatened that unless he confessed, they would proceed to consider the bill against him. 9 Macaulay 218.

of the alleged offense, but prior to defendant's trial, the last provision (excluding convicted felons from being witnesses) was repealed.

The defendant argued that the retrospective application of the felon witness-competency provision violated the *Ex post facto* Clause. Because of the emphasis the parties (and the dissent) have placed on *Hopt*, it is worth quoting at length this Court's explanation for why it rejected the defendant's argument:

> "Statutes which simply enlarge the class of persons who may be competent to testify in criminal cases are not *ex post facto* in their application to prosecutions for crimes committed prior to their passage; for they do not attach criminality to any act previously done, and which was innocent when done; nor aggravate any crime theretofore committed; nor provide a greater punishment therefor than was prescribed at the time of its commission; nor do they alter the degree, or lessen the amount or measure, of the proof which was made necessary to conviction when the crime was committed.
>
> "The crime for which the present defendant was indicted, the punishment prescribed therefor, and the quantity or the degree of proof necessary to establish his guilt, all remained unaffected by the subsequent statute. Any statutory alteration of the legal rules of evidence which would authorize conviction upon less proof, in amount or degree, than was required when the offence was committed, might, in respect of that offence, be obnoxious to the constitutional inhibition upon *ex post facto* laws. But alterations which do not increase the punishment, nor change the ingredients of the offence or the ultimate facts necessary to establish guilt, but—leaving untouched the nature of the crime and the amount or degree of proof essential to conviction—only remove existing restrictions upon the competency of certain classes of persons as witnesses, relate to modes of procedure only, in which no one can be said to have a vested right, and which the State, upon grounds of public policy, may regulate at pleasure. Such regulations of the mode in which the facts constituting guilt may be placed before the jury, can be made applicable to prosecutions or trials thereafter had, without reference to the date of the commission of the offence charged."

Id., at 589–590, 4 S.Ct. 202 (emphases added).

Thompson v. Missouri, also relied upon by Texas, involved a similar *ex post facto* challenge to the retrospective application of a law permitting the introduction of expert handwriting testimony as competent evidence, where the rule in place at the time of the offense did not permit such evidence to be introduced. Mainly on the authority of *Hopt*, the Court rejected Thompson's *ex post facto* challenge as well.

Texas' reliance on *Hopt* is misplaced. Article 38.07 is simply not a witness competency rule. It does not "simply enlarge the class of persons who may be competent to testify," and it does not "only remove existing restrictions upon the competency of certain classes of persons as witnesses." 110 U.S., at 589–590, 4 S.Ct. 202. Both before and after the amendment, the victim's testimony was competent evidence. Texas Rule of Criminal Evidence 601(a) already prescribes that "[e]very person is competent to be a witness except as otherwise provided in these rules," and Rule 601(a)(2) already contains its own provision respecting child witnesses. As explained earlier, see *supra*, at 1624–1625, 1632–1633, Article 38.07 is a sufficiency of the evidence rule. As such, it does not merely "regulat[e] . . . the mode in which the facts constituting guilt may be placed before the jury," (Rule 601(a) already does that), but governs the sufficiency of those facts for meeting the burden of proof. Indeed, *Hopt* expressly distinguished witness competency laws from those laws that "alter the degree, or lessen the amount or measure, of the proof which was made necessary to conviction when the crime was committed." 110 U.S., at 589, 4 S.Ct. 202; *see also id.*, at 590, 4 S.Ct. 202 (felon witness law "leav[es] untouched . . . the amount or degree of proof essential to conviction").

It is profitable, in this respect, to compare the statutes in *Hopt* and Thompson with the text of Article 38.07. The law in *Hopt* proscribed a "'rul[e] for determining the competency of witnesses'" that stated "'persons . . . convict[ed] of a] felony . . . shall not be witnesses.'" 110 U.S., at 587–588, 4 S.Ct. 202. The statute in Thompson, similarly, specified that "'comparison of a disputed writing . . . shall be permitted to be made by witnesses, and such writings . . . may be submitted to the court and jury as evidence.'" 171 U.S., at 381, 18 S.Ct. 922. Article 38.07, however, speaks in terms of whether "[a] conviction . . . is supportable on" certain evidence. It is Rule 601(a), not Article 38.07, that addresses who is "competent to testify." We think the differences in these laws are plain.

Moreover, a sufficiency of the evidence rule resonates with the interests to which the *Ex post facto* Clause is addressed in a way that a witness competency rule does not. In particular, the elements of unfairness and injustice in subverting the presumption of innocence are directly implicated by rules lowering the quantum of evidence required to convict. Such rules will always run in the prosecution's favor, because they always make it easier to convict the accused. This is so even if the accused is not in fact guilty, because the coercive pressure of a more easily obtained conviction may induce a defendant to plead to a lesser crime rather than run the risk of conviction on a greater crime. Witness competency rules, to the contrary, do not necessarily run in the State's favor. A felon witness competency rule, for example, might help a defendant if a felon is able to relate credible exculpatory evidence.

Nor do such rules necessarily affect, let alone subvert, the presumption of innocence. The issue of the admissibility of evidence is simply different from the question whether the properly admitted evidence is sufficient to convict the defendant. Evidence admissibility rules do not go to the general issue of guilt, nor to whether a conviction, as a matter of law, may be sustained. Prosecutors may satisfy all the requirements of any number of witness competency rules, but this says absolutely nothing about whether they have introduced a quantum of evidence sufficient to convict the offender. Sufficiency of the evidence rules (by definition) do just that—they inform us whether the evidence introduced is sufficient to convict as a matter of law (which is not to say the jury must convict, but only that, as a matter of law, the case may be submitted to the jury and the jury may convict). In the words of Article 38.07, "[a] conviction . . . is supportable" when its requirements are met.

IX

The dissent contends that Article 38.07 is not a sufficiency of the evidence rule. It begins its argument by describing at length how the corroboration requirement "is premised on a legislative judgment that accusations made by sexual assault victims above a certain age are not independently trustworthy." *Post*, at 1645; *see also Post*, at 1645–1647. But it does not follow from that premise that Article 38.07 cannot be a sufficiency of the evidence rule. Surely the legislature can address trustworthiness issues through witness competency rules and sufficiency of the evidence rules alike. Indeed, the statutory history to which the dissent points cuts against its own argument. Article 38.07's statutory antecedent, the dissent says, was a "replac[ement]" for the old common-law rule that seduced females were "'incompetent'" as witnesses. *Post*, at 1646. In 1891, Texas substituted a law stating that "'the female alleged to have been seduced *shall be permitted to testify*; but *no conviction* shall be had upon the testimony of the said female, *unless the same is corroborated*. . . .'" *Post*, at 1646 (emphasis added). That statute was recodified as Article 38.07 in 1965, was repealed in 1973, and then replaced in 1975 by another version of Article 38.07. As reenacted, the law's language changed from "no conviction shall be had" to its current language that "[a] conviction . . . is supportable." We think this legislative history, to the extent it is relevant for interpreting the current law, demonstrates that Texas perceived the issue of witness trustworthiness as *both* an admissibility issue and as a sufficiency question; that it long ago abandoned its rule that victims of these types of crimes are incompetent as witnesses; and that Article 38.07 codifies Texas' sufficiency of the evidence solution to the trustworthiness issue.

Next, the dissent argues that under Texas' law "the prosecution need not introduce the victim's testimony at all, much less any corroboration of that testimony." *Post*, at 1647. Instead, "[u]nder both the old and new versions of the statute, a conviction could be sustained on the testimony of a single third-party witness, on purely circumstantial evidence, or in any number of other ways." *Post*, at 1647. Because other avenues of prosecution—besides the victim's testimony (with or without corroboration or outcry)—remain available to the State, Article 38.07 "did not change the quantity of proof necessary to convict *in every case*." *Post*, at 1647 (emphasis added in part and deleted in part); *see also* post, at 1648 ("Article 38.07 has never dictated what it takes in all cases . . . for evidence to be sufficient to convict" (emphasis added)). Accordingly, the dissent urges, more evidence (in the form of corroboration) is not really *required* under Article 38.07. See post, at 1647, 1654. It is unclear whether the dissent's argument is that laws cannot be sufficiency of the evidence rules unless they apply to *every* conviction for a particular crime, or whether the dissent means that sufficiency rules not applicable in every prosecution for a particular crime do not fall within *Calder*'s fourth category, which refers to less testimony "*required* . . . in order to convict the offender." 3 Dall., at 390 (emphasis added in part and deleted in part). Either way, the argument fails.

Fenwick's case once again provides the guide. The dissent agrees that "[t]he treason statute in effect at the time of John Fenwick's conspiracy, like the Treason Clause of our Constitution, embodied . . . a quantitative sufficiency [of the evidence] rule." *Post*, at 1654. But, it argues, Fenwick's law and the Treason Clause are different from Article 38.07; with the first two laws, "two witnesses [were] necessary to support a conviction," *ibid.* (emphasis added), whereas with Article 38.07, the victim's testimony plus corroboration is not "necessary to convict *in every case*," *Post*, at 1647 (emphasis added). But a closer look at Fenwick's law and at the Treason Clause shows that this supposed distinction is simply incorrect. Fenwick's law stated that no person could be convicted of high treason "but by and upon the Oaths and Testimony of Two lawfull Witnesses . . . *unlesse the Party indicted and arraigned or tryed shall willingly without violence in open Court confesse the same or shall stand Mute or refuse to plead . . .*" See n. 15, *supra* (emphasis added). And the Treason Clause, of course, states that "No Person shall be convicted of Treason unless on the Testimony of two Witnesses to the same overt Act, *or on Confession in open Court*." U.S. Const., Art. III, § 3 (emphasis added). Plainly, in neither instance were two witnesses "*necessary to support a conviction*," as the dissent claims. Accordingly, its assertion that Article 38.07 "is nothing like the two-witness rule on which Fenwick vainly relied" appears erroneous, as does its accusation that our reliance on Fenwick's case "simply will not wash." *Post*, at 1654.

The dissent's final argument relies upon *Hopt* and runs something like this. The "effect" of Article 38.07, it claims, is the same, in certain cases, as a witness credibility rule. See post, at 1646, 1648–1650, 1655. However differently *Hopt*-type laws and Article 38.07 may seem to operate on their face, in practical application (at least in certain instances) their consequences are no different, and, accordingly, they ought to be treated alike. For example, if there were a rule declaring a victim to be incompetent to testify unless she was under a certain age at the time of the offense, or had made an outcry within a specified period of time, or had other corroborating evidence, and the prosecution attempted to rest its case on the victim's testimony alone without satisfying those requirements, the end result would be a judgment of acquittal. *Post*, at 1649–1650. Likewise, under Article 38.07, if the prosecution attempts to rest its case on the victim's testimony alone without satisfying the Article's requirements, the result would also be an acquittal. Thus, *Hopt*-type laws and Article 38.07 should be treated the same way for *ex post facto* purposes.

This argument seeks to make *Hopt* controlling by ignoring what the case says. *Hopt* specifically distinguished laws that "alter the degree, or lessen the amount or measure, of the proof" required to convict from those laws that merely respect what kind of evidence may be introduced at trial. See *supra*, at 1639. The above argument, though, simply denies any meaningful distinction between those types of laws, on the premise that they produce the same results in some situations. See post, at 1649 ("Such a victim is of course not literally forbidden from testifying, but that cannot make the difference for *Ex post facto* Clause purposes between a sufficiency of the evidence rule and a witness competency rule"); Post, at 1653 ("*Hopt* cannot meaningfully be distinguished from the instant case"). In short, the argument finds *Hopt* controlling by erasing the case's controlling distinction.

The argument also pays no heed to the example laid down by Fenwick's case. Surely we can imagine a witness competency rule that would operate in a manner similar to the law in that case (e.g., a witness to a treasonous act is not competent to testify unless corroborated by another witness). Plainly, the imagined rule does not mean that Fenwick's case is not an example of an *ex post facto* law. But if that is so, why should it be any different for Article 38.07? Just as we can imagine a witness competency rule that would operate similarly to the statute in Fenwick's case, the above argument imagines a witness competency rule that operates similarly to Article 38.07. If the former does not change our view of the law in Fenwick's case, why should the latter change our view in the present circumstances?

Moreover, the argument fails to account for what *Calder*'s fourth category actually says, and tells only half the story of what a witness competency rule does. As for what *Calder* says, the fourth category applies to "[e]very law that alters the legal rules of evidence, and receives less, or different, testimony, than the law required at the time of the commission of the offence, in order to convict the offender." 3 Dall., at 390 (emphasis deleted). The last six words are crucial. The relevant question is whether the law affects the quantum of evidence required to convict; a witness competency rule that (in certain instances at least) has the practical effect of telling us what evidence would result in acquittal does not really speak to *Calder*'s fourth category.

As for relating only half the story, the dissent's argument rests on the assertion that sometimes a witness competency rule will result in acquittals in the same instances in which Article 38.07 would also demand an acquittal. That may be conceded, but it is only half the story—and, as just noted, not the most relevant half. The other half concerns what a witness competency rule has to say about the evidence "required . . . in order to convict the offender." The answer is, nothing at all. As mentioned earlier, see *supra*, at 1640, prosecutors may satisfy all the requirements of any number of witness competency rules, but this says absolutely nothing about whether they have introduced a quantum of evidence sufficient to convict the offender. Sufficiency of the evidence rules, however, tell us precisely that.

X

For these reasons, we hold that petitioner's convictions on counts 7 through 10, insofar as they are not corroborated by other evidence, cannot be sustained under the *Ex post facto* Clause, because Texas' amendment to Article 38.07 falls within *Calder*'s fourth category. It seems worth remembering, at this point, Joseph Story's observation about the Clause:

> "'If the laws in being do not punish an offender, let him go unpunished; let the legislature, admonished of the defect of the laws, provide against the commission of future crimes of the same sort. The escape of one delinquent can never produce so much harm to the community, as may arise from the infraction of a rule, upon which the purity of public justice, and the existence of civil liberty, essentially depend.'" 3 Commentaries on the Constitution § 1338, at 211, n. 2.

And, of course, nothing in the *Ex post facto* Clause prohibits Texas' prospective application of its amendment. Accordingly, the judgment of the Texas Court of Appeals is reversed, and the case is remanded for further proceedings not inconsistent with this opinion.

It is so ordered.

Justice GINSBURG, with whom THE CHIEF JUSTICE, Justice O'CONNOR, and Justice KENNEDY join, dissenting.

The Court today holds that the amended version of Article 38.07 of the Texas Code of Criminal Procedure reduces the amount of proof necessary to support a sexual assault conviction, and that its retroactive application therefore violates the *Ex post facto* Clause. In so holding, the Court misreads both the Texas statute and our precedents concerning the *Ex post facto* Clause. Article 38.07 is not, as the Court would have it, most accurately characterized as a "sufficiency of the evidence rule"; it is in its essence an evidentiary provision dictating the circumstances under which the jury may credit victim testimony in sexual offense prosecutions. The amended version of Article 38.07 does nothing more than accord to certain victims of sexual offenses full testimonial stature, giving them the same undiminished competency to testify that Texas extends to witnesses generally in the State's judicial proceedings. Our precedents make clear that such a witness competency rule validly may be applied to offenses committed before its enactment. I therefore dissent.

* * *

II

The *Ex Post Facto* Clause, this Court has said repeatedly, furthers two important purposes. First, it serves "to assure that legislative Acts give fair warning of their effect and permit individuals to rely on their meaning until explicitly changed." *Weaver v. Graham*, 450 U.S. 24, 28–29, 101 S.Ct. 960, 67 L.Ed.2d 17 (1981). Second, it "restricts governmental power by restraining arbitrary and potentially vindictive legislation." *Id.*, at 29, 101 S.Ct. 960; *see also Landgraf v. USI Film Products*, 511 U.S. 244, 267, 114 S.Ct. 1483, 128 L.Ed.2d 229 (1994); *Miller v. Florida*, 482 U.S. 423, 429–430, 107 S.Ct. 2446, 96 L.Ed.2d 351 (1987). The latter purpose has much to do with the separation of powers; like its textual and conceptual neighbor the Bill of Attainder Clause, the *Ex post facto* Clause aims to ensure that legislatures do not meddle with the judiciary's task of adjudicating guilt and innocence in individual cases. Weaver, 450 U.S., at 29, n. 10, 101 S.Ct. 960.

The Court does not even attempt to justify its extension of the Clause in terms of these two fundamental purposes. That is understandable, for today's decision serves neither purpose. The first purpose (fair warning and reliance), vital as it is, cannot tenably be relied upon by Carmell. He had ample notice that the conduct in which he engaged was illegal. He certainly cannot claim to have relied in any way on the preamendment version of Article 38.07: He tendered no reason to anticipate that K.M. would not report the assault within the outcry period, nor any cause to expect that corroborating evidence would not turn up sooner or later. Nor is the Clause's second purpose relevant here, for there is no indication that the Texas Legislature intended to single out this defendant or any class of defendants for vindictive or arbitrary treatment. Instead, the amendment of Article 38.07 simply brought the rules governing certain victim testimony in sexual offense prosecutions into conformity with Texas law governing witness testimony generally.

Notes and Questions

1. What sources does the Court use to draw its conclusions?

2. Is it not clear that Carmell deserves to be convicted? Can you argue that there is a basis for a constitutional challenge to the Texas legislature's restriction of testimony?

3. Note the unusual lineup of justices in the majority and dissent.

4. If Texas law at the time of the offense provided that testimony of the victim was inadmissible, unless corroborated, would a subsequent repeal of the corroboration requirement have been *ex post facto* if applied to the defendant?

5. This was obviously a very close case. What lesson do you draw as a future advocate?

6. Is extension of a period of sex offender registration *ex post facto*? Compare *Gonzalez v. State*, 980 N.E.2d 312 (Ind. 2013) with *State v. Trosclair*, 89 So. 3d 340, 341 (La. 2012). How about imposing registration for previously non-registrable offense? *See Doe v. Dep't of Pub. Safety & Corr. Servs.*, 62 A.3d 123 (2013).

7. If some conduct takes place before an increase in penalty, and some after, may a defendant properly be convicted? *Miller v. Commonwealth*, 391 S.W.3d 857, 863 (Ky. 2013).

---

2. Due Process Retroactivity

The *ex post facto* clauses, by their terms, do not apply to the actions of courts. Nevertheless, judicial decisions can result in unfair surprise; imagine, for example, that a state supreme court had invalidated a criminal prohibition on hunting without a license, or held that the statute did not apply in a particular state park, and then retroactively reversed itself. People who relied on the judicial decision would justly feel deceived. For this reason, the due process clauses of the Fifth and Fourteenth Amendments impose some limitations on retroactive judicial decisions.

Harris v. Booker

United States District Court, E.D. Michigan
738 F.Supp.2d 734 (2010)

MEMORANDUM AND ORDER
GRANTING HABEAS RELIEF ON DUE PROCESS CLAIM

AVERN COHN, District Judge.

I. INTRODUCTION

This is a habeas case under 28 U.S.C. § 2254. Michigan parolee Erwin Harris ("Petitioner") was convicted of two counts of armed robbery and two counts of possession of a firearm during the commission of a felony following a jury trial in the Washtenaw County Circuit Court in 1999. He was sentenced to concurrent terms of 10 to 20 years on the armed robbery convictions and to concurrent terms of two years imprisonment on the felony firearm convictions, to be served consecutively to the armed robbery sentences.

In his habeas application, Petitioner raised claims challenging the sufficiency of the evidence for one of the armed robbery convictions and for both of the felony firearm convictions, as well as a due process claim. On October 16, 2006, 2006 WL 2946771, the Court issued a Memorandum and Order denying Petitioner relief on his insufficient evidence claims, and dismissing the due process claim without prejudice to allow him to properly exhaust that issue in the state courts. See Dkt. # 24. Petitioner completed his remedies in the state courts and has returned to the Court to proceed on the now-exhausted due process claim. The parties have filed supplemental papers in support of their positions. The matter is ready for decision. For the reasons that follow, Petitioner is entitled to habeas relief on his due process claim.

* * *

III. RELEVANT FACTS

Petitioner's convictions arise from an incident in which he and Eugene Mays robbed two people at a gas station in Washtenaw County, Michigan on September 28, 1998. The Michigan Supreme Court described the facts, which are presumed correct on habeas review, see *Monroe v. Smith*, 197 F.Supp.2d 753, 758 (E.D.Mich.2001), aff'd 41 Fed.Appx. 730 (6th Cir.2002), as follows:

> Harris drove Eugene Mays to a gasoline station. Mays had a sawed-off shotgun in the vehicle. Harris first entered the store on the pretense of asking for directions. After leaving the store, he reentered moments later followed by Mays, who was wielding the shotgun. While Mays pointed the gun at the clerk, Harris approached a customer from behind and proceeded to remove the customer's wallet and other items from his pockets. The clerk refused to give Mays any money and pushed a button that locked the cash register. Although Harris repeatedly directed Mays to "pop," or shoot, the clerk after he locked the register, the two men left the store without physically harming either the clerk or the customer.
>
> Defendant Harris was convicted by a jury on two counts of armed robbery, two counts of felony-firearm on an aiding and abetting theory, and one count of fleeing and eluding the police.

People v. Moore, 470 Mich. 56, 60–61, 679 N.W.2d 41 (2004) (footnotes omitted).

As part of his direct appeal, Petitioner challenged the sufficiency of the evidence to support his felony firearm convictions asserting that the prosecution failed to present evidence that he assisted Mays in obtaining or retaining the firearm used during the robberies. Michigan's felony firearm statute provides, in relevant part:

> A person who carries or has in his or her possession a firearm when he or she commits or attempts to commit a felony . . . is guilty of a felony, and shall be imprisoned for 2 years.

Mich. Comp. Laws § 750.227b(1). The purpose of the felony firearm statute is to enhance the penalty for possessing firearms during the commission of felonies and to deter the use of guns. See *Wayne Co. Prosecutor v. Recorder's Ct. Judge*, 406 Mich. 374 391, 280 N.W.2d 793 (1979), overruled in part on other grounds, *People v. Robideau*, 419 Mich. 458, 355 N.W.2d 592 (1984). The aiding and abetting statute provides:

> Every person concerned in the commission of an offense, whether he directly commits the act constituting the offense or procures, counsels, aids, or abets in its commission may hereafter be prosecuted, indicted, tried and on conviction shall be punished as if he had directly committed such offense.

Mich. Comp. Laws § 767.39. The purpose of the aiding and abetting statute is to abolish the distinction between accessories and principals to an offense so that both may be punished equally upon conviction for the crime. See *People v. Palmer*, 392 Mich. 370, 378, 220 N.W.2d 393 (1974).

In *People v. Johnson*, 411 Mich. 50, 303 N.W.2d 442 (1981), the Michigan Supreme Court held that a person could be convicted of aiding and abetting felony firearm only if he or she aided the principal in either "obtaining" or "retaining" possession of the firearm used during the attempted or completed felony. *Johnson*, 411 Mich. at 54, 303 N.W.2d 442. That standard was in effect at the time of Petitioner's crimes.

Citing *Johnson*, the Michigan Court of Appeals ruled that the prosecution presented sufficient evidence to support Petitioner's felony firearm convictions under an aiding and abetting theory. The court relied on evidence that Petitioner drove his armed accomplice, Mays, to the robbery and encouraged him to use the gun during the robbery. See *People v. Harris*, No. 222468, 2001 WL 849867 (Mich.App. July 27, 2001) (unpublished).

The Michigan Supreme Court disagreed, finding that the prosecution failed to present sufficient evidence to support Petitioner's felony firearm convictions under the existing *Johnson* standard for aiding and abetting felony firearm, i.e., the prosecution failed to show that Petitioner assisted Mays in obtaining or retaining possession of the gun, and stating that Petitioner's felony firearm convictions would be reversed under that standard. See *Harris*, 470 Mich. at 65–66, 679 N.W.2d 41. The Michigan Supreme Court then overruled *Johnson*, finding that its holding was overly narrow, and held that while a person may still be convicted of aiding and abetting felony firearm upon proof that he or she aided the principal in obtaining or retaining the firearm, a person may also be convicted of aiding and abetting felony firearm upon proof that he or she "aided and abetted another in carrying or having in his possession a firearm while that other commits or attempts to commit a felony." *Harris*, 470 Mich. at 68, 679 N.W.2d 41. The court went on to apply general aiding and abetting principles to the facts of Petitioner's case, stated that "[i]mplicit in the use of a firearm is the possession of that firearm," *id.* at 71, 679 N.W.2d 41, and concluded that, under the new standard, the prosecution presented sufficient evidence to support Petitioner's felony firearm convictions under an aiding and abetting theory. *Id.* at 73–74, 679 N.W.2d 41. Justices Cavanagh, Kelly, and Taylor dissented from the four-person majority opinion.

IV. DISCUSSION

A.

Petitioner asserts that he is entitled to habeas relief because the Michigan Supreme Court's decision in his case overruling prior precedent, People v. *Johnson*, 411 Mich. 50, 303 N.W.2d 442 (1981), and imposing a new and retroactively applicable test for aiding and abetting felony firearm in Michigan violates due process and runs contrary to *Bouie v. City of Columbia*, 378 U.S. 347, 354–55, 84 S.Ct. 1697, 12 L.Ed.2d 894 (1964) (retroactively applying an unforeseeable state court interpretation of a criminal statute violates due process). Petitioner relatedly asserts that, under the old test for aiding and abetting felony firearm, the prosecution presented insufficient evidence to support his felony firearm convictions such that those convictions must be overturned. Respondent contends that the due process claim lacks merit because the Michigan Supreme Court's interpretation of the statute was based upon the language of the statute and was foreseeable and requests that habeas relief be denied.

B.

On post-conviction review, the state trial court denied Petitioner relief on his due process claim finding that the Michigan Supreme Court's decision "did not amount to an unexpected or indefensible interpretation of MCL 767.39." *People v. Harris,* No. 98–11081–FC (Washtenaw Co. Cir. Ct. May 18, 2007). The court further explained:

> [The] testimony showed that [Harris] drove his accomplice, Mays, to the gas station. Harris 'cased' the interior of the store. Harris left the store and re-entered with Mays. Harris used Mays' possession of the firearm to intimidate and rob a store customer. Harris also encouraged Mays to 'pop' or shoot the store clerk when the clerk locked the register and refused to hand over the money. [Harris] ultimately drove away with Mays and the firearm.

> Harris did in fact counsel, aid, or abet Mays in the commission of a felony firearm.

Id. The Michigan Court of Appeals denied leave to appeal because Petitioner "failed to meet the burden of establishing entitlement to relief under MCR 6.508(D)." See *People v. Harris,* No. 280406 (Mich.Ct.App. Dec. 13, 2007). The Michigan Supreme Court similarly denied leave to appeal. *People v. Harris,* 482 Mich. 880, 752 N.W.2d 464 (2008).

C.

The Court concludes that the state court decisions denying relief on this claim are contrary to or an unreasonable application of United States Supreme Court precedent. The United States Supreme Court has clearly established that an unforeseeable judicial enlargement of a criminal statute, applied retroactively, violates the federal due process right to fair warning of what constitutes criminal conduct. *See Bouie*, 378 U.S. at 354–55, 84 S.Ct. 1697; *see also Marks v. United*

States, 430 U.S. 188, 191–92, 97 S.Ct. 990, 51 L.Ed.2d 260 (1977) (stating that people have a fundamental right to fair warning of conduct which will give rise to criminal penalties and "that right is protected against judicial action by the Due Process Clause of the Fifth Amendment"). The constitutionality of judicial action turns on the traditional due process principles of "notice, foreseeability, and, in particular, the right to fair warning." *Bouie*, 378 U.S. at 358–59, 84 S.Ct. 1697; *see also Hooks v. Sheets*, 603 F.3d 316, 321 (6th Cir.2010) (citing *Bouie*).

In *Rogers v. Tennessee*, 532 U.S. 451, 462, 121 S.Ct. 1693, 149 L.Ed.2d 697 (2001), the Supreme Court clarified Bouie when it ruled that "judicial alteration of a common law doctrine of criminal law violates the principles of fair warning, and hence must not be given retroactive effect, only where it is unexpected and indefensible by reference to the law which had been expressed prior to the conduct at issue." *Id.* at 462, 121 S.Ct. 1693; *see also United States v. Barton*, 455 F.3d 649, 654 (6th Cir.2006) (interpreting *Rogers* and stating that "when addressing ex post facto-type due process concerns, questions of notice, foreseeability, and fair warning are paramount").

The resolution of Petitioner's due process claim thus rests on whether the Michigan Supreme Court's decision overruling its prior precedent in *Johnson*, *supra*, and imposing a broader construction of aiding and abetting felony firearm in Michigan was foreseeable, *i.e.* not "unexpected or indefensible," in light of pre-existing law. As noted, the state trial court concluded that the new interpretation was foreseeable. This Court disagrees.

In *Johnson*, the Michigan Supreme Court considered the issue of whether a person who does not possess a firearm during a crime could even be convicted under the felony firearm statute as an aider and abetter in order to resolve a conflict within the Michigan Court of Appeals. *See Harris,* 470 Mich. at 63, 679 N.W.2d 41. While some lower courts had previously ruled that a person could be convicted of aiding and abetting felony firearm, several had ruled that a person could not be convicted of aiding and abetting felony firearm because the statute required "personal" possession. *Id.* at 63, n. 12, 679 N.W.2d 41 (noting prior conflicting cases). Against this backdrop, the Michigan Supreme Court ruled that a person could be convicted of aiding and abetting felony firearm, but only if he or she aided the principal in either "obtaining" or "retaining" the firearm used during the attempted or completed felony. *Johnson*, 411 Mich. at 54, 303 N.W.2d 442. The ruling in *Johnson* was a unanimous 7–0 decision. The court also denied the prosecution's motion for reconsideration.

For more than 20 years after Johnson was decided, the Michigan Supreme Court and the Michigan Court of Appeals applied the Johnson standard consistently. In fact, those courts reversed and vacated criminal defendants' aiding and abetting felony firearm convictions in at least 13 cases during that time period.

* * *

In Petitioner's case on direct appeal, however, the Michigan Supreme Court overruled *Johnson*, finding that its holding was overly narrow, and held that while a person may still be convicted of aiding and abetting felony firearm upon proof that he or she aided the principal in "obtaining or retaining" the firearm, a person may also be convicted of aiding and abetting felony firearm upon proof that he or she "aided and abetted another in carrying or having in his possession a firearm while that other commits or attempts to commit a felony." *Harris*, 470 Mich. at 68, 679 N.W.2d 41.

The Michigan Supreme Court's decision was not foreseeable for several reasons. While it may have advanced the general purposes of the felony firearm and aiding and abetting statutes, it went well beyond the Michigan Supreme Court's own previous and clear interpretation of those statutes in the context of aiding and abetting felony firearm, as well as the Michigan Court of Appeals' historically consistent application of the *Johnson* standard in factually-similar cases. See discussion *supra*. In fact, this Court was unable to find any Michigan cases or legal treatises which challenged or criticized the *Johnson* ruling or its application in state criminal proceedings—until the Michigan Supreme Court revisited the issue in Petitioner's case on direct appeal.

Moreover, following the *Johnson* decision, the Michigan Legislature re-enacted the felony firearm statute without changing its language. Under the re-enactment rule, the Michigan Legislature is presumed to be aware of the Michigan Supreme Court's judicial construction of the felony firearm statute and to adopt that interpretation. *See Harris*, 470 Mich. at 76–80, 679 N.W.2d 41 (Cavanagh, J. dissenting) (citing *Lorillard, a Div. of Loew's Theatres, Inc. v. Pons*, 434 U.S. 575, 580, 98 S.Ct. 866, 55 L.Ed.2d 40 (1978)). Thus, it could be said that the Michigan Supreme Court's decision in Petitioner's case contradicted the intent of the Michigan Legislature. At the very least, the re-enactment of the felony statute without a language change or other clarification supports Petitioner's claim that the Michigan Supreme Court's decision on direct appeal was unforeseeable.

The *Bouie* line of cases are concerned with situations when a court applies a clear criminal statute in a way that a defendant could not anticipate or applies a vague criminal statute in a new and unexpected fashion. *See United States v. Mitra*, 405 F.3d 492, 496 (7th Cir.2005); *see also Rabe v. Washington*, 405 U.S. 313, 315, 92 S.Ct. 993, 31 L.Ed.2d 258 (1972) (holding that Washington Supreme Court's broadening of obscenity statute, which by its terms did not proscribe defendant's conduct, did not provide fair notice and was unexpected). The Michigan Supreme Court did just that in this case. Petitioner had no reason to anticipate that the Michigan Supreme Court would alter its 20–year course and broadly construe the felony firearm statute to essentially make participation in the underlying crime in which a firearm is used sufficient to convict a person of the felony firearm offense as well. The Michigan Supreme Court completely changed its prior interpretation of what constitutes sufficient action to aid and abet felony firearm and failed to provide Petitioner with fair warning that his conduct could subject him to criminal prosecution as an aider and abettor to felony firearm. Federal habeas courts have found such action to violate due process as articulated in Bouie and subsequent Supreme Court cases. *See, e.g., Rathert v. Galaza*, 203 Fed.Appx. 97, 98–99 (9th Cir.2006) (ruling that habeas relief was warranted under Bouie and Rogers where California Supreme Court retroactively abrogated specific intent requirement established by a decade old, uncontradicted, and controlling appellate court case); *Devine v. New Mexico Dept. of Corr.,* 866 F.2d 339, 346–47 (10th Cir.1989) (finding that New Mexico Supreme Court's decision regarding habeas petitioner's parole eligibility was unforeseeable in light of published sources of state law); *Moore v. Wyrick*, 766 F.2d 1253, 1259 (8th Cir.1985) (Missouri Supreme Court decision expanding scope of felony murder statute was constitutionally unforeseeable and could not be retroactively applied where no intervening case challenged or weakened prior controlling decision).

This is not a case where a state appellate court has interpreted a criminal provision for the very first time, *see, e.g., Niederstadt v. Nixon*, 505 F.3d 832, 837 (8th Cir.2007) (habeas petitioner's due process rights were not violated by Missouri Supreme Court's first-time construction of forcible compulsion element of sodomy statute), overruled a "plainly incorrect" lower court's interpretation of a statute, *see, e.g., Hagan v. Caspari*, 50 F.3d 542, 546–47 (8th Cir.1995) (denying habeas relief on double jeopardy claim where Missouri Supreme Court overruled intermediate appellate court's decision which was contrary to clear statutory language), clarified prior or vague rulings, *see, e.g., Webster v. Woodford*, 369 F.3d 1062 (9th Cir.2004) (denying habeas relief upon finding that California Supreme Court's construction of "immediate presence" in robbery statute and "lying in wait" in murder statute did not violate due process), resolved a disagreement among the courts in interpreting state law, *see, e.g., Evans v. Ray*, 390 F.3d 1247, 1253–54 (10th Cir.2004) (ruling that retroactive application of state appellate court decision to resolve conflict among prior decisions was "eminently predictable" and did not violate due process and denying habeas relief), or applied a statutory provision to a new set of facts, *see, e.g., Ortiz v. New York State Parole in Bronx, N.Y.,* 586 F.3d 149, 158–60 (2d Cir.2009) (denying habeas relief on due process challenge to state courts' interpretation of riot statute where courts had not previously considered same factual situation).

To the contrary, in Petitioner's case, the Michigan Supreme Court overruled its own prior, long-established precedent to criminalize conduct which, by its own admission, was not considered criminal under the felony firearm statute at the time of its commission. Such action violates due process. *See Bouie*, 378 U.S. at 354–55, 84 S.Ct. 1697; *Webb v. Mitchell*, 586 F.3d 383, 393 (6th Cir.2009) (discussing the Bouie line of cases and stating that all of those cases involved judicial decisions that "retroactively converted an innocent act into a crime"); *see also Douglas v. Buder*, 412 U.S. 430, 432, 93 S.Ct. 2199, 37 L.Ed.2d 52 (1973). To be sure, the United States Supreme Court has held that a court overruling its own precedent is unforeseeable for the purposes of due process. *See Marks*, 430 U.S. at 192–96, 97 S.Ct. 990.

Respondent argues that the Michigan Supreme Court's decision overruling *Johnson* and retroactively applying its new interpretation to Petitioner does not violate due process because the new interpretation is consistent with the broad language of the felony firearm and aiding and abetting statutes. This argument ignores one crucial fact—the Michigan Supreme Court was not writing on a clean slate in this case. It had previously given the felony firearm statute, in the context of aiding and abetting, a more narrow interpretation—that a person must assist the principal in "obtaining or retaining" possession of the firearm to be convicted of aiding and abetting felony firearm. To then broaden that long-employed interpretation, without warning or prior notice, was neither foresee-able nor fair. *See Clark v. Brown*, 450 F.3d 898, 912, 916 (9th Cir.2006) (stating that the California Supreme Court's interpretation of felony murder special circumstance statute would not have violated due process had it been written on a "clean slate," but finding that it did so precisely because it deviated from the court's prior, narrower interpretation).

The Michigan Supreme Court's new interpretation of the felony firearm statute in the context of aiding and abetting, and its retroactive application to Petitioner's conduct, are inconsistent with the demands of due process and the United States Constitution. As one justice of the United States Supreme Court has aptly stated:

> It is simply not fair to prosecute someone for a crime that has not been defined until the judicial decision that sends him to jail. 'How can the public be expected to know what the statute means when the judges and prosecutors themselves do not know, or must make it up as they go along?'

Sorich v. United States, 555 U.S. 1204, 129 S.Ct. 1308, 1310, 173 L.Ed.2d 645 (2009) (citation omitted) (Scalia, J. dissenting from denial of certiorari). Petitioner was denied due process and the right to a fair proceeding by the Michigan Supreme Court's decision on direct appeal of his convictions. The state court decisions finding otherwise and denying him relief are contrary to and/or an unreasonable application of Bouie and its progeny. Habeas relief is warranted on this claim.

V. CONCLUSION

For the reasons stated, the Court concludes that Petitioner is entitled to habeas relief on his supplemental due process claim. Accordingly, the Court GRANTS the petition as to this claim.

Given the Court's conclusion that the Michigan Supreme Court's revised interpretation and retroactive application of the felony firearm statute in the context of aiding and abetting does not pass constitutional muster, and given that the Michigan Supreme Court has already ruled that the prosecution failed to present sufficient evidence to support Petitioner's felony firearm convictions under the *Johnson* standard, Petitioner is entitled to have his felony firearm convictions vacated. Respondent is directed to take such action forthwith. Should Respondent timely appeal this decision to the United States Court of Appeals for the Sixth Circuit, the order to vacate Petitioner's felony firearm convictions is stayed pending the resolution of that appeal.

SO ORDERED.

Notes and Questions

1. Be sure you understand what was required for aider and abetter liability under the *Johnson* case, and what is required under *Harris*.

2. What, according to the court, is the test for whether retroactive application of a judicial decision violates due process? Which, to you, seems more restrictive on changes in legal rules, the *ex post facto* clause, or the due process test?

B. Void for Vagueness

In addition to being on the books before the conduct at issue, a law must be reasonably clear. The void for vagueness doctrine invalidates some statutes which are difficult to understand.

Papachristou v. City of Jacksonville

Supreme Court of the United States
405 U.S. 156 (1972)

Mr. Justice DOUGLAS delivered the opinion of the Court.

This case involves eight defendants who were convicted in a Florida municipal court of violating a Jacksonville, Florida, vagrancy ordinance.[1] * * *

At issue are five consolidated cases. Margaret Papachristou, Betty Calloway, Eugene Eddie Melton, and Leonard *Johnson* were all arrested early on a Sunday morning, and charged with vagrancy—'prowling by auto.'

Jimmy Lee Smith and Milton Henry were charged with vagrancy—'vagabonds.'

Henry Edward Heath and a codefendant were arrested for vagrancy—'loitering' and 'common thief.'

Thomas Owen Campbell was charged with vagrancy—'common thief.'

Hugh Brown was charged with vagrancy—'disorderly loitering on street' and 'disorderly conduct—resisting arrest with violence.'

The facts are stipulated. Papachristou and Calloway are white females. Melton and *Johnson* are black males. Papachristou was enrolled in a job-training program sponsored by the State Employment Service at Florida Junior College in Jacksonville. Calloway was a typing and shorthand teacher at a state mental insti-

---

1   Jacksonville Ordinance Code § 26—57 provided at the time of these arrests and convictions as follows: 'Rogues and vagabonds, or dissolute persons who go about begging, common gamblers, persons who use juggling or unlawful games or plays, common drunkards, common night walkers, thieves, pilferers or pickpockets, traders in stolen property, lewd, wanton and lascivious persons, keepers of gambling places, common railers and brawlers, persons wandering or strolling around from place to place without any lawful purpose or object, habitual loafers, disorderly persons, persons neglecting all lawful business and habitually spending their time by frequenting houses of ill fame, gaming houses, or places where alcoholic beverages are sold or served, persons able to work but habitually living upon the earnings of their wives or minor children shall be deemed vagrants and, upon conviction in the Municipal Court shall be punished as provided for Class D offenses.' Class D offenses at the time of these arrests and convictions were punishable by 90 days' imprisonment, $500 fine, or both. Jacksonville Ordinance Code s 1—8 (1965). The maximum punishment has since been reduced to 75 days or $450. § 304.101 (1971). We are advised that that downward revision was made to avoid federal right-to-counsel decisions. The Fifth Circuit case extending right to counsel in misdemeanors where a fine of $500 or 90 days' imprisonment could be imposed is Harvey v. Mississippi, 340 F.2d 263 (1965). We are advised that at present the Jacksonville vagrancy ordinance is § 330.107 and *id*.ntical with the earlier one except that 'juggling' has been eliminated.

tution located near Jacksonville. She was the owner of the automobile in which the four defendants were arrested. Melton was a Vietnam war veteran who had been released from the Navy after nine months in a veterans' hospital. On the date of his arrest he was a part-time computer helper while attending college as a full-time student in Jacksonville. *Johnson* was a tow-motor operator in a grocery chain warehouse and was a lifelong resident of Jacksonville.

At the time of their arrest the four of them were riding in Calloway's car on the main thoroughfare in Jacksonville. They had left a restaurant owned by *Johnson*'s uncle where they had eaten and were on their way to a nightclub. The arresting officers denied that the racial mixture in the car played any part in the decision to make the arrest. The arrest, they said, was made because the defendants had stopped near a used-car lot which had been broken into several times. There was, however, no evidence of any breaking and entering on the night in question.

Of these four charged with 'prowling by auto' none had been previously arrested except Papachristou who had once been convicted of a municipal offense.

Jimmy Lee Smith and Milton Henry (who is not a petitioner) were arrested between 9 and 10 a.m. on a weekday in downtown Jacksonville, while waiting for a friend who was to lend them a car so they could apply for a job at a produce company. Smith was a part-time produce worker and part-time organizer for a Negro political group. He had a common-law wife and three children supported by him and his wife. He had been arrested several times but convicted only once. Smith's companion, Henry, was an 18-year-old high school student with no previous record of arrest.

This morning it was cold, and Smith had no jacket, so they went briefly into a dry cleaning shop to wait, but left when requested to do so. They thereafter walked back and forth two or three times over a two-block stretch looking for their friend. The store owners, who apparently were wary of Smith and his companion, summoned two police officers who searched the men and found neither had a weapon. But they were arrested because the officers said they had no *id*.ntification and because the officers did not believe their story.

Heath and a codefendant were arrested for 'loitering' and for 'common thief.' Both were residents of Jacksonville, Heath having lived there all his life and being employed at an automobile body shop. Heath had previously been arrested but his codefendant had no arrest record. Heath and his companion were arrested when they drove up to a residence shared by Heath's girl friend and some other girls. Some police officers were already there in the process of arresting another man. When Heath and his companion started backing out of the driveway, the officers signaled to them to stop and asked them to get out of the car, which they did. Thereupon they and the automobile were searched. Although no contraband or incriminating evidence was found, they were both arrested, Heath being charged with being a 'common thief' because he was reputed to be a thief. The codefendant was charged with 'loitering' because he was standing in the driveway, an act which the officers admitted was done only at their command.

Campbell was arrested as he reached his home very early one morning and was charged with 'common thief.' He was stopped by officers because he was traveling at a high rate of speed, yet no speeding charge was placed against him.

Brown was arrested when he was observed leaving a downtown Jacksonville hotel by a police officer seated in a cruiser. The police testified he was reputed to be a thief, narcotics pusher, and generally opprobrious character. The officer called Brown over to the car, intending at that time to arrest him unless he had a good explanation for being on the street. Brown walked over to the police cruiser, as commanded, and the officer began to search him, apparently preparatory to placing him in the car. In the process of the search he came on two small packets which were later found to contain heroin. When the officer touched the pocket where the packets were, Brown began to resist. He was charged with 'disorderly loitering on street' and 'disorderly conduct—resisting arrest with violence.' While he was also charged with a narcotics violation, that charge was nolled.

Jacksonville's ordinance and Florida's statute were 'derived from early English law,' *Johnson* v. State, 202 So.2d, at 854, and employ 'archaic language' in their definitions of vagrants. *Id.*, at 855. The history is an often-told tale. The break-up of feudal estates in England led to labor shortages which in turn resulted in the Statutes of Laborers, designed to stabilize the labor force by prohibiting increases in wages and prohibiting the movement of workers from their home areas in search of improved conditions. Later vagrancy laws became criminal aspects of the poor laws. The series of laws passed in England on the subject became increasingly severe. But 'the theory of the Elizabethan poor laws no longer fits the facts,' *Edwards v. California*, 314 U.S. 160, 174, 62 S.Ct. 164, 167, 86 L.Ed. 119. The conditions which spawned these laws may be gone, but the archaic classifications remain.

This ordinance is void for vagueness, both in the sense that it 'fails to give a person of ordinary intelligence fair notice that his contemplated conduct is forbidden by the statute,' *United States v. Harriss*, 347 U.S. 612, 617, 74 S.Ct. 808, 812, 98 L.Ed. 989, and because it encourages arbitrary and erratic arrests and convictions. *Thornhill v. Alabama*, 310 U.S. 88, 60 S.Ct. 736, 84 L.Ed. 1093; *Herndon v. Lowry*, 301 U.S. 242, 57 S.Ct. 732, 81 L.Ed. 1066.

Living under a rule of law entails various suppositions, one of which is that '(all persons) are entitled to be informed as to what the State commands or forbids.' *Lanzetta v. New Jersey*, 306 U.S. 451, 453, 59 S.Ct. 618, 619, 83 L.Ed. 888.

* * *

The Jacksonville ordinance makes criminal activities which by modern standards are normally innocent. 'Nightwalking' is one. Florida construes the ordinance not to make criminal one night's wandering, *Johnson* v. State, 202 So.2d, at 855, only the 'habitual' wanderer or, as the ordinance describes it, 'common night walkers.' We know, however, from experience that sleepless people often walk at night, perhaps hopeful that sleep-inducing relaxation will result.

Luis Munoz-Marin, former Governor of Puerto Rico, commented once that 'loafing' was a national virtue in his Commonwealth and that it should be encouraged. It is, however, a crime in Jacksonville.

'(P)ersons able to work but habitually living upon the earnings of their wives or minor children'—like habitually living 'without visible means of support'—might implicate unemployed pillars of the community who have married rich wives.

'(P)ersons able to work but habitually living upon the earnings of their wives or minor children' may also embrace unemployed people out of the labor market, by reason of a recession or disemployed by reason of technological or so-called structural displacements.

Persons 'wandering or strolling' from place to place have been extolled by Walt Whitman and Vachel Lindsay. The qualification 'without any lawful purpose or object' may be a trap for innocent acts. Persons 'neglecting all lawful business and habitually spending their time by frequenting . . . places where alcoholic beverages are sold or served' would literally embrace many members of golf clubs and city clubs.

Walkers and strollers and wanderers may be going to or coming from a burglary. Loafers or loiterers may be 'casing' a place for a holdup. Letting one's wife support him is an intra-family matter, and normally of no concern to the police. Yet it may, of course, be the setting for numerous crimes.

The difficulty is that these activities are historically part of the amenities of life as we have known them. They are not mentioned in the Constitution or in the Bill of Rights. These unwritten amenities have been in part responsible for giving our people the feeling of independence and self-confidence, the feeling of creativity. These amenities have dignified the right of dissent and have honored the right to be nonconformists and the right to defy submissiveness. They have encouraged lives of high spirits rather than hushed, suffocating silence.

* * *

This aspect of the vagrancy ordinance before us is suggested by what this Court said in 1876 about a broad criminal statute enacted by Congress: 'It would certainly be dangerous if the legislature could set a net large enough to catch all possible offenders, and leave it to the courts to step inside and say who could be rightfully detained, and who should be set at large.' *United States v. Reese*, 92 U.S. 214, 221, 23 L.Ed. 563.

While that was a federal case, the due process implications are equally applicable to the States and to this vagrancy ordinance. Here the net cast is large, not to give the courts the power to pick and choose but to increase the arsenal of the police. In *Winters v. New York*, 333 U.S. 507, 68 S.Ct. 665, 92 L.Ed. 840, the Court struck down a New York statute that made criminal the distribution of a magazine made up principally of items of criminal deeds of bloodshed or lust so massed as to become vehicles for inciting violent and depraved crimes against the person. The infirmity the Court found was vagueness—the absence of 'ascertainable standards of guilt' (id., at 515, 68 S.Ct., at 670) in the sensitive First Amendment area. Mr. Justice Frankfurter dissented. But concerned as he, and many others, had been over the vagrancy laws, he added:

'Only a word needs to be said regarding *Lanzetta v. New Jersey*, 306 U.S. 451, 59 S.Ct. 618, 83 L.Ed. 888. The case involved a New Jersey statute of the type that seek to control 'vagrancy.' These statutes are in a class by themselves, in view of the familiar abuses to which they are put. . . . Definiteness is designedly avoided so as to allow the net to be cast at large, to enable men to be caught who are vaguely undesirable in the eyes of police and prosecution, although not chargeable with any particular offense. In short, these 'vagrancy statutes' and laws against 'gangs' are not fenced in by the text of the statute or by the subject matter so as to give notice of conduct to be avoided.' *Id.*, at 540, 68 S.Ct., at 682.

Where the list of crimes is so all-inclusive and generalized[10] as the one in this ordinance, those convicted may be punished for no more than vindicating affronts to police authority:

---

10   President Roosevelt, in vetoing a vagrancy law for the District of Columbia, said: 'The bill contains many provisions that constitute an improvement over existing law. Unfortunately, however, there are two provisions in the bill that appear objectionable. 'Section 1 of the bill contains a number of clauses defining a 'vagrant.' Clause 6 of this section would include within that category 'any able-bodied person who lives in *id.*eness upon the wages, earnings, or property of any person having no legal obligation to support him.' This definition is so broadly and loosely drawn that in many cases it would make a vagrant of an adult daughter or son of a well-to-do family who, though amply provided for and not guilty of any improper or unlawful conduct, has no occupation and is dependent upon parental support. 'Under clause 9 of said section 'any person leading an *id.*e life . . . and not giving a good account of himself' would incur guilt and liability to punishment unless he could prove, as required by section 2, that he has lawful means of support realized from a lawful occupation or source. What constitutes 'leading an *id.*e life' and 'not giving a good account of oneself' is not indicated by the statute but is left to the determination in the first place of a police officer and eventually of a judge of the police court, subject to further review in proper cases. While this phraseology may be suitable for general purposes as a definition of a vagrant, it does not conform with accepted standards of legislative practice as a definition of a criminal offense. I am not willing to agree that a person without lawful means of support, temporarily or otherwise, should be subject to the risk of arrest and punishment under provisions as indefinite and uncertain in their meaning and application as those employed in this clause. 'It would hardly be a satisfactory answer to say that the sound judgment and decisions of the police and prosecuting officers must be trusted to invoke the law only in proper cases. The law itself should be so drawn as not to make it applicable to cases which obviously should not be comprised within its terms.' H.R.Doc. No. 392, 77th Cong., 1st Sess.

'The common ground which brings such a motley assortment of human troubles before the magistrates in vagrancy-type proceedings is the procedural laxity which permits 'conviction' for almost any kind of conduct and the existence of the House of Correction as an easy and convenient dumping-ground for problems that appear to have no other immediate solution.' Foote, *Vagrancy-Type Law and Its Administration*, 104 U.Pa.L.Rev. 603, 631.[11]

Another aspect of the ordinance's vagueness appears when we focus, not on the lack of notice given a potential offender, but on the effect of the unfettered discretion it places in the hands of the Jacksonville police. . . Arresting a person on suspicion, like arresting a person for investigation, is foreign to our system, even when the arrest is for past criminality. Future criminality, however, is the common justification for the presence of vagrancy statutes. See Foote, *supra*, at 625. Florida has, indeed, construed her vagrancy statute 'as necessary regulations,' inter alia, 'to deter vagabondage and prevent crimes.' *Johnson v. State*, Fla., 202 So.2d 852; *Smith v. State, Fla.*, 239 So.2d 250, 251.

A direction by a legislature to the police to arrest all 'suspicious' persons would not pass constitutional muster. A vagrancy prosecution may be merely the cloak for a conviction which could not be obtained on the real but undisclosed grounds for the arrest. . . .

Those generally implicated by the imprecise terms of the ordinance—poor people, nonconformists, dissenters, *id*.ers—may be required to comport themselves according to the life style deemed appropriate by the Jacksonville police and the courts. Where, as here, there are no standards governing the exercise of the discretion granted by the ordinance, the scheme permits and encourages an arbitrary and discriminatory enforcement of the law. It furnishes a convenient tool for 'harsh and discriminatory enforcement by local prosecuting officials, against particular groups deemed to merit their displeasure.' *Thornhill v. Alabama*, 310 U.S. 88, 97–98, 60 S.Ct. 736, 742, 84 L.Ed. 1093. It results in a regime in which the poor and the unpopular are permitted to 'stand on a public sidewalk . . . only at the whim of any police officer.' *Shuttlesworth v. Birmingham*, 382 U.S. 87, 90, 86 S.Ct. 211, 213, 15 L.Ed.2d 176. . . .

A presumption that people who might walk or loaf or loiter or stroll or frequent houses where liquor is sold, or who are supported by their wives or who look suspicious to the police are to become future criminals is too precarious for a rule of law. The implicit presumption in these generalized vagrancy standards—

---

11 Thus, 'prowling by auto,' which formed the basis for the vagrancy arrests and convictions of four of the petitioners herein, is not even listed in the ordinance as a crime. But see Hanks v. State, 195 So.2d 49, 51, in which the Florida District Court of Appeal construed 'wandering or strolling from place to place' as including travel by automobile.

that crime is being nipped in the bud—is too extravagant to deserve extended treatment. Of course, vagrancy statutes are useful to the police. Of course, they are nets making easy the roundup of so-called undesirables. But the rule of law implies equality and justice in its application. Vagrancy laws of the Jacksonville type teach that the scales of justice are so tipped that even-handed administration of the law is not possible. The rule of law, evenly applied to minorities as well as majorities, to the poor as well as the rich, is the great mucilage that holds society together.

The Jacksonville ordinance cannot be squared with our constitutional standards and is plainly unconstitutional.

Reversed.

City of Chicago v. Morales

Supreme Court of the United States
527 U.S. 41 (1999)

Justice STEVENS announced the judgment of the Court and delivered the opinion of the Court with respect to Parts I, II, and V, and an opinion with respect to Parts III, IV, and VI, in which Justice SOUTER and Justice GINSBURG join.

In 1992, the Chicago City Council enacted the Gang Congregation Ordinance, which prohibits "criminal street gang members" from "loitering" with one another or with other persons in any public place. The question presented is whether the Supreme Court of Illinois correctly held that the ordinance violates the Due Process Clause of the Fourteenth Amendment to the Federal Constitution.

I

Before the ordinance was adopted, the city council's Committee on Police and Fire conducted hearings to explore the problems created by the city's street gangs, and more particularly, the consequences of public loitering by gang members. Witnesses included residents of the neighborhoods where gang members are most active, as well as some of the aldermen who represent those areas. Based on that evidence, the council made a series of findings that are included in the text of the ordinance and explain the reasons for its enactment.

The council found that a continuing increase in criminal street gang activity was largely responsible for the city's rising murder rate, as well as an escalation of violent and drug related crimes. It noted that in many neighborhoods throughout the city, "'the burgeoning presence of street gang members in public places has intimidated many law abiding citizens.'" 177 Ill.2d 440, 445, 227 Ill. Dec. 130, 687 N.E.2d 53, 58 (1997). Furthermore, the council stated that gang members "'establish control over *id.*ntifiable areas . . . by loitering in those areas and intimidating others from entering those areas; and . . . [m]embers of criminal street gangs avoid arrest by committing no offense punishable under existing laws when they know the police are present. . . .'" *Ibid.* It further found that "'loitering in public places by criminal street gang members creates a justifiable fear for the safety of persons and property in the area'" and that "'[a]ggressive action is necessary to preserve the city's streets and other public places so that the public may use such places without fear.'" Moreover, the council concluded that the city "'has an interest in discouraging all persons from loitering in public places with criminal gang members.'" *Ibid.*

The ordinance creates a criminal offense punishable by a fine of up to $500, imprisonment for not more than six months, and a requirement to perform up to 120 hours of community service. Commission of the offense involves four predicates. First, the police officer must reasonably believe that at least one of the two or more persons present in a "'public place'" is a "'criminal street gang membe[r].'" Second, the persons must be "'loitering,'" which the ordinance defines as "remain[ing] in any one place with no apparent purpose." Third, the officer must then order "'all'" of the persons to disperse and remove themselves "'from the area.'" Fourth, a person must disobey the officer's order. If any person, whether a gang member or not, disobeys the officer's order, that person is guilty of violating the ordinance. *Ibid.*[2]

---

2   The ordinance states in pertinent part:

"(a) Whenever a police officer observes a person whom he reasonably believes to be a criminal street gang member loitering in any public place with one or more other persons, he shall order all such persons to disperse and remove themselves from the area. Any person who does not promptly obey such an order is in violation of this section.

" (b) It shall be an affirmative defense to an alleged violation of this section that no person who was observed loitering was in fact a member of a criminal street gang.

"(c) As used in this Section:

"(1) 'Loiter' means to remain in any one place with no apparent purpose.

"(2) 'Criminal street gang' means any ongoing organization, association in fact or group of three or more persons, whether formal or informal, having as one of its substantial activities the commission of one or more of the criminal acts enumerated in paragraph (3), and whose members individually or collectively engage in or have engaged in a pattern of criminal gang activity.

. . . . .

"(5) 'Public place' means the public way and any other location open to the public, whether publicly or privately owned.

"(e) Any person who violates this Section is subject to a fine of not less than $100 and not more than $500 for each offense, or imprisonment for not more than six months, or both.

Two months after the ordinance was adopted, the Chicago Police Department promulgated General Order 92–4 to provide guidelines to govern its enforcement. That order purported to establish limitations on the enforcement discretion of police officers "to ensure that the anti-gang loitering ordinance is not enforced in an arbitrary or discriminatory way." Chicago Police Department, General Order 92–4, reprinted in App. to Pet. for Cert. 65a. The limitations confine the authority to arrest gang members who violate the ordinance to sworn "members of the Gang Crime Section" and certain other designated officers,[4] and establish detailed criteria for defining street gangs and membership in such gangs. *Id.*, at 66a–67a. In addition, the order directs district commanders to "designate areas in which the presence of gang members has a demonstrable effect on the activities of law abiding persons in the surrounding community," and provides that the ordinance "will be enforced only within the designated areas." *Id.*, at 68a–69 a. The city, however, does not release the locations of these "designated areas" to the public.

II

During the three years of its enforcement, the police issued over 89,000 dispersal orders and arrested over 42,000 people for violating the ordinance. In the ensuing enforcement proceedings, 2 trial judges upheld the constitutionality of the ordinance, but 11 others ruled that it was invalid. In respondent Youkhana's case, the trial judge held that the "ordinance fails to notify individuals what conduct is prohibited, and it encourages arbitrary and capricious enforcement by police."

* * *

We granted certiorari, 523 U.S. 1071, 118 S.Ct. 1510, 140 L.Ed.2d 664 (1998), and now affirm. Like the Illinois Supreme Court, we conclude that the ordinance enacted by the city of Chicago is unconstitutionally vague.

* * *

IV

"It is established that a law fails to meet the requirements of the Due Process Clause if it is so vague and standardless that it leaves the public uncertain as to the conduct it prohibits. . . ." *Giaccio v. Pennsylvania*, 382 U.S. 399, 402–403, 86 S.Ct. 518, 15 L.Ed.2d 447 (1966). The Illinois Supreme Court recognized that the

---

"In addition to or instead of the above penalties, any person who violates this section may be required to perform up to 120 hours of community service pursuant to section 1–4–120 of this Code." Chicago Municipal Code § 8–4–015 (added June 17, 1992), reprinted in App. to Pet. for Cert. 61a–63a.

4   Presumably, these officers would also be able to arrest all nongang members who violate the ordinance.

term "loiter" may have a common and accepted meaning, 177 Ill.2d, at 451, 227 Ill.Dec. 130, 687 N.E.2d, at 61, but the definition of that term in this ordinance— "to remain in any one place with no apparent purpose"—does not. It is difficult to imagine how any citizen of the city of Chicago standing in a public place with a group of people would know if he or she had an "apparent purpose." If she were talking to another person, would she have an apparent purpose? If she were frequently checking her watch and looking expectantly down the street, would she have an apparent purpose?

Since the city cannot conceivably have meant to criminalize each instance a citizen stands in public with a gang member, the vagueness that dooms this ordinance is not the product of uncertainty about the normal meaning of "loitering," but rather about what loitering is covered by the ordinance and what is not. The Illinois Supreme Court emphasized the law's failure to distinguish between innocent conduct and conduct threatening harm.[24] Its decision followed the precedent set by a number of state courts that have upheld ordinances that criminalize loitering combined with some other overt act or evidence of criminal intent. However, state courts have uniformly invalidated laws that do not join the term "loitering" with a second specific element of the crime.

The city's principal response to this concern about adequate notice is that loiterers are not subject to sanction until after they have failed to comply with an officer's order to disperse. "[W]hatever problem is created by a law that criminalizes conduct people normally believe to be innocent is solved when persons receive actual notice from a police order of what they are expected to do." We find this response unpersuasive for at least two reasons.

First, the purpose of the fair notice requirement is to enable the ordinary citizen to conform his or her conduct to the law. "No one may be required at peril of life, liberty or property to speculate as to the meaning of penal statutes." *Lanzetta v. New Jersey*, 306 U.S. 451, 453, 59 S.Ct. 618, 83 L.Ed. 888 (1939). Although it is true that a loiterer is not subject to criminal sanctions unless he or she disobeys a dispersal order, the loitering is the conduct that the ordinance is designed to prohibit. If the loitering is in fact harmless and innocent, the dispersal order itself is an unjustified impairment of liberty. If the police are able to decide arbitrarily which members of the public they will order to disperse, then the Chicago ordinance becomes indistinguishable from the law we held invalid

---

24 177 Ill.2d, at 452, 227 Ill.Dec. 130, 687 N.E.2d, at 61. One of the trial courts that invalidated the ordinance gave the following illustration: "Suppose a group of gang members were playing basketball in the park, while waiting for a drug delivery. Their apparent purpose is that they are in the park to play ball. The actual purpose is that they are waiting for drugs. Under this definition of loitering, a group of people innocently sitting in a park discussing their futures would be arrested, while the 'basketball players' awaiting a drug delivery would be left alone." *Chicago v. Youkhana*, Nos. 93 MCI 293363 et al. (Ill. Cir. Ct., Cook Cty., Sept. 29, 1993), App. to Pet. for Cert. 48a–49a.

in *Shuttlesworth v. Birmingham*, 382 U.S. 87, 90, 86 S.Ct. 211, 15 L.Ed.2d 176 1965).[29] Because an officer may issue an order only after prohibited conduct has already occurred, it cannot provide the kind of advance notice that will protect the putative loiterer from being ordered to disperse. Such an order cannot retroactively give adequate warning of the boundary between the permissible and the impermissible applications of the law.

Second, the terms of the dispersal order compound the inadequacy of the notice afforded by the ordinance. It provides that the officer "shall order all such persons to disperse and remove themselves from the area." App. to Pet. for Cert. 61a. This vague phrasing raises a host of questions. After such an order issues, how long must the loiterers remain apart? How far must they move? If each loiterer walks around the block and they meet again at the same location, are they subject to arrest or merely to being ordered to disperse again? As we do here, we have found vagueness in a criminal statute exacerbated by the use of the standards of "neighborhood" and "locality." *Connally v. General Constr. Co.*, 269 U.S. 385, 46 S.Ct. 126, 70 L.Ed. 322 (1926). We remarked in *Connally* that "[b]oth terms are elastic and, dependent upon circumstances, may be equally satisfied by areas measured by rods or by miles." *Id.*, at 395, 46 S.Ct. 126.

Lack of clarity in the description of the loiterer's duty to obey a dispersal order might not render the ordinance unconstitutionally vague if the definition of the forbidden conduct were clear, but it does buttress our conclusion that the entire ordinance fails to give the ordinary citizen adequate notice of what is forbidden and what is permitted. The Constitution does not permit a legislature to "set a net large enough to catch all possible offenders, and leave it to the courts to step inside and say who could be rightfully detained, and who should be set at large." *United States v. Reese*, 92 U.S. 214, 221, 23 L.Ed. 563 (1876). This ordinance is therefore vague "not in the sense that it requires a person to conform his conduct to an imprecise but comprehensible normative standard, but rather in the sense that no standard of conduct is specified at all." *Coates v. Cincinnati*, 402 U.S. 611, 614, 91 S.Ct. 1686, 29 L.Ed.2d 214 (1971).

V

The broad sweep of the ordinance also violates "'the requirement that a legislature establish minimal guidelines to govern law enforcement.'" *Kolender v. Lawson*, 461 U.S., at 358, 103 S.Ct. 1855. There are no such guidelines in the ordinance. In any public place in the city of Chicago, persons who stand or sit in the company of a gang member may be ordered to disperse unless their

---

15 "Literally read . . . this ordinance says that a person may stand on a public sidewalk in Birmingham only at the whim of any police officer of that city. The constitutional vice of so broad a provision needs no demonstration." 382 U.S., at 90, 86 S.Ct. 211

purpose is apparent. The mandatory language in the enactment directs the police to issue an order without first making any inquiry about their possible purposes. It matters not whether the reason that a gang member and his father, for example, might loiter near Wrigley Field is to rob an unsuspecting fan or just to get a glimpse of Sammy Sosa leaving the ballpark; in either event, if their purpose is not apparent to a nearby police officer, she may—indeed, she "shall"—order them to disperse.

Recognizing that the ordinance does reach a substantial amount of innocent conduct, we turn, then, to its language to determine if it "necessarily entrusts lawmaking to the moment-to-moment judgment of the policeman on his beat." *Kolender v. Lawson*, 461 U.S., at 360, 103 S.Ct. 1855 (internal quotation marks omitted). As we discussed in the context of fair notice, see *supra*, at 1859–1860, this page, the principal source of the vast discretion conferred on the police in this case is the definition of loitering as "to remain in any one place with no apparent purpose."

* * *

Nevertheless, the city disputes the Illinois Supreme Court's interpretation, arguing that the text of the ordinance limits the officer's discretion in three ways. First, it does not permit the officer to issue a dispersal order to anyone who is moving along or who has an apparent purpose. Second, it does not permit an arrest if individuals obey a dispersal order. Third, no order can issue unless the officer reasonably believes that one of the loiterers is a member of a criminal street gang.

. . . That the ordinance does not apply to people who are moving—that is, to activity that would not constitute loitering under any possible definition of the term—does not even address the question of how much discretion the police enjoy in deciding which stationary persons to disperse under the ordinance.[32] Similarly, that the ordinance does not permit an arrest until after a dispersal order has been disobeyed does not provide any guidance to the officer deciding whether such an order should issue. The "no apparent purpose" standard for making that decision is inherently subjective because its application depends on whether some purpose is "apparent" to the officer on the scene.

Presumably an officer would have discretion to treat some purposes—perhaps a purpose to engage in idle conversation or simply to enjoy a cool breeze on a warm evening—as too frivolous to be apparent if he suspected a different

---

16   32 It is possible to read the mandatory language of the ordinance and conclude that it affords the police no discretion, since it speaks with the mandatory "shall." However, not even the city makes this argument, which flies in the face of common sense that all police officers must use some discretion in deciding when and where to enforce city ordinances.

ulterior motive. Moreover, an officer conscious of the city council's reasons for enacting the ordinance might well ignore its text and issue a dispersal order, even though an illicit purpose is actually apparent.

It is true, as the city argues, that the requirement that the officer reasonably believe that a group of loiterers contains a gang member does place a limit on the authority to order dispersal. That limitation would no doubt be sufficient if the ordinance only applied to loitering that had an apparently harmful purpose or effect, or possibly if it only applied to loitering by persons reasonably believed to be criminal gang members. But this ordinance, for reasons that are not explained in the findings of the city council, requires no harmful purpose and applies to nongang members as well as suspected gang members.[34] It applies to everyone in the city who may remain in one place with one suspected gang member as long as their purpose is not apparent to an officer observing them. Friends, relatives, teachers, counselors, or even total strangers might unwittingly engage in forbidden loitering if they happen to engage in *id*.e conversation with a gang member.

Ironically, the definition of loitering in the Chicago ordinance not only extends its scope to encompass harmless conduct, but also has the perverse consequence of excluding from its coverage much of the intimidating conduct that motivated its enactment. As the city council's findings demonstrate, the most harmful gang loitering is motivated either by an apparent purpose to publicize the gang's dominance of certain territory, thereby intimidating nonmembers, or by an equally apparent purpose to conceal ongoing commerce in illegal drugs. As the Illinois Supreme Court has not placed any limiting construction on the language in the ordinance, we must assume that the ordinance means what it says and that it has no application to loiterers whose purpose is apparent. The relative importance of its application to harmless loitering is magnified by its inapplicability to loitering that has an obviously threatening or illicit purpose.

Finally, in its opinion striking down the ordinance, the Illinois Supreme Court refused to accept the general order issued by the police department as a sufficient limitation on the "vast amount of discretion" granted to the police in its enforcement. We agree. *See Smith v. Goguen*, 415 U.S. 566, 575, 94 S.Ct. 1242, 39 L.Ed.2d 605 (1974). That the police have adopted internal rules limiting their enforcement to certain designated areas in the city would not provide a defense to a loiterer who might be arrested elsewhere. Nor could a person who knowingly

---

17   34 Not all of the respondents in this case, for example, are gang members. The city admits that it was unable to prove that Morales is a gang member but justifies his arrest and conviction by the fact that Morales admitted "that he knew he was with criminal street gang members." Reply Brief for Petitioner 23, n. 14. In fact, 34 of the 66 respondents in this case were charged in a document that only accused them of being in the presence of a gang member. Tr. of Oral Arg. 34, 58.

loitered with a well-known gang member anywhere in the city safely assume that they would not be ordered to disperse no matter how innocent and harmless their loitering might be.

* * *

Accordingly, the judgment of the Supreme Court of Illinois is Affirmed.

[Justices O'CONNOR, KENNEDY and BREYER concurred in part and concurred in the judgment; Chief Justice REHNQUIST and Justices SCALIA and THOMAS dissented.]

Notes and Questions

1. As the facts of *Papachristou* suggest, vagrancy laws were often used for purposes of racial oppression. The plurality in Morales noted:

> Petitioner cites historical precedent against recognizing what it describes as the "fundamental right to loiter." Brief for Petitioner 12. While antiloitering ordinances have long existed in this country, their pedigree does not ensure their constitutionality. In 16th-century England, for example, the "'Slavery acts'" provided for a 2–year enslavement period for anyone who "'liveth *id*.y and loiteringly, by the space of three days.'" Note, *Homelessness in a Modern Urban Setting*, 10 Ford. Urb. L.J. 749, 754, n. 17 (1982). In *Papachristou* we noted that many American vagrancy laws were patterned on these "Elizabethan poor laws." 405 U.S., at 161–162, 92 S.Ct. 839. These laws went virtually unchallenged in this country until attorneys became widely available to the indigent following our decision in *Gideon v. Wainwright*, 372 U.S. 335, 83 S.Ct. 792, 9 L.Ed.2d 799 (1963). See Recent Developments, *Constitutional Attacks on Vagrancy Laws*, 20 Stan. L.Rev. 782, 783 (1968). In addition, vagrancy laws were used after the Civil War to keep former slaves in a state of quasi slavery. In 1865, for example, Alabama broadened its vagrancy statute to include "'any runaway, stubborn servant or child'" and "'a laborer or servant who loiters away his time, or refuses to comply with any contract for a term of service without just cause.'" T. Wilson, Black Codes of the South 76 (1965). The Reconstruction-era vagrancy laws had especially harsh consequences on African–American women and children. L. Kerber, No Constitutional Right to be Ladies:

Women and the Obligations of Citizenship 50–69 (1998). Neither this history nor the scholarly compendia in Justice THOMAS' dissent persuades us that the right to engage in loitering that is entirely harmless in both purpose and effect is not a part of the liberty protected by the Due Process Clause.

City of Chicago v. Morales, 527 U.S. 41, 54, 119 S. Ct. 1849, 1858, 144 L. Ed. 2d 67 (1999)

2. Is there an argument that *Papachristou* is really an equal protection case?

PRACTICE EXERCISE

Read the following excerpts from actual cases and decide whether the statutes/ regulations are unconstitutionally vague. Refer to *Papachristou* and *Morales* as authority.

■ *Desertrain v. City of Los Angeles*, 754 F.3d 1147, 1149 (9th Cir. 2014):

In 1983, the City of Los Angeles enacted Municipal Code Section 85.02:

USE OF STREETS AND PUBLIC PARKING LOTS FOR HABITATION.

No person shall use a vehicle parked or standing upon any City street, or upon any parking lot owned by the City of Los Angeles and under the control of the City of Los Angeles or under control of the Los Angeles County Department of Beaches and Harbors, as living quarters either overnight, day-by-day, or otherwise.

On September 23, 2010, Los Angeles officials held a "Town Hall on Homelessness" to address complaints of homeless individuals with vehicles living on local streets in Venice. Present at the meeting were a member of the City Council, the Chief of the LAPD, the Chief Deputy to the City Attorney, and the Assistant Director of the Los Angeles Bureau of Sanitation. City officials repeated throughout the meeting that their concern was not homelessness generally, but the illegal dumping of trash and human waste on city streets that was endangering public health. To address this concern, officials announced a renewed commitment to enforcing Section 85.02.

Within the week, the LAPD created the Venice Homelessness Task Force (the "Task Force"). The Task Force's twenty-one officers were to use Section 85.02 to cite and arrest homeless people using their automobiles as "living quarters," and were also to distribute to such people information concerning providers of shelter and other social services.

Defendant Captain Jon Peters ran the Task Force, which included Defendant Officers Randy Yoshioka, Jason Prince, and Brianna Gonzales. Task Force officers received informal, verbal training, as well as internal policy memoranda, on how to enforce Section 85.02. Supervisors instructed officers to look for vehicles containing possessions normally found in a home, such as food, bedding, clothing, medicine, and basic necessities. According to those instructions, an individual need not be sleeping or have slept in the vehicle to violate Section 85.02. Supervisors directed officers to issue a warning and to provide information concerning local shelters on the first instance of a violation, to issue a citation on the second instance, and to make an arrest on the third.

- *United States v. Parrel*, 2:12-CR-00244-KJM, 2013 WL 2302306 (E.D. Cal. May 24, 2013)

To determine whether a law is void for vagueness, the court first examines the language of the regulation itself. Wyatt, 408 F.3d at 1260. Section 1.218(a)(3) provides:

> Preservation of property. The improper disposal of rubbish on property; the spitting on the property; the creation of any hazard on property to persons or things; the throwing of articles of any kind from a building; the climbing upon the roof or any part of the building, without permission; or the willful destruction, damage, or removal of Government property or any part thereof, without authorization, is prohibited. The destruction, mutilation, defacement, injury, or removal of any monument, gravestone, or other structure within the limits of any national cemetery is prohibited.

Parrel argues that the regulation is inherently ambiguous because it refers only to the "improper" disposal of rubbish. (ECF 29 at 6.) He avers that, to determine whether placing a cigarette butt on the ground is improper, he could rely only on environmental cues. (Id.) And the environmental cues—the presence of many butts all around him, the officer's ambiguous gesture toward a trash can, and the prior similar acts of others without legal consequence—suggested that putting a butt on the ground was not improper. (*Id.*)

The government counters that the regulation consists of "common words" that are easily understandable by people of ordinary intelligence. (Appellee's Br. at 4, ECF 30.) Littering is commonly understood to be improper; Parrel's own witness, the government argues, proved this when he testified that he did not know of a place in the United States where throwing cigarette butts on the ground is legal. (*Id.* at 4–5 (citing ER 31).) The plain language of the regulation, in other words, contradicts any conclusion that Parrel might have gleaned from environmental cues that throwing a cigarette butt on the ground is proper. (*Id.* at 5.)

- *State v. Doe*, 148 Idaho 919, 923, 231 P.3d 1016, 1020 (2010):

John Doe, a minor, was a passenger in a vehicle stopped at 1:30 a.m. for a traffic violation. Doe was supposed to be staying at a friend's house, but sneaked out with two friends to look for a party. Doe was cited for a violation of Wendell City Ordinance No. 442 ("Ordinance"), a curfew ordinance, which provides:

SECTION 1. CURFEW HOURS, VIOLATIONS, AND EXCEPTIONS

A. NIGHT TIME CURFEW: It shall be unlawful for any minor person under the age of eighteen (18) years to loiter, idle, wander, stroll, play, or otherwise be upon the public streets, highways, roads, sidewalks, alleys, parks, playgrounds, or other public grounds, or public places, building, or other property generally open to public use, or vacant lots within the City of Wendell, between the hours of 11:00 o'clock p.m. and 5:00 o'clock a.m.

B. EXCEPTIONS: The provisions of this section do not apply to a minor accompanied by his or her parents or legal guardians, or where the minor is upon an emergency errand or other legitimate business directed by his or her parents or legal guardian or custodian or school, having in their possession some form of documentation as to the business to be performed.

. . . .

SECTION 5. PENALTIES

Any person in violation of any section or provision of this ordinance shall be guilty of a misdemeanor and upon conviction thereof shall be punished as provided in Ordinance Number 192 of the City of Wendell, Idaho. Each violation of any section of this ordinance shall constitute a separate offense.

Doe sought to dismiss the citation in juvenile court, asserting the Ordinance was facially unconstitutional. Specifically, Doe argued that the Ordinance was void for vagueness in violation of the Due Process Clause, was overbroad in violation of the First Amendment, denied Doe equal protection of the laws in violation of the Fourteenth Amendment . . .

1. Substantive Due Process

Even laws which are quite clear can be unconstitutional if they violate the substance of a protection granted by some provision of a state or federal constitution.

C. First Amendment

On occasion, the protection of freedom of speech limits the state's ability to prosecute even an ordinary seeming crime. *Bonner* describes an example of such a limitation.

State v. Bonner

Court of Appeals of Idaho
138 Idaho 254, 61 P.3d 611 (2003)

LANSING, Judge.

Gary Bonner appeals from his judgment of conviction for sexual battery of a minor. Because we conclude that the subsection of the sexual battery statute under which Bonner was prosecuted is unconstitutional, we reverse the judgment.

I.

FACTS AND PROCEDURE

Bonner was apprehended by police standing outside the home where a sixteen-year-old girl resided. He had in his possession a video camera and a small stepstool. Police determined that he had secretly videotaped the girl in various states of undress by standing on the stepstool to make a videotape recording through a gap in the blinds covering a window. Bonner was charged with sexual battery of a minor child of the age of sixteen or seventeen years, Idaho Code § 18–1508A(1)(d).

Bonner moved for dismissal of the case, arguing that the subsection of the statute under which he was charged was unconstitutionally overbroad and vague. The district court denied the motion. Thereafter, Bonner entered a conditional guilty plea pursuant to Idaho Criminal Rule 11 and reserved the right to appeal the denial of his dismissal motion. On appeal, Bonner renews his assertion that I.C. § 18–1508A(1)(d) violates the Idaho and United States Constitutions because it is overbroad on its face and void for vagueness.

II.

ANALYSIS

Where the issue presented involves the constitutionality of a statute, we review the district court's determination de novo. State v. Richards, 127 Idaho 31, 34, 896 P.2d 357, 360 (Ct.App.1995).

The statute at issue here is subsection (1)(d) of I.C. § 18–1508A, which provides:

(1) It is a felony for any person at least five (5) years of age older than a minor child who is sixteen (16) or seventeen (17) years of age, who, with the intent of arousing, appealing to or gratifying the lust, passion, or sexual desires of such person, minor child, or third party, to:

. . . .

(d) Make any photographic or electronic recording of such minor child.

Bonner does not contend that I.C. § 18–1508A(1)(d) is unconstitutional as applied to his own conduct. Rather, he makes a facial challenge to the statute, contending that it is overbroad because it impermissibly proscribes a substantial amount of constitutionally protected conduct and is therefore incapable of any constitutional application. *See generally, Broadrick v. Oklahoma,* 413 U.S. 601,

609–13, 93 S.Ct. 2908, 2914–17, 37 L.Ed.2d 830, 838–41 (1973); *State v. Goodrick*, 102 Idaho 811, 812, 641 P.2d 998, 999 (1982). Bonner submits that the statute runs afoul of the First Amendment because the proscription against photographs and electronic recordings is not limited to those with sexual content or those that were made under circumstances likely to be harmful to children. Rather, he points out, the statute is so broad that the creation of photos or recordings with entirely innocent content is criminalized based solely upon the intent or thoughts of the person creating them. Bonner argues that the statute thus infringes upon First Amendment rights and may have a chilling effect upon constitutionally protected expression.

Facial attacks for overbreadth are not favored in the law and are allowed only in limited circumstances. *Broadrick*, 413 U.S. at 613, 93 S.Ct. at 2914, 37 L.Ed.2d at 840; *Goodrick*, 102 Idaho at 812, 641 P.2d at 999. If a statute can be constitutionally applied to the defendant's individual conduct, the defendant ordinarily cannot complain that the statute violates the constitutional rights of third persons who do not stand accused. *Broadrick*, 413 U.S. at 610, 93 S.Ct. at 2914, 37 L.Ed.2d at 838; *Goodrick*, 102 Idaho at 812, 641 P.2d at 999. Such challenges are allowed, however, where the statute in question might impermissibly infringe upon speech or conduct protected by the First Amendment. *Broadrick*, 413 U.S. at 612, 93 S.Ct. at 2916, 37 L.Ed.2d at 840. The United States Supreme Court has explained:

> In those cases, an individual whose own speech or expressive conduct may validly be prohibited or sanctioned is permitted to challenge a statute on its face because it also threatens others not before the court—those who desire to engage in legally protected expression but who may refrain from doing so rather than risk prosecution or undertake to have the law declared partially invalid.

Brockett v. Spokane Arcades, Inc., 472 U.S. 491, 503, 105 S.Ct. 2794, 2801, 86 L.Ed.2d 394, 405 (1985).

The overbreadth doctrine is aimed at statutes which, though designed to prohibit legitimately regulated conduct, include within their prohibitions constitutionally protected freedoms. *Cantwell v. Connecticut*, 310 U.S. 296, 303–04, 60 S.Ct. 900, 903–04, 84 L.Ed. 1213, 1217–18 (1940); *Schwartzmiller v. Gardner*, 752 F.2d 1341, 1346 (9th Cir.1984). Where a facial overbreadth challenge is presented, our inquiry is to "determine whether the enactment reaches a substantial amount of constitutionally protected conduct." *Hoffman Estates v. Flipside, Hoffman Estates*, 455 U.S. 489, 494, 102 S.Ct. 1186, 1191, 71 L.Ed.2d 362, 369 (1982). *See also State v. Newman*, 108 Idaho 5, 11, 696 P.2d 856, 862 (1985). "If the overbreadth is 'substantial,' the law may not be enforced against anyone, including the party before the court, until it is narrowed to reach only unprotected activity, whether by legislative action or by judicial construction or partial invalidation." *Brockett*, 472 U.S. at 503–04, 105 S.Ct. at 2801–02, 86 L.Ed.2d at 405–06. *See also Sec'y of State of Maryland v. J.H. Munson Co.*, 467 U.S. 947, 964–65, 104 S.Ct. 2839, 2850–51, 81 L.Ed.2d 786, 800–01 (1984). Overbreadth is not substantial if, "despite some possibly impermissible application, the 'remainder of the statute . . . covers a whole range of easily identifiable and constitutionally proscribable . . . conduct . . . .'" *Id.*, quoting *United States Civil Serv. Comm'n v. Letter Carriers*, 413 U.S. 548, 580–81, 93 S.Ct. 2880, 2898, 37 L.Ed.2d 796, 817 (1973). The test may be otherwise stated as whether the statute is unconstitutional in a substantial portion of the cases to which it applies. *Regan v. Time, Inc.*, 468 U.S. 641, 650, 104 S.Ct. 3262, 3267, 82 L.Ed.2d 487, 495 (1984).

Although the State argues to the contrary, it is clear that the creation of photographs, paintings, and other nonverbal productions is expressive activity that ordinarily qualifies for First Amendment protection. *Kaplan v. California*, 413 U.S. 115, 119–20, 93 S.Ct. 2680, 2684–85, 37 L.Ed.2d 492, 496–97 (1973) (stating that "pictures, films, paintings, drawings and engravings . . . have First Amendment protection" if not obscene). *See also Massachusetts v. Oakes*, 491 U.S. 576, 591–92, 109 S.Ct. 2633, 2642–43, 105 L.Ed.2d 493, 506–07 (1989) (photographs); Schad v. Mount Ephraim, 452 U.S. 61, 66, 101 S.Ct. 2176, 2181, 68 L.Ed.2d 671, 678 (1981) (stating that "nude dancing is not without its First Amendment protections from official regulation"); *Ashcroft v. Free Speech Coalition*, 535 U.S. 234, 122 S.Ct. 1389, 152 L.Ed.2d 403 (2002) (computer-generated images and photographs). Nevertheless, there are categories of such "speech" that may be prohibited without offending the First Amendment. Forms of unprotected speech include obscenity, *Memoirs v. Massachusetts*, 383 U.S. 413, 86 S.Ct. 975, 16 L.Ed.2d 1 (1966); *Roth v. United States*, 354 U.S. 476, 77 S.Ct. 1304, 1 L.Ed.2d 1498 (1957), and child pornography, *New York v. Ferber*, 458 U.S. 747, 102 S.Ct. 3348, 73 L.Ed.2d 1113 (1982).

Speech may be banned as obscene only if it meets the definition of obscenity set forth in *Miller v. California*, 413 U.S. 15, 93 S.Ct. 2607, 37 L.Ed.2d 419 (1973), which limits that appellation to "works which, taken as a whole, appeal to the prurient interest in sex, which portray sexual conduct in a patently offensive way, and which, taken as a whole, do not have serious literary, artistic, political, or scientific value." *Id.* at 24, 93 S.Ct. at 2615, 37 L.Ed.2d at 430. Child pornography is also outside the scope of First Amendment protection, regardless of whether it meets the Miller standard for obscenity. *Ferber*, 458 U.S. 747, 102 S.Ct. 3348, 73 L.Ed.2d 1113. In Ferber, the United States Supreme Court held that the compelling public interest in preventing the sexual exploitation and abuse of children justified the prohibition of child pornography because the use of children as subjects of pornographic photos, films or other recordings "is harmful to the physiological, emotional and mental health of the child." *Id.* at 758, 102 S.Ct. at 3355, 73 L.Ed.2d at 1123. Because such harm may occur regardless of whether the resulting work meets the Miller obscenity test, a sexually explicit depiction of a child may be barred even if the work possesses legitimate literary, artistic, political or scientific value. *Id.* at 761, 102 S.Ct.at 3357, 73 L.Ed.2d at 1125.

Nevertheless, because legislation banning child pornography, like that prohibiting obscenity, regulates speech, it must be carefully crafted to limit its reach. The conduct to be prohibited must be adequately defined, the prohibition must be limited to works that visually depict sexual conduct by children below a specified age, the forms of "sexual conduct" must be suitably limited and described, and criminal responsibility may not be imposed without some element of scienter on the part of the defendant. *Ferber*, 458 U.S. at 764–65, 102 S.Ct. at 3358–59, 73 L.Ed.2d at 1127–28. The production and distribution of descriptions or other depictions of sexual conduct by children, if not obscene and if not involving live performance or photographic or other reproduction of live performance, retain First Amendment protection. *Id.* at 764–65, 102 S.Ct. at 3358–59, 73 L.Ed.2d at 1127–28.

Recently, in *Free Speech Coalition*, the Supreme Court reemphasized that it is the governmental interest in preventing physical and psychological harm arising from the use of real children in child pornography that underlies the exemption of child pornography from First Amendment protection. The Court there held that this legitimate interest does not similarly justify prohibitions against sexually explicit images that appear to be children but do not, in fact, involve the use of children in their production. The legislation under scrutiny in *Ashcroft* was the Child Pornography Prevention Act, 18 U.S.C. § 2251, *et seq.* (the CPPA), which proscribed any visual depiction that is, or appears to be, of a minor engaging in sexually explicit conduct, including computer-generated images and photos or films of adults who appear to be minors. The Supreme Court held that this provision of the CPPA violated the First Amendment because the proscription was not limited to obscenity as defined in *Miller* or true child pornography, which entails the use of real children. Because the proscription of the CPPA was not limited to obscenity, the Court said, it prohibited speech that possessed "serious literary, artistic, political, or scientific value." *Free Speech Coalition*, 535 U.S. at 246, 122 S.Ct. at 1400. The Court observed that themes of teenage sexual activity and sexual abuse of children "have inspired countless literary works," including films based on William Shakespeare's Romeo and Juliet and recent academy award-winning movies, the possession of which could be subject to severe punishment under the CPPA without inquiry into the work's redeeming value. *Id.* at 247–248, 122 S.Ct. at 1400–1401.

The Supreme Court rejected the government's stance that the speech prohibited by the CPPA is indistinguishable from child pornography, which may be banned without regard to whether it possesses literary or artistic merit. The Court explained that the prohibition of child pornography is constitutional because child pornography inflicts injury upon the children used in its production and "[t]he fact that a work contain[s] serious literary, artistic, or other value [does] not excuse the harm it caused to its child participants." *Id.* at 249, 122 S.Ct. at 1401. In child pornography, the Court said, "the images are themselves the product of child sexual abuse," and its distribution and sale, as well as its production, may be banned because those acts are intrinsically related to the sexual abuse of children and exacerbate the harm to the child victims. *Id.* In contrast, the Court said, the CPPA prohibited speech that recorded no crime and created no victims by its production. Therefore, the Court concluded, the CPPA found no support in *Ferber*, which had reaffirmed that speech which is neither obscene nor the product of sexual abuse retains First Amendment protection. *Id.* at 251, 122 S.Ct. at 1402.

The *Free Speech Coalition* court was likewise unpersuaded by the government's argument that "virtual" child pornography stimulates the appetites of pedophiles and may encourage them to engage in illegal conduct. This rationale would not sustain the CPPA because "[t]he mere tendency of speech to encourage unlawful acts is not a sufficient reason for banning it." *Id.* at 253, 122 S.Ct. at 1403.

The Supreme Court's reasoning in *Free Speech Coalition* illuminates the issue before us. Like the CPPA provisions challenged in *Free Speech Coalition*, I.C. § 18–1508A(1)(d) bars the creation of photographs or electronic recordings without regard to whether those materials are obscene or constitute child pornography. Indeed, the statute's proscription extends to photographs or electronic recordings of minors having no sexual or offensive content at all. Nor is the statute focused to proscribe only photographs and recordings that harm the child subjects; it sweeps within its prohibition even photographs of innocuous content which are taken without the child's knowledge and which are not distributed or otherwise used in a manner that could inflict physical or psychological injury on the child. Such an undifferentiating ban is inconsistent with the First Amendment. Because the sweep of § 18–1508A(1) (d) is not limited as to the content of the proscribed photographs and recordings of minors, it may chill much protected expression.

We are mindful that § 18–1508A(1)(d) purports to prohibit only photographs and recordings made with the particular intent of arousing lust, passion or sexual desires. This limitation, however, does not save the statute. With its ban on photos and recordings unlimited as to content, the provision of § 18–1508A(1)(d) that narrows the statute's scope is, in essence, a prohibition of particular thoughts. Such legislation is impermissible. In *Stanley v. Georgia*, 394 U.S. 557, 565–66, 89 S.Ct. 1243, 1248–49, 22 L.Ed.2d 542, 549–50 (1969), where the Supreme Court struck down a state statute prohibiting private possession of obscene materials, the Court rejected the notion that "the State has the right to control the moral content of a person's thoughts." Said the Court, "To some, this may be a noble purpose, but is wholly inconsistent with the philosophy of the First Amendment. . . . Whatever the power of the state to control public dissemination of *id.*as inimical to the public morality, it cannot constitutionally premise legislation on the desirability of controlling a person's private thoughts." *Id.* In *Free Speech Coalition*, the Supreme Court again cautioned that "First Amendment freedoms are most in danger when the government seeks to control thoughts or to justify its laws for that impermissible end." *Free Speech Coalition*, 535 U.S. at 253, 122 S.Ct. at 1403. Moreover, because the requisite offensive intent can be easily hypothesized and ascribed to an accused by prosecuting authorities, the mental element of § 18–1508A(1)(d) does little to prevent a chilling effect on entirely innocent, protected expression.

We do not suggest that the conduct attributed to Bonner may not be legislatively prohibited by a properly crafted statute. Our state legislature has enacted statutes directed at child pornography, I.C. §§ 18–1507, 18–1507A, obscenity, I.C. §§ 18–4101, *et seq.*; 18–1513, 18–1514, and trespass of privacy (window peeping), I.C. § 18–7006. We hold only that the statute under which Bonner was charged in this case does not provide a permissible vehicle for his prosecution. Section 18–1508A(1)(d) regulates a vast amount of expressive activity and is not sufficiently narrow to avoid criminalizing an intolerable range of constitutionally protected conduct. That I.C. § 18–1508A(1)(d) criminalizes expression only when such expression is accompanied by an illegitimate and ignoble intent does not limit the statute's scope in such a way as to render it constitutional. Because I.C. § 18–1508A(1)(d) is unconstitutional on its face, it cannot be applied to punish Bonner's conduct.

Accordingly, the judgment of conviction is reversed.

Chief Judge PERRY and Judge GUTIERREZ concur.

———————

Notes and Questions

1. Would it be permissible for a state to criminally punish any person "who publicly advertises, offers, or holds himself or herself out as offering that he or she will intentionally and actively assist another person in the commission of suicide and commits any overt act to further that purpose is guilty of a felony"? Assume the state has not criminalized assisted suicide in general. *See Final Exit Network v. Georgia*, 290 Ga. 508, 722 S.E.2d 722 (2012).

2. Does the following describe a crime that can constitutionally be punished?

> ... On or about and between February 22, 2010 and April 11, 2010, while employed at the Nassau County District Attorney's Office ... as an Assistant District Attorney, I received a series of telephone voice mail recordings from defendant, Nicolas Pierre–Louis. ... In the voice mails, Nicolas Pierre–Louis yells, screams and uses profanity, stating in part, "I'm coming at you with fury," and, "piece of shit faggot fucking cock sucking cock," and "bitch, you will lose your fucking job," and "I got all the juice enough to make sure that you're holding a can in the fucking street," and "and I will keep calling until you arrest Jessy Pierre–Louis, so do your fucking job" and "when you lose your job bitch, don't say I didn't warn you," and "I will rain hell on your office and make sure heads roll," you racist bitch" and "you assholes" and "you motherfuckers." Nicolas Pierre–Louis says many other profane and offensive comments left recorded on my office voice mail that are alarming and annoying. The repeated calls left by Nicolas Pierre–Louis caused me to fear for my safety and the safety of [another] Assistant District Attorney ... because of the screaming outbursts of rage and anger directed toward [the other ADA] ... and I [sic] and the content of what he was saying during his many calls.

> *People v. Nicolas Pierre–Louis*, 34 Misc.3d 703, 927 N.Y.S.2d 592 (Dist. Ct. 2011).

D. State Constitutional Protections

State v. Adkins

Supreme Court of Nebraska
241 N.W.2d 655 (1976)

BRODKEY, Justice.

The county attorney of Platte County has brought consolidated error proceedings * * * to test the constitutionality of subsection (1)(g) of section 28—4,127, R.S.Supp., 1974, as contained in the Nebraska Controlled Substances Act. That portion of the statute reads as follows: '(1) It shall be unlawful for any person: * * * (g) To visit or to be in any room, dwelling house, vehicle, or place where any controlled substance is being used contrary to the provisions of sections 28—459 and 28—4,115 to 28—4,142, if the person has knowledge that such activity is occurring; * * *.' The numbered sections referred to in subsection (1)(g) constitute the entire Nebraska Controlled Substances Act, and a violation of subsection (1)(g) is a misdemeanor.

Neither subsection (1)(g), above quoted, nor any equivalent thereof, appears in the Uniform Controlled Substances Act which was approved by the National Conference of Commissioners on Uniform State Laws in 1970. See 9 Uniform Laws Annotated (Master Ed.), 145, and particularly section 402, pp. 298, 299, and 301. Nor does that language, or its equivalent, appear in the present federal Drug Abuse Prevention and Control Laws. Title 21 U.S.C.A., s. 801, et seq. A review of the legislative history of Laws 1971, L.B. 326, the Nebraska Controlled Substances Act, is of no assistance in determining the reason for the Nebraska Legislature including the language contained in subsection (1)(g), as there is no discussion of that particular subsection in the record of the committee hearings or of the floor debates. Therefore, our decision as to the constitutionality of subsection (1)(g) will be determined strictly upon the merits of the statute itself, and not upon the intention of the Legislature in enacting the provision.

The factual background of these cases, as reflected by the record, is meager. Appellees, James E. Adkins and Daniel J. Sutherland, were each charged in the county court of Platte County, in separate cases, with being present where controlled substances were being used, in violation of section 28—4,127(1) (g). The separate complaints charged that on or about February 20, 1975, in Platte County, Nebraska, each of them was unlawfully present in the same 1968 Chevrolet automobile in which controlled substances were being used, each of them knowing full well that such activity was occurring. It appears that both individuals, and certain casual acquaintances, were present in the same automobile at the same time and occasion, and under the same circumstances.

Prior to trial, counsel for each appellee moved for a dismissal of the charges, claiming that the statute was unconstitutionally vague and overbroad on its face in contravention of the Due Process and Equal Protection Clauses of the Fourteenth Amendment to the United States Constitution, and sections 1, 3, and 5 of Article I of the Nebraska Constitution. The county court sustained each motion, quashed the complaints, and dismissed the actions. The Platte County attorney appealed to the District Court for Platte County, which affirmed the ruling of the county court and held that section 28—4,127(1)(g) was unconstitutionally vague and overbroad on its face. The cases were consolidated for purposes of appeal, and the Platte County attorney brought error proceedings to this court from the District Court's order dismissing and quashing the complaints and affirming the county court's ruling. The appellees had not been in jeopardy. We affirm the judgment of the District Court.

The crux of appellees' argument that the statute under consideration is unconstitutionally vague and overbroad is that it encompasses within its express language what may essentially be innocent conduct.

Under the express terms of section 28—4,127(1)(g) only three things are necessary to constitute a crime. A person need only (1) be in a place, (2) where a violation of the Controlled Substances Act is being committed, and (3) with knowledge that such activity is occurring. It is evident that the statute as written is broad enough to encompass entirely innocent behavior. Individuals may find themselves in situations such as at parties, theaters, dance halls, hotel lobbies, buses, apartments, taxis, or even in private automobiles, where their conduct has no relation to the acts of others who may be disposed to use controlled drugs. In such situations, must they either immediately leave because of fear of prosecution under the statute under consideration; or perhaps force the others to discontinue the use of the controlled substance; or perhaps have the others arrested. Must a host expel his guest if he discovers the guest is in possession of or using a controlled substance?

Could a college student be convicted under the statute if he merely continued to reside with a roommate whom he knew illegally possessed marijuana? What action would a passenger in a car take when he learns that others in the car have drugs on their persons although they are not at that time using the drugs? Must the passenger demand that he be let out of the car or that the others dispose of anything illegal in their pockets? How about the status of relatives, priests, or doctors attempting to discourage continued violations? What if a person were engaged in a constitutionally protected activity, such as attending a public meeting or voting, when he inadvertently discovers that another person at the meeting or at the polls is in possession of a controlled substance? All the above situations would appear to be covered by the express language of the statute itself, and would result in the imposition of criminal liability upon a person merely because of his or her presence at the scene of the offense with knowledge that such illegal activity was taking place. We do not believe the Legislature intended to make such innocent conduct criminal, and yet by virtue of the overbreadth of the language used, as commonly understood, criminal liability might well result.

There are certain well-established rules for the interpretation of criminal statutes which are applicable in the present case. The general rule as to vagueness is well summarized in *State v. Adams*, 180 Neb. 542, 143 N.W.2d 920 (1966), where this court stated: 'It is a fundamental requirement of due process of law that a criminal statute be reasonably clear and definite. *Markham v. Brainard*, 178 Neb. 544, 134 N.W.2d 84. A crime must be defined with sufficient definiteness and there must be ascertainable standards of guilt to inform those subject thereto as to what conduct will render them liable to punishment thereunder. *State v. Nelson*, 168 Neb. 394, 95 N.W.2d 678. The dividing line between what is lawful and unlawful cannot be left to conjecture.'

A penal statute creating an offense must be sufficiently explicit to inform those who are subject to it what conduct on their part will render them liable to its penalties. Any statute which forbids the doing of an act in terms so vague that men of common intelligence must necessarily guess at its meaning, and differ as to its application, violates the first essential of due process of law. *State v. Adams, supra*, citing *Connally v. General Constr. Co.*, 269 U.S. 385, 46 S.Ct. 126, 70 L.Ed. 322; *State v. Nelson*, 168 Neb. 394, 95 N.W.2d 678; State v. Pocras, 166 Neb. 642, 90 N.W.2d 263; *State ex rel. English v. Ruback*, 135 Neb. 335, 281 N.W. 607. Other cases stating the same rule, with minor variations, are *Markham v. Brainard*, 178 Neb. 544, 134 N.W.2d 84 (1965); *Heywood v. Brainard*, 181 Neb. 294, 147 N.W.2d 772 (1967).

In *State ex rel. English v. Ruback, supra*, the court quoted from *Fairmont Creamery Co. v. Minnesota*, 274 U.S. 1, 10, 47 S.Ct. 506, 71 L.Ed. 893, indicating the invalidity of overbroad criminal statutes, stating: 'It is not permissible to enact a law which, in effect, spreads an all-inclusive net for the feet of everybody, upon the chance that, while the innocent will surely be entangled in its meshes, some wrong-doers also may be caught.' See, also, State v. Pocras, *supra*.

In *Markham v. Brainard, supra*, the court ruled that a penal law which makes criminal an act which the utmost care and circumspection would not enable one to avoid is invalid. In *Heywood v. Brainard, supra*, this court declared unconstitutional a Nebraska statute making it unlawful for the operator of a motor vehicle to flee in the vehicle in an effort to avoid arrest for violating any law of this state and further stating that the operation of such vehicle in an otherwise lawful manner shall not constitute fleeing to avoid arrest. In pointing out the ambiguity inherent in that statute the court stated: 'Does the statute mean that the operator fleeing to avoid arrest must have violated some traffic regulation such as speeding or running a stop sign or some similar violation previous to the pursuit? The Revisor of Statutes may have placed this interpretation on it in the catch line phrase 'operating motor vehicle in violation of law.' This may be a plausible interpretation, but the statute does not appear to be so restricted. The statute says 'for violating any law of this state.' It does not say for violating a law while operating a motor vehicle. Does the statute mean that if a law has been violated and the operator in fleeing from arrest does not violate any traffic regulation, the statute does not apply? This might raise a question as to whether it is possible to operate a vehicle in a lawful manner while fleeing to avoid arrest. There are many other questions that might be raised as to the meaning of the statute, but these are sufficient to point up the problem.'

In declaring that statute unconstitutional, the court cited the test quoted from *State v. Adams*, supra. The court concluded that the phrase: "Operation of such motor vehicle in an otherwise lawful manner shall not constitute fleeing to avoid arrest' makes section 6–430.02, R.S.Supp., 1965, vague and uncertain and requires men of ordinary intelligence to speculate on its meaning.'

Our court, has laid down guidelines to assist in determining whether a statute defining an offense is void for uncertainty. In *State ex rel. English v. Ruback*, supra, [test] is quoted as follows: "The test to determine whether a statute defining an offense is void for uncertainty (1) is whether the language may apply not only to a particular act about which there can be little or no difference of opinion, but equally to other acts about which there may be radical differences, thereby devolving on the court the exercise of arbitrary power of discriminating between the several classes of acts. (Citing case.) (2) The dividing line between what is lawful and what is unlawful cannot be left to conjecture." See, also, *Connally v. General Construction Co.*, 269 U.S. 385, 46 S.Ct. 126, 70 L.Ed. 322; *Lanzetta v. New Jersey*, 306 U.S. 451, 59 S.Ct. 618, 83 L.Ed. 888.

In our opinion, the statute under consideration contains both of the above flaws, and is also vulnerable to attack on the ground that the language employed therein is so general and indefinite as to embrace not only acts commonly recognized as reprehensible, but also others which it is unreasonable to presume were intended to be made criminal. Section 28–4,127(1)(g) offers no guidance as to how one can avoid violating the law and is not sufficiently clear so that a person of ordinary intelligence has fair notice of what exactly is forbidden conduct under the statute.

Appellant points out, however, that three jurisdictions, Massachusetts, California, and Florida, have interpreted similar statutes to avoid in the problems inherent in subsection (1)(g). They have, in effect, done this by the expedient of providing through interpretation exceptions to the application of the statute. See, for example, *Commonwealth v. Tirella*, 356 Mass. 271, 249 N.E.2d 573 (1969); *People v. Brim*, 257 Cal.App.2d 839, 65 Cal.Rptr. 265 (1968); *People v. Cressey*, 2 Cal.3d 836, 87 Cal.Rptr. 699, 471 P.2d 19 (1970); *Jolley v. City of Jacksonville*, 281 So.2d 901 (Fla.App., 1973). Generally speaking, they have done this by interjecting these additional requirements or some combination thereof: (1) Control of the premises or automobile by the person activity; (3) acquiescence or fellowship on activity; (3) acquiescence or fellowship on the part of the accused, including the failure to leave or take other action, within a reasonable time after becoming aware of such illegal activities; and, on occasion, (4) other acts of the accused constituting violations of the Controlled Substances Act.

We point out, however, that these decisions have themselves resulted in further questions of interpretation of their respective statutes. For example, in *In re Elisabeth H.*, 20 Cal.App.3d 323, 97 Cal.Rptr. 565 (1971), the court decried the 'legal quagmire' created by *People v. Cressey*, supra, and expressed the hope that subsequent decisions would remove some of the uncertainty from the application of the statute. In the opinion of that court, the only thing really clear at the time of that decision was that mere knowledge and presence were not sufficient to constitute a violation. The problems created by the *Cressey* case in California are illustrated in a law review article entitled *'No Place for 'Being in a Place': The Vanishing of Health and Safety Code Section 11,556,'* 23 Stan.L.Rev. 1009 (1971). See, also, *Commonwealth v. Flaherty*, 358 Mass. 817, 266 N.E.2d 875 (1971).

It is not the court's duty, nor is it within its province, to read a meaning into a statute that is not warranted by the legislative language. *Wessel v. City of Lincoln*, 145 Neb. 357, 16 N.W.2d 476 (1944). This is especially true in the absence of any evidence of legislative intent. In *State v. Adams*, supra, the court had before it the Nebraska statute providing that: 'Any person or persons who shall operate a vehicle upon any highway in such a manner as to (1) endanger the safety of others or (2) cause immoderate wear or damage to any highway, shall be deemed guilty of a misdemeanor * * *.' In holding the statute unconstitutional and void, the court stated: 'As pointed out by the defendant, in a broad sense the mere operation of a motor vehicle endangers the safety of others to some extent. Although it is unlikely that the [Legislature] intended such a broad application, there is no language in the statute which limits it to a more specific application.' We are faced with the same situation in this case. Even assuming that subsection (1)(g) was intended to accomplish a socially desirable objective, if drastic surgery is necessary to preserve it, the surgery should, in our opinion, be performed by the Legislature and not by the court.

We conclude that section 28–4,127(1)(g), R.S.Supp., 1974, as presently constituted is vague and overbroad and in contravention of the United States and Nebraska Constitutions and we affirm the judgment of the District Court.

AFFIRMED.

SPENCER, Justice (dissenting).

I respectfully dissent for the reason that all the courts which have heretofore construed this particular statute have found it to be constitutional. I feel it is our duty to find a statute to be constitutional, if, by a proper construction we can reasonably do so. California, Florida, and Massachusetts have done so with this specific statute.

As the United States Supreme Court said in *Rose v. Locke* (1975), 423 U.S. 48, 96 S.Ct. 243, 46 L.Ed.2d 185: (The) "prohibition against excessive vagueness does not invalidate every statute which a reviewing court believes could have been drafted with greater precision. [Many] statutes will have some inherent vagueness, for '(i)n most English words and phrases there lurk uncertainties.'"

In *United States v. Powell* (1975), 423 U.S. 87, 96 S.Ct. 316, L.Ed.2d 228, the Supreme Court of the United States held: 'That Congress might have chosen 'clearer and more precise language' equally capable of achieving its objective does not mean that the statute is unconstitutionally vague.' Further, 'While doubts as to the applicability of the language in marginal fact situations may be conceived, we think that the statute gave respondent adequate warning * * *. Even as to more doubtful cases than that of respondent, we have said that 'the law is full of instances where a man's fate depends on his estimating rightly, that is, as the jury subsequently estimates it, some matter of degree.'"

CLINTON, Justice (responding to the dissent of SPENCER, J.)

The dissent of Spencer, J., calls for a brief response on two points. First, the primary constitutional deficiency of the provision of the statute in question is that it is overbroad, not that it is vague. The majority opinion amply demonstrates this overbreadth. Second, the Massachusetts, California, and Florida cases upon which the dissent relies completely disregard proper judicial functions and simply rewrite the statute. If we are to do that then we violate the principle of separation of powers of our own Constitution by a completely unwarranted intrusion into the legislative domain. We have said many times in somewhat varying language that: 'A court cannot, under the guise of its powers of construction, rewrite a statute, supply omissions, or make other changes . . . .' *Bessey v. Board of Educational Lands & Funds*, 185 Neb. 801, 178 N.W.2d 794.

It is far more important that we adhere to our own salutary principles of statutory construction, which are a recognition of the fundamental constitutional doctrine of separation of powers, than that we defend the police power of the state by arbitrarily restricting the operation of the general words of our present statute.

We cannot remedy the overbreadth short of rewriting the statute. If we can do that in this case, we can do it in any other. That is beyond our constitutional power as a court.

E. Drugs and Alcohol

An often-litigated issue was whether the constitutions of the United States or the States protect the right to drink alcohol or use other psychoactive substances. At one time, there was respectable authority that individuals did have such a right. Over time, courts revisited that position.

Herman v. State

Supreme Court of Indiana
8 Ind. 545 (1855)

PERKINS, J.

Herman was arrested upon a charge of having violated the liquor act of 1855. He obtained a writ of *habeas corpus,* pursuant to which he is now brought before us at chambers, with the cause of his detention in custody.

His counsel moves for his discharge on the ground that said liquor act is unconstitutional and void.

* * *

Counsel on both sides concede in argument that the record presents the question of the validity of, at least, what is alleged to be the prohibitory portion of said liquor act, and that question will, therefore, without inquiry upon the point, be considered.

We approach it with all the caution and solicitude its nature is calculated to inspire, and that intention of careful investigation its importance demands, feeling that the consequences of the principles we are about to assert will not be confined in their operation to this case alone. Preliminary to the discussion of the main questions involved, however, the course of argument of counsel requires that we should say a word by way of fairly setting forth the duty this Court has to perform in the premises, viz., the simply declaring the constitutionality or unconstitutionality of the law, with an assignment of the reasons upon which the declaration is based.

It will not be for us to inquire whether it be a good or bad law, in the abstract, unless the fact, as it might turn out to be, should become of some consequence in determining a doubtful point on the main question. It not unfrequently becomes the duty of courts to enforce injudicious acts of the legislature because they are constitutional, and to strike down such as, at first view, appear to be judicious, because they are in conflict with the constitution.

With these remarks, we proceed to the examination of the feature of the liquor act of 1855, now more especially presented to the Court. We shall not spend time upon the inquiry whether, on the day it came into force, there were existing unsold manufactured products in the hands of the distillers and brewers upon which it operated, rendering them valueless, or whether such products had all been disposed of between the passage and taking effect of the law. We shall direct our investigation to the character of its operation upon the future manufacture, sale, and consumption of intoxicating liquors. And—

First. Is it prohibitory?

* * *

We assume it as established, then, that the liquor act in question is absolutely prohibitory of the manufacture, sale, and use as a beverage, by the people of this State, of whisky, ale, porter, and beer.

* * *

The question now presents itself—

Secondly. Could the legislature of this State enact the prohibitory liquor law under consideration?

Few, if any, judicial decisions will be found to aid us in investigating this question, as no such law, in a country possessed of a judiciary and a constitution limiting the legislative power, has, till of late, been enacted. Some twelve hundred years ago *Mahomet* made such a law a part of his religious creed in opposition to the *Jewish* and *Christian* systems which recommended the moderate, but forbade the excessive use of intoxicating liquors. This law of *Mahomet*, (Koran, pp. 25 and 93,) was perhaps the first prohibitory act, but it does not appear to have been adopted by civilized nations till its late revival, in some shape or other, in one or more of our sister states. Hence, it has not often, if at all, as to this point, passed under judicial consideration.

A number of European writers on natural, public, and civil law are cited by counsel on behalf of the State to show the extent of legislative power; but those writers, respectable, able, and instructive upon some subjects as they are admitted to be, are not authority here upon this point. They are dangerous—indeed, utterly blind guides to follow in searching for the landmarks of legislative power in our free and limited government; for they had in view when writing, governments as existing when and where they wrote; under which they lived and had been educated, and which had no written constitutions limiting their powers—governments the theory of which was that they were paternal in character—that all power was in them by divine right, and they, hence, absolute; that the people of a country had no rights except what the government of that country graciously saw fit to confer upon them, and that it was its duty, like as a father towards his children, to command whatever it deemed expedient for the public good without first, in any manner, consulting that public, or recognizing in its members any individual rights.

Indeed, the discovery of the great doctrine of rights in the people as against the government, had not been made when the writers above referred to lived. Such governments as those described, could adopt the maxim quoted by counsel, that the safety of the people is the supreme law, and act upon it; and being severally the sole judges of what their safety, in the countries governed, respectively required, could prescribe what the people should eat and drink, what political, moral and religious creeds they should believe in, and punish heresy by burning at the stake, all for the public good. Even in *Great Britain,* esteemed to have the most liberal constitution on the Eastern continent, *Magna Charta* is not of sufficient potency to restrain the action of Parliament, as the judiciary do not, as a settled rule, bring laws to the test of its provisions. Laws are there overthrown only occasionally by judicial construction. But here, we have written constitutions which are the supreme law, which our legislators are sworn to support, within whose restrictions they must limit their action for the public welfare, and whose barriers they cannot overleap, under any pretext of supposed safety of the people; for along with our written constitutions, we have a judiciary whose duty it is, as the only means of securing to the people safety from legislative aggression, to annul all legislative action without the pale of those instruments. This duty of the judicial department in this country, was demonstrated by Chief Justice MARSHALL in *Marbury v. Madison,* 1 Cranch 137, and has since been recognized as settled American law. The maxim above quoted, therefore, as applied to legislative power, is here without meaning.

Nor does it prove the power of the State legislature to enact the law in question, to show that the Supreme Court of the *United States* has decided that it cannot declare such a State law inoperative; for that Court can only declare void such State laws as conflict with the restrictions imposed upon State power by the constitution of the *United States;* and if, in that constitution, the states are not restrained from passing laws in violation of the natural rights of the citizen, the Supreme Court of the *United States* cannot act upon such laws when passed, because they do not fall within its jurisdiction. Hence, that Court has decided that a state may deprive its citizens of property without making compensation, and of the right of trial by jury (*Barron v. The Mayor, &c.,* 7 Pet. 243); may pass laws depriving them of vested rights in property, and of the benefit of judgments they may have obtained in courts, and the like (*Satterlee v. Mathewson,* 2 Pet. 380, and the license cases in 5 How. 504); and no redress be obtainable in the *United States* Courts because there are no provisions in the *United States* constitution prohibiting the passage of such state laws. But the Supreme Court of this State has decided that, under our State constitution, the legislature cannot enact a law for the taking of private property without making compensation; cannot deprive the citizen of the right of trial by jury; and cannot set aside the judgment of a court, &c. *Young v. The State Bank,* 4 Ind. R. 301.—*McCormick v. Lafayette,* 1 *id.* 48.—*The State v. Mead,* 4 Blackf. 309.

It does not, therefore, follow that because the constitution of the *United States* does not prohibit state legislation infringing the natural rights of the citizen, such legislation is valid. The constitution of the *United States* may not, but that of the State may, inhibit it. And so, indeed, according to many eminent judges, may principles of natural justice, independently of all constitutional restraint. This doctrine has been asserted here. In *Andrews v. Russell,* 7 Blackf. 474, Judge DEWEY says: "We have said that the only provisions in the federal or State constitution restrictive of the power of the legislature, ... are," &c. "There are certain absolute rights, and the right of property is among them, which in all free governments must of necessity be protected from legislative interference, irrespective of constitutional checks and guards."

Should we find, however, in the course of this investigation that the constitution of our free State does, in fact, sufficiently protect natural rights from legislative interference, as it surely does, or it is grievously defective, it will not become necessary for us to inquire whether, in any event, it might be proper to fall back upon the doctrine above so unhesitatingly asserted.

Does our constitution, then, prohibit the passage of such an act as that now being considered? A *dictum* is quoted by counsel from the opinion in *Bepley v. The State,* 4 Ind. R. 264, that "it is competent for the legislature to declare any practice deemed injurious to the public a nuisance, and to punish it accordingly;" and hence, it is reasoned, any property; but *dicta,* as counsel well know, are not necessarily law—are, in fact, generally unconsidered first impressions which, all legal experience proves, are thrown out by all judges in giving opinions, as habitually and thoughtlessly as violations of the constitution are perpetrated by the legislature in enacting laws, and infinitely more excusably. Scarcely an elaborate opinion is written not containing them. This the profession will understand, and hence, are not misled by them if erroneous.

And it must be manifest to every one, on a moment's consideration, that the doctrine just quoted cannot be taken for law, and could not have been so intended, in an unlimited sense, by the learned judge who uttered it. The legislature cannot declare any practice it may deem injurious to the public a nuisance and punish it accordingly. It cannot so declare the practice of reading the Bible, though, perhaps, the government of *Spain* once did. It cannot so declare the practice of worshipping God according to the dictates of one's own conscience, though perhaps *Massachusetts,* in the days of *Roger Williams,* did it. It cannot so declare the practice of teaching schools, though perhaps *Virginia* might have done so in 1674, when Governor *Berkly* wrote from that colony: "I thank God there are no free schools nor printing; and I hope we shall not have these hundred years; for learning has brought disobedience and heresy and sects into the world, and printing has divulged them, and libels against the best government. God keep us from both." It cannot so declare the holding of political meetings and making speeches, the bearing of arms, publishing of newspapers, &c., &c., however injurious to the public the legislature might deem such practices to be; and why? Because the constitution forbids such declaration and punishment, and permits the people to use these practices. So with property: the legislature cannot interfere with it further, at all events, than the constitution permits. In short, the legislature cannot forbid and punish the doing of that which the constitution permits; and cannot take from the citizen that which the constitution says he shall have and enjoy. If it can, then we think all will admit that the constitution itself is worthless, the liberties of the people a dream, and our government as despotic as any on earth.

And we may here remark that the legislature can add nothing to its power over things by declaring them nuisances. A public nuisance is that which is noxious—offensive to all the people who may come in contact with it—and the offensive quality is in the thing itself, or the particular manner of its use, and is neither increased nor diminished by a legislative declaration. What the legislature has a right by the constitution to prohibit and punish, even to the forfeiture of property, it may thus deal with without first declaring the matter a nuisance; and whatever it has not a right by the constitution to prohibit and punish, it cannot thus deal with, even though it first fix upon it that odious name. To illustrate: The legislature has power, perhaps unlimited, over the public highways. It provides for opening, repairing, and vacating them. They are not the private property of the citizen. The legislature, therefore, may declare what obstructions shall be permitted, and what removed, whether they be in fact nuisances or not. So with Congress, in relation to the national highways for commerce. These are public for purposes of navigation, and are, perhaps, completely under the legislative power. So the legislature, when the practice was to license houses for the exclusive retail of spirituous liquors, that is, the sale of them in particular quantities at particular places, could impose conditions upon which the license should be granted, and could make the violation of the conditions cause of forfeiture, whether it was such as rendered the retailing house a nuisance or not, and whether it was so denominated or not.

But the legislature cannot declare the path from my house to my barn, nor any obstruction I may place in it, a nuisance, and order it discontinued; nor can it declare my store-room and stock of goods a nuisance, prohibit my selling them, and order them destroyed; because such acts would invade private property which the constitution protects. Still, the fact may be that the path and the store-room are nuisances which I have no right to maintain; for while I have the right to use my own property, still I must not so use it as to injure others. So all trades, practices, and property, may, by the manner, time, or place of use, become nuisances in fact, in quality; and subject, consequently, to forfeiture and abatement: for example, slaughter-houses in cities, or some descriptions of retailing houses; and this the legislature may have inquired into, and, if the fact of nuisance be found, may have the forfeiture and abatement adjudged and executed. And it is the province of the judiciary to conduct the inquiry, and declare the fact, or deny it, as the truth may turn out to be. Many things, by such proceedings, have already become established nuisances at common law. By this mode, when a party loses his trade or property, he does so because of his own fault, and this according to the judgment of his peers, and the provision of the general law of the land, and not by the tyranny of the legislature whose enactment may not be the law of the land. See numerous cases collected on this point in the first chapter of *Blackwell on Tax Titles.*

In accordance with this doctrine, we find that the criminal code of this State has ever contained the general provision that any person who erected or maintained a nuisance should be fined, &c., and that the nuisance might be abated (2 R. S. pp. 428, 429, ss. 8 and 9)—a provision that submits it to the country, to-wit, a jury under the charge of the court, to decide the fact of nuisance. This provision the courts have been daily enforcing against various noxious subjects; and if breweries and casks of liquor are nuisances, why have they not been prosecuted and abated also? What was the need of this special law upon the subject? We have assumed thus far, upon this branch of the case, that the constitution protects private property and pursuits, and the use of private property by way of beverage as well as medicine. It may be necessary, at this day, to demonstrate the fact.

The first section of the first article declares, that all men are endowed by their Creator with certain unalienable rights; that among these are life, liberty, and the pursuit of happiness. Under our constitution, then, we all have some natural rights that have not been surrendered, and which government cannot deprive us of, unless we shall first forfeit them by our crimes; and to secure to us the enjoyment of these rights, is the great end and aim of the constitution itself.

It thus appears conceded that rights existed anterior to the constitution— that we did not derive them from it, but established it to secure to us the enjoyment of them; and it here becomes important to ascertain with some degree of precision what these rights, natural rights, are.

Chancellor KENT, following BLACKSTONE, says: (vol. 2, p. 1.) "The absolute [or natural] rights of individuals may be resolved into the right of personal security, the right of personal liberty, and the right to acquire and enjoy property;" not some property, or one kind of property, but, at least, whatsoever the society organizing government, recognizes as property. How much does this right embrace, how far does it extend? It undoubtedly extends to the right of pursuing the trades of manufacturing, buying, and selling, and to the practice of using. These acts are but means of acquiring and enjoying, and are absolutely necessary and incidental to them. What, we may ask, is the right of property worth, stripped of the right of producing and using? "The right of property is equally invaded by obstructing the free employment of the means of production, as by violently depriving the proprietor of the product of his land." Say's Pol. Econ. 133.

In *Arrowsmith v. Burlingim*, 4 McLean, on p. 497, it is said: "A freeman may buy and sell at his pleasure. This right is not of society, but from nature. He never gave it up. It would be amusing to see a man hunting through our law books for authority to buy or sell or make a bargain." To the same effect Lord *Coke*, in 2 Inst. ch. 29, p. 47. Rutherforth's Inst. p. 20. This great natural right of using our liberty in pursuing trade and business for the acquisition of property, and of pursuing our happiness in using it, though not secure in *Europe* from the invasions of omnipotent parliaments, or executives, is secured to us by our constitutions. For in addition to the first section which we have quoted, and aside from the fact that the very purpose of establishing the constitution was such security, by section 11, article 1, it is declared that we shall be secure in our "persons, houses, papers, and effects, against unreasonable search and seizure." By section 21, we have the right to devote our labor to our own advantage, and to keep our property or its value for our own use, as they cannot be taken from us without being paid for. And by section 12, it is declared that "every man, for injury done to him in his person, property, or reputation, shall have remedy by due course of law." These sections, fairly construed, will protect the citizen in the use of his industrial faculties, and in the enjoyment of his acquisitions. This doctrine is not new in this Court. In *Doe v. Douglass*, 8 Blackf. 10, in speaking of the limitations in our constitution upon the legislative power, it is said, "they restrain the legislature from passing a law impairing the obligation of a contract, from the performance of a judicial act, and from any flagrant violation of the right of private property. This last restriction we think clearly contained in the first and 24th sections of the first article of our constitution,"—that of 1816.

We lay down this proposition, then, as applicable to the present case; that the right of liberty and pursuing happiness secured by the constitution, embraces the right, in each *compos mentis* individual, of selecting what he will eat and drink, in short, his beverages, so far as he may be capable of producing them, or they may be within his reach, and that the legislature cannot take away that right by direct enactment. If the constitution does not secure this right to the people, it secures nothing of value. If the people are subject to be controlled by the legislature in the matter of their beverages, so they are as to their articles of dress, and in their hours of sleeping and waking. And if the people are incompetent to select their own beverages, they are also incompetent to determine anything in relation to their living, and should be placed at once in a state of pupilage to a set of government sumptuary officers; eulogies upon the dignity of human nature should cease; and the doctrine of the competency of the people for self-government be declared a deluding rhetorical flourish. If the government can prohibit any practice it pleases, it can prohibit the drinking of cold water. Can it do that? If not, why not? If we are right in this, that the constitution restrains the legislature from passing a law regulating the diet of the people, a sumptuary law, (for that under consideration is such, no matter whether its object be morals or economy, or both,) then the legislature cannot prohibit the manufacture and sale, for use as a beverage, of ale, porter, beer, &c., and cannot declare those manufactured, kept and sold for that purpose, a nuisance, if such is the use to which those articles are put by the people. It all resolves itself into this, as in the case of printing, worshipping God, &c. If the constitution does not protect the people in the right, the legislature may probably prohibit; if it does, the legislature cannot. We think the constitution furnishes the protection. If it does not in this particular, it does, as we have said, as to nothing of any importance, and tea, coffee, tobacco, corn-bread, ham and eggs, may next be placed under the ban. The very extent to which a concession of the power in this case would carry its exercise, shows it cannot exist. We are confirmed in this view when we consider that at the adoption of our present constitution, there were in the State fifty distilleries and breweries, in which a half a million of dollars was invested, and five hundred men were employed; which furnished a market annually for two million bushels of grain, and turned out manufactured products to the value of a million of dollars, which were consumed by our people, to a great extent, as a beverage. With these facts existing, the question of incorporating into the constitution the prohibitory principle was repeatedly brought before the constitutional convention, and uniformly rejected. Debates in the Conv. vol. 2 p. 1,434 and others. We are further strengthened in this opinion when we notice, as we will as matter of general knowledge, the universality of the use of these articles as a beverage. It shows the judgment of mankind as to their value. "This use may be traced in several parts of the ancient world. *Pliny,* the naturalist, states that in his time it was in general use amongst all the several nations who inhabited the western part of *Europe;* and, according to him, it was not confined to those northern countries whose climate did not permit the successful cultivation of the grape. He mentions that the inhabitants of *Egypt* and *Spain* used a kind of ale; and says that, though it was differently named in different countries, it was universally the same liquor. See Plin. Nat. Hist. lib. 14, c. 22. *Herodotus,* who wrote five hundred years before *Pliny,* tells us that the *Egyptians* used a liquor made of barley. (2, 77.) *Dion Cassius* alludes to a similar beverage among the people inhabiting the shores of the *Adriatic.* Lib. 49, *De Pannoniis. Tacitus* states that the ancient *Germans,* for their drink, used a liquor from barley or other grain, and fermented it so as to make it resemble wine. *Tacitus De Mor. Germ. c.* 23. Ale was also the favorite liquor of the *Anglo-Saxons* and *Danes.'*If the accounts given by *Isidorus* and *Orosius* of the method of making ale amongst the ancient *Britons* be correct, it is evident that it did not essentially differ from our modern brewing. They state 'that the grain is steeped in water and made to germinate; it is then dried and ground; after which it is infused in a certain quantity of water, which is afterwards fermented.' Henry's Hist. of Eng. vol. 2, p. 364.'In early periods of the history of *England,* ale and bread appear to have been considered equally victuals or absolute necessaries of life.""""

In Biblical history we are told that the "vine, a plant which bears clusters of grapes, out of which wine is pressed," so abounded in *Palestine* that almost every family had a vineyard. *Solomon,* said to be the wisest man, had extensive vineyards which he leased to tenants. Song 8. verse 12; and *David,* in his 104th psalm, in speaking of the greatness, power, and works of God, says, verses 14 and 15, "He causeth grass to to grow for the cattle, and herb for the service of man; and wine that maketh glad the heart of man, and oil to make his face shine, and bread which strengtheneth man's heart."

It thus appears, if the inspired psalmist is entitled to credit, that man was made to laugh as well as weep, and that these stimulating beverages were created by the Almighty expressly to promote his social hilarity and enjoyment. And for this purpose have the world ever used them, they have ever given, in the language of another passage of scripture, strong drink to him that was weary and wine to those of heavy heart. The first miracle wrought by our Saviour, that at *Cana* of *Galilee,* the place where he dwelt in his youth, and where he met his followers after his resurrection, was to supply this article to increase the festivities of a joyous occasion; that he used it himself is evident from the fact that he was called by his enemies a winebibber; and he paid it the distinguished honor of being the eternal memorial of his death and man's redemption.

From *De Bow's* compendium of the census of 1850, p. 182, we learn that at that date there were in the *United States* 1,217 distilleries and breweries, with a capital of 8,507,574 dollars, consuming some 18,000,000 bushels of grain and apples, 1,294 tons of hops, and 61,675 hogsheads of molasses, and producing some 83,000,000 gallons of liquor.

From the Secretary of the Treasury's report of the commerce and navigation of the *United States* for 1850, we gather that there were imported into the *United States,* in that year, about 15,000,000 gallons of various kinds of liquors.

By the National Cyclopædia, vol. 12, p. 934, we are informed that for the year ending *January* 5, 1850, there were imported into *Great Britain* and *Ireland* 7,970,067 gallons of wine, 4,950,781 of brandy, and 5,123,148 of rum; and that there were manufactured in the same period, in that kingdom, in round numbers, 25,000,000 gallons.

In the 6th vol. of the same work, p. 328, it is said:

"The vine is one of the most important objects of cultivation in *France.* The amount of land occupied by this culture is about 5,000,000 *English* acres. The average yearly product is about 926,000,000 *English* gallons, of which about one-sixth is converted into brandy. The annual produce of the vineyards is estimated at about £28,500,000 sterling, [near 140,000,000 dollars,] of which ten-elevenths is consumed in *France.*" Wine is the common beverage of the people of *France,* and yet Professor *Silliman,* of *Yale* College, on the 17th of *April,* 1851, then at *Chalons,* writes:

"In traveling more than 400 miles through the rural districts of *France,* we have seen only a quiet, industrious population, peaceable in their habits, and, as far as we had intercourse with them, courteous and kind in their manners. We have seen no rudeness, no broil or tumult—have observed no one who was not decently clad, or who appeared to be ill fed. We are told, however, that the *French* peasantry live upon very small supplies of food, and in their houses are satisfied with very humble accommodations. Except in *Paris,* we have seen no instance of apparent suffering, and few even there; nor have we seen a single individual intoxicated or without shoes and stockings." Vol. 1, p. 185, of his Visit to Europe.

We have thus shown, from what we will take notice of historically, that the use of liquors, as a beverage, and article of trade and commerce, is so universal that they cannot be pronounced a nuisance. The world does not so regard them, and will not till the Bible is discarded, and an overwhelming change in public sentiment, if not in man's nature, wrought. And who, as we have asked before, is to force the people to discontinue the use of beverages?

Counsel say the maxim that you shall so use your own as not to injure another, justifies such a law by the legislature. But the maxim is misapplied; for it contemplates the free use, by the owner, of his property, but with such care as not to trespass upon his neighbor; while this prohibitory law forbids the owner to use his own in any manner, as a beverage. It is based on the principle that a man shall not use at all for enjoyment what his neighbor may abuse, a doctrine that would, if enforced by law in general practice, annihilate society, make eunuchs of all men, or drive them into the cells of the monks, and bring the human race to an end, or continue it under the direction of licensed county agents.

Such, however, is not the principle upon which the Almighty governs the world. He made man a free agent, and to give him opportunity to exercise his will, to be virtuous or vicious as he should choose, he placed evil as well as good before him, he put the apple into the garden of *Eden,* and left upon man the responsibility of his choice, made it a moral question, and left it so. He enacted as to that, a moral, not a physical prohibition. He could have easily enacted a physical prohibitory law by declaring the fatal apple a nuisance and removing it. He did not. His purpose was otherwise, and he has since declared that the tares and wheat shall grow together to the end of the world. Man cannot, by prohibitory law, be robbed of his free agency. See Milton's Areopagitica, or Speech for Liberty of Unlicensed Printing, Works vol. 1, p. 166.

But notwithstanding the legislature cannot prohibit, it can, by enactments within constitutional limits, so regulate the use of intoxicating beverages, as to prevent most of the abuses to which the use may be subject. We do not say that it can all; for under our system of government, founded in a confidence in man's capacity to direct his own conduct, designed to allow to each individual the largest liberty consistent with the welfare of the whole, and to subject the private affairs of the citizen to the least possible governmental interference, some excesses will occur, and must be tolerated, subject only to such punishment as may be inflicted. This itself will be preventive in its influence. The happiness enjoyed in the exercise of general, reasonably regulated liberty by all, overbalances the evil of occasional individual excess. Order must not be made to reign here as once at *Warsaw,* by the annihilation of all freedom of action, crushing out, indeed, the spirit itself of liberty. With us, in the language of the then illustrious *Burke,* when defending the revolting *American* colonies, something must be pardoned to the spirit of liberty.

What regulations of the liquor business would be constitutional, it is not for us to indicate in advance; but those which the legislature may from time to time prescribe can be brought by the citizen to the constitutional test before the judiciary, and it will devolve upon that department to decide upon their consistency with the organic law; in fact, the question of power, of usurpation, between the people and the people's representatives; and in doing this, so far as it may devolve upon us, we shall cheerfully throw every doubt in favor of the latter, and of stringent regulations. Such is the constitution of our government. *Maize v. The State,* 4 Ind. R. 342.—*Thomas v. The Board of Commissioners of Clay county,* 5 *id.* 557.—*Greencastle Township v. Black,* 5 *id.* 557.—*Larmer v. The Trustees of Albion,* 5 Hill, 121.—*Dunham v. The Trustees of Rochester,* 5 Cow. 462.—*Cotter v. Doty,* 5 Ohio R. 395.

It is like the case of laws for the collection of debts. The constitution prohibits the passage of an act impairing the obligation of a contract; yet the legislature may regulate the remedy upon contracts, but must regulate within such limits as not substantially to impair the remedy, as that would indirectly impair the obligation of the contract itself. *Gantly's Lessee v. Ewing,* 3 How. U. S. 707.

Regulations within constitutional limits, we have no doubt, if efficiently enforced, will accomplish, as we have said, nearly all that can reasonably be desired.

The legislature, we will add, may undoubtedly require the forfeiture of such particular portions of liquor as shall be kept for use in violation of proper regulations, as in the case of gunpowder stored in a populous city, and this forfeiture will be adjudged by the judiciary (see *Cotter v. Doty, supra*); but neither all the gunpowder nor liquor in the State, accompanied by the prohibition of the further manufacture and use of the article, can be forfeited on account of the improper use of a given quantity, because the entirety of neither of the articles is a nuisance. It is not pretended to be so as to gunpowder, and we think we have shown it is not so as to liquor.

So, it is doubtless competent for the legislature to establish proper police regulations to prevent the introduction of foreign paupers, &c.; for there is a palpable difference between excluding a foreign, and expelling a citizen, pauper. The constitutional convention thought it might have power to prohibit the ingress of foreign, while it might not to compel the egress of resident, negroes.

So, by such regulations, may the introduction of nuisances be prevented; for there is a wide difference between assuming to declare that a given thing is a nuisance, and the prohibiting of the introduction of what is conceded, or shall turn out to be, a nuisance.

And, in fact, the restrictions in the constitution upon the legislative power may operate for the benefit of those living under, and in some sense a party to, its provisions, and not for that of strangers. It will not be denied that but for the constitution and laws of the *United States* which impose the restriction, the State, as an independent sovereignty, might exclude from her borders all foreign liquors, whether nuisances, or not, unless, indeed, the doctrine upon which *Great Britain* was defended in forcing trade with *China* at the cannon's mouth be correct—that in this day of Christian civilization, it is the duty of all nations to admit universal reciprocal trade and commerce—a doctrine not yet, we think, incorporated into the code of international law.

And it would not follow that, because the State might prohibit the introduction of foreign wheat, she could, therefore, prohibit the cultivation of it within the State by her own citizens. The right of the State to prevent the introduction of foreign objects does not depend upon the fact of their being nuisances, or offensive otherwise; but she does it, when not restrained by the constitution or laws of the *United States,* in the exercise of her sovereign will.

This, however, is a topic involving questions of power between the state and federal governments which we do not intend discussing in the present opinion. We limit ourselves here to the question of the power of the legislature over the property and pursuits of the citizen under the State constitution. The restrictions which we have examined upon the legislative power of the State were inserted in the constitution to protect the minority from the oppression of the majority, and all from the usurpation of the legislature, the members of which, under our plurality system of elections, may be returned by a minority of the people. They should, therefore, be faithfully maintained. They are the main safeguards to the persons and property of the State.

It is easy to see that when the people are smarting under losses from depreciated bank paper, a feeling might be aroused that would, under our plurality system, return a majority to the legislature, which would declare all banks a nuisance, confiscate their paper and the buildings from which it issues.

So with railroads, when repeated wholesale murders are perpetrated by some of them; and, in Great Britain and France, we have examples of the confiscation of the property of the churches even; which, here, the same constitution that protects the dealer in beer, would render safe from invasion by the legislative power.

In our opinion for the reasons given above, the liquor act of 1855 is void. Let the prisoner be discharged.

———————————

Territory v. Ah Lim

Supreme Court of Washington
24 P. 588 (1890)

DUNBAR, J.

The defendant was indicted at the August term of the district court for King county for the crime of smoking opium as follows, to-wit, (omitting the formal part of the indictment:) "The said Ah Lim, on the 27th day of September, A. D. 1889, in the county of King, in the district aforesaid, then and there being, did then and there, willfully and unlawfully, smoke opium, by then and there burning said opium, and inhaling the fumes thereof through an instrument commonly known as an 'opium pipe,' contrary to the form of the statute," etc. To this indictment the defendant interposed a demurrer specifying several grounds, but the one relied upon by defendant, and the one to be considered here, is that the statute upon which the indictment is based is unconstitutional, as being in violation of the in alienable rights to life, liberty, and pursuit of happiness, and that it involves a deprivation of liberty and property, through a limitation upon the means and ways of enjoyment, without due process of law.

The duty of passing upon the constitutionality of a law should be approached by the court with the utmost caution, and demands the most solemn, thoughtful, and painstaking consideration, and in view of the consequences to society from the annulling of laws made by the representatives of the people, and presumed to have been enacted in response to the express desire of the people, it becomes the gravest question with which courts have to deal; and we believe it has been the uniform conviction of the courts that they ought not, and cannot, in justice to a coordinate department of the state government, declare a law to be void without a strong and earnest conviction, divested of all reasonable doubt, of its invalidity. The following quotation from an opinion rendered by Chief Justice MARSHALL in the case of *Fletcher v. Peck*, 6 Cranch, 87, commends itself to our approbation as resting upon sound principles of propriety and right. Said the judge: "The question whether a law be void for its repugnancy to the constitution is at all times a question of much delicacy, which ought seldom, if ever, to be decided in the affirmative in a doubtful case. The court, when impelled by a duty to render such a judgment, would be unworthy of its station could it be unmindful of the solemn obligations which that station imposes. But it is not on slight implication and vague conjecture that the legislature is to be pronounced to have transcended its powers, and its acts to be considered as void."

The organic act extends the power of the territorial legislature to all rightful subjects of legislation; and, when once we concede the rightfulness of the subject, the extent and character of the legislation on that subject cannot be called in question by the court. It has a right to take a comprehensive view in determining the necessity of the law, and the character of the purpose to be accomplished by it. This is the especial function of the legislature, and, in the investigation of legislative power, courts have nothing to do with questions of policy or expediency; for, as a learned author says: "The constitution has created the legislative and the judicial departments,-the one to make the law, the other to construe and administer it. It may be mischievous in its effects, burdensome upon the people, conflict with our conceptions of natural right, abstract justice, or pure morality, and of doubtful propriety, in numerous respects, and yet we would not be justified to hold that it was not within the scope of legislative authority for such reason; and, has as been well said by Mr. Cooley in his work on Constitutional Limitations, it must be evident to any one that the power to declare a legislative enactment void is one which the judge, conscious of the fallibility of human judgment, will shrink from exercising in any case where he can conscientiously, and with due regard to duty and official oath, decline the responsibility. Page 192. The legislative and judicial are co-ordinate departments of the government, of equal dignity. Each is alike supreme in the exercise of its proper functions, and cannot, directly or indirectly, while acting within the limit of its authority, be subjected to the control or supervision of the other without an unwarrantable assumption by that other power which by the constitution is not conferred upon it."

* * *

It is its peculiar duty to keep the first lines of the constitution clear, and not to stretch its power in order to correct legislative or executive abuses. Every branch of the government, the judicial included, does injustice for which there is no remedy, because everything human is imperfect. The legislative power "may be unwisely exercised or abused, yet it is a power intrusted by the constitution to the legislature, which, while exercised within the scope of the grant, is subject alone to their discretion; with which the judicial tribunals have no right to interfere because, in their judgment, the action of the legislature is contrary to the principles of natural justice." *Williams v. Cammack*, 27 Miss. 209.

In the case at bar, no special constitutional limitation or inhibition is pointed out with which the law in question is in conflict; but it is contended by the defense that the right of liberty, and pursuit of happiness, is violated by the prohibition of any act which does not involve direct and immediate injury to another. Counsel for appellant says in his brief that the parent may be compelled to send the child to school so many months in the year; the state may prescribe his studies, and may tax the people to the verge of bankruptcy to mould the infant's mind to their liking; but this right, he urges, is on the ground that the child is the ward of the state, and that such jurisdiction ceases when it becomes of age. It is difficult to see how the question of inalienable rights can be affected by age, when the law prescribes the age at which the ward arrives at his majority, and the time at which the inalienable rights attach. Doubtless the true theory on which compulsory education is sustained is that the state has an interest in the intellectual condition of each of its citizens, recognizing the fact that society is but an aggregation of individuals, and that the moral or intellectual plane of society is elevated or degraded in proportion to the plane occupied by its individual members, and that the education is not compelled for the benefit of the child during its minority, or for its exclusive benefit after its majority. The state has an undisputed right to, and does, provide gymnasium attachments to its schools, and prescribes calisthenic exercises for the muscular development of school children. The object to be attained is not for the exclusive benefit of the child. The state has an interest in the health of its citizens, and has a right to see to it that its citizens are self-supporting. It is burdened with taxation to build and maintain jails and penitentiaries for the safe-keeping of its criminals, and to protect its law-abiding subjects from their ravages. It is taxed to maintain insane asylums for the safe-keeping and care of those who become insane through vicious habits or otherwise. It is compelled to maintain hospitals for its sick, and poor-houses for the indigent and helpless; and surely it ought to have no small interest in, and no small control over, the moral, mental, and physical condition of its citizens. If the state concludes that a given habit is detrimental to either the moral, mental, or physical well-being of one of its citizens, to such an extent that it is liable to become a burden upon society, it has an undoubted right to restrain the citizen from the commission of that act; and fair and equitable consideration of the rights of other citizens make it not only its right, but its duty, to restrain him. If a man willfully cuts off his hand, or maims himself in such a way that he is liable to become a public charge, no one will doubt the right of the state to punish him; and if he smokes opium, thereby destroying his intellect, and shattering his nerves, it is difficult to see why a limitation of power should be imposed upon the state in such a case. But it is urged by the defense that a moderate use of opium, or that the moderate use of an opium pipe, is not deleterious, and consequently cannot be prohibited. We answer that this is a question of fact, which can only be inquired into by the legislature. Smoking opium is a recognized evil in this country. It is a matter of general information that it is an insidious and dangerous vice, a loathsome, disgusting, and degrading habit, that is becoming dangerously common with the youth of the country, and that its usual concomitants are imbecility, pauperism, and crime. It has been regarded as a proper subject of legislation in every western state; and it is admitted by counsel in defense, in the argument of this case, that the statute in relation to the suppression of joints kept for the purpose of smoking opium was constitutional and right.

Granted that this is a proper subject for legislative enactment and control, no limit can be placed on the legislative discretion. It is for the legislature to place on foot the inquiry as to just in what degree the use is injurious, to collate all the information, and to make all the needful and necessary calculations. These are questions of fact, with which the court cannot deal. The constitutionality of laws is not thus to be determined.

* * *

It is common to indulge in a great deal of loose talk about natural rights and liberties, as if these were terms of well-defined and unchangeable meaning. There is no such thing as an absolute or unqualified right or liberty guarantied to any member of society. Natural rights and liberties of a subject are relative expressions, and have relative or changeable meanings. What would be a right of liberty in one state of society would be an undue license in another. The natural rights of the subject, or his rightful exercise of liberty in the pursuit of happiness, depends largely upon the amount of protection which he receives from the government. Governments, in their earlier existence, afforded but little protection to their subjects. Consequently the subject had a right to pursue his happiness without much regard to the rights of the government. The reciprocal relations were not large. He yielded up but little, and received but little. If he was strong enough to buffet successfully with the world, all well and good. If not, he must live on the charity of individuals, or die, neglected, on the highway. But now all civilized governments make provisions for their unfortunates, and progress in this direction has been wonderful even since noted sages like Blackstone lectured upon the inalienable rights of man. Not only is the protection of individual property becoming more secure, but the vicious are restrained and controlled, and the indigent and unfortunate are maintained, at the expense of the government, in comfort and decency; and the natural liberties and rights of the subject must yield up something to each one of these burdens which advancing civilization is imposing upon the state. It is not an encroachment upon the time-honored rights of the individual, but it is simply an adjustment of the relative rights and responsibilities incident to the changing condition of society.

Our conclusion is that the law in question involves no inalienable right. It may be radical, injudicious, and wrong; but, as we have before indicated, these are questions solely for legislative investigation and discretion, and, as has been said by Judge Story: "Judges should regard it as their duty to interpret laws, and not to wander off into speculations upon their policy." The judgment of the court below is affirmed.

ANDERS, C. J., and HOYT, J., concur.

SCOTT, J., (*dissenting.*)

I cannot agree with the decision rendered in this case. That part of the act upon which the indictment is founded is, in my opinion, void. It is as follows: "Any person or persons who shall smoke or inhale opium *** shall be deemed guilty of a misdemeanor," etc. Sess. Laws 1883, p. 30. It is amendatory of section 2073 of chapter 149 of the Code of 1881. The chapter is entitled, "Smoking and Inhaling Opium," and apparently was mainly intended to prohibit the keeping of resorts for the smoking of opium, and to this extent was a legitimate exercise of police powers. The purpose for which the amendment was adopted is not declared either in the entitling, or in the body of the act, and cannot easily be arrived at. The acts prohibited therein have no reference to the keeping of a resort. The only other legislation we have found upon this subject is contained in the act approved November 6, 1877, which amends section 13 of an act approved November 12, 1875, entitled "An act defining nuisances and securing remedies." The chapter in the Code does not refer in any way to this act. All these laws were passed by our various legislatures while we were under a territorial form of government.

The offense charged in this case cannot be held to be a nuisance, for it relates purely to the private action or conduct of the individual, and must not be confounded with those acts which directly affect the public. It is thought that the act in question is *sui generis;* that there is none other of a similar nature in force in this country, or one that has ever been sustained by the courts since we became an independent nation, although there may be occasional instances somewhat closely allied to it. Legislation, however, has ordinarily been confined to those cases where the act of the person directly and clearly affected the public in some manner. But here a single inhalation of opium, even by a person in the seclusion of his own house, away from the sight, and without the knowledge of any other person, constitutes a criminal offense under this statute; and this regardless of the actual effect of the particular act upon the individual, whether beneficial or injurious. It is urged that there could be no conviction in such a case, for the want of proof. But the difficulty or impossibility of conviction could not affect the criminality of the act; also, the evidence might sometimes be furnished by the admission or confession of the guilty party, if in no other way. It is admitted that this law can only be sustained upon some one or more of the following grounds, viz.: That smoking or inhaling opium injures the health of the individual, and in this way weakens the state; that it tends to the increase of pauperism; that it destroys the moral sentiment, and leads to the commission of crime. In other words, that it has an injurious effect upon the individual, and consequently results indirectly in an injury to the community. And it is claimed that we must presume that the legislature had some one or more of these objects in view in enacting the law, although there is nothing upon the face of the act to indicate the legislative intention. This is going to a very great and dangerous extent to sustain legislation in this most important branch of our social structure.

* * *

It is the one great principle of our form of government, expressed throughout that soul-inspiring document, our national constitution, that the individual right of self-control is not to be limited, only to that extent which is necessary to promote the general welfare; and these are not only questions of natural right but of constitutional right as well. It is none the less a constitutional guaranty because general in its nature, or implied in the bill of rights, or because each particular act wherein the will of the citizen should not be interfered with is not pointedly and specifically guaranteed. Such particularity would be impossible. When one becomes a member of society, he necessarily parts with some rights or privileges which as an individual, not affected by his relations to others, he might retain. A body politic is a social compact by which the whole people covenant with each citizen, and each citizen with the whole people, that all shall be governed by certain laws for the common good. This does not confer power upon the whole people to control rights which are purely and exclusively private; but it does authorize the establishing of laws requiring each citizen to so conduct himself, and so use his own property, as not unnecessarily to injure another. This is the very essence of government. See *Munn v. Illinois*, 94 U. S. 114.

It is contended here that the legislature, being the sole and absolute judge of the effect upon the individual of the act forbidden, has decided every act of smoking or inhaling opium to be injurious to the person so doing, no matter how long or how short the duration, or how great or how small the quantity, or under what conditions or circumstances the same might have been used, and that there is no right of appeal to the courts in this particular. Such a construction of the law makes the legislature the sole judge of the constitutionality of its own acts of this character. There must be a right of review or control, to some extent, in the courts. Each citizen is entitled to the protection of all the branches of the government. A declaration by the legislature as to what the law shall be is not necessarily a conclusion reached by the state. The legislature is not the state, although a very important or essential part of it. The power to protect the rights of the citizen from the wrongful effect of such legislation is peculiarly adapted to, and within the province of, the judicial branch of the government, and can be exercised in one of two ways. Either the scope of such legislation should be limited to those instances where injury results as a matter of fact, and resorting to a trial in court to prove that fact in each individual instance; or if this would render an enforcement of the law impracticable, and a few must suffer for the public good by being prevented from regulating their own personal conduct in some matters beneficial or not harmful to them, in order that another class may be prevented from like actions, which to such persons would be harmful, then by recognizing a discretionary power in the legislature to prohibit such acts entirely, and at the same time recognizing the duty of the courts to correct abuses thereof when the act prohibited should have no real relation or tendency to produce any of the results sought to be avoided. To declare any private act or omission of the citizen to be crime, which does not result in any injury to the person, and could not possibly affect society under any other possible view except the last one, would be an unwarranted infringement of individual rights, and therefore unconstitutional. Individual desires are too sacred to be ruthlessly violated where only acts are involved which purely appertain to the person, and which do not clearly result in an injury to society, unless, possibly, thus rendered necessary in order to prevent others from like actions, which to them are injurious.

A great principle is involved in this character of legislation. Suppose the legislature had forbidden the use of opium in any manner. If the unqualified right to prohibit its use in one way exists, this carries with it the right to prohibit its use entirely. Substitute any other substance, whether commonly used as medicine, food, or drink, and still such a statute must be upheld, if the courts have no right of review. It is no answer to say that the legislature would do nothing unreasonable. No man knows as to this. The question is, has it the arbitrary power and right? Neither is it a sufficient answer to say that an appeal may be had to a subsequent legislature for redress; that where such laws are wrongfully passed the remedy must be sought in this way; and that until another legislature is convened, the citizen must tamely submit to, and obey, the restrictions and commands of every conceivable law relating to his personal conduct that, through some possible legislative caprice or inadvertence, might find its way upon the statute-books, before the question could be again submitted to another legislature, and its constitutionality again be tried by it, as that is virtually what the question would be. If it tended to promote the public welfare in any of the ways specified, it would be constitutional; and, if it did not do so, it would then be unconstitutional and void. And under such a view the legislature must decide this.

* * *

Whichever view is taken of the duty of the courts in the premises-whether to hold such laws must be limited to instances where injury results to the particular person, or otherwise-the act in question should be held void. It is altogether too sweeping in its terms. I make no question but that the habit of smoking opium may be repulsive and degrading; that its effect would be to shatter the nerves, and destroy the intellect; and that it may tend to the increase of pauperism and crime. But there is a vast difference between the commission of a single act and a confirmed habit. There is a distinction to be recognized between the use and abuse of any article or substance. It is also a well-known fact that opium, in its different forms, is frequently administered as a medicine, and with beneficial results; and, while it may not be customary to administer it by way of inhalation, yet the legislature should not arbitrarily prevent its use in such a manner. If this act must be held valid, it is hard to conceive of any legislative action affecting the personal conduct or privileges of the individual citizen that must not be upheld. We have been cited to no law, which has been sustained, that goes to the extent that this one does. It has no reference to the manufacture or sale of the substance. It is not based upon any pernicious example that the commission of the act might be to others. The prohibited act cannot affect the public in any way except through the primary personal injury to the individual, if it occasions him any injury. It looks like a new and extreme step, under our government, in the field of legislation, if it really was passed for any of the purposes upon which that character of legislation can be sustained, if at all. An act somewhat similar to it was held void in Re *Ah Jow*, 29 Fed. Rep. 181.

In former times, laws were sometimes passed limiting individual conduct in ways that are now considered ridiculous, such as regarding the number of courses permissible at dinner, the length of pikes that might be worn on the shoes, etc. But these were founded on the pique or whims of an exacting and tyrannical aristocracy rather than on reason, or, as in the case of the Connecticut Blue Laws, upon views of propriety or religion that do not now obtain with anything like the former degree of strictness. Judge Cooley, in his admirable work on Constitutional Limitations, at page 385, says: "In former times, sumptuary laws were sometimes passed, and they were even deemed essential in republics to restrain the luxury so fatal to that species of government. But the ideas which suggested such laws are now exploded, utterly, and no one would seriously attempt to justify them in the present age. The right of every man to do what he will with his own, not interfering with the reciprocal right of others, is accepted among the fundamentals of our law. The instances of attempt to interfere with it have not been numerous since the early colonial days. A notable instance of an attempt to substitute the legislative judgment for that of the proprietor, regarding the manner in which he should use and employ his property, may be mentioned. In the state of Kentucky, at an early day, an act was passed to compel the owners of wild lands to make certain improvements upon them within a specified time; and it declared them forfeited to the state in case the statute was not complied with. It would be difficult to frame, consistently with the general principles of free government, a plausible argument in support of such a statute. It was not an exercise of the right of eminent domain, for that appropriates property to some specific public use on making compensation. It was not taxation, for that is simply an apportionment of the burden of supporting the government. It was not a police regulation, for that could not go beyond preventing an improper use of the land with reference to the due exercise of rights and enjoyment of legal privileges by others. It was purely and simply a law to forfeit a man's property if he failed to improve it according to a standard which the legislature had pre-scribed. To such a power, if possessed by the government, there could be no limit but the legislative discretion; and, if defensible on principle, then a law which should authorize the officer to enter a man's dwelling, and seize and confiscate his furniture if it fell below, or his food if it exceeded, an established legal stan-dard, would be equally so. But, in a free country, such laws, when mentioned, are condemned instinctively." This statute, referred to, was subsequently declared unconstitutional in Gaines v. Buford, 1 Dana, 484, as appears in the note in said work. In *Mugler v. Kansas*, 123 U. S. 623, 8 Sup. Ct. Rep. 273, which was a case arising under the prohibitory liquor laws of that state, the court in its opinion discussed the question, somewhat, as to whether the state could prohibit a man from manufacturing liquor for his own personal use, and concluded it could do so if it affected the rights and interests of the community. As to where the power rested to decide as to this, the court said: "But by whom, or by what authority, is it to be determined whether the manufacture of particular articles of drink, either for general use or for the personal use of the maker, will injuriously affect the public? Power to determine such questions so as to bind all must exist some-where, else society will be at the mercy of the few, who, regarding only their own appetites or passions, may be willing to imperil the peace and security of the many, provided only they are permitted to do as they please. Under our system that power is lodged with the legislative branch of the government. It belongs to that department to exert what are known as the 'police powers of the state,' and to determine primarily what measures are appropriate or needful for the protec-tion of the public morals, the public health, or the public safety. It does not at all follow that every statute enacted ostensibly for the promotion of these ends is to be accepted as a legitimate exertion of the police powers of the state. There are, of necessity, limits beyond which legislation cannot rightfully go. While every possible presumption is to be indulged in favor of the validity of a statute, *** the courts must obey the constitution rather than the law-making department of government, and must, upon their own responsibility, determine whether, in any particular case, these limits have been passed." Here a discretionary power in the legislature is distinctly recognized, and also a final revisory or restraining power in the courts to correct what may appear to be abuses. The court further said, quoting partly from *Marbury v. Madison*, 1 Cranch, 137: "To what purpose are powers limited, and to what purpose is that limitation committed to writing, if these limits may at any time be passed by those intended to be restrained? The distinction between a government with limited and unlimited powers is abolished if those limits do not confine the persons on whom they are imposed, and if acts prohibited and acts allowed are of equal obligation. The courts are not bound by mere forms, nor are they to be misled by mere pretenses. They are at liberty, indeed, are under a solemn duty, to look at the substance of things, whenever they enter upon the inquiry whether the legislature has transcended the limits of its authority. If, therefore, a statute purporting to have been enacted to protect the public health, the public morals, or the public safety has no real or substantial relation to those objects, or is a palpable invasion of rights secured by the fundamental law, it is the duty of the courts to so adjudge, and thereby give effect to the constitution."

From the best investigation I have been able to give this subject, I am forced to the conclusion that the judgment of the court below should have been reversed, and the defendant discharged.

STILES, J., concurs with SCOTT, J.

Notes and Questions

1. In *Ex Parte Yung Jon*, 28 F. 308 (D. Or. 1886), Judge Deady denied that the defendant had a constitutional right to use opium. Do you see the basis for another constitutional claim in the opinion:

> True, we permit the indiscriminate use of alcohol and tobacco, both of which are classed by science as poisons, and doubtless destroy many lives annually. But the people of this country have been accustomed to the manufacture and use of these for many generations, and they are produced and possessed under the common and long-standing impression that they are legitimate articles of property, which the owner is entitled to dispose of without any unusual restraint; and even now it is pretty well settled that the legislature may absolutely prohibit the future manufacture and use of these articles, and may also prohibit the sale and use of the stock in hand, on making compensation to the owners for the loss occasioned thereby. On the other hand, the use of opium, otherwise than as this act allows, as a medicine, has but little, if any, place in the experience or habits of the people of this country, save among a few aliens. Smoking opium is not our vice, and therefore it may be that this legislation proceeds more from a desire to vex and annoy the 'Heathen Chinee' in this respect, than to protect the people

from the evil habit. But the motives of legislators cannot be the subject of judicial investigation for the purpose of affecting the validity of their acts. It is the duty of the law-maker, as far as his power extends, to enact laws for the conservation of the morals of society, and to promote the growth of right thinking and acting in all matters affecting the physical or mental well-being of its members. In the exercise of this power, and the discharge of this duty, this act to regulate the disposition and use of opium, considered as a dangerous drug, which the weak and unwary, unless prevented, may use to their physical and mental ruin, appears to have been passed. The subject of the act is sufficiently expressed in the title, and the use of the article is not thereby restrained, so as to destroy its value as a medicine or remedial agent, the only use of which is generally considered and accepted as a proper one in this country. *State v. Ah Chew,* 16 Nev. 50.

2. Keep your eyes open for other constitutional problems. Some state constitutions, for example, require that bills deal only with a single subject or properly display their topic in the title, and if they fail to do so, courts will later strike them down. *See, e.g., Missouri Health Care Association v. Attorney General,* 953 S.W.2d 617 (Mo. 1997) (invalidating statute which, among other things, created a felony, because it dealt with more than one subject).

United States v. Clary

United States District Court, E.D. Missouri, Eastern Division
846 F. Supp. 768 (1994)

FINDINGS AND CONCLUSIONS OF LAW

CAHILL, District Judge.

Defendant Edward Clary was arrested for possession with intent to distribute 67.76 grams of cocaine base. Clary pled guilty to possession with intent to distribute cocaine base ("crack cocaine"), pursuant to 21 U.S.C. § 841(b)(1)(A)(iii) (hereinafter referred to as the "crack statute"), punishable by a mandatory minimum sentence of 10 years imprisonment. Prior to sentencing, Clary, a black male, filed a motion challenging the constitutionality of the crack statute and contended, *inter alia,* that the sentence enhancement provisions contained in it and United States Sentencing Guidelines (U.S.S.G.) § 2D1.1 violated his equal protection rights guaranteed by the Fifth Amendment.

The Court scheduled this case for hearing on the motion for a downward departure and the motion challenging the constitutionality of the statute. After extended hearings the Court took this matter under advisement and gave it detailed and exhaustive consideration. Upon evaluating the evidence and legal arguments, the Court issues this memorandum.

Specifically, defendant Clary asserts that the penalty differential of the "100 to 1" ratio of cocaine to cocaine base contained in both the crack statute and the United States Sentencing Guidelines has a disproportionate impact on blacks because blacks are more likely to possess cocaine base than whites who are more likely to possess cocaine powder. Therefore, defendant's argument continues, providing longer sentences for possession of cocaine base than for the identical amount of cocaine powder treats a similarly situated defendant in a dissimilar manner, which violates his right to equal protection under the law.

The Problem Before The Court

Before this Court are two different sentencing provisions contained within the same statute for possession and distribution of different forms of the same drug. The difference—the key difference—is that possession and distribution of 50 grams of crack cocaine carries the same mandatory minimum sentence of 10 years imprisonment as possession and distribution of 5000 grams of powder cocaine. Both provisions punish the same drug, but penalize crack cocaine 100 times more than powder cocaine!

Congress tells us that the rationale for this sentencing dichotomy which produces harsher punishment for involvement with crack cocaine is because it is so much more dangerous than powder cocaine. As "proof," Congress relied upon endless media accounts of crack's increased threat to society. While Congress may have had well-intentioned concerns, the Court is equally aware that this one provision, the crack statute, has been directly responsible for incarcerating nearly an entire generation of young black American men for very long periods, usually during the most productive time of their lives. Inasmuch as crack and powder cocaine are really the same drug (powder cocaine is "cooked" with baking soda for about a minute to make crack), it appears likely that race rather than conduct was the determining factor.

Although both statutory provisions purport to punish criminal activity for both crack and powder cocaine, the blacks using crack are punished with much longer sentences than whites using the same amount of powder cocaine. This disparity is so significantly disproportional that it shocks the conscience of the Court and invokes examination.

* * *

The Challenge To The Court

The Court is faced with the task of resolving whether the crack statute violated defendant Clary's equal protection rights. The equal protection component of the Fifth Amendment Due Process clause commands that similarly situated people must be treated alike. The Court's basic understanding of this constitutional rule is that when one group of people violates the same type of laws as other people similar to them, they should be punished in the same manner.

To determine whether a law treats similarly situated people in a dissimilar manner, a violation of equal protection under the U.S. Constitution, the Court must first determine the appropriate type of judicial review to apply. Judicial review is conducted under one of three different levels of scrutiny depending upon the seriousness of the constitutional violation that triggers the review.

The Court conducts the lowest level of constitutional scrutiny, a *rational basis review,* to determine whether a law that causes disparate treatment among similarly situated persons serves a rational state or governmental purpose. "Equal protection does not require that all persons be dealt with identically . . . [but] it does require that a distinction [that is] made have some relevance to the purpose for which the classification is made." *Baxstrom v. Herold,* 383 U.S. 107, 111, 86 S.Ct. 760, 763, 15 L.Ed.2d 620 (1966).

The next level of review, *intermediate scrutiny,* applies when the Court must determine whether the classification scheme included in the law must "fairly be viewed as furthering a substantial interest of the state." *Plyler v. Doe,* 457 U.S. 202, 217–18, 102 S.Ct. 2382, 2395, 72 L.Ed.2d 786 (1982). "Under this standard, although a law does not involve a facially invidious classification, it will be reviewed if it gives rise to recurring constitutional difficulties." *Id.*

The highest form of constitutional review that the Court evokes, *strict scrutiny,* is mandated when the legislative classification incorporates presumptively suspect factors, such as race, or fundamental individual liberties, such as religion. In such cases, once the suspect classification is revealed, the government must prove that the classification is narrowly tailored to further a compelling government interest. For example, racist statutes which on their face and in their direct language created segregated facilities such as restrooms and drinking fountains were struck down by the United States Supreme Court under strict scrutiny.

The difficult situation that a Court must face is to determine whether a statute which is facially neutral was enacted for racial reasons and would thereby have a disparate impact on a particular racial group. Whether or not racial discrimination was involved in legislative action that resulted in a law which, although facially neutral, still has a racially disparate impact "demands a sensitive inquiry into such circumstantial evidence of intent as may be available." *Arlington Heights v. Metropolitan Housing Development Corporation,* 429 U.S. 252, 266, 97 S.Ct. 555, 564, 50 L.Ed.2d 450 (1977).

Under *Arlington,* the Supreme Court set forth key factors to evaluate whether a law was motivated by racial discrimination. These factors included the presence of disparate impact, the overall historical context of the legislation, the legislative history of the challenged law, and departures from the normal legislative process. Additional legal precedent has provided the Court with more criteria for its review, such as foreseeability of the consequences of the legislation; however, *Arlington* provides the Court with the major benchmark to discover the presence of racial influence in the legislative decision making process.

These various levels of constitutional review evolved as a response to the manner in which racism in America has manifested itself within the legal system. Overt racism, evidenced by such occurrences as "Jim Crow Laws," allowed legislators to enact racist laws without reprisals. As civil rights for *all* Americans became a reality, continued attempts to maintain racial barriers took on the form of more subtle, covert, facially neutral legislation. Examples of this type of legislation included zoning, voting and housing laws.

Today most legislation would not contain overtly racist referrals and, indeed, would eliminate the slightest allusion to racial factors in the words of the legislation itself. But today, despite the fact that a law may be racially neutral on its face, there still may be factors derived from unconscious racism that affect and infiltrate the legislative result.

A History Of Racism in Criminal Punishment

That black people have been punished more severely for violating the same law as whites is not a new phenomenon. A dual system of criminal punishment based on racial discrimination can be traced back to the time of slavery. In order to understand the role that racism has played in enacting the penalty enhancement for using crack cocaine, one must first take note of America's history of racially tainted criminal laws, particularly drug laws. Race has often served as a significant contributing factor to the enhancement of penalties for crime.

Early in our nation's history, legislatures were motivated by racial discrimination to differentiate between crimes committed by whites and crimes committed by blacks. For example, "An Act Against Stealing Hogs" provided a penalty of 25 lashes on a bare back or a 10 pound fine for white offenders, while nonwhites (slave and free) would receive 39 lashes, with no chance of paying a fine to avoid the whipping. In 1697, Pennsylvania passed death sentence legislation for black men who raped white women and castrated them for attempted rape. White men who committed the same offense would be fined, whipped, or imprisoned for one year.

During Reconstruction, Southern legislatures sought to maintain control of freed slaves by passing criminal laws directed at blacks that treated petty crimes as serious offenses. A Georgia law passed in 1875 made hog stealing a felony. A Missouri "pig law" defined the theft of property worth more than $10 as grand larceny and provided for punishment of up to five years of hard labor. As a result, Southern prisons swelled and became, for the first time, predominantly black. The prison population in Georgia alone tripled within two years.

Prior to the civil rights era, Congress repeatedly imposed severe criminal sanctions on addictive substances once they became popular with minorities.9 Historically, a consortium of reactionary media and a subsequently inflamed constituency have combined to influence Congress to impose more severe criminal sanctions for use of narcotics once they became popular with minorities.

Media accounts and inaccurate data influenced public opinion about opium smoking. "Ambivalence and outright hostility" toward Chinese coupled with the concern that opium smoking was spreading to the upper classes, provided the foundation for the passage of the 1909 Smoking Opium Exclusion Act. "Yellow Peril" was a term used in the years between the Great Wars to express the fear that the huge population of the Far East posed a military threat to the West. This fear induced an aversion to the opium usage believed to be prevalent in Chinese communities and foisted anti-opium legislation.

The Harrison Act of 1914, the first federal law to prohibit distribution of cocaine and heroin, was passed on the heels of overblown media accounts depicting heroin-addicted black prostitutes and criminals in the cities. The author of the Act, Representative Francis Harrison, moved to include coca leaves in the bill "since [the leaves] make Coca–Cola and Pepsi–Cola and all those things are sold to Negroes all over the South." At one point the bill appeared to be facing defeat until Dr. Hamilton Wright, the American delegate to the Hague Opium Conference, 1911–1912, submitted an official report in which he warned Congress of the drug crazed blacks in the South whose drug habits *"threaten[ed] to creep into the higher social ranks of the country"* [emphasis added]. The images of narcotics and a black rebellion in the South and images of black addicts involved with white women were central to the hysteria that motivated legislative enactments. His report, amplified and personalized by the news media and photographs, helped to shape public opinion regardless of the factual basis. True or not, the black addict became a stereotype not synonymous with most black men.

The Marijuana Tax Act was signed into law on August 2, 1937, after a successful media campaign orchestrated by Harry J. Anslinger, then the Commissioner of the Treasury Department's Bureau of Narcotics. Using the media as his forum, Anslinger graphically depicted the alleged insane violence which he alleged resulted from marijuana use.

In later decades cocaine became associated with exotic groups such as Hollywood entertainers and jazz musicians. It earned the moniker of the "rich man's drug." In the early 1960s and 1970s, cocaine began to move into mainstream society, and became the "drug of the eighties." Even with the widespread use of powder cocaine, no new drug laws were enacted to further criminalize or penalize cocaine possession. The "war on drugs" with respect to powder cocaine was concentrated on impeding international import of the drug or targeted large scale financiers. The social history is clear that so long as cocaine powder was a popular amusement among young, white professionals, law enforcement policy prohibiting cocaine was weakly enforced.

Almost every major drug has been, at various times in America's history, treated as a threat to the survival of America by some minority segment of society. Panic based on media reports which incited racial fears has been used historically in this country as the catalyst for generating racially biased legislation. The association of illicit drug use with minorities and the threat of it "spreading to the higher ranks" is disturbingly similar to the events which culminated in the "100 to 1" ratio enhancement in the crack statute.

* * *

Unconscious Racism

Thus, the root of racism has been implanted in our collective unconscious and has biased the ideas that Americans accept about the significance of race. Racism goes beyond prejudicial discrimination and bigotry. It arises from outlooks, stereotypes, and fears of which we are vastly unaware. Our historical experience has made racism an integral part of our culture even though society has more recently embraced an ideal that rejects racism as immoral. When an individual experiences conflict between racist ideas and the social ethic that condemns those ideas, the mind excludes his racism from his awareness.

Conjointly, the root of unconscious racism can be found in the latent psyches of white Americans that were inundated for centuries with myths and fallacies of their superiority over the black race. So deeply embedded are these ideas, that their acceptance and socialization from generation to generation have become a mere routine.

Unconscious racism existed in some limited form during slavery. As outright discrimination against blacks became increasingly politically and socially unacceptable, and, in 1954, in some measure *illegal*, racist actions metamorphized into more subtle forms of discrimination. As more well-educated blacks flowed into America's mainstream, whites even began to differentiate between the kind of blacks who reflected white values and who were not like "those other" blacks akin to the inner city stereotype.

A benign neglect for the harmful impact or fallout upon the black community that might ensue from decisions made by the white community for the "greater good" of society has replaced intentional discrimination. In the "enlightened and politically correct 90s," whites have become indignant at the suggestion that they harbor any ill-will towards blacks or retain any vestiges of racism. After all, they have black friends. They work with black people every day. They enjoy black entertainers on their favorite television programs every night.

Similarly, police and law enforcement authorities responded that they were also protecting black neighborhoods and black citizens from the scourges of crime and drugs by using harsh "get tough" laws to arrest crack dealers and other criminal perpetrators who lurked in the ghetto. Therefore, the logic continued, it really did not matter what happened to those blacks who did not fit the mold as long as white America was kept protected and safe from them. Hardly any law or measure was too harsh to deal with them, including the crack statute.

When counsel first argued that overt racism was really the basis for the discriminatory crack penalties, this Court rejected that approach out-of-hand, for the Court did not believe that such outrageous and outmoded ideas would affect the legislators of this day and age. But upon reflection, the Court recognizes that while intentional discrimination is unlikely today, unconscious feelings of difference and superiority still live on even in well-intentioned minds. There is a realization that most Americans have grown beyond the evils of overt racial malice, but still have not completely shed the deeply rooted cultural bias that differentiates between "them" and "us."

The illustration of unconscious racism is patently evident in the crack cocaine statutes. Had the same type of law been applied to powder cocaine, it would have sentenced droves of young whites to prison for extended terms. Before the enactment of such a law, it would have been much more carefully and deliberately considered. After all, in these days when "toughness on crime" is a political virtue, the simplest and fairest solution would have been to make the severe punishment for powder cocaine the same as for crack cocaine. But when the heavy punishment is inflicted only upon those in the weak and unpopular minority community, it is an example of benign neglect arising from unconscious racism.

Psychoanalytic theory explains the processes which govern the mind and control mental behavior as primary and secondary. The primary process, *the Id,* consists of wishes, desires and instincts that strive for gratification, and which occur outside of our awareness. The secondary process, *the Ego,* happens under conscious control and is bound by logic and reason. "The Ego is required to respect the demands of reality and to conform to ethical and moral laws." The thoughts and desires generated by the Id will not reach our conscious control until screened by the Ego where they are "criticized, rejected or modified" by defense measures. In the case of a conflict, the information from the Id will not pass, thereby remaining in the unconscious, or will pass by "disguising forbidden wishes and making them palatable."

Racism is irrational. It is socially and politically unacceptable. Because the "Ego must adapt to cultural order," ideas, attitudes, and behavior based upon racial prejudice will be repressed and relegated to the unconscious by the Ego and not allowed to pass to the conscious until they reshape or restructure to be disguised as morally and socially acceptable. When an individual cannot live up to the aspirations and standards of his own conscience, he will rationalize his unexplained conflict in his emotions with a legitimate reason. Hence, racism is forced into the unconscious mind. A person who feels benign toward blacks will nevertheless make decisions and take actions that will harm minorities "because of" their race and consequently create racial stereotypes.

Cognitive theorists promote that "categorization" is a common source of racial stereotypes. Because too many events occur daily for the mind to address them on an individual basis, the mind categorizes experiences in order to make sense of them. The more particular the categorization of groups of people, the more likely the person is to sharply distinguish the characteristics of individuals belonging to the group. Social categories are created through assimilation, which "entails learning and internalizing preferences and evaluations "[footnote omitted]. Stereotyping, assimilating and internalizing occur early in life, usually from parents or television. Becoming fearful of blacks, perceiving blacks as dangerous, different or subordinate, are lessons learned and internalized completely outside of our awareness, and are reinforced by the media generated stereotyping [footnote ommitted].

Studies of the impact of race on white decision making nearly always explain disparate effects by focusing on negative assessments of, or undesirable outcomes for, nonwhites, rather than positive results for whites. That is, they adopt a conceptual framework in which unconscious race discrimination is triggered by stereotyping.

Whites are rarely introduced to the image of blacks as criminals through direct experience; generally, the media serves to provide and promote these racial caricatures. A fearful white class afraid to encounter a black man results from never being exposed to positive images of black America [footnote ommitted]. Given the racially segregated nature of American economic and social life, the media has played an important role in the construction of a national image of black male youth as "the criminal" in two significant respects which served to enhance penalties for crack cocaine violators: 1) generating public panic regarding crack cocaine; and 2) associating black males with crack cocaine. Ergo, the decision maker who is unaware of this selection perception that has produced his stereotype will believe that his actions **are not** motivated by racial prejudice.

The influence of "unconscious racism" on legislative decisions has never been presented to any court in this context. Constitutional redress to racial discrimination has resulted primarily from judicial vigilance directed toward correcting overt and facially discriminatory legislation forged first by slavery and followed by continuing racial animosity toward blacks and other ethnic minorities. Remaining still is a more pernicious, albeit intangible, form of race discrimination in the individual's unconscious thoughts that influences the decision making process. As a result, "individuals . . . ubiquitously attach a significance to race that is irrational and often used outside their awareness." *McClesky v. Kemp,* 481 U.S. 279, 332, 107 S.Ct. 1756, 1788, 95 L.Ed.2d 262 (1987) (Brennan, J. dissenting) * * *

Consequently, the focus on "purposeful" discrimination is inadequate as a response to more subtle and deeply buried forms of racism. In 1909, the United States Supreme Court acknowledged that "[racial] [b]ias or prejudice is such an elusive condition of the mind that it is most difficult, if not impossible, to always recognize its existence." *Crawford v. United States,* 212 U.S. 183, 196, 29 S.Ct. 260, 265, 53 L.Ed. 465 (1909). Eighty-three years later, *Crawford* holds: the inquiry to determine racial bias is still "difficult, if not impossible." Without consideration of the influences of unconscious racism, the standard of review set forth in *Washington v. Davis,* 426 U.S. 229, 96 S.Ct. 2040, 48 L.Ed.2d 597 (1976) is a "crippling burden of proof." *Batson v. Kentucky,* 476 U.S. 79, 92, 106 S.Ct. 1712, 1721, 90 L.Ed.2d 69 (1985).

The concomitant twin of racism is class oppression. Race and class bias have always worked together to reinforce systems of social control and economic distribution. Arguably, most forms of overt racism have been eliminated. However, those who choose to discriminate on the basis of race find it easier to achieve the same results by basing their distinctions on class. Ergo, identification of race bias has become more complex, more divisive, and morally more problematic.

On average, blacks experience significantly worse economic conditions than whites, and historically the criminal justice system has dealt more harshly with those who are economically weak. Black people constitute a disproportionate share of persons who exist in absolute poverty. In 1990, there were 33.6 million persons in poverty in the U.S. Although blacks comprise only 12% of the nation's population, 29% of those poverty stricken were black—2.4 times the rate of the general population [footnote ommitted]. This mixture of race and economic discrimination has diminished the bright line of overt racism. "The . . . distorting effects of racial discrimination and poverty continue to be painfully visible" in decisions to mete out criminal punishment. *Godfrey v. Georgia,* 446

U.S. 420, 439, 100 S.Ct. 1759, 1770, 64 L.Ed.2d 398 (1980) (Marshall, J. concurring) [footnote omitted].

It is against this background that the Court considers the merits of defendant's challenge.

Equal Protection Analysis

A current equal protection analysis must therefore take into account the unconscious predispositions of people, including legislators, who may sincerely believe that they are not making decisions on the basis of race. This predisposition is a pertinent factor in determining the existence of a racially discriminatory motive. Racial influences which unconsciously seeped into the legislative decision making process are no less injurious, reprehensible, or unconstitutional. Although intent *per se* may not have entered Congress' enactment of the crack statute, its failure to account for a foreseeable disparate impact which would affect black Americans in grossly disproportionate numbers would, nonetheless, violate the spirit and letter of equal protection.

The equal protection component of the Fifth Amendment Due Process clause commands that similarly situated people be treated alike. *Bolling v. Sharpe,* 347 U.S. 497, 74 S.Ct. 693, 98 L.Ed. 884 (1954); *Plyler v. Doe,* 457 U.S. 202, 216, 102 S.Ct. 2382, 2394, 72 L.Ed.2d 786 (1982). A criminal defendant who alleges an equal protection violation must prove that the "invidious quality" of governmental action claimed to be racially discriminatory "must ultimately be traced to a racially discriminatory purpose." *Washington v. Davis,* 426 U.S. 229, 240, 96 S.Ct. 2040, 2048, 48 L.Ed.2d 597 (1976). Absent direct evidence of intent to discriminate, the defendant can make a prima facie case "by showing [that] the totality of the relevant facts gives rise to an inference of discriminatory purpose." *Id.* In deciding whether the defendant has carried the burden of persuasion, a court must undertake a "sensitive inquiry into such circumstantial evidence of intent as may be available." *Arlington,* 429 U.S. 252, 266, 97 S.Ct. 555, 564, 50 L.Ed.2d 450 (1977).

In *Arlington,* the Supreme Court listed circumstantial evidentiary sources for judicial review of legislative or executive motivation to determine whether a racially discriminatory purpose exists. The "subjects of proper inquiry," are:

(1) adverse racial impact of the official action,

(2) historical background of the decisions,

(3) specific sequence of events leading up to the challenged decision,

(4) departures from normal procedure sequence,

(5) substantive departure from routine decisions,

(6) contemporary statements made by the decision makers, *Davis,* 426 U.S. at 252, 96 S.Ct. at 2053, and

(7) the inevitability or foreseeability of the consequence of the law, *Personnel Admin. of Mass. v. Feeney,* 442 U.S. 256, 266, 99 S.Ct. 2282, 2289, 60 L.Ed.2d 870 (1979).

The Court explicitly stated that the list of evidentiary sources was not exhaustive. *Arlington* 429 U.S. at 268, 97 S.Ct. at 565. Therefore, this Court will proceed with its examination by reviewing the circumstantial evidence, including the *Arlington* factors, to determine whether race influenced the legislature's actions.

Enactment of the Crack Statute

Crack cocaine eased into the mainstream of the drug culture about 1985 and immediately absorbed the media's attention. Between 1985 and 1986, over 400 reports had been broadcast by the networks. Media accounts of crack-user horror stories appeared daily on every major channel and in every major newspaper. Many of the stories were racist. Despite the statistical data that whites were prevalent among crack users, rare was the interview with a young black person who had avoided drugs and the drug culture, and even rarer was any media association with whites and crack. Images of young black men daily saturated the screens of our televisions. These distorted images branded onto the public mind and the minds of legislators that young black men were *solely* responsible for the drug crisis in America. The media created a stereotype of a crack dealer as a young black male, unemployed, gang affiliated, gun toting, and a menace to society. These stereotypical descriptions of drug dealers may be accurate, but not all young black men are drug dealers. The broad brush of uninformed public opinion paints them all as the same.

Legislators used these media accounts as informational support for the enactment of the crack statute. The *Congressional Record,* prior to enactment of the statute, is replete with news articles submitted by members for their colleagues' consideration which labeled crack dealers as black youths and gangs.48 Members of Congress also introduced into the record media reports containing language that was either overtly or subtly racist, and which exacerbated white fears that the "crack problem" would spill out of the ghettos.

These stereotypical images undoubtedly served as the touchstone that influenced racial perceptions held by legislators and the public as related to the "crack epidemic." The fear of increased crime as a result of crack cocaine fed white society's fear of the black male as a crack user and as a source of social disruption. The prospect of black crack migrating to the white suburbs led the legislators to reflexively punish crack violators more harshly than their white, suburban, powder cocaine dealing counterparts. The ultimate outcome resulted in the legislators drafting the crack statute with its Draconian punishment.

Arlington decided that departures from normal procedures are relevant in determining the existence of invidious influences. Defendant presented evidence that there were significant departures from prior substantive and procedural sequences, which point toward invidious discriminatory purpose.

The media reports associating blacks with the horrors of crack cocaine caused the Congress to react irrationally and arbitrarily. The evolution of the 100 to 1 crack to powder ratio mandatory minimum sentence was a direct result of a "frenzied" Congress that was moved to action based upon an unconscious racial animus. The "frenzied" state of Congress led members to depart from normal and substantive procedures that are *routinely* considered a part of the legislative process.

The 1986 Controlled Substances Act followed an extraordinarily hasty and truncated legislative process. * * *

Few hearings were held in the House on the enhanced penalties for crack offenders. Despite the lack of fact-gathering about crack, "the 100:1 cocaine to crack ratio . . . was originally a 50:1 ratio in the Crime Subcommittee's bill, H.R. 5394, . . . arbitrarily doubled simply to symbolize redoubled Congressional seriousness." *Id.* at 4.

When the Senate considered the legislation, many Senators fruitlessly cautioned against undue haste in light of the House's abbreviated consideration of the bill, to little avail. Tossing caution to the wind, the Senate conducted a single hearing between 9:40 a.m. to 1:15 p.m., including recesses. Attendance was intermittent. *"Crack" Cocaine: Hearing Before the Permanent Subcommittee on Investigations of the Committee on Governmental Affairs,* United States Senate, 99th Cong.2d Sess. (July 15, 1986) ("Crack Hearing").

The Supreme Court has addressed the issue of foreseeability in the disparate impact context as follows:

> [A]ctions having foreseeable and anticipated disparate impact are relevant evidence to prove the ultimate fact, forbidden purpose. . . . Adherence to a particular policy or practice, "with full knowledge of the predictable effects of such adherence upon racial imbalance . . . may be considered by a court in determining whether an inference of [discriminatory] intent should be drawn."

Columbus Bd. of Education v. Penick, 443 U.S. 449, 464–65, 99 S.Ct. 2941, 2950, 61 L.Ed.2d 666 (1979), [citations omitted]; *See Feeney,* 442 U.S. at 279, n. 25, 99 S.Ct. at 2296, n. 25.

What cannot be clearly gleaned from the transcripts of floor discussions among congressional members may well be inferred from the exhibits that were introduced into the record. Legions of newspaper and magazine articles regarding the crack cocaine epidemic depicted racial imagery of heavy involvement by blacks in crack cocaine. Practically every newspaper account featured a black male either using crack, selling crack, involved in police contact due to crack, or behind bars because of crack.

Media pictures and stories emphasized that the "crack problem" was a "black problem" that needed to be isolated and prevented from "spreading" to white suburban areas. The intent to contain the crack problem and prevent it from entering the "mainstream" or the "suburbs" is evident from the articles cited in the *Congressional Record.* To keep crack out of suburbia meant to keep crack users and dealers out of suburban neighborhoods. While it may not have been intentional, it was foreseeable that the harsh penalties imposed upon blacks would be clearly disproportional to the far more lenient sentences given whites for use of the same drug—cocaine.

Circumstantial evidence of invidious intent may include proof of disproportionate impact. *Davis,* 426 U.S. at 242, 96 S.Ct. at 2048. "Impact of the official action—whether it 'bears more heavily on one race than another,'" *id.,* is important evidence.

Defendant's evidence that the impact of the crack statute "bears more heavily" on blacks than whites is undisputed. 98.2 percent of defendants convicted of crack cocaine charges in the Eastern District of Missouri between the years 1988 and 1992 were black. Nationally, 92.6 percent of the defendants convicted during 1992 of federal crack cocaine violations were black and 4.7 percent of the defendants were white. In comparison, 45.2 percent of defendants sentenced for powder cocaine were white, as opposed to 20.7 percent of black defendants. All of the defendants sentenced for simple possession of crack cocaine were black. The national figures comport to essentially the same percentage as the Missouri statistics.

According to a *U.S.A. Today* report which investigated the racial disparity caused by the "100 to 1 ratio" and the mandatory minimum sentencing practices in the country, although only 12 percent of the population, blacks accounted for 42 percent of all drug arrests in 1991. The 1992 federal figures indicate that blacks comprise 1.6 million of the illegal drug use population while 8.7 million whites admit to illegal drug use. Yet, blacks are four times as likely as whites to be arrested on drug charges in this country. Notably, in the Eastern District blacks are eight times as likely to be arrested.

According to the U.S. Sentencing Commission, blacks receive sentences at or above the mandatory minimum more often than whites arrested on the same charge. The disparate application appears to be related to race, and the disparity is constant even when variables such as nature of the offense and prior criminal record are considered.

Moreover, overcrowding in the Federal Bureau of Prisons reflects the disparity in a dramatic way. An estimated 90 percent increase in the prison population during the last several years is directly related to the mandatory minimum drug sentences and the sentencing guidelines. As of July 1993, 60.4 percent of the inmates in the Bureau of Prisons are there for drug related offenses. "Attorney General Reno told the Judicial Conference this past summer that the federal prisons are filling faster than new prisons can be built, and the Bureau of Prison faces gridlock within three years." *U.S. v. Fleming,* 8 F.3d. 1264, 1267 (8th Cir.1993)

(HEANEY, J., dissenting).

Clary argues that the statistical disparity is overwhelming proof of discrimination, and that in cases where statistical evidence of disparity is "stark," statistics alone have been accepted as the sole source of proof of an equal protection violation. *Arlington,* 429 U.S., at 266, 97 S.Ct. at 563. This Court agrees that the statistical evidence of disparate impact resulting from crack cocaine sentences is compelling. In one of the first in a long line of cases which interpreted the equal protection clause, the Supreme Court ruled that the effect of a law may be so harsh or adverse in its weight against a particular race that an intent to discriminate is not only a permissible inference, but a necessary one. *Yick Wo v. Hopkins,* 118 U.S. 356, 6 S.Ct. 1064, 30 L.Ed. 220 (1886). This appears to be the effect of the crack statute challenged in this court.

Objective evidence supports the belief that racial animus was a motivating factor in enacting the crack statute. Congress' decision was based, in large part, on the racial imagery generated by the media which connected the "crack problem" with blacks in the inner city. Congress deviated from procedural patterns, departed from a thorough, rational discussion of the "crack issue" and reacted to it in a "frenzy" initiated by the media and emotionally charged constituents. Under *Arlington,* all of these factors may be considered by the Court to infer intent.

Prosecutorial and Law Enforcement Discretion

The crack statute in conjunction with the resultant mandatory minimum sentence, standing alone, may not have spawned the kind and degree of racially disparate impact that warrants judicial review but for the manner of its application by law enforcement agencies. The law enforcement practices, charging policies, and sentencing departure decisions by prosecutors constitute major contributing factors which have escalated the disparate outcome.

Prosecutors do have broad discretion in determining who will be charged with a crime. All that is required for the prosecutor to have probable cause is to believe that the accused committed an offense defined by statute. "The decision whether or not to prosecute, and what charge to file . . . generally rests within his discretion." *Bordenkircher v. Hayes,* 434 U.S. 357, 364, 98 S.Ct. 663, 668, 54 L.Ed.2d 604. While the prosecutor does have broad discretion, it is not unlimited. For example, the prosecutor may not base the decision to prosecute upon impermissible factors such as race, religion, or other arbitrary and unjustified classifications. *Id.,* at 364, 98 S.Ct. at 668.

Prosecutorial discretion as it relates to crack cocaine cases should be exercised in a manner that is responsive to Congress' expressed intent to target "kingpins" and "high level traffickers." It would seem to be economically sensible to devote scarce government resources to reducing the large ingress and wholesale distribution of powder cocaine by major traffickers which would consequently reduce the existence of crack as a derivative product. Without cocaine, there could be no crack.

However, both national and local statistical data do not show that the prosecution is targeting the upper echelons in the drug trade. Few kingpins are prosecuted. Review of the cases that have been prosecuted in this district reflects a clear pattern of disparate impact. Out of 57 convictions in the Eastern District of Missouri, 55 of the defendants were black, one was white, one was Hispanic, and not one kingpin among them. Three of the 56 defendants were jointly charged with having 944 grams, three others had 454 grams between them, and one had 451 grams. The other 50 had a total of less than 2000 grams, averaging less than 40 grams each. Eight defendants had less than 10 grams. Five of them had less than a gram, barely enough to detect or to utilize. The total amount of crack cocaine for 56 of the 57 defendants (the amount for one defendant was not determined) was less than 4,000 grams. Powder cocaine is usually imported into this country by boats, trucks, and planes, and in huge quantities. Kingpin dealers are then able to transport the drug in brick-like packages referred to as "kilos." A kilogram weighs 1,000 grams. Thus, it appears clear that the removal of this small quantity of drugs would hardly reduce the supply of crack cocaine in St. Louis or impede its flow.

The issue of prosecutorial venue is so intertwined with the racial impact flowing from the crack and mandatory minimum statute that it requires careful scrutiny. Generally, federal prosecutions are much more likely to result in conviction, with more severe punishment. In cases where there is joint jurisdiction of similar offenses, careful discernment by conscientious state and federal prosecutors can carefully select among the charges (state and federal) the ones that more nearly result in the most appropriate penalty. There would be inefficiency in double prosecutions, so a choice ought to be made. While various factors would be considered in selecting federal or state actions, certainly a decision based upon race would not be appropriate. And yet—when an examination of the crack cocaine violations in the district court is made, they are nearly all black (55 of 57). Where conviction is a certainty, harsh penalties inevitable, and nearly all defendants are black, suspicion will arise.

The Court notes that a close examination of many of the 57 files involving crack cocaine in this district shows that federal prosecution occurs with both state and federal law officers making the arrests. Generally, those arrested by state officers had very small amounts of crack cocaine. For example, nine of the 57 crack cocaine defendants were assigned to this Court and most of them had only tiny quantities of crack cocaine. All but one was black. All of them, even though arrested by state law officers, were prosecuted in the federal court. Even a disinterested inquirer would wonder why the tremendous expense of federal prosecution and subsequent incarceration should be wasted on relatively minor offenders. The following tables (Def.Ex. 12B) are a descriptive list of the 57 persons prosecuted for crack cocaine violations in the Eastern District of Missouri during 1989–92. Fifty-five defendants were black, one was Hispanic, and one was white. Those defendants in boldface were assigned to this Court for trial. That is why this Court can produce greater detail garnered from its own files. The defendants who were assigned to this Court were all arrested by state officials and then transferred to the federal courts when charged.

* * *

Perhaps there were other reasons for charging those with "dust amounts," and then, perhaps they were *all* charged in the federal court because they had crack and were black. The failure by the prosecutors to explain these and other discrepancies adds a telling ingredient to the argument that the crack statute was constitutionally infirm and further exhibited the unconscious racism proffered here, generally, and as applied to this defendant. After all, while the Eastern District of Missouri includes the City of St. Louis with its large black population, it also includes St. Louis County with a white population four or five times larger. Surely if the prosecution were really free of racism, unconscious or not, there would be more than one white defendant convicted for crack violations in the federal courts of the Eastern District of Missouri in three years.

Without explanation, the logical inference to be drawn is that the prosecutors in the federal courts are selectively prosecuting black defendants who were involved with crack, no matter how trivial the amount, and ignoring or diverting whites when they do the same thing.

There may be rational explanations for these disproportionate figures. That is why this Court repeatedly requested the U.S. Attorney's Office to make available its standards or principles for the selection of crack cocaine cases. But the prosecutor refused to divulge this information (an *in camera* submission would have been sufficient), citing prosecutorial discretion. The Court is not sure that it has the authority to demand such an explanation from the prosecutor. But failure to divulge the standards used during 1989–92 raises an inference that unconscious racism may have influenced the decision to severely punish blacks for violations involving their form of cocaine while hardly touching whites who utilize another form of the same drug—both are forms of cocaine.

The focus on the prosecution of numerous low level crack dealers appears to be part of a national policy, perhaps designed to give the impression of great victories in the War on Drugs. Such a misguided approach to the elimination of drug traffic has resulted in the necessity for expensive prisons, has destroyed the lives of many young first offenders, and most importantly, has not reduced the quantity of drugs saturating the nation. In the St. Louis area there is a greater amount of cocaine available than in 1980 and it is cheaper. Small-time dealers grow like dandelions and are immediately and easily replaced, which further establishes the authority of the drug kingpins and dilutes the police resources available to curtail kingpin drug dealers.

This Court has known and respected the staff of the United States Attorney's Office for many years, and does not believe that overt racism would influence their decisions. The national statistics comport with the data from the Eastern District of Missouri. What is more likely is that the subliminal influence of unconscious racism has permeated federal prosecution throughout the nation. After all, even U.S. prosecutors are not immune from unconscious racism.

Level of Judicial Scrutiny

As with all instances of judicial review of federal legislation, the Court should not lightly set aside the considered judgment of a coordinate branch. *See, Metro Broadcasting, Inc. v. FCC,* 497 U.S. 547, 605, 110 S.Ct. 2997, 3030, 111 L.Ed.2d 445 (1990) (O'Connor, J. dissenting). In *Arlington,* the Supreme Court acknowledged that the legislature was entitled to judicial deference to its constitutionally ordained legislative power from the beginning. But once there is proof that a discriminatory motive is afoot, "judicial deference is no longer justified." 429 U.S. at 265–266, 97 S.Ct. at 563.

A law which burdens blacks disproportionately and whose influence has been traced to racial considerations, even if unconscious, warrants the most rigorous scrutiny. Such a law can survive only if the classification which is suspect is narrowly tailored to further a compelling governmental interest. *McDaniel v. Paty,* 435 U.S. 618, 628, 98 S.Ct. 1322, 1328, 55 L.Ed.2d 593 (1978). Consistent with the history of criminalizing behavior among minority groups in this country, at the very least, the crack statute in its application has created a "de facto suspect classification" to which strict scrutiny must apply. Under this standard, the crack statute is defective.

The totality of the facts in this case converge to support the conclusion that racial discriminatory influences, at least unconsciously, played an appreciable role in promulgating the enhanced statutory scheme for possession and distribution of crack. Legislators' unconscious racial aversion towards blacks, sparked by unsubstantiated reports of the effects of crack, reactionary media prodding, and an agitated constituency, motivated the legislators to enhance the punishment scheme to produce a dual system of punishment in the application of this statute.

To rebut defendant's claim that racial animus played a role in penalizing crimes involving cocaine base more severely than crimes involving powder cocaine, the Government offered evidence that members of Congress considered crack to be more dangerous because of its potency, its highly addictive nature, its affordability, and increasing prevalence. Ample evidence has been presented to this Court that contradicts many of Congress' claims.

Congress had no hard evidence before it to support the contentions that crack was 100 times more potent or dangerous than powder cocaine. Even Senator Hawkins, among the first of the members of Congress to initiate dialogue about crack cocaine, noted that "the dividing line between crack and powder cocaine is indistinct and arbitrary." Ex. 17, 132 Cong.Rec. S9788 (daily ed. July 29, 1986) (statement of Senator Hawkins). Dr. Robert Byck, Professor of Psychiatry and Pharmacology of the Yale University School of Medicine, testified at the Crack Cocaine Hearing before the Senate Subcommittee on Governmental Affairs and acknowledged that there was no reliable evidence at that time that crack cocaine was more addictive or dangerous than powder cocaine. [Crack Hearing at 21]; [Schwartz Testimony: Transcript, Vol. II at 50:14–51:3.] Today, there is no reliable medical evidence that crack cocaine is more addictive than powder cocaine. [Schwartz Testimony: Transcript, Vol. II at 49:20–50:6.]

Crack's purported greater potency was not supported by the evidence. The testimony of Dr. Byck provided little more than a layman's explanation of methods of ingestion and *unsupported* conclusions of crack cocaine's "dangerousness." Dr. Charles R. Shuster, Director of the National Institute on Drug Abuse, provided testimony that supported the dangers of cocaine and gave statistical data on cocaine related deaths. He further testified that cocaine related deaths had increased. His reports did not distinguish among smoking cocaine, smoking crack, or freebasing cocaine. He did state, however, that both the ingestion of cocaine in the form of crack or in liquid form intravenously equally provided rapid and euphoric responses for the user. In comparison, Dr. Schwartz testified that there were far more deaths from ingestion of cocaine nasally. [Transcript, Vol. II 55:6.] He also testified that the intravenous route was far more dangerous than any other method of ingestion. [Transcript, Vol. II 62; and *see,* Def.Ex. 4(M) and 4(N).]

There is no evidence that the use of crack makes the user physiologically or psychologically more prone to violence or other antisocial behavior than does the use of powder cocaine. [Schwartz testimony.] *See Substance Abuse: A Comprehensive Textbook,* "Cocaine (and Crack): Neurology" (Gold, Miller, Jonas, M.D.s) p. 225 [Def.Exh. 4V.] Moreover, researchers have concluded that the short-term and long-term effects of crack and powder cocaine are identical. *See,* Peterson, David, *Powder, Crack Effects Called Same,* Minneapolis Star Tribune, Oct. 18, 1991, at 1B (Remarks of Dr. Dorothy Hatsukami, Professor of Psychiatry at the University of Minnesota), *cited* in *U.S. v. Willis,* 967 F.2d 1220, 1226 (8th Cir.1992) (Heaney, J. dissenting).

According to the market approach, crack cocaine can be distributed in small packets at a low unit price. Crack is no cheaper than cocaine powder because cocaine is the essential product of crack. But all forms of cocaine are available today in greater quantity and at lower prices than a few years ago.

Poor and powerless black people are vulnerable to every form of exploitation. Drugs flow in their community because of desperate economic need meeting rare economic opportunity. There is little other enterprise for these people to turn to in pursuit of the American Dream except the narcotics industry, which is a rare "equal opportunity employer" without concern for educational requirements or previous work performance. Unlike their white suburban counterparts, poverty of blacks brings their illegal activity into open areas that is both annoying to the public and easily targeted by police. It is quite easy for police to sweep them off the streets like grains of sand, only to be replaced by tides of unemployed youths. The sensible course is to direct resources to attack the source of crack: powder cocaine.

If the "100 to 1" ratio were reversed to penalize powder cocaine possession of 50 grams with a 10 year mandatory minimum, Congress would be encouraged to respond with more creative and effective ways to wage the drug war. The uproar from their constituencies would be deafening, and politicians would be moved to action much more quickly. As sad as it may sound, and as much as the Court feels discomfort in pointing it out, if young white males were being incarcerated at the same rate as young black males, the statute would have been amended long ago.

The record does not support the fact that Congress had a reasonable basis to make the harsh distinction between penalties for powder and crack cocaine. It is not difficult to understand the pressures upon Congress to react to the abundance of elements regarding the imminent arrival of crack cocaine, and the political expediency of exploiting its presumed dangers. But the frenzied, irrational response to criminalize crack at 100 times greater than powder cocaine, in a manner that would disproportionately affect blacks, is unjustified.

Even were the Congress' interests compelling, the statute was not drafted in narrow terms to accomplish those interests. Why not punish the possession and distribution of powder cocaine with equal severity as crack cocaine? COCAINE IS COCAINE. Neither should be punished less than or more than the other: they are equal in their harm to society and destruction of individual lives and the punishment should be the same for both. To impose a more severe penalty on a derivative source of an illegal narcotic while the principal source of the drug is tolerated is illogical. To the extent that the source dries up, the derivative must necessarily wither upon the vine. If any enhancement would be justified, it would be to penalize cocaine more severely. Hence, the absence of narrow tailoring corroborates the constitutional infirmity of the statute.

* * *

FINDINGS AND CONCLUSIONS

In summary, the Court, after careful consideration, reluctantly concludes that the pertinent sections of 21 U.S.C. § 841 which mandate punishment to be 100 times greater for crack cocaine than for powder cocaine are constitutionally invalid, both generally and *as applied* in this case. The Court finds that there is no material difference between the chemical properties of crack and powder cocaine, and that they are one and the same drug. The Court further finds that this defendant has been denied equal protection of the laws when the punishment assessed against him is 100 times greater than the punishment assessed for the same violation but involving powder cocaine.

The Court further finds that the "symbolic" action of the Congress in raising the original 50 to 1 ratio to 100 to 1 is yet another indication of its irrational and arbitrary actions, and further evidences the failure of the Congress to narrowly tailor its provisions as required by law in suspect class cases.

The Court further finds that the Congress enacted this law in an arbitrary and irrational manner, without the testimony of adequate scientific and professional advice, and without providing sufficient time for subcommittee hearings and debate.

The Court further finds that the statistics offered by the defendant, both local and national, show that the disparate impact upon blacks is so great as to shock the conscience of the court. Ratios as high as 55 to 1 appear in the Eastern

District of Missouri; even greater disparities are evident on the national level. These ratios are apparent in arrest levels, convictions, and the prosecutorial acts which mitigate or eliminate punishment for whites while maximizing punishment for blacks. The Court finds that the actions of Congress and the prosecuting officials were influenced and motivated by unconscious racism, causing great harm and injury to black defendants because of their race inasmuch as whites are rarely arrested, prosecuted, or convicted for crack cocaine offenses.

The Court further finds that the Office of the U.S. Attorney for the Eastern District of Missouri only convicted one white person for crack cocaine violations during the years 1989–92 while convicting 55 blacks and one Hispanic. In the absence of explanation by the prosecutors, these disproportionate figures give rise to a strong inference that only blacks are being prosecuted in the federal courts for crack cocaine violations. Prosecution based on race is obviously discriminatory even if it is occasioned by *unconscious* racism.[75]

Invalidation of the Crack Statute

Therefore, this Court concludes that the disproportionate penalties for crack cocaine as specified in all of the pertinent sections of 21 U.S.C. § 841 violate the Equal Protection Clause of the U.S. Constitution generally and as applied in this case. The Court further holds that the prosecutorial selection of cases on the basis of race is constitutionally impermissible as applied to this defendant in this case.

Accordingly, the Court has sentenced the defendant to a prison term in conformity with this memorandum.

Dated this 11th day of February, 1994.

United States v. Clary

United States Court of Appeals, Eighth Circuit
34 F.3d 709 (1994)

JOHN R. GIBSON, Senior Circuit Judge.

The United States appeals from the sentence imposed upon Edward James Clary for possession with intent to distribute cocaine base in violation of 21 U.S.C. § 841(b)(1)(A)(iii). Clary entered a guilty plea to the charge which called for a ten-year mandatory minimum sentence. After conducting a four-day hearing, the district court sentenced Clary to four years. The court held that the 100 to 1 ratio for crack cocaine to powder cocaine was disproportionate and in violation of the Equal Protection Clause both generally and as applied, and that the selective prosecution of crack cases on the basis of race was constitutionally impermissible as applied to Clary. The United States essentially argues that these issues have been repeatedly decided and there was no equal protection violation or selective prosecution of Clary. We reverse and remand for resentencing in accord with the applicable statutes and guidelines.

After Clary's guilty plea but before sentencing, he filed a motion arguing that the ten-year mandatory minimum sentence contained in the crack cocaine statute, 21 U.S.C. § 841(b)(A)(iii), and United States Sentencing Guideline section 2D1.1, violated his Equal Protection rights guaranteed by the Fifth Amendment.1 Clary presented eleven witnesses who testified about the profound impact of the crack statute and its ten year mandatory minimum sentence on African Americans. The district court determined that in spite of earlier decisions from this court stating that the differentiation between the treatment of powder cocaine and crack cocaine was constitutional and did not violate the Equal Protection Clause, we invited arguments presenting new facts and legal analysis in *United States v. Marshall*, 998 F.2d 634, 635 n. 2 (8th Cir.1993).

The district court began its factual analysis by examining the role that racism has played in criminal punishment in this country since the late seventeenth century. *United States v. Clary*, 846 F.Supp. 768, 774-782 (E.D.Mo.1994). The district court touched on such recent events as the turmoil of the 1960's and the "cataclysmic economic change" in the 1980's. *Id*. at 777-78. The court also examined unemployment levels, which the court concluded impacted African Americans more than the general population. *Id*. at 777. According to the court, African Americans' anger and frustration led to increased drug traffic and associated violence. *Id*. at 777-78.

The district court also discussed the unconscious predisposition of legislators, and reasoned that although overt racial animus may not have led to Congress' enactment of the crack statute, its failure to account for a substantial and foreseeable disparate impact would violate the spirit and letter of equal protection. *Id*. at 782. Accordingly, it concluded that the statute should be reviewed under strict scrutiny and the rules announced in *Arlington Heights v. Metropolitan Housing Development Corp.*, 429 U.S. 252, 266, 97 S.Ct. 555, 564, 50 L.Ed.2d 450 (1977). The court listed the seven factors outlined by *Arlington* as circumstantial evidence of a racially-discriminatory legislative purpose. The factors are: (1) adverse racial impact, (2) historical background, (3) specific sequence of events leading up to the decision, (4) departure from normal procedure sequence, (5) substantive departure from routine decision, (6) contemporary statements made by decisionmakers, and (7) the inevitability or foreseeability of the consequence of the law. 846 F.Supp. at 783.

The court outlined the events leading up to passage of the crack statute. The court cited several news articles submitted by members of Congress for publication in the *Congressional Record* which portrayed crack dealers as unemployed, gang-affiliated, gun-toting, young black males. *Id.* at 783-84. Legislators, the court reasoned, used these media accounts as informational support for the statute. The district court also pointed to perceived procedural irregularities surrounding Congress' approval of the crack sentencing provisions. *Id.* at 784-85. For instance, few hearings were held in the House on the enhanced penalties for crack. *Id.* at 785. While many Senators called for a more measured response, the Senate committee conducted a single morning hearing. *Id.* at 784-85. Finally, although the penalties were originally set at 50 to 1, they were arbitrarily doubled. *Id.* at 784.

The district court also observed that 98.2 percent of defendants convicted of crack cocaine charges in the Eastern District of Missouri between the years 1988 and 1992 were African American. *Id.* at 786. Nationally, 92.6 percent of those convicted of crack cocaine charges were African American, as opposed to 4.7 percent who were white. 786. With respect to powder cocaine, the percentages were largely reversed. *Id.* The court found that this statistical evidence demonstrated both the disparate impact of the 100 to 1 ratio and the probability that "the subliminal influence of unconscious racism ha[d] permeated federal prosecution throughout the nation." *Id.* at 791.

While the government directed the court to evidence that Congress considered crack to be more dangerous because of its potency, addictiveness, affordability and prevalence, the court found evidence in the record contradicting many of the legislators' beliefs. *Id.* at 781-92. In particular, the court questioned Congress' conclusion that crack was 100 times more potent or dangerous than powder cocaine, referring to testimony that there is no reliable medical evidence that crack cocaine is more addictive than powder cocaine. *Id.* In light of these factors, the court found the punishment of crack at 100 times greater than powder cocaine to be a "frenzied, irrational response." *Id.* at 792. The court repeatedly stressed that "cocaine is cocaine." *Id.* at 793.

The district court held the portions of 21 U.S.C. section 841 mandating punishment 100 times greater for crack than powder cocaine to be constitutionally invalid generally and as applied in this case.

We believe that this case could well be decided on the basis of past decisions by this court. *See United States v. Maxwell,* 25 F.3d 1389, 1396-97 (8th Cir.1994);

* * *

In *Lattimore,* Chief Judge Arnold carefully examined earlier authority holding that Congress clearly had rational motives for creating the distinction between crack and powder cocaine. 974 F.2d at 974-75. Among the reasons were "the potency of the drug, the ease with which drug dealers can carry and conceal it, the highly addictive nature of the drug, and the violence which often accompanies trade in it." *Id.* at 975. *Lattimore* squarely rejects the argument that crack cocaine sentences disparately impact on African Americans. *Id.* Citing *Personnel Administrator of Massachusetts v. Feeney,* 442 U.S. 256, 99 S.Ct. 2282, 60 L.Ed.2d 870 (1979), we observed that even if a neutral law has a disproportionate adverse impact on a racial minority, it is unconstitutional only if that effect can be traced to a discriminatory purpose. *Lattimore,* 974 F.2d at 975. Discriminatory purpose "implies that the decisionmaker, in this case [Congress], selected or reaffirmed a particular course of action at least in part 'because of' not merely 'in spite of,' its adverse effects upon an identifiable group." *Id.* (quoting *Feeney,* 442 U.S. at 279, 99 S.Ct. at 2296). We concluded that there was no evidence that Congress or the Sentencing Commission had a racially discriminatory motive when it crafted the Guidelines with extended sentences for crack cocaine felonies. *Lattimore,* 974 F.2d at 975.

* * *

The district court's painstakingly-crafted opinion demonstrates the careful consideration it gave not only to the testimony before it, but also to the voluminous documents introduced by Clary, including both law review and text materials. This case undoubtedly presents the most complete record on this issue to come before this court. Nevertheless, we are satisfied that both the record before the district court and the district court's findings fall short of establishing that Congress acted with a discriminatory purpose in enacting the statute, and that Congress selected or reaffirmed a particular course of action "at least in part 'because of,' not merely 'in spite of' its adverse effects upon an identifiable group." *Lattimore,* 974 F.2d at 975 (quoting *Feeney*), 442 U.S. at 279, 99 S.Ct. at 2296. While impact is an important starting point, *Arlington Heights* made clear that impact alone is not determinative absent a pattern as stark as that in *Gomillion v. Lightfoot,* 364 U.S. 339, 81 S.Ct. 125, 5 L.Ed.2d 110 (1960), or *Yick Wo v. Hopkins,* 118 U.S. 356, 6 S.Ct. 1064, 30 L.Ed. 220 (1886). 429 U.S. at 266, 97 S.Ct. at 564.

We first question the district court's reliance on "unconscious racism." 846 F.Supp. at 778-782. The court reasoned that a focus on purposeful discrimination will not show more subtle and deeply-buried forms of racism. *Id.* at 781. The court's reasoning, however, simply does not address the question whether Congress acted with a discriminatory purpose. Similar failings affect the court's statement that although intent per se may not have entered into Congress' enactment of the crack statutes, Congress' failure to account for a substantial and foreseeable disparate impact on African Americans nonetheless violates the spirit and letter of equal protection.

We also question the court's reliance on media-created stereotypes of crack dealers and its conclusion that this information "undoubtedly served as the touchstone that influenced racial perceptions held by legislators and the public as related to the 'crack epidemic.'" *Id.* at 784. Although the placement of newspaper and magazine articles in the *Congressional Record* indicates that this information may have affected at least some legislators, these articles hardly demonstrate that the stereotypical images "undoubtedly" influenced the legislators' racial perceptions. It is too long a leap from newspaper and magazine articles to an inference that Congress enacted the crack statute because of its adverse effect on African American males, instead of the stated purpose of responding to the serious impact of a rapidly-developing and particularly-dangerous form of drug use. Similarly, the evidence of the haste with which Congress acted and the action it took is as easily explained by the seriousness of the perceived problem as by racial animus.

The district court's final conclusion that objective evidence supports the belief that racial animus was a motivating factor in enacting the crack statute further belies the weakness of its position. A belief that racial animus was a motivating factor, based on disproportionate impact, is simply not enough since the Equal Protection Clause is violated "only if that impact can be traced to a discriminatory purpose." *Feeney,* 442 U.S. at 272, 99 S.Ct. at 2293. The chain of reasoning of the district court simply will not support a conclusion or a finding that the crack statutes were passed "because of, not merely in spite of" the adverse effect upon an identifiable group. *Id.* at 279, 99 S.Ct. at 2296.

* * *

The district court also found it "likely . . . that the subliminal influence of unconscious racism has permeated federal prosecution throughout the nation." 846 F.Supp. at 791. Clary concedes he "did not claim below that he was selectively prosecuted because of his race . . . [because he] was mindful of the even more difficult burden of proof he would have had to carry." Appellees's Brief at 43. To prevail on such a claim, a defendant "must establish that the decision to bring the federal charges against him, and not against others who committed federal crack violations and thus were similarly situated, itself had a racially discriminatory effect." *United States v. Brown,* 9 F.3d 1374, 1376 (8th Cir.1993), *cert. denied,* 511 U.S. 1043, 114 S.Ct. 1568, 128 L.Ed.2d 213 (1994). Even more to the point, Clary presented only statistical evidence and offered nothing else to show selective prosecution. As we held in *Brown,* this is simply not enough. *Id.*

We reverse and remand to the district court for resentencing consistent with this opinion.

Notes and Questions

President Obama recently granted clemency to people serving long sentences for crack offenses. *See* Charlie Savage, *Obama Commutes Sentences for 8 in Crack Cocaine Cases*, N.Y. Times, Dec. 19, 2013 http://www.nytimes.com/2013/12/20/us/obama-commuting-sentences-in-crack-cocaine-cases.html. Margaret Colgate Love, former U.S. Pardon Attorney, has urged that others be granted relief. *President Obama's Crack Commutations: What's Next, Mr. President?*, ACS Blog, January 16, 2014 http://www.acslaw.org/acsblog/president-obama%E2%80%99s-crack-commutations-what%E2%80%99s-next-mr-president

PRACTICE EXERCISE

After reading *Herman*, *Ah Lim*, and *Clary*, how would you vote on the following initiatives in your state? Please be prepared to discuss why you arrived at your conclusion, and what possible negative ramifications could exist for your decision.

Initiative 1

It shall now be legal to use any drug or substance previously deemed illegal.

Initiative 2

It shall be legal to possess any quantity of an illicit substance as long as the possessor has no intention of selling it.

Initiative 3

It shall be legal to possess any quantity of an illicit substance as long as the possessor has no intention of selling or distributing it.

Initiative 4

It shall be legal to consume any quantity of an illicit substance as long as the consumer never possesses it. Doctors may not be held criminally liable for possession of an illicit substance.

Initiative 5

The age for legal consumption of alcohol is abolished. Anyone may drink alcohol legally.

Initiative 6

The age for legal consumption of alcohol is reduced to 18 years old.

Initiative 7

The age for legal consumption of alcohol is reduced to 16 years old.

Initiative 8

There is no age limit for legal consumption of alcohol as long as the otherwise under-age person is consuming alcohol in the presence of an adult.

Initiative 9

There is no age limit for legal consumption of alcohol as long as the otherwise under-age person is consuming alcohol in the presence of his or her parent or guardian.

Initiative 10

Any person previously convicted of an alcohol or drug related offense may never possess or consume that same type of alcohol or drug again.

Initiative 11

Marijuana is no longer illegal to possess or consume.

Initiative 12

Marijuana is no longer illegal to consume or possess. A $200 state surcharge shall be assessed per half pound of Marijuana sold by any dealer.

Initiative 13

Marijuana is no longer illegal to consume or possess. A $500 state surcharge shall be assessed per half pound of Marijuana sold by any dealer. Monies collected will used solely to monitor and regulate the use and distribution of marijuana to ensure quality and safety.

F. Proof Beyond a Reasonable Doubt

In *In re Winship*, 397 U.S. 358, 364 (1970), the Supreme Court "explicitly" held "that the Due Process Clause protects the accused against conviction except upon proof beyond a reasonable doubt of every fact necessary to constitute the crime with which he is charged." This case applies that standard to a conviction on appeal.

Monroe v. State

Supreme Court of Delaware
652 A.2d 560 (1995)

VEASEY, Chief Justice:

In this appeal we consider the contention of defendant below-appellant Bobby L. Monroe ("Monroe") that there was insufficient evidence to sustain his convictions for Burglary Third Degree1 and Theft Felony. This case presents the questions of whether: (i) latent fingerprints of defendant on the outside door to a burglarized, commercial building is sufficient to convict in the absence of any other evidence in the State's case-in-chief; and (ii) the failure of defendant to move for judgment of acquittal at the conclusion of the State's case bars him from raising sufficiency of evidence claims on appeal. For the reasons set forth below, we hold that: (i) the Superior Court committed plain error in not entering *sua sponte* a judgment of acquittal based on insufficient evidence linking Monroe to the offenses; (ii) the trial court's error is reversible; and (iii) the Double Jeopardy Clauses of the United States Constitution and the Delaware Constitution require that we remand the case for an entry of a judgment of acquittal.

I. FACTS

In the early morning hours of July 4, 1991, the American Appliance Center (the "appliance center"), located in Wilmington, Delaware, was burglarized. When the manager of the appliance center arrived at the crime scene, he observed that the lower half of the front plexiglass door was broken. Upon inspection, he found that seven camcorders and four video cassette recorders were missing.

When officers from the Wilmington Police Evidence Detection Unit arrived at the scene, they surmised that a steel pipe found nearby was used to break the plexiglass door, which they concluded was the point-of-entry ("POE"). Though the officers could not lift any fingerprints from the pipe due to its rough surface, they were able to remove several sets of latent prints from nearby pieces of shattered plexiglass. The police later matched some of these prints to Monroe. The other prints, both identifiable and unidentifiable, could not be matched. Based on the print match, the police obtained and executed a warrant to search Monroe's house. They did not, however, uncover any stolen goods or other incriminating evidence.

The police nonetheless procured an arrest warrant for Monroe. Upon his arrest, Monroe denied his involvement in the burglary and told the arresting officer that he was with his brother at the time of the burglary.

On August 5, 1991, Monroe was charged with Burglary Third Degree and Theft Felony. A jury trial commenced on January 7, 1992. The State presented testimony from several witnesses, including Officer John Ciritella ("Officer Ciritella"), who originally lifted the fingerprints from the plexiglass shards, and Officer Thomas Liszkiewicz ("Officer Liszkiewicz"), a fingerprint expert who examined the prints.

After the State rested, Monroe put on his defense. As part of his defense, Monroe presented an alibi. He offered the testimony of his former girlfriend, Latonya Roundtree, who testified that she went to a movie with Monroe and that they window-shopped at the appliance center on July 3, 1991. Though she stated initially that they saw the movie "Boys 'N the Hood" that night, when confronted on cross-examination with evidence indicating that the movie had yet to open in Delaware as of July 3, 1991, she conceded that she might have been mistaken about the date she saw the movie with Monroe.

On January 9, 1992, the jury returned a guilty verdict as to both counts. Monroe did not move to dismiss the indictment at the end of the State's case, or for a judgment of acquittal either before or after the verdict. On May 1, 1992, the Superior Court sentenced Monroe to three years of incarceration for Burglary Third Degree and two years of suspended incarceration for Theft Felony. Monroe did not file a timely appeal.

Subsequently, Monroe filed a successful motion for post-conviction relief from the time limit for filing a direct appeal, resulting, *inter alia,* in a renewal of that time period. On November 24, 1993, Monroe timely filed this direct appeal, contending that the State presented insufficient evidence at trial to sustain his convictions. In an Order dated September 20, 1994, this Court ordered supplemental briefing and scheduled the case for oral argument. The Court heard oral argument on December 6, 1994.

II. MONROE'S WAIVER IS EXCUSED

As an initial matter, the State argues that Monroe waived his insufficiency of evidence claims by failing to move timely for a judgment of acquittal in the Superior Court. Though we find that Monroe did waive his insufficiency claims, we hold that the waiver should be excused under the circumstances of this case.

A motion for judgment of acquittal must be presented either before a case is submitted to a jury or within seven days of the jury's discharge. Super.Ct.Crim.R. 29 ("Rule 29"). A claim of insufficiency of evidence is reviewable only if the defendant first presented it to the trial court, either in a motion for a directed verdict or a Rule 29 motion for judgment of acquittal. Absent any such motion, the claim is waived. *Gordon v. State,* Del.Supr., 604 A.2d 1367, 1368 (1992); *see* Supr.Ct.R. 8 ("Rule 8"). This Court may excuse a waiver, however, if it finds that the trial court committed plain error requiring review in the interests of justice. Supr.Ct.R. 8; *e.g., Davis v. State,* Del.Supr., No. 283, 1993, *slip op.* at 2-3, 1994 WL 10980, Moore, J. (Jan. 12, 1994) (ORDER).

In the instant case, Monroe did not move for a directed verdict or a judgment of acquittal. Rule 8, however, requires only that a "question[ ] [be] fairly presented to the trial court[.]" Supr.Ct.R. 8. Monroe presented the insufficiency claim to the trial court in his post-conviction motion under Superior Court Criminal Procedure Rule 61. In that motion, he sought relief from his counsel's failure to heed his request to file an appeal within the time-frame provided for in Supreme Court Rule 6(a)(ii) ("Rule 6(a)(ii)"). In granting relief from the dereliction of Monroe's trial counsel, the Superior Court renewed the time to file a direct appeal. Such renewal, however, placed Monroe in only as good a position as he would have been absent the trial counsel's dereliction with regard to the filing of the appeal. *See Dixon v. State,* Del.Supr., 581 A.2d 1115, 1117 (1990). Though the Superior Court granted Monroe a fresh opportunity to meet the requirements of Rule 6(a)(ii), which he did, the failure to move originally for a judgment of acquittal under the time-frame provided for in Rule 29 was not excused. Nonetheless, the Court finds that, in view of its holding *infra* that Monroe would have been entitled to an entry of a judgment of acquittal if that motion had been made at the conclusion of the State's case, the interests of justice require that we review Monroe's claims on a plain error scope of review. *See, e.g., Davis, slip op.* at 2-3.

III. STANDARD OF REVIEW FOR INSUFFICIENCY OF EVIDENCE CLAIMS

The standard of review in assessing an insufficiency of evidence claim is "whether *any* rational trier of fact, viewing the evidence in the light most favorable to the State, could find [a] defendant guilty beyond a reasonable doubt." *Robertson v. State,* Del.Supr., 596 A.2d 1345, 1355 (1991); *accord Shipley v. State,* Del.Supr., 570 A.2d 1159, 1170 (1990); *Skinner v. State,* Del.Supr., 575 A.2d 1108, 1121 (1990). In making this determination, "[t]he fact that most of the State's evidence [is] circumstantial is irrelevant; 'the Court does not distinguish between direct and circumstantial evidence.'" *Robertson,* 596 A.2d at 1355 (quoting *Shipley,* 570 A.2d at 1170).

In the instant case, the State's evidence, though purely circumstantial, was sufficient to sustain the jury's finding that the appliance center was burglarized. The key issue, however, is whether the fingerprint evidence presented here was sufficient to establish, *prima facie* during the State's case, the identity of Monroe as the burglar. As to that issue, we agree with Monroe that no rational trier of fact could have concluded that he committed the charged offenses based on the evidence presented during the State's case.

IV. INSUFFICIENCY OF EVIDENCE CLAIMS

Monroe argues that his convictions and sentence should be reversed because of an insufficiency of evidence as to each charged offense. The State responds that, although the evidence against Monroe is only circumstantial, it is sufficient to sustain the guilty verdicts.

Although we have not previously addressed the question before the Court in this case-whether fingerprint evidence under circumstances such as those presented here is sufficient to establish a perpetrator's identity-other jurisdictions have dealt with similar issues. A substantial number of jurisdictions appear to have adopted the following rule in one form or another: a conviction cannot be sustained solely on a defendant's fingerprints being found on an object at a crime scene unless the State demonstrates that the prints could have been impressed only at the time the crime was committed. * * *

Evidence may be sufficient to sustain a conviction, however, where the circumstances surrounding a defendant's fingerprints create a strong inference that the defendant was the perpetrator. These surrounding circumstances include, but are not limited to, the following: whether the prints were found in a private or public structure (*i.e.,* whether the object in question was generally-accessible); whether the defendant had any special access to the object in question which may provide an alternative explanation for the presence of the prints; and whether the manner of placement of the prints on the object is supportive of the defendant having placed them there while committing the charged offense.

Representative cases where convictions were not set aside on an insufficiency of evidence basis include: *Taylor v. Stainer,* 9th Cir., 31 F.3d 907, 908-09 (1994) (defendant's fingerprints found on inside of POE window sill of private home; no special access); *Carter,* 118 Ariz. at 563, 578 P.2d at 992 (prints on inside surface of POE window of private home; no special access); *State v. Crosby,* 196 Conn. 185, 491 A.2d 1092, 1094 (1985) (prints on glass door of wall unit inside store from which jewelry was stolen; door was cleaned with solution that removed all fingerprints from surface and store was inaccessible from time of cleaning until burglary); *State v. Thorpe,* 188 Conn. 645, 453 A.2d 88, 89-90 (1982) (prints on jewelry box locat-ed inside business premises from which jewelry was stolen; box was cleaned and not accessible to defendant before burglary); *Hawkins v. United States,* D.C.App., 329 A.2d 781, 782 (1974) (prints on dresser drawer inside bedroom of burglarized home; no special access); *Woods,* 167 Ill.Dec. at 1097-98, 588 N.E.2d at 1227-28 (prints on glass shard from broken POE window in private residence; no proof of special access); *Colvin,* 472 A.2d at 964-65 (prints on glass shards of POE, inacces-sible basement door, broken to gain entry to burglarized private home; defendant found in possession of stolen items); *Deutschmann,* 392 S.W.2d at 282 (prints on coin box located behind counter of burglarized business; not generally-accessible); *Ouellette,* 484 A.2d at 1150 (prints on certain papers taken from dispenser located behind counter of burglarized store; no special access); *Giordano,* 440 A.2d at 746-47 (prints on air conditioner unit inside premises that was unsuccessful target of burglary; unit was thoroughly cleaned before burglary and there was no public access to premises between time of cleaning and burglary); *Ricks,* 237 S.E.2d at 812 (prints on jar inside bedroom of burglarized private home; no special access).

Applying the above standards, the courts in each of the following cases reversed a defendant's conviction due to lack of sufficient evidence linking the defendant to the charged offenses. *Payne,* 440 A.2d at 282-83 (prints on outside of a driver side, front door window of generally-accessible car in which victim was robbed); *J.C.M.,* 502 A.2d at 473-75 (prints on can of air freshener, gener-ally accessible before purchase by victim, and located near POE window of bur-glarized private home; stolen property not recovered); *Townsley v. United States,* D.C.App., 236 A.2d 63, 65 (1967) (prints on glass shard from smashed POE front door of burglarized business; glass piece located inside premises); *White,* 312 S.E.2d at 713-14 (defendant's fingerprints on window shattered while gaining entry to victim's private home; defendant claimed special access); *Commonwealth v. Cichy,* 227 Pa.Super. 480, 323 A.2d 817, 818 (1974) (prints on cigarette pack-age's cellophane wrapper, found inside burglarized gas station which defendant had visited on at least one prior occasion). In such cases, a defendant has no obligation to offer a credible, lawful explanation for the existence of his or her fingerprints on the object in question. *E.g., Payne,* 440 A.2d at 282 n. 3; *White,* 312 S.E.2d at 714. *But see Woods,* 167 Ill.Dec. at 1098, 588 N.E.2d at 1228 (reject-ing defendant's unsupported theory on appeal that his prints could have been impressed at time other than during commission of burglary).

We find the treatment of this issue by other jurisdictions useful in analyzing the insufficiency of evidence claims presented here. In the instant case, the State presented the following fingerprint evidence in attempting to satisfy its burden of linking Monroe to the burglary:

(1) Officer Ciritella testified that, based on his past experience, fingerprints on a large piece of glass that was dangling at the POE indicates that the print's owner moved the glass piece aside to more easily enter the store. He admitted, however, that he was speculating as to what may have actually occurred.

(2) Upon being recalled to the stand, Officer Ciritella conceded that "[t]he only latent lift that I can determine that came from inside is [that from] the [dangling] pane of glass that I took out of the door," and that he could not identify those particular prints to be Monroe's. He stated that Officer Liszkiewicz was responsible for making the latter identification.

(3) Officer Liszkiewicz presented extensive testimony relating to the prints. Aggregately, he identified eight prints as Monroe's and seventeen prints which belonged to others. As to the latter, he did not know whether they belonged to more than one person, or the identity of their owner(s). He also found an additional fourteen prints which he classified as unidentifiable, that is, of insufficient quality to make a comparison.

(4) Officer Liszkiewicz continued that he had no knowledge regarding whether the fingerprints he matched to those of Monroe were removed from one or more pieces of glass, or whether they were removed from glass pieces that were inside or outside the store.

(5) hough he initially stated that he could not "form some rough hypotheses as to how [Monroe's] fingerprint was left behind," Officer Liszkiewicz later opined that, based on his "experience on the streets," "the known fingerprints of [Monroe] and the unknown fingerprints left behind by this other person or persons, and the smudges, [were] consistent with someone pulling shards of Plexiglass out of a door frame and moving them out of the way[.]" He conceded that the prints were also consistent with "somebody just touching the surface of the door[.]"

(6) Officer Liszkiewicz also conjectured that, based on his training and experience, an area on the door between the ground and the handle (which was the POE and from where the pieces of glass yielded the prints) is less likely to be touched in the normal use of a door than the area adjacent to the door handle.

The State's reliance on the above testimony of the two officers to satisfy its burden of making out a *prima facie* case is unpersuasive. Regarding the testimony relating to the prints on the inside of the dangling plexiglass shard, what is saliently absent from the testimony is any match-up of the prints on that shard and those of Monroe. That is, Officer Ciritella could testify only that he found someone's prints on the inside shard and Officer Liszkiewicz could not match those prints on that piece of glass to Monroe's prints. Officer Liszkiewicz, in fact, did not know whether the fingerprints were all from one piece of shattered plexiglass or several, or whether any particular prints he tested were from shards found inside or outside the appliance center. Thus, even assuming that finding Monroe's prints on the inside surface of the glass piece dangling from the door is somehow more inculpatory than finding them on the outside,[8] the State failed to establish that the prints on the inside were indeed Monroe's.

The plexiglass pieces came from the front door of the appliance center, which was generally accessible to the public. *See Townsley*, 236 A.2d at 65. There was no evidence that Monroe's prints were placed on the glass at the time the door was shattered to gain entry. *See id.; Cichy*, 323 A.2d at 818; *White*, 312 S.E.2d at 713-14. Both Officers Ciritella and Liszkiewicz testified that they could not determine on which day or at what time any of the prints were left on the door. None of the items stolen were found in Monroe's possession upon execution of the search warrant. *See Colvin*, 472 A.2d at 964-65. The only explanation that Officer Liszkiewicz could attribute to the existence of the several sets of identifiable but unmatched, as well as the several unidentifiable, fingerprints on the glass pieces was that a door is a type of object that, in its natural use, tends to accumulate many fingerprints. That explanation is demonstratively indicative of the weakness in the State's case.[9]

---

8 The Court notes that this is not self-evident, given that both the inside and outside surfaces of the door were generally accessible to the public. *See Townsley*, 236 A.2d at 65. *But see White*, 608 N.E.2d at 1225-26 (focusing on prints being on inside surface of porch door; reasoning that, because door was to private home to which defendant had no special access, there was no innocent explanation for presence of prints). The only reason that inside prints would be more inculpatory here would be if the Court considered Monroe's failed alibi. As part of his alibi, Monroe claimed he had never been inside the store, in which case there would be no innocent explanation for the presence of the prints on the inside surface of the glass piece. Thus, even had the State established that Monroe's prints were on the inside surface of a generally-accessible, public door, because this evidence would not have been sufficient for the State to have established identity as part of its case-in-chief, the apparent mendacity of Monroe's alibi is irrelevant to deciding whether the Superior Court erred in not *sua sponte* dismissing the indictment at the conclusion of the State's case. *See White*, 312 S.E.2d at 714; *Townsley*, 236 A.2d at 65. The Court finds unpersuasive the State's reliance on *Wright v. West*, 505 U.S. 277, 112 S.Ct. 2482, 120 L.Ed.2d 225 (1992), in arguing to the contrary. That case held that a jury is entitled to consider the implausibility of a defendant's alibi in determining guilt, *Wright*, 505 U.S. at — - ——, 112 S.Ct. at 2492-93, whereas the specific issue here is whether the Superior Court erred *ex ante* in allowing the case to go to the jury where the State failed to produce sufficient, *prima facie* evidence establishing identity.

9 As to the State's theory that the location of the POE prints was not indicative of them having been left there in the normal use of a door, presented via speculation by Officers Ciritella and Liszkiewicz, this represents, at

Though the State no longer needs to disprove every possible innocent explanation in pure circumstantial evidence cases, *Williams v. State,* Del.Supr., 539 A.2d 164, 167, *cert. denied,* 488 U.S. 969, 109 S.Ct. 500, 102 L.Ed.2d 536 (1988), the range of abundant, innocent explanations for the presence of Monroe's prints on the plexiglass shards is too vast for "any rational trier of fact" to have found beyond a reasonable doubt an essential element of both charged offenses-namely, identity. *See Payne,* 440 A.2d at 282; *White,* 312 S.E.2d at 713-14; *Townsley,* 236 A.2d at 65; *Cichy,* 323 A.2d at 819.

The Court holds that the Superior Court committed plain error in not *sua sponte* granting a judgment of acquittal upon the State's completion of its case. Given the self-evident importance of establishing identity, this error, though perhaps understandable in view of Monroe's failure to raise the question, cannot be said to be harmless. Our holding is limited to the facts before us today. We express no opinion on the sufficiency of fingerprint evidence to establish guilt in cases involving different circumstances. We hold only that the evidence the State presented at trial in this case fell short of the reasonable doubt requirement.

V. DISPOSITION OF THIS CASE

The final issue before the Court is the proper disposition of this case. Where an appellate court overturns a jury's guilty verdict on insufficiency of evidence grounds, the Double Jeopardy Clause of the United States Constitution bars retrial of the defendant. *Burks v. United States,* 437 U.S. 1, 11, 18, 98 S.Ct. 2141, 2147, 2150-51, 57 L.Ed.2d 1 (1978); *Greene v. Massey,* 437 U.S. 19, 24, 98 S.Ct. 2151, 2154, 57 L.Ed.2d 15 (1978) (applying *Burks* to state criminal prosecution). The *Burks* court reasoned: "The Double Jeopardy Clause forbids a second trial for the purpose of affording the prosecution another opportunity to supply evidence which it failed to muster in the first proceeding." 437 U.S. at 11, 98 S.Ct. at 2147. Any other regime of law would "afford the government an opportunity for the proverbial 'second bite at the apple.'" *Id.* at 17, 98 S.Ct. at 2150. Thus, given our holding above that the State did not sufficiently establish identity in its case-in-chief, the federal Double Jeopardy Clause would bar retrial of Monroe for the conduct in question here. *See Greene,* 437 U.S. at 24, 98 S.Ct. at 2154.

The Double Jeopardy Clause of the Delaware Constitution also requires that Monroe be acquitted. "[T]he double jeopardy provisions in the United States Constitution and the Delaware Constitution are similar." *E.g., State v. Pusey,* Del. Supr., 600 A.2d 32, 36 n. 2 (1991). Delaware has codified double jeopardy analysis in 11 *Del.C.* § 207(1) ("§ 207(1)"), which reads in relevant part:

---

best, a scintilla of inculpatory, circumstantial evidence. The Court finds that, as such, it is insufficient to sustain Monroe's convictions.

> When a prosecution is for a violation of the same statutory provisions and is based upon the same facts as a former prosecution, it is barred by the former prosecution [when] ... [t]he former prosecution resulted in an acquittal. ... There is an acquittal if the prosecution resulted ... in a determination by the court that there was insufficient evidence to warrant a conviction.

Once there is a finding of an "acquittal" under § 207(1), then Delaware's Double Jeopardy Clause bars retrial. *See Chao v. State,* Del.Supr., 604 A.2d 1351, 1360 (1992) (Delaware's Double Jeopardy Clause "'protects against a second prosecution for the same offense after acquittal'") (citation omitted); *accord State v. Cook,* Del.Supr., 600 A.2d 352, 354 (1991); *Pusey,* 600 A.2d at 35. Where the basis for acquittal is a lack of sufficient evidence, this Court must remand the case for an entry of a judgment of acquittal. *Weber v. State,* Del.Supr., 547 A.2d 948, 959-61 (1988) (finding meritorious an insufficiency of evidence claim; reversing denial of directed verdict motion and remanding for entry of a judgment of acquittal).

In the instant case, as earlier stated, the Superior Court erred in *sua sponte* failing to make at the end of the State's case "a determination ... that there was insufficient evidence to warrant a conviction." *See* 11 *Del.C.* § 207(1). Had the trial court made the requisite determination, then the "former prosecution [would have] resulted in an acquittal." *See id.* Upon being so acquitted, Monroe could not have been retried under Delaware's Double Jeopardy Clause. *See id.; Chao,* 604 A.2d at 1360; *Cook,* 600 A.2d at 354; *Pusey,* 600 A.2d at 35. Thus, because we reverse Monroe's convictions based on a lack of sufficient evidence, the federal and State Double Jeopardy Clauses require that we remand the case for an entry of a judgment of acquittal.

VI. CONCLUSION

By failing to move for a directed verdict or a judgment of acquittal in the trial court, Monroe waived his right to raise an insufficiency claim on appeal. The Court finds, however, that the interests of justice mandate review. On the merits, because there was insufficient evidence linking Monroe to the charged offenses, the Superior Court committed plain error in failing *sua sponte* to enter a judgment of acquittal in favor of Monroe. We REVERSE the judgment of conviction and REMAND the case to the Superior Court for an ENTRY OF A JUDGMENT OF ACQUITTAL in favor of Monroe as to the Burglary Third Degree and Theft Felony counts.

Notes and Questions

1. It is clear that the prosecution bears the burden of proving guilt beyond a reasonable doubt. This can arise in several contexts. First, juries apply this standard in rendering their verdicts. Second, a judge may apply this standard when deciding a motion to discuss the case for insufficiency of the evidence, as occurred in *Evans v. Michigan*, or when serving as the trier of fact in a bench trial. Third, a court may apply this standard on appeal following a guilty verdict by a judge or jury. It is relatively unusual for an appellate court to overrule the decision of a factfinder. If a judge or jury finds that the prosecution has not met its burden, or if a reviewing court finds that the evidence is insufficient, then the prosecution ends and cannot be pursued again because of double jeopardy.

2. The standard is also important when attorneys argue and when judges instruct. Certain arguments and instructions have been held to "shift the burden" and therefore constitute error requiring a new trial, even if the evidence is sufficient. *See, e.g., People v. Carbajal*, 2013 IL App (2d) 111018 (reversing where prosecutor argued, about defendant's testimony "it does not prove the defendant's innocence in any way."); *State v. Abdi*, 248 P.3d 209 (Ariz. Ct. App. 2011) (reversing where, in self-defense case, jury was instructed that conduct by homeowner-victim was presumed to be reasonable). Does it shift the burden for the prosecutor to argue that the only way the defendant can be acquitted is if the prosecution witnesses are lying or mistaken? *Paul v. State*, 980 So. 2d 1282 (Fla. App. 2008); *State v. Fleming*, 921 P.2d 1076 (Wash. App. 1996). Does it shift the burden in a DUI case if the Court instructs, in accordance with a statute addressing admissibility, that a chemical test "shall be considered valid" if it is done in accordance with the statutory requirements? *Bailey v. State*, 747 S.E.2d 210 (Ga. App. 2013) (*citing Muir v. State*, 545 S.E.2d 176 (Ga. App. 2001)).

3. While it is clear that the Constitution forbids conviction except upon proof beyond a reasonable doubt, it is not so clear what "beyond a reasonable doubt" means. As the great California Supreme Court Justice Stanley Mosk argued, "all attempts to define the phrase 'beyond a reasonable doubt' are at once futile and unnecessary. They are futile because . . . the definition is more complicated than the phrase itself and results in confusing rather than enlightening the jury; and they are unnecessary because 'beyond a reasonable doubt' is not a technical legal term requiring learned explanation, but a phrase of common meaning and usage that is known to and understood by the average juror."

People v. Brigham, 599 P.2d 100, 116 (Cal. 1979). Nevertheless, some instructions are error. What do you think the Supreme Court found insufficient in this instruction?

> If you entertain a reasonable doubt as to any fact or element necessary to constitute the defendant's guilt, it is your duty to give him the benefit of that doubt and return a verdict of not guilty. Even where the evidence demonstrates a probability of guilt, if it does not establish such guilt beyond a reasonable doubt, you must acquit the accused. This doubt, however, must be a reasonable one; that is one that is founded upon a real tangible substantial basis and not upon mere caprice and conjecture. It must be such doubt as would give rise to a grave uncertainty, raised in your mind by reasons of the unsatisfactory character of the evidence or lack thereof. A reasonable doubt is not a mere possible doubt. It is an actual substantial doubt.

Cage v. Louisiana, 498 U.S. 39, 40, 111 S. Ct. 328, 329, 112 L. Ed. 2d 339 (1990) *disapproved of on other grounds, Estelle v. McGuire*, 502 U.S. 62, 112 S. Ct. 475, 116 L. Ed. 2d 385 (1991).

4. Some jurisdictions also have special sufficiency rules based on their constitutions, statutes, or common law.

   A. *Accomplice Testimony.* On the ground that admitted criminals are inherently untrustworthy and, in hopes of obtaining leniency, have strong incentives to implicate others, truthfully or not, some jurisdictions prohibit convictions based solely on the uncorroborated testimony of an accomplice. *See, e.g.*, Minn. Stats. § 634.04 ("A conviction cannot be had upon the testimony of an accomplice, unless it is corroborated by such other evidence as tends to convict the defendant of the commission of the offense, and the corroboration is not sufficient if it merely shows the commission of the offense or the circumstances thereof."); N.Y. Crim. Proc. L. 60.22(1) ("A conviction cannot be had upon the testimony of an accomplice, unless it is corroborated by such other evidence as tends to convict the defendant of the commission of the offense, and the corroboration is not sufficient if it merely shows the commission of the offense or the circumstances thereof."); *Williams v. State*, 72 So.3d 721 (Ala. Ct. App. 2010); *Gilmore v. State*, 726 S.E.2d 584 (Ga. Ct. App. 2012); *State v. Foster*, 188 P.3d 440 (Or. Ct. App. 2008).

   B. *Corpus Delicti.* Some jurisdictions apply the "corpus delicti" rule, prohibiting conviction based on a defendant's uncorroborated confession without independent proof of the crime. The purpose is to ensure that no one is committed unless it is clear that a crime actually occurred. *See, e.g., State v. Nieves*, 87 P.3d 851 (Ariz. Ct. App. 2004); *People v. Harris*, 986 N.E.2d 496 (Ill. Ct. App. 2010); *State v. Smith*, 669 S.E.2d 299 (N.C. 2008); *Hacker v. State*, 389 S.W.2d 860 (Tex. Crim. App. 2013); *Allen v. Commonwealth*, 2014 WL 92183 (Va. Jan. 10, 2014); *see also People v. Alvarez*, 46 P.3d 372 (Cal. 2002) (corpus delicti rule applies in California).

C. *Circumstantial Evidence*. Some jurisdictions impose special limits on convictions based solely on circumstantial evidence. Thus, for example in Florida, "where a conviction is based wholly upon circumstantial evidence, a special standard of review applies. The special standard requires that the circumstances lead to a reasonable and moral certainty that the accused and no one else committed the offense charged. It is not sufficient that the facts create a strong probability of, and be consistent with, guilt. They must be inconsistent with innocence." *Lindsey v. State*, 14 So. 3d 211, 214-15 (Fla. 2009) (citations omitted). *See generally* Irene Merker Rosenberg & Yale L. Rosenberg, *"Perhaps What Ye Say Is Based Only on Conjecture"-Circumstantial Evidence*, Then and Now, 31 Hous. L. Rev. 1371 (1995).

D. *Weight of the Evidence/Thirteenth Juror Reversals*. Some jurisdictions allow trial courts to grant new trials or appellate courts to reverse convictions where the evidence is legally sufficient but where conviction is against the "weight of the evidence." *State v. Thompkins*, 1997-Ohio-52, 78 Ohio St. 3d 380, 387, 678 N.E.2d 541, 546 (1997) ("Although a court of appeals may determine that a judgment of a trial court is sustained by sufficient evidence, that court may nevertheless conclude that the judgment is against the weight of the evidence."). *See also, e.g., Velloso v. State*, 117 So.3d 903 (Fla. Dist. Ct. App. 2013); *People v. Cornelius*, 1996 WL 33358107 (Mich. Ct. App. Sept. 20, 2996); *People v. Peters*, 911 N.Y.S.2d 719 (App. Div. 2010); *Commonwealth v. Brown*, 648 A.2d 1177 (Pa. 1994).

Some jurisdictions address these issues with jury instructions in addition to, or instead of, special sufficiency rules.

5. Some statutes also have special sufficiency provisions. For example, many jurisdictions provide in perjury prosecutions that if a defendant made irrec-

oncilably inconsistent statements under oath, a conviction may be had without proving which, in particular, was false. *See, e.g.,* 18 U.S.C. § 1623(c).

G. Elements Versus Defenses

A persistent question in interpreting statutes is whether an exception or exemption is an element of the offense, which the prosecution must disprove, or a defense, which the defendant must prove, or at least raise with some evidence. The following cases address that question.

People v. Neidinger

Supreme Court of California
40 Cal.4th 67, 146 P.3d 502 (2006)

CHIN, J.

Penal Code section 278.5 provides in subdivision (a) that it is a crime when a person "takes, entices away, keeps, withholds, or conceals a child and maliciously deprives a lawful custodian of a right to custody, or a person of a right to visitation . . . ." Section 278.7, subdivision (a) (section 278.7(a)), provides, however, that section 278.5 does not apply to a person who has a right to custody of the child and acts "with a good faith and reasonable belief that the child, if left with the other person, will suffer immediate bodily injury or emotional harm . . . ." This case requires us to examine the relationship between these two provisions. We conclude that the defendant bears the burden of raising a reasonable doubt regarding whether section 278.7(a) applies. Because the trial court instructed the jury that defendant had to prove section 278.7(a)'s facts by a preponderance of the evidence, and because the error was prejudicial, we affirm the judgment of the Court of Appeal, which had reversed the trial judgment.

I. FACTS AND PROCEDURAL HISTORY

We take these facts largely from the Court of Appeal opinion. Defendant, William Neidinger, and Olga Neidinger (Olga) were married in 1998. They have two children, a son born in October 1998, and a daughter born in November 1999. As the Court of Appeal describes it, "The relationship between defendant and Olga was tumultuous; they had many arguments that escalated to physical altercations. Olga and defendant each claimed the other was the aggressor. Olga testified defendant was physically abusive; defendant testified that Olga became quite angry after the birth of [their daughter], and would take out her aggressions by hitting him or damaging his personal property." Eventually, after one altercation, Olga and the children moved into an apartment in West Sacramento. On September 5, 2001, at Olga's request, the Sacramento County Superior Court issued an order restraining defendant from contacting Olga or the children.

In December 2001, Olga filed a petition for legal separation. Later, the court granted Olga and defendant joint legal and physical custody of the children and gave defendant supervised and then unsupervised visitation rights. Pursuant to stipulation, the custody order was modified on February 21, 2002. The new order granted Olga and defendant joint legal custody with primary physical custody to Olga. Defendant was granted visitation with the children on each Saturday and Sunday from 9:00 a.m. to 7:00 p.m.

Defendant testified that after he began to see the children more frequently, he became concerned about their well-being, as they had regressed into a state of near autism. They were lethargic, detached, and almost catatonic. He said he made over 20 complaints to child protective service agencies about the children's well-being without receiving a satisfactory response. Defendant's concern culminated in an incident on March 5, 2002, that, he testified, caused him to decide to take the children from Olga's care for their own safety. During this time, defendant was trying to conclude all court proceedings in California and to initiate a new proceeding in Nevada because, he testified, "[n]obody was living in Sacramento whatsoever," and he had maintained his residency in Nevada even after he had moved to Sacramento to complete a job. On March 7, 2002, defendant filed an application in a Nevada court for an order for protection against domestic violence.

Defendant picked up his children for his regular visitation on Saturday, March 9, 2002. He testified he drove to the police station in West Sacramento to inform them of his plans to remove the children, but the station was closed. A woman in civilian clothes told him that the police did not get into such matters and did not care. Through third parties, he communicated to Olga that he would not return the children because he had moved to Nevada, which would be a better place for them. Olga called the police. While a police officer was interviewing her, defendant telephoned her. He told her that he had an order granting custody issued by a Nevada court on March 8, 2002, but he declined to fax a copy of the order to the officer.

Officer Ricky Gore, the investigating officer, left a message on defendant's cellular telephone the evening of March 9, 2002, to which defendant replied with a lengthy message of his own. Officer Gore testified that defendant said he was fed up with the California court system; he had "gotten rid" of all actions in California; he had tried, unsuccessfully, to serve Olga with court papers; and the children were safe. Officer Gore returned defendant's call the next morning, and defendant reiterated the concerns he had stated in his earlier message. The day after that, Monday, March 11, 2002, Officer Gore again spoke with defendant by telephone, who reiterated his frustration with the California courts and said he was concerned about his children's welfare. Defendant said he would not return the children to California, but he agreed to fax the Nevada court order to Officer Gore. Officer Gore obtained an arrest warrant for defendant, and Nevada police arrested him later that same day while he was faxing the Nevada order to Officer Gore.

Defendant was charged with two counts of maliciously depriving a lawful custodian of the right to custody of a child in violation of section 278.5, subdivision (a), one count for each of the two children.3 At trial, defendant claimed that he had a reasonable and good faith belief that removal of the children from Olga's care was necessary for their physical and emotional well-being under section 278.7(a). The court instructed the jury on this defense. As part of this instruction, the court told the jury that defendant had the burden of proving the facts necessary to establish this defense by a preponderance of the evidence.

The jury found defendant guilty on both counts. The trial court suspended imposition of sentence and placed defendant on probation for four years on the condition that he serve 240 days in jail and have no contact with Olga and the children.

Defendant appealed. He argued that the trial court erred in imposing on him the burden of proving section 278.7(a)'s factual requirements by a preponderance of the evidence. The Court of Appeal held that the preponderance-of-the-evidence instruction was proper. But it also held that the trial court erred by not additionally giving an instruction "which clarified the relationship between the good faith defense and the element of malice, so that it was clear to the jury that, to the extent the evidence regarding the good faith defense also showed that defendant acted without malice, he need raise only a reasonable doubt as to that element of the offense." It found the error prejudicial and reversed the judgment.

We granted the Attorney General's petition for review.

II. DISCUSSION

In criminal cases, it is well settled, indeed, virtually axiomatic, that the prosecution has the burden of proof beyond a reasonable doubt. (E.g., *In re Winship* (1970) 397 U.S. 358, 364, 90 S.Ct. 1068, 25 L.Ed.2d 368; § 1096.) Accordingly, in this case, the prosecution had the burden of proving beyond a reasonable doubt every element of the crime stated in section 278.5, subdivision (a). No one questions this basic proposition. But it is constitutionally permissible to place on the defendant the burden of proving affirmative defenses by a preponderance of the evidence, as long as the defendant is not required to negate an element of the offense. (*Dixon v. U.S.* (2006) 548 U.S. 1, 126 S.Ct. 2437, 165 L.Ed.2d 299 [interpreting federal statutes as requiring defendant to prove duress by a preponderance of the evidence]; *Martin v. Ohio* (1987) 480 U.S. 228, 107 S.Ct. 1098, 94 L.Ed.2d 267 [Ohio law may permissibly require defendants charged with murder to prove self-defense by a preponderance of the evidence]; *Moss v. Superior Court* (1998) 17 Cal.4th 396, 71 Cal.Rptr.2d 215, 950 P.2d 59 [person charged with criminal contempt for failure to comply with a child support order must prove inability to comply with the order by a preponderance of the evidence].)

In this case, defendant was convicted of violating section 278.5, subdivision (a), which provides:

> "Every person who takes, entices away, keeps, withholds, or conceals a child and maliciously deprives a lawful custodian of a right to custody, or a person of a right to visitation," is guilty of a crime. At trial, he relied on section 278.7(a), which provides: "Section 278.5 does not apply to a person with a right to custody of a child who, with a good faith and reasonable belief that the child, if left with the other person, will suffer immediate bodily injury or emotional harm, takes, entices away, keeps, withholds, or conceals that child."

We must decide how section 278.7(a)'s belief defense interacts with section 278.5. Specifically, we must decide who has the burden of proof regarding this belief, and what that burden is. Within limits, this is a question of state law. "[D]efining the elements of an offense and the procedures, including the burdens of producing evidence and of persuasion, are matters committed to the state." (*Moss v. Superior Court, supra,* 17 Cal.4th at p. 425, 71 Cal.Rptr.2d 215, 950 P.2d 59, citing *Martin v. Ohio, supra,* 480 U.S. at p. 232, 107 S.Ct. 1098, and *Patterson v. New York* (1977) 432 U.S. 197, 97 S.Ct. 2319, 53 L.Ed.2d 281; *see also Dixon v. U.S., supra,* 548 U.S. at pp. 6–8, 126 S.Ct. at p. 2442.) There are, of course, limits on what the state may do in this regard. "[T]he state may not label as an affirmative defense a traditional element of an offense and thereby make a defendant presumptively guilty of that offense unless the defendant disproves the existence of that element." (*Moss v. Superior Court, supra,* at p. 426, 71 Cal.Rptr.2d 215, 950 P.2d 59.) "Due process does not require that the state prove the nonexistence of a constitutionally permissible affirmative defense, however." (*Ibid.*) Defendant does not argue that section 278.7's good faith belief is a traditional element of an offense that cannot be made an affirmative defense. Accordingly, we turn to state law to decide these questions.

We recently decided similar questions regarding a different offense. (*People v. Mower* (2002) 28 Cal.4th 457, 122 Cal.Rptr.2d 326, 49 P.3d 1067 (*Mower*).)

Mower was charged with possessing and cultivating marijuana in violation of Health and Safety Code sections 11357 and 11358. He relied on the defense established by Proposition 215, approved in 1996, entitled Medical Use of Marijuana. Specifically, Health and Safety Code section 11362.5, subdivision (d), provides: "Section 11357, relating to the possession of marijuana, and Section 11358, relating to the cultivation of marijuana, shall not apply to a patient, or to a patient's primary caregiver, who possesses or cultivates marijuana for the personal medical purposes of the patient upon the written or oral recommendation or approval of a physician." As here, we had to decide who had the burden of proving the facts underlying this medical use provision and what that burden was. Also as in this case, "the trial court instructed that defendant bore the burden of proof as to the facts underlying this defense, and that he was required to prove those facts by a preponderance of the evidence." (*Mower, supra,* at p. 476, 122 Cal.Rptr.2d 326, 49 P.3d 1067.)

We began by explaining that two related but distinct issues are involved. The first issue is which party, the prosecution or the defendant, bears the burden of proof regarding the facts underlying the defense. The second issue is exactly what that burden is. (*Mower, supra,* 28 Cal.4th at p. 476, 122 Cal.Rptr.2d 326, 49 P.3d 1067.) As to the first issue, we placed the burden on the defendant. Our reasoning applies equally to this case. We relied primarily on the "so-called rule of convenience and necessity," which "declares that, unless it is 'unduly harsh or unfair,' the 'burden of proving an exonerating fact may be imposed on a defendant if its existence is "peculiarly" within his personal knowledge and proof of its nonexistence by the prosecution would be relatively difficult or inconvenient.'" (*Mower, supra,* 28 Cal.4th at p. 477, 122 Cal.Rptr.2d 326, 49 P.3d 1067.) This rule supports placing the burden on defendant in this case, just as it did in *Mower*. The facts underlying section 278.7(a)'s belief requirement are peculiarly within defendant's personal knowledge, and it would be relatively difficult or inconvenient for the prosecution to prove their nonexistence. It would not be unduly harsh or unfair to place the burden of proving those facts on the defendant.

Additionally, we explained that the medical marijuana statute, Health and Safety Code section 11362.5, subdivision (d), "constitutes an exception" to the criminal statutes because it provides that the criminal statutes "'*shall not apply*'" when the medical requirements are met. (*Mower, supra,* 28 Cal.4th at p. 477, 122 Cal.Rptr.2d 326, 49 P.3d 1067.) The same is true here. Section 278.7(a) uses the phrase "does not apply" rather than "shall not apply," but we see no difference in meaning. "'It is well established that where a statute first defines an offense in unconditional terms and then specifies an exception to its operation, the exception is an affirmative defense to be raised and proved by the defendant.'" (*People v. George* (1994) 30 Cal.App.4th 262, 275, 35 Cal.Rptr.2d 750, quoting *In re Andre*

R. (1984) 158 Cal.App.3d 336, 341, 204 Cal.Rptr. 723.) Here, section 278.7(a) is an exception to section 278.5, which supports the conclusion it is an affirmative defense that the defendant must raise.

Both of the reasons we cited in *Mower, supra,* 28 Cal.4th at page 477, 122 Cal.Rptr.2d 326, 49 P.3d 1067, for placing on defendant the initial burden regarding the medical marijuana defense apply equally here. Accordingly, we conclude that defendant has the initial burden regarding the facts underlying section 278.7(a).

Our conclusion that defendant bears this burden raises the second question, which is how heavy that burden is. Here we come to the main contested issue. The Attorney General argues that the defendant must prove the facts underlying section 278.7(a) by a preponderance of the evidence. Defendant argues he need only raise a reasonable doubt regarding these facts.

We noted in *Mower, supra,* 28 Cal.4th at page 478, 122 Cal.Rptr.2d 326, 49 P.3d 1067, that the rule of convenience and necessity is equally consistent with requiring the defendant merely to raise a reasonable doubt as it is with requiring the defendant to prove the defense by a preponderance of the evidence. Moreover, the fact that section 278.7(a) states an affirmative defense does not decide this question. For example, over a century ago, in a murder case, we considered a statute that "casts upon the defendant the burden of proving circumstances of mitigation, or that justify or excuse the commission of the homicide." (*People v. Bushton* (1889) 80 Cal. 160, 164, 22 P. 549.) We held that this statute only required the defendant "to produce such evidence as will create in the minds of the jury a reasonable doubt of his guilt of the offense charged." (*Ibid.*) Accordingly, to resolve the second question, we "must look elsewhere." (*Mower, supra,* at p. 478, 122 Cal.Rptr.2d 326, 49 P.3d 1067.)

In *Mower,* we began with Evidence Code section 501 which, we explained, "provides that, when a statute allocates the burden of proof to a defendant on any fact *relating to his or her guilt,* the defendant is required merely to raise a reasonable doubt as to that fact." (*Mower, supra,* 28 Cal.4th at p. 479, 122 Cal.Rptr.2d 326, 49 P.3d 1067, italics added.) We noted that with respect to many defenses, the defendant need only raise a reasonable doubt. (*Ibid.; see also id.,* at p. 479, fn. 7, 122 Cal.Rptr.2d 326, 49 P.3d 1067 [giving several examples].) These defenses, we explained, "relate to the defendant's guilt or innocence *because they relate to an element of the crime in question.*" (*Id.* at p. 480, 122 Cal.Rptr.2d 326, 49 P.3d 1067.) We also noted that "[w]hen a statute allocates the burden of proof to a defendant as to a fact collateral to his or her guilt, however, the defendant may be required to prove that fact by a preponderance of the evidence." (*Ibid.*) We said that "[s]uch defenses are collateral to the defendant's guilt or innocence *because they are collateral to any element of the crime in question.*" (*Ibid.*)

Applying this test, we concluded that the defendant need only raise a reasonable doubt as to the facts underlying the medical marijuana defense. "This defense plainly relates to the defendant's guilt or innocence." (*Mower, supra,* 28 Cal.4th at pp. 481–482, 122 Cal.Rptr.2d 326, 49 P.3d 1067.) "As a result of the enactment of [Health and Safety Code] section 11362.5[, subdivision] (d), the possession and cultivation of marijuana is no more criminal—so long as its conditions are satisfied—than the possession and acquisition of any prescription drug with a physician's prescription." (*Id.* at p. 482, 122 Cal.Rptr.2d 326, 49 P.3d 1067.) "In sum, the defense provided by [Health and Safety Code] section 11362.5[, subdivision] (d) relates to the defendant's guilt or innocence, *because it relates to an element of the crime of possession* or *cultivation of marijuana.* Thus, this defense negates the element of the *possession or cultivation* of marijuana *to the extent that the element requires that such possession or cultivation be unlawful.*" (*Ibid.*)

As we explain, we reach the same conclusion in this case that we did in *Mower*—defendant need only raise a reasonable doubt regarding the facts underlying the section 278.7(a) defense. Two Courts of Appeal interpreting two predecessor versions of crimes similar to, but in some ways different than, the crime involved here reached differing results.

In *People v. Beach* (1987) 194 Cal.App.3d 955, 240 Cal.Rptr. 50, the court construed former section 278.5, subdivision (a), which provided in pertinent part: "Every person who in violation of a custody decree takes, retains after the expiration of a visitation period, or conceals the child from his legal custodian" is guilty of a crime. (Former § 278.5, as added by Stats.1976, ch. 1399, § 11, p. 6316; see *People v. Beach, supra,* at p. 962, 240 Cal.Rptr. 50.) At that time section 278.7(a) did not exist. The trial court had instructed the jury on the general, nonstatutory defense of necessity. The Court of Appeal rejected the contention that the court should have instructed the jury that defendant need only raise a reasonable doubt regarding this defense. It concluded, "The necessity defense does not negate any element of the crime but represents a public policy decision not to punish such an individual despite the proof of all the elements of the crime." (*People v. Beach, supra,* at p. 973, 240 Cal.Rptr. 50.) Accordingly, the Court of Appeal held, "The trial court properly refused to instruct the jury [the defendants] had to raise only a reasonable doubt as to the necessity justifying the commission of their crimes." (*Ibid.*)

In *People v. Dewberry* (1992) 8 Cal.App.4th 1017, 10 Cal.Rptr.2d 800, the court construed former section 277, which provided in pertinent part: "In the absence of a court order determining rights of custody or visitation to a minor child, every person having a right of custody of the child who maliciously takes, detains, conceals, or entices away that child within or without the state, *without good cause,* and with the intent to deprive the custody right of another person or a public agency also having a custody right to that child," is guilty of a crime. (Former § 277, as amended by Stats.1990, ch. 400, § 1, p. 2177; italics added.) As relevant, the statute defined "good cause," as "a good faith and reasonable belief that the taking, detaining, concealing, or enticing away of the child is necessary to protect the child from immediate bodily injury or emotional harm." (*Ibid.;* see *People v. Dewberry, supra,* at p. 1020, 10 Cal.Rptr.2d 800.) This definition of "good cause" is similar to the current section 278.7(a) defense. The *Dewberry* court focused on the italicized words in former section 277, "without good cause," and concluded that the absence of good cause was an element of the offense. Accordingly, it held that the defendant need only raise a reasonable doubt regarding this element. (*People v. Dewberry, supra,* at pp. 1020–1021, 10 Cal.Rptr.2d 800.)

* * *

In sum, the key differences between the statutes at issue here and the one in *People v. Beach, supra,* 194 Cal.App.3d 955, 240 Cal.Rptr. 50, are that in *Beach* the statute had no malice requirement and the section 278.7(a) defense did not exist. The key differences between the statutes here and the one in *People v. Dewberry, supra,* 8 Cal.App.4th 1017, 10 Cal.Rptr.2d 800, is that in *Dewberry,* but not here, the absence of good cause was an element of the crime, the statute here requires malice, and the separate section 278.7(a) defense did not exist in *Dewberry.* We must now apply the analysis of *Mower, supra,* 28 Cal.4th 457, 122 Cal.Rptr.2d 326, 49 P.3d 1067, to decide which rule prevails after these changes.

We think that, for these purposes, the current statutory scheme is closer to that of *People v. Dewberry, supra,* 8 Cal.App.4th 1017, 10 Cal.Rptr.2d 800, than that of *People v. Beach, supra,* 194 Cal.App.3d 955, 240 Cal.Rptr. 50. The *Beach* statute had neither a malice requirement nor a separate defense like that of section 278.7(a). Instead, the trial court instructed the jury on the judicially-created necessity defense. This defense was created in other contexts, primarily to provide a defense against a charge of escape from lawful custody. (See, e.g., *People v. Lovercamp* (1974) 43 Cal.App.3d 823, 118 Cal.Rptr. 110.) This defense is similar in some respects to the section 278.7(a) defense, and courts have, indeed, held that a defendant must prove the facts underlying this necessity defense by a preponderance of the evidence. (See *Mower, supra,* 28 Cal.4th at p. 480, fn. 8, 122 Cal.Rptr.2d 326, 49 P.3d 1067.) But the statute here is quite different than the escape statutes or the one in *Beach.* The current section 278.5 requires that the person act "maliciously." Section 7, subdivision 4, states that this word "import[s] a wish to vex, annoy, or injure another person, or an intent to do a wrongful act . . . ." The parties debate at length exactly how this definition fits in with section 278.7(a)'s belief requirement. The two concepts are not identical. But, in effect, the section 278.7(a) defense provides a specific example of when the person does not act maliciously.

Although the Legislature replaced the absence-of-good-cause element of the *Dewberry* statute with a malice element and the separate section 278.7(a) defense, we see no indication it intended to place a greater burden on the defendant to establish good cause than had existed before the statutory change. We think the *Dewberry* rule should still apply. The malice requirement and the section 278.7(a) defense are intertwined, not entirely separate. Section 278.7(a) is not entirely collateral to the elements of the offense but relates to the element of malice and thus to the person's guilt. (Cf. *Mower, supra,* 28 Cal.4th at pp. 479–480, 122 Cal. Rptr.2d 326, 49 P.3d 1067.)

We conclude that a defendant need only raise a reasonable doubt whether the facts underlying the section 278.7(a) defense exist. Thus, the trial court erred in requiring defendant to prove those facts by a preponderance of the evidence. The Court of Appeal had found the preponderance-of-the-evidence instruction correct but found error in not clarifying the relationship between section 278.7(a)'s belief defense and the element of malice. It found that error prejudicial. We conclude that the more serious error that we have found—placing an erroneously high burden on defendant to prove the section 278.7(a) defense—was prejudicial. The Attorney General does not argue that any error was harmless. In *Mower, supra,* 28 Cal.4th at pages 484–485, 122 Cal.Rptr.2d 326, 49 P.3d 1067, we did not decide which standard of prejudice applies to this kind of error because we found the error prejudicial even under the more lenient test for state law error. (See *People v. Watson* (1956) 46 Cal.2d 818, 299 P.2d 243.) We reach the same conclusion here. The jury obviously did not believe defendant had proven by a preponderance of the evidence that he had met the requirements of the section 278.7(a) defense. But, as the Court of Appeal found, the evidence in this regard was reasonably close. Moreover, as in *Mower,* the error "went to the heart of the case against defendant." (*Mower, supra,* at p. 464, 122 Cal.Rptr.2d 326, 49 P.3d 1067.) Accordingly, we find a reasonable probability the result would have been more favorable to defendant in the absence of the error. (*Id.* at p. 484, 122 Cal. Rptr.2d 326, 49 P.3d 1067; *People v. Watson, supra,* at p. 836, 299 P.2d 243.)

III. CONCLUSION

We affirm the judgment of the Court of Appeal.

GEORGE, C.J., KENNARD, BAXTER, WERDEGAR, MORENO, and CORRIGAN, JJ., concur.

Notes and Questions

1. Jurisdictions vary in their allocation of burdens. In general, the defendant bears the burden of production, introducing some evidence that a defense or statutory exception applies. The defendant can satisfy this burden with evidence from the prosecution's case. Thus, if a prosecution witness testifies to facts suggesting a defense of self-defense or entrapment, that would be sufficient to satisfy the defendant's burden of production. States vary on where they place the burden of persuasion on a defense once the burden of production is met. They range from requiring the defendant to *prove* a defense by clear and convincing evidence, *United States v. Amos*, 803 F.3d 419 (8th Cir. 1986) (insanity), to requiring the prosecution to disprove the defense beyond a reasonable doubt. This may be the effect of Neidinger for the defense involved in that case (can you see why?). Of course, "[i]n assigning the burden of proof" jurisdictions are in effect "determining the 'risk of error' faced by the subject of the proceedings." *Heller v. Doe by Doe*, 509 U.S. 312, 322, 113 S. Ct. 2637, 2644, 125 L. Ed. 2d 257 (1993). The "beyond a reasonable doubt" standard is based on the idea that we have a strong preference for false negatives (mistaken acquittals of the guilty) rather than false positives (mistaken convictions of the innocent). The classic exposition of the idea is this: "Blackstone (1753-1765) maintains that 'the law holds that it is better that ten guilty persons escape than that one innocent suffer.' 2 Bl. Comm. c. 27, marg. p. 358, ad finem." *Coffin v. United States*, 156 U.S. 432, 456, 15 S. Ct. 394, 403, 39 L. Ed. 481 (1895)

2. In *Beach*, the court placed the burden of proof on the defendant to establish the defense of necessity. The necessity defense, also known as choice of evils, offers a defense if the crime was committed to avoid a greater harm. *See, e.g.,* MPC 3.02(1)(1) ("Conduct that the actor believes to be necessary to avoid a harm or evil to himself or to another is justifiable, provided that . . . the harm or evil sought to be avoided by such conduct is greater than that sought to be prevented by the law defining the offense charged."). But if the defense of necessity exists in a particular situation, is the defendant not just as "not guilty" as if one of the elements are missing? Therefore, why is a reasonable doubt insufficient with the necessity defense but sufficient for others?

The next case addresses the scope of legislative authority to change elements of the offense into defenses, and placing the burden on defendants to disprove them.

State v. Adkins

Supreme Court of Florida
96 So.3d 412 (2012)

CANADY, J.

In this case we consider the constitutionality of the provisions of chapter 893, Florida Statutes (2011), the Florida Comprehensive Drug Abuse Prevention and Control Act, that provide that knowledge of the illicit nature of a controlled substance is not an element of any offenses under the chapter but that the lack of such knowledge is an affirmative defense.

Based on its conclusion that section 893.13, Florida Statutes (2011)—which creates offenses related to the sale, manufacture, delivery, and possession of controlled substances—is facially unconstitutional under the Due Process Clauses of the Florida and the United States Constitutions, the circuit court for the Twelfth Judicial Circuit issued an order granting motions to dismiss charges filed under section 893.13 in forty-six criminal cases. The circuit court reasoned that the requirements of due process precluded the Legislature from eliminating knowledge of the illicit nature of the substance as an element of the offenses under section 893.13. On appeal, the Second District Court of Appeal certified to this Court that the circuit court's judgment presents issues that require immediate resolution by this Court because the issues are of great public importance and will have a great effect on the proper administration of justice throughout the State. We have jurisdiction. *See* art. V, § 3(b)(5), Fla. Const.

For the reasons explained below, we conclude that the circuit court erred in determining the statute to be unconstitutional. Accordingly, we reverse the circuit court's order granting the motions to dismiss.

I. BACKGROUND

Section 893.13, part of the Florida Comprehensive Drug Abuse Prevention and Control Act, provides in part that except as otherwise authorized "it is unlawful for any person to sell, manufacture, or deliver, or possess with intent to sell, manufacture, or deliver, a controlled substance" or "to be in actual or constructive possession of a controlled substance." § 893.13(1)(a), (6)(a), Fla. Stat. (2011). Depending on the controlled substance involved and the circumstances of the offense, a violation of section 893.13 can be punished as a misdemeanor, a third-degree felony, a second-degree felony, or a first-degree felony. *See, e.g.,* § 893.13(1)(a)(1), (1)(a)(2), (1)(a)(3), (1)(b), Fla. Stat. (2011).

Section 893.13 itself does not specify what mental state a defendant must possess in order to be convicted for selling, manufacturing, delivering, or possessing a controlled substance. In *Chicone v. State,* 684 So.2d 736 (Fla.1996), this Court addressed whether section 893.13 should be interpreted to include a mens rea—that is, a "guilty mind"—element. In reviewing a conviction for possession of cocaine, this Court determined that "guilty knowledge" was one of the elements of the crime of possession of a controlled substance and that the State was required to prove that Chicone knew he possessed the substance and knew of the illicit nature of the substance in his possession. *Id.* at 738–41. This Court reasoned that the common law typically required "scienter or mens rea [as] a necessary element in the indictment and proof of every crime" and that the penalties facing defendants convicted under chapter 893, Florida Statutes, were much harsher than the usual penalties for crimes where a knowledge element is not required. *Chicone,* 684 So.2d at 741. This Court further reasoned that the Legislature "would have spoken more clearly" if it had intended to not require proof of guilty knowledge to convict under section 893.13. *Chicone,* 684 So.2d at 743.

More recently, in *Scott v. State,* 808 So.2d 166 (Fla.2002), this Court clarified that the "guilty knowledge" element of the crime of possession of a controlled substance contains two aspects: knowledge of the presence of the substance and knowledge of the illicit nature of the substance. 808 So.2d at 169. In addition, this Court clarified that the presumption of knowledge set out in *State v. Medlin,* 273 So.2d 394 (Fla.1973), and reiterated in *Chicone*—that a defendant's knowledge of the illicit nature of a controlled substance can be presumed from evidence that the defendant had possession of the controlled substance—can be employed only in cases in which the State proves actual, personal possession of the controlled substance. *Scott,* 808 So.2d at 171–72.

In response to this Court's decisions, the Legislature enacted a statute now codified in section 893.101, Florida Statutes (2011). Section 893.101 provides in full:

(1) The Legislature finds that the cases of *Scott v. State,* Slip Opinion No. SC94701 [808 So.2d 166] (Fla.2002)[,] and *Chicone v. State,* 684 So.2d 736 (Fla.1996), holding that the state must prove that the defendant knew of the illicit nature of a controlled substance found in his or her actual or constructive possession, were contrary to legislative intent.

(2) The Legislature finds that *knowledge of the illicit nature of a controlled substance is not an element* of any offense under this chapter. *Lack of*

knowledge of the illicit nature of a controlled substance is an affirmative defense to the offenses of this chapter.

(3) In those instances in which a defendant asserts the affirmative defense described in this section, the possession of a controlled substance, whether actual or constructive, shall give rise to a permissive presumption that the possessor knew of the illicit nature of the substance. It is the intent of the Legislature that, in those cases where such an affirmative defense is raised, the jury shall be instructed on the permissive presumption provided in this subsection.

(Emphasis added.) The statute thus expressly eliminates knowledge of the illicit nature of the controlled substance as an element of controlled substance offenses and expressly creates an affirmative defense of lack of knowledge of the illicit nature of the substance. The statute does not eliminate the element of knowledge of the presence of the substance, which we acknowledged in *Chicone,* 684 So.2d at 739–40, and *Scott,* 808 So.2d at 169.

Since the enactment of section 893.101, each of the district courts of appeal has ruled that the statute does not violate the requirements of due process. *See Harris v. State,* 932 So.2d 551 (Fla. 1st DCA 2006); *Burnette v. State,* 901 So.2d 925 (Fla. 2d DCA 2005); *Taylor v. State,* 929 So.2d 665 (Fla. 3d DCA 2006); *Wright v. State,* 920 So.2d 21 (Fla. 4th DCA 2005); *Lanier v. State,* 74 So.3d 1130 (Fla. 5th DCA 2011).

[Nevertheless,] the circuit court in this case concluded that section 893.13 is facially unconstitutional because it violates the Due Process Clauses of article I, section 9 of the Florida Constitution and the Fourteenth Amendment to the United States Constitution. The circuit court reasoned that the Legislature did not have authority to dispense with a mens rea element for a serious felony crime.

The State now appeals the circuit court's decision in this Court. The State asserts that section 893.13, as modified by section 893.101, is facially constitutional and that the circuit court therefore erred in granting the motions to dismiss.

II. ANALYSIS

In the following analysis, after acknowledging the applicable standard of review, we first consider the case law that discusses the broad authority of the legislative branch to define the elements of criminal offenses as well as the case law that recognizes that due process ordinarily does not preclude the creation of an offense without a guilty knowledge element. We then examine the limited circumstances in which the absence of a guilty knowledge element has resulted in a holding that the requirements of due process were not satisfied. Finally, we explain our conclusion that sections 893.13 and 893.101 do not violate due process.

"The constitutionality of a statute is a question of law subject to de novo review." *Crist v. Ervin,* 56 So.3d 745, 747 (Fla.2011). In considering a challenge to the constitutionality of a statute, this Court is "obligated to accord legislative acts a presumption of constitutionality and to construe challenged legislation to effect a constitutional outcome whenever possible." *Fla. Dep't of Revenue v. City of Gainesville,* 918 So.2d 250, 256 (Fla.2005) (quoting *Fla. Dep't of Revenue v. Howard,* 916 So.2d 640, 642 (Fla.2005)). "[A] determination that a statute is facially unconstitutional means that no set of circumstances exists under which the statute would be valid." *Id.*

"Enacting laws—and especially criminal laws—is quintessentially a legislative function." *Fla. House of Representatives v. Crist,* 999 So.2d 601, 615 (Fla.2008). "[T]he Legislature generally has broad authority to determine any requirement for intent or knowledge in the definition of a crime." *State v. Giorgetti,* 868 So.2d 512, 515 (Fla.2004). We thus have recognized that generally "[i]t is within the power of the Legislature to declare an act a crime regardless of the intent or knowledge of the violation thereof." *Coleman v. State ex rel. Jackson,* 140 Fla. 772, 193 So. 84, 86 (1939). "The doing of the act inhibited by the statute makes the crime[,] and moral turpitude or purity of motive and the knowledge or ignorance of its criminal character are immaterial circumstances on the question of guilt." *Id.*

Given the broad authority of the legislative branch to define the elements of crimes, the requirements of due process ordinarily do not preclude the creation of offenses which lack a guilty knowledge element. This point was recognized long ago in *United States v. Balint,* 258 U.S. 250, 251, 42 S.Ct. 301, 66 L.Ed. 604 (1922), where the Supreme Court considered the imposition of criminal penalties—fines of up to $2000 or imprisonment for up to five years, or both—under section 9 of the Narcotic Act of 1914 where the indictment "failed to charge that [the defendants] had sold the inhibited drugs knowing them to be such." The Narcotic Act required "every person who produces, imports, manufactures, compounds, deals in, dispenses, sells, distributes, or gives away" a substance containing opium or coca leaves to register and pay a tax. Narcotic Act of Dec. 17, 1914, ch. 1, § 1, 38 Stat. 785 (1914). The Narcotic Act prohibited possession of the specified drugs by any unregistered person, subject to certain exceptions—including an exception for persons to whom the drugs "have been prescribed in good faith" by a registered medical professional. Narcotic Act of Dec. 17, 1914, ch. 1, § 8, 38 Stat. 785 (1914). The Act also provided that "possession or control" of the specified drugs "shall be presumptive evidence of a violation" of the statute. *Id* As recognized by the Supreme Court, the statute did not make "knowledge an element of the offense." *Balint,* 258 U.S. at 251, 42 S.Ct. 301. Despite the substantial penalty for noncompliance with the Narcotic Act, the Supreme Court declined either to read a mens rea element into the Narcotic Act or to conclude that the lack of such an element in the Narcotic Act was unconstitutional.

The *Balint* court specifically rejected the argument that "punishment of a person for an act in violation of law when ignorant of the facts making it so, is an absence of due process of law." *Id.* at 252, 42 S.Ct. 301. The Supreme Court observed that "the state may in the maintenance of a public policy provide 'that he who shall do [proscribed acts] shall do them at his peril and will not be heard to plead in defense good faith or ignorance.'" *Id.* at 252, 42 S.Ct. 301 (quoting *Shevlin–Carpenter Co. v. Minnesota,* 218 U.S. 57, 70, 30 S.Ct. 663, 54 L.Ed. 930 (1910)). The Supreme Court explained that offenses lacking such a knowledge element were commonly "found in regulatory measures in the exercise of what is called the police power where the emphasis of the statute is evidently upon achievement of some social betterment rather than the punishment of crimes as in cases of mala in se." *Id.*

The *Balint* court thus gave effect to the "manifest purpose" of the Narcotic Act—that is, "to require every person dealing in drugs to ascertain at his peril whether that which he sells comes within the inhibition of the statute, and if he sells the inhibited drug in ignorance of its character, to penalize him." 258 U.S. at 254, 42 S.Ct. 301. The Supreme Court recognized that the statutory purpose was properly based at least in part on "considerations as to the opportunity of the seller to find out the fact and the difficulty of proof of knowledge." *Id.*

Since the Supreme Court's decision in *Balint,* both the Supreme Court and this Court have repeatedly recognized that the legislative branch has broad discretion to omit a mens rea element from a criminal offense. For example, in *Staples,* which reviewed a federal law criminalizing the unregistered possession of certain automatic firearms that did not expressly include or exclude a mens rea element, the Supreme Court explained that whether or not a criminal offense requires proof that a defendant knew of the illegal nature of his act "is a question of statutory construction" and that the "definition of the elements of a criminal offense is entrusted to the legislature, particularly in the case of federal crimes, which are solely creatures of statute." 511 U.S. at 604, 114 S.Ct. 1793 (quoting *Liparota v. United States,* 471 U.S. 419, 424, 105 S.Ct. 2084, 85 L.Ed.2d 434 (1985)). Similarly, in *United States v. Freed,* 401 U.S. 601, 91 S.Ct. 1112, 28 L.Ed.2d 356 (1971), and *United States v. International Minerals & Chemical Corp.,* 402 U.S. 558, 91 S.Ct. 1697, 29 L.Ed.2d 178 (1971), the Supreme Court rejected the view that due process required that mens rea elements be read into public safety statutes regulating the possession of unregistered firearms and the shipping of corrosive liquids.

Likewise in *State v. Gray*, 435 So.2d 816 (Fla.1983), this Court determined that the district court erred by construing a witness tampering statute to include scienter and intent elements, explaining:

> The problem with the district court's analysis is its failure to recognize that unless the law in question directly or indirectly impinges on the exercise of some constitutionally protected freedom, or exceeds or violates some constitutional prohibition on the power of the legislature, courts have no power to declare conduct innocent when the legislature has declared otherwise. *Ah Sin v. Wittman*, 198 U.S. 500, 25 S.Ct. 756, 49 L.Ed. 1142 (1905).

> It is within the power of the legislature to declare conduct criminal without requiring specific criminal intent to achieve a certain result; that is, the legislature may punish conduct without regard to the mental attitude of the offender, so that the general intent of the accused to do the act is deemed to give rise to a presumption of intent to achieve the criminal result. The legislature may also dispense with a requirement that the actor be aware of the facts making his conduct criminal. A recent decision from the district court of appeal has recognized these principles. *State v. Oxx*, 417 So.2d 287 (Fla. 5th DCA 1982).

> The question of whether conviction of a crime should require proof of a specific, as opposed to a general, criminal intent is a matter for the legislature to determine in defining the crime. The elements of a crime are derived from the statutory definition. There are some authorities to the effect that infamous crimes, crimes *mala in se,* or common-law crimes may not be defined by the legislature in such a way as to dispense with the element of specific intent, but these authorities are suspect.

Gray, 435 So.2d at 819–20 (some citations omitted).

In a limited category of circumstances, the omission of a mens rea element from the definition of a criminal offense has been held to violate due process. A salient example of such circumstance is found in the Supreme Court's decision in *Lambert v. California,* 355 U.S. 225, 78 S.Ct. 240, 2 L.Ed.2d 228 (1957), which addressed a Los Angeles municipal code provision requiring that felons present in the municipality for more than five days register with law enforcement. The code provision applied to "a person who has no actual knowledge of his duty to register." *Id.* at 227, 78 S.Ct. 240. In *Lambert,* the Supreme Court concluded that a legislative body may not criminalize otherwise entirely innocent, passive conduct—such as a convicted felon remaining in Los Angeles for more than five days—without sufficiently informing the population of the legal requirement. As a result, the Supreme Court concluded that the registration requirement then at issue could be enforced only when the defendant was aware of the ordinance. Still, the Supreme Court emphasized that in a situation where the lawmaking body seeks to prohibit affirmative acts, it can do so without requiring proof that the actor knew his or her conduct to be illegal:

> We do not go with Blackstone in saying that "a vicious will" is necessary to constitute a crime, for conduct alone without regard to the intent of the doer is often sufficient. *There is wide latitude in the lawmakers to declare an offense and to exclude elements of knowledge and diligence from its definition.* But we deal here with conduct that is wholly passive—mere failure to register. It is unlike the commission of acts, or the failure to act under circumstances that should alert the doer to the consequences of his deed. The rule that "ignorance of the law will not excuse" is deep in our law, as is the principle that of all the powers of local government, the police power is "one of the least limitable."

Lambert, 355 U.S. at 228, 78 S.Ct. 240 (emphasis added) (citations omitted).

In *Giorgetti,* this Court followed the holding of *Lambert* in invalidating Florida's sexual offender registration statutes. Because the defendant's alleged illegal conduct "was similar to the passive conduct discussed in *Lambert,* i.e., relocating residences and failing to notify the State within forty-eight hours," we determined that "as in *Lambert,* knowledge is required here to define the wrongful conduct, i.e., the defendant's failure to comply with a statutory requirement." *Giorgetti,* 868 So.2d at 519.

The Supreme Court has also concluded that the omission of a scienter element from the definition of a criminal offense can result in a due process violation where the omission results in criminalizing conduct protected by the First Amendment of the United States Constitution. For example, in *Smith v. California,* 361 U.S. 147, 80 S.Ct. 215, 4 L.Ed.2d 205 (1959), the Supreme Court determined that a scienter element was required in an ordinance making it illegal for any person to have in his possession any obscene or indecent writing in a place of business where books are sold. The Supreme Court reasoned that without such an element, the ordinance would cause a bookseller "to restrict the books he sells to those he has inspected; and thus the State will have imposed a restriction upon the distribution of constitutionally protected as well as obscene literature." *Id.* at 153, 80 S.Ct. 215. Similarly, in *United States v. X–Citement Video, Inc.,* 513 U.S. 64, 115 S.Ct. 464, 130 L.Ed.2d 372 (1994), the Supreme Court construed the modifier "knowing" in the Protection of Children Against Sexual Exploitation Act to apply to the element of the age of the performers. The Supreme Court explained that because nonobscene, sexually explicit materials involving persons over the age of seventeen are protected by the First Amendment, "a statute completely bereft of a scienter requirement as to the age of the performers would raise serious constitutional doubts," and it was "therefore incumbent upon [the court] to read the statute to eliminate those doubts so long as such a reading is not plainly contrary to the intent of Congress." *Id.* at 78, 115 S.Ct. 464.

In *Schmitt v. State,* 590 So.2d 404, 413 (Fla.1991), we concluded that "a due process violation occurs if a criminal statute's means is not rationally related to its purposes and, as a result, it criminalizes innocuous conduct." Specifically, we considered a statute prohibiting the possession of a depiction involving "actual physical contact with a [minor] person's clothed or unclothed genitals, pubic area, buttocks, or if such person is a female, breast." *Id.* at 408 (quoting § 827.071(1)(g), Fla. Stat. (1987)). We held that the statute violated due process because it criminalized family photographs of innocent caretaker-child conduct, such as bathing the child or changing a diaper. While Florida's civil child abuse statute expressly excluded from the definition of sexual child abuse physical contact that "may reasonably be construed to be a normal caretaker responsibility," the criminal statute declared depictions of such acts to be a felony. *Id.* at 413 (quoting § 415.503(17)(d), Fla. Stat. (1987)).

In *In re Forfeiture 1969 Piper Navajo,* 592 So.2d 233, 235 n. 6 (Fla.1992), this Court concluded that the Legislature could not authorize the confiscation of airplanes based on the presence of additional fuel capacity—where extra fuel capacity was not "the exclusive domain of drug smugglers." This Court reasoned that such an action would impinge on protected property rights. *Id.* at 236. Similarly, this Court determined that statutes criminalizing the possession of embossing machines, lawfully obtained drugs not in their original packaging, and spearfishing equipment—without requiring proof of intent to use the items illegally—were not reasonably related to achieving a legitimate legislative purpose and interfered with the property rights of individuals who used those items for noncriminal purposes. *See State v. Saiez,* 489 So.2d 1125 (Fla.1986); *State v. Walker,* 444 So.2d 1137 (Fla. 2d DCA), *aff'd,* 461 So.2d 108 (Fla.1984) (adopting district court of appeal's opinion); *Delmonico v. State,* 155 So.2d 368 (Fla.1963).

The provisions of chapter 893 at issue in the present case are readily distinguishable from those cases in which definitions of particular criminal offenses were found to violate the requirements of due process. The rationale for each of those cases is not applicable to the context of controlled substance offenses under Florida law.

Sections 893.13 and 893.101 do not trigger the concern raised in *Lambert* and *Giorgetti.* The statutes do not penalize without notice a "failure to act [that absent the statutes] otherwise amounts to essentially innocent conduct," such as living in a particular municipality without registering. *Giorgetti,* 868 So.2d at 517 (quoting *Oxx,* 417 So.2d at 290). Rather than punishing inaction, to convict under section 893.13 the State must prove that the defendant engaged in the affirmative act of selling, manufacturing, delivering, or possessing a controlled substance. The controlled substance statutes are further distinguishable from the statutes in *Lambert* and *Giorgetti*—which would impose criminal liability for failing to register regardless of the defendant's knowledge of the regulation and his or her status—because in section 893.101 the Legislature has expressly provided that a person charged under chapter 893 who did not have knowledge of the illegality of his or her conduct may raise that fact as an affirmative defense.

Furthermore, sections 893.13 and 893.101—unlike the provisions we invalidated in *Schmitt, 1969 Piper Navajo, Saiez, Walker,* and *Delmonico*—are rationally related to the Legislature's goal of controlling substances that have a high potential for abuse, and the statutes do not interfere with any constitutionally protected rights. The Legislature tailored section 893.13 to permit legitimate, medical uses of controlled substances but to prohibit non-medically necessary uses of those substances. Section 893.13 expressly excludes from criminal liability individuals who possess a controlled substance that "was lawfully obtained from a practitioner or pursuant to a valid prescription," § 893.13(6)(a), Fla. Stat. (2011), and the following persons and entities who handle medically necessary controlled substances as part of their profession: pharmacists, medical practitioners, hospital employees, government officials working in their official capacity, common carriers, pharmaceutical companies, and the employees and agents of the above, § 893.13(9), Fla. Stat. (2011).

Because there is no legally recognized use for controlled substances outside the circumstances identified by the statute, prohibiting the sale, manufacture, delivery, or possession of those substances without requiring proof of knowledge of the illicit nature of the substances does not criminalize innocuous conduct or "impinge[ ] on the exercise of some constitutionally protected freedom." *Gray,* 435 So.2d at 819. Because the statutory provisions at issue here do not have the potential to curtail constitutionally protected speech, they are materially distinguishable from statutes that implicate the possession of materials protected by the First Amendment, such as those at issue in *Smith* and *X–Citement Video.* There is no constitutional right to possess contraband. "[A]ny interest in possessing contraband cannot be deemed 'legitimate.'" *Illinois v. Caballes,* 543 U.S. 405, 408, 125 S.Ct. 834, 160 L.Ed.2d 842 (2005) (quoting *United States v. Jacobsen,* 466 U.S. 109, 123, 104 S.Ct. 1652, 80 L.Ed.2d 85 (1984)).

Nor is there a protected right to be ignorant of the nature of the property in one's possession. *See Turner v. United States,* 396 U.S. 398, 417, 90 S.Ct. 642, 24 L.Ed.2d 610 (1970) ("'Common' sense tells us that those who traffic in heroin will inevitably become aware that the product they deal in is smuggled, *unless they practice a studied ignorance to which they are not entitled.*") (emphasis added) (citation and footnotes omitted); *Balint,* 258 U.S. at 254, 42 S.Ct. 301 (upholding as constitutional a statute that "require[d] every person dealing in drugs to ascertain at his peril whether that which he sells comes within the inhibition of the statute"). Just as "common sense and experience" dictate that a person in possession of Treasury checks addressed to another person should be "aware of the high probability that the checks were stolen," a person in possession of a controlled substance should be aware of the nature of the substance as an illegal drug. *Barnes v. United States,* 412 U.S. 837, 845, 93 S.Ct. 2357, 37 L.Ed.2d 380 (1973). Because controlled substances are valuable, common sense indicates that they are generally handled with care. As a result, possession without awareness of the illicit nature of the substance is highly unusual. *See United States v. Bunton,* No. 8:10–cr–327–T–30EAJ, 2011 WL 5080307, at *8 (M.D.Fla. Oct. 26, 2011) ("It bears repeating that common sense dictates, given the numerous drug polic[i]es that are designed to discourage the production, distribution, and consumption of illegal drugs, that one can reasonably infer guilty knowledge when a defendant is in possession of an illegal substance and knows of the substance's presence. In other words, having knowledge of the presence of the substance should alert the defendant to the probability of strict regulation.").

Any concern that entirely innocent conduct will be punished with a criminal sanction under chapter 893 is obviated by the statutory provision that allows a defendant to raise the affirmative defense of an absence of knowledge of the illicit nature of the controlled substance. In the unusual circumstance where an individual has actual or constructive possession of a controlled substance but has no knowledge that the substance is illicit, the defendant may present such a defense to the jury.

Because we conclude that the Legislature did not exceed its constitutional authority in redefining section 893.13 to not require proof that the defendant knew of the illicit nature of the controlled substance, we likewise conclude that the Legislature did not violate due process by defining lack of such knowledge as an affirmative defense to the offenses set out in chapter 893. The Legislature's decision to treat lack of such knowledge as an affirmative defense does not unconstitutionally shift the burden of proof of a criminal offense to the defendant.

In *Patterson v. New York,* 432 U.S. 197, 207, 97 S.Ct. 2319, 53 L.Ed.2d 281 (1977), the Supreme Court concluded that the New York legislature's decision to define extreme emotional disturbance as an affirmative defense to the crime of murder was permissible because the defense did "not serve to negative any facts of the crime which the State is to prove in order to convict of murder" but instead "constitute[d] a separate issue on which the defendant is required to carry the burden of persuasion." The Supreme Court explained that because the fact constituting the affirmative defense was not logically intertwined with a fact necessary to prove guilt, the affirmative defense did not "unhinge the proce-dural presumption of innocence." *Id.* at 211 n. 13, 97 S.Ct. 2319 (quoting *People v. Patterson,* 39 N.Y.2d 288, 383 N.Y.S.2d 573, 347 N.E.2d 898, 909 (1976) (Breitel, C.J., concurring), *aff'd,* 432 U.S. 197, 97 S.Ct. 2319, 53 L.Ed.2d 281 (1977)).

This Court applied similar reasoning in *State v. Cohen,* 568 So.2d 49 (Fla.1990). In *Cohen,* this Court reviewed a statutory affirmative defense to Florida's witness-tampering statute. The affirmative defense required Cohen to prove that he engaged in lawful conduct and that his sole intention was to encourage, induce, or cause the witness to testify truthfully. *Id.* at 51. This Court concluded that the supposed affirmative defense was merely an illusory affirmative defense. This Court explained that the purported affirmative defense was illusory because Cohen could not logically both raise the affirmative defense and concede the elements of the crime. By attempting to prove the affirmative defense that he had acted lawfully with the intent to encourage the witness to testify truthfully, Cohen would necessarily negate the State's theory that he illegally contacted a witness, as opposed to conceding the State's charges. Thus, the purported affirmative defense unconstitutionally placed a burden on Cohen—as a defendant—to refute the State's case. *Id.* at 52.

Here, the Legislature's decision to make the absence of knowledge of the illicit nature of the controlled substance an affirmative defense is constitutional. Under section 893.13, as modified by section 893.101, the State is not required to prove that the defendant had knowledge of the illicit nature of the controlled substance in order to convict the defendant of one of the defined offenses. The conduct the Legislature seeks to curtail is the sale, manufacture, delivery, or possession of a controlled substance, regardless of the defendant's subjective intent. As a result, the defendant can concede all elements of the offense but still coherently raise the "separate issue," *Patterson,* 432 U.S. at 207, 97 S.Ct. 2319, of whether the defendant lacked knowledge of the illicit nature of the controlled substance. The affirmative defense does not ask the defendant to disprove something that the State must prove in order to convict, but instead provides a defendant with an opportunity to explain why his or her admittedly illegal conduct should not be punished. "It is plain enough that if [the sale, manufacture, delivery, or possession of a controlled substance] is shown, the State intends to deal with the defendant as a [criminal] unless he demonstrates the mitigating circumstances." *Patterson,* 432 U.S. at 206, 97 S.Ct. 2319. Thus, the affirmative defense does not improperly shift the burden of proof to the defendant.

III. CONCLUSION

In enacting section 893.101, the Legislature eliminated from the definitions of the offenses in chapter 893 the element that the defendant has knowledge of the illicit nature of the controlled substance and created the affirmative defense of lack of such knowledge. The statutory provisions do not violate any requirement of due process articulated by this Court or the Supreme Court. In the unusual circumstance where a person possesses a controlled substance inadvertently, establishing the affirmative defense available under section 893.101 will preclude the conviction of the defendant. Based on the foregoing, we conclude that the circuit court erred in granting the motions to dismiss and we reverse the circuit court's order.

It is so ordered.

PARIENTE, J., concurring in result.

Forty-eight states, either by statute or judicial decision, require that knowledge of a controlled substance—mens rea ("guilty mind")—be an element of a criminal narcotics offense.[1] Despite the Legislature's elimination of knowledge of the illicit nature of the controlled substance as an element of a drug-related offense, conviction for such an offense under the Florida Comprehensive Drug Abuse Prevention Act (Act) can subject a defendant to staggering penalties, ranging from punishment of up to fifteen years' imprisonment to life in prison for recidivists.

I share Justice Perry's concerns about the Act's harsh application to a potentially blameless defendant, but in my view, these legitimate concerns do not render the Act facially unconstitutional; that is, under no set of circumstances can the Act be constitutionally applied. Although I concur in the result reached by the majority, I write separately to emphasize the very narrow basis for my concurrence.

The Act is facially constitutional only because it (1) continues to require the State to prove that a defendant had knowledge of the presence of the controlled substance as an element of drug-related offenses and (2) expressly authorizes a defendant to assert lack of knowledge of the illicit nature of the controlled substance as an affirmative defense. Both aspects reduce the likelihood that a defendant will be punished for what could otherwise be considered innocent possession and save this Act from facial invalidity. However, because of genuine

---

1   A national survey reveals that Florida's drug law is clearly out of the mainstream. Except for Washington, which eliminates mens rea for simple drug possession offenses, and now Florida, the remaining forty-eight states require knowledge to be an element of a narcotics possession law, either by statute or by judicial decision. *See State v. Bradshaw*, 152 Wash.2d 528, 98 P.3d 1190, 1196 (2004) (Sanders, J., dissenting) (noting that at least forty-eight states have adopted the Uniform Controlled Substance Act and all but two expressly require knowledge to be proved as an element of unlawful possession); *Dawkins v. State*, 313 Md. 638, 547 A.2d 1041, 1045, 1046 n. 10 (1988) ("In surveying the law of other states that have adopted the Uniform Controlled Substances Act, we note that the overwhelming majority of states, either by statute or by judicial decision, require that the possession be knowing"; "Most states addressing the issue of possession of controlled substances hold that the accused must not only know of the presence of the substance but also of the general character of the substance.").

constitutional concerns that notwithstanding the availability of an affirmative defense, the Act could be unconstitutionally applied to a specific defendant by criminalizing innocent conduct while subjecting him or her to a substantial term of imprisonment, I would not foreclose an individual defendant from raising an as-applied challenge to the Act on due process grounds. In short, it would be difficult to uphold the Act, which codifies felony offenses with substantial penalties, against a constitutional attack when mounted by a person who possessed a controlled substance unwittingly or without knowledge of its illicit nature.

Being one among a distinct minority of states to eliminate an element traditionally included in criminal offenses does not, of course, render Florida's drug law unconstitutional. After all, this Court's task is not to decide whether the Legislature has made a wise choice—or even one in keeping with the overwhelming majority of jurisdictions—when defining the elements of drug-related offenses. Rather, we must determine whether the Legislature deprived defendants of due process of law under the United States and Florida Constitutions by omitting knowledge of the illicit nature of a controlled substance as an element of the offense. When reviewing the constitutional validity of a statute, we must remain mindful of the United States Supreme Court's consistent recital of the notion that the "existence of a mens rea is the rule of, rather than the exception to, the principles of Anglo–American criminal jurisprudence."[3] The inclusion of mens rea as an essential element of an offense is a mechanism that safeguards against the criminalization of innocent conduct. As this Court has recognized, "scienter is often necessary to comport with due process requirements," and the elimination of this element "from a criminal statute must be done within constitutional constraints." *State v. Giorgetti,* 868 So.2d 512, 518, 520 (Fla.2004). Therefore, laws that dispense with the requirement of mens rea require very close judicial scrutiny to ensure their compliance with what the Constitution commands.

Initially, I recognize, as does the majority, that the Legislature's 2002 amendment to the Act abrogated only the requirement that the State prove a defendant had knowledge of the illicit nature of the controlled substance. *See* ch.2002–258, § 1, Laws of Fla. (codified at § 893.101(2), Fla. Stat. (2002)). Significantly, the State still bears the burden of proving a defendant's knowledge of presence in order to establish a defendant's actual or constructive possession of the controlled substance. *See Maestas v. State,* 76 So.3d 991, 994–95 (Fla. 4th DCA 2011). Therefore, I agree that "the statute does not punish strictly an unknowing possession or delivery," *id.* at 995, thereby saving the Act from being unconstitutionally applied to defendants where knowledge of the *presence* of the substance is

---

3   *United States v. U.S. Gypsum Co.,* 438 U.S. 422, 436, 98 S.Ct. 2864, 57 L.Ed.2d 854 (1978) (quoting *Dennis v. United States,* 341 U.S. 494, 500, 71 S.Ct. 857, 95 L.Ed. 1137 (1951)); *see also Staples v. United States,* 511 U.S. 600, 605, 114 S.Ct. 1793, 128 L.Ed.2d 608 (1994) (reciting the same).

unknown. *Cf. United States v. Garrett,* 984 F.2d 1402, 1411 (5th Cir.1993) (noting that "a serious due process problem would be raised by application of [a statute criminalizing gun possession on an aircraft], which carries fairly substantial penalties, to someone who did not know and had no reason to know that he was carrying a weapon").

On the other hand, I disagree with the majority's broad pronouncement that due process will not ordinarily preclude the Legislature from creating criminal offenses that dispense with the mens rea requirement. *See* majority op. at 417. The majority's analysis upholding the constitutionality of the Act is flawed because it appears to be based on whether the Legislature has a rational basis for imposing criminal liability. In fact, there are constitutional limitations on the Legislature's ability to create crimes that dispense with mens rea and in effect criminalize actions that could be characterized as innocent conduct where such crimes carry substantial penalties.

The majority's reliance on several cases from the United States Supreme Court to reach that broad pronouncement is misplaced and fails to discuss the fact that courts and commentators have expressed serious concerns about the constitutionality of criminal statutes that eliminate mens rea as an element of a criminal offense.

The majority affords great significance to the Supreme Court's 1922 decision in *United States v. Balint,* 258 U.S. 250, 42 S.Ct. 301, 66 L.Ed. 604 (1922), as standing for the proposition that due process does not, as a general matter, preclude the creation of offenses lacking a guilty knowledge element. *See* majority op. at 417–18. But unlike the drug law at issue here criminalizing clandestine drug deals, the public welfare Narcotic Act of 1914 under scrutiny in *Balint* was a "taxing act" that regulated and taxed the legal distribution of drugs to secure "a close supervision of the business of dealing in these dangerous drugs." 258 U.S. at 253–54, 42 S.Ct. 301. There, the defendants knew they were distributing drugs (a derivative of opium and coca leaves), they just did not know that the substances at issue were regulated as narcotics and had to be distributed pursuant to a written order form. *See id.* at 251, 42 S.Ct. 301. Knowledge that the substances seeking to be distributed were in fact regulated was not an element of the offense. *See id.; see also Staples v. United States,* 511 U.S. 600, 606, 114 S.Ct. 1793, 128 L.Ed.2d 608 (1994) (acknowledging that the Narcotic Act discussed in *Balint* "required proof only that the defendant knew he was selling drugs, not that he knew that the specific items he had sold were 'narcotics' within the ambit of the statute").

The Supreme Court upheld the Narcotic Act, rejecting the argument that "punishment of a person for an act in violation of law when ignorant of the facts making it so" violated due process. *Balint,* 258 U.S. at 252, 42 S.Ct. 301. The Court in *Balint* reasoned that the act was much more similar to "regulatory measures" designed for "social betterment" than to those designed for "punishment." *Id.* Concluding that knowledge was not an aspect of this element of the offense, the Court held that the "manifest purpose" of the act was "to require every person dealing in drugs to ascertain at his peril whether that which he sells comes within the inhibition of the statute, and if he sells the inhibited drug in ignorance of its character, to penalize him," using a criminal penalty merely "to secure recorded evidence of the disposition of such drugs as a means of taxing and restraining the traffic." *Id.* at 254, 42 S.Ct. 301.

Notably, when examining the statute in *Balint* contextually, at least one court has more recently observed that *Balint* no longer has any application as a case about strict liability and narcotics given the serious nature of contemporary drug laws:

> [T]he statute must be understood in context. It predated the era during which all possession and sale of drugs came to be regarded as serious crimes. Aside from its penalty, it fairly can be characterized as a regulation. It required manufacturers and distributors of certain narcotics to register with the IRS, pay a special tax of one dollar per year and record all transactions on forms provided by the IRS. [Narcotic Act of 1914, Pub.L. No. 223,] §§ 1–3 and 8[, 38 Stat. 784 (1914)].
>
> As a case about strict liability and narcotics, *Balint* has no application today. Prior to the [Narcotic] Act narcotics had been freely available without prescription. This change by tax statute was a first modest transitional step towards the present complex and serious criminal statutes dealing with narcotics offenses. They have come to be treated as among the most serious of crimes in the federal criminal code. *See, e.g.,* 21 U.S.C. §§ 960 (mandatory minimum sentences as high as 10 years for certain drug offenses); 848(e) (possible sentence of death for drug offenses in which killing results).

United States v. Cordoba–Hincapie, 825 F.Supp. 485, 507 (E.D.N.Y.1993).

The majority similarly relies upon *United States v. Freed,* 401 U.S. 601, 91 S.Ct. 1112, 28 L.Ed.2d 356 (1971), and *United States v. International Minerals and Chemical Corp.,* 402 U.S. 558, 91 S.Ct. 1697, 29 L.Ed.2d 178 (1971), for the conclusion that the Supreme Court has rejected the view that due process mandates that a mens rea element be read into public safety statutes regulating the possession of unregistered firearms and the shipping of corrosive liquids. However, the matters involved in *Freed* and *International Minerals*—and even *Balint*—placed those cases squarely within the realm of traditional public welfare offenses regulating conduct of a particular nature.

By contrast, in *Staples,* another decision cited by the majority, the Supreme Court declined to apply the public welfare rationale to the statute under review due in part to the fact that it imposed a penalty of up to ten years' imprisonment for a felony offense. *See* 511 U.S. at 616–18, 114 S.Ct. 1793. Indeed, the Court in *Staples* specifically distinguished "the cases that first defined the concept of the public welfare offense," which "almost uniformly involved statutes that provided for only light penalties such as fines or short jail sentences, not imprisonment in the state penitentiary." *Id.* at 616, 114 S.Ct. 1793.

Unlike the possession or delivery of substances one does not know to be illicit (an innocent act), certain items of property regulated by public welfare statutes, such as unlicensed hand grenades (*Freed*), corrosive liquids (*International Minerals*), and legalized narcotics (*Balint*), by their very nature suggest that a reasonable person should know the item is subject to public regulation and may seriously threaten the community's health or safety. *See Liparota v. United States,* 471 U.S. 419, 432–33, 105 S.Ct. 2084, 85 L.Ed.2d 434 (1985) (describing "public welfare offenses" as rendering "criminal a type of conduct that a reasonable person should know is subject to stringent public regulation or may seriously threaten the community's health or safety" and citing *Freed, International Materials,* and *Balint* for support).

Accordingly, *Freed, International Minerals,* and *Balint* are of limited precedential value because the Act at issue in the present case could not, in my view, be deemed a public welfare statute as that term has been used and imposes substantial felony penalties for drug-related offenses where the accused might be unaware of the illicit nature of the substance of which he or she is in possession. *See Cordoba–Hincapie,* 825 F.Supp. at 497 (concluding that modern, anti-drug offenses could no longer be characterized as public welfare offenses); *Dawkins,* 547 A.2d at 1047 (concluding that the prohibition against possessing a controlled dangerous substance, such as heroin or cocaine, "is regarded as a most serious offense," the purpose of which was not to regulate conduct but to punish and deter behavior). *But see United States v. Bunton,* No. 8:10–cr–327–T–30EAJ, 2011 WL 5080307, at *8 (M.D.Fla. Oct. 26, 2011) (concluding that because the criminal offenses enumerated in Florida's drug law are public welfare offenses, mens rea was not a required element).

I recognize that "[t]here is wide latitude in the lawmakers to declare an offense and to exclude elements of knowledge and diligence from its definition." *Lambert v. California,* 355 U.S. 225, 228, 78 S.Ct. 240, 2 L.Ed.2d 228 (1957). This discretion is not unbridled, however. The complementary principle is that legislative bodies must "act within any applicable constitutional constraints" when defining the elements of an offense. *Liparota,* 471 U.S. at 424 n. 6, 105 S.Ct. 2084; *see also Giorgetti,* 868 So.2d at 518, 520.

Although neither the United States Supreme Court nor any other court "has undertaken to delineate a precise line or set forth comprehensive criteria for distinguishing between crimes that require a mental element and crimes that do not," *Staples,* 511 U.S. at 620, 114 S.Ct. 1793 (quoting *Morissette v. United States,* 342 U.S. 246, 260, 72 S.Ct. 240, 96 L.Ed. 288 (1952)), the requirement that an accused act with a culpable mental state is an axiom of criminal jurisprudence that must be emphasized. As Justice Jackson stated when writing for the Supreme Court in *Morissette:*

> The contention that an injury can amount to a crime only when inflicted by intention is no provincial or transient notion. It is as universal and persistent in mature systems of law as belief in freedom of the human will and a consequent ability and duty of the normal individual to choose between good and evil. A relation between some mental element and punishment for a harmful act is almost as instinctive as the child's familiar exculpatory 'But I didn't mean to,' and has afforded the rational basis for a tardy and unfinished substitution of deterrence and reformation in place of retaliation and vengeance as the motivation for public prosecution. Unqualified acceptance of this doctrine by English common law in the Eighteenth Century was indicated by Blackstone's sweeping statement that to constitute any crime there must first be a 'vicious will.' Common-law commentators of the Nineteenth Century early pronounced the same principle. . . .

342 U.S. at 250–51, 72 S.Ct. 240 (footnotes omitted).

Since *Morissette,* the Supreme Court has oft repeated that the "existence of a *mens rea* is the rule of, rather than the exception to, the principles of Anglo–American criminal jurisprudence." *U.S. Gypsum Co.,* 438 U.S. at 436, 98 S.Ct. 2864 (quoting *Dennis,* 341 U.S. at 500, 71 S.Ct. 857); *see also Staples,* 511 U.S. at 605, 114 S.Ct. 1793 (reciting the same). And in applying this principle, the Supreme Court has likewise recognized that offenses dispensing with mens rea are generally disfavored. *Staples,* 511 U.S. at 606, 114 S.Ct. 1793. Therefore, the Supreme Court's reluctance to devise a precise line does not mean that limitations do not exist where the criminal laws of a state are non-regulatory in nature and have the potential to subject a defendant to substantial punishment for conduct that might be entirely innocent or where the defendant lacks culpability.

In fact, some state courts over the years have pointed out the constitutional dimension of mens rea when confronting drug laws similar to the one the Court addresses in this case, stressing that due process would prevent the sanctioning of blameless conduct. *See, e.g., State v. Brown,* 389 So.2d 48, 50–51 (La.1980) (declaring a portion of a state statute criminalizing the "unknowing" possession of a dangerous controlled substance unconstitutional because there could be a circumstance where a conviction would result notwithstanding the accused never being aware of the nature of the substance); *Walker v. State,* 356 So.2d 672,

674 (Ala.1977) (reading into the state's controlled substances statute a knowledge component because "the desirability of efficient enforcement of regulatory statutes must give way to the traditional requirement that criminal sanction be imposed only for blameworthy conduct in order to comply with the requirements of due process of law").[5]

Absent from the statutes addressed by the courts in *Brown* and *Walker,* however, was the availability of any affirmative defense like the one available under Florida's drug law. Notably, the two states that have gone further than Florida by eliminating knowledge, including knowledge of possession, entirely from the offense of possession of a controlled substance—Washington and North Dakota—have recognized that allowing a defendant to raise the affirmative defense of lack of knowledge spares those state statutes from constitutional attack. *See City of Kennewick v. Day,* 142 Wash.2d 1, 11 P.3d 304, 309 (2000) (observing that the "unwitting possession defense is unique to Washington and North Dakota").

Before the North Dakota law was amended to include willfulness, the state supreme court held that the pre-amended version of North Dakota's controlled substance law, which prohibited possession of a controlled substance with intent to deliver, was constitutional despite imposing strict liability. *See State v. Michlitsch,* 438 N.W.2d 175, 178 (N.D.1989). In adhering to this conclusion that the Legislature intended the possession of a controlled substance and possession with intent to deliver to constitute strict liability offenses, the court did note that as applied, "*it would be difficult to sustain these statutory provisions, the violation of which are punishable as felonies in many circumstances, against a constitutional attack when mounted by a person who possessed the controlled substance unwittingly.*" *Id.* (emphasis added). Thus, the court in *Michlitsch* held that an affirmative defense that the defendant unwittingly or unknowingly possessed the controlled substance was "a logical accommodation which recognizes the reasons for both the legislative designation of the crimes as strict liability offenses and the constitutional interests of the accused." *Id.; see also State v. Holte,* 631

---

5   Professor LaFave, who is considered to be a leading authority in the area of criminal law, has also offered in his substantive criminal law treatise the observation that "some authority is to be found to the effect that a strict-liability criminal statute is unconstitutional if (1) the subject matter of the statute does not place it 'in a narrow class of public welfare offenses,' (2) the statute carries a substantial penalty of imprisonment, or (3) the statute imposes an unreasonable duty in terms of a person's responsibility to ascertain the relevant facts." 1 W. LaFave, *Substantive Criminal Law* § 5.5(b) at 389–90 (2d ed. 2003) (footnotes omitted). In addition, some federal precedent holds that a felony statute prescribing substantial penalties for conviction will subject the defendant to significant social stigma and violates due process unless it requires the State to prove intent or knowledge. *See, e.g., United States v. Wulff,* 758 F.2d 1121, 1125 (6th Cir.1985) (holding that a felony provision of the Migratory Bird Treaty Act, which did not require proof of scienter, violated due process because the crime was not one known at common law, had a maximum penalty of two years' imprisonment or fine of $2,000, and created a felony conviction that irreparably damages reputation).

N.W.2d 595, 599 (N.D.2001) (holding that because it was possible for a person to be convicted of the strict liability offense of violating a domestic violence protection order based on innocent or mistaken conduct, a *Michlitsch*-type affirmative defense instruction could be given under appropriate circumstances).

Like the Supreme Court of North Dakota, the Supreme Court of Washington has rejected the argument that a mens rea element must be read into that state's drug possession statute. *See Bradshaw,* 98 P.3d at 1195. However, as in North Dakota, in Washington unwitting possession is an affirmative defense in simple possession cases because such a defense "ameliorates the harshness of the almost strict criminal liability [the] law imposes for unauthorized possession of a controlled substance." *State v. Cleppe,* 96 Wash.2d 373, 635 P.2d 435, 439 (1981) (reaffirmed by *Bradshaw,* 98 P.3d at 1195). The affirmative defense in Washington "is supported by one of two alternative showings: (1) that the defendant did not know he was in possession of the controlled substance; or (2) that the defendant did not know the nature of the substance he possessed." *Day,* 11 P.3d at 310 (citations omitted).

I agree with the reasoning of the North Dakota and Washington state courts. As has been articulated, it would be "fundamentally unsound to convict a defendant for a crime involving a substantial term of imprisonment without giving him the opportunity to prove that his action was due to an honest and reasonable mistake of fact or that he acted without guilty intent." LaFave, *supra* § 5.5(d) at 393 n. 51 (quoting Francis B. Sayre, *Public Welfare Offenses,* 33 Colum. L.Rev. 55, 82 (1933)).

An affirmative defense that affords the defendant with an opportunity to place his or her culpability at issue hampers the concerns of innocent criminalization and a violation of due process. Similar to the judicially recognized affirmative defenses of mistake of fact in North Dakota and Washington, where the accused believes he or she possesses or is delivering an innocuous substance in Florida, the accused may—but is not required to—assert the affirmative defense enumerated under section 893.101(2), Florida Statutes (2011), of "lack of knowledge of the illicit nature" of the controlled substance. Moreover, when this defense is asserted, the trial court must then instruct the jurors to find the defendant "not guilty" if they "have a reasonable doubt on the question of whether [the defendant] knew of the illicit nature of the controlled substance." Fla. Std. Jury Instr. (Crim.) 25.2. That is, if the defense is raised, the State has the burden to overcome the defense by proving beyond a reasonable doubt that the defendant knew of the illicit nature of the substance.

Therefore, although the Act is not a public welfare statute like the statutes reviewed in *Balint, Freed,* or *International Minerals,* and it imposes harsh penalties, this statutorily authorized affirmative defense, when read in conjunction with the applicable jury instruction, ameliorates the concern that the statute criminalizes truly innocent conduct and saves the Act from a *facial* due process challenge.[237] In short, the Act does not codify true strict liability crimes because the Legislature has expressly allowed the defendant to place his or her lack of knowledge of the illicit nature of the substance at issue as a complete defense.

But, there is an important caveat. Given that the jury is also permitted to presume the defendant was aware of the illicit nature of the controlled substance just because he or she was in possession of that substance, even when the affirmative defense is raised, *see* Fla. Std. Jury Instr. (Crim.) 25.2, I do not foreclose the possibility for a defendant to claim on an as-applied basis that his or her innocent possession of an illicit substance was criminalized. A serious due process problem would be raised by application of the Act to this latter scenario. *Cf. Liparota,* 471 U.S. at 426, 105 S.Ct. 2084 (construing a statute to include mens rea, noting that "to interpret the statute otherwise would be to criminalize a broad range of apparently innocent conduct").

In sum, I concur in upholding the statute against a facial challenge because the Act continues to require the State to prove knowledge of presence of the illicit controlled substance and authorizes an affirmative defense of lack of knowledge of the illicit nature of that substance. However, I would not foreclose an as-applied challenge to the Act on due process grounds.

PERRY, J., dissenting.

I respectfully dissent. I cannot overstate my opposition to the majority's opinion. In my view, it shatters bedrock constitutional principles and builds on a foundation of flawed "common sense."

INNOCENT POSSESSION

The majority pronounces that "common sense and experience" dictate that "a person in possession of a controlled substance should be aware of the nature of the substance as an illegal drug" and further that, "[b]ecause controlled substances are valuable, common sense indicates that they are generally handled

---

7   I emphasize that requiring the defendant to establish lack of knowledge of the illicit nature of the controlled substance, as opposed to requiring the State to prove the presence of such knowledge, does not impermissibly shift the burden of proof to the defendant. A state cannot require a defendant to prove the absence of a fact necessary to constitute a crime, *see Mullaney v. Wilbur,* 421 U.S. 684, 684–85, 701, 95 S.Ct. 1881, 44 L.Ed.2d 508 (1975), and the State must prove each element of the charged crime beyond a reasonable doubt, *see In re Winship,* 397 U.S. 358, 362, 90 S.Ct. 1068, 25 L.Ed.2d 368 (1970). However, removing a component of mens rea from the offense does not amount to shifting the burden of proof; rather, the Legislature has chosen to redefine what conduct amounts to an offense under the Act. *See Stepniewski v. Gagnon,* 732 F.2d 567, 571 (7th Cir.1984) (concluding that by removing the element of intent from a criminal statute, the state legislature did not impermissibly shift the burden of proof because the legislature simply redefined the conduct that violates the statute).

with care. As a result, possession without awareness of the illicit nature of the substance is highly unusual." Majority op. at 421–22.

But common sense to me dictates that the potential for innocent possession is not so "highly unusual" as the majority makes it out to be.

> [T]he simple acts of possession and delivery are part of daily life. Each of us engages in actual possession of all that we have on our person and in our hands, and in constructive possession of all that we own, wherever it may be located. Each of us engages in delivery when we hand a colleague a pen, a friend a cup of coffee, a stranger the parcel she just dropped.

State v. Washington, 18 Fla. L. Weekly Supp. 1129, 1133 (Fla. 11th Cir.Ct. Aug. 17, 2011) (footnote omitted), *rev'd,* ––– So.3d –––– (Fla. 3d DCA 2012). "[C]arrying luggage on and off of public transportation; carrying bags in and out of stores and buildings; carrying book bags and purses in schools and places of business and work; transporting boxes via commercial transportation—the list extends *ad infinitum.*" *Shelton v. Sec'y, Dep't of Corr.,* 802 F.Supp.2d 1289, 1305 (M.D.Fla.2011).

Given this reality, "[i]t requires little imagination to visualize a situation in which a third party hands [a] controlled substance to an unknowing individual who then can be charged with and subsequently convicted . . . without ever being aware of the nature of the substance he was given." *State v. Brown,* 389 So.2d 48, 51 (La.1980) (finding that such a situation offends the conscience and concluding that "the 'unknowing' possession of a dangerous drug cannot be made criminal"). For example,

> [c]onsider the student in whose book bag a classmate hastily stashes his drugs to avoid imminent detection. The bag is then given to another for safekeeping. Caught in the act, the hapless victim is guilty based upon the only two elements of the statute: delivery (actual, constructive, or attempted) and the illicit nature of the substance. *See* FLA. STAT. §§ 893.02(6), 893.13(1)(a). The victim would be faced with the Hobson's choice of pleading guilty or going to trial where he is presumed guilty because he is in fact guilty of the two elements. He must then prove his innocence for lack of knowledge against the permissive presumption the statute imposes that he does in fact have guilty knowledge. Such an outcome is not countenanced under applicable constitutional proscriptions.

Shelton, 802 F.Supp.2d at 1308. The trial court order presently under review provides even more examples of innocent possession: a letter carrier who delivers a package containing unprescribed Adderall; a roommate who is unaware that the person who shares his apartment has hidden illegal drugs in the common areas of the home; a mother who carries a prescription pill bottle in her purse, unaware that the pills have been substituted for illegally obtained drugs by her teenage daughter, who placed them in the bottle to avoid detection. *State v. Adkins,* Nos. 2011 CF 002001, et al., slip op. at 14 (Fla. 12th Cir.Ct. Sept. 14, 2011).

> As the examples illustrate, even people who are normally diligent in inspecting and organizing their possessions may find themselves unexpectedly in violation of this law, and without the notice necessary to defend their rights. The illegal drugs subject to the statute include tablets which can also be and are commonly and legally prescribed. A medicine which is legally available, can be difficult for innocent parties to recognize as illegal, even if they think they know the contents. For example, the mother of the teenage daughter carries the pill bottle, taking it at face value as a bottle for the pills it ought to contain, even during the traffic stop at which she consents to [a] search of her belongings, confident in her own innocence. These examples represent incidents of innocence which should be protected by the requirement of [a] *mens rea* element, particularly given the serious penalties for the crime of drug possession required under Florida law.

Id. at 14–15. Other examples of innocent possession spring easily and immediately to mind: a driver who rents a car in which a past passenger accidentally dropped a baggie of marijuana under the seat; a traveler who mistakenly retrieves from a luggage carousel a bag identical to her own containing Oxycodone; a helpful college student who drives a carload of a friend's possessions to the friend's new apartment, unaware that a stash of heroin is tucked within those possessions; an ex-wife who is framed by an ex-husband who planted cocaine in her home in an effort to get the upper hand in a bitter custody dispute. The list is endless.

The majority nevertheless states that there is not "a protected right to be ignorant of the nature of the property in one's possession," elaborating that "'[c]ommon' sense tells us that those who traffic in heroin will inevitably become aware that the product they deal in is smuggled, *unless they practice a studied ignorance to which they are not entitled.*" Majority op. at 421 (quoting *Turner v. United States,* 396 U.S. 398, 417, 90 S.Ct. 642, 24 L.Ed.2d 610 (1970)). But the above examples, and surely countless others, do not involve such a "studied ignorance." Rather, they involve genuinely innocent citizens who will be snared in the overly broad net of section 893.13. And therein lies the point:

> Section 893.13 does not punish the drug dealer who possesses or delivers controlled substances. It punishes *anyone* who possesses or delivers controlled substances—however inadvertently, however accidentally, however unintentionally. . . . What distinguishes innocent possession and innocent

delivery from guilty possession and guilty delivery is not merely what we possess, not merely what we deliver, *but what we intend.* As to that—as to the state of mind that distinguishes non-culpable from culpable possession or delivery— § 893.13 refuses to make a distinction. The speckled flock and the clean are, for its purposes, all one.

Washington, 18 Fla. L. Weekly Supp. at 1133.

PRESUMPTION OF INNOCENCE AND BURDEN OF PROOF

The majority rather cavalierly offers that, "[i]n the unusual circumstance where a person possesses a controlled substance inadvertently, establishing the affirmative defense available under section 893.101 will preclude the conviction of the defendant." Majority op. at 423. As discussed at length above, I do not agree that innocent possession is such an "unusual circumstance." Moreover, the majority's passing reference to simply "establishing the affirmative defense" implies that it is an inconsequential and easy thing to do. The majority further minimizes the enormity of the task, making it seem even friendly, in stating that "[t]he affirmative defense does not ask the defendant to disprove something that the State must prove in order to convict, but instead provides a defendant with an opportunity to explain why his or her admittedly illegal conduct should not be punished." *Id.* at 423.

But the affirmative defense at issue is hardly a friendly opportunity; rather, it is an onerous burden that strips defendants—including genuinely innocent defendants—of their constitutional presumption of innocence. "The principle that there is a presumption of innocence in favor of the accused is the undoubted law, axiomatic and elementary, and its enforcement lies at the foundation of the administration of our criminal law." *Coffin v. United States,* 156 U.S. 432, 453, 15 S.Ct. 394, 39 L.Ed. 481 (1895). It is as ancient as it is profound:

> Numerius [was on trial and] contented himself with denying his guilt, and there was not sufficient proof against him. His adversary, Delphidius, "a passionate man," seeing that the failure of the accusation was inevitable, could not restrain himself, and exclaimed, "Oh, illustrious Caesar! if it is sufficient to deny, what hereafter will become of the guilty?" to which Julian replied, "If it suffices to accuse, what will become of the innocent?"

Id. at 455, 15 S.Ct. 394. "What will become of the innocent?" The answer to that question in the present context is as inevitable as it is disturbing. Under the majority's decision and the above examples, the innocent will from the start be presumed guilty. The innocent will be deprived of their right to simply deny the charges and hold the State to its burden of proving them guilty beyond a reasonable doubt. The innocent will instead be forced to assert an affirmative defense, whereupon "the possession of a controlled substance, whether actual or constructive, shall give rise to a permissive presumption that the possessor knew of the illicit nature of the substance." § 893.101(3), Fla. Stat. (2011).

The innocent will then have no realistic choice but to shoulder the burden of proof and present evidence to overcome that presumption. *See generally Stimus v. State,* 995 So.2d 1149, 1151 (Fla. 5th DCA 2008) (recognizing that a defendant who raised an affirmative defense "had the burden to establish the defense and present evidence" regarding same). The innocent will thus have to bear the considerable time and expense involved in conducting discovery, calling witnesses, and otherwise crafting a case for their innocence—all while the State, with its vastly superior resources, should be bearing the burden of proving their guilt.

The innocent will then hear their jury instructed on the permissive presumption that they knew of the illicit nature of the substance in question. § 893.101(3), Fla. Stat. (2011). Finally, the innocent—in I fear far too many cases—may be found guilty, convicted, and sentenced to up to life in prison. *See Shelton,* 802 F.Supp.2d at 1302 ("Sentences of fifteen years, thirty years, and life imprisonment [possible under section 893.13] are not by any measure 'relatively small.'").

Such convictions and sentences will be a disgrace when, on a profoundly foundational level, "the law holds that it is better that ten guilty persons escape than that one innocent suffer." *Coffin,* 156 U.S. at 456, 15 S.Ct. 394 (quoting 2 William Blackstone, Commentaries *357). The majority opinion breaks that sacred law and, as discussed below, threatens bedrock principles of the presumption of innocence and burden of proof in contexts well beyond the one at hand.

SLIPPERY SLOPE

As in the present case, the effect of the trial court order in *Washington* would be the dismissal of charges against all the defendants at issue "the overwhelming majority of whom may have known perfectly well that their acts of possession or delivery were contrary to law." 18 Fla. L. Weekly Supp. at 1133.

Viewed in that light, these movants are unworthy, utterly unworthy, of this windfall exoneration. But as no less a constitutional scholar than Justice Felix Frankfurter observed, "It is easy to make light of insistence on scrupulous regard for the safeguards of civil liberties when invoked on behalf of the unworthy. It is too easy. History bears testimony that by such disregard are the rights of liberty extinguished, heedlessly at first, then stealthily, and brazenly in the end."

Id. (quoting *Davis v. United States,* 328 U.S. 582, 597, 66 S.Ct. 1256, 90 L.Ed. 1453 (1946) (Frankfurter, J., dissenting)). In this vein, the court in *Shelton* noted with some consternation that

> if the Florida legislature can by edict and without constitutional restriction eliminate the element of *mens rea* from a drug statute with penal-

ties of this magnitude, it is hard to imagine what other statutes it could not similarly affect. Could the legislature amend its murder statute such that the State could meet its burden of proving murder by proving that a Defendant touched another and the victim died as a result, leaving the Defendant to raise the absence of intent as a defense, overcoming a permissive presumption that murder was the Defendant's intent? Could the state prove felony theft by proving that a Defendant was in possession of an item that belonged to another, leaving the Defendant to prove he did not take it, overcoming a permissive presumption that he did?

802 F.Supp.2d at 1308 n. 12 (citation omitted); *see also* Norman L. Reimer, *Focus on Florida: A Report and a Case Expose a Flawed Justice System,* The Champion, Sept. 2011, at 7, 8 ("The singularly extraordinary effort by the Florida Legislature to strip intent requirements from one of the most serious of felony offenses [under section 893.13] was an extreme example of the trend toward the dilution of intent requirements.") (footnote omitted). Making similar observations, the court in *Washington* lamented, "Oh brave new world!" 18 Fla. L. Weekly Supp. at 1134 n. 14.

CONCLUSION

"Brave" indeed, in the most foreboding sense of that word. The majority opinion sets alarming precedent, both in the context of section 893.13 and beyond. It makes neither legal nor common sense to me, offends all notions of due process, and threatens core principles of the presumption of innocence and burden of proof. I would find section 893.13 facially unconstitutional and affirm the trial court order under review.

Notes and Questions

1. Do you agree with the law student who commented: "The criminalizing net cast by DAPCA is simply too wide, too unfair, too unclear, and wholly unconstitutional"? Erika Concetta Pagano, Note, *Freedom of Contact Without Fear of Criminal Misconduct: The Constitutionality of Florida's Drug Abuse Prevention and Control Act,* 67 U. Miami L. Rev. 277, 301 (2012).

2. Based on its decision in *Neidinger,* how would the California Supreme Court have ruled on this statute?

3. In *Patterson v. New York*, 432 U.S. 197, 210, 97 S. Ct. 2319, 2327, 53 L. Ed. 2d 281 (1977), the Court held that states have some discretion to decide whether particular matters should be elements or defenses.

> But there are obviously constitutional limits beyond which the States may not go in this regard. "(I)t is not within the province of a legislature to declare an individual guilty or presumptively guilty of a crime." *McFarland v. American Sugar Rfg. Co.*, 241 U.S. 79, 86, 36 S.Ct. 498, 500, 60 L.Ed. 899 (1916). The legislature cannot "validly command that the finding of an indictment, or mere proof of the identity of the accused, should create a presumption of the existence of all the facts essential to guilt." *Tot v. United States*, 319 U.S. 463, 469, 63 S.Ct. 1241, 1246, 87 L.Ed. 1519 (1943).

> Is this language consistent with the Florida statute?

4. A frequently litigated question is whether absence of a permit or license is an element of unlawful possession of a weapon, or is, instead, an affirmative defense. Courts are split. Some jurisdictions require proof of the absence of a license. *State v. Vick*, 566 A.2d 531 (N.J. 1989); *State v. Hodges*, 305 S.E.2d 278 (W. Va. 1983); *see also United States v. Serrano*, 406 F.3d 1208, 1212 (10th Cir. 2005) (prosecutions bears the burden of showing that the firearm "was not registered to Defendant."). Others impose on the defense at least a burden of production. *Commonwealth v. Gouse*, 965 N.E.2d 774 (Mass. 2012). *See also Powell v. Tompkins*, 926 F.Supp.2d 367 (D. Mass. 2013).

H. Presumptions and Inferences

Assuming that a particular relevant fact is an element rather than a defense, the prosecution bears the burden of proving it beyond a reasonable doubt. Yet, there is a procedure by which the state may prove a fact without evidence, namely, a "presumption." A presumption is created when a statute, or, less commonly, a judicial decision, determines that the jury may presume that an element exists based on proof of specified facts. The following cases deal with the permissibility of presumptions.

Sandstrom v. Montana

Supreme Court of the United States
442 U.S. 510, 99 S. Ct. 2450 (1979)

Mr. Justice BRENNAN delivered the opinion of the Court.

The question presented is whether, in a case in which intent is an element of the crime charged, the jury instruction, "the law presumes that a person intends the ordinary consequences of his voluntary acts," violates the Fourteenth Amendment's requirement that the State prove every element of a criminal offense beyond a reasonable doubt.

I

On November 22, 1976, 18-year-old David Sandstrom confessed to the slaying of Annie Jessen. Based upon the confession and corroborating evidence, petitioner was charged on December 2 with "deliberate homicide," Mont.Code Ann. § 45–5–102 (1978), in that he "purposely or knowingly caused the death of Annie Jessen." App. 3.[2] At trial, Sandstrom's attorney informed the jury that, although his client admitted killing Jessen, he did not do so "purposely or knowingly," and was therefore not guilty of "deliberate homicide" but of a lesser crime. *Id.*, at 6–8. The basic support for this contention was the testimony of two court-appointed mental health experts, each of whom described for the jury petitioner's mental state at the time of the incident. Sandstrom's attorney argued that this testimony demonstrated that petitioner, due to a personality disorder aggravated by alcohol consumption, did not kill Annie Jessen "purposely or knowingly."

The prosecution requested the trial judge to instruct the jury that "[t]he law presumes that a person intends the ordinary consequences of his voluntary acts." Petitioner's counsel objected, arguing that "the instruction has the effect of shifting the burden of proof on the issue of" purpose or knowledge to the defense, and that "that is impermissible under the Federal Constitution, due process of law." *Id.*, at 34. He offered to provide a number of federal decisions in support of the objection, including this Court's holding in *Mullaney v. Wilbur*, 421 U.S.

---

2   The statute provides:

"45–5–101. Criminal homicide. (1) A person commits the offense of criminal homicide if he purposely, knowingly, or negligently causes the death of another human being.

"(2) Criminal homicide is deliberate homicide, mitigated deliberate homicide, or negligent homicide.

"45–5–102. Deliberate homicide. (1) Except as provided in 45–5–103(1), criminal homicide constitutes deliberate homicide if:

"(a) it is committed purposely or knowingly . . . .

684, 95 S.Ct. 1881, 44 L.Ed.2d 508 (1975), but was told by the judge: "You can give those to the Supreme Court. The objection is overruled." App. 34. The instruction was delivered, the jury found petitioner guilty of deliberate homicide, *id.*, at 38, and petitioner was sentenced to 100 years in prison.

Sandstrom appealed to the Supreme Court of Montana, again contending that the instruction shifted to the defendant the burden of disproving an element of the crime charged, in violation of *Mullaney v. Wilbur, supra, In re Winship*, 397 U.S. 358, 90 S.Ct. 1068, 25 L.Ed.2d 368 (1970), and *Patterson v. New York*, 432 U.S. 197, 97 S.Ct. 2319, 53 L.Ed.2d 281 (1977). The Montana court conceded that these cases did prohibit shifting the burden of proof to the defendant by means of a presumption, but held that the cases "do not prohibit allocation of *some* burden of proof to a defendant under certain circumstances." 176 Mont. 492, 497, 580 P.2d 106, 109 (1978). Since in the court's view, "[d]efendant's sole burden under instruction No. 5 was to produce *some* evidence that he did not intend the ordinary consequences of his voluntary acts, not to disprove that he acted 'purposely' or 'knowingly,' . . . the instruction does not violate due process standards as defined by the United States or Montana Constitution . . . ." *Ibid.* (emphasis added).

Both federal and state courts have held, under a variety of rationales, that the giving of an instruction similar to that challenged here is fatal to the validity of a criminal conviction. We granted certiorari, 439 U.S. 1067, 99 S.Ct. 832, 59 L.Ed.2d 31 (1979), to decide the important question of the instruction's constitutionality. We reverse.

<h2 style="text-align:center">II</h2>

The threshold inquiry in ascertaining the constitutional analysis applicable to this kind of jury instruction is to determine the nature of the presumption it describes. See *Ulster County Court v. Allen*, 442 U.S. 140, 157–163, 99 S.Ct. 2213, 2224–2227, 60 L.Ed.2d 777 (1979). That determination requires careful attention to the words actually spoken to the jury, see *id.*, at 157–159, n. 16, 99 S.Ct., at 2225, for whether a defendant has been accorded his constitutional rights depends upon the way in which a reasonable juror could have interpreted the instruction.

Respondent argues, first, that the instruction merely described a permissive inference—that is, it allowed but did not require the jury to draw conclusions about defendant's intent from his actions—and that such inferences are constitutional. Brief for Respondent 3, 15. These arguments need not detain us long, for even respondent admits that "it's possible" that the jury believed they were required to apply the presumption. Tr. of Oral Arg. 28. Sandstrom's jurors were told that "[t]he law presumes that a person intends the ordinary consequences of his voluntary acts." They were not told that they had a choice, or that they might infer that conclusion; they were told only that the law presumed it. It is clear that a reasonable juror could easily have viewed such an instruction as mandatory. See generally *United States v. Wharton*, 139 U.S.App.D.C. 293, 298, 433 F.2d 451, 456 (1970); *Green v. United States*, 132 U.S.App.D.C. 98, 99, 405 F.2d 1368, 1369 (1968).

In the alternative, respondent urges that, even if viewed as a mandatory presumption rather than as a permissive inference, the presumption did not conclusively establish intent but rather could be rebutted. On this view, the instruction required the jury, if satisfied as to the facts which trigger the presumption, to find intent *unless* the defendant offered evidence to the contrary. Moreover, according to the State, all the defendant had to do to rebut the presumption was produce "some" contrary evidence; he did not have to "prove" that he lacked the required mental state. Thus, "[a]t most, it placed a *burden of production* on the petitioner," but "did not shift to petitioner the *burden of persuasion* with respect to any element of the offense . . . ." Brief for Respondent 3 (emphasis added). Again, respondent contends that presumptions with this limited effect pass constitutional muster.

We need not review respondent's constitutional argument on this point either, however, for we reject this characterization of the presumption as well. Respondent concedes there is a "risk" that the jury, once having found petitioner's act voluntary, would interpret the instruction as automatically directing a finding of intent. Tr. of Oral Arg. 29. Moreover, the State also concedes that numerous courts "have differed as to the effect of the presumption when given as a jury instruction without further explanation as to its use by the jury," and that some have found it to shift more than the burden of production, and even to have conclusive effect. Brief for Respondent 17. Nonetheless, the State contends that the only authoritative reading of the effect of the presumption resides in the Supreme Court of Montana. And the State argues that by holding that "[d]efendant's sole burden under instruction No. 5 was to produce *some* evidence that he did not intend the ordinary consequences of his voluntary acts, not to disprove that he acted 'purposely' or 'knowingly,'" 176 Mont., at 497–498, 580 P.2d at 109 (emphasis added), the Montana Supreme Court decisively established that the presumption at most affected only the burden of going forward with evidence of intent—that is, the burden of production.[5]

---

[5]   For purposes of argument, we accept respondent's definition of the production burden when applied to a defendant in a criminal case. We note, however, that the burden is often described quite differently when it rests upon the prosecution. See *United States v. Vuitch*, 402 U.S. 62, 72 n. 7, 91 S.Ct. 1294, 1299, 28 L.Ed.2d 601 (1971) ("evidence from which a jury could find a defendant guilty beyond a reasonable doubt"); C. McCormick, Evidence § 338, p. 790, and n. 33 (2d ed. 1972), p. 101, and n. 34.1 (Supp.1978). We also note that the effect of a failure to meet the production burden is significantly different for the defendant and prosecution. When the pros-

The Supreme Court of Montana is, of course, the final authority on the legal weight to be given a presumption under Montana law, but it is not the final authority on the interpretation which a jury could have given the instruction. If Montana intended its presumption to have only the effect described by its Supreme Court, then we are convinced that a reasonable juror could well have been misled by the instruction given, and could have believed that the presumption was not limited to requiring the defendant to satisfy only a burden of production. Petitioner's jury was told that "*[t]he law presumes* that a person intends the ordinary consequences of his voluntary acts." They were not told that the presumption could be rebutted, as the Montana Supreme Court held, by the defendant's simple presentation of "some" evidence; nor even that it could be rebutted at all. Given the common definition of "presume" as "to suppose to be true without proof," Webster's New Collegiate Dictionary 911 (1974), and given the lack of qualifying instructions as to the legal effect of the presumption, we cannot discount the possibility that the jury may have interpreted the instruction in either of two more stringent ways.

First, a reasonable jury could well have interpreted the presumption as "conclusive," that is, not technically as a presumption at all, but rather as an irrebuttable direction by the court to find intent once convinced of the facts triggering the presumption. Alternatively, the jury may have interpreted the instruction as a direction to find intent upon proof of the defendant's voluntary actions (and their "ordinary" consequences), unless *the defendant* proved the contrary by some quantum of proof which may well have been considerably greater than "some" evidence—thus effectively shifting the burden of persuasion on the element of intent. Numerous federal and state courts have warned that instructions of the type given here can be interpreted in just these ways. See generally *United States v. Wharton*, 139 U.S.App.D.C. 293, 433 F.2d 451 (1970); *Berkovitz v. United States*, 213 F.2d 468 (CA5 1954); *State v. Roberts*, 88 Wash.2d 337, 341–342, 562 P.2d 1259, 1261–1262 (1977) (en banc); *State v. Warbritton*, 211 Kan. 506, 509, 506 P.2d 1152, 1155 (1973); *Hall v. State*, 49 Ala.App. 381, 385, 272 So.2d 590, 593 (Crim.App.1973). *See also United States v. Chiantese*, 560 F.2d 1244, 1255 (CA5 1977). And although the Montana Supreme Court held to the contrary in this case, Montana's own Rules of Evidence expressly state that the presumption at issue here may be overcome only "by a preponderance of evidence contrary to the presumption." Montana Rule of Evidence 301(b)(2). Such a requirement shifts

---

ecution fails to meet it, a directed verdict in favor of the defense results. Such a consequence is not possible upon a defendant's failure, however, as verdicts may not be directed against defendants in criminal cases. *United States v. Martin Linen Supply Co.*, 430 U.S. 564, 572–573, 97 S.Ct. 1349, 1355, 51 L.Ed.2d 642 (1977); *Carpenters v. United States*, 330 U.S. 395, 408, 67 S.Ct. 775, 782, 91 L.Ed. 973 (1947); *Mims v. United States*, 375 F.2d 135, 148 (CA5 1967).

not only the burden of production, but also the ultimate burden of persuasion on the issue of intent.

We do not reject the possibility that some jurors may have interpreted the challenged instruction as permissive, or, if mandatory, as requiring only that the defendant come forward with "some" evidence in rebuttal. However, the fact that a reasonable juror could have given the presumption conclusive or persuasion-shifting effect means that we cannot discount the possibility that Sandstrom's jurors actually did proceed upon one or the other of these latter interpretations. And that means that unless these kinds of presumptions are constitutional, the instruction cannot be adjudged valid. *Ulster County Court v. Allen*, 442 U.S., at 159–160, n. 17, 99 S.Ct., at 2226, and at 175–176, 99 S.Ct., at 2234 (POWELL, J., dissenting); *Bachellar v. Maryland*, 397 U.S. 564, 570–571, 90 S.Ct. 1312, 1315–1316, 25 L.Ed.2d 570 (1970); *Leary v. United States*, 395 U.S. 6, 31–32, 89 S.Ct. 1532, 1545–1546, 23 L.Ed.2d 57 (1969); *Carpenters v. United States*, 330 U.S. 395, 408–409, 67 S.Ct. 775, 782, 91 L.Ed. 973 (1947); *Bollenbach v. United States*, 326 U.S. 607, 611–614, 66 S.Ct. 402, 404–405, 90 L.Ed. 350 (1946). It is the line of cases urged by petitioner, and exemplified by *In re Winship*, 397 U.S. 358, 90 S.Ct. 1068, 25 L.Ed.2d 368 (1970), that provides the appropriate mode of constitutional analysis for these kinds of presumptions.

III

In *Winship*, this Court stated:

> "Lest there remain any doubt about the constitutional stature of the reasonable-doubt standard, we explicitly hold that the Due Process Clause protects the accused against conviction except upon proof beyond a reasonable doubt *of every fact* necessary to constitute the crime with which he is charged." *Id.*, at 364, 90 S.Ct. at 1073 (emphasis added).

Accord, *Patterson v. New York*, 432 U.S., at 210, 97 S.Ct. at 2327. The petitioner here was charged with and convicted of deliberate homicide, committed purposely or knowingly, under Mont.Code Ann. § 45–5–102(a) (1978). See App. 3, 42. It is clear that under Montana law, whether the crime was committed purposely or knowingly is a fact necessary to constitute the crime of deliberate homicide. Indeed, it was the lone element of the offense at issue in Sandstrom's trial, as he confessed to causing the death of the victim, told the jury that knowledge and purpose were the only questions he was controverting, and introduced evidence solely on those points. App. 6–8. Moreover, it is conceded that proof of defendant's "intent" would be sufficient to establish this element. Thus, the question before this Court is whether the challenged jury instruction had the effect of relieving the State of the burden of proof enunciated in *Winship* on the critical question of petitioner's state of mind. We conclude that under either of the two possible interpretations of the instruction set out above, precisely that effect would result, and that the instruction therefore represents constitutional error.

We consider first the validity of a conclusive presumption. This Court has considered such a presumption on at least two prior occasions. In *Morissette v. United States*, 342 U.S. 246, 72 S.Ct. 240, 96 L.Ed. 288 (1952), the defendant was charged with willful and knowing theft of Government property. Although his attorney argued that for his client to be found guilty, "'the taking must have been with felonious intent'," the trial judge ruled that "'[t]hat is presumed by his own act.'" *Id.*, at 249, 72 S.Ct. at 243. After first concluding that intent was in fact an element of the crime charged, and after declaring that "[w]here intent of the accused is an ingredient of the crime charged, its existence is . . . a jury issue," *Morissette* held:

> "*It follows that the trial court may not withdraw or prejudge the issue by instruction that the law raises a presumption of intent from an act.* It often is tempting to cast in terms of a 'presumption' a conclusion which a court thinks probable from given facts. . . . [But] [w]e think presumptive intent has no place in this case. *A conclusive presumption which testimony could not overthrow would effectively eliminate intent as an ingredient of the offense.* A presumption which would permit but not require the jury to assume intent from an isolated fact would prejudge a conclusion which the jury should reach of its own volition. A presumption which would permit the jury to make an assumption which all the evidence considered together does not logically establish would give to a proven fact an artificial and fictional effect. In either case, *this presumption would conflict with the overriding presumption of innocence with which the law endows the accused and which extends to every element of the crime.*" *Id.*, at 274–275, 72 S.Ct. at 255–256. (Emphasis added; footnote omitted.)

Just last Term, in *United States v. United States Gypsum Co.*, 438 U.S. 422, 98 S.Ct. 2864, 57 L.Ed.2d 854 (1978), we reaffirmed the holding of *Morissette*. In that case defendants, who were charged with criminal violations of the Sherman Act, challenged the following jury instruction:

> "The law presumes that a person intends the necessary and natural consequences of his acts. Therefore, if the effect of the exchanges of pricing information was to raise, fix, maintain and stabilize prices, then the parties to them are presumed, as a matter of law, to have intended that result." 438 U.S., at 430, 98 S.Ct., at 2869.

After again determining that the offense included the element of intent, we held:

> "[A] defendant's state of mind or *intent is an element of a criminal antitrust offense which . . . cannot be taken from the trier of fact through reliance on a legal presumption* of wrongful intent from proof of an effect on prices. Cf. *Morissette v. United States* . . . .

> "Although an effect on prices may well support an inference that the defendant had knowledge of the probability of such a consequence at the time he acted, the jury must remain free to consider additional evidence before accepting or rejecting the inference. . . . [U]ltimately the decision on the issue of intent must be left to the trier of fact alone. The instruction given invaded this factfinding function." *Id.*, at 435, 446, 98 S.Ct. at 2872, 2878 (emphasis added).

> *See also Hickory v. United States*, 160 U.S. 408, 422, 16 S.Ct. 327, 332, 40 L.Ed. 474 (1896).

As in *Morissette* and *United States Gypsum Co.*, a conclusive presumption in this case would "conflict with the overriding presumption of innocence with which the law endows the accused and which extends to every element of the crime," and would "invade [the] factfinding function" which in a criminal case the law assigns solely to the jury. The instruction announced to David Sandstrom's jury may well have had exactly these consequences. Upon finding proof of one element of the crime (causing death), and of facts insufficient to establish the second (the voluntariness and "ordinary consequences" of defendant's action), Sandstrom's jurors could reasonably have concluded that they were directed to find against defendant on the element of intent. The State was thus not forced to prove "beyond a reasonable doubt . . . every fact necessary to constitute the crime . . . charged," 397 U.S., at 364, 90 S.Ct. at 1073, and defendant was deprived of his constitutional rights as explicated in *Winship*.

A presumption which, although not conclusive, had the effect of shifting the burden of persuasion to the defendant, would have suffered from similar infirmities. If Sandstrom's jury interpreted the presumption in that manner, it could have concluded that upon proof by the State of the slaying, and of additional facts not themselves establishing the element of intent, the burden was shifted to the defendant to prove that he lacked the requisite mental state. Such a presumption was found constitutionally deficient in *Mullaney v. Wilbur*, 421 U.S. 684, 95 S.Ct. 1881, 44 L.Ed.2d 508 (1975). In *Mullaney*, the charge was murder, which under Maine law required proof not only of intent but of malice. The trial court charged the jury that "'malice aforethought is an essential and indispensable element of the crime of murder.'" *Id.*, at 686, 95 S.Ct. at 1883. However, it also instructed that if the prosecution established that the homicide was both intentional and unlawful, malice aforethought was to be implied unless the defendant proved by a fair preponderance of the evidence that he acted in the heat of passion on sudden provocation. *Ibid.* As we recounted just two Terms ago in *Patterson v. New York*, "[t]his Court . . . unanimously agreed with the Court of Appeals that Wilbur's due process rights had been invaded by the presumption casting upon him the burden of proving by a preponderance of the evidence that he had acted in the heat of passion upon sudden provocation." 432 U.S., at 214, 97 S.Ct. at 2329. And *Patterson* reaffirmed that "a State must prove every ingredient of an offense beyond a reasonable doubt, and . . . may not shift the burden of proof to the defendant" by means of such a presumption. *Id.*, at 215, 97 S.Ct. at 2330.

Because David Sandstrom's jury may have interpreted the judge's instruction as constituting either a burden-shifting presumption like that in *Mullaney*, or a conclusive presumption like those in *Morissette* and *United States Gypsum Co.*, and because either interpretation would have deprived defendant of his right to the due process of law, we hold the instruction given in this case unconstitutional.

* * * Accordingly, the judgment of the Supreme Court of Montana is reversed, and the case is remanded for further proceedings not inconsistent with this opinion.

It is so ordered.

Mr. Justice REHNQUIST, with whom THE CHIEF JUSTICE joins, concurring. [omitted]

---

1. Presumption of Possession

County Court of Ulster County, New York v. Samuel Allen

Supreme Court of the United States
442 U.S. 140 (1979)

Mr. Justice STEVENS delivered the opinion of the Court.

A New York statute provides that, with certain exceptions, the presence of a firearm in an automobile is presumptive evidence of its illegal possession by all persons then occupying the vehicle.[1] The United States Court of Appeals for the Second Circuit held that respondents may challenge the constitutionality of this statute in a federal habeas corpus proceeding and that the statute is "unconstitutional on its face." 568 F.2d 998, 1009. We granted certiorari to review these holdings and also to consider whether the statute is constitutional in its application to respondents. 439 U.S. 815, 99 S.Ct. 75, 58 L.Ed.2d 106.

Four persons, three adult males (respondents) and a 16-year-old girl (Jane Doe, who is not a respondent here), were jointly tried on charges that they possessed two loaded handguns, a loaded machinegun, and over a pound of heroin found in a Chevrolet in which they were riding when it was stopped for speeding on the New York Thruway shortly after noon on March 28, 1973. The two large-caliber handguns, which together with their ammunition weighed approximately six pounds, were seen through the window of the car by the investigating police officer. They were positioned crosswise in an open handbag on either the front floor or the front seat of the car on the passenger side where Jane Doe was sitting. Jane Doe admitted that the handbag was hers. The machine gun and the heroin were discovered in the trunk after the police pried it open. The car had been borrowed from the driver's brother earlier that day; the key to the trunk could not be found in the car or on the person of any of its occupants, although there was testimony that two of the occupants had placed something in the trunk before embarking in the borrowed car. The jury convicted all four of possession of the handguns and acquitted them of possession of the contents of the trunk.

Counsel for all four defendants objected to the introduction into evidence of the two handguns, the machinegun, and the drugs, arguing that the State had not adequately demonstrated a connection between their clients and the contraband. The trial court overruled the objection, relying on the presumption of possession created by the New York statute. Tr. 474–483. Because that presumption does not apply if a weapon is found "upon the person" of one of the occupants of the car, see n. 1, *supra,* the three male defendants also moved to dismiss the charges relating to the handguns on the ground that the guns were found on

---

1   New York Penal Law § 265.15(3) (McKinney 1967):

"The presence in an automobile, other than a stolen one or a public omnibus, of any firearm, defaced firearm, firearm silencer, bomb, bombshell, gravity knife, switchblade knife, dagger, dirk, stiletto, billy, blackjack, metal knuckles, sandbag, sandclub or slungshot is presumptive evidence of its possession by all persons occupying such automobile at the time such weapon, instrument or appliance is found, except under the following circumstances:

"(a) if such weapon, instrument or appliance is found upon the person of one of the occupants therein;
"(b) if such weapon, instrument or appliance is found in an automobile which is being operated for hire by a duly licensed driver in the due, lawful and proper pursuit of his trade, then such presumption shall not apply to the driver; or (c) if the weapon so found is a pistol or revolver and one of the occupants, not present under duress, has in his possession a valid license to have and carry concealed the same."

the person of Jane Doe. Respondents made this motion both at the close of the prosecution's case and at the close of all evidence. The trial judge twice denied it, concluding that the applicability of the "upon the person" exception was a question of fact for the jury. Tr. 544–557, 589–590.

At the close of the trial, the judge instructed the jurors that they were entitled to infer possession from the defendants' presence in the car. He did not make any reference to the "upon the person" exception in his explanation of the statutory presumption, nor did any of the defendants object to this omission or request alternative or additional instructions on the subject.

Defendants filed a post-trial motion in which they challenged the constitutionality of the New York statute as applied in this case. The challenge was made in support of their argument that the evidence, apart from the presumption, was insufficient to sustain the convictions. The motion was denied, *id.*, at 775–776, and the convictions were affirmed by the Appellate Division without opinion. *People v. Lemmons*, 49 A.D.2d 639, 370 N.Y.S.2d 243 (1975). The New York Court of Appeals also affirmed. *People v. Lemmons*, 40 N.Y.2d 505, 387 N.Y.S.2d 97, 354 N.E.2d 836 (1976). It rejected the argument that as a matter of law the guns were on Jane Doe's person because they were in her pocketbook. Although the court recognized that in some circumstances the evidence could only lead to the conclusion that the weapons were in one person's sole possession, it held that this record presented a jury question on that issue. Since the defendants had not asked the trial judge to submit the question to the jury, the Court of Appeals treated the case as though the jury had resolved this fact question in the prosecution's favor. It therefore concluded that the presumption did apply and that there was sufficient evidence to support the convictions. *Id.*, at 509–512, 387 N.Y.S.2d, at 99–101, 354 N.E.2d, at 839–841. It also summarily rejected the argument that the presumption was unconstitutional as applied in this case. See *infra*, at 2222–2223.

Respondents filed a petition for a writ of habeas corpus in the United States District Court for the Southern District of New York contending that they were denied due process of law by the application of the statutory presumption of possession. The District Court issued the writ, holding that respondents had not "deliberately bypassed" their federal claim by their actions at trial and that the mere presence of two guns in a woman's handbag in a car could not reasonably give rise to the inference that they were in the possession of three other persons in the car. App. to Pet. for Cert. 33a–36a.

The Court of Appeals for the Second Circuit affirmed, but for different reasons. First, the entire panel concluded that the New York Court of Appeals had decided respondents' constitutional claim on its merits rather than on any independent state procedural ground that might have barred collateral relief.

Then, the majority of the court, without deciding whether the presumption was constitutional as applied in this case, concluded that the statute is unconstitutional on its face because the "presumption obviously sweeps within its compass (1) many occupants who may not know they are riding with a gun (which may be out of their sight), and (2) many who may be aware of the presence of the gun but not permitted access to it." Concurring separately, Judge Timbers agreed with the District Court that the statute was unconstitutional as applied but considered it improper to reach the issue of the statute's facial constitutionality. 568 F.2d, at 1011–1012.

The petition for a writ of certiorari presented three questions: (1) whether the District Court had jurisdiction to entertain respondents' claim that the presumption is unconstitutional; (2) whether it was proper for the Court of Appeals to decide the facial constitutionality issue; and (3) whether the application of the presumption in this case is unconstitutional. We answer the first question in the affirmative, the second two in the negative. We accordingly reverse.

I

[The Court found that the claim was reviewable in federal court.]

II

Although 28 U.S.C. § 2254 authorizes the federal courts to entertain respondents' claim that they are being held in custody in violation of the Constitution, it is not a grant of power to decide constitutional questions not necessarily subsumed within that claim. Federal courts are courts of limited jurisdiction. They have the authority to adjudicate specific controversies between adverse litigants over which and over whom they have jurisdiction. In the exercise of that authority, they have a duty to decide constitutional questions when necessary to dispose of the litigation before them. But they have an equally strong duty to avoid constitutional issues that need not be resolved in order to determine the rights of the parties to the case under consideration. E. g., New York Transit Authority v. Beazer, 440 U.S. 568, 582–583, 99 S.Ct. 1355, 1363–1364, 59 L.Ed.2d 587.

A party has standing to challenge the constitutionality of a statute only insofar as it has an adverse impact on his own rights. As a general rule, if there is no constitutional defect in the application of the statute to a litigant, he does not have standing to argue that it would be unconstitutional if applied to third parties in hypothetical situations. Broadrick v. Oklahoma, 413 U.S. 601, 610, 93 S.Ct. 2908, 2914, 37 L.Ed.2d 830 (and cases cited). A limited exception has been recognized for statutes that broadly prohibit speech protected by the First Amendment. Id., at 611–616, 93 S.Ct., at 2915–2918. This exception has been justified by the overriding interest in removing illegal deterrents to the exercise of the right of free speech. E. g., Gooding v. Wilson, 405 U.S. 518, 520, 92 S.Ct. 1103, 1105, 31 L.Ed.2d 408;

Dombrowski v. Pfister, 380 U.S. 479, 486, 85 S.Ct. 1116, 1120, 14 L.Ed.2d 22. That justification, of course, has no application to a statute that enhances the legal risks associated with riding in vehicles containing dangerous weapons.

In this case, the Court of Appeals undertook the task of deciding the constitutionality of the New York statute "on its face." Its conclusion that the statutory presumption was arbitrary rested entirely on its view of the fairness of applying the presumption in hypothetical situations—situations, indeed, in which it is improbable that a jury would return a conviction,[28] or that a prosecution would ever be instituted. We must accordingly inquire whether these respondents had standing to advance the arguments that the Court of Appeals considered decisive. An analysis of our prior cases indicates that the answer to this inquiry depends on the type of presumption that is involved in the case.

Inferences and presumptions are a staple of our adversary system of fact-finding. It is often necessary for the trier of fact to determine the existence of an element of the crime—that is, an "ultimate" or "elemental" fact—from the existence of one or more "evidentiary" or "basic" facts. *E. g., Barnes v. United States*, 412 U.S. 837, 843–844, 93 S.Ct. 2357, 2361–2362, 37 L.Ed.2d 380; *Tot v. United States*, 319 U.S. 463, 467, 63 S.Ct. 1241, 1244, 87 L.Ed.2d 1519; *Mobile, J. & K. C. R. Co. v. Turnipseed*, 219 U.S. 35, 42, 31 S.Ct. 136, 137, 55 L.Ed. 78. The value of these evidentiary devices, and their validity under the Due Process Clause, vary from case to case, however, depending on the strength of the connection between the particular basic and elemental facts involved and on the degree to which the device curtails the factfinder's freedom to assess the evidence independently. Nonetheless, in criminal cases, the ultimate test of any device's constitutional validity in a given case remains constant: the device must not undermine the factfinder's responsibility at trial, based on evidence adduced by the State, to find the ultimate facts beyond a reasonable doubt. See *In re Winship*, 397 U.S. 358,

---

28 Indeed, in this very case the permissive presumptions in § 265.15(3) and its companion drug statute, N.Y.Penal Law § 220.25(1) (McKinney Supp. 1978), were insufficient to persuade the jury to convict the defendants of possession of the loaded machinegun and heroin in the trunk of the car notwithstanding the supporting testimony that at least two of them had been seen transferring something into the trunk that morning. See n. 3, *supra.*

The hypothetical, even implausible, nature of the situations relied upon by the Court of Appeals is illustrated by the fact that there are no reported cases in which the presumption led to convictions in circumstances even remotely similar to the posited situations. In those occasional cases in which a jury has reached a guilty verdict on the basis of evidence insufficient to justify an inference of possession from presence, the New York appellate courts have not hesitated to reverse. *E. g., People v. Scott*, 53 App.Div.2d 703, 384 N.Y.S.2d 878 (1976); *People v. Garcia*, 41 App.Div.2d 560, 340 N.Y.S.2d 35 (1973).

In light of the improbable character of the situations hypothesized by the Court of Appeals, its facial analysis would still be unconvincing even were that type of analysis appropriate. This Court has never required that a presumption be accurate in every imaginable case. See *Leary v. United States*, 395 U.S., at 53, 89 S.Ct., at 1557.

364, 90 S.Ct. 1068, 1072, 25 L.Ed.2d 368; *Mullaney v. Wilbur*, 421 U.S., at 702–703 n. 31, 95 S.Ct., at 1891–1892 n. 31.

The most common evidentiary device is the entirely permissive inference or presumption, which allows—but does not require—the trier of fact to infer the elemental fact from proof by the prosecutor of the basic one and which places no burden of any kind on the defendant. See, *e. g., Barnes v. United States, supra*, 412 U.S., at 840 n. 3, 93 S.Ct., at 2360 n. 3. In that situation the basic fact may constitute prima facie evidence of the elemental fact. See, *e. g., Turner v. United States*, 396 U.S. 398, 402 n. 2, 90 S.Ct. 642, 645, n. 2, 24 L.Ed.2d 610. When reviewing this type of device, the Court has required the party challenging it to demonstrate its invalidity as applied to him. *E. g., Barnes v. United States, supra*, 412 U.S., at 845, 93 S.Ct., at 2362; *Turner v. United States, supra*, 396 U.S., at 419–424, 90 S.Ct., at 653–656. *See also United States v. Gainey*, 380 U.S. 63, 67–68, 69–70, 85 S.Ct. 754, 757–758, 758–759, 13 L.Ed.2d 658. Because this permissive presumption leaves the trier of fact free to credit or reject the inference and does not shift the burden of proof, it affects the application of the "beyond a reasonable doubt" standard only if, under the facts of the case, there is no rational way the trier could make the connection permitted by the inference. For only in that situation is there any risk that an explanation of the permissible inference to a jury, or its use by a jury, has caused the presumptively rational factfinder to make an erroneous factual determination.

A mandatory presumption is a far more troublesome evidentiary device. For it may affect not only the strength of the "no reasonable doubt" burden but also the placement of that burden; it tells the trier that he or they *must* find the elemental fact upon proof of the basic fact, at least unless the defendant has come forward with some evidence to rebut the presumed connection between the two facts. *E.g., Turner v. United States, supra*, at 401–402, and n. 1, 90 S.Ct., at 644–645, and n. 1; *Leary v. United States*, 395 U.S. 6, 30, 89 S.Ct. 1532, 1545, 23 L.Ed.2d 57; *United States v. Romano*, 382 U.S. 136, 137, and n. 4, 138, 143, 86 S.Ct. 279, 280, and n. 4, 281, 283, 15 L.Ed.2d 210; *Tot v. United States, supra*, 319 U.S., at 469, 63 S.Ct., at 1245.[16] In this situation, the Court has generally examined the presumption on

---

16 This class of more or less mandatory presumptions can be subdivided into two parts: presumptions that merely shift the burden of production to the defendant, following the satisfaction of which the ultimate burden of persuasion returns to the prosecution; and presumptions that entirely shift the burden of proof to the defendant. The mandatory presumptions examined by our cases have almost uniformly fit into the former subclass, in that they never totally removed the ultimate burden of proof beyond a reasonable doubt from the prosecution. *E. g., Tot v. United States*, 319 U.S., at 469, 63 S.Ct., at 1245. See *Roviaro v. United States*, 353 U.S. 53, 63, 77 S.Ct. 623, 629, 1 L.Ed.2d 639, describing the operation of the presumption involved in *Turner, Leary*, and *Romano*.

To the extent that a presumption imposes an extremely low burden of production—*e. g.*, being satisfied by "any" evidence—it may well be that its impact is no greater than that of a permissive inference, and it may be proper to analyze it as such. See generally *Mullaney v. Wilbur*, 421 U.S. 684, 703 n. 31, 95 S.Ct. 1881, 1892 n. 31, 44 L.Ed.2d 508.

its face to determine the extent to which the basic and elemental facts coincide. *E. g., Turner v. United States, supra*, 396 U.S., at 408–418, 90 S.Ct., at 648–653; *Leary v. United States, supra*, 395 U.S., at 45–52, 89 S.Ct., at 1552–1553; *United States v. Romano, supra*, 382 U.S., at 140–141, 86 S.Ct., at 281–282; *Tot v. United States*, 319 U.S., at 468, 63 S.Ct., at 1245. To the extent that the trier of fact is forced to abide by the presumption, and may not reject it based on an independent evaluation of the particular facts presented by the State, the analysis of the presumption's constitutional validity is logically divorced from those facts and based on the presumption's accuracy in the run of cases. It is for this reason that the Court has held it irrelevant in analyzing a mandatory presumption, but not in analyzing a purely permissive one, that there is ample evidence in the record other than the presumption to support a conviction. *E. g., Turner v. United States*, 396 U.S., at 407, 90 S.Ct., at 647; *Leary v. United States*, 395 U.S., at 31–32, 89 S.Ct., at 1545–1546; *United States v. Romano*, 382 U.S., at 138–139, 86 S.Ct., at 280–281.

Without determining whether the presumption in this case was mandatory, the Court of Appeals analyzed it on its face as if it were. In fact, it was not, as the New York Court of Appeals had earlier pointed out. 40 N.Y.2d, at 510–511, 387 N.Y.S.2d, at 100, 354 N.E.2d, at 840.

The trial judge's instructions make it clear that the presumption was merely a part of the prosecution's case, that it gave rise to a permissive inference available only in certain circumstances, rather than a mandatory conclusion of possession, and that it could be ignored by the jury even if there was no affirmative proof offered by defendants in rebuttal.[20] The judge explained that possession could be actual or constructive, but that constructive possession could not exist without the intent and ability to exercise control or dominion over the weapons.[21] He also carefully instructed the jury that there is a mandatory presumption of innocence in favor of the defendants that controls unless it, as the exclusive trier of fact, is satisfied beyond a reasonable doubt that the defendants possessed the handguns in the manner described by the judge.[22] In short, the instructions

---

* * *

20 "Our Penal Law also provides that the presence in an automobile of any machine gun or of any handgun or firearm which is loaded is presumptive evidence of their unlawful possession.

21 "As so defined, possession means actual physical possession, just as having the drugs or weapons in one's hand, in one's home or other place under one's exclusive control, or constructive possession which may exist without personal dominion over the drugs or weapons but with the intent and ability to retain such control or dominion." *Id.*, at 742.

22 "[Y]ou are the exclusive judges of all the questions of fact in this case. That means that you are the sole judges as to the weight to be given to the evidence and to the weight and probative value to be given to the testimony of each particular witness and to the credibility of any witness." *Id.*, at 730.

"Under our law, every defendant in a criminal trial starts the trial with the presumption in his favor that he is innocent, and this presumption follows him throughout the entire trial and remains with him until such

plainly directed the jury to consider all the circumstances tending to support or contradict the inference that all four occupants of the car had possession of the two loaded handguns and to decide the matter for itself without regard to how much evidence the defendants introduced.[23]

Our cases considering the validity of permissive statutory presumptions such as the one involved here have rested on an evaluation of the presumption as applied to the record before the Court. None suggests that a court should pass on the constitutionality of this kind of statute "on its face." It was error for the Court of Appeals to make such a determination in this case.

III

As applied to the facts of this case, the presumption of possession is entirely rational. Notwithstanding the Court of Appeals' analysis, respondents were not "hitchhikers or other casual passengers," and the guns were neither "a few inches in length" nor "out of [respondents'] sight." See n. 4, *supra*, and accompanying text. The argument against possession by any of the respondents was predicated solely on the fact that the guns were in Jane Doe's pocketbook. But several circumstances—which, not surprisingly, her counsel repeatedly emphasized in his questions and his argument, *e. g.*, Tr. 282–283, 294–297, 306—made it highly improbable that she was the sole custodian of those weapons.

Even if it was reasonable to conclude that she had placed the guns in her purse before the car was stopped by police, the facts strongly suggest that Jane Doe was not the only person able to exercise dominion over them. The two guns were too large to be concealed in her handbag. The bag was consequently open, and part of one of the guns was in plain view, within easy access of the driver of the car and even, perhaps, of the other two respondents who were riding in the rear seat.

Moreover, it is highly improbable that the loaded guns belonged to Jane Doe or that she was solely responsible for their being in her purse. As a 16-year-old girl in the company of three adult men she was the least likely of the four to

---

time as you, by your verdict, find him or her guilty beyond a reasonable doubt or innocent of the charge. If you find him or her not guilty, then, of course, this presumption ripens into an established fact. On the other hand, if you find him or her guilty, then this presumption has been overcome and is destroyed." *Id.*, at 734.

"Now, in order to find any of the defendants guilty of the unlawful possession of the weapons, the machine gun, the .45 and the .38, you must be satisfied beyond a reasonable doubt that the defendants possessed the machine gun and the .45 and the .38, possessed it as I defined it to you before." *Id.*, at 745.

23 The verdict announced by the jury clearly indicates that it understood its duty to evaluate the presumption independently and to reject it if it was not supported in the record. Despite receiving almost identical instructions on the applicability of the presumption of possession to the contraband found in the front seat and in the trunk, the jury convicted all four defendants of possession of the former but acquitted all of them of possession of the latter. See n. 14, *supra*.

be carrying one, let alone two, heavy handguns. It is far more probable that she relied on the pocketknife found in her brassiere for any necessary self-protection. Under these circumstances, it was not unreasonable for her counsel to argue and for the jury to infer that when the car was halted for speeding, the other passengers in the car anticipated the risk of a search and attempted to conceal their weapons in a pocketbook in the front seat. The inference is surely more likely than the notion that these weapons were the sole property of the 16-year-old girl.

Under these circumstances, the jury would have been entirely reasonable in rejecting the suggestion—which, incidentally, defense counsel did not even advance in their closing arguments to the jury—that the handguns were in the sole possession of Jane Doe. Assuming that the jury did reject it, the case is tantamount to one in which the guns were lying on the floor or the seat of the car in the plain view of the three other occupants of the automobile. In such a case, it is surely rational to infer that each of the respondents was fully aware of the presence of the guns and had both the ability and the intent to exercise dominion and control over the weapons. The application of the statutory presumption in this case therefore comports with the standard laid down in *Tot v. United States*, 319 U.S., at 467, 63 S.Ct., at 1244, and restated in *Leary v. United States, supra*, 395 U.S., at 36, 89 S.Ct., at 1548. For there is a "rational connection" between the basic facts that the prosecution proved and the ultimate fact presumed, and the latter is "more likely than not to flow from" the former.

Respondents argue, however, that the validity of the New York presumption must be judged by a "reasonable doubt" test rather than the "more likely than not" standard employed in *Leary*. Under the more stringent test, it is argued that a statutory presumption must be rejected unless the evidence necessary to invoke the inference is sufficient for a rational jury to find the inferred fact beyond a reasonable doubt. See *Barnes v. United States*, 412 U.S., at 842–843, 93 S.Ct., at 2361–2362. Respondents' argument again overlooks the distinction between a permissive presumption on which the prosecution is entitled to rely as one not necessarily sufficient part of its proof and a mandatory presumption which the jury must accept even if it is the sole evidence of an element of the offense.[29]

In the latter situation, since the prosecution bears the burden of establishing guilt, it may not rest its case entirely on a presumption unless the fact proved is sufficient to support the inference of guilt beyond a reasonable doubt. But in

---

[29] The dissenting argument rests on the assumption that "the jury [may have] rejected all of the prosecution's evidence concerning the location and origin of the guns." *Post*, at 2234. Even if that assumption were plausible, the jury was plainly told that it was free to disregard the presumption. But the dissent's assumption is not plausible; for if the jury rejected the testimony describing where the guns were found, it would necessarily also have rejected the only evidence in the record proving that the guns were found in the car. The conclusion that the jury attached significance to the particular location of the handguns follows inexorably from the acquittal on the charge of possession of the machinegun and heroin in the trunk.

the former situation, the prosecution may rely on all of the evidence in the record to meet the reasonable-doubt standard. There is no more reason to require a permissive statutory presumption to meet a reasonable-doubt standard before it may be permitted to play any part in a trial than there is to require that degree of probative force for other relevant evidence before it may be admitted. As long as it is clear that the presumption is not the sole and sufficient basis for a finding of guilt, it need only satisfy the test described in *Leary*.

The permissive presumption, as used in this case, satisfied the *Leary* test. And, as already noted, the New York Court of Appeals has concluded that the record as a whole was sufficient to establish guilt beyond a reasonable doubt. The judgment is reversed.

So ordered.

Mr. CHIEF JUSTICE BURGER, concurring.

I join fully in the Court's opinion reversing the judgment under review. In the necessarily detailed step-by-step analysis of the legal issues, the central and controlling facts of a case often can become lost. The "underbrush" of finely tuned legal analysis of complex issues tends to bury the facts.

On this record, the jury could readily have reached the same result without benefit of the challenged statutory presumption; here it reached what was rather obviously a compromise verdict. Even without relying on evidence that two people had been seen placing something in the car trunk shortly before respondents occupied it, and that a machinegun and a package of heroin were soon after found in that trunk, the jury apparently decided that it was enough to hold the passengers to knowledge of the two handguns which were in such plain view that the officer could see them from outside the car. Reasonable jurors could reasonably find that what the officer could see from outside, the passengers within the car could hardly miss seeing. Courts have long held that in the practical business of deciding cases the factfinders, not unlike negotiators, are permitted the luxury of verdicts reached by compromise.

Mr. Justice POWELL, with whom Mr. Justice BRENNAN, Mr. Justice STEWART and Mr. Justice MARSHALL join, dissenting.

I agree with the Court that there is no procedural bar to our considering the underlying constitutional question presented by this case. I am not in agreement, however, with the Court's conclusion that the presumption as charged to the jury in this case meets the constitutional requirements of due process as set forth in our prior decisions. On the contrary, an individual's mere presence in an automobile where there is a handgun does not even make it "more likely than not" that the individual possesses the weapon.

I

In the criminal law, presumptions are used to encourage the jury to find certain facts, with respect to which no direct evidence is presented, solely because other facts have been proved.[1] See, *e. g., Barnes v. United States*, 412 U.S. 837, 840 n. 3, 93 S.Ct. 2357, 2360 n. 3, 37 L.Ed.2d 380 (1973); *United States v. Romano*, 382 U.S. 136, 138, 86 S.Ct. 279, 280, 15 L.Ed.2d 210 (1965). The purpose of such presumptions is plain: Like certain other jury instructions, they provide guidance for jurors' thinking in considering the evidence laid before them. Once in the juryroom, jurors necessarily draw inferences from the evidence—both direct and circumstantial. Through the use of presumptions, certain inferences are commended to the attention of jurors by legislatures or courts.

Legitimate guidance of a jury's deliberations is an indispensible part of our criminal justice system. Nonetheless, the use of presumptions in criminal cases poses at least two distinct perils for defendants' constitutional rights. The Court accurately identifies the first of these as being the danger of interference with "the factfinder's responsibility at trial, based on evidence adduced by the State, to find the ultimate facts beyond a reasonable doubt." *Ante*, at 2224. If the jury is instructed that it must infer some ultimate fact (that is, some element of the offense) from proof of other facts unless the defendant disproves the ultimate fact by a preponderance of the evidence, then the presumption shifts the burden of proof to the defendant concerning the element thus inferred.

But I do not agree with the Court's conclusion that the only constitutional difficulty with presumptions lies in the danger of lessening the burden of proof the prosecution must bear. As the Court notes, the presumptions thus far reviewed by the Court have not shifted the burden of persuasion, see *ante*, at 2224, n. 16; instead, they either have required only that the defendant produce some evidence to rebut the inference suggested by the prosecution's evidence, see *Tot v. United States*, 319 U.S. 463, 63 S.Ct. 1241, 87 L.Ed.2d 1519 (1943), or merely have been suggestions to the jury that it would be sensible to draw certain conclusions on the basis of the evidence presented. See *Barnes v. United States, supra,* 412 U.S., at 840 n. 3, 93 S.Ct., at 2360 n. 3. Evolving from our decisions, therefore, is a second standard for judging the constitutionality of criminal presumptions which is based—not on the constitutional requirement that the State be put to its proof—but rather on the due process rule that when the jury is encouraged to make factual inferences, those inferences must reflect

---

1   Such encouragement can be provided either by statutory presumptions, see, *e. g.,* 18 U.S.C. § 1201(b), or by presumptions created in the common law. See, *e. g., Barnes v. United States*, 412 U.S. 837, 93 S.Ct. 2357, 37 L.Ed.2d 380 (1973). Unless otherwise specified, "presumption" will be used herein to "permissible inferences," as well as to "true" presumptions. See F. James, Civil Procedure § 7.9 (1965).

some valid general observation about the natural connection between events as they occur in our society.

* * *

In sum, our decisions uniformly have recognized that due process requires more than merely that the prosecution be put to its proof. In addition, the Constitution restricts the court in its charge to the jury by requiring that, when particular factual inferences are recommended to the jury, those factual inferences be accurate reflections of what history, common sense, and experience tell us about the relations between events in our society. Generally, this due process rule has been articulated as requiring that the truth of the inferred fact be more likely than not whenever the premise for the inference is true. Thus, to be constitutional a presumption must be at least more likely than not true.

II

In the present case, the jury was told:

> "Our Penal Law also provides that the presence in an automobile of any machine gun or of any handgun or firearm which is loaded is presumptive evidence of their unlawful possession. In other words, [under] these presumptions or this latter presumption upon proof of the presence of the machine gun and the hand weapons, you may infer and draw a conclusion that such prohibited weapon was possessed by each of the defendants who occupied the automobile at the time when such instruments were found. The presumption or presumptions is effective only so long as there is no substantial evidence contradicting the conclusion flowing from the presumption, and the presumption is said to disappear when such contradictory evidence is adduced."

Undeniably, the presumption charged in this case encouraged the jury to draw a particular factual inference regardless of any other evidence presented: to infer that respondents possessed the weapons found in the automobile "upon proof of the presence of the machine gun and the hand weapon" and proof that respondents "occupied the automobile at the time such instruments were found." I believe that the presumption thus charged was unconstitutional because it did not fairly reflect what common sense and experience tell us about passengers in automobiles and the possession of handguns. People present in automobiles where there are weapons simply are not "more likely than not" the possessors of those weapons.

Under New York law, "to possess" is "to have physical possession or otherwise to exercise dominion or control over tangible property." N.Y.Penal Law § 10.00(8) (McKinney 1975). Plainly, the mere presence of an individual in an automobile—without more—does not indicate that he exercises "dominion or control over" everything within it. As the Court of Appeals noted, there are countless situations in which individuals are invited as guests into vehicles the contents of which they know nothing about, much less have control over. Similarly, those who invite others into their automobile do not generally search them to determine what they may have on their person; nor do they insist that any handguns be identified and placed within reach of the occupants of the automobile. Indeed, handguns are particularly susceptible to concealment and therefore are less likely than are other objects to be observed by those in an automobile.

In another context, this Court has been particularly hesitant to infer possession from mere presence in a location, noting that "[p]resence is relevant and admissible evidence in a trial on a possession charge; but absent some showing of the defendant's function at the [illegal] still, its connection with possession is too tenuous to permit a reasonable inference of guilt—'the inference of the one from proof of the other is arbitrary . . . .' *Tot v. United States*, 319 U.S. 463, 467, 63 S.Ct. 1241, 1245, 87 L.Ed.2d 1519." *United States v. Romano*, 382 U.S., at 141, 86 S.Ct., at 282. We should be even more hesitant to uphold the inference of possession of a handgun from mere presence in an automobile, in light of common experience concerning automobiles and handguns. Because the specific factual inference recommended to the jury in this case is not one that is supported by the general experience of our society, I cannot say that the presumption charged is "more likely than not" to be true. Accordingly, respondents' due process rights were violated by the presumption's use.

As I understand it, the Court today does not contend that in general those who are present in automobiles are more likely than not to possess any gun contained within their vehicles. It argues, however, that the nature of the presumption here involved requires that we look, not only to the immediate facts upon which the jury was encouraged to base its inference, but to the other facts "proved" by the prosecution as well. The Court suggests that this is the proper approach when reviewing what it calls "permissive" presumptions because the jury was urged "to consider all the circumstances tending to support or contradict the inference." *Ante*, at 2227.

It seems to me that the Court mischaracterizes the function of the presumption charged in this case. As it acknowledges was the case in *Romano, supra*, the "instruction authorized conviction even if the jury disbelieved all of the testimony except the proof of presence" in the automobile. *Ante*, at 2225 n. 16. The Court nevertheless relies on all of the evidence introduced by the prosecution and argues that the "permissive" presumption could not have prejudiced defendants. The possibility that the jury disbelieved all of this evidence, and relied on the presumption, is simply ignored.

I agree that the circumstances relied upon by the Court in determining the plausibility of the presumption charged in this case would have made it reasonable for the jury to "infer that each of the respondents was fully aware of the presence of the guns and had both the ability and the intent to exercise dominion and control over the weapons." But the jury was told that it could conclude that respondents possessed the weapons found therein from proof of the mere fact of respondents' presence in the automobile. For all we know, the jury rejected all of the prosecution's evidence concerning the location and origin of the guns, and based its conclusion that respondents possessed the weapons solely upon its belief that respondents had been present in the automobile. For purposes of reviewing the constitutionality of the presumption at issue here, we must assume that this was the case. See *Bollenbach v. United States*, 326 U.S. 607, 613, 66 S.Ct. 402, 405, 90 L.Ed. 350 (1946); cf. *Leary v. United States*, 395 U.S., at 31, 89 S.Ct., at 1545.

The Court's novel approach in this case appears to contradict prior decisions of this Court reviewing such presumptions. Under the Court's analysis, whenever it is determined that an inference is "permissive," the only question is whether, in light of all of the evidence adduced at trial, the inference recommended to the jury is a reasonable one. The Court has never suggested that the inquiry into the rational basis of a permissible inference may be circumvented in this manner. Quite the contrary, the Court has required that the "evidence *necessary to invoke the inference* [be] sufficient for a rational juror to find the inferred fact . . . ." *Barnes v. United States*, 412 U.S., at 843, 93 S.Ct., at 2362 (emphasis supplied). See *Turner v. United States*, 396 U.S. 398, 407, 90 S.Ct. 642, 647, 24 L.Ed.2d 610 (1970). Under the presumption charged in this case, the only evidence necessary to invoke the inference was the presence of the weapons in the automobile with respondents—an inference that is plainly irrational.

In sum, it seems to me that the Court today ignores the teaching of our prior decisions. By speculating about what the jury may have done with the factual inference thrust upon it, the Court in effect assumes away the inference altogether, constructing a rule that permits the use of any inference—no matter how irrational in itself—provided that otherwise there is sufficient evidence in the record to support a finding of guilt. Applying this novel analysis to the present case, the Court upholds the use of a presumption that it makes no effort to defend in isolation. In substance, the Court—applying an unarticulated harmless-error standard—simply finds that the respondents were guilty as charged. They may well have been but rather than acknowledging this rationale, the Court seems to have made new law with respect to presumptions that could seriously jeopardize a defendant's right to a fair trial. Accordingly, I dissent.

Notes and Questions

Are there other grounds upon which it could be argued that presumptions such as this are improper or unnecessary?

People v. Nix

Criminal Court, City of New York Bronx County
960 N.Y.S.2d 299 (2013)

JOHN H. WILSON, J.

Defendant is charged with one count of Permits for Possession or Purchase of Rifles or Shotguns (AC Sec. 10–303). Under AC Sec. 10–310, this charge is a violation.

By omnibus motion dated January 7, 2013, Defendant seeks dismissal of the sole charge, asserting that the People's complaint is facially insufficient and suppression of all physical evidence seized by law enforcement personnel.

The Court has reviewed the Court file, Defendant's motion, and the People's Response dated January 25, 2013. For the reasons stated below, the motion to dismiss is granted to the extent of ordering the People to provide a superseding information to the Court and defense within 30 days of the publication of this decision to the parties.

* * *

STATEMENT OF THE FACTS

Pursuant to the Criminal Court Complaint dated October 27, 2012, on or about October 26, 2012, at approximately 5:40 PM, Police Officer Sean McGuire observed Defendant seated in the front passenger seat of a Honda Accord stopped outside of 1852 Archer Street, Bronx, New York. The officer states that "he observed in the custody and control of the defendant. . .in the trunk of said vehicle with the butt of the item exposed causing the trunk to remain partially open, one (1) pump action 12 gauge shotgun."

The complaint also alleges that "said shotgun was defaced in that the section of said shotgun where the serial number exited (sic) had been concealed so that said serial number was unreadable." See, Criminal Court Complaint dated October 27, 2012, p. 2.

LEGAL ANALYSIS

Under CPL Sec. 100.15, every accusatory instrument is required to contain two elements; 1) an accusatory portion designating the offense charged, and 2) a factual portion containing evidentiary facts which support or tend to support the charges stated in the accusatory portion of the instrument. These facts must provide reasonable cause to believe that the defendant has committed the crime alleged in the accusatory portion of the accusatory instrument. See, *People v. Dumas,* 68 N.Y.2d 729, 506 N.Y.S.2d 319, 497 N.E.2d 686 (1986).

* * *

On a motion to dismiss, this Court's review is limited to whether or not the People's allegations as stated in the Criminal Court Complaint are facially sufficient. The facts alleged need only establish the existence of a *prima facie* case, even if those facts would not be legally sufficient to prove guilt beyond a reasonable doubt. See, *People v. Jennings,* 69 N.Y.2d 103, 115, 512 N.Y.S.2d 652, 504 N.E.2d 1079 (1986).

Applying these principles to the instant matter, the factual allegations contained in the complaint before this Court are not sufficient.

Under AC Sec. 10–303, "it shall be unlawful for any person to have in his or her possession any rifle or shotgun unless said person is the holder of a permit for the possession and purchase of rifles and shotguns."

At the outset of our analysis, it must be noted that the complaint does not include any statement regarding whether or not Defendant, or the driver of the vehicle, is the holder of any permit for the possession of rifles or shotguns. On this basis alone, then, the complaint must be superceded. However, a more significant issue is presented by the People's insufficient allegations.

PL Sec. 265.15(3) states that "(t)he presence in an automobile. . . .of any. . . defaced rifle or shotgun. . .is presumptive evidence of its possession by all persons occupying such automobile at the time such weapon, instrument or appliance is found."

Known as the "Automobile Presumption", "the statutory presumption establishes a prima facie case against defendant, which presumption he may rebut by offering evidence." Generally, "the presumption will remain in the case for the jury to weigh even if contrary proof is offered, (but) it may be nullified if the contrary evidence is strong enough to make the presumption incredible." See, *People v. Wilt,* 105 A.D.2d 1089, 1090, 482 N.Y.S.2d 629 (4th Dept., 1984), citing *People v. Lemmons,* 40 N.Y.2d 505, 510, 387 N.Y.S.2d 97, 354 N.E.2d 836 (1976).

The People allege that "said shotgun was defaced in that the section of said shotgun where the serial number exited (sic) had been concealed so that said serial number was unreadable." See, Criminal Court Complaint dated October 27, 2012, p. 2. Thus, on this basis, the automobile presumption can be applied to the weapon recovered here. However, the finding of the presence of this element does not conclude our analysis.

The presumption has been applied to the driver of an automobile when a gun was discovered in the glove compartment. See, *People v. Wade,* 122 Misc.2d 50, 469 N.Y.S.2d 571 (S. Ct., Kings Cty., 1983). To a gun recovered from between a defendant's feet on the floor of the driver's side of an automobile. See, *People v., Sanchez,* 110 A.D.2d 665, 487 N.Y.S.2d 584 (2d Dept., 1985), *app. den.,* 65 N.Y.2d 986, 494 N.Y.S.2d 1056, 484 N.E.2d 686 (1985). To a gun which lay on the back ledge of an automobile in which a defendant was seated, "within the immediate control and reach of the (defendant) and his companions." See, *People v. Russo,* 278 A.D. 98, 101, 103 N.Y.S.2d 603 (1st Dept., 1951) (citation omitted), *aff.,* 303 N.Y. 673, 102 N.E.2d 834 (1951). To a defendant seated "directly behind that portion of the front bench seat under which the sawed-off shotgun and revolver were secreted. . .under these circumstances, it is surely rational to infer that defendant had both the ability and intent to exercise dominion and control over the weapons." See, *People v. Davis,* 104 A.D.2d 1046, 1046–1047, 480 N.Y.S.2d 954 (2d Dept., 1984).

In each of the cases cited above, it was reasonable on the face of the allegations to infer that the defendant knew that a weapon was present in the vehicle. This Court has been unable to locate any case where the presumption has been applied to a weapon located in the trunk of a vehicle without a *prima facie* showing that the defendant knew, or reasonably should have known, that said weapon was there.

"Under PL Sec. 15.00(2); 15.10 the mental culpability required for a crime of possession is, at the very least, awareness of the possession." See, *People v. Sanchez,* 110 A.D.2d 665, 487 N.Y.S.2d 584 (2d Dept., 1985), app. den., 65 N.Y.2d 986, 494 N.Y.S.2d 1056, 484 N.E.2d 686 (1985) (citations omitted). Where "'there is no rational connection' between the discovery of the gun in the trunk and defendant's presumed possession," "the statutory presumption of (PL Sec. 265.15(3) is) unconstitutional as applied." See, *Wilt,* 105 A.D.2d at 1090, 482 N.Y.S.2d 629, citing *Leary v. United States,* 395 U.S. 6, 33, 89 S.Ct. 1532, 23 L.Ed.2d 57 (1969).

"The People reason that the defendant's presence in the car constitutes dominion and control over, and hence possession of, the vehicle and its contents (PL Sec. 10.00(8)). . .(w)hile this argument is appealing, it must fail because it rests upon an impermissible elision between two separate and distinct elements necessary to sustain a charge of criminal possession. In order to prove the charge there must first be evidence of possession, whether actual or constructive, personal or accessorial. Second, there must be evidence of scienter, that is, actual knowledge. . .that the gun was indeed in (defendant's) possession." See, *People v. Porter,* 133 Misc.2d 584, 586, 507 N.Y.S.2d 572 (S. Ct., N.Y. Cty., 1986) (citations omitted).

Porter states the test for satisfaction of the automobile presumption; "whether the nexus or connection between the accused and the contraband is sufficient for a rational conclusion that he or she in fact exercised dominion or control over it." 133 Misc.2d at 589, 507 N.Y.S.2d 572 (citations omitted).

In the instant complaint, the People's allegations fail to provide *prima facie* evidence of the Defendant's knowing commission of the alleged crime. On the face of the complaint, there is no inference possible that this Defendant had knowledge of the defaced shotgun in the trunk. There is only a bald statement that the Defendant was seated in the front passenger seat of a motor vehicle, and that the officer observed "in the trunk of said vehicle with the butt of the item exposed causing the trunk to remain partially open, one (1) pump action 12 gauge shotgun." Nothing connects Defendant to the contraband, other than his mere presence in the vehicle.[3]

Thus, the allegations made herein are facially insufficient. * * *

Conley v. United States

District of Columbia Court of Appeals
79 A.3d 270 (2013)

GLICKMAN, Associate Judge:

In 2009, the Council of the District of Columbia enacted a statute, D.C.Code § 22–2511 (2012 Repl.), making it a felony offense for a person to be present in a motor vehicle if the person knows that the vehicle contains a

---

3   The fact that the "butt of the item (was) exposed causing the trunk to remain partially open" does not establish that Defendant knew that the trunk was partially open, or had viewed the contents of the trunk.

firearm ("PMVCF"), even if the person has no connection to or control over the weapon and is not involved in any wrongdoing whatsoever. This is the first appeal of a PMVCF conviction to come before this court. Appellant Antwaun Conley, joined by the Public Defender Service as *amicus curiae,* contends that the law is unconstitutional and that the trial court plainly erred in allowing the jury to convict him of this crime.

We agree that the PMVCF statute violates due process. We reach that conclusion for two reasons. First, the essence of the offense is the defendant's voluntary presence in a vehicle after he learns that it contains a firearm. Yet instead of requiring the government to prove that the defendant's continued presence was voluntary, § 22–2511 requires the defendant to shoulder the burden of proving, as an affirmative defense, that his presence in the vehicle was involuntary. This shifting of the burden of persuasion with respect to a critical component of the crime is incompatible with due process.

Were that the only defect in the statute, it would not necessarily be fatal, for we might sever the constitutionally invalid affirmative defense and construe the remainder of § 22–2511 as imposing on the government the burden to prove that the defendant stayed in the vehicle voluntarily after he learned that it contained a firearm. But burden-shifting is not the statute's only constitutional defect; it offends due process in another way. As the Supreme Court explained in *Lambert v. California,* [355 U.S. 225, 78 S.Ct. 240, 2 L.Ed.2d 228 (1957)] it is incompatible with due process to convict a person of a crime based on the failure to take a legally required action—a crime of omission—if he had no reason to believe he had a legal duty to act, or even that his failure to act was blameworthy. The fundamental constitutional vice of § 22–2511 is that it criminalizes entirely innocent behavior—merely remaining in the vicinity of a firearm in a vehicle, which the average citizen would not suppose to be wrongful (let alone felonious)—without requiring the government to prove that the defendant had notice of any legal duty to behave otherwise. This is a defect that we cannot cure by interpreting the statutory language. Accordingly, we are obliged to hold that § 22–2511 is unconstitutional on its face and that appellant's conviction for violating that statute must be reversed.[2]

I. FACTUAL BACKGROUND

This case began on July 24, 2010, with an early-morning traffic stop by officers of the Metropolitan Police Department of a Honda Accord on Stanton Road

---

2   Our conclusion that § 22–2511 violates due process in the respects described above renders it unnecessary for us to address other constitutional challenges levied against the statute by appellant and amicus-for example, that it infringes on rights secured by the First and Fifth Amendments to receive information, to associate with others, and to travel freely.

in Southeast, Washington, D.C. Appellant was in the driver's seat and a second man, Kendra Allen, was in the front passenger seat. The police took the two occupants to the rear of the vehicle and held them there while officers shone their flashlights into the passenger compartment. When they did so, they observed a handgun in plain view in the center console between the two front seats. The weapon was loaded. A crime scene search officer later dusted the gun and bullets for fingerprints, but no prints were recovered.

In due course, appellant was charged by indictment with four possessory offenses—unlawful possession of a firearm, [D.C.Code § 22–4503(a)(1) (2012 Repl.)] carrying a pistol without a license, [D.C.Code § 22–4504(a) (2012 Repl.)] possession of an unregistered firearm [D.C.Code § 7–2502.01 (2012 Repl.)] and unlawful possession of ammunition [D.C.Code § 7–2506.01(3) (2012 Repl.)]— plus the non-possessory offense of PMVCF, in violation of D.C.Code § 22–2511. He pleaded not guilty. At trial, his defense was that he neither possessed the gun nor knew it was in the car, and that the weapon must have been placed in the console after he exited the vehicle by either Mr. Allen or one of the police officers.7 Appellant did not challenge the constitutionality of his prosecution for PMVCF.

The judge defined PMVCF for the jury as follows:

> The elements of unlawful presence in a motor vehicle containing a firearm, each of which the Government must prove beyond a reasonable doubt, are that one, Mr. Conley was voluntarily in a motor vehicle; two, a firearm was in the motor vehicle; three, Mr. Conley knew the firearm was in [the] motor vehicle; and four, the firearm was not lawfully carried or lawfully transported.

The jury acquitted appellant of all the possessory offenses. It found him guilty only of PMVCF. For that offense, the judge sentenced appellant to thirty-four months in prison.

II. THE STATUTORY OFFENSE

D.C.Code § 22–2511, the PMVCF statute, reads in pertinent part as follows:

> (a)It is unlawful for a person to be voluntarily in a motor vehicle if that person knows that a firearm is in the vehicle, unless the firearm is being lawfully carried or lawfully transported.

> (b) It shall be an affirmative defense to this offense, which the defendant must prove by a preponderance of the evidence, that the defendant, upon learning that a firearm was in the vehicle, had the specific intent to

immediately leave the vehicle, but did not have a reasonable opportunity under the circumstances to do so.

The offense is a felony, punishable by up to five years in prison.

The statute was enacted as part of the Omnibus Public Safety and Justice Amendment Act of 2009. As the Council's Committee on Public Safety and the Judiciary explained in its report on the legislation, the new offense of PMVCF was created in order to allow convictions to be obtained when a firearm is found in a car with more than one occupant and the government cannot prove who possessed it:

> The issue that this provision seeks to address is when a car is stopped with multiple occupants and a firearm is present in the vehicle—the police are unable to prove who was in possession of the firearm. Even if the police believe they know who possessed the firearm—constructive possession with multiple occupants in the car is very difficult to prove at trial. The proposal therefore seeks to make it illegal for every occupant to be present in the vehicle as opposed to just the occupant that possessed the weapon.

As originally proposed, subsection (a) of the PMVCF statute would have made it "unlawful for a person to be in a motor vehicle if that person knows that a firearm is in the vehicle" without regard to whether the person is in the vehicle voluntarily, and the statute did not include an affirmative defense of involuntariness such as that which now appears in subsection (b). The Public Defender Service for the District of Columbia and the D.C. Association of Criminal Defense Lawyers opposed the legislation, among other reasons because it would make felons of citizens who wanted nothing to do with the firearm and were innocent of any wrongdoing. In response to the criticisms, the Committee on Public Safety and the Judiciary revised the statute to its current form. The alterations, which included adding the word "voluntarily" to subsection (a) and creating the affirmative defense now set forth in subsection (b), were intended "to ensure," *inter alia,* that the PMVCF statute would "not be used against those who . . . had no ability to safely distance themselves from the firearm." "In addition," the Committee stated, its "recommended language makes it clear that there must be some deliberate decision on the part of the accused to be in a vehicle with an illegal firearm present."

* * *

IV. LEGAL DISCUSSION

A. The Constitutionality of § 22–2511

* * * A facial challenge imposes a "heavy burden" on the claimant to establish that "the law is unconstitutional in all of its applications." We look only to whether the statute properly proscribes criminal conduct; we do not examine whether appellant's conduct could have been criminalized under a hypothetical statute. Thus, in a facial challenge, "the claimed constitutional violation inheres in the terms of the statute, not its application." In deciding whether the challenge is meritorious, appellant's "personal situation becomes irrelevant." It is enough that "'[w]e have only the [statute] itself' and the 'statement of basis and purpose that accompanied its promulgation.'" Appellant must demonstrate that the terms of the statute, "measured against the relevant constitutional doctrine, and independent of the constitutionality of particular applications, contain[ ] a constitutional infirmity that invalidates the statute in its entirety." Accordingly, if § 22–2511 fails to require the government to prove everything the Constitution requires it to prove for a criminal sanction to be imposed, as appellant contends, and if the legislative design and the limits of the judicial function do not permit us to read the critical missing elements into the statute, then appellant has carried his burden of showing that every application of § 22–2511 is unconstitutional—even if a validly written statute could have reached appellant's particular conduct.

We begin by considering the argument that § 22–2511 unconstitutionally shifts the burden of persuasion to the defense with respect to an essential element of the offense, i.e., the defendant's voluntary presence in the vehicle. Assuming that it is possible to overcome this argument by a suitable construction of the statute, we go on to consider whether § 22–2511 nonetheless fails to pass constitutional muster under the principles explained by the Supreme Court in *Lambert* [*v. California*, 355 U.S. 225, 78 S.Ct. 240, 2 L.Ed.2d 228 (1957).]

1. Shifting the Burden of Persuasion

Subsection (a) of § 22–2511 makes it unlawful for a person to "voluntarily be" in a motor vehicle if the person knows there is a firearm in the vehicle, unless the firearm is being carried or transported lawfully. In response to appellant's criticism that the offense defined in the statute lacks the essential component of a prohibited *actus reus* (culpable *conduct* of some kind),[29] the government explains

---

29 "In the criminal law, both a culpable *mens rea* and a criminal *actus reus* are generally required for an offense to occur." *United States v. Apfelbaum*, 445 U.S. 115, 131, 100 S.Ct. 948, 63 L.Ed.2d 250 (1980). *See also Powell v. Texas*, 392 U.S. 514, 533, 88 S.Ct. 2145, 20 L.Ed.2d 1254 (1968) (plurality opinion) ("[C]riminal penalties may be inflicted only if the accused has committed some act, has engaged in some behavior, which society has an interest in preventing, or perhaps in historical common law terms, has committed some *actus reus*."); *Rose v. United*

that subsection (a) creates a valid *crime of omission*—the essence of which is a failure to perform an act that one has a legal duty to perform under the circumstances. Specifically, the government argues, criminalizing voluntary presence in a car by one who knows it contains a firearm is equivalent to criminalizing the voluntary failure to leave the car when one knows there is a firearm in it. In other words, according to the government, "[t]he statute criminalizes failing to leave a car as soon as reasonably possible once one learns that a firearm is present where the firearm is not being lawfully carried or transported."

But if the offense created in § 22–2511(a) is the voluntary failure to leave a motor vehicle as soon as reasonably possible after learning that it contains a firearm, subsection (b) creates a problem. Subsection (b) requires the defendant to prove by a preponderance of the evidence the affirmative defense that he remained in the vehicle against his will because he had no reasonable opportunity to leave it. This seems to mean that instead of the government having to prove that the defendant remained in the vehicle voluntarily, the defendant has to *disprove* it, i.e., to prove that he remained involuntarily. This apparent shift in the burden of proof with respect to the element of voluntary presence implicates fundamental principles of due process.

The Due Process Clause "protects the accused against conviction except upon proof beyond a reasonable doubt of every fact necessary to constitute the crime with which he is charged." [*In re Winship*, 397 U.S. 358, 364, 90 S.Ct. 1068, 25 L.Ed.2d 368 (1970).] This means it is up to the prosecution "to prove beyond a reasonable doubt all of the elements included in the definition of the offense. . . ." [*Patterson v. New York*, 432 U.S. 197, 210, 97 S.Ct. 2319, 53 L.Ed.2d 281 (1977).] The defendant therefore may not be required to "prove the critical fact in dispute," [*Mullaney v. Wilbur*, 421 U.S. 684, 701, 95 S.Ct. 1881, 44 L.Ed.2d 508 (1975)] and "the burden of persuasion may not be shifted to the defendant with respect to a defense that serves only to negate an element of the offense that the government is required to prove." [*Hatch*, 35 A.3d at 1121 (citing *Patterson*, 432 U.S. at 207, 97 S.Ct. 2319).] Thus, because voluntary presence is an undisputed element of the offense of PMVCF, the Due Process Clause forbids shifting the burden to the defendant to negate that element by proving that his presence was not voluntary.

Before we conclude that § 22–2511 impermissibly shifts the burden of persuasion with respect to the element of voluntary presence, we must consider further whether the respective burdens of persuasion may coexist. This depends on

---

States, 535 A.2d 849, 852 (D.C.1987) ("It is a fundamental principle of our system of criminal justice that an individual will be punished only for bad conduct, not bad intentions."); *Trice v. United States*, 525 A.2d 176, 187 n. 5 (D.C.1987) (Mack, J., dissenting) ("An *'actus reus,'* or act, is an essential element of every crime. . . . [T]he common law crimes are defined in terms of act or omission to act, and statutory crimes are unconstitutional unless so defined.") (quoting W.R. LAFAVE & A.W. SCOTT, JR., CRIMINAL LAW § 25 (1972) (internal quotation marks omitted)).

how we construe the government's burden under subsection (a) to prove that the defendant "voluntarily" remained in the vehicle. If there are circumstances in which the government could prove beyond a reasonable doubt that the defendant "voluntarily" remained in the vehicle, yet the defendant could prove by a preponderance of the evidence that he would have left but had no reasonable opportunity to do so, then the respective burdens of persuasion would not be incompatible and there would not be an unconstitutional burden-shifting with respect to the element of voluntariness.

What is meant by the word "voluntarily" in subsection (a)? The word is "susceptible to different meanings," so to answer that question, we must consider the statutory context and the purpose of the statute. As a matter of abstract logic, there is one possible interpretation of "voluntarily" that, if acceptable, would avoid the due process problem. If, to prove voluntariness, all the government needs to show is that it would have been *physically possible* for the defendant to leave the vehicle—regardless of the danger, difficulty, inconvenience, or adverse consequences of doing so, and however reluctantly the defendant chose not to leave in light of such impediments—then the affirmative defense would not be inconsistent with the government's burden of persuasion. The respective burdens would be compatible because the government would simply have to prove that the defendant had *an opportunity* to leave, while the defense could prove that it was not a *reasonable opportunity* in the circumstances.

A hypothetical raised at oral argument in this case illustrates the distinction. Imagine an elderly defendant who sees a gun in the center console of the vehicle she entered as a passenger but decides to stay in the vehicle until it is closer to a bus stop that is still a mile away because she has a bad knee. On such facts, the government could prove that the defendant "voluntarily" remained in the vehicle in the sense that she had an opportunity to leave it. But the defendant could prove that in light of her bad knee and consequent inability to walk a mile, the opportunity she had to exit the vehicle right away was not a reasonable opportunity.

Although this broad construction of the word "voluntarily" would manage to avoid the logical incompatibility of subsections (a) and (b), we are not persuaded that it is a plausible construction. No one, of course, can be held criminally liable "for failing to do an act that he is physically incapable of performing." The word "voluntarily" would be superfluous if it was inserted in subsection (a) merely to make that basic jurisprudential point. The law was not meant to target innocent persons like the elderly woman with the bad knee in the hypothetical, who remain unwillingly only because they have no reasonable opportunity to leave. Only in the most technical sense would one say of such a person that she "voluntarily" stayed in the car. In common parlance, we think one would say she did not voluntarily remain.

Relatedly, a difficult-to-accept consequence of construing the word "voluntarily" to mean only that the defendant had the physical ability to leave would be to increase the risk of convicting innocent defendants—persons who genuinely wanted to leave a vehicle containing a firearm but who had no reasonable opportunity to do so. That such persons would have the opportunity to avoid being convicted by proving the affirmative defense set forth in subsection (b) of the statute does not eliminate that risk, because shifting the burden of persuasion with respect to an essential element from the government to the defendant makes conviction more likely: There is a material difference between requiring the government to prove the existence of a reasonable opportunity to leave beyond a reasonable doubt in order to obtain a conviction and requiring the defendant to prove the absence of such an opportunity by a preponderance of the evidence in order to secure an acquittal. We do not lightly attribute to the Council the intent to increase the risk of convicting the innocent.

Thus, we are persuaded that subsection (a) requires the government to prove beyond a reasonable doubt that the defendant forsook a reasonable opportunity to leave the vehicle; yet subsection (b) places the burden on the defendant to prove by a preponderance of the evidence that he had no such opportunity. The inconsistency is stark.[40] We therefore are led to conclude that § 22–2511, read as a whole, unconstitutionally shifts the burden of persuasion from the prosecution to the defense with respect to voluntary presence, an essential element of the offense.

* * *

2. Criminalizing the Failure to Perform a Highly Unusual and Unforeseeable Duty

Even if § 22–2511 is construed to avoid an unconstitutional shifting of the burden of persuasion, appellant argues that the statute still violates due process because it creates an unusual legal duty previously unknown in the District of Columbia—the duty to leave a motor vehicle if it contains a firearm—without requiring proof that the defendant knew or should have known he had such a duty. As appellant recognizes, such proof ordinarily is not required; "[it] is a common maxim, familiar to all minds, that ignorance of the law will not excuse any person, either civilly or criminally. . . ." In unusual circumstances, however,

---

40 *Cf. Hatch v. United States,* 35 A.3d 1115, 1122 (D.C.2011) (explaining that an affirmative defense of consent to a prosecution for forcible sexual abuse "makes sense only in the unusual case," because ordinarily "it is 'difficult to conceive [how] the government could establish force beyond a reasonable doubt yet the [defendant] could prove consent by a preponderance of the evidence'") (quoting *Gaynor v. United States,* 16 A.3d 944, 948 (D.C.2011)).

that maxim conflicts with "one of the bedrock principles of American law": the principle that "[i]t is wrong to convict a person of a crime if he had no reason to believe that the act for which he was convicted *was* a crime, or even that it was wrongful." Under such unusual circumstances, either the maxim or the principle must yield. In *Lambert v. California,* the case on which appellant principally relies, the Supreme Court confronted the question of when a legislature may impose criminal liability for failure to perform an unknown legal duty.

Lambert, like the present case, involved a crime of unlawful presence based on an obscure local enactment. A municipal ordinance made it unlawful for convicted felons "to be or remain" in Los Angeles for more than five days without registering with the police. Ms. Lambert, who had resided there for seven years, was found guilty of having violated this ordinance by failing to register following her conviction in Los Angeles of forgery (a felony under California law). The state courts rejected her contention that the ordinance denied her due process of law because it neither required proof that the defendant's failure to register was willful (i.e., that the defendant disregarded a known legal obligation to register) nor recognized ignorance of the registration requirement as a defense.

The Supreme Court reversed Ms. Lambert's conviction. The Court readily acknowledged that legislators have "wide latitude . . . to declare an offense and to exclude elements of knowledge and diligence from its definition." So too, the Court agreed, "[t]he rule that 'ignorance of the law will not excuse' is deep in our law, as is the principle that of all the powers of local government, the police power is 'one of the least limitable.'" Nonetheless, the Court reasoned, the requirement of notice embodied in due process "places some limits" on the application of these tenets when a law criminalizes "conduct that is wholly passive . . . [and] unlike the commission of acts, or the failure to act under circumstances that should alert the doer to the consequences of his deed."

The ordinance in *Lambert* met this description, as it made "mere presence" in the city unlawful in the complete absence of "circumstances which might move one to inquire as to the necessity of registration. . . ." Moreover, the Court noted, "this appellant on first becoming aware of her duty to register was given no opportunity to comply with the law and avoid its penalty, even though her default was entirely innocent." To convict someone under such an ordinance, the Court held, due process requires the government to prove the defendant's "actual knowledge of the duty to register or . . . the probability of such knowledge and subsequent failure to comply. . . ."

As this court has stated, *Lambert* is "a rare instance" in which the Supreme Court has held that knowledge of the law is a constitutionally required prerequisite to criminal liability. While *Lambert* is not limited exclusively to registration statutes, it clearly does not stand for the proposition that ignorance of the law is a defense to every crime of omission, and it suggests "no general requirement that a State take affirmative steps to inform its citizenry of their obligations under a particular statute before imposing legal sanctions for violation of that statute." Rather, *Lambert* recognizes that "[t]he State's power to impose sanctions on individuals is to be tested in part against the rationality of the proposition that those individuals were or could have been aware of their legal obligations." *Lambert* applies only when an unusual statute is "triggered in circumstances so commonplace, that an average citizen would have no reason to regard the triggering event as calling for a heightened awareness of one's legal obligations."56 In other words, only legal "duties of a highly unusual and unforeseeable nature" trigger *Lambert*.57 But when such novel and unanticipated duties are in question, it is no answer to say that the law is on the books, the books are in the public library, and anyone can go read them.[58]

Criminal laws seldom impose unusual and unforeseeable duties on the average person. In most cases in which courts have confronted the issue, they have found it fair to charge people with knowing their legal obligations because the circumstances put them on, at least, inquiry notice. Many of these cases involve "public welfare offenses" created by "statutes that regulate potentially harmful or injurious items" like drugs, highly dangerous weapons like machine guns and grenades, or noxious waste materials.[59] In those cases, the Supreme Court has "reasoned that as long as a defendant knows that he is dealing with a dangerous device of a character that places him 'in responsible relation to a public danger,' he should be alerted to the probability of strict regulation, and [the Court has] assumed that in such cases Congress intended to place the burden on the defendant to 'ascertain at his peril whether [his conduct] comes within the inhibition of the statute.'"[60]

This court has followed that reasoning. In *McNeely*, for instance, we rebuffed a *Lambert* challenge to a provision of the "Pit Bull Act" making it a crime to own a pit bull that has injured or killed a human being or another domestic animal

---

58 As Judge Posner has written,

> We want people to familiarize themselves with the laws bearing on their activities. But a reasonable opportunity doesn't mean being able to go to the local law library and read Title 18. It would be preposterous to suppose that [the average individual] is able to take advantage of such an opportunity.

United States v. Wilson, 159 F.3d 280, 295 (7th Cir.1998) (Posner, J., dissenting).

59 *Staples v. United States*, 511 U.S. 600, 607, 114 S.Ct. 1793, 128 L.Ed.2d 608 (1994); *see also, e.g., Freed*, 401 U.S. at 609, 91 S.Ct. 1112 (declining to extend *Lambert* to the possession of hand grenades, for "one would hardly be surprised to learn that possession of hand grenades is not an innocent act").

60 *Staples*, 511 U.S. at 607, 114 S.Ct. 1793 (citations omitted) (quoting *United States v. Dotterweich*, 320 U.S. 277, 281, 64 S.Ct. 134, 88 L.Ed. 48 (1943)). We note that the *mens rea* issue in *Staples* was not whether the government had to prove the defendant's knowledge of the law, but rather whether it had to prove his knowledge of the critical fact that brought him within the law's application.

without provocation. We held that given the well-known dangerous proclivities of the breed, the owner's "knowledge that his dogs were pit bulls should have moved him to inquire into his heightened obligations under the Act."61 Similarly, in *McIntosh v. Washington,* we rejected a *Lambert* claim that the District's firearms laws denied due process by imposing criminal penalties on those who fail to register their firearms, "regardless of their knowledge of the duty to register." "[W]here dangerous or deleterious devices or products are involved," we explained, "the probability of regulation is so great that anyone who is aware that he is either in possession of or dealing with them must be presumed to be aware of the regulation."

Courts also have rejected *Lambert* challenges to statutes imposing legal obligations on persons with other particular reasons to be on notice of them, as in prosecutions for violating 18 U.S.C. § 922(g)(9) and 18 U.S.C. § 922(g)(8) (statutes that prohibit the possession of firearms by persons who have been convicted of misdemeanor domestic violence offenses or who are subject to a judicial anti-harassment or anti-stalking order) and for failing to register as required by the Sex Offender Registration and Notification Act ("SORNA"), 18 U.S.C. § 2250(a). (Judge Thompson's concurrence cites a provision of the District's old Narcotic Vagrancy statute (repealed in 1981) that, in a somewhat similar vein, made it a crime for "any person who is a narcotic drug user or who has been convicted of a narcotic offense" to be "found in any place . . . in which any illicit narcotic drugs are kept, found used or dispensed.")

The statute before us in this case, § 22–2511, is similar to the ordinance in *Lambert:* It criminalizes the "wholly passive" state of "mere presence" in a particular location—a motor vehicle—without requiring proof of "actual knowledge" of a legal duty to absent oneself if the vehicle contains a firearm or "proof of the probability of such knowledge and subsequent failure to comply." Nor does the statute require proof of any conduct beyond mere presence that would traditionally and foreseeably subject a person to criminal sanction, such as handling or concealing the firearm, constructively possessing it, or aiding and abetting someone else's possession or use of it. And it cannot be maintained (nor does the government contend) that penalizing mere presence is permissible because anyone who knowingly enters or stays in a car after learning it contains a gun must be embarked on a criminal venture of some sort. On the contrary, people harboring no evil intent of any kind may find themselves, inadvertently or otherwise, riding with a gun in a car, taxi cab, or truck for any number of innocent reasons—and, in doing so, they reasonably may perceive no necessity (let alone a legal obligation) to interrupt and discontinue their journey abruptly in order to make a premature exit just because there is a gun present. Indeed, given the "long tradition of widespread lawful gun ownership by private individuals in this country," and the recent definitive recognition of a Second Amendment right to possess guns for self-protection,[69] individuals (especially visitors from other jurisdictions) who do not happen to be well-versed in the intricacies of the District's firearms laws may not see anything wrong in the presence of a gun or realize that the local law may proscribe its possession or transportation.[70]

Moreover, unlike § 22–2511, laws that survive *Lambert* challenges target those who are on inquiry notice of the legal duties imposed on them by the nature of the activities in which they have chosen to engage. It is fair to say that persons who choose to own, possess, transport, or otherwise deal with firearms are or should be aware that their activities are highly regulated by law and that they must be alert to ascertain and comply with their attendant legal obligations. Such persons are on notice that they may incur criminal penalties if they are not careful. But § 22–2511 requires no proof of firearm ownership, possession, transportation, or dealing by the defendant.[71] The statute targets persons who are not engaged in any of those activities and who therefore have no reason to be familiar with the firearms laws or to investigate whether those laws impose any duties on *them*. And the existence of § 22–2511, or any law regulating simple presence in the vicinity of a firearm, is certainly not common knowledge.

The critical question, then, is whether merely finding oneself riding in a motor vehicle with a gun is in itself a "circumstance[ ] which might move one to inquire as to the [legal] necessity" of exiting the vehicle; or, to put it more finely, whether the average person should know that he may be committing a felony offense merely by remaining in the vehicle, even if the gun belongs to someone else and he has nothing to do with it. We think not. Section 22–2511 is an anomaly, a unique departure from the fundamental and intuitive premise of our legal system that one does nothing wrong and does not become a criminal

---

69 *See McDonald v. City of Chicago,* ––– U.S. ––––, 130 S.Ct. 3020, 3049, 177 L.Ed.2d 894 (2010); *District of Columbia v. Heller,* 554 U.S. 570, 635, 128 S.Ct. 2783, 171 L.Ed.2d 637 (2008).

70 Although we do not decide the question, we note that § 22–2511 does not appear to require the government to prove knowledge that the firearm was carried or transported unlawfully. On the other hand, the Committee on Public Safety and the Judiciary did state that its revisions to the proposed enactment would "ensure that the charge will not be used against those who . . . legitimately believed the possession of the firearm was lawful. . . ." Committee Report, at 4. In any event, even if we were to agree with Judge Thompson's view that § 22–2511 should be construed to require proof that the defendant knew or should have known the firearm was carried or transported unlawfully, *see post,* at 290–91, it would not alter our analysis of the statute's unconstitutionality, as the statute would remain subject to the due process defects we identify. It would still suffer from the shift in the burden of proof with respect to voluntariness. And, more fundamentally, the problem would remain that the PMVCF statute would still criminalize a failure to perform a highly unusual and unknown legal duty.

71 We do not agree with the suggestion, *post* at 294, that merely remaining in the presence of a firearm is the equivalent, for *Lambert* purposes, of being "in possession or dealing with" a firearm, as we used those words in *McIntosh v. Washington,* 395 A.2d 744, 756 (D.C.1978).

merely by being a bystander to a crime.[73] It is a legal truism that, absent voluntary participation of some kind in criminal activity, "mere presence" in the vicinity of such activity is normally not culpable and is not subject to a criminal sanction.[74] That proposition, we believe, expresses a widely held expectation in our society—an expectation reinforced by the understanding that our Constitutional liberties include "the right to remove from one place to another according to one's inclination" and the "individual's decision to remain in a public place of his choice." The freedom to move around as we see fit and be where we want to be with minimal legal constraint is indeed "part of our heritage."

Statutes criminalizing trespass or knowing presence in an illegal establishment[79] can be cited as exceptions to the generalization that "mere presence" is not a sufficient basis for criminal punishment. But the important point, for present purposes, is that those statutes raise no *Lambert* notice issue—the average citi-

---

73 *Cf.* LAFAVE § 6.2, at 435 n. 4 (noting that there is generally a "reluctance to enact" statutes imposing a duty to act, since "a governmental demand to perform is significantly more intrusive than a command to refrain from harmful action") (quoting 1 P. ROBINSON, CRIMINAL LAW DEFENSES § 86(b) (1984)). Indeed, we are hard-pressed to find a comparable statute anywhere in the United States. However, in *State v. Adkins*, 196 Neb. 76, 241 N.W.2d 655 (1976), the Supreme Court of Nebraska did have occasion to consider an analogous law, which made it "unlawful for any person . . . to visit or to be in any room, dwelling house, vehicle, or place where any controlled substance is being used contrary to [specified laws] if the person has knowledge that such activity is occurring." *Id.* at 656. The court held the statute unconstitutionally vague and overbroad. *Id.* at 659–60. Courts in a few other jurisdictions have salvaged similar enactments by construing them to require proof of additional elements beyond mere knowing presence at the scene of illegal activity. *See People v. Cressey*, 2 Cal.3d 836, 87 Cal.Rptr. 699, 471 P.2d 19, 28–29 (1970) (requiring proof that the defendant controlled the premises); *Commonwealth v. Tirella*, 356 Mass. 271, 249 N.E.2d 573, 575–76 (1969) (requiring the state to prove "acquiescent association" and "an absence of prompt and adequate objection" in addition to presence); *Jolley v. City of Jacksonville*, 281 So.2d 901, 903 (Fla.Dist.Ct.App.1973) (requiring the government to prove aiding or abetting in addition to presence).

74 *See, e.g., Rivas v. United States*, 783 A.2d 125, 130 (D.C.2001) (en banc) (reversing the conviction of an automobile passenger for constructive possession of narcotics in the vehicle, stating: "There must be something to prove that the individual was not merely an incidental bystander. It may be foolish to stand by when others are acting illegally, or to associate with those who have committed a crime. Such conduct or association, however, *without more,* does not establish the offenses here charged.") (quoting *United States v. Pardo*, 636 F.2d 535, 549 (D.C.Cir.1980)); *Bailey v. United States*, 416 F.2d 1110, 1113–14 (D.C.Cir.1969) (reversing a conviction for robbery, stating: "An inference of criminal participation cannot be drawn merely from presence; a culpable purpose is essential. . . . [T]he accused's presence is a circumstance from which guilt may be deduced if that presence is meant to assist the commission of the offense or is pursuant to an understanding that he is on the scene for that purpose. And . . . mere presence would be enough if it is intended to and does aid the primary actors. Presence is thus equated to aiding and abetting when it is shown that it designedly encourages the perpetrator, facilitates the unlawful deed—as when the accused acts as a lookout—or where it stimulates others to render assistance to the criminal act. But presence without these or similar attributes is insufficient to identify the accused as a party to the criminality." (internal quotation marks, citation, and footnotes omitted)).

79 As mentioned in Judge Thompson's concurrence, a former statute in this jurisdiction made it a crime for a person to be "found" in "a gambling establishment or an establishment where intoxicating liquor is sold without a license or any narcotic drug is sold, administered, or dispersed without a license," if the person "knew that it was such an establishment and if he is unable to give a good account of his presence in the establishment." D.C.Code § 22–1515(a) (1967). The United States Court of Appeals for the District of Columbia Circuit held this statute to be unconstitutionally vague in *Holly v. United States,* 464 F.2d 796, 798–99 (D.C.Cir.1972) (*per curiam*), reversing this court's decision holding otherwise in *United States v. McClough,* 263 A.2d 48, 52 (D.C.1970).

zen hardly would be unaware of the wrongfulness of trespassing or patronizing criminal enterprises, or surprised to learn of legal duties to avoid trespassing and frequenting illegal establishments. The PMVCF statute is in a different category.

Indeed, the anomaly and unforeseeability of § 22–2511 are exacerbated by the peculiarity that it is only a crime to remain in the presence of a firearm when inside a motor vehicle. Nowhere else in the District of Columbia does one incur a legal duty to distance oneself upon learning of the presence of a gun on the premises or within one's immediate proximity. Similarly, one who knows a friend is illegally carrying a firearm on his person may remain in the friend's company all day long, pursuing a wide range of normal activities—for instance, walking on the street, going shopping, eating at a restaurant, seeing a movie, visiting the gym, conducting business, and so forth—without violating the law; yet under § 22–2511, if one takes the equally innocuous additional step of accompanying the friend in a car, truck, or bus, one suddenly and without warning commits a felony. Who, not previously informed of it, would anticipate such a volte-face exception?

And to expand on a point made earlier, the duty created by § 22–2511 not to be in any motor vehicle containing a firearm is even more extraordinary and unimaginable because it is so unqualified—the existence of legitimate, innocent reasons for being in the vehicle voluntarily despite knowing that a firearm is present *do not matter.* Illustratively, the doctor who enters the car to minister to a sick or injured occupant, the friend who drives that person to the hospital, the parent who seeks to take a child from the car, the person who desires only to retrieve his personal property from the vehicle—all are subject to § 22–2511; all are felons under the law if they act with knowledge that a firearm is in the vehicle. Again, who not previously informed of this statute would conceive of such a state of affairs?

Although, as Judge Thompson argues, motor vehicles are subject to "pervasive schemes of regulation," we are aware of no vehicular regulation or regulatory scheme that would alert an innocent person to a legal duty to leave a vehicle if it contains a firearm. To say, for example, that passengers are on notice of regulations clearly connected to the consequences of their riding in a car—for example, regulations requiring them to wear seatbelts for their own protection in the event of an accident—does not imply they are legally responsible for the car's contents (not their own) or put them on notice of a duty to leave a car depending on what objects happen to be in it. Few (if any) motor vehicle regulations impose duties on passengers based on the actions of other occupants. Similarly, we think it immaterial that (as the concurrence argues) motor vehicle passengers may be detained along with the driver in a traffic stop and, "if contraband is observed anywhere in the vehicle, may have their purses, backpacks, and similar contain-

ers searched." That is true enough, but it is beside the point—it does not put innocent passengers on notice of the legal duty created by § 22–2511. The same is true
of the self-evident fact, also mentioned in the concurrence, that the presence of a
firearm increases the risk of harm if the motor vehicle is used to commit a crime.

The average person surely does know that guns are dangerous and subject
to regulation, and that while "guns generally can be owned in perfect innocence,"
they also often are possessed illegally and used to commit crimes. In many circumstances, prudent, law-abiding persons naturally may be uncomfortable in
the presence of firearms and wish not to be associated with them. Those facts
are not enough, however, to put ordinary people on notice that merely being in a
motor vehicle containing a gun is subject to the "strict regulation" that § 22–2511
imposes—that the simple sight of a handgun triggers a novel legal duty to leave
a motor vehicle at once, or to refrain from entering one.

We are compelled to conclude that this case, like *Lambert,* presents the
"rare instance" in which due process forbids the imposition of a criminal sanction
unless the government is required to prove that the defendant had "actual knowledge" of the law or "the probability of such knowledge." By its terms, § 22–2511
does not require proof that the defendant knew it was a crime to enter or remain
in a motor vehicle knowing it contains a firearm; there is no ambiguity in the
statute that could be construed as requiring such proof. Because the statute
therefore purports to allow the government, in every case, to obtain a conviction by proving only what cannot by itself be a crime, § 22–2511, as written, is
facially unconstitutional.

We do not believe we properly can undertake to "cure" this facial defect by
judicially decreeing that the statute means something other than what it says. As
this court has stated on more than one occasion, "[i]t is not within the judicial
function . . . to rewrite the statute, or to supply omissions in it, in order to make it
more fair." Furthermore, this is not the more usual situation courts have faced in
which a criminal statute that omits an intent element may be construed in light
of "an interpretive presumption that *mens rea* is required." There is a difference
between *mens rea* (as to which the statute is not silent) and knowledge of the
law. There is no background presumption that a knowledge-of-the-law element
is required by a criminal statute; *au contraire,* the starting point of our analysis
has been "the well-established tenet that ignorance of the law [normally] is not
a defense to criminal prosecution." Nor do we have warrant to infer a requirement that the government prove the defendant's knowledge of the law in order
to effectuate the goal of the statute. Adding such a requirement would thwart
the Council's intent to alleviate the government's burden of proof. Of course, the
Council remains free, if it wishes, to amend § 22–2511 so as avoid the constitutional defects we have identified.

As a result, we hold that § 22–2511 is unconstitutional on its face and that the trial court erred in allowing appellant to be convicted of violating that statute.

* * *

V.

Because D.C.Code § 22–2511 is unconstitutional on its face and the requirements of plain error review are satisfied, appellant's conviction under that statute cannot stand. As appellant was acquitted of all the other offenses with which he was charged, we remand with directions that his conviction be vacated and that the charge of violating § 22–2511 be dismissed with prejudice.

So ordered.

Opinion by Associate Judge THOMPSON, concurring in the judgment.
THOMPSON, Associate Judge, concurring in the judgment:

In reporting the legislation that is now codified as D.C.Code § 22–2511 (2012 Repl.), the Council of the District of Columbia Committee on Public Safety and the Judiciary explained that the legislation would "ensure that the charge [of presence in a motor vehicle containing a firearm ("PMVCF")] will not be used against those who . . . legitimately believed the possession of the firearm was lawful. . . ." D.C. Council Comm. on Pub. Safety & Judiciary, Comm. Report on Bill 18–151, "Omnibus Public Safety and Justice Amendment Act of 2009," at 4 (June 26, 2009) ("Committee Report"). Under the principles that "[t]he words of a statute are 'a primary index but not the sole index to legislative intent'" and that "the words 'cannot prevail over strong contrary indications in the legislative history,'"[1] I believe we must construe § 22–2511 to impose on the government a burden of proving that a defendant charged with PMVCF knew or had reason to know that possession of the firearm was unlawful. *Cf. United States v. McClough*, 263 A.2d 48, 55 (D.C.1970) (applying statute, D.C.Code § 33–416a (b)(1)(B) (1967), that made it unlawful for a narcotic drug user or a person who had been convicted of a narcotic offense to be present in a vehicle or structure where illicit narcotic drugs are kept, found, used, or dispensed, and holding that "by construing [the statute] to require knowledge on the part of the defendant of the presence of narcotic drugs in the place where he is, the statute can be constitutionally upheld"). Because the jury instructions in this case, described *ante*

---

1   *Grayson v. AT & T Corp.*, 15 A.3d 219, 238 (D.C.2011); *see also Sandwick v. District of Columbia*, 21 A.3d 997, 1000 (D.C.2011) (agreeing that "a mental element must be read into the statute" since it was "'inconceivable that the legislature intended that punishment would be imposed for failure to follow the course of conduct outlined, if the operator of the vehicle was ignorant of the happening of an accident'").

at 273–74, did not inform the jury of that required element of proof, I concur in the judgment that appellant Conley is entitled to reversal of his conviction * * *.

However, I am unable to join the opinion for the court, because I do not agree that § 22–2511 is unconstitutional on its face, i.e., that "every application of [it] is unconstitutional." *Ante,* 277. *A fortiori,* I do not agree that it is plainly unconstitutional.

First, I disagree with my colleagues' conclusion that § 22–2511 violates due process by shifting to the criminal defendant and away from the government the burden of proving that his presence in the motor vehicle was voluntary. Judge Glickman's opinion attempts to answer the hypothetical that I posed at oral argument, but does not succeed in doing so. My hypothetical: I have a bad knee and, after seeing what I'm pretty sure must be an illegal gun in the center console of the vehicle I have entered as a passenger, I decide to stay in the vehicle until it is close to a bus stop, now many blocks away, because I know that we are in an area where taxicabs pass infrequently, and I am without a cell phone or device that might enable me to summon a taxi or car service (and, perhaps, I am apprehensive about standing alone in the area). In other words, to use the language that the Committee Report employed to describe what must be proven for a PMVCF conviction, I make a "deliberate decision . . . to be in the vehicle [a little while longer] with an illegal firearm present." Committee Report at 4. Unfortunately for me, the vehicle is pulled over for a traffic infraction after we've gone just a block, the officer sees the gun in the console, and the driver and I are arrested, me for PMVCF. On these facts, the government would be able to prove that I voluntarily remained in the vehicle, as required by § 22–2511(a); my action *was* voluntary, because I was physically capable of getting out of the vehicle and of communicating to the driver, "please stop the car; I need to get out" (or, perhaps, "I can't ride with you, grandson, if you're going to bring that gun along"), and because no one threatened me with harm if I should try to exit.[5] But, in my (affirmative) defense, I would have the opportunity to explain that in light of my bad knee, the difficulty I would have encountered in trying to walk several blocks to the bus stop, and the other circumstances described above, the opportunity I

---

[5]   That is, I did not lack the ability to "safely distance [myself] from the firearm." Committee Report at 4. And, unlike the individuals in Judge Glickman's example about the doctor who is in the car ministering to a sick or injured occupant and the friend who drives that person to the hospital, *ante,* 288, my continued presence in the vehicle was not because of an exigent circumstance.

As the government points out, § 22–2511 is not the only criminal statute in the D.C. Code that reaches conduct that is "legal until an individual learns something and fails to act." For example, the unlawful entry statute, D.C.Code § 22–3302 (2012), makes it unlawful to "refuse to quit the [property] on the demand of the lawful occupant" even if the defendant entered the property lawfully.

had to get out of the vehicle right away was not a reasonable opportunity—matters I am "in the best position to prove [.]"[6]

In my view, the foregoing (quite realistic) hypothetical offers an entirely plausible construction of the word "voluntarily" as used in § 22–2511(a) and one that avoids any "logical incompatibility" of subsections (a) and (b). This hypothetical shows that there *are*, in Judge Glickman's words, "circumstances in which the government could prove beyond a reasonable doubt that the defendant 'voluntarily' remained in the vehicle, yet the defendant could prove by a preponderance of the evidence that [s]he would have left but had no reasonable opportunity to do so," and thus that "the respective burdens of persuasion would not be incompatible and there would not be an unconstitutional burden-shifting with respect to the element of voluntariness." *Ante,* 279.

Nor, in my opinion, does the PMVCF statute offend due process for the reasons discussed in *Lambert v. California,* 355 U.S. 225, 78 S.Ct. 240, 2 L.Ed.2d 228 (1957). In *Lambert,* the Supreme Court considered the validity of an ordinance that made it a criminal offense for a convicted felon to remain in the city of Los Angeles for five days without registering with the chief of police. *Id.* at 226, 78 S.Ct. 240. The Court "assume[d] that [convicted felon Lambert, a seven-year resident of Los Angeles] had no actual knowledge of the requirement that she register under this ordinance." *Id.* at 227, 78 S.Ct. 240. Although acknowledging that "[t]he rule that 'ignorance of the law will not excuse' . . . is deep in our law," *id.* at 228, 78 S.Ct. 240 (citation omitted), the Court held that it was incompatible with due process to convict her of a crime of omission where "circumstances which might move one to inquire as to [any applicable legal duty were] completely lacking" and where the law "'punished conduct which would not be blameworthy in the average member of the community.'" *Id.* at 229, 78 S.Ct. 240.

As courts (including this one) have observed, the Supreme Court "has steadfastly resisted efforts to extend *Lambert's* reach, . . . and has gone so far as to suggest that the *Lambert* dissent correctly characterized the majority opinion as 'an isolated deviation from the strong current of precedents[.]'" *United States v. Meade,* 175 F.3d 215, 225 (1st Cir.1999) (internal citation omitted) (quoting *Texaco, Inc. v. Short,* 454 U.S. 516, 537 n. 33, 102 S.Ct. 781, 70 L.Ed.2d 738 (1982) (observing that *Lambert's* "application has been limited, lending some credence to Justice Frankfurter's colorful prediction in dissent that the case would stand

---

6   *United States v. McArthur,* 108 F.3d 1350, 1355 (11th Cir.1997) ("[C]ourts determining whether a statutory exception is an element of the crime or an affirmative defense often consider whether the government or the defendant is in the best position to prove facts necessary to trigger the exception. Where defendants are better equipped to prove facts that would allow them to take advantage of a statutory exception, we ordinarily view that exception as an affirmative defense."); *see also Dixon v. United States,* 548 U.S. 1, 8, 126 S.Ct. 2437, 165 L.Ed.2d 299 (2006) (citing the doctrine that "where the facts with regard to an issue lie peculiarly in the knowledge of a party, that party has the burden of proving the issue").

as . . . 'a derelict on the waters of the law'")); *see also McNeely v. United States*, 874 A.2d 371, 384 (D.C.2005) ("*Lambert* is thus a rare instance in which the Supreme Court has held that, contrary to the well-established tenet that ignorance of the law is not a defense to criminal prosecution, . . . actual knowledge of the law is a prerequisite to criminal liability.") (internal citation omitted).

There is no reason to extend *Lambert's* reach in this case, where circumstances of the type that led the Supreme Court to deviate from the well-established tenet about ignorance of the law are not present. "Engrained in our concept of due process is the requirement of notice." *Lambert*, 355 U.S. at 228, 78 S.Ct. 240. I believe it is fair to say that our populace does not lack notice that the law significantly curtails their freedoms as passengers in a motor vehicle and that motor vehicles are a regular focus of crime-reduction efforts. Motor vehicles are subject to "pervasive schemes of regulation" (which "necessarily lead to reduced expectations of privacy"). *California v. Carney*, 471 U.S. 386, 392, 105 S.Ct. 2066, 85 L.Ed.2d 406 (1985). In addition, the law is clear that, upon a traffic stop even for an infraction as minor as a broken tail light, passengers in a motor vehicle may be stopped along with the driver, may be asked to step out of the vehicle, and, if contraband is observed anywhere in the vehicle, may have their purses, backpacks, and similar containers searched. Further, it can come as a surprise to no one that (as the Committee Report described) motor vehicles frequently "are used to facilitate a quick escape or enable swift implementation of [a] crime" and that there is an "escalation of harm due to the combination of the presence of a firearm and the use of a motor vehicle." Committee Report at 4.

As the majority opinion notes, in *McIntosh v. Washington*, 395 A.2d 744, 756 (D.C.1978), this court rejected a *Lambert* claim that the District's firearms laws denied due process by imposing criminal penalties on those who fail to register their firearms, "regardless of their knowledge of the duty to register." We explained that "where dangerous or deleterious devices or products are involved, the probability of regulation is so great that anyone who is aware that he is either in possession of *or dealing with them* must be presumed to be aware of the regulation." *Id.* (italics added). That principle seems equally applicable here. Given the District of Columbia's longstanding law treating guns as dangerous weapons, I believe it is fair to say that the average member of our community who voluntarily and knowingly is in a vehicle with an illegal firearm "knows that he is dealing with a dangerous device of a character that places him 'in responsible relation to a public danger,'" and thus is "alerted to the probability of strict regulation." *Staples v. United States*, 511 U.S. 600, 607, 114 S.Ct. 1793, 128 L.Ed.2d 608 (1994); *see also, e.g., Speaks v. United States*, 959 A.2d 712, 715 (D.C.2008) (citing cases recognizing that a gun is a "dangerous weapon"); *cf. Wells*, 281 A.2d at 227, 227 n. 1 (applying statute that penalized presence in "an establishment where . . . any narcotic drug is sold [or] administered," and rejecting argument by Wells (who claimed that he "was at the apartment [where drugs and distribution paraphernalia were found] to pick up a minor child who was present there") that to obtain a conviction, the government must prove that he was present in the apartment "with an intent to participate in the illegal activity").

To borrow the language of one of those who testified on the bill that became the PMVCF statute, the message of the legislation is, "If there is a gun illegally in the car, you should not be." Committee Report, Attachment, Statement of Patricia Riley, Spec. Counsel to U.S. Att'y for D.C., at 18. That message cannot be a surprise to anyone. As to the visitor from another jurisdiction who is unaware that local law generally proscribes possession of a firearm in a vehicle (to use Judge Glickman's example), it would likely be difficult for the government to prove that the genuinely clueless visitor lacked a legitimate belief that the firearm was lawful. Thus, construed in accordance with the legislative history (i.e., construed to include as an element of the offense a requirement that the defendant know or be charged with knowledge that the firearm is being carried unlawfully), the PMVCF statute would not offend due process. Because we have "a duty to construe statutes in a way which avoids declaring them unconstitutional," *Berg v. United States,* 631 A.2d 394, 398 (D.C.1993), that is the construction we should apply. With it, there is no reason why we should rest on the example of the uninformed visitor to conclude that § 22–2511 is unconstitutional.

Continuing with my discussion of why the circumstances here are unlike those in *Lambert,* I reject my colleagues' suggestion that the PMVCF statute punishes conduct that would not be blameworthy in the average member of the community. The District of Columbia has long had some of the most restrictive gun laws in the nation; as a result, the public policy against carrying firearms on the streets of the District of Columbia is well-known to our populace. At the same time, it is common knowledge that gun violence has ravaged our city, and common knowledge that firearms are dangerous in our urban environment, certainly at least as dangerous as pit bulls. *Cf. McNeely,* 874 A.2d at 384 (holding that, given the well-known dangerous proclivities of the breed, the owner's "knowledge that his dogs were pit bulls should have moved him to inquire into his heightened obligations under the Act"). Further, an individual's voluntary entry into or continued presence in a motor vehicle that he knows to contain a firearm being carried unlawfully can reasonably be thought to encourage unlawful conduct,[11] in that it enables the person in possession of the gun to carry or possess it in the vehicle without losing companionship (or, perhaps, without losing a paying passenger). An individual's presence in a motor vehicle containing an illegal firearm also hampers law enforcement, in that, as the Committee Report explains, "when a car is stopped with multiple occupants and a firearm is present in the vehicle

. . . police are unable to prove who was in possession of the firearm." Committee Report at 3. Until the PMVCF statute was enacted, the conduct it describes was not illegal (and it is no longer illegal after the court's decision today). But, in light of the foregoing facts, it surely goes too far to say that an individual's voluntary entry into or continued presence in a motor vehicle that he knows to contain a firearm being carried unlawfully is "entirely innocent behavior." *Ante,* 273. It most certainly is not. *Cf. McClough,* 263 A.2d at 52 (reasoning that knowing presence in an illegal establishment "is not presumptively innocent behavior").

For the foregoing reasons, I cannot join my colleagues in declaring that § 22–2511 is facially unconstitutional.

---

2. Presumption of Intent

State v. Taylor

Supreme Court of Nebraska
282 Neb. 297, 803 N.W.2d 746 (2011)

McCORMACK, J.

I. NATURE OF CASE

Trevelle J. Taylor was convicted in Douglas County District Court of first degree murder and use of a deadly weapon to commit a felony. He was sentenced to serve a term of life imprisonment on the murder conviction and a consecutive term of 10 years' imprisonment on the weapon conviction. Taylor appeals. For the following reasons, we reverse, and remand for a new trial.

II. BACKGROUND

Justin Gaines was shot and killed outside his residence on September 19, 2009. The gunshot entered Gaines' back and fatally penetrated his lungs and heart. Taylor was arrested nine blocks from the scene of the shooting. He was tried before a jury and convicted of first degree murder and use of a deadly weapon to commit a felony. The following evidence was adduced at trial:

In the early afternoon on September 19, 2009, Gaines was driving near his residence on Curtis Avenue in Omaha, when he noticed his friend, Catrice Bryson, standing near her car, which was parked in his driveway. Gaines parked his car in the driveway behind Bryson's and spoke with Bryson through his open driver's-side window while he remained in his car. Gaines asked Bryson to write down her telephone number, and she walked to her car to retrieve a pen. Bryson then heard numerous gunshots before she was able to return to Gaines' car. She observed two men shooting guns at Gaines, who remained seated in his car. Bryson retreated toward the residence and heard Gaines yell that he had been shot in the back. Bryson then observed the two men run from the scene in opposite directions.

Bryson described the two suspects she witnessed at the scene. She described the first suspect as an African–American male, "[s]kinny with a brush cut in a brown shirt with orange on it," and holding a gun. Bryson described the second suspect as an African–American male, light complected with shoulder-length braids, wearing a white T-shirt with a basketball jersey, and also holding a gun.

At the scene of the crime, near the end of the driveway where Gaines' car was parked, the police collected 16 spent shell casings from a 9–mm handgun. Local residents told police that they heard the sounds of two different guns. Police also eventually recovered a 9–mm handgun near the area of the shooting. A neighbor told police that the day of the shooting, he heard the gunshots and witnessed a black male run through the area where the 9–mm handgun was found.

At trial, several local residents testified as to what they witnessed on September 19, 2009. One such witness testified that, prior to the shooting, she was standing on her porch when she witnessed a black male jog past her house wearing a white T-shirt and baggy denim shorts and that the man had long braids and a goatee. The man proceeded, alone, toward 45th Street and Curtis Avenue. The witness went inside her home and then heard a series of gunshots coming from the area near Gaines' residence. The witness identified a photograph of Joshua Nolan as the man she saw jogging past her house.

Another such witness testified that she heard the gunshots from her residence near 44th Street and Curtis Avenue. She went outside when she heard the shots, and then witnessed a black male running east on Curtis Avenue, then north through the yards of homes across the street from her. She described the man as wearing a brown T-shirt and having a "brush cut" hairstyle.

A third such witness also testified that she witnessed a black male running east on Curtis Avenue, and through her yard. She testified that the man was wearing a brown T-shirt and blue shorts.

A fourth witness testified that she was driving home at the time of the shooting. She witnessed a man run past her car and huddle behind some bushes. The man was wearing a tan shirt and blue shorts, and she overheard him speaking on a cellular telephone, telling someone to "come get [him]." The witness identified Taylor as the man she saw that afternoon.

Officer Joel Strominger was on duty on the afternoon that Gaines was shot. Strominger heard a broadcast regarding the shooting which described the suspects' vehicle as a small, white four-door car without hubcaps. Strominger observed a parked white vehicle matching this description in the area of 40th Street and Redick Avenue. A black male was sitting in the driver's seat, and a black male wearing a white T-shirt and black shorts was standing outside the car, holding what appeared to be a brown T-shirt. Strominger then observed the driver make a U-turn and drive west on Redick Avenue, while the individual outside the car walked east on Redick Avenue. Strominger followed the car, ran a license plate check and determined the car was stolen. He then stopped the car, which was being driven by Joshua Kercheval.

Officer Jarvis Duncan had also responded to the broadcast regarding the shooting, and on his patrol of the area, he came upon a black male running north on 37th Street near Redick Avenue. Duncan and his partner witnessed the individual throw a brown shirt to the ground. Duncan and his partner ordered him to stop, arrested him, and took his cellular telephone into possession. The individual was later identified as Taylor. Strominger identified Taylor as the man he observed standing outside of the car driven by Kercheval. Taylor was transported to the Omaha Police Department's headquarters, where his hands and arms were swabbed for gunshot residue. Police also seized the brown T-shirt Duncan and his partner observed Taylor throw to the ground. Bryson identified the shirt seized as the one that was worn by one of the shooters.

Nolan was stopped by police for a traffic violation 8 days after the homicide. The car Nolan was driving was registered in his name. Nolan was in possession of a .44–caliber Smith & Wesson revolver, with a laser sight, which was hidden in his waistband. Nolan was arrested, and his car was impounded and searched by police. The search produced four spent 9–mm shell casings.

Kercheval testified at trial. He stated that on the morning of the shooting, he was at his home when Taylor and Nolan arrived in a white car. Kercheval had never seen the car before, and the three agreed to ride around for a while with Kercheval driving. They drove to the area of 45th Street and Curtis Avenue, and Kercheval noticed a man sitting in a parked car talking to a woman in a driveway. Taylor told him to stop the car and said, "There's the weedman." Kercheval pulled over and parked near 45th and Vernon Streets.

Kercheval testified that he remained in the car at all times, but that Taylor got out of the car on 44th Street and that Nolan got out of the car after it was parked on 45th Street. Kercheval then heard a series of gunshots, and he started to leave when he noticed Nolan running up the street. Nolan entered the car, and the two men drove east toward 42nd Street. Nolan then jumped out of the car, and Kercheval made a U-turn and was then stopped by Strominger. Kercheval did not see Taylor between the time Taylor exited the car and when the police brought Taylor to where Strominger had stopped Kercheval in the car.

Kercheval was in custody during his testimony, which he gave only after his arrest on a bench warrant for failure to appear when subpoenaed to testify earlier in the trial. Kercheval stated that he received a telephone call from Taylor the Friday prior to the scheduled trial date. During that telephone call, Taylor told Kercheval not to come to court, and Kercheval testified that he subsequently failed to appear because he felt threatened. The telephone call from Taylor to Kercheval was recorded by a system at the jail. A recording of the call was received into evidence and played for the jury. During the call, Taylor stated, among other things: "leave this shit alone"; "don't let me go out like this"; "if I don't come home, man, this shit is gonna go places where it don't even need to go, man"; and "make sure you stay out [of] the way." Prior to receiving the telephone call, Kercheval had told the prosecutor on two separate occasions that he would appear and testify.

* * *

The district court also gave jury instruction No. 9 over Taylor's objection. That instruction provided:

> You have heard evidence regarding [Taylor's] alleged attempt to prevent [Kercheval] from testifying in this case. A defendant's attempt to prevent a state's witness from testifying may be evidence of the defendant's "conscious guilt" that a crime has been committed and serves as a basis for an inference that the defendant is guilty of the crimes charged. Such evidence may be considered by you in determining whether the [S]tate has proved the elements of each of the crimes charged beyond a reasonable doubt.

The jury found Taylor guilty of murder in the first degree and use of a deadly weapon to commit a felony. Taylor was sentenced to life imprisonment on the murder conviction and a consecutive term of 10 years' imprisonment on the weapon conviction. Taylor appeals.

III. ASSIGNMENTS OF ERROR

Taylor assigns, renumbered and restated, that the district court erred in (1) giving jury instruction No. 9, regarding an inference of guilt; (2) giving jury instruction No. 4, a step instruction regarding the lesser-included offenses; (3) giving jury instruction No. 8, regarding the definition of premeditation; (4) receiving expert opinion testimony regarding the presence of gunshot residue on Taylor's hands, in violation of rule 403; and (5) admitting cellular telephone records purporting to prove contacts between Taylor and his codefendant Nolan, on the basis of insufficient foundation.

IV. STANDARD OF REVIEW

Whether jury instructions are correct is a question of law, which an appellate court resolves independently of the lower court's decision.

In proceedings where the Nebraska Evidence Rules apply, the admissibility of evidence is controlled by the Nebraska Evidence Rules; judicial discretion is involved only when the rules make such discretion a factor in determining admissibility. Where the Nebraska Evidence Rules commit the evidentiary question at issue to the discretion of the trial court, the admissibility of evidence is reviewed for an abuse of discretion.

The exercise of judicial discretion is implicit in the determinations of relevancy under rule 403, and a trial court's decisions regarding them will not be reversed absent an abuse of discretion.

A court must determine whether there is sufficient foundation evidence for the admission of physical evidence on a case-by-case basis. Because authentication rulings are necessarily fact specific, a trial court has discretion to determine whether evidence has been properly authenticated. We review a trial court's ruling on authentication for abuse of discretion.

V. ANALYSIS

1. Jury Instructions

Taylor assigns as error the giving of jury instructions Nos. 4, 8, and 9. Whether jury instructions are correct is a question of law, which an appellate court resolves independently of the lower court's decision.

(a) Inference of Guilt Based on Taylor's Alleged Attempt to Prevent State's Witness From Testifying

The district court gave jury instruction No. 9 over Taylor's objection. The instruction provided:

> You have heard evidence regarding [Taylor's] alleged attempt to prevent [Kercheval] from testifying in this case. A defendant's attempt to prevent a state's witness from testifying may be evidence of the defendant's "conscious guilt" that a crime has been committed and serves as a basis for an inference that the defendant is guilty of the crimes charged. Such evidence may be considered by you in determining whether the [S]tate has proved the elements of each of the crimes charged beyond a reasonable doubt.

Taylor argues that because the instruction did not explain to the jury that it had the option of not drawing the specified inference, it created an improper presumption of guilt.

* * *

The U.S. Supreme Court has determined that jury instructions which create mandatory presumptions are improper, but that those which create merely permissive presumptions are allowed. In *Sandstrom v. Montana,* an appeal from a prosecution for deliberate homicide, the Court held that because the jury, which was instructed that the law presumes a person intends the ordinary consequences of his voluntary acts, might have interpreted the presumption as conclusive or as shifting the burden of persuasion, and because either interpretation would have violated the 14th Amendment's requirement that the state prove every element of a criminal offense beyond a reasonable doubt, the instruction was unconstitutional.

In Nebraska, instructions as to presumptions in criminal cases must also conform to the requirements of Neb. Evid. R. 303(3), which states:

Whenever the existence of a presumed fact against the accused is submitted to the jury, the judge shall give an instruction that the law declares that the jury may regard the basic facts as sufficient evidence of the presumed fact but does not require it to do so. In addition, if the presumed fact establishes guilt or is an element of the offense or negatives a defense, the judge shall instruct the jury that its existence must, on all the evidence, be proved beyond a reasonable doubt.

Here, the challenged instruction is based on a common-law inference rather than a presumption. However, we have previously determined that references to "presumptions" in rule 303 necessarily include "inferences" in criminal cases as well. Although frequent reference is made to "presumptions" in criminal cases, a presumption that relieves the State of its burden of proof beyond a reasonable doubt on any essential element of a crime violates a defendant's due process rights and is constitutionally impermissible.

In *State v. Parks,* [511 N.W.2d 774 (Neb. 1994)] a theft-by-receiving case, we interpreted the propriety of an instruction which provided, "'[P]ossession of recently stolen property, if not satisfactorily explained, is ordinarily a circumstance from which you may reasonably draw the inference and find, in the light of the surrounding circumstances shown by the evidence in the case, that the person in possession knew the property had been stolen.'" We reversed the conviction based on that instruction. We held that when a trial court instructs a jury on an inference regarding a specific fact or set of facts, the instruction must specifically include a statement explaining to the jury that it may regard the basic facts as sufficient evidence of the inferred fact, but that it is not required to do so. And the instruction must explain that the existence of the inferred fact must, on all the evidence, be proved beyond a reasonable doubt. Failure to meet these requirements constitutes reversible error.

In *Parks,* the jury might have interpreted the instruction as conclusive that the State had proved one element of the crime charged. But here in Taylor's case, in the context of the "conscious guilt" doctrine, the instruction allowed the jury to presume that the defendant was guilty of the crimes charged. Here, the district court included the requirement that the inferred fact must be proved beyond a reasonable doubt, but the instruction failed to specify that the jury was not required to make the inference of guilt. Rule 303(3) is couched in mandatory terms. The instruction, as given in Taylor's case, failed to inform the jury that it was not required to draw the inference of guilt. This omission in the court's instruction No. 9 is fatal to the constitutional validity of that instruction. Accordingly, the district court's failure to comply with the requirements of rule 303(3) is a ground for reversal of Taylor's convictions.

* * *

VI. CONCLUSION

For the foregoing reasons, the district court committed reversible error in giving jury instruction No. 9. Accordingly, we reverse, and remand the cause for a new trial. * * *

REVERSED AND REMANDED FOR A NEW TRIAL.

PRACTICE EXERCISE

You are a legislator for the State. The following people have met with you and told you the following narratives. Each person wants you to introduce a bill changing the current law so that possession of a pocket knife creates a presumption of intent to injure or kill. The requested change does not make it illegal to possess a pocket knife. The current law contains a result element. Make a decision.

8:00 am appointment.
Mother of Lolita Rodriguez. Via translator.

My daughter was a beautiful little girl, full of life and with a pure heart. She was stabbed through the temple with a pocket knife brought to her school by a well-known bully; she is now blind in one eye, and has suffered some brain damage. She has a learning disability and spent five months in the hospital. My bills now total $2 million; I cannot pay it because I work as a waitress and have no health insurance. That little f----- had picked on her incessantly for weeks. I called the principal, but he just told me to stay out of his way, "because the school is not in your neighborhood, if you know what I mean." I told my daughter, "You stay with your friends at all times and call the police if you have any problems." The day she went to school and was stabbed, her phone was taken from her by her first period teacher. She was reprimanded in front of the class. In the hallway after class, the bully made fun of her for getting caught. He then waived his pocket knife in front of her face to intimidate her, and overreached and stabbed her right behind her left eye socket. The court said that no one can prove the bully wanted to stab her. This is ridiculous and this f----- school and country will rot in hell for allowing such depraved behavior. This bully had punched a kid the previous day, knocking out three teeth! Now my daughter is permanently disabled. She used to be the smartest in her class.

8: 30 am appointment.

Lobbyists from "Citizens against Violence."

The data is clear. In 2011, there were 15,000 stabbings in the State, according to police statistics. 5,000 of those stabbings resulted from pocket knives. 3,000 caused serious bodily injury, and of those 1,000 resulted in deaths. Of those 1,000 deaths, there were 500 acquittals because the prosecution was unable to show the *mens rea* element. With a change in the law, the state would not bear this burden of proof, and more criminals would be brought to justice. Just think, there are 500 murderers out there right now who got away because of this high standard!

9:00 am appointment.

Lobbyists from "National Association of Crime Fighters."

Deterrence is key. If criminals knew they would be punished, they'd stop doing bad things. Reducing the burden of proof, by creating a presumption that possession of a pocket knife is intent to injure or kill, does just that: it tells criminals that they can't hide from the law. Think of it this way: no innocent person will be punished because innocent people don't hurt one another with pocket knives. It's only when a person hurts someone else does the lesser burden of proof trigger. This law is perfect because it makes it easier to capture the bad guys, those who harm others, not those who "knick their finger" carving a stick. We're talking about murderers hiding shanks and knives in their socks and sleeves. Let justice be done!

CHAPTER FOUR

Statutory Interpretation

THE MEANING of a criminal statute defining an offense, defense, or sentencing provision often disposes of the case. In principle, this should make criminal law fairly straightforward; lawyers and judges need only read the statute to determine what it means. However, in practice it is not that simple. Criminal statutes are often incomplete. The Supreme Court long ago recognized that the language of the statute itself might not be enough to identify the elements of an offense: "In an indictment upon a statute, it is not sufficient to set forth the offence in the words of the statute, unless those words of themselves fully, directly, and expressly, without any uncertainty or ambiguity, set forth all the elements necessary to constitute the offence intended to be punished." *United States v. Carll*, 105 U.S. 611, 26 L. Ed. 1135 (1881). That is, a statute's description of an offense might be partial; other essential elements might be required. In addition, the Court has recognized that "most statutes are ambiguous to some degree." *Dean v. United States*, 556 U.S. 568, 129 S.Ct. 1849, 173 L.Ed.2d 785 (2009) (quoting *Muscarello v. United States*, 524 U.S. 125, 138, 118 S.Ct. 1911, 141 L.Ed.2d 111 (1998)). Effective prosecutors and defense attorneys read statutes with an eye to identifying ambiguities and determining how they can be turned to their advantage.

Because of its critical importance in the practice of law in all contexts, statutory interpretation has drawn enormous scholarly and judicial attention. *See, e.g.*, Guido Calabresi, *A Common Law for the Age of Statutes* (1982); William N. Eskridge, Jr., Philip P. Frickey & Elizabeth Garrett, *Cases and Materials on Statutory Interpretation* (2012); Linda D. Jellum, *Mastering Statutory Interpretation* (2d ed. 2013); Abner J. Mikva & Eric Lane, *An Introduction to Statutory Interpretation and the Legislative Process* (1997); Richard A. Posner,

Reflections on Judging (2013); Antonin Scalia & Bryan A. Garner, *Reading Law: The Interpretation of Legal Texts* (2012).

While the theoretical approaches are complex and varied, it might be fair to say that there are, broadly speaking, two main schools of thought. One approach, "textualism", focuses on the plain meaning of the statute based on its language. This approach, famously embraced by Justice Antonin Scalia, relies on contemporary dictionaries to understand the meaning of words in a law. It eschews the use of legislative history, such as committee reports and statements by legislators, both because such things is manipulable and because legislative history does not represent the views of Congress or the state legislature as a whole.

Another approach, what might be called "purposive" or "intentionalist" interpretation, is more willing to look at legislative history and other sources to determine what a legislature was trying to accomplish in cases where the text itself is ambiguous.

Both approaches agree with the "plain meaning rule", the principle that unambiguous textual language normally must simply be applied as it appears in the statute. Both approaches are also willing to rely on canons of construction, rules of thumb identified by courts and scholars used as general principles in interpreting statutes. A number of these principles applied by the federal courts appear in Yule Kim, *Congressional Research Service, Statutory Interpretation: General Principles and Recent Trends* (2008), a government document available on the internet and well worth reading.

Many lawyers and judges will claim to have identified the best reading of the statute. Very few will claim, however, that there are methods, canons, rules or principles which can be asserted uncontroversially to achieve clearly correct results in every case. That is, while many cases raising questions of statutory interpretation are unanimous, many are decided by divided courts, each making reasonable arguments supported by applicable precedent. Many cases are close, hard and debatable.

With respect to each case in this chapter, ask yourself the following questions: What provision of the claim or defense is at issue? Why does it matter? What position does each party take? What does the court decide, and, given the court's decision, what facts are necessary and sufficient to prove the offense or defense at issue? And what principles of interpretation or decision does the court apply? While answering each question is essential to understanding the case, the last is particularly important. You should make a list of the interpretive techniques courts employ. This will be an inventory of tools you can use in practice (and on exams) to advocate on behalf of your clients.

A. Legislative Purpose and Strict Construction

When dealing with a case in a particular jurisdiction, you should know whether the legislature has adopted a statute addressing how statutes in general, or criminal statutes in particular, are to be construed. A number of states by statute or common law provide that criminal statutes must be strictly construed. For example, Florida provides: "The provisions of this code and offenses defined by other statutes shall be strictly construed; when the language is susceptible of differing constructions, it shall be construed most favorably to the accused." Fla. Stat. Ann. § 775.021 (1) (West). *See also, e.g.,* Ohio Rev. Code § 2901.04(A); 1 Pa. Cons. Stat. Ann. § 1928 (West).

Other jurisdictions reject the principle of strict construction. For example, California law provides:

> *Construction of the Penal Code.* The rule of the common law, that penal statutes are to be strictly construed, has no application to this Code. All its provisions are to be construed according to the fair import of their terms, with a view to effect its objects and to promote justice.

Cal. Penal Code § 4 (West). Similarly, Louisiana's law states:

> The articles of this Code cannot be extended by analogy so as to create crimes not provided for herein; however, in order to promote justice and to effect the objects of the law, all of its provisions shall be given a genuine construction, according to the fair import of their words, taken in their usual sense, in connection with the context, and with reference to the purpose of the provision.

La. Rev. Stat. Ann. § 14:3. Similarly, the following is Washington's rule:

> (1) The general purposes of the provisions governing the definition of offenses are:
>
> (a) To forbid and prevent conduct that inflicts or threatens substantial harm to individual or public interests;
>
> (b) To safeguard conduct that is without culpability from condemnation as criminal;
>
> (c) To give fair warning of the nature of the conduct declared to constitute an offense;

(d) To differentiate on reasonable grounds between serious and minor offenses, and to prescribe proportionate penalties for each.

(2) The provisions of this title shall be construed according to the fair import of their terms but when the language is susceptible of differing constructions it shall be interpreted to further the general purposes stated in this title.

Wash. Rev. Code Ann. § 9A.04.020 (West).

United States v. Giles

Supreme Court of the United States
300 U.S. 41, 57 S.Ct. 340, 81 L.Ed. 493 (1937)

Mr. Justice McREYNOLDS delivered the opinion of the Court.

Section 5209, R.S., as amended * * * provides:

'Any officer, director, agent, or employee of any Federal reserve bank, or of any member bank * * * who makes any false entry in any book, report, or statement of such Federal reserve bank or member bank, with intent in any case to injure or defraud such Federal reserve bank or member bank, or any other company, body politic or corporate, or any individual person, or to deceive any officer of such Federal reserve bank or member bank, or the Comptroller of the Currency, or any agent or examiner appointed to examine the affairs of such Federal reserve bank or member bank, or the Federal Reserve Board * * * shall be deemed guilty of a misdemeanor, and upon conviction thereof in any district court of the United States shall be fined not more than $5,000 or shall be imprisoned for not more than five years, or both, in the discretion of the court.'

Count 3 of an indictment in the United States District Court, Western District of Texas, charged that respondent, Giles, while employed as teller by the Commercial National Bank of San Antonio, Tex., a member of the Federal Reserve National Bank of Dallas, did 'unlawfully, knowingly, wilfully, fraudulently, and feloniously make and cause to be made in a book of the said The Commercial National Bank of San Antonio, Texas, known as the Individual Ledger, in the account designated 'S.A. Public Service Company,' under date of 'Jul 25 '33' in the column bearing the printed heading 'Balance,' being the fifth entry from the top of the column aforesaid, and directly opposite the machine printed date thereon 'July 25 33,' a certain false entry in the following figures, to wit, '7,874.07,' which said entry so made as aforesaid, purports to show and does in substance and effect indicate and declare that The Commercial National Bank of San Antonio, Texas, was indebted and liable to the San Antonio Public Service Company in the amount of Seven Thousand Eight Hundred Seventy-Four Dollars and Seven Cents ($7,874.07) on July 25, 1933, whereas in truth and in fact said indebtedness and liability on said date was a different and much larger amount.'

Count 4 made a like charge relative to the account of the National Life & Accident Insurance Company.

He was tried, found guilty, and sentenced under both counts. The point for our decision is whether the trial court erred in refusing to direct a verdict of not guilty. The essential facts are not in dispute.

From the evidence it appears—

Giles, once bookkeeper for the Commercial National Bank, became first paying and receiving teller with custody each day of some $35,000 cash. His duty was to receive deposits and place accompanying slips or tickets where they would reach the bookkeepers for entry. Eighteen months prior to the alleged offense, he discovered shortage in his cash but made no report to his superiors. To cover up the shortage he resorted to the practice of withholding selected deposit slips for three or four days before permitting them to reach the bookkeeping department. This caused the ledger to show false balances. Other shortages occurred; July 25, 1933, the total stood at $2,650.

On that day he accepted deposits with proper tickets from San Antonio Public Service Company and National Life & Accident Insurance Company for $1,985.79 and $663.27, respectively, accompanied by cash and checks. Together these approximated his shortage. He withheld both tickets from the place where they should have gone and secreted them. If placed as usual and as his duty required, they would have reached the bookkeeper during the day. Entries on the ledger would have shown the depositors' true balances.

The Bank closed July 29th. The slips never reached the bookkeeper. The individual ledger accounts at the end of the 25th and thereafter understated the liability of the Bank to the depositors.

The respondent acknowledged his purpose in withholding the deposit tickets was to prevent officers and examiners from discovering his shortage. * * *

At the conclusion of the evidence counsel moved for a directed verdict of not guilty. This was denied. The jury found guilt under both counts; an appeal, with many assignments of error, went to the Circuit Court of Appeals.

That court declared: 'The serious question presented for decision is whether the law will support a conviction on an indictment charging that defendant caused the false entries to be made.'

'Of course, in a sense, one who makes a false entry causes it to be made. If he makes an entry himself or directs another to make it, an allegation in the indictment that he caused it to be made may be treated as surplusage and harmless, but where the defendant has neither made a false entry nor directed another to do so, the same allegation is material and injurious. A charge that one has caused a false entry to be made is very much broader than the charge that he made it.' 'We consider the allegation of the indictment, that defendant did 'cause to be made a certain false entry in a book of the bank,' charged a degree and classification of the offense not within the letter or intent of the law.' 'The evidence in the record conclusively shows that defendant neither made the false entries nor did anything that could be considered as a direction to the bookkeeper to make them. Without the charge that he caused the entries to be made he could not have been convicted. It follows that it was prejudicial error to overrule the motion for a directed verdict of acquittal.'

Dissenting, one judge said:

'This statute plainly intends to punish the falsification of bank records with intent to deceive or defraud. If false entries are deliberately produced, although through an ignorantly innocent agent, the bank employee who concocts the plan and achieves the result is, in my opinion, guilty. This innocent bookkeeper was the teller's real though unconscious agent in making the entries; as truly so as if the false entries had been requested in words.' 'The present case is not one of a mere failure to prevent a consequence, but is one of contriving that consequence and so fathering it as to make it wholly the contriver's own. The bookkeeper in making these false entries was doing the will of the teller, though he did not know it. The false entries are in law the acts of the teller who planned them and did all he needed to do to produce them.'

Counsel for the respondent now affirm: 'There is no dispute as to the facts.' 'The act committed by the defendant was the withholding by him and the failure by him to turn over to the Bookkeeping Department in the usual course of the bank's business a deposit slip.' He did not cause any false entry to be made. Personally he made no such entry; he did not affirmatively direct one. By withholding the ticket he prevented an entry; he caused none.

The rule, often announced, that criminal statutes must be strictly construed does not require that the words of an enactment be given their narrowest meaning or that the lawmaker's evident intent be disregarded. *United States v. Corbett*, 215 U.S. 233, 242, 30 S.Ct. 81, 54 L.Ed. 173. Here the purpose to insure the correctness of bank records by prescribing punishment for any employee who, with intent to deceive, etc., deliberately brings about their falsification is plain enough. The statute denounces as criminal one who with intent, etc., 'makes any false entry.' The word 'make' has many meanings, among them 'To cause to exist, appear or occur,' Webster's International Dictionary, (2d Ed.). To hold the statute broad enough to include deliberate action from which a false entry by an innocent intermediary necessarily follows gives to the words employed their fair meaning and is in accord with the evident intent of Congress. To hold that it applies only when the accused personally writes the false entry or affirmatively directs another so to do would emasculate the statute—defeat the very end in view.

Morse v. United States, 174 F. 539, 547, 553, 20 Ann.Cas. 938—Circuit Court of Appeals, Second Circuit—gave much consideration to an indictment and conviction under R.S. § 5209. The court said: 'It is true that the defendant did not make any of the entries in the books or reports with his own pen. All of them were made by the employees of the bank as part of their routine work. If it were necessary to prove against a director that he actually made the entry charged to be false, conviction under the statute would be impossible, as these entries are invariably made by subordinates in the executive department. Congress was not seeking to punish the ignorant bookkeeper who copies items into the books as part of his daily task, but the officers who conceived and carried out the fraudulent scheme which the false entry was designed to conceal. It is wholly immaterial whether such officer acts through a pen or a clerk controlled by him.' It seems to us that defendant is as fully responsible for any false entries which necessarily result from the presentation of these pieces of paper which he caused to be prepared as he would if he had given oral instructions in reference to them or had written them himself.'

We agree with the view so expressed in that opinion. *United States v. McClarty* (D.C.) 191 F. 518 and 523, apparently is in conflict with our conclusion.

The record leaves us in no doubt that the false entries on the ledger were the intended and necessary result of respondent's deliberate action in withholding the deposit tickets. Within the statute he made them.

The judgment of the Circuit Court of Appeals must be reversed. The District Court will be affirmed.

Reversed.

Notes and Questions

How could the principle of strict construction not control here, especially given that several judges thought that the defendant was not guilty? Why was the defendant not charged with theft? Assuming it is also a crime to steal from a national bank, what do you make of the fact that there are two statutes potentially covering what the defendant did?

United States v. Campos-Serrano

Supreme Court of the United States
404 U.S. 293, 92 S.Ct. 471, 30 L.Ed.2d 457 (1971)

Mr. Justice STEWART delivered the opinion of the Court.

The respondent was convicted in a federal district court of possession of a counterfeit alien registration receipt card in violation of 18 U.S.C. § 1546,[1] and sentenced to a three-year prison term. The Court of Appeals reversed the conviction, 430 F.2d 173, holding that because of the circumstances under which Government agents had acquired the card from the respondent, it had been unconstitutionally admitted against him at the trial under *Miranda v. Arizona*, 384 U.S. 436, 86 S.Ct. 1602, 16 L.Ed.2d 694. We granted certiorari. 401 U.S. 936, 91 S.Ct. 926, 28 L.Ed.2d 215. We do not reach the constitutional issue, however, for we have concluded that the judgment of the Court of Appeals must be affirmed upon a discrete statutory ground. *See Ashwander v. Tennessee Valley Authority*, 297 U.S. 288, 347, 56 S.Ct. 466, 483, 80 L.Ed. 688 (Brandeis, J., concurring).[3] We hold that possession of a counterfeit alien registration receipt card is not an act punishable under 18 U.S.C. § 1546.

The statutory provision in question prohibits, inter alia, the counterfeiting or alteration of, or the possession, use, or receipt of an already counterfeited or altered 'immigrant or nonimmigrant visa, permit, or other document required for entry into the United States.' This offense originated in Section 22(a) of the Immigration Act of 1924, which covered only an 'immigration visa or permit.' The words 'other document required for entry into the United States,' were added in 1952 as part of the Immigrant and Nationality Act. § 402(a), 66 Stat. 275. The legislative history of the 1952 Act, however, does not make clear which 'other' entry documents the Congress had in mind.

Alien registration receipt cards were first issued in 1941. They are small, simple cards containing the alien's picture and basic identification information. They have no function whatsoever in facilitating the initial entry into the United

---

1   The applicable portion of § 1546 reads as follows:

'Whoever . . . knowingly forges, counterfeits, alters, or falsely makes any immigrant or nonimmigrant visa, permit, or other document required for entry into the United States, or utters, uses, attempts to use, possesses, obtains, accepts, or receives any such visa, permit, or document, knowing it to be forged, counterfeited, altered, or falsely made, or to have been procured by means of any false claim or statement, or to have been otherwise procured by fraud or unlawful obtained . . . . 'Shall be fined not more than $2,000 or imprisoned not more than five years, or both.'

3   'The Court will not pass upon a constitutional question although properly presented by the record, if there is also present some other ground upon which the case may be disposed of.'

States. Rather, they are issued after an alien has entered the country and taken up residence. Their essential purpose is to effectuate the registration requirement for all resident aliens established in the Alien Registration Act of 1940.

Until 1952, alien registration receipt cards could not even be used to facilitate re-entry into the United States by a resident alien who had left temporarily. Such an alien was required to obtain special documents authorizing his re-entry into the country, such as a visa or a re-entry permit. However, in 1952—less than a month before final enactment of the Immigration and Nationality Act—the Immigration and Naturalization Service promulgated a regulation that allowed resident aliens to use their registration receipt cards for re-entry purposes as a permissible substitute for the specialized documents. The apparent reason for this regulation was to minimize paper work and streamline administrative procedures by giving resident aliens the option of using for re-entry a document already issued and serving other purposes. Thus, the registration receipt cards may now be used in lieu of a visa or a re-entry permit on condition that the holder is returning to the United States after a temporary absence of not more than one year.

The Court of Appeals held that the limited, merely permissible, re-entry function of the alien registration receipt card is sufficient to make it a 'document required for entry into the United States' under § 1546. 430 F.2d, at 175. We cannot agree. It has long been settled that 'penal statutes are to be construed strictly,' *Federal Communications Comm'n v. American Broadcasting Co.*, 347 U.S. 284, 296, 74 S.Ct. 593, 601, 98 L.Ed. 699, and that one 'is not to be subjected to a penalty unless the words of the statute plainly impose it,' *Keppel v. Tiffin Savings Bank*, 197 U.S. 356, 362, 25 S.Ct. 443, 445, 49 L.Ed. 790. '(W)hen choice has to be made between two readings of what conduct Congress has made a crime, it is appropriate, before we choose the harsher alternative, to require that Congress should have spoken in language that is clear and definite.' *United States v. Universal C.I.T. Credit Corp.*, 344 U.S. 218, 221—222, 73 S.Ct. 227, 229, 97 L.Ed. 260. In § 1546, Congress did speak in 'clear and definite' language. But, taken literally and given its plain and ordinary meaning, that language does not impose a criminal penalty for possession of a counterfeited alien registration receipt card. Alien registration receipt cards may be used for re-entry by certain persons into the United States. They are not required for entry.

The canon of strict construction of criminal statutes, of course, 'does not mean that every criminal statute must be given the narrowest possible meaning in complete disregard of the purpose of the legislature.' *United States v. Bramblett*, 348 U.S. 503, 510, 75 S.Ct. 504, 508, 99 L.Ed. 594. If an absolutely literal reading of a statutory provision is irreconcilably at war with the clear congressional purpose, a less literal construction must be considered. In this spirit, we read s 1546 in conjunction with 8 U.S.C. § 1101(a)(13)—another part of the 1952 Immigration and Nationality Act—which provides that, under most circumstances, an 'entry' into the United States is defined to include a 're-entry.' We have held in the past that Congress did not intend these terms to be taken entirely synonymously. *Rosenberg v. Fleuti*, 374 U.S. 449, 83 S.Ct. 1804, 10 L.Ed.2d 1000. But Congress clearly did intend a significant overlap, and we cannot say that a document usable for 'entry' into the United States under § 1546 does not include some documents usable for 're-entry.' Nor do we hold that § 1546 applies only to those documents absolutely 'required' in order to enter or re-entry the country. To do so would undermine the congressional purpose behind § 1546, since the Immigration and Naturalization Service has not required that presentation of any one particular document be the exclusive condition of crossing our borders.

While the apparent congressional purpose underlying § 1546 would thus seem to bar an uncompromisingly literal construction, the precise language of the provision must not be deprived of all force. The principle of strict construction of criminal statutes demands that some determinate limits be established based upon the actual words of the statute. Accordingly, a 'document required for entry into the United States' cannot be construed to include any document whatsoever that the Immigration and Naturalization Service, from time to time, decides may be presented for re-entry at the border. The language of § 1546 denotes a very special class of 'entry' documents—documents whose primary raison d'etre is the facilitation of entry into the country. The phrase, 'required for entry into the United States,' is descriptive of the nature of the documents; it is not simply a open-ended reference to future administrative regulations.

If, for example, the Immigration and Naturalization Service were to allow the presentation of identification such as a driver's license at the border, the nature of such a license would not suddenly change so that it would fall into the category of a 'document required for entry into the United States' under § 1546. To be sure, if a counterfeit driver's license were presented to secure entry or re-entry into the country, the bearer could be prosecuted under 8 U.S.C. § 1325, which provides for the punishment of '(a)ny alien who . . . obtains entry to the United States by a willfully false or misleading representation . . . .' But mere possession of a counterfeit driver's license, far from the border, could not be prosecuted under § 1546. The reason is that a driver's license is not essentially an 'entry' document. Rather, its primary purpose is to allow its bearer lawfully to drive a car, and the bearer's possession of a counterfeit license, far from the border, could not be assumed to be related to the policies underlying the 1952 Immigration and Nationality Act.

The same analysis applies to the alien registration receipt card. Its essential purpose is not to secure entry into the United States, but to identify the bearer as a lawfully registered alien residing in the United States. It is issued to an alien after he has taken up residence in this country. It is intended to govern his activities and presence within this country. The card has been given a convenient, additional function as a permissible substitute for a visa or re-entry permit in facilitating reentry into the United States by a resident alien. But, unlike a visa or a re-entry permit,[12] an alien registration receipt card serves this function in only a secondary way. Unlike a visa or a re-entry permit, it is not, by its nature, a 'document required for entry into the United States' under § 1546.

This construction of the language of § 1546 is conclusively supported by that section's statutory context. In the 1952 Immigration and Nationality Act, Congress clearly regarded alien registration receipt cards as serving policies separate and distinct from those served by pure 'entry' documents. Although, in 1952, those cards could be used as substitutes for visas or re-entry permits, the Congress chose to deal with them separately. In 8 U.S.C. § 1306(c) and § 1306(d), it specifically provided for the punishment of one 'who procures or attempts to procure registration of himself or another person through fraud' and of one who counterfeits an alien registration receipt card. The fact that the Congress did not rely on § 1546 to ensure the integrity of alien registration receipt cards indicates that it did not believe that they were covered by that section. Moreover, there is a very specific overlap between § 1546 and § 1306. Both sections explicitly prohibit counterfeiting, and both explicitly prohibit fraud in the acquisition of documents.[13] Unless we assume that § 1306 is mere surplusage, we must conclude

---

12   Visas and re-entry permits are the specialized 'entry' documents for which the alien registration receipt card is a permissible substitute under present INS regulations. *See* n. 10, *supra*. Border-crossing identification cards are like visas and re-entry permits, and unlike alien registration receipt cards, in that they are specialized documents whose sole purpose and function is to regulate the crossing of our national borders. Hence, the likelihood that Congress in 1952 wished to expand the coverage of § 1546 to reach border-crossing identification cards, see n. 6, *supra*, supports our holding. The expansion mandated by Congress was simply within the class of specialized 'entry' documents.

13   The prohibition of counterfeiting in § 1546 is contained in the first paragraph of that section. *See* n. 1, *supra*. The prohibition of fraud in the acquisition of documents is contained in the third paragraph of § 1546, which reads as follows:

> 'Whoever, when applying for an immigrant or nonimmigrant visa, permit, or other document required for entry into the United States, or for admission to the United States personates another, or falsely appears in the name of a deceased individual, or evades or attempts to evade the immigration laws by appearing under an assumed or fictitious name without disclosing his true identity . . . .

> 'Shall be fined not more than $2,000 or imprisoned not more than five years, or both.'

that § 1546 covers only specialized 'entry' documents, and not alien registration receipt cards specifically covered in § 1306.[14]

For these reasons the judgment is affirmed.

Affirmed.

Mr. Justice BLACKMUN, with whom THE CHIEF JUSTICE and Mr. Justice WHITE join, dissenting.

The Court today affirms the judgment of the Court of Appeals 'upon a discrete statutory ground' and does not reach the questions with respect to which certiorari was granted. This statutory ground was rejected by the District Court when it denied a defense motion to dismiss the indictment. It was also rejected by the Court of Appeals. 430 F.2d 173, at 175—176. I would reject it here.

The statutory issue to which the Court retreats is whether an alien registration card is a 'document required for entry into the United States,' within the meaning of 18 U.S.C. § 1546. The Court holds, somewhat to the surprise of the litigants I am sure, that the card is not such a document, and that Campos-Serrano's indictment, therefore, charged no offense under the statute. I feel that this conclusion has no support either in the statutory language and meaning or in the legislative history, and is certainly not supported by the practice, long in effect, at our Nation's borders.

I

The parent of § 1546 is § 22(a) of the Immigration Act of 1924. 43 Stat. 165. That statute did not refer to 'any immigrant or nonimmigrant visa, permit, or other document required for entry into the United States,' as § 1546 does today. Instead, it spoke only of 'any immigrant visa or permit.' Nevertheless, even under the definition of 'permit' in this order and narrower statute, Congress specifically included a temporary re-entry paper issued to and used by a resident alien who wished to leave the country for a period of less than one year. Clearly, therefore, the statutory scheme, as far back as 1924, contemplated that knowing possession of an altered document useful only for reentering the United States was punishable as a felony.

The registration card came into being with Title III of the Alien Registration Act of 1940, 54 Stat. 673. At first it served only for identification of the alien who had complied with the registration requirements. Section 30 of the 1940 Act, however, authorized the use of a separate 'border-crossing identification card'

---

14 "(A) statute ought, upon the whole, to be so construed that, if it can be prevented, no clause, sentence, or word shall be superfluous, void, or insignificant." *Market Co. v. Hoffman*, 101 U.S. 112, 115—116, 25 L.Ed. 782. *See Jarecki v. G. D. Searle & Co.*, 367 U.S. 303, 307—308, 81 S.Ct. 1579, 1582, 6 L.Ed.2d 859. To be sure, the overlap between § 1546 and § 1306 is only partial, since § 1546 goes farther than § 1306—prohibiting the possession of counterfeit documents as well as the counterfeiting of documents. But the Congress would hardly have thought it necessary to create any overlap at all, if it had believed alien registration receipt cards were covered by § 1546.

by a resident alien in order to enable him to return to the United States after temporary travel to a contiguous country.

An INS regulation filed May 29, 1952, provided that a registration card, issued on or after September 10, 1946, 'shall constitute a resident alien's border crossing card' and could be used by the alien in effecting re-entry into the United States provided he had not visited any foreign territory other than Canada or Mexico. 17 Fed.Reg. 4921—4922. This was the first time a registration card, as such, was recognized as a re-entry document. But it was so recognized. Five years later its use was expanded with respect to re-entry from nations that were not contiguous. 22 Fed.Reg. 6377 (1957). Its use for this purpose has continued to the present time. 8 CFR § 211.1(b) (1971).

In addition to this administrative practice, the statutory language itself was expanded. Section 22(a) of the 1924 Act was repealed in 1948 and simultaneously re-enacted without significant change as 18 U.S.C. § 1546 and as part of that year's general recodification of the federal criminal laws. 62 Stat. 771, 865. Finally, § 1546 was amended to its present form by § 402(a) of the Immigration and Nationality Act of 1952. 66 Stat. 275.

There is no room for dispute that the 1952 change served to broaden, not to contract, the number of documents within the prohibition of § 1546. The 1924 reference to 'any immigration visa or permit' is obviously but a lesser part of the later and still current phrase, 'any immigrant or nonimmigrant visa, permit, or other document required for entry.' *See United States v. Rodriguez*, 182 F.Supp. 479, 484 n. 3 (SD Cal.1960), rev'd in part on other grounds, sub nom. *Rocha v. United States*, 288 F.2d 545 (CA9), cert. denied, 366 U.S. 948, 81 S.Ct. 1902, 6 L.Ed.2d 1241 (1961). From 1924 until the 1952 legislation, narrower statutory language nevertheless had covered a document used solely for re-entry. Surely nothing in the expanded language of 1952 suggests congressional intent thenceforth to confine the statute to initial-entry documents. Indeed, congressional intent to the contrary, that is, to enlarge the coverage of § 1546, is evident not only from the statute's words but, as well, from the definition of 'entry' in the 1952 Act, § 101(a)(13), 66 Stat. 167, 8 U.S.C. § 1101(a)(13):

> 'The term 'entry' means any coming of an alien into the United States, from a foreign port or place or from an outlying possession, whether voluntarily or otherwise, except . . . .' (Emphasis supplied.)

From this it inevitably follows that the phrase 'document required for entry' embraces a document used for re-entry into the United States. One document of that kind is the alien registration card.[3]

---

3   The face of the card, Form I—151, bears the recital, 'This card will be honored in lieu of a visa and passport on condition that the rightful holder is returning to the United States after a temporary absence of not more than one year and is not subject to exclusion under any provision of the immigration laws.'

This brief but clear administrative and legislative history, it seems to me, reveals and proves the intent of Congress and the meaning and reach of the statute. The alien registration card, Form I—151, became one of a number of documents specified and accepted and required for re-entry.

The Court's opinion, as I read it, seems to accept most of all this, that is, that there is no § 1546 distinction between 'entry' and 're-entry,' and that an alien registration card is a document 'required' for entry into the United States. *Ante*, at 475.

Having made this broad and, to me, sensible reading of § 1546, the Court, however, then reverses direction and conveniently restricts § 1546 to 'a very special class of 'entry' documents—documents whose primary raison d'etre is the facilitation of entry into the country,' and it accuses the INS of standing to gain 'an open-ended reference to future administrative regulations' if the Government were to prevail here. The reasons for this change of direction are not apparent to me. The Court's comparison of the registration card to a driver's license in this context is wide of the mark. A driver's license has nothing to do with immigration. A registration card has everything to do with immigration. It is authorized under the immigration statutes. It is required of a resident alien. 8 U.S.C. §§ 1301—1306. And for almost two decades it has been a re-entry document.

II

The fact that there may be some overlapping between § 1546 and 8 U.S.C. § 1306(d) does not prevent the application of § 1546 to the alien registration card. Section 1306(d) came into being as § 266(d) of the 1952 Act, 66 Stat. 226. It does refer specifically to 'an alien registration receipt card,' whereas § 1546 has no such specific reference. The two sections, however, have different purposes and relate to different aspects of immigration. Section 266(d) was a part of the Act's chapter that concerned 'Registration of Aliens.' It has to do with the implementation and protection of the alien registration scheme. It reached counterfeiting alone. Section 1546, on the other hand, is concerned with entry into the country and with the integrity of documents used in effecting entry. It is not restricted to counterfeiting. It also reaches knowing possession and alternation. The Court's exclusion of the alien registration card from the reach of § 1546 leaves entirely free from punishment the alteration of a card and the possession of a card with knowledge of its altered or counterfeit character. Surely Congress did not intend to leave that loophole.[5]

---

5   The loophole is not closed by 8 U.S.C. § 1325, as the respondent would assert. Section 1325 concerns a very different offense, namely, the actual misuse of the entry document in obtaining entry to the United States. Section 1546, on the other hand, relates to potential misuse of the entry document after gaining entry to the country.

I therefore dissent from the Court's affirmance of the judgment of the Court of Appeals upon the 'discrete statutory ground.' I would decide that issue as the Court of Appeals decided it and I would go on to reach the questions we anticipated when we granted the petition for certiorari.

Notes and Questions

1. Why does strict construction control here, when it failed in *Giles*?

2. The issue Court wanted to avoid, whether *Miranda* violations could lead to the suppression of tangible objects, was ultimately answered in the negative. *See Oregon v. Elstead*, 470 U.S. 298, 105 S. Ct. 1285 (1985). What does this case tell you about the number of issues you should raise?

Begay v. United States

Supreme Court of the United States
553 U.S. 137 (2008)

Justice BREYER delivered the opinion of the Court.

The Armed Career Criminal Act imposes a special mandatory 15–year prison term upon felons who unlawfully possess a firearm and who also have three or more previous convictions for committing certain drug crimes or "violent felon[ies]." 18 U.S.C. § 924(e)(1) (2000 ed., Supp. V). The question in this case is whether driving under the influence of alcohol is a "violent felony" as the Act defines it. We conclude that it is not.

I

A

Federal law prohibits a previously convicted felon from possessing a firearm. § 922(g)(1) (2000 ed.). A related provision provides for a prison term of up to 10 years for an ordinary offender. § 924(a)(2). The Armed Career Criminal Act imposes a more stringent 15–year mandatory minimum sentence on an offender who has three prior convictions "for a violent felony or a serious drug offense." § 924(e)(1) (2000 ed., Supp. V).

The Act defines a "violent felony" as "any crime punishable by imprisonment for a term exceeding one year" that

"(i) has as an element the use, attempted use, or threatened use of physical force against the person of another; or

"(ii) is burglary, arson, or extortion, involves use of explosives, or otherwise involves conduct that presents a serious potential risk of physical injury to another." § 924(e)(2)(B) (2000 ed.).

We here consider whether driving under the influence of alcohol (DUI), as set forth in New Mexico's criminal statutes, falls within the scope of the second clause.

B

The relevant background circumstances include the following: In September 2004, New Mexico police officers received a report that Larry Begay, the petitioner here, had threatened his sister and aunt with a rifle. The police arrested him. Begay subsequently conceded he was a felon and pleaded guilty to a federal charge of unlawful possession of a firearm in violation of § 922(g)(1). Begay's presentence report said that he had been convicted a dozen times for DUI, which under New Mexico's law, becomes a felony (punishable by a prison term of more than one year) the fourth (or subsequent) time an individual commits it. *See* N.M. Stat. Ann. §§ 66–8–102(G) to (J) (Supp.2007). The sentencing judge consequently found that Begay had at least three prior convictions for a crime "punishable by imprisonment for a term exceeding one year." 377 F.Supp.2d 1141, 1143 (NM 2005). The judge also concluded that Begay's "three felony DUI convictions involve conduct that presents a serious potential risk of physical injury to another." *Id.*, at 1145. The judge consequently concluded that Begay had three or more prior convictions for a "violent felony" and should receive a sentence that reflected a mandatory minimum prison term of 15 years. *Ibid.*

Begay, claiming that DUI is not a "violent felony" within the terms of the statute, appealed. The Court of Appeals panel by a vote of 2 to 1 rejected that claim. 470 F.3d 964 (C.A.10 2006). Begay sought certiorari, and we agreed to decide the question.

II

A

New Mexico's DUI statute makes it a crime (and a felony after three earlier convictions) to "drive a vehicle within [the] state" if the driver "is under the influence of intoxicating liquor" (or has an alcohol concentration of .08 or more in his blood or breath within three hours of having driven the vehicle resulting from "alcohol consumed before or while driving the vehicle"). §§ 66–8–102(A), (C). In determining whether this crime is a violent felony, we consider the offense generically, that is to say, we examine it in terms of how the law defines the offense and not in terms of how an individual offender might have committed it on a particular occasion. *See Taylor v. United States*, 495 U.S. 575, 602, 110 S.Ct. 2143, 109 L.Ed.2d 607 (1990) (adopting this "categorical approach"); *see also James v. United States*, 550 U.S. 192, 208-209, 127 S.Ct. 1586, 1597, 167 L.Ed.2d 532 (2007) (attempted burglary is a violent felony even if, on *some* occasions, it can be committed in a way that poses no serious risk of physical harm).

We also take as a given that DUI does not fall within the scope of the Act's *clause (i)* "violent felony" definition. DUI, as New Mexico defines it, nowhere "has as an element the use, attempted use, or threatened use of physical force against the person of another." 18 U.S.C. § 924(e)(2)(B)(i).

Finally, we assume that the lower courts were right in concluding that DUI involves conduct that "presents a serious potential risk of physical injury to another." § 924(e)(2)(B)(ii). Drunk driving is an extremely dangerous crime. In the United States in 2006, alcohol-related motor vehicle crashes claimed the lives of more than 17,000 individuals and harmed untold amounts of property. National Highway Traffic Safety Admin., *Traffic Safety Facts*, 2006 Traffic Safety Annual Assessment—Alcohol–Related Fatalities 1 (No. 810821, Aug. 2007), http://www-nrd.nhtsa.dot.gov/Pubs/810821.PDF (as visited Apr. 11, 2008, and available in Clerk of Court's case file). Even so, we find that DUI falls outside the scope of clause (ii). It is simply too unlike the provision's listed examples for us to believe that Congress intended the provision to cover it.

B

1

In our view, the provision's listed examples—burglary, arson, extortion, or crimes involving the use of explosives—illustrate the kinds of crimes that fall within the statute's scope. Their presence indicates that the statute covers only *similar* crimes, rather than *every* crime that "presents a serious potential risk of physical injury to another." § 924(e)(2)(B)(ii). If Congress meant the latter, *i.e.*, if it meant the statute to be all-encompassing, it is hard to see why it would have needed to include the examples at all. Without them, clause (ii) would cover *all* crimes that present a "serious potential risk of physical injury." *Ibid.* Additionally, if Congress meant clause (ii) to include *all* risky crimes, why would it have included clause (i)? A crime which has as an element the "use, attempted use, or threatened use of physical force" against the person (as clause (i) specifies) is likely to create "a serious potential risk of physical injury" and would seem to fall within the scope of clause (ii).

Of course, Congress *might* have included the examples solely for quantitative purposes. Congress might have intended them to demonstrate no more than the degree of risk sufficient to bring a crime within the statute's scope. But were that the case, Congress would have likely chosen examples that better illustrated the "degree of risk" it had in mind. Our recent case, *James v. United States*—where we considered only matters of degree, *i.e.*, whether the amount of risk posed by attempted burglary was comparable to the amount of risk posed by the example crime of burglary—illustrates the difficulty of interpreting the examples in this respect. Compare 550 U.S., at 203–207, 127 S.Ct., at 1594–1597, with *id.*, at 215, 218–219, 229, 127 S.Ct., at 1601, 1603–1604, 1609 (SCALIA, J., dissenting). Indeed, the examples are so far from clear in respect to the degree of risk each poses that it is difficult to accept clarification in respect to degree of risk as Congress' only reason for including them. *See id.*, at 229, 127 S.Ct. at 1598–99 ("Congress provided examples [that] . . . have little in common, most especially with respect to the level of risk of physical injury that they pose").

These considerations taken together convince us that, "'to give effect . . . to every clause and word'" of this statute, we should read the examples as limiting the crimes that clause (ii) covers to crimes that are roughly similar, in kind as well as in degree of risk posed, to the examples themselves. *Duncan v. Walker*, 533 U.S. 167, 174, 121 S.Ct. 2120, 150 L.Ed.2d 251 (2001) (quoting *United States v. Menasche*, 348 U.S. 528, 538–539, 75 S.Ct. 513, 99 L.Ed. 615 (1955); some internal quotation marks omitted); *see also Leocal v. Ashcroft*, 543 U.S. 1, 12, 125 S.Ct. 377, 160 L.Ed.2d 271 (2004) (describing the need to interpret a statute in a way that gives meaning to each word).

The concurrence complains that our interpretive approach is insufficiently specific. *See post*, at 1589–1590 (SCALIA, J., concurring in judgment). But the concurrence's own approach demands a crime-by-crime analysis, uses a standard of measurement (comparative degree of risk) that even the concurrence admits is often "unclear," *post*, at 1590, requires the concurrence to turn here to the still less clear "rule of lenity," *post*, at 1591, and, as we explain, is less likely to reflect Congress' intent. *See, e.g., post*, at 1590–1591 (recognizing inability to measure quantitative seriousness of risks associated with DUI).

The statute's history offers further support for our conclusion that the examples in clause (ii) limit the scope of the clause to crimes that are similar to the examples themselves. Prior to the enactment of the current language, the Act applied its enhanced sentence to offenders with "three previous convictions for robbery or burglary." *Taylor*, 495 U.S., at 581, 110 S.Ct. 2143 (internal quotation marks omitted). Congress sought to expand that definition to include both crimes against the person (clause (i)) and certain physically risky crimes against property (clause (ii)). *See* H.R.Rep. No. 99–849, p. 3 (1986) (hereinafter H.R. Rep.). When doing so, Congress rejected a broad proposal that would have covered *every* offense that involved a substantial risk of the use of "'physical force against the person or property of another.'" *Taylor, supra*, at 583, 110 S.Ct. 2143 (quoting S. 2312, 99th Cong., 2d Sess. (1986); H.R. 4639, 99th Cong., 2d Sess. (1986)). Instead, it added the present examples. And in the relevant House Report, it described clause (ii) as including "State and Federal felonies against property such as burglary, arson, extortion, use of explosives and *similar* crimes as predicate offenses where the conduct involved presents a serious risk of injury to a person." H.R. Rep., at 5 (emphasis added).

Of course, the statute places the word "otherwise," just after the examples, so that the provision covers a felony that is one of the example crimes "or *otherwise* involves conduct that presents a serious potential risk of physical injury." § 924(e)(2)(B)(ii) (emphasis added). But we cannot agree with the Government that the word "otherwise" is *sufficient* to demonstrate that the examples do not limit the scope of the clause. That is because the word "otherwise" *can* (we do not say *must*, cf. *post*, at 1589–1590 (SCALIA, J., concurring in judgment)) refer to a crime that is similar to the listed examples in some respects but different in others—similar say in respect to the degree of risk it produces, but different in respect to the "way or manner" in which it produces that risk. Webster's Third New International Dictionary 1598 (1961) (defining "otherwise" to mean "in a different way or manner").

2

In our view, DUI differs from the example crimes—burglary, arson, extortion, and crimes involving the use of explosives—in at least one pertinent, and important, respect. The listed crimes all typically involve purposeful, "violent," and "aggressive" conduct. 470 F.3d, at 980 (McConnell, J., dissenting in part); see, *e.g., Taylor, supra*, at 598, 110 S.Ct. 2143 ("burglary" is an unlawful or unprivileged entry into a building or other structure with "intent to commit a crime"); ALI Model Penal Code § 220.1(1) (1985) ("arson" is causing a fire or explosion with " the purpose of," *e.g.*, "destroying a building . . . of another" or "damaging any property . . . to collect insurance"); *id.*, § 223.4 (extortion is "purposely"

obtaining property of another through threat of, *e.g.*, inflicting "bodily injury");
Leocal, supra, at 9, 125 S.Ct. 377 (the word "'use' . . . most naturally suggests a
higher degree of intent than negligent or merely accidental conduct" which fact
helps bring it outside the scope of the statutory term "crime of violence"). That
conduct is such that it makes more likely that an offender, later possessing a
gun, will use that gun deliberately to harm a victim. Crimes committed in such
a purposeful, violent, and aggressive manner are "potentially more dangerous
when firearms are involved." 470 F.3d, at 980 (McConnell, J., dissenting in part).
And such crimes are "characteristic of the armed career criminal, the eponym
of the statute." *Ibid.*

By way of contrast, statutes that forbid driving under the influence, such as
the statute before us, typically do not insist on purposeful, violent, and aggressive
conduct; rather, they are, or are most nearly comparable to, crimes that impose
strict liability, criminalizing conduct in respect to which the offender need not
have had any criminal intent at all. The Government argues that "the knowing
nature of the conduct that produces intoxication combined with the inherent
recklessness of the ensuing conduct more than suffices" to create an element of
intent. Brief for United States 35. And we agree with the Government that a drunk
driver may very well drink on purpose. But this Court has said that, unlike the
example crimes, the conduct for which the drunk driver is convicted (driving
under the influence) need not be purposeful or deliberate. *See Leocal,* 543 U.S.,
at 11, 125 S.Ct. 377 (a DUI offense involves "accidental or negligent conduct");
see also 470 F.3d, at 980 (McConnell, J., dissenting in part) ("[D]runk driving is a
crime of negligence or recklessness, rather than violence or aggression").

When viewed in terms of the Act's basic purposes, this distinction matters
considerably. As suggested by its title, the Armed Career Criminal Act focuses
upon the special danger created when a particular type of offender—a violent
criminal or drug trafficker—possesses a gun. *See Taylor, supra,* at 587–588, 110
S.Ct. 2143; 470 F.3d, at 981, n. 3 (McConnell, J., dissenting in part) ("[T]he title
[of the Act] was not merely decorative"). In order to determine which offenders
fall into this category, the Act looks to past crimes. This is because an offender's
criminal history is relevant to the question whether he is a career criminal, or,
more precisely, to the kind or degree of danger the offender would pose were he
to possess a gun.

In this respect—namely, a prior crime's relevance to the possibility of future
danger with a gun—crimes involving intentional or purposeful conduct (as
in burglary and arson) are different than DUI, a strict liability crime. In both
instances, the offender's prior crimes reveal a degree of callousness toward risk,
but in the former instance they also show an increased likelihood that the offender is the kind of person who might deliberately point the gun and pull the trig-

ger. We have no reason to believe that Congress intended a 15–year mandatory prison term where that increased likelihood does not exist.

Were we to read the statute without this distinction, its 15–year mandatory minimum sentence would apply to a host of crimes which, though dangerous, are not typically committed by those whom one normally labels "armed career criminals." See, *e.g.,* Ark.Code Ann. § 8–4–103(a)(2)(A)(ii) (2007) (reckless polluters); 33 U.S.C. § 1319(c)(1) (individuals who negligently introduce pollutants into the sewer system); 18 U.S.C. § 1365(a) (individuals who recklessly tamper with consumer products); § 1115 (seamen whose inattention to duty causes serious accidents). We have no reason to believe that Congress intended to bring within the statute's scope these kinds of crimes, far removed as they are from the deliberate kind of behavior associated with violent criminal use of firearms. The statute's use of examples (and the other considerations we have mentioned) indicate the contrary.

The dissent's approach, on the other hand, would likely include these crimes within the statutory definition of "violent felony," along with any other crime that can be said to present a "'potential risk of physical injury.'" *Post*, at 1592 (opinion of ALITO, J.). And it would do so because it believes such a result is compelled by the statute's text. *See ibid.* But the dissent's explanation does not account for a key feature of that text—namely, the four example crimes intended to illustrate what kind of "violent felony" the statute covers. The dissent at most believes that these examples are relevant only to define the requisite serious risk associated with a "crime of violence." *Post*, at 1595. But the dissent does not explain how to identify the requisite level of risk, nor does it describe how these various examples might help determine what other offenses involve conduct presenting the same level of risk. If they were in fact helpful on that score, we might expect more predictable results from a purely risk-based approach. Compare *post*, at 1588, 1591–1592 (SCALIA, J., concurring in judgment), with *post*, at 1592–1594 (dissenting opinion). Thus, the dissent's reliance on these examples for a function they appear incapable of performing reads them out of the statute and, in so doing, fails to effectuate Congress' purpose to punish only a particular subset of offender, namely, career criminals.

The distinction we make does not minimize the seriousness of the risks attached to driving under the influence. Nor does our argument deny that an individual with a criminal history of DUI might later pull the trigger of a gun. (Indeed, we may have such an instance before us. 470 F.3d, at 965.) Rather, we hold only that, for purposes of the particular statutory provision before us, a prior record of DUI, a strict liability crime, differs from a prior record of violent and aggressive crimes committed intentionally such as arson, burglary, extortion, or crimes involving the use of explosives. The latter are associated with a likelihood of future violent, aggressive, and purposeful "armed career criminal" behavior in a way that the former are not.

We consequently conclude that New Mexico's crime of "driving under the influence" falls outside the scope of the Armed Career Criminal Act's clause (ii) "violent felony" definition. And we reverse the judgment of the Court of Appeals in relevant part and remand the case for proceedings consistent with this opinion. *It is so ordered.*

Justice SCALIA, concurring in the judgment.

The statute in this case defines "violent felony" in part as "any crime punishable by imprisonment for a term exceeding one year . . . that . . . is burglary, arson, or extortion, involves the use of explosives, or otherwise involves conduct that presents a serious potential risk of physical injury to another." 18 U.S.C. § 924(e)(2)(B)(ii). Contrary to the Court, I conclude that the residual clause unambiguously encompasses *all* crimes that present a serious risk of injury to another. But because I cannot say that drunk driving clearly poses such a risk (within the meaning of the statute), the rule of lenity brings me to concur in the judgment of the Court.

* * * I can do no more than guess as to whether drunk driving poses a more serious risk than burglary, and I will not condemn a man to a minimum of 15 years in prison on the basis of such speculation. *See Ladner v. United States*, 358 U.S. 169, 178, 79 S.Ct. 209, 3 L.Ed.2d 199 (1958). Applying the rule of lenity to a statute that demands it, I would reverse the decision of the Court of Appeals.

Justice ALITO, with whom Justice SOUTER and Justice THOMAS join, dissenting.

The statutory provision at issue in this case—the so-called "residual clause" of 18 U.S.C. § 924(e)(2)(B)(ii)—calls out for legislative clarification, and I am sympathetic to the result produced by the Court's attempt to craft a narrowing construction of this provision. Unfortunately, the Court's interpretation simply cannot be reconciled with the statutory text, and I therefore respectfully dissent.

In September 2004, after a night of heavy drinking, petitioner pointed a rifle at his aunt and threatened to shoot if she did not give him money. When she replied that she did not have any money, petitioner repeatedly pulled the trigger, but the rifle was unloaded and did not fire. Petitioner then threatened his sister in a similar fashion.

At the time of this incident, petitioner was a convicted felon. He had 12 prior convictions in New Mexico for driving under the influence of alcohol (DUI). While DUI is generally a misdemeanor under New Mexico law, the offense of DUI after at least three prior DUI convictions is a felony requiring a sentence of 18 months' imprisonment. N.M. Stat. Ann. § 66–8–102(G) (Supp.2007).

Petitioner pleaded guilty to possession of a firearm by a convicted felon, in violation of 18 U.S.C. § 922(g)(1). A violation of that provision generally carries a maximum term of imprisonment of 10 years, see § 924(a)(2), but the District Court and the Court of Appeals held that petitioner was subject to a mandatory minimum sentence of 15 years because he had at least three prior convictions for the New Mexico felony of DUI after being convicted of DUI on at least three prior occasions. 377 F.Supp.2d 1141, 1143–1145 (NM 2005); 470 F.3d 964, 966–975, 977 (C.A.10 2006). The lower courts concluded that these offenses were crimes "punishable by imprisonment for a term exceeding one year" and "involve[d] conduct that present[ed] a serious potential risk of physical injury to another." 18 U.S.C. § 924(e)(2)(B).

The Court does not hold that the maximum term of imprisonment that petitioner faced on his felony DUI convictions was less than one year. Nor does the Court dispute that petitioner's offenses involved a "potential risk of physical injury to another." *Ibid.* The only remaining question, therefore, is whether the risk presented by petitioner's qualifying DUI felony convictions was "serious," *i.e.*, "significant" or "important." See, *e.g.*, Webster's Third New International Dictionary 2073 (2002) (hereinafter Webster's); 15 Oxford English Dictionary 15 (def. 6(a)) (2d ed.1989) (hereinafter OED). In my view, it was.

Statistics dramatically show that driving under the influence of alcohol is very dangerous. Each year, approximately 15,000 fatal alcohol-related crashes occur, accounting for roughly 40% of all fatal crashes. Approximately a quarter million people are injured annually in alcohol-related crashes. The number of people who are killed each year by drunk drivers is far greater than the number of murders committed during any of the crimes specifically set out in the statutory provision at issue here, § 924(e)(2)(B)(ii)—burglary, arson, extortion, and offenses involving the use of explosives.

Petitioner's qualifying offenses, moreover, fell within the statute only because he had been convicted of DUI on at least three prior occasions. As noted, petitioner had *a dozen* prior DUI convictions. Persons who repeatedly drive drunk present a greatly enhanced danger that they and others will be injured as a result. In addition, it has been estimated that the ratio of DUI incidents to DUI arrests is between 250 to 1 and 2,000 to 1. Accordingly, the risk presented by a 10th, 11th, and 12th DUI conviction may be viewed as the risk created by literally thousands of drunk-driving events. That risk was surely "serious," and therefore petitioner's offenses fell squarely within the language of the statute.

Moreover, taking the statutory language to mean what it says would not sweep in all DUI convictions. Most DUI convictions are not punishable by a term of imprisonment of more than one year and thus fall outside the scope of the statute. Petitioner's convictions qualified only because of his extraordinary—and, I would say, extraordinarily dangerous—record of drunk driving.

The Court holds that an offense does not fall within the residual clause unless it is "roughly similar, in kind as well as in degree of risked posed," *ante*, at 1585, to the crimes specifically listed in 18 U.S.C. § 924(e)(2)(B), *i.e.*, burglary, extortion, arson, and crimes involving the use of explosives. These crimes, according to the Court, "all typically involve purposeful, 'violent,' and 'aggressive' conduct." *Ante*, at 1586 (quoting 470 F.3d, at 980 (McConnell, J., dissenting)).

This interpretation cannot be squared with the text of the statute, which simply does not provide that an offense must be "purposeful," "violent," or "aggressive" in order to fall within the residual clause. Rather, after listing burglary, arson, extortion, and explosives offenses, the statute provides (in the residual clause) that an offense qualifies if it "otherwise involves conduct that presents a serious potential risk of physical injury to another." Therefore, offenses falling within the residual clause must be similar to the named offenses in one respect only: They must "otherwise"—which is to say, "in a different manner," 10 OED 984 (def. B(1)); *see also* Webster's 1598—"involv[e] conduct that presents a serious potential risk of physical injury to another." Requiring that an offense must also be "purposeful," "violent," or "aggressive" amounts to adding new elements to the statute, but we "ordinarily resist reading words or elements into a statute that do not appear on its face." *Bates v. United States*, 522 U.S. 23, 29, 118 S.Ct. 285, 139 L.Ed.2d 215 (1997).

Each part of this additional, judicially added requirement presents other problems as well.

Purposeful. At least one State's DUI law requires proof of purposeful conduct. *See Tam v. State*, 232 Ga.App. 15, 15-16, 501 S.E.2d 51, 52 (1998) (requiring proof of the intent to drive). In addition, many States recognize involuntary intoxication as a defense. *See* 4 R. Essen & R. Erwin, Defense of Drunk Driving Cases: Criminal—Civil § 44.04 (2007). And even in States that do not require purposefulness, I have no doubt that the overwhelming majority of DUI defendants purposefully drank before getting behind the wheel and were purposefully operating their vehicles at the time of apprehension. I suspect that many DUI statutes do not require proof of purposefulness because the element is almost always present, requiring proof of the element would introduce an unnecessary complication, and it would make no sense to preclude conviction of those defendants who were so drunk that they did not even realize that they were behind the wheel.

Violent. It is clear that 18 U.S.C. § 924(e)(2)(B) is not limited to "violent" crimes, for if it were, it would be redundant. The prior subparagraph, § 924(e)(2)(A), includes offenses that have as an element the use or threatened use of violence.

Aggressive. The concept of "aggressive" crimes is vague, and in any event, it is hardly apparent why DUI—not to mention the species of felony DUI recidivism that resulted in petitioner's predicament—is not "aggressive." Driving can certainly involve "aggressive" conduct. Indeed, some States have created the offense of "aggressive driving." *See* M. Savage, M. Sundeen, & A. Teigen, *Transportation Series, Traffic Safety and Public Health: State Legislative Action 2007,* p. 17, and App. J,(NCSL, No. 32, Dec. 2007), online at http://www. ncsl. org/print/transportation/07trafficsafety.pdf. Most States have a toll-free telephone number to call to report "aggressive" driving. *See Campaign Safe & Sober, Phone Numbers for Reporting Impaired, Aggressive, or Unsafe Driving,* online at http://www.nhtsa.dot.gov/people/outreach/safesobr/16 qp/phone.html.

The Court defends its new statutory element on the ground that a defendant who merely engages in felony drunk driving is not likely to be "the kind of person who might deliberately point the gun and pull the trigger." *Ante,* at 1587. The Court cites no empirical support for this conclusion, and its accuracy is not self-evident. Petitioner's pattern of behavior may or may not be typical of those defendants who have enough DUI convictions to qualify under N.M. Stat. Ann. § 66–8–102(G) and 18 U.S.C. § 924(e)(2)(B), but the example of his behavior in this case—pointing a gun at his aunt's head and repeatedly pulling the trigger—should surely be enough to counsel against uncritical reliance on stereotypes about "the type" of people who commit felony DUI violations.

Defendants who qualify for an enhanced sentence under § 924(e) (2000 ed. and Supp. V) based (in whole or in part) on felony DUI convictions share at least three characteristics that are relevant for present purposes. First, they are persons who, in the judgment of Congress, cannot be trusted to use a firearm responsibly. In order to qualify for an enhanced sentence under § 924(e), a defendant must of course be convicted of violating the felon-in-possession statute, § 922(g) (2000 ed.). The felon-in-possession statute necessarily rests on the judgment that a person with a prior felony conviction cannot be trusted with a firearm. *See Caron v. United States,* 524 U.S. 308, 315, 118 S.Ct. 2007, 141 L.Ed.2d 303 (1998) ("Congress meant to keep guns away from all offenders who, the Federal Government feared, might cause harm . . ."). And there is no dispute that a prior felony DUI conviction qualifies as a felony under the felon-in-possession law. If Congress thought that a person with a prior felony DUI conviction is not "the kind of person" who is likely to use a gun unlawfully, why would Congress have made it a crime for such a person to possess a gun?

Second, defendants with DUI convictions that are counted under 18 U.S.C. § 924(e)(2)(B) are likely to have serious alcohol abuse problems. As previously mentioned, ordinary DUI convictions are generally not counted under § 924(e) because they are not punishable by imprisonment for more than a year. Such penalties are generally reserved for persons, like petitioner, with a record of repeated DUI violations. *See* National Conference of State Legislatures, *supra*. Such individuals are very likely to have serious alcohol abuse problems and a propensity to engage in irresponsible conduct while under the influence. Alcohol use often precedes violent crimes, see, *e.g.*, Roizen, *Epidemiological Issues in Alcohol–Related Violence, in 13 Recent Developments in Alcoholism 7*, 8–9 (M. Galanter ed.1997), and thus there is reason to worry about the misuse of firearms by defendants whose alcohol abuse problems are serious enough to result in felony DUI convictions.

Third, defendants with DUI convictions that are counted under § 924(e)(2)(B) have either (1) such serious alcohol abuse problems that they have at least three prior felony DUI convictions or (2) both one or two felony DUI convictions and one or two offenses that fall under § 924(e)(2)(B)(i) (offenses that have "as an element the use, attempted use, or threatened use of physical force") or that are specifically set out in § 924(e)(2)(B)(ii) (burglary, arson, extortion, or an explosives offense). Defendants with three felony DUI convictions are likely to be super-DUI-recidivists like petitioner. Defendants with a combination of felony DUI and other qualifying convictions—for example, convictions for assault or burglary—are persons who, even by the Court's lights, could be classified as "the kind of person who might deliberately point [a] gun and pull the trigger."

Unlike the Court, I cannot say that persons with these characteristics are less likely to use a gun illegally than are persons convicted of other qualifying felonies.

Justice SCALIA's concurrence takes a different approach, but his analysis is likewise flawed. Justice SCALIA would hold (1) that an offense does not fall within the residual clause unless it presents a risk that is at least as great as that presented by the least dangerous of the enumerated offenses; (2) that burglary is the least dangerous of the enumerated offenses; (3) that the relevant measure of risk is the risk that the typical burglary, DUI, etc. would result in injury; and (4) that the risk presented by an incident of DUI is less than the risk presented by a burglary.

Justice SCALIA, like the Court, does not follow the statutory language. The statute says that offenses falling within the residual clause must present "a serious potential risk of physical injury to another." The statute does not say that these offenses must present at least as much risk as the enumerated offenses.

The statute also does not say, as Justice SCALIA would hold, that the relevant risk is the risk that each incident of DUI will result in injury. I see no basis for concluding that Congress was not also concerned with the risk faced by potential victims, particularly since the statute explicitly refers to "potential risk." Drunk driving is regarded as a severe societal problem in large measure because of the very large number of victims it produces each year.

Finally, Justice SCALIA's conclusion that burglary is the least risky of the enumerated offenses is based on a procrustean reading of § 924(e)(2)(B)(ii). This provision refers, without qualification, to "extortion." In his dissent in *James v. United States*, 550 U.S. 192, 127 S.Ct. 1586 (2007), Justice SCALIA concluded that many forms of extortion are "inherently *unlikely* to cause physical harm." *Id.*, at 223, 127 S.Ct., at 1594–95 (emphasis in original). Only by finding that the term "extortion" in § 924(e)(2)(B)(ii) really means only certain forms of extortion was Justice SCALIA able to come to the conclusion that burglary is the least risky of the enumerated offenses.

For all these reasons, I would affirm the decision of the Tenth Circuit.

———————

B. Legislative History

18 U.S.C. § 228 provides:

(a) Offense.— Any person who—

(1) willfully fails to pay a support obligation with respect to a child who resides in another State, if such obligation has remained unpaid for a period longer than 1 year, or is greater than $5,000;

(2) travels in interstate or foreign commerce with the intent to evade a support obligation, if such obligation has remained unpaid for a period longer than 1 year, or is greater than $5,000; or

(3) willfully fails to pay a support obligation with respect to a child who resides in another State, if such obligation has remained unpaid for a period longer than 2 years, or is greater than $10,000;

shall be punished as provided in [18 U.S.C. § 228(c)].

(b) Presumption.— The existence of a support obligation that was in effect for the time period charged in the indictment or information creates a rebuttable presumption that the obligor has the ability to pay the support obligation for that time period.

United States v. Kramer

United States Court of Appeals, Seventh Circuit
225 F.3d 847 (2000)

RIPPLE, Circuit Judge.

Robert Herbert Kramer was found guilty of the willful failure to pay a past due child support obligation in violation of the Child Support Recovery Act ("CSRA"), 18 U.S.C. § 228. On appeal, Mr. Kramer claims that he did not receive service of process in the state action seeking the child support order and that his federal conviction based on his noncompliance with that state order is therefore invalid. For the reasons set forth in the following opinion, we reverse Mr. Kramer's conviction and remand to the district court for further proceedings consistent with this opinion.

I

BACKGROUND

A.

Mr. Kramer, while a resident of Minnesota, worked as an over-the-road truck driver for Mayflower Van Lines, Inc. ("Mayflower"). In January 1980, when he first started working for Mayflower, he attended three weeks of training sessions in Indianapolis, Indiana. While in Indianapolis, he had a brief sexual relationship with Janice Jacobs, a resident of Indiana. By January 30, at the latest, Mr. Kramer left Indiana to return to Minnesota. On November 25, 1980, Ms. Jacobs gave birth to a son, and she claims that Mr. Kramer is the father. When the child was born, Mr. Kramer received a call from his dispatcher, telling him that he was a father.

In late 1982, Jacobs informed Mr. Kramer that she intended to file a paternity suit against him. She then filed a paternity action in the Marion County Circuit Court of Indiana. Mr. Kramer never appeared at any of the proceedings; Mr. Kramer submits that he never received either formal service of process or informal notification of the paternity proceedings. The state court file does not show that process was served, and neither party asserts that Mr. Kramer received service of process. In December 1982, the Indiana court established Mr. Kramer's paternity by default and directed him to pay $25 per week in child support.

Mr. Kramer insists that he first learned of the Indiana child support order in the fall of 1990. At that time, Mayflower informed him that an Indiana court had ordered it to withhold $50 from each two-week paycheck. This was required, Mayflower told Mr. Kramer, because of an outstanding child support order. Due to the attachment of his wages, Mr. Kramer hired an attorney to contest the default judgment establishing his paternity. Mr. Kramer failed to appear at his hearing dates, and his attorney eventually withdrew from representing him. After his attorney's withdrawal from representation, Mr. Kramer did not pursue this collateral attack on the default judgment. Then, in January 1992, Mr. Kramer stopped working for Mayflower. He left Mayflower because he had failed to renew his trucker's license and because he was suffering from both asthma and self-diagnosed depression. This depression, he claims, was caused in part by his worries over the outstanding child support order.

Starting in June 1993, Mr. Kramer worked for Lenneman Transport. While at Lenneman Transport, none of his wages were attached due to the child support order. However, he injured his back while at work and left Lenneman Transport in February 1994. Since that time, Mr. Kramer has not worked at all because he does not believe that he could pass a physical examination due to his bad back, his asthma, and his depression.

Mr. Kramer moved to the State of Washington in September 1996. Then, in July 1998, he was visited by an FBI agent about the outstanding child support order. Mr. Kramer informed the agent that, although he might be able to return to work, he did not see any reason to do so until the support order was cleared up because he would "just be attacked all the time." Tr.I at 41. A federal grand jury thereafter indicted Mr. Kramer on October 15, 1998, for the willful failure to pay, between October 1993 and December 1995, a past due support obligation with respect to a child residing in Indiana.

B.

The United States District Court for the Southern District of Indiana conducted a bench trial on the criminal charge against Mr. Kramer. At the close of the Government's case, Mr. Kramer moved for a judgment of acquittal, asserting that the Government had failed to prove that the underlying child support order was valid. He claimed that the order was invalid because he did not receive service of process and that the state court therefore did not have personal jurisdiction over him. The district court reserved its decision until the completion of the trial.

At the end of the trial, the court found Mr. Kramer guilty of the willful failure to pay a past due support obligation in violation of 18 U.S.C. § 228. The court first stated that the Government needed to prove beyond a reasonable doubt (1) that Mr. Kramer acted willfully, (2) in failing to pay, (3) a past due support obligation, (4) with respect to a child who resided in another state. The court found that, although "Kramer may not have learned of the lawsuit or the entry of the default judgment in 1982, it is clear that he understood by at least 1990 that such an order had been entered against him." R.20 at 7. Next, the court found that Mr.

Kramer had failed to pay the $25 per week mandated by the court order during the period of the indictment. The court also found that, during the time stated in the indictment, the child covered by the support order resided in Indiana and Mr. Kramer resided in Minnesota. "Therefore," the court concluded, "the evidence establishes beyond a reasonable doubt that Kramer knew prior to October 1993 that an Indiana state court had ordered him to pay child support for a child that resided in a different state than him and that he failed to do so." *Id.* at 8.

The court next discussed the element of willfulness and stated: "We harbor no hesitancy in concluding that Kramer acted willfully in not paying the support amount due." *Id.* The court noted that Mr. Kramer had challenged the support order when it served his interest to do so. But then, when he left Mayflower and was no longer subject to the attachment of his wages, he no longer believed that he owed support. "Indeed," the court stated, "we do not credit Kramer's assertion that he simply forgot that an outstanding support order existed, as other testimony he provided revealed that the outstanding matter caused him such discomfort as to contribute to his ongoing 'depression.'" *Id.* at 9.

The court also addressed Mr. Kramer's argument that the underlying support order was invalid because the state court lacked personal jurisdiction over him. The court characterized Mr. Kramer's defense as a collateral attack on the state court default judgment. First, the court held that federal courts do not need to question the validity of support orders issued by state courts before entering a judgment of conviction under § 228. The court relied upon *United States v. Bailey*, 115 F.3d 1222, 1232 (5th Cir.1997), for the proposition that the language of § 228 does not require a federal court to look beyond the four corners of the state child support order or permit a collateral attack on the state court order in federal court. Mr. Kramer, the court explained, should have challenged the state court default judgment through state channels, of which he was aware, as evidenced by his attempted collateral attack in 1991. His failure to complete that process, continued the court, does not invalidate the support obligation element of § 228.

Next, the court held that Mr. Kramer had been afforded sufficient due process in his federal prosecution. According to the court, Mr. Kramer had argued that, because he did not receive due process in the state default judgment, he was denied due process in the federal conviction because it relied on the state default judgment. According to the court, the Supreme Court in *United States v. Mendoza–Lopez*, 481 U.S. 828, 107 S.Ct. 2148, 95 L.Ed.2d 772 (1987), required the availability of meaningful review of a decision of an administrative proceeding as a necessary condition before a court imposed criminal sanctions based on that administrative decision. The court stated, however, that Mr. Kramer possessed an opportunity to seek review of the state default judgment before the imposition of his criminal sanction. Moreover, the court explained, "[a]ny putative due process violation occurring in 1982 was cured by the Indiana state court's granting Kramer a hearing to challenge that default judgment in late 1991." R.20 at 12.

For these reasons, the court found Mr. Kramer guilty of the willful failure to pay a past due child support obligation for the period between October 1993 and December 1995. The court sentenced Mr. Kramer to one year of probation, with 60 days community confinement as a condition of his probation, and it ordered him to pay $19,750.00 in restitution.

II

DISCUSSION

A.

Mr. Kramer submits that he cannot be found guilty under the CSRA because the Government did not establish that the Indiana court that issued the support order had personal jurisdiction over him. He contends, as he did in the district court, that he was never served process nor notified of the state paternity proceeding which produced the support obligation. Without such notice and opportunity to be heard, he submits, the Indiana court did not have personal jurisdiction over him, *see Mullane v. Central Hanover Bank*, 339 U.S. 306, 313, 70 S.Ct. 652, 94 L.Ed. 865 (1950), and the default judgment issued by the Indiana state court does not constitute a valid "support obligation" under the CSRA.

The Government has another view. It submits that it needed to prove beyond a reasonable doubt only the existence of the support order. Mr. Kramer's position, it contends, is an impermissible collateral attack on the state court child support order. Relying on our decision in *United States v. Black*, 125 F.3d 454 (7th Cir.1997), the Government argues that a federal court cannot revise the domestic relationship decided by a state court. Therefore, the Government submits, Mr. Kramer's conviction should be upheld.

B.

1.

We begin, as we must, with the wording of the statute. The CSRA punishes any person who "willfully fails to pay a support obligation with respect to a child who resides in another State, if such obligation has remained unpaid for a period longer than 1 year, or is greater than $5,000." 18 U.S.C. § 228(a). The term "support obligation" is defined as "any amount determined under a court order or an order of an administrative process pursuant to the law of a State . . . to be due from a person for the support and maintenance of a child or of a child and the parent with whom the child is living." 18 U.S.C. § 228(f)(3). Nothing in this definition suggests that a defendant may defend a prosecution under this statute by contesting the substantive merits of the underlying support obligation. Indeed, courts interpreting the CSRA, including this one, have spoken with one voice on that issue. *See United States v. Brand*, 163 F.3d 1268, 1275–76 (11th Cir.1998); *United States v. Black*, 125 F.3d 454, 463 (7th Cir.1997); *United States v. Bailey*, 115 F.3d 1222, 1232 (5th Cir.1997); *United States v. Johnson*, 114 F.3d 476, 481 (4th Cir.1997); *United States v. Sage*, 92 F.3d 101, 107 (2d Cir.1996).

The question remains, however, whether a defendant in a federal CSRA prosecution may defend on the limited ground that the underlying state support obligation was imposed by a court that did not have personal jurisdiction over the defendant. The general rule for default judgments in civil actions is that the judgment may be attacked collaterally on the narrow ground that the judgment was void because the rendering court lacked the requisite nexus with the defaulting party or gave inadequate notice of the support action to that party. *See Burnham v. Superior Ct. of Cal.*, 495 U.S. 604, 609–11, 110 S.Ct. 2105, 109 L.Ed.2d 631 (1990); *Kulko v. Superior Ct. of Cal.*, 436 U.S. 84, 91, 98 S.Ct. 1690, 56 L.Ed.2d 132 (1978); *see also World–Wide Volkswagen Corp. v. Woodson*, 444 U.S. 286, 291, 100 S.Ct. 559, 62 L.Ed.2d 490 (1980). To sustain the Government's position therefore, we must ascertain that Congress, in enacting the CSRA, intended to establish an approach different from the rule that usually applies.

2.

In an effort to demonstrate that Congress intended to permit a successful CSRA prosecution without a showing that the underlying support judgment had been issued by a court properly exercising personal jurisdiction over the defendant, the Government invites our attention to *Custis v. United States*, 511 U.S. 485, 114 S.Ct. 1732, 128 L.Ed.2d 517 (1994), and *Lewis v. United States*, 445 U.S. 55, 100 S.Ct. 915, 63 L.Ed.2d 198 (1980). We shall examine each of these cases in chronological order.

In *Lewis*, the defendant was charged with being a felon in possession of a firearm in violation of 18 U.S.C. § 1202(a)(1). *See* 445 U.S. at 57, 100 S.Ct. 915. In defending against the charge, he attempted to attack collaterally the prior state conviction that was the basis for prosecuting him as a felon in possession of a firearm. He claimed that this state conviction was invalid because he had not been represented by counsel, and, therefore, the conviction had been obtained in violation of his Sixth and Fourteenth Amendment rights. *See id.* at 57–58, 100 S.Ct. 915. The Supreme Court rejected his argument. The Court stated that the statute forbidding a felon to possess a firearm did not permit a collateral attack on the underlying conviction on constitutional grounds. *See id.* at 65, 100 S.Ct. 915 (discussing 18 U.S.C. § 1202(a)(1)). The Court explained that the plain language of the statute contained no exceptions to the definition of "prior conviction." *Id.* at 60, 100 S.Ct. 915. Moreover, continued the Court, Congress would have made such an exception explicit because, in other sections of the same statute, it had explicitly made exceptions to liability for those individuals who, despite a felony conviction, could be entrusted with a firearm under limited circumstances. *See id.* at 61–62, 100 S.Ct. 915 (listing sections). Other statutes, the Court continued, explicitly permitted a defendant to challenge, by way of defense, the validity or constitutionality of the predicate felony. *See id.* at 62, 100 S.Ct. 915 (listing statutes). The Court further noted that the legislative history did not indicate any intent by Congress to permit a felon to contest the validity of the underlying conviction. *See id.* at 62–63, 100 S.Ct. 915. Indeed, the Court noted that the legislative history made clear that Congress intended a "sweeping prophylaxis" against the misuse of firearms. *Id.* at 63, 100 S.Ct. 915. Additionally, other sections forbade the reception of a firearm by someone indicted for a felony even if he was subsequently acquitted. *See id.* at 64, 100 S.Ct. 915. Finally, the Court noted that the convicted felon is not without relief; he could have had the underlying conviction removed by a qualifying pardon or could have challenged the prior conviction in the state court. *See id.* As the Court concluded, "Congress clearly intended that the defendant clear his status *before* obtaining a firearm." *Id.*

The later Supreme Court case of *Custis* involved an interpretation of the Armed Career Criminal Act, 18 U.S.C. § 924(e), which provides for the enhancement of a sentence of a convicted firearms possessor who "has three previous convictions . . . for a violent felony or a serious drug offense." 511 U.S. at 487, 114 S.Ct. 1732. Interpreting the statute before it, the Supreme Court held that there was no indication that Congress had intended to permit the defendant to challenge the predicate convictions on the ground that they were procured through errors of constitutional magnitude. *See id.* Notably, the Court grounded its analysis on the text and the structure of the particular statute before it, the Armed Career Criminal Act. *See id.* at 490–91, 114 S.Ct. 1732. "The statute focuses on the fact of the conviction and nothing suggests that the prior final conviction may be subject to collateral attack for potential constitutional errors before it may be counted." *Id.* at 490–91, 114 S.Ct. 1732. Moreover, noted the Court, the statute affirmatively provides that no conviction "which has been . . . set aside" may be counted and therefore "creates a clear negative implication that courts may count a conviction that has *not* been set aside." *Id.* at 491, 114 S.Ct. 1732. The Court also noted that Congress had enacted other statutes that expressly permit repeat offenders to challenge convictions that are used for enhancement purposes. *See id.* at 491–92, 114 S.Ct. 1732.

Although the Court in *Custis* held that a defendant could not attack collaterally the merits of the underlying conviction, the Court also held that a defendant could attack collaterally a state court conviction when the defendant had been convicted in violation of his right to counsel under the Sixth Amendment. The Court deemed such a violation akin to a "jurisdictional defect," *see id.* at 496, 114 S.Ct. 1732, that raised questions about the court's power to render a decision at all and stated that "this Court [has] attributed a jurisdictional significance to the failure to appoint counsel," *id.* at 494, 114 S.Ct. 1732.

> "If the accused, however, is not represented by counsel and has not competently and intelligently waived his constitutional right, the Sixth Amendment stands as a jurisdictional bar to a valid conviction and sentence depriving him of his life or his liberty. . . . The judgment of conviction pronounced by a court without jurisdiction is void, and one imprisoned thereunder may obtain release by *habeas corpus.*"

Id. (quoting *Johnson v. Zerbst,* 304 U.S. 458, 468, 58 S.Ct. 1019, 82 L.Ed. 1461 (1938)). The Court concluded that the "failure to appoint counsel for an indigent defendant was a unique constitutional defect," and none of the other constitutional defects "rises to the level of a jurisdictional defect resulting from the failure to appoint counsel at all." *Id.* at 496, 114 S.Ct. 1732.

Although these cases are somewhat helpful guides in deciding the case before us, their value is not the one that the Government ascribes to them. The analysis of the Supreme Court in *Lewis* and in *Custis* does not suggest that it is proper in every situation involving the use of an earlier procured judgment to refuse to allow an inquiry into the validity of that underlying judgment. To the contrary—and here we believe is the true value of *Lewis* and *Custis* to our present decision—these cases make clear that, in determining whether we should look into the validity of the underlying judgment, we must focus on the particular statutory scheme at issue and decide whether Congress expected courts to evaluate the validity of the underlying judgment. In *Lewis* and in *Custis*, the Court also made clear that we must focus on the language of the statute and the intent of Congress. *See Custis*, 511 U.S. at 490–92, 114 S.Ct. 1732; *Lewis*, 445 U.S. at 60–61, 100 S.Ct. 915. In each case, the Court reached the issues that it did reach because of its interpretation of the congressional will in the particular statutory schemes. *See Custis*, 511 U.S. at 493, 114 S.Ct. 1732; *Lewis*, 445 U.S. at 64–65, 100 S.Ct. 915. Repeatedly in *Lewis* and in *Custis*, the Supreme Court contrasted the firearms statutes at issue with other sections of the criminal code that permitted the sort of collateral attack that the Court found impermissible under the statutes in those cases. It is also of great significance that, even when the Court in *Custis* determined that the statutory scheme did not permit the scrutiny of the merits of the underlying conviction, the Court did permit the examination of the jurisdictional basis of the underlying judgment.

3.

As we already have noted, we have no quarrel with those courts that have held that Congress did not intend that a defendant could raise the correctness of the underlying support judgment as a defense. Indeed, as we previously have pointed out, this court is among those circuits that have so held. *See Black*, 125 F.3d at 454. In this case, however, our focus must be on whether Congress intended to prevent the defendant from raising as a defense to his CSRA prosecution that the state court rendered the support judgment without jurisdiction. To determine whether the general rule that allows a defendant to contest a default judgment on jurisdictional grounds has been abrogated by Congress in a prosecution under the CSRA, we must focus on that particular statute and the circumstances surrounding its passage.

The issue of the enforcement of support orders has been a focal point of legislative activity at both the national and state levels. Support obligations are part of the law of domestic relations and therefore are a significant responsibility of state government. Nevertheless, because so many of these obligations transcend state borders, interstate cooperation is vital, and, in recent years, the federal government has found it necessary to play a larger role in improving the overall national situation. As we noted in *Black*, "Congress has expressly recognized that collecting past due child support obligations from out-of-state deadbeat parents has outgrown state enforcement mechanisms." 125 F.3d at 458.

In 1988, Congress created the U.S. Commission on Interstate Child Support ("the Commission") and charged the Commission to "submit a report to Congress that contains recommendations for (A) improving the interstate establishment and enforcement of child support awards, and (B) revising the Uniform Reciprocal Enforcement of Support Act." *Family Support Act of 1988*, Pub.L. No. 100–485, § 126, 102 Stat. 2343, 2355 (1988) (codified at 42 U.S.C. § 666).

The Commission submitted its report to Congress in 1992. In its report, the Commission discussed the inefficiencies prevalent in the current system for the enforcement of interstate child support orders. *See Supporting Our Children: A Blueprint for Reform,* U.S. *Commission on Interstate Child Support's Report to Congress XII* (1992) [hereinafter Blueprint for Reform]. The Commission noted that almost $5 billion went uncollected in child support cases in 1989. *See id.* Moreover, the report explained, three out of every ten child support cases are interstate, yet only $1 of every $10 is collected in interstate cases. *See id.* Due to the poor rate of collection on interstate child support cases, the Commission sought to reform the old system of collection for a more effective one. *See id.*

While the Commission was conducting its study, the prevailing statute governing interstate collection of past due support obligations was the Uniform Reciprocal Enforcement of Support Act ("URESA"), which contained both civil and criminal provisions. This model act was enacted throughout the United States, although in a variety of forms. *Blueprint for Reform*, at 16. The differences in URESA among the states contributed to delay and inefficiency. *See id.* Under URESA's civil provisions, a person seeking support for a child had two options for obtaining jurisdiction over a defendant. First, the plaintiff could transmit the appropriate legal documents to the defendant's state. The defendant's state would then take action to establish or enforce the support order against the defendant. Oftentimes, multiple orders would be issued. *See id.* at 228–31. Or, the plaintiff's state could exert its long-arm jurisdiction over the defendant. The reach of long-arm jurisdiction varied by state, increasing the difficulties in enforcing the support orders. Although URESA addressed the need for jurisdiction over the defendant and for service of process, the Commission report explained that the requirements for jurisdiction and notice varied by state and that oftentimes the requirements of one state would not be effective in a different state. *See id.* at 92–93.

URESA also contained criminal provisions to facilitate the extradition of a defendant who had been charged with criminal nonsupport. *See id.* at 17. The uniform act required the governor of a defendant's state to surrender the defendant, unless the defendant was complying with an existing support order, the defendant had prevailed on a previous support action, or the governor believed that civil remedies would be effective. *See id.* This process under URESA, however, remained a "tedious, cumbersome and slow method of collection." H.R. Rep. No. 102–771, 1992 WL 187429 (1992).

When the Commission wrote its report, it discussed extensively the importance of obtaining jurisdiction over the parties. *See Blueprint for Reform*, at 79–85. It explained that a court or agency can establish a child support obligation only if it has authority over the person. *See id.* at 79. It also discussed the obligation that states give full faith and credit to the support orders of sister states. It then recommended to Congress that it "provide for the interstate recognition and enforcement of child support orders, including ongoing orders, that are based on the valid exercises of jurisdiction up to constitutionally permissible limits." *Id.* at 91 (emphasis added).

The Commission also discussed a new uniform act for the states to follow. Rather than merely revising URESA, the Commission advocated the implementation of the radically different Uniform Interstate Family Support Act ("UIFSA"). *See id.* at 231. The basic premise behind UIFSA is that "there should be one support order between parties that is controlling at any given point in time." *Id.* at 232. Under this proposition, only one state controls the support obligation, and once that state obtains jurisdiction, it then has continuing, exclusive jurisdiction over the parties. *See id.* According to the Commission, to obtain jurisdiction over the parties, UIFSA contains a new provision for long-arm jurisdiction as well as retaining the two-state process introduced in URESA. *See id.* The Commission recommended that, "[s]ubject to the risk of losing federal funding, states shall adopt verbatim the [ ] drafting committee's final version of UIFSA." *Id.* at 236. By requiring the adoption of UIFSA verbatim, the Commission hoped to avoid the difficulties that had been attendant to the myriad versions of the old uniform act that the states had enacted. *See id.*

Of particular importance to Mr. Kramer's case, the Commission also specifically discussed the role of service of process in interstate child support cases. The Commission noted that a support action begins with service of process to the defendant in order to perfect personal jurisdiction and to notify the defendant of the action. *See id.* at 92. It also explained that each affected party is entitled to receive notice and that a party who is not served properly with notice later may challenge jurisdiction. *See id.* Then, the Commission recommended that each state observe other states' service of process laws. *See id.* at 94. Also, the Commission wrote that "States shall have and use laws that provide that: . . . Notice required for the exercise of jurisdiction over an individual outside the forum state must be given in a manner reasonably calculated to give actual notice." *Id.*

The language of UIFSA itself also focuses on the importance of jurisdiction in child support cases. First, to establish a support order, the act states: "Upon finding, after notice and opportunity to be heard, that an obligor owes a duty of support, the tribunal shall issue a support order directed to the obligor. . . ." UIFSA § 401(c). If a support order has been issued already in another state, then the receiving state "shall recognize and enforce, but may not modify, a registered order *if the issuing tribunal had jurisdiction.*" *Id.* § 603(c) (emphasis added). Also, the receiving tribunal shall notify the defendant of the registration of the support order issued by another state. *See id.* § 605(a). Although a defendant may not plead lack of parentage as a defense to a support obligation once another tribunal has established parentage, *see id.* § 315, the defendant may contest the validity or enforcement of the support order on the grounds that "the issuing tribunal lacked personal jurisdiction over the contesting party," *id.* § 607(a)(1).

Congress acted on the recommendations of the Commission with a variety of legislative efforts. In the *Full Faith and Credit for Child Support Orders Act,* Pub.L. No. 103–383, § 3(a), 108 Stat. 4063, 4064 (1994) (codified at 28 U.S.C. § 1738B), Congress provided that each state "shall enforce according to its terms a child support order made consistently with this section by a court of another State." *Id.* § 3(a)(1). It further provided that

A child support order is made consistently with this section if—

(1) a court that makes the order, pursuant to the laws of the State in which the court is located—

(A) has subject matter jurisdiction to hear the matter and enter such an order; and

(B) has personal jurisdiction over the contestants; and

(2) reasonable notice and opportunity to be heard is given to the contestants.

Id. § 3(c), 108 Stat. at 4065. Furthermore, Congress has mandated that each state enact UIFSA or lose federal funding.

The Commission report also emphasized the importance of state criminal nonsupport statutes and recommended that all states enact them. *See Blueprint for Reform*, at 178. It stressed that felony penalties should be "reserved for the especially egregious cases of nonsupport" and that "criminal enforcement is a last resort enforcement device." *Id.* "Civil enforcement techniques should be tried before prosecuting [a defendant] for criminal nonsupport," the Commission warned. *Id.* The Commission recommended that there should be a federal criminal nonsupport statute to coexist with the state criminal nonsupport statutes. *See id.* The Commission explained that, although a state court's criminal jurisdiction over an out-of-state defendant is not clear cut, the federal government's jurisdiction is nationwide. *See id.* Then, the report states, "[t]he Commission encourages Congress to pass a statute that would make it a federal crime to willfully fail to pay support." *Id.* at 179.

The CSRA itself started through Congress before the Commission released its final report. The Act was developed, however, in consultation with the Commission and was based on a preliminary recommendation made by the Commission. *See* 138 Cong. Rec. H7324–01, H7325 (daily ed. Aug. 4, 1992) (statement of then–Rep. Schumer). The House Report revealed that, in August 1992, 42 states already had made willful failure to pay child support a crime, although the ability to enforce the criminal statutes diminished significantly once the nonpaying parent crossed state lines. *See* H.R. Rep. No. 102–771. Representative Hyde, who spearheaded the movement for the CSRA, stated that, although URESA was necessary, it was a poor substitute for a state's internal enforcement mechanism. *See* 138 Cong. Rec. H7324–01, H7326 (statement of Rep. Hyde). He also stressed that the CSRA's goal was to strengthen, not supplant, state enforcement efforts. *See id.*

During the House debates, one of the sponsors of the bill explained that:

The bill would create a simple and straightforward criminal statute that would punish any person who willfully fails to pay a past-due support obligation to a child who resides in another State.

The bill also creates a grant program under which the Bureau of Justice Assistance may make grants to States and local entities to develop and implement this legislation and coordinate criminal interstate child support enforcement efforts.

... Many of our States have done their best, and they have made willful failure to pay child support a crime punishable in some States by up to 10 years in prison. But the ability of those States to enforce such laws outside their own boundaries is hobbled by a labyrinth of extradition laws and snarls of red tape. As a result, skipping out on child support is one of the easiest crimes to get away with in America today.

Id. at H7325 (statement of then-Rep. Schumer). Another representative, Representative Schiff, stated that "existing reciprocal support statutes between States are simply bogged down and unable to perform with the efficiency we would like to see." *Id.* at H7326 (statement of Rep. Schiff). No mention is made of jurisdiction or the validity of the underlying state support obligation in the legislative history of the CSRA.

4.

When we scrutinize the entire legal landscape surrounding the CSRA, it is clear that this criminal provision is only a small component in a nation-wide effort to deal with the need to enforce support orders. In addressing this problem, it is clear that, as Congress legislated, it was well aware of the longstanding rule, both in federal and state jurisprudence, that a default judgment in a civil case is void if there is no personal jurisdiction over the defendant and that a judgment may be attacked collaterally on that basis. Additionally, in addressing the problem of nonpayment of support orders, the Commission emphasized the importance of jurisdiction and service of process in procuring support obligations. Although the problem of enforcement of child support orders has been the focus of both national and state legislative efforts for well over a decade, there is no indication that the Commission or Congress ever intended to abrogate the traditional rule that a default judgment procured without personal jurisdiction is a nullity. More precisely, the prevailing uniform act at the time of the CSRA's passage, URESA, allowed the defendant to attack collaterally the earlier state order on jurisdictional grounds. The new order of mutually supportive federal and state legislation continued the same adherence to traditional jurisdictional standards. Notably, the new uniform act, UIFSA, also allowed a defendant to attack collaterally the earlier state order on the limited ground that it was procured without jurisdiction. The related civil statutes that Congress enacted in the wake of the Commission's report accept the general rule that a defendant may attack collaterally the underlying support order because it was procured without jurisdiction over his person. *See, e.g.*, 28 U.S.C. § 1738B.

Subjecting Mr. Kramer to criminal penalties for non-compliance with the state support judgment without allowing him to challenge the state court's personal jurisdiction would permit the federal criminal law to accomplish what the states forbid in their own civil and criminal courts and, indeed, what Congress has forbidden in the civil remedies it has created. In a carefully coordinated statutory scheme that places great emphasis on federal-state cooperation, such a result makes no sense. Because the CSRA itself, its legislative history, the Commission's report, the old and new uniform acts, and the federal statutes stemming from the Commission's report contain no indication that Congress intended to alter the traditional rule that a defendant may challenge on collateral attack a default judgment that is entered without personal jurisdiction, Mr. Kramer should be able to attack the Indiana child support order that formed the basis for his federal conviction for the willful failure to pay a past due support obligation. The failure of the district court to afford him the opportunity to do so constitutes reversible error.

C.

There is another reason, firmly embedded in the statutory language, for permitting Mr. Kramer to argue that he ought not be criminally sanctioned without an opportunity to demonstrate that that judgment is a nullity because it was procured without jurisdiction. It is important to note that the statute proscribes only the willful disobedience of a state support order. Indeed, the legislative history of the statute makes clear that Congress intended that, in this statute, the term "willfully" be given the same meaning that it is given in the criminal tax statutes. *See* H.R. Rep. No. 102–771. Therefore, Congress, in enacting this statute, was well aware that, by using the term "willfully," the Government would be required to prove "an intentional violation of a known legal duty." *Id.* Indeed, quoting the Supreme Court's decision in *United States v. Bishop*, 412 U.S. 346, 361, 93 S.Ct. 2008, 36 L.Ed.2d 941 (1973), the House Report noted that the word "willfully" under the tax felony statute "imports a bad purpose or evil motive." *See* H.R. Rep. No. 102–771.

Under traditional principles, an individual can ignore a default judgment procured without jurisdiction and raise that lack of jurisdiction when the judgment creditor attempts enforcement. Mr. Kramer was denied the right to have his jurisdictional contention ever considered by the district court. Certainly, the maintenance of a meritorious jurisdictional defense would negate the element of willfulness.

CONCLUSION

The district court erroneously held that Mr. Kramer's contention that the underlying judgment was procured without jurisdiction was not a defense to the charge. Accordingly, the judgment of the district court is reversed and the case is remanded for proceedings consistent with this opinion.

REVERSED and REMANDED.

Notes and Questions

1. Could Congress criminalize failing to pay child support if a defendant did not even know about the judgment?

2. What does the court say is the import of the offense using the term "willfully"? Does this mean that if a defendant had a good faith belief that an order was void, he would be not guilty?

C. Practice and Policy

District of Columbia v. Clawans

Supreme Court of the United States
300 U.S. 617 (1937)

Mr. Justice STONE delivered the opinion of the Court.

Respondent was convicted in the District of Columbia police court of engaging, without a license, in the business of a dealer in secondhand personal property, to wit, the unused portions of railway excursion tickets, in violation of section 7, par. 39, of the Act of Congress, approved July 1, 1902, 32 Stat. 622, 627, c. 1352, as amended by the Act of July 1, 1932, 47 Stat. 550, 558, c. 366. On arraignment she demanded a jury trial, which was denied, and on conviction she was sentenced to pay a fine of $300 or to be confined in jail for sixty days. The case was brought to the Court of Appeals for the District of Columbia by writ of error to review the denial of the respondent's request for a jury, and other rulings of the trial court which, it was claimed, had deprived her of a fair trial. The Court of Appeals reversed the judgment, holding that a jury trial was guaranteed to petitioner by the Constitution, but that the trial had been fair in other respects. 66 App.D.C. 11, 84 F.(2d) 265. We granted certiorari, 299 U.S. 524, 57 S.Ct. 14, 81 L.Ed. 386.

The statute under which petitioner was convicted provides that the offense may be prosecuted in the District of Columbia police court and is punishable by a fine of not more than $300 or imprisonment for not more than ninety days. The Code of the District of Columbia (1929) Tit. 18, § 165, provides that prosecutions in the police court shall be on information and that the trial shall be by jury in all cases 'in which, according to the Constitution of the United States, the accused would be entitled to a jury trial,' and that, 'in all cases where the accused would not by force of the Constitution of the United States be entitled to a trial by jury, the trial shall be by the court without a jury, unless in * * * cases wherein the fine or penalty may be more than $300, or imprisonment as punishment for the offense may be more than ninety days, the accused shall demand a trial by jury, in which case the trial shall be by jury.' Article 3, section 2, clause 3, of the Constitution, provides that 'the Trial of all Crimes, except in Cases of Impeachment, shall be by Jury.' The Sixth Amendment declares that 'in all criminal prosecutions, the accused shall enjoy the right to a speedy and public trial, by an impartial jury of the State and district wherein the crime shall have been committed.'

It is settled by the decisions of this Court, which need not now be discussed in detail, that the right of trial by jury, thus secured, does not extend to every criminal proceeding. At the time of the adoption of the Constitution there were numerous offenses, commonly described as 'petty,' which were tried summarily without a jury, by justices of the peace in England, and by police magistrates or corresponding judicial officers in the Colonies, and punished by commitment to jail, a workhouse, or a house of correction.[1] We think, as the Court of Appeals held and respondent concedes, that, apart from the prescribed penalty, the offense of which petitioner was convicted is, by its nature, of this class, and that were it not for the severity of the punishment, the offender could not, under our decisions, claim a trial by jury as of right. *Schick v. United States*, 195 U.S. 65, 24 S.Ct. 826, 49 L.Ed. 99, 1 Ann.Cas. 585; and *see Callan v. Wilson*, 127 U.S. 540, 552, 555, 8 S.Ct. 1301, 32 L.Ed. 223; *Natal v. Louisiana*, 139 U.S. 621, 624, 11

---

[1]   4 Blackstone, Commentaries, 280, 281; McNamara's Paley on Summary Convictions (4th Ed.1856) 10-12; Dillon, Municipal Corporations, § 433 (5th Ed.1911, § 750). A comprehensive collection of the statutes, English and American, will be found in *Petty Federal Offenses and the Constitutional Guaranty of Trial by Jury*, 39 Harv.L.Rev. 917, 922-965, 983-1019.

S.Ct. 636, 35 L.Ed. 288; *District of Columbia v. Colts*, 282 U.S. 63, 72, 73, 51 S.Ct. 52, 53, 75 L.Ed. 177.

Engaging in the business of selling secondhand property without a license was not indictable at common law. Today it is at most but an infringement of local police regulations, and its moral quality is relatively inoffensive. But this Court has refused to foreclose consideration of the severity of the penalty as an element to be considered in determining whether a statutory offense, in other respects trivial and not a crime at common law, must be deemed so serious as to be comparable with common-law crimes, and thus to entitle the accused to the benefit of a jury trial prescribed by the Constitution. *See Schick v. United States, supra*, 195 U.S. 65, 67, 68, 24 S.Ct. 826, 49 L.Ed. 99, 1 Ann.Cas. 585.

We are thus brought to the question whether the penalty, which may be imposed for the present offense, of ninety days in a common jail, is sufficient to bring it within the class of major offenses, for the trial of which a jury may be demanded. The court below thought, as we do, that the question is not free from doubt, but concluded, in view of the fact that the statute allows no appeal as of right from the conviction for the offense, and in view of its own estimate of the severity of the penalty, that three months' imprisonment is a punishment sufficiently rigorous to place respondent's delinquency in the category of major offenses.

If we look to the standard which prevailed at the time of the adoption of the Constitution, we find that confinement for a period of ninety days or more was not an unusual punishment for petty offenses, tried without a jury. Laying aside those for which the punishment was of a type no longer commonly employed, such as whipping, confinement in stocks, and the like, and others, punished by commitment for an indefinite period, we know that there were petty offenses, triable summarily under English statutes, which carried possible sentences of imprisonment for periods from three to twelve months. At least sixteen statutes, passed prior to the time of the American Revolution by the Colonies, or shortly after by the newlycreated states, authorized the summary punishment of petty offenses by imprisonment for three months or more. And at least eight others were punishable by imprisonment for six months.

In the face of this history, we find it impossible to say that a ninety-day penalty for a petty offense, meted out upon a trial without a jury, does not conform to standards which prevailed when the Constitution was adopted, or was not then contemplated as appropriate notwithstanding the constitutional guarantee of a jury trial. This conclusion is unaffected by the fact that respondent is not entitled to an appeal as of right. Code of the District of Columbia (1929) Tit. 18, § 28. The safeguards of an appeal are different in nature and purpose from those of a jury trial. At common law there was no review of criminal cases as of right. Due process does not comprehend the right of appeal. *McKane v. Durston*, 153 U.S. 684, 687, 14 S.Ct. 913, 38 L.Ed. 867. The early statutes providing for summary trial often did not allow it. And in any case it cannot be assumed that the authority to allow an appeal, given to the justices of the Court of Appeals by the District laws, will not be exercised in a proper case. We are aware that those standards of action and of policy which find expression in the common and statute law may vary from generation to generation. Such change has led to the abandonment of the lash and the stocks, and we may assume, for present purposes, that commonly accepted views of the severity of punishment by imprisonment may become so modified that a penalty once thought to be mild may come to be regarded as so harsh as to call for the jury trial, which the Constitution prescribes, in some cases which were triable without a jury when the Constitution was adopted. *See Schick v. United States, supra*, 195 U.S. 65, 67, 68, 24 S.Ct. 826, 49 L.Ed. 99, 1 Ann.Cas. 585; compare *Weems v. United States*, 217 U.S. 349, 373, 30 S.Ct. 544, 54 L.Ed. 793, 19 Ann.Cas. 705; *District of Columbia v. Colts, supra*, 282 U.S. 63, 74, 51 S.Ct. 52, 53, 75 L.Ed. 177; *Powell v. Alabama*, 287 U.S. 45, 71-73, 53 S.Ct. 55, 65, 77 L.Ed. 158, 84 A.L.R. 527; *United States v. Wood*, 299 U.S. 123, 141 et seq., 57 S.Ct. 177, 183, 81 L.Ed. 78. But we may doubt whether summary trial with punishment of more than six months' imprisonment, prescribed by some pre-Revolutionary statutes, is admissible, without concluding that a penalty of ninety days is too much. Doubts must be resolved, not subjectively by recourse of the judge to his own sympathy and emotions, but by objective standards such as may be observed in the laws and practices of the community taken as a gauge of its social and ethical judgments.

Congress itself, by measuring the punishment in this case in conformity to the commonly accepted standard when the Constitution was adopted, and declaring that it should be applied today unless found to transgress constitutional limitations, has expressed its deliberate judgment that the punishment is not too great to be summarily administered. A number of states have continued in force statutes providing for trial, without a jury, of violations of municipal ordinances, and sundry petty statutory offenses, punishable by commitment for three months or more. Convictions under such legislation have been upheld many times in the state courts, despite objections to the denial of a jury trial. In England many acts of Parliament now in force, authorizing ninety day punishments, call for summary trials.

This record of statute and judicial decision is persuasive that there has been no such change in the generally accepted standards of punishment as would overcome the presumption that a summary punishment of ninety days' imprisonment, permissible when the Constitution was adopted, is permissible now. Respondent points to no contrary evidence. We cannot say that this penalty, when attached to the offense of selling secondhand goods without a license, gives it the character of a common-law crime or of a major offense, or that it so offends the public sense of propriety and fairness as to bring it within the sweep of a constitutional protection which it did not previously enjoy.

Although we conclude that respondent's demand for a jury trial was rightly denied, there must be a new trial because of the prejudicial restriction, by the trial judge, of cross-examination by respondent. * * * The judgment of the Court of Appeals will be affirmed, that of the police court reversed, and the case will be remanded with instructions for a new trial without a jury.

Affirmed.

Separate opinion of Mr. Justice McREYNOLDS and Mr. Justice BUTLER.

Mr. Justice BUTLER and I approve the conclusion of the Court of Appeals concerning respondent's right to trial by jury; also we accept the supporting opinion announced there as entirely adequate.

The Sixth Amendment-In all criminal prosecutions, the accused shall enjoy the right to a speedy, and public trial, by an impartial jury of the state and district wherein the crime shall have been committed, which district shall have been previously ascertained by law, and to be informed of the nature and cause of the accusation; to be confronted with the witnesses against him; to have compulsory process for obtaining witnesses in his favor; and to have the assistance of counsel for his defense.

The Seventh Amendment-In suits at common law, where the value in controversy shall exceed $20, the right of trial by jury shall be preserved and no fact tried by a jury shall be otherwise re-examined in any court of the United States than according to the rules of the common law.

We cannot agree that when a citizen is put on trial for an offense punishable by 90 days in jail or a fine of $300, the prosecution is not criminal within the Sixth Amendment. In a suit at common law to recover above $20, a jury trial is assured. And to us, it seems improbable that while providing for this protection in such a trifling matter the framers of the Constitution intended that it might be denied where imprisonment for a considerable time or liability for fifteen times $20 confronts the accused.

In view of the opinion just announced, it seems permissible to inquire what will become of the other solemn declarations of the Amendment. Constitutional guarantees ought not to be subordinated to convenience, nor denied upon questionable precedents or uncertain reasoning. *See Boyd v. United States*, 116 U.S. 616, 635, 6 S.Ct. 524, 29 L.Ed. 746; In re *Debs* et al., 158 U.S. 564, 594, 15 S.Ct. 900, 39 L.Ed. 1092.

We concur in the conclusion of the Court concerning unfairness of the trial and the necessity for a new one.

This cause shows the grave danger to liberty when one accused must submit to the uncertain judgment of a single magistrate.

Notes and Questions

1. Is there any way to interpret "all criminal prosecutions" as meaning "some criminal prosecutions"?

2. [At least one of] the authors predict that the Court will extend the right to jury trial to include all criminal cases because of the increasing collateral consequences of misdemeanor convictions. *See, e.g.*, John D. King, *Beyond "Life and Liberty": The Evolving Right to Counsel*, 48 Harv. Civ. Rts.-Civ. Libs. L. Rev. 1 (2013); Alexandra Natapoff, *Misdemeanors*, 85 S. Cal. L. Rev. 1313 (2012); Jenny Roberts, *Why Misdemeanors Matter: Defining Effective Advocacy in the Lower Criminal Courts*, 45 U.C. Davis L. Rev. 277 (2011).

D. Common Law Antecedents of Modern Statutes

Carter v. United States

Supreme Court of the United States
530 U.S. 255 (2000)

Justice THOMAS delivered the opinion of the Court.

In *Schmuck v. United States,* 489 U.S. 705, 109 S.Ct. 1443, 103 L.Ed.2d 734 (1989), we held that a defendant who requests a jury instruction on a lesser offense under Rule 31(c) of the Federal Rules of Criminal Procedure must demonstrate that "the elements of the lesser offense are a subset of the elements of the charged offense." *Id.,* at 716, 109 S.Ct. 1443. This case requires us to apply this elements test to the offenses described by 18 U.S.C. §§ 2113(a) and (b) 1994 ed. and Supp. IV). The former punishes "[w]hoever, by force and violence, or by intimidation, takes . . . from the person or presence of another . . . any . . . thing of value belonging to, or in the . . . possession of, any bank. . . ." The latter, which entails less severe penalties, punishes, *inter alia,* "[w]hoever takes and carries away, with intent to steal or purloin, any . . . thing of value exceeding $1,000 belonging to, or in the . . . possession of, any bank. . . ." We hold that § 2113(b) requires an element not required by § 2113(a)—three in fact—and therefore is not a lesser included offense of § 2113(a). Petitioner is accordingly prohibited as a matter of law from obtaining a lesser included offense instruction on the offense described by § 2113(b).

I.

On September 9, 1997, petitioner Floyd J. Carter donned a ski mask and entered the Collective Federal Savings Bank in Hamilton Township, New Jersey. Carter confronted a customer who was exiting the bank and pushed her back inside. She screamed, startling others in the bank. Undeterred, Carter ran into the bank and leaped over the customer service counter and through one of the teller windows. One of the tellers rushed into the manager's office. Meanwhile, Carter opened several teller drawers and emptied the money into a bag. After having removed almost $16,000 in currency, Carter jumped back over the counter and fled from the scene. Later that day, the police apprehended him.

A grand jury indicted Carter, charging him with violating § 2113(a). While not contesting the basic facts of the episode, Carter pleaded not guilty on the theory that he had not taken the bank's money "by force and violence, or by intimidation," as § 2113(a) requires. Before trial, Carter moved that the court instruct the jury on the offense described by § 2113(b) as a lesser included offense of the offense described by § 2113(a). The District Court, relying on *United States v. Mosley,* 126 F.3d 200 (C.A.3 1997), denied the motion in a preliminary ruling. At the close of the Government's case, the District Court denied Carter's motion for a judgment of acquittal and indicated that the preliminary ruling denying the lesser included offense instruction would stand. The jury, instructed on § 2113(a) alone, returned a guilty verdict, and the District Court entered judgment pursuant to that verdict.

The Court of Appeals for the Third Circuit affirmed in an unpublished opinion, relying on its earlier decision in *Mosley.* Judgment order reported at 185 F.3d 863 (1999). While the Ninth Circuit agrees with the Third that a lesser offense instruction is precluded in this context, see *United States v. Gregory,* 891 F.2d 732, 734 (C.A.9 1989), other Circuits have held to the contrary, see *United States v. Walker,* 75 F.3d 178, 180 (C.A.4 1996); *United States v. Brittain,* 41 F.3d 1409, 1410 (C.A.10 1994). We granted certiorari to resolve the conflict, 528 U.S. 1060, 120 S.Ct. 613, 145 L.Ed.2d 508 (1999), and now affirm.

II.

In *Schmuck, supra*, we were called upon to interpret Federal Rule of Criminal Procedure 31(c)'s provision that "[t]he defendant may be found guilty of an offense necessarily included in the offense charged." We held that this provision requires application of an elements test, under which "one offense is not 'necessarily included' in another unless the elements of the lesser offense are a subset of the elements of the charged offense." 489 U.S., at 716, 109 S.Ct. 1443. The elements test requires "a textual comparison of criminal statutes," an approach that, we explained, lends itself to "certain and predictable" outcomes. *Id.*, at 720, 109 S.Ct. 1443.

Applying the test, we held that the offense of tampering with an odometer, 15 U.S.C. §§ 1984 and 1990c(a) (1982 ed.), is not a lesser included offense of mail fraud, 18 U.S.C. § 1341. We explained that mail fraud requires two elements—(1) having devised or intending to devise a scheme to defraud (or to perform specified fraudulent acts), and (2) use of the mail for the purpose of executing, or attempting to execute, the scheme (or specified fraudulent acts). The lesser offense of odometer tampering, however, requires the element of knowingly and willfully causing an odometer to be altered, an element that is absent from the offense of mail fraud. Accordingly, the elements of odometer tampering are not a subset of the elements of mail fraud, and a defendant charged with the latter is not entitled to an instruction on the former under Rule 31(c). *Schmuck, supra*, at 721–722, 109 S.Ct. 1443.

Turning to the instant case, the Government contends that three elements required by § 2113(b)'s first paragraph are *not* required by § 2113(a): (1) specific intent to steal; (2) asportation; and (3) valuation exceeding $1,000. The statute provides:

"§ 2113. Bank robbery and incidental crimes

"(a) Whoever, by force and violence, or by intimidation, takes, or attempts to take, from the person or presence of another, or obtains or attempts to obtain by extortion any property or money or any other thing of value belonging to, or in the care, custody, control, management, or possession of, any bank, credit union, or any savings and loan association. . .

. . . . .

"Shall be fined under this title or imprisoned not more than twenty years, or both.

"(b) Whoever takes and carries away, with intent to steal or purloin, any property or money or any other thing of value exceeding $1,000 belonging to, or in the care, custody, control, management, or possession of

> any bank, credit union, or any savings and loan association, shall be
> fined under this title or imprisoned not more than ten years, or both; or

"Whoever takes and carries away, with intent to steal or purloin, any property or money or any other thing of value not exceeding $1,000 belonging
to, or in the care, custody, control, management, or possession of any bank,
credit union, or any savings and loan association, shall be fined not more
than $1,000 or imprisoned not more than one year, or both."

A "textual comparison" of the elements of these offenses suggests that the
Government is correct. First, whereas subsection (b) requires that the defendant act "with intent to steal or purloin," subsection (a) contains no similar
requirement. Second, whereas subsection (b) requires that the defendant "tak[e]
and carr[y] away" the property, subsection (a) only requires that the defendant
"tak[e]" the property. Third, whereas the first paragraph of subsection (b) requires
that the property have a "value exceeding $1,000," subsection (a) contains no
valuation requirement. These extra clauses in subsection (b) "cannot be regarded
as mere surplusage; [they] mea[n] something." *Potter v. United States*, 155 U.S.
438, 446, 15 S.Ct. 144, 39 L.Ed. 214 (1894).

Carter urges that the foregoing application of *Schmuck's* elements test is too
rigid and submits that ordinary principles of statutory interpretation are relevant
to the *Schmuck* inquiry. We do not dispute the latter proposition. The *Schmuck*
test, after all, requires an exercise in statutory interpretation before the comparison of elements may be made, and it is only sensible that normal principles of
statutory construction apply. We disagree, however, with petitioner's conclusion
that such principles counsel a departure in this case from what is indicated by a
straightforward reading of the text.

III.

We begin with the arguments pertinent to the general relationship between
§§ 2113(a) and (b). Carter first contends that the structure of § 2113 supports the
view that subsection (b) is a lesser included offense of subsection (a). He points to
subsection (c) of § 2113, which imposes criminal liability on a person who knowingly "receives, possesses, conceals, stores, barters, sells, or disposes of, any property or money or other thing of value which has been taken or stolen from a bank
... in violation of *subsection (b)*." (Emphasis added.) It would be anomalous, posits
Carter, for subsection (c) to apply—as its text plainly provides—only to the fence
who receives property from a violator of subsection (b) but not to the fence who
receives property from a violator of subsection (a). The anomaly disappears, he
concludes, only if subsection (b) is always violated when subsection (a) is violated—*i.e.*, only if subsection (b) is a lesser included offense of subsection (a).

But Carter's anomaly—even if it truly exists—is only an anomaly. Petitioner does not claim, and we tend to doubt, that it rises to the level of absurdity. Cf. *Green v. Bock Laundry Machine Co.*, 490 U.S. 504, 509–511, 109 S.Ct. 1981, 104 L.Ed.2d 557 (1989); *id.*, at 527, 109 S.Ct. 1981 (SCALIA, J., concurring in judgment). For example, it may be that violators of subsection (a) generally act alone, while violators of subsection (b) are commonly assisted by fences. In such a state of affairs, a sensible Congress may have thought it necessary to punish only the fences of property taken in violation of subsection (b). Or Congress may have thought that a defendant who violates subsection (a) usually—if not inevitably— also violates subsection (b), so that the fence may be punished by reference to that latter violation. In any event, nothing in subsection (c) purports to redefine the elements required by the text of subsections (a) and (b).

Carter's second argument is more substantial. He submits that, insofar as subsections (a) and (b) are *similar* to the common-law crimes of robbery and larceny, we must assume that subsections (a) and (b) require the *same* elements as their common-law predecessors, at least absent Congress' affirmative indication (whether in text or legislative history) of an intent to displace the common-law scheme. While we (and the Government) agree that the statutory crimes at issue here bear a close resemblance to the common-law crimes of robbery and larceny, see Brief for United States 29 (citing 4 W. Blackstone, Commentaries *229, *232); accord, *post,* at 2173–2174, that observation is beside the point. The canon on imputing common-law meaning applies only when Congress makes use of a statutory *term* with established meaning at common law, and Carter does not point to any such term in the text of the statute.

This limited scope of the canon on imputing common-law meaning has long been understood. In *Morissette v. United States*, 342 U.S. 246, 72 S.Ct. 240, 96 L.Ed. 288 (1952), for example, we articulated the canon in this way:

> "[W]here Congress borrows *terms* of art in which are accumulated the legal tradition and meaning of centuries of practice, it presumably knows and adopts the cluster of ideas that were attached to each borrowed *word* in the body of learning from which it was taken and the meaning its use will convey to the judicial mind unless otherwise instructed. In such case, absence of contrary direction may be taken as satisfaction with widely accepted definitions, not as a departure from them." *Id.*, at 263, 72 S.Ct. 240 (emphasis added).

In other words, a "cluster of ideas" from the common law should be imported into statutory text only when Congress employs a common-law *term*, and not when, as here, Congress simply describes an offense analogous to a common-law crime without using common-law terms.

We made this clear in *United States v. Wells*, 519 U.S. 482, 117 S.Ct. 921, 137 L.Ed.2d 107 (1997). At issue was whether 18 U.S.C. § 1014—which punishes a person who "knowingly makes any false statement or report . . . for the purpose of influencing in any way the action" of a Federal Deposit Insurance Corporation insured bank "upon any application, advance, . . . commitment, or loan"—requires proof of the materiality of the "false statement." The defendants contended that since materiality was a required element of "false statement"-type offenses at common law, it must also be required by § 1014. Although Justice STEVENS in dissent thought the argument to be meritorious, we rejected it:

> "[F]undamentally, we disagree with our colleague's apparent view that any term that is an element of a common-law crime carries with it every other aspect of that common-law crime when the term is used in a statute. Justice STEVENS seems to assume that because 'false statement' is an element of perjury, and perjury criminalizes only material statements, a statute criminalizing 'false statements' covers only material statements. By a parity of reasoning, because common-law perjury involved statements under oath, a statute criminalizing a false statement would reach only statements under oath. It is impossible to believe that Congress intended to impose such restrictions *sub silentio*, however, and so *our rule on imputing common-law meaning to statutory terms does not sweep so broadly*." 519 U.S., at 492, n. 10, 117 S.Ct. 921 (emphasis added; citation omitted).

Similarly, in *United States v. Turley*, 352 U.S. 407, 77 S.Ct. 397, 1 L.Ed.2d 430 (1957), we declined to look to the analogous common-law crime because the statutory term at issue—"stolen"—had no meaning at common law. *See id.*, at 411–412, 77 S.Ct. 397 ("[W]hile 'stolen' is constantly identified with larceny, the term was never at common law equated or exclusively dedicated to larceny" (internal quotation marks omitted)).

By contrast, we have not hesitated to turn to the common law for guidance when the relevant statutory text does contain a term with an established meaning at common law. In *Neder v. United States*, 527 U.S. 1, 119 S.Ct. 1827, 144 L.Ed.2d 35 (1999), for example, we addressed whether materiality is required by federal statutes punishing a "scheme or artifice to defraud." *Id.*, at 20, and 20–21, nn. 3–4, 119 S.Ct. 1827 (citing 18 U.S.C. §§ 1341, 1343, 1344). Unlike the statute in *Wells*, which contained no common-law term, these statutes did include a common-law term—"defraud." 527 U.S., at 22, 119 S.Ct. 1827. Because common-law fraud required proof of materiality, we applied the canon to hold that these federal statutes implicitly contain a materiality requirement as well. *Id.*, at 23, 119 S.Ct. 1827. Similarly, in *Evans v. United States*, 504 U.S. 255, 261–264, 112 S.Ct.

1881, 119 L.Ed.2d 57 (1992), we observed that "extortion" in 18 U.S.C. § 1951 was a common-law term, and proceeded to interpret this term by reference to its meaning at common law.

Here, it is undisputed that "robbery" and "larceny" are terms with established meanings at common law. But neither term appears in the text of § 2113(a) or § 2113(b).[5] While the term "robbery" does appear in § 2113's title, the title of a statute "'[is] of use only when [it] shed[s] light on some ambiguous word or phrase'" in the statute itself. *Pennsylvania Dept. of Corrections v. Yeskey*, 524 U.S. 206, 212, 118 S.Ct. 1952, 141 L.Ed.2d 215 (1998) (quoting *Brotherhood of R.R. Trainmen v. Baltimore & Ohio R. Co.*, 331 U.S. 519, 528–529, 67 S.Ct. 1387, 91 L.Ed. 1646 (1947) (modifications in original)). And Carter does not claim that this title illuminates any such ambiguous language. Accordingly, the canon on imputing common-law meaning has no bearing on this case.

IV.

We turn now to Carter's more specific arguments concerning the "extra" elements of § 2113(b). While conceding the absence of three of § 2113(b)'s requirements from the text of § 2113(a)—(1) "intent to steal or purloin"; (2) "takes *and carries away*," *i.e.*, asportation; and (3) "value exceeding $1,000" (first paragraph)—Carter claims that the first two should be deemed implicit in § 2113(a), and that the third is not an element at all.

A.

As to "intent to steal or purloin," it will be recalled that the text of subsection (b) requires a specific "intent to steal or purloin," whereas subsection (a) contains no explicit *mens rea* requirement of any kind. Carter nevertheless argues that such a *specific intent* requirement must be deemed implicitly present in § 2113(a) by virtue of "our cases interpreting criminal statutes to include broadly applicable scienter requirements, even where the statute by its terms does not contain them." *United States v. X–Citement Video, Inc.*, 513 U.S. 64, 70, 115 S.Ct. 464, 130 L.Ed.2d 372 (1994). Properly applied to § 2113, however, the presumption in favor of scienter demands only that we read subsection (a) as requiring proof of *general intent*—that is, that the defendant possessed knowledge with respect to the *actus reus* of the crime (here, the taking of property of another by force and violence or intimidation).

---

5   Congress could have simply punished "robbery" or "larceny" as some States have done (and as Congress itself has done elsewhere, see, *e.g.*, 18 U.S.C. §§ 2112, 2114, 2115), thereby leaving the definition of these terms to the common law, but Congress instead followed the more prevalent legislative practice of spelling out elements of these crimes. *See* 2 W. LaFave & A. Scott, Substantive Criminal Law § 8.11, p. 438, n. 6 (1986).

Before explaining why this is so under our cases, an example, *United States v. Lewis*, 628 F.2d 1276, 1279 (C.A.10 1980), cert. denied, 450 U.S. 924, 101 S.Ct. 1375, 67 L.Ed.2d 353 (1981), will help to make the distinction between "general" and "specific" intent less esoteric. In *Lewis*, a person entered a bank and took money from a teller at gunpoint, but deliberately failed to make a quick getaway from the bank in the hope of being arrested so that he would be returned to prison and treated for alcoholism. Though this defendant knowingly engaged in the acts of using force and taking money (satisfying "general intent"), he did not intend permanently to deprive the bank of its possession of the money (failing to satisfy "specific intent"). *See generally* 1 W. LaFave & A. Scott, Substantive Criminal Law § 3.5, p. 315 (1986) (distinguishing general from specific intent).

The presumption in favor of scienter requires a court to read into a statute only that *mens rea* which is necessary to separate wrongful conduct from "otherwise innocent conduct." *X–Citement Video, supra*, at 72, 115 S.Ct. 464. In *Staples v. United States*, 511 U.S. 600, 114 S.Ct. 1793, 128 L.Ed.2d 608 (1994), for example, to avoid criminalizing the innocent activity of gun ownership, we interpreted a federal firearms statute to require proof that the defendant knew that the weapon he possessed had the characteristics bringing it within the scope of the statute. Id., at 611–612, 114 S.Ct. 1793. *See also, e.g., Liparota v. United States*, 471 U.S. 419, 426, 105 S.Ct. 2084, 85 L.Ed.2d 434 (1985); *Morissette*, 342 U.S., at 270–271, 72 S.Ct. 240. By contrast, some situations may call for implying a specific intent requirement into statutory text. Suppose, for example, a statute identical to § 2113(b) but without the words "intent to steal or purloin." Such a statute would run the risk of punishing seemingly innocent conduct in the case of a defendant who peaceably takes money believing it to be his. Reading the statute to require that the defendant possess general intent with respect to the *actus reus—i.e.*, that he know that he is physically taking the money—would fail to protect the innocent actor. The statute therefore would need to be read to require not only general intent, but also specific intent—*i.e.*, that the defendant take the money with "intent to steal or purloin."

In this case, as in *Staples*, a general intent requirement suffices to separate wrongful from "otherwise innocent" conduct. Section 2113(a) certainly should not be interpreted to apply to the hypothetical person who engages in forceful taking of money while sleepwalking (innocent, if aberrant activity), but this result is accomplished simply by requiring, as *Staples* did, general intent—*i.e.*, proof of knowledge with respect to the *actus reus* of the crime. And once this mental state and *actus reus* are shown, the concerns underlying the presumption in favor of scienter are fully satisfied, for a forceful taking—even by a defendant who takes under a good-faith claim of right—falls outside the realm of the "otherwise innocent." Thus, the presumption in favor of scienter does

not justify reading a specific intent requirement—"intent to steal or purloin"—
into § 2113(a).

Independent of his reliance upon the presumption in favor of scienter,
Carter argues that the legislative history of § 2113 supports the notion that an
"intent to steal" requirement should be read into § 2113(a). Carter points out that,
in 1934, Congress enacted what is now § 2113(a), but with the adverb "feloniously" (which all agree is equivalent to "intent to steal") modifying the verb
"takes." Act of May 18, 1934, ch. 304, § 2(a), 48 Stat. 783. In 1937, Congress added
what is now § 2113(b). Act of Aug. 24, 1937, ch. 747, 50 Stat. 749. Finally, in 1948,
Congress made two changes to § 2113, deleting "feloniously" from what is now
§ 2113(a) and dividing the "robbery" and "larceny" offenses into their own separate subsections. 62 Stat. 796.

Carter concludes that the 1948 deletion of "feloniously" was merely a stylistic change, and that Congress had no intention, in deleting that word, to drop
the requirement that the defendant "feloniously" take the property—that is, with
intent to steal. Such reasoning, however, misunderstands our approach to statutory interpretation. In analyzing a statute, we begin by examining the text, see,
e.g., Estate of Cowart v. Nicklos Drilling Co., 505 U.S. 469, 475, 112 S.Ct. 2589,
120 L.Ed.2d 379 (1992), not by "psychoanalyzing those who enacted it," *Bank
One Chicago, N.A. v. Midwest Bank & Trust Co.,* 516 U.S. 264, 279, 116 S.Ct. 637,
133 L.Ed.2d 635 (1996) (SCALIA, J., concurring in part and concurring in judgment). While "feloniously" no doubt would be sufficient to convey a specific
intent requirement akin to the one spelled out in subsection (b), the word simply
does not appear in subsection (a).

Contrary to the dissent's suggestion, *post,* at 2176–2177, this reading is not a
fanciful one. The absence of a specific intent requirement from subsection (a), for
example, permits the statute to reach cases like *Lewis, see supra,* at 2168, where
an ex-convict robs a bank because he wants to be apprehended and returned to
prison. (The Government represents that indictments on this same fact pattern
(which invariably plead out and hence do not result in reported decisions) are
brought "as often as every year," Brief for United States 22, n. 13.) It can hardly be
said, therefore, that it would have been absurd to delete "feloniously" in order to
reach such defendants. And once we have made that determination, our inquiry
into legislative motivation is at an end. Cf. *Bock Laundry Machine Co.,* 490 U.S.,
at 510–511, 109 S.Ct. 1981.

B.

Turning to the second element in dispute, it will be recalled that, whereas
subsection (b) requires that the defendant "tak[e] and carr[y] away the property,"
subsection (a) requires only that the defendant "tak[e]" the property. Carter con-

tends that the "takes" in subsection (a) is equivalent to "takes and carries away" in subsection (b). While Carter seems to acknowledge that the argument is at war with the text of the statute, he urges that text should not be dispositive here because nothing in the evolution of § 2113(a) suggests that Congress sought to discard the asportation requirement from that subsection.

But, again, our inquiry focuses on an analysis of the textual product of Congress' efforts, not on speculation as to the internal thought processes of its Members. Congress is certainly free to outlaw bank theft that does not involve asportation, and it hardly would have been absurd for Congress to do so, since the taking-without-asportation scenario is no imagined hypothetical. *See, e.g., State v. Boyle*, 970 S.W.2d 835, 836, 838–839 (Mo.Ct.App.1998) (construing state statutory codification of common-law robbery to apply to defendant who, after taking money by threat of force, dropped the money on the spot). Indeed, a leading treatise applauds the deletion of the asportation requirement from the elements of robbery. *See* 2 LaFave & Scott, Substantive Criminal Law § 8.11, at 439. No doubt the common law's decision to require asportation also has its virtues. But Congress adopted a different view in § 2113(a), and it is not for us to question that choice.

C.

There remains the requirement in § 2113(b)'s first paragraph that the property taken have a "value exceeding $1,000"—a requirement notably absent from § 2113(a). Carter, shifting gears from his previous arguments, concedes the textual point but claims that the valuation requirement does not affect the *Schmuck* elements analysis because it is a *sentencing factor*, not an element. We disagree. The structure of subsection (b) strongly suggests that its two paragraphs—the first of which requires that the property taken have "value exceeding $1,000," the second of which refers to property of "value not exceeding $1,000"—describe distinct offenses. Each begins with the word "[w]hoever," proceeds to describe identically (apart from the differing valuation requirements) the elements of the offense, and concludes by stating the prescribed punishment. That these provisions "stand on their own grammatical feet" strongly suggests that Congress intended the valuation requirement to be an element of each paragraph's offense, rather than a sentencing factor of some base § 2113(b) offense. *Jones v. United States*, 526 U.S. 227, 234, 119 S.Ct. 1215, 143 L.Ed.2d 311 (1999). Even aside from the statute's structure, the "steeply higher penalties"—an enhancement from a 1–year to a 10–year maximum penalty on proof of valuation exceeding $1,000— leads us to conclude that the valuation requirement is an element of the first paragraph of subsection (b). *See Castillo v. United States*, 530 U.S. 120, 127, 120 S.Ct. 2090, 147 L.Ed.2d 94; *Jones*, 526 U.S., at 233, 119 S.Ct. 1215. Finally, the constitutional questions that would be raised by interpreting the valuation requirement to be a sentencing factor persuade us to adopt the view that the valuation requirement is an element. *See id.,* at 239–252, 119 S.Ct. 1215.

The dissent agrees that the valuation requirement of subsection (b)'s first paragraph is an element, but nonetheless would hold that subsection (b) is a lesser included offense of subsection (a). *Post,* at 2178–2180. The dissent reasons that the "value *not* exceeding $1,000" component of § 2113(b)'s *second* paragraph is not an element of the offense described in that paragraph. Hence, the matter of value does not prevent § 2113(b)'s second paragraph from being a lesser included offense of § 2113(a). And if a defendant wishes to receive an instruction on the first paragraph of § 2113(b)—which entails more severe penalties than the second paragraph, but is a more realistic option from the jury's standpoint in a case such as this one where the value of the property clearly exceeds $1,000—the dissent sees no reason to bar him from making that election, even though the "value exceeding $1,000" element of § 2113(b)'s first paragraph is clearly absent from § 2113(a).

This novel maneuver creates a problem, however. Since subsection (a) contains no valuation requirement, a defendant indicted for violating that subsection who requests an instruction under subsection (b)'s first paragraph would effectively "waive . . . his [Fifth Amendment] right to notice by indictment of the 'value exceeding $1,000' element." *Post,* at 2179. But this same course would not be available to the prosecutor who seeks the insurance policy of a lesser included offense instruction under that same paragraph after determining that his case may have fallen short of proving the elements of subsection (a). For, whatever authority defense counsel may possess to waive a defendant's constitutional rights, see generally *New York v. Hill,* 528 U.S. 110, 120 S.Ct. 659, 145 L.Ed.2d 560 (2000), a prosecutor has no such power. Thus, the prosecutor would be disabled from obtaining a lesser included offense instruction under Rule 31(c), a result plainly contrary to *Schmuck,* in which we explicitly rejected an interpretive approach to the Rule that would have permitted "the defendant, by in effect waiving his right to notice, . . . [to] obtain a lesser [included] offense instruction in circumstances where the constitutional restraint of notice to the defendant would prevent the prosecutor from seeking an identical instruction," 489 U.S., at 718, 109 S.Ct. 1443.* * *

We hold that § 2113(b) is not a lesser included offense of § 2113(a), and therefore that petitioner is not entitled to a jury instruction on § 2113(b). The judgment of the Third Circuit is affirmed.

It is so ordered.

Justice GINSBURG, with whom Justice STEVENS, Justice SOUTER, and Justice BREYER join, dissenting.

At common law, robbery meant larceny *plus* force, violence, or putting in fear. Because robbery was an aggravated form of larceny at common law, larceny was a lesser included offense of robbery. Congress, I conclude, did not depart from that traditional understanding when it rendered "Bank robbery and incidental crimes" federal offenses. Accordingly, I would hold that petitioner Carter is not prohibited as a matter of law from obtaining an instruction on bank larceny as a lesser included offense. The Court holds that Congress, in 18 U.S.C. § 2113, has dislodged bank robbery and bank larceny from their common-law mooring. I dissent from that determination.

I.

The Court presents three reasons in support of its conclusion that a lesser included offense instruction was properly withheld in this case under the elements-based test of *Schmuck v. United States*, 489 U.S. 705, 109 S.Ct. 1443, 103 L.Ed.2d 734 (1989). First, the Court holds that bank larceny contains an "intent to steal" requirement that bank robbery lacks. *Ante*, at 2168–2170. Second, the Court concludes that larceny contains a requirement of carrying away, or "asportation," while robbery does not. *Ante*, at 2170–2171. And third, the Court states that the "value exceeding $1,000" requirement in the first paragraph of the larceny statute is an element for which no equivalent exists in the robbery statute. *Ante*, at 2171 and this page. The Court's first and second points, I conclude, are mistaken. As for the third, I agree with the Court that the "value exceeding $1,000" requirement is an element essential to sustain a conviction for the higher degree of bank larceny. I would hold, however, that Carter was not disqualified on that account from obtaining the lesser included offense instruction he sought.

I note at the outset that the structure of § 2113 points strongly toward the conclusion that bank larceny is a lesser included offense of bank robbery. Section 2113(c) imposes criminal liability on any person who knowingly "receives, possesses, conceals, stores, barters, sells, or disposes of, any property or money or other thing of value which has been taken or stolen from a bank . . . in violation of subsection (b)." If bank larceny, covered in § 2113(b), contains an intent or asportation element not included in bank robbery, covered in § 2113(a), then § 2113(c) creates an anomaly. As the Court concedes, *ante*, at 2166, under today's decision the fence who gets his loot from a bank larcenist will necessarily receive property "stolen . . . in violation of subsection (b)," but the one who gets his loot from a bank robber will not. Once it is recognized that bank larceny is a lesser included offense of bank robbery, however, the anomaly vanishes. Because anyone who violates § 2113(a) necessarily commits the lesser included offense described in § 2113(b), a person who knowingly receives stolen property from a bank robber is just as guilty under § 2113(c) as one who knowingly receives stolen property from a bank larcenist.[1]

I emphasize as well that the title of § 2113 is "Bank robbery and incidental crimes." This Court has repeatedly recognized that "'the title of a statute and the heading of a section' are 'tools available for the resolution of a doubt' about the meaning of a statute." *Almendarez–Torres v. United States*, 523 U.S. 224, 234, 118 S.Ct. 1219, 140 L.Ed.2d 350 (1998) (quoting *Brotherhood of R.R. Trainmen v. Baltimore & Ohio R. Co.*, 331 U.S. 519, 528–529, 67 S.Ct. 1387, 91 L.Ed. 1646 (1947)).[2] Robbery, all agree, was an offense at common law, and this Court has consistently instructed that courts should ordinarily read federal criminal laws in accordance with their common-law origins, if Congress has not directed otherwise. *See Neder v. United States*, 527 U.S. 1, 21, 119 S.Ct. 1827, 144 L.Ed.2d 35 (1999) ("[W]here Congress uses terms that have accumulated settled meaning under the common law, a court must infer, unless the statute otherwise dictates, that Congress means to incorporate the established meaning of these terms." (internal quotation marks and modifications omitted)); *Evans v. United States*, 504 U.S. 255, 259, 112 S.Ct. 1881, 119 L.Ed.2d 57 (1992) ("It is a familiar 'maxim that a statutory term is generally presumed to have its common-law meaning.'") (quoting *Taylor v. United States*, 495 U.S. 575, 592, 110 S.Ct. 2143, 109 L.Ed.2d 607 (1990)); *United States v. Turley*, 352 U.S. 407, 411, 77 S.Ct. 397, 1 L.Ed.2d 430 (1957) ("We recognize that where a federal criminal statute uses a common-law term of established meaning without otherwise defining it, the general practice is to give that term its common-law meaning."). As we explained in *Morissette v. United States*, 342 U.S. 246, 72 S.Ct. 240, 96 L.Ed. 288 (1952):

> "[W]here Congress borrows terms of art in which are accumulated the legal tradition and meaning of centuries of practice, it presumably knows and adopts the cluster of ideas that were attached to each borrowed word in the body of learning from which it was taken and the meaning its use will convey to the judicial mind unless otherwise instructed. In such case, absence

---

1   I further note, and the Court does not dispute, that under today's holding the Double Jeopardy Clause would not bar the Government from bringing a bank larceny prosecution against a defendant who has already been acquitted—or, indeed, convicted—by a jury of bank robbery on the same facts. *See Blockburger v. United States*, 284 U.S. 299, 52 S.Ct. 180, 76 L.Ed. 306 (1932) (Double Jeopardy Clause does not bar consecutive prosecutions for a single act if each charged offense requires proof of an element that the other does not); Tr. of Oral Arg. 46–47 (in response to Court's inquiry, counsel for the Government stated that, under the Government's construction of § 2113, if a jury acquitted a defendant on an indictment for bank robbery, it would be open to the prosecution thereafter to seek the defendant's reindictment for bank larceny).

2   The majority says that courts may use a statutory title or heading only to "shed light on some ambiguous word or phrase," but not as a guide to a statute's overall meaning. *See ante,* at 2168. Our cases have never before imposed such a wooden and arbitrary limitation, and for good reason: A statute's meaning can be elusive, and its title illuminating, even where a court cannot pinpoint a discrete word or phrase as the source of the ambiguity.

of contrary direction may be taken as satisfaction with widely accepted definitions, not as a departure from them." *Id.,* at 263, 72 S.Ct. 240.

In interpreting § 2113, then, I am guided by the common-law understanding of "robbery and incidental crimes."

At common law, as the Government concedes, robbery was an aggravated form of larceny. Specifically, the common law defined larceny as "the felonious taking, and carrying away, of the personal goods of another." 4 W. Blackstone, Commentaries on the Laws of England 230 (1769) (Blackstone) (internal quotation marks omitted). Robbery, in turn, was larceny effected by taking property from the person or presence of another by means of force or putting in fear. Brief for United States 29–30 (citing 2 W. LaFave & A. Scott, Substantive Criminal Law § 8.11, pp. 437–438 (1986) (LaFave & Scott)). Larceny was therefore a lesser included offense of robbery at common law. *See* 4 Blackstone 241 (robbery is "[o]pen and violent larceny from the person" (emphasis deleted)); 2 E. East, Pleas of the Crown § 124, p. 707 (1803) (robbery is a species of "aggravated larceny"); 2 W. Russell & C. Greaves, Crimes and Misdemeanors *101 ("robbery is an aggravated species of larceny").

Closer inspection of the common-law elements of both crimes confirms the relationship. The elements of common-law larceny were also elements of robbery. First and most essentially, robbery, like larceny, entailed an intentional taking. *See* 4 Blackstone 241 (robbery is "the felonious and forcible taking, from the person of another, of goods or money to any value, by putting him in fear"); 2 East, *supra*, at 707 (robbery is the "felonious taking of money or goods, to any value, from the person of another, or in his presence, against his will, by violence or putting him in fear"). Second, as the above quotations indicate, the taking in a robbery had to be "felonious," a common-law term of art signifying an intent to steal. *See* 4 Blackstone 232 ("This taking, and carrying away, must also be *felonious*; that is, done *animo furandi* [with intent to steal]: or, as the civil law expresses it, *lucri causa* [for the sake of gain]."); Black's Law Dictionary 555 (5th ed. 1979) ("Felonious" is "[a] technical word of law which means done with intent to commit crime"). And third, again like larceny, robbery contained an asportation requirement. *See* 2 LaFave & Scott § 8.11, at 439 ("Just as larceny requires that the thief both 'take' (secure dominion over) and 'carry away' (move slightly) the property in question, so too robbery under the traditional view requires both a taking and an asportation (in the sense of at least a slight movement) of the property." (footnotes omitted)). Unlike larceny, however, robbery included one further essential component: an element of force, violence, or intimidation. *See* 4 Blackstone 242 ("[P]utting in fear is the criterion that distinguishes robbery from other larcenies.").

Precedent thus instructs us to presume that Congress has adhered to the altogether clear common-law understanding that larceny is a lesser included offense of robbery, unless Congress has affirmatively indicated its design, in codifying the crimes of robbery and larceny, to displace their common-law meanings and relationship.

Far from signaling an intent to depart from the common law, the codification of § 2113's predecessor statute suggests that Congress intended to adhere to the traditional ranking of larceny as a lesser included offense of robbery. There is no indication at any point during the codification of the two crimes that Congress meant to install new conceptions of larceny and robbery severed from their common-law foundations.

Prior to 1934, federal law did not criminalize bank robbery or larceny; these crimes were punishable only under state law. Congress enacted the precursor to § 2113(a) in response to an outbreak of bank robberies committed by John Dillinger and others who evaded capture by state authorities by moving from State to State. *See Jerome v. United States*, 318 U.S. 101, 102, 63 S.Ct. 483, 87 L.Ed. 640 (1943) (1934 Act aimed at "interstate operations by gangsters against banks—activities with which local authorities were frequently unable to cope"). In bringing federal law into this area, Congress did not aim to reshape robbery by altering the common-law definition of that crime. On the contrary, Congress chose language that practically jumped out of Blackstone's Commentaries:

> "Whoever, by force and violence, or by putting in fear, feloniously takes, or feloniously attempts to take, from the person or presence of another any property or money or any other thing of value belonging to, or in the care, custody, control, management, or possession of, any bank shall be fined not more than $5,000 or imprisoned not more than twenty years, or both." Act of May 18, 1934, ch. 304, § 2(a), 48 Stat. 783.

It soon became apparent, however, that this legislation left a gap: It did not reach the thief who intentionally, though not violently, stole money from a bank. Within a few years, federal law enforcers endeavored to close the gap. In a letter to the Speaker of the House, the Attorney General conveyed the Executive Branch's official position: "The fact that the statute is limited to robbery and does not include larceny and burglary has led to some incongruous results." *See* H.R.Rep. No. 732, 75th Cong., 1st Sess., 1 (1937) (reprinting letter). In particular, the Attorney General cited the example of a thief apprehended after taking $11,000 from a bank while a teller was temporarily absent. *Id.*, at 1–2. He therefore asked Congress to amend the bank robbery statute, specifically to add a larceny provision shorn of any force, violence, or fear requirement. *Id.*, at 2. Congress responded by passing an Act "[t]o amend the bank robbery statute to include burglary and larceny." Act of Aug. 24, 1937, ch. 747, 50 Stat. 749. The Act's new larceny provision, which Congress placed in the very same section as the robbery provision, punished "whoever shall take and carry away, with intent to steal or purloin," property, money, or anything of value from a bank. *Ibid.* There is not the slightest sign that, when this new larceny provision was proposed in terms tracking the common-law formulation, the Attorney General advocated any change in the definition of robbery from larceny *plus* to something less. Nor is there any sign that Congress meant to order such a change. The Act left in place the 1934 Act's definition of bank robbery, which continued to include the word "feloniously," requiring (as the Court concedes, *ante*, at 2169–2170) proof by the Government of an intent to steal. 50 Stat. 749.

In its 1948 codification of federal crimes, Congress delineated the bank robbery and larceny provisions of §§ 2113(a) and 2113(b) and placed these provisions under the title "Bank robbery and incidental crimes." Act of June 25, 1948, § 2113, 62 Stat. 796–797. In this codification, Congress deleted the word "feloniously" from the robbery provision, leaving the statute in substantially its present form.

II.

That 1948 deletion forms the basis of the Government's prime argument against characterizing § 2113(b) as a lesser included offense of § 2113(a), namely, that robbery, unlike larceny, no longer requires a specific intent to steal. The Government concedes that to gain a conviction for robbery at common law, the prosecutor had to prove the perpetrator's intent to steal. The Government therefore acknowledges that when Congress uses the terms "rob" or "robbery" "without further elaboration," Congress intends to retain the common-law meaning of robbery. Brief for United States 16, n. 9. But the Government contends that the 1948 removal of "feloniously" from § 2113(a) showed Congress' purpose to dispense with any requirement of intent to steal.

It is true that the larceny provision contains the words "intent to steal" while the current robbery provision does not.[4] But the element-based comparison called for by *Schmuck* is not so rigid as to require that the compared statutes contain identical words. Nor does *Schmuck* counsel deviation from our traditional practice of interpreting federal criminal statutes consistently with their common-law origins in the absence of affirmative congressional indication to the contrary. Guided by the historical understanding of the relationship between robbery and larceny both at common law and as brought into the federal criminal code, I conclude that the offense of bank robbery under § 2113(a), like the offense of bank larceny under § 2113(b), has always included and continues to include a requirement of intent to steal.

---

4   Notably, the Court would read a requirement of intent to steal into § 2113(b) even if that provision did not contain such words. *Ante*, at 2169.

This traditional reading of the robbery statute makes common sense. The Government agrees that to be convicted of robbery, the defendant must resort to force and violence, or intimidation, to accomplish his purpose. But what purpose could this be other than to steal? The Government describes two scenarios in which, it maintains, a person could commit bank robbery while nonetheless lacking intent to steal. One scenario involves a terrorist who temporarily takes a bank's money or property aiming only to disrupt the bank's business; the other involves an ex-convict, unable to cope with life in a free society, who robs a bank because he wants to be apprehended and returned to prison. Brief for United States 22, n. 13.

The Government does not point to any cases involving its terrorist scenario, and I know of none. To illustrate its ex-convict scenario, the Government cites *United States v. Lewis*, 628 F.2d 1276 (C.A.10 1980), which appears to be the only reported federal case presenting this staged situation. The facts of *Lewis*—a case on which the Court relies heavily, see *ante*, at 2168–2169, 2170—were strange, to say the least. Hoping to be sent back to prison where he could receive treatment for his alcoholism and have time to pursue his writing hobby, Lewis called a local detective and informed him of his intention to rob a bank. 628 F.2d, at 1277. He also discussed his felonious little plans with the police chief, undercover police officers, and a psychologist. *Ibid.* He even allowed his picture to be taken so that it could be posted in local banks for identification. *Ibid.* Following his much-awaited heist, Lewis was arrested in the bank's outer foyer by officers who had him under surveillance. *Id.*, at 1278.

I am not sure whether a defendant exhibiting this kind of "bizarre behavior," *ibid.*, should in fact be deemed to lack a specific intent to steal. (The Tenth Circuit, I note, determined that specific intent was present in *Lewis*, for "[t]he jury, charged with the duty to infer from conflicting evidence the defendant's intent, could have concluded that if Lewis was not arrested he would have kept the money and spent it." *Id.*, at 1279.) But whatever its proper disposition, this sort of case is extremely rare—the Government represents that, nationwide, such indictments are brought no more than once per year. Brief for United States 22, n. 13. Moreover, unlike a John Dillinger who foils state enforcers by robbing banks in Chicago and lying low in South Bend, the thief who orchestrates his own capture at the hands of the local constable hardly poses the kind of problem that one would normally expect to trigger a federal statutory response. In sum, I resist the notion—apparently embraced by the Court, see *ante*, at 2170—that Congress' purpose in deleting the word "feloniously" from § 2113(a) was to grant homesick ex-convicts like Lewis their wish to return to prison. Nor can I credit the suggestion that Congress' concern was to cover the Government's fictional terrorist, or the frustrated account holder who "withdraws" $100 by force or violence, believing the money to be rightfully his, or the thrill seeker who holds up a bank with the intent of driving around the block in a getaway car and then returning the loot, or any other defendant whose exploits are seldom encountered outside the pages of law school exams.

Indeed, there is no cause to suspect that the 1948 deletion of "feloniously" was intended to effect any substantive change at all. Nothing indicates that Congress removed that word in response to any assertion or perception of prosecutorial need. Nor is there any other reason to believe that it was Congress' design to alter the elements of the offense of robbery. Rather, the legislative history suggests that Congress intended only to make "changes in phraseology." H.R.Rep. No. 304, 80th Cong., 1st Sess., A135 (1947). *See Prince v. United States*, 352 U.S. 322, 326, n. 5, 77 S.Ct. 403, 1 L.Ed.2d 370 (1957) ("The legislative history indicates that no substantial change was made in this [1948] revision" of § 2113); *Morissette*, 342 U.S., at 269, n. 28, 72 S.Ct. 240 ("The 1948 Revision was not intended to create new crimes but to recodify those then in existence."). As the Third Circuit has recognized, "it seems that the deletion of 'feloniously' was a result of Congress' effort to delete references to felonies and misdemeanors from the code, inasmuch as both terms were defined in 18 U.S.C. § 1," a statute that has since been repealed. *United States v. Mosley*, 126 F.3d 200, 205 (C.A.3 1997). *See* also *United States v. Richardson*, 687 F.2d 952, 957 (C.A.7 1982) (giving the same account of the 1948 revision). I would not attribute to Congress a design to create a robbery offense stripped of the requirement of larcenous intent in the absence of any affirmative indication of such a design.

Our decision in *Prince* supports this conclusion. The petitioner in that case had entered a bank, displayed a revolver, and robbed the bank. He was convicted of robbery and of entering the bank with the intent to commit a felony, both crimes prohibited by § 2113(a). The trial judge sentenced him, consecutively, to 20 years for the robbery and 15 years for the entering-with-intent crime. 352 U.S., at 324, 77 S.Ct. 403. This Court reversed the sentencing decision. The entering-with-intent crime, we held, merges with the robbery crime once the latter crime is consummated. Thus, we explained, the punishment could not exceed 20 years, the sentence authorized for a consummated robbery. *Id.*, at 329, 77 S.Ct. 403. In reaching our decision in *Prince*, we noted that, when the federal bank robbery proscription was enlarged in 1937 to add the entering-with-intent and larceny provisions, "[i]t was manifestly the purpose of Congress to establish lesser offenses." *Id.*, at 327, 77 S.Ct. 403. We further stated that the "heart of the [entering] crime is the intent to steal," and that "[t]his mental element merges into the completed crime if the robbery is consummated." *Id.*, at 328. *Prince* thus conveys the Court's comprehension that an intent to steal is central not only to the entry and larceny crimes, but to robbery as well.

United States v. Wells, 519 U.S. 482, 117 S.Ct. 921, 137 L.Ed.2d 107 (1997), relied on by the Court, *ante*, at 2166–2167, is not in point. In that case, we held that the offense of making a false statement to a federally insured bank, 18 U.S.C. § 1014, did not include a requirement of materiality. We reached that holding only after concluding that the defendants in that case had not "come close to showing that at common law the term 'false statement' acquired any implication of materiality that came with it into § 1014." 519 U.S., at 491, 117 S.Ct. 921. Indeed, the defendants made "no claims about the settled meaning of 'false statement' at common law." *Ibid.* Moreover, we held that "Congress did not codify the crime of perjury or comparable common-law crimes in § 1014; . . . it simply consolidated 13 statutory provisions relating to financial institutions" to create a single regulatory offense. *Ibid.* Three of those 13 provisions, we observed, had contained express materiality requirements and lost them in the course of consolidation. *Id.*, at 492–493, 117 S.Ct. 921. From this fact, we inferred that "Congress deliberately dropped the term 'materiality' without intending materiality to be an element of § 1014." *Id.*, at 493, 117 S.Ct. 921. Here, by contrast, it is clear that Congress' aim was to codify the common-law offenses of bank robbery and bank larceny; that intent to steal was an element of common-law robbery brought into § 2113(a) via the word "feloniously"; and that Congress' deletion of that word was not intended to have any substantive effect, much less to dispense with the requirement of intent to steal.

Having accepted the Government's argument concerning intent to steal, the Court goes on to agree with the Government that robbery, unlike larceny, does not require that the defendant carry away the property. As with intent to steal, the historical linkage of the two crimes reveals the Court's error. It is true that § 2113(b) includes the phrase "takes and carries away" while § 2113(a) says only "takes." Both crimes, however, included an asportation requirement at common law. *See supra*, at 2174. Indeed, the text of §§ 2113(a) and (b)—which the Court maintains must be the primary focus of lesser included offense analysis—mirrors the language of the common law quite precisely. At common law, larceny was typically described as a crime involving both a "taking" and a "*carrying away*." *See* 4 Blackstone 231 (helpfully reminding us that "*cepit et asportavit* was the old law-latin"). Robbery, on the other hand, was often defined in "somewhat undetailed language," LaFave & Scott § 8.11, at 438, n. 6, that made no mention of "carrying away," see 4 Blackstone 231, but was nevertheless consistently interpreted to encompass an element of asportation. The Court overlooks completely this feature of the common-law terminology. I note, moreover, that the asportation requirement, both at common law and under § 2113, is an extremely modest one: even a slight movement will do. *See* LaFave & Scott § 8.11, at 439; 2 Russell & Greaves, Crimes and Misdemeanors, at *152–*153. The text of §§ 2113(a) and (b) thus tracks the common law. The Court's conclusory statement notwithstanding, nothing in the evolution of the statute suggests that "Congress adopted a different view in § 2113(a)," *ante*, at 2171, deliberately doing away with the minimal asportation requirement in prosecutions for bank robbery. I would hold, therefore, that both crimes continue to contain an asportation requirement.

Finally, the Court concludes that the "value exceeding $1,000" requirement of the first paragraph of § 2113(b) is an element of the offense described in that paragraph. I agree with this conclusion and with the reasoning in support of it. *See ante*, at 2171. It bears emphasis, however, that the lesser degree of bank larceny defined in § 2113(b)'s second paragraph contains no dollar value element even arguably impeding its classification as a lesser included offense of bank robbery. The Government does not contend that the "value not exceeding $1,000" component of that paragraph is an element of the misdemeanor offense, and such a contention would make scant sense. Surely Congress did not intend that a defendant charged only with the lower grade of bank larceny could successfully defend against that charge by showing that he stole *more* than $1,000. In other words, if a defendant commits larceny without exhibiting the distinguishing characteristics of robbery (force and violence, or intimidation), he has necessarily committed at least the lesser degree of larceny, whether he has taken $500 or $5,000. Under *Schmuck*, then, a defendant charged with bank robbery in violation of § 2113(a) is not barred as a matter of law from obtaining a jury instruction on bank larceny as defined in the second paragraph of § 2113(b).

I see no reason why a defendant charged with bank robbery, which securely encompasses as a lesser included offense the statutory equivalent of petit larceny, should automatically be denied an instruction on the statutory equivalent of grand larceny if he wants one. It is clear that petit and grand larceny were two grades of the same offense at common law. *See* 4 Blackstone 229 (petit and grand larceny are "considerably distinguished in their punishment, but not otherwise"). And, as earlier explained, *supra*, at 2173–2174, robbery at common law was an aggravated form of that single offense. One of the key purposes of *Schmuck's* elements test is to allow easy comparison between two discrete crimes. *See* 489 U.S., at 720–721, 109 S.Ct. 1443. That purpose would be frustrated if an element that exists only to distinguish a more culpable from a less culpable grade of the same crime were sufficient to prevent the defendant from getting a lesser included offense instruction as to the more culpable grade. I would therefore hold that a defendant charged with the felony of bank robbery is not barred as a matter of law from requesting and receiving an instruction describing as a lesser included offense the felony grade of bank larceny.

To be sure, any request by the defendant for an instruction covering the higher grade of bank larceny would be tantamount to a waiver of his right to notice by indictment of the "value exceeding $1,000" element. *See Stirone v. United States*, 361 U.S. 212, 215, 80 S.Ct. 270, 4 L.Ed.2d 252 (1960) (Fifth Amendment requires the Government to get a grand jury indictment before it may prosecute any felony). The constitutional requirement of notice would likely prevent the prosecution from obtaining the same instruction without the defendant's consent. I would limit any such asymmetry, however, to the unusual circumstance presented here, where an element serves only to distinguish a more culpable from a less culpable grade of the very same common-law crime and where the less culpable grade is, in turn, a lesser included offense of the crime charged.

* * *

In sum, I would hold that a defendant charged with bank robbery as defined in 18 U.S.C. § 2113(a) is not barred as a matter of law from obtaining a jury instruction on bank larceny as defined in 18 U.S.C. § 2113(b). In reaching the opposite conclusion, the Court gives short shrift to the common-law origin and statutory evolution of § 2113. The Court's woodenly literal construction gives rise to practical anomalies, see *supra*, at 2172–2173, and n. 1, and effectively shrinks the jury's choices while enlarging the prosecutor's options. I dissent.

E. In Pari Materia

The Latin phrase, *in para materia*, literally means "upon the same subject." Courts look to statutes drafted on the same subject as having been motivated by a common purpose.

United States v. Scharton

Supreme Court of the United States
285 U.S. 518 (1932)

Mr. Justice ROBERTS delivered the opinion of the Court.

The appellee was indicted under section 1114(b) of the Revenue Act of 1926, [1] the charge being attempts to evade taxes for 1926 and 1927 by falsely understating taxable income. In bar of the action he pleaded that the face of the indictment showed the offenses were committed more than three years prior to the return of a true bill. The plea was sustained and the indictment quashed, on the ground that the period of limitations is fixed by the first clause of section 1110(a) of the act, [2] and not, as the appellant contended, in the proviso thereof. The basis of this ruling was that the offense defined by use of the words 'evade or defeat' does not involve defrauding, or attempting to defraud, within the intent of the proviso.

The appellant contends fraud is implicit in the concept of evading or defeating; and asserts that attempts to obstruct or defeat the lawful functions of any department of the government (*Haas v. Henkel*, 216 U. S. 462, 479-480, 30 S. Ct. 249, 54 L. Ed. 569, 17 Ann. Cas. 1112), or to cheat it out of money to which it is entitled (*Capone v. United States* (C. C. A.) 51 F. (2d) 609, 615, 76 A. L. R. 1534) are attempts to defraud the United States, if accompanied by deceit, craft, trickery, or other dishonest methods or schemes, *Hammerschmidt v. United States*, 265 U. S. 182, 188, 44 S. Ct. 511, 68 L. Ed. 968. Any effort to defeat or evade a tax is said to be tantamount to and to possess every element of an attempt to defraud the taxing body.

We are required to ascertain the intent of Congress from the language used and to determine what cases the proviso intended to except from the general statute of limitations applicable to all offenses against the internal revenue laws. Section 1114(a), 26 USCA § 1265, makes willful failure to pay taxes, to make return, to keep necessary records, or to supply requisite information, a misdemeanor; and section 1114(c), 26 USCA § 1267 provides that willfully aiding, assisting, procuring, counselling, or advising preparation or presentation of a false or fraudulent return, affidavit, claim, or document shall be a felony. Save

---

1 U. S. Code, Supp. V, title 26, § 1266 (26 USCA § 1266): 'Any * * * person who willfully attempts in any manner to evade or defeat any tax imposed by this title or the payment thereof, shall * * * be guilty of a felony. * * *'

2 U. S. Code, Supp. V, title 18, § 585 (18 USCA § 585): 'No person shall be prosecuted, tried, or punished for any of the various offenses arising under the internal revenue laws of the United States unless the indictment is found or the information instituted within three years next after the commission of the offense: Provided, That for offenses involving the defrauding or attempting to defraud the United States or any agency thereof, whether by conspiracy or not, and in any manner, the period of limitation shall be six years. * * *' [now in effect as amended at 26 U.S.C. § 6531– eds.]

for that under consideration, these are the only sections in the Revenue Act of 1926 defining offenses against the income tax law. There are, however, numerous statutes expressly making intent to defraud an element of a specified offense against the revenue laws. Under these, an indictment failing to aver that intent would be defective; but under section 1114(b) such an averment would be surplusage, for it would be sufficient to plead and prove a willful attempt to evade or defeat. Compare *United States v. Noveck*, 271 U. S. 201, 203, 46 S. Ct. 476, 477, 70 L. Ed. 904.

As said in the *Noveck* Case, statutes will not be read as creating crimes or classes of crimes unless clearly so intended, and obviously we are here concerned with one meant only to fix periods of limitation. Moreover, the concluding clause of the section, though denominated a proviso, is an excepting clause, and therefore to be narrowly construed. *United States v. McElvain*, 272 U. S. 633, 639, 47 S. Ct. 219, 71 L. Ed. 451. And, as the section has to do with statutory crimes, it is to be liberally interpreted in favor of repose, and ought not to be extended by construction to embrace so-called frauds not so denominated by the statutes creating offenses. *United States v. Hirsch*, 100 U. S. 33, 25 L. Ed. 539; *United States v. Rabinowich*, 238 U. S. 78, 87-88, 35 S. Ct. 682, 59 L. Ed. 1211; *United States v. Noveck, supra*; *United States v. McElvain, supra*. The purpose of the proviso is to apply the six-year period to cases 'in which defrauding or an attempt to defraud the United States is an ingredient under the statute defining the offense.' *United States v. Noveck, supra*.

F. Absurd Results

Sorrells v. United States

Supreme Court of the United States
287 U.S. 435 (1932)

Mr. Chief Justice HUGHES delivered the opinion of the Court.

Defendant was indicted on two counts (1) for possessing and (2) for selling, on July 13, 1930, one-half gallon of whisky in violation of the National Prohibition Act (27 USCA). He pleaded not guilty. Upon the trial he relied upon the defense of entrapment. The court refused to sustain the defense, denying a motion to direct a verdict in favor of defendant and also refusing to submit the issue of entrapment to the jury. The court ruled that 'as a matter of law' there was no entrapment. Verdict of guilty followed, motions in arrest, and to set aside the verdict as contrary to the law and the evidence, were denied, and defendant was sentenced to imprisonment for eighteen months. The Circuit Court of Appeals affirmed the judgment (57 F. (2d) 973), and this Court granted a writ of certiorari limited to the question whether the evidence was sufficient to go to the jury upon the issue of entrapment. 287 U.S. 584, 53 S.Ct. 19, 77 L.Ed. 511.

The government, while supporting the conclusion of the court below, also urges that the defense, if available, should have been pleaded in bar to further proceedings under the indictment and could not be raised under the plea of not guilty. This question of pleading appropriately awaits the consideration of the nature and grounds of the defense.

The substance of the testimony at the trial as to entrapment was as follows: For the government, one Martin, a prohibition agent, testified that having resided for a time in Haywood county, N.C., where he posed as a tourist, he visited defendant's home near Canton, on Sunday, July 13, 1930, accompanied by three residents of the county who knew the defendant well. He was introduced as a resident of Charlotte who was stopping for a time at Clyde. The witness ascertained that defendant was a veteran of the World War and a former member of the Thirtieth Division A.E.F. Witness informed defendant that he was also an ex-service man and a former member of the same Division, which was true. Witness asked defendant if he could get the witness some liquor and defendant stated that he did not have any. Later there was a second request without result. One of those present, one Jones, was also an ex-service man and a former member of the Thirtieth Division, and the conversation turned to the war experiences of the three. After this, witness asked defendant for a third time to get him some liquor, whereupon defendant left his home and after a few minutes came back with a half gallon of liquor for which the witness paid defendant $5. Martin also testified that he was 'the first and only person among those present at the time who said anything about securing some liquor,' and that his purpose was to prosecute the defendant for procuring and selling it. The government rested its case on Martin's testimony.

Defendant called as witnesses the three persons who had accompanied the prohibition agent. In substance, they corroborated the latter's story but with some additions. Jones, a railroad employee, testified that he had introduced the agent to the defendant 'as a furniture dealer of Charlotte,' because the agent had so represented himself; that witness told defendant that the agent was 'an old 30th Division man' and the agent thereupon said to defendant that he 'would like to get a half gallon of whisky to take back to Charlotte to a friend' of his that was in the furniture business with him, and that defendant replied that he 'did not fool with whisky'; that the agent and his companions were at defendant's home 'for probably an hour or an hour and a half and that during such time the agent asked the defendant three or four or probably five times to get him, the agent, some liquor.' Defendant said 'he would go and see if he could get a half gallon of liquor,' and he returned with it after an absence of 'between twenty and thirty minutes.' Jones added that at that time he had never heard of defendant being in the liquor business, that he and the defendant were 'two old buddies,' and that he believed 'one former war buddy would get liquor for another.'

Another witness, the timekeeper and assistant paymaster of the Champion Fibre Company at Canton, testified that defendant was an employee of that company and had been 'on his job continuously without missing a pay day since March, 1924.' Witness identified the time sheet showing this employment. This witness and three others who were neighbors of the defendant and had known him for many years testified to his good character.

To rebut this testimony, the government called three witnesses who testified that the defendant had the general reputation of a rum runner. There was no evidence that the defendant had ever possessed or sold any intoxicating liquor prior to the transaction in question.

It is clear that the evidence was sufficient to warrant a finding that the act for which defendant was prosecuted was instigated by the prohibition agent, that it was the creature of his purpose, that defendant had no previous disposition to commit it but was an industrious, law-abiding citizen, and that the agent lured defendant, otherwise innocent, to its commission by repeated and persistent solicitation in which he succeeded by taking advantage of the sentiment aroused by reminiscences of their experiences as companions in arms in the World War. Such a gross abuse of authority given for the purpose of detecting and punishing crime, and not for the making of criminals, deserves the severest condemnation; but the question whether it precludes prosecution or affords a ground of defense, and, if so, upon what theory, has given rise to conflicting opinions.

It is well settled that the fact that officers or employees of the government merely afford opportunities or facilities for the commission of the offense does not defeat the prosecution. Artifice and stratagem may be employed to catch those engaged in criminal enterprises. *Grimm v. United States*, 156 U.S. 604, 610, 15 S.Ct. 470, 39 L.Ed. 550; *Goode v. United States*, 159 U.S. 663, 669, 16 S.Ct. 136, 40 L.Ed. 297 * * * The appropriate object of this permitted activity, frequently essential to the enforcement of the law, is to reveal the criminal design; to expose the illicit traffic, the prohibited publication, the fraudulent use of the mails, the illegal conspiracy, or other offenses, and thus to disclose the would-be violators of the law. A different question is presented when the criminal design originates with the officials of the government, and they implant in the mind of an innocent person the disposition to commit the alleged offense and induce its commission in order that they may prosecute.

The Circuit Court of Appeals reached the conclusion that the defense of entrapment can be maintained only where, as a result of inducement, the accused is placed in the attitude of having committed a crime which he did not intend to commit, or where, by reason of the consent implied in the inducement, no crime has in fact been committed. 57 F.(2d) page 974. As illustrating the first class, reference is made to the case of a sale of liquor to an Indian who was disguised so as to mislead the accused as to his identity. *United States v. Healy* (D.C.) 202 F. 349; *Voves v. United States* (C.C.A.) 249 F. 191. In the second class are found cases such as those of larceny or rape where want of consent is an element of the crime. * * * There may also be physical conditions which are essential to the offense and which do not exist in the case of a trap, as, for example, in the case of a prosecution for burglary where it appears that by reason of the trap there is no breaking. *Rex v. Egginton*, 2 Leach, C.C. 913; *Regina v. Johnson*, Car. & Mar. 218; *Saunders v. People*, 38 Mich. 218; *People v. McCord*, 76 Mich. 200, 42 N.W. 1106; *Allen v. State*, 40 Ala. 334, 91 Am.Dec. 477; *Love v. People*, 160 Ill. 501, 43 N.E. 710, 32 L.R.A. 139. But these decisions applying accepted principles to particular offenses, do not reach, much less determine, the present question. Neither in reasoning nor in effect do they prescribe limits for the doctrine of entrapment.

While this Court has not spoken on the precise question (see *Casey v. United States*, 276 U.S. 413, 419, 423, 48 S.Ct. 373, 72 L.Ed. 6323), the weight of authority in the lower federal courts is decidedly in favor of the view that in such case as the one before us the defense of entrapment is available. * * * The federal courts have generally approved the statement of Circuit Judge Sanborn in the leading case of *Butts v. United States*, [273 F. 35, 38 (8th Cir. 1921)], as follows: 'The first duties of the officers of the law are to prevent, not to punish crime. It is not their duty to incite to and create crime for the sole purpose of prosecuting and punishing it. Here the evidence strongly tends to prove, if it does not conclusively do so, that their first and chief endeavor was to cause, to create, crime in order to punish it, and it is unconscionable, contrary to public policy, and to the established law of the land to punish a man for the commission of an offense of the like of which he had never been guilty, either in thought or in deed, and evidently never would have been guilty of if the officers of the law had not inspired, incited, persuaded, and lured him to attempt to commit it.' The judgment in that case was reversed because of the 'fatal error' of the trial court in refusing to instruct the jury to that effect. In *Newman v. United States*, [299 F. 128, 131 (4th Cir. 1924)] the applicable principle was thus stated by Circuit Judge Woods: 'It is well settled that decoys may be used to entrap criminals, and to present opportunity to one intending or willing to commit crime. But decoys are not permissible to ensnare the innocent and lawabiding into the commission of crime. When the criminal design originates, not with the accused, but is conceived in the mind of the government officers, and the accused is by persuasion, deceitful representation, or inducement lured into the commission of a criminal act, the government is estopped by sound public policy from prosecution therefor.' These quotations sufficiently indicate the grounds of the decisions above cited.

The validity of the principle as thus stated and applied is challenged both upon theoretical and practical grounds. The argument, from the standpoint of principle, is that the court is called upon to try the accused for a particular offense which is defined by statute and that, if the evidence shows that this offense has knowingly been committed, it matters not that its commission was induced by officers of the government in the manner and circumstances assumed. It is said that where one intentionally does an act in circumstances known to him, and the particular conduct is forbidden by the law in those circumstances, he intentionally breaks the law in the only sense in which the law considers intent. *Ellis v. United States*, 206 U.S. 246, 257, 27 S.Ct. 600, 51 L.Ed. 1047, 11 Ann.Cas. 589. Moreover, that as the statute is designed to redress a public wrong, and not a private injury, there is no ground for holding the government estopped by the conduct of its officers from prosecuting the offender. To the suggestion of public policy the objectors answer that the Legislature, acting within its constitutional authority, is the arbiter of public policy and that, where conduct is expressly forbidden and penalized by a valid statute, the courts are not at liberty to disregard the law and to bar a prosecution for its violation because they are of the opinion that the crime has been instigated by government officials.

It is manifest that these arguments rest entirely upon the letter of the statute. They take no account of the fact that its application in the circumstances under consideration is foreign to its purpose; that such an application is so shocking to the sense of justice that it has been urged that it is the duty of the court to stop the prosecution in the interest of the government itself, to protect it from the illegal conduct of its officers and to preserve the purity of its courts. *Casey v. United States*, supra. But can an application of the statute having such an effect-creating a situation so contrary to the purpose of the law and so inconsistent with its proper enforcement as to invoke such a challenge-fairly be deemed to be within its intendment?

Literal interpretation of statutes at the expense of the reason of the law and producing absurd consequences or flagrant injustice has frequently been condemned. In *United States v. Palmer*, 3 Wheat. 610, 631, 4 L.Ed. 471, Chief Justice Marshall, in construing the Act of Congress of April 30, 1790, section 8 (1 Stat. 113), relating to robbery on the high seas, found that the words 'any person or persons' were 'broad enough to comprehend every human being,' but he concluded that 'general words must not only be limited to cases within the jurisdiction of the state, but also to those objects to which the legislature intended to apply them.' In *United States v. Kirby*, 7 Wall. 482, 19 L.Ed. 278, the case arose under the Act of Congress of March 3, 1825 (4 Stat. 104, s 9), providing for the conviction of any person who 'shall, knowingly and wilfully, obstruct or retard the passage of the mail, or of any driver or carrier * * * carrying the same.' Considering the purpose of the statute, the Court held that it had no application to the obstruction or retarding of the passage of the mail or of its carrier by reason of the arrest of the carrier upon a warrant issued by a state court. The Court said: 'All laws should receive a sensible construction. General terms should be so limited in their application as not to lead to injustice, oppression, or an absurd consequence. It will always, therefore, be presumed that the legislature intended exceptions to its language, which would avoid results of this character. The reason of the law in such cases should prevail over its letter.' And the Court supported this conclusion by reference to the classical illustrations found in *Puffendorf* and *Plowden*. Id., pages 486, 487 of 7 Wall.

Applying this principle in *Lau Ow Bew v. United States*, 144 U.S. 47, 12 S.Ct. 517, 518, 36 L.Ed. 340, the Court decided that a statute requiring the permission of the Chinese government, and identification by certificate, of 'every Chinese person, other than a laborer,' entitled by treaty or the act of Congress to come within the United States, did not apply to Chinese merchants already domiciled in the United States, who had left the country for temporary purposes, animo revertendi, and sought to re-enter it on their return to their business and their homes. And in *United States v. Katz*, 271 U.S. 354, 362, 46 S.Ct. 513, 516, 70 L.Ed. 986, construing title 2, section 10 of the National Prohibition Act (27 USCA § 22) so as to avoid an unreasonable application of its words, if taken literally, the Court again declared that 'general terms descriptive of a class of persons made subject to a criminal statute may and should be limited, where the literal application of the statute would lead to extreme or absurd results, and where the legislative purpose gathered from the whole act would be satisfied by a more limited interpretation.'[7] *See,* to the same effect, *Heydenfeldt v. Daney Gold & S. Min. Company*, 93 U.S. 634, 638, 23 L.Ed. 995; * * *

---

7   In *Hawaii v. Mankichi*, 190 U.S. 197, 214, 23 S.Ct. 787, 789, 47 L.Ed. 1016, the court referred with approval to the following language of the Master of the Rolls (afterwards Lord Esher) in *Plumstead Board of Works v. Spackman*, L.R. 13 Q.B.D. 878, 887: "If there are no means of avoiding such an interpretation of the statute' (as will amount to a great hardship), 'a judge must come to the conclusion that the legislature by inadvertence has committed an act of legislative injustice; but, to my mind, a judge ought to struggle with all the intellect that he has, and with all the vigor of mind that he has, against such an interpretation of an act of Parliament; and, unless he is forced to come to a contrary conclusion, he ought to assume that it is impossible that the legislature could have as intended."

We think that this established principle of construction is applicable here. We are unable to conclude that it was the intention of the Congress in enacting this statute that its processes of detection and enforcement should be abused by the instigation by government officials of an act on the part of persons otherwise innocent in order to lure them to its commission and to punish them. We are not forced by the letter to do violence to the spirit and purpose of the statute. This, we think, has been the underlying and controlling thought in the suggestions in judicial opinions that the government in such a case is estopped to prosecute or that the courts should bar the prosecution. If the requirements of the highest public policy in the maintenance of the integrity of administration would preclude the enforcement of the statute in such circumstances as are present here, the same considerations justify the conclusion that the case lies outside the purview of the act and that its general words should not be construed to demand a proceeding at once inconsistent with that policy and abhorrent to the sense of justice. This view does not derogate from the authority of the court to deal appropriately with abuses of its process and it obviates the objection to the exercise by the court of a dispensing power in forbidding the prosecution of one who is charged with conduct assumed to fall within the statute.

We are unable to approve the view that the court, although treating the statute as applicable despite the entrapment, and the defendant as guilty, has authority to grant immunity, or to adopt a procedure to that end. It is the function of the court to construe the statute, not to defeat it as construed. Clemency is the function of the Executive. Ex parte *United States*, 242 U.S. 27, 42, 37 S.Ct. 72, 74, 61 L.Ed. 129, L.R.A. 1917E, 1178, Ann. Cas. 1917B, 355. In that case, this Court decisively denied such authority to free guilty defendants, in holding that the court had no power to suspend sentences indefinitely. The Court, speaking by Chief Justice White, said: 'If it be that the plain legislative command fixing a specific punishment for crime is subject to be permanently set aside by an implied judicial power upon considerations extraneous to the legality of the conviction, it would seem necessarily to follow that there could be likewise implied a discretionary authority to permanently refuse to try a criminal charge because of the conclusion that a particular act made criminal by law ought not to be treated as criminal. And thus it would come to pass that the possession by the judicial department of power to permanently refuse to enforce a law would result in the destruction of the conceded powers of the other departments, and hence leave no law to be enforced.' And while recognizing the humane considerations which had led judges to adopt the practice of suspending sentences indefinitely in certain cases, the Court found no ground for approving the practice 'since its exercise, in the very nature of things, amounts to a refusal by the judicial power to perform a duty resting upon it, and, as a consequence thereof, to an interference with both the legislative and executive authority as fixed by the Constitution.' Id., pages 51, 52 of 242 U.S., 37 S.Ct. 72, 78. Where defendant has been duly indicted for an offense found to be within the statute, and the proper authorities seek to proceed with the prosecution, the court cannot refuse to try the case in the constitutional method because it desires to let the defendant go free.

Suggested analogies from procedure in civil cases are not helpful. When courts of law refuse to sustain alleged causes of action which grow out of illegal schemes, the applicable law itself denies the right to recover. Where courts of equity refuse equitable relief because complainants come with unclean hands, they are administering the principles of equitable jurisprudence governing equitable rights. But in a criminal prosecution, the statute defining the offense is necessarily the law of the case.

To construe statutes so as to avoid absurd or glaringly unjust results, foreign to the legislative purpose, is, as we have seen, a traditional and appropriate function of the courts. Judicial nullification of statutes, admittedly valid and applicable, has, happily, no place in our system. The Congress by legislation can always, if it desires, alter the effect of judicial construction of statutes. We conceive it to be our duty to construe the statute here in question reasonably, and we hold that it is beyond our prerogative to give the statute an unreasonable construction, confessedly contrary to public policy, and then to decline to enforce it.

The conclusion we have reached upon these grounds carries its own limitation. We are dealing with a statutory prohibition and we are simply concerned to ascertain whether in the light of a plain public policy and of the proper administration of justice, conduct induced as stated should be deemed to be within that prohibition. We have no occasion to consider hypothetical cases of crimes so heinous or revolting that the applicable law would admit of no exceptions. No such situation is presented here. The question in each case must be determined by the scope of the law considered in the light of what may fairly be deemed to be its object.

Objections to the defense of entrapment are also urged upon practical grounds. But considerations of mere convenience must yield to the essential demands of justice. The argument is pressed that if the defense is available it will lead to the introduction of issues of a collateral character relating to the activities of the officials of the government and to the conduct and purposes of the defendant previous to the alleged offense. For the defense of entrapment is not simply that the particular act was committed at the instance of government officials. That is often the case where the proper action of these officials leads to the revelation of criminal enterprises. *Grimm v. United States, supra.* The predisposition and criminal design of the defendant are relevant. But the issues raised and the evidence adduced must be pertinent to the controlling question whether the defendant is a person otherwise innocent whom the government is seeking to punish for an alleged offense which is the product of the creative activity of its own officials. If that is the fact, common justice requires that the accused be permitted to prove it. The government in such a case is in no position to object to evidence of the activities of its representatives in relation to the accused, and if the defendant seeks acquittal by reason of entrapment he cannot complain of an appropriate and searching inquiry into his own conduct and predisposition as bearing upon that issue. If in consequence he suffers a disadvantage, he has brought it upon himself by reason of the nature of the defense.

What has been said indicates the answer to the contention of the government that the defense of entrapment must be pleaded in bar to further proceedings under the indictment and cannot be raised under the plea of not guilty. This contention presupposes that the defense is available to the accused and relates only to the manner in which it shall be presented. The government considers the defense as analogous to a plea of pardon or of autrefois convict or autrefois acquit. It is assumed that the accused is not denying his guilt but is setting up special facts in bar upon which he relies regardless of his guilt or innocence of the crime charged. This, as we have seen, is a misconception. The defense is available, not in the view that the accused though guilty may go free, but that the government cannot be permitted to contend that he is guilty of a crime where the government officials are the instigators of his conduct. The federal courts in sustaining the defense in such circumstances have proceeded in the view that the defendant is not guilty. The practice of requiring a plea in bar has not obtained. Fundamentally, the question is whether the defense, if the facts bear it out, takes the case out of the purview of the statute because it cannot be supposed that the Congress intended that the letter of its enactment should be used to support such a gross perversion of its purpose.

We are of the opinion that upon the evidence produced in the instant case the defense of entrapment was available and that the trial court was in error in holding that as a matter of law there was no entrapment and in refusing to submit the issue to the jury.

The judgment is reversed, and the cause is remanded for further proceedings in conformity with this opinion.
Judgment reversed.

Mr. Justice McREYNOLDS is of the opinion that the judgment below should be affirmed.

Mr. Justice ROBERTS.

The facts set forth in the court's opinion establish that a prohibition enforcement officer instigated the commission of the crime charged. The courts below held that the showing was insufficient, as matter of law, to sustain the claim of entrapment, and that the jury were properly instructed to ignore that defense in their consideration of the case. A conviction resulted. The government maintains that the issue of entrapment is not triable under the plea of not guilty, but should be raised by plea in bar or be adjudicated in some manner by the court rather than by the jury, and as the trial court properly decided the question, the record presents no reversible error. I think, however, the judgment should be reversed, but for reasons and upon grounds other than those stated in the opinion of the court.

Of late the term 'entrapment' has been adopted by the courts to signify instigation of crime by officers of government. The cases in which such incitement has been recognized as a defense have grown to an amazing total [footnote omitted]. The increasing frequency of the assertion that the defendant was entrapped is doubtless due to the creation by statute of many new crimes (*e.g.,* sale and transportation of liquor and narcotics) and the correlative establishment of special enforcement bodies for the detection and punishment of offenders. The efforts of members of these forces to obtain arrests and convictions have too often been marked by reprehensible methods.

Society is at war with the criminal classes, and courts have uniformly held that in waging this warfare the forces of prevention and detection may use traps, decoys, and deception to obtain evidence of the commission of crime. Resort to such means does not render an indictment thereafter found a nullity nor call for the exclusion of evidence so procured. But the defense here asserted involves more than obtaining evidence by artifice or deception. Entrapment is the conception and planning of an offense by an officer, and his procurement of its commission by one who would not have perpetrated it except for the trickery, persuasion, or fraud of the officer. Federal and state courts have held that substantial proof of entrapment as thus defined calls for the submission of the issue to the jury and warrants an acquittal. The reasons assigned in support of this procedure have not been uniform. Thus it has been held that the acts of its officers estop the government to prove the offense. The result has also been justified by the mere statement of the rule that where entrapment is proved the defendant is not guilty of the crime charged. Often the defense has been permitted upon grounds of public policy, which the courts formulate by saying they will not permit their process to be used in aid of a scheme for the actual creation of a crime by those whose duty is to deter its commission.

This court has adverted to the doctrine, but has not heretofore had occasion to determine its validity, the basis on which it should rest, or the procedure to be followed when it is involved. The present case affords the opportunity to settle these matters as respects the administration of the federal criminal law.

There is common agreement that where a law officer envisages a crime, plans it, and activates its commission by one not theretofore intending its perpetration, for the sole purpose of obtaining a victim through indictment, conviction and sentence, the consummation of so revolting a plan ought not to be permitted by any self respecting tribunal. Equally true is this whether the offense is one at common law or merely a creature of statute. Public policy forbids such sacrifice of decency. The enforcement of this policy calls upon the court, in every instance where alleged entrapment of a defendant is brought to its notice, to ascertain the facts, to appraise their effect upon the administration of justice, and to make such order with respect to the further prosecution of the cause as the circumstances require.

This view calls for no distinction between crimes mala in se and statutory offenses of lesser gravity; requires no statutory construction, and attributes no merit to a guilty defendant; but frankly recognizes the true foundation of the doctrine in the public policy which protects the purity of government and its processes. Always the courts refuse their aid in civil cases to the perpetration and consummation of an illegal scheme. Invariably they hold a civil action must be abated if its basis is violation of the decencies of life, disregard of the rules, statutory or common law, which formulate the ethics of men's relations to each other. Neither courts of equity nor those administering legal remedies tolerate the use of their process to consummate a wrong. The doctrine of entrapment in criminal law is the analogue of the same rule applied in civil proceedings. And this is the real basis of the decisions approving the defense of entrapment, though in statement the rule is cloaked under a declaration that the government is estopped or the defendant has not been proved guilty.

A new method of rationalizing the defense is now asserted. This is to construe the act creating the offense by reading in a condition or proviso that if the offender shall have been entrapped into crime the law shall not apply to him. So, it is said, the true intent of the legislature will be effectuated. This seems a strained and unwarranted construction of the statute; and amounts, in fact, to judicial amendment. It is not merely broad construction, but addition of an element not contained in the legislation. The constituents of the offense are enumerated by the statute. If we assume the defendant to have been a person of upright purposes, law abiding, and not prone to crime,-induced against his own will and better judgment to become the instrument of the criminal purpose of another,-his action, so induced, none the less falls within the letter of the law and renders him amenable to its penalties. Viewed in its true light entrapment is not a defense to him; his act, coupled with his intent to do the act, brings him within the definition of the law; he has no rights or equities by reason of his entrapment. It cannot truly be said that entrapment excuses him or contradicts the obvious fact of his commission of the offense. We cannot escape this conclusion by saying that where need arises the statute will be read as containing an implicit condition that it shall not apply in the case of entrapment. The effect of such construction is to add to the words of the statute a proviso which gives to the defendant a double defense under his plea of not guilty, namely, (a) that what he did does not fall within the definition of the statute, and (b) entrapment. This amounts to saying that one who with full intent commits the act defined by law as an offense is nevertheless by virtue of the unspoken and implied mandate of the statute to be adjudged not guilty by reason of someone else's improper conduct. It is merely to adopt a form of words to justify action which ought to be based on the inherent right of the court not to be made the instrument of wrong.

It is said that this case warrants such a construction of the applicable act, but that the question whether a similar construction will be required in the case of other or more serious crimes is not before the court. Thus no guide or rule is announced as to when a statute shall be read as excluding a case of entrapment; and no principle of statutory construction is suggested which would enable us to say that it is excluded by some statutes and not by others.

The doctrine rests, rather, on a fundamental rule of public policy. The protection of its own functions and the preservation of the purity of its own temple belongs only to the court. It is the province of the court and of the court alone to protect itself and the government from such prostitution of the criminal law. The violation of the principles of justice by the entrapment of the unwary into crime should be dealt with by the court no matter by whom or at what stage of the proceedings the facts are brought to its attention. Quite properly it may discharge the prisoner upon a writ of habeas corpus. Equally well may it quash the indictment or entertain and try a plea in bar. But its powers do not end there. Proof of entrapment, at any stage of the case, requires the court to stop the prosecution, direct that the indictment be quashed, and the defendant set at liberty. If in doubt as to the facts it may submit the issue of entrapment to a jury for advice. But whatever may be the finding upon such submission the power and the duty to act remain with the court and not with the jury.

Such action does not grant immunity to a guilty defendant. But to afford him as his right a defense founded not on the statute, but on the court's view of what the legislature is assumed to have meant, is to grant him unwarranted immunity. If the court may construe an act of Congress so as to create a defense for one whose guilt the act pronounces, no reason is apparent why the same statute may not be modified by a similar process of construction as to the penalty prescribed. But it is settled that this may not be done. Ex parte *United States*, 242 U.S. 27, 37 S.Ct. 72, 61 L.Ed. 129, L.R.A. 1917E, 1178, Ann. Cas. 1917B, 355. The broad distinction between the refusal to lend the aid of the court's own processes to the consummation of a wrong and the attempt to modify by judicial legislation the mandate of the statute as to the punishment to be imposed after trial and conviction is so obvious as not to need discussion.

Recognition of the defense of entrapment as belonging to the defendant and as raising an issue for decision by the jury called to try him upon plea of the general issue, results in the trial of a false issue wholly outside the true rule which should be applied by the courts. It has been generally held, where the defendant has proved an entrapment, it is permissible for the government to show in rebuttal that the officer guilty of incitement of the crime had reasonable cause to believe the defendant was a person disposed to commit the offense. This procedure is approved by the opinion of the court. The proof received in rebuttal usually amounts to no more than that the defendant had a bad reputation, or that he had been previously convicted. Is the statute upon which the indictment is based to be further construed as removing the defense of entrapment from such a defendant?

Whatever may be the demerits of the defendant or his previous infractions of law these will not justify the instigation and creation of a new crime, as a means to reach him and punish him for his past misdemeanors. He has committed the crime in question, but, by supposition, only because of instigation and inducement by a government officer. To say that such conduct by an official of government is condoned and rendered innocuous by the fact that the defendant had a bad reputation or had previously transgressed is wholly to disregard the reason for refusing the processes of the court to consummate an abhorrent transaction. It is to discard the basis of the doctrine and in effect to weigh the equities as between the government and the defendant when there are in truth no equities belonging to the latter, and when the rule of action cannot rest on any estimate of the good which may come of the conviction of the offender by foul means. The accepted procedure, in effect, pivots conviction in such cases, not on the commission of the crime charged, but on the prior reputation or some former act or acts of the defendant not mentioned in the indictment.

The applicable principle is that courts must be closed to the trial of a crime instigated by the government's own agents. No other issue, no comparison of equities as between the guilty official and the guilty defendant, has any place in the enforcement of this overruling principle of public policy.

The judgment should be reversed and the cause remanded to the District Court with instructions to quash the indictment and discharge the defendant.

Mr. Justice BRANDEIS and Mr. Justice STONE concur in this opinion.

Notes and Questions

1. Congress has never acted to overrule this decision, notwithstanding that the Court has continued to apply it. *See Sherman v. United States*, 356 U.S. 369 (1958); *Jacobson v. United States*, 503 U.S. 540 (1992). Does this mean the majority correctly divined the intent of Congress?

2. If it exists only as a matter of statutory interpretation, could Congress or a state abolish the entrapment defense?

3. There is a debate in the states between those taking an objective approach, focusing on the conduct of the police rather than the predisposition of the defendant to commit the offense, and those focusing on the subjective question of predisposition.

G. Constitutional Doubt

United States v. X–Citement Video, Inc.

Supreme Court of the United States
513 U.S. 64 (1994)

Chief Justice REHNQUIST delivered the opinion of the Court.

The Protection of Children Against Sexual Exploitation Act of 1977, as amended, prohibits the interstate transportation, shipping, receipt, distribution, or reproduction of visual depictions of minors engaged in sexually explicit conduct. 18 U.S.C. § 2252. The Court of Appeals for the Ninth Circuit reversed the conviction of respondents for violation of this Act. It held that the Act did not require that the defendant know that one of the performers was a minor, and that it was therefore facially unconstitutional. We conclude that the Act is properly read to include such a requirement.

Rubin Gottesman owned and operated X–Citement Video, Inc. Undercover police posed as pornography retailers and targeted X–Citement Video for investigation. During the course of the sting operation, the media exposed Traci Lords for her roles in pornographic films while under the age of 18. Police Officer Steven Takeshita expressed an interest in obtaining Traci Lords tapes. Gottesman complied, selling Takeshita 49 videotapes featuring Lords before her 18th birthday. Two months later, Gottesman shipped eight tapes of the underage Traci Lords to Takeshita in Hawaii.

These two transactions formed the basis for a federal indictment under the child pornography statute. The indictment charged respondents with one count each of violating 18 U.S.C. §§ 2252(a)(1) and (a)(2), along with one count of conspiracy to do the same under 18 U.S.C. § 371. Evidence at trial suggested that Gottesman had full awareness of Lords' underage performances. *United States v. Gottesman*, No. CR 88–295KN, Findings of Fact ¶ 7 (CD Cal., Sept. 20, 1989), App. to Pet. for Cert. 39a ("Defendants knew that Traci Lords was underage when she made the films defendant's [sic] transported or shipped in interstate commerce"). The District Court convicted respondents of all three counts. On appeal, Gottesman argued, *inter alia*, that the Act was facially unconstitutional because it lacked a necessary scienter requirement and was unconstitutional as applied because the tapes at issue were not child pornography. The Ninth Circuit remanded to the District Court for reconsideration in light of *United States v. Thomas*, 893 F.2d 1066 (CA9), cert. denied, 498 U.S. 826, 111 S.Ct. 80, 112 L.Ed.2d 53 (1990). In that case, the Ninth Circuit had held § 2252 did not contain a scienter requirement, but had not reached the constitutional questions. On remand, the District Court refused to set aside the judgment of conviction.

On appeal for the second time, Gottesman reiterated his constitutional arguments. This time, the court reached the merits of his claims and, by a divided vote, found § 2252 facially unconstitutional. The court first held that 18 U.S.C. § 2256 met constitutional standards in setting the age of majority at age 18, substituting lascivious for lewd, and prohibiting actual or simulated bestiality and sadistic or masochistic abuse. 982 F.2d 1285, 1288–1289 (CA9 1992). It then discussed § 2252, noting it was bound by its conclusion in *Thomas* to construe the Act as lacking a scienter requirement for the age of minority. The court concluded that case law from this Court required that the defendant must have knowledge at least of the nature and character of the materials. 982 F.2d, at 1290, citing *Smith v. California*, 361 U.S. 147, 80 S.Ct. 215, 4 L.Ed.2d 205 (1959); *New York v. Ferber*, 458 U.S. 747, 102 S.Ct. 3348, 73 L.Ed.2d 1113 (1982); and

Hamling v. United States, 418 U.S. 87, 94 S.Ct. 2887, 41 L.Ed.2d 590 (1974). The court extended these cases to hold that the First Amendment requires that the defendant possess knowledge of the particular fact that one performer had not reached the age of majority at the time the visual depiction was produced. 982 F.2d, at 1291. Because the court found the statute did not require such a showing, it reversed respondents' convictions. We granted certiorari, 510 U.S. 1163, 114 S.Ct. 1186, 127 L.Ed.2d 536 (1994), and now reverse.

Title 18 U.S.C. § 2252 (1988 ed. and Supp. V) provides, in relevant part:

"(a) Any person who—

"(1) knowingly transports or ships in interstate or foreign commerce by any means including by computer or mails, any visual depiction, if—

"(A) the producing of such visual depiction involves the use of a minor engaging in sexually explicit conduct; and

"(B) such visual depiction is of such conduct;

"(2) knowingly receives, or distributes, any visual depiction that has been mailed, or has been shipped or transported in interstate or foreign commerce, or which contains materials which have been mailed or so shipped or transported, by any means including by computer, or knowingly reproduces any visual depiction for distribution in interstate or foreign commerce or through the mails, if—

"(A) the producing of such visual depiction involves the use of a minor engaging in sexually explicit conduct; and

"(B) such visual depiction is of such conduct;

. . . .

"shall be punished as provided in subsection (b) of this section."

The critical determination which we must make is whether the term "knowingly" in subsections (1) and (2) modifies the phrase "the use of a minor" in subsections (1)(A) and (2)(A). The most natural grammatical reading, adopted by the Ninth Circuit, suggests that the term "knowingly" modifies only the surrounding verbs: transports, ships, receives, distributes, or reproduces. Under this construction, the word "knowingly" would not modify the elements of the minority of the performers, or the sexually explicit nature of the material, because they are set forth in independent clauses separated by interruptive punctuation. But we do not think this is the end of the matter, both because of anomalies which result from this construction, and because of the respective presumptions that some form of scienter is to be implied in a criminal statute even if not expressed, and that a statute is to be construed where fairly possible so as to avoid substantial constitutional questions.

If the term "knowingly" applies only to the relevant verbs in § 2252—transporting, shipping, receiving, distributing, and reproducing—we would have to conclude that Congress wished to distinguish between someone who knowingly transported a particular package of film whose contents were unknown to him, and someone who unknowingly transported that package. It would seem odd, to say the least, that Congress distinguished between someone who inadvertently dropped an item into the mail without realizing it, and someone who consciously placed the same item in the mail, but was nonetheless unconcerned about whether the person had any knowledge of the prohibited contents of the package.

Some applications of respondents' position would produce results that were not merely odd, but positively absurd. If we were to conclude that "knowingly" only modifies the relevant verbs in § 2252, we would sweep within the ambit of the statute actors who had no idea that they were even dealing with sexually explicit material. For instance, a retail druggist who returns an uninspected roll of developed film to a customer "knowingly distributes" a visual depiction and would be criminally liable if it were later discovered that the visual depiction contained images of children engaged in sexually explicit conduct. Or, a new resident of an apartment might receive mail for the prior resident and store the mail unopened. If the prior tenant had requested delivery of materials covered by § 2252, his residential successor could be prosecuted for "knowing receipt" of such materials. Similarly, a Federal Express courier who delivers a box in which the shipper has declared the contents to be "film" "knowingly transports" such film. We do not assume that Congress, in passing laws, intended such results. *Public Citizen v. Department of Justice*, 491 U.S. 440, 453–455, 109 S.Ct. 2558, 2566–67, 105 L.Ed.2d 377 (1989); *United States v. Turkette*, 452 U.S. 576, 580, 101 S.Ct. 2524, 2527, 69 L.Ed.2d 246 (1981).

Our reluctance to simply follow the most grammatical reading of the statute is heightened by our cases interpreting criminal statutes to include broadly applicable scienter requirements, even where the statute by its terms does not contain them. The landmark opinion in *Morissette v. United States*, 342 U.S. 246, 72 S.Ct. 240, 96 L.Ed. 288 (1952), discussed the common-law history of *mens rea* as applied to the elements of the federal embezzlement statute. That statute read: "Whoever embezzles, steals, purloins, or knowingly converts to his use or the use of another, or without authority, sells, conveys or disposes of any record, voucher, money, or thing of value of the United States . . . [s]hall be fined." 18 U.S.C. § 641, cited in *Morissette*, 342 U.S., at 248, n. 2, 72 S.Ct., at 242, n. 2. Perhaps even more obviously than in the statute presently before us, the word "knowingly" in its isolated position suggested that it only attached to the verb "converts," and required only that the defendant intentionally assume dominion over the property. But the Court used the background presumption of evil intent to conclude that the term "knowingly" also required that the defendant have knowledge of the facts that made the taking a conversion—*i.e.*, that the property belonged to the United States. *Id.*, at 271, 72 S.Ct., at 254. *See also United States v. United States Gypsum Co.*, 438 U.S. 422, 438, 98 S.Ct. 2864, 2874, 57 L.Ed.2d 854 (1978) ("[F]ar more than the simple omission of the appropriate phrase from the statutory definition is necessary to justify dispensing with an intent requirement").

Liparota v. United States, 471 U.S. 419, 105 S.Ct. 2084, 85 L.Ed.2d 434 (1985), posed a challenge to a federal statute prohibiting certain actions with respect to food stamps. The statute's use of "knowingly" could be read only to modify "uses, transfers, acquires, alters, or possesses" or it could be read also to modify "in any manner not authorized by [the statute]." Noting that neither interpretation posed constitutional problems, *id.*, at 424, n. 6, 105 S.Ct., at 2087, n. 6, the Court held the scienter requirement applied to both elements by invoking the background principle set forth in *Morissette*. In addition, the Court was concerned with the broader reading which would "criminalize a broad range of apparently innocent conduct." 471 U.S., at 426, 105 S.Ct., at 2088. Imposing criminal liability on an unwitting food stamp recipient who purchased groceries at a store that inflated its prices to such purchasers struck the Court as beyond the intended reach of the statute.

The same analysis drove the recent conclusion in *Staples v. United States*, 511 U.S. 600, 114 S.Ct. 1793, 128 L.Ed.2d 608 (1994), that to be criminally liable a defendant must know that his weapon possessed automatic firing capability so as to make it a machine gun as defined by the National Firearms Act. Congress had not expressly imposed any *mens rea* requirement in the provision criminalizing the possession of a firearm in the absence of proper registration. 26 U.S.C. § 5861(d). The Court first rejected the argument that the statute described a public welfare offense, traditionally excepted from the background principle favoring scienter. *Morissette, supra*, 342 U.S., at 255, 72 S.Ct., at 246. The Court then expressed concern with a statutory reading that would criminalize behavior that a defendant believed fell within "a long tradition of widespread lawful gun ownership by private individuals." *Staples*, 511 U.S., at 610, 114 S.Ct., at 1799. The Court also emphasized the harsh penalties attaching to violations of the statute as a "significant consideration in determining whether the statute should be construed as dispensing with *mens rea*." *Id.*, at 616, 114 S.Ct., at 1802.

Applying these principles, we think the Ninth Circuit's plain language reading of § 2252 is not so plain. First, § 2252 is not a public welfare offense. Persons do not harbor settled expectations that the contents of magazines and film are generally subject to stringent public regulation. In fact, First Amendment constraints presuppose the opposite view. Rather, the statute is more akin to the common-law offenses against the "state, the person, property, or public morals," *Morissette, supra*, 342 U.S., at 255, 72 S.Ct., at 246, that presume a scienter requirement in the absence of express contrary intent.[2] Second, *Staples*' concern with harsh penalties looms equally large respecting § 2252: Violations are punishable by up to 10 years in prison as well as substantial fines and forfeiture. 18 U.S.C. §§ 2252(b), 2253, 2254. *See also Morissette, supra*, at 260, 72 S.Ct., at 248.

Morissette, reinforced by *Staples*, instructs that the presumption in favor of a scienter requirement should apply to each of the statutory elements that criminalize otherwise innocent conduct. *Staples* held that the features of a gun as technically described by the firearm registration Act was such an element. Its holding rested upon "the nature of the particular device or substance Congress has subjected to regulation and the expectations that individuals may legitimately have in dealing with the regulated items." *Staples, supra*, at 619, 114 S.Ct., at 1804. Age of minority in § 2252 indisputably possesses the same status as an elemental fact because non-obscene, sexually explicit materials involving persons over the age of 17 are protected by the First Amendment. *Alexander v. United States*, 509 U.S. 544, 549–550, 113 S.Ct. 2766, 2771, 125 L.Ed.2d 441 (1993); *Sable Communications of Cal., Inc. v. FCC*, 492 U.S. 115, 126, 109 S.Ct. 2829, 2836–37, 106 L.Ed.2d 93 (1989); *FW/PBS, Inc. v. Dallas*, 493 U.S. 215, 224, 110 S.Ct. 596, 604, 107 L.Ed.2d 603 (1990); *Smith v. California*, 361 U.S., at 152, 80 S.Ct., at 218.[17] In the light of these decisions, one would reasonably expect to be free from regulation when trafficking in sexually explicit, though not obscene,

---

2   *Morissette's* treatment of the common-law presumption of *mens rea* recognized that the presumption expressly excepted "sex offenses, such as rape, in which the victim's actual age was determinative despite defendant's reasonable belief that the girl had reached age of consent." 342 U.S., at 251, n. 8, 72 S.Ct., at 244, n. 8. But as in the criminalization of pornography production at 18 U.S.C. § 2251, see *infra*, at 471, n. 5, the perpetrator confronts the underage victim personally and may reasonably be required to ascertain that victim's age. The opportunity for reasonable mistake as to age increases significantly once the victim is reduced to a visual depiction, unavailable for questioning by the distributor or receiver. Thus we do not think the common-law treatment of sex offenses militates against our construction of the present statute.

3   In this regard, age of minority is not a "jurisdictional fact" that enhances an offense otherwise committed with an evil intent. *See, e.g., United States v. Feola*, 420 U.S. 671, 95 S.Ct. 1255, 43 L.Ed.2d 541 (1975). There, the Court did not require knowledge of "jurisdictional facts"—that the target of an assault was a federal officer. Criminal intent serves to separate those who understand the wrongful nature of their act from those who do not, but does not require knowledge of the precise consequences that may flow from that act once aware that the act is wrongful. *Id.*, at 685, 95 S.Ct., at 1264. Cf. *Hamling v. United States*, 418 U.S. 87, 120, 94 S.Ct. 2887, 2909, 41 L.Ed.2d 590 (1974) (knowledge that the materials at issue are legally obscene not required).

materials involving adults. Therefore, the age of the performers is the crucial element separating legal innocence from wrongful conduct.

The legislative history of the statute evolved over a period of years, and perhaps for that reason speaks somewhat indistinctly to the question whether "knowingly" in the statute modifies the elements of subsections (1)(A) and (2)(A)—that the visual depiction involves the use of a minor engaging in sexually explicit conduct—or merely the verbs "transport or ship" in subsection (1) and "receive or distribute . . . [or] reproduce" in subsection (2). In 1959, we held in *Smith v. California, supra*, that a California statute that dispensed with any *mens rea* requirement as to the contents of an obscene book would violate the First Amendment. *Id.*, at 154, 80 S.Ct., at 219. When Congress began dealing with child pornography in 1977, the content of the legislative debates suggest that it was aware of this decision. *See, e.g.*, 123 Cong.Rec. 30935 (1977) ("It is intended that they have knowledge of the type of material . . . proscribed by this bill. The legislative history should be clear on that so as to remove any chance it will lead into constitutional problems"). Even if that were not the case, we do not impute to Congress an intent to pass legislation that is inconsistent with the Constitution as construed by this Court. *Yates v. United States*, 354 U.S. 298, 319, 77 S.Ct. 1064, 1077, 1 L.Ed.2d 1356 (1957) ("In [construing the statute] we should not assume that Congress chose to disregard a constitutional danger zone so clearly marked"). When first passed, § 2252 punished one who "knowingly transports or ships in interstate or foreign commerce or mails, for the purpose of sale or distribution for sale, any *obscene* visual or print medium" if it involved the use of a minor engaged in sexually explicit conduct. Pub.L. 95–225, 92 Stat. 7 (emphasis added). Assuming awareness of *Smith*, at a minimum, "knowingly" was intended to modify "obscene" in the 1978 version.

In 1984, Congress amended the statute to its current form, broadening its application to those sexually explicit materials that, while not obscene as defined by *Miller v. California*, 413 U.S. 15, 93 S.Ct. 2607, 37 L.Ed.2d 419 (1973),[4] could be restricted without violating the First Amendment as explained by *New York v. Ferber*, 458 U.S. 747, 102 S.Ct. 3348, 73 L.Ed.2d 1113 (1982). When Congress eliminated the adjective "obscene," all of the elements defining the character and content of the materials at issue were relegated to subsections (1)(A) and (2)(A). In this effort to expand the child pornography statute to its full constitutional limits, Congress nowhere expressed an intent to eliminate the *mens rea* requirement that had previously attached to the character and content of the material through the word obscene.

---

4 The *Miller* test for obscenity asks whether the work, taken as a whole, "appeals to the prurient interest," "depicts or describes [sexual conduct] in a patently offensive way," and "lacks serious literary, artistic, political, or scientific value." *Miller*, 413 U.S., at 24, 93 S.Ct., at 2615.

The Committee Reports and legislative debate speak more opaquely as to the desire of Congress for a scienter requirement with respect to the age of minority. An early form of the proposed legislation, S. 1011, was rejected principally because it failed to distinguish between obscene and non-obscene materials. S.Rep. No. 95–438, p. 12 (1977) U.S.Code Cong. & Admin.News 1978, pp. 40, 49. In evaluating the proposal, the Justice Department offered its thoughts:

> "[T]he word 'knowingly' in the second line of section 2251 is unnecessary and should be stricken. . . . Unless 'knowingly' is deleted here, the bill might be subject to an interpretation requiring the Government to prove the defendant's knowledge of everything that follows 'knowingly', including the age of the child. We assume that it is not the intention of the drafters to require the Government to prove that the defendant knew the child was under age sixteen but merely to prove that the child was, in fact, less than age sixteen. . . .

> "On the other hand, the use of the word 'knowingly' in subsection 2252(a)(1) is appropriate to make it clear that the bill does not apply to common carriers or other innocent transporters who have no knowledge of the nature or character of the material they are transporting. To clarify the situation, the legislative history might reflect that the defendant's knowledge of the age of the child is not an element of the offense but that the bill is not intended to apply to innocent transportation with no knowledge of the nature or character of the material involved." *Id.*, at 28–29.

Respondents point to this language as an unambiguous revelation that Congress omitted a scienter requirement. But the bill eventually reported by the Senate Judiciary Committee adopted some, but not all, of the Department's suggestions; most notably, it restricted the prohibition in § 2251 to obscene materials. *Id.*, at 2. The Committee did not make any clarification with respect to scienter as to the age of minority. In fact, the version reported by the Committee eliminated § 2252 altogether. *Ibid.* At that juncture, Senator Roth introduced an amendment which would be another precursor of § 2252. In one paragraph, the amendment forbade any person to "knowingly transport [or] ship . . . [any] visual medium depicting a minor engaged in sexually explicit conduct." 123 Cong.Rec. 33047 (1977). In an exchange during debate, Senator Percy inquired:

> "Would this not mean that the distributor or seller must have either, first, actual knowledge that the materials do contain child pornographic depictions or, second, circumstances must be such that he should have had such actual knowledge, and that mere inadvertence or negligence would not alone be enough to render his actions unlawful?" *Id.*, at 33050.

Senator Roth replied:

> "That is absolutely correct. This amendment, limited as it is by the phrase 'knowingly,' insures that only those sellers and distributors who are consciously and deliberately engaged in the marketing of child pornography . . . are subject to prosecution. . . ." *Ibid.*

The parallel House bill did not contain a comparable provision to § 2252 of the Senate bill, and limited § 2251 prosecutions to obscene materials. The Conference Committee adopted the substance of the Roth amendment in large part, but followed the House version by restricting the proscribed depictions to obscene ones. The new bill did restructure the § 2252 provision somewhat, setting off the age of minority requirement in a separate subclause. S.Conf.Rep. No. 95–601, p. 2 (1977). Most importantly, the new bill retained the adverb "knowingly" in § 2252 while simultaneously deleting the word "knowingly" from § 2251(a). The Conference Committee explained the deletion in § 2251(a) as reflecting an "intent that it is not a necessary element of a prosecution that the defendant knew the actual age of the child." *Id.*, at 5.[5] Respondents point to the appearance of "knowingly" in § 2251(c) and argue that § 2252 ought to be read like § 2251. But this argument depends on the conclusion that § 2252(c) does not include a knowing requirement, a premise that respondents fail to support. Respondents offer in support of their premise only the legislative history discussing an intent to exclude a scienter requirement from *§ 2251(a)*. Because §§ 2251(a) and 2251(c) were passed at different times and contain different wording, the intent to exclude scienter from § 2251(a) does not imply an intent to exclude scienter from § 2251(c).

The legislative history can be summarized by saying that it persuasively indicates that Congress intended that the term "knowingly" apply to the requirement that the depiction be of sexually explicit conduct; it is a good deal less clear from the Committee Reports and floor debates that Congress intended that the requirement extend also to the age of the performers. But, turning once again to the statute itself, if the term "knowingly" applies to the sexually explicit conduct depicted, it is emancipated from merely modifying the verbs in subsections (1) and (2). And as a matter of grammar it is difficult to conclude that the word

---

5   The difference in congressional intent with respect to § 2251 versus § 2252 reflects the reality that producers are more conveniently able to ascertain the age of performers. It thus makes sense to impose the risk of error on producers. *United States v. United States District Court for Central District of California*, 858 F.2d 534, 543, n. 6 (CA9 1988). Although producers may be convicted under § 2251(a) without proof they had knowledge of age, Congress has independently required both primary and secondary producers to record the ages of performers with independent penalties for failure to comply. 18 U.S.C. §§ 2257(a) and (i) (1988 ed. and Supp. V); *American Library Assn. v. Reno*, 33 F.3d 78 (CADC 1994).

"knowingly" modifies one of the elements in subsections (1)(A) and (2)(A), but not the other.

A final canon of statutory construction supports the reading that the term "knowingly" applies to both elements. Cases such as *Ferber*, 458 U.S., at 765, 102 S.Ct., at 3359 ("As with obscenity laws, criminal responsibility may not be imposed without some element of scienter on the part of the defendant"); *Smith v. California*, 361 U.S. 147, 80 S.Ct. 215, 4 L.Ed.2d 205 (1959); *Hamling v. United States*, 418 U.S. 87, 94 S.Ct. 2887, 41 L.Ed.2d 590 (1974); and *Osborne v. Ohio*, 495 U.S. 103, 115, 110 S.Ct. 1691, 1699, 109 L.Ed.2d 98 (1990), suggest that a statute completely bereft of a scienter requirement as to the age of the performers would raise serious constitutional doubts. It is therefore incumbent upon us to read the statute to eliminate those doubts so long as such a reading is not plainly contrary to the intent of Congress. *Edward J. DeBartolo Corp. v. Florida Gulf Coast Building & Constr. Trades Council*, 485 U.S. 568, 575, 108 S.Ct. 1392, 1397, 99 L.Ed.2d 645 (1988).

For all of the foregoing reasons, we conclude that the term "knowingly" in § 2252 extends both to the sexually explicit nature of the material and to the age of the performers.

* * *

The judgment of the Court of Appeals is
Reversed.

Justice STEVENS, concurring.

In my opinion, the normal, commonsense reading of a subsection of a criminal statute introduced by the word "knowingly" is to treat that adverb as modifying each of the elements of the offense identified in the remainder of the subsection. Title 18 U.S.C. § 2252(a)(1) (1988 ed. and Supp. V) reads as follows:

> "(a) Any person who—
>
> "(1) *knowingly* transports or ships in interstate or foreign commerce by any means including by computer or mails, any visual depiction, if—
>
>> "(A) the producing of such visual depiction involves the use of a minor engaging in sexually explicit conduct; and
>> "(B) such visual depiction is of such conduct." (Emphasis added.)

Surely reading this provision to require proof of scienter for each fact that must be proved is far more reasonable than adding such a requirement to a statutory offense that contains no scienter requirement whatsoever. Cf. *Staples v. United States*, 511 U.S. 600, 624, 114 S.Ct. 1793, 1806, 128 L.Ed.2d 608 (1994) (STEVENS,

J., dissenting). Indeed, as the Court demonstrates, *ante*, at 467–468, to give the statute its most grammatically correct reading, and merely require knowledge that a "visual depiction" has been shipped in interstate commerce, would be ridiculous. Accordingly, I join the Court's opinion without qualification.

Justice SCALIA, with whom Justice THOMAS joins, dissenting.

Today's opinion is without antecedent. None of the decisions cited as authority support interpreting an explicit statutory scienter requirement in a manner that its language simply will not bear. *Staples v. United States*, 511 U.S. 600, 114 S.Ct. 1793, 128 L.Ed.2d 608 (1994), discussed *ante*, at 468, and *United States v. United States Gypsum Co.*, 438 U.S. 422, 98 S.Ct. 2864, 57 L.Ed.2d 854 (1978), discussed *ante*, at 468, applied the background common-law rule of scienter to a statute that said *nothing* about the matter. *Morissette v. United States*, 342 U.S. 246, 72 S.Ct. 240, 96 L.Ed. 288 (1952), discussed *ante*, at 467–468, applied that same background rule to a statute that *did* contain the word "knowingly," in order to conclude that "knowingly converts" requires knowledge not merely of the fact of one's assertion of dominion over property, but also knowledge of the fact that that assertion *is* a conversion, *i.e.*, is wrongful.* *Liparota v. United States*, 471 U.S. 419, 105 S.Ct. 2084, 85 L.Ed.2d 434 (1985), discussed *ante*, at 468, again involved a statute that did contain the word "'knowingly,'" used in such a fashion that it could reasonably and grammatically be thought to apply (1) only to the phrase "'uses, transfers, acquires, alters, or possesses'" (which would cause a defendant to be liable without wrongful intent), or (2) also to the later phrase "'in any manner not authorized by [the statute].'" Once again applying the background rule of scienter, the latter reasonable and permissible reading was preferred.

There is no way in which any of these cases, or all of them in combination, can be read to stand for the sweeping proposition that "the presumption in favor of a scienter requirement should apply to each of the statutory elements that criminalize otherwise innocent conduct," *ante*, at 469, *even when the plain text of the statute says otherwise.* All those earlier cases employ the presumption as a rule of interpretation which applies when Congress has not addressed the question of criminal intent (*Staples* and *Gypsum*), or when the import of what it has said on that subject is ambiguous (*Morissette* and *Liparota*). Today's opinion converts the rule of interpretation into a rule of law,

---

* The case did not involve, as the Court claims, a situation in which, "even more obviously than in the statute presently before us, the word 'knowingly' in its isolated position suggested that it only attached to the verb 'converts,'" *ante*, at 468, and we nonetheless applied it as well to another word. The issue was simply the meaning of "knowingly converts."

contradicting the plain import of what Congress has specifically prescribed regarding criminal intent.

In *United States v. Thomas*, 893 F.2d 1066, 1070 (CA9), *cert. denied*, 498 U.S. 826, 111 S.Ct. 80, 112 L.Ed.2d 53 (1990), the Ninth Circuit interpreted 18 U.S.C. § 2252 to require knowledge of neither the fact that the visual depiction portrays sexually explicit conduct, nor the fact that a participant in that conduct was a minor. The panel in the present case accepted that interpretation. *See* 982 F.2d 1285, 1289 (CA9 1992). To say, as the Court does, that this interpretation is "the most grammatical reading," *ante*, at 468, or "[t]he most natural grammatical reading," *ante*, at 467, is understatement to the point of distortion—rather like saying that the ordinarily preferred total for two plus two is four. The Ninth Circuit's interpretation is in fact and quite obviously *the only grammatical reading*. If one were to rack his brains for a way to express the thought that the knowledge requirement in subsection (a)(1) applied only to the transportation or shipment of visual depiction in interstate or foreign commerce, and not to the fact that that depiction was produced by use of a minor engaging in sexually explicit conduct, and was a depiction of that conduct, *it would be impossible* to construct a sentence structure that more clearly conveys that thought, and that thought alone. The word "knowingly" is contained, not merely in a distant phrase, but in an entirely separate clause from the one into which today's opinion inserts it. The equivalent, in expressing a simpler thought, would be the following: "Anyone who knowingly double-parks will be subject to a $200 fine if that conduct occurs during the 4:30–to–6:30 rush hour." It could not be clearer that the scienter requirement applies only to the double-parking, and not to the time of day. So also here, it could not be clearer that it applies only to the transportation or shipment of visual depiction in interstate or foreign commerce. There is no doubt. There is no ambiguity. There is no possible "less natural" but nonetheless permissible reading.

I have been willing, in the case of civil statutes, to acknowledge a doctrine of "scrivener's error" that permits a court to give an unusual (though not unheard-of) meaning to a word which, if given its normal meaning, would produce an absurd and arguably unconstitutional result. *See Green v. Bock Laundry Machine Co.*, 490 U.S. 504, 527, 109 S.Ct. 1981, 1994, 104 L.Ed.2d 557 (1989) (SCALIA, J., concurring). Even if I were willing to stretch that doctrine so as to give the problematic text a meaning it cannot possibly bear; and even if I were willing to extend the doctrine to criminal cases in which its application would produce conviction rather than acquittal; it would still have no proper bearing here. For the *sine qua non* of any "scrivener's error" doctrine, it seems to me, is that the meaning genuinely intended but inadequately expressed must be absolutely clear; otherwise we might be rewriting the statute rather than correcting a technical mistake. That condition is not met here.

The Court acknowledges that "it is a good deal less clear from the Committee Reports and floor debates that Congress intended that the requirement [of scienter] extend . . . to the age of the performers." *Ante,* at 471. That is surely so. In fact, it seems to me that the dominant (if not entirely uncontradicted) view expressed in the legislative history is that set forth in the statement of the Carter Administration Justice Department which introduced the original bill: "[T]he defendant's knowledge of the age of the child is not an element of the offense but . . . the bill is not intended to apply to innocent transportation with no knowledge of the nature or character of the material involved." S.Rep. No. 95–438, p. 29 (1977), U.S.Code Cong. & Admin.News 1978, p. 64. As applied to the final bill, this would mean that the scienter requirement applies to the element of the crime that the depiction be of "sexually explicit conduct," but not to the element that the depiction "involv[e] the use of a minor engaging" in such conduct. *See* 18 U.S.C. §§ 2252(a)(1)(A) and (a)(2)(A). This is the interpretation that was argued by the United States before the Ninth Circuit. *See* 982 F.2d, at 1289.

The Court rejects this construction of the statute for two reasons: First, because "as a matter of grammar it is difficult to conclude that the word 'knowingly' modifies one of the elements in subsections (1)(A) and (2)(A), but not the other." *Ante,* at 472. But as I have described, "as a matter of grammar" it is also difficult (nay, impossible) to conclude that the word "knowingly" modifies *both* of those elements. It is really quite extraordinary for the Court, fresh from having, as it says, *ibid.,* "emancipated" the adverb from the grammatical restriction that renders it inapplicable to the *entire* conditional clause, suddenly to insist that the demands of syntax must prevail over legislative intent—thus producing an end result that accords *neither* with syntax *nor* with supposed intent. If what the statute says must be ignored, one would think we might settle at least for what the statute was meant to say; but alas, we are told, what the statute says prevents this.

The Court's second reason is even worse: "[A] statute completely bereft of a scienter requirement as to the age of the performers would raise serious constitutional doubts." *Ante,* at 472. In my view (as in the apparent view of the Government before the Court of Appeals) that is not true. The Court derives its "serious constitutional doubts" from the fact that "sexually explicit materials involving persons over the age of 17 are protected by the First Amendment," *ante,* at 469. We have made it entirely clear, however, that the First Amendment protection accorded to such materials is not as extensive as that accorded to other speech. "[T]here is surely a less vital interest in the uninhibited exhibition of material that is on the borderline between pornography and artistic expression than in the free dissemination of ideas of social and political significance. . . ."

Young v. American Mini Theatres, Inc., 427 U.S. 50, 61, 96 S.Ct. 2440, 2448, 49 L.Ed.2d 310 (1976). *See also id.*, at 70–71, 96 S.Ct., at 2452–53 ("[E]ven though we recognize that the First Amendment will not tolerate the total suppression of erotic materials that have some arguably artistic value, it is manifest that society's interest in protecting this type of expression is of a wholly different, and lesser, magnitude than the interest in untrammeled political debate . . .") (opinion of STEVENS, J., joined by BURGER, C.J., and WHITE and REHNQUIST, JJ.). Cf. *FCC v. Pacifica Foundation*, 438 U.S. 726, 743, 98 S.Ct. 3026, 3037, 57 L.Ed.2d 1073 (1978) (While some broadcasts of patently offensive references to excretory and sexual organs and activities may be protected, "they surely lie at the periphery of First Amendment concern"). Let us be clear about what sort of pictures are at issue here. They are not the sort that will likely be found in a catalog of the National Gallery or the Metropolitan Museum of Art. "'[S]exually explicit conduct,'" as defined in the statute, does not include mere nudity, but only *conduct* that consists of "sexual intercourse . . . between persons of the same or opposite sex," "bestiality," "masturbation," "sadistic or masochistic abuse," and "lascivious exhibition of the genitals or pubic area." *See* 18 U.S.C. § 2256(2). What is involved, in other words, is not the clinical, the artistic, nor even the risqué, but hard-core pornography. Indeed, I think it entirely clear that all of what is involved constitutes not merely pornography but fully proscribable obscenity, except to the extent it is joined with some other material (or perhaps some manner of presentation) that has artistic or other social value. *See Miller v. California*, 413 U.S. 15, 24, 93 S.Ct. 2607, 2614–15, 37 L.Ed.2d 419 (1973). (Such a requirement cannot be imposed, of course, upon fully protected speech: one can shout "Down with the Republic!," "Hooray for Mozart!," or even "Twenty–Three Skidoo!," *whether or not* that expression is joined with something else of social value.) And whereas what is on one side of the balance in the present case is this material of minimal First Amendment concern, the Court has described what is on the other side—"prevention of sexual exploitation and abuse of children"—as "a government objective of surpassing importance." *New York v. Ferber*, 458 U.S. 747, 757, 102 S.Ct. 3348, 3354–55, 73 L.Ed.2d 1113 (1982).

I am not concerned that holding the purveyors and receivers of this material absolutely liable for supporting the exploitation of minors will deter any activity the United States Constitution was designed to protect. But I am concerned that the Court's suggestion of the unconstitutionality of such absolute liability will cause Congress to leave the world's children inadequately protected against the depredations of the pornography trade. As we recognized in *Ferber, supra,* at 766, n. 19, 102 S.Ct., at 3359, n. 19, the producers of these materials are not always readily found, and are often located abroad; and knowledge of the performers' age by the dealers who specialize in child pornography, and by the purchasers who sustain that market, is obviously hard to prove. The First Amendment will lose none of its value to a free society if those who knowingly place themselves in the stream of pornographic commerce are obliged to make sure that they are not subsidizing child abuse. It is no more unconstitutional to make persons who knowingly deal in hard-core pornography criminally liable for the underage character of their entertainers than it is to make men who engage in consensual fornication criminally liable (in statutory rape) for the underage character of their partners.

I would dispose of the present case, as the Ninth Circuit did, by reading the statute as it is written: to provide criminal penalties for the knowing transportation or shipment of a visual depiction in interstate or foreign commerce, and for the knowing receipt or distribution of a visual depiction so transported or shipped, if that depiction was (whether the defendant knew it or not) a portrayal of a minor engaging in sexually explicit conduct. I would find the statute, as so interpreted, to be unconstitutional since, by imposing criminal liability upon those not knowingly dealing in pornography, it establishes a severe deterrent, not narrowly tailored to its purposes, upon fully protected First Amendment activities. *See Smith v. California*, 361 U.S. 147, 153–154, 80 S.Ct. 215, 218–19, 4 L.Ed.2d 205 (1959). This conclusion of unconstitutionality is of course no ground for going back to reinterpret the statute, making it say something that it does not say, but that *is* constitutional. Not every construction, but only "'every *reasonable* construction must be resorted to, in order to save a statute from unconstitutionality.'" *Edward J. DeBartolo Corp. v. Florida Gulf Coast Building & Constr. Trades Council*, 485 U.S. 568, 575, 108 S.Ct. 1392, 1397, 99 L.Ed.2d 645 (1988) (quoting *Hooper v. California*, 155 U.S. 648, 657, 15 S.Ct. 207, 211, 39 L.Ed. 297 (1895)) (emphasis added). "Although this Court will often strain to construe legislation so as to save it against constitutional attack, it must not and will not carry this to the point of perverting the purpose of a statute . . ." or judicially rewriting it.'" *Commodity Futures Trading Comm'n v. Schor*, 478 U.S. 833, 841, 106 S.Ct. 3245, 3251, 92 L.Ed.2d 675 (1986) (quoting *Aptheker v. Secretary of State*, 378 U.S. 500, 515, 84 S.Ct. 1659, 1668, 12 L.Ed.2d 992 (1964)). Otherwise, there would be no such thing as an unconstitutional statute. As I have earlier discussed, in the present case no reasonable alternative construction exists, neither any that can be coaxed from the text nor any that can be substituted for the text on "scrivener's error" grounds. I therefore agree with the Ninth Circuit that respondents' conviction cannot stand.

I could understand (though I would not approve of) a disposition which, in order to uphold this statute, departed from its text as little as possible in order to sustain its constitutionality—*i.e.*, a disposition applying the scienter requirement to the pornographic nature of the materials, but not to the age of the performers. I can neither understand nor approve of the disposition urged by the United States before this Court and adopted today, which not only rewrites the statute, but (1) rewrites it more radically than its constitutional survival demands, and (2) raises baseless constitutional doubts that will impede congressional enactment of a law providing greater protection for the child-victims of the pornography industry. The Court today saves a single conviction by putting in place a relatively toothless child-pornography law that Congress did not enact, and by rendering congressional strengthening of that new law more difficult. I respectfully dissent.

Notes and Questions

1. Why was the government arguing that the statute required more proof, and the defendant arguing that it required less?

2. Justice Stevens' idea that the express mens rea term applies to all of the elements is reflected in many statutes; for example, New York Penal Law § 15.15(1) provides that when a mens rea term "appears in a statute defining an offense, it is presumed to apply to every element of the offense unless an intent to limit its application clearly appears." This is the Model Penal Code approach. *See* MPC 2.02(5). *See also e.g., Flores-Figueroa v. United States*, 556 U.S. 646, 660 (2009) (Alito J., concurring) ("In interpreting a criminal statute . . . I think it is fair to begin with a general presumption that the specified mens rea applies to all the elements of an offense, but it must be recognized that there are instances in which context may well rebut that presumption.").

H. Lenity

Arthur Andersen LLP v. United States

Supreme Court of the United States
544 U.S. 696 (2005)

Chief Justice REHNQUIST delivered the opinion of the Court.

As Enron Corporation's financial difficulties became public in 2001, petitioner Arthur Andersen LLP, Enron's auditor, instructed its employees to destroy documents pursuant to its document retention policy. A jury found that this action made petitioner guilty of violating 18 U.S.C. §§ 1512(b)(2)(A) and (B). These sections make it a crime to "knowingly us[e] intimidation or physical force, threate[n], or corruptly persuad[e] another person . . . with intent to . . . cause" that person to "withhold" documents from, or "alter" documents for use in, an "official proceeding." The Court of Appeals for the Fifth Circuit affirmed. We hold that the jury instructions failed to convey properly the elements of a "corrup[t] persua[sion]" conviction under § 1512(b), and therefore reverse.

Enron Corporation, during the 1990's, switched its business from operation of natural gas pipelines to an energy conglomerate, a move that was accompanied by aggressive accounting practices and rapid growth. Petitioner audited Enron's publicly filed financial statements and provided internal audit and consulting services to it. Petitioner's "engagement team" for Enron was headed by David Duncan. Beginning in 2000, Enron's financial performance began to suffer, and, as 2001 wore on, worsened.[2] On August 14, 2001, Jeffrey Skilling, Enron's Chief Executive Officer (CEO), unexpectedly resigned. Within days, Sherron Watkins, a senior accountant at Enron, warned Kenneth Lay, Enron's newly reappointed CEO, that Enron could "implode in a wave of accounting scandals." Brief for United States 2. She likewise informed Duncan and Michael Odom, one of petitioner's partners who had supervisory responsibility over Duncan, of the looming problems.

On August 28, an article in the Wall Street Journal suggested improprieties at Enron, and the SEC opened an informal investigation. By early September, petitioner had formed an Enron "crisis-response" team, which included Nancy Temple, an in-house counsel.[3] On October 8, petitioner retained outside counsel to represent it in any litigation that might arise from the Enron matter. The next day, Temple discussed Enron with other in-house counsel. Her notes from that meeting reflect that "some SEC investigation" is "highly probable." *Id.*, at 3.

On October 10, Odom spoke at a general training meeting attended by 89 employees, including 10 from the Enron engagement team. Odom urged every-

---

2 During this time, petitioner faced problems of its own. In June 2001, petitioner entered into a settlement agreement with the Securities and Exchange Commission (SEC) related to its audit work of Waste Management, Inc. As part of the settlement, petitioner paid a massive fine. It also was censured and enjoined from committing further violations of the securities laws. In July 2001, the SEC filed an amended complaint alleging improprieties by Sunbeam Corporation, and petitioner's lead partner on the Sunbeam audit was named.

3 A key accounting problem involved Enron's use of "Raptors," which were special purpose entities used to engage in "off-balance-sheet" activities. Petitioner's engagement team had allowed Enron to "aggregate" the Raptors for accounting purposes so that they reflected a positive return. This was, in the words of petitioner's experts, a "black-and-white" violation of Generally Accepted Accounting Principles. Brief for United States 2.

one to comply with the firm's document retention policy.[4] He added: "'[I]f it's destroyed in the course of [the] normal policy and litigation is filed the next day, that's great. . . . . [W]e've followed our own policy, and whatever there was that might have been of interest to somebody is gone and irretrievable.'" 374 F.3d 281, 286 (C.A.5 2004). On October 12, Temple entered the Enron matter into her computer, designating the "Type of Potential Claim" as "Professional Practice— Government/Regulatory Inv[estigation]." App. JA–127. Temple also e-mailed Odom, suggesting that he "'remin[d] the engagement team of our documentation and retention policy.'" Brief for United States 6.

On October 16, Enron announced its third quarter results. That release disclosed a $1.01 billion charge to earnings.[5] The following day, the SEC notified Enron by letter that it had opened an investigation in August and requested certain information and documents. On October 19, Enron forwarded a copy of that letter to petitioner.

On the same day, Temple also sent an e-mail to a member of petitioner's internal team of accounting experts and attached a copy of the document policy. On October 20, the Enron crisis-response team held a conference call, during which Temple instructed everyone to "[m]ake sure to follow the [document] policy." Brief for United States 7 (brackets in original). On October 23, Enron CEO Lay declined to answer questions during a call with analysts because of "potential lawsuits, as well as the SEC inquiry." *Ibid.* After the call, Duncan met with other Andersen partners on the Enron engagement team and told them that they should ensure team members were complying with the document policy. Another meeting for all team members followed, during which Duncan distributed the policy and told everyone to comply. These, and other smaller meetings, were followed by substantial destruction of paper and electronic documents.

On October 26, one of petitioner's senior partners circulated a New York Times article discussing the SEC's response to Enron. His e-mail commented that "the problems are just beginning and we will be in the cross hairs. The mar-

---

4   The firm's policy called for a single central engagement file, which "should contain only that information which is relevant to supporting our work." App. JA–45. The policy stated that, "[i]n cases of threatened litigation, . . . no related information will be destroyed." *Id.*, at JA–44. It also separately provided that, if petitioner is "advised of litigation or subpoenas regarding a particular engagement, the related information should not be destroyed. *See* Policy Statement No. 780—Notification of Litigation." *Id.*, at JA–65 (emphasis deleted). Policy Statement No. 780 set forth "notification" procedures for whenever "professional practice litigation against [petitioner] or any of its personnel has been commenced, has been threatened or is judged likely to occur, or when governmental or professional investigations that may involve [petitioner] or any of its personnel have been commenced or are judged likely." *Id.*, at JA–29 to JA–30.

5   The release characterized the charge to earnings as "non-recurring." Brief for United States 6, n. 4. Petitioner had expressed doubts about this characterization to Enron, but Enron refused to alter the release. Temple wrote an e-mail to Duncan that "suggested deleting some language that might suggest we have concluded the release is misleading." App. JA–95.

ketplace is going to keep the pressure on this and is going to force the SEC to be tough." *Id.*, at 8. On October 30, the SEC opened a formal investigation and sent Enron a letter that requested accounting documents.

Throughout this time period, the document destruction continued, despite reservations by some of petitioner's managers. On November 8, Enron announced that it would issue a comprehensive restatement of its earnings and assets. Also on November 8, the SEC served Enron and petitioner with subpoenas for records. On November 9, Duncan's secretary sent an e-mail that stated: "Per Dave—No more shredding . . . . We have been officially served for our documents." *Id.*, at 10. Enron filed for bankruptcy less than a month later. Duncan was fired and later pleaded guilty to witness tampering.

In March 2002, petitioner was indicted in the Southern District of Texas on one count of violating §§ 1512(b)(2)(A) and (B). The indictment alleged that, between October 10 and November 9, 2001, petitioner "did knowingly, intentionally and corruptly persuade . . . other persons, to wit: [petitioner's] employees, with intent to cause" them to withhold documents from, and alter documents for use in, "official proceedings, namely: regulatory and criminal proceedings and investigations." App. JA–139. A jury trial followed. When the case went to the jury, that body deliberated for seven days and then declared that it was deadlocked. The District Court delivered an "*Allen* charge," *Allen v. United States*, 164 U.S. 492, 17 S.Ct. 154, 41 L.Ed. 528 (1896), and, after three more days of deliberation, the jury returned a guilty verdict. The District Court denied petitioner's motion for a judgment of acquittal.

The Court of Appeals for the Fifth Circuit affirmed. 374 F.3d, at 284. It held that the jury instructions properly conveyed the meaning of "corruptly persuades" and "official proceeding"; that the jury need not find any consciousness of wrongdoing; and that there was no reversible error. Because of a split of authority regarding the meaning of § 1512(b), we granted certiorari. 543 U.S. 1042, 125 S.Ct. 823, 160 L.Ed.2d 609 (2005).

Chapter 73 of Title 18 of the United States Code provides criminal sanctions for those who obstruct justice. Sections 1512(b)(2)(A) and (B), part of the witness tampering provisions, provide in relevant part:

> "Whoever knowingly uses intimidation or physical force, threatens, or corruptly persuades another person, or attempts to do so, or engages in misleading conduct toward another person, with intent to . . . cause or induce any person to . . . withhold testimony, or withhold a record, document, or other object, from an official proceeding [or] alter, destroy, mutilate, or conceal an object with intent to impair the object's integrity or availability for use in an official proceeding . . . shall be fined under this title or imprisoned not more than ten years, or both."

In this case, our attention is focused on what it means to "knowingly . . . corruptly persuad[e]" another person "with intent to . . . cause" that person to "withhold" documents from, or "alter" documents for use in, an "official proceeding."

"We have traditionally exercised restraint in assessing the reach of a federal criminal statute, both out of deference to the prerogatives of Congress, *Dowling v. United States*, 473 U.S. 207, 105 S.Ct. 3127, 87 L.Ed.2d 152 (1985), and out of concern that 'a fair warning should be given to the world in language that the common world will understand, of what the law intends to do if a certain line is passed,' *McBoyle v. United States*, 283 U.S. 25, 27, 51 S.Ct. 340, 75 L.Ed. 816 (1931)." *United States v. Aguilar*, 515 U.S. 593, 600, 115 S.Ct. 2357, 132 L.Ed.2d 520 (1995).

Such restraint is particularly appropriate here, where the act underlying the conviction—"persua[sion]"—is by itself innocuous. Indeed, "persuad[ing]" a person "with intent to . . . cause" that person to "withhold" testimony or documents from a Government proceeding or Government official is not inherently malign. Consider, for instance, a mother who suggests to her son that he invoke his right against compelled self-incrimination, see U.S. Const., Amdt. 5, or a wife who persuades her husband not to disclose marital confidences, see *Trammel v. United States*, 445 U.S. 40, 100 S.Ct. 906, 63 L.Ed.2d 186 (1980).

Nor is it necessarily corrupt for an attorney to "persuad[e]" a client "with intent to . . . cause" that client to "withhold" documents from the Government. In *Upjohn Co. v. United States*, 449 U.S. 383, 101 S.Ct. 677, 66 L.Ed.2d 584 (1981), for example, we held that Upjohn was justified in withholding documents that were covered by the attorney-client privilege from the Internal Revenue Service (IRS). *See id.*, at 395, 101 S.Ct. 677. No one would suggest that an attorney who "persuade[d]" Upjohn to take that step acted wrongfully, even though he surely intended that his client keep those documents out of the IRS' hands.

"Document retention policies," which are created in part to keep certain information from getting into the hands of others, including the Government, are common in business. *See generally* Chase, *To Shred or Not to Shred: Document Retention Policies and Federal Obstruction of Justice Statutes*, 8 Ford. J. Corp. & Fin. L. 721 (2003). It is, of course, not wrongful for a manager to instruct his employees to comply with a valid document retention policy under ordinary circumstances.

Acknowledging this point, the parties have largely focused their attention on the word "corruptly" as the key to what may or may not lawfully be done in the situation presented here. Section 1512(b) punishes not just "corruptly persuad[ing]" another, but "*knowingly* (3)27 corruptly persuad[ing]" another. (Emphasis added.) The Government suggests that "knowingly" does not modify "corruptly persuades," but that is not how the statute most naturally reads. It provides the *mens rea*—"knowingly"—and then a list of acts—"uses intimidation or physical force, threatens, or corruptly persuades." We have recognized with regard to similar statutory language that the *mens rea* at least applies to the acts that immediately follow, if not to other elements down the statutory chain. *See United States v. X-Citement Video, Inc.*, 513 U.S. 64, 68, 115 S.Ct. 464, 130 L.Ed.2d 372 (1994) (recognizing that the "most natural grammatical reading" of 18 U.S.C. §§ 2252(a)(1) and (2) "suggests that the term 'knowingly' modifies only the surrounding verbs: transports, ships, receives, distributes, or reproduces"); *see also Liparota v. United States*, 471 U.S. 419, 105 S.Ct. 2084, 85 L.Ed.2d 434 (1985). The Government suggests that it is "questionable whether Congress would employ such an inelegant formulation as 'knowingly . . . corruptly persuades.'" Brief for United States 35, n. 18. Long experience has not taught us to share the Government's doubts on this score, and we must simply interpret the statute as written.

The parties have not pointed us to another interpretation of "knowingly . . . corruptly" to guide us here. In any event, the natural meaning of these terms provides a clear answer. *See Bailey v. United States*, 516 U.S. 137, 144–145, 116 S.Ct. 501, 133 L.Ed.2d 472 (1995). "[K]nowledge" and "knowingly" are normally associated with awareness, understanding, or consciousness. *See Black's Law Dictionary* 888 (8th ed.2004) (hereinafter Black's); *Webster's Third New International Dictionary* 1252–1253 (1993) (hereinafter Webster's 3d); *American Heritage Dictionary of the English Language* 725 (1981) (hereinafter Am. Hert.). "Corrupt" and "corruptly" are normally associated with wrongful, immoral, depraved, or evil. *See* Black's 371; Webster's 3d 512; Am. Hert. 299–300. Joining these meanings together here makes sense both linguistically and in the statutory scheme. Only persons conscious of wrongdoing can be said to "knowingly . . . corruptly persuad [e]." And limiting criminality to persuaders conscious of their wrongdoing sensibly allows § 1512(b) to reach only those with the level of "culpability . . . we usually require in order to impose criminal liability." *United States v. Aguilar*, 515 U.S., at 602, 115 S.Ct. 2357; *see also Liparota v. United States, supra*, at 426, 105 S.Ct. 2084.

The outer limits of this element need not be explored here because the jury instructions at issue simply failed to convey the requisite consciousness of wrongdoing. Indeed, it is striking how little culpability the instructions required. For example, the jury was told that, "even if [petitioner] honestly and sincerely believed that its conduct was lawful, you may find [petitioner] guilty." App. JA–213. The instructions also diluted the meaning of "corruptly" so that it covered innocent conduct. *Id.*, at JA–212.

The parties vigorously disputed how the jury would be instructed on "corruptly." The District Court based its instruction on the definition of that term found in the Fifth Circuit Pattern Jury Instruction for § 1503. This pattern instruction defined "corruptly" as "'knowingly and dishonestly, with the specific intent to subvert or undermine the integrity'" of a proceeding. Brief for Petitioner 3, n. 3 (emphasis deleted). The Government, however, insisted on excluding "dishonestly" and adding the term "impede" to the phrase "subvert or undermine." Ibid. (internal quotation marks omitted). The District Court agreed over petitioner's objections, and the jury was told to convict if it found petitioner intended to "subvert, undermine, or impede" governmental factfinding by suggesting to its employees that they enforce the document retention policy. App. JA–212.

These changes were significant. No longer was any type of "dishonest[y]" necessary to a finding of guilt, and it was enough for petitioner to have simply "impede[d]" the Government's factfinding ability. As the Government conceded at oral argument, "' [i]mpede'" has broader connotations than "'subvert'" or even "'[u]ndermine,'" see Tr. of Oral Arg. 38, and many of these connotations do not incorporate any "corrupt[ness]" at all. The dictionary defines "impede" as "to interfere with or get in the way of the progress of" or "hold up" or "detract from." Webster's 3d 1132. By definition, anyone who innocently persuades another to withhold information from the Government "get[s] in the way of the progress of" the Government. With regard to such innocent conduct, the "corruptly" instructions did no limiting work whatsoever.

The instructions also were infirm for another reason. They led the jury to believe that it did not have to find *any* nexus between the "persua[sion]" to destroy documents and any particular proceeding. In resisting any type of nexus element, the Government relies heavily on § 1512(e)(1), which states that an official proceeding "need not be pending or about to be instituted at the time of the offense." It is, however, one thing to say that a proceeding "need not be pending or about to be instituted at the time of the offense," and quite another to say a proceeding need not even be foreseen. A "knowingly . . . corrup[t] persaude[r]" cannot be someone who persuades others to shred documents under a document retention policy when he does not have in contemplation any particular official proceeding in which those documents might be material.

We faced a similar situation in *Aguilar, supra.* Respondent Aguilar lied to a Federal Bureau of Investigation agent in the course of an investigation and was convicted of "'corruptly endeavor[ing] to influence, obstruct, and impede [a] . . . grand jury investigation'" under § 1503. 515 U.S., at 599, 115 S.Ct. 2357. All the Government had shown was that Aguilar had uttered false statements to an investigating agent "who might or might not testify before a grand jury." *Id.*, at 600, 115 S.Ct. 2357. We held that § 1503 required something more—specifically, a "nexus" between the obstructive act and the proceeding. *Id.*, at 599–600, 115 S.Ct. 2357. "[I]f the defendant lacks knowledge that his actions are likely to affect the judicial proceeding," we explained, "he lacks the requisite intent to obstruct." *Id.*, at 599, 115 S.Ct. 2357.

For these reasons, the jury instructions here were flawed in important respects. The judgment of the Court of Appeals is reversed, and the case is remanded for further proceedings consistent with this opinion.

It is so ordered.

I. Actus Reus

State v. Eaton

Supreme Court of Washington
168 Wash.2d 476, 229 P.3d 704 (2010)

CHAMBERS, J.

Thomas Eaton was arrested for driving under the influence (DUI) and taken by police to the Clark County Jail. At the jail, Eaton was searched by staff who discovered a small bag of methamphetamine taped to his sock. The State charged Eaton with DUI and possession of methamphetamine and sought a sentencing enhancement for possessing a controlled substance in a jail or prison. A jury convicted Eaton on both charges and found by special verdict that Eaton possessed methamphetamine while in a jail. The trial court imposed an enhanced sentence.

At issue is whether a sentencing enhancement for possession of a controlled substance in a jail or prison requires a finding that that defendant took a volitional act to place himself in the enhancement zone. We hold that the enhancement does require a volitional act and affirm the Court of Appeals.

FACTS AND PROCEDURAL HISTORY

On September 22, 2005, Vancouver Police Department Officer Jeff Starks saw Eaton driving with his headlights turned off and made a routine traffic stop. After performing field sobriety tests Officer Starks concluded that Eaton was impaired and arrested him for DUI. Eaton was read his *Miranda* rights and was taken to jail. There he was searched and officers found "what appeared to be a plastic bag taped to the top of [Eaton's] sock." I Report of Proceedings at 99. The contents of the bag tested positive for methamphetamine.

The State charged Eaton with one count of DUI and one count of possession of a controlled substance. Because the methamphetamine was discovered on

Eaton while he was in the county jail the State sought a sentence enhancement. The jury found Eaton guilty of both counts and, by special verdict, found that Eaton possessed methamphetamine in a county jail. Eaton's standard sentencing range would have been 0 to 6 months, but with the sentence enhancement, his range became 12 to 18 months. The trial court sentenced Eaton to 12 months and 1 day.

The Court of Appeals reversed the trial court's imposition of the sentencing enhancement, reasoning that the State failed to prove Eaton acted voluntarily. *State v. Eaton*, 143 Wash.App. 155, 164–65, 177 P.3d 157 (2008). The court held that the sentencing enhancement statute was not intended to punish defendants for their involuntary acts. *Id.* at 164, 177 P.3d 157. Eaton's convictions for DUI and possession of a controlled substance are not before us; we are reviewing only the sentencing enhancement for possession of methamphetamine in a jail.

ANALYSIS

Questions of statutory interpretation are reviewed de novo. *State v. Wadsworth*, 139 Wash.2d 724, 734, 991 P.2d 80 (2000). Our purpose in interpreting a statute is to determine and carry out the intent of the legislature. *State v. Cromwell*, 157 Wash.2d 529, 539, 140 P.3d 593 (2006). We must construe statutes consistent with their underlying purposes while avoiding constitutional deficiencies. *State v. Crediford*, 130 Wash.2d 747, 755, 927 P.2d 1129 (1996). In construing a statute, we presume the legislature did not intend absurd results. *State v. J.P.*, 149 Wash.2d 444, 450, 69 P.3d 318 (2003).

CRIMINAL RESPONSIBILITY

As the Court of Appeals correctly observed: "as a general rule, every crime must contain two elements: (1) an actus reus and (2) a mens rea." *Eaton*, 143 Wash. App. at 160, 177 P.3d 157 (citing *State v. Utter*, 4 Wash.App. 137, 139, 479 P.2d 946 (1971)). Actus reus is defined as "'[t]he wrongful deed that comprises the physical components of a crime,'" *Id.* (alteration in original) (quoting BLACK'S LAW DICTIONARY 39 (8th ed.2004)), and the mens rea is "'[t]he state of mind that the prosecution . . . must prove that a defendant had when committing a crime.'" *Id.* (alteration in original) (quoting BLACK'S LAW DICTIONARY 1006 (8th ed.2004)). At common law it was said that "to constitute a crime against human laws, there must be, first, a vitious will; and, secondly, an unlawful act consequent upon such vitious will." WILLIAM BLACKSTONE, 5 COMMENTARIES *21. "An involuntary act, as it has no claim to merit, so neither can it induce any guilt: the concurrence of the will, when it has [its] choice either to do or to avoid the fact in question, being the only thing that renders human actions either praiseworthy or culpable." *Id.*

Although most criminal laws since codified still adhere to this general principle, we now recognize that the "legislature has the authority to create a crime without a mens rea element." *State v. Bradshaw*, 152 Wash.2d 528, 532, 98 P.3d 1190 (2004) (citing *State v. Anderson*, 141 Wash.2d 357, 361, 5 P.3d 1247 (2000)). Though they are disfavored, these "strict liability" crimes criminalize unlawful conduct regardless of whether the actor possesses a culpable mental state. *State v. Rivas*, 126 Wash.2d 443, 452, 896 P.2d 57 (1995); *see also Morissette v. United States*, 342 U.S. 246, 256 n. 14, 72 S.Ct. 240, 96 L.Ed. 288 (1952). In this way, the legislature seeks to deter harmful conduct by creating harsh penalties that focus on the defendant's actions and their consequences. "The law threatens certain pains if you do certain things, intending thereby to give you a new motive for not doing them." O.W. HOLMES, Jr., THE COMMON LAW 40 (Mark DeWolfe Howe ed., Harvard Univ. Press, 1967) (1881).

Fundamental to our notion of an ordered society is that people are punished only for their own conduct. Where an individual has taken no volitional action she is not generally subject to criminal liability as punishment would not serve to further any of the legitimate goals of the criminal law.[2] We punish people for what they do, not for what others do to them. We do not punish those who do not have the capacity to choose. Where the individual has not voluntarily acted, punishment will not deter the consequences.

As these principles suggest, although an individual need not possess a culpable mental state in order to commit a crime, there is "a certain minimal mental element required in order to establish the actus reus itself." *Utter*, 4 Wash.App. at 139, 479 P.2d 946. Movements must be willed; a spasm is not an act. HOLMES, *supra*, at 45–46. It is this volitional aspect of a person's actions that renders her morally responsible and her actions potentially deterrable. To punish an individual for an involuntary act would run counter to the principle that "a person cannot be morally responsible for an outcome unless the outcome is a consequence of that person's action." A.P. Simester, *On the So-called Requirement for Voluntary Action*, 1 BUFF. CRIM. L. REV. 403, 405 (1998). It would create what Simester has called "situational liability," penalizing a defendant for a situation she simply finds herself in. *Id.* at 410. "Unless there is a requirement of voluntariness, situational offenses are at odds with the deepest presuppositions of the criminal law." *Id.* at 412. As Holmes tells us, the "reason for requiring an act is, that an act implies a choice, and that it is felt to be impolitic and unjust to make a man answerable for harm, unless he might have chosen otherwise." HOLMES, *supra*, at 46. "[T]he choice [to act] must be made with a chance of contemplating

---

2   Of course, the legislature has legitimately criminalized the failure to act in some instances. *See e.g.* RCW 9A.76.030 (refusing to summon aid for a peace officer); RCW 9A.84.020 (failure to disperse). Importantly, under these crimes, it is the defendant's choice not to act that renders him criminally liable.

the consequence complained of, or else it has no bearing on responsibility for that consequence." *Id.* A person cannot be answerable for a state of affairs unless she could have done something to avoid it.[4] Simester, *supra*, at 412.

THE ENHANCEMENT

The purpose of sentencing enhancements is to provide legislative guidance to courts in calibrating the appropriate punishment for crimes based on relevant circumstances surrounding the underlying conduct. "Zone" enhancements direct courts to sentence offenders beyond the standard range if they are found committing some designated crime in a particular area. For example, the legislature has enacted statutes creating mandatory increased penalties for individuals convicted of possession with intent to deliver controlled substances in a variety of "zones," including near schools, parks, bus stops, and on public transport vehicles. RCW 69.50.435. In this case, Eaton was convicted of possession of methamphetamine and his sentence was enhanced because the police found the methamphetamine while he was in a jail, which has been designated an enhancement zone. RCW 9.94A.533(5).

The Court of Appeals held that Eaton committed no actus reus amounting to voluntary possession of methamphetamine in the enhancement zone. *Eaton*, 143 Wash.App. at 157, 177 P.3d 157. RCW 69.50.4013(1) states that "[i]t is unlawful for any person to possess a controlled substance." In addition, RCW 9.94A.533(5) requires courts to impose a sentencing enhancement under certain circumstances. The statute states in relevant part:

> The following additional times shall be added to the standard sentence range if the offender or an accomplice committed the offense while in a county jail or state correctional facility and the offender is being sentenced for one of the crimes listed in this subsection.
>
> . . . .
>
> (c) Twelve months for offenses committed under RCW 69.50.4013.
>
> For the purposes of this subsection, all of the real property of a state correctional facility or county jail shall be deemed to be part of that facility or county jail.
>
> RCW 9.94A.533(5).

---

4   As a cautionary example, Simester references the notorious English case of *Rex v. Larsonneur* where the defendant, a French woman, was convicted of being in the United Kingdom when permission to enter had previously been refused. Simester, *supra*, at 410–11 (citing *Rex v. Larsonneur*, 149 L.T. 542 (1933)). Larsonneur was convicted despite the fact that she had been brought to the United Kingdom from Ireland by the police, against her will. *Larsonneur*, 149 L.T. at 544.

The State argues that the plain language of the statute does not contain a volitional element, that one should not be inferred, and that the sentencing enhancement should be upheld. The State is correct that the language of RCW 9.94A.533(5) is silent on whether a volitional act is required before imposing an enhancement. The statute simply requires that the State show the defendant was in a jail or correctional facility while possessing a controlled substance. However, as noted above, we attempt to construe statutes in a way that is consistent with their underlying purpose. *Crediford*, 130 Wash.2d at 755, 927 P.2d 1129. As the Court of Appeals concluded, the State's application of the enhancement statute would lead "to an unlikely, absurd, and strained consequence, imposing a strict liability sentence enhancement for *involuntary* possession of a controlled substance in a county jail or state correctional facility." *Eaton*, 143 Wash.App. at 161, 177 P.3d 157. Once Eaton was arrested, he no longer had control over his location. From the time of arrest, his movement from street to jail became involuntary: involuntary not because he did not wish to enter the jail, but because he was forcibly taken there by State authority. He no longer had the ability to choose his own course of action. Nor did he have the ability through some other course of action to avoid entering the area that would increase the penalty for the underlying crime.[5] We doubt the legislature intended to grant the police such broad authority to affect the defendant's punishment after arrest. Additional punishment for being in an enhancement zone serves no logical purpose unless we presume that its infliction was intended only where the defendant could have avoided being there.[6] The act may be as simple as choosing to put one foot in front of the other and running the risk of entering an enhancement zone. But it must be a choice made free from the kind of authority the State exercises when it makes an arrest.[7] For these reasons we hold that RCW 9.94A.533(5) encompasses a volitional element that the State must prove beyond a reasonable doubt. *Cf. State v. Boyer*, 91

---

[5]   The State is concerned that requiring a volitional element calls into question the State's ability to seek harsher punishments for "zone" enhancements generally. The State appears to be under the misapprehension that requiring volition is the same as requiring intent. But nothing in our opinion should be read as requiring that the State prove a defendant intended to be in the enhancement zone or even that she knew she was in the enhancement zone. The State must simply demonstrate that the defendant took some voluntary action that placed him in the zone.

[6]   The dissent suggests that its strict interpretation of the sentencing enhancement statute creates incentives for admitting possession to the arresting officer before being taken to jail. Dissent at 712. In other words, if Eaton wished to avoid a more severe punishment, he should have offered up the evidence that would eventually convict him of illegal possession. Such an application of the enhancement statute may have implications on the Fifth Amendment right against self-incrimination.

[7]   The dissent suggests that our holding eliminates the State's ability to seek a sentencing enhancement under RCW 9.94A.533(5) even where the controlled substance is discovered several days after a defendant is booked. Dissent at 713. It does not. At some point, when the defendant retains possession despite the opportunity to do otherwise, possession within the zone becomes voluntary. The State simply bears the burden of proving this has occurred.

Wash.2d 342, 344, 588 P.2d 1151 (1979) (finding an implied element of guilty knowledge in the crime of delivery of a controlled substance); *see also State v. Hall*, 54 Wash. 142, 144, 102 P. 888 (1909).

Cases from other jurisdictions support our conclusion that the legislature did not intend to hold individuals criminally liable for being in some designated place when forced there involuntarily by an arresting officer. *Martin v. State*, 31 Ala.App. 334, 335, 17 So.2d 427 (1944) (accusation of public intoxication cannot be established where an intoxicated defendant was involuntarily and forcibly carried onto the street by an arresting officer); *Fontaine v. State*, 135 Md.App. 471, 762 A.2d 1027 (2000) (holding that after a defendant was arrested in Delaware and taken to Maryland by the police, the evidence failed to prove he intended to distribute marijuana in his possession while in Maryland); *State v. Tippetts*, 180 Or.App. 350, 43 P.3d 455 (2002) (holding that conviction for supplying contraband in a correctional facility requires a showing the defendant voluntarily introduced the contraband). Echoing Holmes the *Tippetts* court noted "the concept of fault ordinarily implies the ability to choose." *Id.* at 355, 43 P.3d 455. Where, as here, the defendant is forcibly transported by police to the area giving rise to additional punishment, he did not have the requisite ability to choose.

The State argues that the above cited cases are distinguishable from the case before us because RCW 9.94A.533(5) is an enhancement statute and not a separate crime. As the State points out, Eaton was convicted of possession of a controlled substance, a crime that does require a volitional act of possession. Under the State's theory, once every element has been proved for the underlying offense, a defendant may receive additional punishment based on any circumstance she finds herself in after the time of arrest, regardless of whether those circumstances were brought about by her own volition. The State suggests that requiring a separate volitional act for the sentencing enhancement "adds additional elements that were never contemplated by the legislature." Pet. for Review at 7. We disagree. Allowing the State to bootstrap additional punishments to the underlying crime where the defendant has done nothing to create the aggravating circumstance would run counter to the notions of justice that serve as the backdrop for our criminal law. While the enhancement in this case was not, strictly speaking, a separate crime, it still requires proof that the defendant did something separate.

While the State bears the burden of proving each element beyond a reasonable doubt, we hold that when a person is found within an enhancement zone in possession of a controlled substance, the State is entitled to a permissive inference that the person is within the zone of his own volition. *See State v. Cantu*, 156 Wash.2d 819, 822, 132 P.3d 725 (2006) (permissive inferences permitted because they do not relieve the State of its burden of proof). "'[D]ue process is not offended if the prosecution shows that the inference more likely than not flows from the proven fact.'" *Id.* at 826, 132 P.3d 725 (quoting *State v. Deal*, 128 Wash.2d 693, 700, 911 P.2d 996 (1996)). However, while possession within the enhancement zone allows a fact finder to infer volition, the inference alone may not be enough for the State to meet its burden. *State v. Hanna*, 123 Wash.2d 704, 710, 871 P.2d 135 (1994). Here it was not. The facts clearly establish that Eaton was arrested outside the enhancement zone and was transported to the jail by Officer Starks. After he was arrested, there was nothing he could have reasonably done to avoid being taken to jail. The State failed to meet its burden of proof that Eaton volitionally possessed drugs inside the enhancement zone.

Eaton made a choice to possess methamphetamine. That is properly subject to punishment under the laws of our State. The State is seeking to subject Eaton to additional punishment based on circumstances it created. Eaton could not have chosen to avoid the enhancement zone. We hold that RCW 9.94A.533(5) was not intended to create criminal liability for one forced into an enhancement zone against his own will.

CONCLUSION

We hold that RCW 9.94A.533(5) requires that a defendant took some voluntary act to be placed within the enhanced zone in order to subject the defendant to an enhanced sentence. The defendant need not intend or even know he is entering an enhanced zone. The volitional element may be as simple as choosing to put one foot in front of the other to enter the zone, but it must be a choice freely made. The fact that a defendant is found within an enhancement zone gives rise to a reasonable inference that the defendant is there volitionally. The permissive inference does not relieve the State of its burden of proof that the defendant was within the enhancement zone volitionally. Where, as here, the defendant is arrested and taken to the enhancement zone, the volitional component of the actus reus cannot be met. Eaton did not enter the jail volitionally. We affirm the Court of Appeals.

WE CONCUR: Justice CHARLES W. JOHNSON, Justice GERRY L. ALEXANDER, Justice RICHARD B. SANDERS, Justice DEBRA L. STEPHENS.

FAIRHURST, J. (dissenting).

The issue in this case is whether the plain words of RCW 9.94A.533(5) mean what they say. RCW 9.94A.533(5) provides that a sentence enhancement must be added to the standard sentence range for certain drug crimes, including possession of a controlled substance, RCW 69.50.4013(1), if the defendant "committed the offense while in a county jail or state correctional facility." The majority holds that RCW 9.94A.533(5) applies only if the State proves, beyond a reasonable doubt, "that a defendant took some voluntary act to be placed within the enhanced zone." Majority at 710.

The majority is wrong for at least four reasons. First, the statute's plain meaning does not support the majority's interpretation of RCW 9.94A.533(5). Second, the majority undermines the statute's purpose of deterring drug crimes in county jails and state correctional facilities because RCW 9.94A.533(5) will no longer apply to prisoners—none of whom enter jail or prison voluntarily. Third, the majority ignores the difference between a person's conduct and the circumstances surrounding that conduct. Fourth, the majority's reasoning casts doubt on the meaning of other statutes imposing sentence enhancements.

I respectfully dissent.

I. FACTS

Thomas Harry Eaton was arrested and taken to the Clark County Jail on suspicion of driving under the influence. Upon Eaton's arrival, the jail staff asked Eaton to remove his shoes and take his socks off. Eaton removed his shoes but hesitated to remove his socks. Staff asked him a second time to remove his socks. Eaton removed the sock from his left foot. Eaton then asked the jail staff if he could use the bathroom. After they said no and instructed him to remove the other sock, Eaton took off the sock on his right foot. The staff noticed a plastic bag taped to the top of the sock. When the staff moved forward to retrieve the bag, Eaton refused to relinquish the bag and had to be tackled. The bag fell to the floor, and an officer picked it up. The contents tested positive for methamphetamine. For possessing a controlled substance, Eaton was charged and convicted of violating RCW 69.50.4013(1). For being in a county jail at the time of the offense, Eaton received a 12–month sentence enhancement pursuant to RCW 9.94A.533(5).

II. ANALYSIS

Statutory interpretation begins and usually ends with the statute's plain meaning. Because statutes are the creation of the people's elected representatives in the legislature, the "fundamental objective" of statutory interpretation "is to ascertain and carry out the Legislature's intent." *Dep't of Ecology v. Campbell & Gwinn, LLC*, 146 Wash.2d 1, 9, 43 P.3d 4 (2002) (citing *State v. J.M.*, 144 Wash.2d 472, 480, 28 P.3d 720 (2001)). Under the plain meaning rule, "if the statute's meaning is plain on its face, then the court *must* give effect to that plain meaning as an expression of legislative intent." *Id.* at 9–10, 43 P.3d 4 (emphasis added) (citing *J.M.*, 144 Wash.2d at 480, 28 P.3d 720). When a statute does not define a word it uses, as here, the word's plain meaning includes its dictionary definition. *State v. Sullivan*, 143 Wash.2d 162, 175, 19 P.3d 1012 (2001). "[T]he plain meaning rule requires courts to consider legislative purposes or policies appearing on the face of the statute as part of the statute's context." 2A Norman J. Singer & J.d. Shambie Singer, Statutes and Statutory Construction § 48A:16, at 918 (7th ed.2007); *accord State ex rel. Faulk v. CSG Job Ctr.*, 117 Wash.2d 493, 500, 816 P.2d 725 (1991) (stating, "a statute is to be interpreted in a manner that is consistent with its underlying purpose" (citing *In re Det. of Cross*, 99 Wash.2d 373, 382, 662 P.2d 828 (1983))). Although a statute's plain meaning usually ends the debate, this court will look beyond the face of the statute if following the plain meaning would yield absurd results. *See State v. J.P.*, 149 Wash.2d 444, 450, 69 P.3d 318 (2003).

A. The words of RCW 9.94A.533(5)

RCW 9.94A.533(5) provides:

> The following additional times shall be added to the standard sentence range if the offender or an accomplice committed the offense while in a county jail or state correctional facility and the offender is being sentenced for one of the crimes listed in this subsection. . . .

> . . . .

> (c) Twelve months for offenses committed under RCW 69.50.4013.

The majority concludes that RCW 9.94A.533(5) "requires that a defendant took some *voluntary act to be placed* within the enhanced zone." Majority at 710 (emphasis added). But, as the majority acknowledges, "the language of RCW 9.94A.533(5) is silent on whether a volitional act is required before imposing an enhancement." Majority at 708. The words "voluntary," "volitional," "willful," and their kind do not appear in the statute. Words such as "entered" and "be placed" are conspicuously absent, showing that the legislature did not intend to include an actus reus. The majority adds words to the statute even though "[w]e cannot add words or clauses to an unambiguous statute when the legislature has chosen not to include that language." *State v. Delgado*, 148 Wash.2d 723, 727, 63 P.3d 792 (2003).

The dictionary definitions of the words actually in RCW 9.94A.533(5) do not support a requirement of a voluntary act. The dictionary defines "commit" as to "DO" or "PERFORM," with the usage example of "convicted of *committing* crimes against the state." WEBSTER'S THIRD NEW INTERNATIONAL DICTIONARY 457 (2002). A dictionary definition of "while" is "during the time that." *Id.* at 2604. With these definitions, RCW 9.94A.533(5) says that a sentence enhancement applies "if the offender or an accomplice [did] the offense [during the time that] [the offender was] in a county jail or state correctional facility."

The plain language of RCW 9.94A.533(5) does not evidence legislative intent to include an element of a voluntary act.[1] The words relate only to the circumstances surrounding the criminal offense defined in other statutes.

B. The Purpose of RCW 9.94A.533(5)

Besides ignoring the words of RCW 9.94A.533(5), the majority's interpretation undermines the statute's purpose and leads to absurd results. On its face, the statute's purpose is to deter people from selling, buying, using, or possessing drugs in a jail or state correctional facility. But the majority's interpretation narrows the class of offenders subject to a sentence enhancement under the statute. Because voluntary entrance into the enhancement zone is an element of RCW 9.94A.533(5), according to the majority, RCW 9.94A.533(5) will no longer apply to arrestees or prisoners—all of whom are forced into jail or prison against their will. Only employees and visitors enter a jail or prison voluntarily. In Eaton's case, even if Eaton's methamphetamine had not been discovered by jail staff until several days after he was booked, RCW 9.94A.533(5) would not apply because he did not enter the Clark County Jail on his own volition.[2] That result contradicts the statute's overall purpose of reducing the number of drug crimes in jails and prisons.

By contrast, the plain meaning of RCW 9.94A.533(5) advances the statute's purpose in at least three ways. First, a prisoner who is already in a jail or state correctional facility would think twice before having anything to do with illegal drugs. Second, before being taken to jail, an arrestee possessing drugs would have an incentive to either get rid of the drugs or admit possession to the arresting officer. A person so admitting would be subject to a possession charge but not the enhancement. Without the 12–month enhancement, however, the arrestee is better off keeping quiet or lying. There would be a chance that the drugs would not be detected by the booking officer, and even if the arrestee's drugs are noticed eventually by the jail staff, the maximum sentence would be the same as if the drugs had been discovered outside the jail. Because the penalty for possession inside the jail would be the same as for possession outside the jail, the arrestee,

---

1   Further, the Court of Appeals, the parties, and the majority have not pointed to anything in the legislative history discussing whether the sentence enhancement requires a finding the offender was volitionally in the jail or prison.

2   The majority dismisses this concern, claiming, "At some point, when the defendant retains possession despite the opportunity to do otherwise, possession within the zone becomes voluntary." Majority at 709 n. 7. But the majority holds that the prosecution must prove beyond a reasonable doubt "that a defendant took some voluntary act to be placed within the enhanced zone." *Id.* at 710. The majority's interpretation conditions RCW 9.94A.533(5) on the defendant taking some affirmative, voluntary step to enter a county jail or state prison.

When these statements are taken together, the majority seems to say that by passing a few days in jail, an incarcerated person takes "some voluntary act to be placed within" the jail, in satisfaction of the majority's interpretation of RCW 9.94A.533(5). But how can an inmate's presence in jail suddenly become voluntary?

in the hope of avoiding being punished altogether, would be more likely to try to sneak the drugs past the jail staff unnoticed. But with the 12–month enhancement, trying to maintain possession unnoticed is a riskier proposition, and the arrestee is much more likely to try to get rid of the drugs or admit to their presence, making the presence of drugs in jail less likely. Third and finally, a non-incarcerated person who might otherwise consider possessing drugs would be less likely to commit possession in the first instance, because there is always the risk of being arrested and booked into jail.

C. The Concept of Attendant Circumstances

The majority's fundamental error is to ignore the difference between a person's conduct and the circumstances surrounding that conduct. In criminal law, liability is often predicated on a combination of mental state, conduct, the conduct's results, *and* attendant circumstances—the facts surrounding the conduct. *See* 1 WAYNE R. LAFAVE & AUSTIN W. SCOTT, JR., SUBSTANTIVE CRIMINAL LAW § 1.2(c), at 12 (1986) ("The totality of these various items—conduct, mental fault, plus attendant circumstances and specified result when required by the definition of a crime—may be said to constitute the 'elements' of the crime."). The majority is right that criminal liability usually does not attach when the conduct is involuntary. But the same is not true for attendant circumstances.

This point is illustrated by a different statute. RCW 46.20.342(1) makes it a crime "for any person to drive a motor vehicle in this state while that person is in a suspended or revoked status." The conduct is the act of driving. An attendant circumstance is a suspended or revoked license. Rarely will a person voluntarily have his or her license suspended or revoked. The Department of Licensing usually does this *against* the licensee's will. But that does not matter. Criminal liability flows from the conduct of driving at the same time that the attendant circumstance—a suspended or revoked driver's license—is present, even though the attendant circumstance is usually involuntary.

Sentence enhancements typically relate to attendant circumstances. As the majority observes correctly, "The purpose of sentencing enhancements is to provide legislative guidance to courts in calibrating the appropriate punishment for crimes based on *relevant circumstances surrounding the underlying conduct.*" Majority at 707 (emphasis added). And as the Court of Appeals noted in its opinion, a "sentence enhancement is not a separate sentence of a separate substantive crime." *State v. Eaton*, 143 Wash.App. 155, 160, 177 P.3d 157 (2008). Instead, an enhancement statute presupposes the defendant committed a crime involving conduct—in this case, possession of methamphetamine—and increases the sentencing range when an attendant circumstance is present. *See State v. Barnes*, 153 Wash.2d 378, 385, 103 P.3d 1219 (2005).

RCW 9.94A.533(5) follows this pattern. To the contrary of what the majority suggests, RCW 9.94A.533(5) does not deal with conduct, namely the act of entering a particular area. Rather, RCW 9.94A.533(5) describes a circumstance—the offender's location—attending the conduct prohibited by another statute. When a person violates RCW 69.50.4013(1) by possessing a controlled substance "while in a county jail or state correctional facility," the legislature requires the sentencing court to impose a sentence enhancement of 12 months to the standard sentence range. RCW 9.94A.533(5). In this way, RCW 9.94A.533(5) "provide[s] legislative guidance to courts in calibrating the appropriate punishment for crimes based on relevant circumstances surrounding the underlying conduct." Majority at 707. The statute indicates that possession of illegal drugs is already culpable, but it becomes even more culpable when done at a given location. RCW 9.94A.533(5) is unconcerned with how a person got to jail. Rather, RCW 9.94A.533(5) provides additional punishment for a person's voluntary misconduct once there.

In this case, although Eaton did not bring about the attendant circumstance defined in RCW 9.94A.533(5), the underlying criminal conduct of possessing drugs is a justifiable basis for criminal liability. Possession is a continuing offense "lasting as long as the act of possession does," 1 Wayne R. LaFave, *Substantive Criminal Law* § 6.1(d), at 430 n. 46 (2d ed.2003), and Eaton voluntarily continued his possession. This case would be very different if Eaton were arguing that his possession became involuntary due to the arrest or transport of him to jail. But he does not make that argument, and Eaton does not contest his conviction under RCW 69.50.4013(1). So the majority is wrong to suggest that Eaton was punished for involuntary conduct.

The majority claims that Eaton "did not have the requisite ability to choose." Majority at 709. But criminal liability was still within Eaton's control; he could have simply ceased possessing drugs. Eaton did not choose to enter the Clark County Jail, but he had a choice about his course of conduct upon his arrival. By continuing his possession while he was in jail, rather than relinquishing the methamphetamine beforehand, Eaton subjected himself to the 12–month enhancement provided in RCW 9.94A.533(5). The location of the offense was an attendant circumstance triggering additional punishment for the predicate crime.

D. Effect On Other Sentence Enhancements

The majority's logic and sweeping language also raises doubts about how other sentence enhancements should be read. For instance, several subsections in RCW 69.50.435(1) subject an offender to a sentence enhancement for selling drugs "to a person" who is "[i]n a school," "[w]ithin one thousand feet of the perimeter of the school grounds," "[i]n a public park," "[i]n a public transit stop shelter," or located in another such place. As in RCW 9.94A.533(5), the statute levies an additional punishment for a person who commits a drug offense while in a specific location. As in RCW 9.94A.533(5), the statute merely describes an attendant circumstance accompanying a substantive crime defined in another statute. Under the logic of the majority, however, RCW 69.50.435 presumably would not apply unless the prosecution affirmatively proves beyond a reasonable doubt that the defendant voluntarily entered the enhancement zone.

III. CONCLUSION

I would hold that the plain meaning of RCW 9.94A.533(5) does not include a requirement that the offender was voluntarily in a jail or prison. Because the Court of Appeals reversed Eaton's sentence based on this argument, the court did not address Eaton's other arguments on appeal. I would reverse and remand to the Court of Appeals to address Eaton's other claims.

WE CONCUR: Chief Justice BARBARA A. MADSEN, Justice SUSAN OWENS, Justice JAMES M. JOHNSON.

PRACTICE EXERCISE

This exercise requires three people: one judge, one prosecutor, and one defense counsel. The judge will have two minutes to issue a decision that cites particular portions of each side's argument as effective, after a maximum of 5 minutes of oral argument per side. The following scenario is taken from *State v. Scott*, 429 N.J. Super. 1, 3, 55 A.3d 728, 729 (N.J. Super. Ct. App. Div. 2012). Each side may use its discretion to decide what method and means of argument to use, but use the above-mentioned cases as authority—majority or dissent. This exercise is intended to test both your ability to discern possible winning arguments for your side and your ability to persuasively argue:

Several people participated in the murder of a victim following a dispute over drugs. One individual requested that defendant retrieve a handgun that had been stashed in an old mattress lying in a nearby alley. Defendant retrieved the gun from the mattress and handed it to another individual who shot and killed the victim. The rusty gun was known to the several participants, available for anyone to access, and had been stored in the mattress for approximately a year and a half.

* * *

The Legislature has indicated that

> [the] words and phrases shall be read and construed with their context, and shall, unless inconsistent with the manifest intent of the legislature or unless another or different meaning is expressly indicated, be given their generally accepted meaning, according to the approved usage of the language. [N.J.S.A. 1:1–1.]

* * *

Specifically, N.J.S.A. 2C:39–4a(2) provides that

> [a]ny person who *possesses, receives[,] or transfers a community gun* is guilty of a crime of the second degree and shall be sentenced to a term of imprisonment by the court. The term of imprisonment shall include the imposition of a minimum term. The minimum term shall be fixed at one-half of the sentence imposed by the court or three years, whichever is greater and during which the defendant shall be ineligible for parole. *As used in this paragraph, "community gun" means a firearm that is transferred among, between [,] or within any association of two or more persons who, while possessing that firearm, engage in criminal activity or use it unlawfully against the person or property of another.* [(Emphasis added).]

* * *

In 2007, the Legislature amended N.J.S.A. 2C:39–4a to add subsection a(2), the community gun offense.*** Before the amendment, the statute provided:

2C:39–4. Possession of weapons for unlawful purposes

a. *Firearms.* Any person who has in his possession any firearm *with a purpose to use it unlawfully* against the person or property of another is guilty of a crime of the second degree.

b. *Explosives.* Any person who has in his possession or carries any explosive substance *with a purpose to use it unlawfully* against the person or property of another is guilty of a crime of the second degree.

c. *Destructive devices.* Any person who has in his possession any destructive device *with a purpose to use it unlawfully* against the person or property of another is guilty of a crime of the second degree.

d. *Other weapons.* Any person who has in his possession any weapon, except a firearm, *with a purpose to use it unlawfully* against the person or property of another is guilty of a crime of the third degree.

e. *Imitation firearms.* Any person who has in his possession an imitation firearm under circumstances that would lead an observer to reasonably believe that it is possessed for an *unlawful purpose* is guilty of a crime of the fourth degree.

[*N.J.S.A.* 2C:39–4 (emphasis added).]

In each pre-amendment subsection of *N.J.S.A.* 2C:39–4, the Legislature expressly required, as an element of the offense, that the State prove that a defendant possessed a weapon with a purpose to use it unlawfully. When it amended the statute, however, the Legislature did not include the culpability requirement it had expressly stated in subsections a(1), b, c, d, and e. In subsection a(2), the Legislature omitted any express mens rea requirement that a defendant must know that the weapon is "a firearm that is transferred among, between[,] or within any association of two or more persons who, while possessing that firearm, engage in criminal activity or use it unlawfully against the person or property of another," N.J.S.A. 2C:39–4a(2). Therefore, the Legislature treated the community gun offense differently than firearms, explosives, destructive devices, other weapons, and imitation firearms offenses.

CHAPTER FIVE

Crimes Against the Person

IN MANY CRIMINAL law classes, the most frequently discussed crime against the person is homicide. In fact, historically, criminal law classes considered only the crime of homicide. Homicide is useful to study as it involves all the potential types of elements that define crimes. To prove homicide, the prosecution must show that there was a voluntary act (or, in some cases, an omission), which must be accompanied by a culpable mental state, death must follow from this act or omission, and the defendant's act must be the proximate cause of the death. By focusing primarily on homicide statutes, criminal law courses have rightly assumed that students will gain experience interpreting each type of element they will encounter in other crimes. Such an approach, however, fails to give students an understanding of how to go about building, or attacking, other types of charges. The types of facts used to prove that a defendant *knew* he was taking a life are very different that the types of facts used to prove that a defendant *knew* he was in possession of drugs. This book takes a broader approach than is typically taken and provides an introduction to the crimes most commonly prosecuted.

In this chapter, we consider a variety of conduct that harms, could harm, or put another in fear of harm. This chapter will certainly devote considerable attention to the crime of homicide. We will consider the crime itself and also unsuccessful efforts to kill—attempt, conspiracy, and solicitation in this context of homicide. We will also consider crimes which, under appropriate circumstances, could be charged as lesser-included offenses to homicide, including assault and reckless endangerment. Finally we will consider the crimes of rape and kidnapping.

A. Homicide

To prove homicide, the prosecution must demonstrate that the defendant:

(1) engaged in conduct (or failed to perform an act he had a legal duty to perform);

(2) with a culpable state of mind; that

(3) caused a death.

The first and third requirements are binary considerations; either there was a voluntary act that caused a death or that wasn't. There are, however, a variety of mental states in homicide law and the defendant's punishment for causing a death turns on which mental state he had.

The fact that the first and third requirements are binary considerations does not mean that they are necessarily easy to consider, as you will discover. It means only that there are only two possible answers. A defendant's criminal liability for a death does not turn on *how* voluntary his actions were or the *extent* to which the defendant's actions caused his victim's death. The law simply decides *whether* he acted in a voluntary manner and *whether* his actions were the cause of the death. Every state requires these two criteria to be satisfied for a homicide conviction and very similar principles prevail in all the states.

The degree of the defendant's liability is determined by examining the second requirement for homicidal crimes. There are a variety of culpable mental states used to determine the type of homicide a defendant has committed. You are likely already familiar with the idea of grading homicide. Based on watching a number of television shows and movies, and listening to more than a few Johnny Cash songs, you are doubtlessly already familiar with one grade of homicide, murder in the first-degree. Many states have this category of homicide with most of these states having two forms of murder, first- and second-degree. A few states define a category of homicide as third degree murder. Some states have only one category of murder. Each state then has degrees of homicide less serious than murder and they are defined by a variety of terms. We will consider the various ways states have decided how to decide which homicides are more serious than the other.

1. Voluntary Acts and Crimes of Omission

In order to obtain a homicide conviction, the prosecution must demonstrate that the defendant either committed an act that produced another's death, or failed to engage in an act he has a duty to perform that would have prevented a death.

a. Consciousness of Action

Hinckle, the case that follows, in many ways raises more questions than it answers. It articulates the requirement of voluntariness rather nicely, as you will see. As we discussed in the introductory chapter, a crime must be voluntarily committed and, as you would expect, there is no exception to this rule for homicide. As you read this case, ask yourself exactly what was wrong with the proceedings in the trial court and how does the West Virginia Supreme Court in *Hinckle* fix this problem?

State v. Hinckle

Supreme Court of West Virginia
489 S.E.2d 257 (1996)

CLECKLEY, Justice:

The defendant below and appellant herein, Charles Rhea Hinkle, appeals a verdict by a jury in the Circuit Court of Pleasants County of guilty of involuntary manslaughter. By order dated May 17, 1995, the circuit court denied the defendant's motions for a judgment of acquittal and a new trial, and sentenced him to one year in the Pleasants County jail. This appeal ensued.

I.

FACTUAL AND PROCEDURAL HISTORY

On June 12, 1993, the defendant finished his work shift at the Ormet Corporation, an aluminum plant in Hannibal, Ohio, at approximately 4:00 p.m. He obtained a ride to the Village Inn tavern in Paden City, West Virginia. At the tavern, the defendant made several telephone calls attempting to locate someone to give him a ride to his car. The defendant also ordered a can of beer, and drank approximately one-third of the beer. While at the tavern, the defendant complained of not feeling well, dizziness, and double vision. The tavern owner's daughter then agreed to take the defendant to retrieve his car. As he was leaving the bar, the defendant took an unopened can of beer with him.

At approximately 7:30 p.m., the defendant was traveling north on Route 2 in St. Marys, West Virginia. Robert Barrett was driving south on Route 2 with his wife, Charlotte Ann Barrett. It appears the defendant's car gradually crossed the centerline and traveled in a straight line for approximately two hundred yards in the southbound lane before it collided head-on with the Barrett automobile. As a result of the accident, the defendant and Mr. Barrett suffered severe injuries.

Mrs. Barrett also sustained serious injuries, and died as a result of those injuries. Eyewitnesses reported the defendant crossed the centerline in a consistent, even fashion without attempting to swerve, brake, change directions, or stop. Witnesses also indicated that both the defendant and Mr. Barrett were traveling at the posted speed limit.

* * *

While treating the defendant's injuries, he was given a Magnetic Resonance Imaging [MRI] scan to determine whether he had sustained any head injuries. The MRI results indicated the defendant had an undiagnosed brain disorder in the portion of his brain that regulates consciousness.

On September 13, 1993, a Pleasants County grand jury returned an indictment charging the defendant with the misdemeanor offense of involuntary manslaughter while driving a motor vehicle in an unlawful manner in violation of W. Va.Code, 61-2-5 (1923). The defendant stood trial, by jury, for this charge in Pleasants County on March 1, 1995. During the trial, the defendant's son testified that the defendant had been having memory loss for several months prior to the accident, and that he believed the defendant had seen a doctor in New Martinsville, West Virginia. Similarly, the tavern owner stated the defendant had complained of feeling ill during the months preceding the collision, and he had complained of dizziness, memory loss, and double vision on the night of the accident. She, too, believed the defendant recently had been treated by a physician.

Defense witness, Ronald Washburn, M.D., reported the defendant's MRI scan showed an undiagnosed brain disorder affecting the reticular activating system of his brain. Dr. Washburn reasoned that because this portion of the brain affects one's consciousness, this disorder could have caused the defendant to suddenly lose consciousness immediately before the collision. He also indicated the defendant had developed this brain abnormality approximately four to eight months prior to the accident, and the disease was not caused by chronic alcohol abuse. Testifying further, Dr. Washburn surmised the defendant's prior memory loss was a symptom of his brain disorder, but his other complaints of not feeling well, dizziness, and blurred or double vision were not related to this disease. Concluding his opinion, Dr. Washburn determined the defendant's brain disorder would not have been diagnosed if he had not had an MRI scan after the accident. Finally, both the defendant and Mr. Barrett testified they could not recall any details of the automobile accident.

* * *

---

10   It does not appear the defendant ever had lost consciousness prior to the accident of June 12, 1993.

[T]he trial court directed the jury to find that the defendant suffered from a brain disorder affecting the consciousness-regulating portion of his brain. The court further instructed the jury:

"[O]ne who suffers from an as yet undiagnosed disease or defect cannot be convicted of involuntary manslaughter for a death resulting from his operation of an automobile unless the State proves beyond a reasonable doubt that:

"1. The driver knew or should reasonably have known of the existence of his physical or mental condition, disease or defect; and,

"2. The driver should reasonably have foreseen that his condition, disease or defect would impair his ability to drive an automobile to such a degree so as to endanger human life; and,

"3. The driver's condition, disease or defect did contribute to the accident resulting in death; and,

"4. His decision to drive an automobile at the date and time and in the place set forth in the indictment was negligence so gross, wanton and culpable as to show a reckless disregard of human life; and,

"5. Indicated a conscious indifference to the probable dangerous consequences of driving so impaired.

"If the evidence fails to prove any of these matters beyond a reasonable doubt, then you shall find the defendant, Charles Rhea Hinkle, not guilty of involuntary manslaughter as charged in the indictment.

"If the evidence proves each of these matters beyond a reasonable doubt then you may find the defendant, Charles Rhea Hinkle, guilty of involuntary manslaughter as charged in the indictment."

* * *

II.

DISCUSSION

Despite the additional issues raised, disposition of this appeal begins and ends with an inquiry into whether the jury instructions were inadequate. Thus, the appeal in this case has been limited to one issue: Whether the jury was instructed properly as to the defense of unconsciousness. The defendant claims the trial court committed reversible error when it refused to give his insanity instruction. On the other hand, the State contends the instruction offered by the defendant was imperfect, and the evidence did not support an insanity instruction. Moreover, the State urges the instructions offered were more than adequate to cover the defense of unconsciousness. This case requires us to harmonize a conflict between the defense of unconsciousness and that of insanity.

* * *

ANALYSIS

The defendant argues he was entitled to an insanity instruction. Of course, the State contends otherwise. We agree partially with the State that technically the defense was one of unconsciousness as opposed to insanity. The law on the notion of unconsciousness in West Virginia is terribly undeveloped. This is, no doubt, the reason why the defendant requested an insanity instruction in this case, since that is where our older cases seem to place this claim. *See State v. Painter*, 135 W.Va. 106, 63 S.E.2d 86 (1950); *State v. Alie*, 82 W.Va. 601, 96 S.E. 1011 (1918). Indeed, there is only a paucity of American appellate courts that have discussed this defense. With regard to those jurisdictions, Section 44 of Wayne R. LaFave & Austin W. Scott, Jr., *Criminal Law* (1972), one of the few treatises that gives this defense any extensive coverage, states: "A defense related to but different from the defense of insanity is that of unconsciousness, often referred to as automatism: one who engages in what would otherwise be criminal conduct is not guilty of a crime if he does so in a state of unconsciousness or semi-consciousness." *Id.* at 337.

Interpreting this defense, the weight of authority in this country suggests that unconsciousness, or automatism as it is sometimes called, is not part of the insanity defense for several reasons. First, unconsciousness does not necessarily arise from a mental disease or defect. Although always containing a mental component in the form of loss of cognitive functioning, the causes and conditions are diverse; examples include epilepsy, concussion, gunshot wounds, somnambulism, coronary episodes, and certain brain disorders, as here. *See generally* LaFave & Scott, *supra*, at 339-40. Additionally, these unconscious disorders tend to be acute, unlike most cases of insanity which are typically chronic. Because cases of unconsciousness are temporary, they do not normally call for institutionalization, which is the customary disposition following a successful insanity defense. *Id.* at 338.

. . . .[U]nconsciousness eliminates one of the basic elements of the crime-either the mental state or the voluntary nature of the act. As such, once the issue of unconsciousness or automatism is raised by the defense, the State must disprove it beyond a reasonable doubt in order to meet its burden of proof with respect to the elements of the crime. . . .

Unconsciousness is thus a separate and distinct defense from insanity. . . . In order to keep this distinction conceptually clear, it is better to view unconsciousness as eliminating the voluntary act requirement rather than negating the mental component of crimes. Thinking of unconsciousness in this conceptual fashion helps to avoid the temptation to collapse it into insanity which, of course, also deals with mental conditions. The defense of unconsciousness should be recognized in a criminal trial and equated with epilepsy rather than insanity. We believe this is the way the claim of unconsciousness should be viewed jurisprudentially in West Virginia.

Accordingly, we hold that unconsciousness (or automatism) is not part of the insanity defense, but is a separate claim which may eliminate the voluntariness of the criminal act. Moreover, the burden of proof on this issue, once raised by the defense, remains on the State to prove that the act was voluntary beyond a reasonable doubt. An instruction on the defense of unconsciousness is required when there is reasonable evidence that the defendant was unconscious at the time of the commission of the crime. In the instant case, it is contended the defendant was, in fact, rendered unconscious at the time of the commission of the crime by reason of an undiagnosed brain disorder affecting the reticular activating system of his brain.

Even if the trier of fact believes the defendant was unconscious at the time of the act, there is another consideration which occasionally arises. If the defendant was sufficiently apprised and aware of the condition and experienced recurring episodes of loss of consciousness, e.g., epilepsy, then operating a vehicle or other potentially destructive implement, with knowledge of the potential danger, might well amount to reckless disregard for the safety of others. Therefore, the jury should be charged that even if it believes there is a reasonable doubt about the defendant's consciousness at the time of the event, the voluntary operation of a motor vehicle with knowledge of the potential for loss of consciousness can constitute reckless behavior.

The next questions are whether the evidence in the present case was sufficient to justify an unconsciousness instruction, and, if so, whether the instruction given by the court was adequate.

* * *

[A]lthough the trial court instructed the jury that the defendant was suffering from a brain disorder, no further instruction was given (on insanity or otherwise) which required the jury carefully to focus on how the nature of the defendant's brain disorder related to the elements of the crime. The jury should have been told that, in light of the evidence of the defendant's brain disorder and apparent blackout, he could not be convicted unless the State proved beyond a reasonable doubt that his act was *voluntary and that he acted in reckless disregard of the safety* of others.

The instructions were not wholly wanting in this regard, for the trial court did tell the jury that it could nevertheless convict the defendant, in spite of his brain disorder, if it concluded that he "knew *or should reasonably have known* of the existence of his . . . condition" and he " *should reasonably have foreseen* that his condition, disease or defect would impair his ability to drive an automobile to such a degree as to endanger human life." (Emphasis added). This portion of the instruction, however, suffers from the infirmity that it is phrased in the language of civil negligence rather than gross negligence or recklessness. Later, in the same instruction, the trial court did refer to "negligence so gross, wanton and culpable as to show a reckless disregard for human life" which "indicated a conscious indifference to the probable consequences." Nevertheless, viewing the instruction as a whole, as we must, the jury may well have been misguided with respect to the appropriate standard by which to measure the defendant's liability. An instruction more faithful to the relevant standard of voluntariness (or recklessness) would require a finding that the defendant *knew* of his condition and *knew* it could impair his ability to drive.

[I]rrespective of the foregoing, we would be inclined to reverse the defendant's conviction based on the absence of evidence justifying the "should have known" language in the charge. There is virtually no evidence in the record to indicate that the defendant knew (or reasonably should have known) of the serious nature of his brain disorder or that he knew (or reasonably should have known) that it would impair his ability to drive an automobile so as to endanger human life.[29] We would be inclined to reverse for lack of sufficient evidence, which would bar retrial on double jeopardy grounds, as opposed to the weight of the evidence, which does not bar retrial, except for the fact that the State was not

---

29 The defendant had suffered from other symptoms such as dizziness and blurred vision, but he had not previously experienced a blackout.

given an adequate opportunity to meet the defendant's unconsciousness claim as we have outlined it above.

III.

CONCLUSION

Based on the foregoing, the judgment of the Circuit Court of Pleasants County is reversed, and this case is remanded for a new trial.

Reversed and Remanded.

Notes and Questions

1. The jury was told that if Charles Hinckle "should have known" of his disorder impairing his ability to drive, he could be convicted of involuntary manslaughter. The Court concludes that the instruction is incorrect, that Hinckle can only be convicted only if he *knew* he had the disorder that prevented him from being able to safely operate the car. So the problem that the Court sees with this case is that the State of West Virginia was too easily able to show that Mr. Hinckle was aware of a risk he posed to other motorists. That must be why the Court is requiring the State to prove that Mr. Hinckle *knew*, not just that he *should have known*, of a medical condition that posed a risk to others with his driving, right?

2. Isn't the Court's opinion then inconsistent with this conclusion? The Court then concludes that the State of West Virginia failed to present evidence that Mr. Hinckle knew, or even *should have known* about the serious nature of his brain disorder that caused the fatal crash. The Court concludes that the case would have reversed for lack of sufficient evidence, which would have prevented a retrial, rather than on jury instruction grounds, "except for the fact that the State was not given an opportunity to meet the defendant's unconsciousness claim as we have outlined it above." But Justice Cleckley concluded that the trial court's instructions made it too easy for the State to prove Mr. Hinckle committed involuntary manslaughter. He then concludes that the State of West Virginia failed to present adequate evidence to satisfy the too lax burden that he voluntarily caused this fatal crash. If the State's evidence was insufficient to prove even the trial court's lax standard of voluntariness, why would the State be afforded an opportunity to meet the more stringent standard of voluntariness the Supreme Court of West Virginia required? As illogical as this conclusion seems, even at this point in your legal education,

you should be realizing a practice pointer about the type of role judges prefer to play in criminal cases and how this reality affects the way lawyers should present cases. Appellate courts far prefer to remand decisions for further proceedings, citing some legal error (usually in the jury instructions), than declare that the defendant should be released because there is insufficient evidence for the conviction.

PRACTICE EXERCISE

Imagine you're the Assistant District Attorney assigned to handle the *Hinckle* case after it is remanded to the Circuit Court of Pleasants County, West Virginia. Hinckle's defense lawyer comes to you and asks you dismiss the charge against his client. What sort of information do you want to know before you make this decision? What information would you request of the defense attorney and what sort of information would you instruct your investigator to gather?

b. Homicide by Omission

As a general matter, American law imposes no duty on individuals to protect one another. This legal generalization formed the basis of the final episode of *Seinfeld*. When the primary cast members of the show were charged with violating a newly enacted Good Samaritan Law for failing to assist the victim of a robbery, their attorney, Jackie Chiles, responded, "You don't have to help anybody. That's what this country is all about. That's deplorable, unfathomable, improbable."

There are, however, some exceptions to this generalization. Parents do owe a duty to protect their children; spouses owe a duty to protect one another; those who contract to protect one another owe such a duty (for instance doctors, nurses, innkeepers, security personnel); and those whom courts impose a duty upon (universities housing students, for instance).

The duties are often fairly straight forward, except when the prosecution attempts to extend duties to non-traditional relationships (as you will see in the *Leet* case in this section), or as in the following case, where parents claim a religious basis for not seeking medical treatment for their children. Christian Scientists are among the religious groups associated with the rejection of medical treatment. The church was founded, and has their headquarters in Massachusetts, the location of our next case.

i. Interpreting the Nature of the Duty

As you read the *Twitchell* case, ask yourself what you would have told the parents of the child if you had been called and asked your legal opinion about their duty to seek medical attention in Massachusetts.

Commonwealth v. Twitchell

Supreme Judicial Court of Massachusetts
617 N.E.2d 609 (1993)

WILKINS, Justice.

David and Ginger Twitchell appeal from their convictions of involuntary manslaughter in connection with the April 8, 1986, death of their two and one-half year old son Robyn. Robyn died of the consequences of peritonitis caused by the perforation of his bowel which had been obstructed as a result of an anomaly known as Meckel's diverticulum. There was evidence that the condition could be corrected by surgery with a high success rate.

The defendants are practicing Christian Scientists who grew up in Christian Science families. They believe in healing by spiritual treatment. During Robyn's five-day illness from Friday, April 4, through Tuesday, April 8, they retained a Christian Science practitioner, a Christian Science nurse, and at one time consulted with Nathan Talbot, who held a position in the church known as the "Committee on Publication."[3] As a result of that consultation, David Twitchell read a church publication concerning the legal rights and obligations of Christian Scientists in Massachusetts. That publication quoted a portion of G.L. c. 273, § 1, as then amended, which, at least in the context of the crimes described in that section, accepted remedial treatment by spiritual means alone as satisfying any parental obligation not to neglect a child or to provide a child with physical care. We shall subsequently discuss this statute in connection with the defendants'

---

3   The "Committee on Publication" for each State is a one-person committee authorized by the church's founder, Mary Baker Eddy, to explain Christian Science to the community and to give advice to practitioners. Talbot was head of all the Committees on Publication in the country.

claim, rejected by the trial judge, that the spiritual treatment provision in G.L. c. 273, § 1, protects them from criminal liability for manslaughter.[4]

We need not recite in detail the circumstances of Robyn's illness. The jury would have been warranted in concluding that Robyn was in considerable distress and that, in the absence of their belief in and reliance on spiritual treatment, the parents of a child in his condition would normally have sought medical treatment in sufficient time to save that child's life. There was also evidence that the intensity of Robyn's distress ebbed and flowed, perhaps causing his parents to believe that prayer would lead to the healing of the illness. On the other hand, the jury would have been warranted in finding that the Twitchells were wanton or reckless in failing to provide medical care for Robyn, if parents have a legal duty to provide a child with medical care in such circumstances and if the spiritual treatment provision of G.L. c. 273, § 1, did not protect them from manslaughter liability.

Christian Science Center, Boston, MA.

We shall conclude that parents have a duty to seek medical attention for a child in Robyn's circumstances, the violation of which, if their conduct was wanton or reckless, could support a conviction of involuntary manslaughter and that the spiritual healing provision in G.L. c. 273, § 1, did not bar a prosecution for manslaughter in these circumstances. We further conclude, however, that special circumstances in this case would justify a jury's finding that the Twitchells reasonably believed that they could rely on spiritual treatment without fear of criminal prosecution. This affirmative defense should have been asserted and presented to the jury. Because it was not, there is a substantial risk of a miscarriage of justice in this case, and, therefore, the judgments must be reversed.

1. We shall first consider whether the law generally imposes a parental duty to provide medical services to a child, the breach of which can be the basis of a conviction for involuntary manslaughter. We thus put aside temporarily the

---

4   The spiritual treatment provision then read, as it does now, as follows: "A child shall not be deemed to be neglected or lack proper physical care for the sole reason that he is being provided remedial treatment by spiritual means alone in accordance with the tenets and practice of a recognized church or religious denomination by a duly accredited practitioner thereof." G.L. c. 273, § 1 (1992 ed.).

question of what, if any, application the spiritual treatment provision in G.L. c. 273, § 1, has to this case.

The Commonwealth presented its case on the theory that each defendant was guilty of involuntary manslaughter because the intentional failure of each to seek medical attention for their son involved such "a high degree of likelihood that substantial harm will result to" him as to be wanton or reckless conduct. *Commonwealth v. Welansky*, 316 Mass. 383, 399, 55 N.E.2d 902 (1944). Our definition of involuntary manslaughter derives from the common law. A charge of involuntary manslaughter based on an omission to act can be proved only if the defendant had a duty to act and did not do so. *Commonwealth v. Welansky*, *supra*. That duty, however, is not limited to those duties whose violation would create civil liability. *Commonwealth v. Godin*, *supra* 374 Mass. at 126–127, 371 N.E.2d 438.

The Commonwealth claims that the defendants owed an affirmative duty of care to their son which they wantonly or recklessly failed to perform. The duty to provide sufficient support for a child is legally enforceable in a civil proceeding against a parent. A breach of that duty is a misdemeanor. G.L. c. 273, § 1 (1992 ed.). Where necessary to protect a child's well-being, the Commonwealth may intervene, over the parents' objections, to assure that needed services are provided. More important, for our current purposes, a parental duty of care has been recognized in the common law of homicide in this Commonwealth. *See Commonwealth v. Hall*, 322 Mass. 523, 528, 78 N.E.2d 644 (1948) (conviction of murder in the second-degree based on withholding of food and liquids).

The defendants argue, however, that any common law duty of care does not include a duty to provide medical treatment and that there is no statute imposing such a duty except G.L. c. 273, § 1, which, in turn, in their view, provides them with complete protection against any criminal charge based on their failure to seek medical treatment for their son. In their argument that the common law of the Commonwealth does not include a duty to provide medical treatment, the defendants overlook *Commonwealth v. Gallison*, 383 Mass. 659, 421 N.E.2d 757 (1981). In that case, we upheld a conviction of manslaughter, saying that a parent who "made no effort to obtain medical help, knowing that her child was gravely ill," could be found guilty of wanton or reckless involuntary manslaughter for her child's death caused by her omission to meet her "duty to provide for the care and welfare of her child." *Id.* at 665, 421 N.E.2d 757. The *Gallison* opinion did not rely on § 1 as the basis of the parent's duty to provide medical care. It relied rather on the more general duty of care underlying civil and criminal liability. *Commonwealth v. Gallison*, *supra* 383 Mass. at 665, 421 N.E.2d 757. There is, consequently, quite apart from § 1, a common law duty to provide medical services for a child, the breach of which can be the basis, in the appropriate circumstances, for the conviction of a parent for involuntary manslaughter.

2. We, therefore, consider the impact, if any, of G.L. c. 273, § 1, on this case. The defendants argue that the spiritual treatment provision in § 1 bars any involuntary manslaughter charge against a parent who relies, as they did, on spiritual treatment and who does not seek medical attention for his or her child, even if the parent's failure to seek such care would otherwise be wanton or reckless conduct. We disagree.

* * *

Section 1 of G.L. c. 273 provides no complete protection to a parent against a charge of involuntary manslaughter that is based on the parent's wanton or reckless failure to provide medical services to a child.[6] Section 1 concerns child support and care in a chapter of the General Laws that deals not so much with the punishment of criminal conduct as with motivating parents to fulfil their natural obligations of support. On the other hand, the principle underlying involuntary manslaughter is the Commonwealth's "interest that persons within its territory should not be killed by the wanton and reckless conduct of others." *Commonwealth v. Godin*, 374 Mass. 120, 126, 371 N.E.2d 438 (1977). It is unlikely that the Legislature placed the spiritual treatment provision in § 1 to provide a defense to, or to alter any definition of, common law homicide. [7] There is no history to § 1 that suggests that the spiritual treatment provision carries any message beyond § 1 itself. * * * The act that added the spiritual treatment provision was entitled "An Act defining the term 'proper physical care' under the law relative to care of children by a parent." St.1971, c. 762. The amendment's concern

---

6   At the time of Robyn Twitchell's death, the relevant parts of G.L. c. 273, § 1, read as follows:

"Any spouse or parent who without just cause deserts his spouse or minor child, whether by going into another town in the commonwealth or into another state, and leaves them or any or either of them without making reasonable provision for their support, and any spouse or parent who unreasonably neglects or refuses to provide for the support and maintenance of his spouse, whether living with him or living apart from him for justifiable cause, or of his minor child, and any spouse or parent who abandons or leaves his spouse or minor child in danger of becoming a burden upon the public, and any parent of a minor child or any guardian with care and custody of a minor child, or any custodian of a minor child, who willfully fails to provide necessary and proper physical, educational or moral care and guidance, or who permits said child to grow up under conditions or circumstances damaging to the child's sound character development, or who fails to provide proper attention for said child, shall be punished by a fine of not more than five hundred dollars or by imprisonment for not more than two years, or both. A child shall not be deemed to be neglected or lack proper physical care for the sole reason that he is being provided remedial treatment by spiritual means alone in accordance with the tenets and practice of a recognized church or religious denomination by a duly accredited practitioner thereof." G.L. c. 273, § 1

2   General Laws c. 265, § 13 (1992 ed.), which fixes the penalty for common law manslaughter, would be the logical place for any such recognition of spiritual treatment as barring a charge of involuntary manslaughter.

seems focused on the subject matter of § 1 and certainly not directed toward changing the common law of homicide. Indeed, that was the view expressed at the time by a representative of the Christian Science Church.

The spiritual treatment provision refers to neglect and lack of proper physical care, which are concepts set forth earlier in § 1, as then amended, as bases for punishment: (1) neglect to provide support and (2) wilful failure to provide necessary and proper physical care. These concepts do not underlie involuntary manslaughter. Wanton or reckless conduct is not a form of negligence. *See Commonwealth v. Godin, supra* 374 Mass. at 127, 371 N.E.2d 438. Wanton or reckless conduct does not involve a wilful intention to cause the resulting harm. *See Commonwealth v. Welansky*, 316 Mass. 383, 397–398, 55 N.E.2d 902 (1944). An involuntary manslaughter verdict does not require proof of wilfulness. *See Commonwealth v. Catalina*, 407 Mass. 779, 789, 556 N.E.2d 973 (1990). Thus, by its terms, the spiritual treatment provision in § 1 does not apply to involuntary manslaughter.

* * *

[The Court granted a new trial on other grounds.—Eds.]

Notes and Questions

1. Strong policy reasons obviously encourage the Court to interpret the law to require parents to seek medical treatment necessary to save the lives of their children. Does the court, however, have to strain the reading of the statute to reach this conclusion? Would an ordinary person reading the statute relied on by the parents believe they had a duty to act contrary to their religious beliefs? The court reasons that the statute in question was codified "in a chapter of the General Laws that deals not so much with the punishment of criminal conduct as with motivating parents to fulfill their natural obligations of support." An ordinary person, lacking legal training, is required to ask where a statute, that fairly clearly permits the conduct at issue, is *codified*?

2. Then consider the court's analysis of the statute itself. The court reasoned: (1) Child neglect shall not be deemed to have occurred if the parents "acted in accordance with tenets and practice of a recognized church or religious denomination." (2) Child neglect occurs if there was neglect or "willful failure to provide necessary and proper care." (3) The parents were convicted of involuntary manslaughter, which does not involve negligence or willful conduct—it involves wanton or reckless conduct. (4) Therefore, the statute pro-

vides no defense to the parents' failure to get treatment for their child that led to her death. But, of course, it was the willful act of following the tenets of the Christian Science Church that led the parents not to seek medical attention— and doing so amounted to taking a wanton and reckless risk with their child's life. Is there any way to justify this decision as a matter of statutory interpretation? Is this not just a decision on the basis of (an admitted very legitimate) policy?

3. While the Christian Science Church has its headquarters in Boston, the Commonwealth of Massachusetts is certainly not the only jurisdiction to adopt a statute permitting parents to refrain from seeking medical treatment on the basis of religious convictions. Courts elsewhere have similarly been unwilling to allow those statutes to exonerate parents who allow their children to die for want of medical care. *See State v. McKown*, 475 N.W.2d 63 (Minn. 1991) (spiritual treatment provision did not apply manslaughter statute); *Walker v. Superior Court*, 47 Cal.3d 112, 134 (1988) ("Prayer treatment will be accommodated as an acceptable means of attending to the needs of a child only insofar as serious physical harm or illness is not at risk); *People in the Interest of D.L.E.*, 645 P.2d 271 (Colo. 1982) ("[W]here the child is deprived of medical care necessary to prevent a life-endangering condition [epileptic seizures], the child may be adjudicated dependent and neglected under the statutory scheme."); *Hall v. State*, 493 N.E.2d 433, 435 (Ind. 1986) ("Prayer is not permitted as a defense when a caretaker engages in omissive conduct which results in the child's death.").

---

ii. Determining Who Has a Duty

One of the harder questions courts face in a world of increasingly non-traditional families is: Who has a duty to protect a child from harm? The *Leet* case presents an all-too-common issue in American courts.

Leet v. State

District Court of Appeal of Florida, Second District
595 So.2d 959 (1991)

ALTENBERND, Judge.

Raymond Earl Leet appeals his convictions for child abuse and third-degree felony murder. §§ 827.04(1), Fla.Stat. (Supp.1988), 782.04(4), Fla.Stat. (1987).

Although this case presents two difficult issues, we affirm. First, the state's evidence was sufficient to create a jury question concerning Mr. Leet's legal obligation to prevent his girlfriend's abuse of her child while the child was living in Mr. Leet's home on a permanent basis. Second, even though the physical injuries which ultimately caused the child's death were inflicted by the child's mother in Mr. Leet's absence, the state's evidence established circumstances prior to the final beating from which a jury could properly find Mr. Leet culpably negligent. In deference to the valid concerns expressed by the special concurrence and the need to assure statewide uniformity on issues relating to the protection of Florida's children, we certify an issue to the Florida Supreme Court.

I. A Brief Biography of Joshua Collins.

The victim, Joshua Collins, was born on January 31, 1987, to Mary Lee Collins. Ms. Collins was incarcerated at the time of Joshua's birth. The child was immediately given to Joanna Hay to raise until Ms. Collins was released.

About one month after Ms. Collins was released from jail, when Joshua was four months old, she returned for the child. She kept him for about three weeks and then returned him to Ms. Hay. In January 1988, when the child was about one year old, Ms. Collins again retrieved her son.

Mr. Leet met Ms. Collins in that same month. Shortly thereafter, Ms. Collins, Joshua and Nathan, Joshua's older brother, moved into Mr. Leet's home in Zephyrhills, Florida. Ms. Collins became pregnant with Mr. Leet's child.

In April 1988, HRS investigated a child abuse complaint concerning Joshua. Ms. Hay had reported this claim after seeing Mr. Leet bathing Joshua while Joshua was bleeding from his nose. Although Joshua had facial bruises, the report was classified as unfounded when Ms. Collins explained that the child had fallen down a flight of stairs. Her story was confirmed by her brother.

In May 1988, a neighbor friend took photographs of Joshua showing extensive facial bruises. On June 8, 1988, HRS conducted another investigation concerning an abrasion over Joshua's left eye. This report was classified as unfounded when Ms. Collins claimed that Joshua had fallen into some concrete blocks.

On June 18, 1988, Mr. Leet took Joshua and Ms. Collins to the hospital because Joshua had multiple bruises on his head, trunk, and extremities. These injuries occurred while Mr. Leet was at work. Ms. Collins claimed that Joshua had fallen against a tombstone in a cemetery. On this occasion, Ms. Collins was arrested and charged with child abuse.

Joshua and his brother were then placed in the custody of their maternal grandmother. Both boys were returned to their mother, with the acquiescence of HRS and the circuit court, before the criminal charges were resolved. Apparently, Nathan was returned in August and Joshua in early October.

By early November 1988, there is evidence that Joshua was once again abused. Mr. Leet knew that the child had received a black eye "from something" in this period. It is noteworthy that this abuse resumed when Ms. Collins was nine months pregnant and her criminal case concerning the prior child abuse reached sentencing. A day or two before the fatal incident, Ms. Collins was sentenced to probation for the prior abuse.

On Monday or Tuesday during the week of November 20–26, 1988, the week of Joshua's death, Joshua sustained large bruises on his chest. When Mr. Leet asked about the bruises, Ms. Collins claimed that Nathan had closed a car door on Joshua. Nathan is a small child. He was sometimes rough with his younger brother. According to Mr. Leet, Nathan admitted that he closed the car door on Joshua. Nevertheless, the autopsy photographs display graphic bruises from this incident. A jury could decide that the ordinary reasonable person would not believe that these bruises were caused by a car door.

On Wednesday, Joshua had a black eye when Mr. Leet returned from work. Ms. Collins explained that Joshua had caused this injury by either poking his own eye or rubbing it too much. The autopsy photographs, however, were sufficient evidence to permit a reasonable jury to believe that any reasonable person would have rejected this explanation.

Mr. Leet worked nights and slept during the morning. On Thursday, November 24, 1988, when he got up in the afternoon, he noticed that Joshua had some swelling near his jaw. Ms. Collins claimed this was caused by an infected tooth. Mr. Leet accepted this explanation and went to work. After the child's death, Mr. Leet told the police that the child appeared fine on Thursday afternoon. Mr. Leet's brother saw this injury and testified that the swelling was the size of a man's fist.

It is unclear from the evidence whether Ms. Collins beat Joshua again on Thursday afternoon or evening. Because the child already had extensive marking on his upper chest and head, it is difficult to determine if an additional beating occurred. An additional beating, however, is consistent with the medical testimony and the child's near comatose state on Friday.

At approximately 2 a.m. on Friday, November 25, 1988, Ms. Collins came to Mr. Leet's work place with Joshua and Nathan. She explained that she was in labor. Mr. Leet drove Ms. Collins to Tampa General Hospital while Joshua slept in the back seat. When Ms. Collins entered the hospital to have his child, Mr. Leet did not encourage the child's mother to request any medical treatment for Joshua. Mr. Leet and the two boys returned home at sunrise. Mr. Leet took care of Joshua and Nathan on this day. Joshua slept a large part of the day, did not eat, and vomited at least once during the day.

On Friday evening, Mr. Leet returned to the hospital to pick up Ms. Collins. Joshua stayed in the back seat of the car while Ms. Collins was checking out. When she got into the car, she discovered that Joshua was not breathing. He was taken to the emergency room and died shortly thereafter.

II. The Cases Against Ms. Collins and Mr. Leet.

Ms. Collins' responsibility for Joshua's death is not at issue in this case. She pled guilty to aggravated child abuse and first-degree felony murder and received a life sentence. Both her legal and moral responsibility for the death of her own child are beyond question.

This case concerns the more troublesome issue of Mr. Leet's criminal responsibility. Ms. Collins did not testify at Mr. Leet's trial. It is noteworthy that Mr. Leet was not charged as a principal concerning the aggravated child abuse by Ms. Collins. *See* § 777.011, Fla.Stat. (1987). Instead, the state charged him with simple child abuse and third-degree felony murder. *McDaniel v. State*, 566 So.2d 941 (Fla. 2d DCA 1990).

> Section 827.04(1), Florida Statutes (Supp.1988), states:
>
> Whoever, willfully or by culpable negligence, deprives a child of, or allows a child to be deprived of, necessary food, clothing, shelter, or medical treatment, or who, knowingly or by culpable negligence, inflicts or permits the infliction of physical or mental injury to the child, and in so doing causes great bodily harm, permanent disability, or permanent disfigurement to such child, shall be guilty of a felony of the third degree, punishable as provided in s. 775.082, s. 775.083, or s. 775.084.

Section 782.04(4) states that third-degree murder requires proof of "the unlawful killing of a human being, when perpetrated without any design to effect death, by a person engaged in the perpetration of, or in the attempt to perpetrate, any felony. . . ."[1]

We note that the state did not charge Mr. Leet with personally depriving Joshua of medical treatment on Friday while the child was in his sole custody. Whether this was an accidental or intentional prosecutorial decision is unclear. Medically, any failure to obtain care on Friday may not have been a cause of Joshua's death. By that time, it may have been too late to save this child. Thus, the state maintains that Monday through Thursday of the last week of the child's life is the critical period in which Mr. Leet permitted child abuse by culpable negligence.

---

1   The statute further explains that certain felonies cannot be the underlying offense for third-degree felony murder. Child abuse is not one of those felonies.

III. The Jury Could Determine That Mr. Leet Owed A Duty To Protect Joshua Under Section 827.04(1).

The state argues that Mr. Leet is a "whoever" that "by culpable negligence . . . permit[ted] . . . physical . . . injury" to this child. The state suggests that the broad language of the statute creates a duty to protect a child that applies to many adults in addition to the natural parents of the child. Mr. Leet argues that he is not this child's father, did not assume the role of a father, and had no legal authority to regulate the mother's discipline. Therefore, he concludes that he could not, as a matter of law, "permit" the abuse.

* * *

In this case, there is evidence that Mr. Leet allowed the mother and child to move into his home on a permanent basis. They shared various expenses and shared the same living space. Although the mother was primarily responsible for child care and discipline, there is evidence that Mr. Leet bathed Joshua, played with him, and took him for car rides. Indeed, Ms. Collins left the child in Mr. Leet's sole care for the last day of the child's life.

We recognize that common law marriage is no longer a viable doctrine in Florida. § 741.211, Fla.Stat. (1987). If this couple had separated, Mr. Leet would not owe child support to Ms. Collins for Joshua. It is not entirely clear that Mr. Leet had created a total *in loco parentis* relationship with Joshua by November 1988. *See generally* 67A C.J.S. *Parent and Child* §§ 53–60 (1978); 59 Am.Jur.2d *Parent and Child* §§ 75–79 (1987). He may not have been able to authorize medical treatment for Joshua. We do not, however, regard these circumstances as dispositive.

Under circumstances similar to this, it has been held that a boyfriend may be a person "in a position of familial, custodial, or official authority" for purposes of sexual battery on a child. *Coleman v. State*, 485 So.2d 1342 (Fla. 1st DCA 1986). "Although appellant was neither the victim's natural father nor her stepfather, nor does the evidence disclose his status as in loco parentis to the victim at the time of the offense charged, appellant did live with the child and her mother in the same household. . . ." *Coleman*, 485 So.2d at 1345. Likewise, we conclude that the jury was entitled to determine that Mr. Leet had temporarily assumed responsibility for Joshua's well-being when he established a family-like relationship with Joshua and his mother for an extended and indefinite period.

IV. The Jury Could Determine That Mr. Leet's Conduct Constituted Culpable Negligence.

* * *

Apparently, Mr. Leet was never home when Ms. Collins abused Joshua. As explained earlier, his conduct on the Friday the child died cannot be the source of the finding of culpable negligence. Instead, the issue in this case is whether Mr. Leet followed a course of conduct between Monday and Thursday of the week of Joshua's death that he reasonably should have known was likely to cause death or great bodily injury to Joshua.

Mr. Leet was approximately thirty years old at the time of these events. He had been previously married and had three children by his first wife. Although he had not been extensively involved in the upbringing of his own children, he had lived with them when they were Joshua's age. Despite his limited education, a jury could determine that he knew the difference between normal childhood scrapes and bruises, and the kind of physical abuse involved in this case.

From the problems in May and June, Mr. Leet knew that Ms. Collins was capable of making excuses to cover her acts of child abuse. The bruises on Joshua and the excuses of Ms. Collins in November were comparable to those in the spring. This is not a case involving isolated child abuse; it concerns a return to a prior pattern of abuse. The pattern returned when Ms. Collins was under two obvious sources of stress. A jury could reasonably conclude that Mr. Leet simply closed his eyes to clear evidence of the most severe acts of child abuse.

The jury could decide that a reasonable person, living with this child and the mother, would not have accepted three suspicious explanations for physical injuries to the child in the span of a few days. It could disbelieve Mr. Leet's testimony that Nathan had caused Joshua's chest bruises and determine that even a lay person would have known that the bruises were not caused by a car door, but were consistent with physical abuse. Likewise, the jury could also determine that Mr. Leet should not have accepted Ms. Collins' explanation that Joshua caused his black eye by poking it or rubbing it too much.

The involvement of HRS is an interesting factor in this case. Arguably, Mr. Leet could assume that HRS and the circuit court would not have returned Joshua to his mother if they believed the problem would reoccur. On the other hand, Mr. Leet knew the criminal case was ongoing. He could easily have called HRS or the court on Tuesday or Wednesday to explain the evidence of child abuse that existed in his home. He did not. Admittedly, he was faced with a dilemma. If he reported Ms. Collins, he knew there could be new criminal charges and, perhaps, the woman he loved would be sent back to jail. If he did not report the problem, Joshua might be severely injured. He chose to leave

Joshua at risk. The law does not protect that choice merely because he did not wish to jeopardize Ms. Collins.

In *Jakubczak v. State*, 425 So.2d 187 (Fla. 3d DCA 1983), a mother was convicted of child abuse because she left her child with her husband who was mentally ill. The child had previously suffered unexplained injuries while in his care. If a mother can be culpably negligent for leaving a child with its father, Mr. Leet can be equally negligent for taking no action to protect the child from its mother in his household. Section 827.04 applies to acts of omission as well as acts of commission. *See generally State v. Harris*, 537 So.2d 1128 (Fla. 2d DCA 1989); *Nicholson v. State*, 579 So.2d 816 (Fla. 1st DCA 1991).

We share the concern of the special concurrence that child abuse is a very emotional topic and that juries may be tempted to shift a defendant's standard of care from culpable negligence to mere negligence, or to lower the state's burden of proof. The state must prove a crime beyond a reasonable doubt, not merely an immoral or unethical omission by a preponderance of the evidence. Nevertheless, when the state has met its prima facia burden, the issues must be submitted to a jury. *State v. Law*, 559 So.2d 187 (Fla.1989). In this case, we conclude that the state fulfilled its burden and the decision of guilt was properly left to the jury to determine. Annotation, *Validity and Construction of Penal Statute Prohibiting Child Abuse*, 1 A.L.R. 4th 1 (1980).

Once the jury determined that Mr. Leet was guilty of child abuse, the evidence was sufficient to permit them to further conclude that his actions constituted third-degree felony murder. § 782.04(4), Fla.Stat. (1987). We find Mr. Leet's remaining points on appeal without merit.

PATTERSON, Judge, concurring specially.

I concur with reservations as to whether Mr. Leet can be guilty of the offense as charged. Section 827.04(1), Florida Statutes (Supp.1988), proscribes both acts of commission and acts of omission. Mr. Leet is charged with an act of omission, i.e., failing to prevent Collins from abusing her child in his absence. Count II of the information, which alleges child abuse, reads in pertinent part:

> RAYMOND E. LEET . . . between the 1st day of April and the 25th day of November . . . [1988] . . . did then and there knowingly or by culpable negligence, permit physical injury to a child, Joshua Collins, and in so doing caused great bodily harm, permanent disability, or permanent disfigurement to said child; . . . .

As is acknowledged by the majority, Mr. Leet was not charged as a principal in the aggravated child abuse committed by the child's mother or for any act of commission of child abuse on Friday, November 25, 1988, the day of Joshua's death—a day during which Joshua was in Mr. Leet's sole custody.

Section 827.04(1) describes the class of persons to which it applies as "whoever," an all encompassing term of no limitation. This term, or its equivalent, "any person," is used throughout the criminal statutes and is appropriate in regard to all acts of commission. It is not appropriate, however, for criminal acts of omission which depend on the violation of a duty owed between parties by reason of a relationship existing between them. Mr. Leet was not married to Joshua's mother, was not his natural father or other blood relative, and his uncontroverted testimony refuted an *in loco parentis* relationship with Joshua. He had no legal standing in regard to Joshua whatsoever. [4]

Mr. Leet is charged with having permitted the abuse to occur. "To permit" implies the legal ability "to prevent." Mr. Leet holds no such legal authority in his own right which he could exercise over Joshua or the child's mother. His only recourse would be to *attempt* to prevent further abuse by reporting the child's recurring injuries to the police, to HRS, or to some other authority. In my view, Mr. Leet could not, *by himself,* legally prevent the abuse and, therefore, in like manner, could not have permitted it to occur.

I concur rather than dissent because of section 415.504, Florida Statutes (Supp.1988). [5] This section requires "any person" who knows or suspects of child

---

4   There is no Florida case thus far which has extended the act of omission provision of section 827.04(1) to a live-in boyfriend or girlfriend. The majority in this regard cites to *Coleman v. State*, 485 So.2d 1342 (Fla. 1st DCA 1986). *Coleman*, however, is a sexual abuse case and is to be distinguished from child abuse arising from the violation of a separate statute. *See D.A.O. v. Dept. of Health & Rehab. Serv.*, 561 So.2d 380 (Fla. 1st DCA 1990). Other jurisdictions confronted with this question have come to varying conclusions. *See Annotation, Validity and Construction of Penal Statute Prohibiting Child Abuse*, 1 A.L.R. 4th 38 (1980).

5   415.504 Mandatory reports of child abuse or neglect; mandatory reports of death; central abuse registry and tracking system.—

(1) Any person, including, but not limited to, any:

(a) Physician, osteopath, medical examiner, chiropractor, nurse, or hospital personnel engaged in the admission, examination, care, or treatment of persons;

(b) Health or mental health professional other than one listed in paragraph (a);

(c) Practitioner who relies solely on spiritual means for healing;

(d) School teacher or other school official or personnel;

(e) Social worker, day care center worker, or other professional child care, foster care, residential, or institutional worker; or

(f) Law enforcement officer, who knows, or has reasonable cause to suspect, that a child is an abused or neglected child shall report such knowledge or suspicion to the department in the manner prescribed in subsection (2).

The violation of this section constitutes an act of omission and in such regard the use of the term "any person" suffers from the same type of infirmities which I have noted in regard to the use of the term "whoever" in section 827.04(1). It has been construed to be subject to some limitations, but not in the context of the facts of this case. *See State v. Groff*, 409 So.2d 44 (Fla. 2d DCA 1981).

abuse to report it to HRS. Mr. Leet did not do this, and his failure to report constitutes a second-degree misdemeanor under section 415.513, Florida Statutes (Supp.1988). If the violation of this statutory duty is construed to be "permitting" the abuse to continue and if such omission rises to the level of culpable negligence, then an affirmance of Mr. Leet's conviction is proper. If not, he should be discharged. * * *

Notes and Questions

1. This case introduces you to an issue alluded to in the introduction of this section. The prosecution chose not to contend that Raymond Earl Leet failed to obtain medical treatment from Joshua Collins on the Friday Joshua died. The prosecution argued only that Leet was liable only for his failure to obtain treatment only on those days preceding the death when he did not actually have sole custody of Joshua. Why did the prosecution not include Leet's omission on that Friday?

2. What exactly did the majority expect Mr. Leet to do? Is the concurrence correct that Mr. Leet's only omission was failing to report the acts of child abuse by his girlfriend? If that is his failing, does he not have a causation defense based on the Joshua's earlier experience with the Florida Department of Health and Rehabilitative Services?

3. What facts suggest that Raymond Earl Leets was not the paradigm example of a live-in boyfriend who ought to be convicted for his girlfriend's abuse of her child? What facts would you develop for the defense in negotiating this case with the prosecutor, or for arguing the case to the jury? How would these facts be used differently in a negotiation than in an argument to the jury?

4. The existence of a duty in this case is premised upon the Court's view of the relationship between the parties. Raymond Earl Leet does not stand in the shoes of the parent, he is not *in loco parentis*, as the Court observed, but the Court clearly sees something akin to a parent-like relationship between Leet and Joshua Collins. Parents are not the only category of persons who owe duties to others. Spouses, innkeepers, landowners, doctors, lifeguards, and a host of others owe duties to protect others based on either their inherent relationship with others, or as a result of contractual duties voluntarily undertaken. Legislatures also impose duties on categories of persons to render aid, such as those involved in automobile accidents, a specific example of a doctrine

frequently recognized by courts to render aid to those an individual harms. The *Leet* case demonstrates that courts are willing to expand on the categories recognized by public law (statutes) and private law (contracts) to recognize that duties are owed by those who almost fit into a category of persons owing a duty to others. Consider how the logic of the *Leet* case might be extended to other persons almost fitting into other traditional categories of persons owing duties to others. *See* LaFave, Criminal Law § 6.2(a).

---

2. Mental State

Depending on the mental state with which the defendant killed, he is either guilty of murder or manslaughter, though some states use different names for crimes fitting into this latter category—reckless homicide or criminally negligent homicide are offenses in some jurisdictions that would map onto a form of manslaughter in other jurisdictions. As George Constanza's character in *Seinfeld* insightfully noted, manslaughter should sound worse to us than murder, but it is not. As Costanza observed, the *lesser* form of homicide is after all, the slaughter of a man. While many popular conceptions about the law are incorrect, it is certainly true that in every state murder is the most serious form of unlawful killing.

Most states divide murder into degrees depending on the defendant's state of mind. States provide a number of definitions of first-degree murder, but in every jurisdiction with the distinction between first- and second-degree murder (or, in three states, first, second, and third degree murder), a killing resulting from a contemplated desire to kill constitutes the most egregious form of murder. In some states, there are additional ways the prosecution can demonstrate that this is first-degree murder. Identifying the line that separates degrees of murder is seldom easy as you will discover. Of course many states do not differentiate degrees of murder.

Manslaughter most commonly has two forms—voluntary and involuntary. Voluntary manslaughter occurs when someone intends to takes a life, but was provoked by something that would provoke a person of reasonable sensibility. For years, the paradigm example of voluntary manslaughter involved a killing immediately following discovery of marital infidelity. More recent authorities have not permitted this theory of voluntary manslaughter, finding the justification to be based on an antiquated conception of gender relations. A stabbing during a fistfight may be the new paradigm case of voluntary manslaughter.

Involuntary manslaughter involves a killing in which a death follows from an unreasonable risk taken by the defendant. Some jurisdictions divide this form of homicide into multiple degrees, depending on whether the defendant was actually aware of the risk. Another line drawing problem arises as we try to distinguish between forms of murder less than first-degree and involuntary manslaughter.

Obviously, we have no way to reliably read human minds. So these states of mind that determine where a defendant falls on the homicide spectrum often have to be evaluated using circumstantial evidence. We look at the circumstances surrounding the defendant's act to determine whether he intended the death, was very reckless in the risk he took with another's life, or was simply reckless. Often the defendant's statements will provide evidence of his state of mind—when the defendant says he wanted to kill his victim. This is the only way direct evidence can be offered on a defendant's intent. Far more often than you would think, defendants waive their protections against self-incrimination provided by the case of *Miranda v. Arizona* and provide statements giving the prosecution evidence on their states of mind.

The next few sections offer the various definitions of the degrees of homicide and show the type of proof required to satisfy the various definitions.

a. Degrees of Murder

Many states divide murder into two types, first- and second-degree. A fair number of states make no distinction between forms of murder. Three states have three classes murder; first, second and third degree. Of course the real question is the definition states provide for each of these degrees and what range of penalties attach to each degree.

i. Representative Examples of Murder Statutes with Only One Degree of Culpability

Georgia Code Annotated § 16-5-1:

(a) A person commits the offense of murder when he unlawfully and with malice aforethought, either express or implied, causes the death of another human being

(b) Express malice is that deliberate intention unlawfully to take the life of another human being which is manifested by external circumstances capable of proof. Malice shall be implied where no considerable provocation appears and where all the circumstances of the killing show an abandoned and malignant heart.

(c) A person also commits the offense of murder when, in the commission of a felony, he causes the death of another human being irrespective of malice.

(d) A person convicted of the offense of murder shall be punished by death, by imprisonment for life without parole, or by imprisonment for life.

17 Maine Revised Statute Annotated § 201

A person is guilty of murder if the person:

A. Intentionally or knowingly causes the death of another human being;

B. Engages in conduct that manifests a depraved indifference to the value of human life and that in fact causes the death of another human being; or

C. Intentionally or knowingly causes another human being to commit suicide by the use of force, duress or deception.

ii. Representative Examples of Murder Statutes with Two Degrees of Culpability

Alaska Statute § 11.41.100-110

A person commits the crime of murder in the first degree if

(1) with intent to cause the death of another person, the person

    (A) causes the death of any person; or

    (B) compels or induces any person to commit suicide through duress or deception;

(2) the person knowingly engages in conduct directed toward a child under the age of 16 and the person with criminal negligence inflicts serious physical injury on the child by at least two separate acts, and one of the acts results in the death of the child;

(3) acting alone or with one or more persons, the person commits or attempts to commit a sexual offense against or kidnapping of a child under 16 years of age and, in the course of or in furtherance of the offense or in immediate flight from that offense, any person causes the death of the child; in this paragraph, "sexual offense" means an offense defined in AS 11.41.410-- 11.41.470;

(4) acting alone or with one or more persons, the person commits or attempts to commit criminal mischief in the first degree under AS

11.46.475 and, in the course of or in furtherance of the offense or in immediate flight from that offense, any person causes the death of a person other than one of the participants; or

(5) acting alone or with one or more persons, the person commits terroristic threatening in the first degree under AS 11.56.807 and, in the course of or in furtherance of the offense or in immediate flight from that offense, any person causes the death of a person other than one of the participants.

A person commits the crime of murder in the second degree if

(1) with intent to cause serious physical injury to another person or knowing that the conduct is substantially certain to cause death or serious physical injury to another person, the person causes the death of any person;

(2) the person knowingly engages in conduct that results in the death of another person under circumstances manifesting an extreme indifference to the value of human life;

(3) under circumstances not amounting to murder in the first degree under AS 11.41.100(a)(3), while acting either alone or with one or more persons, the person commits or attempts to commit arson in the first degree, kidnapping, sexual assault in the first degree, sexual assault in the second degree, sexual abuse of a minor in the first degree, sexual abuse of a minor in the second degree, burglary in the first degree, escape in the first or second degree, robbery in any degree, or misconduct involving a controlled substance under AS 11.71.010(a), 11.71.020(a), 11.71.030(a)(1) or (2), or 11.71.040(a)(1) or (2) and, in the course of or in furtherance of that crime or in immediate flight from that crime, any person causes the death of a person other than one of the participants;

(4) acting with a criminal street gang, the person commits or attempts to commit a crime that is a felony and, in the course of or in furtherance of that crime or in immediate flight from that crime, any person causes the death of a person other than one of the participants; or

(5) the person with criminal negligence causes the death of a child under the age of 16, and the person has been previously convicted of a crime involving a child under the age of 16 that was

(A) a felony violation of AS 11.41;

(B) in violation of a law or ordinance in another jurisdiction with elements similar to a felony under AS 11.41; or

(C) an attempt, a solicitation, or a conspiracy to commit a crime listed in (A) or (B) of this paragraph.

California Penal Code §§ 187, 189

Murder is the unlawful killing of a human being, or a fetus, with malice aforethought.

All murder which is perpetrated by means of a destructive device or explosive, a weapon of mass destruction, knowing use of ammunition designed primarily to penetrate metal or armor, poison, lying in wait, torture, or by any other kind of willful, deliberate, and premeditated killing, or which is committed in the perpetration of, or attempt to perpetrate, arson, rape, carjacking, robbery, burglary, mayhem, kidnapping, train wrecking, or any act punishable under Section 206, 286, 288, 288a, or 289, or any murder which is perpetrated by means of discharging a firearm from a motor vehicle, intentionally at another person outside of the vehicle with the intent to inflict death, is murder of the first degree. All other kinds of murders are of the second degree.

Louisiana Revised Statutes 14:30-30.1

First degree murder is the killing of a human being:

(1) When the offender has specific intent to kill or to inflict great bodily harm and is engaged in the perpetration or attempted perpetration of aggravated kidnapping, second degree kidnapping, aggravated escape, aggravated arson, aggravated rape, forcible rape, aggravated burglary, armed robbery, assault by drive-by shooting, first degree robbery, second degree robbery, simple robbery, terrorism, cruelty to juveniles, or second degree cruelty to juveniles.

(2) When the offender has a specific intent to kill or to inflict great bodily harm upon a fireman, peace officer, or civilian employee of the Louisiana State Police Crime Laboratory or any other forensic laboratory engaged in the performance of his lawful duties, or when the spe-

cific intent to kill or to inflict great bodily harm is directly related to the victim's status as a fireman, peace officer, or civilian employee.

(3) When the offender has a specific intent to kill or to inflict great bodily harm upon more than one person.

(4) When the offender has specific intent to kill or inflict great bodily harm and has offered, has been offered, has given, or has received anything of value for the killing.

(5) When the offender has the specific intent to kill or to inflict great bodily harm upon a victim who is under the age of twelve or sixty-five years of age or older.

(6) When the offender has the specific intent to kill or to inflict great bodily harm while engaged in the distribution, exchange, sale, or purchase, or any attempt thereof, of a controlled dangerous substance listed in Schedules I, II, III, IV, or V of the Uniform Controlled Dangerous Substances Law.

(7) When the offender has specific intent to kill or to inflict great bodily harm and is engaged in the activities prohibited by R.S. 14:107.1(C)(1).

(8) When the offender has specific intent to kill or to inflict great bodily harm and there has been issued by a judge or magistrate any lawful order prohibiting contact between the offender and the victim in response to threats of physical violence or harm which was served on the offender and is in effect at the time of the homicide.

(9) When the offender has specific intent to kill or to inflict great bodily harm upon a victim who was a witness to a crime or was a member of the immediate family of a witness to a crime committed on a prior occasion and:

(a) The killing was committed for the purpose of preventing or influencing the victim's testimony in any criminal action or proceeding whether or not such action or proceeding had been commenced; or

(b) The killing was committed for the purpose of exacting retribution for the victim's prior testimony.

(10) When the offender has a specific intent to kill or to inflict great bodily harm upon a taxicab driver who is in the course and scope of his employment. For purposes of this Paragraph, "taxicab" means a motor vehicle for hire, carrying six passengers or less, including the driver thereof, that is subject to call from a garage, office, taxi stand, or otherwise.

(11) When the offender has a specific intent to kill or inflict great bodily harm and the offender has previously acted with a specific intent to kill or inflict great bodily harm that resulted in the killing of one or more persons.

Second degree murder is the killing of a human being:

(1) When the offender has a specific intent to kill or to inflict great bodily harm; or

(2) When the offender is engaged in the perpetration or attempted perpetration of aggravated rape, forcible rape, aggravated arson, aggravated burglary, aggravated kidnapping, second degree kidnapping, aggravated escape, assault by drive-by shooting, armed robbery, first degree robbery, second degree robbery, simple robbery, cruelty to juveniles, second degree cruelty to juveniles, or terrorism, even though he has no intent to kill or to inflict great bodily harm.

(3) When the offender unlawfully distributes or dispenses a controlled dangerous substance listed in Schedules I through V of the Uniform Controlled Dangerous Substances Law, or any combination thereof, which is the direct cause of the death of the recipient who ingested or consumed the controlled dangerous substance.

(4) When the offender unlawfully distributes or dispenses a controlled dangerous substance listed in Schedules I through V of the Uniform Controlled Dangerous Substances Law, or any combination thereof, to another who subsequently distributes or dispenses such controlled dangerous substance which is the direct cause of the death of the person who ingested or consumed the controlled dangerous substance.

Tennessee Code Annotated § 39-13-202, 210

First degree murder is:

(1) A premeditated and intentional killing of another;

(2) A killing of another committed in the perpetration of or attempt to perpetrate any first degree murder, act of terrorism, arson, rape, robbery, burglary, theft, kidnapping, aggravated child abuse, aggravated child neglect, rape of a child, aggravated rape of a child or aircraft piracy; or

(3) A killing of another committed as the result of the unlawful throwing, placing or discharging of a destructive device or bomb.

No culpable mental state is required for conviction under subdivision (a)(2) or (a)(3), except the intent to commit the enumerated offenses or acts in those subdivisions.

Second degree murder is:

(1) A knowing killing of another; or

(2) A killing of another that results from the unlawful distribution of any Schedule I or Schedule II drug, when the drug is the proximate cause of the death of the user.

In a prosecution for a violation of this section, if the defendant knowingly engages in multiple incidents of domestic abuse, assault or the infliction of bodily injury against a single victim, the trier of fact may infer that the defendant was aware that the cumulative effect of the conduct was reasonably certain to result in the death of the victim, regardless of whether any single incident would have resulted in the death.

West Virginia Code § 61-2-1

Murder by poison, lying in wait, imprisonment, starving, or by any willful, deliberate and premeditated killing, or in the commission of, or attempt to commit, arson, kidnapping, sexual assault, robbery, burglary, breaking and entering, escape from lawful custody, or a felony offense of manufacturing or delivering a controlled substance as defined in article four, chapter sixty-a of this code, is murder of the first degree. All other murder is murder of the second degree.

iii. Representative Examples of Statute with Three Degrees of Culpability

Minnesota Statutes Annotated § 609.185, 609.19, 609.195

Murder in the First Degree:

(a) Whoever does any of the following is guilty of murder in the first degree and shall be sentenced to imprisonment for life:

(1) causes the death of a human being with premeditation and with intent to effect the death of the person or of another;

(2) causes the death of a human being while committing or attempting to commit criminal sexual conduct in the first or second degree with force or violence, either upon or affecting the person or another;

(3) causes the death of a human being with intent to effect the death of the person or another, while committing or attempting to commit burglary, aggravated robbery, kidnapping, arson in the first or second degree, a drive-by shooting, tampering with a witness in the first degree, escape from custody, or any felony violation of chapter 152 involving the unlawful sale of a controlled substance;

(4) causes the death of a peace officer or a guard employed at a Minnesota state or local correctional facility, with intent to effect the death of that person or another, while the peace officer or guard is engaged in the performance of official duties;

(5) causes the death of a minor while committing child abuse, when the perpetrator has engaged in a past pattern of child abuse upon a child and the death occurs under circumstances manifesting an extreme indifference to human life;

(6) causes the death of a human being while committing domestic abuse, when the perpetrator has engaged in a past pattern of domestic abuse upon the victim or upon another family or household member and the death occurs under circumstances manifesting an extreme indifference to human life; or

(7) causes the death of a human being while committing, conspiring to commit, or attempting to commit a felony crime to further terrorism and the death occurs under circumstances manifesting an extreme indifference to human life.

Murder in the Second Degree:

Subdivision 1. Intentional murder; drive-by shootings. Whoever does either of the following is guilty of murder in the second degree and may be sentenced to imprisonment for not more than 40 years:

(1) causes the death of a human being with intent to effect the death of that person or another, but without premeditation; or

(2) causes the death of a human being while committing or attempting to commit a drive-by shooting in violation of section 609.66, subdivision 1e, under circumstances other than those described in section 609.185, clause (3).

Subd. 2. Unintentional murders. Whoever does either of the following is guilty of unintentional murder in the second degree and may be sentenced to imprisonment for not more than 40 years:

(1) causes the death of a human being, without intent to effect the death of any person, while committing or attempting to commit a felony offense other than criminal sexual conduct in the first or second degree with force or violence or a drive-by shooting; or

(2) causes the death of a human being without intent to effect the death of any person, while intentionally inflicting or attempting to inflict bodily harm upon the victim, when the perpetrator is restrained under an order for protection and the victim is a person designated to receive protection under the order. As used in this clause, "order for protection" includes an order for protection issued under chapter 518B; a harassment restraining order issued under section 609.748; a court order setting conditions of pretrial release or conditions of a criminal sentence or juvenile court disposition; a restraining order issued in a marriage dissolution action; and any order issued by a court of another state or of the United States that is similar to any of these orders.

Murder in the Third Degree:

(a) Whoever, without intent to effect the death of any person, causes the death of another by perpetrating an act eminently dangerous to others and evincing a depraved mind, without regard for human life, is guilty of murder in the third degree and may be sentenced to imprisonment for not more than 25 years.

(b) Whoever, without intent to cause death, proximately causes the death of a human being by, directly or indirectly, unlawfully selling, giving away, bartering, delivering, exchanging, distributing, or administering a controlled substance classified in Schedule I or II, is guilty of murder in the third degree and may be sentenced to imprisonment for not more than 25 years or to payment of a fine of not more than $40,000, or both.

As you can tell from this list, legislatures have come up with a variety of factors to distinguish one form of homicide from another. To generalize from the statutes you just read, they use roughly three criteria to define more serious types of killing:

1) a thought-out desire that the victim die;

2) commission of a dangerous crime in addition to any risk the defendant took with the victim's life

3) taking a unreasonable risk with the life of a person in a protected class, such as children, law enforcement officers, fireman, or, in New Hampshire, a candidate for President of the United States.

These degrees of murder matter. In many jurisdictions dividing the most serious form of homicide (murder) into multiple degrees, first-degree murder is punished with a mandatory minimum life sentence, and in many of these jurisdictions there is no parole for that offense. Typically, though certainly there are exceptions, jurisdictions recognizing only one category of murder give judges considerable discretion to determine the sentence. The prosecutor's charging decision in a homicide case in Pennsylvania, where first-degree murder carries a mandatory sentence of life without parole, is therefore a more significant act than it is in Alaska, where judges have the discretion to give first-degree murderers a sentence between 20 and 99 years. Outside the context of capital cases, no jurisdiction informs a jury what type of sentence each degree of homicide will carry. A jury that finds a defendant guilty of first-degree murder is ensuring that he will spend his natural life in prison in Pennsylvania. No amount of mitigating evidence in the world can spare the defendant from a life sentence in such jurisdictions once a jury has determined he satisfied one of the statutory criteria defining first-degree murder. This would not be such a terrible state of affairs if premeditated murderers—or those who killed police officers—were categorically worse than killers who had not premeditated or killed accountants. Real cases, however, present reasons for leniency that judges in these jurisdiction are unable to account for. We will consider later in this chapter the story of a man found guilty of first-degree murder in North Carolina who shot his father, who lay suffering in a hospital bed of a painful terminal illness that likely would have killed him within a day.

The amount of discretion given to the sentencing judge upon conviction is thus undeniably significant for defendants who go to trial in each jurisdiction, but it is far more significant for defendants considering plea offers. Defendants face a certain life sentence in Pennsylvania if jurors find they committed a premeditated killing. Prosecutors are able to threaten life sentences in jurisdictions like Pennsylvania in a way that there are not able to in Alaska. If a life sentence does not automatically follow from a first-degree murder conviction, then a defendant going to trial has a lesser risk of a life sentence than he does in jurisdictions in which judges have no discretion to determine how first-degree murderers should be sentenced. This is particularly true if the circumstances of the offense, or the defendant's life history, suggest that a life sentence is inappropriate. Other things being equal, a plea offer in a jurisdiction giving the sentencing judge discretion in sentencing first-degree murderers would have to be more generous than a plea offer in a jurisdiction providing for an automatic life sentence. With 95% of all criminal cases being resolved through guilty pleas, the impact substantive criminal law has on plea bargaining is far more important than the impact it has on trials or appeals.

As you consider homicide cases, indeed as you consider all the crimes in this book, consider what factors about the defendant and his crime are given to the jury or the judge to decide. Or to pose the issue in a more nuanced fashion, consider to what extent factors about the defendant and his crimes can be considered by juries and judges. Those factors not given to juries and judges are left alone in the hands of prosecutors who decide what to charge. Homicide statutes give judges varying ranges of discretion as we've considered. Homicide statutes also provide juries with varying ranges of discretion. Some jurisdictions, for instance, conclude that premeditation can be formed in an instant, leaving jurors little wiggle room to find anything but the highest form of murder if there is any evidence of intent to kill.

In criminal law, as in the study of all aspects of law, you will be considering a legal term in relation to its nearest cousin. When considering whether a homicide is first-degree murder, you will most often be asking whether it is first- or second-degree murder. Second-degree murder is defined in a wide variety of ways as you saw in the statutes. Most states recognize that taking an unreasonable and extraordinarily high degree of risk of killing, or an intent to inflict serious bodily injury, amounts to this form of homicide, if death results. Other definitions of second-degree murder involve categories that are similar to some definitions of first-degree murder. Many states define second-degree murder as a death occurring during certain types of crimes, such as drug distribution—or causing the death of a person in a protected category. The interpretive tools you learn in considering first-degree murder will obviously be useful in evaluating the very similar provisions in second-degree murder provisions.

PRACTICE EXERCISE

Alfonse and Beatrice work at "The Sell Mart," where they meander the store aisles as salespersons, each with the title of "Customer Service Representative." They are 18 years old. Bored and hoping to avoid talking to customers, they decide to "clean" the warehouse, a large section of the building accessible only to employees.

They each grab brooms and begin sweeping, but mostly chatting about the lack of pay and the lousy hours each is required to work. "Isn't the scheduler, Clarence, such a jerk?" says Beatrice, "He scheduled me for 30 hours last week when my maximum hours are supposed to be 20."

Alfonse responds, "Yeah, I wish he'd have our job, and really know how ridiculous it is to have to talk to customers. I don't know who I dislike more, customers or Clarence."

Clarence's office is located in the warehouse, in a walled portion with a window looking at the time-punch clock and onto the warehouse floor. Seeing Alfonse and Beatrice leaning on their brooms and chatting, Clarence marches out of the office and yells at them: "You will both be reported to management if you don't get out to that sales floor and start providing quality customer service!" Beatrice smirks, flips him off, and yells back, "I'm pacing myself, jerk! I have to work this stupid shift because of you, so I'm taking a minute to sweep back here!"

Alfonse laughs at Beatrice's gesture, and joins in: "Tick-tock Clarence, why don't you get back to your office and track your own time? When's the last time you did anything but make other's miserable?" Clarence, in a furious rage, walks forward and yells in Alfonse's face: "Your time is up at Sell Mart!" He then turns to Beatrice and slaps her in the face, "How's that for a gesture?"

Clarence then stomps away toward the manager's office, adjacent to his own office, finds the door locked, swears to himself, kicks the door in anger, and marches into his own office.

Alfonse and Beatrice, equally "steamed," quickly comport and decide to teach Clarence a lesson.

Alfonse whispers to Beatrice while Clarence marches into his office: "Let's get him in the cardboard bailer and lock him there for a shift; he won't fall in to the compactor because it has such a long shoot, but it will scare him to death." Beatrice's lips curl in devious glee. "I'll flush him out of his office and get him to unlock the compactor. Then, when I open the door, shove him in and lock it." Alfonse thinks to himself, "I wouldn't mind him getting smashed, the lazy a**hole."

The plan succeeds: Clarence is flushed from his office after five minutes of apologies from Beatrice, the compactor is unlocked, Clarence is shoved in by Alfonse, and the door is locked by Beatrice. "Go to hell!" screams Beatrice. "We'll get him out next break," says Alfonse, as they walk away.

Before the next break, Drexel punches the button initiating the compactor because the weight gauge for the factor shoot reads "heavy," which usually means the shoot is full of cardboard and ready to be compacted. Initiating the compactor without physically checking the shoot is a violation of company policy and state law. Clarence, exhausted and disoriented in the darkness, is jarred from the shoot into the compactor basin, where he is killed.

You are a Minnesota prosecutor charged with bringing Alfonse, Beatrice, and Drexel to justice. Draft an indictment using the Minnesota statute above as a basis for your charges. List the facts which support your charge. Then prepare a press release explaining your decision.

---

b. Mental States Often Defining the Most Serious Form of Murder

i. Contemplated Killings

Virtually all states that identify degrees of murder conclude that a defendant's conscious decision to kill makes his killing particularly reprehensible. Some statutes define methods of killing that themselves involve a deliberative process. Examples include poisoning, lying in wait, dueling, and committing or suborning perjury that causes the execution of an innocent person. Far more common are statutes that attempt to describe a contemplative process. Words like intent, purpose, premeditation, and deliberation are used to explain this mental state. At best, one can describe American courts as mercurial in their application of the deliberation requirement. At worst, this way of defining first-degree murder requires the most stringent punishment on the basis of a virtually unknowable momentary thought process, the moral culpability of which is indistinguishable from the thought process yielding a lesser punishment. Some jurisdictions require that the jury find that there was an "exercise of reflection and judgment" in order to find that deliberation occurred. Other jurisdictions conclude that the intent to kill can be formed in an instant.

Of course the difficulty of defining a contemplated killing lies in distinguishing it from a killing that is not contemplated. Thoroughly planned killings—serial killings, for instance—are obviously intentional, deliberate, and premeditated killings. The difficulty in defining categories of killing (or anything) is not in identifying a paradigm example of something fitting within the category, but in distinguishing one category from another. What is the line separating a premeditated killing from one in which the killer has decided to take life but his action is not premeditated? The cases illustrate the difficulty of distinguishing these contemplated killings from a slightly less serious category of killing.

(a) Can the Intent to Kill be Formed in an Instant?

State v. Guthrie

Supreme Court of West Virginia
461 S.E.2d 163 (1995)

CLECKLEY, Justice:

The defendant, Dale Edward Guthrie, appeals the January, 1994, jury verdict of the Circuit Court of Kanawha County finding him guilty of first degree murder. In May of 1994, the defendant was sentenced to serve a life sentence with a recommendation of mercy. . .

I.

FACTS AND PROCEDURAL BACKGROUND

It is undisputed that on the evening of February 12, 1993, the defendant removed a knife from his pocket and stabbed his co-worker, Steven Todd Farley, in the neck and killed him. The two men worked together as dishwashers at Danny's Rib House in Nitro and got along well together before this incident. On the night of the killing, the victim, his brother, Tracy Farley, and James Gibson were joking around while working in the kitchen of the restaurant. The victim was poking fun at the defendant who appeared to be in a bad mood. He told the defendant to "lighten up" and snapped him with a dishtowel several times. Apparently, the victim had no idea he was upsetting the defendant very much. The dishtowel flipped the defendant on the nose and he became enraged.

The defendant removed his gloves and started toward the victim. Mr. Farley, still teasing, said: "Ooo, he's taking his gloves off." The defendant then pulled a knife from his pocket and stabbed the victim in the neck. He also stabbed Mr. Farley in the arm as he fell to the floor. Mr. Farley looked up and cried: "Man, I was just kidding around." The defendant responded: "Well, man, you should have never hit me in my face." The police arrived at the restaurant and arrested the defendant. He was given his *Miranda* rights. The defendant made a statement at the police station and confessed to the killing.[1] The police officers described him as calm and willing to cooperate.

It is also undisputed that the defendant suffers from a host of psychiatric problems. He experiences up to two panic attacks daily and had received treatment for them at the Veterans Administration Hospital in Huntington for more than a year preceding the killing. He suffers from chronic depression (dysthymic disorder), an obsession with his nose (body dysmorphic disorder), and border-line personality disorder. The defendant's father shed some light on his nose fixation. He stated that dozens of times a day the defendant stared in the mirror and turned his head back and forth to look at his nose. His father estimated that 50 percent of the time he observed his son he was looking at his nose. The defendant repeatedly asked for assurances that his nose was not too big. This

---

1   The confession, which was read to the jury, stated, in part:

"I arrived at work, at 4:00 o'clock, and was looking forward to another evening of work, I was looking forward to it, because I do enjoy working at Danny's Rib House. Upon my arrival at work I immediately observed the verbal and physical aggression of Mr. Farley. During the evening of work I heard him calling certain employee's 'Boy' and during the evening he referred to me as 'Boy' many times, I did and said nothing, continuing my work, letting it pass. He was really loud, and obnoxious, as I'm sure many employee's noticed. As the evening was coming to a close Mr. Farley walked very close by me and said 'that I had an "attitude problem."' It was verbal, I let it pass, continuing my work. After bringing some dishes to the cook, I walked back to the dishwasher to begin drying off some dishes, Mr. Farley approached me and made a sarcastic comment about me being a quiet person, he walked ever closer, to me until he was in my face, as I was trying to carry out my responsibilities. After all these things were said, and even though he was exhibiting physical aggression by coming up to my face, and putting forth what I interpreted to be a challenge, again I did nothing, continuing to carry out my responsibilities. Standing a few inches from my face he took his wet dishrag and hit me once, on the forearm, I did nothing continuing my work. Standing in the same area, he hit me again on the forearm, obviously wanting a confrontation, I gave him none, continuing my work. Standing in the same place he hit me, hard, two times in the face, it really hurt, it was soaking wet, and it stung, as he brought it to bear upon my face, at that moment I thought he was going to go further and hit me, so I reached in my right pants pocket, and retrieved my lock blade knife, that I use for skinning rabbits and squirrells [*sic*] during hunting season. I swung at Mr. Farley with my right hand in which was my knife, he backed up, so I didn't swing twice, he slowly sunk to [the] floor, I ran to the front of the restaurant and yelled out, call the ambulance. All I came to work for, was to work, and carry out my obligations, having ill will toward no one, and I still have none, but I feel I had the right to respond, finally, to this act of aggression that was perpetrated against me, I do not exhibit aggressive, violent behavior but I felt I had no alternative, or recourse."

obsession began when he was approximately seventeen years old. The defendant was twenty-nine years old at the time of trial.

The defendant testified he suffered a panic attack immediately preceding the stabbing. He described the attack as "intense"; he felt a lot of pressure and his heart beat rapidly. In contrast to the boisterous atmosphere in the kitchen that evening, the defendant was quiet and kept to himself. He stated that Mr. Farley kept irritating him that night. The defendant could not understand why Mr. Farley was picking on him because he had never done that before. Even at trial, the defendant did not comprehend his utter overreaction to the situation. In hindsight, the defendant believed the better decision would have been to punch out on his time card and quit over the incident. However, all the witnesses related that the defendant was in no way attacked, as he perceived it, but that Mr. Farley was playing around. The defendant could not bring himself to tell the other workers to leave him alone or inform them about his panic attacks.

In contrast to his written statement, the defendant testified he was unable to recall stabbing the victim. After he was struck in the nose, he stated that he "lost it" and, when he came to himself, he was holding the knife in his hand and Mr. Farley was sinking to the floor.

A psychiatrist, Dr. Sidney Lerfald, testified on behalf of the defendant. He diagnosed the various disorders discussed above. Dr. Lerfald felt the defendant's diagnoses "may have affected his perception somewhat." Nevertheless, it was his opinion the defendant was sane at the time of the offense because he was able to distinguish between right and wrong and could have conformed his actions accordingly.

* * *

II.

DISCUSSION

In his appeal, the defendant raises several assignments of error: (1) whether the evidence was sufficient to support the verdict; (2) whether the trial court erred in giving instructions covering first degree murder. . .

A.

Sufficiency of the Evidence

First, the defendant strives to persuade us that the record in this case does not support the verdict of guilty of first degree murder beyond a reasonable doubt. Because this exhortation challenges the sufficiency of evidence to support a jury's verdict, our authority to review is limited.

* * *

In summary, a criminal defendant challenging the sufficiency of the evidence to support a conviction takes on a heavy burden. An appellate court must review all the evidence, whether direct or circumstantial, in the light most favorable to the prosecution and must credit all inferences and credibility assessments that the jury might have drawn in favor of the prosecution.

* * *

We begin by emphasizing that our review is conducted from a cold appellate transcript and record. For that reason, we must assume that the jury credited all witnesses whose testimony supports the verdict. The essential facts of this case-those that the jury was unquestionably entitled to find-are rather simple: The defendant became irritated with the "horseplay" of the victim; when the victim in jest hit the defendant with a wet dishtowel on his nose, the defendant became angry and drew a four-inch-long lock blade knife from his pocket and stabbed the victim fatally in the neck. After the defendant was confronted with his deed, he made a statement that could be interpreted to mean he was not remorseful but, to the contrary, was unconcerned about the welfare of the victim.[10] In addition to the jury hearing testimony from eyewitnesses to the killing, the defendant confessed.

There is no doubt what inferences and findings of fact the jury had to draw in order to convict the defendant of first degree murder. The jury must have believed that: (1) The "horseplay" provocation was not sufficient to justify a deadly attack; (2) the defendant was under no real fear of his own from being

---

10   On cross-examination, the prosecuting attorney asked the defendant if, upon learning of the victim's death, he replied to the police officer: "That's too bad, buddy. Do you think it'll snow?" This Court does not suggest this evidence should have been admitted. However, when reviewing a sufficiency of the evidence claim, an appellate court is entitled to review all the evidence that was actually admitted rightly or wrongly. *See Lockhart v. Nelson,* 488 U.S. 33, 109 S.Ct. 285, 102 L.Ed.2d 265 (1988).

attacked; (3) the stabbing was intentional; and (4) the time it took the defendant to open his knife and inflict the mortal wound was sufficient to establish premeditation.[11]

The difficult factual question must have been the mental state of the defendant at the time of the stabbing. The evidence was somewhat conflicting on this point. While the evidence offered by the defendant is not impossible to believe, some of his explanations seem unlikely. Guilt beyond a reasonable doubt cannot be premised on pure conjecture. However, a conjecture consistent with the evidence becomes less and less conjecture and moves gradually toward proof, as alternative innocent explanations are discarded or made less likely. The beyond a reasonable doubt standard does not require the exclusion of every other hypothesis or, for that matter, every other *reasonable* hypothesis. It is enough if, after considering all the evidence, direct and circumstantial, a reasonable trier of fact could find the evidence established guilt beyond a reasonable doubt.

After reviewing the record, this Court has some doubt as to whether this is a first degree murder case; but, at this point, *Jackson's* own objective standard turns against the defendant. It makes absolutely no difference whether we on the appellate bench as jurors would have voted to convict the defendant of a lesser-included offense or whether we would have thought there was some reasonable doubt. To the contrary, the question posed by *Jackson* [*v. Virginia*, 443 U.S. 307 (1979)] is whether any rational jury could on the evidence presented think the defendant premeditated and intentionally killed the victim. We do not find the evidence so weak as to render the verdict irrational. A rational jury may well have found the defendant guilty of some lesser-included crime without violating its oath; but, drawing all favorable inferences in favor of the prosecution, a rational jury could also convict. We end by suggesting that variations in human experience suggest it is not unexpected to see a considerable range of reasonable verdicts or estimates about what is likely or unlikely. . .

B.

Jury Instructions

The principal question before us under this assignment of error is whether our instructions on murder when given together deprive a criminal defendant of due process or are otherwise wrong and confusing. * * *

---

11 The evidence shows the victim's actions were irritating to the defendant well before the stabbing took place. His anger was building with each comment and flip of the towel. Furthermore, witnesses testified the defendant attempted to stab the victim a second time as he fell to the ground. The evidence shows the victim was slashed in the arm during this attempt. Finally, the defendant's statement that he "had the right to respond, finally, to this act of aggression that was perpetrated against [him]" is considered probative evidence of premeditation and deliberation.

The jury was instructed that in order to find the defendant guilty of murder it had to find five elements beyond a reasonable doubt: "The Court further instructs the jury that murder in the first degree is when one person kills another person unlawfully, willfully, maliciously, deliberately and premeditatedly[.]"[18] In its effort to define these terms, the trial court gave three instructions. State's Instruction No. 8, commonly referred to as the *Clifford* instruction, stated:

> "The Court instructs the jury that to constitute a willful, deliberate and premeditated killing, it is not necessary that the intention to kill should exist for any particular length of time prior to the actual killing; it is only necessary that such intention should have come into existence for the first time at the time of such killing, or at any time previously."

See State v. Clifford, 59 W.Va. 1, 52 S.E. 981 (1906). State's Instruction No. 10 stated: "The Court instructs the jury that in order to constitute a 'premeditated' murder an intent to kill need exist only for an instant." State's Instruction No. 12 stated: "The Court instructs the jury that what is meant by the language willful, deliberate and premeditated is that the killing be intentional." State's Instruction Nos. 10 and 12 are commonly referred to as *Schrader* instructions. *See State v. Schrader*, 172 W.Va. 1, 302 S.E.2d 70 (1982).

While many jurisdictions do not favor the distinction between first and second degree murder,[22] given the doctrine of separation of powers, we do not have the judicial prerogative to abolish the distinction between first and second degree murder and rewrite the law of homicide for West Virginia; unless, of course, we were to declare this classification a violation of due process and force the Legislature to rewrite the law-a bold stroke that we refuse to do. On the other hand, we believe within the parameters of our current homicide statutes the *Schrader* definition of premeditation and deliberation is confusing, if not meaningless. To allow the State to prove premeditation and deliberation by only

---

18   As to the other offenses, the jury instruction stated:

"[M]urder in the second degree is when one person kills another person unlawfully and maliciously, but not deliberately or premeditatedly; that voluntary manslaughter is the intentional, unlawful and felonious but not deliberate or malicious taking of human life under sudden excitement and heat of passion; that involuntary manslaughter is where one person while engaged in an unlawful act, unintentionally causes the death of another person, or when engaged in a lawful act unlawfully causes the death of another person."

22   The Model Penal Code and many of the modern state criminal codes abolish the first and second degree murder distinction in favor of classifications based on more meaningful criteria. Interestingly, defining premeditation in such a way that the formation of the intent to kill and the killing can result from successive impulses, *see Schrader, supra* (intent equals premeditation formula), grants the jury complete discretion to find more ruthless killers guilty of first degree murder regardless of actual premeditation. History teaches that such unbridled discretion is not always carefully and thoughtfully employed, and this case may be an example. In 1994, the Legislature raised the penalty for second degree murder to ten-to-forty years (from five-to-eighteen years), making it less important to give juries the unguided discretion to find the aggravated form of murder in the case of more ruthless killings, irrespective of actual premeditation. The penalties are now comparable.

showing that the intention came "into existence for the first time at the time of such killing" completely eliminates the distinction between the two degrees of murder. Hence, we feel compelled in this case to attempt to make the dichotomy meaningful by making some modifications to our homicide common law.

Premeditation and deliberation should be defined in a more careful, but still general way to give juries both guidance and reasonable discretion. Although premeditation and deliberation are not measured by any particular period of time, there must be some period between the formation of the intent to kill and the actual killing, which indicates the killing is by prior calculation and design. As suggested by the dissenting opinion in *Green v. State*, 1 Tenn.Crim.App. 719, 735, 450 S.W.2d 27, 34 (1970): "True, it is not necessary to prove premeditation existed for any definite period of time. But it is necessary to prove that it did exist." This means there must be an opportunity for some reflection on the intention to kill after it is formed. The accused must kill purposely after contemplating the intent to kill. Although an elaborate plan or scheme to take life is not required, our *Schrader*'s notion of instantaneous premeditation and momentary deliberation is not satisfactory for proof of first degree murder. In *Bullock v. United States*, 74 App.D.C. 220, 221, 122 F.2d 213, 214 (1941), *cert. denied*, 317 U.S. 627, 63 S.Ct. 39, 87 L.Ed. 507 (1942), the court discussed the need to have some appreciable time elapse between the intent to kill and the killing:

> "To speak of premeditation and deliberation which are instantaneous, or which take no appreciable time, is a contradiction in terms. It deprives the statutory requirement of all meaning and destroys the statutory distinction between first and second degree murder. At common law there were no degrees of murder. If the accused had no overwhelming provocation to kill, he was equally guilty whether he carried out his murderous intent at once or after mature reflection. Statutes like ours, which distinguish deliberate and premeditated murder from other murder, reflect a belief that one who meditates an intent to kill and then deliberately executes it is more dangerous, more culpable or less capable of reformation than one who kills on sudden impulse; or that the prospect of the death penalty is more likely to deter men from deliberate than from impulsive murder. The deliberate killer is guilty of first degree murder; the impulsive killer is not. The quoted part of the charge was therefore erroneous."

Thus, there must be some evidence that the defendant considered and weighed his decision to kill in order for the State to establish premeditation and deliberation under our first degree murder statute.[23] This is what is meant by a ruthless,

---

23 In the absence of statements by the accused which indicate the killing was by prior calculation and design, a jury must consider the circumstances in which the killing occurred to determine whether it fits into the first

cold-blooded, calculating killing. Any other intentional killing, by its spontane-ous and nonreflective nature, is second degree murder.[24]

To the extent that the *Schrader* opinion is inconsistent with our holding today, it is overruled. * * *

[W]e feel obligated to discuss what instruction defining premeditation is now acceptable. What came about as a mere suggestion in *Hatfield*, we now approve as a proper instruction under today's decision. Note 7 of *Hatfield*, 169 W.Va. at 202, 286 S.E.2d at 410, states:

> "A more appropriate instruction for first degree murder, paraphrased from 2 Devitt and Blackmar, *Federal Jury Practice and Instructions* § 41.03, at 214, is:

>> "'The jury is instructed that murder in the first degree consists of an intentional, deliberate and premeditated killing which means that the killing is done after a period of time for prior consideration. The duration of that period cannot be arbitrarily fixed. The time in which to form a deliberate and premeditated design varies as the minds and temperaments of people differ, and according to the circumstances in which they may be placed. Any interval of time between the form-ing of the intent to kill and the execution of that intent, which is of sufficient duration for the accused to be fully conscious of what he intended, is sufficient to support a conviction for first degree murder.'"

* * *

WORKMAN, Justice, concurring:

I concur with the holding of the majority, but write this separate opinion to reiterate that the duration of the time period required for premeditation can-not be arbitrarily fixed. Neither the jury instruction approved by the majority,

---

degree category. Relevant factors include the relationship of the accused and the victim and its condition at the time of the homicide; whether plan or preparation existed either in terms of the type of weapon utilized or the place where the killing occurred; and the presence of a reason or motive to deliberately take life. No one factor is controlling. Any one or all taken together may indicate actual reflection on the decision to kill. This is what our statute means by "willful, deliberate and premeditated killing."

24 As examples of what type of evidence supports a finding of first degree murder, we identify three categories: (1) "planning" activity-facts regarding the defendant's behavior prior to the killing which might indicate a design to take life; (2) facts about the defendant's prior relationship or behavior with the victim which might indicate a motive to kill; and (3) evidence regarding the nature or manner of the killing which indicate a deliberate intention to kill according to a preconceived design. The California courts evidently require evidence of all three categories or at least extremely strong evidence of planning activity or evidence of category (2) in conjunction with either (1) or (3). *See People v. Anderson*, 70 Cal.2d 15, 73 Cal.Rptr. 550, 447 P.2d 942 (1968). These examples are illustrative only and are not intended to be exhaustive.

created from our past decisions in *State v. Clifford*, 59 W.Va. 1, 52 S.E. 981 (1906) and *State v. Hatfield*, 169 W.Va. 191, 286 S.E.2d 402 (1982) (as amplified by the majority opinion), nor the new instruction approved in the majority opinion affix any specific amount of time which must pass between the formation of the intent to kill and the actual killing for first degree murder cases. Given the majority's recognition that these concepts are necessarily incapable of being reduced formulaically, I am concerned that some of the language in the opinion may indirectly suggest that some appreciable length of time must pass before premeditation can occur.

I agree with the majority in its conclusion that our decision in *State v. Schrader*, 172 W.Va. 1, 302 S.E.2d 70 (1982), incorrectly equated premeditation with intent to kill. However, I must point out that the majority's suggested basis for defining premeditation and deliberation in terms of requiring some "appreciable time elapse between the intent to kill and the killing" and "some period between the formation of the intent to kill and the actual killing which indicates that the killing is by prior calculation and design" may create confusion in suggesting that premeditation must be the deeply thoughtful enterprise typically associated with the words reflection and contemplation. * * * The majority's interpretation may create ambiguity, if not clarified, by adding arguably contradictory factors to the law enunciated by the majority in the approved instruction, as well as the language in the *Hatfield* and *Dodds* cases that the majority upholds. *See Hatfield*, 169 W.Va. at 202, 286 S.E.2d at 410 n. 7; *see also State v. Dodds*, 54 W.Va. 289, 297-98, 46 S.E. 228, 231 (1903).

Accordingly, it is necessary to make abundantly clear that premeditation is sufficiently demonstrated as long as "[a]ny interval of time[, no matter how short that interval is, lapses] between the forming of the intent to kill and the execution of that intent[.]" *See Hatfield*, 169 W.Va. at 202, 286 S.E.2d at 410 (quoting 2 Devitt and Blackmar, *Federal Jury Practice and Instructions* § 41.03, at 214).

Notes and Questions

1. The majority objects that an instruction that premeditation can be formed in an instant undermines the distinction between first- and second-degree murder. Does the majority's opinion, however, reject the idea that premeditation can be formed this quickly? Certainly the concurrence does not seem to think the Court has rejected such a notion. What, then, is the majority doing to dif-

ferentiate between first- and second-degree murder? How is it even changing the rule announced in *Shrader*?

2. The majority appears to disapprove of a distinction between first- and second-degree murder but is the Court advocating a single punishment for all persons committing killings that are labeled murder? Notice in footnote 22 that the Court finds the existence of a vague distinction between first- and second-degree less problematic now that the West Virginia Legislature has modified the punishment from 5-18 years (the punishment for second-degree murder in West Virginia at the time the defendant in *Ohler v. Boles* was sentenced, (*see* page 99) to 10 to 40 years. First-degree murder in West Virginia, at the time of the *Guthrie* case, was punished by life imprisonment. The Court was certainly correct to observe that criminal law cannot be analyzed solely in terms of the elements of crimes. The sentencing consequences that flow from the definition of crimes are essential to understanding the real impact of the terms defined by criminal statutes. The improvement Justice Cleckley appears to see with the modification to the law is that a jury's incorrect assessment that a crime is second-degree, rather than first-degree murder, can be remedied by a judge sentencing the defendant to a very lengthy term. Judges, unlike juries, consider many factors in determining how to sentence, while jurors are limited to determining whether premeditation existed in deciding how a defendant ought to be punished. Looking at the flip side of Justice Cleckley's perceived improvement, what happens when a jury incorrectly finds that the defendant committed first-degree murder? The ability of a court to remedy this problem depends on the power of a court to suspend a portion of a defendant's sentence. If the judge has such power, then he or she can correct this error just as a jury's incorrect finding of second-degree murder can be corrected. Justice Cleckley can therefore be seen to support either greater judicial power to sentence defendants *or* determinations, by judges or juries, on the basis of more information than simply whether premeditation was present.

3. In considering the defendant's argument that there was insufficient evidence for a first-degree murder conviction, the Court concluded that it was not sure that this was a first-degree case, but that it could not conclude that no reasonable jury could find that it was not a first-degree case. There is a division of labor between legislatures, judges, and juries. Judges, based on statutes created by legislatures, fashion instructions for juries. Only when juries are completely unreasonable in applying those instructions do courts reverse their conclusions. Courts far more readily find that juries have been incorrectly instructed than they find their interpretations of instructions have been whol-

ly unreasonable. What do you think caused the Court to have some doubt that this may be a first-degree murder case?

4. Perhaps the most useful thing the Court did in this case was offer methods of demonstrating premeditation in notes 23 and 24. Notice, though, that the Court is announcing standards for the jury to apply upon which courts, like the one in *Guthrie*, will largely leave unchecked. *Guthrie* thus makes clear that the differentiation between first- and second-degree murder is primarily a jury function, one judges become a part of only when the jury's assessment is unreasonable. Arguments prosecutors and defense lawyers offer to the jury about the inference that can be drawn about the defendant's mental state are therefore far more substantial than the lines appellate courts draw between first- and second-degree murder. There are few legal limitations on the types of arguments that lawyers can make during their closings. Professional organizations, both for the prosecution and defense, regularly host seminars on the sorts of arguments that are the most effective, but the inferences lawyers draw in their closing, that juries use to arrive at their decisions, are subject to little oversight.

PRACTICE EXERCISE

Most often a defendant's statement is helpful to the prosecution, which is in part why defendants are given the right under *Miranda v. Arizona*, about which you will learn more in criminal procedure, to refuse to answer any questions during police interrogation. The defendant's statement in *Guthrie*, however, cuts in both directions. Sketch out closing arguments for both the prosecution and defense using the defendant's statement. For the purpose of this exercise you may assume that the prosecution is seeking first-degree murder while defense is seeking only to negate first-degree murder—in other words, the defense is seeking to do no more than demonstrate that the defendant is, at worst, guilty of only second-degree murder in West Virginia. Include in your arguments references to the jury instructions *Guthrie* describes as appropriate.

Even though the decision to kill can be formed in a short period of time, there must be *some* evidence that the defendant formed the intent to kill, regardless of how long it took, as the Supreme Court of New Mexico demonstrates in *State v. Tafoya*. As you read this case, note the various ways the Court suggests that prosecution can demonstrate that the defendant deliberated about his decision to kill.

(b) General Principles for Establishing Deliberation

The portion of the *Tafoya* case offered below examines the Court's analysis of the defendant's mental state for an *attempted* murder. We will cover attempts later, but the Court's analysis of the defendant's mental state for an attempted murder is the same as it would be if this victim had died from her wounds. Notice how the Court recognizes the policy of reserving first-degree murder as a category of the most serious offenses.

State v. Tafoya

Supreme Court of New Mexico
285 P.3d 604 (2012)

SERNA, Justice.

On the night of November 15, 2008, while aimlessly driving around Roswell, New Mexico, Julian Tafoya (Defendant) shot and killed Andrea Larez, and shot and injured Crystal Brady. Larez and Brady were sitting in the front of the car and Defendant and his girlfriend, Kaprice Conde, were sitting in back. Defendant was convicted by a jury of first degree felony murder with the predicate felony of "shooting at or from a motor vehicle," NMSA 1978, § 30–3–8(B) (1993), attempted first degree murder, and tampering with evidence. The trial court also found Defendant guilty of being a felon in possession of a firearm after the jury issued a special verdict finding that Defendant committed the above crimes with a firearm. Defendant was sentenced to life imprisonment plus seventeen and one-half years.

* * *

Defendant . . . argues that there was insufficient evidence of deliberation to support his conviction for attempted first degree murder. We agree, and seeing no dispute that the evidence supports a finding on the lesser included offense of attempted second degree murder, we remand the case for entry of judgment for second degree murder.

* * *

I. BACKGROUND

Crystal Brady, Andrea Larez, and Kaprice Conde picked Defendant up at an Allsup's Convenience Store in Roswell the night of November 15, 2008. Conde and Defendant were dating, and Brady, Conde, and Defendant had been hanging out at a motel together earlier that day. Brady testified that she was addicted to methamphetamine (meth) at the time, and that before the shooting the three of them had been smoking meth and marijuana, and drinking alcohol. Conde testified that she had been up for five days partying, was high on meth at the time, and was also addicted to the drug. Bloodwork done during Larez's autopsy revealed she had also been using meth.

After picking Defendant up, the four proceeded to cruise around the city listening to loud music. Brady testified that during this time she and the other occupants of the car were smoking meth and marijuana and drinking alcohol. Brady was driving the car, which belonged to Larez. The car had a standard transmission, which was unfamiliar to Brady, and at one point "[she] heard a loud sound, and [the car] stalled out." Right after the car stalled, Defendant shot Larez. Conde and Brady both testified that there was a sudden gunshot followed by more shots. An officer in the area described the gunfire as multiple shots in fairly rapid succession, possibly with a short pause between the fourth and fifth shot.

After the first shot, Brady observed that Larez had been shot and appeared to have died instantly from the wound. When asked what Brady was thinking after she saw that Larez had been shot, she testified that "[she] didn't [think]—it was all so sudden." Brady further testified that upon seeing that Larez had been shot, she turned toward the back of the car screaming and was shot in the face. Brady testified that she only remembers Defendant's face, does not remember him saying anything, that "he looked like a scared little punk," and that she thought Defendant was really high. After being shot, Brady was able to exit the car and crawl away for help. Defendant and Conde also exited the car and ran away, ultimately taking separate paths.

Physical evidence presented at trial showed that Larez and Brady were both shot only once: Larez through the back of the neck and Brady in the face through her right nostril.

* * *

New Mexico's statutory scheme provides for two categories of intentional killings: "those that are willful, deliberate, and premeditated; and those that are committed without such deliberation and premeditation but with knowledge that the killer's acts create a strong probability of death or great bodily harm." *Garcia*, 114 N.M. at 273, 837 P.2d at 866. This Court has in the past articulated this categorical distinction as whether a killing was "deliberate and premeditated, or [whether it was] only rash and impulsive[.]" *Id.* "Thus, if the state merely proves that the accused acted rashly or impulsively, rather than deliberately, and if the accused acted intentionally and without justification or provocation, then the facts would only support second-degree murder." *State v. Adonis*, 2008–NMSC–059, ¶ 16, 145 N.M. 102, 194 P.3d 717.

Although a seemingly straightforward distinction to draw, time has shown that sometimes this is far from the case. *See id.* ¶ 13 (acknowledging the inherent difficulty in articulating and applying the distinction between first and second degree murder and noting the importance of proper application to the fair administration of criminal justice). Well settled, however, is the principle that "[f]irst-degree murder is reserved for the most heinous and reprehensible of killings, and therefore deserving of the most serious punishment under this state's law." *Id.* ¶ 15 (quoting *Garcia*, 114 N.M. at 272, 837 P.2d at 865) (internal quotation marks and alteration omitted). Also well settled is the understanding that, due to the steep penalty reserved for first degree murder convictions, the Legislature did not mean for first degree murder to serve as a catch-all category for every intentional killing. *See generally Adonis*, 2008–NMSC–059, ¶¶ 15, 16, 145 N.M. 102, 194 P.3d 717; *Garcia*, 114 N.M. at 272, 837 P.2d at 865.

* * *

The notion that careful reasoning can occur in a short period of time seems somewhat counterintuitive, and rash and impulsive killings are far more likely to be the product of an expedited decision-making process than are carefully contemplated killings. This Court has in the past entertained the question of how to quantify this complex temporal consideration. *See Garcia*, 114 N.M. at 275, 837 P.2d at 868 ("[W]hat is a short period of time? A second or two? If so, then it is hard to see any principled distinction between an impulsive killing and one that is deliberate and premeditated."). *See generally* Leo M. Romero, *A Critique of the Willful, Deliberate, and Premeditated Formula for Distinguishing Between First and Second Degree Murder in New Mexico*, 18 N.M.L.Rev. 73, 87 (1988) ("By informing the jury that a deliberate intent can be formed in a short time, the instruction fails to recognize the relationship between the thought processes involved in deliberation and the time sufficient to engage them.").

Based on a common understanding of the amount of time it would reasonably take to carefully weigh options for or against doing anything, the only logical way to read this advisement, and the way it has been interpreted in passing within our case law, is to recognize that it is *possible* in certain cases for a jury to reasonably infer from evidence presented that the deliberative process occurred within a short period of time—the crucial element being the presentation of other evidence. *See generally State v. Bingham*, 105 Wash.2d 820, 719 P.2d 109, 113 (1986) (en banc) (observing that allowing the mere "opportunity to deliberate" to serve alone as sufficient evidence of deliberate intent has been criticized as "obliterat[ing] the distinction between first and second degree murder."). Cases that have affirmed first degree murder convictions where the killing(s) occurred within a short period of time have relied on evidence beyond the temporal aspect of the crime in order to find sufficient evidence of deliberation. *See, e.g., State v. Lucero*, 88 N.M. 441, 443, 541 P.2d 430, 432 (1975) (relying on evidence that the defendant went with a loaded gun to a treatment center, where he was not a patient, confronted a known confidential informant and his wife, initiated a fight with the informant and called him a rat, and shot informant and his wife); *see also State v. Blea*, 101 N.M. 323, 325, 681 P.2d 1100, 1102 (1984) (relying on evidence that the defendant got into an argument with the two victims in a bar and shot one victim, chased the other victim out of the bar and shot him, and then returned to shoot the first victim again).

This Court has in the past concluded that, while sufficient time elapsed for the defendant to theoretically form deliberate intent, insufficient indicia of deliberation was presented where "nothing in the evidence enabled the jury to infer . . . that [the defendant] *ever* formed such an intent." *Garcia*, 114 N.M. at 275, 837 P.2d at 868. In *Garcia*, the defendant and victim were fighting in the back yard of a home, appeared to reconcile, and then were later found fighting in the front yard. *Id.* at 270, 837 P.2d at 863. During the front-yard fighting, Defendant stabbed the victim multiple times. *Id.* Although we stated that the defendant *could have* formed deliberate intent in the ten to fifteen minutes between the fighting in the back yard and the fighting-turned-stabbing in the front, no evidence was presented to support such a formation. *Id.* at 275, 837 P.2d at 868.

This Court rejected a similar argument in *State v. Adonis*, a case where the defendant, upon witnessing someone who regularly parked in the defendant's assigned parking space re-offend, ran out of his apartment and fired multiple shots, killing the victim. 2008–NMSC–059, ¶¶ 3–4, 145 N.M. 102, 194 P.3d 717. . . *Adonis* . . . held that there was no evidence to support a finding of deliberative intent—no evidence that the defendant had complained about people parking in his spot in the past or that he had ever before threatened anyone for doing so. *Id.*

¶ 21. While we conceded that the retrieval of a gun within his apartment before running outside to shoot the victim *could* have provided sufficient time for the defendant to form deliberative intent, the State did not produce evidence that "tend[ed] to show that [the defendant] actually did so." *Id.* ¶ 22. Although the State theorized that the defendant was waiting for the victim to park in his spot, or that the defendant had otherwise prepared for this occasion, *Adonis* held that these formulations were nothing more than conjecture. *Id.* ¶ 21.

In this case, the evidence showed that Defendant and the victims spent at least that day, if not also the preceding days, drinking and taking drugs. While aimlessly driving around Roswell drinking and doing more drugs, Defendant, without any evidence of motive, shot Larez and then in very quick succession shot Brady. Brady testified that she had seen Defendant earlier in the day with a gun but clarified that it was normal for the type of people she hung out with to regularly carry guns.

Brady testified that she had no time to think about what had just happened, because it was "all so sudden . . . . it was just too quick." All testimony regarding the succession of shots supported the inference that the shots were all fired in a row, possibly with a very short pause in between the fourth or fifth shot. Although the testimony supports the inference that multiple shots were fired, both Larez and Brady were shot only once.

Brady testified that she started screaming after Larez was shot, turned around, and then Defendant shot her. Brady testified that she did not recall Defendant saying anything to her, but that she thought he was really high.[4] Although the State theorized that Defendant made the conscious decision to kill Brady after shooting Larez in order to eliminate a potential eyewitness, as in *Adonis*, without any evidence to support the argument, this was nothing more than conjecture.

Although both *Garcia* and *Adonis* ultimately held that the evidence presented was inadequate to support a finding of deliberation, both cases, unlike the present case, involved *some* evidence to review. For example, although we held in *Garcia* and *Adonis* that the temporal element of the killing was insufficient in itself to show deliberation, the facts of both cases establish that there was potentially enough time for deliberation. In this case, the evidence only establishes that the shots were fired in quick succession, and there may have been a very short pause between shots. Further, although the testimony presented in *Adonis* and *Garcia* was held to be too inferential, without more, to support deliberation, both cases involved at least some other evidence to consider. Testimony established that the defendant in *Adonis* told the victim's brother after-the-fact

---

4   The State attempted to establish that Brady told a detective in the hospital that Defendant said "now, plot on that, bitch" prior to shooting her. Brady testified that she did not "remember him saying a damn thing."

that this would "teach this guy a lesson not to park in my place no more." 2008–NMSC–059, ¶ 4, 145 N.M. 102, 194 P.3d 717. Under a lesser burden of proof, we held the evidence presented regarding deliberate intent in *Adonis* to be insufficient. *Id.* ¶ 11. Testimony similarly established that the defendant in *Garcia* commented earlier in the day that the victim needed to be removed "away from [the defendant] or you're not going to be seeing him for the rest of the day." 114 N.M. at 275, 837 P.2d at 868. Testimony also established that the defendant in *Garcia* made the post-killing statement that "I told my brother that I did him and I'd do him again." *Id.*

In this case, after hearing the above evidence, the trial court granted the directed verdict motion as to the theory of first degree murder for the killing of Larez. In doing so, the trial court remarked on the evidence, noting that:

> These people were apparently consuming drugs and alcohol for some period of time. And their level of paranoia may have reached a point where one or more of them was unable to control their behavior. I don't know. But in any event, it seems to me that [it] is at least as likely in this case that as opposed to a deliberate contemplated act by [Defendant] that it was as likely a rash or impulse to shoot [Larez].

The trial court ultimately found, however, that because the State presented evidence that Defendant shot Brady after he shot Larez, "once he committed that act, it seems . . . that the next shooting that he engages in, the likelihood of impulse of just a reaction or something like that is less likely simply because she turns around and looks at him and there [are] some comments." Brady only testified that she started screaming, however, and that Defendant said nothing. Certainly, no evidence was presented that Defendant and Brady exchanged words before Defendant shot Brady.

The only evidence that served to support the attempted first degree murder charge, therefore, was time: the passage of perhaps a second or two at most between Defendant's shooting of Larez and Brady. As mentioned above, although the State attempted to establish a motive by theorizing that Defendant decided to kill Brady because of her potential role as a witness against him, there was no evidence whatsoever to support such speculation. There was similarly no circumstantial evidence of earlier confrontation, threats, debts owed, or other common areas of friction leading to violence, nor was there physical evidence that would support the formation of deliberation. *See generally State v. Flores*, 2010–NMSC–002, ¶ 21, 147 N.M. 542, 226 P.3d 641 (reviewing premeditated first degree murder case law discussed in *State v. Duran*, 2006–NMSC–035, ¶ 11, 140 N.M. 94, 140 P.3d 515, and this Court's prior determinations that rational juries could draw an inference of deliberation, for example, from "the large number of wounds, the evidence of a prolonged struggle, the evidence of the defendant's attitude toward the victim, and the defendant's own statements.").

This lack of evidence undoubtedly influenced the trial court in its decision to grant Defendant's directed verdict motion on the count of first degree murder, but it is equally applicable to the attempted murder charge. The only distinction that can be drawn between the shooting of Larez and the shooting of Brady is that one happened immediately before the other, and that Brady started yelling or screaming between the two shootings. Without evidence that the screaming had a communicative purpose, this piece of evidence suggests nothing more than a very brief expression of shock. The void of evidence to support deliberate intent in this case is filled with evidence of rash and impulsive behavior, however. Testimony established the fact that the passengers of the car were addicts, that they had been drinking and doing drugs earlier in the day, and they were drinking and doing drugs at the time of the shootings. They were listening to loud music and driving around town, and then Defendant suddenly shot Larez and then Brady.

Although, as we have established, the law allows for a jury to infer that a short amount of time can be sufficient to form deliberate intent, without other evidence supporting the inference that deliberate intent was actually formed, it would be difficult to ever make a "principled distinction between an impulsive killing and one that is deliberate and premeditated." *Garcia*, 114 N.M. at 275, 837 P.2d at 868. With the complete absence of other evidence to support deliberation, we cannot hold that Defendant proceeded from the rash impulsive murder of Larez to the willful, deliberate and premeditated attempted murder of Brady simply because a second or two *might* have elapsed between the shots.

While we do not find sufficient evidence to support Defendant's conviction for attempted first degree murder, there is substantial evidence in the record that Defendant knowingly created a strong probability of death or great bodily injury and Defendant does not argue otherwise on appeal. We therefore hold that the elements of attempted second degree murder have been met and remand the case for entry of judgment on the lesser included offense of attempted second degree murder. . . .

Notes and Questions

1. Notice that the New Mexico Supreme Court asserts that it is attempting to interpret the legislature's distinction between first- and second-degree murder to identify "the most heinous and reprehensible of killings, and therefore deserving of the most serious punishment. . . ." As you looked at the decisions cited, did you have the sense that New Mexico courts were considering

anything other than evidence of deliberation in deciding whether there was sufficient evidence for a first-degree murder conviction? To ask the question another way, have New Mexico courts arrived at a meaningful way to determine whether a defendant deliberated and decided to kill? Could you explain to a non-lawyer why the *Adonis* and *Garcia* were decided as they were?

2. While the jury is not required to demonstrate that the defendant deliberated for any particular period of time to be guilty of first-degree murder, it is clearly more difficult for the prosecution to show deliberation in a small space of time. The Court, however, seems to suggest that while a small period of contemplation cannot preclude a first-degree murder conviction, a long period of time may be sufficient, observing "in *Garcia* and *Adonis* that the temporal element of the killing was insufficient in itself to show deliberation." The logical inference is that enough time for deliberation can be enough for the jury to conclude that the defendant did deliberate. Does this make sense?

3. The Court in this case concluded that the defendant was guilty of attempted second-degree murder of the victim considered in this portion of the opinion. A number of jurisdictions do not recognize the crime of attempted second-degree murder as those jurisdictions conclude that the nature of attempt is that one intends the act and, as second-degree murder does not require proof of intent, one may not attempt it. New Mexico is in the minority of jurisdictions to recognize this crime.

4. Compare *Tafoya*, and the cases considered in the *Tafoya* case, with *Guthrie*. The *Guthrie* Court concluded that the evidence in that case was sufficient for a jury to find that the slaying in that case was murder in the first-degree. Does it appear that the New Mexico Supreme Court in 2012 would have come to the same conclusion? If not, do you have any thoughts about why the two courts might have arrived at different conclusions? In other words, what might have led the New Mexico Supreme Court in 2012 to exercise more supervision over jury verdicts than the West Virginia Supreme Court did in 1995? Consider this: the jury in the *Guthrie* case had the option of finding first-degree murder and recommending mercy, which prompted the trial court to sentence the defendant to life with a recommendation of mercy. Under West Virginia law, this meant that the defendant was eligible for parole in 15 years. Judges and juries in West Virginia both retained power to mitigate the harshness of first-degree murder conviction when there were mitigating facts. Under New Mexico law in 2012, and at the time of all the cases cited in *Tafoya*, a jury's finding of first-degree murder, which requires a jury to find only that the

defendant formed the intent to kill and did so, automatically meant a minimum of a life sentence with no possibility of parole regardless of any mitigating factors.

5. Consider some of the various ways the New Mexico Supreme Court concludes the prosecution can demonstrate deliberation: a large number of wounds, evidence of a prolonged struggle, and evidence of the defendant's attitude toward the victim. How helpful are these facts in demonstrating a defendant's contemplation of a killing? Are multiple wounds consistent with a design to kill or an act that is only "rash and impulsive"? The victims in this case were each shot once at close range in the face and neck. Were drugs not involved in this case, would such single shots not be very probative of the decision to kill? Is a prolonged struggle evidence of deliberation or mutual combat? What about the relationship between the defendant and the victim? Under the same ambiguous facts, should a defendant's killing of a lifelong enemy be punished differently than his killing of a stranger? It is easy to surmise a situation in which evidence in each one of the *Tafoya* Court's categories would not even be sufficient for a jury to conclude that the defendant premeditated, deliberated or intended the killing. The Court's categories therefore serve at most as a guide for how lawyers ought to argue cases to juries and subsequent courts ought to review first-degree murder convictions based on the defendant's contemplation.

6. In searching for evidence of a defendant's intent, notice that the Court observes that a defendant's post-killing statements can be used to establish his mental state at the time of the killing. We saw the prosecution use Dale Edward Guthrie's statements for this purpose in the previous case. Recall also that we observed in the *Guthrie* case that a defendant has the right not to speak with officers who wish to interrogate him after he is arrested. In homicide cases, a defendant's statements to the police are more frequently used to demonstrate his state of mind than establish his identity as the killer.

7. The Court does not appear to directly reduce the degree of the defendant's culpability because he was high on methamphetamine, but how would a court interpret these facts if the defendant had not been on drugs? What other than a sober person's thought-out decision to kill another would explain firing a weapon into another's face at close range?

8. *Tafoya* is representative of how courts address the line between deliberated killings and those that are not deliberated. As you will see, courts often

describe a hodgepodge of different ways that the prosecution may show deliberation. Rarely is there anything like a complete list offered. California courts have, however, offered a systematic ways to describe what the prosecution must generally show to establish deliberation—planning, motive, and method—but California courts observe that there are circumstances where all of the criteria won't be satisfied.

> Generally, there are three categories of evidence that are sufficient to sustain a premeditated and deliberated murder: evidence of planning, motive, and method. When evidence of all three categories is not present, we require either very strong evidence of planning, or some evidence of motive in conjunction with planning or a deliberate manner of killing. But these categories of evidence . . . are descriptive not normative. They are simply an aid for reviewing courts in assessing whether the evidence is supportive of an inference that the killing was the result of preexisting reflection and weighing of considerations rather than mere unconsidered or rash impulse.

People v. Elliot, 37 Cal.4th 453, 470-71 (Cal. 2005).

Most state courts describe a variety of single factors such as motive, or multiple wounds, as potentially being alone sufficient, with no exhaustive list ever being offered.

9. Many have thought that the distinction between murder that is contemplated (whether that is described as deliberated, intended, or premeditated), and that which is not, is not well defined. Benjamin Cardozo was one of those people. He wrote in 1931:

> I think the distinction is much too vague to be continued in our law. There can be no intent unless there is a choice, yet by the hypothesis, the choice without more is enough to justify the inference that the intent was deliberate and premeditated. The presence of a sudden impulse is said to mark the dividing line, but how can an impulse be anything but sudden when the time for its formation is measured by the lapse of seconds? Yet the decisions are to the effect that seconds may be enough. What is meant, as I understand it, is that the impulse must be the product of an emotion or passion so swift and overmastering as to sweep the mind from its moorings. A metaphor, however, is, to say the least, a shifting test whereby to measure degrees of guilt that mean the difference between life and death. I think the students of the mind should make it clear to the lawmakers that the statute

is framed along the lines of a defective and unreal psychology. If intent is deliberate and premeditated whenever there is a choice, then in truth it is always deliberate and premeditated, since choice is involved in the hypothesis of intent. What we have is merely a privilege offered to the jury to find the lesser degree when the suddenness of the intent, the vehemence of the passion, seems to call irresistibly for the exercise of mercy. I have no objection to giving them this dispensing power, but it should be given to them directly and not in mystifying clouds of words. The present distinction is so obscure that no jury hearing it for the first time can fairly be expected to assimilate and understand it. I am not at all sure that I understand it myself after trying to apply it for many years and after diligent study of what has been written in the books. Upon the basis of this fine distinction with its obscure and mystifying psychology, scores of men have gone to their death.

Benjamin Cardozo, *Law and Literature and Other Essays and Addresses* 99-101 (1931). Based on the *Tafoya* case, and the cases discussed in it, is Cardozo's criticism correct or is there a meaningful line dividing contemplated killings from those that are not?

10. A quick note on the burden of proof. You are probably aware, just from having lived in this country, that the prosecution has to prove every element of a crime beyond a reasonable doubt. How sure are you of a jury's ability to *ever* determine whether a defendant thought about his decision to kill? Now consider the burden of proof. How sure are you that these jurors can do so *beyond a reasonable doubt*? This is a task the Supreme Court of New Mexico gives to the jury if there is evidence of motive to kill, animosity between the defendant and the victim, a number of wounds, or a number of other circumstances suggesting the defendant deliberated, a term Benjamin Cardozo suggests is itself meaningless.

PRACTICE EXERCISE

Draft a statute defining murder (and its punishments) in your jurisdiction, using the statutes above as a reference. *Remember that statutes are the elemental basis for jury instructions.* Consider the following:

(1) How long would you make it? Does a long, specific statute make the punitive scheme more or less confusing? Is it possible to remove all ambiguity from a statute?

(2) How many degrees of murder would you include? What would define each degree?

(3) What punishment(s) would you attach to each degree? If you have only one degree, would you create a mandatory sentencing scheme, or only draft "recommendations" for the judiciary to consider?

(4) Finally, ask yourself whether the legislature (statutes) or the judiciary (case law) is better equipped to handle the drafting of criminal law in your jurisdiction, and how your resolution of that consideration affects your drafting approach.

(c) Planning—Obtaining and Using a Weapon

Courts frequently find that when a defendant obtains a weapon to kill and then kills that the killing has been contemplated. Some even conclude that the *use* of a weapon is sufficient to demonstrate that the slayer sufficiently deliberated to be convicted of first-degree murder. Consider whether the following two cases, each justified in part by the fact that the defendant procured a weapon, achieve the goal stated by the New Mexico Supreme Court of reserving first-degree murder for "the most heinous and reprehensible of killings."

People v. Sanchez

Colorado Court of Appeals, Div. II
253 P.3d 1260 (2010)

Opinion by Judge FURMAN.

Defendant, Adrian Enrique Sanchez, appeals his conviction following a jury trial. The jury found him guilty of first degree murder after deliberation, two counts of attempted first degree murder after deliberation, first degree assault under the heat of passion, and second degree assault under the heat of passion. We affirm.

Testimony at trial revealed the following facts.

A group of about thirty people, including defendant, attended an overnight party at a campground. During the night, R.M. left his tent and noticed C.R. inside of his boss's Jeep and defendant standing outside the Jeep. R.M. approached the

Jeep and saw C.R. holding a camera that belonged to R.M.'s boss. R.M. asked what C.R. and defendant were doing and told them to get out of the Jeep. R.M. was angry, pointed his finger at C.R. and defendant, and accused them of stealing. Defendant told R.M., "We're ready for this," and, "You don't want to do this."

Defendant stabbed R.M. in the chest with a folding knife, and then stabbed S.P. and D.C., two onlookers, as D.C. fought C.R. R.M. and D.C. survived, but S.P. died from his stab wound.

After the stabbings, defendant ran from the campground. The police later found him hiding in a trailer.

On appeal, defendant contends . . . the evidence of intent after deliberation supporting the first degree murder conviction and the two attempted first degree murder convictions was insufficient. . .

The first degree murder and attempted first degree murder charges required the prosecution to prove defendant deliberated before stabbing the victims. *See* §§ 18–2–101(1), 18–3–102(1)(a), C.R.S.2009. "The term 'after deliberation' means not only intentionally but also that the decision to commit the act has been made after the exercise of reflection and judgment concerning the act. An act committed after deliberation is never one which has been committed in a hasty or impulsive manner." § 18–3–101(3), C.R.S.2009. The length of time required for deliberation, however, is not long. *People v. Bartowsheski*, 661 P.2d 235, 242 (Colo.1983).

"The element of deliberation, like intent, can rarely be proven other than through circumstantial or indirect evidence." *People v. Dist. Court*, 926 P.2d 567, 571 (Colo.1996). "Such evidence may include the use of a deadly weapon, the manner in which it was used, and the existence of hostility or jealousy between the accused and the victim." *People v. Dist. Court*, 779 P.2d 385, 388 (Colo.1989).

Viewed in the light most favorable to the prosecution, the circumstances surrounding the stabbings are sufficient to show defendant acted after exercising reflection and judgment. *Id.* First, the jury reasonably could have inferred defendant acted after exercising reflection because he unfolded the knife before the stabbings. Second, the jury also reasonably could have inferred defendant exercised judgment from the locations of the stabbings—R.M.'s chest; S.P.'s neck; and D.C.'s back—because of the degree of harm that may result from stabbing a person in those places. Finally, before the stabbings, defendant stated, "We're ready for this," and, "You don't want to do this." From these statements, the jury reasonably could have inferred that defendant consciously decided to stab the victims.

Commonwealth v. Coleman

Supreme Judicial Court of Massachusetts
747 N.E.2d 666 (2001)

MARSHALL, C.J.

The defendant was convicted of murder in the first degree on a theory of deliberate premeditation, and of unlawful possession of a firearm.

The jury could have found that at approximately 2 A.M. on May 25, 1997, the defendant was involved in an altercation involving several persons outside a nightclub in Worcester. The fight began when two men attacked the defendant. At some point during or after the fight in which several persons had thrown punches, the defendant left the brawl and went to a nearby automobile where he retrieved a gun from the trunk. He then turned in the direction from which he had come and shot the victim at close range. There was evidence that the victim had followed the defendant to the automobile, but no evidence that the victim was armed at the time of the shooting. There was evidence that the defendant also shot the victim a second time as he lay on the ground. After the shooting, the defendant and three other men jumped into an automobile and sped away.

Paramedics arrived at the scene shortly after the shooting and found the victim with a gunshot wound to his chest. The victim was transported to a hospital, where he died approximately two hours later. A medical examiner located a single bullet that killed the victim lodged in his lower right chest. The gun used in the shooting was not recovered.

The defendant asserts that the evidence was insufficient to permit the jury to find that the element of deliberate premeditation had been proved beyond a reasonable doubt because there was insufficient time for the defendant to have planned the killing. For the same reason (insufficiency of the evidence to establish the element of deliberate premeditation) the defendant argues that his murder conviction was obtained in violation of his Federal due process rights. *Jackson v. Virginia*, 443 U.S. 307, 318-319, 99 S.Ct. 2781, 61 L.Ed.2d 560 (1979). There was no error.

The Commonwealth was required to establish beyond a reasonable doubt that the defendant "reflected on his resolution to kill," *Commonwealth v. Ruci*, 409 Mass. 94, 96, 564 N.E.2d 1000 (1991), and cases cited, and that the defendant's decision to kill was the product of "cool reflection," *Commonwealth v. Davis*, 403 Mass. 575, 582, 531 N.E.2d 577 (1988). * * * "'Cool reflection' merely requires that 'the purpose [be] resolved upon and the mind determined to do it before the blow is struck [;] then it is, within the meaning of the law, deliberately premeditated malice aforethought.'" *Id.*, quoting *Commonwealth v. Tucker*, 189 Mass. 457, 494, 76 N.E. 127 (1905).

The defendant recognizes that no particular period of reflection is required, and that a plan to murder may be formed in seconds. . . . He argues that, because the fighting started when two men attacked the defendant and thereafter "everything was spontaneous," there was not enough time for the defendant to plan the killing. We disagree. Three witnesses testified that, during or after a brief fistfight, the defendant walked to the trunk of a nearby automobile and obtained a gun. One witness testified that, as the defendant walked toward an automobile, he overheard another man say, "It ain't over. It ain't over. Pop the trunk. Pop the trunk." This witness saw the trunk pop open, and the man hand something to the defendant, who then turned toward and shot the victim. A rational jury could infer that as the defendant walked toward the automobile, he formed the plan to kill. *See Commonwealth v. Whipple*, 377 Mass. 709, 714-715, 387 N.E.2d 575 (1979) (sufficient evidence of premeditation where defendant disengaged from fistfight, obtained gun from nearby automobile, returned and shot victim).

One witness also testified that, after the defendant shot at the victim once, the victim fell to the ground, and the defendant "stepped back like a foot or so, and . . . shot at him again." Other witnesses also heard more than one shot. Because only one bullet wound was located in the victim's body and the victim fell to the ground after the first shot, the defendant argues that this evidence cannot support a finding of deliberate premeditation, as the fatal shot had already been fired. But the jury could have inferred in these circumstances that the multiple shots fired at the victim were evidence of deliberate premeditation, even if only one shot killed the victim. *Commonwealth v. Good*, 409 Mass. 612, 618, 568 N.E.2d 1127 (1991) (evidence that defendant approached victim and at close range fired three bullets at victim sufficient to support finding that "before the shooting, the defendant at least briefly reflected on his resolution to kill"). *See Commonwealth v. Watkins*, 373 Mass. 849, 852, 370 N.E.2d 701 (1977). The placement of the fatal wound, fired at close range into the victim's chest would also support a finding of deliberate premeditation. *Commonwealth v. Robertson, supra* (placement of bullet wound supports jury's finding of deliberate premeditation).

The defendant points to testimony that he claims undermines the evidence of deliberate premeditation, namely that the victim chased the defendant as he approached the automobile from which he obtained the gun. But there was no evidence that the victim was armed, or that the defendant shot the victim to protect himself from the victim. In any event, the defendant's reliance on contradictory evidence is misplaced. "Once sufficient evidence is presented to warrant submission of the charges to the jury, it is for the jury alone to determine what weight will be accorded to the evidence." *Commonwealth v. Ruci, supra* at 97, 564 N.E.2d 1000, quoting *Commonwealth v. Hill*, 387 Mass. 619, 624, 442 N.E.2d 24 (1982).

Because we conclude that there was sufficient evidence to support a finding of deliberate premeditation, there is no merit to the defendant's due process claim premised on the same theory.

Notes and Questions

1. These cases that regard the acquisition of a weapon to be sufficient to show deliberation mark perhaps the thinnest point in the line separating first- and second-degree murder. Unless the defendant killed his victim with his bare hands (a difficult task with one blow and if multiple blows are involved, this itself might show deliberation), then he would have had to have obtained the weapon. In *Sanchez* and *Guthrie* the defendants merely opened knives already in their possession. Consider this quotation from the late former Senator Arlen Specter who was at the time of this quote the District Attorney for Philadelphia:

   The dictum that "justice and liberty are not the subjects of bargaining and barter" does not fit the realities of a typical barroom killing . . . . There is ordinarily sufficient evidence of malice and deliberation in such cases for the jury to find the defendant guilty of murder in the first degree, which [in Pennsylvania] carries either life imprisonment or death in the electric chair. Or, the conceded drinking by the defendant may be sufficient to nullify specific intent or malice to make the case second degree murder, which calls for a maximum of 10 to 20 years in jail. From all the prosecutor knows by the time the cold carbon copies of the police reports reach the District Attorney's office, the defendant may have acted in "hot blood," which makes the offense only voluntary manslaughter with a maximum penalty of 6 to 12 years. And, the defense invariably produces testimony showing that the killing was pure self-defense. When such cases are submitted to juries, a variety of verdicts are returned, which leads to the inescapable conclusion of variable guilt. Most of those trials result in convictions for second degree murder or voluntary manslaughter. The judges generally impose sentences with a minimum range of 5 to 8 years and a maximum of 10 to 20 years. That distilled experience enables the assistant district attorney and the defense lawyer to bargain on the middle ground of what experience has shown to be "justice" without the defense running the risk of the occasional first degree conviction. . . and without the Commonwealth tying up a jury room for 3 to 5 days and running the risk of acquittal.

See Albert W. Alschuler, *The Prosecutor's Role in Plea Bargaining*, 36 U. Chi. L. Rev. 50, 76-77 (1968-69). Were then-District Attorney Specter and then-Judge Cardozo saying the same things about the distinctions between first- and second-degree murder but from their differing vantage points in the criminal justice system?

2. As we discovered in *Guthrie*, courts only rarely rule that a jury has incorrectly concluded that a defendant is guilty of first-degree murder. The bulk of the decisions defining the line between first- and second-degree murder are therefore made by jurors considering matters unlike anything they've previously seen and using criteria that, according to Benjamin Cardozo and a lot of others, is difficult to understand. When juries decide the appropriate sentence in a capital case, when they decide whether a defendant should live or die, they are similarly considering circumstances they have likely never previously encountered. Capital juries are expressly given the power to reject a death sentence even if the legal criteria required for this penalty has been satisfied. Juries, however, have no context for understanding whether the killings they have considered should receive the ultimate penalty. For this reason, a number of states require appellate courts to ensure that juries have not imposed a sentence disproportionate to the defendant's crime, that is to ensure that an individual jury has not reached an idiosyncratic conclusion. While appellate courts do, with some frequency, find that the legal criteria for a death sentence has not been met, they rarely conclude that the jury has inappropriately exercised its discretion and disproportionately punished a defendant. Appellate courts, by contrast, very rarely find jury verdicts of first-degree murder are legally unsound and there is no mechanism for a court to conclude that the jury inappropriately failed to grant the mercy of a second-degree conviction, as Cardozo describes such a verdict. When you study constitutional law, you will discover an interesting analogy to this sort of unchecked power of juries to essentially define the law. In an obscenity prosecution, a jury is required to conclude that pornography is obscene by the standards of the local community. *See Miller v. California*, 413 U.S. 15 (1973). In a similar fashion, jurors alone, for the overwhelming majority of murder cases, as members of the community appear to have the power to decide how they feel a particular type of murder ought to be punished—and their views may or may not be representative.

(d) Planning, Activity, Motive and Nature of Killing

It is hornbook law that the prosecution is not required to demonstrate a killer's motive to convict him of first-degree murder. As the California Supreme Court described in the *Elliot* case, however, the prosecution, in a paradigm case of first-degree murder, is able to demonstrate planning, motive, and method. Most states, unlike California, do not even mention the role of motive in evaluating the proof of premeditation and deliberation. While not required, motive is far from irrelevant to the prosecution case. In all American jurisdictions, reviewing courts will consider evidence of motive as adding to the proof that there was deliberation—and certainly evidence of motive will make jurors more inclined to convict.

State v. Moore

Supreme Court of Minnesota
846 N.W.2d 83 (2014)

PAGE, Justice.

Appellant Prince Oliver Moore, Jr., was found guilty after a jury trial of one count of first-degree premeditated murder in violation of Minn.Stat. § 609.185(a)(1) (2012), and one count of first-degree domestic-abuse murder in violation of Minn.Stat. § 609.185(a)(6) (2012). The trial court convicted Moore of first-degree premeditated murder and sentenced him to life in prison without the possibility of release. On appeal, Moore [challenges the sufficiency of the evidence demonstrating premeditation].

* * *

At trial, the following evidence was presented. In the early morning hours of September 13, 2011, Moore called 911 to report that his wife Mauryn had attacked him with a knife while he was sleeping. Moore said that he grabbed the knife from Mauryn and stabbed her. Moore said that he did not believe Mauryn was alive. When officers arrived at the Moores' apartment, they found Mauryn's body lying in the couple's bedroom with approximately 64 sharp-force injuries. Near her body was a knife that Moore concedes likely came from the kitchen. After the officers observed cuts on Moore's chest and neck, he was transported to a hospital. Moore's treating physician testified that in his professional opinion

Moore's injuries were not life threatening and it was possible that the injuries were self-inflicted.

The Hennepin County Medical Examiner's Office conducted an autopsy on Mauryn's body. The autopsy revealed that Mauryn had approximately 64 sharp-force injuries. These injuries included a 2–inch deep laceration on the front of her neck that cut her trachea, right carotid artery, right jugular vein, and esophagus. According to the medical examiner, that laceration was not a survivable wound. Mauryn also had several lacerations on her fingers and hands, which may have been defensive wounds. She had multiple stab wounds to her back, two of which had very little hemorrhage, indicating that they were likely inflicted after Mauryn had died or lost a significant amount of blood.

A neighbor of the Moores testified that he heard the Moores argue at least every week and that on the morning of the killing he heard them having an unusually serious argument. At one point, he heard what he described as a "scramble" and a female voice yell, "Stop."

Over Moore's objection, Moore's former wife testified. She testified that Moore was a jealous and controlling husband; that he did not like it when she would talk with other men or get rides to work from men; that he would get upset, which led to them arguing, which sometimes escalated to physical fights; and that he both physically and sexually abused her during their marriage. She also testified that Moore's abuse started while the couple was living in Liberia and continued after they moved to Minnesota.

Several of Mauryn's friends testified pursuant to Minn. R. Evid. 807, the residual hearsay exception. This testimony revealed that Mauryn complained that Moore was controlling and abusive, and that Mauryn wanted to leave the marriage. The testimony also disclosed that Mauryn complained that Moore hit her and she once had to go to the hospital because of the abuse. One of Mauryn's friends testified that when she and Mauryn were studying Moore would call every few minutes to check in on Mauryn. Another friend testified that Moore would stare at Mauryn through a window at Mauryn's work. Moore declined to testify in his own defense.

The next question presented is whether the circumstantial evidence produced at trial was sufficient to support the jury's finding of premeditation. "Premeditation is a state of mind generally proved circumstantially by drawing inferences from a defendant's words and actions in light of the totality of the circumstances." *State v. Brocks*, 587 N.W.2d 37, 42 (Minn.1998). We apply a two-step analysis in determining whether circumstantial evidence is sufficient to support a guilty verdict. *State v. Andersen*, 784 N.W.2d 320, 329–30 (Minn.2010). The first step is to identify the circumstances proved. *Id.* at 329. The second step is to "determine whether the circumstances proved are 'consistent with guilt and inconsistent with any rational hypothesis except that of guilt.'" *State v. Palmer*, 803 N.W.2d 727, 733 (Minn.2011) (quoting *Andersen*, 784 N.W.2d at 330).

* * *

Viewing the evidence in the light most favorable to the verdict, the circumstances proved here include the following. Moore was a jealous and controlling husband. Moore and Mauryn had weekly arguments that sometimes turned physical. Mauryn wanted a divorce. On the night of the killing, the couple fought for over an hour. During that argument, a downstairs neighbor heard a woman yell, "Stop." Mauryn was cut in vital areas of her body, including a 2–inch deep cut along her throat and numerous stab wounds to her chest and back. Mauryn's body was found in the couple's bedroom, but the weapon was procured from the kitchen. Moore continued to stab Mauryn after she was dead or had lost a significant amount of blood. Moore's injuries were not life threatening and were self-inflicted.[2]

We have recognized three categories of evidence that are relevant to an inference of premeditation—planning activity, motive, and the nature of the killing. *E.g., State v. Hughes*, 749 N.W.2d 307, 313 (Minn.2008). We address each in turn and conclude that the circumstances proved are consistent with a reasonable inference that Moore premeditated Mauryn's killing and inconsistent with any rational hypothesis except that of guilt.

With respect to planning activity, in *State v. Merrill* we addressed a fact pattern similar to the one here. 274 N.W.2d 99, 103–04 (Minn.1978). In *Merrill*, the defendant admitted to "going into the kitchen to search for a knife, finding a knife, and then returning to the bedroom and stabbing the victim 17 times." *Id.* at 112. Merrill argued that the evidence was insufficient to support the jury's finding of premeditation. *Id.* at 111. We disagreed, concluding that Merrill's "actions in going into the kitchen [from the bedroom], obtaining the knife, returning to the bedroom, and stabbing the victim numerous times" demonstrated premeditation. *Id.* at 112.

This case presents nearly identical facts. Although Moore did not admit that he retrieved the knife from the kitchen, the circumstances proved support an inference that he did so. The knife used to kill Mauryn was one normally found in a kitchen. The kitchen was roughly 10 feet from the door to the bedroom and was separated by a hallway. Moore continued to stab Mauryn after she was dead or had lost a significant amount of blood. Moore's injuries were self-inflicted. The

---

2   We acknowledge that Moore claimed that Mauryn inflicted his injuries. However, in identifying the circumstances proved, we must resolve the factual dispute regarding the source of Moore's injuries in a manner consistent with the jury's verdict. *See Tscheu*, 758 N.W.2d at 858.

circumstances proved are inconsistent with a rational hypothesis that Moore grabbed the knife from Mauryn and stabbed her in self-defense and are consistent with a reasonable inference that Moore retrieved the knife from the kitchen and then returned to the bedroom where he stabbed Mauryn approximately 64 times. We conclude that the evidence of Moore's planning activity supports the jury's finding on premeditation.

Moore argues that there was no motive evidence that could support premeditation. While "[e]vidence of motive is unnecessary to a finding of premeditation," *Palmer*, 803 N.W.2d at 735, we note that, contrary to Moore's argument, there was evidence of motive in this case. We have found motive evidence when the "defendant's relationship with the victim had deteriorated and [the] defendant was angry with [the victim,]" including "evidence that defendant and the victim had argued the night before the killing." *State v. Lodermeier*, 539 N.W.2d 396, 398 (Minn.1995); *see also State v. Pendleton*, 759 N.W.2d 900, 910 (Minn.2009). We have also relied on the defendant's expressions of jealousy in finding premeditation. *State v. Hurd*, 819 N.W.2d 591, 601 (Minn.2012).

Here, the circumstances proved establish the following. Moore was jealous, controlling, and abusive, and Mauryn wanted a divorce. Before the murder, Moore and Mauryn argued for over an hour. This argument was more serious than normal. The anger sparked by the deterioration of the couple's relationship and Moore's jealousy provided a motive to kill, which supports the jury's premeditation determination. *See Lodermeier*, 539 N.W.2d at 398.

Finally, we conclude that the nature of the killing also supports the jury's finding of premeditation. In *State v. Chomnarith*, we concluded that wounds placed deliberately on vital areas of the body show premeditation. 654 N.W.2d 660, 665 (Minn.2003) (holding that stab wounds puncturing a lung, penetrating a rib bone, and severing an artery support a finding of premeditation). Moreover, we have said that 40 stab wounds on the victim were probative of premeditation. *State v. Smith*, 367 N.W.2d 497, 501 (Minn.1985). We have also observed that a prolonged, severe attack may show premeditation. *State v. Cooper*, 561 N.W.2d 175, 180 (Minn.1997); *State v. Martin*, 261 N.W.2d 341, 345 (Minn.1977) (concluding that a brutal killing, including the infliction of post-mortem wounds, supports a premeditated murder verdict).

Here, Mauryn was cut in vital areas of her body, including a 2–inch deep laceration on her neck that cut her trachea, right carotid artery, right jugular vein, and esophagus. That laceration was not survivable. Mauryn also had stab wounds to her back, resulting in two collapsed lungs. Some of the 64 wounds appear to have been inflicted after Mauryn's heart had stopped beating or she had lost a significant amount of blood, which suggests a prolonged attack. We conclude that the nature of the killing supports the jury's finding of premeditation.

In sum, the evidence of Moore's planning activity, motive, and the nature of the killing all support the jury's finding of premeditation. We therefore hold that the State presented sufficient evidence to support Moore's first-degree premeditated murder conviction.

(e) Method—Abuse/Multiple Blows

Recall that the New Mexico Supreme Court in *Tafoya* said that multiple wounds could demonstrate deliberation. What about multiple non-lethal blows? The *Midgett* case takes up this issue.

Midgett v. State

Supreme Court of Arkansas
729 S.W.2d 410 (1987)

NEWBERN, Justice.

This child abuse case resulted in the appellant's conviction of first degree murder. The sole issue on appeal is whether the state's evidence was sufficient to sustain the conviction. We hold there was no evidence of the ". . . premeditated and deliberated purpose of causing the death of another person . . ." required for conviction of first degree murder by Ark.Stat.Ann. § 41–1502(1)(b) (Repl.1977). However, we find the evidence was sufficient to sustain a conviction of second degree murder, described in Ark.Stat.Ann. § 41–1503(1)(c) (Repl.1977), as the appellant was shown to have caused his son's death by delivering a blow to his abdomen or chest ". . . with the purpose of causing serious physical injury. . . ." The conviction is thus modified from one of first degree murder to one of second degree murder and affirmed.

The facts of this case are as heart-rending as any we are likely to see. The appellant is six feet two inches tall and weighs 300 pounds. His son, Ronnie Midgett, Jr., was eight years old and weighed between thirty-eight and forty-five pounds. The evidence showed that Ronnie Jr. had been abused by brutal beating over a substantial period of time. Typically, as in other child abuse cases, the bruises had been noticed by school personnel, and a school counselor as well as a SCAN worker had gone to the Midgett home to inquire. Ronnie Jr. would not say how he had obtained the bruises or why he was so lethargic at school except to blame it all, vaguely, on a rough playing little brother. He did not even complain to his siblings about the treatment he was receiving from the appellant. His mother, the wife of the appellant, was not living in the home. The other children apparently were not being physically abused by the appellant.

Ronnie Jr.'s sister, Sherry, aged ten, testified that on the Saturday preceding the Wednesday of Ronnie Jr.'s death their father, the appellant, was drinking whiskey (two to three quarts that day) and beating on Ronnie Jr. She testified that the appellant would "bundle up his fist" and hit Ronnie Jr. in the stomach and in the back. On direct examination she said that she had not previously seen the appellant beat Ronnie Jr., but she had seen the appellant choke him for no particular reason on Sunday nights after she and Ronnie Jr. returned from church. On cross-examination, Sherry testified that Ronnie Jr. had lied and her father was, on that Saturday, trying to get him to tell the truth. She said the bruises on Ronnie Jr.'s body noticed over the preceding six months had been caused by the appellant. She said the beating administered on the Saturday in question consisted of four blows, two to the stomach and two to the back.

On the Wednesday Ronnie Jr. died, the appellant appeared at a hospital carrying the body. He told hospital personnel something was wrong with the child. An autopsy was performed, and it showed Ronnie Jr. was a very poorly nourished and underdeveloped eight-year-old. There were recently caused bruises on the lips, center of the chest plate, and forehead as well as on the back part of the lateral chest wall, the soft tissue near the spine, and the buttocks. There was discoloration of the abdominal wall and prominent bruising on the palms of the hands. Older bruises were found on the right temple, under the chin, and on the left mandible. Recent as well as older, healed, rib fractures were found.

The conclusion of the medical examiner who performed the autopsy was that Ronnie Jr. died as the result of intra-abdominal hemorrhage caused by a blunt force trauma consistent with having been delivered by a human fist. The appellant argues that in spite of all this evidence of child abuse, there is no evidence that he killed Ronnie Jr. having premeditated and deliberated causing his death. We must agree.

* * *

The appellant argues, and we must agree, that in a case of child abuse of long duration the jury could well infer that the perpetrator comes not to expect death of the child from his action, but rather that the child will live so that the abuse may be administered again and again. Had the appellant planned his son's death, he could have accomplished it in a previous beating.

In this case the evidence might possibly support the inference that the blows which proved fatal to Ronnie Jr. could have been struck with the intent to cause his death developed in a drunken, misguided, and overheated attempt at disciplining him for not having told the truth. Even if we were to conclude there was substantial evidence from which the jury could fairly have found the appellant intended to cause Ronnie Jr.'s death in a drunken disciplinary beating on that Saturday, there would still be no evidence whatever of a premeditated and deliberated killing.

In *Ford v. State*, 276 Ark. 98, 633 S.W.2d 3, *cert. den.* 459 U.S. 1022, 103 S.Ct. 389, 74 L.Ed.2d 519 (1980), we held that to show the appellant acted with a premeditated and deliberated purpose, the state must prove that he (1) had the conscious object to cause death, (2) formed that intention before acting, and (3) weighed in his mind the consequences of a course of conduct, as distinguished from acting upon sudden impulse without the exercise of reasoning power. Viewing the evidence most favorable to the appellee, the circumstances of this case are not substantial evidence the appellant did (2) and (3), as opposed to acting on impulse or with no conscious object of causing death. The jury was thus forced to resort to speculation on these important elements.

A clear exposition of the premeditation and deliberation requirement which separates first degree from second degree murder is found in 2 W. LaFave and A. Scott, Jr., *Substantive Criminal Law* § 7.7 (1986):

> Almost all American jurisdictions which divide murder into degrees include the following two murder situations in the category of first degree murder: (1) intent-to-kill murder where there exists (in addition to the intent to kill) the elements of premeditation and deliberation, and (2) felony murder where the felony in question is one of five or six listed felonies, generally including rape, robbery, kidnapping, arson and burglary. Some states instead or in addition have other kinds of first degree murder.

> (a) Premeditated, Deliberate, Intentional Killing. To be guilty of this form of first degree murder the defendant must not only intend to kill but in addition he must premeditate the killing and deliberate about it. It is not easy to give a meaningful definition of the words "premeditate" and "deliberate" as they are used in connection with first degree murder. Perhaps the best that can be said of "deliberation" is that it requires a cool mind that is capable of reflection, and of "premeditation" that it requires that the one with the cool mind did in fact reflect, at least for a short period of time before his act of killing.

* * *

The evidence in this case supports only the conclusion that the appellant intended not to kill his son but to further abuse him or that his intent, if it was to kill the child, was developed in a drunken, heated, rage while disciplining the child. Neither of those supports a finding of premeditation or deliberation.

Perhaps because they wish to punish more severely child abusers who kill their children, other states' legislatures have created laws permitting them to go beyond second degree murder. For example, Illinois has made aggravated battery one of the felonies qualifying for "felony murder," and a child abuser can be convicted of murder if the child dies as a result of aggravated battery. *See People v. Ray*, 80 Ill.App.3d 151, 35 Ill.Dec. 688, 399 N.E.2d 977 (1979). Georgia makes "cruelty to children" a felony, and homicide in the course of cruelty to children is "felony murder." *See Bethea v. State*, 251 Ga. 328, 304 S.E.2d 713 (1983). Idaho has made murder by torture a first degree offense, regardless of intent of the perpetrator to kill the victim, and the offense is punishable by the death penalty. *See State v. Stuart*, 110 Idaho 163, 715 P.2d 833 (1985). California has also adopted a murder by torture statute making the offense murder in the first degree without regard to the intent to kill. *See People v. Demond*, 59 Cal.App.3d 574, 130 Cal. Rptr. 590 (1976). *Cf. People v. Steger*, 16 Cal.3d 539, 128 Cal.Rptr. 161, 546 P.2d 665 (1976), in which the California Supreme Court held that the person accused of torture murder in the first degree must be shown to have had a premeditated intent to inflict extreme and prolonged pain in order to be convicted.

All of this goes to show that there remains a difference between first and second degree murder, not only under our statute, but generally. Unless our law is changed to permit conviction of first degree murder for something like child abuse or torture resulting in death, our duty is to give those accused of first degree murder the benefit of the requirement that they be shown by substantial evidence to have premeditated and deliberated the killing, no matter how heinous the facts may otherwise be. We understand and appreciate the state's citation of *Burnett v. State, supra*, but, to the extent it is inconsistent with this opinion, we must overrule it.

The dissenting opinion begins by stating the majority concludes that one who starves and beats a child to death cannot be convicted of murder. That is not so, as we are affirming the conviction of murder; we are, however, reducing it to second degree murder. The dissenting opinion's conclusion that the appellant starved Ronnie Jr., must be based solely on the child's underdeveloped condition which could, presumably, have been caused by any number of physical malfunctions. There is no evidence the appellant starved the child. The dissenting opinion says it is for the jury to determine the degree of murder of which the appellant is guilty. That is true so long as there is substantial evidence to support the jury's choice. The point of this opinion is to note that there was no evidence of premeditation or deliberation which are required elements of the crime of first degree murder. The dissenting opinion cites two child abuse cases in which first degree murder convictions have been affirmed. One is *Morris v. State, supra*, with which we dealt earlier in this opinion. The other is *Lindsey v. State*, 501 S.W.2d 647 (Tex.Crim.App.1973), in which the opinion does not say the conviction was for first degree murder. In fact, the issue there was whether the killing occurred with "intent and malice" which are obviously not the same as premeditation and deliberation.

In this case we have no difficulty with reducing the sentence to the maximum for second degree murder. *Dixon v. State*, 260 Ark. 857, 545 S.W.2d 606 (1977). The jury gave the appellant a sentence of forty years imprisonment which was the maximum for first degree murder, and we reduce that to twenty years which is the maximum imprisonment for second degree murder. Just as walking away from the victim in the water-filled ditch in *House v. State, supra*, after a protracted fight, and the "overkill" and mutilation of the body in *Weldon v. State, supra*, were circumstances creating substantial evidence of premeditation and deliberation, the obvious effect the beatings were having on Ronnie Jr. and his emaciated condition when the final beating occurred are circumstances constituting substantial evidence that the appellant's purpose was to cause serious physical injury, and that he caused his death in the process. That is second degree murder, § 41–1503(1)(c). Therefore, we reduce the appellant's sentence to imprisonment for twenty years.

Affirmed as modified.

HICKMAN, Justice, dissenting.

* * *

In this case the majority, with clairvoyance, decides that this parent did not intend to kill his child, but rather to keep him alive for further abuse. This is not a child neglect case. The state proved Midgett starved the boy, choked him, and struck him several times in the stomach and back. The jury could easily conclude that such repeated treatment was intended to kill the child.

* * *

The facts in this case are substantial to support a first degree murder conviction. The defendant was in charge of three small children. The victim was eight years old and had been starved; he weighed only 38 pounds at the time of his death. He had multiple bruises and abrasions. The cause of death was an internal hemorrhage due to blunt force trauma. His body was black and blue from repeated blows. The victim's sister testified she saw the defendant, a 30 year old man, 6'2" tall, weighing 300 pounds, repeatedly strike the victim in the stomach and back with his fist. One time he choked the child.

The majority is saying that as a matter of law a parent cannot be guilty of intentionally killing a child by such deliberate acts. Why not? Is it because it is inconceivable to rational people that a parent would intend to kill his own child? Evidently, this is the majority's conclusion, because they hold the intention of Midgett was to keep him alive for further abuse, not kill him. How does the majority know that? How do we ever know the actual or subliminal intent of a defendant? "If the *act* appellant intended was criminal, then the law holds him accountable, even though such *result* was not intended." *Hankins v. State*, 206 Ark. 881, 178 S.W.2d 56 (1944); *see also Black v. State*, 215 Ark. 618, 222 S.W.2d 816 (1949). There is no difference so far as the law is concerned in this case than in any other murder case. It is simply a question of proof. This parent killed his own child, and the majority cannot accept the fact that he intended to do just that.

Undoubtedly, the majority could accept it if the child were murdered with a bullet or a knife; but they cannot accept the fact, and it is a fact, that this defendant beat and starved his own child to death. His course of conduct could not have been negligent or unintentional.

Other states have not hesitated to uphold a conviction for first degree murder in such cases. *Morris v. State*, 270 Ind. 245, 384 N.E.2d 1022 (1979); *Lindsey v. State*, 501 S.W.2d 647 (Tex.1973). The fact that some states (California and Idaho) have passed a murder by torture statute is irrelevant. Those statutes may make it easier to prosecute child murderers, but they do not replace or intend to replace the law of murder. Whether murder exists is a question of the facts—not the method. The majority spends a good deal of effort laboring over the words "premeditation and deliberation," ignoring what the defendant did. Oliver Wendell Holmes said: "We must think things not words . . ." Holmes, "Law in Science and Science in Law," *Collected Legal Papers*, p. 238 (1921). If what Midgett did was deliberate and intentional, and that is not disputed, and he killed the child, a jury can find first degree murder.

I cannot fathom how this father could have done what he did; but it is not my place to sit in judgment of his mental state, nor allow my human feelings to color my judgment of his accountability to the law. The law has an objective standard of accountability for all who take human life. If one does certain acts and the result is murder, one must pay. The jury found Midgett guilty and, according to the law, there is substantial evidence to support that verdict. That should end the matter for us. He is guilty of first degree murder in the eyes of the law. His moral crime as a father is another matter, and it is not for us to speculate why he did it.

I would affirm the judgment.

HAYS and GLAZE, JJ., join in the dissent.

Notes and Questions

1. The idea that this crime is not among the most serious forms of homicide probably does not sit well with many students reading this opinion. The Arkansas Legislature was also not comfortable with this decision. It modified its statute to make death by child abuse a form of first-degree murder. One month after the *Midgett* decision the Arkansas Legislature modified its first-degree statute to include "knowingly causing the death of a person age fourteen or younger under circumstances manifesting cruel and malicious indifference to the value of human life." *See Davis v. State,* S.W.2d 768, 773 (Ark. 1996).

2. Is the issue in this case as simple as the majority suggests? Repeated blows in the middle of a bar fight may not suggest anything about the defendant's decision to kill, but can the same thing be said about repeated blows to a four year old child? Is there not something more than the repeated blows in this case that casts light on the mental state of Ronnie Midgett? We draw certain inferences from a defendant's conduct. If he points a loaded gun at a person's face and pulls the trigger, it is hard to conclude that he did not contemplate the death he brought about. How can we conclude that Ronnie Midgett did not also intend the natural and probable consequence of such a severe beating?

PRACTICE EXERCISE

Read the following set of facts, then read the instructions.

Cyla's testimony to be presented at trial:

Amberleigh offered to drive her three friends to the mountains that weekend, to enjoy some skiing and tobogganing after a week of snow had made conditions "perfect." Amberleigh borrowed her parent's mini-van, and shuttled her three friends up to the mountains. The conversation was light and optimistic en route: school was almost over for the semester, the day was completely open for whatever they felt like doing, and the scenery was "magical." The conversation was littered with the usual jokes and jabs about old relationships and break-ups, but the four were good friends and "took it in stride."

Amberleigh did not "take it in stride." She resented the fact that her love interest Bronson had invited a mutual friend, Cyla, who Amberleigh perceived as a threat to her chances of being with Bronson. But Amberleigh appeared to bury her resentments and tried to have a good time. After hours on the slopes, hanging out at the lodge and drinking too much beer, the weather turned. Despite feeling tired and woozy, Amberleigh told everyone, "Saddle up. I don't want to get stuck up here when the roads freeze over." The four piled into the van.

As they were descending the mountain, "the snow started to fall fast and heavy. And it dropped twenty degrees in some places, where the sun had not shown on that side of the mountain all day." Amberleigh drove very cautiously, especially when they hit black ice (a thin sheet of near-invisible ice that can form on roadways during cold, wet conditions).

"But this is where it gets weird." Just before a hairpin turn on the mountainside, Amberleigh slowed the vehicle almost to a stop, unbuckled her seatbelt, stepped out of the van, and slammed her driver's door shut. The van rolled forward "because it was in 'drive,'" missed the guardrail by inches, and plummeted off the mountainside into a ravine two hundred feet below. Cyla alone survived. Bronson and Ella died of their injuries.

Instructions:

You are Amberleigh's defense attorney. Using California Penal Code Sections 187 and 189 (p. 627), and California's *Elliot* standard (p. 597), for delineating deliberate from non-deliberate killings, draft a jury instruction using the facts. Consider: balance your goal of reducing your client's liability against producing an instruction that is reasonable enough to be adopted and withstand appellate review.

ii. Felony Murder

Many states recognize a type of homicide known as felony murder. Under this doctrine, a very severe version of homicide liability attaches if a death occurs when the defendant is engaging in conduct that is defined as a felony.

The felony murder doctrine is heavily criticized because even without the felony murder rule, the underlying felony is punishable and the defendant is punishable for the homicide depending on his mental state in the killing. Those felons who manage to commit their crimes without anyone dying are thus punished only for a non-lethal felony. Those unlucky felons, whose felonious activities lead to the death of others, are punished for a very serious degree of homicide, even if the defendants were merely negligent in causing the death.

The felony murder rule is justified on utilitarian grounds. If felons are aware that they are strictly liable for deaths that occur during their crimes, they will be more careful during their crimes. Of course we would prefer that people not engage in felonies in the first place—and the felony murder rule imposes extraordinary liability (in many cases a life sentence, in some states a potential death sentence) on those, who by virtue of little more than chance, have killed during the commission of their crimes.

As you might imagine, there are a number of issues that come up with the felony murder rule that are resolved differently in various jurisdictions. We consider some of these issues below.

(a) Is Felony Murder a Fair Way to Punish?

Rarely do courts second-guess the decisions made by legislatures about how to punish. As you saw in our consideration of strict liability offenses, when courts are considering ambiguous circumstances, they look at equitable considerations to determine what a reasonable legislature must have meant. In the *Armstrong* case that follows, the legislature's intent to have a felony murder rule that applied to the facts of the defendant's case was unmistakably clear. The defendant was therefore left with an argument that was statistically much less successful—he is left to argue that the scheme the legislature created violates the United States Constitution and/or the Washington Constitution. Do not become too bogged down in the discussion about the levels of scrutiny that apply to various types of constitutional challenges, but focus instead on the types of arguments the defendant made against the felony murder rule. Understand that these types of arguments are considerably more successful when used to argue that the statute the legislature created should be interpreted to extend to the facts of the defendant's case—but this type of argument requires that the statute have some ambiguity that requires judicial interpretation.

State v. Armstrong

Court of Appeals of Washington
178 P.3d 1048 (2008)

COX, J.

Anthony T. Armstrong appeals his conviction of second degree felony murder based on the predicate felony of second degree assault. He claims the conviction violates his right to equal protection under the state and federal constitutions.

Those convicted of second degree felony murder under the current version of RCW 9A.32.050 do not constitute a suspect or semisuspect class.[1] Moreover, physical liberty is an important, but not a fundamental right.[2] Accordingly, the proper standard of review here is rational basis review.[3] Applying that standard to the felony murder statute that is at issue in this case, we hold that the statute does not violate the constitutional right to equal protection. We affirm.

A brief statement of relevant facts provides the context for our resolution of the legal question whether the felony murder statute violates the right to equal protection. Testimony at trial indicated that Armstrong shot the victim, Mychal Alexander, following a physical altercation between the two near a Seattle playground area. Alexander was on the ground at the time of the shooting.

Armstrong claimed self-defense. He based his defense on the assertion that he believed that Alexander was also armed and was going to shoot first. Alexander died from gunshot wounds shortly after the altercation with Armstrong.

The State charged Armstrong with second degree murder, alleging both means under the current version of the statute, RCW 9A.32.050(1)(a) and (b). Specifically, the State charged intentional murder under one subsection of the statute.[4] It also charged felony murder based on the predicate crime of second degree assault under the other subsection of the statute.[5] The assault allegation

---

1   See *State v. Manussier*, 129 Wash.2d 652, 673 & n. 79, 921 P.2d 473 (1996).

2   *Id.* at 673–74 & n. 77, 921 P.2d 473.

3   See *id.* at 674, 921 P.2d 473 (citing *State v. Phelan*, 100 Wash.2d 508, 514, 671 P.2d 1212 (1983), *superseded by statute on other grounds by* RCW 9.94A.728).

4   See RCW 9A.32.050(1)(a) ("A person is guilty of murder in the second degree when: With intent to cause the death of another person but without premeditation, he or she causes the death of such person or of a third person. . . .").

5   See RCW 9A.32.050(1)(b) ("A person is guilty of murder in the second degree when: He or she commits or attempts to commit any felony, including assault, other than those enumerated in RCW 9A.32.030(1)(c), and, in the course of and in furtherance of such crime or in immediate flight therefrom, he or she, or another participant, causes the death of a person other than one of the participants. . . .").

was based on the assertion that Armstrong was armed with a deadly weapon during the shooting.

During trial, the court instructed the jury that it need not be unanimous as to which of the two alternative means of second degree murder Armstrong committed in order to find him guilty. The jury found him guilty of second degree murder and also found that he was armed with a deadly weapon during the commission of the crime. The trial judge sentenced him to 183 months of confinement, the low end of the standard range, plus a mandatory deadly weapon enhancement.

Armstrong appeals.

Equal Protection And Felony Murder

Armstrong argues that the felony murder statute violates his right to equal protection. We disagree.

Article I, section 12 of the Washington Constitution and the Fourteenth Amendment to the United States Constitution guarantee that similarly situated persons must receive like treatment under the law.[6] Our supreme court has consistently construed the federal and state equal protection clauses identically and considered claims arising under them to be one issue.[7]

When courts analyze equal protection claims, they apply one of three standards of review—strict scrutiny, intermediate or heightened scrutiny, or rational basis review.[8] Rational basis review, or the rational relationship test, is the most relaxed level of scrutiny. It applies when a statutory classification does not involve a suspect or semisuspect class and does not threaten a fundamental right.[9]

When a statutory classification only affects a physical liberty interest, our courts apply the deferential rational relationship test.[10] To satisfy this test, the challenged law must rest upon a legitimate state objective, and the law must be rationally related to, and not wholly irrelevant to, achieving that objective.[11] As our state supreme court has explained:

> "The burden is on the party challenging the classification to show that it is 'purely arbitrary'." The rational basis test requires only that the means

---

6   *Manussier*, 129 Wash.2d at 672, 921 P.2d 473 (citing *State v. Schaaf*, 109 Wash.2d 1, 17, 743 P.2d 240 (1987)).

7   *Id.* (citing *State v. Smith*, 117 Wash.2d 263, 281, 814 P.2d 652 (1991)).

8   *Id.* at 672–73, 921 P.2d 473.

9   *Id.* at 673, 921 P.2d 473 (citing *State v. Shawn P.*, 122 Wash.2d 553, 560, 859 P.2d 1220 (1993)).

10   *State v. Coria*, 120 Wash.2d 156, 171, 839 P.2d 890 (1992) (rejecting intermediate scrutiny when physical liberty interest is involved, but no semisuspect class is affected).

11   *Madison v. State*, 161 Wash.2d 85, 103, 163 P.3d 757 (2007); *Manussier*, 129 Wash.2d at 673, 921 P.2d 473; *Coria*, 120 Wash.2d at 171, 839 P.2d 890.

employed by the statute be rationally related to a legitimate State goal, and not that the means be the best way of achieving that goal. "[T]he Legislature has broad discretion to determine what the public interest demands and what measures are necessary to secure and protect that interest."[12]

* * *

The essence of Armstrong's argument is that it is unfair and overly harsh to punish equally for two crimes, felony murder and intentional murder. This is an argument grounded on whether the felony murder statute makes sound policy. That question is better directed to the legislature, which has consistently rejected this policy argument in adhering to Washington's retention of the felony murder rule.

Armstrong also expresses concern that even negligent assaults can now lead to convictions for second-degree murder.[32] Again, this is a policy choice better directed to the legislature, not this court.

Armstrong further argues that he was disadvantaged in this case. He argues that the jury would have had to deadlock or acquit on both alternative means of murder before being allowed to consider a lesser included instruction of manslaughter for the charge of intentional murder. Armstrong contends that a prosecutor's ability to charge both alternative means of intentional murder and felony murder-assault in a given case proves that the decision is arbitrary. We disagree.

In this case, the prosecutor charged both alternatives of second degree murder. That the facts in this case and others arguably support more than one alternative means of committing the crime does not make the distinction in this statute arbitrary. If the State believes sufficient evidence supports charging both means, it may do so without offending the constitution. And, as the supreme court held in *Wanrow*, the State's ability to charge in this way does not fall within the prohibited category of improper purposes that the court identified in that case.

Armstrong heavily relies on the supreme court's opinion in *Andress*[33] to support his equal protection arguments in this case. That reliance is misplaced.

There, the supreme court concluded that the legislature did not intend to include assault as a predicate for felony murder.[34] Accordingly, it granted the personal restraint petition and reversed the conviction of second degree felony

---

12   *Manussier*, 129 Wash.2d at 673, 921 P.2d 473 (quoting *Coria*, 120 Wash.2d at 171–73, 839 P.2d 890; *State v. Ward*, 123 Wash.2d 488, 516, 869 P.2d 1062 (1994)) (internal footnotes omitted).

32   Appellant's Brief at 22 (citing *Tamalini*, 134 Wash.2d at 746 n. 17, 953 P.2d 450 (Sanders, J., dissenting)).

33   147 Wash.2d 602, 56 P.3d 981.

34   *Id.* at 616, 56 P.3d 981.

murder in that case. *Andress* is of little or no value in resolving the constitutional question now before us.

First, as the *Andress* majority expressly noted in its opinion, it did not reach any of the constitutional challenges advanced by the petitioner in that case, deciding the matter on statutory grounds only.[35] Thus, the case simply did not address whether the former version of the felony murder statute violated equal protection.

Second, the legislature expressly rejected the *Andress* court's legislative intent analysis, subsequently amending the felony murder statute to expressly include assault as a predicate offense to felony murder.[36] The *Andress* opinion, then, represents nothing more than the supreme court's then view that assault should not qualify as a predicate felony for felony murder. Given the legislature's rejection of the supreme court's view, we see nothing in the analysis in *Andress* to assist us in the case now before us.

We affirm the judgment and sentence.

Notes and Questions

1. Is Anthony Armstrong wrong? Without the felony murder statute, the prosecutor in this case would have had to demonstrate that Armstrong intended to kill to achieve this sentence. By using the felony murder statute, however, the prosecutor was only required to show that Armstrong intended to *assault* his victim and that death followed. A killing will almost always involve an assault (i.e., an unwanted touching), except in those type of homicides involving culpable omissions. Does the court's decision in *Armstrong* not effectively change the *mens rea* for murder in Washington from intent to kill to intent to assault?

2. Notice the court says that the defendant is inappropriately relying on the *Andress* case in which the court appears to have considered similar reasoning to find that an assault was not an appropriate predicate felony for felony murder. Following the *Andress* decision, the Washington Legislature made clear that the state supreme court had misinterpreted its intent. You will consider this issue much more thoroughly in Constitutional Law, but given the strength of the argument Anthony Armstrong makes, does it make sense that the legislature would get the final word on this question so long as it clear in its intent?

---

35 *Id.* at 605, 56 P.3d 981.

36 RCW 9A.32.050(1)(b); Laws of 2003, ch. 3, § 1.

(b) Inherently Dangerous Felonies

There is language in cases suggesting that the felony murder rule is justified by one of two different policies—deterring would-be criminals from engaging in crimes that take lives or encouraging criminals engaging in felonies to take care to make sure that death does not occur during their crimes. At the same time, it is frequently recognized that the felony murder rule is problematic in that it severely punishes a defendant for a death for which he may have had minimal, or in some cases no culpability. As a result of the severe penalties that this statute mandates—that will be imposed on the unfortunate and the malicious alike—courts have limited the application of the rule. A majority of jurisdictions limit the felonies that can be a predicate to a felony murder conviction to felonies that are inherently dangerous, those that in the ordinary course of events pose a threat to life. *Anderson* considers the question of whether a shooting by a felon in possession of a weapon, which is itself a felony, occurs during an inherently dangerous felony. The argument in this case should remind you of the argument in *Staples* (p. 30), where the Supreme Court considered whether possession of a semi-automatic weapon was sufficiently dangerous that its owner should be on notice about the risk that it has been converted to an automatic weapon. At its core, this case turns on one's view of how dangerous guns themselves are.

State v. Anderson

Supreme Court of Minnesota
666 N.W.2d 696 (2003)

BLATZ, Chief Justice.

In this pretrial appeal, appellant Jerrett Lee Anderson challenges the court of appeals' decision reversing the district court's dismissal of the charge of unintentional second-degree felony murder for lack of probable cause. Anderson argues that, when the second-degree felony-murder statute is read in conjunction with our prior holdings, the court of appeals' decision must be reversed. We agree and hold that the predicate offenses of felon in possession of a firearm[1] and possession of a stolen firearm cannot support the charge of unintentional second-degree felony murder.

---

1   Minnesota Statutes section 624.713, which defines this offense, is entitled "Certain Persons Not to Have Pistols or Semiautomatic Military-Style Assault Weapons." For ease of reference we will adopt the parties' description of this offense for the purposes of this opinion.

The facts giving rise to this appeal are not in dispute. On February 26, 2002, Jerrett Lee Anderson arrived at Blake Rogers' residence in Minneapolis and, at about 10:45 p.m., joined Rogers and a friend of Rogers in Rogers' bedroom. While there, Anderson showed them a 12-gauge shotgun, which was missing its rifle stock, and stated that the shotgun had been stolen. Rogers' friend handled the shotgun, and all three noticed that the shotgun was loaded. As the shotgun was returned to Anderson, Rogers was kneeling in front of his stereo system, inserting compact discs. Anderson then pointed the shotgun at Rogers, and it discharged, killing Rogers. Anderson and Rogers' friend fled the residence.

Anderson was charged with second-degree unintentional felony murder, in violation of Minn.Stat. § 609.19, subd. 2(1) (2002), and third-degree murder ("depraved mind" killing), in violation of Minn.Stat. § 609.195(a) (2002). The district court dismissed the second-degree felony-murder charge, ruling that felon in possession of a firearm and possession of a stolen firearm are not proper predicate offenses for second-degree felony murder.

The state appealed under Minn. R.Crim. P. 28.04, subd. 1, which permits appeals from pretrial orders of the trial court. In a 2-1 decision, the court of appeals concluded that possession of a loaded, stockless shotgun pointed at the victim was inherently dangerous. *State v. Anderson*, 654 N.W.2d 367, 372 (Minn.App.2002). Accordingly, the court of appeals held that the district court erred in dismissing the second-degree felony-murder charge. *Id.* The dissenting judge argued that there is nothing inherently dangerous about the two predicate unlawful firearm possession offenses. *Id.* at 373. Viewing the majority holding as an unwarranted extension of the felony-murder doctrine to "status" offenses,[2] the dissenting judge explained that she "would [have affirmed] the trial court's pretrial order dismissing the unintentional murder in the second-degree (felony-murder) charge on the grounds that the 'status' offenses of unlawful possession of a firearm and possession of a stolen firearm cannot serve as predicate offenses to felony-murder." *Id.* at 372, 375. It is from this court of appeals' decision that Anderson appeals.

The single issue presented by this case is whether the offenses of felon in possession of a firearm and possession of a stolen firearm are proper predicate offenses for a charge of unintentional second-degree felony murder. This issue is a question of law, subject to de novo review. *Frost-Benco Elec. Ass'n v. Minnesota Pub. Utils. Comm'n*, 358 N.W.2d 639, 642 (Minn.1984). Whether a statute has been properly construed is also a question of law, reviewed de novo. *State v. Stevenson*, 656 N.W.2d 235, 238 (Minn.2003).

---

2   The dissenting judge explained that "each of these offenses is *malum prohibitum*-a crime because it is prohibited by statute-rather than *malum in se*-an inherently immoral act." *Anderson*, 654 N.W.2d at 373.

We begin with the statutory provisions at issue. The felon-in-possession statute provides that a person who has been adjudicated delinquent of a crime of violence shall not be entitled to possess a firearm for 10 years following restoration of civil rights or expiration of his or her sentence, and a violator is subject to a penalty of up to 15 years imprisonment or a $30,000 penalty, or both.[3] Minn. Stat. § 624.713, subds. 1(b), 2 (2002). Similarly, the receiving stolen property statute provides that the offense of possession of a stolen firearm is subject to up to 20 years confinement or a fine of $100,000, or both. Minn.Stat. §§ 609.53, subd. 1 (2002); 609.52, subd. 3(1) (2002). The second-degree felony-murder statute, under which Anderson was charged, provides that a person who "causes the death of a human being, without intent to effect the death of any person, while committing or attempting to commit a felony offense other than criminal sexual conduct in the first or second degree with force or violence or a drive-by shooting" may be sentenced to imprisonment for not more than forty years. Minn.Stat. § 609.19, subd. 2(1). This statutory provision does not define what constitutes "a felony offense."

To understand the felony-murder statute, it is helpful to review the historical backdrop surrounding its enactment as well as our case law. To begin, Minnesota's second-degree felony-murder statute codifies the common law felony-murder rule: "'if one intends to do another felony, and undesignedly kills a man, this is also murder.'" Rudolph J. Gerber, *The Felony Murder Rule: Conundrum Without Principle*, 31 Ariz. St. L.J. 763, 765 (1999) (quoting Sir William Blackstone, *Commentaries on the Laws of England* 947 (George Chase ed., 4th ed. 1938)). Viewed in historical context, the common law felony-murder rule, though stated broadly, was limited in scope and consequence because there were few felonies[4] at common law-all were *malam in se*[5] and most were life-endangering-and because all were punishable by death. James J. Tomkovicz, *The Endurance of the Felony-Murder Rule: A Study of the Forces that Shape Our Criminal Law*, 51 Wash. & Lee L.Rev. 1429, 1445-46 (1994). As a result, application of the felony-murder rule at common law was consistent with the requirement of mens rea because the malice required for murder could be imputed from

---

3   In 1998, Anderson was adjudicated delinquent for the crime of riot in the second degree, a "crime of violence" pursuant to Minn.Stat. § 624.712, subd. 5 (2002). It is a felony for one who is adjudicated delinquent of a crime of violence to possess a firearm. Minn.Stat. § 624.713, subds. 1(b), 2.

4   The felonies that traditionally supported a felony-murder conviction were: "homicide, mayhem, rape, arson, robbery, burglary, larceny, prison breach, and rescue of a felon." *State v. Aarsvold*, 376 N.W.2d 518, 521 (Minn. App.1985).

5   *Malum in se* means "a wrong in itself[.] * * * An act is said to be *malum in se* when it is inherently and essentially evil, that is, immoral in its nature and injurious in its consequences, without any regard to the fact of its being noticed or punished by the law of the state." *Black's Law Dictionary* 959 (6th ed. 1990). In comparison, *malum prohibitum* means "a thing which is wrong *because* [it is] prohibited; an act which is not inherentlyimmoral, but becomes so because its commission is expressly forbidden by positive law." *Id.* at 960.

the wrongful mental attitude for the predicate felony, and "it made little differ-
ence whether the felon was hanged for the felony or for the murder." 2 Wayne R.
LaFave & Austin W. Scott, Jr., *Substantive Criminal Law* § 7.5, at 207 n. 4 (1986);
State v. Branson, 487 N.W.2d 880, 881 (Minn.1992).

More recently, because the number of felonies has increased and many
comparatively minor offenses are classified as felonies, malice is imputed from
crimes that are much less severe than murder. *Branson,* 487 N.W.2d at 882. For
this reason, many courts have judicially limited the application of the doctrine
so that not every felony offense serves as a predicate felony for a felony-murder
charge. *Id.; see also* 2 LaFave & Scott, Jr., *supra,* § 7.5, at 206-11.

In Minnesota, prior to 1981, predicate felonies for felony murder were
those felonies "committed upon or affecting the person whose death was
caused." 40 Minn.Stat. Ann. § 609.195 at 333, 1963 advisory committee cmt.
(West 2003). This language limited the application of the felony-murder statute
so that "a purely property crime would not fall within the clause [as a proper
predicate felony]." *Id.* In *State v. Nunn,* we stated that the justification for this
limitation was to "isolate for special treatment those felonies that involve some
special danger to human life." 297 N.W.2d 752, 753 (Minn.1980). Accordingly,
district courts were to determine whether an offense involved a special danger
to human life by examining the offense in the abstract together with the facts
of the particular case, including the circumstances in which the felony was
committed. *Id.* at 754.

In 1981, the legislature amended Minnesota's felony-murder statute, increasing the severity of the offense from third-degree murder to second-degree murder and deleting the limiting language, "a felony upon or affecting the person
whose death was caused." Act of May 19, 1981, ch. 227, §§ 10 and 11, 1981 Minn.
Laws 1006, 1010 (amending Minn.Stat. §§ 609.19, 609.195 (1980) and codified
at Minn.Stat. § 609.19, subd. 2 (1982)). In *State v. Back,* decided after the 1981
amendment was adopted, we held that even a property offense can be used as an
underlying felony *when a special danger to human life is present.* 341 N.W.2d 273,
276-77 (Minn.1983). In essence, in interpreting the 1981 statutory amendment,
we concluded that the possible universe of predicate offenses was expanded to
include property offenses but that the previous limitation—that "a special danger
to human life" be present—was not abandoned.

In recent years, Minnesota courts have continued to consider both the elements of the predicate felony in the abstract and the totality of the circumstances
in determining whether the predicate felony involves a special danger to human
life. *See State v. Cole,* 542 N.W.2d 43, 53 (Minn.1996) ("When determining if the
underlying felony involves a special danger to life, we not only consider the elements of the underlying felony in the abstract, but also the facts of the particular

case and the circumstances under which the felony was committed."). In *Cole*, we concluded a special danger to human life existed where the defendant, armed with a loaded gun, entered a department store to exchange stolen goods for cash. *Id*. at 46, 53. To avoid arrest for the felony theft charge, the defendant shot and killed a police officer. *Id*. at 47. We determined that both the property crime of theft and the second-degree assault were proper predicate offenses because "the circumstances of this case clearly demonstrate that special danger existed." *Id*. at 53. Furthermore, we noted that the assault itself was a proper predicate felony to a felony-murder conviction because assault is not a property crime but a crime against the person. *Id*.

In the instant case, the state argues that Anderson's felon-in-possession and possession of a stolen firearm offenses support a charge of felony murder. In support of its position, the state first contends that under the plain meaning of the second-degree felony-murder statute, any felony, except those expressly excluded by the statute, can serve as a predicate felony.

The plain language of the second-degree felony-murder statute punishes perpetrators of all unintentional deaths caused during the commission of "a felony," with the exception of crimes that are predicates for first-degree murder:

> Whoever does * * * the following is guilty of unintentional murder in the second degree and may be sentenced to imprisonment for not more than 40 years:

> (1) causes the death of a human being, without intent to effect the death of any person, while committing or attempting to commit a felony offense other than criminal sexual conduct in the first or second degree with force or violence or a drive-by shooting * * *.

Minn.Stat. § 609.19, subd. 2(1). Admittedly, under its plain language, except for the three specified exceptions, the statute appears to apply to all other felonies. *In re Welfare of M.D.S.*, 345 N.W.2d 723, 729 (Minn.1984).

However, this interpretation ignores the history of our court's judicial limitation of the felony-murder rule as set forth in precedent. We have recognized that when the legislature does not amend our construction of a statute, the court's construction stands. *Western Union Telegraph Co. v. Spaeth*, 232 Minn. 128, 131-32, 44 N.W.2d 440, 441-42 (Minn.1950) ("The 'judicial construction of a statute, so long as it is unreversed, is as much a part thereof as if it had been written into it originally'" and quoting 6 Dunnell, Dig. & Supp. § 8936b); *see also* Minn.Stat. § 645.17 (2002) (providing that "when a court of last resort has construed the language of a law, the legislature in subsequent laws on the same subject matter intends the same construction to be placed upon such language").

Therefore, our post-1981 case law, read in conjunction with the statutory language, is dispositive.

In 1980-before the 1981 amendment-we adopted the "special danger to human life" standard which, in Minnesota, requires consideration of the elements of the underlying felony in the abstract *and* the circumstances under which the felony was committed.[6] *Nunn,* 297 N.W.2d at 753-54. Post-amendment, in 1983 and 1996 respectively, we decided *Back,* 341 N.W.2d 273, and *Cole,* 542 N.W.2d 43. *See also M.D.S.,* 345 N.W.2d at 729-30 (citing, in 1984, *Nunn's* special danger to human life standard). In *Back,* we cited *Nunn's* special danger to human life standard and recognized that if a property offense involved special danger to human life, it could support a felony-murder conviction. *Back,* 341 N.W.2d at 277. Our court advanced *Nunn* again in *Cole* by rejecting Cole's argument that the district court had mistakenly relied upon *Back. Cole,* 542 N.W.2d at 52. In concluding that felony theft and second-degree assault were proper predicate felonies for second-degree felony murder, we noted that the special danger standard requires consideration not only of "the elements of the underlying felony in the abstract, but also the facts of the particular case and the circumstances under which the felony was committed." *Id.* at 53. In summary, our post-1981 cases consistently have recognized *Nunn's* special danger to human life two-part standard to limit the application of the felony-murder rule in Minnesota, and the legislature has not legislated otherwise.[7]

Applying the statute as previously interpreted by us to this record, we conclude that the predicate offenses of felon in possession of a firearm and possession of a stolen firearm are not inherently dangerous. While the use of a firearm can pose significant danger to human life, simple possession-standing alone-does not. In other words, there is nothing about a felon's possession of a firearm, or of a stolen firearm—in the abstract—that in and of itself involves a special danger to human life. As the district court below explained:

---

6   We reject the state's argument that the standard to determine whether an underlying felony can support a charge of second-degree felony murder is a one-part inquiry-whether the offense involves a special danger to human life *as committed*. Minnesota's special danger to human life standard is not merely a totality of the circumstances standard but rather a two-part inquiry into the inherent danger of the offense *and* the danger of the offense as committed. Looking only at the circumstances of a particular case-i.e. the facts-would eviscerate the special danger to human life standard because the predicate offense would always be found to have been committed in a particularly dangerous manner if a death occurs.

7   Contrary to the implications set forth in the dissent, we are not writing on a clean slate. We cannot, and should not, ignore our precedent interpreting Minnesota's felony-murder statute in order to render an opinion reaching a different result. While in the future the legislature may choose to amend the statute to clarify or to change the statute's reach, the fact remains that, to date, despite our existing precedent interpreting the statute, it has not.

While a felon in possession of a firearm or stolen firearm creates a dangerous situation, there is a material distinction between the level of imminency and probability of the special danger to human life in that situation than
in a situation involving the traditional felony predicates. The predicate
felony in this case does not require an act of violence in carrying out the
crime. Nor can it be persuasively argued that death would be the natural
and probable consequence of the Defendant's conduct in carrying out the
predicate offense.

Because felon in possession of a firearm and possession of a stolen firearm are
not dangerous in the abstract, these predicate felonies fail the special danger to
human life standard. Accordingly, we hold that the predicate offenses of felon
in possession of a firearm and possession of a stolen firearm cannot support the
charge of unintentional second-degree felony murder.[8]

Reversed.

GILBERT, Justice (dissenting).

I respectfully dissent from the majority opinion and would affirm the court
of appeals. The majority adopts the reasoning of the dissenting judge in the court
of appeals panel, which would have affirmed a district court's dismissal of this
charge. The district court dismissed this charge in part because, in its reasoning,
"[t]he felony offense of felon in possession is more akin to the criminalization of
the status of a person, namely, one who is a felon and who possesses a firearm or
stolen firearm. Such felony offense is *malum prohibitum* as opposed to *malum in
se*." The majority wisely avoids adopting the status offense rationale of the district
court but still appears to be intrigued by the district court's reasoning. Rather
than reverting to an exercise in Latin, we should deal with the realities of this
situation, including the clear intent of the legislature.

The majority acknowledges that the appellant was a felon in possession of a
firearm, in fact a stolen firearm. This firearm happened to be a loaded, shortened
12-gauge shotgun. *See* Minn.Stat. § 609.67, subd. 1(c) (2002). Furthermore, this
appellant had already been adjudicated a delinquent of riot in the second degree,
which is a crime of violence under Minn.Stat. § 624.712, subd. 5 (2002). It also
appears to be undisputed that the appellant pointed the shotgun at the victim, it
discharged, and Rogers was shot in the head.

The majority candidly admits that "under its plain language, except for
the three specified exceptions, the statute appears to apply to all other felonies."

---

8   Because we reverse on these grounds, we do not reach Anderson's argument that the court of appeals should
be reversed because the required causal relationship between the predicate offense and the resulting death is lacking.

Accordingly, the majority concedes that the felon in possession statute and felon in possession of stolen goods are predicate acts under Minn.Stat. § 609.19, subd. 2(1) (2002). The majority then holds, "we conclude that the predicate offenses of felon in possession of a firearm and possession of a stolen firearm are not inherently dangerous." I disagree. This case involves exactly the inherently dangerous situation the legislature envisioned.

The appellant had already been adjudicated delinquent of a crime of violence. The majority summarily concludes that "there is nothing about a felon's possession of a firearm, or of a stolen firearm-in the abstract-that in and of itself involves a special danger to human life." First of all, we should not decide this case in the abstract. Second, we must recognize that a felon in possession of a firearm is not one of those "many comparatively minor offenses [that] are classified as felonies" noted by the majority. The legislature has determined that felons and firearms are not a good mix. Likewise, the crime of riot in the second degree is a serious crime of violence, which had been recently committed by appellant. Now, the appellant has not only been adjudicated delinquent, but also acts to possess a stolen gun, which is loaded and had been shortened. Shortly upon entering the house of the victim, this gun, which the appellant was feloniously possessing, was pointed at the victim and used to shoot him in the head. Possession of a loaded gun in these circumstances is indeed the type of felony that is inherently dangerous and represents a special danger to human life. As the majority states, "we noted that the special danger standard requires consideration not only of 'the elements of the underlying felony in the abstract, but also the facts of the particular case and the circumstances under which the felony was committed.'" (quoting *State v. Cole*, 542 N.W.2d 43, 53 (Minn.1996)). While I agree with the majority that we must be careful in the application of the felony murder doctrine so that not every felony offense serves as a predicate felony for a felony-murder charge, the legislature wisely included the felonies in issue here within the felony-murder statute.

The majority casts away the clear legislative directive of this enhanced crime by summarily concluding that the offenses of felon in possession of a firearm and possession of a stolen firearm are not felonies sufficiently dangerous to support a felony-murder conviction. The majority opinion effectively amends the statute and discounts the legislative process's recognition of the obvious inherent danger of convicted felons possessing firearms. This is precisely the especially dangerous situation that the legislature may have anticipated in expanding the felony-murder statute to include all but a few designated felonies under this statute. The dangerous combination of a felon and an illegally possessed gun made it possible for the most serious of felonies to be committed; that of wrongfully taking an individual's life.

Notes and Questions

1. As noted earlier, judicial disagreement about whether the crime of being a felon in possession is an inherently dangerous felony should remind you of the discussion in *United States v. Staples*. In *Staples*, the Supreme Court Justices' view of the appropriateness of a strict liability offense for possessing a machine gun appeared to track their general views of the Second Amendment. Would you guess the justices in the majority of *Anderson* generally align with gun control advocates while those in the dissent would typically align with gun rights advocates? Are there reasons to think this might not be case? Imagine you were employed by the National Rifle Association as legal counsel and asked to write a memo on the position that organization ought to take in the *Anderson* case as it was pending before the Minnesota Supreme Court. What would you recommend and why?

2. States are split on whether a court should look just to the elements of an offense, or the circumstances of the commission of the offense to determine whether the felony is inherently dangerous. Consider the breadth of the felony murder rule when the felony is not required to be dangerous in the abstract. In *People v. Phillips*, 414 P.2d 353 (Cal. 1966), the California Supreme Court ruled that a chiropractor, who convinced a family to withdraw traditional medical treatment for their daughter diagnosed with cancer, could be convicted of felony murder when he convinced the family to instead pay for his alternative treatment. The chiropractor's underlying felony was grand theft, the elements of which do not involve actions that threaten life. Of course the manner in which the defendant committed his theft in *Phillips* was not only dangerous to life, but highly offensive—it is hard to feel much sympathy for the defendant in *Phillips*. But doesn't the theory of liability in *Anderson* and *Phillips* extend the doctrine of felony murder to any death occurring during any felony?

———————————

(c) Must the Felony Be for an Act Other than the One Producing Death?

In the *Armstrong* case, the defendant's best argument was that the statute did not identify assault as a predicate felony giving rise to felony murder, but that argument had been foreclosed to him. The following case addresses the issue Anthony Armstrong would have preferred to have been able to argue. In the *Contreras* case that follows, the defendant was charged with felony murder as a death occurred in the course of a burglary he was committing. By way of background to this case, you need to know a bit about the crime of burglary, which we will study more in depth later. The version of it with which you are most familiar involves entry into a building for the purpose of stealing something in the building. Burglary actually criminalizes a much broader range of criminal conduct—it is defined most commonly as the entry into a building with the intention of committing a felony in the building. In *Contreras*, the prosecution established the burglary by showing that the defendant entered the building in question for the purpose of committing a battery on the victim whose death led to this prosecution. *Contreras* therefore asks whether felony murder be established by showing that the defendant carried out an action to assault the victim.

State v. Contreras

Supreme Court of Nevada
46 P.3d 661 (2002)

BECKER, J.

The State appeals from a district court pretrial order granting respondents' motion to dismiss a first-degree felony-murder charge. The district court dismissed that part of the information charging first-degree murder under the felony-murder rule. The district court held that a felony-murder charge is inappropriate when the underlying felony is a burglary committed with the intent to commit a battery. We reverse the district court order.

FACTS

This case arises out of an incident at the Roundhouse Motel in Carson City on August 23, 1998. Based on the limited record submitted, it appears that prior to the incident resulting in the charged crimes, respondent Evans was involved in a separate altercation at the motel. The police arrived and investigated that incident. Later that evening, apparently in retaliation for the previous altercation, respondent Evans allegedly gathered the other respondents, and they proceeded back to the motel with metal and wooden clubs. Respondents knocked on a motel room door, and when the door opened, rushed into the room and proceeded to beat Samuel Resendiz and Carlos Lainez. Resendiz died as a result of his injuries.

The State charged respondents with open murder with the use of a deadly weapon, battery with the use of a deadly weapon, burglary, and conspiracy to commit battery. One of the two specified alternatives in the open murder charge was first-degree felony murder. On this charge, the State alleged that the defendants:

> [D]id, acting in concert and by preexisting plan, willfully and unlawfully, with malice aforethought, kill and murder one SAMUEL RESENDIZ, a human being, *during the perpetration of a burglary, by entering a motel room with the intent then and there to apply force and violence with wooden or metal clubs and/or fists* against the person of some or all of the occupants therein.

(Emphasis added.) Respondents filed a motion to dismiss the first-degree felony-murder charge based on the merger doctrine. The district court granted respondents' motion to dismiss the felony-murder charge. The State appeals.

DISCUSSION

Nevada's statutory scheme has long recognized the felony-murder rule. NRS 200.030(1)(b) defines first-degree felony murder as a murder that is committed in the perpetration or attempted perpetration of certain enumerated crimes, including burglary. The felonious intent involved in the underlying felony is deemed, by law, to supply the malicious intent necessary to characterize the killing as a murder, and because felony murder is defined by statute as first-degree murder, no proof of the traditional factors of willfulness, premeditation, or deliberation is required for a first-degree murder conviction.

In this case, the prosecutor charged both traditional second-degree murder, requiring proof of malicious intent (without premeditation and deliberation), and first-degree felony murder, based on the allegation that the defendants entered the premises "with the intent then and there to apply force and violence" and thereby alleging the felony of burglary. The district court relied on the merger doctrine to dismiss the felony-murder charge, holding that the burglary merged into the homicide because both involved the same intent—the defendants' intent to apply force and violence to the victims.

In so holding, the district court relied on the California Supreme Court's decision in *People v. Wilson*.[3] In *Wilson*, the defendant was charged with felony murder based on burglary.[4] The burglary was alleged to have occurred when the defendant broke into his wife's home with the intent to assault her with a deadly weapon.[5] The California court stated:

> [T]he only basis for finding a felonious entry is the intent to commit an assault with a deadly weapon. When, as here, the entry would be nonfelonious but for the intent to commit the assault, and the assault is an integral

---

3   1 Cal.3d 431, 82 Cal.Rptr. 494, 462 P.2d 22 (1969).

4   *Id.* at 27.

5   *Id.*

part of the homicide and is included in fact in the offense charged, utilization of the felony-murder rule extends that doctrine "'beyond any rational function that it is designed to serve.'" We have heretofore emphasized "that the felony-murder doctrine expresses a highly artificial concept that deserves no extension beyond its required application."[6]

The California court concluded that the purpose of the felony-murder rule, to deter felons from killing negligently or accidentally, was not met when the underlying felony has the same general mental purpose as the homicide—to physically harm the victim.[7] Therefore, in *Wilson*, the California Supreme Court merged the two crimes and held that a felony-murder conviction was not appropriate because the intent in committing the burglary was the same as the intent in committing the homicide.[8]

The California Supreme Court's decision in *Wilson* was an extension of the merger doctrine as previously applied by California and other states. California and many other states have applied the merger doctrine as a limitation on felony murder when a prosecutor has attempted to charge felony murder based on a felonious assault or battery that culminates in a homicide.[9] In these cases, the courts have held that the battery merges into the homicide. Absent such merger, virtually every homicide would be felony murder, and the traditional factors of willfulness, premeditation and deliberation would never be required for a first-degree murder conviction.[10] This application of the merger doctrine has not been considered in Nevada because NRS 200.030(1)(b), the felony-murder statute, does not include assault or battery as crimes that support a felony-murder charge.

Not all courts, however, have followed California's approach in felony-murder cases based on burglary with intent to assault. For example, the New York Court of Appeals in *People v. Miller* held that any burglary, including one based on intent to assault, justifies application of the felony-murder rule.[11] The New York court's rationale was that homicide is more likely to result when the

---

6 *Id.* at 28 (quoting *People v. Phillips*, 64 Cal.2d 574, 51 Cal.Rptr. 225, 414 P.2d 353, 360 & n. 5 (1966) (quoting *People v. Washington*, 62 Cal.2d 777, 44 Cal.Rptr. 442, 402 P.2d 130, 134 (1965)), *overruled on other grounds by People v. Flood*, 18 Cal.4th 470, 76 Cal.Rptr.2d 180, 957 P.2d 869 (1998)).

7 *Id.*

8 *Id.* at 28–29.

9 Robert L. Simpson, Annotation, *Application of Felony–Murder Doctrine Where the Felony Relied upon Is an Includible Offense with the Homicide*, 40 A.L.R.3d 1341, 1345–46 (1971 & Supp.2001).

10 *See People v. Moran*, 246 N.Y. 100, 158 N.E. 35, 36 (1927).

11 32 N.Y.2d 157, 344 N.Y.S.2d 342, 297 N.E.2d 85, 87–88 (1973).

assault is committed within the victim's home rather than in the street, even if the criminal intent in both locations is the same.[12] The court stated:

> It should be apparent that the Legislature, in including burglary as one of the enumerated felonies as a basis for felony murder, recognized that persons within domiciles are in greater peril from those entering the domicile with criminal intent, than persons on the street who are being subjected to the same criminal intent. . . . When the assault takes place within the domicile, the victim may be more likely to resist the assault; the victim is also less likely to be able to avoid the consequences of the assault, since his paths of retreat and escape may be barred or severely restricted by furniture, walls and other obstructions incidental to buildings. Further, it is also more likely that when the assault occurs in the victim's domicile, there will be present family or close friends who will come to the victim's aid and be killed. Since the purpose of the felony-murder statute is to reduce the disproportionate number of accidental homicides which occur during the commission of the enumerated predicate felonies by punishing the party responsible for the homicide not merely for manslaughter, but for murder, the Legislature, in enacting the burglary and felony-murder statutes, did not exclude from the definition of burglary, a burglary based upon the intent to assault, but intended that the definition be "satisfied if the intruder's intent, existing at the time of the unlawful entry or remaining, is to commit *any crime*."[13]

* * *

Although Nevada's statutory scheme is basically the same as California's, and the purpose of the felony-murder statute has been stated to be the same,[16] we find the reasoning of the New York court on this issue more persuasive. The Nevada Legislature has specifically included burglary as one of the crimes that can escalate a homicide to first-degree murder without the necessity of proving premeditation and deliberation. There is a rational basis for including burglary in the felony-murder statute, even when the criminal intent behind the burglary is assault or battery. In *People v. Wilson*, the California court minimizes the impact of the location of an assault.[17] Yet the likelihood of harm to individuals

---

12   *Id.* at 87.

13   *Id.* at 87–89 (footnote and citations omitted).

16   *See Payne v. State*, 81 Nev. 503, 506, 406 P.2d 922, 924 (1965) (citing California law regarding the purpose of the felony-murder rule).

17   462 P.2d at 28.

is greater when they are encountered in a dwelling or an enclosed space where escape or outside intervention is less likely than if they are encountered on the street. In the instant case, it certainly appears that the attack in a motel room held greater risk of homicide for the victims than if they had been outside and better able to escape or receive help.

We do not believe it is appropriate to apply the merger doctrine to felony murder when the underlying felony is burglary, regardless of the intent of the burglary. The legislative language is clear, and we are not persuaded that any policy considerations should override the legislature's determination that burglary should be one of the enumerated felonies appropriate to elevate a homicide to felony murder. We, therefore, hold that the district court was incorrect in dismissing the felony-murder charge against the respondents.

Accordingly, the order of the district court is reversed, and the case remanded for further proceedings consistent with this opinion.

SHEARING, J., with whom ROSE and LEAVITT, JJ., agree, dissenting.

I would affirm the judgment of the district court dismissing the first-degree felony-murder charge. The intent required to make the entry into the motel room a burglary, namely, the intent to apply force and violence to the victims, is the same intent that supports the felony-murder charge. The felony-murder rule raises a homicide to first-degree murder without requiring the State to prove the traditional first-degree murder elements of willfulness, premeditation, and deliberation. The felonious intent involved in the underlying felony is regarded as sufficient intent to raise the resulting homicide to first-degree murder. When the felonious intent involved in committing the burglary is the same intent involved in the resulting homicide, the felony-murder rule is expanded beyond the reason for its existence.

I agree with the California Supreme Court in *People v. Wilson* when it said:

[T]he only basis for finding a felonious entry is the intent to commit an assault with a deadly weapon. When, as here, the entry would be nonfelonious but for the intent to commit the assault, and the assault is an integral part of the homicide and is included in fact in the offense charged, utilization of the felony-murder rule extends that doctrine "'beyond any rational function that it is designed to serve.'" We have heretofore emphasized "that the felony-murder doctrine expresses a highly artificial concept that deserves no extension beyond its required application." [1]

---

1   1 Cal.3d 431, 82 Cal.Rptr. 494, 462 P.2d 22, 28 (1969) (quoting *People v. Phillips*, 64 Cal.2d 574, 51 Cal.Rptr. 225, 414 P.2d 353, 360 & n. 5 (1966) (quoting *People v. Washington*, 62 Cal.2d 777, 44 Cal.Rptr. 442, 402 P.2d 130, 134 (1965)), *overruled on other grounds by People v. Flood*, 18 Cal.4th 470, 76 Cal.Rptr.2d 180, 957 P.2d 869 (1998)).

The California court concluded that the purpose of the felony-murder rule, to deter felons from killing negligently or accidentally, is not met when the underlying felony has the same general mental purpose as the homicide—to physically harm the victim.[2] The court went on to say:

> In [*People v. Ireland*[3]], we rejected the bootstrap reasoning involved in taking an element of a homicide and using it as the underlying felony in a second degree felony-murder instruction. We conclude that the same boot-strapping is involved in instructing a jury that the intent to assault makes the entry burglary and that the burglary raises the homicide resulting from the assault to first degree murder without proof of malice aforethought and premeditation. To hold otherwise, we would have to declare that because burglary is not technically a lesser offense included within a charge of murder, burglary constitutes an independent felony which can support a felony-murder instruction. . . . [A] burglary based on intent to assault with a deadly weapon is included in fact within a charge of murder, and cannot support a felony-murder instruction.[4]

In *Payne v. State*, this court agreed with California as to the purpose of the felony-murder rule, stating:

> The original purpose of the felony-murder rule was to deter felons from killing negligently or accidentally by holding them strictly responsible for the killings that are the result of a felony or an attempted one. *People v. Washington*, [62 Cal.2d 777,] 44 Cal.Rptr. 442, 402 P.2d 130 (1965). In the majority of jurisdictions, such a homicide acquires first degree murder status without the necessity of proving premeditation and deliberation. The heinous character of the felony is thought to justify the omission of the requirements of premeditation and deliberation.[5]

Here, when the defendants entered the building with the intent to harm the victims, the purpose of the felony-murder rule was not implicated because the subsequent harm to the victims was not negligent or accidental; harm to the victims was the very reason for the defendants' entry into the motel room.

In *Wilson*, the California court reached a similar result, concluding that the felony-murder rule does not apply to a murder that follows from an assault with a

---

2   *Id.*

3   70 Cal.2d 522, 75 Cal.Rptr. 188, 450 P.2d 580 (1969).

4   *Wilson*, 462 P.2d at 28–29 (citation omitted).

5   81 Nev. 503, 506, 406 P.2d 922, 924 (1965).

deadly weapon.[6] The California court based its decision on the merger doctrine.[7] Although I agree with the California court's conclusion, I do not agree that the merger doctrine applies.

Here, as NRS 205.070 specifically provides, each crime, the burglary and the homicide, can be charged separately. However, because the burglary and the homicide share the same underlying intent, the felony-murder rule should not apply. Application of the rule would bootstrap the homicide into first-degree murder simply because of the location of the homicide. Where, as here, the intent in both the underlying felony and the homicide is the same, application of the felony-murder rule does not further the rule's intended purpose, to prevent accidental or negligent killing, but rather, extends the rule unjustly.

Felony murder itself is an anomaly in that, unlike most felonies, it does not require that the defendant intend the resulting harm; on the contrary, it addresses accidental or unintentional killing. Application of the felony-murder rule when the underlying felony involves the intent to do serious bodily harm defeats the purpose of the rule and unfairly elevates a crime to first-degree murder without requiring the State to prove willfulness, deliberation, and premeditation. The State here has every opportunity to prove second-degree murder.

Notes and Questions

1. As the dissent noted, the defendant could have been charged with both burglary and malice murder. And judges have broad discretion to sentence defendants to concurrent or consecutive terms. The penalties for the separate crimes of malice murder and burglary each carry very substantial penalties, but less severe than the penalties provided for felony murder. This should remind you of the *Batchelder* case in the introductory chapter in which the Supreme Court held that prosecutors were entitled to select among various offenses describing the same offense, even though they carried very different penalties.

2. Suppose the Nevada Legislature had defined felony murder as a death resulting from the commission of any felony and this death occurred on the sidewalk rather than in a motel room. In other words, assume the underlying felony charge was an actual assault, not just an entry with intent to assault. How would these judges have resolved the issue that Anthony Armstrong would have liked to have been able to raise? What would the majority and the dissent say about a prosecution for attempted murder based on the fact that a death occurred while the defendant was committing the crime of aggravated assault?

---

6   462 P.2d at 28–29.

7   *Id.* at 29–30.

3. Is there any limit to the felony murder doctrine under the majority's reasoning? How do you imagine the Nevada Supreme Court would have resolved the issue in *Anderson*?

4. Think back to David Harris' article, *Punishment that Leaves Something to Chance* (p. 48). Just like punishing murder more severely than attempted murder, the felony murder rule establishes a very different penalty for robbery or burglary, depending on whether someone died during the commission of the crime. An accidental discharge of a gun could take a defendant from a crime punishable by a few years in prison to a crime punishable by life or death. From the perspective of Harris' article, isn't the difference in punishment created by the felony murder rule *less* problematic when the defendant intends the result of his burglary, or arson, to be the death of another rather than just the theft of goods or the destruction of property? Yet this less problematic application of the felony murder rule is frequently forbidden.

5. The dissent "reject[s] the bootstrap reasoning involved in taking an element of homicide and using it in a . . . felony murder instruction." This is a very important line to understanding the dissent and, more generally, objections often made to the felony murder rule. What exactly does the line mean?

————————————

(d) Must the Defendant, or His Agent, be the Triggerman?

Imagine police respond to a robbery in progress at a convenience store. A firefight ensues and a policeman's bullet strikes and kills the clerk, or one of the defendant's confederates. Should the defendant be held liable for this killing? The *Dekens* case that follows addresses this issue and observes two different theories of liability under the felony murder rule—the proximate cause theory and the agency theory. Under the agency theory, the defendant can be liable only for his own actions and the actions of those working with him. Under the proximate cause theory, so long as the death is sufficiently connected to the defendant's actions, he can be held criminally liable for felony murder even if neither he, nor any of his confederates, were the triggermen.

————————————

People v. Dekens

Supreme Court of Illinois
695 N.E.2d 474 (1998)

Justice MILLER delivered the opinion of the court:

This appeal presents the question whether a defendant may be charged with first degree murder, on a felony-murder theory, when the decedent is a cofelon who is killed by an intended victim of the defendant and cofelon.

The defendant was charged in the circuit court of Kankakee County with murder, criminal drug conspiracy, and attempted armed robbery. Prior to trial, the defendant moved to dismiss the murder charge, which was based on a felony-murder theory. The defendant contended that he could not be charged with that offense because the decedent in this case was a cofelon, who was shot and killed by the victim of the robbery attempt. For purposes of resolving the defendant's motion, the prosecution and the defense stipulated to the facts underlying the case. According to the parties' stipulation, an undercover police officer arranged to buy drugs from the defendant at a residence in Kankakee on January 5, 1996. Prior to the meeting, the defendant and the decedent, Peter Pecchenino, formulated a plan to rob the officer. During the drug transaction, the defendant pointed a shotgun at the officer and threatened him. In response, the officer fired several shots at the defendant. As the officer was leaving the residence, he was grabbed by Pecchenino. The officer shot Pecchenino, who later died as a result of those wounds. The defendant was subsequently charged with Pecchenino's murder, under a felony-murder theory. 720 ILCS 5/9-1(a)(3) (West 1996).

The trial judge granted the defendant's motion to dismiss the murder charge. The judge believed that he was required to follow the appellate court opinion in *People v. Morris*, 1 Ill.App.3d 566, 274 N.E.2d 898 (1971), which had held that a defendant could not be liable under a felony-murder theory for the death of a cofelon when the act causing the cofelon's death was not done in furtherance of the common design to commit the felony. The State appealed the dismissal of the charge pursuant to Supreme Court Rule 604(a)(1) (145 Ill.2d R. 604(a)(1)), and the appellate court affirmed the trial judge's ruling. In an unpublished order, the appellate court relied on a rationale different from the one used by the trial judge yet reached the same result. From a review of the case law in this area, the appellate court believed that liability under a felony-murder theory could extend only to innocent victims. We allowed the State's petition for leave to appeal (166 Ill.2d R. 315(a)), and we now reverse the judgments of the courts below and remand the cause to the circuit court of Kankakee County for further proceedings.

In *People v. Lowery*, 178 Ill.2d 462, 227 Ill.Dec. 491, 687 N.E.2d 973 (1997), this court recently reviewed the nature of the felony-murder doctrine and the opposing theories on which liability may be based. As *Lowery* explains, Illinois follows the "proximate cause" theory of liability for felony murder. Under that theory, liability attaches "for any death proximately resulting from the unlawful activity-notwithstanding the fact that the killing was by one resisting the crime." *Lowery*, 178 Ill.2d at 465, 227 Ill.Dec. 491, 687 N.E.2d 973. The other principal theory of liability under the felony-murder doctrine is the agency theory, which is followed by a majority of jurisdictions. Under the agency theory, "'the doctrine of felony murder does not extend to a killing, although growing out of the commission of the felony, if directly attributable to the act of one other than the defendant or those associated with him in the unlawful enterprise.' [Citations.]" *Lowery*, 178 Ill.2d at 466, 227 Ill.Dec. 491, 687 N.E.2d 973. There is no liability under the agency theory when the homicide is committed by a person resisting the felony. *Morris*, relied on by the trial judge in this case, is an expression of the agency theory of liability.

* * *

We believe that a charge of felony murder is appropriate in these circumstances. In [*People v. Lowery*, 667 N.E.2d 973 (1997)] we determined that a defendant may be charged with the offense when an intended victim mistakenly shoots and kills a bystander. Here, the intended victim shot and killed the defendant's cofelon. We do not believe that the defendant should be relieved from liability for the homicide simply because of the decedent's role in the offense. Nor do we believe that application of the doctrine depends on whether or not the decedent was an innocent party. To hold otherwise would import the agency theory of felony murder into our law. As we have noted, Illinois has long followed the proximate cause theory. Consistent with that view, then, we conclude that a defendant may be charged with murder under a felony-murder theory when an intended victim of the felony shoots and kills a cofelon of the defendant. We note that other states that adhere to the proximate cause theory also recognize liability for felony murder when the decedent is a cofelon of the defendant. *See State v. Baker*, 607 S.W.2d 153 (Mo.1980); *State v. Oimen*, 184 Wis.2d 423, 516 N.W.2d 399 (1994).

* * *

The defendant further suggests that his proposed limitation is consistent with the purposes of the felony-murder doctrine. [W]e do not agree. In explaining the intended scope of the doctrine in Illinois, the committee comments to section 9-1 of the Criminal Code of 1961 state:

"It is immaterial whether the killing in such a case is intentional or accidental, or is committed by a confederate without the connivance of the
defendant * * * or even by a third person trying to prevent the commission
of the felony." 720 ILCS Ann. 5/9-1, Committee Comments-1961, at 12-13
(Smith-Hurd 1993).

We believe that denying liability when the decedent is a cofelon would conflict with the legislature's adoption of the proximate cause theory.

For the reasons stated, the judgments of the appellate court and of the circuit court of Kankakee County are reversed, and the cause is remanded to the
circuit court of Kankakee County for further proceedings.

*Appellate court judgment reversed; circuit court judgment reversed; cause
remanded.*

Justice BILANDIC, dissenting:

I dissent. Unlike my colleague Justice Heiple, I do not believe that this court
should now abandon its adoption of the proximate cause theory of liability for
felony murder. In this case, however, the majority applies this theory without
any consideration of the purposes sought to be achieved by the felony-murder
doctrine. I would hold that the felony-murder doctrine does not apply to render
a surviving felon guilty of murder where a cofelon is killed by a nonparticipant
in the felony.

As codified in Illinois, the felony-murder doctrine permits a defendant to be
convicted of first degree murder if, "in performing the acts which cause the death
* * * he is attempting or committing a forcible felony." 720 ILCS 5/9-1(a)(3) (West
1996). Under this doctrine, the defendant need not have intended, nor even contemplated, causing anyone's death. Rather, the defendant's culpability for murder
rests solely on his commission or attempt of one of a list of felonies. Accordingly,
the ramifications of the felony-murder doctrine are harsh; a defendant who, it
is conceded, intended only to commit a far less serious offense than murder is
nonetheless made guilty of first degree murder. This is no small matter. First
degree murder in this state carries with it a sentence ranging from 20 to 60 years'
imprisonment to natural life imprisonment. 730 ILCS 5/5-8-1(a) (West 1996).

The justification for the felony-murder rule is that forcible felonies are so
"inherently dangerous" that a death occurring in the course thereof is strongly
probable. *Lowery,* 178 Ill.2d at 469, 227 Ill.Dec. 491, 687 N.E.2d 973. Obviously,
the "inherent danger" referred to here is the danger to the victims of the felonies,
or to bystanders or intervenors. It certainly was not the potential danger to the
participants in the forcible felony which prompted the legislature to codify this
form of murder. As this court stated recently in *Lowery,* the felony-murder rule
reflects the legislature's concern for "protecting the general populace." *Lowery,*

178 Ill.2d at 469, 227 Ill.Dec. 491, 687 N.E.2d 973. Given the harsh consequences of the felony-murder doctrine, I believe that it should be limited to those situations in which its application achieves the purpose underlying the rule. Extending the doctrine to render a defendant guilty of first degree murder when his cofelon is killed by the intended victim of the attempted felony so dilutes the justification for the felony-murder doctrine as to make it absurd and unfair.

There is no dispute in this case that Pecchenino, the decedent, was a willing and active participant in the attempted armed robbery. According to the stipulated facts, defendant and Pecchenino together planned the crime. Defendant did not intend Pecchenino's death, nor did defendant perform the acts which caused his death. Rather, the stipulated facts reveal that Pecchenino was shot and killed by the undercover officer after Pecchenino grabbed the officer as he was attempting to leave. Thus, the only basis for rendering defendant guilty of murder in this case is defendant's participation in the attempted armed robbery, the same attempted armed robbery which Pecchenino himself planned and carried out.

The majority concludes that, because defendant's attempt to commit the armed robbery "set in motion a chain of events" which resulted in Pecchenino's death, defendant may rightly be charged with murder for Pecchenino's death. When a defendant's commission of a forcible felony proximately results in the death of an innocent party, I agree that charging the defendant with murder may comport with notions of justice and fairness. There is, however, simply a qualitative difference between that situation and the situation presented here, where the death which resulted was that of a coparticipant in the underlying felony. As one renowned treatise on criminal law has noted:

> "[I]t is now generally accepted that there is no felony murder liability when one of the felons is shot and killed by the victim, a police officer, or a bystander * * *. * * *
>
> A more plausible explanation [for this conclusion] is the feeling that it is not justice (though it may be poetic justice) to hold the felon liable for murder on account of the death, which the felon did not intend, of a co-felon willingly participating in the risky venture. It is true that it is no defense to intentional homicide crimes that the victim voluntarily placed himself in danger of death at the hands of the defendant * * *. But with unintended killings it would seem proper to take the victim's willing participation into account * * *." W. LaFave & A. Scott, 2 Substantive Criminal Law § 7.5, at 217-18 (1986).

The majority provides no explanation for how the purpose of the felony-murder doctrine is served by applying it in cases such as this. Rather, the majority's holding is simply that the proximate cause theory "compels" this result. The only question, according to the majority, is "whether the decedent's death is the direct and proximate result of the defendant's felony." 182 Ill.2d at 252, 230 Ill. Dec. at 987, 695 N.E.2d at 477.

* * *

The majority * * * refers to an excerpt from the committee comments to section 9-1. Those comments do not address the question presented in this case, whether felony murder applies where the decedent is a cofelon killed by a third party. Those comments merely state that it is immaterial whether the killing was *performed* by the defendant or by a third person trying to prevent the commission of the felony. 720 ILCS Ann. 5/9-1(a), Committee Comments-1961, at 12-13 (Smith-Hurd 1993). The comments are silent with regard to the identity of the decedent.

Accordingly, no prior precedent of this court or any expression of legislative intent "compels" any particular resolution of the issue presented in this case. The majority therefore should have engaged in an analysis of whether, consonant with notions of justice and fairness, liability for first degree murder should be imposed in the circumstances presented by this case. The majority's failure to conduct such an analysis has led it to reach what I consider to be an unjust result. I therefore dissent.

Justice HEIPLE, also dissenting:

Although I joined this court's opinion in *People v. Lowery*, 178 Ill.2d 462, 227 Ill.Dec. 491, 687 N.E.2d 973 (1997), I have changed my view of the matter. For the reasons given below, I believe the court should reexamine and reject the proximate cause theory of liability in felony-murder cases.

The felony-murder doctrine originated in England to impose liability for murder upon a criminal defendant whose conduct in committing or attempting a felony brought about an unintended death. *State v. Branson*, 487 N.W.2d 880, 881 (Minn.1992). At the time the doctrine was conceived, few offenses were classified as felonies, and all felonies were punishable by death. *Branson*, 487 N.W.2d at 881-82. Since the advent of the felonymurder doctrine, however, many less serious offenses have been added to the felony category. In response, many American jurisdictions have narrowed the doctrine's application, while England has abandoned the doctrine altogether. *Branson*, 487 N.W.2d at 882 & n. 3.

In Illinois, the only type of first degree murder which does not require proof of a specific *mens rea*, or intent, on the part of the defendant is felony murder. *See* 720 ILCS 5/9-1(a) (West 1996). The felony-murder doctrine thus stands as a substitute for intent in cases where the defendant's commission of a felony causes another person's death. This principle is sound when the death actually results from an action taken by the defendant. When the death is caused by the conduct of a third person, however, the rationale for the felony-murder doctrine fails, because the doctrine operates as a rule of intent, not of causation. As one court held on facts similar to those of the instant case, "the thing which is imputed to a felon for a killing incidental to his felony is malice and not the act of killing." (Emphasis omitted.) *Commonwealth v. Redline*, 391 Pa. 486, 495, 137 A.2d 472, 476 (1958). In other words, although the State, to obtain a conviction for felony murder, need not prove intent to kill or knowledge that bodily harm will result, it still must prove that the defendant performed the acts which caused the death.

This analysis applies with particular force to the Illinois felony-murder statute, which provides as follows:

> "A person who *kills an individual* without lawful justification commits first degree murder if, *in performing the acts which cause the death:*
>
> * * *
>
> (3) he is attempting or committing a forcible felony other than second degree murder." (Emphasis added.) 720 ILCS 5/9-1(a)(3) (West 1996).
>
> This language clearly requires the State to prove that the defendant personally killed the decedent by "performing the acts which cause[d] the death."

The majority cites a passage from the committee comments on section 9-1 to support its reading of the statute. 182 Ill.2d at 254, 230 Ill.Dec. at 988, 695 N.E.2d at 478. This passage states that the death upon which a felony-murder conviction is based may have been caused "even by a third person trying to prevent the commission of the felony." 720 ILCS Ann. 5/9-1, Committee Comments-1961, at 12-13 (Smith-Hurd 1993). The only authority given by the Committee for this statement is this court's opinion in *People v. Payne*, 359 Ill. 246, 194 N.E. 539 (1935). In *Payne*, this court held that the defendant could be found guilty of murder even if the shot that killed the decedent had been fired by another victim of the underlying felony. *Payne*, 359 Ill. at 255, 194 N.E. 539. This court's holding in *Payne*, however, is flawed for the same reason as is the majority's analysis in the instant case: namely, the State failed to prove that the defendant performed the acts which caused the death. Other than this brief reference by a nonlegislative committee to an opinion of this court, there is no evidence that the General Assembly intended to sanction a conviction for felony murder where the death was caused by the actions of a person other than the defendant. Moreover, comments on a statute cannot alter the plain language of the statute. Giving the statute a fair reading, I cannot see how the comments could have been made in the first place, and I certainly do not see how those comments can now be given any validity or weight.

As the majority notes, most United States jurisdictions have rejected the proximate cause standard in favor of an agency theory of liability. Under the agency theory, "the doctrine of felony murder does not extend to a killing, although growing out of the commission of the felony, if directly attributable to the act of one other than the defendant or those associated with him in the unlawful enterprise." *State v. Canola*, 73 N.J. 206, 211-12, 374 A.2d 20, 23 (1977). Illinois also should adopt the agency theory, not because the majority of other states have done so, but rather because that theory represents a reasonable and just interpretation of the law. For this reason, I respectfully dissent.

Notes and Questions

1. How exactly do you explain Justice Bilandic's opinion in this case? He claims not to be abandoning the proximate cause view of felony murder liability in favor of the agency theory, about which you will learn more in the next case. What exactly is he relying on to arrive at his conclusion? Is he relying on a doctrine of unclean hands that the majority rejects? Recall that Bilandic wrote, "It is illogical to conclude that the same degree of guilt should attach where a defendant's felony results in the death of an innocent party and where a defendant's felony results in the death of an innocent party and where it results in the death of an active participant in the felony." Does his reasoning seem more like one you would expect from a prosecutor rather than a judge?

2. Justice McMorrow is quite critical of the statutory analysis the majority conducted. Do you agree with his plain reading of the statute? Can you, however, dismiss as unpersuasive the committee comments as based on an unpersuasive case? Even if the comments to the statute are *less* suggestive of the legislature's intent, do the committee's comments embracing even an opinion Justice McMorrow finds to be flawed not have *some* significance?

3. The majority of American jurisdictions embrace the agency theory of felony murder, but Illinois is part of a strong minority of jurisdictions to adopt the proximate cause theory.

PLEA BARGAINING EXERCISE

Instructions

You will be paired with another student. You will both read the statement of the case. Your instructor will provide each side with confidential facts. One will be a defense attorney, accessing only the defense attorney's confidential facts. The other will be a prosecutor, accessing only the prosecutor's confidential facts. You will have 20 minutes for this negotiation, after reading the facts and taking a few minutes to outline your negotiation plan. Based on your confidential facts, you will attempt to come to an agreement with the other side.

Statement of the Case

It is the third day of trial, and things are moving slowly. Defense counsel is putting up a stiff fight for the client, Anfirney, who is charged with first-degree felony murder, robbery, and larceny. First-degree murder carries punishment of 15 years to life imprisonment, robbery 10 to 30 years imprisonment, and larceny 5 to 20 years imprisonment.

The prosecution is attempting to tell the jury the following story at trial: Anfirney is a bad person, having failed to pay his child support three separate times, been cited for public drunkenness twice, and according to friends, solicits prostitutes on a regular basis. Short on cash to satisfy his unsavory habits, Anfirney and two others entered a convenience store, where Anfirney's companions each held the clerk at gunpoint, and forced him to open the cash register. Anfirney held the bag for the clerk, who dumped the money into the bag. The store was empty except for Anfirney, the other two assailants, and the clerk. As they were leaving—Anfirney carrying the cash—the clerk pulled a handgun from under his counter and began firing at Anfirney and the other two assailants. Anfirney ducked behind an ice cream chest, while his companions wheeled around and returned fire. The clerk was killed instantly by a bullet to the head, from one of the assailant's gunshots. The two shooters ran out of the store, and Anfirney, after hearing the gunshots stop, stood up and ran for the door. The money was found in a mailbox directly between where Anfirney was arrested and where the robbery took place, and Anfirney was jogging up that same street away from both the mailbox and the store. Anfirney's clothes matched the man in the video hiding behind the ice cream freezer, except for a hat and a big overcoat.

Therefore, Anfirney stole the money to satisfy his bad desires and hid it in a mailbox while running from the scene, and took off his hat and overcoat to hide his identity.

The following evidence is emphasized at trial by defense counsel: it cannot be concluded "beyond a reasonable doubt" who actually entered and robbed the clerk because Anfirney and the other assailants wore sock masks. Anfirney was arrested one mile away, jogging down the street without the money, which was found in a mail box for a vacant, for-sale house—no one knows whether the money is from the robbery down the street because it cannot be proved how much money was in the cash drawer at the time of the robbery. No money of any kind was found on Anfirney while he was jogging on the street. While felony murder in this jurisdiction takes a proximate cause theory of felony murder, Anfirney (if the man in the surveillance video) did not take sufficient part in the shooting because it was provoked by the clerk and Anfirney did not have a gun. Plus, it's just plain unfair to hold Anfirney responsible for shooting the clerk and being responsible for the other two when Anfirney (if the man in the surveillance video) didn't pull the trigger, and the other two have not been found. Lastly, Anfirney did not use a gun to take the money, so he shouldn't be guilty of robbery, which requires a forced taking.

After the third day of trial, defense counsel has contacted the prosecutor "to talk."

(e) In the Course of the Felony?

The *Dekens* case was an example of a felony murder prosecution in a state that uses the proximate cause test rather than the agency test for murder. Regardless of which test a state uses for first-degree murder, however, there is a limitation on the scope of felony murder prosecutions—they have to have been committed in the course of the felony. A defendant who commits a felony at some point in his life cannot be permanently susceptible to a first-degree murder prosecution for an accidental death he subsequently causes for the rest of his life. *Pierce* lays out the principles to be analyzed in determining how for this liability should extend.

State v. Pierce

Supreme Court of Tennessee
23 S.W.3d 289 (2000)

DROWOTA, J., delivered the opinion of the court, in which ANDERSON, C.J., BIRCH, HOLDER and BARKER, JJ. joined.

The appellant, Lon Mitchell Pierce, Jr., was fleeing from law enforcement officials in a van that another person had stolen in Florida twenty days earlier when the stolen van he was driving collided with a Sullivan County deputy's patrol car. The deputy died almost immediately from injuries he sustained in the collision. As a result of the deputy's death, the appellant was charged with and convicted of first degree murder in the perpetration of a theft. . . .

BACKGROUND

The events giving rise to this appeal began on November 2, 1995, in Orlando, Florida. On that day, Nora Comacho and her husband stopped their blue 1995 Dodge Caravan at a 7–11 convenience store for gasoline. Passengers in the van included their fourteen-year-old daughter, Sarah Comacho, the appellant, fifteen-year-old Lon Mitchell Pierce, Jr., his sixteen-year-old girlfriend, April Worley, and an unidentified four-year-old child who was temporarily in Worley's care.

Ms. Comacho went into the convenience store and bought her daughter a soft drink. When Ms. Comacho returned to the vehicle, Sarah became upset because the soft drink was in a cup rather than a bottle and she and her mother argued. Apparently as a result of this argument, Sarah jumped into the driver's seat of the van while her father was inside the store and her mother was pumping gasoline. She then hit the automatic door locks and sped away from the convenience store, tearing the hose from the gasoline pump.

* * *

About twenty minutes after taking the van, Sarah, realizing her inexperience as a driver, pulled over and asked the appellant to drive. The appellant agreed, and immediately drove the four-year-old child to the child's home. Worley then suggested that the trio drive to Bristol, Virginia to visit her grandmother. Worley and the appellant alternated driving and arrived in Bristol, Virginia from Orlando, Florida, approximately twelve hours later.

For the next approximately three weeks, the three teenagers stayed either with Worley's grandmother at her residence in the Rice Terrace Apartments or at local motels. The three spent their time "mostly [riding] around . . . to different cities [in Tennessee]." During this period, "Sarah [Comacho] got caught shoplifting a Notre Dame jacket from K–Mart in Kingsport." Although the trio was able to escape, they believed that store personnel had obtained the license number of the van. As a result, they located a van of the same color and type as the stolen vehicle they were driving, stole the license plate from that van, and "threw the old plate in the dumpster at a mini-market."

On November 22, 1995, twenty days after Sarah had taken the van from her parents in Orlando, Florida, police officers in Bristol, Virginia, received information that a possible stolen blue Dodge van was located in the Rice Terrace area. At approximately 3:15 p.m., two Bristol, Virginia officers located a vehicle matching that description parked on Buckner Street near the Rice Terrace Apartments. The officers observed for about ten minutes what they believed to be an unoccupied van. When the van pulled out of the parking lot, the officers followed the van, activated their blue lights, and attempted to make a traffic stop when the van failed to stop at an intersection before turning right. Rather than stopping for the officers, the van accelerated, crossed the double line, and passed a school bus that was unloading children. A three minute pursuit ensued through Bristol, Virginia, during which the van driven by the appellant violated numerous traffic laws. When the van crossed out of Virginia into Tennessee, the Virginia officers terminated their pursuit and notified law enforcement authorities in Bristol, Tennessee that the van was approaching.

Locating the fleeing vehicle, Bristol, Tennessee police officer James Breuer activated his emergency lights and sirens and continued the pursuit. Officer Breuer described his pursuit as a low speed chase, approximately forty-five miles per hour in a twenty-five mile per hour speed zone. According to Officer Breuer, the van "would slow down almost to a stop to allow vehicles in front of him to pull over." As the chase continued, Officer Breuer was joined by Lieutenant Danny Baines of the Bristol police department. Once outside the city limits, Captain Daryll Chambers of the Sullivan County Sheriff's Department took the lead in the pursuit. While the Bristol officers continued to follow the van, they deactivated their emergency equipment.

The chase continued through Sullivan County on Route 44 at speeds of twenty-five to sixty-five miles per hour. . . . Approximately fourteen miles into the chase, Sullivan County Deputy Steve Mullins notified Captain Chambers that he was located in front of the pursuit, traveling in the opposite direction and that he would "try to cut them off" somewhere ahead. Shortly thereafter, Captain Chambers was able to see the blue lights from Deputy Mullins' patrol car, approximately four-tenths of a mile ahead. Deputy Mullins had positioned his patrol car diagonally across the roadway to set up a "road block." The front portion of Deputy Mullins' patrol car extended approximately two feet over the center line into the lane of oncoming traffic, but enough space remained in that lane for a vehicle to safely maneuver around the patrol car. After creating the "road block," Deputy Mullins exited his car, leaned across the hood, and pointed his service revolver at the approaching van driven by the appellant.

The record does not clearly establish the precise movements of the van after the "road block" became visible. Captain Chambers, immediately behind the van, testified that it slowed down when Deputy Mullins first came into view, and he initially thought the van was going to stop, but in the end, the van drove straight into the front of the patrol car and veered off to the right on impact. Lieutenant Baines, who was the second police car in the pursuit, approximately ten to twelve car lengths from Captain Chambers, testified that the van appeared to veer to the right, away from the patrol car, before impact. Officer Breuer, located in the rear of the pursuit, testified that the van made a sharp turn to the left into Deputy Mullins' patrol car right before the collision occurred.

In any event, when the van struck the patrol car, Deputy Mullins was thrown several feet into the air. His body hit a civilian vehicle that was parked behind the patrol car and then landed hard on the paved roadway. Deputy Mullins died almost immediately of severe head injuries. Following the collision, the van veered off the roadway, rolled onto its side, and came to rest in a field. The appellant, April Worley, and Sarah Comacho were arrested.

Following his arrest, the appellant told police that "[t]he reason I didn't stop was because I was scared . . . all I wanted to do was get on the interstate and get out of the van and leave it there and get away from it. . . ." With respect to the collision, the appellant stated as follows:

> I saw the police car pull out across the road in front of me. He was across his lane and in my lane just a little bit, but I had enough room to go around him in my lane. I was trying to go around him and that's what I wanted to do.
>
> I saw the police officer open his door and he pointed a . . . pistol at the van. . . .
>
> When I saw the pistol, I thought I put my foot on the brake, I'm not sure if I did or not. I let go of the steering wheel and ducked straight down with my arms covering my face. I then heard and felt the crash and knew I'd hit something. I thought I was swerving to the right and would miss the police officer when I ducked my head.

Worley gave a similar account of the accident during her testimony at trial indicating that the appellant yelled, "Duck!" just before the van hit Deputy Mullins' patrol car.

DISCUSSION

The statute under which the appellant was convicted defines felony murder as "[a] killing of another committed *in the perpetration of* or attempt to perpetrate any first degree murder, arson, rape, robbery, burglary, theft, kidnapping, aggravated child abuse or aircraft piracy." Tenn.Code Ann. § 39–13–202(a)(2) (emphasis added). The felony supporting the appellant's conviction of felony murder is theft. In Tennessee "[a] person commits theft of property if, with intent to deprive the owner of property, the person knowingly obtains or exercises control over the property without the owner's effective consent." Tenn.Code Ann. § 39–14–103.

* * *

This Court has previously considered how the statutory phrase, "in the perpetration of," should be defined in the felony murder context. *See, e.g., State v. Buggs*, 995 S.W.2d 102, 107 (Tenn.1999); *Farmer v. State*, 201 Tenn. 107, 296 S.W.2d 879 (1956). For example, in *Farmer*, this Court explained that for a killing to occur "in the perpetration of" a felony so that the felony murder rule applies, the killing must be done "in pursuance of the [felony], and not collateral to it. In other words, the killing must have had an intimate relation and close connection with the felony . . . and not be separate, distinct, and independent from it. . . ." *Farmer*, 201 Tenn. at 115–16, 296 S.W.2d at 883 (internal quotations and citations omitted). In addition, there must be a causal connection between the felony and the killing. *Farmer*, 201 Tenn. at 117, 296 S.W.2d at 884.

More recently we recognized that when determining whether a killing is "in the perpetration of" a felony courts in Tennessee have considered such factors as time, place, and causal connection. *Buggs*, 995 S.W.2d at 106. We stressed in *Buggs* that a killing "may precede, coincide with, or follow a felony and still be considered as occurring 'in the perpetration of' the felony, so long as there is a connection in time, place, and continuity of action." *Id.*

Our research reveals that when determining whether a killing was committed "in the perpetration of" a felony, the majority of courts in other jurisdictions also consider whether the killing and the felony are closely connected in time, place, causation, and continuity of action. One of the most important factors to consider in determining whether there has been a break in the chain of events that would preclude application of the felony murder rule is whether the felon has reached a place of temporary safety. *See* LaFave & Scott, *Substantive Criminal Law*, § 7.5(f)(1). If the felon has gained a place of temporary safety after commission of the felony and before the killing, the felony murder rule generally does not apply. Accordingly, in resolving the issue in this appeal, we must evaluate the sufficiency of the evidence to determine if the fatal collision resulting in Deputy

Mullins' death and the felony of theft are closely connected in time, place, and causation, and continuity of action.

The State asserts that the killing and felony in this case occurred at the same time and place because the appellant was committing theft by exercising control over the van when the fatal collision occurred. The State also says that the killing and theft are causally connected because the appellant was attempting to evade arrest for the theft when the fatal collision occurred. Essentially, the State argues that the felony murder rule can be applied when the underlying felony is theft even if the killing is completely separate from and collateral to the initial *taking* of the property. The State's position is that no period of time or intervening events can break the chain between the felony and the killing when the underlying felony is theft. According to the State, so long as a defendant is exercising control over an article of stolen property when an accidental or unintentional killing occurs, that defendant can be convicted of felony murder even if the property was initially stolen twenty years before the accidental or unintentional killing.[6]

We disagree and conclude that in determining whether the evidence is sufficient to support a conviction of first degree murder in the perpetration of theft, a court must determine whether the killing is closely connected to the initial *taking* of the property in time, place, causation, and continuity of action. . . .

CONCLUSION

Applying our holding to the facts in this case, we conclude that the evidence is not sufficient to support the defendant's conviction of felony murder. Clearly, the killing in this case was not closely connected in time or place to the taking of the vehicle. The State has never claimed that the appellant initially took the vehicle. Indeed, there is no question that Sarah Comacho actually stole the vehicle more than twenty days prior to the fatal collision from a location more than six hundred miles away from the site of the collision that resulted in Deputy Mullins' death. According to the proof in the record, the appellant and Worley were completely unaware that Sarah intended to take the vehicle without her parents' consent. In addition, there was a break in the chain of events between the initial taking and the killing. As previously stated, one of the most important factors in determining whether there has been a break in the chain of events is whether or not the felon has reached a place of temporary safety. In this case, the appellant reached a place of temporary safety when he arrived and resided in the Bristol, Virginia area for twenty days prior to the killing. The appellant was not being actively and continuously pursued by police during this time, nor was

---

6　According to the State's position, the felony murder rule can be applied to a person who steals a piece of jewelry, retains it in his or her possession for twenty years, and is involved in a car accident twenty years later which results in the death of a police officer. According to the State, so long as the person has the stolen jewelry in his or her possession at the time of the car accident, the felony murder rule applies.

he attempting to hide from the police. Indeed, he, along with Worley and Sarah, were daily driving the stolen vehicle to various cities in Tennessee. Clearly, they had reached a place of safety before the killing occurred. While there was an attenuated causal connection between the initial taking of the vehicle and the killing since the appellant was attempting to evade arrest for theft of the vehicle when the collision occurred,[9] this tenuous causal connection was insufficient in light of the fact that the killing was completely unconnected to the initial taking of the vehicle in time, place, and continuity of action. After considering the evidence in light of the relevant factors, we are constrained to conclude that the evidence is insufficient to support the appellant's conviction of felony murder. Accordingly, the judgment of the Court of Criminal Appeals is reversed. The appellant's conviction of felony murder is vacated, and the case is remanded for a new trial. Costs of this appeal are taxed to the State of Tennessee.

Notes and Questions

1. The Court gives us nothing to suggest that this fact matters, but the defendant in this case was 15 years old at the time of his crime and, by virtue of his age, could not have had much experience in handling vehicles at high rates of speed. You will be learning about a variety of homicide offenses that are less severe than first-degree murder. These lesser homicide charges consider whether the defendant showed extreme indifference to human life, was recklessly disregarded the safety of others, or was negligent in his regard for others. The degree of risk a defendant takes does not change with his youth or experience but they are factors that those with the power to exercise discretion certainly can take into account. Appeals to these equitable factors can be made indirectly to the jury but can be made quite openly to prosecutors in plea negotiations. What other factors do you see in the facts that the court seems to be suggesting that the prosecution consider in offering a plea when this case is remanded?

2. Under the state's interpretation, when is a larceny complete? Could a defendant ever be guilty of larceny, as opposed to attempted larceny, under attempted larceny, under that state's theory?

----

9   The killing was most causally connected to the offense of evading arrest which is not listed as one of the felonies that will support a conviction of first degree murder.

C

PRACTICE EXERCISE

Read the following statutes, fact pattern, and procedural history, then read the instructions.

§ 17.200 Purpose

It shall be the intent of the Legislature of the State of Walaska in the passage of the "Crime Enhancement and Prevention Act" (§§ 17.200-.500) to further the ends of justice by deterring crime through punishment.

§ 17.201 Murder Defined

A person is guilty of first degree murder, a Class A felony, if the person:

> A. Intentionally or knowingly causes the death of another human being; or

> B. Causes the death of another human being during the course of a dangerous felony.

A person is guilty of second degree murder, a Class B felony, if the person:

> C. Engages in conduct that manifests a depraved indifference to the value of human life and causes the death of another human being; or

> D. Intentionally or knowingly causes another human being to commit suicide by the use of force, duress or deception.

§ 17.401 Felonies

A person is guilty of a Class C felony if the person:

A. Commits any of the common law crimes against the person, including arson, assault, burglary, sexual assault, robbery, or theft.

B. Possesses or uses a weapon of any kind while intoxicated. A hunting rifle is not a weapon when it is used for hunting.

C. Operates a motor vehicle while intoxicated.

D. Knowingly enters any Walaska Wildlife Refuge and traps, entangles, impedes, injures, or kills a species which is not in season.

Facts

Akron, Bethanne, Chip and Dixie were good friends who decided to take a trip to Walaska, where Akron had a remote cabin in Walaska State Park. Chip and Dixie are brother and sister. While hanging out at the cabin, the four decided it was time to put their hunting skills to the test. Akron, an avid hunter, had a closet full of hunting rifles and ammunition, "because hunting keeps it real." Because of their remote location and the relaxed, vacation atmosphere, the four decided to partake in some "tasty beverages" before heading out into the hills to "hunt some deer." Each was certifiably drunk by the time they set out for the hills. Bethanne asked, "Don't we need hunting licenses or something?" Chip responded, "Nah, we won't get caught out here." Akron sincerely stated, "The deer are in season anyway." The deer are not in season.

Having fanned out, each stalked quietly in the same direction, hoping to spook a deer. Akron spotted a beautiful buck, but decided to pull a prank on Chip, located to his left, to show off his sharpshooting skills to Bethanne and Dixie, located to right. "Plus, since that idiot doesn't see that buck, he deserves a good scare," thought Akron. Thus, Akron decided to have Chip run from left to right 50 yards in front of Akron's current position in order to spook the deer from behind, causing it to run directly across Akron's path, where he could get a shot at it while it was at full speed. Akron whispered as loud as he could to Chip, "We're changing direction, run up fifty yards then start running right." Desensitized by the alcohol, Chip blindly agreed, began running, and did not see the deer until he changed directions, when he realized he had spooked a magnificent buck. Akron was ready, but due to the intoxication, delayed his shot by a half second, pulled his aim to the left, and missed the buck by at least twenty feet. Akron's bullet struck Chip, who was running at full speed approximately 50 yards ahead. Chip instantly died.

Shocked and mortified by what had just happened to her brother, Dixie screamed and ran toward Chip's body. When Akron arrived at Chip's body, Dixie swore through her tears, "Akron, you f* * * ing murderer!" "You killed him!" She lifted her rifle and aimed it at Akron, "Why should I let you live? This is all your fault!" Bethanne stepped in between Dixie and Akron to intervene. Dixie stepped sideways to maintain her aim at Akron, and stumbled slightly on a rock. Dixie shot Bethanne as a result of her automatic reflex to steady her grip on the gun. Dixie then screamed as Bethanne crumpled to the ground, gripping her abdomen. "Why? Oh, why? I wasn't really going to shoot anyone," mourned Dixie. Akron ran for help.

Akron arrived at the cabin minutes later, jumped in his Superb Off-Road Vehicle (SOV) and sped off for the nearest ranger's station. Akron did not return in time.

Bethanne died. The park rangers arrested Akron and Dixie, who were still intoxicated at the time of arrest.

Procedure

The Walaska state prosecutor has obtained the following indictments.

(1) Akron: violation of every single statute listed above, with the exception of § 17.200, for the deaths of both Chip and Bethanne.

(2) Dixie: violation of §§ 17.201(B) (killing during the course of a dangerous felony), 17.201(C) (depraved heart killing), 17.401(A) (assault), 17.401(B) (possession of weapon while intoxicated), and 17.401(D) (entering Walaska Wildlife Refuge and impeding species not in season), for the deaths of both Chip and Bethanne.

The cases are about to proceed to trial, and the judge has requested proposed jury instructions from both sides in each case. The state will follow the pattern instructions which mirror the statutes. The judge will expect policy arguments for your proposed jury instructions, because Walaska has not determined whether: (1) to follow agency theory or proximate cause theory for felony murder liability; (2) to follow the merger doctrine for felony murder liability; and (3) if § 17.201(B) ("dangerous felony") includes all § 17.401 felonies mentioned above.

Instructions

You are the defense attorney for both Akron and Dixie because you are desperate for work, despite the conflict of interest which could emerge in handling both cases simultaneously. Your task is to (1) draft jury instructions for Akron and Dixie on the primary issue (as you see it) in each indictment using the elements of the statutes and the facts, and (2) provide policy arguments for your proposed instructions, where relevant (as you see it), on (a) agency/proximate cause theories, (b) the merger doctrine, and (c) the dangerous felony limitation.

Consider: is it more fair that Akron or Dixie is punished?

iii. Special Victims

A number of states make the killing of a particular type of person first-degree murder. In some jurisdictions, the killing of persons in a special class can also be a type of second-degree murder. Common examples of special categories of persons include police officers, firefighters, and children under a certain age.

The *Murry* decision considers whether the defendant had to be aware that his victim was a member of one of these classes to fall within the definition of such a statute, the most frequently litigated issue with a special victim element. In *Murry*, the Alabama Supreme Court is looking at a capital murder statute, not simply a first-degree murder statute, but the issue is obviously analogous to the one raised when a first-degree murder statute defines the killing of a particular sort of person.

Ex Parte Murry

Supreme Court of Alabama
455 So.2d 72 (1984)

PER CURIAM.

Petitioner asserts that the capital offense of murder of a police officer requires knowledge of the officer's status and that a trial judge should not be allowed, under the sentencing provisions of the Alabama Criminal Code, to impose a sentence of death after a jury recommends life without parole.

Paul Edward Murry was indicted on February 5, 1982, the grand jury charging that he

> "did intentionally cause the death of Mary Pearl McCord by shooting the said Mary Pearl McCord with a pistol while the said Mary Pearl McCord was on duty as a Police Officer for the City of Montgomery, Alabama. . . ."

Murry pleaded not guilty at his arraignment. The case came to trial on May 17, 1982. On May 19 the jury pronounced Murry guilty of capital murder. . . .

. . . Murry made statements immediately after the incident and at trial that he did not know the people he shot were police officers, but thought they were trying to rob him. The trial judge refused to charge the jury that the offense of capital murder of a police officer required the defendant to know that the victim was a police officer on duty.

The statute under which Murry was convicted and sentenced is the 1981 capital offense statute. 1981 Acts of Alabama, Act No. 81-178; Code 1975, §§ 13A-5-39 through—59 (1982 replacement volume). He was indicted under the following provision of § 13A-5-40:

> "(a) The following are capital offenses:
>
> " . . .

"(5) Murder of any police officer, sheriff, deputy, state trooper, federal law enforcement officer or any other state or federal peace officer of any kind, or prison or jail guard, *while such officer or guard is on duty or because of some official or job-related act or performance of such officer or guard . . . .*" [Emphasis added.]

This case squarely raises the issue of whether this statute requires that the accused know that the victim was a peace officer in order for the murder to be a capital offense.

Clearly, a murder "because of some official or job-related act" requires that the perpetrator know the victim is a peace officer and is or was performing an official act. A reading of § 13A-5-40 shows two similar offenses: murder of a public official which "stems from or is caused by or is related to [the victim's] official position, act, or capacity," § 13A-5-40(a)(11); and murder of a witness "when the murder stems from, is caused by, or is related to the capacity or role of the victim as a witness," § 13A-5-40(a)(14). The causal elements of these provisions require that the defendant have knowledge of the specified status or act and intend to murder the victim because of the status or act.

To determine whether the clause "while such officer or guard is on duty" similarly requires an intent to murder with knowledge that the victim is an officer on duty, or at least a reckless disregard of facts which should inform the offender of the victim's status, we must examine the criminal code for an expression of legislative intent.

* * *

. . . The question before us is whether a *mens rea* in addition to the intent to murder, i.e., a culpable mental state regarding the status of a police officer on duty, is required in order for an intentional murder of a victim who is such an officer to sustain a capital conviction.

* * *

We turn to the Alabama Criminal Code to ascertain whether the legislature has created an offense without regard to criminal intent, as the State contends.

* * *

Section 13A-2-4 provides in part as follows:

"(a) When a statute defining an offense prescribes as an element thereof a specified culpable mental state, such mental state is presumed to apply to every element of the offense unless the context thereof indicates to the contrary.

"(b) Although no culpable mental state is expressly designated in a statute defining an offense, an appropriate culpable mental state may nevertheless be required for the commission of that offense, or with respect to some or all of the material elements thereof, if the proscribed conduct necessarily involves such culpable mental state. A statute defining a crime, unless clearly indicating a legislative intent to impose strict liability, states a crime of mental culpability."

This statute supports the construction of § 13A-5-40(a)(5) advanced by Murry for three reasons: (1) paragraph (a) suggests that the "intentional" element of the murder applies to the element of the capital offense that the victim was a police officer on duty; (2) the first sentence of paragraph (b) pertains to the extent that the "proscribed conduct," murder punishable as a capital offense, "necessarily involves" a culpable mental state; and (3) the second sentence of paragraph (b) applies because § 13A-5-40(a)(5) says nothing "clearly indicating a legislative intent to impose strict liability," such as "whether or not the defendant knew that the victim was a police officer on duty or intended to kill the victim for that reason."

While the reasons we have listed as (1) and (3) in the previous paragraph are general rules of construction provided by the criminal code itself and tending to require a culpable mental state in addition to an intent to murder for a crime to be a capital offense rather than non-capital murder, reason (2) triggers an analysis more specific and more designed to resolve the issue on its merits. The question may be posed as, "Does a capital offense require a culpable mental state in addition to the intent to murder taken from the non-capital murder statute?"

The first approach is to survey the crimes deemed capital offenses in § 13A-5-40(a). The offenses numbered (1) through (4) and (8) prescribe capital offenses of "[m]urder by the defendant during [specified felonies] or an attempt thereof committed by the defendant." These offenses clearly require additional culpable mental states: the felonious intent to kidnap, rob, rape, etc. Offense number (6) is murder while the defendant is under sentence of life imprisonment, and number (13) is murder by a defendant who has been convicted of murder within the previous 20 years. These two crimes address the recidivist or habitual offender, who is put on notice that he will be punished more harshly for subsequent offenses.

Offense number (7) is murder for profit or for hire, involving a particularly odious criminal intent. Offense number (9) includes murder during arson, similar to the first group of offenses above, and murder by means of explosives, an abnormally dangerous means which readily implies knowledge or at least recklessness on the part of the offender regarding the fact that he is at least potentially placing persons other than the intended victim in unreasonable danger. Offense number (10) requires multiple intentional murders. Offenses (11) and (14) were mentioned above as requiring intent to murder officials and witnesses because of their capacity or acts. Finally, offense number (12) is murder during an aircraft hijacking, which requires the intent to exert unlawful control over the aircraft.

All of these offenses, in short, require an element in addition to murder of which the defendant must have at least knowledge, and in most cases an additional criminal intent. Under the trial court's refusal to instruct the jury that Murry had to know that the deceased was a police officer, Murry was convicted of capital murder with no more of a mens rea requirement than that of the intent to kill in the non-capital murder statute. Although controverted, Murry's testimony was that he did not know the two he shot were police officers, but thought they were attempting to rob him.

The statute as applied by the trial court cannot have the effect of protecting police officers. If the defendant does not know the victim is a police officer, how is the escalation of the murder of a police officer to a capital offense supposed to deter him?

The state argues that the issue here is one of proof: the only time this issue is likely to arise is when an undercover, plainclothes police officer is shot while on duty. In such situations, argues the state, the assailant is likely to be the only surviving witness, and will of course testify that he did not know the victim was a police officer. We cannot speculate that the legislature intended to create a unique strict liability capital offense on the basis of this reasoning, especially not in this case, where the surviving officer, Burks, contradicted Murry's testimony and said that both he and Officer McCord identified themselves as police.

The trial court submitted the questions of provocation, justification, and self-defense to the jury, so it might be said that the jury disbelieved Murry's claim that he did not know the victims were police officers. It is just as possible, however, that the jury found that legal provocation existed but Murry's use of deadly force was unwarranted or that his claim of self-defense could not stand because he did not retreat when he had the opportunity.

"[C]riminal statutes are to be strictly construed in favor of those persons sought to be subjected to their operation, i.e., defendants." *Clements v. State*, 370 So.2d 723, 725 (Ala.1979), citing *Schenher v. State*, 38 Ala.App. 573, 90 So.2d 234, *cert. denied*, 265 Ala. 700, 90 So.2d 238 (1956). We are bound to resolve the ambiguity regarding the peace officer offense in Murry's favor, especially in light of the rules of construction found in the criminal code militating against the creation of strict liability offenses by implication.

Our conclusion that the legislature did not intend to create a strict liability capital offense is bolstered by the fact that this would be such an extreme change from prior law. Under prior law, a homicide by one resisting an unlawful arrest could not be more than manslaughter, unless the resistance was in enormous disproportion to the threatened injury. *Dodd v. State*, 251 Ala. 130, 36 So.2d 474 (1948); *Spooney v. State*, 217 Ala. 219, 115 So. 308 (1928); *Brown v. State*, 109 Ala. 70, 20 So. 103 (1895); *Catrett v. State*, 31 Ala.App. 326, 16 So.2d 725, cert. denied, 245 Ala. 336, 16 So.2d 727 (1944); *Shine v. State*, 44 Ala.App. 171, 204 So.2d 817 (1967). Under these authorities, if the officer did not disclose his authority, the arrest was not lawful. If the legislature intended to create a capital offense for what might have been limited to manslaughter under traditional law, it should have been more explicit.

We are mindful that the legislature in 1967 passed an act creating the crime of assault with a deadly instrument upon a police officer in performance of his duties:

> "Whenever any peace officer or other law enforcement officer of this state or any political subdivision of this state shall be engaged in the active discharge of his lawful duty or duties, it shall be unlawful for any person to commit any assault with a deadly instrument upon such officer, and any person guilty of such assault with a deadly instrument shall be guilty of a felony, and upon conviction shall be imprisoned in the penitentiary for not less than two years nor more than twenty years."

1967 Ala. Acts p. 1600, Act No. 746, § 3; Code 1940 (Recomp. 1958, 1973 cum. supp.), t. 14, § 374(20).

In *McKinney v. State*, 50 Ala.App. 271, 274, 278 So.2d 719, 722 (1973), cert. den., 291 Ala. 789, 278 So.2d 724, cert. den., 414 U.S. 1027, 94 S.Ct. 456, 38 L.Ed.2d 320, the Court of Criminal Appeals held that

> "[t]o read into this statute the additional elements of scienter, murderous intent, and the use of the instrumentality in such manner as to reflect an evil intent, is unwarranted. The statute falls in the class of *malum prohibitum* and not *malum in se*. It was enacted to protect a class of citizens engaged in ferreting out crime and in the enforcement of the criminal laws of the State and thereby for the ultimate protection of society."

Without reaching the discrepancy between the opinion in *McKinney* that officers are protected without a knowledge requirement and our observation above to the contrary, we decline to follow the holding in *McKinney* in a death penalty case. The statute at issue in that case increased the punishment for assault with a deadly instrument against a police officer without a *mens rea* requirement other than that required for the ordinary crime of assault with a deadly instrument, but the increase in punishment was qualitatively different from that involved herein. Under the criminal code's own presumptions against strict liability crimes, it would be a preposterous result to increase punishment, from a term of years or life with possibility of parole, to life without parole or the death penalty, with the sole difference being an element making no reference to the mental culpability of the defendant.

The United States Supreme Court, in *Enmund v. Florida,* 458 U.S. 782, 102 S.Ct. 3368, 73 L.Ed.2d 1140 (1982), reversed the death sentence of an accomplice to a robbery who had no intent to kill. . . .

* * *

The Court in *Enmund* analyzed the felony murder statutes of the various states and concluded that "the current legislative judgment . . . weighs on the side of rejecting capital punishment for the crime at issue." *Id.,* 102 S.Ct. at 3374. We have similarly analyzed the death penalty provisions of the states which have death penalty statutes. Thirty-two states have "murder of a peace officer" offenses similar to the one at issue here. Of these states, seventeen have statutes which require that the offender know, or in some cases "should know," the status of the peace officer, and fifteen are silent on the subject.

Of the states which make no specific requirement of knowledge of the status of the victim as a peace officer, only Missouri has specifically ruled that no such requirement will be inferred. *State v. Baker,* 636 S.W.2d 902 (Mo.1982). . . .

We decline to follow the reasoning of the Missouri Supreme Court whereby that court refused to interpret the statute to require that the accused know the victim to be a peace officer, basing its decision only on its conclusion that "[t] he evidence was sufficient for a rational trier of fact to find beyond a reasonable doubt that appellant knew Erson was a police officer." *State v. Baker, supra,* 636 S.W.2d at 907. Because the trier of fact was never asked to make a finding on the issue of knowledge, the possibility that such a finding would have been sustainable is irrelevant. Nor do we see the logic of holding that no finding of knowledge is required on the ground that such a finding could have been made in the case at bar. Moreover, the Missouri Supreme Court "decline[d] to address the unscrutable [sic] question of *mens rea,* [citing] *Morrisette v. United States,* 342 U.S. 246, 72 S.Ct. 240, 96 L.Ed. 288 (1952); [and] *Powell v. Texas,* 392 U.S. 514, 88 S.Ct. 2145, 20 L.Ed.2d 1254 (1968)." *Id.* The *mens rea* issue is the very heart of the case, especially under a statute such as we have here, where the only element differentiating the capital offense from non-capital murder is the identity of the victim.

Of the fifteen states, not including Alabama, which have statutory provisions regarding murder of a peace officer but making no mention of the perpetrator's knowledge of the identity of the victim, thirteen include such provisions among the aggravating circumstances to be considered by the sentencer, not as elements of the offense of capital murder. Thus, the possibility of applying an element which makes no reference to criminal intent could only arise after the defendant has been convicted of a capital crime. Even assuming some of these states other than Missouri would refuse to infer a knowledge requirement, the identity of the victim as an aggravating circumstance is only one of the circumstances to be considered in deciding whether the defendant is to be punished by life imprisonment without parole (in most cases) or by death. This is unlike the situation in Alabama, where the offense is necessarily raised from a non-capital one to a capital one without any distinct criminal intent.

For the reasons discussed above, we hold that the trial court erred in failing to instruct the jury in accordance with Murry's requested instructions that, in the event the jury found him guilty of murder, the murder could be raised to a capital offense only if Murry knew that the victim was a peace officer on duty. We note that the *mens rea* analysis above would allow an instruction that the offense could be raised to a capital one even if the State did not prove beyond a reasonable doubt that the defendant knew the victim was a peace officer, so long as the State proved a mentally culpable state regarding the victim's status, such as reckless disregard of facts which should put the offender on notice that the victim was a peace officer. Without any such instruction, however, Murry has been convicted of a capital offense without proof of "a consciousness materially more 'depraved' than that of any person guilty of murder." *Enmund v. Florida, supra*. We cannot hold that the legislature intended to impose such a strict liability offense merely by implication.

For the reasons stated, the judgment of the Court of Criminal Appeals is reversed and the cause remanded.

REVERSED AND REMANDED.

TORBERT, C.J., and JONES, ALMON, SHORES, EMBRY and BEATTY, JJ., concur.

MADDOX, FAULKNER and ADAMS, JJ., dissent.

MADDOX, Justice (dissenting).

I am of the opinion that the Court errs in holding that the § 13A-5-40(a)(5) capital offense requires the State to prove that the defendant knew the person he was murdering was a law enforcement officer on duty.

Applying principles of statutory construction, I conclude that the obvious purpose the legislature sought to obtain when it enacted § 13A-5-40(a)(5) was protection of law enforcement officers while in the performance of their duties.

Since the legislative intent behind § 13A-5-40(a)(5) is to protect law enforcement officers by providing severe punishment, even death, for anyone who murders an officer on duty, I am of the opinion that no knowledge requirement should be read into the law. The State should only be required to prove that a defendant intentionally killed a law enforcement officer while that officer was in the performance of his duty. To require more interferes with the protection of law enforcement officers which the legislature sought to provide.

We can take judicial knowledge of the fact that many police officers are killed while in the performance of their duties, and that many of these policemen perform their duties in plain clothes. The majority decision, which requires that the State prove beyond a reasonable doubt that the defendant knew at the time that his victim was a law enforcement officer, puts a burden on the State which the legislature did not impose and creates a problem of proof, especially in cases involving the murder of a policeman in plain clothes who is acting as an undercover officer. The only surviving witness to the situation that preceded the murder of a plain-clothes or undercover officer might be the murderer himself, who could always claim that he did not know he was murdering an officer. The officer would not be able to testify that he identified himself to the defendant, because the officer would be dead.

In the present case, there was a surviving eyewitness, Officer Burks, who did live to testify that he and Officer McCord had identified themselves to the defendant; however, that happened only because Officer Burks survived the gunshot wound the defendant inflicted on him. Had the defendant's aim been better, he would have murdered two officers and how could the State, under those circumstances, prove that the defendant knew the two persons he killed were police officers performing their duty? Here, the State may be able to meet the burden placed upon it, but what about all those cases where there are no witnesses to prove the knowledge of the defendant? I believe the legislature was aware of this problem and deliberately did not put a knowledge requirement in the statute. I recognize that criminal statutes should be narrowly construed, but a strict construction rule should not be substituted for "common sense, precedent, and legislative history." *United States v. Standard Oil Co.*, 384 U.S. 224, 225, 86 S.Ct. 1427, 16 L.Ed.2d 492 (1966).

The canon of strict construction is but one of many rules of statutory construction, and as this Court itself has noted, "[a]ll rules for construing statutes must be regarded as subservient to the end of determining legislative intent." *State ex rel. Moore v. Strickland*, 289 Ala. 488, 493, 268 So.2d 766, 770 (1972). The clear and obvious legislative intent behind § 13A-5-40(a)(5) is to protect all law enforcement officers by inflicting the supreme penalty on those who murder them while they are performing their duties. That intent can only be effectuated insofar as plain-clothes officers are concerned by not reading a status scienter requirement into the statute.

The United States Supreme Court has addressed a very similar issue concerning 18 U.S.C. § 111, the modern statute which prohibits obstructing or assaulting a federal officer. *United States v. Feola*, 420 U.S. 671, 95 S.Ct. 1255, 43 L.Ed.2d 541 (1975), involved a conviction under that statute which grew out of an assault on drug purchasers who turned out to be undercover narcotics agents. It was undisputed that defendants were unaware that their victims were federal officers. 420 U.S. at 674-675, 95 S.Ct. at 1258-1259. The trial court charged the jury that status scienter was not required, and the court of appeals reversed on that ground. *Id.*, at 675, 95 S.Ct. at 1259. After determining that the purpose of the statute was to protect federal officers, the Supreme Court reinstated the convictions, holding:

> "We conclude, from all this, that in order to effectuate the congressional purpose of according maximum protection to federal officers by making prosecution for assaults upon them cognizable in the federal courts, § 111 cannot be construed as embodying an unexpressed requirement that an assailant be aware that his victim is a federal officer. *All the statute requires is an intent to assault, not an intent to assault a federal officer. A contrary conclusion would give insufficient protection to the agent enforcing an unpopular law, and none to the agent acting under cover.*

> "This interpretation poses no risk of unfairness to defendants. It is no snare for the unsuspecting. Although the perpetrator of a narcotics 'rip-off,' such as the one involved here, may be surprised to find that his intended victim is a federal officer in civilian apparel, he nonetheless knows from the very outset that his planned course of conduct is wrongful. *The situation is not one where legitimate conduct becomes unlawful solely because of the identity of the individual or agency affected. In a case of this kind the offender takes his victim as he finds him. . . .*"

420 U.S. at 684, 685, 95 S.Ct. at 1263, 1264 (emphasis added) (footnote omitted).

Likewise, § 13A-5-40(a)(5) does not involve legitimate conduct which becomes unlawful solely because of the identity of the individual affected-murder is illegitimate conduct regardless of the victim's identity. I would hold that "the offender takes his victim as he finds him." *Id.*, at 685, 95 S.Ct. at 1264. Consequently, I must respectfully dissent.

FAULKNER and ADAMS, JJ., concur.

Notes and Questions

1. The majority has a two-prong approach to its argument. First, canons of statutory interpretation and the presumption that attaches to criminal statutes require a showing of a culpable mental state. But the majority has a fallback position. The provision in question differentiates first-degree murder from capital murder, which makes the defendant eligible for the death penalty. The majority reasons the state should particularly be required to show a degree of culpability for that which differentiates a crime carrying even a life sentence from a crime with a potential death sentence. There is therefore use that both the prosecution and defense can make of the *Murry* decision in interpreting ordinary first-degree murder statutes that identify categories of persons whose killing amounts to first-degree murder.

2. Who do you think had the better end of this argument? Look back to our discussion on strict liability crimes in the first chapter. The dissent is surely correct to note that the prosecution may have a difficult time in demonstrating the defendant knew a plain-clothed officer was in fact an officer and this difficulty of proof is a reason for interpreting a statute, or a portion of it, as not requiring a culpable mental state. What factors from that discussion suggest that this should not be regarded as a strict liability provision? Think back to the *Thompson* case, p. 21.

3. Very shortly after the *Murry* decision, the Alabama legislature amended its capital murder statutes to remove the requirement that the defendant be aware that his victim is a law enforcement officer.

> The legislature hereby finds that law enforcement officers are the foot soldiers of society's defense of ordered liberty; that they literally risk their lives on a continuous basis to preserve the rights and defend the interests of law-abiding citizens and to maintain the order which is essential to our society; and that they deserve special protection when performing their duties. The legislature further finds that the protection law enforcement officers deserve and need is not provided by an interpretation of Code of Alabama 1975, § 13A-5-40(a)(5) which results in capital punishment being available in a case involving the intentional murder of an officer on duty only if it can be proven that the murderer knew that the person whom he was intentionally murdering was an officer on duty. The legislature finds that such an interpretation provides little or no protection to undercover or plain clothes officers and also reduces the protection provided officers in

other situations. The legislature further finds that the amendment effected in section 3 is necessary to achieve the amount of protection of law enforcement officers which it deems essential.

Act No. 87-709, Ala. Acts 1987 (modifying § 13A-5-40(a)(5)).

4. You should see the dissenting opinion as another application of the "in for a penny, in for a pound" doctrine—the defendant unlawfully shot a woman. The court had to decide whether the legislature required a *mens rea* term for the identity of the victim of an unlawful shooting. This should remind you of a number of cases in which courts have permitted a strict liability term once the defendant crossed the threshold of criminality. We first saw this principle at play in the *Dean* case in which the defendant accidentally discharged a weapon during a robbery (*see* p. 40). We just finished studying the felony murder doctrine. We will see this principle at play when courts consider a defendant's liability for the amount, or type, of drugs a defendant possessed. Courts are much more willing to permit a defendant to be held strictly liable for the element of a crime once it is established that he is already acting in a criminal manner.

---

iv. Universal Malice

States that differentiate degrees of murder typically recognize a form of homicide less than first-degree murder (i.e., second-degree murder) often defined as depraved heart murder. In essence this form of murder involves an action that takes an extraordinarily great risk of death that comes to pass. Consider below one of Colorado's definitions of first-degree murder. If a defendant's conduct, "[u]nder circumstances evidencing an attitude of universal malice manifesting extreme indifference to the value of human life generally, he knowingly engages in conduct which creates a grave risk of death to a person, or persons," causes a death, then he is guilty of first-degree murder. *People v. Jefferson* addresses the defendant's claim that this definition of the crime cannot be distinguished from second-degree murder, defined as a knowing killing in Colorado.

This definition of first-degree murder appears to be unique to Colorado, but serves as a nice segue into our discussion of second-degree murder. Consider whether Colorado's distinction between the universal malice form of first-degree murder and second-degree murder is any more or less easy to defend than the distinction between a premeditated and deliberated killing and second-degree murder.

People v. Jefferson

Supreme Court of Colorado
748 P.2d 1223 (1988)

ROVIRA, Justice.

These two cases on appeal raise an identical issue: The constitutionality of Colorado's "extreme indifference" murder statute, section 18-3-102(1)(d), 8B C.R.S. (1986). In both cases, the district court held the statute facially unconstitutional as violative of defendants' equal protection rights under article II, section 25 of the Colorado Constitution because it could not be rationally distinguished from Colorado's second-degree murder statute, section 18-3-103(1)(a), 8B C.R.S. (1986).

* * *

III.
A.

In considering the motions to dismiss both district courts found the extreme indifference murder statute indistinguishable from the second-degree murder statute. They concluded that prosecution under the former statute violated the defendants' rights to equal protection of the laws, under article II, section 25 of the Colorado Constitution.

Equal protection assures that those who are similarly situated will be afforded similar treatment.... When two criminal statutes prescribe different punishment for the same acts, a defendant convicted and sentenced under the harsher statute is denied equal protection of the laws.... Similarly, separate statutes proscribing with different penalties what ostensibly might be different acts, but offering no intelligent standard for distinguishing the proscribed conduct, run afoul of equal protection under state constitutional doctrine.

Equal protection of the laws requires that statutory classifications of crimes be based on differences that are real in fact and reasonably related to the general purposes of criminal legislation. The General Assembly may, however, prescribe more severe penalties for acts it perceives to have graver social consequences, even if the differences are only a matter of degree.... The constitution does not demand symmetry of punishment where valid classifications, based on varieties of evil, exist.... Nor is equal protection offended simply because the conduct in question violates more than one statutory proscription....

Section 18-3-102(1)(d) provides that a person commits the crime of murder in the first-degree if:

Under circumstances evidencing an attitude of universal malice manifesting extreme indifference to the value of human life generally, he knowingly
engages in conduct which creates a grave risk of death to a person, or persons, other than himself, and thereby causes the death of another.

By comparison, section 18-3-103(1)(a) provides that a person commits the crime
of murder in the second degree if "[h]e causes the death of a person knowingly,
but not after deliberation." If these two crimes cannot be sufficiently distinguished so that a person of average intelligence could understand the difference
between them, then the defendant who engages in identical conduct proscribed
by both statutes but is sentenced under the harsher penalty accompanying a conviction for first-degree murder, would be denied the equal protection of the laws.

* * *

A comparison of the two statutes reveals that extreme indifference murder
contains an element in addition to those required for second-degree murder. A
person commits the crime of extreme indifference murder if: (1) under circumstances evidencing an attitude of universal malice manifesting extreme indifference to the value of human life generally; (2) he knowingly engages in conduct
which creates a grave risk of death to a person, or persons, and (3) thereby causes
the death of another. § 18-3-102(1)(d). By comparison, a person commits the
crime of second-degree murder if he: (1) knowingly causes the death of a person,
but (2) not after deliberation. § 18-3-103(1)(a).

The presence of this additional element in the definition of extreme indifference murder requires the prosecution to prove that the defendant's conduct
manifested extreme indifference to the value of human life generally, and that
the circumstances evidence an attitude of universal malice. § 18-1-503(4);
§ 18-1-501(6). . . .

It is rational for the legislature to differently punish knowing conduct of
a type directed against a particular individual, and knowing, killing conduct-
aggravated recklessness or cold-bloodedness-which by its very nature evidences
a willingness to take human life without regard to the victim. . . .

Because a single criminal transaction may give rise to the violation of more
than one statute, it is for the trier of fact to decide whether the facts of the individual case justify a finding that the defendant is guilty of extreme indifference,
as opposed to second-degree, murder. . . .

* * *

QUINN, Chief Justice, dissenting:
. . . We have held on numerous occasions that separate statutes proscribing
with different penalties what ostensibly might be different acts, but offering no

intelligent standard for distinguishing the proscribed conduct, run afoul of equal protection under state constitutional doctrine. *E.g., People v. Marcy*, 628 P.2d 69 (Colo.1981) . . . Because I am satisfied that the 1981 amendment to the extreme indifference murder statute does not remove the equal protection impediments recognized by this court in *Marcy*, 628 P.2d 69, I respectfully dissent.

I.

In *Marcy*, decided in 1981, we held that the statutory proscription of extreme indifference murder in section 18-3-102(1)(d), 8 C.R.S. (1978), violated equal protection of the laws under the Colorado Constitution because it could not reasonably be distinguished from the lesser offense of second degree murder. The pre-1981 version of section 18-3-102(1)(d), which was at issue in *Marcy*, stated that a person commits the crime of murder in the first degree if:

> Under circumstances manifesting extreme indifference to the value of human life, he knowingly engages in conduct which creates a grave risk of death to a person other than himself, and thereby causes the death of another.

Section 18-3-103(1)(a), 8 C.R.S. (1978), stated that a person commits the crime of murder in the second degree if "[h]e causes the death of a person knowingly, but not after deliberation." Since the evil consequence proscribed by both statutory offenses was the death of a person, we stated in *Marcy* that if a valid basis exists for distinguishing these offenses, it must be found in either the culpability element of each offense or in the added component required for extreme indifference murder of acting "under circumstances manifesting extreme indifference to the value of human life." *Marcy*, 628 P.2d at 75.

After initially scrutinizing the culpability elements of each offense-knowingly engaging in conduct which creates a grave risk of death in the case of extreme indifference murder and knowingly causing the death of a person in the case of murder in the second degree-we concluded in *Marcy* that no rational basis of distinction existed between these two offenses. We explicated the rationale for our conclusion as follows:

> Under the statutory definition of "knowingly", the culpable mental state for extreme indifference murder is that the offender be aware that his conduct creates a grave risk of death to another. This culpability, however, is certainly no greater than that required for second degree murder. We considered the *mens rea* of second degree murder in *People v. Mingo*, 196 Colo. 315, 317, 584 P.2d 632, 633 (1978), and held that under the 1977 amendment "[s]econd-degree murder . . . is a general intent crime which entails being aware that one's actions are practically certain to result in another's death."

While, as a matter of conceptual possibility, one might be aware that his conduct creates a grave risk of death to another, as required for extreme indifference murder, and simultaneously lack that awareness required for second degree murder-that his actions are practically certain to result in another's death-it would be a most bizarre psychological state and certainly not a basis on which to structure the momentous variations and sanctions. . . . The distinction, if any, between the culpable mental state for the two offenses is one without a sufficiently pragmatic difference to permit an intelligent and uniform application of the law.

628 P.2d at 78.

We then turned to the requirement that the conduct occur "under circumstances manifesting extreme indifference to the value of human life" and determined that this language was the equivalent of acting "knowingly," the very same culpability required for murder in the second degree. *Marcy*, 628 P.2d at 79-80. Drawing on our 1974 decision in *People ex rel. Russel v. District Court*, 185 Colo. 78, 521 P.2d 1254, we reaffirmed the proposition that the term "extreme indifference to the value of human life" is clearly a more culpable standard of conduct than recklessness, which requires a conscious disregard of a substantial and unjustifiable risk of death. *See* § 18-1-501(8), 8B C.R.S. (1986). After pointing out the equally obvious truth that "[b]efore a person can *consciously* disregard a risk, he must be aware of that risk," *Marcy*, 628 P.2d at 79 (emphasis in original), we then concluded:

> . . . In the context of criminal homicide, therefore, acting under circumstances manifesting extreme indifference to the value of human life must mean acting with the awareness that one's actions are practically certain to cause the death of another-in other words, acting knowingly, the very same culpability required for murder in the second degree under the existing statutory scheme.

Id. at 79-80 (citations omitted).

II.

Subsequent to our decision in *Marcy*, the General Assembly amended the statutory definition of extreme indifference murder in the following manner:

(1) A person commits the crime of murder in the first degree if:

* * *

(d) Under circumstances *evidencing an attitude of universal malice* manifesting extreme indifference to the value of human life *generally,* he knowingly engages in conduct which creates a grave risk of death to a person, *or persons,* other than himself, and thereby causes the death of another.

Ch. 212, sec. 4, § 18-3-102, 1981 Colo.Sess.Laws 972, 973 (currently codified at § 18-3-102(1)(d), 8B C.R.S. (1986)) (emphasis reflects 1981 amendment). Even with this new terminology, however, the crime of extreme indifference murder, which is a class 1 felony punishable by life imprisonment or death, is not sufficiently distinguishable from murder in the second degree, a class 2 felony punishable by a presumptive sentence of 8-24 years, to overcome the equal protection problem identified in *Marcy.*

The majority turns its decision on the concept of "universal malice," which was the forerunner of the modern concept of extreme indifference to human life. "Universal malice," as the majority notes, is evinced by conduct greatly dangerous to the lives of other persons and manifesting a depraved mind not directed against the life of a particular person but against human life in general, without care or concern as to who the ultimate victim may be. Maj op. at 1231-1232. The fact remains, however, that the pre-1981 statutory terminology of "extreme indifference to the value of human life" encompasses the very same type of conduct embodied in the concept of "universal malice." *See Marcy,* 628 P.2d at 76; *Longinotti v. People,* 46 Colo. 173, 178-81, 102 P. 165, 167-68 (1909); O. Warren & B. Bilas, 1 Warren on Homicide § 78, at 366 (perm. ed. 1914). The majority's purported distinction between "universal malice" in the present statutory definition of extreme indifference murder and the pre-1981 concept of "extreme indifference to the value of human life" is a distinction without any intelligible difference. The statutory terminology "evidencing an attitude of universal malice" is simply a restatement of "extreme indifference to the value of human life," and, as such, adds up to nothing more than a statutory redundancy. "To base a substantial differential in penalty 'upon the shifting sands of these semantics does not constitute substantial justice.'" *Marcy,* 628 P.2d at 78 (quoting *People v. Calvaresi,* 188 Colo. at 282, 534 P.2d at 319).

I also find no significance in the additional words "generally" and "or persons" in the 1981 amendment. It has always been implicit in the pre-1981 version of extreme indifference murder that the "extreme indifference" be directed generally to the value of human life, rather than to the life of a particular person. *See People ex rel. Russel,* 185 Colo. at 83, 521 P.2d at 1256. The proscription of conduct creating a grave risk of death to "persons" as well as to "a person" also fails to contribute any objective basis to the purported distinction between extreme indifference murder and murder in the second degree. Indeed, this court's 1977 decision in *People v. Jones,* 193 Colo. 250, 565 P.2d 1333, made quite clear that extreme indifference murder encompassed conduct which creates a grave risk to either a single person or many persons. *Id.* at 254, 565 P.2d at 1336.

In sum, as long as second degree murder requires that the offender "knowingly" cause the death of another-that is, that he act with an awareness that his conduct is practically certain to result in death, *Mingo*, 196 Colo. at 317, 584 P.2d at 633—and as long as extreme indifference murder, as presently defined, also requires that the offender knowingly engage in conduct which creates a grave risk of death to another "under circumstances evidencing an attitude of universal malice manifesting extreme indifference to the value of human life generally," then, in my view, any purported distinction between these two offenses will necessarily fail to pass constitutional muster under an equal protection analysis.

Notes and Questions

1. Recall that when we considered the distinction between premeditated first-degree murder and second-degree murder, we observed that the distinction was only difficult in borderline cases, and that there were cases that were clear examples of a premeditated killing. Ted Bundy, John Wayne Gacy, Jeffrey Dahmer, and Osama bin Laden all clearly contemplated their killings in ways that clearly define their crimes as first-degree murders and not simply second-degree murder. Our inability to draw a meaningful line between premeditated murder and second-degree murder is problematic, but there are certainly cases that are, beyond any debate, first-degree murder cases. Are there any cases that clearly fit into Colorado's definition of universal malice? If a serial killer is a paradigm example of a premeditated killer, what is the paradigm example of a killer who acts with universal malice?

2. The majority's argument rests on a very thin reed. It concludes that the legislature can differently punish conduct directed against a particular individual and conduct "evidencing a willingness to take human life without regard to the victim. . ." Shooting a stranger, under this rationale, is somehow worse than shooting a known person. In some ways, the prosecution seems to be reprising *Batchelder* (see p. 102). The majority observes that a "single criminal transaction may give rise to the violation of more than one statute," and that it is for the trier of fact to decide which crime was committed. *Batchelder*, of course, dealt with the power of the prosecutor to choose which of two substantively identical statutes to charge. In *Batchelder*, it was the prosecutor who chose between statutes. The majority in *Jefferson* appears to suggest that juries can similarly decide between two statutes, with very different penalties, that cover the same conduct. The dissent observes that the Colorado Supreme

Court had previously rejected the possibility that juries can exercise that role. If that is true, why should it be true that prosecutors are permitted to pick among substantively identical offenses, with different penalties, but jurors should be denied this opportunity.

---

c. Mental States Often Defining Second Degree Murder

Second-degree murder is something of a catch-all. It is defined in a number of ways: depraved heart, malice, and a knowing killing. A number of states define second-murder occurs when the slayer intended great bodily harm, but not death, to his victim. A few states define second-degree murder as an intentional killing done without premeditation or deliberation. Then there are variety of statutes defining second-degree murder as the unintentional killing of victims with a special status and felony murder (or a subcategory of felony murder). Some states conclude that an unlawful killing is presumed to be second-degree murder.

To understand how a degree of homicide is defined, we most often must consider it in comparison to either the degree of above or below. In the sections above, we have come to have a decent understanding of second-degree murder. A killing on the border between first- and second-degree murder that does not satisfy the requirements for murder in the first-degree is second-degree.

The *Standiford* case that follows nicely lays out many of the various theories of homicide typically associated with second degree murder. As the case illustrates, however, it is often difficult distinguish between degrees of murder.

State v. Standiford

Supreme Court of Utah
769 P.2d 254 (1988)

STEWART, Justice:

Defendant Fred W. Standiford was convicted of second degree murder for the fatal stabbing of Hisae Wood. . . .

Defendant argues that the jury instructions on second degree murder violated his right to a unanimous jury verdict under article I, section 10 of the Utah Constitution because they did not specifically require jury unanimity as to whether the mens rea found by the jury was intent to kill, intent to cause grievous bodily harm, or knowing conduct that created a grave risk of death with depraved indifference to human life. *State v. Russell*, 733 P.2d 162 (Utah 1987), held that a jury does not have to be unanimous in deciding which of the three culpable mental states it finds in convicting of second degree murder, as long as the jurors are unanimous that one or another form of second degree murder was committed. That holding was based on the historical development of the crime of murder with malice aforethought[1] and on the similarity of the culpability required by the three alternatives. Compare *State v. Tillman*, 750 P.2d 546, 577–80, 585–88 (Utah 1988) (Stewart, J., concurring and concurring in the result and Durham, J., concurring and dissenting), where a majority of the Court held that jury unanimity is necessary as to all other elements in criminal cases. *See also State v. Rasmussen*, 92 Utah 357, 68 P.2d 176 (1937).

Standiford asserts that the trial court erred in failing to instruct the jury that second degree murder required proof of "malice aforethought." Prior to the adoption of Utah's current criminal code in 1973, murder was defined as "the unlawful killing of a human being with malice aforethought." Utah Code Ann. § 76–30–1 (1953) (repealed 1973). Defendant relies on *Farrow v. Smith*, 541 P.2d 1107, 1109 (Utah 1975), for the proposition that the trial court should have instructed on malice aforethought. In *Farrow*, the Court stated in dictum:

---

1   The commentary to the Model Penal Code summarizes the common law concept of malice aforethought:

At common law, murder was defined as the unlawful killing of another human being with "malice aforethought." Whatever the original meaning of that phrase, it became over time an "arbitrary symbol" used by judges to signify any of a number of mental states deemed sufficient to support liability for murder. Successive generations added new content to "malice aforethought" until it encompassed a variety of mental attitudes bearing no predictable relation to the ordinary sense of the two words. . . .

Various authorities have given different summaries of the several meanings of "malice aforethought." Generally, these definitions converge on four constituent states of mind. First and foremost, there was intent to kill. Common-law authorities included in the notion of intent to kill awareness that the death of another would result from one's actions, even if the actor had no particular desire to achieve such a consequence. Thus, intentional or knowing homicide was murder unless the actor killed in the heat of passion engendered by adequate provocation, in which case the crime was manslaughter. A second species of murder involved intent to cause grievous bodily harm. Again, knowledge that conduct would cause serious bodily injury was generally assimilated to intent and was deemed sufficient for murder if death of another actually resulted. A third category of murder was sometimes called depraved-heart murder. This label derived from decisions and statutes condemning as murder unintentional homicide under circumstances evincing a "depraved mind" or an "abandoned and malignant heart." Older authorities may have described such circumstances as giving rise to an "implied" or "presumed" intent to kill or injure, but the essential concept was one of extreme recklessness regarding homicidal risk. Thus, a person might be liable for murder absent any actual intent to kill or injure if he caused the death of another in a manner exhibiting a "wanton and willful disregard of an unreasonable human risk" or, in confusing elaboration, a "wickedness of disposition, hardness of heart, cruelty, recklessness of consequences, and a mind regardless of social duty." The fourth kind of murder was based on intent to commit a felony. This is the origin of the felony-murder rule, which assigns strict liability for homicide committed during the commission of a felony. These four states of mind exhausted the meaning of "malice aforethought"; the phrase had no residual content.

Model Penal Code, § 210.2 comment 1 at 13–15 (Official Draft and Revised Comments 1980) (footnotes omitted; citations omitted).

For many years the definition of second degree murder has been the unlawful killing of a human being with malice aforethought, and . . . manslaughter was the unlawful killing of a human being without malice. In our opinion the new criminal code has not changed those definitions.
In at least one other case, this Court has also referred to "malice aforethought." *State v. Norman,* 580 P.2d 237, 240 (Utah 1978).

The present criminal code abandoned the common law terminology of malice aforethought and adopted more descriptive and precise language describing the requisite culpable mental states in defining the various crimes. Since the term "malice aforethought" is a confusing carry-over from prior law and can lead to confusion, if not error, it should no longer be used. The present second degree murder statute sets forth the necessary mental states required for each type of second degree murder, except as modified by case law. *See State v. Bolsinger,* 699 P.2d 1214 (Utah 1985); *State v. Fontana,* 680 P.2d 1042 (Utah 1984). The statute provides:

> Murder in the second degree—(1) Criminal homicide constitutes murder in the second degree if the actor:
>
>> (a) intentionally or knowingly causes the death of another;
>>
>> (b) intending to cause serious bodily injury to another, he commits an act clearly dangerous to human life that causes the death of another;
>>
>> (c) acting under circumstances evidencing a depraved indifference to human life, he engages in conduct which creates a grave risk of death to another and thereby causes the death of another; or
>>
>> (d) while in the commission, attempted commission, or immediate flight from the commission or attempted commission of [certain enumerated felonies], [the actor] causes the death of another person other than a party. . . .

Utah Code Ann. § 76–5–203 (Supp.1988).

Thus, the culpable mental states included in the second degree murder statute are (1) an intent to kill, (2) an intent to inflict serious bodily harm, (3) conduct knowingly engaged in and evidencing a depraved indifference to human life, and (4) intent to commit a felony other than murder.

These terms are comparable to the old malice aforethought, but are much more precise and less confusing. The statute treats these forms of homicide as having similar culpability. Second degree murder is based on a very high degree of moral culpability. That culpability arises either from an actual intent to kill or from a mental state that is essentially equivalent thereto—such as intending grievous bodily injury and knowingly creating a very high risk of death. The risk of death in the latter two instances must be so great as to evidence such an indifference to life as to be tantamount to that evidenced by an intent to kill. In contrast, the felony-murder provision of the second degree murder statute is something of an exception to the above principle, as it does not require an intent to kill or any similar mental state.

The trial court framed its second degree murder and manslaughter instructions in the statutory language and correctly refused to give defendant's requested malice aforethought and absence of malice instructions. *See Bolsinger*, 699 P.2d 1214; *Fontana*, 680 P.2d 1042. To the extent that *Farrow v. Smith, State v. Norman*, and any other cases have perpetuated the use of malice aforethought with respect to second degree murder, they are disapproved.

Notes and Questions

The Utah statute is quite representative of the variety of ways second-degree murder in defined in the states. Sometimes this definition occurs by statute, as it does in Utah, and sometimes it occurs only in common law. Pennsylvania, for instance, defines third-degree murder (a category analogous to second-degree murder in most jurisdictions as second-degree murder in Pennsylvania is felony murder alone) as a form of murder not elsewhere defined. In such a jurisdiction, one would necessarily have to rely on common law to fill in the definition.

i. Intentional (But Not Premeditated or Deliberated) Killing

Before you read the *Gillespie* case, recall that the *Jefferson* case observes that there must be some meaningful distinction between the degrees of homicide. So if a defendant formed an intent to kill, how could he do so without deliberating over the matter?

State v. Gillespie

Supreme Court of Rhode Island
960 A.2d 969 (2008)

Chief Justice WILLIAMS, for the Court.

The defendant, Clyde Gillespie (defendant), appeals his convictions for second-degree murder and for failing to report a death with the intention of concealing a crime. He alleges that the trial justice erred in: (1) instructing the jury that premeditation is not an element of second-degree murder; [and] (2) instructing the jury on second-degree murder where, as the defendant contends, such a charge was not supported by the evidence. . . For the reasons hereinafter set forth, we affirm the judgment of the Superior Court.

I

Facts and Travel

On November 24, 1998, police responded to an unoccupied apartment in Providence, Rhode Island, where a cleaning crew had discovered a decomposing body wrapped in bedding and curtains in an attic crawl space accessible through a padlocked closet. Further investigation by the police revealed that defendant and his wife, Betty Sue Gillespie, were the last tenants to occupy the apartment.

After locating defendant, the police initially questioned him about his wife's whereabouts without disclosing that a body had been found in his former apartment. The defendant claimed that he had not seen Betty Sue since July, when she left him following an argument over another woman. He admitted, and bank records confirmed, that he since had been using Betty Sue's ATM card to withdraw money from her credit-union account. After the police informed him that they had discovered a body in the apartment, defendant acknowledged that the body was indeed that of Betty Sue. He explained that he had found her dead in bed one morning in July after a night during which she had been smoking crack cocaine. According to defendant, he wrapped Betty Sue's body in bed sheets, hid it in the attic crawl space, and padlocked shut the closet door after panicking over the thought that he would be held accountable for her death. A subsequent autopsy confirmed that the body was that of Betty Sue, but it also indicated that the cause of death was manual strangulation.

Doctor [Elizabeth] Laposata testified for the state regarding the condition of Betty Sue's body. She described the body as having been wrapped in three layers of sheets and draperies and noted the peculiar manner in which it was clothed: both the bra and underwear were inside out. Doctor Laposata testified that her examination of Betty Sue's body had revealed that Betty Sue had sustained injuries to her neck contemporaneously with her death, including a fractured hyoid bone and hemorrhaging in the upper neck tissue. According to Dr. Laposata, a fractured hyoid bone is "a classic marker for death by manual strangulation." She also testified that any other potential physical injuries were obscured by the body's advanced state of decomposition. Although toxicology tests had revealed the presence of cocaine and alcohol in Betty Sue's system, Dr. Laposata concluded to a reasonable degree of scientific certainty that the cause of death was asphyxia caused by manual strangulation.

The defendant did not testify or present any evidence at trial. The trial justice instructed the jury on both the crime of first-degree murder and the lesser-included offense of second-degree murder. The trial justice's jury instructions stated in relevant part:

> "I will now address the elements of the crime of murder and you must know that to convict of murder, the State must prove each of the elements beyond a reasonable doubt. Murder generally is the unlawful killing of a human being with malice aforethought. A willful, malicious and premeditated killing is murder in the first degree. In order to convict the defendant of first degree murder, the State must prove beyond a reasonable doubt that within the dates in question, the defendant, Clyde Gillespie, killed Betty Sue Gillespie by manual strangulation and that he did so willfully, deliberately, maliciously and with premeditation. An act is done willfully if done voluntarily and intentionally and not by mistake or accident. The terms 'deliberate' and 'voluntary' are actions resulting from the defendant's prior consideration of the act of killing itself. Such a prior consideration, however, must have existed in the mind of the defendant for more than simply a moments [sic] duration. In other words, the defendant must have deliberated and already fixed in his mind for more than a mere moment an intention to kill before the killing occurred. Perhaps, the best that can be said of deliberation is that it requires a cool mind that is capable of reflection and premeditation, that it requires that one with a cool mind did in fact reflect for more than a moment before the killing. Malice may be expressed or implied. Malice can arise from either an expressed intent to kill or to inflict great bodily harm. Malice may be implied or inferred from all the surrounding circumstances.

> " * * *

"Our law also recognizes murder in the second degree as a lesser included offense to the charge of murder. To prove the defendant guilty of murder in the second degree, the State must prove beyond a reasonable doubt that he killed Betty Sue Gillespie by manual strangulation within the dates in question and that he did so intentionally and maliciously. Unlike first degree murder, however, second degree murder does not require the State to prove beyond a reasonable doubt that the defendant killed with premeditation and deliberation. If a person's conscious intent or design to kill existed only amount [sic] momentarily or fleetingly, or if you are not convinced beyond a reasonable doubt that it existed for more than a moment or deliberately, it is second degree murder. On the other hand, if such a conscious design or intent existed for more than a mere moment and was a product of the deliberation, then the crime rises to the level of first degree murder. Just as with the instructions that I have given you as to first degree murder, as with second degree murder as well, there must be proof of malice and that malice may be expressed or implied.

"* * *

"In this case, therefore, if the State satisfies you beyond a reasonable doubt that the defendant, Clyde Gillespie, killed Betty Sue Gillespie, between the dates of June 1st, 1998 and November 24, 1998 by manual strangulation and that he did so intentionally and maliciously and with deliberation and premeditation, then you may return a verdict of guilty on the charge of first degree murder. If you find that the State has failed to prove beyond a reasonable doubt that such a killing was premeditated or deliberate, but you nonetheless determine that Clyde Gillespie intentionally and maliciously killed Betty Sue Gillespie, then you may return a verdict of guilty on the lesser included offense of second degree murder."

The defendant then proceeded to object on two grounds to the jury instructions cited above. First, defendant argued that it was improper to instruct the jury on second-degree murder because the proposed cause of death was manual strangulation, which he argued required the deliberation and premeditation that occurs only with first-degree murder. Secondly, defendant contended that the trial justice erred in instructing the jury that premeditation is not an element of second-degree murder. Rejecting both objections, the trial justice declined to amend her jury instructions.

On January 13, 2006, the jury convicted defendant of second-degree murder and of failing to report a death with the intention of concealing a crime. The defendant subsequently filed a motion for a new trial, in which he again challenged the second-degree murder jury instructions. The trial justice denied defendant's motion for a new trial and sentenced him to life imprisonment for the murder conviction and five years imprisonment for the conviction on failing to report a death, to be served consecutively.

II

ANALYSIS

A

Elements of Second-Degree Murder

The defendant argues that the trial justice committed reversible error when she declined to instruct the jury that premeditation is an element of second-degree murder. He cites a line of cases from this Court in which we either impliedly or expressly have stated that premeditation is an element of second-degree murder.

Section 11-23-1 defines murder as "[t]he unlawful killing of a human being with malice aforethought" and separates it into two degrees. "Every murder perpetrated by poison, lying in wait, or any other kind of willful, deliberate, malicious, and premeditated killing * * * is murder in the first degree. Any other murder is murder in the second degree."[4] *Id.* "In other words, murder in the second-degree 'is any killing of a human being committed with malice aforethought that is not defined by statute as first-degree murder.'" *State v. Texieira*, 944 A.2d 132, 142 (R.I.2008) (quoting *State v. Parkhurst*, 706 A.2d 412, 421 (R.I.1998)).

Although § 11-23-1 imports the old common-law definition of murder as a killing committed with malice aforethought, its delineation of murder into degrees is a statutory creation. Unfortunately, however, § 11-23-1 goes no further in distinguishing between first- and second-degree murder or in defining such terms as "deliberate" or "premeditated." The onus, therefore, has fallen on the judiciary to interpret this distinction; admittedly, we have not fulfilled our duty in that regard with the greatest clarity. We hope that this opinion will rectify any confusion about the distinction between first- and second-degree murder.

As § 11-23-1 indicates, a murder must be "willful, deliberate, malicious, and premeditated" for it to rise to the level of first-degree murder. Because § 11-23-1 defines first-degree murder as a "willful, deliberate, malicious, and premeditated killing," and second-degree murder as "[a]ny other murder," it necessarily follows that second-degree murder does not encompass "willful, deliberate, malicious, and premeditated" killings. Rather, the only requirement for a killing to qualify as second-degree murder is that it be committed with malice aforethought.

---

4   First-degree murder also includes felony murder for felonies specifically listed in G.L. 1956 § 11-23-1.

We have defined malice aforethought as "an unjustified disregard for the possibility of death or great bodily harm and an extreme indifference to the sanctity of human life." *Texieira*, 944 A.2d at 142. Malice aforethought arises either from "an express intent to kill or to inflict great bodily harm or from a hardness of the heart, cruelty, wickedness of disposition, recklessness of consequence, and a mind dispassionate of social duty."[5] *Id.*

Thus, we have recognized three theories of second-degree murder, each grounded in a different aspect of malice aforethought. *State v. Iovino*, 554 A.2d 1037, 1039 (R.I.1989). The first, which is the theory upon which the trial justice instructed the jury in this case, involves those killings in which the defendant formed a momentary intent to kill contemporaneous with the homicide. A second theory includes felony murder for inherently dangerous felonies that are not expressly listed within the statutory definition of first-degree murder. Finally, second-degree murder may be charged where the defendant killed with wanton recklessness or "conscious disregard for the possibility of death or of great bodily harm."

Again, the issue in this case is the distinction between the premeditation characteristic of first-degree murder and the momentary intent to kill involved in second-degree murder. Regrettably, our overly liberal use of the term "premeditation" in some past decisions has contributed to a certain amount of confusion regarding the required elements of second-degree murder. As defendant correctly notes, on various occasions we either have implied or expressly stated that premeditation is an element of second-degree murder.

Despite this semantic incongruity, we nonetheless have remained consistent in our application of the legal principle underlying the distinction between first- and second-degree murder. In all of our cases, regardless of the terminology employed, we have acted in accordance with § 11-23-1 and have held that the distinction between first-degree and momentary-intent-based second-degree murder is the *duration* of the defendant's intent to kill. First-degree murder requires that the defendant harbored a more-than-momentary intent to kill prior to committing the homicide-in essence, that he or she acted with premeditation. In contrast, the momentary-intent theory of second-degree murder involves a fleeting intent that is contemporaneous with the murder. Let there be no further

---

5   Our definition of "malice aforethought" comports with the common-law definition of the phrase. *See 2 Wharton's Criminal Law*, § 139 at 246-47 (Torcia 15th ed. 1994). The defendant argues that use of the term "aforethought" imports premeditation into the definition of murder. It is true that at early English common law, the word "aforethought" was used to signify premeditation-a requirement for murder at that time. Wayne R. LaFave, *Criminal Law*, § 14.1 at 725 (4th ed. 2003). However, as courts in England, and later in the United States, began to recognize other forms of murder absent premeditation, "aforethought" lost its meaning. *Id.* at 725-26. Today, "since malice need exist only at the time the homicidal act is committed, the term 'aforethought' has come to be superfluous." *2 Wharton's Criminal Law*, § 139 at 246.

confusion: premeditation is not a requirement of malice aforethought and thus is not an element of second-degree murder.

In the case at bar, the trial justice correctly instructed the jury on the elements of second-degree murder and its distinction from murder in the first degree. Before discussing the degrees of murder, she explained, consistent with § 11-23-1, that "[m]urder generally is the unlawful killing of a human being with malice aforethought." The trial justice then explained that, in order to convict defendant of first-degree murder, the jury would have to find beyond a reasonable doubt that he had killed his wife willfully, deliberately, maliciously, and with premeditation. After stating that second-degree murder does not require proof of premeditation or deliberation, the trial justice then proceeded to instruct on the momentary-intent theory:

> "If a person's conscious intent or design to kill existed only amount [sic] momentarily or fleetingly, or if you are not convinced beyond a reasonable doubt that it existed for more than a moment or deliberately, it is second degree murder. On the other hand, if such a conscious design or intent existed for more than a mere moment and was the product of the deliberation, then the crime rises to the level of first degree murder."

This instruction is entirely consistent with the momentary-intent theory of second-degree murder that we have recognized as inherent in § 11-23-1. The instruction clearly distinguished for the jury the momentary-intent concept from the premeditation required for first-degree murder. There was no error.

B

Appropriateness of the Trial Justice's Instruction on Second-Degree Murder

The defendant next argues that the trial justice erred by instructing the jury on the lesser-included offense of second-degree murder because, he contends, it was unsupported by the evidence. Based on Dr. Laposata's testimony that manual strangulation requires several minutes to accomplish, defendant asserts that it inherently requires premeditation and deliberation. Thus, he concludes, evidence of manual strangulation never can support an instruction for second-degree murder.

In determining the appropriateness of a trial justice's instruction on a lesser-included offense, we look to see if such an instruction is warranted by the evidence. "[T]here must be an actual and adequate factual dispute concerning the element that distinguishes the greater from the lesser offense" to justify an instruction on both. *Vorgvongsa*, 692 A.2d at 1197.

"There is no question that second-degree murder is a lesser included offense of the crime of murder in the first degree." *Vorgvongsa*, 692 A.2d at 1196. "[I]f the state proceeds on a theory of an intent to kill and the duration of the intent to kill is questionable, an instruction on both first- and second-degree murder should be given." *Parkhurst*, 706 A.2d at 421.

We never have held that convictions for manual strangulation are limited to murder in the first degree.[6] In fact, on numerous occasions, we have affirmed second-degree murder convictions where the cause of death was manual strangulation. *See, e.g., State v. Gomes*, 881 A.2d 97, 99 (R.I.2005) (where the defendant both strangled and stabbed the victim in the neck); *State v. Diaz*, 521 A.2d 129, 130 (R.I.1987) (where the evidence suggested that the defendant manually strangled the victim in an attempt to quiet her during an argument); *State v. Danahey*, 108 R.I. 291, 292, 294, 274 A.2d 736, 737, 738 (1971) (where the defendant strangled the victim with a necktie).[7]

Our decisions in these cases are consistent with our interpretation of premeditation and first-degree murder. As we explained above, premeditation constitutes a more-than-momentary period of intent formed in the defendant's mind *before* commission of the homicidal act. This is different from the amount of time that it takes the defendant to actually perpetrate the homicide. As the trial justice aptly observed, the most that can be gleaned from the fact that the cause of death was manual strangulation is that a defendant had the *opportunity* to premeditate and deliberate. *See id.*[8] We likewise have said that "[t]he act of killing, of itself, is not sufficient to give rise to a presumption that it was premeditated and deliberate. Indeed, although a homicide without additional evidence is presumed to be murder, the presumption ordinarily rises no higher than murder in the second degree." *Mattatall*, 603 A.2d at 1106 (quoting 2 *Wharton's Criminal Law*, § 140 at 182, 184-85 (Torcia 14th ed. 1979)). In the absence of additional evidence clearly indicating that a defendant did indeed premeditate and deliberate, an instruction on the lesser-included offense of second-degree murder is appropriate.

The defendant cites two cases in which we upheld a trial justice's refusal to instruct on second-degree murder on the grounds that the evidence supported only the conclusion that the defendant killed with premeditation and

---

6   We also note that the General Assembly chose not to list manual strangulation in the murder statute alongside murders perpetrated by poison and by lying in wait, which acts are statutorily classified as exclusively first-degree murder. *See* § 11-23-1.

7   We even have upheld a manslaughter conviction where the cause of death was manual strangulation. *See State v. Cohen*, 93 R.I. 215, 216, 218, 172 A.2d 737, 738, 739 (1961), *overruled on other grounds, State v. Caruolo*, 524 A.2d 575, 585 n. 3 (R.I.1987).

8   In fact, the facts of past cases demonstrate that manual strangulation is possible even absent any intent to kill. *See State v. Diaz*, 521 A.2d 129, 130 (R.I.1987) (evidence indicated that the strangulation might have been the result of the defendant trying to quiet the victim during an argument); *Randall v. State*, 760 So.2d 892, 901-02 (Fla.2000) (evidence suggested that the defendant strangled the victims for his own sexual gratification during consensual sex, not with an intent to kill).

deliberation. *See State v. Brown*, 898 A.2d 69, 84-85 (R.I.2006); *Sosa*, 839 A.2d at 526-27. Both cases, however, easily are distinguishable from the case at bar because of the extensive evidence in each case of premeditation and deliberation. *See Brown*, 898 A.2d at 73, 84-85 (victim slowly asphyxiated after the defendant sexually assaulted her, stabbed her in the neck several times, disconnected the telephone cord, and used it to bind her arms and strangle her); *Sosa*, 839 A.2d at 526-27 (shooting death of victim followed: (1) an altercation with the defendant days before the murder; (2) verbal threats from the defendant minutes before the murder; and (3) the defendant's departure from the scene of the threats to retrieve a gun before returning and shooting the victim).

In the case at bar, the limited evidence concerning the circumstances of Betty Sue's strangulation illustrates that the jury could have had reasonable doubt about whether defendant harbored the premeditation required for first-degree murder. As Dr. Laposata testified, the advanced state of decomposition of Betty Sue's body obscured any evidence of other physical injuries that might have reinforced the notion that the murder was premeditated. In contrast, other evidence, such as the haphazard manner in which Betty Sue was clothed, militates against the theory that the murderer acted with premeditation. Accordingly, the trial justice did not err in instructing the jury on the lesser-included offense of second-degree murder.

Notes and Questions

1. Is Rhode Island's perspective on time and premeditation consistent with many of the other cases we've read? Notice that many states conclude that premeditation can be formed in an instant. Even the *Guthrie* decision (p. 607) seems to conclude that premeditation can be formed in an instant, even if the West Virginia Supreme Court called on trial courts to be somewhat less explicit about this point in their instructions to juries. Recall that the New Mexico Supreme Court in *Tafoya* (p. 618) also observed that premeditation could be formed in an instant, but the prosecution had a much more difficult task when the defendant had only a short period to contemplate his killing. The Rhode Island Supreme Court in *Gillespie* expressly says that when the defendant only has moments to deliberate, his killing is not first-degree murder. How do you explain Rhode Island's rule, especially in light of the fact that the notion that "premeditation can be formed in an instant" is often regarded as hornbook law?

2. In considering the answer to the last question, consider the principle assumed to be true in *Jefferson* (p. 698), that there must be a differentiation between the

degrees of homicide. First-degree murder in Rhode Island requires intent plus premeditation, but an intentional killing is one of Rhode Island's definitions of second-degree murder.

---

ii. Intent to Cause Serious Bodily Injury

Most but certainly not all of the cases we consider that define the substance of criminal statutes involve one of three types of claimed errors: (1) challenges to the sufficiency of the evidence to prove one or more of the elements of the crime; (2) challenges to jury instructions that define one or more of the elements of the crime; (3) challenges to the trial court's decision to admit or reject evidence on the basis of its interpretation that the elements of a statute make the evidence relevant or irrelevant. The Utah Supreme Court's decision in *Fisher* fleshes out the definition of one way of proving second-degree murder (intent to cause serious bodily injury) but does so in a non-traditional way.

This case involves the appropriateness of the prosecutor's argument and the court observes that even if the prosecutor's comments were inappropriate, this would have been harmless error because there was overwhelming evidence supporting the conviction. The prosecution represented in its opening argument that it would present evidence on the defendant's intent to kill the victim, which we just learned is one way of demonstrating second-degree murder. The trial testimony was not, however, as strong on intent as the prosecutor suggested that it should be. The court found that error to be harmless because there was more than sufficient evidence on another method of proving second-degree murder— intent to cause serious bodily injury.

State v. Fisher

Supreme Court of Utah
680 P.2d 35 (1984)

OAKS, Justice:

A jury convicted defendant of second degree murder for the strangulation death of Jolene Scott, a prostitute who defendant believed was having a homosexual affair with his wife. On appeal, defendant claims that he was denied a fair trial because the prosecutor's opening statement outlined damaging testimony that was never produced at trial.

According to defendant's signed statement and trial testimony, he and Scott drove around Salt Lake City for seven or eight hours on July 7, 1980, while she "worked" at two truck stops. Thereafter, when he confronted her about his wife's whereabouts, she told him she did not know. He called her a liar and struck her. She made an inflammatory remark about the affections of his wife. A fight ensued, during which Scott "went wild." Defendant strangled her "to get her to go unconscious." As he did so, he felt her neck snap. Defendant claims he never intended to kill her.

In his opening statement to the jury, the prosecutor outlined the anticipated testimony of defendant's friend, Edward Houser:

> Mr. Houser will testify that on several occasions after Howard Fisher's wife had left him, Howard Fisher had threatened the life of Jolene Scott, making the statement that he felt if in fact he could do away with Jolene Scott that his wife, Zacoma, would come back to him. And he indicated to Mr. Houser on not one but several occasions different methods by which he would do away with Jolene Scott and that some of those ways included strangulation.

Houser had testified at the preliminary hearing, but not to all of the matters described above. At the time of the opening statement, he had been subpoenaed to testify and was present at trial. Thereafter, he refused to testify due to threats he had received from fellow inmates at the Utah State Penitentiary. When defendant learned of Houser's refusal, he moved for a mistrial. The motion was denied. Defendant contends that Houser's failure to testify as described in the opening statement denied him his right to confront and cross-examine the "witness."

Where the State does not produce a witness whose testimony was outlined during its opening statement, we look at two factors to determine whether the conviction should be reversed. "The controlling question should be the good faith or lack of good faith of counsel in saying what he said in his opening statement and the likelihood that the opening statement was unfairly prejudicial to the defendant." *State v. Williams*, Utah, 656 P.2d 450, 452 (1982), *quoting Gladden v. Frazier*, 388 F.2d 777, 779 (9th Cir.1968).

Defendant does not contend that this prosecutor lacked good faith in his description of the anticipated testimony. Nothing in the record indicates that the prosecutor knew Houser would refuse to testify. After he learned of Houser's refusal, he made no further reference to the testimony.

Defendant relies on the second ground, insisting that he was prejudiced by the prosecutor's statements. The critical inquiry under this ground is whether the statements would have so influenced the jury that without them there was "a reasonable likelihood of a more favorable result for the defendant." *State v.*

Fontana, Utah, 680 P.2d 1042, 1048 (1984), *quoting State v. Hutchison*, Utah, 655 P.2d 635, 637 (1982). That question turns on the nature of the statements and their relationship to the evidence introduced at trial.

Because of defendant's signed confession, which he verified on the witness stand, most of the facts surrounding the killing were not in dispute at the trial. The contested issue was defendant's intent. Houser's anticipated testimony, outlined by the prosecutor, bore directly on that vital issue. It indicated (1) that defendant had threatened Scott's life on several occasions, (2) that he had a motive for killing her, and (3) that he had planned the murder in advance, including strangulation as one possible method.

The prosecution presented the testimony of Linda Calvin, Houser's sister.[1] She testified that defendant had threatened to kill Scott on at least two occasions and that on another occasion defendant struck Scott and had to be physically restrained. Thus, Calvin's testimony covered the first portion of Houser's expected testimony—defendant's threats to kill the victim—but not the second two portions. Calvin's testimony gave the jury a basis to infer defendant's intent to kill Jolene Scott, but that basis was not as strong as it would have been under the anticipated testimony of Houser.

Defendant was charged with three variations of second degree murder: intent to kill, intent to cause serious bodily injury, and acting under circumstances evidencing a depraved indifference to human life. U.C.A., 1953, § 76–5–203(1)(a), (b), and (c). Intent to kill is a necessary element of only one of these three variations. The jury was instructed on each alternative, as well as on the lesser included offenses of manslaughter and negligent homicide. Counsel did not request separate verdict forms, *see* Utah R.Crim.P. § 77–35–21(d); *State v. Anderson*, 27 Utah 2d 276, 278, 495 P.2d 804, 805 (1972), and the general verdict did not specify which variation of second degree murder the jury relied upon.

Disregarding for a moment the possible effect of the prosecutor's statement, we conclude that there was ample independent, credible evidence to support a jury verdict on the first variation, that defendant intended to kill Scott.[2]

More importantly, defendant admitted each element of the second variation of second degree murder, where death results from an act "clearly dangerous to human life" committed with the intent "to cause serious bodily injury . . . ." "Serious bodily injury" is "bodily injury that creates or causes . . . protracted loss

---

1 Defendant argues that Calvin had "serious problems of credibility." All of the witness's infirmities were brought out at trial. It was for the jury, not this Court, to judge her credibility.

2 For example, in *Cato v. State*, Tex.Cr.App., 534 S.W.2d 135, 137–38 (1976), a defendant was convicted of intentionally or knowingly causing his wife's death by strangulation, notwithstanding his testimony that he never intended to kill her. The only evidence of intent to kill in *Cato* was the fact of strangulation itself.

or impairment of the function of any bodily member or organ or creates a substantial risk of death." § 76–1–601(9). Defendant's conduct falls squarely within this variation of second degree murder. He testified that he intentionally placed his hands on the victim's neck, that he intentionally squeezed her throat, and that he intended to "get her to go unconscious." In other words, defendant intentionally committed an act that is dangerous to human life (strangulation), intending to cause serious bodily injury (protracted loss or impairment of both the heart and the brain, i.e., unconsciousness). Our holding that strangulation constitutes "serious bodily injury" is consistent with the case law on this question, cited in the footnote.[3]

Where the evidence overwhelmingly supports a conviction under one variation of a crime submitted to the jury, we need not reverse a conviction even if there were erroneous instructions on another variation. *State v. Fontana, supra,* at 1048–49, and cases cited therein. Similarly, a defendant who has made "no request for an instruction which would enable him to know which theory the jury adopted" cannot complain of insufficiency of the evidence for one theory of first degree murder when there was ample evidence under either theory. *State v. Anderson,* 27 Utah 2d at 278, 495 P.2d at 805.

By analogy, the likelihood of prejudice from an opening statement as to one variation of a crime is to be considered in light of the quantum of evidence that supports another variation. Here, the evidence, including defendant's testimony and sworn statement, is adequate for his conviction of second degree murder under the variation charging intent to kill and is virtually conclusive of his conviction under the variation charging intent to inflict serious bodily injury. In light of that fact, we are unable to say that there is any reasonable likelihood that the outcome of defendant's trial would have been different without the remarks in the opening statement. Defendant was not denied his right to a fair trial.

---

3 *State v. Blakeney,* 137 Vt. 495, 408 A.2d 636 (1979) (strangulation constituted "serious bodily injury" for purposes of aggravation element in aggravated assault conviction); *Commonwealth v. Watson,* 494 Pa. 467, 474, 431 A.2d 949, 952 (1981) ("it is beyond question that manual strangulation can result in serious bodily injury, if not death"). *Cf. State v. King,* Utah, 604 P.2d 923 (1979) (jury justified in finding "serious bodily injury" where defendant strangled victim into unconsciousness and stabbed her with a pair of scissors); *Houck v. State,* Okl. Cr.App., 563 P.2d 665 (1977) (death by strangulation constituted second degree murder).

Notes and Questions

1. Is there not something artificial about the category of intent to cause serious bodily harm that the court describes here? Can you imagine a person strangling a person merely with the intent that the person become unconscious? Or can you imagine a person acting with the intent of causing unconsciousness that did not create an extraordinary risk to the life to his victim? Professor Wayne LaFave has observed that there is an argument there is "no need for the separate category of intent-to-do-serious-bodily-harm murder . . . that such cases are properly encompassed within the depraved-heart murder and reckless manslaughter categories, depending upon on the facts of the particular case." Wayne R. LaFave, *Criminal Law* 778, § 14.3 (5th ed. 2010). This argument seems especially compelling when it is realized that serious bodily injury "means something close to, though of course less than, death." *Id.* at 779.

2. Courts have, however, found that serious bodily injury can be demonstrated by acts that do not seem to threaten life. *See Baker v. State*, 246 Ga. 317, 271 S.E.2d 360 (1980) (broken nose and bruises); *People v. Caliendo*, 84 Ill.App.3d 987, 40 Ill.Dec. 41, 405 N.E.2d 1133 (1980) (fractured ribs and lacerations); *People v. Rickman*, 73 Ill.App.3d 755, 29 Ill.Dec. 431, 391 N.E.2d 1114 (1979) (broken ankle); *State v. Colomy*, 407 A.2d 1115 (Me.1979) (contusion of the kidney); *State v. Fuger*, 170 Mont. 442, 554 P.2d 1338 (1976) (broken nose and fractured pallet); *Commonwealth v. Alexander, Aplnt.*, 237 Pa.Super. 111, 346 A.2d 319 (1975) (broken nose and blackened eyes).

iii. Depraved Heart

The most commonly used form of second-degree murder is described using a variety of terms, including malice, malice aforethought, extreme indifference to human life, and, as you will see in *Windham*, depraved heart. Practically speaking, this form of homicide requires the state to prove that the defendant created an extraordinarily high risk of death, with many states requiring the state prove that the defendant created a virtual certainty of death.

As we observed, the line between premeditated first-degree murder and the depraved heart version of second-degree murder is a blurry one at best. We considered the line between these two when we considered first-degree murder. Premeditated first-degree murder and depraved heart second-degree murder are, in theory anyway, separated by a difference in kind not degree. Depraved heart second-degree murder is distinguished from the less serious homicide offense, typically known as involuntary manslaughter, only by a difference in degree.

Windham reveals how conceptually difficult it is to distinguish between depraved heart murder and involuntary manslaughter, even if the result is one that as a juror you might find quite acceptable. *Windham* thus again demonstrates the prominent role of the jury in defining the law of homicide. Procedurally, *Windham* argues that the jury should not have been instructed on the depraved heart version of murder because, given the lack of distinction between depraved heart murder and involuntary manslaughter, the depraved heart instruction effectively prevented the jury from considering the involuntary manslaughter count.

Windham v. State

Supreme Court of Mississippi
602 So.2d 798 (1992)

PRATHER, Justice, for the Court:

I. INTRODUCTION

A. Procedural History

In November 1985, the Kemper County Grand Jury indicted 21-year-old Otis Lee Windham under Miss.Code Ann. §§ 97-3-19 & 97-3-21 (1972) for the June 1985 murder of 79-year-old Albert Thurston Calvert.

At the Kemper County Circuit Court, a jury found Windham guilty, and the trial judge sentenced him to life imprisonment. On appeal, this Court reversed and remanded for a new trial.

On remand, another jury found Windham guilty of murder, and Judge Robert W. Bailey sentenced him to life imprisonment. Windham appealed. This Court affirms.

B. Facts

The facts or evidence adduced in the second trial is essentially the same as that adduced in the first trial. *See Windham v. State*, 520 So.2d 123, 124 (Miss.1988). The following is a summary of this evidence viewed in a light most favorable to the State.

Albert Calvert and his wife, Betty, owned and operated a small grocery store in the Zion Community of Kemper County. Albert was seventy-nine years old and had no right arm; it had been cut off at the shoulder. Betty was seventy-eight years old. On June 26, 1985, around 6:00 to 6:30 p.m., twenty-one-year-old Otis Lee Windham pulled into Calvert's Grocery to buy gas.

No one disputes that, as Otis pumped gas, he and Albert argued over a debt Otis owed Calvert's Grocery. Betty walked to the scene and noticed Otis gripping her husband's arm. She immediately attempted to pry Otis' grip loose, but she did not succeed. Wanda Hampton, while fishing in the Calverts' nearby pond, overheard Betty say: "If you don't leave him alone, I'll call the sheriff." When Windham refused to release Albert, Betty struck Otis in the face with her hand. Otis then reached through his car window, retrieved a carpenter's hammer, and hit her head hard enough to render her unconscious. According to Otis, Albert "never hit me but he started back in the store and that's when I grabbed him and throwed him." Meanwhile, Betty regained consciousness and witnessed her husband's body fall "limber as a dishrag" in front of her. The State contended—and the jury obviously believed—that Otis had assaulted Albert with the hammer,[1] which resulted in his death a short time later.

II. ANALYSIS

1.

Otis presents two contentions. He contends that Instruction S-3, a "depraved heart" murder instruction should not have been granted: (1) because it (Instruction S-3) "amounted to a denial, or substantial diminishing of a manslaughter consideration"; and (2) because it was "not supported by the facts." * * *

Specifically, Instruction S-3 provides:

The Court instructs the Jury that, if you believe from the evidence in this case, beyond a reasonable doubt, that on the 26th day of June, 1985, in Kemper County, Mississippi, the deceased, Albert Thurston Calvert, was a living person, and the Defendant, Otis Lee Windham, did wilfully, unlawfully and feloniously act in a manner eminently dangerous to Albert Thurston Calvert and others, evincing a depraved heart, regardless of human life, by beating Albert Thurston Calvert with a Hammer which resulted in the death of Albert Thurston Calvert, then you shall find the Defendant guilty of murder.

Vol. I, at 61. Otis contends that this instruction should not have been granted because it "amounted to a denial, or substantial diminishing of a manslaughter consideration." At the trial level, Otis phrased his objection accordingly: "I object

---

1   Albert contended that he merely "grabbed [him] and pushed him and got into [his] car and left." Vol. II, at 119–20. An autopsy, however, revealed that Albert's injuries were inconsistent with a mere fall to the ground. Albert sustained scalp lacerations, skull fractures, and extensive brain injury—all of which the pathologist opined were caused by a "blow" from a blunt object such as a hammer. As metaphorically described by the pathologist, the blows reflected "home run hits." *Id.* at 58.

to S-3 . . . [because it] is designed to deprive the defendant of manslaughter-or any manslaughter or any excusable homicide instruction." In essence, Otis' contention is that the crime of depraved-heart murder as defined by Section 97-3-19(1)(b) is indistinguishable from culpable-negligence manslaughter as defined in Miss.Code Ann. Section 97-3-47.

Instruction S-3 derives its authority specifically from statutory law, which provides in part:

(1) The killing of a human being without the authority of law by any means or in any manner shall be murder in the following cases:

(b) When done in the commission of an act eminently dangerous to others and evincing a *depraved heart*, regardless of human life, although without any premeditated design to effect the death of any particular individual. . . .

MISS.CODE ANN. § 97-3-19(1)(b) (1991 Supp.) (emphasis added).

The familiar manslaughter statute, which Otis contends is diminished by Instruction S-3, provides:

Every other killing of a human being, by the act, procurement, or culpable negligence of another, and without authority of law, not provided for in this title, shall be manslaughter.

MISS.CODE ANN. § 97-3-47 (1972). Countering Otis' contention, the State asserts that § 97-3-47 "specifically excludes homicides falling under § 97-3-19(1) (b)." "Therefore," the State concludes, "depraved-heart murder and culpable-negligence manslaughter are mutually exclusive; by the express terms of the Mississippi Code, they do not overlap."

Otis' contention is unpersuasive. Depraved-heart murder and culpable-negligence manslaughter are distinguishable simply by degree of mental state of culpability. In short, depraved-heart murder involves a higher degree of recklessness from which malice or deliberate design may be implied. *See, e.g.*, W. LAFAVE & A. SCOTT, CRIMINAL LAW §§ 30 & 70 (1972); *United States v. Browner*, 889 F.2d 549, 552 (5th Cir.1989).

In sum, Instruction S-3 did not "amount[ ] to a denial, or substantial diminishing, of a manslaughter consideration" by the jury. This conclusion is consistent with this Court's decision in at least one other case in which a depraved-heart murder instruction and a culpable-negligence manslaughter instruction were properly granted. *See Johnson v. State*, 475 So.2d 1136, 1139-40 & 1148 (Miss.1985); *accord State v. Smith*, 415 A.2d 562 (Me.1980) (depraved-heart and culpable-negligence instructions given in this case involving death from "brutal and senseless beating"); *State v. Goodall*, 407 A.2d 268 (Me.1979) (same). Thus, Otis' contention is deemed devoid of merit.

2.

Next, Otis contends that Instruction S-3 should not have been granted because it was "not supported by the facts." Otis' contention is devoid of merit. The evidence clearly establishes the existence of actual or implied malice or deliberate design. More specifically, the evidence establishes the possibility that Otis could have killed Calvert "while acting in a manner eminently dangerous to others [*i.e.*, the Calverts] and evincing a depraved heart, regardless of human life." *Compare with Johnson v. State*, 475 So.2d 1136, 1139-40 (Miss.1985).

* * *

Under the traditional view, death which resulted from a reckless act directed toward a *particular* individual would not be deemed to be within the scope of depraved-heart murder statutes. To constitute depraved-heart murder, the act must have manifested a reckless indifference to human life in general. *See* F. WHARTON, THE LAW OF HOMICIDE § 129 (3rd ed. 1907). For example, an unjustified shooting at a passing train or into a house, which generally poses a risk to a group of individuals and which results in death, is a familiar example of traditional depraved-heart murder. *See People v. Jernatowski*, 238 N.Y. 188, 144 N.E. 497 (1924) (shooting into a room); *Banks v. State*, 85 Tex.Crim. 165, 211 S.W. 217 (1919) (shooting into caboose of passing train).

The traditional view has since evolved. An act which poses a risk to only one individual and which results in that individual's death may also be deemed depraved-heart murder. * * *

In *Johnson v. State*, 475 So.2d 1136 (Miss.1985), this Court left no question regarding the view to which Mississippi adheres. That is, this Court construed Miss.Code Ann. § 97-3-19(1)(b) (Supp.1984)-the depraved-heart murder statute-in a manner which encompasses a reckless and eminently dangerous act directed toward a single individual. Indeed, this Court can perceive no rationale for characterizing a horrendously-violent act, like the one committed by Otis, as manslaughter rather than depraved-heart murder, simply because, under the traditional view, the act must have been directed toward " *human life in general*" as opposed to *one individual in particular*. A distinction between the risk of death to one particular individual and the risk of death to more than one individual is a senseless and outmoded one which this Court properly discarded six years ago in *Johnson v. State*. *See* R. PERKINS, CRIMINAL LAW 32 (1957) (Under the depraved-heart theory, "a wanton and reckless disregard of an obvious human risk is with malice aforethought even if there was no actual intent to kill or injure."); *cf.* O.W. HOLMES, THE COMMON LAW 53 (1881) ("[K]nowledge that the act will probably cause death . . . is enough in murder as in tort."); *Commonwealth v. Chance*, 174 Mass. 245, 252, 54 N.E. 551, 554 (1899) (As Justice Holmes further explained: "[I]t is possible to commit murder without any actual intent to kill or to do grievous bodily harm, and that, reduced to its lowest terms, 'malice,' in murder, means knowledge of such circumstances that according to common experience there is a plain and strong likelihood that death will follow the contemplated act, coupled perhaps with an implied negation of any excuse or justification. 'The criterion in such cases is to examine whether common social duty would, under the circumstances, have suggested a more circumspect conduct.'") (quoting case law).

3.

In sum, the judge granted instructions on various theories of culpability—including simple murder, depraved-heart murder, inexcusable manslaughter, and excusable manslaughter. The jury found Otis guilty of "murder"—which means the jury accepted a simple-murder theory or a depraved-heart murder theory. In either event, the evidence or facts justified an instruction on, and a finding of, depraved-heart murder. This conclusion is consistent with case law in this State as well as the modern view espoused in other jurisdictions. *See generally Annotation, Validity and Construction of Statute Defining Homicide By Conduct Manifesting "Depraved Indifference,"* 435 A.L.R.4th 311 (1983 & 1990 Supp.); *see* W. LAFAVE & A. SCOTT, CRIMINAL LAW § 70 (1972); R. PERKINS, CRIMINAL LAW 32 (1957). This Court therefore affirms on this issue.

III. CONCLUSION

Otis Lee Windham has been afforded two trials by jury. In each case, the jury concluded: (1) that the evidence proves beyond a reasonable doubt the existence of the element of malice-actual or implied; and (2) that no justifiable or mitigating circumstance existed to support a finding of manslaughter.

This Court is convinced beyond a reasonable doubt that the evidence supports the jury verdict. A third trial is not warranted. The murder conviction is therefore AFFIRMED.

HAWKINS, Presiding Justice, concurring:

I concur in affirming, but with serious misgivings. As the majority notes, in *Johnson v. State*, 475 So.2d 1136 (Miss.1985). . ., this Court crossed the bridge upon which I have concern. I should have dissented then.

Miss.Code Ann. § 97-3-19 (1972) states:

§ 97-3-19. Homicide-murder defined.

. . . . .

(a) When done with deliberate design to effect the death of the person killed, or of any human being;

(b) When done in the commission of an act eminently dangerous to others, and evincing a depraved heart, regardless of human life, although without any premeditated design to effect the death of any particular individual;

(c) When done without any design to effect death, by any person engaged in the commission of the crime of rape, burglary, arson, or robbery, or in any attempt to commit such felonies.

We are only dealing with subparagraphs (a) and (b) above. Subparagraph (a) deals, of course, with a killing in which A intentionally slays B. It is that simple.

Subparagraph (b) is something quite different.[1] It states that *while* A is engaged in an act that is very dangerous *to others* he happens to kill B, and he had a "depraved heart" in committing this extremely dangerous act, then he is guilty of murder even though he had no actual design to kill any particular person. Classic examples of this type of murder are shooting into an occupied building or bus, or putting a bomb in a building or car. *Gentry v. State*, 92 Miss. 141, 45 So. 721, 721 (1908):

It is, of course, a well-known general principle that if one fires into a crowd of persons with a spirit of malignity and utter recklessness of human life, and kills any one in the crowd, he is guilty of murder, because of the recklessness and willfulness and malignity of the shooting generally.

* * *

[I]f Windham did not actually *intend* to kill Mr. Calvert, what are the possibilities in his state of mind? It could have been that Windham was afraid Mr. Calvert was about to reach into the store and get that rifle or his pistol, as he

---

1   My guess is that the authors meant "imminently" rather than "eminently" dangerous to others. "Imminently" suggests something that is likely to occur at any moment. The word "eminently," however, has been in this code section at least since 1848.

testified. Or, it could have been anger, rape, ignorance, stupidity, and perhaps mean to boot. But *depraved*? After this incident Windham drove straight to the sheriff's office and reported what had happened. Was this the act of a man with a "depraved heart?"

I cannot recall of reading or ever hearing of any man who planted a bomb, blew up a bridge, or shot into an occupied bus going to a sheriff or policeman and telling him what he had just done. * * *

On the question of "depraved heart," the Court makes no distinction whatever, gives no guide to the jury, between a subparagraph (b) slaying and manslaughter. . . .

If we read the statute as the Legislature manifestly meant it to be read, we would encounter no difficulty. This statute says quite simply that a person who (1) engages in some act extremely dangerous to others and (2) who does so with an evil state of mind- *e.g.,* placing a bomb in a building-this meets the requirement. If we would leave it at that, we would have no problem. We had none in the first 150 years we had the statute. It is when a Court seeks to expand the statute to mean something else that we run into trouble.

ROBERTSON, Justice, concurring:

* *. *

I see no rational distinction in criminal culpability between acts regardless of human life when compared with an act regardless of a particular human life. Practical people are not concerned with fine lines between states of mind when each act creates great risk of grave harm to another person. Do we not hold "A" for murder where he shoots at "B" intending to kill "B" but misses "B" and instead strikes and kills "C"? *See, e.g., Ross v. State*, 158 Miss. 827, 831-32, 131 So. 367, 368 (1930). This, of course, leads quickly to the point that Subsection (1)(b) "eminently dangerous" murder engulfs and subsumes Subsection (1)(a) "deliberate design" murder, and it does. They are concentric circles around conduct with (1)(a) the smaller within. Can anyone find a case in our reports where a defendant has been convicted of Subsection 1(a) "deliberate design" murder and where, had the prosecution proceeded solely under Subsection 1(b) "eminently dangerous" murder, we would not reject on appeal a challenge to the weight and sufficiency of the evidence? And, so a deliberate reading together of (1)(a) and (1)(b) renders intent-malice aforethought-if you must, a bit of lagniappe.

We are told this would cut into manslaughter's domain. . . (Hawkins, P.J., concurring, p. 805) That is certainly true, and it may indeed, in practical effect, deny a trial court the power to direct a verdict that the defendant is at most guilty of manslaughter. What we are not told is how and why this would be a loss to the law or the society it serves.

BANKS, Justice, dissenting:

I agree with Justice Hawkins that the "depraved heart" provision in our murder statute does not reach acts directed at a single person. One is presumed to intend the natural consequences of one's acts. *Johnson v. State*, 461 So.2d 1288, 1293-94 (Miss.1984) quoting *Lee v. State*, 244 Miss. 813, 146 So.2d 736, 738 (1962). Conduct directed at a single individual which is likely to produce death may evince a deliberate design to kill. *Berry v. State*, 575 So.2d 1, 12 (Miss.1990). To the extent that the jury finds that it does not, the perpetrator is, or may be, guilty of manslaughter. *Mease v. State*, 539 So.2d 1324 (Miss.1989).

The "depraved heart" provision is designed to reach different conduct, undirected as to a single individual or the individual harmed as fully explained in Justice Hawkins' opinion. As Justice Robertson incisively notes, the majority reading of "depraved heart" murder subsumes both deliberate design murder and most, if not all, of our various manslaughter statutes. That's the problem. While it may be difficult to explain why this would be a loss to society, the power of the legislature to define crimes includes the power to make distinctions. Our duty to construe statutes to give effect to all of their provisions compels us to recognize such distinctions.

Because the jury here was allowed to convict on "depraved heart" murder, I dissent.

DAN M. LEE, P.J., joins this dissent.

Notes and Questions

1. Is Justice Hawkins correct when he suggests that the only possible inference from the defendant's conduct is that he intended to kill Mr. Calvert? Can you imagine the defendant actually having utter indifference to whether his actions killed Mr. Calvert but not actually consciously desiring Calvert's death?

2. Recall that Colorado uses the distinction between creating great risk to one person and a great risk to more than one, a difference Justice Robertson says practical people are not concerned with, to separate first-degree (universal malice) murder from second-degree (depraved heart) murder. *See People v. Jefferson*, p. 698. In Mississippi, as in Colorado, however, reasonable peo-

ple differ over whether there is a meaningful distinction between killing a known person and killing with complete indifference to the identity of the vicitm. The opinions of Justice Prather and Justice Robertson find the distinction meaningless. Justice Hawkins' and Justice Banks' opinions, by contrast, approve of a definition of depraved heart.

3. Justice Hawkins' concurrence stressed his concern that courts are given no way to rule at the close of the evidence that a crime is no more than manslaughter—that there is no practical way to distinguish manslaughter from depraved heart second-degree murder. By extension, he is concerned there is no way for appellate courts to conclude that a jury incorrectly found a defendant was guilty of second-degree (depraved heart) murder when the evidence supported only a finding of manslaughter. In essence, Justice Hawkins is concluding that there is something wrong with leaving the degree of homicide to juries alone to decide, but he does not tell us what that problem is.

4. By contrast, Justice Robertson recognizes that there may be no way for courts to identify a difference between second-degree depraved heart murder and manslaughter, but he notes, "What we are not told is how and why this would be a loss to the law or the society it serves." He implicitly approves of juries having exclusive authority over determining the seriousness of homicide. There, however, seem to be two problems with this trust in juries. Juries typically learn all the facts of exactly one case and thus have no point of comparison to determine which homicide should be viewed as worse than the other if the law does not provide them with adequate guidance on which one is more serious than the other. Further, unless juries are told the consequences of a conviction for each type of offense, then they are simply picking between two terms which equally describe the defendant's actions.

————————

Courts vary in their degree to which they police the boundaries between categories of murder. The *Kelly* case demonstrates a court much more actively supervising the lines between second-degree murder and the lesser form of homicide. Instead of depraved heart murder, Tennessee's criminal code defines second-degree murder as a knowing killing. The Tennessee Code, which in this way tracks the Model Penal Code, concludes that a defendant knows that the prohibited results will occur when those results are practically certain to occur from his actions. Tennessee, following the Model Penal Code in this regard as well, does not have the crime of involuntary manslaughter, but instead has the crime of reckless homicide, which requires that the defendant consciously disregarded an unreasonable risk to human life. Notice in the *Kelly* case that the court is trying to define a line between these forms of homicide that Justice Robertson found in *Windham* to be non-existent and bad policy to try to fashion.

State v. Kelly

Court of Criminal Appeals of Tennessee, at Nashville
1998 WL 712268

[The defendant, George Blake Kelly, highly agitated from marital troubles, drove down a two-lane country road at night with a blood alcohol level of 0.28 and, as he was attempted to pass a car on a curve, collided with an oncoming vehicle, killing its passenger.]

The relevant definition of second-degree murder is the "knowing killing of another." Tenn.Code Ann. § 39-13-210(a)(1) (1991). The defendant claims the evidence is insufficient to support the conclusion he knowingly killed Ginny Prince. He argues that murder is a crime defined by its results; therefore, the state must prove that he knew a killing would result from his conduct. On the other hand, the state argues that the proof shows that the killing was knowing, and further, that the relevant inquiry is not solely into defendant's mental state with respect to result of the his actions but alternatively into his mental state with respect to his conduct. Thus, the state argues, if he knowingly or intentionally drank and drove, he is guilty of second-degree murder for the result of the unlawful drinking and driving.

We find insufficient evidence of a knowing killing to sustain the defendant's conviction of second-degree murder.

Under our Criminal Code, murder is an offense defined by the result, not by the offender's conduct or by the circumstances surrounding the conduct. *See, e.g., State v. Freeman*, 943 S.W.2d 25, 29 (Tenn.Crim.App.1996), *perm. app. denied* (Tenn.1997). "A person acts knowingly with respect to a result of a person's conduct when the person is aware that the conduct is reasonably certain to cause the result." Tenn.Code Ann. § 39-11-302(b) (1997). Thus, to establish second-degree murder, the state must prove that the defendant was "aware that the conduct is reasonably certain" to cause death.

In a case of this type, the offending activity may arguably occur at a given point in a sequence of events or along a continuum of time. A reviewing court must determine during which event or at what point in time the critical "conduct" occurred. The state would have us choose an event or time very early in the sequence-that is, when the intoxicated defendant began to drive his vehicle in violation of the DUI laws. Certainly, under the pre-1989 Code, this theory would support a finding of implied malice which was the underpinning for a long line of Tennessee cases which, before 1989, approved second-degree murder convictions in vehicular-homicide situations. *See, e.g., State v. Durham*, 614 S.W.2d 815 (Tenn.Crim.App.1981). Malice was implied from the defendant's decision to drive a motor vehicle while intoxicated. Under the pre-1989 law, the facts of this case would have demonstrated actions which are *malum in se* and which evince "willful recklessness," *State v. Johnson*, 541 S.W.2d 417 (Tenn.1976), and, as such, they would have supported a finding of implied malice which, in turn, would have authorized a conviction for second-degree murder. However, the 1989 Criminal Code removed malice as an element of murder, relegated the old implied-malice formula to crimes proscribing killings resulting from reckless conduct, *see* Tenn.Code Ann. § 39-13-210(a)(1) (1991), and inserted the *mens rea* of a knowing killing as an element of second-degree murder. Moreover, as we have said, it is not conduct, but a result, that is proscribed by the current second-degree murder statute. Therefore, for purposes of second-degree murder, we must reject the argument that the critical time for judging the defendant's actions is when he climbed behind the wheel of his vehicle.

Alternatively, the state suggests that the critical time for judging the defendant's conduct is the point in time after he passed the Perry vehicle when, instead of returning to his lane of travel, he veered left, further into the path of the victims' car. Mr. Perry is the only witness to this movement of the defendant's vehicle, and we have examined carefully his testimony. We do not find that this testimony provides meaningful evidence of the defendant's knowledge, awareness or intent at that point in time. The perceived veering of the defendant's truck could have been an evasive maneuver, and moreover, in light of the defendant's blood alcohol content of .28 percent, his full consciousness at the critical time is arguably in doubt. We believe that the critical conduct for which the defendant must be judged occurred prior to the instant just before the collision.

The critical conduct occurred when the intoxicated defendant passed another vehicle on a curve in a no-passing zone and his presence in the opposing lane of traffic became irreversible. As such, the record is devoid of any proof of the defendant's knowledge that death was reasonably certain to result before the events were irretrievably set into motion by this conduct. The defendant's outrageously reckless conduct is analogous to a person firing a pistol from inside a windowless building out through the open doorway. The person cannot see whether someone may be walking outside along the front of the building, about to pass the doorway, and he knows of no one present outside. The "conduct" is commenced by the firing of the weapon and must be judged at that time because the conduct is then irreversible. Under our Criminal Code, such conduct is, as is the conduct in the present case, reckless. This reckless conduct, however egregious, is distinguishable from a hypothesis where the person is firing the pistol through the doorway when he is aware that a moving line of people is filing in close order past the open door. In that hypothesis, death is reasonably certain to result from the conduct, even *before* the bullet is fired, such that a death resulting from the shot is, at least, knowing. As seen in this analogy, the facts in the present case do not support a finding of a knowing killing which is necessary to a conviction of second-degree murder.

The case at bar presents an egregious picture of an individual who drove while intoxicated and after his driver's license had been revoked. He drove with his vehicle full of personal belongings, which may have impaired his ability to see out of the right side of the vehicle. He attempted to pass a vehicle in a no passing zone. Tragically, the defendant's blatant, unjustifiable disregard for the rules of the road and the safety of others resulted in the death of a young woman and the permanent bodily injury of a young man. Nonetheless, the facts when viewed in the light most favorable to the state do not support a conclusion beyond a reasonable doubt that he was aware that his actions were reasonably certain to cause the victim's death. *See* Tenn.Code Ann. § 39-11-302(b) (1997). On the other hand, however, the defendant's conduct was clearly reckless, and, as he concedes, he is guilty of the crime of vehicular homicide.

* * *

As senseless as the defendant's crimes are, we are constrained to follow the dictates of and observe the limitations imposed by the legislature. Given the legislature's substitution of a "knowing" killing in place of malice as the basis for second-degree murder, and our finding that the facts in the present case, even in the light most favorable to the state, do not support a knowing killing, we are bound to reverse the second-degree murder conviction, even though such a reversal relegates this offense to a gradation of vehicular homicide which the legislature has recently decided was inadequately sanctioned at the time the defendant committed the crime.

In accord with the relevant law, we modify the defendant's conviction for second-degree murder to a conviction of vehicular homicide by intoxication.

Notes and Questions

1. Do you find the court's reasoning persuasive? The court concludes that because Tennessee's second-degree murder statute, since 1989, requires a *mens rea* of knowing, unlike the previous version of the law which required malice, that the defendant's mental state must be evaluated at the moment he decided to pass, not at the moment he decided to drive. The court recognized, however, that the *mens rea* of knowledge was a term of art and that the defendant knew death would follow from his actions if he was "reasonably certain" he would cause a death. Does this standard sound terribly different than the depraved heart version of second-degree murder we've seen in the previous cases? The defendant got behind the wheel of an automobile with a blood alcohol level of 0.28 and passed a car at night on the curve of a dark country road. In Tennessee, as in most states, a defendant is presumed impaired with a BAL of 0.08 and death occurs between 0.35 and 0.40. Do you agree that there was no "reasonable certainty" that the defendant would kill someone on that road?

2. Has the court improperly atomized its analysis? The court concludes that we have to consider the defendant's culpability only at the point at which he tried to pass a car on the two lane road. But isn't the defendant's cupability determined by his level of intoxication and informed by the degree of care he took in his other traffic maneuvers that evening? Does it make sense to just look at the moment when he chose to pass the car in front of him in evaluating his level of fault in this accident?

3. The distinction between second-degree murder and reckless homicide was not purely an academic one. As a result of the modification of the defendant's conviction, his 25-year sentence for second-degree murder was replaced with a 6-year sentence for reckless homicide.

4. From a defendant's perspective, once he has one felony conviction, the number of years he is required to serve is the most important consideration. Assuming that the court arrived at the right conclusion, there is now a way a defendant like this one could suffer a penalty very similar to the one initially imposed. The court observed in a part of the opinion not abstracted above that this case occurred at a time when it was widely believed that the penalties for vehicular homicide were too lenient and had the defendant committed these crimes at the time the opinion was written, he could have been charged under a newly enacted vehicular homicide provision that would have, because of his level of

intoxication, produced the same penalty range. Obviously this modification in the law moots this arguably incorrect interpretation of the law.

———————

The resolution of the *Kelly* case is not typical. While courts require more carelessness than is involved in simply driving home from a bar slightly intoxicated for a finding that the defendant was guilty of second-degree murder, the aggravated facts of *Kelly* would lead courts in most jurisdictions to affirm a conviction of second-degree murder. The *Jeffries* case provides a much more typical analysis of a second-degree murder charge predicated on an intoxicated collision.

Jeffries v. State

Court of Appeals of Alaska
90 P.3d 185 (2004)

MANNHEIMER, Judge.

This appeal requires us to examine the distinction between two degrees of criminal homicide: manslaughter as defined in AS 11.41.120(a)(1), which requires proof of the defendant's recklessness; and second-degree murder as defined in AS 11.41.110(a)(2), which requires proof of a recklessness so heightened as to constitute "an extreme indifference to the value of human life".

In prior cases, we have upheld second-degree murder convictions for intoxicated drivers who killed other people. But in each of those instances, the defendant drove in ways that were manifestly extremely dangerous (even leaving aside the fact that the defendant's perceptions and reactions were impaired due to intoxication). In the present case, the defendant's physical acts of driving included only one reported lapse: he made a left turn directly in front of an oncoming car.

To prove Jeffries's "extreme indifference to the value of human life", the State relied heavily on evidence that Jeffries had numerous prior convictions for driving while intoxicated, that his license had been revoked for the previous ten years, that he had been drinking all day in violation of the conditions of his probation, and that he had previously refused several times to participate in court-ordered alcohol treatment programs. On appeal, Jeffries argues that this is an improper way to prove "extreme indifference". He asserts that extreme indifference must be proved solely by the quality of the defendant's conduct during the episode in question.

Jeffries contends that his particular act of careless driving—the dangerous left turn—was not particularly egregious compared to the acts of careless driving that would typically lead to manslaughter convictions. Because Jeffries's physical conduct involved only a single dangerous left turn, he argues that he should have been convicted only of manslaughter.

For the reasons explained here, we conclude that Jeffries's suggested construction of the second-degree murder statute is too narrow. We have examined court decisions from jurisdictions that (like Alaska) have second-degree murder statutes derived from the Model Penal Code. We have also examined court decisions from jurisdictions that retain a common-law definition of murder—a definition that requires proof of "malice". Both of these groups of jurisdictions have upheld second-degree murder convictions in cases where the government's proof of extreme recklessness rested primarily on an intoxicated driver's persistent recidivism and failures at rehabilitation.

We, too, now hold that "extreme indifference to the value of human life" can be proved in this fashion. When a jury deliberates whether an intoxicated driver is guilty of second-degree murder or only manslaughter, the jury can lawfully consider the defendant's past convictions for driving while intoxicated, the defendant's refusals to honor license suspensions or abide by the conditions of probation in those prior DWI cases, and the defendant's past refusals to engage in alcohol treatment programs. We therefore affirm Jeffries's conviction for second-degree murder.

Underlying facts

On February 8, 2000, Michael V. Jeffries spent most of the day drinking. Viewing the evidence presented at trial in the light most favorable to the State, Jeffries downed approximately twenty beers over the course of several hours. In the mid-afternoon, Jeffries and his long-time girlfriend, Beulah Dean, arrived at the Veterans of Foreign Wars club in Mountain View. They stayed there until approximately 8:00 p.m., with Jeffries continuing to drink beer. Jeffries and Dean then left the VFW to go home; Jeffries was driving.

Some fifteen minutes later, at the corner of DeBarr Road and Columbine Street, Jeffries made a left turn directly in front of an oncoming car. The other driver, who was traveling on DeBarr Road at a lawful speed of approximately 45 miles per hour, "had [just] enough warning to take [his] foot off the gas" before he collided with the passenger side of Jeffries's vehicle. When the paramedics arrived a few minutes later, Beulah Dean was bleeding from her head and was completely unresponsive. She was taken to the hospital, where she died a short time later.

When the police contacted Jeffries at the scene, he staggered when he walked, he leaned on his car for balance, and he smelled of alcoholic beverages. Jeffries's blood alcohol level tested at .27 percent.

Jeffries had six prior convictions for driving while intoxicated, and his driver's license had been revoked for the ten years preceding this incident. (Jeffries was not eligible to obtain a driver's license until 2018.) Jeffries was on probation, and one of his conditions of probation was to refrain from drinking alcoholic beverages. Four times previously, Jeffries had refused to participate in court-ordered alcohol treatment programs.

Jeffries was initially charged with manslaughter for causing Dean's death, but the State later re-indicted Jeffries for second-degree murder. Following a jury trial, Jeffries was convicted of this charge (as well as driving while intoxicated and driving while his license was suspended or revoked).

The Distinction Between "Recklessness" and "Extreme Indifference to the Value Of Human Life"

Under AS 11.41.120(a)(1), the crime of manslaughter consists of causing the death of another human being while acting at least recklessly with respect to this result. The term "recklessly" is defined in AS 11.81.900(a)(3):

> [A] person acts "recklessly" with respect to a result . . . when the person is aware of and consciously disregards a substantial and unjustifiable risk that the result will occur . . .; the risk must be of such a nature and degree that disregard of it constitutes a gross deviation from the standard of conduct that a reasonable person would observe in the situation; a person who is unaware of a risk of which the person would have been aware had that person not been intoxicated acts recklessly with respect to that risk[.]

In contrast, the crime of second-degree murder defined in AS 11.41.110(a)(2) requires proof that the defendant "knowingly engage[d] in conduct that result[ed] in the death of another person under circumstances manifesting an extreme indifference to the value of human life".

Alaska's criminal code does not contain an express definition of "extreme indifference to the value of human life". However, this Court defined this phrase in *Neitzel v. State*, 655 P.2d 325 (Alaska App.1982). We concluded that "extreme indifference to the value of human life" was intended to codify the common-law concept of "reckless murder".[1]

As we explained in *Neitzel*, murder was defined at common law as a homicide committed with "malice".[2] Generally speaking, "malice" referred to any

---

1   *Neitzel*, 655 P.2d at 327.

2   *Id.*

intentional homicide that was not justified, excused, or mitigated.[3] However, [the] [c]ommon-law courts permitted a jury to find malice [even] in the absence of a specific intent to kill [when the defendant's] act was done with such heedless disregard of a harmful result, foreseen as a likely possibility, that it differ[ed] little in the scale of moral blameworthiness from an actual intent to [kill]. . . . Typical examples of this kind of murder are: shooting . . . into a home, room, train, or automobile in which others are known to be or might be. *Neitzel*, 655 P.2d at 327.[4]

The Model Penal Code contains a provision— § 210.2(1)(b)—that declares a homicide to be murder if "it is committed recklessly under circumstances manifesting extreme indifference to the value of human life".[5] The drafters of the Model Penal Code intended this provision to apply to "[the] kind of reckless homicide that cannot fairly be distinguished [in terms of blameworthiness] from homicides committed purposely or knowingly".[6] As explained in the Commentary to this provision of the Model Penal Code,

> [R]isk [is always] a matter of degree[,] and the motives for risk creation may be infinite in variation[.] . . . [If] the actor's conscious disregard of the risk, given the circumstances of the case, so far departs from acceptable behavior that it constitutes a "gross deviation from the standard of conduct that a law-abiding person would observe in the actor's situation . . .", [this culpable mental state is] sufficient for a conviction of manslaughter. . . . In a prosecution for murder, however, the [Model Penal] Code calls for the further judgment [of] whether the actor's conscious disregard of the risk, under the circumstances, manifests extreme indifference to the value of human life. . . . Whether [the actor's] recklessness is so extreme that it demonstrates [extreme] indifference [to the value of human life] is not a question . . . that can be further clarified. It must be left directly to the trier of fact under instructions which make it clear that [a] recklessness that can fairly be [likened] to purpose or knowledge should be treated as murder and that less extreme recklessness should be punished as manslaughter. American Law Institute, *Model Penal Code and Commentaries* (1980), Part II, § 210.2, pp. 21–22.[7]

---

3   *Id.*

4   Quoting Rollin M. Perkins, *Criminal Law* (2nd edition 1969), § 1, pp. 36 & 768.

5   Quoted in *Neitzel*, 655 P.2d at 332.

6   American Law Institute, *Model Penal Code and Commentaries* (1980), Part II, § 210.2, p. 21, quoted in *Neitzel*, 655 P.2d at 335.

7   Quoted in *Neitzel*, 655 P.2d at 335–36.

This provision of the Model Penal is the source of our "extreme indifference" provision, AS 11.41.110(a)(2).[8] After reviewing the statutory history of this language, we concluded in *Neitzel* that the Alaska Legislature intended AS 11.41.110(a)(2) to apply to cases where the defendant "knowingly engage[s] in conduct . . . which[,] in light of the circumstances [,] is reckless to the point that it manifests an extreme indifference to the value of human life".[9]

The word "reckless" in that last sentence is used in its technical sense—*i.e.*, the sense defined in AS 11.81.900(a)(3). When *Neitzel* was litigated, the State argued that the phrase "extreme indifference to the value of human life" referred to "an objective standard" of dangerousness, and that this concept was therefore "similar to negligence rather than . . . recklessness" in the sense that the State did not have to prove the defendant's subjective awareness of the risk.[10] This Court rejected the State's interpretation of the statute; we held that "extreme indifference to the value of human life" is an extreme form of recklessness, not an extreme form of negligence.[11]

Neitzel lists four factors that a jury should weigh when deciding whether a defendant's conduct manifested "recklessness" or "extreme indifference to the value of human life": the "social utility of the actor's conduct", the "magnitude of the risk [that the defendant's] conduct create[d], including both the nature of the foreseeable harm and the likelihood that the conduct [would] result in that harm"; "the [extent of the] actor's knowledge of the risk"; and "any precautions [that] the actor [took] to minimize the risk."[12]

Neitzel actually lists the third factor as "the actor's knowledge of the risk". But this passage from *Neitzel* is addressed to the broader issue of how a jury should differentiate *three* levels of culpability: criminal negligence, recklessness, and extreme indifference to the value of human life.[13] As the *Neitzel* opinion points out, the actor's knowledge of the risk is the factor that generally distinguishes "criminal negligence" from "recklessness".[14]

When the jury is debating "recklessness" versus "extreme indifference to the value of human life", both of these levels of culpability presuppose that the

---

8   *Id.* at 335.

9   *Id.* at 332–33.

10   *Id.* at 332. *Compare* AS 11.81.900(a)(3) (the definition of "recklessly") *with* AS 11.81.900(a)(4) (the definition of "criminal negligence").

11   *Neitzel*, 655 P.2d at 334.

12   *Id.* at 336–37.

13   *Id.* at 336.

14   *Id.* at 337.

defendant was aware of the risk (or that the defendant would have been aware of the risk but for intoxication). Therefore, in distinguishing between reckless-ness and extreme indifference to the value of human life, the pertinent question is not whether the actor was "aware of the risk [of death]"—for, leaving aside instances of intoxication, the actor must have been subjectively aware of this risk to support a finding of either recklessness or extreme indifference. Rather, the pertinent question is whether the defendant's level of awareness of the risk exceeded the level of awareness necessary to establish the defendant's reckless-ness as defined in AS 11.81.900(a)(3).

Jeffries's argument that the State's evidence is insufficient, as a matter of law, to support a conviction for second-degree murder

Jeffries contends that a drunk-driving homicide should typically lead to a manslaughter conviction, and that a conviction for second-degree murder is justified only in extreme cases. We agree with this contention.

In *St. John v. State*, this Court held that "evidence that a defendant drove while intoxicated and, as a result, caused the death of another person" is suf-ficient to establish "a prima facie case of the recklessness necessary for a finding that the defendant committed manslaughter".[15] And in *Neitzel*, we suggested that an intoxicated driver should not be convicted of "extreme indifference" murder unless the driver's actions "create [d] a much greater risk [of] death" than the risk that is created by simply driving home from a bar in an intoxicated condition.[16]

Thus, our case law supports Jeffries's contention that a typical drunk driv-ing homicide should be prosecuted as manslaughter. But Jeffries's appeal requires us to examine and clarify what is meant by a "typical" drunk driving homicide.

Jeffries argues that defendants who commit drunk driving homicides can not properly be convicted of "extreme indifference" second-degree murder unless their handling of the motor vehicle on the occasion in question mani-fested an extreme degree of overt dangerousness or heedlessness—a degree of overt dangerousness or heedlessness far exceeding the type of careless driving that one might expect from an intoxicated person who was apparently trying to drive safely. Jeffries asserts that "extreme indifference to human life" can not be established in the way that the State sought to prove this element at his trial—to wit, by showing that Jeffries had a history of past convictions for driving while intoxicated, that Jeffries had repeatedly refused to engage in rehabilitative treat-ment, and that Jeffries had for years continued to drive and to drink even though

---

15 715 P.2d 1205, 1209 (Alaska App.1986).

16 *Neitzel*, 655 P.2d at 337.

he knew that he was prohibited by law from doing either (because his license was revoked and his conditions of probation prohibited him from drinking).

In several of our past cases dealing with vehicular homicide charged as second-degree murder, the defendant's conduct has fit the definition suggested by Jeffries. That is, the defendants engaged in egregiously dangerous driving— much more dangerous than simply taking control of a vehicle while intoxicated and then driving carelessly.

For instance, in *Foxglove v. State*, 929 P.2d 669 (Alaska App.1997), the defendant intentionally drove his snow machine at a speed of 70 miles per hour through a crowd of people gathered around a bonfire.[17] In *Ratliff v. State*, 798 P.2d 1288(Alaska App.1990), the defendant weaved across the road, forcing one oncoming car completely off the road and into a snowbank, and forcing another car to veer almost off the road in order to avoid a head-on collision. Ratliff then entered the wrong side of a divided highway, passing two pairs of large signs that warned him he was going the wrong way. Driving in excess of the speed limit, and disregarding the efforts of motorists who flashed their lights to get his attention, Ratliff drove for two miles before colliding head-on with another car.[18] In *Stiegele v. State*, 714 P.2d 356 (Alaska App.1986), the defendant spun his truck around 360 degrees, then headed up a road on the left side. Shortly afterwards, the police observed the defendant's truck traveling down the wrong side of the road at approximately 85 miles per hour, then leave the road and crash into the woods. Witnesses testified that, before the crash, the passengers in the truck were screaming for Stiegele to stop.[19] And in *Pears v. State*, 672 P.2d 903 (Alaska App.1983), the defendant repeatedly exceeded the speed limit and ran through stop signs and red lights, disregarding the warnings of his passenger. He then dropped off his passenger and continued driving. Just before the fatal collision, Pears saw that the cars in front of him were stopping for a red light, so he drove around those cars in the right-turn lane, then entered the intersection without slowing down. Pears collided with one of the cars entering the intersection on the green light; he knocked this other car 146 feet.[20]

On the other hand, some of our prior cases involving intoxicated drivers convicted of second-degree murder have arisen from episodes in which the physical actions of the intoxicated drivers were fairly typical of what one might expect from an intoxicated person. In both *Richardson v. State*, 47 P.3d 660, 661

---

17 *Foxglove*, 929 P.2d at 670.

18 *Ratliff*, 798 P.2d at 1289–90.

19 *Stiegele*, 714 P.2d at 358–59.

20 *Pears*, 672 P.2d at 909.

(Alaska App.2002), and *Puzewicz v. State*, 856 P.2d 1178, 1179 (Alaska App.1993), the defendants crossed the center line and collided with an oncoming car.

In particular, the facts of *Puzewicz* are similar in most respects to the facts of Jeffries's case. Puzewicz spent most of the day drinking beer, and then he went driving in the evening and killed two people.[21] Although Puzewicz claimed to have drunk only four or five beers in the hours preceding the collision, his blood alcohol level was .219 percent.[22]

Puzewicz had three prior convictions for driving while intoxicated, and he was on probation from his third DWI conviction when he committed the murders.[23] Puzewicz was not supposed to be driving at all—because, as a result of his third DWI conviction, Puzewicz's driver's license had been revoked for ten years.[24] Moreover, Puzewicz had failed to undertake the residential treatment program that was required as part of his sentence for that prior conviction, and the district court had issued an unserved warrant for his arrest.[25]

However, the *Puzewicz* decision has little precedential value on the issue raised by Jeffries in this case. Puzewicz only pursued a sentence appeal, so this Court did not reach the question of whether the above-described evidence was legally sufficient to support Puzewicz's murder convictions.

Nevertheless, decisions from other states that have murder statutes based on the Model Penal Code suggest that the facts of *Puzewicz* are sufficient to support a conviction for "extreme indifference" murder.

Kentucky has an "extreme indifference" murder statute similar to Alaska's.[26] In *Estep v. Commonwealth*, 957 S.W.2d 191 (Ky.1997), the Supreme Court of Kentucky held that an intoxicated motorist who crossed the center line and collided with an oncoming vehicle could be convicted of murder under this statute based primarily on evidence of her extreme intoxication:

> [Kentucky Statute] 507.020(1)(b) permits a conviction for wanton murder for the operation of a motor vehicle under circumstances manifesting extreme indifference to human life.... [C]onduct such as Estep's has been held to constitute wanton murder under such a statutory standard. *Walden v. Commonwealth*, Ky., 805 S.W.2d 102 (1991), held that a wanton murder conviction was proper because the conduct of the defendant amounted

---

21 *Puzewicz*, 856 P.2d at 1179.

22 *Id.*

23 *Id.* at 1180.

84 *Id.*

25 *Id.*

26 *See* Kentucky Stats. § 507.020(1)(b) (Baldwin 2003).

to more than a typical automobile accident by virtue of the extreme rate of speed and level of intoxication. . . . [T]his Court concluded that . . . the extreme nature of the intoxication was sufficient evidence from which a jury could infer wantonness so extreme as to manifest extreme indifference to human life. *Id.*

The evidence in this case demonstrated that Estep was driving her truck at a high rate of speed in an improper manner under the influence of drugs. Blood tests revealed the existence of five different types of drugs in Estep's body: Xanax, Elavil, Soma, Valium and Hydrocodone.

. . .

Eyewitnesses testified that Estep was seen passing at a rate of speed greater than 50 miles per hour in a no-passing zone near a curve in the road. The testimony indicated that after she completed passing one automobile, she failed to return to the proper lane and collided with a car on the wrong side of the road. One of the passengers in the other vehicle testified that . . . Estep was slumped over in her seat and that she raised her head only seconds before the fatal crash. There was evidence that[,] when Estep was taken to the hospital for observation following the accident[,] she kept passing out and appeared "pretty zonked." [This] was sufficient evidence that Estep was operating a motor vehicle under circumstances manifesting extreme indifference to human life and she wantonly engaged in conduct which created a grave risk of death and caused the death of another person. *Estep,* 957 S.W.2d at 192–93.

The Alabama Court of Criminal Appeals reached a similar conclusion in *Allen v. State,* 611 So.2d 1188 (Ala.Crim.App.1992). Quoting the Kentucky court's decision in *Walden* with approval, the Alabama court agreed that "[d]epending on the situation, drunk driving may be . . . a circumstance that a jury could find to 'manifest[ ] extreme indifference to human life.'"[27] The Alabama court then upheld a murder conviction for an intoxicated driver whose careless driving was manifested primarily by an inability to keep his vehicle within the proper lane of travel:

[T]he "situation" that will support a conviction for reckless murder must involve something more than simply driving after having consumed alcohol and becoming involved in a collision. As noted above, [Alabama's reckless murder statute] contemplates conduct that is the culpable equivalent of intentional murder.

. . .

In the present case, . . . the testimony of the State's witnesses [showed] that the appellant was driving his vehicle in a reckless manner by weaving in his own lane; by swerving into the oncoming lane; by running off the surface of the road onto a low shoulder and attempting to return in an unsafe manner; or by

27   *Allen,* 611 So.2d at 1192.

engaging in a combination of any of the three. The prosecution also presented evidence . . . that the appellant was legally intoxicated while driving his car in a reckless manner. Although it is a close question, we find that there was sufficient evidence from which the jury could have concluded that the appellant's overall conduct was so grossly wanton that it manifested an extreme indifference to human life. *Allen*, 611 So.2d at 1192–93.

The decision in *Allen* conforms to two earlier Alabama decisions, *Patterson v. State*, 518 So.2d 809 (Ala.Crim.App.1987),[28] and *Slaughter v. State*, 424 So.2d 1365 (Ala.Crim.App.1982).

The defendant in *Patterson* had previously undergone alcohol abuse treatment, and he had been arrested for driving while intoxicated within the previous year.[29] During the twelve hours preceding the homicide, Patterson drank three bottles of wine; his blood alcohol level was .30 percent.[30] Patterson's car jumped the median of a divided road, crossed into the oncoming lanes, and struck two vehicles.[31] Under these facts, the court affirmed Patterson's conviction for extreme indifference murder.[32]

The defendant in *Slaughter*, who had been arrested at least four times previously for driving while intoxicated, spent the day drinking and then he went driving.[33] During the drive, Slaughter either passed out from intoxication or fell asleep; his car crossed the roadway, jumped the curb, and killed a woman who was working in her front yard.[34] On appeal, the Alabama court held that these facts were sufficient to establish extreme indifference murder.[35]

Likewise, in *State v. Schultz*, 141 N.H. 101, 677 A.2d 675, 678 (1996), the New Hampshire Supreme Court held that "extreme indifference [murder] does not require proof of particularly vicious conduct. Rather, the critical factor is the degree to which the defendant disregards the risk of death to another."

We now turn to jurisdictions that retain the common-law definition of murder (*i.e.*, those jurisdictions that define murder as a homicide committed with "malice"). As explained above, the common law recognized extreme recklessness

---

28 Overruled on other grounds in *Fore v. State*, 858 So.2d 982, 990 (Ala.Crim.App.2003).

39 518 So.2d at 816.

40 *Id.* at 811–12.

31 *Id.* at 810–11.

32 *Id.* at 816.

33 424 So.2d at 1367

34 *Id.* at 1366.

35 *Id.* at 1367.

as a category of malice. And courts applying the common-law definition of murder have affirmed murder convictions for homicides committed by intoxicated drivers.

Many of these court decisions involved defendants who engaged in egregiously dangerous driving.[36] However, some of these "reckless murder" cases involved driving that one might typically expect of an intoxicated driver: impatiently attempting to pass a slower vehicle, inability to keep their vehicle traveling in a straight line, failing to see traffic signs and road markings, miscalculating distances, or misjudging the motion of other vehicles.

For instance, in *Geter v. State*, 219 Ga. 125, 132 S.E.2d 30 (1963), the court upheld the murder conviction of a defendant who, driving while intoxicated, attempted to pass the cars ahead of him on an uphill grade, at a place where the roadway was marked with a "no passing" double yellow line. As the defendant crested the hill on the wrong side of the road, he struck an oncoming vehicle and killed three of its occupants.[37] Similarly, in *Shiflet v. State*, 216 Tenn. 365, 392 S.W.2d 676 (1965), the court upheld the murder conviction of an intoxicated driver who veered into the oncoming lane of traffic and struck another vehicle.[38] In *State v. Goodman*, 149 N.C.App. 57, 560 S.E.2d 196 (2002)[39], the court upheld the murder conviction of an intoxicated driver who struck another vehicle when he ran a red light (apparently after passing out, with his "head and arm hanging out of the driver's side window").[40] A major factor in the court's decision was the fact that the defendant had numerous prior convictions for driving while intoxicated and other traffic offenses.[41] And in *Commonwealth v. Taylor*, 461 Pa. 557, 337 A.2d 545 (1975), the court upheld the murder conviction of an intoxicated driver who passed another car at a high rate of speed and struck two boys who were bicycling along the other side of the road.[42] The court stated:

> The intoxicated condition of the driver, the excessive rate of speed [at] which he was traveling, the distance the bodies and bicycles were propelled upon impact, his awareness that this was an area where children were likely to traverse, the absence of any physical or climatic condition which could explain or contribute to the happening of the accident and the appel-

---

36 *See, e.g., United States v. Fleming*, 739 F.2d 945 (4th Cir.1984); *State v. Boone*, 294 Or. 630, 661 P.2d 917, 920–22 (1983).

37 *Geter*, 132 S.E.2d at 31, 35.

38 *Shiflet*, 392 S.W.2d at 678.

39 Reversed on other grounds, *State v. Goodman*, 357 N.C. 43, 577 S.E.2d 619 (2003).

40 *Goodman*, 560 S.E.2d at 198.

41 *Id.* at 199–200.

42 *Taylor*, 337 A.2d at 546.

lant's failure to stop immediately after impact, all exhibit the wickedness of disposition, the hardness of heart, cruelty and recklessness associated with murder in the second degree. *Taylor*, 337 A.2d at 548.

Based on these authorities, we hold that in cases of homicide caused by an intoxicated driver, the element of "extreme indifference to the value of human life" required for conviction of second-degree murder under AS 11.41.110(a)(2) can be established not only through evidence that the defendant engaged in egregiously dangerous driving, but also through evidence of the defendant's extreme intoxication, the defendant's decision to ignore warnings not to drive, the defendant's past convictions for driving while intoxicated, the defendant's refusal to participate in court-ordered treatment for alcohol abuse imposed as part of the defendant's sentence or conditions of probation from previous DWI convictions, and the defendant's decision to drive despite a license suspension or revocation stemming from previous DWI convictions.

The presence of some or all of these factors does not necessarily prove that the defendant acted with extreme indifference to the value of human life. However, the jury is entitled to consider these factors when deciding whether the government has proved that the defendant acted with the extreme degree of recklessness that will support a murder conviction under AS 11.41.110(a)(2).

Notes and Questions

1. *Jeffries* is more representative of the approach of courts in dealing with their oversight of the line between second-degree murder and involuntary manslaughter than is either Justice Robertson's view in *Windham*, that largely left grades of homicide to juries, or Judge Witt's result in *Kelly* that very readily second-guessed a jury. Do not expect to find the amount of caselaw you saw in *Jeffries* for most types of second-degree murder cases, however. Deaths occurring by drivers have similar facts and courts can more easily compare the severity of defendants actions when there is a large pool of cases with similar facts.

2. Think a bit about the types of *mens rea* involved in these cases. Regardless of how a jurisdiction defines its version of depraved heart second-degree murder, the upshot is essentially the same. A knowing killing requires a practical certainty of death, a standard very similar to extreme indifference, or any of the other variations states use to define second-degree murder. Judge Witt's analysis of Tennessee's second-degree murder is really out of sync with the overwhelming majority of cases considering second-degree murder cases,

regardless of whether courts are using the Model Penal Code formulation or the various other formulations that states use. Courts are unable to determine what was in the mind of drunken motorists, or other types of killers. In evaluating whether the defendant engaged in a conscious disregard of an unreasonable risk, or something more serious, courts are obviously looking at how egregious the *facts* of the case are, not the defendant's mental state in the abstract. While *mens rea* is ostensibly about mental state, notice how a crime goes from one that is less serious to one that is more serious on the basis of what the defendant *did*, not what he *thought*.

---

iv. Involuntary Manslaughter/Reckless Homicide and Criminally Negligent Homicide

(a) Representative Example of an Involuntary Manslaughter Statute

Georgia Code Annotated § 16-5-3

(a) A person commits the offense of involuntary manslaughter in the commission of an unlawful act when he causes the death of another human being without any intention to do so by the commission of an unlawful act other than a felony. A person who commits the offense of involuntary manslaughter in the commission of an unlawful act, upon conviction thereof, shall be punished by imprisonment for not less than one year nor more than ten years.

(b) A person commits the offense of involuntary manslaughter in the commission of a lawful act in an unlawful manner when he causes the death of another human being without any intention to do so, by the commission of a lawful act in an unlawful manner likely to cause death or great bodily harm. A person who commits the offense of involuntary manslaughter in the commission of a lawful act in an unlawful manner, upon conviction thereof, shall be punished as for a misdemeanor.

(b) Representative Example of Reckless Homicide Statute

Tennessee Code Annotated § 39-13-215

Reckless homicide is a reckless killing of another.

(c) Representative Example of Criminally Negligent Homicide Statute

Tennessee Code Annotated § 39-13-212

Criminally negligent conduct that results in death constitutes criminally negligent homicide.

While the cases in the previous section considered the line between second-degree murder and involuntary manslaughter, *Standiford* considers the line between reckless homicide and criminally negligent homicide. Reckless homicide and involuntary manslaughter are roughly the same crime—rarely will a jurisdiction have both a crime of involuntary manslaughter and reckless homicide. Reckless homicide uses the Model Penal Code's definition for this level of offense while involuntary manslaughter uses the common law's definition. Jurisdictions with reckless homicide typically also have a crime of criminally negligent homicide. Most often, when a jury is instructed on reckless homicide, it will also be instructed on criminally negligent homicide. *Standiford* is a rare decision in that the court found that an instruction on reckless homicide was appropriate but not an instruction on criminally negligent homicide.

State v. Standiford

Supreme Court of Utah
769 P.2d 254 (1988)

Defendant Fred W. Standiford was convicted of second degree murder for the fatal stabbing of Hisae Wood. He appeals the conviction on a variety of grounds. We affirm.

I. THE FACTS

Sometime between 3:00 a.m. and 4:00 a.m. on April 27, 1984, Hisae Wood was stabbed to death in an assault during which 107 stab wounds were inflicted on her body. Earlier that night, Standiford had been in his garage with his friend, Joey Granato, painting Granato's Jeep. Twice during the evening, Standiford and Granato went to Wood's residence to purchase cocaine. After each trip, Standiford and Granato freebased the cocaine and then resumed painting the Jeep. Around 4:00 a.m., Standiford told Granato that he was going to a convenience store to buy cigarettes. Although he was gone longer than necessary for that errand, his behavior was not unusual when he returned. When Standiford revealed that he had more cocaine, Granato asked if Standiford had returned to the Woods' residence. Standiford replied that he had not and indicated that he had merely saved the cocaine from one of their earlier purchases.

The next day, Standiford contacted Granato and asked if he had heard that Mrs. Wood had been murdered. Later that day, Standiford was questioned by the police. Afterwards, he told Granato that they were both in trouble and that if the police asked, Granato should tell the police that he and Standiford had not left the garage all night. Granato became concerned, contacted the police, and volunteered a statement about his and Standiford's whereabouts and their cocaine purchases. Based on Granato's statement, the police searched Standiford's house and garage and found incriminating evidence.

When confronted with Granato's statement, Standiford confessed to killing Mrs. Wood but claimed that he had acted in self-defense. He asserted that Mrs. Wood came after him with a gun, screaming in Japanese, and grabbed him. He seized the closest weapon, a kitchen knife, intending only to scare her, and since the threat of the knife did not stop her, he just started swinging the knife. After he realized that Mrs. Wood was dead, Standiford went into the kitchen and washed his hands and the knife, wiped off his fingerprints with a kitchen towel, and turned off the lights in the house. He then took a bag of cocaine, the knife, and the gun allegedly brandished by Mrs. Wood and left. After disposing of the knife, he stopped at a convenience store and then returned home, where he changed his clothes and hid the evidence. The gun he said he took was not found.

Another of Standiford's friends, Don Bendixen, testified that several days prior to the incident, Standiford had mentioned to him that Mrs. Wood's husband was going to be out of town and that it would be easy to "knock her out and possibly kill her and take everything she has." When Bendixen commented that that was "crazy thinking," Standiford replied that he was only joking.

After Standiford was charged, defense counsel contacted Dr. Lincoln Clark, a psychiatrist, and asked him to evaluate Standiford's case to determine whether he could assist the defense. Counsel gave Dr. Clark defendant's file, which consisted of police reports and a transcript of Standiford's taped confession. Defendant asserts that it may have also contained a handwritten statement of facts prepared by Standiford for his attorney, although Dr. Clark testified that he did not remember reviewing any handwritten statement. The next day, Dr. Clark informed counsel that his opinion would not help the defense and that the file could be picked up. At trial, Dr. Clark testified on behalf of the prosecution and in rebuttal to defendant's expert that Standiford's drug abuse was not a significant factor in committing the homicide.

* * *

Instruction on Lesser Included Offense of Negligent Homicide

Finally, defendant attacks the trial judge's refusal to give defendant's requested instruction on the lesser included offense of negligent homicide. *State v. Baker*, 671 P.2d 152, 157–59 (Utah 1983), held that a defendant's requested lesser included offense instruction must be given when there is some evidence which supports the theory asserted by defendant. The requirement is more than a procedural nicety; it is rooted in defendant's constitutional right to a jury trial. A defendant is entitled to have his legal theory of the case placed before the jury if it would not be superfluous to do so because of an absence of any evidence to support the theory. Sometimes prosecutors overcharge, and sometimes expected evidence just does not materialize. In such cases, instructions on lesser offenses may be essential to avoid injustice. Furthermore, juries should not be precluded from determining how criminal conduct should be characterized and judged. In all events, a defendant has an absolute right to have the jury instructed on a lesser crime, as long as there is some evidence to support it.

Negligent homicide is conceptually related to reckless manslaughter. Reckless manslaughter requires that a defendant be aware of the risk of death. Negligent homicide requires only that a defendant "ought to be aware of a substantial and unjustifiable" risk of death. Utah Code Ann. § 76–2–103(4) (1978). The sole difference between reckless manslaughter and negligent homicide is whether the defendant actually knew of the risk of death or simply was not, but should have been, aware. *Boggess v. State*, 655 P.2d 654, 656–58 (Utah 1982) (Stewart, J., concurring). In both cases, a defendant's conduct must be "a gross deviation" from the standard of care exercised by an ordinary person. Thus, ordinary negligence, which is the basis for a civil action for damages, is not sufficient to constitute criminal negligence.

Here, 107 stab wounds bespeak at least a knowledge of the risk of death, if not an actual intent to kill. Although the line between the risks that a person is in fact aware of and the risks that he ought to be aware of may well be imprecise in some cases, that is not so here. Even if the jury had believed that defendant did not know of the great risk of death because of drug intoxication, that would not have relieved him of liability for manslaughter. In short, on the facts of this case, there was no evidence that would support defendant's theory of negligent homicide. Furthermore, since the jury convicted of second degree murder despite the fact that an instruction was given on the lesser included offense of manslaughter, failure to give a negligent homicide instruction was, at the very best, harmless error.

Notes and Questions

Notice how the difference between reckless and negligent manslaughter has to be evaluated—from objective criteria. We obviously have no way of knowing what a person is thinking and must infer their thoughts from the circumstances. Here, the court concluded that the defendant was at least aware of the risk of death from the 107 stab wounds. Even if we could read minds, it would be difficult to differentiate between the state of mind of one who was aware of a risk of death, as opposed to a risk of death that the defendant should have been aware of but was not. You should be getting the sense that the mental state, the *mens rea*, of homicide offenses has less to do with the actual workings of the defendant's mind and more to do with risk the defendant's actions took with the victim's life.

----

d. *Murder Mitigated By Provocation: Voluntary Manslaughter*

An intentional killing is regarded as less serious if the defendant acted under reasonable provocation, often described in the heat of passion, and the passion had no adequate opportunity to cool. *Girouard* considers what sorts of things constitute reasonable provocation.

Girouard v. State

Court of Appeals of Maryland
583 A.2d 718 (1991)

COLE, Judge.

In this case we are asked to reconsider whether the types of provocation sufficient to mitigate the crime of murder to manslaughter should be limited to the categories we have heretofore recognized, or whether the sufficiency of the provocation should be decided by the factfinder on a case-by-case basis. Specifically, we must determine whether words alone are provocation adequate to justify a conviction of manslaughter rather than one of second degree murder.

The Petitioner, Steven S. Girouard, and the deceased, Joyce M. Girouard, had been married for about two months on October 28, 1987, the night of Joyce's death. Both parties, who met while working in the same building, were in the army. They married after having known each other for approximately three months. The evidence at trial indicated that the marriage was often tense and strained, and there was some evidence that after marrying Steven, Joyce had resumed a relationship with her old boyfriend, Wayne.

On the night of Joyce's death, Steven overheard her talking on the telephone to her friend, whereupon she told the friend that she had asked her first sergeant for a hardship discharge because her husband did not love her anymore. Steven went into the living room where Joyce was on the phone and asked her what she meant by her comments; she responded, "nothing." Angered by her lack of response, Steven kicked away the plate of food Joyce had in front of her. He then went to lie down in the bedroom.

Joyce followed him into the bedroom, stepped up onto the bed and onto Steven's back, pulled his hair and said, "What are you going to do, hit me?" She continued to taunt him by saying, "I never did want to marry you and you are a lousy fuck and you remind me of my dad." The barrage of insults continued with her telling Steven that she wanted a divorce, that the marriage had been a mistake and that she had never wanted to marry him. She also told him she had seen his commanding officer and filed charges against him for abuse. She then asked Steven, "What are you going to do?" Receiving no response, she continued her verbal attack. She added that she had filed charges against him in the Judge Advocate General's Office (JAG) and that he would probably be court martialed.

When she was through, Steven asked her if she had really done all those things, and she responded in the affirmative. He left the bedroom with his pillow in his arms and proceeded to the kitchen where he procured a long handled kitchen knife. He returned to Joyce in the bedroom with the knife behind the pillow. He testified that he was enraged and that he kept waiting for Joyce to say she was kidding, but Joyce continued talking. She said she had learned a lot from the marriage and that it had been a mistake. She also told him she would remain in their apartment after he moved out. When he questioned how she would afford it, she told him she would claim her brain-damaged sister as a dependent and have the sister move in. Joyce reiterated that the marriage was a big mistake, that she did not love him and that the divorce would be better for her.

After pausing for a moment, Joyce asked what Steven was going to do. What he did was lunge at her with the kitchen knife he had hidden behind the pillow and stab her 19 times. Realizing what he had done, he dropped the knife and went to the bathroom to shower off Joyce's blood. Feeling like he wanted to die, Steven went back to the kitchen and found two steak knives with which he slit his own wrists. He lay down on the bed waiting to die, but when he realized that

---

1   There was some testimony presented at trial to the effect that Joyce had never gotten along with her father, at least in part because he had impregnated her when she was fourteen, the result of which was an abortion. Joyce's aunt, however, denied that Joyce's father was the father of Joyce's child.

2   Joyce lied about filing the charges against her husband.

he would not die from his self-inflicted wounds, he got up and called the police, telling the dispatcher that he had just murdered his wife.

When the police arrived they found Steven wandering around outside his apartment building. Steven was despondent and tearful and seemed detached, according to police officers who had been at the scene. He was unconcerned about his own wounds, talking only about how much he loved his wife and how he could not believe what he had done. Joyce Girouard was pronounced dead at the scene.

At trial, defense witness, psychologist, Dr. William Stejskal, testified that Steven was out of touch with his own capacity to experience anger or express hostility. He stated that the events of October 28, 1987, were entirely consistent with Steven's personality, that Steven had "basically reach[ed] the limit of his ability to swallow his anger, to rationalize his wife's behavior, to tolerate, or actually to remain in a passive mode with that. He essentially went over the limit of his ability to bottle up those strong emotions. What ensued was a very extreme explosion of rage that was intermingled with a great deal of panic." Another defense witness, psychiatrist, Thomas Goldman, testified that Joyce had a "compulsive need to provoke jealousy so that she's always asking for love and at the same time destroying and undermining any chance that she really might have to establish any kind of mature love with anybody."

Steven Girouard was convicted, at a court trial in the Circuit Court for Montgomery County, of second degree murder and was sentenced to 22 years incarceration, 10 of which were suspended. Upon his release, Petitioner is to be on probation for five years, two years supervised and three years unsupervised. The Court of Special Appeals affirmed the judgment of the circuit court in an unreported opinion. We granted certiorari to determine whether the circumstances of the case presented provocation adequate to mitigate the second degree murder charge to manslaughter.

Petitioner relies primarily on out of state cases to provide support for his argument that the provocation to mitigate murder to manslaughter should not be limited only to the traditional circumstances of: extreme assault or battery upon the defendant; mutual combat; defendant's illegal arrest; injury or serious abuse of a close relative of the defendant's; or the sudden discovery of a spouse's adultery. Petitioner argues that manslaughter is a catchall for homicides which are criminal but that lack the malice essential for a conviction of murder. Steven argues that the trial judge did find provocation (although he held it inadequate to mitigate murder) and that the categories of provocation adequate to mitigate should be broadened to include factual situations such as this one.

The State counters by stating that although there is no finite list of legally adequate provocations, the common law has developed to a point at which it may be said there are some concededly provocative acts that society is not prepared to recognize as reasonable. Words spoken by the victim, no matter how abusive or taunting, fall into a category society should not accept as adequate provocation. According to the State, if abusive words alone could mitigate murder to manslaughter, nearly every domestic argument ending in the death of one party could be mitigated to manslaughter. This, the State avers, is not an acceptable outcome. Thus, the State argues that the courts below were correct in holding that the taunting words by Joyce Girouard were not provocation adequate to reduce Steven's second degree murder charge to voluntary manslaughter.

* * *

There are certain facts that may mitigate what would normally be murder to manslaughter. For example, we have recognized as falling into that group: (1) discovering one's spouse in the act of sexual intercourse with another; (2) mutual combat; (3) assault and battery. *See State v. Faulkner,* 301 Md. at 486, 483 A.2d 759. There is also authority recognizing injury to one of the defendant's relatives or to a third party, and death resulting from resistance of an illegal arrest as adequate provocation for mitigation to manslaughter. *See, e.g.,* 40 C.J.S. *Homicide* § 48 at 913 (1944) and 40 C.J.S. *Homicide* § 50 at 915–16 (1944). Those acts mitigate homicide to manslaughter because they create passion in the defendant and are not considered the product of free will. *State v. Faulkner,* 301 Md. at 486, 483 A.2d 759.

In order to determine whether murder should be mitigated to manslaughter we look to the circumstances surrounding the homicide and try to discover if it was provoked by the victim. Over the facts of the case we lay the template of the so-called "Rule of Provocation." The courts of this State have repeatedly set forth the requirements of the Rule of Provocation:

1. There must have been adequate provocation;

2. The killing must have been in the heat of passion;

3. It must have been a sudden heat of passion—that is, the killing must have followed the provocation before there had been a reasonable opportunity for the passion to cool;

4. There must have been a causal connection between the provocation, the passion, and the fatal act.

We shall assume without deciding that the second, third, and fourth of the criteria listed above were met in this case. We focus our attention on an examination of the ultimate issue in this case, that is, whether the provocation of Steven by Joyce was enough in the eyes of the law so that the murder charge against

Steven should have been mitigated to voluntary manslaughter. For provocation to be "adequate," it must be "'calculated to inflame the passion of a reasonable man and tend to cause him to act for the moment from passion rather than reason.'" *Carter v. State*, 66 Md.App. at 572, 505 A.2d 545 quoting R. Perkins, *Perkins on Criminal Law* at p. 56 (2d ed. 1969). The issue we must resolve, then, is whether the taunting words uttered by Joyce were enough to inflame the passion of a *reasonable* man so that that man would be sufficiently infuriated so as to strike out in hot-blooded blind passion to kill her. Although we agree with the trial judge that there was needless provocation by Joyce, we also agree with him that the provocation was not adequate to mitigate second degree murder to voluntary manslaughter.

Although there are few Maryland cases discussing the issue at bar, those that do hold that words alone are not adequate provocation. Most recently, in *Sims v. State*, 319 Md. 540, 573 A.2d 1317, we held that "[i]nsulting words or gestures, no matter how opprobrious, do not amount to an affray, and standing alone, do not constitute adequate provocation." *Id.* at 552, 573 A.2d 1317. That case involved the flinging of racial slurs and derogatory comments by the victim at the defendant. That conduct did not constitute adequate provocation.

In *Lang v. State*, 6 Md.App. 128, 250 A.2d 276, *cert. denied*, 396 U.S. 971, 90 S.Ct. 457, 24 L.Ed.2d 438 (1969), the Court of Special Appeals stated that it is "generally held that mere words, threats, menaces or gestures, however offensive and insulting, do not constitute adequate provocation." *Id.* at 132, 250 A.2d 276. Before the shooting, the victim had called the appellant "a chump" and "a chicken," dared the appellant to fight, shouted obscenities at him and shook his fist at him. *Id.* The provocation, again, was not enough to mitigate murder.

The court in *Lang* did note, however, that words can constitute adequate provocation if they are accompanied by conduct indicating a present intention and ability to cause the defendant bodily harm. *Id.* Clearly, no such conduct was exhibited by Joyce in this case. While Joyce did step on Steven's back and pull his hair, he could not reasonably have feared bodily harm at her hands. This, to us, is certain based on Steven's testimony at trial that Joyce was about 5'1" tall and weighed 115 pounds, while he was 6'2" tall, weighing over 200 pounds. Joyce simply did not have the size or strength to cause Steven to fear for his bodily safety. Thus, since there was no ability on the part of Joyce to cause Steven harm, the words she hurled at him could not, under the analysis in *Lang*, constitute legally sufficient provocation.

[*The court observed that every jurisdiction but one to consider the issue has concluded that words alone are insufficient for prosecution.*]

We are unpersuaded by that one case awash in a sea of opposite holdings, especially since a Maryland case counters *Nelson* by stating that "the long-smoldering grudge . . . may be psychologically just as compelling a force as the sudden impulse but it, unlike the impulse, is a telltale characteristic of premeditation." *Tripp v. State*, 36 Md.App. at 471–72, 374 A.2d 384. Aside from the cases, recognized legal authority in the form of treatises supports our holding. *Perkins on Criminal Law*, at p. 62, states that it is "with remarkable uniformity that even words generally regarded as 'fighting words' in the community have no recognition as adequate provocation in the eyes of the law." It is noted that:

> mere words or gestures, however offensive, insulting, or abusive they may be, are not, according to the great weight of authority, adequate to reduce a homicide, although committed in a passion provoked by them, from murder to manslaughter, especially when the homicide was intentionally committed with a deadly weapon[.] (Footnotes omitted)

40 C.J.S. *Homicide* § 47, at 909 (1944). *See also*, 40 Am.Jur.2d *Homicide* § 64, at 357 (1968).

Thus, with no reservation, we hold that the provocation in this case was not enough to cause a reasonable man to stab his provoker 19 times. Although a psychologist testified to Steven's mental problems and his need for acceptance and love, we agree with the Court of Special Appeals speaking through Judge Moylan that "there must be not simply provocation in psychological fact, but one of certain fairly well-defined classes of provocation recognized as being adequate as a matter of law." *Tripp v. State*, 36 Md.App. at 473, 374 A.2d 384. The standard is one of reasonableness; it does not and should not focus on the peculiar frailties of mind of the Petitioner. That standard of reasonableness has not been met here. We cannot in good conscience countenance holding that a verbal domestic argument ending in the death of one spouse can result in a conviction of manslaughter. We agree with the trial judge that social necessity dictates our holding. Domestic arguments easily escalate into furious fights. We perceive no reason for a holding in favor of those who find the easiest way to end a domestic dispute is by killing the offending spouse.

We will leave to another day the possibility of expansion of the categories of adequate provocation to mitigate murder to manslaughter. The facts of this case do not warrant the broadening of the categories recognized thus far.

———————————

Notes and Questions

1. What exactly does this reasonableness standard mean in this context? It appears to mean (with the exception of spousal infidelity) that the defendant had to fear physical harm. But wouldn't that be self-defense? You will discover when we get to self-defense that a killing because of an unreasonable fear for one's life—or serious bodily injury—is manslaughter. Does this seems to be the only circumstance the Court would describe as creating reasonable provocation?

2. The Court is clearly concerned about sanctioning violence as a response to an insult to one's dignity. The Court was just as clearly interested in limiting violence. How then do you explain the spousal infidelity exception? If this exception seems out of sync with the other categories, so did the Maryland Legislature which eliminated spousal infidelity as reasonable provocation.

---

e. Death Must Be Cause of Defendant's Actions

In order to be guilty of a homicide, the defendant must have caused the death—this is always an element of any homicide offense, though often causation is not at issue. Like any other element of a crime, it must be proven beyond a reasonable doubt. The *Rose* case lays out the basic doctrine—you cannot kill a dead man—and the subsequent cases address thornier questions where the actions of multiple actors could have, or did, contribute to the victim's death.

See State v. Rose, p. 60, and the accompanying discussion.

PLEA BARGAINING EXERCISE

John Forrest was charged with murder of his father, Clyde Forrest, Sr., on December 24, 1985 in Pinehurst, North Carolina and convicted. The facts are offered below. You will assume that conviction was reversed because of a problem with the composition of the jury, a matter thar will not affect the retrial.

According to Frances Foster, a nurse's assistant at Moore Memorial Hospital, Clyde Forrest was a patient at the hospital on December 24, 1985. Foster had seen him the day before and knew at that time, his status was critical. She first saw him at 7:15 am on the 24th when she checked his temperature and was not in his room for more than five minutes. She asked Forrest how he felt and he told her that he was feeling better. She was again in Forrest's room at 10:45 am and at noon to take his temperature. She testified that he tried to feed himself at lunchtime but did not eat much. She continued to check in on Mr. Forrest during the day to "see if he was breathing all right." While he had an oxygen mask, he was breathing on his own. He was not coughing or groaning. When she entered the room at 2:30, John Forrest was also there, and she emptied his Foley bag. John Forrest said to her, "There is no need in doing that. He's dying." She responded, "Well, I think he's better." John Forrest "was sniffing as if he was crying." Foster went to the nurse's station and asked Alice Lanza, a registered nurse, to come into Forrest's room, explaining that John Forrest seemed "uncomfortable about his father" and perhaps "needs somebody to talk to him."

Ms. Lazra asked John Forrest if he had talked to his father's doctors and that they would be happy to answer any questions at the nurse's station. Lanza had not worked on this hallway in the past three weeks. She had seen Clyde Forrest earlier in the day and described him as alert, awake and oriented. She observed that he had an oxygen mask, an IV, and a Foley catheter, but was "in no obvious distress." His condition had not changed over the course of the day. She testified that the reason for the catheter was not an inability to urinate but, "[p]robably because he did have the respiratory problems they insert the catheter so he would not have to make the effort of getting up to go to the bathroom or to use the urinal." Ms. Lazra did recall, however, that Clyde Forrest's chart indicated a "no code," meaning that no heroic measures, such as CPR were to be performed to save his life.

At Ms. Foster's request, Ms. Lazra came into Clyde Forrest's room and said to John Forrest, "I don't think your father is as sick as you think he is." She testified that John Forrest said to her, "Go to hell. I've been taking care of him for years. I'll take care of him." Ms. Lazra said to him, "You don't have to talk to me like that. Have you talked to his doctor about his condition?" She noticed that John Forrest was crying and said to him, "If you have any questions for the doctors or nurses just come to the nurse's station. We'll be glad to talk to you." As she was leaving the room, John Forrest said to her, "You go to hell. You all go to hell." Ms. Lazra did not remember Clyde coughing, wheezing, or making any gurgling sounds when she was in the room with him. Ms. Foster reported that Clyde Forrest "was still in bed, but seemed to be breathing all right" when the two left the room.

Five or ten minutes later, the sound of four gunshots were heard. Bernice Chavis, then a nurse's assistant came to the door of Clyde Forrest's room where she saw John Forrest mumbling something to himself and crying. Ms. Chavis reported that John threw something in his hand to the ground and said "there wasn't no help for his father and now he was out of his misery." She smelled gunpowder and noticed the very small gun on the floor. She also described the gun as looking like a toy. John did not threaten Ms. Chavis, or anyone else. He "[j]ust stood there mumbling, crying. . ." and made no attempt to run away.

L.O. Pruden was working that day as a security guard. When he got to Clyde Forrest's room, there was a male nurse standing beside John Forrest and a gun lying on the floor. He wrapped the gun in a handkerchief and put it in his pocket. Pruden reported that the gun was small enough to put in the palm of his hand. Pruden saw Clyde Forrest in the bed with four distinct bullet holes. As Pruden came out Clyde's room, he heard John Forrest say that "we could put him in jail, lock him up. We could do anything we wanted to with him, but his father wouldn't have to suffer any longer."

Joe Prusser was employed in the hospital's maintenance department. Maintenance and security had been summoned stat to Clyde Forrest's room. He went to the nurse's station where he was told that a man had been shot. He saw John Forrest leaning against the wall out in the hallway crying. He heard Forrest say, "I killed my daddy. He won't have to suffer anymore." Prusser asked Forrest if he would "just go with us quietly, if he would go to the quiet room," a room also known as the nurses' lounge. Prusser described John Forrest as cooperative and nice. Once they arrived, John said, "I know they can burn me for it, but my dad will not have to suffer anymore." John further related that his father had blood clots that could not be treated because he could not take a blood thinner because he had an ulcer. He said, "I know the doctors couldn't do it, but I could," and that he had promised his father that he would not suffer, and that "his last day at home I stayed with him and cleaned up after him and looked after him."

Danny Brown, who worked for the Pinehurst Police Department, went to the hospital that afternoon and was asked to take custody of John Forrest. The officer went to the nurses' lounge where he found Forrest who "was making statement about it was the hardest thing he ever done in his life. He didn't think he could do it. He just couldn't stand to see his daddy suffer anymore. He said his dad told him: 'If you have an animal that was suffering put it out of its misery. He said he loved his dad. He was glad he did it. If he had it to do over he would do it again. He said, 'They could do whatever they want to with me. They can electrocute me, hang me, put me in prison, whatever. All I know it's like a heavy load has been lifted off my shoulders.'"

The officer reported that Forrest continued to make these and similar statements over and over.

When they arrived at the Moore County Jail, Forrest talked with Officer Brown about his life experiences with his father and repeated that he was glad that he did it and that his father was not suffering. He talked about his experience in the service and his experience as a truck driver. The officer described John Forrest as totally cooperative and polite.

On December 26, Patrolman Brown made John Forrest aware of his *Miranda* rights, which he waived, and provided a statement which Brown reduced to writing and Forrest signed. The statement read:

> The last day my dad, Clyde Forrest, was at home was Sunday, December 22, 1985. My son and I stayed with him at his home practically all day. My mother, Josephine Forrest, went to her daughter's house while my son and I stayed with my dad. My dad wasn't able to get out of bed so I helped him do what he had to and looked after him. As the day went on, he became progressively worse and seemed disoriented. That night we called the rescue squad and he was transported to Moore Memorial Hospital where he was admitted. That same night I called my bossman and advised him that my dad was in the hospital again, but he was not in intensive care. I advised my bossman that I would be at work unless my dad got worse. The next morning, Monday, December 23rd, 1985, I left home at approximately five o'clock A.M. accompanied by my son to make my deliveries. After my first delivery I called my brother, Doug and spoke to his wife, Betty. She advised me that my dad had been moved to intensive care. I gave her, Betty, my telephone number at work to call in case he, my dad, became worse. I then made my next delivery and called my brother again. Doug advised me that dad had a blood clot in his lung and the doctor could not give him a blood thinner would cause the bleeding ulcer to start bleeding again. Doug also stated that the doctor told him, Doug, that the family had a choice of putting dad on a life support system and letting him live for a few days or putting him, daddy, in a comfortable room out of intensive care to die. After talking to Doug I made my last delivery and went home. When I reached home I advised my son that I didn't want to see anyone or talk to anyone on the telephone. I told my son to take messages if anyone called and be sure to tell me when they called to tell me that my dad was dead. I then went to the bedroom to be alone. I kept waiting to hear the phone ring to tell me that my dad was dead, but the phone didn't ring. I cried most of the time because I

knew my dad was suffering and drowning in his own blood. The next day, Tuesday, December 24th, 1985, I called Doug, and Betty answered the phone. I asked Betty which room dad was in, and she stated Room 224. After finding out dad's room number I went to Moore Memorial Hospital. I was by myself. I went to Room 224 and walked in. Dad was lying there by himself, no family in the room with him. I started crying at this point, walked over to the bed and told dad that I loved him. He started coughing. There was gurgling and rattling noise.

He then made a second statement to Patrolman Brown on December 27, which read:

I bought a pistol approximately four years ago for my protection because I drive a long distance truck. I bought the pistol from Dan Phillips, Bennett, North Carolina, for $110.00. The pistol was a .22 caliber, five shot revolver. I don't remember the brand name of the revolver. I kept it with me all the time. On Tuesday, December 24, 1985, I had the revolver in my pocket of my pants. I went to Moore Memorial Hospital at approximately 2:00 P.M., Tuesday, December 24, 1985, to see my dad, Clyde Forrest, a patient at the hospital. I went to Room 224, Moore Memorial Hospital. The room was located on the second floor. My dad was in Room 224. I had thought about putting him out of his misery because I knew he was suffering. I walked in his room and he was alone. I spoke to him and I started crying and said to him, "Daddy, I love you." I told him I loved him two or three times, and he, my dad, opened his eyes and looked straight ahead. I stood there beside his bed, and I was still crying and a nurse came in. The nurse said, "He's not in that bad of shape." I was upset and I told her to go to hell because I knew he was dying. The nurse put a plastic mask over his, my dad's, nose and mouth, and I assumed it was oxygen he was receiving. The nurse then left. I stood sort of behind the bed for a while. I don't know how long. He, my dad, began to cough very badly and had several coughing spells. I was still crying during this time. I then pulled my revolver out of my right front pants pocket with my right hand, stuck the revolver which was a single action revolver to my dad, Clyde Forrest's right temple, cocked the hammer back, and pulled the trigger. The revolver went off, and I knew I had shot him, my dad. After the first shot went off I quickly shot him, my dad, several more times. I don't remember how many because I didn't want my dad to hurt anymore. I then immediately left the room. I walked out in the hall and I heard a woman scream. I threw the revolver on the floor of the hallway. I can't remember anything else that happened until the police came.

Ms. Foster saw John Forrest after the shooting and heard him say, "You can't do anything to him now. He's out of his suffering."

During the proceedings, Dr. Stuber testified the Clyde Forrest, Sr., died of four gunshots to the head. He also testified to further findings:

> I found evidence of severe heart disease, and in the lungs of the major finding was the large number of pulmonary emboli in both lungs. The other major finding included the gastrointestinal tract where I demonstrated that he had a peptic ulcer. . . . Mr. Forrest's major cardiovascular problem was severe disease in the coronary arteries.
>
> Mr. Forrest's major cardiovascular problem was severe disease in the coronary arteries. I'm sure you've all heard of hardening of the arteries or arteriosclerosis, athrosclerosis, by these names. The major problem in this condition is that the inside diameter of the coronary vessels is decreased and this diminishes bloody supply to the heart. In its most severe form this results in death of heart muscle or what is commonly called in lay terms heart attack or myocardial infarction in medical terms. So the major condition that Mr. Forrest was suffering from was severe arteriosclerosis. I was going to point out that Mr. Forrest's left ventricle which is the major pump portion of the heart that supplies blood to your body—he had evidence of an old heart attack in his left ventricle which I could see a scar which was a bit larger than one inch. So he not only had a severe coronary disease, but he showed evidence of having had a heart attack in the past.
>
> He also had other cardiac conditions which I haven't mentioned yet. One of these: He showed evidence of high blood pressure. I of course can't take his blood pressure at autopsy, but by examining the left ventricle one can tell by the thickness and the overall weight of the heart. These are beyond certain limits, and the Pathologist can also diagnose high blood pressure in life. Mr. Forrest did have an enlarged heart in the left ventricle so I know that he also had hypertension. In two of his heart valves I could demonstrate some thickening and areas of calcification. This was not terribly severe, but compounded with some of the other difficulties he had, could be of some significance. The heart valves control the flow of blood between the four chambers, and if these valves are thickened or if

they have calcification that function can be altered somewhat. Finally, not directly related to the heart, he also had a thoracic aneurysm. An aneurysm is a dilatation of a vessel. In this case he had a dilated aorta in the chest. This is a potentially hazardous condition.

The major problem in the lungs was a large number—large in number and large in size of pulmonary emboli which were present in both lungs. They were more severely involved in the left lung, but there was also a large number of emboli in the right one as well.

Pulmonary emboli implies a clot in the blood which occurs somewhere in the lower part of the body. Almost always it occurs in the legs, in the large veins in the leg. If they stay in the leg that's good. If they break off they are carried by the circulation through the heart and then pumped out into the lungs. In this instance when they are pumped up to the vessels in the lungs they eventually reach a point where they can no longer go any further and they stop circulation to the lung on that basis.

Dr. Stuber further testified that had "seen less involvement of pulmonary embolism, less than Mr. Forrest had, and be the cause of death." Based on the autopsy, he further concluded that Mr. Forrest would have been in a "great deal of distress [or pain]" before his death. He finally concluded that "Mr. Forrest was a very critically ill person. . . . [I]t would not have surprised me if he would have died very shortly, within 24 hours." The cause of death, according to Dr. Stuber, was nevertheless the gunshot wounds.

You will be divided into teams, with half of you acting as prosecutors and half of you acting as defense counsel. Assume this case was overturned and sent back to the trial court for a retrial—and assume that all of these witnesses are still available to testify and forgotten none of the details. Some of the teams will assume the case occurred in North Carolina, as it actually did. Other teams will be asked to assume that the case occurred in Maine. The prosecutors and defense lawyers will meet and try to work out a disposition of the case to avoid a retrial. At the conclusion of your meeting, the prosecutors will draft a press release explaining the offer the prosecution made that will be given to the press in the event the defendant accepts it. The defense will draft a letter to the client explaining the offer and making a recommendation on whether the deal ought to be accepted.

3. Complicity and Conspiracy to Kill

a. Mens Rea: Can an Unintentional Killing Trigger Complicity Liability?

We considered complicity in the introductory chapter where we discovered that those who encourage, assist, or aid a crime are as guilty as those who committed the crimes themselves. But in order to be liable for the crimes, the aider or abettor must *intend* that the crime occur. What about crimes that do not require intent, such as a reckless killing? The majority in *Simmons*, as you will see, concludes that a defendant may encourage the reckless conduct that leads to the death and thus be liable for the homicide. The dissent, however, concludes that the one may not intend to commit a crime that does not require intent.

Ex Parte Simmons

Supreme Court of Alabama
649 So.2d 1282 (1994)

PER CURIAM.

Michael Anthony Simmons was convicted of reckless murder, pursuant to Ala.Code 1975, § 13A–6–2(a)(2). The Court of Criminal Appeals held that the trial court had erred in charging the jury on aiding and abetting, so that court reversed the conviction and remanded the case for a new trial. *Simmons v. State*, 649 So.2d 1279 (Ala.Cr.App.1992). Both the State and Simmons petitioned this Court for certiorari review. We granted both petitions. The State contends that the Court of Criminal Appeals erred in reversing the judgment of conviction, because it argues that it was not error to charge the jury on aiding and abetting. Simmons argues that the Court of Criminal Appeals erred in not rendering a judgment for him, because he contends that there was insufficient evidence to support a conviction of reckless murder.

A three-year-old child was killed by a bullet fired from a gun while he was a passenger in his mother's automobile. The mother testified that she was driving down a public street when she noticed several men in a pickup truck shooting guns in her direction. She stated that she recognized the man on the back of the truck as the defendant, Simmons. She also testified that she observed several other people on the street, one of whom she recognized as Vernon "Blue" Peterson. She testified that Peterson appeared to be the target of the gunfire. At some point during the gunfire, the child was killed when a bullet entered the car and struck him in the head.

The bullet that killed the child exited the back of his head and was not recovered. Another bullet was recovered from the car in which the child was riding, and an expert witness testified that it was either a 9 mm., a .38 caliber, or a .357 caliber bullet. The expert witness testified that the fatal shot could have been fired from a weapon having any one of those three calibers. A total of 11 expended 9 mm. cartridge cases and 6 expended .38 special cartridge cases were found at the scene; some were found in the bed of the pickup truck and some were found on the street. An expert witness testified that the 9 mm. cartridges had been fired by two different weapons and that at least three different weapons had been fired at the scene. He further stated that, based upon his expertise, he believed that the bullet that killed the child could have been fired from any of the revolvers and semi-automatic pistols that were used in the shoot-out. However, it could not be determined from the evidence presented which of the men fired the fatal shot.

Although he was indicted for murder on two different theories, Simmons was eventually tried and convicted pursuant to Ala.Code 1975, § 13A–6–2(a)(2). In charging a violation of that section, the State alleged that Simmons

> "did, under circumstances manifesting extreme indifference to human life, recklessly engage in conduct which created a grave risk of death to a person other than himself, to-wit: by firing a gun numerous times on a crowded street and in the direction of said crowd, and thereby caused the death of another person, to-wit: Leonard Rivers. . . ."

The State proceeded under a theory of accomplice liability. The State conceded at trial and on appeal that it could not prove that Simmons fired the shot that killed the child. However, it contends that the evidence proves that Simmons aided and abetted in the reckless conduct that resulted in the death of the child.

I.

(State's Petition—No. 1920431)

The Court of Criminal Appeals held that the trial court erroneously instructed the jury that Simmons could be convicted of reckless murder on a theory of complicity. Essentially, the court held that it is "incompatible within the same charged offense" to say that one intends to promote or assist the commission of reckless conduct. 649 So.2d at 1281. We disagree.

Section § 13A–6–2(a)(2) provides:

> "(a) A person commits the crime of murder if:
>
> ". . . .

"(2) Under circumstances manifesting extreme indifference to human life, he recklessly engages in conduct which creates a grave risk of death to a person other than himself, and thereby causes the death of another person. . . ."

This section deals with "reckless murder" or, as it is sometimes called, "universal malice murder" or "depraved heart murder." It requires the prosecution to prove conduct that manifests an extreme indifference to human life and not to the life of any particular person. The purpose of § 13A–6–2(a)(2) is to embrace those homicides caused by such acts as shooting a firearm into a crowd, throwing a timber from a roof onto a crowded street, or driving an automobile in a grossly wanton manner. *See Northington v. State*, 413 So.2d 1169 (Ala.Cr.App.1981), *writ quashed*, 413 So.2d 1172 (Ala.1982). This section was written in an attempt to define a degree of recklessness "that cannot be fairly distinguished from homicides committed purposely or knowingly." Model Penal Code and Commentaries, § 210.02, comment 4 (1980), as quoted in *Ex parte Weems*, 463 So.2d 170, 172 (Ala.1984). Under the concept of reckless murder, the actor perceives a substantial and unjustified risk, but consciously disregards the risk of death.

Alabama's complicity statute, § 13A–2–23, provides:

"A person is legally accountable for the behavior of another constituting a criminal offense if, with the intent to promote or assist the commission of the offense:

"(1) He procures, induces or causes such other person to commit the offense; or

"(2) He aids or abets such other person in committing the offense; or

"(3) Having a legal duty to prevent the commission of the offense, he fails to make an effort he is legally required to make."

This section provides the basic principles for determining criminal liability that is based upon the behavior of another person. It sets out the type of action required and the necessary mental state.

In *Ex parte Howell*, 431 So.2d 1328 (Ala.1983), this Court addressed the issue of accomplice liability. There, the defendant, the victim, and the co-defendant were in a room together. The co-defendant was showing the victim a pistol when the defendant exploded some firecrackers in the house. The pistol fired and the bullet struck the victim, killing him. The defendant was charged with manslaughter, but was convicted of the lesser included offense of criminally negligent homicide. The Court of Criminal Appeals affirmed the conviction. On certiorari review, the only issue before this Court was whether a conviction of criminally negligent homicide by way of complicity was inconsistent.

This Court held that a defendant could not be convicted of criminally negligent homicide under a complicity theory, because, it said, complicity and criminally negligent homicide are "fundamentally inconsistent." *Howell*, supra, at 1330. The Court further said that it is logically impossible to be an accomplice to a criminally negligent homicide. However, *Howell* does not stand for the proposition that it is logically or legally impossible to be an accomplice to a reckless homicide.

Here, we are not concerned so much with a failure to "perceive a substantial and unjustifiable risk" (criminally negligent homicide, § 13A–6–4) as we are with an offense in which the principal actor does perceive, but consciously disregards, the risk of death. Therefore, we find it to be both logically and legally consistent to impose liability on one whose conduct aids or encourages another who is aware of, and who consciously disregards, a substantial risk of death.

Accomplice liability does not require that the accomplice intend for the principal to act in a reckless manner. Rather, accomplice liability requires only that the accomplice intend to promote or to assist the principal, having knowledge that the principal is engaging in, or is about to engage in, criminal conduct. *See* § 13A–2–23, Committee Comments. The mental state required for complicity is the intent to aid the principal in the criminal act or conduct, not the intent of the principal that death occur either intentionally or recklessly. In other words, for a person to be guilty of reckless murder as an accomplice, he need not know or decide whether the principal will act intentionally (§ 13A–6–2(a)(1)) or recklessly (§ 13A–6–2(a)(2)); rather, the accomplice need only have knowledge that the principal is engaging in reckless conduct and intentionally assist or encourage that conduct with the intent to promote or facilitate its commission.

In further support of our conclusion that complicity is consistent with recklessness, we point out that this Court has held that one can be an accomplice to manslaughter, which is also a reckless crime.[1] See generally 2 W. LaFave and A. Scott, *Substantive Criminal Law* § 6.7(e) (1986). *Morris v. State*, 146 Ala. 66, 41 So. 274 (1906); *Ferguson v. State*, 141 Ala. 20, 37 So. 448 (1904); *Martin v. State*, 89 Ala. 115, 8 So. 23 (1890). In *Martin*, this Court held that two brothers were equally guilty of manslaughter, regardless of which brother fired the fatal shot:

> "The jury were not without testimony from which they could draw the
> inference that the two Martins had a common purpose to set the law at

---

1   The difference between murder and manslaughter is one of degree (of recklessness) and not of kind. *Ex parte Weems*, 463 So.2d 170 (Ala.1984).

defiance, and to use whatever force might be necessary to accomplish their object; and that each was ready to assist and encourage the other, if assistance and encouragement should become necessary. [This being so], each was accountable for the act of the other, whether such act was previously intended or not, if it grew naturally and proximately out of the unlawful purpose they had in view." 89 Ala. at 120, 8 So. at 25.

We note that the facts of this case are unusual in that one cannot determine who fired the fatal shot. However, we hold that Simmons could legally be found guilty of reckless murder as an accomplice. He was a principal actor in complicity with the reckless conduct of the other shooters on this occasion. He knowingly advanced and participated in reckless behavior (even though we do not know the identity of the person who fired the fatal shot), and that reckless behavior resulted in the death of a three-year-old child who was traveling on a public street where the shooting occurred. In other words, one could conclude from the evidence that Simmons's conduct aided and encouraged another who was aware of, and who consciously disregarded, a substantial risk of death. *See Martin v. State*, supra. Therefore, the Court of Criminal Appeals erred in reversing the conviction on the holding that Simmons could not aid and abet in the commission of reckless murder.

* * *

REVERSED AND REMANDED.

MADDOX, HOUSTON, STEAGALL, INGRAM and COOK, JJ., concur.
ALMON, SHORES and KENNEDY, JJ., dissent.

ALMON, Justice (dissenting).

I respectfully dissent from the majority opinion. I would affirm the judgment of the Court of Criminal Appeals, because I agree that it was error for the circuit court to charge the jury on aiding and abetting, although I would limit the holding to the facts of this case. Simmons was tried only under § 13A–6–2(a)(2), Ala.Code 1975, which reads:

"(a) A person commits the crime of murder if:

"....

"(2) Under circumstances manifesting extreme indifference to human life, he recklessly engages in conduct which creates a grave risk of death to a

person other than himself, and thereby causes the death of another person;
. . . ."

Our complicity statute, § 13A–2–23 states:

"A person is legally accountable for the behavior of another constituting a criminal offense if, with the *intent to promote or assist the commission of the offense*:

"(1) He procures, induces or causes such other person to commit the offense; or

"(2) He aids or abets such other person in committing the offense; . . . ."

(Emphasis added).

The Court of Criminal Appeals held, essentially, that it is "incompatible within the same charged offense" to say that one *intends* to promote or assist the commission of *reckless* conduct. *See* the definitions of "Intentionally" and "Recklessly" at Ala.Code 1975, § 13A–2–2(1) and (3). I agree with the majority that there may be some circumstances under which one person can intentionally promote or assist in the commission of a murder under § 13A–6–2(a)(2), such as where two persons jointly shoot into a crowd, or one drives a vehicle while encouraging the other as a passenger to shoot into groups of people on the street, or similar fact situations.[2] However, under the facts of this case, I agree with the Court of Criminal Appeals that it was error to submit a charge of aiding and abetting or complicity in the commission of the murder of Leonard Rivers.

The problem arises here because § 13A–6–2(a)(2) does not apply to the evidence in this case at all. It has been held that this provision applies to conduct showing extreme indifference "directed toward human life in general," not to conduct evidencing an intent to injure or kill a particular individual. *Ex parte McCormack*, 431 So.2d 1340 (Ala.1983); *Leverett v. State*, 611 So.2d 481 (Ala. Crim.App.1992); *Thomas v. State*, 517 So.2d 640 (Ala.Crim.App.1987); *Free v. State*, 455 So.2d 137 (Ala.Crim.App.1984), appeal after remand, 495 So.2d 1147 (Ala.Crim.App.1986); *Northington v. State*, 413 So.2d 1169 (Ala.Crim.App.1981), cert. quashed, 413 So.2d 1172 (Ala.1982). All of the evidence here supports only the conclusion that Simmons or someone else in the truck was shooting at and

---

2   However, I reserve judgment on the applicability of *Morris v. State*, 146 Ala. 66, 41 So. 274 (1906); *Ferguson v. State*, 141 Ala. 20, 37 So. 448 (1904); and *Martin v. State*, 89 Ala. 115, 8 So. 23 (1890), to the question of aiding and abetting in the commission of manslaughter under current law. These cases were decided long before our current Criminal Code, Ala.Code 1975, § 13A–1–1 et seq., was enacted. I would consider carefully whether these cases would properly apply under the Code definition of "complicity" at § 13A–2–23 and the Code definition of "manslaughter" at § 13A–6–3(a)(1), before reaffirming them in the context of the Criminal Code.

attempting to kill Peterson or another person with Peterson, Antonio Pearson. If Simmons was aiding and abetting others in the truck in any offense, it was in the attempt to kill Peterson or Pearson. Thus, when the State for some reason decided to prosecute Simmons for "recklessly" killing Rivers, it forced itself into the untenable position of asking the trial court to instruct the jury that Simmons "intended to promote or assist" in the reckless murder of Rivers.

As I view this case, it appears that the State should have tried Simmons under either § 13A–6–2(a)(1) or § 13A–6–2(a)(3):

"(a) A person commits the crime of murder if:

"(1) With intent to cause the death of another person, he causes the death of that person *or of another person*; or

"....

"(3) He commits or attempts to commit arson in the first degree, burglary in the first or second degree, escape in the first degree, kidnapping in the first degree, rape in the first degree, robbery in any degree, sodomy in the first degree or any other felony clearly dangerous to human life and, in the course of and in furtherance of the crime that he is committing or attempting to commit, or in immediate flight therefrom, he, *or another participant* if there be any, causes the death of *any person*."

(Emphasis added.) The district attorney stated that he could not prove that "Simmons fired the shot that killed Leonard Rivers." However, if he could have proved, even by circumstantial evidence, that the fatal shot was fired by Simmons or by one of the persons with him in the truck, Simmons could be found guilty under § 13A–6–2(a)(1) pursuant to the complicity statute, because he apparently intended to aid and abet his companions in causing the murder of Peterson. Section 13A–6–2(a)(1) allows the intent to kill Peterson to be "transferred" to Rivers, so I see no reason why the aiding and abetting of the attempt to kill Peterson cannot support a conviction for the intentional murder of Rivers.

Alternatively, if the district attorney could have proved that Simmons or one of his companions fired the shot that killed Rivers, Simmons could be found guilty under § 13A–6–2(a)(3) without even invoking the complicity statute. It seems clear that Simmons and his companions were attempting to murder Peterson; the murder of Peterson would be a felony that is "clearly dangerous to human life," as required under § 13A–6–2(a)(3). Thus, the attempt to murder Peterson would support a conviction of Simmons for the murder of Rivers if

Simmons or one of the other participants in the attempt to murder Peterson caused the death of Rivers.

If the State was unable to prove even circumstantially that the shot that killed Rivers came from the truck in which Simmons was riding, I cannot see how Simmons can be found guilty of murder. If the evidence equally supports the inference that Peterson shot Rivers, Simmons cannot be found guilty under the complicity statute and § 13A–6–2(a)(1), because there is no evidence that, with the "intent to promote or assist the commission of" the murder of Rivers, Simmons induced or caused Peterson to kill Rivers (§ 13A–2–23(1)) or aided and abetted Peterson in killing Rivers (§ 13A–2–23(2)). Nor, under such a state of the evidence, could Simmons be found guilty of murder under § 13A–6–2(a)(3), because Peterson was not a "participant" in the felony that Simmons and his companions were attempting; Peterson was the intended *victim* of the underlying felony, not a participant. It does seem that a jury could find Simmons guilty of the attempted murder of Peterson, a class A felony. *See* Ala.Code 1975, § 13A–4–2.

I would hold that the evidence in this case does not support an instruction stating that Simmons could be found guilty of murder for aiding and abetting the reckless murder of Rivers; therefore, I would affirm the judgment of the Court of Criminal Appeals.

SHORES, J., concurs.

Notes and Questions

1. Doctrinally, the dissent's position certainly makes sense. Look back to complicity in the introductory chapter. To be guilty of aiding and abetting, a defendant must intend the crime he is aiding to come to fruition. Reckless homicide is not a crime that requires intent; the crime is completed when a harmful result occurs as a result of recklessness. Those guilty of reckless homicide may, or may not, have desired the death—but in no case does the prosecution have to prove that one committing this crime desired the death he caused. How, then, can A be guilty of intending to assist B in bringing about a result that B himself did not intend? A number of jurisdictions, tracking the dissent's reasoning, conclude that it is indeed not possible to be guilty of another's crimes through a complicity theory, unless the crime itself requires intent.

2. Unless the majority's position is accepted, however, a very strange set of affairs exists. If A encourages B to engage in a crime that requires B to intend a certain result, then A is just as guilty as B. If, however, A encourages B to

utterly disregard another's life, and B does so because of A's encouragement, then A has no liability for the death that results. The majority concludes that all that A must do is encourage B to engage in the *conduct* that led to the death. For another, very well-reasoned decision arriving at this conclusion, *see Commonwealth v. Roebuck* p. 90. This reasoning is, however, problematic because under the Alabama law the court cites, a person is liable for another's offenses if "with the intent to promote or assist the commission of *the offense*" he"aids or abets such other person in committing *the offense*." (This is, by the way, a very standard description of complicity liability.) The offense at issue, reckless homicide, is not a crime that proscribes *conduct*, it is an offense that proscribes a *result*.

3. Courts have, however, also used another principle to arrive at this same result. Refer back to complicity in the introductory chapter. Many states recognize the doctrine of natural and probable consequences. Once a defendant has encouraged another's criminal conduct, in these states, he is liable for the natural and probable consequences of the conduct. In these jurisdictions, the prosecution could allege that he encouraged another to engage in illegal conduct, aggravated assault for instance, the natural and foreseeable consequences of which led to a death. *See People v. Prettyman*, 926 P.2d 103 (Cal. 1996). But *see Sharma v. State*, 56 P.3d 868 (Nev. 2002) (rejecting such a theory of liability).

---

b. *The Relationship Between Conspiracy and Complicity*

A defendant who is *complicit* in a crime—because he aids or abets the crime—is guilty of the crime itself. Conspiracy is an agreement to commit a crime, not the crime itself. The agreement is itself a different, and less serious, offense. Complicity and conspiracy are typically proven by the same evidence. The existence of an agreement to kill must be established either through a confession by the defendant, the testimony of conspirators, or concerted action from which the agreement of the conspirators can be inferred. The same type of evidence will also be used to show that a defendant aided another in the killing.

Additionally, conspiracy and complicity leave defendants liable for crimes beyond those aided or agreed to. As discussed in the notes to *Simmons*, many states recognize that those who aid or abet are liable for the natural and foreseeable consequences of those crimes—the scope of which varies by jurisdiction, as you would expect. In many jurisdictions, defendants are similarly liable for acts "in furtherance" of conspiracies they join. *See Pinkerton v. United States*, 328 U.S. 640 (1946).

In the *Marquez* case that follows, you will see many of the issues involved in complicity and conspiracy. We are discussing homicides, so naturally this case involves a death. (A quick note on terminology: Pennsylvania uses the term "natural and probable consequence" in describing the scope of co-conspirator liability, just as it does for the scope of liability for an aider and abettor.)

Marquez addresses several issues in play when conspiracy and complicity are used to show liability in homicide cases. *Marquez* involves a prosecution for malice (depraved heart) murder and a conspiracy to commit this crime. The prosecution alleged that Marquez was liable on the basis of his acts alone, as well as under a complicity theory. It is very common in homicide cases involving multiple actors for the prosecution to allege that the defendant is liable under both theories—especially common when death occurs by shooting and the identity of the shooter is in question.

The majority finds that the defendant is liable for conspiracy to commit murder as well as complicity for the murder itself. Judge Klein's concurring and dissenting opinion concludes that the defendant was liable for only conspiracy to assault and that a murder is not a natural and probable consequence of the assault that defendant agreed to commit. Judge Klein apparently concluded that there was no basis for holding the defendant liable for the malice murder under a complicity theory. Judge Cleland's concurring and dissenting opinion similarly concludes that the defendant was not guilty of conspiracy, but nevertheless concludes that he was guilty of the crime of third degree murder. Judge Cleland thus views this as one of the rare cases in which a defendant *aided* (or actually *committed*) a crime that he did not *agree* to participate in.

Commonwealth v. Marquez

Superior Court of Pennsylvania
980 A.2d 145 (2009)

OPINION BY MUSMANNO, J.

Edwin Marquez ("Marquez")[1] appeals from the judgment of sentence imposed after he was convicted of third-degree murder and criminal conspiracy.[2] We affirm.

---

1   We note that Marquez is also known as Edwin Jiminez.

2   18 Pa.C.S.A. §§ 2502, 903.

The pertinent facts of this case are as follows:

The instant matter arose out of the burglary of [Marquez's] home on May 22, 2005. On that date, [Marquez] and his brother, . . . Carlos Jiminez ["Jiminez"], arrived home, after going to a nearby store, and found three men in the home they shared.

At least one of the men was armed. The intruders ran from the home but not before [Jiminez] disarmed one of them.

After the intruders were gone, the police were summoned and, based on the descriptions provided them, they apprehended a suspect. [Jiminez] did not tell the police about the gun he had taken from one of the men.

Two days later, Carlos Alicea, ["the decedent"], his sister, Melanie Cales, his cousin, Rosa Ayala, and her cousin, Grisel Rivera were waiting together for a bu[s] at 5th & Cambria Streets when [Marquez] and another male walked by them. [Marquez] was speaking to someone on a cell phone and was overheard saying "He is here, he is in the store" all the while imploring the person to whom he was speaking to hurry up and get there. [Marquez] then entered the store where he grabbed the decedent, who had just gone inside it, because he believed that the decedent had been one of the men who had entered his home two days earlier. The two men began tussling. This continued for a short while both inside the store and outside it. Eventually, [Marquez] got the decedent in a "full nelson" hold outside the store. When he did, [Jiminez], who had just driven up, ran up to the decedent and shot the decedent in the chest from close range while he still was in the grasp of [Marquez] with the gun he had taken from one of the intruders two days earlier. [Marquez] immediately let go of the decedent[,] who stumbled away. When he did so, [Jiminez] fired a second shot at him. The decedent then fell to the ground at which time [Jiminez] walked over to him and fired a third shot at him.

Following the shooting, both [Marquez] and his brother fled the scene. They both eventually went to Florida where they were arrested on June 7, 2005 and returned to Philadelphia.

The decedent was taken to a nearby hospital where he died shortly after arriving there. An autopsy revealed that the decedent suffered two gunshot wounds to his upper body. The bullets that entered his body damaged his heart, lungs, and liver.

Trial Court Opinion, 4/26/07, at 2–3.

Marquez was charged with murder generally, criminal conspiracy and various weapons offenses. Marquez and Jiminez were tried, as co-defendants, by a jury in October/November 2006. The jury convicted Marquez of third-degree murder and criminal conspiracy. On January 18, 2007, the trial court sentenced Marquez to a prison term of seventeen and one-half to thirty-five years on the murder conviction and a concurrent prison term of ten to twenty years on the conspiracy conviction. Marquez then filed a timely Notice of appeal. The trial court ordered that Marquez file a Concise Statement of matters complained of on appeal, pursuant to Pennsylvania Rule of Appellate Procedure 1925(b), within fourteen days from the date the notes of testimony became available.[3] Marquez filed a Concise Statement on April 10, 2007.

Marquez raises the following issues on appeal:

1. Is [Marquez] entitled to an arrest of judgment on the charges of murder in the third degree and criminal conspiracy where there is insufficient evidence to sustain the verdict and where the Commonwealth did not prove its case beyond a reasonable doubt?

2. Is [Marquez] entitled to a new trial where he requested a charge on the issue of voluntary manslaughter (unreasonable self-defense) and where the evidence would have justified such a charge, but where the court refused to give that charge?

Brief for Appellant at 3.

Marquez first contends that he is entitled to an arrest of judgment on his convictions of third-degree murder and criminal conspiracy. Marquez argues that there is nothing in the record that would indicate that he agreed with Jiminez to shoot or kill the decedent. Marquez also asserts that he was not acting with the *mens rea* of malice at the time of the shooting. Further, Marquez argues that he was not an accomplice to the decedent's murder.

* * *

Third-degree murder is defined "all other kinds of murder" other than first degree murder or second degree murder. 18 Pa.C.S. § 2502(c). "The elements of third-degree murder, as developed by case law, are a killing done with legal malice." *Commonwealth v. MacArthur*, 427 Pa.Super. 409, 629 A.2d 166, 167–68 (1993).

Malice exists where there is a particular ill-will, and also where "there is a wickedness of disposition, hardness of heart, wanton conduct, cruelty, recklessness of consequences and a mind regardless of social duty."

---

3   The record before us does not indicate the date upon which the notes of testimony became available.

Melechio, 658 A.2d at 1388 (citations omitted).

"A person is guilty of [criminal] conspiracy with another person or persons . . . if with the intent of promoting or facilitating" the commission of a crime, he:

(1) agrees with such other person or persons that they or one or more of them will engage in conduct which constitutes such crime or an attempt or solicitation to commit such crime; or

(2) agrees to aid such other person or persons in the planning or commission of such crime or of an attempt or solicitation to commit such crime.

18 Pa.C.S.A. § 903(a). In addition, a person will be found to be an accomplice "of another person in the commission of an offense if:"

(1) with the intent of promoting or facilitating the commission of the offense, he:

(i) solicits such other person to commit it; or

(ii) aids or agrees or attempts to aid such other person in planning or committing it. . . .

18 Pa.C.S.A. § 306(c).

Our review of the evidence of record reveals, *inter alia*, that Rosa Ayala ("Ayala") testified that, prior to the shooting, while at the bus stop, she heard a man she identified as Marquez tell someone, while using his cell phone, to "hurry up, come over here, he is here, hurry up." N.T., 10/31/06, at 106. This testimony was corroborated by that of Grisel Rivera ("Rivera"), another eyewitness. N.T., 11/1/06, at 11, 15. Ayala further testified that Marquez then followed the decedent into the grocery store. N.T., 10/31/06, at 106. As the decedent was coming out of the store, Marquez put him in a headlock and held him in that position. *Id.* at 109, 115; *see also* N.T., 11/1/06, at 15. While Marquez was holding the decedent in a headlock outside of the grocery store, Jiminez came down Cambria Street, "took the gun and shot [the decedent]." N.T., 10/31/06, at 114; *see also* N.T., 11/1/06, at 18. After Jiminez shot the decedent, Marquez "moved back," and the decedent fell. N.T., 10/31/06, at 115.

Commonwealth witness Anthony Fox ("Fox") testified that he observed the fight that occurred between the decedent and a "larger man" prior to the shooting. N.T., 11/1/06, at 43–45. Fox testified that the larger man had the decedent in a headlock, at which time another man came across the street with an automatic hand weapon, approached the decedent, and shot him from very close range. *Id.* at 46. Fox indicated that the larger man "definitely" had the decedent in a headlock until after the first shot was fired. *Id.* at 46–47. After the first shot was fired, the larger man "let go" of the decedent. *Id.* at 47. The shooter then shot the victim a second time, and the decedent fell to the ground on his hands and knees. *Id.* at 48. The shooter then stood over the decedent and shot him a third time from above. *Id.*

At trial, Fox could not specifically identify the shooter or the man who had the decedent in a headlock because "[e]verything happened so fast." *Id.* at 49–50. However, prior to trial, on May 31, 2005, Fox picked a photo of Jiminez from a photo array and identified him as the shooter. *Id.* at 57. Fox also picked a photo of Marquez from another photo array as looking "somewhat like the guy I picked from the first set of pictures. . . ." *Id.* at 59.

Viewing the evidence adduced at trial in the light most favorable to the Commonwealth, as required under our standard of review, we conclude that it was sufficient to establish the elements of the crimes of third-degree murder and criminal conspiracy. From the Commonwealth's evidence, the jury could infer that Marquez acted with malice by seeking out the decedent, calling someone to let them know that "he is here," and holding the decedent in a headlock until after Jiminez shot him. Thus, the evidence was sufficient to establish Marquez's guilt of third-degree murder.

Further, the evidence was sufficient to establish that Marquez was guilty of criminal conspiracy. The evidence revealed that Marquez was a larger man than the decedent, which casts doubt on Marquez's assertion that he restrained the decedent only to ensure his arrest by the police. Fox indicated that Marquez was heavier and taller than the decedent, and as a result, Marquez easily overpowered the decedent in the scuffle that lasted less than a minute. N.T., 11/01/06, at 44–45. Given Marquez's size advantage, it is doubtful that Marquez reasonably expected difficulty holding the decedent until the police arrived. Nonetheless, Marquez called Jiminez to urge his presence at the scene.

Fox testified further that Jiminez arrived with his gun drawn, charging it in preparation to fire in full view of Marquez, as he crossed the street toward the decedent. *Id.* at 45–46. Marquez continued to restrain the decedent until Jiminez shot him in the chest from a distance of three feet. *Id.* at 46–47. Jiminez subsequently shot the decedent two more times. *Id.*[4]

Marquez showed no surprise and did not release the decedent until he had been shot. If Marquez were truly ignorant of his brother's plans to shoot the

---

4   Marquez did nothing to prevent Jiminez from shooting the decedent two more times, which would militate against a conspiracy to commit assault, as espoused by the dissent.

decedent, one would not expect him to continue holding the decedent in place as Jiminez approached, wielding a loaded weapon. Instead, Marquez restrained the decedent long enough to be shot. He then immediately fled the scene with his brother, failing to remain and provide assistance to the decedent or the police.

This Court has repeatedly held that flight, along with other circumstantial evidence, supports the inference of a criminal conspiracy. *See Commonwealth v. Davalos*, 779 A.2d 1190 (Pa.Super.2001); *Commonwealth v. Hatchin*, 709 A.2d 405 (Pa.Super.1998). Flight is one aspect of the web of evidence that as a whole points to the existence of a criminal conspiracy. *Commonwealth v. Davenport*, 307 Pa.Super. 102, 452 A.2d 1058 (1982).

Marquez's flight to Florida with his brother, Carlos Jiminez, after the murder, suggested an attempt to avoid prosecution. Likewise, his flight from the scene of the crime and from the Commonwealth established he was not an innocent pawn, unaware of his brother's murderous designs. Indeed, when viewed in the totality of the circumstances, Marquez's conduct showed consciousness of his guilt and a desire to escape prosecution for his part in the murder. Flight was the logical conclusion of their criminal confederation.

The web of circumstantial evidence, taken as a whole, points to the existence of a criminal conspiracy carried out by the two brothers. Marquez's assertions that he restrained the decedent only in anticipation of police intervention, oblivious to Jiminez's criminal intentions, were unsupported by the factual record. The evidence provided at trial was sufficient to allow the jury to conclude there was a criminal conspiracy.

Marquez's contrary claims, *i.e.*, that he did not act with malice, that he did not engage in a conspiracy to commit murder, and that he was not an accomplice to the murder, are based on his own testimony and that of Jiminez. Thus, those claims go to the weight of the evidence and the credibility of the witnesses, which were within the province of the jury as fact-finder. *See Commonwealth v. Troy*, 832 A.2d 1089, 1092 (Pa.Super.2003) (stating that, "the trier of fact[,] while passing upon the credibility of witnesses and the weight of the evidence produced, is free to believe all, part or none of the evidence;" the Commonwealth may sustain its burden of proof by means of circumstantial evidence); *Melechio*, 658 A.2d at 1387 (holding that, on a motion in arrest of judgment, the trial court "cannot make a redetermination of credibility and weight of the evidence"). Here, the jury chose to believe the testimony of the Commonwealth's witnesses. Thus, we conclude that Marquez's claim that he was entitled to an arrest of judgment lacks merit.

* * *

Judgment of sentence affirmed.

CONCURRING AND DISSENTING OPINION BY KLEIN, J.:

I agree with the majority that the trial court properly refused to charge the jury on self-defense. I also agree that the evidence was sufficient to establish criminal conspiracy, although I believe the only conspiracy proven was a conspiracy to commit assault against the victim, not a conspiracy to commit murder. However, I disagree with the majority's conclusion that there was sufficient evidence to support the third-degree murder conviction. Therefore, I respectfully dissent on that issue.

Under Pennsylvania law, if you conspire with another person to conduct a robbery, and, unbeknownst to you, your co-conspirator has a gun, pulls out the gun, and kills someone, the murder would qualify as a natural and probable consequence of the conspiracy for which you could be criminally liable as a co-conspirator. *See Commonwealth v. Johnson*, 719 A.2d 778, 786 (Pa.Super.1998) (*en banc*). However, a defendant may not be found guilty of homicide simply because it appears some kind of confrontation was about to take place and another participant, without knowledge, request, or encouragement of the defendant, radically alters the nature of incident by a using deadly weapon that the defendant did not know the participant had. *See Commonwealth v. Menginie*, 477 Pa. 156, 383 A.2d 870, 873 (1978). Our Court has stated that a defendant may not be liable as a co-conspirator when he or she "had no expectation that a minor scuffle would unexpectedly explode into murder." *Johnson*, 719 A.2d at 786.

In this case, the record established that some type of conspiracy did exist between Marquez and his brother, Carlos Jiminez.[1] However, the evidence showed nothing more than a conspiracy between the two men to apprehend the victim and presumably beat him up in retaliation for a prior burglary. In my view, it is pure conjecture to conclude that Marquez and his brother shared any intent other than to assault the victim. I do not believe it was a natural and probable consequence of that conspiracy that Marquez's coconspirator would come along from a separate location and shoot the victim in front of a crowd of people, shooting Marquez in the process. Under these circumstances, I would conclude that the Commonwealth failed to prove beyond a reasonable doubt that the victim's murder was a natural and probable consequence of the conspiracy to assault him.

To establish a conspiracy, the Commonwealth must show that the defendant (1) entered into an agreement to commit or aid in an unlawful act with another person or persons, (2) with shared criminal intent, and (3) an overt act

---

1   Though not mentioned in the majority's opinion, a third brother, Orlando Jiminez, was the person who initially called Marquez to tell him that he had seen Alicea at 5th and Cambria Streets. Orlando was not a co-defendant in this case.

was done in furtherance of the conspiracy. *Commonwealth v. Bricker*, 882 A.2d 1008, 1017 (Pa.Super.2005). The conduct of the parties and the circumstances surrounding such conduct may create a web of evidence linking the accused to the alleged conspiracy. *Id.* An agreement may also be inferred from the relation between the parties, their knowledge of and participation in the crime, and the circumstances and conduct of the parties surrounding the crime. *Id.*

The majority concludes that from the Commonwealth's evidence, the jury could have inferred that Marquez and Jiminez agreed to commit murder or that Marquez agreed to aid Jiminez in committing murder. (Majority Op. at 149.) I disagree. I believe the prior communication between the brothers regarding Alicea's location and physical description, coupled with Marquez's attack of the victim, established nothing more than a conspiracy to commit assault.

It is evident that a conspiracy existed between Marquez and Jiminez. The testimony showed that when he was informed of Alicea's location, Marquez called someone and told that person to "hurry up" and "come over here." (N.T. Trial, 10/31/06, at 106.) Marquez and Jiminez arrived in the area of 5th and Cambria Streets within minutes of each other, further suggesting that a common plan existed between them. (*Id.* at 122.) Although Marquez and Jiminez testified that they merely wanted to hold Alicea for the police, the fact that neither brother called the police, despite having cell phones, contradicts this argument. (*Id.*, 11/2/06, at 40, 48, 84, 98.)

Still, I do not believe this evidence comes close to proving that the brothers had formed a conspiracy to commit murder. Pennsylvania law provides that a person found to be a co-conspirator in a minor crime that develops into a more serious crime is liable for the more serious crime if such crime was a natural and probable consequence of the original conspiracy. *See* Johnson, supra (defendant who conspired to commit violent attacks with baseball bats is liable for conspiracy to commit third-degree murder because death is natural and probable consequence of such attack, regardless of whether defendant participated in killing); *Commonwealth v. La*, 433 Pa.Super. 432, 640 A.2d 1336 (1994) (defendant convicted of conspiracy to commit murder for providing knives used in killing, even though defendant only participated in fight and not in killing itself); *Commonwealth v. Bigelow*, 416 Pa.Super. 449, 611 A.2d 301 (1992) (defendant convicted of third-degree murder and criminal conspiracy when he and three co-conspirators fought victim and one co-conspirator used 3 1/2-foot stick to kill victim).

The evidence in this case does not establish that Alicea's murder was a natural and probable consequence of the conspiracy between Marquez and Jiminez. There is no evidence that Marquez had any knowledge that Jiminez had a gun in his possession. (*See* N.T. Trial, 11/2/06, at 96, 117.) When Jiminez obtained the gun after the burglary, Marquez was not even present in the home. (*Id.* at 116.)

Jiminez did not reveal to police that he had a gun, choosing to keep the gun hidden in his car instead. (*Id.* at 46, 47.) Without any inclination on Marquez's part that Jiminez had a gun, Alicea's murder cannot be a natural and probable consequence of the conspiracy to assault him. While it may be inferred that Marquez and Jiminez shared an intent to engage in an assault, it cannot be inferred that the two brothers shared a criminal intent to commit murder.

Furthermore, Jiminez shot and killed Alicea in front of a large number of witnesses, and even shot Marquez in the process. (*Id.* at 108.) Under these facts, and even viewing the evidence in the light most favorable to the Commonwealth, I cannot conclude beyond a reasonable doubt that murder was a natural and probable consequence of the conspiracy to assault Alicea. In *Johnson, supra*, this Court specifically distinguished the fact that the defendant had provided the deadly weapons used to kill the victim from a situation where a defendant "had no expectation that a minor scuffle would unexpectedly explode into murder." 719 A.2d at 786. Here, there is no evidence that Marquez had any expectation that his scuffle with Alicea would result in murder. In fact, eyewitness Anthony Fox's testimony that "[e]verything happened so fast" (N.T. Trial, 11/1/06, at 50), supports Marquez's claim that Jiminez acted suddenly and unexpectedly in pulling out the gun and shooting Alicea.

It is true that in some cases, criminal liability has been extended to a defendant for the acts of his co-conspirators that were committed in furtherance of a common criminal design. *See, e.g., Commonwealth v. Lambert*, 795 A.2d 1010 (Pa.Super.2002) (defendant convicted of second-degree murder, burglary, and criminal conspiracy for driving co-conspirator to victim's house, waiting while co-conspirator broke into house, and remaining in car as co-conspirator shot victim in defendant's presence); *Commonwealth v. Baskerville*, 452 Pa.Super. 82, 681 A.2d 195 (1996) (defendant convicted of second-degree murder and criminal conspiracy when co-conspirator shot and killed victim during armed robbery).

These cases, however, are distinguishable from the situation before us. In each one, the defendant's involvement in the actions leading up to the more serious crime supports the notion that the more serious crime arose as a natural and probable consequence of the original crime. Unlike the defendants in *Lambert* and *Baskerville*, Marquez did not arrive at the scene with his coconspirator. There is no evidence that Marquez even conversed with Jiminez prior to the shooting. (*See* N.T. Trial, 11/2/06, at 110.) Furthermore, I believe Alicea's murder arose out of a conspiracy to commit assault, not a conspiracy to commit robbery or burglary, for which murder would be a natural and probable consequence, as was the case in *Lambert* and *Baskerville*.[2]

---

2   One case that did uphold a murder conviction arising out of a conspiracy to commit assault is also distinguishable because the defendant in that case continued to participate in the assault after the deadly act had been

Consequently, the evidence of record is insufficient to show that Alicea's murder was a natural and probable consequence of the conspiracy to assault him. While the Commonwealth proved the existence of a conspiracy to commit assault, it failed to prove a conspiracy to commit murder beyond a reasonable doubt. Accordingly, I dissent from the majority on this issue.

CONCURRING AND DISSENTING OPINION BY CLELAND, J.:

I agree with my colleagues in the majority that the evidence was sufficient to prove Marquez guilty of the crime of third degree murder, and that he was not entitled to a jury charge on the crime of voluntary manslaughter.

To the majority's conclusion that the evidence was sufficient to prove him guilty of conspiracy to commit murder, however, I respectfully dissent.

In my view the evidence was insufficient to establish Marquez entered into an agreement to commit a specific crime—either murder, as the majority concludes, or assault, as Judge Klein concludes. Since the Commonwealth did not prove what crime Marquez and Jiminez agreed to commit, the Commonwealth did not prove the crime of conspiracy to commit murder.

"To prove conspiracy, 'the trier of fact must find that: (1) the defendant *intended to commit* or aid in the commission of the criminal act; (2) the defendant entered into an agreement with another . . . *to engage in the crime*; and (3) the defendant or one of more of the other co-conspirators committed an overt act in furtherance of the agreed upon crime.'" *Commonwealth v. Montalvo*, 598 Pa. 263, 956 A.2d 926, 932 (2008) (quoting *Commonwealth v. Murphy*, 577 Pa. 275, 844 A.2d 1228, 1238 (2004) (emphasis added)).

The Crimes Code provides that a person is "guilty of conspiracy with another person or persons to commit a crime if with the intent of promoting or facilitating its commission he: (1) *agrees* with such other person or persons that they or one or more of them will engage in conduct which constitutes *such crime* or an attempt or solicitation to commit such crime; or (2) agrees with such other person or persons in the planning or commission of *such crime* or of an attempt or solicitation to commit such crime." 18 Pa.C.S. § 903. (emphasis added). Conspiracy, in other words, is not made out simply with evidence that the participants agreed to do something illegal; the Commonwealth must prove they have agreed to commit a specific crime.

---

performed. *See Commonwealth v. Woodward*, 418 Pa.Super. 218, 614 A.2d 239 (1992) (defendant convicted of first-degree murder and conspiracy for continuing to hit victim after co-conspirator had stabbed victim, even though defendant had no knowledge that co-conspirator had a knife). Here, Marquez released Alicea the moment the shots were fired, thus eliminating any evidence of collusive behavior to kill Alicea. (N.T. Trial, 11/2/06, at 90, 109.)

I believe the evidence, as summarized by the majority, is sufficient to prove the defendant entered into an agreement with someone; and I believe the jury could fairly conclude based on the evidence that Marquez's agreement was with Jiminez. Marquez was overheard on his cell phone saying "He is here, he is in the store" and imploring the person on the other end of the call to come. Shortly thereafter, Jiminez arrived on the scene.

Proving the existence of an agreement, however, does not prove the existence of a conspiracy. "Conspiracy" is not synonymous with "agreement." Not all agreements constitute the crime of conspiracy. To prove the crime of conspiracy the Commonwealth must also prove the purpose of the agreement was to commit a specific crime. Here there was simply insufficient evidence to establish what crime it was Marquez and Jiminez agreed to commit.

The majority correctly notes that both an agreement and the purpose of an agreement may be proved either by direct or circumstantial evidence.

The problem with the Commonwealth's case is the insufficiency of evidence—either direct or circumstantial—of what crime Marquez and Jiminez agreed to commit. In essence, the majority concludes from the fact Jiminez murdered the victim that the murder must have been the purpose of the conspiracy. But proof of harm caused by Jiminez's conduct is not a substitute for proof of Marquez's intent. The result caused by the conduct of one party to an agreement may be *some* evidence of the purpose of the agreement, but it does not necessarily follow that the conduct of one of the parties was the conduct agreed to by the other, and that is the essence of the crime of conspiracy.

Conspiracy is an amorphous crime, made so by the historical willingness of courts to accede to the argument that because proving the specific crime the conspirators agreed to commit is so difficult then the Commonwealth should be permitted to bootstrap proof of harm into proof of intent. It is admittedly difficult to prove the specific crime which is the object of the agreement. This difficulty of proof, however, is not a reason to relax the Legislature's definition of the crime of conspiracy.

I do not believe the evidence was sufficient to prove that Marquez agreed with Jiminez that he would murder the victim. Consequently, as to the majority's decision upholding the conviction for conspiracy to commit third degree murder, I respectfully dissent.

Notes and Questions

1. Notice that it is not clear whether the majority, or Judge Cleland, finds the defendant is guilty of the murder on the basis of a complicity theory, or simply on the basis of the malice murder statute itself.

2. Judge Klein recognizes that Pennsylvania has a version of the *Pinkerton* rule, which renders conspirators liable for the "natural and probable consequences" of the conspiracy. Most jurisdictions that adopt this sort of liability hold defendants liable for acts of co-conspirators "in furtherance" of the conspiracy. Pennsylvania obviously has a slightly different formulation of the standard. Judge Klein's opinion is interesting because it recognizes a limit on the scope of this type of liability.

3. Consider Judge Cleland's opinion again. He concludes that Marquez is guilty of malice murder but not conspiracy. What exactly is he concluding about Marquez's state of mind and when is he concluding that state of mind was formed? What element of conspiracy does Cleland believe the prosecution failed to satisfy?

---

c. Attempted Murder

In order to show an attempted murder the prosecution typically must show that the defendant:

(1) intended his victim's death and

(2) that the defendant's efforts came sufficiently close to achieving this goal to find the defendant liable for his crime.

i. *Mens Rea*

In order to convict a defendant of an attempt, the state must demonstrate that the defendant *intended* the forbidden result he is accused of attempting. There are several ways defendants can be guilty of homicide, as we have discovered, but only those unsuccessful efforts for which the defendant desired his victim's death will be punished as an attempted murder in most jurisdictions.

Earp v. State

Court of Special Appeals of Maryland
916 S.W.2d 909 (1988)

ROBERT M. BELL, Judge.

Randall Paul Earp, appellant, was convicted at a bench trial in the Circuit Court for Montgomery County of attempted second degree murder and assault with intent to maim.[1] Having been sentenced to concurrent terms of imprisonment of 25 years and 9 years respectively . . .

* * *

On October 31, 1985, more than one hundred people were in attendance at a Halloween party. The partygoers ran outside when they learned someone had been run over in the middle of Randolph Road. Michael Dwayne Lawrence, one of the partygoers testified[2] that when he went outside he saw forty or fifty people, some using shovels and sticks, engaged in fights, while others were attacking a gold-colored Ford truck with sticks and pipes, trying to get at the driver. Lawrence ran up to the driver and asked whether his truck had struck the man in the street. The driver abruptly shifted into reverse and backed into a car. When he admitted striking the man, Lawrence grabbed the driver and pinned him against the truck while the police, who were 30 feet away, approached.

At this time, appellant grabbed Lawrence by the shoulder, turned him around and attempted to hit the driver saying, "Let me have a piece of him." Lawrence responded that only the police officer was "going to get something from him." Appellant rejoined, "Well, I'll take a piece of you." After Lawrence had turned away from appellant, he felt a punch in his back and, looking over his shoulder, saw a knife handle protruding from it. He then felt the knife being pulled down and saw it being withdrawn. After the knife had been withdrawn, appellant again lunged at Lawrence, but only managed to strike Lawrence's thumb with the knife, because, as Lawrence testified, he was able to block most of the "[a]bout ten to fifteen slices" appellant attempted. Appellant fled as the police approached.

---

1   Appellant was charged with attempted murder in the first degree, attempted murder in the second degree, assault with intent to murder, assault with intent to maim, disfigure or disable, and battery. His initial trial ended in a mistrial when the jury was unable to reach a verdict on any of the counts. At his subsequent trial, the State nol prossed the counts charging assault with intent to murder and battery and proceeded only on the attempted first degree murder, attempted second degree murder and assault with intent to maim counts.

2   Lawrence died of cancer prior to trial. His deposition, however, had been videotaped.

* * *

II.

The appellant challenges the propriety of his conviction of attempted second degree murder. He argues that the trial judge found that he harbored only an intent to do grievous bodily harm, rather than the specific intent to kill. The State argues, on the other hand, that the trial court did not expressly find the absence of a specific intent to kill. Because the trial judge acquitted the appellant of attempted first degree murder, the State concedes that "an inference may be drawn from the court's ruling and explanatory comments that the court had decided the State had failed in its burden of proving that the appellant harbored the specific intent to kill." The State postulates, however, that "an equally rational inference is that the acquittal was based upon the State's failure to prove the premeditation and deliberation requisite to a finding of attempted first degree murder."

An indispensable element of attempted murder, be it first or second degree,[5] and the separate crime of assault with intent to murder, *see State v. Holmes*, 310 Md. 260, 272, 528 A.2d 1279 (1987), is the intent to murder. *Id. See also State v. Jenkins*, 307 Md. 501, 515, 515 A.2d 465 (1986), *Glenn v. State*, 68 Md.App. 379, 388, 511 A.2d 1110, *cert. denied*, 307 Md. 599, 516 A.2d 569 (1986). And, although by application of the aggravating factors prescribed in Maryland Code Ann. art. 27, §§ 407- 410, an accused may be convicted of murder upon proof of an intent other than the specific intent to kill, *Glenn*, 68 Md.App. at 388, 511 A.2d 1110, when the victim does not die, a necessary ingredient of the intent to murder is a specific intent to kill. *Id.*, 68 Md.App. at 388-89, 389-90, 511 A.2d 1110. This is so because:

> Of the four basic types of murder, specific-intent-to-kill murder is the only one wherein there is a conscious and purposeful design to accomplish the death of the victim. None of the others contains, as a necessary element, any intent that the victim die. A depraved-heart murder is a mere general intent crime-the general intent to do the reckless, life-endangering act with wanton disregard of the human consequences. A felony-murder has no necessary specific intent that harm should come to a victim, let alone that the victim should die. There is merely a general intent to perpetrate a felony. Some felonies, of course, include lesser specific intents, but not an intent that death result. With respect to both depraved-heart murder and

---

5 In *Campbell v. State*, 293 Md. 438, 441, 444 A.2d 1034 (1982), the Court of Appeals pointed out that the effect of the enactment of Maryland Code Ann. art. 27, §§ 407-410 was merely to divide the common law crime of murder into degrees and not to create new statutory crimes or, in any way, to affect its definition.

felony-murder, the death of the victim is not only unintended but some-times not even reasonably foreseen.

* * *

In the case of intent-to-do-grievous-bodily-harm murder, on the other hand, the failure of that intent to establish *ipso facto*-by automatic operation of law-the intent to murder is not so immediately apparent. This is so because there is, in these cases, an actual harm specifically intended for the assault victim. Thus, this form of murder is a specific-intent crime rather than a mere general-intent crime. The critical distinction that needs to be made, however, is between *the results specifically intended, not between the presence or absence of a specific intent.* Although there is the purpose or design that the victim should suffer serious physical harm, there is no necessary purpose or design that the victim should die. (Emphasis in original) * * *

Id. Thus, attempted murder is committed only when the perpetrator intended to commit murder. In other words, "one can intend only that type of murder which if done, would be intentional. It is a truism that one cannot intend the unintended." *Glenn*, 68 Md.App. at 397, 511 A.2d 1110.

A conviction for attempted second degree murder may not be sustained upon proof that the accused intended only to commit grievous bodily harm; a conviction for attempted second degree murder may only be sustained if the perpetrator is found to have harbored the intent to kill his victim.

Our first task is to determine what the trial judge found. We do so by review-ing what he said in rendering his decision. Addressing appellant, the court stated:

> With respect to Count four, the assault with intent to maim, the Court finds that the State has carried its burden of proof with respect to that count and finds you guilty.

> With respect to Count two, attempted murder in the second degree, the court finds that the State has carried its burden of proof with respect to that count, and finds you guilty of attempted second degree murder.

> I cite for you, Mr. DeWolfe [defense counsel], the case of State versus Davis,[6] in which they draw the distinction between second degree murder and first degree murder, and I think you are right with respect to the premeditation,

---

6   Although the court cited to *State v. Davis*, it is apparent that it intended to refer either to *Davis v. State*, 237 Md. 97, 205 A.2d 254 (1964) or *Davis v. State*, 204 Md. 44, 102 A.2d 816 (1954). In light of the subsequent refer-ence to the later Davis case in colloquy with defense counsel, it is probable that it was that case upon which the court relied.

deliberation. In the first degree case, you must find that there was a specific intent to kill.

With respect to the first count of this indictment, attempted first degree-murder in the first degree, I find that the inference is insufficient in this case and does not convince the Court beyond a reasonable doubt that the State has carried its burden with respect to attempted murder in the first degree, and I find the Defendant not guilty of the first count.

The court's findings were clarified during a later colloquy with defense counsel. In response to defense counsel's request for clarification of its ruling, specifically, whether it had found that the only necessary intent to support attempted second degree murder was an intent to cause serious bodily harm, the court said, "In second degree murder. It is in the disjunctive, it says or- . . .-to kill or do-inflict serious bodily harm, which could result in death." The court cited *Davis v. State*, 237 Md. at 104, 205 A.2d 254 in support of that statement * * *

The appellant contends that there was no real evidence of malice and that it was prejudicial error for the trial court to deny his motions for a directed verdict of acquittal as to murder. We do not agree. An actual intent to take life is not necessary for a conviction of murder if the intent is to commit grievous bodily harm and death occurred in consequence of the attack. *Webb v. State*, 201 Md. 158, 93 A.2d 80 (1952). The nature of the injuries inflicted upon Farmer of itself was evidence of malice for the jury's consideration. Wharton, *The Law of Homicide* § 95 (3d ed. 1907). The brutality and severity of a beating are evidence of an intent to commit a homicide. *Morrison v. State*, 234 Md. 87, 198 A.2d 246 (1964).

It is clear from the foregoing that the trial court determined that the only intent necessary to support appellant's conviction of attempted second degree murder was the intent to do grievous bodily harm: The court, in addition to referring to deliberation and premeditation, acknowledged that attempted first degree murder requires an intent to kill; the court's response to defense counsel's request for clarification implied that either an intent to kill or an intent to commit grievous bodily harm would support a conviction of attempted second degree murder; aside from the sufficiency of the evidence, the only dispute at trial was whether attempted second degree murder could be found on proof of an intent less than the intent to kill; had the trial court found an intent to kill, it need not have concerned itself with alternative intents.

There is absolutely no issue in this case as to the sufficiency of the evidence to have sustained a finding of a specific intent to kill on the part of appellant. Indeed, the evidence produced by the State overwhelmingly supports such a finding. Unfortunately, the trial court did not see it that way; on the contrary, it found either that appellant did not have the intent to kill or that it had a reasonable doubt on the issue, but, misinterpreting precedent from the Court of Appeals, nevertheless found, on the basis of its finding of an intent to do grievous bodily harm, the evidence to be sufficient to support a conviction for attempted second degree murder. In so doing, the lower court erred.

We have no quarrel with the propositions espoused by the State: an intent to kill certainly could have been inferred by the trial court, *see Jenkins*, 307 Md. at 513-15, 515 A.2d 465; *Davis v. State*, 237 Md. at 103, 205 A.2d 254, *Davis v. State*, 204 Md. at 52, 102 A.2d 816; *Glenn*, 68 Md.App. at 410, 511 A.2d 1110, and a failure of proof of deliberation and premeditation does not preclude a finding by the trier of fact of an intent to kill. *See Ferrell v. State*, 304 Md. 679, 688, 500 A.2d 1050 (1985). We quarrel only with the applicability of those propositions to the case *sub judice*. The court neither inferred the intent to kill from the circumstances nor considered deliberation and premeditation apart from the intent to kill. Here, as we have previously pointed out, the court found that the accused either had no intent to kill or that it had a reasonable doubt as to whether the accused harbored such an intent. Therefore, the fact that the evidence is legally sufficient to support a contrary finding, *i.e.*, that the accused possessed an intent to kill, is simply irrelevant and immaterial.[7]

GARRITY, Judge, dissenting.

I respectfully dissent from the majority's conclusion that the trial judge found evidence of an intent merely to commit grievous bodily harm rather than finding evidence sufficient from which to infer an intent to kill. In explaining my interpretation of the court's finding, it is necessary to briefly revisit the law relating to attempted murder in the second degree.

The common-law crime of attempt is generally defined as the intent to commit a crime, coupled with some overt act beyond mere preparation in furtherance of that crime. *Wiley v. State*, 237 Md. 560, 207 A.2d 478 (1965). In analyzing the crime of attempted murder in the second degree, Judge Cole observed on behalf of the Court in *Hardy v. State*, 301 Md. 124, 482 A.2d 474 (1984):

The crime of attempt, in a literal sense, is an adjunct crime-it cannot exist by itself, but only in connection with another crime. Although it remains a common-law crime, attempt is applicable to any existing crime, statutory or

---

7   The dissent perceives the court's finding to be that "although the evidence failed to show premeditation and deliberation so as to support a conviction of attempted first degree murder, the evidence was sufficient to establish malice, so that, if death had followed the assault, the offense would have been murder in the second degree." It finds relevant to its position the proposition that "the intent to commit grievous bodily harm (which could result in death) serves as a legally sufficient predicate to support the inference of a murderous *mens rea*." This position entirely misses the point.

common law. . . . The crime of attempt by definition expands and contracts and is redefined commensurate with the substantive offense.

If the evidence satisfied the fact finder by proof beyond a reasonable doubt that the conduct of the defendant falls within the proscribed conduct in the statute labeled as first degree murder that did not result in death of the victim, then the crime of attempted murder in the first degree has been established. If the evidence of criminal culpability is something less, the crime proved may be attempted murder in the second degree or attempted voluntary manslaughter. We emphasize that the basic characteristic of an attempt is that it adjusts according to the proof established at trial.

Id. at 139-140, 482 A.2d 474.

In *Glenn v. State*, 68 Md.App. at 385, 511 A.2d 1110, this court enumerated the four types of murder, each of which has its own *mens rea*, as: intent to kill murder; intent to commit grievous bodily harm murder; felony murder; and depraved heart murder. Judge Moylan, writing on our behalf, explained:

> The presence of one of these intents is an indispensable ingredient, although not the only necessary ingredient, of that slippery legal concept known as "malice." Indeed, the text writers have for 300 years referred to the original murderous *mens rea*-the intent to kill-as "express malice." They have also referred to the latter three murderous *mentes reae*-all of which came into homicide law during its rapid evolution in the early seventeenth century-as the three forms of "implied malice." The original legal fiction, of course, was that any of the latter three states of mind "implied" the former; proof of any of the latter three intents was a predicate fact from which the factfinder could permissibly infer the intent to kill. Legal analysis has now reached a point of sophistication, however, where we recognize that each of these four intents is independently blameworthy enough to support a murder conviction. Each is an autonomous murderous *mens rea* in its own right and not a mere evidentiary avenue to one of the others.

Id. (Footnote omitted).

Relevant to the instant case is the principle that the intent to commit grievous bodily harm (which could result in death) serves as a legally sufficient predicate to support the inference of a murderous *mens rea*.

In post trial discussion, the trial judge explained that he had based his finding of guilt as to attempted second degree murder on the law of homicide as explicated in *Davis v. State*, 237 Md. 97, 205 A.2d 254 (1964), wherein the victim had died following a vicious fight. In affirming the judgment, the Court observed that "the brutality and severity of a beating are evidence of an intent to commit a homicide."

The majority acknowledge that the trial judge in the case *sub judice* relied on the principles enunciated in *Davis* as rationale for his finding the appellant guilty of attempted second degree murder. The majority, however, then completely ignore the inference of malice permitted under *Davis* and conclude "[i]t is clear from the foregoing that the trial court determined that the only intent necessary to support appellant's conviction of attempted second degree murder was the intent to do grievous bodily harm. . . ."

As observed by Judge Hammond in *Davis v. State*, 204 Md. 44, 51, 102 A.2d 816 (1954), an assault with intent to murder case wherein the Court remanded upon the refusal of the trial court to instruct on the existence of malice as a predicate to finding an intent to murder, as opposed to its absence, which would indicate manslaughter:

> [M]alice exists not only when there is an actual, express intent to kill, but may be inferred when there is an intent to do or inflict great bodily harm, or when one wilfully does an act or wilfully fails to do a duty and the natural tendency of the act or failure is to cause death or great bodily harm.

Since intent is subjective and, without the cooperation of the accused, cannot be directly and objectively proven, its presence must be shown by established facts which permit a proper inference of its existence. Malice and, so intent to murder, may be inferred from all the facts and circumstances of the occurrence. The deliberate selection and use of a deadly weapon directed at a vital part of the body is a circumstance which indicates a design to kill, since in the absence of evidence to the contrary, the law presumes that one intends the natural and probable consequences of his act.

The testimony established that the appellant had stabbed his victim in the back, inflicting a wound three centimeters in length and six centimeters in depth. According to the examining physician, a stab wound that extends into the chest cavity creates a potential for hemorrhaging which, if not staunched, could be fatal. Only the protection afforded by the victim's shoulder blade prevented further penetration of the knife. In addition, when Lawrence turned, the appellant repeatedly attempted to slash him. The assaults ended only with the arrival of the police.

I think it is clear that the trial judge determined that although the evidence failed to establish premeditation and deliberation so as to support a conviction of attempted first degree murder, the evidence was sufficient to establish malice, *a fortiori*, an inference of a murderous *mens rea*, so that, if death had followed the assault, the offense would have been murder in the second degree. I would affirm the judgment.

Notes and Questions

1. Does Judge Garrity not make a very compelling point, especially in light of the concerns raised in David Lewis' article, *Punishment that Leaves Something to Chance*? Attempted premeditated murder is punished less severely than premeditated murder—there is undeniably a difference between the punishment for attempted premeditated murder and premeditated murder, this was the point of David Lewis' article (see p. 48). Consider though the difference in punishment from a death that occurs from a depraved heart murder and a near-miss in a depraved heart killing. The driver who narrowly misses a head-on collision while driving 90 mph, with a blood alcohol level of 0.29 is guilty of driving while intoxicated, if the accident is not averted, he is guilty of second-degree murder.

2. What explains the majority rule? Often the result is explained linguistically—to attempt something is to intend it. Does that explanation justify the weight that rests upon it? Very dangerous conduct goes unpunished, or goes arguably under-punished, when it does not cause injury and is *only* malicious. Driving while intoxicated is often punished by no jail time or minimal jail time (no more than a couple of days incarceration). As we've seen, when a death follows from this crime, the punishment can be among the most severe known to the criminal justice system.

3. If legislatures find a problem with there being punishment for attempted first-degree murder but not for attempted second-degree murder, there is a fairly easy way to remedy this difference. Some states define first-degree murder as an intentional, but not premeditated killing. Recall *State v. Gillespie*, p. 48. *See also* Wash. Stat. § 9A.32.050.

4. A few states, relying on reasoning much like the dissent in *Earp*, do permit convictions for attempting unintended killings. *See, e.g., State v. Kimbrough*, 924 S.W.2d 888 (Tenn. 1996) (permitting conviction for attempted felony murder); In re Standard Jury Instructions in Criminal Cases—Report No. 2013-02, 137 So.3d 995 (Fla. 2014) ("In order to convict the defendant of Attempted Second Degree Murder, it is not necessary for the State to prove that defendant had an intent to cause death.").

ii. Proximity

In order to show an attempt, the prosecution must demonstrated that the defendant intended to commit the crime he or she attempted and that the attempt came sufficiently close to completion to hold the defendant liable for the attempt. The Model Penal Code's provision on attempts, which many states adopted, permitted a conviction for an attempt with a less proximity than the common law rules had required. The *Reeves* case lays out the standard under each rule.

State v. Reeves

Supreme Court of Tennessee
916 S.W.2d 909 (1996)

DROWOTA, Judge.

The defendant, Tracie Reeves, appeals from the Court of Appeals' affirmance of the trial court's order designating her a delinquent child. The trial court's delinquency order, which was entered following a jury trial, was based on the jury's finding that the defendant had attempted to commit second degree murder—a violation of Tenn.Code Ann. § 39–12–101. The specific issue for our determination is whether the defendant's actions constitute a "substantial step," under § 39–12–101(a)(3), toward the commission of that crime. For the following reasons, we hold that they do, and therefore affirm the judgment of the Court of Appeals.

FACTS AND PROCEDURAL HISTORY

On the evening of January 5, 1993, Tracie Reeves and Molly Coffman, both twelve years of age and students at West Carroll Middle School, spoke on the telephone and decided to kill their homeroom teacher, Janice Geiger. The girls agreed that Coffman would bring rat poison to school the following day so that it could be placed in Geiger's drink. The girls also agreed that they would thereafter steal Geiger's car and drive to the Smoky Mountains. Reeves then contacted Dean Foutch, a local high school student, informed him of the plan, and asked him to drive Geiger's car. Foutch refused this request.

On the morning of January 6, Coffman placed a packet of rat poison in her purse and boarded the school bus. During the bus ride Coffman told another student, Christy Hernandez, of the plan; Coffman also showed Hernandez the packet of rat poison. Upon their arrival at school Hernandez informed her homeroom teacher, Sherry Cockrill, of the plan. Cockrill then relayed this information to the principal of the school, Claudia Argo.

When Geiger entered her classroom that morning she observed Reeves and Coffman leaning over her desk; and when the girls noticed her, they giggled and ran back to their seats. At that time Geiger saw a purse lying next to her coffee cup on top of the desk. Shortly thereafter Argo called Coffman to the principal's office. Rat poison was found in Coffman's purse and it was turned over to a Sheriff's Department investigator. Both Reeves and Coffman gave written statements to the investigator concerning their plan to poison Geiger and steal her car.

Reeves and Coffman were found to be delinquent by the Carroll County Juvenile Court, and both appealed from that ruling to the Carroll County Circuit Court. After a jury found that the girls attempted to commit second degree murder in violation of Tenn.Code Ann. § 39–12–101, the "criminal attempt" statute, the trial court affirmed the juvenile court's order and sentenced the girls to the Department of Youth Development for an indefinite period. Reeves appealed from this judgment to the Court of Appeals, which affirmed the judgment of the trial court. Reeves then applied to this Court for permission to appeal pursuant to Tenn.R.App.P. 11. Because we have not addressed the law of criminal attempt since the comprehensive reform of our criminal law undertaken by the legislature in 1989, we granted that application.

PRIOR AND CURRENT LAW OF CRIMINAL ATTEMPT

Before the passage of the reform legislation in 1989, the law of criminal attempt, though sanctioned by various statutes, was judicially defined. In order to submit an issue of criminal attempt to the jury, the State was required to present legally sufficient evidence of: (1) an intent to commit a specific crime; (2) an overt act toward the commission of that crime; and (3) a failure to consummate the crime. *Bandy v. State*, 575 S.W.2d 278, 281 (Tenn.1979); *Gervin v. State*, 212 Tenn. 653, 371 S.W.2d 449, 451 (1963); *Dupuy v. State*, 204 Tenn. 624, 325 S.W.2d 238, 240 (1959).

Of the elements of criminal attempt, the second, the "overt act" requirement, was by far the most problematic. By attempting to draw a sharp distinction between "mere preparation" to commit a criminal act, which did not constitute the required overt act, and a "direct movement toward the commission after the preparations had been made," *Dupuy*, 325 S.W.2d at 239, 240, which did, Tennessee courts construed the term "overt act" very narrowly. The best example of this extremely narrow construction occurred in *Dupuy*. In that case, the Memphis police sought to lay a trap for a pharmacist suspected of performing illegal abortions by sending a young woman to request these services from him. After the woman had made several attempts to secure his services, he finally agreed to perform the abortion. The pharmacist transported the young woman to a hotel room, laid out his instruments in preparation for the procedure, and asked the woman to remove her clothes. At that point the police came into the room and arrested the pharmacist, who then admitted that he had performed abortions in the past. The defendant was convicted under a statute that made it illegal to procure a miscarriage, and he appealed to this Court.

A majority of this Court reversed the conviction. After admitting that the defendant's "reprehensible" course of conduct would doubtlessly have resulted in the commission of the crime "had he not been thwarted in his efforts by the arrival of the police," *Dupuy*, 325 S.W.2d at 239, the majority concluded that:

> While the defendant had completed his plan to do this crime the element of attempt [overt act] does not appear in this record. The proof shows that he did not use any of the instruments and did not touch the body of the girl in question. Under such facts we do not think that the defendant is guilty under the statute. *Dupuy*, 325 S.W.2d at 240.

To support its holding, the *Dupuy* court quoted a treatise passage concerning actions that constituted "mere preparation," as opposed to actions that would satisfy the overt act requirement:

> In a general way, however, it may be said that preparation consists in devising or arranging the means or measures necessary for the commission of the offense and that the attempt [overt act] is the direct movement toward the commission after the preparations are made. Even though a person actually intends to commit a crime, his procurement of the instrumentalities adapted to that end will not constitute an attempt to commit the crime in the absence of some overt act.

Id. (quoting 14 Am.Jur. § 68 (1940)). To further illustrate the foregoing principle the majority provided the following example: "the procurement by a prisoner of tools adapted to breaking jail does not render him guilty of an attempt to break jail." *Id.*

As indicated above, the sharp differentiation in *Dupuy* between "mere preparation" and "overt act," or the "act itself," was characteristic of the pre–1989 attempt law. *See e.g., Gervin v. State*, 212 Tenn. 653, 371 S.W.2d 449 (1963) (criminal solicitation does not constitute an attempt); *McEwing v. State*, 134 Tenn. 649, 185 S.W. 688 (1915) (conviction for attempted rape affirmed because defendant actually laid hands on the victim). In 1989, however, the legislature enacted a general criminal attempt statute, Tenn.Code Ann. § 39–12–101, as part of its comprehensive overhaul of Tennessee's criminal law. In that statute, the legislature did not simply codify the judicially-created elements of the crime, but utilized language that had up to then been entirely foreign to Tennessee attempt law. Section 39–12–101 provides, in pertinent part, as follows:

(a) A person commits criminal attempt who, acting with the kind of culpability otherwise required for the offense:

(1) Intentionally engages in action or causes a result that would constitute an offense if the circumstances surrounding the conduct were as the person believes them to be;

(2) Acts with intent to cause a result that is an element of the offense, and believes the conduct will cause the result without further conduct on the person's part; or

(3) Acts with intent to complete a course of action or cause a result that would constitute the offense, under the circumstances surrounding the conduct as the person believe them to be, *and the conduct constitutes a substantial step toward the commission of the offense.*

(b) Conduct does not constitute a *substantial step* under subdivision (a)(3) unless the person's entire course of action is corroborative of the intent to commit the offense.

(emphasis added.)

THE SUBSTANTIAL STEP ISSUE

As stated above, our task is to determine whether the defendant's actions in this case constitute a "substantial step" toward the commission of second degree murder under the new statute. The "substantial step" issue has not yet been addressed by a Tennessee court in a published opinion, and the question is made more difficult by the fact that the legislature declined to set forth any definition of the term, preferring instead to "leave the issue of what constitutes a substantial step [to the courts] for determination in each particular case." § 39–12–101, *Comments of Sentencing Commission.*

In addressing this issue, we first note that the legislature, in enacting § 39–12–101, clearly looked to the criminal attempt section set forth in the Model Penal Code. That section provides, in pertinent part, as follows:

(1) Definition of attempt. A person is guilty of an attempt to commit a crime if, acting with the kind of culpability otherwise required for commission of the crime, he:

(a) purposely engages in conduct which would constitute the crime if the attendant circumstances were as he believes them to be; or

(b) when causing a particular result is an element of the crime, does or omits to do anything with the purpose of causing or with the belief that it will cause such result, without further conduct on his part; or

(c) purposely does or omits to do anything which, under the circumstances as he believes them to be, is a *substantial step in a course of conduct planned to culminate in his commission of the crime*

Model Penal Code, Section 5.01 (emphasis added.)

The State argues that the striking similarity of Tenn.Code Ann. § 39–12–101 and the Model Penal Code evidences the legislature's intention to abandon the old law of criminal attempt and instead adopt the Model Penal Code approach. The State then avers that the model code contains examples of conduct which, if proven, would entitle, but not require, the jury to find that the defendant had taken a "substantial step;" and that two of these examples are applicable to this case. The section of the model code relied upon by the State, § 5.01(2), provides, in pertinent part, as follows:

(2) Conduct which may be held substantial step under paragraph (1)(c). Conduct shall not be held to constitute a substantial step under paragraph (1)(c) of this Section unless it is strongly corroborative of the actor's criminal purpose. Without negating the sufficiency of other conduct, the following, if strongly corroborative of the actor's criminal purpose, shall not be held insufficient as a matter of law:

. . . . .

(e) *possession of materials to be employed in the commission of the crime, which are specially designed for such unlawful use or which can serve no lawful purpose of the actor under the circumstances;*

(f) *possession, collection or fabrication of materials to be employed in the commission of the crime, at or near the place contemplated for its commission, where such possession, collection or fabrication serves no lawful purpose of the actor under the circumstances;*

. . . . .

(emphasis added.)

The State concludes that because the issue of whether the defendant's conduct constitutes a substantial step may be a jury question under the model code, the jury was justified in finding her guilty of attempting to commit second degree murder.

The defendant counters by arguing that despite the similarity of Tenn.Code Ann. § 39–12–101 and the Model Penal Code's attempt provision, the legislature intended to retain the sharp distinction between "mere preparation" and the "act itself" characteristic of such decisions as *Dupuy*. She supports this assertion by pointing out that although the legislature could have easily included the examples set forth in § 5.01(2) of the model code, the Tennessee statute does not include the examples. The defendant concludes that the new statute did not substantially change Tennessee attempt law, and that her conviction must be reversed because her actions constitute "mere preparation" under *Dupuy*.

Initially, we cannot accept the argument that the legislature intended to explicitly adopt the Model Penal Code approach, including the examples set forth in § 5.01(2). Although § 39–12–101 is obviously based on the model code, we agree with the defendant that the legislature could have, if it had so desired, simply included the specific examples in the Tennessee statute. That it did not do so prohibits us from concluding that the legislature explicitly intended to adopt the model code approach in all its particulars.

This conclusion does not mean, however, that the legislature intended to retain the distinction between "mere preparation" and the "act itself." Moreover, while we concede that a strong argument can be made that the conviction conflicts with *Dupuy* because the defendant did not place the poison in the cup, but simply brought it to the crime scene, we also are well aware that the *Dupuy* approach to attempt law has been consistently and effectively criticized. One persistent criticism of the endeavor to separate "mere preparation" from the "act itself" is that the question is ultimately not one of kind but of degree;[1] the "act itself" is merely one of the termini on a continuum of criminal activity. Therefore, distinguishing between "mere preparation" and the "act itself" in a principled manner is a difficult, if not impossible, task.[2] *See U.S. v. Dworken*, 855 F.2d 12, 19 (1st Cir.1988); *U.S. v. Brown*, 604 F.2d 347, 350 (5th Cir.1979); Levenbook, *Prohibiting Attempts and Preparations*, 49 U.M.K.C.L.Rev. 41 (1980); Hall, *Criminal Attempt—A Study of Foundations of Criminal Liability*, 40 Yale L.J. 789, 821–22 (1940). The other principal ground of criticism of the *Dupuy* approach bears directly on the primary objective of the law—that of preventing inchoate

---

1   Judge Holmes noted this point by stating: "Preparation is not an attempt. But some preparations may amount to an attempt. *It is a question of degree.*" *Commonwealth v. Peaslee*, 177 Mass. 267, 272, 59 N.E. 55, 56 (1901) (emphasis added).

2   This conclusion was drawn long ago by Judge Learned Hand, who stated that "the decisions [addressing when preparation has become attempt] are too numerous to cite, and would not be much help anyway, for there is, and obviously can be, no definite line." *U.S. v. Coplon*, 185 F.2d 629, 633 (2d Cir.1950). Interestingly, Judge Hand also rejected the defendant's argument that no attempt responsibility attached until the moment of consummation of the criminal act, stating that "[t]o divide 'attempt' from 'preparation' by the very instant of consummation would be to revert to the old [rejected English] doctrine." *Id.*

crimes from becoming full-blown ones. Many courts and commentators have argued that failing to attach criminal responsibility to the actor—and therefore prohibiting law enforcement officers from taking action—until the actor is on the brink of consummating the crime endangers the public and undermines the preventative goal of attempt law. *See People v. Terrell*, 99 Ill.2d 427, 77 Ill. Dec. 88, 92, 459 N.E.2d 1337, 1341 (1984); *U.S. v. Prichard*, 781 F.2d 179, 182 (10th Cir.1986); *U.S. v. Stallworth*, 543 F.2d 1038, 1040 (2d Cir.1976). *See generally* Wechsler, Jones & Korn, *The Treatment of Inchoate Crimes in the Model Penal Code of the American Law Institute: Attempt, Solicitation, and Conspiracy*, 61 Colum.L.Rev. 571, 586–611 (1961).

The shortcomings of the *Dupuy* rule with respect to the goal of prevention are particularly evident in this case. As stated above, it is likely that under *Dupuy* no criminal responsibility would have attached unless the poison had actually been placed in the teacher's cup. This rigid requirement, however, severely undercuts the objective of prevention because of the surreptitious nature of the act of poisoning. Once a person secretly places a toxic substance into a container from which another person is likely to eat or drink, the damage is done. Here, if it had not been for the intervention of the teacher, she could have been rendered powerless to protect herself from harm.

After carefully weighing considerations of *stare decisis* against the persuasive criticisms of the *Dupuy* rule, we conclude that this artificial and potentially harmful rule must be abandoned. We hold that when an actor possesses materials to be used in the commission of a crime, at or near the scene of the crime, and where the possession of those materials can serve no lawful purpose of the actor under the circumstances, the jury is entitled, but not required, to find that the actor has taken a "substantial step" toward the commission of the crime if such action is strongly corroborative of the actor's overall criminal purpose.[3] For the foregoing reasons, the judgment of the Court of Appeals is affirmed.

---

3 This decision is limited to the facts of this case; we do not specifically adopt any of the examples set forth in § 5.01(2) of the Model Penal Code, but simply agree with the reasoning underlying subsections (e) and (f). However, we do note that several courts charged with the responsibility of defining "substantial step" have adopted or applied the examples in the Model Penal Code. *See State v. Walters*, 311 Or. 80, 804 P.2d 1164, 1167 (1991); *Young v. State*, 303 Md. 298, 493 A.2d 352, 358–59 (1985); *Commonwealth v. Prather*, 690 S.W.2d 396, 397 (Ky.1985); *State v. Pearson*, 680 P.2d 406, 408 (Utah 1984); *State v. Latraverse*, 443 A.2d 890, 894–95 (R.I.1982); *State v. Workman*, 90 Wash.2d 443, 584 P.2d 382, 387 (1978); *State v. Woods*, 48 Ohio St.2d 127, 357 N.E.2d 1059, 1063 (1976); *U.S. v. Dworken*, 855 F.2d 12, 19–20 (1st Cir.1988); *U.S. v. Prichard*, 781 F.2d 179, 181–82 (10th Cir.1986); *U.S. v. McFadden*, 739 F.2d 149, 152 (4th Cir.1984); *U.S. v. Joyce*, 693 F.2d 838, 841 (8th Cir.1982); *U.S. v. Mandujano*, 499 F.2d 370, 376–77 (5th Cir.1974).

BIRCH, Justice, concurring and dissenting.

I concur in the majority's statement of the rule to be applied in deciding whether a criminal attempt has occurred. I dissent, however, from their application of that rule to this case.

The applicable standard of review for this case is "[f]indings of guilt in criminal actions whether by the trial court or jury shall be set aside if the evidence is insufficient to support the findings by the trier of fact of guilt beyond a reasonable doubt." Tenn.R.App.P. 13(e); *see also Jackson v. Virginia*, 443 U.S. 307, 319, 99 S.Ct. 2781, 2789, 61 L.Ed.2d 560 (1979) ("[T]he relevant question [in reviewing the sufficiency of the evidence] is whether, after viewing the evidence in the light most favorable to the prosecution, *any* rational trier of fact could have found the essential elements of the crime beyond a reasonable doubt."). Applying this standard of review, I would find that under the test adopted by the majority for determining whether a "substantial step" was taken, the evidence in this case is insufficient as a matter of law.

Tenn.Code Ann. § 39–12–101, the criminal attempt statute, states, in pertinent part:

> (a) A person commits criminal attempt who, acting with the kind of culpability otherwise required for the offense:
>
> . . . . .
>
> (3) Acts with intent to complete a course of action or cause a result that would constitute the offense, under the circumstances surrounding the conduct as the person believes them to be, and the conduct constitutes a substantial step toward the commission of the offense.
>
> (b) Conduct does not constitute a substantial step under subdivision (a)(3) unless the person's *entire* course of action is corroborative of the intent to commit the offense.

(Emphasis added). Based upon this record, I would find that the " *entire* course of action" of these two twelve-year-old girls was not "strongly corroborative" of intent to commit second-degree murder and that the evidence was insufficient as a matter of law. In looking at the "entire course of action," we should remember that these were twelve-year-old girls, not explosive-toting terrorists.

Accordingly, while I concur in the majority's abandonment of the rule stated in *Dupuy v. State*, 204 Tenn. 624, 325 S.W.2d 238 (1959), I dissent from the conclusion of the majority in this case.

Notes and Questions

1. The majority quoted a portion of the section of the Model Penal Code offering examples of a substantial step sufficient for an attempt. This is the complete list provided in that section:

   (a) lying in wait, searching for or following the contemplated victim of the crime;

   (b) enticing or seeking to entice the contemplated victim of the crime to go to the place contemplated for its commission;

   (c) reconnoitering the place contemplated for the commission of the crime;

   (d) unlawful entry of a structure, vehicle or enclosure in which it is contemplated that the crime will be committed;

   (e) possession of materials to be employed in the commission of the crime, that are specially designed for such unlawful use or that can serve no lawful purpose of the actor under the circumstances;

   (f) possession, collection or fabrication of materials to be employed in the commission of the crime, at or near the place contemplated for its commission, if such possession, collection or fabrication serves no lawful purpose of the actor under the circumstances;

   (g) soliciting an innocent agent to engage in conduct constituting an element of the crime.

2. How exactly do you explain Justice Birch's dissent? He clearly includes the girls' ages in determining whether the entire course of their actions were "strongly corroborative" of their intent. How would their age be relevant to such a determination? Suppose they had placed the rat poison in their teacher's coffee cup, she drank it, and died. Would their age be relevant to the question of whether they knowingly killed their teacher? Should it be? Should it be a question for the prosecution to take into consideration in charging either the acts that occurred or the death that would have occurred if she had drank the poison?

3. The drafters of the Model Penal Code, whose handiwork the Tennessee Legislature partially adopted with the new attempt provision, sought to permit

the prosecution to obtain a conviction when the defendant's action were less proximate to the completed crime than was true at common law. The rationale was to deter harmful activity that might lead to actual harm. Why would this rationale not extend to the rule Judge Garrity sought in *Earp* to allow the punishment of very dangerous conduct that is not necessarily intended to kill?

4. It is worth noting that Tennessee did, in fact, embrace the reasoning of Judge Garrity in *Earp v. State*. Notice that the teenagers in *Reeves* were convicted of attempted *second*-degree murder and no theory of second-degree murder in Tennessee requires intent. *See* Tenn. Code. Ann. § 39-13-210.

---

d. *The Line Between Attempt and Solicitation of Murder*

Many of the legal standards we have considered so far have a certain fuzzy quality to them. The reason for this is simple. The facts courts use to decide the cases are unlikely to repeat themselves and the standards courts announce provide only some insight on how to decide cases with different sets of facts. In the second-degree murder context we observed, however, that there was one species of homicide that occurred with sufficient frequency that courts have announced a definitive rule in many jurisdiction, even if the rule varies by jurisdiction. Vehicular homicide cases relating to intoxication (sadly) occur with enough frequency, and involve the same basic set of possible facts, that it is fairly clear whether a death occurring in this manner is second-degree murder or involuntary homicide. (*See* discussion at p. 729-746.)

In the law of attempts, there is similarly an act, that occurs with some frequency, that has a predictable set of variable facts, allowing a prediction of whether a court will view the crime as an attempt, or something short of an attempt. That act, surprisingly enough, is hiring an undercover agent to commit an act of murder. Just as in the vehicular homicide context, courts have come to different conclusions, but a surprising number of courts have weighed in on whether paying money to someone, with the instructions to kill, constitutes an attempt to kill or merely an act of solicitation. *Disanto* lays out the various positions and places them in the context of whether a jurisdiction has adopted the Model Penal Code's attempt rule, which requires less proximity for an attempt conviction.

State v. Disanto

Supreme Court of South Dakota
688 N.W.2d (2004)

KONENKAMP, Justice.

Defendant told several people of his intent to murder his former girlfriend and her new boyfriend. Unknown to defendant, his design was revealed to the authorities and they had a police officer pose as a contract killer to interject himself in the plan. Defendant and the "hit man" discussed the murders, wherein defendant wanted each victim shot twice in the head. He directed the feigned killer to the former girlfriend's address, gave him a picture of her, provided details on what valuables could be obtained during the killings, instructed him to kill a child witness if necessary, and issued a final command to proceed with the murders. Shortly afterwards, however, defendant communicated with an intermediary that he wanted to "halt" the murders, saying "I'm not backing out of it, I just want to put it on hold." In his trial for three counts of attempted first-degree murder, defendant unsuccessfully sought a judgment of acquittal claiming that the evidence was insufficient to establish that he went further than mere preparation for the offenses. The jury convicted him on all three charges. We reverse the convictions because defendant's actions amounted to no more than mere preparation: neither he nor the feigned killer committed an act toward the commission of the offenses.

BACKGROUND

Defendant, Rocco William "Billy" Disanto, and Linda Olson lived together for two years and were engaged for a short time. But their turbulent relationship ended in January 2002. Olson soon began a new friendship with Denny Egemo, and in the next month, they moved in together. Obsessed with his loss, defendant began making threatening telephone calls to Olson and Egemo. He told them and others that he was going to kill them. He also sued Olson claiming that she was responsible for the disappearance of over $15,000 in a joint restaurant venture.

On February 17, 2002, while gambling and drinking at the First Gold Hotel in Deadwood, defendant told a woman that he intended "to shoot his ex-girlfriend, to kill her, to shoot her new lover in the balls so that he would have to live with the guilt, and then he was going to kill himself." As if to confirm his intention, defendant grabbed the woman's hand and placed it on a pistol in his jacket. The woman contacted a hotel security officer who in turn called the police. Defendant was arrested and a loaded .25 caliber pistol was taken from him.

In a plea bargain, defendant pleaded guilty to possession of a concealed pistol without a permit and admitted to a probation violation. For his probation violation, he was sentenced to two years in the South Dakota State Penitentiary with nine months suspended. He received a concurrent one-year jail sentence with all but five days suspended for the offense of carrying a concealed pistol without a permit.

While in the penitentiary, defendant met Stephen Rynders. He told Rynders of his intention to murder Olson and her boyfriend. Rynders gave this information to law enforcement and an investigation began. In June 2002, defendant was released from prison. Upon defendant's release, Rynders, acting under law enforcement direction, picked defendant up and offered him a ride to Lead. Inevitably, the conversation turned to defendant's murder plans. At the suggestion of the investigators, Rynders told defendant that he should hire a contract killer who Rynders knew in Denver.

On the afternoon of June 11, 2002, Rynders and Dale McCabe, a law enforcement officer posing as a killer for hire from Denver, met twice with defendant. Much of their conversation was secretly recorded. Defendant showed McCabe several photos of Olson and gave him one, pointed out her vehicle, led him to the location of her home, and even pointed Olson out to him as she was leaving her home. In between his meetings with McCabe that afternoon, by chance, defendant ran into Olson on the street. Olson exclaimed, "I suppose you're going to kill me." "Like a dog," defendant replied.

Shortly afterwards in their second meeting, defendant told McCabe, "I want her and him dead." "Two shots in the head." With only one shot, he said, "something can go wrong." If Olson's teenage daughter happened to be present, then defendant wanted her killed too: "If you gotta, you gotta, you know what I mean." He wanted no witnesses. He suggested that the murders should appear to have happened during a robbery. Because defendant had no money to pay for the murders, he suggested that jewelry and other valuables in the home might be used as partial compensation. He told McCabe that the boyfriend, Egemo, was known to have a lot of cash. Defendant also agreed to pay for the killings with some methamphetamine he would later obtain.

At 3:00 p.m., defendant and McCabe appeared to close their agreement with the following exchange:

McCabe: So hey, just to make sure, no second thoughts or. . . .

Defendant: No, none.

McCabe: You sure, man?

Defendant: None.

McCabe: Okay.

Defendant: None.

McCabe: The deal's done, man.

Defendant: It's a go.

McCabe: OK. Later. I'll call you tonight.

Defendant: Huh?

McCabe: I'll call you tonight.

Defendant: Thank you.

McCabe would later testify that as he understood their transaction, "the deal was sealed at that point" and the killings could be accomplished "from that time on until whenever I decided to complete the task."

Less than three hours later, however, defendant, seeking to have a message given to McCabe, called Rynders telling him falsely that a "cop stopped by here" and that Olson had spotted McCabe's car with its Colorado plates, that Olson had "called the cops," that defendant was under intense supervision, and that now the police were alerted because of defendant's threat against Olson on the street. All of this was untrue. Defendant's alarm about police involvement was an apparent ruse to explain why he did not want to go through with the killings.

Defendant: So, I suggest we halt this. Let it cool down a little bit. . . .

Rynders: Okay.

* * *

Defendant: So I don't know if that house (Olson's) is being watched, do you know what I'm saying?

Rynders: Okay.

* * *

Defendant: And, ah, the time is not right right now. I'm just telling you, I, I don't feel it. I feel, you know what I mean. I'm not backing out of it, you know what I'm saying.

Rynders: Um hm.

Defendant: But, ah, the timing. You know what I mean. I just got out of prison, right?

* * *

Defendant: So, ah, I'm just telling you right now, put it on hold.

Rynders: Okay.

Defendant: And that's the final word for the simple reason, ah, I don't want nothing to happen to [McCabe], you know what I mean?

* * *

Defendant: Let it cool down. Plus let's let 'em make an offer . . . . [referring to defendant's lawsuit against Olson]

Rynders: Well, I have no clue where [McCabe is] at right now.

Defendant: Oh, God. You got a cell number?

* * *

Defendant: Get it. . . .

Defendant: I just don't feel good about it to be honest and I'll tell 'ya, I've got great intuition.

Rynders: Okay.

* * *

Defendant: So, I mean, just let him [McCabe] know. Alright buddy?

Rynders: Okay.

Defendant: Get to him. He's gonna call me at 11 tonight.

Despite this telephone call, the next day, McCabe, still posing as a contract killer, came to defendant at his place of employment with Olson's diamond ring to verify that the murders had been accomplished. McCabe drove up to defendant and beckoned him to his car.

McCabe: Hey, man. Come here. Come here. Come here. Jump in, man. Jump in, dude.

Defendant: You sure?

McCabe: Jump in.

Defendant: I can't, I can't leave the bakery. I ain't got the key.

McCabe: Fuck, I gotta get the fuck out of here, dude. It's done, man. Fuckin' done, dude.

Defendant: Okay. I don't wanna know nothin' about it.

McCabe: All right. Check this out, man. [Showing him Olson's diamond ring.]

Defendant: No.

McCabe: Here.

Defendant: I don't wanna see nothin'.

McCabe: I got that shit.

Defendant: Good.

* * *

McCabe: Hey. You still owe me some shit, man.

Defendant: Guaranteed.

Defendant was arrested and charged with three counts of attempted murder. He was also charged with one count of simple assault for the threat he made against Olson on the street. The State provided notice that it intended to introduce all the evidence pertaining to defendant's prior arrest and subsequent plea agreement concerning the incident at the First Gold Hotel. Over defendant's objection, the trial court admitted this evidence.

A jury convicted defendant of all charges. He was sentenced to three concurrent thirty-year terms of imprisonment in the South Dakota State Penitentiary. In addition, he received a concurrent 365 days in jail. He was fifty-nine years old at the time. These sentences were consecutive to the unfinished two-year term defendant was to serve for his prior felony conviction.

On appeal, defendant raises the following issues: (1) Whether the trial court erred in denying his motion for judgment of acquittal and motion for judgment notwithstanding the verdict. (2) Whether his sentence was grossly disproportionate to the crime charged in violation of the Eighth Amendment to the United States Constitution and Article VI, § 23 of the South Dakota Constitution. (3) Whether the State's reliance on evidence of acts committed by defendant for which he had already pleaded guilty violated his double jeopardy protections under the Fifth and Fourteenth Amendments to the United States Constitution and Article VI, § 9 of the South Dakota Constitution. We need only reach Issue 1.

ATTEMPTED MURDER BY HIRING CONTRACT KILLER

Defendant argues that the trial court erred in denying his motion for judgment of acquittal because the State failed to offer sufficient evidence to sustain a conviction on the three counts of attempted murder. A motion for judgment of acquittal under SDCL 23A-23-1 (Rule 29(a)) is the proper vehicle for a sufficiency challenge. *Cf.* 2 CHARLES ALAN WRIGHT, FEDERAL PRACTICE AND PROCEDURE § 467 (2d ed 1982). The denial of a motion for judgment of acquittal presents a question of law, and thus our review is de no vo. *See United States v. Staula*, 80 F.3d 596, 604 (1stCir.1996). We must decide anew whether the evidence was sufficient to sustain a conviction. SDCL 23A-23-1 (Rule 29(a)); *State v. Guthrie*, 2001 SD 61, ¶ 47, 627 N.W.2d 401, 420-21; *see also* 2 STEVEN ALAN CHILDRESS & MARTHA S. DAVIS, FEDERAL STANDARDS OF REVIEW § 9.10 (3d ed 1999) (citing *United States v. Scott*, 437 U.S. 82, 100 n. 13, 98 S.Ct. 2187, 2198 n. 13, 57 L.Ed.2d 65 (1978)). In measuring evidentiary sufficiency, we ask "whether, after viewing the evidence in the light most favorable to the prosecution, any rational trier of fact could have found the essential elements of the crime beyond a reasonable doubt." *Jackson v. Virginia*, 443 U.S. 307, 319, 99 S.Ct. 2781, 2789, 61 L.Ed.2d 560 (1979).

In defining the crime of attempt, we begin with our statute. SDCL 22-4-1 states that "Any person who attempts to commit a crime and in the attempt does any act toward the commission of the crime, but fails or is prevented or intercepted in the perpetration thereof, is punishable" as therein provided. To prove an attempt, therefore, the prosecution must show that defendant (1) had the specific intent to commit the crime, (2) committed a direct act toward the commission of the intended crime, and (3) failed or was prevented or intercepted in the perpetration of the crime. *State v. Olson*, 408 N.W.2d 748, 754 (S.D.1987); *State v. Martinez*, 88 S.D. 369, 371-72, 220 N.W.2d 530, 531 (1974); *State v. Judge*, 81 S.D. 128, 131, 131 N.W.2d 573, 574 (1964).

We need not linger on the question of intent. Plainly, the evidence established that defendant repeatedly expressed an intention to kill Olson and Egemo, as well as Olson's daughter, if necessary. As McCabe told the jury, defendant "was a man on a mission to have three individuals murdered."

Defendant does not claim error in any of the court's instructions to the jury. The jury was instructed in part that

Mere preparation, which may consist of planning the offense or of devising, obtaining or arranging the means for its commission, is not sufficient to constitute an attempt; but acts of a person who intends to commit a crime will constitute an attempt when they themselves clearly indicate a certain, unambiguous intent to commit that specific crime, and in themselves are an immediate step in the present commission of the criminal design, the progress of which would be completed unless interrupted by some circumstances not intended in the original design. The attempt is the direct movement toward commission of the crime after the preparations are made.

Once a person has committed acts which constitute an attempt to commit a crime, that person cannot avoid responsibility by not proceeding further with the intent to commit the crime, either by reason of voluntarily abandoning the purpose or because of a fact which prevented or interfered with completing the crime.

However, if a person intends to commit a crime but before the commission [of] any act toward the ultimate commission of the crime, that person freely and voluntarily abandons the original intent and makes no effort to accomplish it, the crime of attempt has not been committed.

Defendant contends that he abandoned any attempt to murder when he telephoned Rynders to "halt" the killings.[1] The State argued to the jury that defendant committed an act toward the commission of first degree murder by giving the "hit-man" a final order to kill, thus making the crime of attempt complete. If he went beyond planning to the actual commission of an act, the State asserted, then a later abandonment would not extricate him from responsibility for the crime of attempted murder. On the other hand, if he only wanted to postpone the crime, then, the State contended, his attempt was merely delayed, not abandoned.

On the question of abandonment, it is usually for the jury to decide whether an accused has already committed an act toward the commission of the murders. Once the requisite act has been committed, whether a defendant later wanted to abandon or delay the plan is irrelevant. As Justice Mosk of the California Supreme Court wrote,

It is obviously impossible to be certain that a person will not lose his resolve to commit the crime until he completes the last act necessary for its accom-

---

1   The Model Penal Code recognizes that a "complete and voluntary renunciation" of criminal purpose is an affirmative defense to a charge of an attempt to commit a crime. *See* Article 5 § 5.01(4).

plishment. But the law of attempts would be largely without function if it could not be invoked until the trigger was pulled, the blow struck, or the money seized. If it is not clear from a suspect's acts what he intends to do, an observer cannot reasonably conclude that a crime will be committed; but when the acts are such that any rational person would believe a crime is about to be consummated absent an intervening force, the attempt is under way, and a last-minute change of heart by the perpetrator should not be permitted to exonerate him.

People v. Dillon, 34 Cal.3d 441, 194 Cal.Rptr. 390, 668 P.2d 697, 703 (1983).

The more perplexing question here is whether there was evidence that, in fulfilling his murderous intent, defendant committed an "act" toward the commission of first degree murder. SDCL 22-4-1. Defendant contends that he never went beyond mere preparation. In *State v. Martinez*, this Court declared that the boundary between preparation and attempt lies at the point where an act "unequivocally demonstrate[s] that a crime is about to be committed." 88 S.D. at 372, 220 N.W.2d at 531 (citing *People v. Miller*, 2 Cal.2d 527, 42 P.2d 308, 310 (1935)). Thus, the term "act" "presupposes some direct act or movement in execution of the design, as distinguished from mere preparation, which leaves the intended assailant only in the condition to commence the first direct act toward consummation of his design." *Miller*, 42 P.2d at 310 (citations omitted). The unequivocal act toward the commission of the offense must demonstrate that a crime is about to be committed unless frustrated by intervening circumstances. *State v. Hanson*, 456 N.W.2d 135, 139 (S.D.1990); *Martinez*, 88 S.D. at 372, 220 N.W.2d at 531; *Judge*, 81 S.D. at 128, 131 N.W.2d at 573. However, this act need not be the last possible act before actual accomplishment of the crime to constitute an attempt. *State v. Miskimins*, 435 N.W.2d 217, 222-23 (S.D.1989).

We have no decisions on point in South Dakota; therefore, we will examine similar cases in other jurisdictions. In murder for hire cases, the courts are divided on how to characterize the offense: is it a solicitation to murder or an act toward the commission of murder? *See generally* Jeffrey F. Ghent, Annotation, *What Constitutes Attempted Murder*, 54 ALR3d 612 (1973). Most courts "take the view that the mere act of solicitation does not constitute an attempt to commit the crime solicited. This issue is particularly significant in a jurisdiction where any crime can be the subject of attempt but only certain crimes can be the subject of solicitation." 4 CHARLES E. TORCIA, WHARTON'S CRIMINAL LAW, § 672 (15th ed Clark Boardman Callaghan 1996). As one commentator explained, "[a]lthough in some jurisdictions solicitations are treated as indictable attempts, either by virtue of judicial decisions failing to distinguish them, or by statutory provisions, the great weight of authority is otherwise. Analytically the two crimes are distinct." Francis Bowes Sayre, *Criminal Attempts*, 41 Harv L Rev 821, 857-58 (1928).

A majority of courts reason that a solicitation to murder is not attempted murder because the completion of the crime requires an act by the one solicited.[2] We will examine cases espousing both the majority and minority view to discern which ones are consistent with South Dakota law and precedent. However, it is important in examining out-of-state authority to confine our review to decisions using definitions of criminal attempt similar to our own.

Typical of the cases following the majority rule is *State v. Davis*, 319 Mo. 1222, 6 S.W.2d 609 (Mo.1928) (superseded by statute). There, the defendant and the wife of the intended victim plotted to kill her husband to collect the life insurance proceeds and then to live together. A police officer, posing as an ex-convict, met with the defendant several times. The defendant gave the undercover officer a map showing where the husband could be found and two photographs of him. He promised to pay the agent $600, and later paid that sum. He wanted the matter handled so that the murder would appear to have been committed in the course of a robbery. Because the agent employed to commit the murder did not act toward the consummation of the intended crime, the court held that the defendant's acts amounted to no more than solicitation or preparation. Similarly, in *People v. Adami*, 36 Cal.App.3d 452, 111 Cal.Rptr. 544 (1973), the defendant gave an undercover police officer $500, a photograph, and a written description of his wife, with instructions to kill her. The court reversed the conviction, finding that the agent, who had only pretended to agree to commit the murder, had performed no act toward the commission of the crime.

In *State v. Otto*, 102 Idaho 250, 629 P.2d 646 (1981), the defendant hired an undercover police officer to kill another police officer investigating the disappearance of the defendant's wife. A divided Idaho Supreme Court reversed the attempted first-degree murder conviction, ruling that the act of soliciting the agent to commit the actual crime, coupled with the payment of $250 and a promise of a larger sum after the crime had been completed, amounted to solicitation to murder rather than attempted murder. The court in *Otto* held that "[t]he solicit[ation] of another, assuming neither solicitor nor solicitee proximately acts toward the crime's commission, cannot be held for an attempt.

---

2   *See also Hobbs v. State*, 548 S.W.2d 884 (Tex.Cr.App.1977); *Hutchinson v. State*, 315 So.2d 546, 548-49 (Fla. App.1975) (holding that solicitation of another to commit murder does not constitute attempt to commit murder because mere solicitation is not overt act toward attempt to commit murder); *Gervin v. State*, 212 Tenn. 653, 371 S.W.2d 449, 451 (1963) (holding that solicitation of another to commit murder does not constitute attempt to commit murder because "[t]o constitute an attempt there must also be an act of perpetration . . . [and] solicitation is preparation rather than perpetration") (internal citations omitted); *Hicks v. Commonwealth*, 86 Va. 223, 9 S.E. 1024 (1889) (defendant purchased strychnine and gave it to agent with instructions to place it in the victim's coffee: these were only preparatory measures and not an attempt).

He does not by his incitement of another to criminal activity commit a dangerously proximate act of perpetration. The extension of attempt liability back to the solicitor destroys the distinction between preparation and perpetration." *Id.* at 650. In sum, "[n]either [the defendant in *Otto*] nor the agent ever took any steps of perpetration in dangerous proximity to the commission of the offense planned." *Id.* at 651.

Requisite to understanding the general rule "is the recognition that solicitation is in the nature of the incitement or encouragement of another to commit a crime in the future [and so] it is essentially preparatory to the commission of the targeted offense." *Id.* at 648 n. 4 (citations omitted). The Idaho Supreme Court made the rather pointed observation that

> [i]t is foreseeable that jurisdictions faced with a general attempt statute and no means of severely punishing a solicitation to commit a felony might resort to the device of transforming the solicitor's urgings into a proximate attempted commission of the crime urged but doing so violates the very essence of the requirement that a sufficient actus reus be proven before criminal liability will attach. *Id.* at 651.[3]

Cases like *Davis, Otto*, and *Adami* are helpful to our analysis because, at the time they were decided, the statutes or case law in those jurisdictions defined attempt in a way identical to our attempt statute. Under this formulation, there must be specific intent to commit the crime and also a direct act done towards its commission, which failed or was intercepted in its perpetration. As the Missouri Supreme Court noted, "[t]his tougher language was couched in terms of preparation and perpetration, and required that '. . . the defendant must have taken steps going beyond mere preparation, by doing something bringing him nearer the crime he intends to commit.'" *State v. Molasky*, 765 S.W.2d 597, 600 (Mo 1989).

To understand the opposite point of view, we will examine cases following the minority rule. But before we begin, we must first consider the definition of attempt under the Model Penal Code, and distinguish cases decided under its formula. In response to court decisions that hiring another to commit murder did not constitute attempted murder, many jurisdictions created, sometimes at the urging of the courts, the offense of solicitation of murder. As an alternative, another widespread response was to adopt the definition of attempt under the Model Penal Code. This is because the Model Penal Code includes in criminal attempt much that was held to be preparation under former decisions. ROLLIN

---

3 This is precisely how the dissenters proceed here. They compare the crime of attempt with the crime of conspiracy and they convert the final solicitation itself into an "act." An attempt to commit a crime is a distinct offense. Defendant was not charged with conspiracy. And a solicitation is still a solicitation even when it comes in the form of a final command for another to proceed. In the end, neither defendant nor McCabe took any "act" toward the perpetration of a crime.

M. PERKINS, CRIMINAL LAW 561 (2d ed 1957). This is clear from the comments accompanying the definition of criminal attempt in Tentative Draft No. 10 (1960) of the American Law Institute's Model Penal Code, Article 5 § 5.01. The intent was to extend the criminality of attempts by drawing the line further away from the final act, so as to make the crime essentially one of criminal purpose implemented by a substantial step highly corroborative of such purpose. MODEL PENAL CODE § 5.01(1) (Proposed Official Draft (1962)).

The Model Penal Code provides in part that "A person is guilty of an attempt to commit a crime if, acting with the kind of culpability otherwise required for commission of the crime, he . . . purposely does or omits to do anything that, under the circumstances as he believes them to be, is an act or omission constituting a *substantial step* in a course of conduct planned to culminate in his commission of the crime." MODEL PENAL CODE § 5.01(1)(c) (1985) (emphasis added).[4] The Code then lists in § 5.01(2) several species of conduct that may constitute a "substantial step." The Model Penal Code treats the solicitation of "an innocent agent to engage in conduct constituting an element of the crime," if strongly corroborative of the actor's criminal purpose, as sufficient satisfaction of the substantial step requirement to support a conviction for criminal attempt. MODEL PENAL CODE § 5.01(2)(g).

Representative of decisions under the Model Penal Code is *State v. Kilgus*, 128 N.H. 577, 519 A.2d 231 (N.H.1986).[5] There, it was held that the defendant's solicitation of a third party to kill the victim constituted attempted murder, where the defendant had completed all the preliminary steps, including setting and paying the contracted for sum, identifying the victim, and instructing the "killer" that the corpse must be found outside the state. The New Hampshire Supreme Court concluded, "[t]his was more than . . . 'mere' or 'naked' solicitation. It was a 'substantial step' toward the commission of capital murder." *Id.* at 236.

Another decision using the Model Penal Code framework in analyzing the offense of attempt is *State v. Burd*, 187 W.Va. 415, 419 S.E.2d 676 (W.Va.1991). In

---

4   Many jurisdictions have adopted the "substantial step" framework from the Model Penal Code. *See* Alaska Stat § 11.31.100 (Supp 1988); Ark Code Ann § 5-3-201 (Michie 1975); Colo Rev Stat § 18-2-101 (2002); Conn Gen Stat § 53a-49 (West 2001); Del Code Ann tit 11, § 531 (1987); Ga Code Ann § 16-4-1 (1988); Haw Rev Stat § 705-500 (1985); Ind Code Ann § 35-41-5-1 (Michie 1985); Me Rev Stat Ann tit 17-A, § 152 (West 1983); Minn Stat Ann § 609.17 (West 1987); Neb Rev Stat § 28-201 (1979); NH Rev Stat Ann § 629:1 (1986); NJ Stat Ann § 2C:5-1 (West 1982); ND Cent Code § 12.1-06-01 (1985); Ohio Rev Code Ann § 2923.02 (West 1986); Or Rev Stat § 161.405 (1985); Pa Stat Ann tit 18, § 901 (West 1983); Wash Rev Code Ann § 9A.28.020 (West 1988); Wyo Stat Ann § 6-1-301 (Michie 1977).

5   Another decision fitting this category is *State v. Sunzar*, 331 N.J.Super. 248, 751 A.2d 627, 632 (1999). By adopting a Model Penal Code type attempt statute the court concluded that "[b]ased on the history outlined above, it appears that our legislature has opted for an expansive version of the attempt law, notwithstanding the 'majority' view, which governs elsewhere." *See also State v. Manchester*, 213 Neb. 670, 331 N.W.2d 776 (1983).

that case, the court ruled that evidence that the defendant solicited the murder of her boyfriend's wife and child, hired the killer, gave him money for a weapon and an advance on the murder contract, drew a map of the residence of the planned victims, and instructed the killer on how to shoot the victims, supported her conviction for attempted murder. What is curious about *Burd* is that at the time of that decision the State of West Virginia had a definition of attempt similar to our own. *Id.* at 679. Nonetheless, the Court seems to have adopted the Model Penal Code "substantial step" analysis from *Kilgus* to conclude that hiring the feigned assassin was a "substantial act" toward commission of the crime of attempted murder. *Id.* at 680. In support of its position, the Court cited several other murder for hire cases decided under the Model Penal Code definition of attempt.

Finally, another attempted murder case decided under Model Penal Code formulation is *State v. Molasky*, 765 S.W.2d at 597. The decision is instructive. There, a conviction for attempted murder was reversed, but only because the conduct consisted solely of conversation, unaccompanied by affirmative acts. *Id.* at 602. Thus, the court reasoned, "a substantial step is evidenced by actions, indicative of purpose, not mere conversation standing alone." *Id.; accord State v. O'Neil*, 262 Conn. 295, 811 A.2d 1288 (2003) (reversing attempted murder conviction under Model Penal Code formulation where defendant sent message from jail to killer to have witness murdered). Acts evincing a defendant's seriousness of purpose to commit murder, the *Molasky* Court suggested, might be money exchanging hands, concrete arrangements for payment, delivering a photograph of the intended victim, providing the address of the intended victim, furnishing a weapon, visiting the crime scene, waiting for the victim, or showing the hit man the victim's expected route of travel. *Molasky*, 765 S.W.2d at 602. Therefore, under the relaxed standards of the Model Penal Code, evidence of an act in furtherance of the crime could include what defendant did here, provide a photograph of the intended victim and point out her home to the feigned killer. *Molasky* crystallizes our sense that without the expansive Model Penal Code definition of attempt, acts such as the ones defendant performed here are not sufficient under our definition to constitute attempt.

Knowing that the Model Penal Code relaxes the distinction between preparation and perpetration, we exclude from our analysis those murder for hire cases using some form of the Code's definition of attempt. Obviously, we cannot engraft a piece of the Model Penal Code onto our statutory definition of attempt, for to do so would amount to a judicial rewriting of our statute. Nonetheless, there are several courts taking the minority position that solicitation of murder can constitute attempted murder, without reference to the Model Penal Code definition. We will now examine those cases.

In *Braham v. State*, 571 P.2d 631 (Alaska 1977), *cert. denied*, 436 U.S. 910, 98 S.Ct. 2246, 56 L.Ed.2d 410 (1978), evidence that the defendant instructed the hired gunman to visit the intended victim in the hospital for purpose of fostering a relationship of trust and confidence was sufficient to establish the required overt act necessary to prove attempted murder requiring an act toward the commission of murder. Alaska's attempt statute at the time is almost identical to ours. The Alaska Supreme Court held that whether an act is merely preparatory or "sufficiently close to the consummation of the crime to amount to attempt, is a question of degree and depends upon the facts and circumstances of a particular case." *Id.* at 637.

In *Duke v. State,* 340 So.2d 727 (Miss.1976), the defendant solicited an employee to kill his business partner. The murder was to take place on a hunting trip. That plan failed and the defendant sought to hire another killer. An FBI agent posed as the killer and collected $11,500 from the defendant after representing to the defendant that the partner was dead. This evidence was held sufficient to sustain the conviction because the court concluded that the defendant's acts went beyond mere preparation.

In *State v. Mandel*, 78 Ariz. 226, 278 P.2d 413 (1954), a woman who made a contract with two pretended accomplices to have her husband murdered, partly executed that contract by paying a portion of the consideration in advance, identified for the intended assassins the home and the car of the intended victim, pointed out a possible site for disposing of the body, and advised them on the time and place where contact could be made for the execution of the murder. The court held that she was properly convicted of attempted murder, stating, "She did everything she was supposed to do to accomplish the purpose. Had it not been for the subterfuge, the intended victim would have been murdered. Under such circumstances she cannot escape by reason of clever, elusive distinctions between preparation, solicitation and acts committed in furtherance of the design." *Id.* at 416.

In *State v. Gay*, 4 Wash.App. 834, 486 P.2d 341 (1971), a wife paid a $1,000 retainer to a feigned killer to assassinate her husband and agreed to pay the killer an additional $9,000 when her husband was dead. She furnished the killer with pictures of her husband so that he would kill the right man and told him about her husband's habits and where he could be found. In upholding her conviction for attempted murder, the court acknowledged that mere solicitation, which involves no more than asking or enticing someone to commit a crime, would not constitute the crime of attempt. However, the court declared that the very act of hiring a contract killer is an overt act directed toward the commission of the target crime. *Id.* at 345. The court ruled that the defendant had done everything that was to be done by her to accomplish the murder of her husband. Since the feigned assassin had made all the contacts and she had no way to contact him, she could not have stopped him after the final planning. The court concluded that the defendant's attempt to murder her husband was clearly established by the following undisputed evidence: (1) the forged assignment of the insurance policy six months before she hired a man to kill her husband, (2) the payment of premiums on her husband's $50,000 life insurance policy after the divorce had commenced, without the knowledge of her husband, and (3) the hiring of the feigned assassin.

The minority view expressed in *Braham, Duke, Gay,* and *Mandel* is epitomized in the dissenting opinion in *Otto,* where it was noted that efforts to distinguish between "acts of preparation and acts of perpetration" are "highly artificial, since all acts leading up to the ultimate consummation of a crime are by their very nature preparatory." *Otto,* 629 P.2d at 653. For these courts, preparation and perpetration are seen merely as degrees on a continuum, and thus the distinction between preparation and perpetration becomes blurred.

In interpreting our law, all "criminal and penal provisions and all penal statutes are to be construed according to the fair import of their terms, with a view to effect their objects and promote justice." SDCL 22-1-1. Under our longstanding jurisprudence, preparation and perpetration are distinct concepts. Neither defendant nor the feigned "hit man" committed an act "which would end in accomplishment, but for . . . circumstances occurring . . . independent of[] the will of the defendant." *Martinez,* 88 S.D. at 371, 220 N.W.2d at 531.

We cannot convert solicitation into attempt because to do so is obviously contrary to what the Legislature had in mind when it set up the distinct categories of solicitation and attempt. Indeed, the Legislature has criminalized other types of solicitations. *See* SDCL 22-43-2 (soliciting commercial bribe); SDCL 22-23-8 (pimping as felony); SDCL 22-11-20 (solicitation by witnesses); SDCL 22-22-24.5 (solicitation of minor for sex); SDCL 16-18-7 (solicitation by disbarred or suspended attorney).

Beyond any doubt, defendant's behavior here was immoral and malevolent. But the question is whether his evil intent went beyond preparation into acts of perpetration. Acts of mere preparation in setting the groundwork for a crime do not amount to an attempt. Under South Dakota's definition of attempt, solicitation alone cannot constitute an attempt to commit a crime. Attempt and solicitation are distinct offenses. To call solicitation an attempt is to do away with the necessary element of an overt act. Worse, to succumb to the understandable but misguided temptation to merge solicitation and attempt only muddles the two concepts and perverts the normal and beneficial development of the criminal law through incremental legislative corrections and improvements. It is for the Legislature to remedy this problem, and not for us through judicial expansion to uphold a conviction where no crime under South Dakota law was committed.

Reversed.

SABERS, Justice (concurring).

I agree because the evidence indicates that this blundering, broke, inept 59-year-old felon, just out of prison, was inadequate to pursue or execute this crime without the motivating encouragement of his "friend from prison" and law enforcement officers. On his own, it would have been no more than a thought.

GILBERTSON, Chief Justice (dissenting).

I respectfully dissent. I would affirm the circuit court.

SDCL 22-4-1 defines what constitutes an attempt:

> Any person who attempts to commit a crime and in the attempt does any act toward the commission of the crime, but fails or is prevented or intercepted in the perpetration thereof,....

Herein the Defendant was convicted of three counts of attempted murder. The issue before us is whether he committed a direct act toward the commission of the intended crime. *See State v. Olson*, 408 N.W.2d 748, 754 (S.D.1987); *State v. Martinez*, 88 S.D. 369, 372, 220 N.W.2d 530, 531 (1974); *State v. Judge*, 81 S.D. 128, 133, 131 N.W.2d 573, 575-76 (1964).

In *State v. Miskimins*, 435 N.W.2d 217, 222-23 (S.D.1989) we analyzed the nature of the requirement that a direct act be committed:

In drawing a distinction between preparation and attempt, this court has held that it is not necessary that the last further act necessary to the actual accomplishment of the crime be taken to be a requisite to make an attempt. The statutes clearly require only that "any" act towards the commission of the crime be done. *State v. Martinez*, 88 S.D. 369, 220 N.W.2d 530 (1974). Any unequivocal act by defendant to insure that the intended result was a crime and not another innocent act constitutes an attempt. "The line between preparation and attempt is drawn at that point where the accused's acts no longer strike the jury as being equivocal but unequivocally demonstrate that a crime is about to be committed." *Martinez*, 88 S.D. at 372, 220 N.W.2d at 531.

We also have previously defined preparation as "devising or arranging the means or measures necessary for the commission of the offense" and attempt as "the direct movement toward the commission after the preparations are made." *Judge*, 81 S.D. at 133, 131 N.W.2d at 575 (quoting *State v. Wood*, 19 S.D. 260, 261, 103 N.W. 25, 26 (1905)). Once "it becomes clear what the actor's intention is and when the acts done show that the perpetrator is actually putting his plan into action," the attempt is complete. *People v. Dillon*, 34 Cal.3d 441, 194 Cal.Rptr. 390, 668 P.2d 697, 702 (1983) (citations omitted). Thus, we must examine the evidence to see whether there was evidence which would allow a jury to find such an act did occur.

> In determining the sufficiency of the evidence on appeal in a criminal case, the issue before this [C]ourt is whether there is evidence in the record which, if believed by the jury, is sufficient to sustain a finding of guilt beyond a reasonable doubt . . . In making our determination, this Court will accept the evidence and the most favorable inferences fairly drawn therefrom, which still support the verdict.

State v. Augustine, 2000 SD 93, ¶ 26, 614 N.W.2d 796, 800 (quoting *State v. Davi*, 504 N.W.2d 844, 856 (S.D.1993) (citations omitted)). As pointed out by the Court, the jury was properly instructed on the difference between mere preparation and acts needed to constitute an attempt.

Herein the Defendant hired McCabe, a hit man, gave him instructions on how to kill the intended victims, provided the hit man with a photo of Olson, showed him the location of Olson's home and personally pointed Olson out to the "hit man." All these acts constitute devising or arranging the murder for hire scheme. The Defendant's acts of arriving at a concrete payment arrangement for the "hit man's" services and issuing the final kill order "[i]t's a go," were direct movements that served to actually put Defendant's plan into action. The consummation of the contract and final kill order were "immediate step[s] in the present commission of the criminal design" as required by the jury instructions used in Defendant's trial. This is far more than mere verbal solicitation of a hit man to accomplish the murders. *See State v. Mandel*, 78 Ariz. 226, 278 P.2d 413, 416 (1954) (holding *that after defendant did everything she was supposed to do to accomplish the purpose of the murder for hire contract* by making partial payment and advising of when and where murder should be conducted, she was beyond the sphere of mere solicitation or preparation) (emphasis added); *State v. Gay*, 4 Wash.App. 834, 486 P.2d 341, 346 (1971) (holding defendant beyond the preparation stage after making final payment arrangements and down payment, furnishing pictures of intended victim to hit man, *issuing final order without means to contact hit man in order to halt the murder* sufficient to sustain a conviction for attempt) (emphasis added).

This evidence, if believed by the jury, was well in excess of the "any act" requirement. It showed Defendant had done everything he could do to carry out his intent to have the killings occur. Defendant had set in motion a course of action that would have resulted in the deaths of two or three individuals "but for" the fact the hit man was in reality an undercover police officer. It appears the only act left was the actual killings themselves. "In analyzing the facts, the jury was well justified in finding defendant's actions had gone 'so far that they would result in the accomplishment of the crime unless frustrated by extraneous circumstances.'" *Miskimins*, 435 N.W.2d at 223 (citing *Martinez*, 88 S.D. at 372, 220 N.W.2d at 531 (quoting *Judge*, 81 S.D. at 133, 131 N.W.2d at 575)).

Defendant argues that the evidence clearly demonstrates that Defendant's actions in June 2002 did not go beyond mere preparation. Defendant cites the police's failure to arrest Defendant after the June 11, 2002 meeting as proof of this proposition. Defendant also notes that his phone call to Rynders "clearly shows the Defendant put a halt to the attempted commission of the crime . . . but chose to do so by remaining friendly and cooperative with the hitman."

Two distinct theories can be drawn from Defendant's telephone conversation. The first, posited by Defendant, is that Defendant wished to extricate himself from an agreed upon murder, but leave the "hit man" with the *perception* that the deal remained in place. However, there is a second equally plausible theory which was presented by the State. That is, Defendant merely wanted to delay the previously planned murder, but leave the "hit man" with the *knowledge* that the deal remained in place.

Both theories were thoroughly argued to the jury. However, the jury chose to believe the State's theory. Therefore, the jury could have properly concluded Defendant's actions were "done toward the commission of the crime . . . the progress of which would be completed unless interrupted by some circumstances not intended in the original design" and not simply mere preparation. (*Supra* at ¶ 17).

Although we do not have any South Dakota cases directly on point, *State v. Kaiser*, 504 N.W.2d 96 (S.D.1993) and *State v. Kaiser*, 526 N.W.2d 722 (S.D.1995) are factually and legally close. Therein Kaiser was convicted of two counts of conspiracy to commit murder on his ex-wife and her new boyfriend under SDCL 22-3-8. Like the case at bar, Kaiser sought to have a hit-man commit the murders with a pistol. The murders were to be disguised so as to appear the result of a robbery for illegal drugs. The murders were halted at the last minute when the hit-man revealed the plot to law enforcement. The hit-man now working with law enforcement was able to obtain admissions by Kaiser over the telephone. On appeal Kaiser argued that there was insufficient evidence to uphold his conviction as he failed to commit an overt act in South Dakota. Based on Kaiser' assisting the hit-man by guiding him to the location of the proposed murder and providing the gun for the murders and other information, we affirmed concluding that Kaiser had committed overt acts required for a conviction of a conspiracy charge.

The Court today enters a lengthy analysis whether the acts constituted preparation or acts in the attempt to commit murder. I find the "majority" position now taken by the Court to be at odds with this Court's prior interpretation of SDCL 22-4-1.

The authorities and texts generally agree that it is often difficult to determine when mere preparation to commit a crime ends, and when the act toward the commission of the crime begins. Each case must be determined by its own facts and circumstances. We are in accord with the view that where the design is shown "courts should not destroy the practical and common sense administration of the law with subtleties as to what constitutes preparation and what an act done toward the commission of a crime."

State v. Pepka, 72 S.D. 503, 508, 37 N.W.2d 189, 191 (1949) (citations omitted). Minute examination between majority and minority views and "preparation" and "perpetration" conflict with the command of SDCL 22-1-1:

The rule of the common law that penal statutes are to be strictly construed has no application to this title. All its criminal and penal provisions and all penal statutes are to be construed according to the fair import of their terms, with a view to effect their objects and promote justice.

Here there was evidence that all that was left was to pull the trigger. As the Court acknowledges "the law of attempts would be largely without function if it could not be invoked until the trigger was pulled." Citing *Dillon,* 194 Cal.Rptr. 390, 668 P.2d at 703.

I also conclude that the two remaining issues raised by the Defendant are without merit and thus would affirm the trial court. Thus, I respectfully dissent.

ZINTER, Justice (dissenting).

I join the Court's legal analysis concerning the distinction between solicitations and attempts to commit murder.[6] Therefore, I agree that Disanto's solicitation of McCabe, in and of itself, was legally insufficient[7] to constitute an attempt to commit murder under SDCL 22-4-1. However, I respectfully disagree with the Court's analysis of the facts, which leads it to find as a matter of law that Disanto "committed [no] act toward the commission of the offense[]." Supra 1. In my judgment, the Court's view of the facts is not supported by the record. On the contrary, even setting aside Disanto's solicitation, he still engaged in sufficient other "acts" toward the commission of the murder such that reasonable jurors could have found that he proceeded "so far that they would result in the accomplishment of the crime unless frustrated by extraneous circumstances." *State v. Martinez,* 88 S.D. 369, 372,

---

6   I also join the Court's analysis of Disanto's defense of abandonment.

7   Technically, this specific argument was not presented to the trial court or raised in the appellate briefs. Thus, the trial court did not have an opportunity to address it, and we would not normally rule upon it. However, the argument is a sub-issue of the preserved issue challenging the sufficiency of the evidence. Because we must address it to rule on the sufficiency of the evidence, it is a proper subject for this appeal.

220 N.W.2d 530, 531 (1974). The intended victims were clearly in more danger then than they were when Disanto first expressed his desire to kill them.

Specifically, Disanto physically provided McCabe with a photograph of the victim, he pointed out her vehicle, and he took McCabe to the victim's home and pointed her out as she was leaving. None of these acts were acts of solicitation. Rather, they were physical "act[s going] toward the commission" of the murder. SDCL 22-4-1.

Although it is acknowledged that the cases discussed by the Court have found that one or more of the foregoing acts can be part of a solicitation, Disanto's case has one significant distinguishing feature. After his solicitation was completed, after the details were arranged, and after Disanto completed the physical acts described above, he then went even further and executed a command to implement the killing. In fact, this Court itself describes this act as the "final command"[8] to execute the murder. Disanto issued the order: "It's a go."[9] This act is not present in the solicitation cases that invalidate attempted murder convictions because they proceeded no further than preparation.[10]

Therefore, when Disanto's final command to execute the plan is combined with his history and other acts, this is the type of case that proceeded further than the mere solicitations and plans found insufficient in the case law. This combination of physical acts would have resulted in accomplishment of the crime absent the intervention of the law enforcement officer. Clearly, the victim was in substantially greater danger after the final command than when Disanto first

---

8   See supra, 1.

9   See supra, 8.

10   This execution order was a significant act toward the commission of the murder after the preparations were made. This act distinguishes the Court's cases: See, *People v. Adami*, 36 Cal.App.3d 452, 111 Cal.Rptr. 544 (1973) (mere acts of preparation did not constitute an overt act: there was only a verbal agreement between defendant and the hired killer, the selection of such person to do the killing, and a payment of a portion of the consideration); *State v. Otto*, 102 Idaho 250, 629 P2d 646, 651 (1981) (agreement reached and payment made, but no other overt act identified); *State v. Davis*, 319 Mo. 1222, 6 S.W.2d 609, 612 (1928) (evidence going no further than developing a verbal arrangement with the agent, the delivery of a certain drawing and two photographs of victim to the agent, and the payment of a portion of the agreed consideration were mere acts of preparation); *State v. Molasky*, 765 SW2d 597, 602 (Mo banc 1989) (only prisoner talk about the killings, but no further act that indicated a seriousness of purpose i.e. payment of money, providing a picture or any other corroborative action); *Gervin v. State*, 212 Tenn. 653, 371 S.W.2d 449, 450 (1963) (indictment insufficient because it merely alleged that defendant hired, persuaded, and procured another to attempt to murder another); *Hobbs v. State*, 548 SW2d 884, 886 (TexCrimApp 1977) (indictment was insufficient because it did nothing more than merely plead a promise to pay a named individual to kill another); *Hicks v. Commonwealth*, 86 Va. 223, 9 S.E. 1024 (1889) (indictment insufficient because it did not charge that agent agreed to administer the poison, or that she did any act towards the commission of the crime, and the mere delivery of poison by one person to another, who refuses to administer it or do any act in furtherance of the homicidal design of the person delivering it, does not constitute an attempt to administer poison).

expressed his desire to kill her. Consequently, there was sufficient evidence to support an attempt conviction.[11]

It bears repeating that none of the various "tests" used by courts in this area of the law can possibly distinguish all preparations from attempts. Therefore, a defendant's entire course of conduct should be evaluated in light of his intent and his prior history in order to determine whether there was substantial evidence from which a reasonable trier of fact could have sustained a finding of an attempt. *People v. Memro*, 38 Cal.3d 658, 214 Cal.Rptr. 832, 860, 700 P.2d 446, 474 (1985). In making that determination, it is universally recognized that the acts of solicitation and attempt are a continuum between planning and perpetration of the offense. Whether acts are so preparatory as to not constitute an attempt or are sufficiently close to consummation of the crime as to constitute an attempt, "is a question of degree and depends upon the facts and circumstances of a particular case." *Braham v. State*, 571 P.2d 631, 637 (Alaska 1977).

However, it is generally the jury's function to determine whether those acts have proceeded beyond mere planning. As this Court itself has noted, where design is shown, "courts should not destroy the practical and common sense administration of the law with subtleties as to what constitutes [the] preparation" to commit a crime as distinguished from acts done towards the commission of a crime. *State v. Pepka*, 72 S.D. 503, 508, 37 N.W.2d 189, 191 (1949). Therefore, it should be a rare case to be decided as a matter of law. Ordinarily this issue would be left to the jury. *State v. Sunzar*, 331 N.J.Super 248, 751 A.2d 627, 630 (Ct.Law Div. 1999). We leave this question to the jury because "[t]he line between preparation and attempt is drawn at that point where the accused's acts *no longer strike the jury* as being equivocal but unequivocally demonstrate that a crime is about to be committed." *State v. Miskimins*, 435 NW2d 217, 223 (SD 1989) (emphasis added) (citing *State v. Martinez*, 88 S.D. 369, 372, 220 N.W.2d 530, 531 (1974)).

I would follow that admonition and affirm the judgment of this jury. Disanto's design, solicitation, physical acts toward commission of the crime and his final command to execute the murder, when considered together, unequivocally demonstrated that a crime was about to be committed. This was sufficient evidence from which the jury could have reasonably found that an attempt had been committed.[12]

---

11 Contrary to the Court's suggestion at n3, supra, the foregoing analysis is not premised upon concepts of conspiracy jurisprudence. However, having said that, it is interesting to note that the purpose of distinguishing between preparations and attempts is the same as the purpose of requiring an overt act in a conspiracy case. "The purpose of the overt act is to afford a locus poenitentiae, when either or all the conspirators may abandon the unlawful purpose." *U.S. v. Olmstead*, 5 F.2d 712, 714 (D.C.Wash.1925) (citing *U.S. v. Britton*, 108 U.S. 199, 2 S.Ct. 531, 27 L.Ed. 698).

12 Disanto's other issues have no merit.

Notes and Questions

1. Is the dissent not correct that the defendant took the final step toward completing this crime? As the majority notes, the defendant's intent is not in question—and it clearly was not formed in an instant or in the heat of passion. If the hit man had not been an undercover agent and had killed as instructed, the defendant would have been on the hook for first-degree murder. How is he not on the hook for attempted murder when he took every step that was necessary on his part to achieve this goal?

2. This case is offered because it provides a fairly exhaustive list of cases dealing with this issue and the majority's analysis really is a study in comparative law. The majority surveys the way murder for hire cases have been handled and comes to the following conclusions: (1) There are cases in jurisdictions using the more prosecution-friendly Model Penal Code attempt standard, which South Dakota has not adopted, and so those cases are regarded as not being persuasive. (2) The majority of jurisdictions not using the MPC standard have concluded that paying a hit man is merely solicitation, not an attempt. Certainly it is better to be consistent with the majority position, but has the court artificially created a majority by discounting the reasoning of jurisdictions using the MPC version of attempt? It is particularly noteworthy that the majority discounts the Connecticut Supreme Court's decision in *O'Neil* which engages in a multi-factored analysis to determine whether the defendants action had proceeded far enough to be regarded as an attempt. Seemingly, South Dakota, having not adopted the MPC's definition of attempt, may require the defendant to have moved further along the continuum toward a killing than the Connecticut Supreme Court would require but how can the court simply dismiss the factors identified in *O'Neil*?

3. The court observed that South Dakota has a crime of attempt and a crime of solicitation—as the defendant did no more than try to get someone to kill, he solicited and to regard this also an attempt would blur the line between solicitation and attempt. Every state the court considered, including those using the MPC version of attempt, has a statute prohibiting solicitation. Justice Zinter contended in dissent, "it is universally recognized that the acts of solicitation and attempt are a continuum between planning and perpetration of the offense." Justice Konenkamp's majority opinion described the *minority* view in murder-for-hire cases as follows: "For these courts, preparation and perpetration are seen merely as degrees on a continuum, and thus the distinction between preparation and perpetration becomes blurred." Based on your study

of criminal law so far, which of these positions is more consistent with criminal statutes and their interpretation?

4. Justice Gilbertson's dissent objects that the majority does not properly comprehend South Dakota's attempt statute, which merely requires that the defendant "commit[] a direct act toward the commission of the crime." As Justice Gilbertson asks, if Disanto did not make a direct act toward hiring someone to kill his wife, her boyfriend, and potentially his son, then what would he have had to do to be guilty of this offense?

5. Justice Zinter concludes that the distinction between attempt and solicitation should be left to juries in typical cases. Do you agree with this assessment? When facts recur with sufficient frequency that appellate courts are in a position to harmonize jury decisions by recognizing factors appropriately considered in determining whether a crime is more or less serious, would they not have a better perspective than a jury comprised of citizens who have, in all likelihood, considered only one criminal case of this kind in their lives—and probably have sat in judgment in only one type of criminal case in their entire lives. In other words, is deference to juries a good idea or merely a matter of necessity in most cases in which unique factual scenarios prevent appellate courts from comparing cases and developing rules assessing degrees of culpability?

PRACTICE EXERCISE

Read the following fact pattern and instructions.

Facts

"X-Man," "Young Killer," and "Z-slayer" are part of a street gang, the "Reapers," whose territory includes the local swimming pool. During the summer the gang runs a lucrative business by controlling admittance to the pool, issuing "safety surcharges," and running a series of food carts and lemonade stands nearby. One gang member, "Watchman," is even a lifeguard at the pool who helps survey the pool area and the area outside the fence, to warn against possible intrusions by rival gangs or persons on the gang's "hit list."

In the middle of a particularly hot day, Watchman sees a rival gang member who is on the top of the Reaper's hit list, for assaulting one of their members two weeks ago over a buy-and-sell exchange of information that had turned out to be faulty. The rival gang member, "T1" (for target one or priority target), is trying to enter the pool area with his family, knowing full well that the pool is Reaper territory. Watchman texts Z-slayer, who is in charge of the pool operations for the day, that T1 wants admittance. Z-slayer is excited to exact revenge on TI, so he texts X-man and Young Killer to put on their swim-suits, permits TI to enter the pool, and then instructs X-man and Young Killer to enter the pool, and "when it gets really busy, and T1 is in the pool, pull him under and drown the f* * * er." X-man texts, "k," but Young Killer texts, "U sure? Many kids." Watchman agrees, "Place all wrong." Z-slayer responds to all, "Doubled monthly bonus. Do it."

X-man and Young Killer wade into the pool amongst the dozens of children and their parents who are wading about and enjoying the water in the hot sun. They come up behind T1, who had entered the pool with his kids, and X-man abruptly pulls T1 under water from behind, while Young Killer floats nearby on a gigantic pool toy, which "takes over that section of the pool." X-man comes up for breath once, and manages to subdue T1. But X-man fails to realize that there is no way of disposing of the body. While Young Killer continues floating on his pool toy, X-man quickly decides to pretend T1 drowned of his own accord by just swimming away. X-man releases the body, which floats to the surface, and causes a stampede for the exits.

An ambulance is called. Watchman, as the lifeguard, is mysteriously absent, and later states in his defense that he "was taking a piss and [I] had no backup" and "how would I know this guy would go face down in the pool?" The emergency responders succeed in resuscitating T1, who suffers permanent brain damage for loss of oxygen to the brain, but does not die. Two pool guests state they saw, "the only lifeguard there," exit the bathroom shortly after the ambulance had arrived.

Upon investigation, X-man's skin was found under T1's fingernails and in T1's mouth, arguably as a result of the struggle under water. The state has taken this evidence, the failed information trade, and the text messages as grounds sufficient to indict Watchman, X-man, Young Killer and Z-slayer for (1) attempted murder, (2) complicity to commit murder, and (3) conspiracy to commit murder. Z-slayer has also been indicted for solicitation to commit murder.

Instructions

You are a prosecutor in charge of the case against Watchman, X-man, Young Killer and Z-slayer. Defense counsel has moved at the end of trial to dismiss for insufficient evidence on each charge, because the evidence at trial is the same as that adduced at the start of trial, listed in the facts above. For this exercise, using your knowledge of each crime (attempt, complicity, conspiracy, solicitation) from the readings, cite the facts in an argument that seeks to overcome the defense's motion. Break down your argument by (1) defendant and (2) alleged crime. If there is an approach to a crime in the readings (majority or dissent) that benefits you as a prosecutor, you may cite that opinion as persuasive authority.

B. Assault

Assault is a lesser included offense to murder. Think back to the *Rose* decision (p. 60) and consider why this is true. Homicide requires an act (that in *some* way ultimately makes contact with the victim) *causing* his death. If the element of causing death is removed, then homicide becomes assault. In the *Rose* case, because causation was very much at issue, the defendant was entitled to an instruction on assault.

Assault can be demonstrated in one of two ways—either by showing that the victim was subjected to offensive and unwanted contact or was placed in reasonable apprehension of harm. Tort law often defines unwanted contact as battery, while criminal statutes tend to use the term "assault" to identify both the unwanted contact that tort law calls "battery" as well as the causing of reasonable apprehension that tort law identifies as "assault". States identify various aggravated versions of assault occur if (1) the defendant was armed; or (2) the victim suffered injury, with the degree of the crime turning on how seriously the victim was injured. We consider here the basic principles of the two ways of demonstrating assault.

1. Causing Reasonable Apprehension

State v. Wilson

Court of Appeals of Tennessee
924 S.W.2d 648 (1996)

WHITE, Justice.

A jury convicted defendant, Mario Lamont Wilson, of three counts of aggravated assault and of felony reckless endangerment and possession of a deadly weapon with the intent to commit a felony. The Court of Criminal Appeals affirmed Wilson's felony reckless endangerment conviction and sentence, but reversed and dismissed the convictions for aggravated assault and possession of a deadly weapon. We granted permission to appeal to consider whether the Court of Criminal Appeals erred when it dismissed Wilson's convictions for aggravated assault. Although we conclude that Wilson's convictions for aggravated assault may not stand, we do not adopt entirely the reasoning of the Court of Criminal Appeals. Rather, we affirm the dismissal of the aggravated assault charges because the evidence is insufficient to prove that Wilson intentionally and knowingly caused another to reasonably fear imminent bodily injury.

An aggravated assault conviction requires proof beyond a reasonable doubt that an accused committed an assault as defined in Tennessee Code Annotated Section 39–13–101[2] and either (a) intentionally, knowingly, or recklessly caused serious bodily injury to another or (b) used or displayed a deadly weapon. Tenn. Code Ann. § 39–13–102(a)(1)(A), (B) (1995 Supp.). The aggravated assault charges against Wilson were based on accusations that Wilson unlawfully, intentionally, or knowingly assaulted the victims by displaying or using a deadly weapon "causing [the victim] to reasonably fear imminent bodily injury." To establish these charges, the state was required to prove beyond a reasonable doubt that Wilson intentionally or knowingly caused the victims to fear imminent bodily injury by his use or display of a weapon.

---

2   A person commits assault who:

(1) Intentionally, knowingly or recklessly causes bodily injury to another;

(2) Intentionally or knowingly causes another to reasonably fear imminent bodily injury; or

(3) Intentionally or knowingly causes physical contact with another and a reasonable person would regard the contact as extremely offensive or provocative. Tenn.Code Ann. § 39–13–101(a) (1991 Repl.).

Two days before defendant fired shots at the residence of Kenneth Hodges, Hodges and defendant had an angry, verbal confrontation. Although the police were called to the scene, no charges were filed. Two days later, on the day of the shooting at issue here, defendant was involved in an argument with Lamont Johnson, Hodges' close friend and next door neighbor. Following this argument, Lamont Johnson shot at defendant as defendant drove down Whitehall Street in Jackson, the street on which Hodges' residence was located.

Shortly after 3:00 p.m. on that day, Kenneth Hodges left his home leaving his brother, James Hodges, his cousin, Gregory Hodges, and three others, Linda Sain, Chandara Haley, and Chequita Sampson at the residence.[3] At approximately 3:30 p.m., Chandara Haley and Chequita Sampson left with their two children to walk to a nearby store. As they were walking back towards the Hodges' home, an older yellow Cutlass Supreme stopped directly in front of the Hodges' residence on the opposite side of the street. One passenger leaned across in front of the driver and began firing shots at the house.[4] The passenger in the rear seat also fired at the house. Haley identified defendant as the passenger in the front seat, David Fenner as the driver, and Turell Robinson as the passenger in the back seat.[5]

When the first shots were fired, James Hodges was in the rear of the house. Linda Sain was in the bedroom. Greg Hodges was in the living room. Just before the first shots were fired, Greg Hodges looked out the front door. The state relies on these facts to establish that defendant committed aggravated assault.

The state has proved beyond a reasonable doubt that defendant fired the shots and that the victims reasonably feared imminent bodily injury. That, however, does not end the inquiry. In addition to those two elements of the offense, known in common-law parlance as the actus reus, or criminal act, the aggravated assault statute requires proof of criminal intent, or mens rea. That criminal intent requires that defendant act either intentionally or knowingly. By requiring that the act be either intentionally or knowingly committed, the legislature has required the state to prove an element in addition to the mere voluntary commission of the criminal act.

One acts intentionally "with respect to the nature of the conduct or to a result of the conduct when it is the person's conscious objective or desire to engage in the conduct or cause the result." Tenn.Code Ann. § 39–11–302(a) (1991 Repl.). A person acts knowingly when, with respect to a result of the person's

---

3   Aris Jones, a friend of Lamont Johnson, testified that he was also in the house. He was not named as a victim in the indictment.

4   Witnesses testified that at least eight shots were fired into the house.

5   Neither David Fenner or Turell Robinson were charged.

conduct, "the person is aware that the conduct is reasonably certain to cause the result." *Id.* at (b). The issue for our determination is whether the facts support a conclusion beyond a reasonable doubt that defendant intentionally or knowingly caused the victims to fear imminent bodily injury.

The state's argument in this case demonstrates some confusion. They vehemently argue that aggravated assault is not a "specific intent" crime. Commentators have noted the confusion engendered by the use of the phrase "specific intent" since "[a]ny specifically required actual intent other than to do the deed which constitutes the *actus reus* of the particular crime, is unquestionably a special mental element; but not every special mental element is a specific intent in the true sense of the word 'intent'." R. Perkins, Criminal Law 751 (1969) (hereafter Perkins, *supra*, at ----). Nonetheless, we have generally used the general intent—specific intent nomenclature in Tennessee. The aggravated assault statute, however, is more correctly characterized as a statute requiring proof of a special mens rea, since it requires proof of a mental element beyond the mere doing of the criminal act.

The state's argument seems to merge the separate concept of mens rea (or special mental element) with the issue of specifically intended victims. For example, the state, in suggesting that the aggravated assault statute does not require a finding of specific intent, observes:

> that is to say it is not necessary for the state to prove that the defendant intended to assault a specific person who was assaulted.

While the state's contention that they are not required to prove that defendant intended to assault "a specific person who was assaulted" is correct, its contention that aggravated assault does not require proof of a special mental element is not.

The subsection of the aggravated assault statute at issue in this case requires proof of either of two specified mental elements. Stated differently, in addition to establishing that defendant voluntarily did the criminal act, the statute requires proof of one of two mental elements, either intentionally or knowingly. In offenses requiring proof of a special mental element, the intent is an essential element of the offense which must be alleged and proved by the prosecution. Perkins, *supra*, at 762–64. When the definition of a crime requires that a defendant act knowingly or intentionally, the burden of proof is on the prosecution to prove the mental element of knowledge beyond a reasonable doubt. *See* J. Miller, *Criminal Law* § 17, at 57 (1934).

The aggravated assault statute under which the state seeks conviction of defendant requires that the state prove either that defendant shot into the Hodges' home (a) for the purpose of causing the victims to fear imminent bodily injury (intentionally) or that defendant was (b) aware that the shooting would cause the victims to fear imminent bodily injury (knowingly). Proving one or the other of these alternative mental elements is not the same as proving that defendant intended to assault a specific person that was assaulted.

Turning to the facts of this case, we find that the state failed to establish the requisite mental element of this crime beyond a reasonable doubt. In order to establish that defendant acted knowingly or intentionally, the proof would have to establish that defendant was aware that persons were inside the Hodges' residence at the time of the shooting. Obviously, defendant could not shoot for the purpose of causing fear or shoot with the reasonable certainty that fear would be caused absent an awareness that someone was inside.

The state poses two arguments for the purpose of satisfying their proof requirement of mens rea. First, the state argues that the previous altercations with Kenneth Hodges and Lamont Johnson establish an intent to harm these two individuals. Defendant's intent to harm these individuals, however, does not establish the mens rea for aggravated assault since there is no proof that defendant thought either of the two were in the Hodges' residence[6] at the time of the shooting.[7]

The state's second argument focuses on the presence of Gregory Hodges at the time of the shooting. The state contends that since he was "right in the front door," defendant must have seen him, thereby making defendant aware that a potential victim was inside. If the evidence established that defendant saw Gregory Hodges (or anyone, for that matter) inside or around the house, the state would be correct. The evidence, however, does not establish that fact.

Gregory Hodges testified that he was standing "right in the front door" of the house between the closed glass storm door and the half-open wooden door. As he turned to leave, Hodges testified that he heard shots and breaking glass. Gregory Hodges saw Chandara Haley approaching the house, but he did not see the yellow Cutlass. He was a "couple of feet" from the door when he heard the first shots. Fortunately, he was not injured in any way and was not struck by flying glass. The demonstrative evidence in the record—photographs—support a conclusion that the interior and storm doors were closed when the shots were

---

6   The evidence establishes that Ken Hodges' automobile was not present at his residence.

7   A further example is present within the facts of this case. When Lamont Johnson shot at defendant as he drove down Whitehall Street, evidence of each of the elements of aggravated assault was present. If Johnson had fired into defendant's house not knowing whether he was inside, and had not actually injured anyone, sufficient evidence would not be present to sustain an aggravated assault conviction.

fired.[8] Had Hodges been standing between or at the two doors at the moment of the shots, he could not have escaped injury.

The shots were fired on a Tuesday afternoon. Neither Lamont Johnson nor Ken Hodges, defendant's assumed targets, were present in the area. Ken Hodges' automobile was gone as well. No testimony pointed to any facts—lights, noises, or other signs—which would indicate to a passerby that the house was occupied.

Without question, defendant acted recklessly and criminally. Had the destructive shots struck anyone, defendant could have been convicted of aggravated assault under Tennessee Code Annotated Section 39–13–101(a)(1) (1991 Repl.) which includes the mens rea of recklessness. Tenn.Code Ann. §§ 39–13–101(a)(1) & 39–13–102(a)(1)(A) (1991 Repl. & 1995 Supp.). Additionally, as this opinion and that of the Court of Criminal Appeals recognizes, defendant's conduct constitutes the offense of felony reckless endangerment. Tenn.Code Ann. § 39–13–103(b) (1991 Repl.).

The statute under which the state opted to prosecute defendant required the state to establish beyond a reasonable doubt that defendant's conduct was intentional or knowing, as defined by the criminal code. The proof that the occupants were justifiably fearful for their lives, while essential to establishing the actus reus of the offense, does not establish in any way the requisite mens rea. For these reasons, we affirm the reversal of defendant's three convictions for aggravated assault and dismiss those charges. The remainder of the Court of Criminal Appeals' decision, including the affirmance of the reckless endangerment conviction and sentence[9] and the dismissal of the weapons charge, is not altered.

Notes and Questions

1. In order to show that the defendant knowingly or *intentionally* placed someone in fear of imminent bodily harm, the *Wilson* case concludes that the defendant must know that someone was in the house at which he shot. When you consider burglary, you will see that courts presume that an unlawful entry into a building is for the purpose of taking items in the building. Why would courts not similarly presume that a defendant who shot into a *house* intended to create fear in someone, even if he did not actually know someone was in the house? As a matter of common sense, why would he shoot into a *house* if not

---

8   The photographs show that the window in the interior door and the glass in the storm door are both completely shattered.

9   Wilson was sentenced to two years for felony reckless endangerment. The trial court ordered him to serve eleven months and twenty-nine days with the remainder to be served on intensive probation.

to frighten or injure someone inside. Under this statute, should it be easier to demonstrate intent than it is knowledge?

2. The court addresses both intent and knowledge, either of which is sufficient to demonstrate assault under this statute, but the court makes the following observation: "Obviously, defendant could not shoot for the purpose of causing fear . . . absent an awareness that someone was inside." The court's conclusion depends on this premise, for which it offers no citation. Is the court's premise obvious? Does it not depend on the meaning of intent? If intent is desire alone, then a defendant could hope with all his heart he scares someone in the home with his shots even if he has no reason to believe that anyone is inside. If, however, one views intent, knowledge, recklessness, and negligence on a continuum of objective risk, then the greater the risk the defendant actually took, the higher on the continuum he falls. Under such an analysis of *mens rea*, knowledge would require a virtual certainly that someone would be frightened by the shot and intent would require something more. Which interpretation makes more sense in this statute?

---

2. Offensive or Unwanted Contact

Criminal law tends to protect people against harm. A basic assault—or simple battery as it is described in tort law—does not itself necessarily involve harm or the threat of harm, at least as that term is understood in the traditional context. The same sort of touching that causes no harm—and would not be objected to—if done accidentally, becomes criminal based entirely on the subjective intent of the defendant in making the contact as the *Dunn* case indicates. Assault does not even require the victim to be offended by the contact, as you will see in *Dunn*. Obviously, the traditional goal of preventing harm is implicated if any type of physical pain or harm is threatened or occurs. Assault, however, can be an injury to dignity alone.

Dunn v. United States

Court of Appeals for the District of Columbia
976 A.2d 217 (2009)

OBERLY, Associate Judge:

Matthew Dunn was convicted of assault in violation of D.C.Code § 22-404 (2001) for shoving a private security officer at an animal rights protest. Dunn appeals, arguing that (1) there was insufficient evidence that he intentionally shoved the officer; (2) the trial judge erroneously convicted Dunn based on the judge's view that a political protester has the propensity to commit assault; and (3) his assault, if any, was *de minimis*. We affirm.

I. FACTS AND PROCEDURAL HISTORY

This is what happened. On February 22, 2008, Matthew Dunn, Adam Ortberg, and Franklin Wade went to 701 Pennsylvania Avenue, N.W., the Navy Memorial Building, to protest against animal cruelty. Wade explained that they were at that address to protest against the pharmaceutical company Novartis; according to Wade, Novartis is "one of the biggest contractors with Huntington Life Sciences, which kills 500 animals every day, including punching beagle puppies in the face in undercover video." Wade testified that his experience as a veteran of more than 100 protests gave him cause to fear "police repression," and so Wade and his co-protesters covered their faces to conceal their identities. Dunn wore a blue bandana which was pulled over his face up to his eyes; a piercing in the shape of upside down bull horns was visible hanging from Dunn's nose.

Mattison Agneu, the security director for 701 Pennsylvania Avenue, had notice that animal rights protesters were coming. Agneu testified that in preparation for the protest, his security team "locked the building down," and Agneu, along with three other security officers, was standing at the door of 701 Pennsylvania Avenue to prevent the protesters from coming into the building. Agneu testified that, following "normal routine," his command center called the Metropolitan Police Department twice to alert the MPD of the protest "just in case" things got out of control. And indeed, although Agneu did not realize it at the time, MPD Detective Norma Horn was across the street, observing the scene for approximately twenty minutes.

Dunn and his confederates arrived at 701 Pennsylvania Avenue at around 1 p.m. They handed out leaflets, chanted, and held signs of a puppy in blood. One of Dunn's friends, Ortberg, yelled through a bullhorn (here, meaning an amplifying device, not a nose piercing) directly into the face and ear of Damien Bonner, a security guard on Agneu's team. Bonner, understandably, moved the bullhorn away from his face. The parties dispute how much force Bonner used-Bonner said he "shoved" the bullhorn, Wade said that Bonner "punched" the bullhorn, and Agneu testified that Bonner "mov[ed]" it—but the precise details are not relevant to this appeal.

What is relevant is what happened next. Having seen Bonner move the bullhorn away from his face, Agneu feared a confrontation. So Agneu came over, "grabbed [Bonner] by his arm, and . . . went to pull him back." "But," Agneu testified, "as I pulled [Bonner] back," Dunn "approached," and, chanting "'all your fault,'" Dunn "kind of—he shoved me." Asked to elaborate, Agneu explained that Dunn was holding a sign "out in front of him, and in one motion, he just thrust forward and, and pushed me back." Dunn's hands, in Agneu's estimation, moved only five to six inches. Nonetheless, Agneu testified, the force of the push was sufficient to move Agneu, a 6'4", 215-pound man, backward. Detective Horn, who had been observing the scene from across the street, largely confirmed Agneu's account. Wade, however, testified that Dunn never got closer than eight feet to Agneu.

Agneu testified that after Dunn pushed him, Agneu asked, "what in the hell are you—do you think you're doing?" In response, according to Agneu, Dunn continued to chant, "'all your fault, all your fault, all your fault.'" Bonner-the security officer whom Agneu pulled back from Ortberg, the protester who was yelling into Bonner's face-did not see Dunn push Agneu. Bonner testified, however, that after Agneu pulled him away from Ortberg, Agneu was "moving backwards" and "telling a guy, 'what are you thinking.'" Agneu then heard "the guy" say, "'well, get your little thug and gangster out of my way then.'" Bonner understood the "thug" moniker to refer to himself.

Wade testified that thereafter Dunn and friends stayed to chant for "several . . . about five more minutes," and then left for the next of three scheduled protest locations for the day. Detective Horn, who had been observing from across the street (it seems in plain clothes), came over, identified herself as a police officer, and informed Agneu that "what had happened out there was an assault." Agneu responded that he had to talk things over with a "higher up," and eventually, a different officer came by and took the assault report. By that time, however, Dunn was gone.

The protesters returned with signs and bullhorns on March 21, 2008, as did Detective Horn, this time in uniform. Horn asked Agneu whether he recognized any of the protesters. Agneu pointed at Dunn who (again wearing a bandana or a scarf) was protesting, beating a white paint bucket with a stick. Agneu told Horn that Dunn was the "guy" who had assaulted him, and predicted that if Horn pulled down the bandana/scarf covering Dunn's face, Dunn's nose piercing would be visible.

Horn then approached Dunn and asked him to uncover his face. Dunn refused, so Horn pulled down the bandana/scarf herself, revealing the nose piercing that Agneu had mentioned. Horn recognized Dunn as the person who pushed Agneu a month earlier, and so Dunn was arrested and taken to the proverbial "downtown" for processing.

The government charged Dunn with assault in violation of D.C.Code § 22-404. After a bench trial, Dunn was convicted and sentenced to seven days' imprisonment, execution of sentence suspended, six months unsupervised probation, and fines totaling $100.

II. DISCUSSION

A. There was sufficient evidence that Dunn assaulted Agneu.

The statute under which Dunn was prosecuted provides: "Whoever unlawfully assaults, or threatens another in a menacing manner, shall be fined not more than $1000 or be imprisoned not more than 180 days, or both." D.C.Code § 22-404(a) (2001). This court has held that there are "three essential elements of the crime of assault: First, there must be an act on the part of the defendant; mere words do not constitute an assault. . . . Secondly, at the time the defendant commits the act, the defendant must have the apparent present ability to injure the victim. Finally, at the time the act is committed, the defendant must have the intent to perform the acts which constitute the assault." *Ray v. United States*, 575 A.2d 1196, 1198 (D.C.1990) (internal quotation marks and citations omitted).

Crucially for this case, "[i]t is firmly established in our case law that the injury resulting from or threatened by an assault may be extremely slight. There need be no physical pain, no bruises, no breaking of the skin, no loss of blood, no medical treatment." *Ray*, 575 A.2d at 1198. That is because "simple assault, as presented here . . . is designed to protect not only against physical *injury*, but against all forms of offensive touching, and even the mere threat of such touching." *Comber v. United States*, 584 A.2d 26, 50 (D.C.1990) (en banc) (internal citations omitted). Thus, "an assault conviction will be upheld when the assaultive act is merely offensive, even though it causes or threatens no physical harm to the victim." *Ray*, 575 A.2d at 1199 (affirming assault conviction of defendant who spat in the face of officer who arrested her); *see also Mahaise v. United States*, 722 A.2d 29, 30 (D.C.1998) (holding that removal of a phone from complainant's left hand and removal of a cigarette from complainant's right hand was sufficient to set out prima facie evidence of two separate assaultive acts).

Dunn's first argument is that "[i]t was clearly erroneous for the trial court to have found Mr. Dunn guilty of the charge." Because Dunn does not cite any factual findings that allegedly were clearly erroneous, we, like the government, understand Dunn to be making a sufficiency of the evidence challenge. And, finding sufficient evidence to sustain the conviction, we reject Dunn's "clearly erroneous" argument.

Although Dunn concedes that both Agneu and Detective Horn testified to having seen him push Agneu, Dunn claims that there was no proof beyond a reasonable doubt that Dunn came into contact with Agneu. In support of this argument, Dunn points out that Bonner, the officer whom Agneu pulled back from the confrontation with Ortberg, answered "no" when asked whether he saw "any physical altercations between any of the protesters and Mr. Agneu." Further, Dunn argues, Wade testified that Dunn got "no closer than eight feet" to Agneu. But Bonner saw Agneu "moving backwards" at the time that Agneu said that he was pushed. And, commenting on Wade's testimony, the trial court said: "I don't think Mr. Wade was necessarily untruthful, but I don't think he had the same immediate opportunity to observe what was happening, at least between the defendant and Agneu. So I credit what Agneu says about the encounter between himself and the defendant." The judge's assessment of this he-said, he-said evidence was reasonable, and so we hold that there was sufficient evidence to find that Dunn came into contact with Agneu. *See Hart v. United States*, 863 A.2d 866, 873 (D.C.2004) ("Contradictions among witnesses at trial are inevitable and are matters for the jury to resolve as they weigh all the evidence, and where there are two permissible views of the evidence, the factfinder's choice between them cannot be clearly erroneous.") (internal quotation marks, citations, and alterations omitted).

Dunn's speculation that he might have been acting unintentionally is just that-speculation that the trial court was not required to accept. It is, of course, possible that, as Dunn argues in his brief, Dunn aimed "to zealously display the sign, not shove Mr. Agneu." But no evidence supports this possibility because Wade did not say that Dunn acted unintentionally and Dunn did not testify to explain his version of events. We cannot infer Dunn's guilt from his failure to testify, but neither are we required to give more credit to the speculation in his brief than to testimony from people who were at the scene and whose testimony is sufficient to show that Dunn acted intentionally.

In a sufficiency challenge we view the evidence in the light most favorable to the government, draw all reasonable inferences in the government's favor, and defer to the factfinder's credibility determinations. *Blakeney v. United States*, 653 A.2d 365, 369 n. 3 (D.C.1995). Applying this standard of review, we hold that there was sufficient evidence from which a reasonable mind might fairly infer that (1) Dunn made contact with Agneu, which contact was offensive to Agneu; (2) no less than the person convicted of assault for spitting in *Ray*, Dunn had the ability to injure (*i.e.*, to offend) Agneu; and (3) Dunn acted intentionally. This is enough to convict for assault. *See Ray*, 575 A.2d 1196.

* * *

C. Dunn's "*de minimis*" argument fails.

Finally, Dunn asks us to overturn his conviction because his violation of the law, if any, was *de minimis*. We decline to do so.

Dunn's argument (and, to some extent, the government's response) conflates two distinct ideas: one, that some trivial violations of the assault statute may be, as Dunn argues, "too slight to constitute a criminal assault," and two, that there should be a *de minimis* defense to assault. The arguments are related, but different. The difference is between arguing that driving at 56 mph in a 55 mph zone is not speeding and arguing that driving at 56 mph in a 55 mph zone is speeding, but does not warrant a fine because, as one might say, "c'mon, judge, it's only one mile over."

The first aspect of the argument is really Dunn's sufficiency argument by another name, and it fails for the same reasons. As mentioned above, it is settled in this jurisdiction that "an assault conviction will be upheld when the assaultive act is merely offensive, even though it causes or threatens no physical harm to the victim." *Ray*, 575 A.2d at 1199. Put differently, just as breaking the speed limit by only one mile per hour is speeding, an assault is an assault, even if it causes no physical injury. Therefore, under our established law, Dunn's shove was an assault even if it did not cause Agneu any physical harm.

Dunn's arguments for why his shove nonetheless does not amount to assault do not withstand scrutiny. As an initial matter, Dunn's claim that the circumstances gave the 6'4", 215-pound Agneu reason only to "feign[ ] offense" at Dunn's pushing him does not do justice to what transpired. Rather, we think that a reasonable mind might fairly conclude, *see Blakeney*, 653 A.2d at 369 n. 3, that Agneu, a security guard who was not employed by the company that allegedly kills beagle puppies, was offended when a masked stranger chanted at and then pushed him without provocation. That inference is supported by the fact that, when he was pushed, Agneu protested: "what in the hell are you-do you think you're doing?" It makes no difference that Dunn moved his hands only five to six inches in striking Agneu. The action was sufficient to move Agneu backward, and there is no reason to doubt that, as a general matter, even a slight hand movement can offend someone.

Dunn also claims that Agneu was not offended by the shove because Agneu did not reach out to police. But Agneu said that he felt no need to call the police because "during these protests, we, we always have plain clothes officers that are somewhere around the area," and, indeed, Detective Horn witnessed the confrontation from across the street. Likewise, Dunn's claims that the police "coached" Agneu to file a claim, and that the litigation was "driven" by the police, not Agneu, are no reasons to reverse. For one thing, there is no evidence in the record that the police "coached" Agneu to file a claim-Agneu expressly denied that anyone from the police pressured him to file a complaint with the police. For another thing, "the judges of [this] court endeavor *not* to decide appeals based on who the litigants are, who their lawyers are, or what we may believe their motives to be." *Severance v. Patterson*, 566 F.3d 490, 493 n. 2 (5th Cir.2009) (responding to dissent's allegation that litigation was driven by ideological interest group), *see id.* at 504-05 (Wiener, J., dissenting). Thus, it is irrelevant whether the police or Agneu instigated the litigation. The question for this court is whether the facts establish that Dunn committed an assault.

Dunn's argument that he should be able to plead a *de minimis* defense-in our earlier example, to be able to say that speeding by one mile per hour, albeit technically a violation, just does not deserve a penalty-also fails. We appreciate that there is no evidence that Dunn frightened Agneu or that Agneu had trouble getting over Dunn's encroachment on his personal space. Similar minor violations of the assault statute may well happen every day, yet it is exceedingly rare for the U.S. Attorney's Office to get involved. Why, then, should Dunn not be able to argue that his shove was too minor to warrant a criminal penalty?

The answer is that Dunn fails to cite any authority for a *de minimis* defense in the District. Some jurisdictions have recognized *de minimis*-type defenses, but they have done so through legislation, not judicial decree. New York, for instance, has a statute that permits trial judges to dismiss certain criminal charges where "some compelling factor, consideration or circumstances clearly demonstrat[es] that conviction or prosecution of the defendant . . . would constitute or result in injustice." N.Y.CRIM. PROC. LAW § 170.40(1) (1979). And a few other states have adopted provisions based on MODEL PENAL CODE § 2.12 (2001), which "authorizes courts to exercise a power inherent in other agencies of criminal justice to ignore merely technical violations of law." *Id.*, Explanatory Note; *see* Stanislaw Pomorski, *On Multiculturalism, Concepts of Crime, and the "De Minimis" Defense*, 1997 B.Y.U. L. REV. 51 & n. 2; *see, e.g.*, N.J. STAT. ANN. 2C:2-11 (2005); ME.REV. STAT. ANN. 17-A, § 12 (2006); 18 PA. CONS.STAT. § 312 (1998). The D.C. Council, however, has not joined ranks with the "very limited" number of states that have adopted the defense. Pomorski, 1997 B.Y.U. L. REV. 51. As a result, we lack the power to give Dunn the relief that he seeks. That the assault was slight is reflected in the minor sentence that Dunn received: seven days' imprisonment, execution of sentence suspended, six months unsupervised probation, and $100 in fines.

III. CONCLUSION

For the foregoing reasons, Dunn's conviction is
Affirmed.

Notes and Questions

Simple assault is perhaps the only crime in which the defendant's intent alone can form the basis of the harm. The court observed in this case that the defendant did not apologize at the time. The victim of this crime did not suffer any real injury. The injury in this case was essentially one to his dignity. This crime can therefore look very different than most crimes we consider. If a defendant accidentally kills another, there is still a substantial injury, but there is no criminal liability because of the defendant's *mens rea*. In *Dunn*, the offense really is the defendant's manifestation of his lack of respect for his victim, not the injury done by his action.

3. Conspiracy to Assault

Conspiracies historically have been established by looking at concerted action. If three men enter a bank wearing ski masks and brandishing weapons, this is all the proof that is needed to establish a conspiracy among the three of them to rob the bank. Unlike corporate charters, plans to commit crimes are not memorialized and filed with the Secretary of State. Sometimes there will be evidence of the agreement itself, rather than just the concert of action that reveals that there must be a conspiracy. Testimony is sometimes offered of one or more of the members that there was an agreement when one of the conspirators is given a deal in exchange for testimony. Sometimes an undercover agent will either surreptitiously record, or simply testify about, an agreement parties entered into. Wiretap evidence can also provide direct evidence of an agreement. And increasingly in a world in which everyone communicates by email, and even more so by text, agreements can be found in the verbatim exchanges of messages that phone companies can retrieve.

Nevertheless, the most common way of demonstrating a conspiracy remains the concerted action of the members of the alleged conspiracy. *Millan* provides an example of a court looking at a fairly rapidly developing situation and trying to determine whether there was an agreement to assault and, if so, when it formed.

State v. Millan

Supreme Court of Connecticut
966 A.2d 699 (2009)

KATZ, J.

The defendant, Cristobal Millan, Jr., appeals from the judgment of conviction, rendered after a jury trial, of assault in the first degree in violation of General Statutes § 53a–59(a)(1)[2] and conspiracy to commit assault in the first degree in violation of General Statutes §§ 53a–48[3] and 53a–59(a)(1). The defendant claims on appeal that: (1) there was insufficient evidence to support the conspiracy conviction under § 53a–59(a)(1); and (2) the admission of uncharged prior misconduct evidence was harmful error. We affirm the trial court's judgment.

The jury reasonably could have found the following facts. On March 21, 2005, Lamarr Sands and his girlfriend, Charie Matos, were staying at the Super 8 Motel (motel) located at the intersection of Scott Road and Schraffts Drive in Waterbury. They had been staying there for several weeks, most recently in room 215. Unbeknownst to Sands and Matos, by coincidence, Darren Madison, a friend with whom Sands recently had had a falling out, was staying in room 214 of the motel on that date. Rooms 214 and 215 are immediately adjacent to each other, their doors only one to two feet apart. The rooms are located on the second floor of the motel and are accessible only by exterior hallways and stairwells.

Sometime during that evening, Sands and Madison encountered each other at the motel. Subsequently, at approximately 10 p.m. that same evening, Jeffrey Smith arrived at the motel to visit Sands and Matos. Smith observed Sands and Madison engaged in a heated argument either in the hallway outside rooms 214 and 215 or inside of room 214. Madison left the motel after making a comment that indicated to Smith and Sands that he was going to return after meeting or picking up his "boys." Smith remained at the motel out of concern that Sands would be outnumbered in a fight upon Madison's return.

---

2   General Statutes § 53a–59(a) provides in relevant part: "A person is guilty of assault in the first degree when: (1) With intent to cause serious physical injury to another person, he causes such injury to such person or to a third person by means of a deadly weapon or a dangerous instrument. . . ."

3   General Statutes § 53a–48 provides: "(a) A person is guilty of conspiracy when, with intent that conduct constituting a crime be performed, he agrees with one or more persons to engage in or cause the performance of such conduct, and any one of them commits an overt act in pursuance of such conspiracy.

"(b) It shall be a defense to a charge of conspiracy that the actor, after conspiring to commit a crime, thwarted the success of the conspiracy, under circumstances manifesting a complete and voluntary renunciation of his criminal purpose."

After Madison left the motel, he drove to the Save–A–Lot store on North Main Street in Waterbury, where the defendant, with whom Madison was friends, worked as a stocker. As a stocker, the defendant regularly used a "cutting blade," commonly referred to as a box cutter (hereinafter knife), that his employer provided for cutting plastic wrapped pallets or boxes. The knife had a retractable razor, with one sharpened edge that came to a point, housed in a thin plastic casing. Madison picked the defendant up following his shift at approximately 10 p.m. and, at some point before the two arrived back at the motel, Madison told the defendant about the previous encounter with Sands. The defendant was carrying his work issued knife in his back pocket. While they were in Madison's car or shortly after they arrived back at the motel, the defendant telephoned Valerie Vicente, a friend with whom he recently had become more intimate. Vicente told the defendant that she was with two male friends. The defendant asked Vicente to come to the motel with the two males.

Soon thereafter, Madison, the defendant, Vicente and her two male friends stood outside of Sands' motel room. At least one of the persons in that group began banging on the door to Sands' room and taunted him to come out. The banging continued for several minutes. When the taunts turned to sexual comments about Matos, Sands could not restrain himself any longer and went into the hallway to confront Madison. Smith followed Sands into the hallway. Sands swung at Madison, and the two started fighting. As the defendant and one of Vicente's male friends moved to join in the fight, Smith told them not to intervene and that the fight was between Sands and Madison. The defendant then swung his fist toward Smith. In response, Smith grabbed the defendant, held him in a "reverse headlock"—the defendant facing Smith with his head down—and punched the defendant with uppercuts, bloodying the defendant's nose. Smith and the defendant fell backwards onto the floor of Sands' motel room, where they stopped fighting and got to their feet. Smith offered the defendant his hand, saying that this was not "their fight. . . ." At that point, one of Vicente's male friends who was in the motel room remarked to the defendant that Smith "had messed [the defendant] up pretty bad." The defendant looked in the mirror, saw his bloodied nose and pulled the knife out of his pocket. Smith took a step back, and the defendant yelled to the other male to hit Smith with a desk chair that was in the room. The male picked up the chair and grazed Smith with it. Smith ducked to avoid being hit by the chair, and his feet became entangled in the comforter hanging from the bed, causing Smith to fall to the floor on his knees and elbows. The defendant then went over to Smith, stood behind and over him and began slashing him with the knife. The other male who had swung the chair at Smith yelled to the defendant, "slash his throat, slash his throat." Smith remained on his knees and tried to protect his throat and face with his arms, as the defendant continued to slash him.

At some point while the defendant and Smith fought, the fight between Sands and Madison ended. The defendant stopped slashing Smith, left the motel room and drove away from the motel with Madison. Madison drove the defendant to a nearby gas station, where the defendant washed up, changed his bloodied shirt into a clean one that Madison gave him and threw away the knife. Thereafter, the defendant fled the state and went to his father's house in Virginia, where police eventually located him.

The morning after the assault, Smith sought treatment at Waterbury Hospital because his wounds would not stop bleeding. An examination revealed that he had sustained seven slash or stab wounds—two to his head, which cut his forehead and ear, one to his chin, one to the back of his head, two to his back and one to his upper abdomen and chest. Some of the cuts went into the subcutaneous tissue, which is below the layer of fatty tissue that lies directly below the skin. One of the cuts to Smith's head had severed his temporal artery. As a result, by the time he arrived at the hospital, Smith had lost approximately two pints of blood, or 15 to 20 percent of his total blood volume.

* * *

The defendant thereafter testified, claiming that he had acted in self-defense when he slashed Smith. Specifically, he testified that Smith had been the initial aggressor and that he had used his knife against Smith while Smith had him in the headlock, after he had been unable to break free and was being choked by the headlock. The jury returned a verdict of guilty on one count of assault in the first degree in violation of § 53a–59(a)(1), with Smith being the victim of the assault, and one count of conspiracy to commit assault in the first degree in violation of §§ 53a–48 and 53a–59(a)(1), with Sands being the victim of the conspiracy. The trial court rendered judgment in accordance with the verdict and imposed a total effective sentence of fourteen years imprisonment and six years special parole. This appeal followed.

The defendant contends that there was insufficient evidence of an agreement to use a dangerous instrument to support the conspiracy charge. . . .

As charged to the jury, the state was required to prove that the defendant was a party to an agreement to assault Sands with a dangerous weapon. The defendant contends that the evidence does not show that anyone else knew, prior to the fight, that he possessed a dangerous instrument, and, therefore, there was no direct or circumstantial evidence of an agreement to carry out an assault with a knife or any other kind of dangerous instrument. The state responds that there was sufficient evidence to support this conviction. In addition to evidence relating to the knife, the state points to evidence that one of the assailants swung a chair at Smith. The state also urges us to adopt the position taken by some jurisdictions, under which body parts can be a dangerous instrument under certain circumstances, and to conclude that the jury properly could have found that the "multiple fists" of the conspirators in the present case constituted a dangerous instrument under General Statutes §§ 53a–3(7) and 53a–59(a)(1). In his reply brief, the defendant contends that we should disregard the state's "multiple fists as a dangerous instrument" argument because the trial court offered no such instruction to the jury.

We conclude that there was sufficient evidence to prove that there was a conspiracy to commit assault with a knife. Therefore, we need not decide whether multiple fists can constitute a dangerous instrument under §§ 53a–3(7) and 53a–59(a)(1), an issue of first impression in this state and one on which the jury did not receive an express instruction in the present case.

* * *

"To establish the crime of conspiracy under § 53a–48 . . . the state must show that there was an agreement between two or more persons to engage in conduct constituting a crime and that the agreement was followed by an overt act in furtherance of the conspiracy by any one of the conspirators. The state must also show intent on the part of the accused that conduct constituting a crime be performed. The existence of a formal agreement between the parties need not be proved; it is sufficient to show that they are knowingly engaged in a mutual plan to do a forbidden act." (Internal quotation marks omitted.) *State v. Padua*, 273 Conn. 138, 181–82, 869 A.2d 192 (2005).

In the present case, "[w]hile the state must prove an agreement [to commit assault with a dangerous weapon], the existence of a formal agreement between the conspirators need not be proved because [i]t is only in rare instances that conspiracy may be established by proof of an express agreement to unite to accomplish an unlawful purpose. . . . [T]he requisite agreement or confederation may be inferred from proof of the separate acts of the individuals accused as coconspirators and from the circumstances surrounding the commission of these acts. . . . Further, [c]onspiracy can seldom be proved by direct evidence. It may be inferred from the activities of the accused persons." (Internal quotation marks omitted.) *State v. Green*, supra, 261 Conn. at 669, 804 A.2d 810. "A conspiracy can be formed [however] in a very short time period. . . ." Id., at 671, 804 A.2d 810.

The record reflects the following evidence. Sands testified that, in a statement to the police, he had identified the defendant as one of his attackers at the Fairmount Projects. [Sometime in 2005, Millan, Madison, and another man had attacked Sands and Madison and stolen a gold bracelet and money at the Fairmount Projects in Waterbury, CT. Eds.] Despite that prior physical assault, testimony from Sands and Smith established that Sands nonetheless confronted

Madison when he first saw him at the motel. The defendant testified that, about one-half hour before he left work, he and Madison had made arrangements for Madison to pick him up from work. He also testified that Madison had told him about the confrontation with Sands. The defendant claimed that he had called Vicente because it was his idea to get "some girls" to come to the motel, yet he also testified that he told Vicente that it was okay for her to bring her two male friends along. Testimony from Smith, Sands and Matos established that, thereafter, the defendant, Madison, Vicente's two male friends and Vicente stood in the hallway outside of Sands' motel room while one or more persons in that group repeatedly knocked on the door to Sands' room and yelled taunts to provoke Sands to come out of his room. Sands testified that someone said: "Come the fuck outside. . . . Just come outside now. We all here now, bitch." Matos testified, on the basis of her knowledge of the previous incident at the Fairmount Projects and the conduct that both preceded and occurred during the fight at the motel, that she believed that "[t]he three of them came to our room to jump [Sands]," apparently referring to Madison, the defendant and one of Vicente's male friends. Smith testified that, after Sands came out from his motel room and started to fight with Madison, the defendant swung his fist at Smith after Smith interfered with the defendant's effort to enter the fray between Sands and Madison. Smith also testified that, when the defendant pulled out his knife, the defendant yelled to one of Vicente's male friends to hit Smith with a chair. The male then attempted to do so, and later yelled to the defendant, "slash his throat, slash his throat." The defendant testified that, after he and Madison left the motel, Madison drove him to a gas station, where the defendant cleaned up and disposed of the knife, and Madison provided the defendant with a clean shirt that he had in his car.

On the basis of this testimony, the jury reasonably could have drawn the following inferences. Before or shortly after the defendant got out of work, the defendant and Madison had formed a plan to go back to the motel to assault Sands. Sands' willingness to confront Madison indicated that he had not been sufficiently intimidated by the earlier assault at the Fairmount Projects. Additionally, Madison had reason to believe that, when he returned to the motel, Smith still would be there with Sands. Therefore, the defendant and Madison reasonably anticipated that greater force than fists would be necessary. The defendant had ready access to the knife that he regularly used for his job and brought it with him to the motel. The defendant telephoned Vicente with the intention of rounding up additional people to confront Sands or formed that intention once he found out that Vicente had two male friends with her. The defendant and Madison had the opportunity to communicate their plan to Vicente's friends before they went to Sands' motel room. The presence of Vicente's two male friends outside of Sands' motel room when one or more persons in Madison's group banged on the door and taunted Sands demonstrated that they were aware of a dispute between Madison and Sands and, at the very least, passively participated in efforts to get Sands out of the room for purposes of the assault. Cf. *State v. Green*, supra, 261 Conn. at 671, 804 A.2d 810 (no evidence of agreement to kill when no evidence that alleged conspirators who shot at victim knew about dispute between victim and defendant).

Most significant, however, was the conduct of the defendant's alleged coconspirators after the defendant pulled the knife out of his pocket. A coconspirator's conduct at the scene can provide the requisite evidence of an agreement. *See State v. Crosswell*, 223 Conn. 243, 256, 612 A.2d 1174 (1992) ("[T]he requisite agreement or confederation may be inferred from proof of the separate acts of the individuals accused as coconspirators and from the circumstances surrounding the commission of these acts. . . . The fact that the defendant stood by silently when a gun was displayed in order to gain entry and then to intimidate the occupants of the premises is evidence from which the jury might reasonably have inferred the defendant's acquiescence in this enlarged criminal enterprise."

* * *

When the defendant pulled out his knife, the unidentified male friend of Vincente who was in the room did not say or do anything to indicate surprise or concern. On the contrary, that male attempted to immobilize Smith by hitting him with the chair to facilitate the defendant's attack and encouraged the defendant to use the knife in a lethal manner, yelling "slash his throat, slash his throat." In addition, the fact that Madison had an extra shirt in the car and aided the defendant in disposing of the knife could support the conclusion that there had been a prearranged plan. In sum, the jury reasonably could have concluded that the coconspirators' intention was to do to Sands what ultimately was done to Smith after Smith had interfered with Madison's assault on Sands. We therefore conclude that the evidence in the present case was sufficient to support a finding that the defendant had conspired with Madison and one of Vicente's male friends to commit assault in the first degree with a dangerous instrument.

* * *

SCHALLER, J., dissenting.

I respectfully dissent because I conclude that the evidence was insufficient to support the defendant's conviction of conspiracy to commit assault in the first degree in violation of General Statutes §§ 53a–48 and 53a–59(a)(1). Accordingly, I would reverse the judgment of conviction as to that offense.

I agree with the majority's statement of the applicable law and the appropriate standard of review for this issue. In addition, I agree for the most part with the majority's statement of the pertinent facts regarding what the jury reasonably could have found. The majority's rendition of the evidence, however, is incomplete, in my view, and its construct of reasonable and logical inferences does not find support in the evidence. Without those unsupportable inferences, the evidence is insufficient to support the defendant's conviction.

At the outset, it is crucial to keep in mind that the conspiracy charge is predicated on an agreement to commit an assault with a dangerous instrument against *Lamarr Sands, rather than Jeffrey Smith.*[2] To this end, the majority selects portions of the evidence that it uses to build the body of inferences that it argues the jury could have drawn "[o]n the basis of this testimony. . . ." In order to establish this prearranged plan to assault Sands with a dangerous instrument, the majority relies on two key inferences: (1) that Darren Madison had an unspecified reason to believe that Smith would still be at the motel with Sands, and that, therefore, "greater force than fists would be necessary";[3] and (2) that Madison had an extra shirt in his car and aided the defendant in disposing of the defendant's box cutter (hereinafter knife). Both of these inferences are nothing more than speculation and cannot be used to support the conviction.

First, the fact that Madison sought additional manpower in the form of assistance from three other males, rather than weapons, belies the notion that "greater force than fists would be necessary." In fact, there is not a shred of evidence that anyone, other than the defendant, was aware of the fact that the defendant possessed a knife until the defendant actually displayed that weapon after his initial altercation with *Smith.* Second, there was no evidence that Madison acquired the spare shirt before he picked up the defendant. The only reasonable inference, therefore, is that Madison already possessed the spare shirt *before* he had his *chance encounter* with Sands. In addition, there was no evidence that Madison had aided the defendant in disposing of the knife. The defendant testified that he and Madison had stopped at a gas station after the incident so that the defendant could buy some water to wash off his face. Although the defendant testified that he had disposed of the knife at the gas station, no evidence was presented that Madison, who exercised his fifth amendment right not to testify, was aware that the defendant did so. Moreover, because there was no evidence that Madison was aware that the defendant originally had possessed the knife,

---

2   With respect to the conspiracy count, the trial court charged the jury that "the object of this assault [and] subject of the conspiracy is . . . Sands and not . . . Smith."

3   During the evening of March 21, 2005, Sands and Madison encountered each other at the motel in which they were both staying. Smith, who was visiting Sands, observed the argument. Later that evening, Madison returned to the motel with the defendant and several other individuals.

the subsequent events at the gas station shed no light on whether there was a *prearranged* plan.

The majority further overlooks other evidence vital to drawing reasonable inferences. As the state conceded in its closing argument at trial, the defendant did not pull out his knife until, in the words of the prosecutor: "[The fight] was over. And [Smith] told you he extended his hand, and instead, there was a second male nearby who made a remark about the defendant's face. He happened to look up. . . . And there is a mirror right there. . . . The defendant looks right up, sees what's happened to his face and just flies into a rage. And . . . Smith tells you [the defendant] pulls out a knife when he catches his image in the mirror and goes to town on [Smith]."

What emerges from this undisputed evidence is that the sudden and unexpected use of the knife at that late, unanticipated stage of the fight was a unilateral action on the part of the defendant, exclusively for purposes of what had now become a personal dispute with *Smith* merely because someone called to the defendant's attention that Smith had bloodied the defendant's face.

Although I agree that evidence regarding this latter, unanticipated event suggests evidence of a conspiracy to commit assault in the first degree, the evidence suggests a conspiracy directed at *Smith*—not *Sands*. As the majority recounts, after the initial altercation between the defendant and Smith, "Smith offered the defendant his hand, saying that this was not 'their fight. . . .' At that point . . . [another male] who was in the motel room remarked to the defendant that Smith 'had messed [the defendant] up pretty bad.' . . . [T]he defendant [then] yelled to the other male to hit Smith with a desk chair. . . ." The other male "attempted to immobilize Smith by hitting him with the chair to facilitate the defendant's [knife] attack and encouraged the defendant to use the knife in a lethal manner." It may well be, therefore, that after the defendant realized that his face had been bloodied, there was evidence to show that the defendant had formed a conspiracy with the other male to assault *Smith* with a dangerous instrument, namely, the knife. *See State v. Green*, 261 Conn. 653, 671, 804 A.2d 810 (2002) ("[a] conspiracy can be formed in a very short time period"). Because the charge to the jury required it to determine whether there was a conspiracy to commit an assault in the first degree directed against *Sands*, and not against Smith, whatever occurred after the initial dispute between the defendant and *Smith* has no bearing whatsoever on the original agreement to assault Sands.[4]

---

4   In *State v. Crosswell*, 223 Conn. 243, 256, 612 A.2d 1174 (1992), we upheld the conviction of a defendant for conspiracy to commit robbery in the first degree because we concluded that the defendant, by standing silently by while another coconspirator brandished a gun during the course of the robbery, acquiesced in what had then become an "enlarged criminal enterprise." In the present case, the state did not assert that brandishing the knife constituted evidence of a then enlarged criminal conspiracy directed at Sands, but, rather, that it had been the

When the full evidentiary picture is taken into account, as it must be, the majority's construct of inferences cannot withstand close scrutiny. There was no evidence that anyone other than the defendant knew that the defendant possessed the knife until he displayed the knife *after* the initial fight was over. *State v. Smith*, 36 Conn.App. 483, 487–88, 651 A.2d 744 (1994) (conspiracy conviction overturned because no evidence that anyone was aware that group member happened to possess gun), cert. denied, 233 Conn. 910, 659 A.2d 184 (1995). Moreover, although the defendant had the opportunity to do so, he did not use the knife during the initial fight between Madison and Sands or when he initially attacked Smith, or even when Smith initially released the defendant after holding him in a headlock. In *State v. Asberry*, 81 Conn.App. 44, 51–52, 837 A.2d 885, cert. denied, 268 Conn. 904, 845 A.2d 408 (2004), the Appellate Court concluded, on the basis of inferences, that the spontaneous finding and use of a brick to assault a victim could support a conviction for conspiracy to commit assault in the first degree. That case, however, turned on the " *immediacy* with which the brick was found and used" in the course of the assault. (Emphasis added.) *Id.* In the present case, the defendant passed up *three opportunities* to use the knife and, instead, pulled the knife only after a chance remark following cessation of the initial fighting.

It bears emphasizing that Madison and the defendant specifically choose to assemble additional manpower to accompany them in their expedition to the motel, rather than bringing weapons. In the absence of evidence or reasonable inferences with regard to weapons, the majority relies on several cases, applied out of context in view of the relevant facts, allowing the use of inferences generally in determining conspiratorial intent. No cases, however, support the use of speculation on the basis of intervening, unplanned and spontaneous events that occur during the course of a confrontation like the one in this case. The initial fight, which took an unexpected turn after it appeared to be finished, was clearly an assault but, just as clearly, was not an assault with a dangerous instrument. Although the defendant should stand convicted of the charged lesser offense of assault in the third degree in violation of General Statutes § 53a–61(a)(1); see footnote 4 of the majority opinion; his conviction for conspiracy to commit assault in the first degree should be reversed. For the foregoing reasons, I respectfully dissent.

---

group's plan all along to use the knife to assault Sands. *Crosswell*, therefore, would support a conviction only if the conspiracy to commit assault was predicated against *Smith*, not Sands.

Notes and Questions

1. The unidentified male who yelled, "slash his throat, slash his throat," is, of course, part of this conspiracy. He is also liable under a complicity theory. As noted earlier, often the evidence that proves conspiracy proves complicity and vice versa.

2. The dissent makes a fairly compelling argument that there was a conspiracy aimed at *Smith not Sands*. Is there sufficient evidence that there was an agreement to use a knife against Sands?

3. Notice how quickly this conspiracy was formed and the circumstances under which it was formed. Within seconds in the middle of a brawl, one of the fighters pulls out a knife and another fighter recommended using it. This seems to better fit the paradigm of complicity—encouragement to use the weapon—than an agreement to use the weapon. Courts have recognized that in the same amount of time, and under very similar circumstances, a defendant can become liable for assault under a theory of complicity. *See State v. Robertson*, 2001 WL 777022 (Ohio App.). Compare the speed, and circumstances, under which this form of liability can attach to the factors courts considered in evaluating premeditation and deliberation. The amount of contemplation required in this context should remind you of second-degree murder statutes that require intent but no premeditation or deliberation.

C

PRACTICE EXERCISE

Read the following set of facts, then read the instructions.

Ashton is new to the neighborhood, but loves to play basketball. Having driven past the neighborhood park a few times, and seeing some intense pick-up games, Ashton decides to play. During his first time out on the courts, Ashton waits for his turn to join a team. The court is busy, and one team has been winning every game that day. Brutus, the best player of that winning team, is aggressive and very big.

No one enters the "paint" under the basket, knowing Brutus will foul hard if he doesn't block the shot. But Ashton wants to prove a point, as the new guy on the block.

During his first game out, Ashton plays well, makes lots of jump shots, and does not venture into the "paint," because he keeps "hitting" his shots. But his team still loses. Because of the respect gained during the first game, Ashton feels confident, and puts together a team for another game to challenge Brutus' team. The second game is a "brawler," with physical play from both sides. Ashton is frustrated, because he is not making his jump shots. So, Ashton starts "driving to the basket," but Brutus starts to foul. During one play, while Ashton is in mid-air laying the ball into the hoop, Brutus shoves him from behind into the metal pole supporting the basket. Ashton calls a foul, according to playground rules, exchanges some heated words with Brutus, and gets the ball back for another possession. To maintain his "respect," Ashton decides to directly challenge Brutus under the basket that play. During Ashton's next attempted lay-up, Brutus hacks Ashton across the arms, takes the ball, and tells Ashton, "B* * * *, get off my f* * * ing court." Ashton is furious, and yells, "You're a f* * * ing cheat! Show me what you really got!"

The next possession, Brutus gets the ball "down low" under the basket, makes a nice move, and dunks on his defender. The playground crowd erupts. While jogging back on defense, Brutus slaps Ashton on the butt, and says, "Oh yeah, I got it." Play continues to "heat up," with players on both sides becoming aggressive and frustrated at the "bad calls" and hard fouls the opposing team makes. Finally, after a hard foul, Brutus and his teammates surround Ashton, cussing at him and threatening to "end him." Brutus states, "If we catch you back here again, my guys will f* * * you up." Infuriated, Ashton leaves the park in the middle of the game.

The police are aware of the increasing territoriality of Brutus and "his guys" at the park. After watching the surveillance footage, officers arrest Brutus the next day at the park, charging him with assault and conspiracy to assault.

Instructions:

You are Brutus' defense attorney. Based on the facts, draft jury instructions using both Tennessee's assault statute in *Wilson* (p. 826) and Connecticut's conspiracy statute in *Millan* (p. 839). Consider: balance your goal of reducing your client's liability against producing an instruction that is reasonable enough to be used and withstand appellate review.

C. Kidnapping and Lesser Included Crimes

1. Abduction

Kidnapping requires abduction, which typically means one of two things: with the intent of prevent the victim's liberation, the defendant (1) secrets the victim away from others, or (2) restrains the victim with force or threat of physical force. The *Stubsjoen* case illustrates how in the case of children, the victim can be hidden in plain view.

State v. Stubsjoen

Washington Court of Appeals
738 P.2d 306 (1987)

SCHOLFIELD, Chief Judge.

Erin Kirsten Stubsjoen appeals her conviction for second degree kidnapping, challenging the sufficiency of the evidence, and assigning error to the exclusion of testimony of a defense witness and to the failure to instruct the jury on the definition of intent. We affirm.

FACTS

Jerry Johnson, Donald Ponis, and Jeanna Bomber were socializing and drinking beer at Johnson's home during the early evening hours of June 11, 1984. They decided to visit Dash Point State Park. They took Jeanna Bomber's 6-month-old daughter, Holly, along with them. On the way, they stopped at a 7–Eleven store, where, according to their testimony, they met Stubsjoen for the first time. Johnson and Ponis invited Stubsjoen along to the park. Stubsjoen joined them, and they drank beer, smoked marijuana and talked in the park for 1 to 2 hours.

When the park was near closing, they drove to a grocery store for more beer and then to a cul-de-sac near 260th and 16th Avenue South. The cul-de-sac was surrounded by sparse woods and underbrush. They sat in the car listening to the radio and drinking beer, Johnson and Stubsjoen in the front seat and Ponis and Bomber in the back seat with Bomber's baby. Not long after they arrived, Ponis and Bomber began to argue, and Johnson asked them to leave the car. They walked some distance away, out of sight of the car.

Johnson testified that, soon afterward, he left the car also, and walked behind some bushes nearby to urinate. He testified that when he returned to the car, Stubsjoen was gone, but it appeared the child was still in her car seat. Bomber and Ponis returned to the car a few minutes later, and the three of them drove to Bomber's house about 5 miles away. It was then that they discovered the baby was missing. According to the testimony, the baby's blankets had been arranged in the car seat to make it appear that the child was still there. They immediately returned to the cul-de-sac, but were unable to find Stubsjoen or the baby, so they contacted the police.

Stubsjoen testified that she was hitchhiking to Bellevue when she was picked up by Johnson, Ponis and Bomber. She told them she was going to Bellevue and that she was unfamiliar with the Federal Way area. Stubsjoen testified she agreed to go along to Dash Point, but with the understanding that afterward, she would be taken to the freeway where she could continue on her way.

After Ponis and Bomber left the car at the cul-de-sac, she said, the baby started crying loudly as if "gasping for air". She took the child into her lap to quiet her, but the baby continued to cry and began "spitting up" on her. At that point, she told the court, Johnson began to make sexual advances toward her. She rebuffed Johnson's advances and told him she wanted to leave, but she did not know where she was. Johnson refused to give her directions. Johnson also refused, she stated, to take the baby from her. Consequently, she got out of the car with the baby and proceeded down a footpath away from the cul-de-sac, calling loudly several times for Ponis and Bomber.

The path eventually led to 16th Avenue South, where a motorist stopped to offer assistance. The man drove her to a fire station in Des Moines. Officer Michael Chaney responded to the call from fire department personnel. Stubsjoen told Chaney her name was Lisa Chapman, that her car had broken down while she was visiting friends in the area, and that she wanted to go to Bellevue. Stubsjoen lied, she testified, because she was afraid the police would find out she was in violation of her parole for drinking and for not maintaining contact with her parole officer.

Officer Chaney arranged for the police department chaplain, Melvin Hinz, to drive Stubsjoen and the baby, whom he assumed belonged to Stubsjoen, to Bellevue. Near the freeway exit to Bellevue, Hinz's pager sounded. When Hinz stopped to telephone back to the police station, Stubsjoen entered a taxi cab with the baby and rode to a nearby establishment called Dave's Place eatery. On cross examination, Stubsjoen admitted that she took the taxi to get away from Hinz because she assumed the police were calling him about the missing baby.

Stubsjoen testified that, while she was at Dave's Place, she called a friend, Eric Jonsson, told him what had happened, and asked him for help. The police, who had traced the taxi to Dave's Place, arrested her a short time later.

At trial, Stubsjoen called Jonsson as a witness. However, the court only permitted him to testify that he had received the phone call, ruling that Stubsjoen's statements were self-serving and that Jonsson's testimony would be inadmissible hearsay. Stubsjoen was convicted, under RCW 9A.40.030, of kidnapping in the second degree.

SUFFICIENCY OF THE EVIDENCE

In a challenge to the sufficiency of the evidence in a criminal case, the test is whether, after viewing the evidence in a light most favorable to the prosecution, any rational trier of fact could have found the essential elements of the crime beyond a reasonable doubt. *State v. Green*, 94 Wash.2d 216, 221, 616 P.2d 628 (1980).

RCW 9A.40.030 defines kidnapping in the second degree:

A person is guilty of kidnapping in the second degree if he intentionally abducts another person under circumstances not amounting to kidnapping in the first degree.

RCW 9A.40.010(2) defines "abduct":

"Abduct" means to restrain a person by either (a) secreting or holding him in a place where he is not likely to be found, or (b) using or threatening to use deadly force.

RCW 9A.40.010(1) defines "restrain":

"Restrain" means to restrict a person's movements without consent and without legal authority in a manner which interferes substantially with his liberty. Restraint is "without consent" if it is accomplished by (a) physical force, intimidation, or deception, or (b) any means including acquiescence of the victim, if he is a child less than sixteen years old or an incompetent person and if the parent, guardian, or other person or institution having lawful control or custody of him has not acquiesced.

Statutes should be construed to avoid strained, unreasonable or illogical results. *Blondheim v. State*, 84 Wash.2d 874, 879, 529 P.2d 1096 (1975). RCW 9A.04.020(2) states:

The provisions of [the Washington Criminal Code] shall be construed according to the fair import of their terms but when the language is susceptible of differing constructions it shall be interpreted to further the general purposes stated in this title.

RCW 9A.04.020(1) requires, moreover, that the provisions of the Washington Criminal Code be construed:

(a) To forbid and prevent conduct that inflicts or threatens substantial harm to individual or public interests;

Stubsjoen contends the evidence here was insufficient for conviction because the State did not prove she secreted or held the baby in a place where she was not likely to be found. She argues that virtually all of the time she had the child, they were in public areas where the child could easily be seen.

Responding to a similar argument to that at bar, the court in *State v. Missmer*, 72 Wash.2d 1022, 435 P.2d 638 (1967) was asked to construe the former kidnapping statute, RCW 9.52.010(2), which read in pertinent part:

Every person who shall wilfully,

* * *

(2) Lead, take, entice away or detain a child under the age of sixteen years with intent to conceal him from his . . . parents . . . shall be guilty of kidnaping in the second degree . . .

The defendant in *Missmer* enticed a 14–year-old girl into his automobile and drove around with her before being apprehended. Missmer argued that there was no evidence of concealment since it was not shown that the child was concealed from her parents because at all times he drove on main, well-traveled thoroughfares in and around the area.

The court held, however, that the State need only prove that the defendant enticed away or detained the child with the intent to conceal her from her parents, and that "the girl could have been as well concealed from her parents in [the] defendant's automobile traveling along one of our high-speed freeways as she could have been in a deserted cabin in the country." *Missmer*, at 1026, 435 P.2d 638.

Likewise, a reasonable interpretation of the current kidnap statute, which is consistent with its purpose, is that a child is abducted when held in areas or under circumstances where it is unlikely those persons directly affected by the victim's disappearance will find the child. Here, such persons were the child's parents, legal guardian or custodian, and law enforcement officers. Stubsjoen in effect concealed the child by acting as though the child was her own.

To adopt Stubsjoen's narrow interpretation of the kidnapping statute would mean that a young child could be taken without the acquiescence of the child's parents or legal guardian, and so long as the child was held in public places and transported in public conveyances such as airlines and buses, there would be no kidnapping within the meaning of the statute. Reasonable statutory interpretation forbids such strained and absurd results. It follows that the evidence here was sufficient to sustain Stubsjoen's conviction.

2. Kidnapping Must Be More Than Incidental to Other Crime

Many crimes involve a defendant restraining the liberty of a victim. While a defendant is robbing his victim, he is restraining his liberty for the period he is exercising force, or threatened force, over him to remove the property. A rapist obviously prevents his victim from leaving while he is committing this crime. The legislature has, however, prescribed penalties for these other crimes.

As part of reform effort in the late 1950s and early 1960s, many legislatures created two types of charges involving unlawfully detaining another. The lesser charge came to be known by a variety of names, such as unlawful restraint or false imprisonment. The *Salamon* case considers whether only the lesser version of the crime is appropriate when the detention that occurred was no more than necessary to commit another crime for which the legislature has provided for separate punishment.

State v. Salamon

Supreme Court of Connecticut
949 A.2d 1092 (2008)

PALMER, J.

A jury found the defendant, Scott Salamon, guilty of one count each of the crimes of kidnapping in the second degree in violation of General Statutes § 53a–94,[1] unlawful restraint in the first degree in violation of General Statutes § 53a–95,[2] and risk of injury to a child in violation of General Statutes (Rev. to

---

1   General Statutes § 53a–94 provides in relevant part: "(a) A person is guilty of kidnapping in the second degree when he abducts another person. . . ."

"'Abduct' means to restrain a person with intent to prevent his liberation by either (A) secreting or holding him in a place where he is not likely to be found, or (B) using or threatening to use physical force or intimidation." General Statutes § 53a–91 (2).

'Restrain' means to restrict a person's movements intentionally and unlawfully in such a manner as to interfere substantially with his liberty by moving him from one place to another, or by confining him either in the place where the restriction commences or in a place to which he has been moved, without consent. As used herein, 'without consent' means, but is not limited to, (A) deception and (B) any means whatever, including acquiescence of the victim, if he is a child less than sixteen years old or an incompetent person and the parent, guardian or other person or institution having lawful control or custody of him has not acquiesced in the movement or confinement." General Statutes § 53a–91 (1).

2   General Statutes § 53a–95 provides in relevant part: "(a) A person is guilty of unlawful restraint in the first degree when he restrains another person under circumstances which expose such other person to a substantial risk of physical injury. . . ."

2001) § 53–21(a)(1).[3] The trial court rendered judgment in accordance with the jury verdict, and the defendant appealed. . . .

The jury reasonably could have found the following facts. In the summer of 2002, the victim, a fifteen year old female, was visiting her aunt and uncle in Tuckahoe, New York. On July 3, 2002, the victim's aunt drove her to Bronx, New York, to visit with other relatives. The following evening, the victim boarded a train in New York, intending to return to the Tuckahoe residence of her aunt and uncle. While on the train, the victim fell asleep. When she awoke sometime between 9:30 and 10 p.m., she realized that she was in Connecticut and that she apparently had taken the wrong train. The victim disembarked the train in Stamford and began walking toward a stairwell in the direction of the main concourse. At that time, the victim noticed the defendant, who was watching her from a nearby platform. As the victim approached the stairwell, she observed that the defendant was following her. The defendant continued to follow the victim as she ascended the stairs. Before the victim reached the top of the stairs, the defendant caught up to her and grabbed her on the back of the neck, causing her to fall onto the steps. The victim, who had injured her elbow as a result of the fall, attempted to get up, but the defendant, who had positioned himself on the steps beside her, was holding her down by her hair. The victim screamed at the defendant to let her go. The defendant then punched the victim once in the mouth and attempted to thrust his fingers down her throat as she was screaming. Eventually, the victim was able to free herself from the defendant's grasp, and the defendant fled. Security personnel were summoned, and, shortly thereafter, the defendant was apprehended and arrested. At the time, the victim told a security guard that she thought that the defendant had been trying to rape her; later, however, the victim indicated that she did not know why the defendant had accosted her. According to the victim, the altercation with the defendant lasted at least five minutes.

On appeal, the defendant claims that his conviction of kidnapping in the second degree must be reversed because, contrary to controlling precedent, the jury should have been instructed to find the defendant not guilty of that charge if it first found that the defendant's restraint of the victim in connection with the kidnapping was incidental to the defendant's restraint of the victim in connection with his assault of the victim. . . .

---

3 General Statutes (Rev. to 2001) § 53–21(a) provides in relevant part: "Any person who (1) wilfully or unlawfully causes or permits any child under the age of sixteen years to be placed in such a situation that the life or limb of such child is endangered, the health of such child is likely to be injured or the morals of such child are likely to be impaired, or does any act likely to impair the health or morals of any such child . . . shall be guilty of a class C felony."

I.

The defendant maintains that our construction of this state's kidnapping statutes has been overly broad, thereby resulting in kidnapping convictions for conduct that the legislature did not contemplate would provide the basis for such convictions. He claims that the legislature did not intend for the enhanced penalties available upon conviction of kidnapping to apply when the restraint involved in the kidnapping is incidental to the commission of another crime or crimes. In support of his claims, the defendant contends: (1) the evolution of the common law predating our kidnapping statutes indicates that a narrower construction is warranted; (2) our prior decisions construing the kidnapping statutes appeared to recognize the propriety of that narrow interpretation, but we subsequently expanded the scope of the offense, without sound reason for doing so, to reflect the literal language of the kidnapping statutes; see footnote 6 of this opinion; (3) our current approach leads to absurd and unconscionable results when the restraint that provides the basis of the kidnapping charge constitutes the same restraint that a defendant necessarily uses to commit the primary, underlying offense; and (4) a significant majority of our sister states have rejected that literalist approach and, instead, have interpreted their kidnapping statutes in accordance with the construction that the defendant urges us to adopt. In response, the state asserts that the defendant has failed to offer cogent reasons for overruling established precedent that permits a conviction for kidnapping when the restraint involved in the commission of that offense is merely incidental to the commission of a separate, underlying offense against the victim. After careful consideration of the competing claims, we are persuaded by the defendant's arguments.

* * *

Kidnapping, a common-law misdemeanor, traditionally was defined as the forcible removal of another individual from the country. *See* W. LaFave, Substantive Criminal Law (2d Ed. 2003) § 18.1, p. 4; *see also* 4 W. Blackstone, *Commentaries on the Laws of England* (1769) p. 219. Early American statutes defining the crime retained the requirement of a boundary crossing but relaxed the requirement by proscribing the victim's forcible removal from the state. *See* note, "From Blackstone to *Innis*: A Judicial Search for a Definition of Kidnapping," 16 Suffolk U. L. Rev. 367, 368 (1982). Over time, however, the scope of proscribed behavior and the penalties attendant to a kidnapping conviction were broadened substantially by state legislatures. *See* W. LaFave, supra, § 18.1, pp. 4–5; *see also* note, "A Rationale of the Law of Kidnapping," 53 Colum. L. Rev. 540 (1953). In the early twentieth century, kidnappings for ransom had become increasingly common, and state lawmakers responded by amending kidnapping statutes to criminalize a wider range of conduct and to authorize more severe sentences upon conviction. *See* note, supra, 53 Colum. L. Rev. 540. This trend intensified in the wake of the highly publicized kidnapping and murder of the young son of famed aviator Charles Lindbergh in 1932 and the public outcry that followed. *See* W. LaFave, supra, § 18.1, p. 4. Among the evils that both the common law and later statutory prohibitions against kidnapping sought to address were the isolation of a victim from the protections of society and the law and the special fear and danger inherent in such isolation.

The evolution of Connecticut's kidnapping statutes tracks these developments. Prior to 1901, our kidnapping statute focused primarily on the unlawful removal of a person from the state, and carried a penalty of a fine and a relatively short period of imprisonment. *See* General Statutes (1887 Rev.) § 1416. In 1901, the definition of kidnapping was expanded to include intrastate abductions for the purpose of extracting ransom, and the maximum penalty was increased to thirty years imprisonment. *See* General Statutes (1902 Rev.) § 1162. In 1937, the statutory definition was broadened again to encompass most types of restriction of a victim's liberty, and the penalties available for a violation of the provision were among the most severe of any penal statute. *See* General Statutes (1949 Rev.) § 8372. Indeed, in cases resulting in the death of the kidnapping victim, the penalty was the same as the penalty for murder, even though the state was not required to prove that the death was either premeditated or the product of a specific intent to kill. *See* General Statutes (1949 Rev.) § 8372. If the victim survived, his kidnapper faced up to fifty years imprisonment. *See* General Statutes (1949 Rev.) § 8372.

Beginning in the 1950s, however, questions surfaced about the propriety of such expansively worded kidnapping statutes. In particular, concerns were expressed that the newly adopted kidnapping statutes permitted the imposition of extremely severe sanctions for abroad and ill defined range of behavior, including relatively trivial types of restraint. *See* W. LaFave, supra, § 18.1, pp. 4–5. Moreover, as one commentator noted, "virtually all conduct within the scope of kidnapping law [was] punishable under some other criminal provision: e.g., extortion, homicide, assault, rape, robbery, statutory rape, [and] contributing to the delinquency of a minor. . . . Consequently, the practical effect of kidnapping law [was] to permit the imposition of additional sanctions when one of [those] other crimes [was] accompanied by a detention and asportation." Note, supra, 53 Colum. L. Rev. 556.

These concerns prompted calls for legislative reform by the drafters of the Model Penal Code. As the drafters stated in the commentary to the proposed code, the goal was "to devise a proper system of grading to discriminate between simple false imprisonment and the more terrifying and dangerous abductions for ransom or other felonious purpose." Model Penal Code § 212. 1, comment 1, p. 11 (Tentative Draft No. 11, 1960). The drafters, noting that "[e]xamples of abusive prosecution for kidnapping [were] common," also sought "to restrict the scope of kidnapping, as an alternative or cumulative treatment of behavior whose chief significance is robbery or rape, because the broad scope of this overlapping offense has given rise to serious injustice. . . ." *Id.*, p. 13. The drafters advocated for statutory schemes that would "minimize opportunities for such injustice by clearly and rationally restricting [prosecutorial] discretion to punish." *Id.*, p. 15.

Contraction of the scope of kidnapping law also was effected through the courts. In the landmark case of *People v. Levy*, 15 N.Y.2d 159, 163–65, 204 N.E.2d 842, 256 N.Y.S.2d 793, cert. denied, 381 U.S. 938, 85 S.Ct. 1770, 14 L.Ed.2d 701 (1965), the New York Court of Appeals rejected a literal application of New York's broadly worded kidnapping statute to the detention and movement of two armed robbery victims during the course of the robbery. The court noted that the provision at issue, which defined kidnapping as "confin[ing] another with intent to cause him . . . to be confined against his will"; (internal quotation marks omitted) *id.*, at 164, 256 N.Y.S.2d 793, 204 N.E.2d 842; "could literally overrun several other crimes, notably robbery and rape, and in some circumstances assault, since detention and sometimes confinement, against the will of the victim, frequently accompany these crimes." *Id.* The court concluded that the legislature did not intend for "restraints, sometimes accompanied by asportation, which are incidents to other crimes and have long been treated as integral parts of other crimes . . . to constitute a separate crime of kidnapping, even though kidnapping might sometimes be spelled out literally from the statutory words." *Id.*; *see also People v. Lombardi*, 20 N.Y.2d 266, 270, 229 N.E.2d 206, 282 N.Y.S.2d 519 (1967) ("the direction of the criminal law has been to limit the scope of the kidnapping statute, with its very substantially more severe penal consequences, to true kidnapping situations and not to apply it to crimes which are essentially robbery, rape or assault and in which some confinement or asportation occurs as a subsidiary incident").

Soon thereafter, the Supreme Court of California, in *People v. Daniels*, 71 Cal.2d 1119, 459 P.2d 225, 80 Cal.Rptr. 897 (1969), a case involving a series of robberies and sexual assaults in which the victims had been forced to move short distances in the moments immediately preceding the commission of those crimes; *see id.*, at 1123–25, 80 Cal.Rptr. 897, 459 P.2d 225; followed the approach of the New York Court of Appeals in *Levy*. *Id.*, at 1134–36, 80 Cal.Rptr. 897, 459 P.2d 225. At the time, kidnapping was defined in the California Penal Code as "the act of one who forcibly steals, takes, or arrests any person in th[e] state, and carries him into another country, state, or county, or into another part of the same county." (Internal quotation marks omitted.) *Id.*, at 1126, 80 Cal.Rptr. 897, 459 P.2d 225. The court overruled its earlier, literal interpretation of the kidnapping provision in light of the contemporaneous "current of common sense in the construction and application of [kidnapping] statutes"; *id.*, at 1127, 80 Cal.Rptr. 897, 459 P.2d 225; and concluded that the statute did not apply to the defendants in that case because their movement of the victims was minimal and incidental to other crimes, that is, those movements were compelled solely to facilitate the commission of the sexual assaults and robberies. *Id.*, at 1130–31, 1134, 1140, 80 Cal.Rptr. 897, 459 P.2d 225. The court found support for its conclusion in the holdings of *Levy* and *Lombardi*, despite differences in the wording of New York's kidnapping statutes, because the reasoning of the New York Court of Appeals was persuasive and representative of the more enlightened, modern approach. *Id.*, at 1134–37, 80 Cal.Rptr. 897, 459 P.2d 225.

This state's current kidnapping statutes were drafted against the foregoing historical backdrop, and as part of a comprehensive revision of the criminal code that was approved by the legislature in 1969. Although the legislative debate surrounding the revision of the code did not focus on the kidnapping statutes, published commentary by the commission to revise the criminal statutes (commission) sheds light on the reasoning underlying the changes that were made to those statutory provisions. That commentary indicates that the commission intended to create a new statutory scheme that recognized varying degrees of unlawful restrictions on a victim's liberty by drawing a distinction between a "restraint," which, standing alone, comprises the crime of unlawful restraint, and an "abduction," which comprises the crime of kidnapping. The goal was to improve on the then-existing statute, which "put all the varying degrees of restriction of liberty under the one umbrella of kidnapping"; Commission to Revise the Criminal Statutes, Connecticut Penal Code Comments (1971) § 53a–91, p. 31, reprinted in 28A Conn. Gen.Stat. Ann. § 53a–91 (West 2007) p. 423; along with the attendant harsh penalties.

We note, finally, that when drafting the revised criminal code, the commission drew generally from comparable provisions of New York's Revised Penal Law and the Model Penal Code. Commission to Revise the Criminal Statutes, supra, tit. 53a, p. 1, reprinted in 28 Conn. Gen.Stat. Ann. tit. 53a (West 2007) p. 289. Overall, the commission sought to create a code that met certain standards: "that it be rational, coherent, cohesive and intelligible; that it take into account modern knowledge and information; that it be based on reason and experience; and that it reflect an enlightened and informed outlook." Commission to Revise the Criminal Statutes, Proposed Connecticut Penal Code (1969) p. 7.

Upon examination of the common law of kidnapping, the history and circumstances surrounding the promulgation of our current kidnapping statutes and the policy objectives animating those statutes, we now conclude the following: Our legislature, in replacing a single, broadly worded kidnapping provision with a gradated scheme that distinguishes kidnappings from unlawful restraints by the presence of an intent to prevent a victim's liberation, intended to exclude from the scope of the more serious crime of kidnapping and its accompanying severe penalties those confinements or movements of a victim that are merely incidental to and necessary for the commission of another crime against that victim. Stated otherwise, to commit a kidnapping in conjunction with another crime, a defendant must intend to prevent the victim's liberation for a longer period of time or to a greater degree than that which is necessary to commit the other crime.

* * *

Our failure previously to recognize such an exclusion largely has eliminated the distinction between restraints and abductions and effectively has merged the statutory scheme such that it now closely resembles the provision that the scheme was intended to replace. Unfortunately, that interpretation has afforded prosecutors virtually unbridled discretion to charge the same conduct either as a kidnapping or as an unlawful restraint despite the significant differences in the penalties that attach to those offenses. Similarly, our prior construction of the kidnapping statutes has permitted prosecutors—indeed, it has encouraged them—to include a kidnapping charge in any case involving a sexual assault or robbery. In view of the trend favoring reform of the law of kidnapping that existed at the time that our statutes were enacted, and in light of the commission's stated goal of creating a modern, informed and enlightened penal code, it is highly likely that our legislature intended to embrace that reform, thereby reducing the potential for unfairness that had been created under this state's prior kidnapping statutes.

Our conclusion is bolstered by the fact that, in the years since *Levy* and *Daniels*, a considerable majority of state courts have followed the lead of New York and California in concluding that the crime of kidnapping does not include conduct involving a restraint that is merely incidental to the commission of some other crime against the victim. See, e.g., *Patzka v. State*, 348 So.2d 520, 523–24 (Ala.Crim.App.1977); *Alam v. State*, 776 P.2d 345, 349 (Alaska App.1989); *Summerlin v. State*, 296 Ark. 347, 350–51, 756 S.W.2d 908 (1988); *People v. Daniels*, supra, 71 Cal.2d at 1130–31, 1134, 80 Cal.Rptr. 897, 459 P.2d 225; *People v. Bridges*, 199 Colo. 520, 528–29, 612 P.2d 1110 (1980); *Tyre v. State*, 412 A.2d 326, 329 n. 5 (Del.1980); *Faison v. State*, 426 So.2d 963, 966 (Fla.1983); *State v. Correa*, 5 Haw. App. 644, 649, 706 P.2d 1321, cert. denied, 68 Haw. 692 (1985); *People v. Cole*, 172 Ill.2d 85, 104, 216 Ill.Dec. 718, 665 N.E.2d 1275, cert. denied, 519 U.S. 1030, 117 S.Ct. 587, 136 L.Ed.2d 517 (1996); *State v. Rich*, 305 N.W.2d 739, 745 (Iowa 1981);

State v. Buggs, 219 Kan. 203, 216, 547 P.2d 720 (1976); *Spencer v. Commonwealth*, 554 S.W.2d 355, 358 (Ky.1977); *State v. Estes*, 418 A.2d 1108, 1113 (Me.1980); *State v. Stouffer*, 352 Md. 97, 112–13, 721 A.2d 207 (1998); *People v. Adams*, 389 Mich. 222, 238, 205 N.W.2d 415 (1973); *State v. Smith*, 669 N.W.2d 19, 32 (Minn.2003); *Cuevas v. State*, 338 So.2d 1236, 1238 (Miss.1976); *State v. Shelton*, 78 S.W.3d 200, 204 (Mo.App.2002); *Wright v. State*, 94 Nev. 415, 417–18, 581 P.2d 442 (1978); *State v. Masino*, 94 N.J. 436, 447, 466 A.2d 955 (1983); *People v. Levy*, supra, 15 N.Y.2d at 164, 256 N.Y.S.2d 793, 204 N.E.2d 842; *State v. Fulcher*, 294 N.C. 503, 523, 243 S.E.2d 338 (1978); *State v. Logan*, 60 Ohio St.2d 126, 135, 397 N.E.2d 1345 (1979); *State v. Garcia*, 288 Or. 413, 423, 605 P.2d 671 (1980); *Commonwealth v. Hughes*, 264 Pa.Super. 118, 125, 399 A.2d 694 (1979); *State v. Innis*, 433 A.2d 646, 655 (R.I.1981), cert. denied, 456 U.S. 930, 102 S.Ct. 1980, 72 L.Ed.2d 447 (1982); *State v. St. Cloud*, 465 N.W.2d 177, 181 (S.D.1991); *State v. Anthony*, 817 S.W.2d 299, 306 (Tenn.1991); *State v. Goodhue*, 175 Vt. 457, 465–66, 833 A.2d 861 (2003); *Brown v. Commonwealth*, 230 Va. 310, 314, 337 S.E.2d 711 (1985); *State v. Miller*, 175 W.Va. 616, 621, 336 S.E.2d 910 (1985).[30] Although these cases involve varying statutory language and analyses, they share a common theme, namely, that it is unlikely that the legislature intended to expose an accused to a kidnapping conviction, and the severe sanctions accompanying such a conviction, when the restraint involved is merely incidental to the commission of a separate, underlying crime. Indeed, this majority view regarding the construction of statutes delineating the crime of kidnapping rightly has been characterized as the "modern" approach; *State v. DeJesus*, 91 Conn.App. 47, 87, 880 A.2d 910 (2005), cert. granted, 279 Conn. 912, 903 A.2d 658 (2006); see *State v. Goodhue*, supra, at 462–63, 833 A.2d 861; the salutary effect of which is to prevent the prosecution of a defendant "on a kidnapping charge in order to expose him to the heavier penalty thereby made available, [when] the period of abduction was brief, the criminal enterprise in its entirety appeared as no more than an offense of robbery or rape, and there was lacking a genuine 'kidnapping' flavor. . . ." (Citation omitted.) *People v. Cassidy*, 40 N.Y.2d 763, 765–66, 358 N.E.2d 870, 390 N.Y.S.2d 45 (1976).

Our holding does not represent a complete refutation of the principles established by our prior kidnapping jurisprudence. First, in order to establish a kidnapping, the state is not required to establish any minimum period of confinement or degree of movement. When that confinement or movement is merely incidental to the commission of another crime, however, the confinement or movement

---

30 A minority of jurisdictions adhere to the view that any movement or confinement of a victim is sufficient to support a kidnapping conviction. See, e.g., *State v. Padilla*, 106 Ariz. 230, 232, 474 P.2d 821 (1970); *Ellis v. State*, 211 Ga.App. 605, 608, 440 S.E.2d 235 (1994); *Wilson v. State*, 253 Ind. 585, 592, 255 N.E.2d 817 (1970); *State v. Smith*, 228 Mont. 258, 263–64, 742 P.2d 451 (1987); *State v. Maeder*, 229 Neb. 568, 572–73, 428 N.W.2d 180 (1988); *State v. Motsko*, 261 N.W.2d 860, 865–67 (N.D.1977); *Hines v. State*, 75 S.W.3d 444, 447–48 (Tex.Crim. App.2002); *Harris v. State*, 78 Wis.2d 357, 366–67, 254 N.W.2d 291 (1977).

must have exceeded that which was necessary to commit the other crime. "[T]he guiding principle is whether the [confinement or movement] was so much the part of another substantive crime that the substantive crime could not have been committed without such acts. . . ." (Internal quotation marks omitted.) *State v. Niemeyer*, 258 Conn. 510, 528, 782 A.2d 658 (2001) (*McDonald, C.J.*, concurring). In other words, "the test . . . to determine whether [the] confinements or movements involved [were] such that kidnapping may also be charged and prosecuted when an offense separate from kidnapping has occurred asks whether the confinement, movement, or detention was merely incidental to the accompanying felony or whether it was significant enough, in and of itself, to warrant independent prosecution." *State v. Goodhue*, supra, 175 Vt. at 464, 833 A.2d 861.

Conversely, a defendant may be convicted of both kidnapping and another substantive crime if, at any time prior to, during or after the commission of that other crime, the victim is moved or confined in a way that has independent criminal significance, that is, the victim was restrained to an extent exceeding that which was necessary to accomplish or complete the other crime. Whether the movement or confinement of the victim is merely incidental to and necessary for another crime will depend on the particular facts and circumstances of each case. Consequently, when the evidence reasonably supports a finding that the restraint was not merely incidental to the commission of some other, separate crime, the ultimate factual determination must be made by the jury. For purposes of making that determination, the jury should be instructed to consider the various relevant factors, including the nature and duration of the victim's movement or confinement by the defendant, whether that movement or confinement occurred during the commission of the separate offense, whether the restraint was inherent in the nature of the separate offense, whether the restraint prevented the victim from summoning assistance, whether the restraint reduced the defendant's risk of detection and whether the restraint created a significant danger or increased the victim's risk of harm independent of that posed by the separate offense. See, e.g., *Virgin Islands v. Berry*, 604 F.2d 221, 227 (3d Cir.1979); *Mendoza v. State*, 122 Nev. 267, 130 P.3d 176, 181 (2006); *State v. LaFrance*, 117 N.J. 583, 588, 569 A.2d 1308 (1990); *State v. Goodhue*, supra, 175 Vt. at 463–64, 833 A.2d 861.

Second, we do not retreat from the general principle that an accused may be charged with and convicted of more than one crime arising out of the same act or acts, as long as all of the elements of each crime are proven. Indeed, because the confinement or movement of a victim that occurs simultaneously with or incidental to the commission of another crime ordinarily will constitute a substantial interference with that victim's liberty, such restraints still may be prosecuted under the unlawful restraint statutes. Undoubtedly, many crimes involving restraints already are prosecuted under those provisions. Moreover, our holding is relatively narrow and directly affects only those cases in which the state cannot establish that the restraint involved had independent significance as the predicate conduct for a kidnapping. We therefore do not anticipate that our holding will force a major shift in prosecutorial decision making.

Finally, in the present case, the defendant claims that he is entitled to a judgment of acquittal on the kidnapping count. The defendant contends that, in light of the evidence adduced at trial, no juror reasonably could conclude that the restraint imposed on the victim was not incidental to the restraint used in connection with the assault of the victim. We disagree.

The evidence established that the defendant came up to the victim from behind her and, while she was walking up a staircase, grabbed her by the back of the neck. The victim fell to the floor, and the defendant held her there. She struggled to free herself from the defendant's grasp and screamed for him to let her go. The defendant continued to hold her down, however, and, when she persisted in screaming and fighting to extricate herself, he punched her once in the mouth and attempted to thrust his fingers down her throat. According to the victim, the defendant forced her to remain on the ground for at least five minutes before she was able to get away.

On the basis of these facts, a juror reasonably could find that the defendant's restraint of the victim was not merely incidental to his assault of the victim. The victim testified that the defendant, after accosting her, forcibly held her down for five minutes or more. Although the defendant punched the victim once and shoved his fingers into her mouth, that conduct was very brief in contrast to the extended duration of the defendant's restraint of the victim. In light of the evidence, moreover, a juror reasonably could find that the defendant pulled the victim to the ground primarily for the purpose of restraining her, and that he struck her and put his fingers in her mouth in an effort to subdue her and to prevent her from screaming for help so that she could not escape.[34] In such cir-

---

34 We acknowledge that it is not clear from the evidence why the defendant accosted and restrained the victim. Nevertheless, on the basis of the evidence presented, a juror reasonably could conclude that the defendant's restraint of the victim was not incidental to his assault of the victim. In other words, a juror reasonably could find that the restraint had significance independent of the assault. The facts of this case, therefore, are readily distinguishable from the facts of other cases in which the restraint imposed on the victim was merely incidental to an underlying crime. For example, in *State v. Sanseverino*, 287 Conn. 608, 949 A.2d 1156 (2008), a case that we also decide today, the defendant, Paolino Sanseverino, the owner of a bakery, followed one of his victims, G, his employee, into a back room of the bakery, where she had gone to retrieve an apron. *Id.*, at 615, 949 A.2d 1167. While alone with G, Sanseverino grabbed G, pushed her against the wall and sexually assaulted her. *Id.* Sanseverino then let G go, and she went into a bathroom and did not come out until she heard another person enter the bakery. *Id.* G then finished her shift and went home. *Id.* After a jury trial, Sanseverino was convicted of kidnapping in the first degree and sexual assault in the first degree. *Id.*, at 616–17, 949 A.2d 1159. Upon application of the rule that we adopt in the present case, we concluded that there was no evidence that Sanseverino had restrained G to any degree or for any period of time greater than that necessary to commit the sexual assault. *Id.*, at 625, 949 A.2d 1167. We therefore concluded that, because no reasonable juror could find that the restraint Sanseverino had imposed on G was not incidental to the commission of the sexual assault against G, Sanseverino

cumstances, we cannot say that the defendant's restraint of the victim necessarily was incidental to his assault of the victim. Whether the defendant's conduct constituted a kidnapping, therefore, is a factual question for determination by a properly instructed jury. For the foregoing reasons, we conclude that the defendant is entitled to a new trial on the charge of kidnapping in the second degree. Furthermore, the jury must be instructed that, if it finds that the defendant's restraint of the victim was merely incidental to the defendant's commission of another crime against the victim, that is, assault, then it must find the defendant not guilty of the crime of kidnapping.[35]

Notes and Questions

1. A common theme in academic commentary on criminal law is overcriminalization—essentially that legislatures have created criminal statutes that cover a wide range range of conduct and carry substantial penalties, giving prosecutors enormous power to threaten severe penalties and thereby obtain plea bargains for penalties that the prosecutors themselves regard as reasonable. *See, e.g.,* William J. Stuntz, *The Pathological Politics of Criminal Justice,* 100 Mich. L. Rev. 505 (2001). The Connecticut court's response to its own previous interpretation of the Connecticut kidnapping statute suggests that the story is somewhat more complicated. As the court noted, Connecticut is far from alone in constricting the scope of the kidnapping statute. The Connecticut Supreme Court was quite explicit in the policy justifying this modification, noting that the previously broad interpretation had afforded prosecutors virtually unbridled discretion to charge the same conduct either as a kidnapping or as an unlawful restraint despite the significant differences in the penalties

---

was entitled to a judgment of acquittal on the kidnapping charge. *See id.* In the present case, by contrast, we cannot say that the evidence requires the conclusion that the defendant restrained the victim solely for the purpose of assaulting her; indeed, a juror reasonably could find that the assaultive conduct in which the defendant engaged was merely incidental to his restraint of the victim.

35 As we noted previously, the defendant ultimately was not tried for assault. We nevertheless conclude that a defendant is entitled to an instruction that he cannot be convicted of kidnapping if the restraint imposed on the victim was merely incidental to the assault, regardless of whether the state elects to try the defendant for assault, because the facts reasonably would support an assault conviction. See, e.g., *Alam v. State,* supra, 776 P.2d at 350 (concluding restraint at issue was incidental to uncharged attempted sexual assault); *People v. Rappuhn,* 78 Mich.App. 348, 354, 260 N.W.2d 90 (1977) (court improperly failed to give incidental instruction with reference to uncharged offense of gross indecency); *People v. Jackson,* 63 A.D.2d 1032, 1032, 406 N.Y.S.2d 345 (1978) (concluding detention of complainant was incidental to commission of uncharged crime of rape). But cf. *People v. Robbins,* 131 Mich.App. 429, 433, 346 N.W.2d 333 (1984) (when no evidence of any other crime, incidental instruction unnecessary). To conclude otherwise would give the state carte blanche to deprive the defendant of the benefit of such an instruction merely by declining to charge him with the underlying crime, which, as in the present case, generally will carry a far less serious maximum possible penalty than the kidnapping charge.

that attach to those offenses: "Similarly, our prior construction of the kidnapping statutes has permitted prosecutors—indeed it has encouraged them—to include a kidnapping charge in any case involving sexual assault or robbery."

2. There are at thus least exceptions to the oft-told tale of unchecked overcriminalization. As the opinion observed, the overwhelming majority of jurisdictions forbid a kidnapping count when the abduction is merely incidental to another crime. Appellate courts are thus, at least in some areas, responding to a legislature transferring power to prosecutors to greatly enhance sentences, or extract pleas.

3. The dissent, which was not reproduced here given the length of the majority opinion, contended that the majority's holding "invades the province of our state's attorneys" and "appears to overlook that defining crimes is the responsibility of the legislature." The majority, in a footnote not reproduced above, quite predictably, contended that it was merely adhering to the legislative intent to create a meaningful distinction between kidnapping and unlawful restraint. The court's willingness to police this boundary between these crimes should have struck you as anomalous. Consider the boundary between first- and second-degree murder, or even Justice Zinter's dissent in *Disanto* (p. 819) in which he trusted juries to police the line between attempt and solicitation of murder. Additionally, this case—and the *trend* of state court to limit the scope of kidnapping –should have struck you as inconsistent with Justice Thurgood Marshall's opinion in *Batchelder* (p. 102) which, on the basis of separation of powers, permitted prosecutors the option of charging defendants under the greater or lesser of two identical weapons crimes. In response, the majority argues that it is demonstrating fidelity to the legislature's intent to create degrees of kidnapping. Who has the better end of this argument?

4. The power a kidnapping charge gave a prosecutor, prior to this decision, over a defendant was quite similar to the power Kentucky's three-strikes law gave the prosecutor over Paul Hayes in *Bordenkircher v. Hayes*. As the Connecticut Supreme Court observed in an omitted footnote, kidnapping carries more severe penalties than the crimes of assault, sexual assault, and robbery. This fact is made even more problematic when one considers that judges have virtually unbridled discretion to sentence defendants to concurrent or consecutive terms when there are multiple convictions. Thus, if a prosecutor knows he is in front of a particularly tough sentencing judge, he can effectively threaten to more than double the defendant's sentence in an ordinary robbery case unless he acquiesces to the maximum penalty the legislature prescribed for robbery.

5. Notice that the court in this case is not, however, itself guarding against over-charging. The court is instructing juries to determine whether the act of kidnapping is merely incidental to another crime.

6. This case should strike you as a fairly radical departure from the way appellate courts have been viewing criminal cases. The court observes in footnote 35 that prosecutors do not have the option of charging the defendant with either the kidnapping or the crime to which the kidnapping is incidental. A prosecutor may not, that is, charge kidnapping but not assault because "this would give the state carte blanche to deprive the defendant of [the instruction forbidding a kidnapping conviction when the act is merely incidental to another crime] by declining to charge him with the underlying crime, which, as in the present case, generally will carry a far less serious maximum possible penalty than the kidnapping charge." Recall that *Batchelder* permitted a prosecutor to elect among *identical* provisions with different punishments.

7. In case you think the quality of argument in appellate courts does not affect outcomes, this case provides a strong counterpoint, if the court is accurately describing its motivations. The court observed that it had never "undertaken an extensive analysis of whether our kidnapping statutes warrant the broad construction that we have given them." By contrast, the court observed "that the parties to the present appeal have thoroughly and thoughtfully briefed this issues, [affording] us the opportunity to conduct a more searching examination of the merits of that issue than we previously have undertaken."

8. Isn't there something ultimately unsatisfactory about the court's limitation on incidental kidnapping prosecutions? The court observes that under Connecticut law, kidnapping is punished more severely than sexual assault. There is, however, no particular time period required for kidnapping. If the kidnapping is no longer than necessary to commit sexual assault, for instance, the jury is to acquit the defendant of kidnapping. But what if the defendant did nothing other detain his victim long enough that he *could* have sexual assaulted her, but did not actually do so? The defendant who holds his victim for a brief period, contemplating raping her, but turns her loose can be convicted of kidnapping her, which carries a greater penalty than sexual assault. But if actually sexually assaults her and does not detain her beyond the period of the assault, he is liable only for the less-severely punished crime of sexual assault.

PLEA BARGAINING EXERCISE

Instructions

You will be paired with another student. You will both read the statement of the case. Your instructor will provide each side with confidential facts. One will be a defense attorney, accessing only the defense attorney's confidential facts. The other will be a prosecutor, accessing only the prosecutor's confidential facts. You will have ten minutes for this negotiation.

Statement of the Case

The indictment reads in relevant part (in italics):

[Section 130 reads as follows and refers only to Sections 130.1-3 as "this Part":

It shall not be a violation of this part if any violation of this part is incidental to a violation not in this part.]

Section 130.1 First Degree Kidnapping
Abella violated section 130.1 when she knowingly carried Bruce, age 5, and Cindy, age 7, away to City Park against the will and knowledge of Erika, the mother of Bruce and Cindy. Witnesses at the park saw Abella leash Bruce and Cindy and walk them about "like dogs."

[Section 130.1 reads as follows:

A) Any person who takes or carries away any other person against that person's will is guilty of First Degree Kidnapping.

B) A violation of this section carries a minimum penalty of 10 years imprisonment.]

Section 130.2 Unlawful Restraint
Abella violated section 130.2 when she knowingly used force to restrain Bruce and Cindy by using various straps and the leashes to prevent their escape against the will of Erika.

[Section 130.2 reads as follows:

A) Any person who unlawfully restrains or confines any person in any manner against that person's will is guilty of Unlawful Restraint.

B) A violation of this section carries a mandatory penalty of 5 years.]

[The relevant authority in your jurisdiction will soon decide whether Unlawful Restraint is a lesser included offense of First Degree Kidnapping, in the case *In re Carried Away*. The decision could be published at any time.]

> Section 130.3 Custodial Interference
> *Abella knowingly and willfully interfered with Erika's custody of her children Billy and Cindy when she carried Bruce and Cindy away to City Park.*

[Section 130.3 reads as follows:

A) Any person who interferes with the rightful custody of a parent or legal guardian over a child is guilty of Custodial Interference.

B) A violation of this section carries a maximum penalty of 1 year imprisonment or 2 years of community service.]

[The authority in your jurisdiction has decided that Custodial Interference is not a lesser included offense of First Degree Kidnapping in the case *In re Past Interference*.]

---

3. Attempts

To show an attempt, the prosecution must demonstrate both proximity and intent.

There have been a few varieties of standards used to determine whether a defendant has come close enough to completing the prohibited conduct to be convicted. One test, which has never been used, is the "last proximate act" test. While no jurisdiction requires this test for an attempt, when the defendant has taken the last proximate step, it is hard to argue that he has not attempted the crime. This was the argument made by Justices Gilbertson and Zinter in the *Disanto* murder-for-hire case (p. 802). Other courts have asked whether the crime would continue to fruition absent some sort of intervening act. Still other courts ask whether the actions taken demonstrate the defendant's unequivocal intent to go forward with the criminal act. Finally, there is the Model Penal Code's test that requires a substantial step that is "strongly corroborative of the actor's criminal purpose." None of these tests, with the exception of the "last proximate act" test, provide much in the way of clarity, but the purpose of the new MPC test was to allow a conviction with less proximity than the previous tests.

For attempts (with very few exceptions noted in the discussion on homicide) the defendant must have the conscious desire to complete the attempted crime.

The first case we consider in this section, *Laster*, considers whether there is adequate proof to demonstrate an attempted kidnapping. The second case, *Sweigert*, looks at whether the defendant's has come close enough to completing the crime of attempted luring a child (a version of kidnapping relaxing the proximity requirement of ordinary kidnapping).

Laster v. State

Texas Court of Criminal Appeals
275 S.W.3d 512 (2008)

KEASLER, J., delivered the opinion of the Court in which KELLER, P.J., MEYERS, WOMACK, and HERVEY, JJ., joined.

I. BACKGROUND

After buying eggs for their mother at a convenience store on January 30, 2005, B.T., who was eight, and her brother, who was ten, began to walk home. While walking on the sidewalk, B.T. pushed a bicycle, and her brother walked beside her. The children saw a man, carrying a closed umbrella, walking toward them. To allow the man to pass, the children leaned against a fence next to the sidewalk. Instead of passing by, the man grabbed B.T.'s arm. The man then put his arm around B.T.'s waist and tried to pull her away. B.T. let go of the bicycle and yelled for help. Her brother grabbed her hand, and a tug of war over B.T. ensued. The man abruptly let go of B.T. when a driver honked the car's horn. The man then continued to walk down the sidewalk toward the store. The children ran home and told their mother that a man tried to take B.T.

B.T.'s mother reported the incident to the police. Later that day, B.T.'s mother saw a man walking down the street. The man, Tommy G. Laster, looked like the man that B.T. had described to the police. B.T.'s mother called the police and continued to follow Laster. The police arrived and arrested Laster based, in part, on the children identifying him as the man who grabbed and pulled B.T. After the police arrested Laster, he gave a written statement describing what happened:

> While [the children] were coming toward me, the voices in my head started telling me that I would be better off dead. As I got closer to the kids and I was watching them, the voices in my head told me to grab the little girl. The voices were telling me to "Get her, get her." I grabbed her using my right arm around her waist. I saw her long hair and the side of her face. I also saw the little boy next to her. That is when I realized that I needed to let go of her because she was a little girl and I knew how that would look to the cars going by. I was thinking to myself, "Did I actually grab her in the broad daylight with all of this traffic[?] I must be nuts." She looked at me. She looked scared and wide eyed. I let her go and hurried my pace to get to the store. . . .

Laster was charged with injury to a child and attempted aggravated kidnapping. The jury convicted him of both counts, and the trial judge sentenced Laster to twenty years' confinement for injuring a child and forty years' confinement for attempting to kidnap B.T.

* * *

B. APPLICABLE LAW

To prove that Laster committed the offense of attempted aggravated kidnapping, the State was required to present sufficient evidence that Laster did "an act amounting to more than mere preparation" with the specific intent to commit aggravated kidnapping. A person commits the offense of aggravated kidnapping if "he intentionally or knowingly abducts another person" and commits an aggravating element. Thus, two elements are required to prove aggravated kidnapping: (1) intent or knowledge to abduct, and (2) commission of an aggravating element.

"'Abduct' means to restrain a person with intent to prevent his liberation by: (A) secreting or holding him in a place where he is not likely to be found; or (B) using or threatening to use deadly force." "Abduct" then includes two elements. First, the defendant must have restrained another, which is the *actus reus* requirement. Second, the defendant must have had the specific intent to prevent liberation, which is the *mens rea* requirement. Secreting or holding another where he or she is unlikely to be found is part of the *mens rea* requirement of the offense—not the *actus reus*. This is an important distinction because the State is not required to prove that the defendant actually secreted or held another. Instead the State must prove that the defendant restrained another with the specific intent to prevent liberation by secreting or holding the person. The offense of kidnapping is legally completed when the defendant, at any time during the restraint, forms the intent to prevent liberation by secreting or holding another in a place unlikely to be found.

A kidnapping is aggravated when a defendant intentionally or knowingly abducts another: (1) with the specific intent to accomplish one of six purposes or (2) "uses or exhibits a deadly weapon during the commission of the offense." The six purposes are as follows:

(1) hold him for ransom or reward;

(2) use him as a shield or hostage;

(3) facilitate the commission of a felony or the flight after the attempt or commission of a felony;

(4) inflict bodily injury on him or violate or abuse him sexually;

(5) terrorize him or a third person; or

(6) interfere with the performance of any governmental or political function.

Here, the State was required to prove that Laster committed an act beyond mere preparation with the intent to secrete or hold B.T. and commit an aggravating element—not that Laster could, or did, actually accomplish this purpose.

C. LEGAL SUFFICIENCY REVIEW

Laster argues that the evidence presented at trial was legally insufficient to support the jury's finding that he intended to hold or secrete B.T. in a place where she was unlikely to be found. We disagree.

In support of his conclusion, Laster points to three circumstances that he contends show that he had no such intent. We will consider each of these arguments in turn.

First, Laster suggests that the State did not prove that he intended to take B.T. because he grabbed her in front of possible eyewitnesses. But the State did not have to prove that he actually accomplished his purpose or even that he could have accomplished his purpose. The State only had to prove that he had such a purpose. Further, as the court of appeals noted, the jury was not precluded from inferring that Laster intended to secrete or hold B.T. in a place where she was unlikely to be found simply because he restrained her in public. We have recognized that a rational factfinder can infer such an intent when a defendant isolates a person from anyone who might be of assistance. B.T. testified that Laster grabbed her around the waist then tried to pull her away. Corroborating B.T.'s testimony, her brother stated that when Laster tried to pull B.T. away, he grabbed her arm and pulled back. The jury could reasonably infer from this testimony that by pulling B.T. away from her brother, the only person available to help her, Laster intended to hold or secrete B.T. in a place where she was unlikely to be found.

... Laster argues that there are other reasonable explanations for why he grabbed B.T. For example, he wanted to steal her bicycle or sexually abuse her. Without proof that one explanation was more reasonable than another, Laster contends ... that the evidence was insufficient. But this reasoning invades the factfinder's role. It is up to the factfinder to "resolve conflicts in the testimony, to weigh the evidence, and to draw reasonable inferences from basic facts to ultimate facts." By focusing on other reasonable alternatives to explain why Laster grabbed B.T., Justice Dauphinot improperly applied the outdated reasonable hypothesis construct, thereby placing herself in the "posture of a 'thirteenth juror.'" As long as the verdict is supported by a reasonable inference, it is within the province of the factfinder to choose which inference is most reasonable. As stated above, the evidence showed that Laster grabbed and then pulled B.T. toward him. Laster continued to pull B.T. after her brother came to her aid. It was not until a driver honked the car's horn that Laster released B.T. A factfinder could reasonably infer from this evidence that Laster was planning to do more than just steal her bike or molest her.

Finally, Laster argues that the evidence showed that he intended only to grab B.T. because his confession did not imply otherwise and he let go of her within a matter of seconds. Contrary to Laster's claim that there is only one interpretation of his confession, there is another rational interpretation. Laster not only said that the voices in his head were telling him to "grab the little girl," but they were also telling him to "'[g]et her, get her.'" He confessed to restraining B.T. until he "saw the little boy next to her" and realized that he "needed to let go of her because she was a little girl and [he] knew how that would look to the cars going by." Even if this evidence was believed, a rational factfinder could infer that Laster formed the intent to take B.T. when he grabbed her and abandoned his plan when he realized that other people were witnessing his actions. Indeed, the evidence presented at trial showed that Laster released B.T. when a driver honked the car's horn. Rather than concluding that Laster released B.T. because he just wanted to grab her, viewed in the light most favorable to the verdict, the evidence showed that Laster formed the intent to take B.T. when he grabbed her and let go because he feared that he may be caught.

* * *

Next, although Laster does not claim that the evidence supporting the aggravating element is insufficient, Judge Cochran claims that it is. But the jury could reasonably infer from Laster's actions that he intended to inflict bodily injury on B.T. Bodily injury is broadly defined in the Penal Code as "physical pain, illness, or any impairment of physical conduction." This definition encompasses even relatively minor physical contact if it constitutes more than offensive touching. Direct evidence that a victim suffered pain is sufficient to show bodily injury. B.T. testified that she felt pain when Laster grabbed her around the waist and pulled her. Because "[o]ne's acts are generally reliable circumstantial evidence of one's intent," the jury could reasonably infer that Laster intended to do exactly what he did—to inflict bodily injury on B.T.

Given the evidence presented at trial, a rational trier of fact, charged with discerning Laster's intent from the surrounding circumstances, could have found beyond a reasonable doubt that Laster intended to inflict bodily injury on B.T. and hold or secrete her in a place she was unlikely to be found. Affording appropriate deference to the jury's verdict, we therefore hold that the evidence supporting Laster's conviction is legally sufficient.

* * *

COCHRAN, J., filed a dissenting opinion in which PRICE, JOHNSON and HOLCOMB, JJ., joined.

I respectfully dissent. I do not agree with the majority of the court of appeals that a rational trier of fact could conclude from the evidence in this case, beyond a reasonable doubt, that appellant (1) had a specific intent to hold or secrete eight-year-old Beatrice in a place where she was unlikely to be found, much less (2) had a specific intent to perform one of the other acts—such as holding her for ransom, using her as a shield, inflicting bodily injury on her or abusing her sexually—that is required for aggravated kidnapping. This is not an attempted kidnapping case. And it is certainly not an attempted aggravated kidnapping case. This is an unlawful restraint case.

I.

A person commits unlawful restraint "if he intentionally or knowingly restrains another person." Restrain means "to restrict a person's movements without consent, so as to interfere substantially with the person's liberty, by moving the person from one place to another or by confining the person." Restraint is "without consent" if "the victim is a child who is less than 14 years of age" and "the parent, guardian, or person or institution acting in loco parentis has not acquiesced in the movement or confinement."

A person commits kidnapping if he "intentionally or knowingly abducts another person." Abduct means "to restrain a person with intent to prevent his liberation by: (A) secreting or holding him in a place where he is not likely to be found; or (B) using or threatening to use deadly force." As noted by the majority, the offense of kidnapping is legally completed when the defendant, at any time during the restraint, forms the intent to prevent liberation by secreting or holding another in a place unlikely to be found.

A person commits aggravated kidnapping if he abducts another person with a further or second specific intent to

(1) hold him for ransom or reward;

(2) use him as a shield or hostage;

(3) facilitate the commission of a felony or the flight after the attempt or commission of a felony;

(4) inflict bodily injury on him or violate or abuse him sexually;

(5) terrorize him or a third person; or

(6) interfere with the performance of any governmental or political function.

A person commits the crime of attempted aggravated kidnapping only if, acting with the specific intent both to abduct another person *and* to hold her for one of the six purposes set out above, he does an act—such as grabbing a child—that amounts to more than mere preparation and that tends, but fails, to effect the commission of the aggravated kidnapping.

But not every grabbing or illegal restraint of a stranger—child or adult—evinces an intent to kidnap.[10] And certainly not every grabbing of a stranger evinces an intent to hold her for ransom, use her as a shield, facilitate the commission of some felony, inflict bodily injury, sexually abuse her or commit one of the other enumerated acts as is required for attempted aggravated kidnapping. Because criminal attempt is an inchoate crime, one that has not actually occurred, the defendant's acts, words, and the attendant circumstances of the attempt should be "strongly corroborative of the actor's criminal purpose." Inchoate crimes balance the goals of law enforcement with the liberty rights of citizens by ensuring that law enforcement may intervene to prevent crime, but only after the actor has formed a specific criminal purpose and has engaged in adequate conduct in furtherance of that specific intent to demonstrate that, if left to his own devices, the attempted crime would likely occur.[11]

---

10 *See Vandiver v. State*, 97 Okla.Crim. 217, 261 P.2d 617, 624 (App.1953) (overruled on other grounds) ("Would the mere fact that the defendant took Mrs. Bridges in his arms and was therefore guilty of assault, force the conclusion *ipso facto* that he was going to kidnap her, (which means to take secretly, confine her against her will) any more than that he was going to murder her there on the spot, or take her for a wild ride in his car, or just sit with her in the car? There was no evidence direct or circumstantial of what the intentions of the defendant were beyond holding Mrs. Bridges in his arms, other than his statement that he asked her to go get a bottle of beer. There are many possible ideas that may have been in his mind. But more than speculation is required. We have sought in vain for evidence to support the judgment, but there is no evidence or circumstances to support the judgment or the conclusion or guess advanced by the Attorney General, which we have heretofore quoted. The law will not presume an intention beyond that realized by the act.").

11"The word 'attempt' means to try; it implies an effort to bring about a desired result. Hence an attempt to commit any crime requires a specific intent to commit that particular offense. If other elements of an attempt are

Some felonies cannot be committed without some restraint of the victim. This Court has stated that the "Legislature did not intend for every crime which involves a victim whose liberty has been interfered with to turn into a kidnapping. It is up to the jury to distinguish between those situations in which a substantial interference with the victim's liberty has taken place and those situations in which a slight interference has taken place."[14] Courts in other jurisdictions have repeatedly recognized that restraint simply incident to other crimes does not support a separate conviction for kidnapping or aggravated kidnapping.[15]

II.

In this case it is undisputed that, at 10:00 a.m., on a Sunday morning, on the sidewalk of a busy street in Fort Worth, appellant grabbed at eight-year-old Beatrice, who, with her ten-year-old brother Raymond, was on the way home after a trip to the store. Raymond had ridden his bike to the store, with Beatrice standing on the back wheel pegs; Beatrice was either riding or walking the bike on their way home. Appellant grabbed her with one hand around the waist, while not himself letting go of the big, red-and-white golf umbrella he was carrying. She screamed, her brother pulled her back toward him and gave appellant a shove, and appellant let her go a few seconds later when a car drove by and its driver honked his horn. Raymond grabbed the bike, and they both ran home. Appellant walked down the street toward the store, and then he stayed in the neighborhood all day,

---

established 'intent is the crucial question.'" ROLLIN M. PERKINS & RONALD N. BOYCE, CRIMINAL LAW 637 (3d ed.1982) (footnotes omitted). *See also* WAYNE R. LAFAVE, SUBSTANTIVE CRIMINAL LAW § 11.3(a) at 213 & n. 25 (2nd ed. 2003) ("It is not enough to show that the defendant intended to do some unspecified criminal act.") (citing *In re Smith*, 3 Cal.3d 192, 90 Cal.Rptr. 1, 474 P.2nd 969 (1970), with a parenthetical stating "where defendant convicted of attempted kidnapping on evidence that he grabbed woman, brandished screwdriver, and said they were going in her car, which he attempted to open, effective counsel might well have argued that this did not show intent to kidnap as opposed to intent to rape or to steal").

14 *Hines v. State*, 75 S.W.3d 444, 448 (Tex.Crim.App.2002) (nothing in the kidnapping statute indicates that the Legislature intended "to bar the prosecution of a kidnapping that is part and parcel of another offense" so long as there is a restriction of a person's movements so as to interfere *substantially* with the person's liberty). *Herrin v. State*, 125 S.W.3d 436, 440–441 (Tex.Crim.App.2002) (kidnapping, or attempted kidnapping not proven when defendant "did not shoot to merely disable or harm Wayne so that he could then abduct him, but shot him at close range in the vital organs in an obvious effort to kill him. In light of appellant's intent to murder Wayne, appellant's moving of Wayne's body after the shooting did not amount to evidence that Wayne was in the course of a kidnapping when the murder took place.").

15 *See State v. Salamon*, 287 Conn. 509, 949 A.2d 1092, 1119–20 (2008) ("[A] considerable majority of state courts have followed the lead of New York and California in concluding that the crime of kidnapping does not include conduct involving a restraint that is merely incidental to the commission of some other crime against the victim. . . . Although these cases involve varying statutory language and analyses, they share a common theme, namely, that it is unlikely that the legislature intended to expose an accused to a kidnapping conviction, and the severe sanctions accompanying such a conviction, when the restraint involved is merely incidental to the commission of a separate, underlying crime. Indeed, this majority view regarding the construction of statutes delineating the crime of kidnapping rightly has been characterized as the 'modern' approach.") (citing cases from numerous jurisdictions).

as if nothing had occurred. Beatrice and Raymond testified that they thought appellant was trying to take Beatrice. Appellant later told the police that voices in his head "started telling me that I would be better off dead." Then the voices told him to "grab the little girl." Appellant had a crack cocaine pipe in his pocket when he was arrested, and the arresting officer thought he was acting "strange," possibly due "to him inducing an illegal narcotic."

Even with fully crediting the testimony of Beatrice and her brother, who were understandably terrified by their encounter with this most peculiar stranger, and discrediting appellant's version, I am nevertheless left with only speculation about what appellant's actual intentions were. Maybe they were nefarious; certainly the children believed that they were. Maybe he intended to secret or hold Beatrice in a place where she would not likely to be found just for "kicks" or because "the voices" told him to. Or maybe (as the jury here found) he intended to secret or hold her in such a place with a second, "aggravated intent," to hold her for the purpose of ransom, or use as a hostage, or to facilitate the commission of a felony such as assault, sexual assault or terrorize her or her brother or mother. Maybe he intended, as the dissent in the court of appeals noted, "to fondle her on the scene, to rape her on the scene, or to steal her bicycle." None of these acts required an intent to abduct Beatrice. Maybe appellant's intentions were not nefarious. Maybe he wanted to put Beatrice on his shoulders or simply grab her and move her out of his way. Maybe he simply intended to follow "the voices" in his head, whatever they told him. But evidence of his intent to do any one of these things is lacking. What we do know is that he intentionally "restrained" Beatrice by grabbing her around the waist, albeit only for a few seconds.[22] And that restraint was, as a matter of law, without consent because Beatrice was less than fourteen years of age and her mother, who was waiting at home to make pancakes for her children, had not "acquiesced in the movement or confinement."

In this case, assuming appellant had the intent to commit rape or some other felony, it would be up the jury to distinguish between whether a substantial interference with the victim's liberty was intended, or just a slight interference.

---

22 The most famous historical test for assessing the sufficiency of evidence to establish an attempt is the so-called "stop the film" test:

If the example may be permitted, it is as though a cinematograph film, which has so far depicted merely the accused person's acts without stating what was his intention, had been suddenly stopped, and the audience were asked to say to what end those acts were directed. If there is only one reasonable answer to this question then the accused has done what amounts to an "attempt" to attain that end. If there is more than one reasonably possible answer, then the accused has not yet done enough. J.W.C. Turner, *Attempts to Commit Crimes*, 5 Cambridge L.J. 120, 237–38 (1934); *see Hamiel v. State*, 92 Wis.2d 656, 285 N.W.2d 639, 645 (1979) (quoting Turner and stating that "in the crime of attempt, it is primarily the acts of the accused which provide evidence of the requisite mental intent. The acts of the accused committed in furtherance of the intended substantive crime '. . . must not be so few or of such an equivocal nature as to render doubtful the existence of the requisite criminal intent.'").

Here, the jury could only speculate which, and, of course, there is no evidence of intent to commit such a felony in the first place. [24]

The evidence is insufficient to support the verdict of the jury. We may conjecture the purpose of the defendant to have been to commit a rape, but, on the facts disclosed, it is conjecture only, and not an inference reasonably drawn from the evidence. The probabilities may be greater that a rape was intended rather than robbery or murder; but mere probability of guilt of a particular crime, and that, too, springing more from instinct than from proved facts, cannot support a verdict of guilty.

There is great danger of improper convictions in cases of this character, and, while the court should not for that reason invade the province of the jury, the danger admonishes us of the necessity of standing firmly upon the right and duty of proper supervision and control of them. *Id.* at 326.

* * *

In this case there is no such evidence of an intent to isolate. There was no car waiting around the corner. There were no ropes in Laster's pocket. He did not even use both hands. He did not spring out from some hiding place to grab Beatrice. He did not state any intention. His conduct—except for grabbing Beatrice around the waist—was wholly ambiguous as to his possible future intent. As the California Supreme Court once noted,

> The reason for requiring evidence of a direct act, however slight, toward consummation of the intended crime, is ... that in the majority of cases up to that time the conduct of the defendant, consisting merely of acts of preparation, has never ceased to be equivocal. ... [S]o long as the equivocal quality remains, no one can say with certainty what the intent of the defendant is. [35]

Oftentimes facts do speak for themselves. But with the offense of criminal attempt, the established facts must be highly indicative of the defendant's intent

---

24 *See e.g., Green v. State*, 67 Miss. 356, 7 So. 326 (1890). In that case, the syllabus states,

The appellant has been convicted of assault with intent to commit rape. The prosecutrix testified that she was riding in the daytime alone and on horse-back along the public road, about two miles from the town of Hazlehurst, when reaching a place where the public road crosses the railroad, she noticed a negro man standing on the crossing. Hearing a train approaching, she stopped and turned the horse's head towards the man, thinking, as she says, that he could assist her if the train frightened her horse. After riding two or three hundred yards beyond the crossing, she noticed that the man was following her on foot, evidently having traveled briskly, and she had ridden but little further when he came hurriedly up behind her and caught her riding-skirt. She immediately uttered an outcry and urged on her horse, and the man, without having spoken, fled in another direction. The prosecutrix on the trial identified the defendant. This was all the evidence. The jury convicted the accused. He moved for a new trial because of the insufficiency of the evidence, and the motion being overruled, appeals. ...

35 *People v. Miller*, 2 Cal.2d 527, 42 P.2d 308, 310 (1935).

to commit a specific crime. These facts, even viewed in the light most generously and favorably to the State, are fatally equivocal and ambiguous. I conclude that no rational juror could find, beyond a reasonable doubt, that, at the moment appellant grabbed Beatrice, he had the specific intent to secrete or hold her in a place where she was unlikely to be found.

Notes and Questions

1. As the dissent observes, the defendant may not be convicted of *kidnapping* if his detention of the victim is merely incidental to another crime—such as assault, robbery, or even rape. But how do we know what exactly the defendant *intended* to do? In the absence of clarity on this issue, can the defendant be convicted of attempted kidnapping even though an actual kidnapping conviction would not stand if incidental to a completed sexual assault.

2. Footnote 24 of Judge Cochran's dissent made reference to the *Green* decision, a case in which an African American man was convicted of assault with intent to rape a woman when he chased after her and fled when she screamed. Like this case, it would seem that the man was up to no good, but convicting him for having the intent to rape was certainly based on nothing more than a stereotype. There could have even been an innocent explanation for the chase in *Green*—and *Green* was certainly not an isolated incident. A number of southern courts affirmed such convictions on the basis of similar evidence. In *McQuirter v. State*, 63 So.2d 388 (Ala. Ct. App. 1953), a black man merely "came toward her from behind a telephone pole." Affirming the conviction, the Alabama Court of Appeals observed that the jury was permitted to infer intent from "social conditions and customs founded upon racial differences." Is there as great a likelihood of innocence in this case?

3. Consider the dissent's characterization of attempt law is very important description of the balance of interests at play. "Inchoate crimes balance the goals of law enforcement with the liberty rights of citizens by ensuring that law enforcement may intervene to prevent crime. . . ." Does society not have a real interest in removing from society the sort of person who would grab children, with whom he has no relationship, and release them only when a car honks its horn at him?

4. Surely the defendant did *something* society wants to discourage with the criminal law. Unlawful restraint, as the dissent suggests, is a misdemeanor. This does not seem like a serious enough a crime to protect society against the sort

of conduct that is at risk in this case. The statute in the *Sweigert* case that follows makes it easier for law enforcement officials to intervene with actors like this—and punish them with something more than a misdemeanor. *Sweigert*, however, really demonstrates the potential reach of the criminal law to punish future conduct—Sweigert was convicted of *attempted* luring of a child.

Quite often, legislatures draft criminal statutes that require less proximity for certain types of attempts, especially when the crime presents a danger that particularly animates the public. Possession of burglar's tools, which we will consider in the chapter on property crimes, is such an example. It is sometimes difficult to demonstrate that a suspicious trespasser has come close enough to entering a home to demonstrate burglary, so the crime of possession of burglar's tools, as you will discover, provides a vehicle to make these convictions easier. Child abduction is certainly an issue that the public reasonably wants to take every step to prevent, not just punish. Some states, like Illinois, have therefore drafted statutes that forbid luring children. *Sweigert* considers an additional step—a charge of *attempted* luring.

People v. Sweigart

Illinois Court of Appeals
985 N.E.2d 1068 (2013)

Justice ZENOFF delivered the judgment of the court, with opinion.

Defendant, Stephen Sweigart, appeals from his conviction of child abduction (720 ILCS 5/10–5(b)(10) (West 2008)). He was charged with attempting to lure a child to his home from a grocery store. Defendant contends that the evidence was insufficient to prove him guilty beyond a reasonable doubt, because there was not a "dangerous proximity of success" when the child's family was nearby and defendant's vehicle was in the parking lot. We affirm.

I. BACKGROUND

Defendant was charged on April 29, 2010, in connection with a December 26, 2009, conversation he had with O.W., who was referred to at trial as "Eddie" and who was eight years old at the time. Defendant was also charged with other offenses related to items found in his van. He pleaded guilty to some of those charges, and others were dismissed by the State. On May 25, 2011, a bench trial was held on the child abduction charge.

At trial, Eddie testified that, on December 26, 2009, defendant approached him in a grocery store. Eddie was sitting on a bench near the self-checkout line and was playing with action figures he had gotten for Christmas. His mother was approximately 10 feet away at the self checkout with Eddie's sister, Mikayla.

According to Eddie, defendant approached him and said, "do you want to come to my house and play with jets or choo-choo trains?" Eddie said "no," and defendant replied, "why not, it is going to be fun." Eddie then heard his mother tell Mikayla to go check on him, and defendant "scurried off away," leaving the store. Mikayla came over to Eddie, but he was scared and unable to talk to her. Defendant never touched Eddie and made no gestures with his hands. Mikayla testified that she saw defendant talking to Eddie, that her mother asked her to see what was wrong, and that Eddie did not answer her.

Eddie told his mother what defendant had said. After speaking to store employees, who took down the license plate number of defendant's van, the family left the store in order to take medicine to a sick relative. The police spoke to the family at their home later that evening. The next day, a television news reporter came to their house, and Eddie said that he found it exciting to talk to the reporter.

Eddie's mother testified that the family was at the store buying Gatorade for a sick relative. She was unable to hear what defendant said to Eddie, but he spoke to Eddie for 30 to 40 seconds, and Eddie looked scared, so she asked Mikayla to go over to him. When Mikayla started to move toward Eddie, defendant walked out the door. Eddie would not say what happened until he was asked five or six times. Eddie's mother did not give defendant permission to ask Eddie to go anywhere with him.

The State played a surveillance DVD of the grocery store. The video showed that Mikayla did not walk all the way up to Eddie. Instead, she walked to the end of the checkout counter, which was a few feet from where Eddie and defendant were located.

The police were called, but the family did not wait for them to come to the store, because they wanted to get back to their sick relative. They waited for defendant to leave the area, but he did not, so store employees escorted them to their car. Eddie's mother said that, while she was driving home, she spoke to Officer Stacey Snyder and told Snyder that she wanted to fill out a police report, but Snyder said that a report could not be made because it was a "he said, she said" situation. The next day, Eddie's mother met with Detective Edward Corral and filled out a police report.

Snyder testified that she was the first responding officer, that she spoke to Eddie's mother by telephone, and that Eddie's mother said she did not want to fill out a report, did not want to come back to the store, and did not want Snyder to come to her home. However, Snyder later went to the family's home and spoke to Eddie and his mother. Snyder testified that Eddie's mother did not want to sign a written statement and indicated that Eddie either had said that nothing happened or had said nothing when Mikayla had asked him what had happened.

Officer Lee Catavau also responded to the call and stopped defendant's van. Catavau said that defendant appeared nervous and shaky. Defendant acknowledged being at the grocery store, but said that he talked to a child in the toy aisle and that he mentioned having some fireman toys at his house. Catavau noticed that the van smelled of cannabis and was littered with items. Defendant gave permission to search his van and, among other items, officers found a loaded handgun, an unloaded handgun, 10 throwing stars, a machete, a cannabis pipe, children's toys, lingerie, wigs, and sex toys, including restraint devices. Defendant's home was approximately 2½ miles away from the grocery store. There, the police recovered two handguns, ammunition, and more throwing stars.

Corral and another detective interrogated defendant. Defendant said that he had talked to a boy in the toy aisle. When Corral asked if that was the same boy defendant talked to near the exit, defendant hesitated and did not respond. Defendant denied asking Eddie to come home with him and said that he told Eddie, "I have a futuristic fire truck at my house and I really want a choo-choo." When Corral pressed defendant for information, defendant changed the subject and talked about irrelevant matters.

When asked if he was attracted to little boys, defendant paused for a couple of seconds, made a noise similar to "uh, uh, uh," and said "I don't think so." Defendant said he was attracted to young girls because of the way they "blossom," "flower," and "put their stuff out there." Defendant was not asked to provide his definition of "young." During the interrogation, defendant also spoke about the Disney character Tinkerbell, stating that he had sexual thoughts about her and masturbated while thinking about her. When asked if he ever role-played or dressed like Tinkerbell, defendant said that nobody could be Tinkerbell, and "only Tinkerbell can be Tinkerbell."

The court found defendant guilty. The court noted that there were inconsistencies in the evidence, stating that Eddie's mother did not look particularly alarmed in the video and that Mikayla did not walk all the way up to Eddie as was claimed. However, the court found Eddie to be focused, articulate, and credible. The court found that the video showed that defendant talked to Eddie near the exit, not in the toy aisle as he claimed, and that defendant's van would have been easily accessible from the exit. The court also noted significant circumstantial evidence based on the incriminating items in the van. Thus, the court found that defendant's contact with Eddie was more than just an innocuous wave, gesture, or comment and was affirmative conduct evincing an intent to lure Eddie out of the store.

Defendant's motion for a new trial was denied, and he was sentenced to three years' incarceration. He appeals.

II. ANALYSIS

Defendant contends that the evidence was insufficient to convict him. Specifically, he argues that the State failed to prove that his conduct brought him in "dangerous proximity of success" for child abduction.

"A criminal conviction will not be set aside unless the evidence is so improbable or unsatisfactory that it creates a reasonable doubt of the defendant's guilt." *People v. Collins*, 106 Ill.2d 237, 261, 87 Ill.Dec. 910, 478 N.E.2d 267 (1985). On a challenge to the sufficiency of the evidence, it is not the function of this court to retry the defendant. *Id.* Rather, "'the relevant question is whether, after viewing the evidence in the light most favorable to the prosecution, *any* rational trier of fact could have found the essential elements of the crime beyond a reasonable doubt.'" (Emphasis in original.) *Id.* (quoting *Jackson v. Virginia*, 443 U.S. 307, 319, 99 S.Ct. 2781, 61 L.Ed.2d 560 (1979)). Under this standard, a court of review must view in the State's favor all reasonable inferences drawn from the record. *People v. Bush*, 214 Ill.2d 318, 326, 292 Ill.Dec. 926, 827 N.E.2d 455 (2005). The trier of fact is responsible for determining the witnesses' credibility, weighing their testimony, and deciding on the reasonable inferences to be drawn from the evidence. *People v. Lamon*, 346 Ill.App.3d 1082, 1089, 281 Ill.Dec. 903, 805 N.E.2d 271 (2004).

A person commits child abduction when he or she "[i]ntentionally lures or attempts to lure a child under the age of 16 into a motor vehicle, building, housetrailer, or dwelling place without the consent of the parent or lawful custodian of the child for other than a lawful purpose." 720 ILCS 5/10–5(b)(10) (West 2008). "The phrase 'other than a lawful purpose' in the child abduction statute implies actions which violate the Criminal Code of 1961 (720 ILCS 5/1–1 *et seq.* (West 2008))." *People v. Velez*, 2012 IL App (1st) 101325, ¶ 30, 359 Ill.Dec. 703, 967 N.E.2d 433. The required showing of "other than a lawful purpose" is a showing of criminal intent, or mens rea, which is a state of mind that is usually inferred from the surrounding circumstances. *Id.* Under section 10–5(b)(10), "the luring or attempted luring of a child under the age of 16 into a motor vehicle, building, housetrailer, or dwelling place without the consent of the parent or lawful custodian of the child shall be prima facie evidence of other than a lawful purpose." 720 ILCS 5/10–5(b)(10) (West 2008).

A person is guilty of attempt when "with intent to commit a specific offense, he [or she] does any act that constitutes a substantial step toward the commission of that offense." 720 ILCS 5/8–4(a) (West 2008). The accused need not have completed the last proximate act to actual commission of a crime, and the defendant's subsequent abandonment of his criminal purpose is no defense. *People v. Hawkins*, 311 Ill.App.3d 418, 424, 243 Ill.Dec. 621, 723 N.E.2d 1222 (2000). However, mere preparation is not enough. *People v. Terrell*, 99 Ill.2d 427, 433, 77 Ill.Dec. 88, 459 N.E.2d 1337 (1984). "The child abduction statute criminalizes the act of luring a child, whether or not the act is successful, in order to protect children from further acts of violence." *Velez*, 2012 IL App (1st) 101325, ¶ 34, 359 Ill.Dec. 703, 967 N.E.2d 433. Under the statute, there is no requirement that a defendant must actually touch or harm the child in order to be guilty of child abduction. *Id.*

This court has looked to section 5.01 of the Model Penal Code (Model Penal Code § 5.01 (1985)) for assistance in determining the types of behavior that constitute an attempt. *People v. Jiles*, 364 Ill.App.3d 320, 333, 301 Ill.Dec. 79, 845 N.E.2d 944 (2006). Under the Model Penal Code, as under section 8–4(a), an attempt has occurred when a person, acting with the required intent, "purposely does or omits to do anything that, under the circumstances as he believes them to be, is an act or omission constituting a substantial step in a course of conduct planned to culminate in his commission of the crime." Model Penal Code § 5.01(1)(c) (1985).

The Model Penal Code lists types of conduct that shall not, as a matter of law, be held insufficient to support an attempt conviction, so long as the act is strongly corroborative of the actor's criminal purpose, including:

"(a) lying in wait, searching for[,] or following the contemplated victim of the crime;

(b) enticing or seeking to entice the contemplated victim of the crime to go to the place contemplated for its commission;

(c) reconnoitering the place contemplated for the commission of the crime; [and]

(d) unlawful entry of a structure, vehicle[,] or enclosure in which it is contemplated that the crime will be committed[.]" Model Penal Code § 5.01(2)(a)-(d) (1985).

This list demonstrates the Model Penal Code's emphasis on the nature of steps taken, rather than on what remains to be done to commit a crime. *Hawkins*, 311 Ill.App.3d at 424, 243 Ill.Dec. 621, 723 N.E.2d 1222. "Precisely what is a substantial step must be determined by evaluating the facts and circumstances of each particular case." *Jiles*, 364 Ill.App.3d at 334, 301 Ill.Dec. 79, 845 N.E.2d 944.

Without some affirmative conduct evincing an intent to lure a child into a building or vehicle, merely waving at a child is insufficient to show an attempt at luring the child. *People v. Wenger*, 258 Ill.App.3d 561, 567, 197 Ill.Dec. 274, 631 N.E.2d 277 (1994). For example, in *Wenger*, there was evidence that the defendant followed children with his vehicle and then waved at them while talking to some other people from the vehicle. The defendant never spoke to the children. The evidence was disputed as to whether he was beckoning the children to come to his vehicle. In that instance, the First District found the evidence insufficient to convict. *Id.* at 566–67, 197 Ill.Dec. 274, 631 N.E.2d 277.

In comparison, in *Velez*, a 14–year–old girl was walking along a sidewalk after school, when the defendant smiled at her from his vehicle, honked his horn, and slowed in order to talk to her. The child then turned a corner and saw the defendant parked up the street. When she neared the vehicle, the defendant asked if she wanted a ride home. The child ignored him and walked faster, but the defendant continued to follow her with his vehicle, called her "baby girl," and again asked her if she wanted a ride home. He also leaned from the driver's seat to the passenger seat, motioning through the window for her to approach the vehicle. The defendant left when the child told him that she saw her mother and began to run toward her mother's car. *Velez*, 2012 IL App (1st) 101325, ¶ 31, 359 Ill.Dec. 703, 967 N.E.2d 433. There was evidence that the defendant then tried to change his appearance by shaving before he spoke to the police about the incident. *Id.* ¶¶ 32, 35. The First District concluded that the evidence was sufficient to convict because the defendant attempted to lure the child to his vehicle. *Id.* ¶ 38.

Likewise, in *People v. Joyce*, 234 Ill.App.3d 394, 399, 174 Ill.Dec. 763, 599 N.E.2d 547 (1992), *overruled on other grounds, People v. Woodrum*, 223 Ill.2d 286, 307 Ill.Dec. 605, 860 N.E.2d 259 (2006), the defendant honked and waved at a child, asked if the child wanted a ride, and said "'[c]ome on, I don't bite.'" The defendant drove away quickly when the child refused. About a month later, the defendant again followed the same child with his vehicle. We held that, under the totality of the circumstances, there was sufficient evidence to convict.

Here, the trial court was entitled to credit Eddie's testimony that defendant asked him if he wanted to come to defendant's home. This was clearly an attempt to lure Eddie to his home. His intent can be inferred from that conduct and, as in *Velez* and *Joyce*, was corroborated by other evidence in the case. Defendant quickly left the scene when Eddie refused and his sister approached, and he lied to the police about where he spoke to Eddie in the store. Further, the items in his vehicle provided circumstantial evidence of his intent.

Defendant contends that the evidence was insufficient because the State did not show that he was in "dangerous proximity of success," and he distinguishes cases such as *Joyce* on the ground that his vehicle was not immediately accessible. It has been said that an attempt requires the defendant to perform acts bringing him in "dangerous proximity" to success in carrying out his intent. See, *e.g., People v. Norris*, 399 Ill.App.3d 525, 532, 341 Ill.Dec. 70, 929 N.E.2d 1149 (2010). This language originates from the dissent of Justice Holmes in *Hyde v. United*

States, 225 U.S. 347, 387–88, 32 S.Ct. 793, 56 L.Ed. 1114 (1912) (Holmes, J., dissenting, joined by Hughes and Lamar, JJ.), where he wrote:

> "An attempt, in the strictest sense, is an act expected to bring about a substantive wrong by the forces of nature. With it is classed the kindred offence where the act and the natural conditions present or supposed to be present are not enough to do the harm without a further act, but where it is so near to the result that, if coupled with an intent to produce that result, the danger is very great. [Citation.] But combination, intention, and overt act may all be present without amounting to a criminal attempt—as if all that were done should be an agreement to murder a man fifty miles away and the purchase of a pistol for the purpose. There must be dangerous proximity to success. But when that exists the overt act is the essence of the offence."

That principle is not wholly inconsistent with the modern rule, reflected in the Model Penal Code, that a substantial step is required in order to prove an attempt. As our supreme court has stated, "[m]ere preparation to commit a crime, of course, does not constitute an attempt to commit it. We feel however that an attempt does exist where a person, with intent to commit a specific offense, performs acts which constitute substantial steps toward the commission of that offense." *People v. Woods*, 24 Ill.2d 154, 158, 180 N.E.2d 475 (1962); *see also Terrell*, 99 Ill.2d at 442, 77 Ill.Dec. 88, 459 N.E.2d 1337 (Simon, J., dissenting, joined by Goldenhersh and Clark, JJ.) (explaining "dangerous proximity" as the difference between mere preparation and attempt). However, the modern rule is substantially different. *See United States v. Farhane*, 634 F.3d 127, 146 (2d Cir.2011) (observing the difference between the "dangerous proximity" test and the Model Penal Code approach). "By shifting the emphasis from what remains to be done to what the actor has already done, the Model Penal Code standards enable a trier of fact to find a 'substantial step' even where the commission of the crime still requires several major steps to be taken. The standards thus broaden the scope of criminal liability beyond that under the 'dangerous proximity' test." *People v. Smith*, 209 Ill.App.3d 795, 801, 155 Ill.Dec. 326, 569 N.E.2d 326 (1991), *rev'd on other grounds*, 148 Ill.2d 454, 170 Ill.Dec. 644, 593 N.E.2d 533 (1992). "The * * * adoption of the expanded scope of 'substantial step' as provided by the Model Penal Code did not abrogate the general rule that mere preparation does not bring a defendant in 'dangerous proximity to success.' [Citation.] Rather, only clearly specific conduct which can only be directed at the specific identified victim or crime if 'strongly corroborative of the actor's criminal purpose' may be held a 'substantial step.'" *Id.* at 801–02, 155 Ill.Dec. 326, 569 N.E.2d 326 (citing Model Penal Code § 5.01(2) (1985)).

Here, defendant seeks to require a strong probability of physical success under the "dangerous proximity" test. But the law does not require such a strong probability of success. Instead, the law requires a "substantial step," and enticing or seeking to entice the contemplated victim of the crime to go to the place contemplated for its commission is a sufficient act to constitute a substantial step. Model Penal Code § 5.01(2)(b) (1985). Defendant did that when he asked Eddie if he wanted to come to his home to play.

Even if we were to ignore the guidance from the Model Penal Code and apply a "dangerous proximity" test, our determination would be the same. As the trial court noted, defendant approached Eddie near the exit of the store. Although his van was outside in the parking lot, it was easily accessible. Further, although Eddie's family was nearby, they were not in earshot. The evidence permits the conclusion that defendant would have successfully abducted Eddie if Eddie had simply agreed to follow him. This readily strikes us as "dangerous proximity."

III. CONCLUSION

The evidence was sufficient to prove defendant guilty beyond a reasonable doubt. Accordingly, the judgment of the circuit court of Kane County is affirmed. Affirmed.

---

4. Conspiracy

Conspiracy, as you have discovered, is in many ways the easiest type of crime for the prosecution to prove. The prosecution does not have to show that the crime came as near to completion as it does to demonstrate an attempt. But with this ease of conviction comes a risk. At what point are harmless thoughts being punished. This is the issue presented in the *Valle* case that alleges a conspiracy to kidnap.

United States v. Valle

U.S. District Court, Southern District of New York
301 F.R.D. 53

PAUL G. GARDEPHE

On March 12, 2013, a jury convicted Defendant Gilberto Valle of conspiracy to commit kidnapping (Count One), in violation of 18 U.S.C. § 1201(c), and of conducting a computer search of a federal database that exceeded his authorized access (Count Two), in violation of 18 U.S.C. § 1030(a)(2)(B). . . . For the reasons set forth below, Valle's motion for a judgment of acquittal will be granted as to Count One but denied as to Count Two. . . .

* * *

BACKGROUND

With respect to the kidnapping conspiracy charge, the primary issue raised in Valle's motion for a judgment of acquittal is whether the evidence and the reasonable inferences that may be drawn from that evidence are such that a rational jury could find that "criminal intent ha[d] crystallized," *United States v. Feola*, 420 U.S. 671, 694 (1975)—that is, that Valle and his alleged co-conspirators entered into a genuine agreement to kidnap certain women and had the specific intent to actually kidnap these woman.

* * *

The Government contended at trial that Valle had conspired with three individuals to commit kidnapping: (1) Michael Van Hise, a New Jersey resident known to Valle only by his email addresses, "mikevanhise81@aol.com" and "rnichael19902135@yahoo.com"; (2) an individual known to Valle as "Aly Khan," who resided in Pakistan or India and used the email address "alisherkhan79@yahoo.com"; and (3) an individual known to Valle as "Moody Blues" or "Christopher Collins," a resident of England whose email address was meatmarketman@rocketmail.com.

According to the Government, the alleged targets of the kidnapping conspiracy were: (1) Kathleen Mangan, Valle's wife; (2) Alisa Friscia, a New York City school teacher and Mangan's former co-worker; (3) Andria Noble, an Ohio prosecutor and college friend of Valle; (4) Kimberly Sauer, also one of Valle's college friends, who was then working as a promotions director for radio stations in the Washington, D.C. area; and (5) Kristen Ponticelli, a 2012 graduate of Valle's high school—Archbishop Malloy—whom Valle had never met.

* * *

On May 31, 2012, Valle ran a search concerning Hartigan's name using a New York City Police Department ("NYPD") software program that queried certain federal, state, and local law enforcement databases. It was undisputed at trial that Valle had no law enforcement purpose for performing this search. That search provided the factual basis for Count Two of the Indictment, which charges Valle with exceeding his authorized access to a federal database.

* * *

I. Valle's Background and Mangan's Discovery of His Internet Activities

Gilberto Valle was raised in Forest Hills, Queens. He graduated from Archbishop Malloy High School and the University of Maryland. After college, Valle returned to New York, and in 2006 he became a police officer in the NYPD. At the time of his arrest six years later in October 2012, Valle worked as a patrol officer in the 26th Precinct on the Upper West Side. There was no evidence at trial that Valle had ever acted violently toward a woman, had ever threatened a woman, had ever been the subject of any misconduct complaint as a police officer, or had ever been involved in criminal activity prior to this case. Kathleen Mangan, Valle's estranged wife, testified that he had never been violent toward her or their child, and that he had no drug or alcohol problems.

* * *

On September 9, 2012, Mangan installed spyware on the couple's MacBook computer. The spyware recorded every keystroke and website entered by the computer's users, and took "pictures every five minutes or so of whatever [was] happening on the computer screen." The next morning, Mangan found several disturbing images captured by the spyware, including "pictures of feet that were not attached to bodies." Mangan was also alarmed by several screen names that Valle had been using to communicate with others, including "girldealer" and "girlmeathunter," as well as websites he had visited' including "[d]arkfetishnet,""sexyamazons,""darkfet," "motherless," and "fetlife."

After confronting Valle a second time about his Internet activities, Mangan left the couple's Queens apartment with their infant daughter and flew to her parents' home in Nevada. Once in Nevada, Mangan further inspected the contents of the MacBook. Using the couple's shared password, she was able to log-in to an email account whose address—"Mhal52@yahoo.com"—she did not recognize. Mangan's review of this email account uncovered Facebook images of herself and several other women she knew. Mangan's search regarding her own name revealed a lurid Internet chat in which Valle discussed butchering her: "I was going to be tied up by my feet and my throat slit and they would have fun watching the blood gush out of me because I was young[.]" Mangan testified that one participant wrote, "[']if she cries, don't listen to her, don't give her mercy. ['] And Gil just said, ['I]t's okay, we will just gag her." In other chats Mangan read, Valle discussed raping and torturing women Mangan knew, including Alisa Friscia, Kimberly Sauer, and Andria Noble. In connection with "the pictures of the girls [Mangan] knew," she also recalled reading, "this is a fantasy[.]"

Shortly after discovering these communications, Mangan contacted the FBI and authorized agents to make a copy of the MacBook's hard drive. She also provided agents with keys to the couple's apartment and authorized them to seize an HP laptop computer that had been used by both Mangan and Valle.

II. Valle's Internet Chats

Valle used his Yahoo! email account to communicate with other members of the DFN ["Dark Fetish Network"]. DFN is a "social media" website with

38,000 registered members worldwide, 4,500 of whom are active users of the site. The website is designed to facilitate communication among those interested in a variety of sexual fetishes and deviant practices, including erotic asphyxiation, cannibalism, rape, necrophilia, and "peril" scenarios (i.e., fantasies that involve "a victim in a dangerous situation"). According to Sergey Merenkov, one of the website's founders, DFN users typically access the site to engage in fantasy "role-playing." Valle began visiting the DFN website in 2010.

By early 2012, Valle began communicating with certain DFN members—including his alleged co-conspirators—on email and Yahoo! messenger, an electronic chat service. One of Valle's alleged co-conspirators—Aly Khan—told Valle that he had been "banned from DFN due to [his] search for real women willing for slaughter or people wil[l]ing to send their women to me." Merenkov testified that DFN would terminate the accounts of individuals who violated the site's terms of service, including by engaging in conversations that sounded like they "could have led to something bad."

A. Agent Walsh's Analysis of Valle's Internet Chats and Emails

* * *

Walsh joined the Bureau after graduating from college with a sociology degree and serving in the United States Army for several years. There is no evidence that Walsh had any prior experience in law enforcement, nor is there any evidence that he had received academic or other specialized training that would have assisted him in distinguishing Internet chats and emails constituting "real" criminal activity from those reflecting fantasy role-play.

* * *

After reviewing "thousands" of Valle's emails and electronic chats, Agent Walsh concluded that nearly all of Valle's communications about kidnapping, sexual assault, murder, and cannibalism "were clearly role-play." Valle's fantasy role-play chats involved twenty-one of the twenty-four individuals with whom he had discussed these topics. Walsh further concluded, however, that forty of Valle's chats and emails "contained elements of real crime[.]" Walsh reached this conclusion—as to these chats and emails—because "[t]hey described dates, names and activities that you would use to conduct a real crime." In these forty chats and emails, Valle corresponded with one of three individuals—Michael Van Hise, Aly Khan, or Moody Blues. Although Walsh testified that Valle's communications with Van Hise, Aly Khan, and Moody Blues reflect an intent to actually commit a kidnapping, he conceded that the "fantasy role-play" chats and emails share many of the same features as the "real" chats and emails that allegedly reflect criminal intent, including discussion of dates for planned kid-nappings, purported past crimes, and real women.

B. Valle's Chats and Emails with Alleged Co-Conspirators

* * *

1. Valle's Communication with Michael Van Hise

* * *

mikevanhise81: [. . .] what i wanna do is make her my slave[,] sex, maid and other wise. i will cause her to play my fantasies and do what i like. if she gets preg. i will kill her if she cheats i will kill her and if she tries to leave first shell get a bad beating second time shell be hung.

Hal M: very very nice . . . . she is a sweet girl. not sure how soon before she would submit. I will abduct her right out of her apartment, stuff her into a large piece of luggage after tying up her hands and feet and off we go. do you want her clothed in what she was wear-ing? or stripped naked?

mikevanhise81:   whatever is better for you and when i get her we[']ll meet somewhere so we can rape her together before i leave with her.

Hal M: excellent! i'll leave her clothes on. I will give you the pleasure of unwrapping your gift

mikevanhise81:   sounds great to me also do you wanna hang her with me just for laughs before we leave

Hal M: its up to you. she is all yours. I really don't mind if she experiences pain and suffering. I will sleep like a baby.

mikevanhise81:   k great anyway gtg for now but wil message later

* * *

Hal M: $5,000 and she is all yours

mikevanhise81:   could we do 4

Hal M: i'm putting my neck on the line here. . . . if some-thing goes wrong some how i am in deep shit.

$5,000 and you need to make sure that she is not found. She will definitely make the news.

mikevanhise81:   no prob shes never leaving the house and also k about the price and would you do a payment plan or full up front

Hal M: full payment due at delivery . . . just so that you know she may be knocked out when I get her to you. I don't know how long the solvent I am using will last but I have to knock her out to get her out of her apartment safely

* * *

Hal M: yeah fill me in a bit on her ordeal. . . i think she will be tough to break, she is kind of feisty and no nonsense

mikevanhise81:   thats fine i can beat her and break her in more than one way also her ordeal is after she fills her purpose or the cops get close she will be raped made to passout by suffocation, tied up drove to somewhere secluded, raped again made to pass out again by strangling than when she comes to hung and raped up the ass while hanging before being buried while i take pies or tape it

Hal M: thats fuckin great. whenever you come here to meet me, it will be absolutely amazing to watch her come out of her school and follow her without her knowing. All the while we both know that her days of freedom are limited. i think you will be happy with what you see. Pictures don't do her justice

mikevanhise81:   i like that and i believe i will be so fucking hapy ill probably fuck her right than and there once we get her in my car

Hal M: it is going to be so hard to restrain myself when i knock her out, but i am aspiring to be a professional kidnapper and that's business. But i will really get off on knocking her out, tying up her hands and bare feet and gagging her. Then she will be stuffed into a large piece of luggage and wheeled out to my van.

* * *

There is no evidence that Valle or Van Hise ever took any steps to kidnap Veronica Bennett; that Van Hise and Valle ever met or made preparations to meet; or that Van Hise knew where Valle lived.

2. Valle's Communications with "Aly Khan"

* * *

alisherkhan79:	I think you are not for real . . . otherwise they would not be living
alisherkhan79:	you are not realy interested in slaughetring them
mhal52:	maybe one day
alisherkhan79:	you are wasting time buddy. I am for real not fantasy.
mhal52:	iam just afraid of getting caugh t
mhal52:	if i were guaranteed to get away with it, i would do it
alisherkhan79:	ok . . . let me tell you. can you please close these phots . . . it makes me hot :)
alisherkhan79:	i can gurantee . . . . i ahve done it before, i ma doing it this month and i will always do it.
mhal52:	you need a plan in little detail
mhal52:	i am a little different though, i am a little more sadistic
mhal52:	i would want to see her suffer
mhal52:	i want to tie her up to a metal frame and slowly roast her alive until she dies

* * *

alisherkhan79:	ok . . . let me ask you one last time before i tell you more.
alisherkhan79:	ARE YOU REALLY RAELLY INTO IT. ARE YOU READY TO SLAUGHTER ONE BEING SAFE
mhal52:	yes
alisherkhan79:	ARE YOU SURE?
mhal52:	definitely
alisherkhan79:	so, when you think you can do it. . .how soon can you gather courage
mhal52:	i dont know. . .

alisherkhan79:   get your mind ready . . . i will guide you rest ok

* * *

At trial, the Government offered evidence that "Andria" is Andria Noble. Noble was then a 27-year-old prosecutor who lived and worked in Columbus, Ohio.

* * *

Andria Noble was never kidnapped, and there is no evidence that Valle took any concrete steps to kidnap her.

3. Valle's Communication with "Moody Blues"

* * *

mhal52:   labor day is sept 3, so i'll go to her place on sept 2

mhal52:   kidnap her from there and we'll get her cooking monday afternoon

meatmarketman: I thought she was for Thanksgiving?

mhal52:   no it will be too cold for a cookout

meatmarketman: Of course. When do you want me over and will I be staying with you?

* * *

There is no discussion of Moody Blues traveling to the United States to help Valle with Andria's kidnapping. In this final chat on September 8, 2012, Valle tells Moody Blues:

mhal52:   I closed out my DFN account

meatmarketman: [.. ..]

mhal52:   Why[?]

mhal52:   Less of a chance of getting caught I figure

meatmarketman: Loll

* * *

DISCUSSION

* * *

3. Requirements to Sustain a Conspiracy Conviction

Conspiracy statutes reflect a societal choice to detect and punish criminal wrongdoing at its inception, before the object of the illegal agreement has been realized or achieved. "The essence of a conspiracy is 'an agreement to commit an unlawful act.'" *United States v. Jimenez Recio*, 537 U.S. 270, 274 (2003) (quoting *Iannelli v. United States*, 420 U.S. 770, 777 (1975)). While "the law does not punish criminal thoughts," in a criminal conspiracy "the criminal agreement itself is the actus reus." *United States v. Shabani*, 513 U.S. 10, 16 (1994).
Conspiracy law is premised on the long-standing belief that criminal agreements themselves warrant punishment separate and apart from the substantive crimes that are their objects. *See United States v. Eppolito*, 543 F.3d 25, 47 (2d Cir. 2008) ("Where there is an agreement to commit an unlawful act, '[t]hat agreement is a distinct evil, which may exist and be punished whether or not the substantive crime ensues.'"). . . . Accordingly, the conspiracy and the substantive crime that is the objective of the conspiracy do not merge, and individuals can be charged with, convicted of, and punished separately for both.

The elements of conspiracy are generally more easily proven than the elements of either a substantive offense or an attempt, the latter of which typically requires proof that a defendant took a "substantial step" toward completing a crime. Conspiracy merely requires proof of "(1) an agreement among the conspirators to commit an offense; (2) specific intent to achieve the objective of the conspiracy; and (3) [here] an overt act to effect the object of the conspiracy." *United States v. Pinckney*, 85 F.3d 4, 8 (2d Cir. 1996) (alteration added) (citation omitted). "'Whether the substantive crime itself is, or is likely to be, committed is irrelevant,'" *United States v. Wallach*, 935 F.2d 445, 470 (2d Cir. 1991) (quoting *United States v. Rose*, 590 F.2d 232, 235 (7th Cir. 1978)), and "'impossibility of success is not a defense.'" Hassan, 578 F.3d at 123 (quoting Jimenez Recio, 537 U.S. at 276). . . .

Moreover, a defendant may be convicted of conspiracy without having entered into a formal or express agreement. "'[I]t is enough that the parties have a tacit understanding to carry out the prohibited conduct.'" *United States v. Rubin*, 844 F.2d 979, 984 (2d Cir. 1988) (quoting *United States v. Wardy*, 777 F.2d 101, 107 (2d Cir. 1985)). A conspiracy may also exist "even if a conspirator does not agree to commit or facilitate each and every part of the substantive offense." *Salinas v. United States*, 522 U.S. 52, 63 (1997) (citation omitted). "The partners in the criminal plan must agree to pursue the same criminal objective and may divide up the work, yet each is responsible for the acts of each other." *Id.* at 63-64 (citing *Pinkerton v. United States*, 328 U.S. 640, 646 (1946)). Because "[s]ecrecy and concealment are essential features of successful conspiracy," prosecutors may prove the "essential nature of the plan and [a defendant's] connections with it" through circumstantial evidence and inferences. *Blumenthal v. United States*, 332 U.S. 539, 557 (1947). . . .

Although the Government may rely on circumstantial evidence and reasonable inferences to establish the elements of a conspiracy, "'because conspiracy is a specific intent crime,'" the Government must demonstrate that the defendant had the specific intent to both engage in the conspiracy and commit the underlying crime. Hassan, 578 F.3d at 123. . . .

"As an added protection to defendants against punishment for mere talk, in some instances an overt act must take place in furtherance of the conspiracy." *United States v. Gigante*, 982 F. Supp. 140, 169 (E.D.N.Y. 1997), aff d, 166 F.3d 75 (2d Cir. 1999) (citation omitted). Where—as here—the applicable conspiracy statute contains an overt act requirement, the purpose of that element is to require the Government to demonstrate that the conspiracy was actually "at work." *Carlson v. United States*, 187 F.2d 366, 370 (10th Cir. 1951) (citation omitted). . . .

Finally, in order to establish proper venue, the Government must demonstrate that at least one overt act in furtherance of the alleged conspiracy was committed within the Southern District of New York. *United States v. Naranjo*, 14 F.3d 145, 147 (2d Cir. 1994). . . .

B. Sufficiency of the Evidence on Count One: Kidnapping Conspiracy

Count One of the Indictment charges Valle with violating 18 U.S.C. § 1201(c). Section 1201(c) provides:

> If two or more persons conspire to violate this section and one or more of such persons do any overt act to effect the object of the conspiracy, each shall be punished by imprisonment for any term of years or for life.18 U.S.C. § 1201(c).

To obtain a conviction under Section 1201(c), the Government was required to demonstrate beyond a reasonable doubt that Valle "agreed with another to commit [one or more kidnappings]; that he knowingly engaged in the conspiracy with the specific intent to commit the [kidnapping or kidnappings] that were the objects of the conspiracy; and that an overt act in furtherance of the conspiracy was committed [in the Southern District of New York]." *United States v. Monaco*, 194 F.3d 381, 386 (2d Cir. 1991). . . .

1. The Government Did Not Demonstrate by Proof Beyond a Reasonable Doubt that Valle's Chats with his Alleged Co-Conspirators Reflect True Criminal Intent as Opposed to Fantasy Role-Play

a. The Government Did Not Offer Sufficient Evidence to Permit a Reasonable Juror to Distinguish the Alleged "Real" Chats from the Conceded Fantasy Chats

At trial, the Government relied almost exclusively on Valle's computer-based activities—chats, emails, searches, and computer-generated documents—to demonstrate his alleged criminal intent to kidnap one or more women. Indeed, the centerpiece of the Government's case was Agent Walsh's analysis of Valle's Internet communications, and his division of these communications into two groups: "real" and fantasy. Given the Government's concession that nearly all of Valle's thousands of online communications about kidnapping, rape, murder, and cannibalism are fantasy role-play, the foundation of the Government's case at trial was its argument that Valle's forty chats and emails with Van Hise, Aly Khan, and Moody Blues are meaningfully different, in that they evince true criminal intent. Stated another way, no reasonable juror could find criminal intent and vote to convict unless the Government demonstrated, by proof beyond a reasonable doubt, that the Van Hise/Aly Khan/Moody Blues chats differ significantly from the fantasy chats in content and/or in surrounding circumstances.

According to Agent Walsh, the differences between the "real" chats and emails and the fantasy chats and emails are as follows:

> In the ones that I believe[d] were fantasy, the individuals said they were fantasy. In the ones that I thought were real, people were sharing, the two people were sharing real details of women, names, what appeared to be photographs of the women, details of past crimes and they also said they were for real. . . .

> [In the "real" chats, the participants] described dates, names and activities that you would use to conduct a real crime. . . .

> [The fantasy chats] didn't seem realistic . . . . They were clearly role-play. [The participants] used the word "fantasy" in the actual chats or emails.

No reasonable juror could have distinguished between the "real" and fantasy chats on this basis, however, because the chats that the Government claims are "real" and the chats that the Government concedes are fantasy share the same elements and characteristics.

For example, in both the alleged "real" chats and the fantasy chats Valle

- transmits Facebook images of real women he knows without their consent (Compare ("Carl Wolfe" fantasy chat) (May 17, 2012, 3:39 a.m. (sharing images of several women, including "Kristen P," "Cecilia," and "Kathleen")) with (Moody Blues "real" chat) (July 9, 2012, 07:38:37-07:46:09 (sharing images of several women, including "Cecilia," "Kathleen," and "Kimberly")));

- offers to kidnap women and sell them on a "cash upon delivery" basis (Compare ("Tim Chase" fantasy chat) (Jan. 23, 2012 (offering to sell "Danielle" for $4,000)) with (Van Hise "real" chat) (Jan. 27, 2012 (offering to sell "Alisa" for $4,000)));

- expresses a desire to kidnap, rape, torture, murder, and/or cannibalize the same real women (Compare ("Jackcrow Two" fantasy chat) (Feb. 27, 2012 (discussing "Andria")) and id. (Apr. 29, 2012 (discussing "Kristen")) and ("Meand Haris" fantasy chat) (July 17, 2012 (discussing "Andria")) with (Moody Blues "real" chat) (Sept. 8, 2012 (discussing "Andria")) and (Moody Blues "real" chat) (Aug. 24, 2012 (discussing "Kristen")) and (Aly Khan "real" chat) (Feb. 9, 2012 (discussing "Andria");

- claims to be surveilling potential victims (Compare ("Meand Haris" fantasy chat) (Apr. 26, 2012, 05:27:26 ("i followed Kristen home")) with (Aly Khan "real" chat) (Feb. 10, 2012, 18:24:57 ("been watchin outside of [Andria's] house")));

- discusses acts of extreme violence in graphic and nearly identical detail (Compare ("Meand Haris" fantasy chat) (Jul. 17, 2012, 08:49:00 ("we are going to tie her onto a rotisserrie and slowly roast her alive over a fire")) with (Aly Khan "real" chat) (Jul. 17, 2012, 08:21:16, 08:23:44 ("we are going to cook her outdoors on the rotissenie in september" and "very slowly cook her alive until she dies")));

- discusses his intention to commit kidnappings on specific dates, all of which pass without incident (Compare ("Tim Chase" fantasy chat) (Jan. 23, 2012, 05:25:30 ("we are a go for the 27th")) with (Aly Khan "real" chat) (Jan. 23, 2012, 05:52:47 ("i can have her there the week of Feb 20"))); and

- explains the means and methods he will use to kidnap women, including chloroform, packing them into suitcases, and tying them up (Compare ("sten9979" fantasy chat) (June 12, 2012, 06:26:15-24 ("some chloroform will do the trick" and "she is small enough to pack into a piece of luggage")) with (Moody Blues "real" chat) (Jul. 9, 2012, 09:29:01-51 (discussing use of chloroform and binding of victim)) and GX 430 (Van Hise "real" chat) (Jan. 27, 2012, 1:40-1:50 p.m. ("I will abduct her right out of her apartment, stuff her into a large piece of luggage after tying up her hands and feet and off we go."))).

Valle's "real" and fantasy chats also contain the same lies. As in the Van Hise/Aly Khan/Moody Blues chats, in the fantasy chats Valle lies about where he lives (claiming to be "2 to 3 hrs" from Erie, Pennsylvania; Forest Hills, where Valle lived, is nearly seven hours from Erie by car))); about whether he owns a house "up in the mountains" with "no one around for a half mile"; about whether he owns a van; about whether he has a basement in his "country house"; about whether he is constructing a "BBQ pit" or a "rotisserie" (claiming to have a "[b]ig back yard away from view" where "I am working on building a BBQ pit")); ("i have all the parts [for the rotisserie] we just have to weld the metal together"))); about whether he is surveilling proposed victims (claiming that a potential kidnapping victim has "been the priority everyday," that "her building has no cameras," and that she "gets home around 5:15, hits the gym and is back around 7:45/8")); and about where the kidnapping targets live (claiming that "Andria" lives in "maryland").

While Agent Walsh testified that he concluded that the Van Hise/Aly Khan/Moody Blues chats as "real" because "they describe[ ] dates, names and activities that you would use to conduct a real crime," the fantasy chats also contain agreed-upon dates for kidnappings, the names of the same real women, and discussion of the same activities—kidnapping, rape, torture, murder, and cannibalization of women. ("Tim Chase" fantasy chat) ("we are a go for the 27th"), ("Meand Haris" fantasy chat) (discussing kidnapping "Andria" the "city prosecutor"), (sten9979 fantasy chat) (discussing cooking and eating "Andria" for "Thanksgiving dinner"). Moreover, as Agent Walsh acknowledged at trial, Valle's fantasy chats—like the "real" chats—are replete with the same graphic descriptions of extreme sexual violence.

The Government defends its "real" versus fantasy categorization by arguing that "Moody Blues, Aly Khan and Van Hise all expressed a genuine desire to kidnap, torture and kill women. . . . ," while "the other individuals with whom Valle communicated identified themselves as fantasists." No reasonable juror could have distinguished between the "real" and fantasy chats on this basis, however.

As an initial matter, many of Valle's fantasy correspondents never state that they are engaged in fantasy. (DX El ("Tim Chase" discussing kidnapping of "Sally"); DX E4 ("Brenda Falcon" discussing kidnapping and cooking of "Andria" on Thanksgiving); DX E6 ("Jackcrow Two" discussing kidnapping and cannibalization of "Andria" on Thanksgiving); DX E12 ("sten9979" discussing kidnapping of "Andria"); DX E13 ("Carl Wolfe" discussing "4th of July Menu" involving several women, including "Kristen P" and "Kathleen")) The Government's claim that the chats it designated as fantasy all contain "explicit assurances" that the participants are engaged in fantasy role-play (Govt. Br. (Dkt. No. 195) at 11) is thus not supported by the evidence.

Moreover, and contrary to Agent Walsh's testimony that he designated as fantasy those chats in which the participants "used the [ ] word 'fantasy' in the actual chats or e-mails," the chats that the Government claims reflect true criminal intent also contain numerous references to fantasy. (See, GX 402 (mhal52 to meatmarketman) (July 9, 2012, 08:36:39 (Valle telling Moody Blues that Sauer has "been one of my favorite victims to fantasize about for almost 10 years now")); GX 408 (meatmarketman to mhal52) (July 17, 2012, 07:36:24 ("When you sit at her table are you going to fantasize that the meal isn't from her but form her!")); GX 410 (mhal52 to meatmarketman) (July 19, 2012, 06:57:41 ("my true fantasy is to cook her whole though until she dies")); GX 413 (mhal52 to meatmarketman) (Aug. 25, 2012, 05:09:56-05:10:10 (Valle stating that "in my fantasies, [Andria] is #1 by far")); GX 417 (alisherkhan to mhal52) (Jan. 23, 2012, 06:38:36 ("what if she agrees for this and we dont have to force her. may be she has a reverse fantasy like us. May be not. . . .")); GX 430 (mikevanhise81 to mhal52) (Jan. 27, 2012, 1:40 p.m. ("i will cause her to play my fantasies and do what i like.")))

Agent Walsh's explanation that he designated as fantasy those chats that "didn't seem realistic" also does not provide a reasonable basis on which to distinguish the alleged "real" chats from the fantasy chats. As discussed above, the chats that the Government has designated as "real" contain a myriad of false, fantastical, and fictional elements, including multiple kidnappings occurring on or about the same day—both inside and outside the United States and the New York-area; a human-size oven and rotisserie; a non-existent soundproofed basement with non-existent pulley apparatus; and the transport of victims in a non-existent van to a non-existent cabin in a remote part of Pennsylvania.

An analysis of Valle's fantasy chats reveals that they are substantively indistinguishable from those chats that the Government claims evince true criminal intent.

* * *

Valle's depraved, misogynistic sexual fantasies about his wife, former college classmates, and acquaintances undoubtedly reflect a mind diseased. But the question before this Court is whether the Government proved beyond a reasonable doubt that (1) Valle entered into genuine agreements with Van Hise, Aly Khan, and Moody Blues to kidnap Mangan, Friscia, Sauer, Noble, or Ponticelli, and (2) Valle had the specific intent to kidnap one or more of these women. An exhaustive analysis of Valle's Internet communications—both the chats that the Government concedes are fantasy and the chats that the Government alleges are "real"—and a careful consideration of the circumstances surrounding those communications—including what happens and what does not happen—demonstrate that the Government has not met its burden.

Accordingly, the jury's verdict on Count One will be vacated, and Count One will be dismissed.

[The conviction for Count Two is upheld—improper use of a police database.]

Notes and Questions

1. Judge Gardephe in *Valle* overturns the jury's conviction of Mr. Valle because of the insufficient evidence that Mr. Valle was involved in anything more than role play. According to Judge Gardephe, no reasonable trier of fact could have found Mr. Valle's behavior satisfied the elements of conspiracy to kidnap beyond a reasonable doubt, because the evidence was too muddled—there was duplicitous evidence the government conceded was "fantasy," which too closely mirrored the evidence deemed "real." Looking back, do you think the prosecution should have admittedly classified so much information as "role play?" Was there any other route for the prosecution to take? Should the prosecution have waited until Mr. Valle kidnapped someone? Would Mr. Valle have kidnapped someone? How much resources should we expect the state to allocate to protect its citizens? What if the state warned the potential victims, and said, "give us a call if something happens, because we can't wait around forever?"

2. You should also consider the values our society places on freedom of thought against the value of preventing and punishing crime. Consider: is it better to prevent crime by punishing thoughts, punishing actions based on thoughts, or only punishing actions regardless of thoughts? Perhaps it should depend on the crime. In *Valle*, 18 U.S.C. § 1201(c) requires some sort of *actus reas* and *mens rea*—real intent to carry out a genuine plan. The state failed to demonstrate the realness of either the plan or intent to carry it out, which appear to be tightly interwoven. Thus, Mr. Valle was acquitted. But as a matter of policy, you should consider whether punishing Mr. Valle for thinking of kidnapping and eating his wife and friends without a real plan would prevent such a tragedy from materializing. If Mr. Valle wasn't really going to do anything, why punish him? Alternatively, would punishing Mr. Valle in such a manner

prevent others from thinking about doing the same or similar? You should consider the value of preventing crime against the value of freedom of thought as you consider the reprehensible mental state of Mr. Valle—"a mind diseased" according to Judge Gardephe. Your evaluation of prevention and freedom of thought, plus questions of right and wrong ("How could Mr. Valle think such things? That's just wrong."), are important questions of policy that frame law-making and statutory interpretation.

D. Sexual Assault

Rape statutes, as you might imagine, have changed more than most criminal statutes in the past 50 years. The common law requirements to prove rape were filled with a number of archaic and offensive provisions. Fear of false rape charges (to be kind) or unmitigated misogyny (to be less kind) appear to explain some of the provisions. Lord Chief Justice Matthew Hale of England stated in 1680 that "rape. . . is an accusation easily made and hard to be proved, and harder to be defended by the party accused, tho never so innocent." Dean Wigmore stated in his famed evidence treatise that any woman claiming she had been raped should be required to submit to a psychiatric examination, the results of which should be admissible in the defendant's criminal trial.

California's rape statute, Penal Code § 261, is reflective of modern statutes:

(a) Rape is an act of sexual intercourse accomplished with a person not the spouse of the perpetrator, under any of the following circumstances:

(1) Where a person is incapable, because of a mental disorder or developmental or physical disability, of giving legal consent, and this is known or reasonably should be known to the person committing the act. . . .

(2) Where it is accomplished against a person's will by means of force, violence, duress, menace, or fear of immediate and unlawful bodily injury on the person or another.

(3) Where a person is prevented from resisting by any intoxicating or anesthetic substance, or any controlled substance, and this condition was known, or reasonably should have been known by the accused.

(4) Where a person is at the time unconscious of the nature of the act, and this is known to the accused. As used in this paragraph, "unconscious of the nature of the act" means incapable of resisting because the victim meets any one of the following conditions:

(A) Was unconscious or asleep.

(B) Was not aware, knowing, perceiving, or cognizant that the act occurred.

(C) Was not aware, knowing, perceiving, or cognizant of the essential characteristics of the act due to the perpetrator's fraud in fact.

(D) Was not aware, knowing, perceiving, or cognizant of the essential characteristics of the act due to the perpetrator's fraudulent representation that the sexual penetration served a professional purpose when it served no professional purpose.

(5) Where a person submits under the belief that the person committing the act is someone known to the victim other than the accused, and this belief is induced by any artifice, pretense, or concealment practiced by the accused, with intent to induce the belief.

(6) Where the act is accomplished against the victim's will by threatening to retaliate in the future against the victim or any other person, and there is a reasonable possibility that the perpetrator will execute the threat. As used in this paragraph, "threatening to retaliate" means a threat to kidnap or falsely imprison, or to inflict extreme pain, serious bodily injury, or death.

(7) Where the act is accomplished against the victim's will by threatening to use the authority of a public official to incarcerate, arrest, or deport the victim or another, and the victim has a reasonable belief that the perpetrator is a public official. As used in this paragraph, "public official" means a person employed by a governmental agency who has the authority, as part of that position, to incarcerate, arrest, or deport another. The perpetrator does not actually have to be a public official.

(b) As used in this section, "duress" means a direct or implied threat of force, violence, danger, or retribution sufficient to coerce a reasonable person of ordinary susceptibilities to perform an act which otherwise would not have been performed, or acquiesce in an act to which one otherwise would not have submitted. The total circumstances, including the age of the victim, and his or her relationship to the defendant, are factors to consider in appraising the existence of duress.

(c) As used in this section, "menace" means any threat, declaration, or act which shows an intention to inflict an injury upon another.

1. Consent

In almost half of the states, statutes define rape simply as sex without the consent of the victim. Other jurisdictions, like California, describe the crime as an act "against a person's will by means of force [or] violence. . . ." Still other jurisdictions, such as New Jersey, omit consent from the statutory language entirely, describing the crime as "the commission of sexual penetration with the use of physical force or coercion." Consent is, however, the critical element under each version of these rape statutes. As the New Jersey Supreme Court stated, "A showing of sexual penetration coupled with a lack of consent would satisfy the elements of the statute." *State in the Interest of M.T.S.*, 609 A.2d 1266, 1269 (N.J. 1992).

a. A Subjective or Objective Standard?

Much is made in the study of substantive criminal law about whether the standard at issue is a subjective or objective one. Under an objective standard, the question in a rape case is whether a reasonable person in the defendant's position would have known that the victim did not consent. Under a subjective standard, the question is whether the defendant himself was aware that that the victim did not consent. Many times this distinction will not make a lot of difference to a jury as the jury will tend to disbelieve the defendant's testimony if it is contrary to what a reasonable person would have believed under the circumstances. In *Newton*, the distinction matters a great deal because the defendant wants to claim that his intoxication prevented him reading the victim's conduct. If a subjective standard is used—which is to say if the defendant's actual perception mattered— then he would be permitted to introduce evidence of intoxication.

People v. Newton

New York Court of Appeals
867 N.E.2d 397 (2007)

READ, J.

On March 19, 2003, defendant James W. Newton, Jr. was indicted for the crimes of sodomy in the first degree (Penal Law § 130.50[1]), sexual abuse in the first degree (Penal Law § 130.65[1]) and sodomy in the third degree (Penal Law § 130.40[3]). The three-count indictment accused defendant of engaging in oral sex with a 19–year–old male by forcible compulsion and without consent (by virtue of something other than incapacity). In light of these allegations, a declaration of delinquency charged defendant with violating the conditions of the sentence of probation imposed upon him in 2000 after his conviction for second-degree assault. Defendant contended that the alleged victim did not resist or otherwise communicate a lack of consent, and that he perceived the sexual act to be consensual. It is undisputed that defendant had been consuming beer steadily in the hours before this incident.

* * *

[T]he court instructed the jury that "intoxication is not a defense under any circumstances" because there was no element of intent or other subjective mental state required for this crime. "Rather, . . . sodomy in the third degree involves an allegation that a reasonable person in the defendant's situation would have understood the . . . alleged victim's words and acts as an expression of a lack of consent." As a result, the court charged the jury that "if the defendant failed to so understand solely as a result of intoxication[,] such would not be a defense under the law" to third-degree sodomy. The jury . . . convicted him of sodomy in the third degree.

* * *

To be guilty of third-degree sodomy under Penal Law § 130.40(3), defendant was required to have engaged in the sexual act "with another person without such person's consent where such lack of consent [was] by reason of some factor other than incapacity to consent." The Sexual Assault Reform Act fleshed out this crime by specially defining "lack of consent" for purposes of third-degree sodomy as

"circumstances under which, at the time of the [sexual act], the victim clearly expressed that he or she did not consent to engage in such act, and a reasonable person in the actor's situation would have understood such person's words and acts as an expression of lack of consent to such act under all the circumstances" (Penal Law § 130.05[2][d]).

This provision was

"designed to address the so-called date rape or acquaintance rape situations [where] there [might] be consent to various acts leading up to the sexual act, but at the time of the act, the victim clearly says no or otherwise expresses a lack of consent, and a reasonable person in the actor's situation would understand that the victim was expressing a lack of consent" (Donnino, Main Volume Supp. Practice Commentary, McKinney's Cons. Laws of N.Y., Book 39, Penal Law art. 130, at 220 [citation and internal quotation marks omitted]).

Further,

"[t]he use of the term 'reasonable person' in the 'actor's situation' imports an objective element into the determination of whether there was a clear expression of non-consent to the [sexual act]. Although the 'reasonable person' must stand in the shoes of the actor, if such a person would understand that the victim was expressing a lack of consent, *then it does not matter that the accused thought otherwise*" (*id.* at 220–221, 473 N.Y.S.2d 966, 462 N.E.2d 143 [emphasis added and citation omitted]).

In short, the proper inquiry for the factfinder is not whether a defendant actually perceives a lack of consent, but whether the victim, by words or actions, clearly expresses an unwillingness to engage in the sexual act in such a way that a neutral observer would have understood that the victim was not consenting. Otherwise, it would not be enough for a victim simply to say "No." Every prosecution would devolve into a dispute over whether the particular defendant might have misapprehended whether "No" really meant "No" for one reason or another. As the People point out, if the Legislature had, in fact, intended to take a defendant's subjective mental state into account, it could have drafted the statute to require the accused to know or have reason to know that the victim was not consenting; or the Legislature could have furnished an accused with an affirmative defense of lack of knowledge (*see e.g.* Penal Law § 130.10[1] [providing for an affirmative defense of lack of knowledge of incapacity where victim's lack of consent is based solely upon incapacity to consent because of mental disability, mental incapacity or physical helplessness]).

Because a defendant's subjective mental state is not an element of the crime of third-degree sodomy, evidence of intoxication at the time of the sexual act is irrelevant. Thus, the trial judge in this case properly declined to instruct the jury on intoxication with respect to the charge of this crime.

Accordingly, the order of the Appellate Division should be affirmed.

---

b. Determining Whether There Was Consent

The following case discusses the intertwining role of the jury, the burden of proof placed upon the state, and the defendant's right to accurate jury instructions, all on the issue of consent to a sexual act. In *Clifton*, the defendant's testimony directly contradicts the victim's testimony. He said there was consent. She said there was no consent. The court addresses whether there is sufficient evidence to convict the defendant on the sole testimony of the victim, and whether the defendant is entitled to an additional instruction clarifying the burden placed on the state regarding the element of lack of consent.

Clifton v. Commonwealth

Court of Appeals of Virginia, Richmond
468 S.E.2d 155 (1996)

WILLIS, Judge.

On appeal from his convictions in a jury trial of breaking and entering with intent to commit rape and of rape, Roger Talley Clifton contends (1) that the evidence is insufficient to support his convictions, and (2) that the trial court erred by refusing to give a jury instruction addressing his perception that the victim consented. We find no error and affirm the judgment of the trial court.

On appeal, we view the evidence in the light most favorable to the Commonwealth, granting to it all reasonable inferences fairly deducible therefrom. *Higginbotham v. Commonwealth*, 216 Va. 349, 352, 218 S.E.2d 534, 537 (1975). "The jury's verdict will not be disturbed on appeal unless it is plainly wrong or without evidence to support it." *Traverso v. Commonwealth*, 6 Va.App. 172, 176, 366 S.E.2d 719, 721 (1988).

"A conviction of rape may be sustained solely upon the credible testimony of the prosecutrix." *Myers v. Commonwealth*, 11 Va.App. 634, 635, 400 S.E.2d 803, 804 (1991). "'[T]he credibility of witnesses and the weight to be given to their testimony are questions exclusively within the province of a jury.'" *Id.* (citation omitted).

The victim testified that on the morning of January 6, 1994, her next door neighbor, Clifton, entered her house. Her husband was at work and her three children were asleep. She testified that she was in the kitchen, dressed only in a nightgown and underclothes, when she heard a "peck." She looked out the window and saw Clifton standing outside pointing at the door. She gestured for him to wait. When she walked into the front room, Clifton was already standing inside the door. He grabbed her and began rubbing her breasts. After she told him "to quit," he twisted her arm behind her back and dragged her to the couch. He bent her over the couch, pulled her panties down, and announced his intention to have sexual intercourse with her. She testified, "I told him no, stop, and I started crying." However, she said that she did not resist, but submitted to sexual intercourse with Clifton because she was afraid for her children and did not want them to be awakened and see what was happening.

During the intercourse, the victim saw her husband drive by and saw Clifton's daughter outside the house. She told Clifton of this, but he continued to have intercourse until he was "finished." When she told Clifton that a black Blazer was pulling into his driveway, he released her and went home. She denied having had intercourse with Clifton previously.

Clifton testified that he and the victim had prior sexual relations in 1991. He testified that on the morning in question, he walked out onto his front porch and saw the victim motioning to him through the window. He walked over to her house and entered through an open door. He testified that she said, "it has been a long time since we did anything." He testified that she pulled the elastic waistband of his pants out, put her hand inside his pants, and fondled him. She then lifted her nightgown, knelt on the couch, reached behind her, grabbed his penis, and inserted it. He testified that while they were having intercourse, the victim saw her husband's car go by outside and became nervous. He assured her that her husband would not arrive for a few minutes and said "[l]et's finish what we started here."

After Clifton left, the victim telephoned her sister-in-law and her husband. The sister-in-law corroborated this, testifying that the victim telephoned her and told her that Clifton had raped her. When the victim's husband arrived home, he called the police. Officer Snodgrass of the Abingdon Police Department testified that when he arrived at the victim's home, she was upset and crying.

The victim was taken to the hospital for a rape examination. Dr. Moore, a medical expert who testified on Clifton's behalf, stated that according to the victim's records, the examination did not disclose injury that would normally be expected to result from forcible sexual penetration.

I.

Clifton acknowledges that he had sexual intercourse with the victim, but contends that it was consensual. He argues that her non-resistance proves her consent. We disagree.

The victim was in her own home when Clifton entered. Her three small children were asleep in their rooms, and her husband was at work. Her account sufficiently described a rape and was not inherently incredible. Her explanation that she did not resist because she was afraid for her children was reasonable. "Her credibility and the weight to be given to her testimony were peculiarly within the province of the jury." *Myers,* 11 Va.App. at 637, 400 S.E.2d at 805.

II.

The trial court gave the following instructions:

Instruction 15.

The defendant is charged with the crime of rape. The Commonwealth must prove beyond a reasonable doubt each of the following elements of that crime:

(1) That the defendant had sexual intercourse with [the victim] who was not then the defendant's spouse; and

(2) That it was against her will and without her consent; and

(3) That it was by force, threat or intimidation. . . .

Instruction B.

The Commonwealth need not show that [the victim] cried out or physically resisted the defendant in order to convict him of the offense for which he is charged, but the absence of such resistance may be considered to show that the act alleged was not against her will.

Instruction C.

Consent by [the victim] is an absolute bar to conviction of rape. If, after consideration of all the evidence, you have a reasonable doubt as to whether [the victim] consented to have intercourse with him, then you shall find him not guilty.

The trial court refused the following jury instruction, which was proposed by Clifton:

> If you find the defendant actually believed that [the victim] was consenting to have sexual intercourse, and if his belief was reasonable, then you shall find him not guilty. The burden is on the Commonwealth to prove beyond a reasonable doubt that the defendant either knew that [the victim] did not consent to sexual intercourse, or that a reasonable person in the position of the defendant would have known that [the victim] did not consent to sexual intercourse.

Contending that the refusal of this instruction was error, Clifton argues that rape is a crime of intent and that the Commonwealth was required to prove that he knew or should have known that the intercourse was accomplished without the victim's consent. We disagree.

Although proof of rape requires proof of intent, the required intent is established upon proof that the accused knowingly and intentionally committed the acts constituting the elements of rape. The elements of rape, as pertinent to this case, consist of engaging in sexual intercourse with the victim, against her will, by force, threat, or intimidation. *See* Code § 18.2–61(A);*Carter v. Commonwealth*, 16 Va.App. 118, 127, 428 S.E.2d 34, 41 (1993). In support of a consent defense, an accused may produce evidence of circumstances, including conduct or statements by the victim, tending to prove consent. He may testify as to his observations or perceptions of statements or conduct by the victim suggesting consent. However, the element to be proven by the Commonwealth is the fact that the intercourse was accomplished against the victim's will. The accused's perception may be evidence bearing on the sufficiency of the proof of this element, but it is not itself an element of the crime. *See Bailey v. Commonwealth*, 82 Va. 107, 111 (1886).[1]

Instructions 15, B, and C properly and fully informed the jury of the elements the Commonwealth was required to prove in order to convict Clifton of rape. Instruction C specifically addressed Clifton's affirmative defense of consent. The jury was instructed that if it had a reasonable doubt whether the victim consented to sexual intercourse with Clifton, it could not convict him of rape.

The judgment of the trial court is affirmed.

Affirmed.

BENTON, Judge, dissenting.

I disagree with the majority's holding that the trial judge did not err in refusing Clifton's proposed jury instruction. The principle is well established that

---

1   Contrary to the assertions in the dissent, we do not hold that the victim's **conduct** is irrelevant, nor do we hold that consent can never be shown in the absence of words indicating a willingness to engage in intercourse. We hold merely that the defendant's state of mind regarding the issue of consent is **not** an element the Commonwealth is required to prove.

"[a] jury must be instructed on any theory or affirmative defense supported by the evidence." *McCoy v. Commonwealth*, 9 Va.App. 227, 229, 385 S.E.2d 628, 629 (1989). Thus, this Court has "held that it was error not to give a separate instruction defining consent when 'consent was vital to [the] defense and was supported by sufficient evidence to make it a jury issue.'" *Morse v. Commonwealth*, 17 Va.App. 627, 637, 440 S.E.2d 145, 151 (1994) (citation omitted). As in Morse, the instruction that Clifton tendered in this case and that was rejected by the trial judge addressed "the meaning of consent." *Id.* Moreover, Clifton's evidence supported the giving of an instruction that would have required the jury, if it accepted Clifton's evidence, to determine whether consent occurred in the absence of a verbal manifestation of consent.

The Commonwealth's evidence proved that Clifton, the complainant's neighbor, entered complainant's residence when she was home with her children. The complainant testified that after Clifton began rubbing her breasts, she told him "to quit." She further testified that she told Clifton "no, stop" when he forcefully grabbed her, moved her to a sofa, and stated that he intended to have sexual intercourse with her. She testified further that her responses were tempered because she did not want her children to awake and witness the assault. She denied any prior sexual relations with Clifton.

In his defense, Clifton testified that the complainant invited him into her residence while she was wearing a nightgown. He testified that the complainant talked about their prior sexual encounters, fondled him, and engaged in consensual sexual intercourse. He testified that she made no statement indicating that she was unwilling to have sexual intercourse. He further testified that the complainant became agitated and disengaged from the act when her husband drove by. She then expressed concern about her husband returning.

Clifton further testified that he had known the complainant for five years and that they had sexual intercourse on two previous occasions when her husband was absent. He also introduced in evidence a photograph of complainant in underwear and testified that she gave it to him.

Clifton's evidence included testimony by a physician that the complainant exhibited no signs of rape. The physician found no bruising marks on her wrists, arms, or body suggesting force. The doctor also testified that the complainant exhibited no signs of stress, emotions, fear, or anger. When she was examined, all of her "vital signs" were normal. The doctor further testified that the examination was "not consistent with what [he had] seen in the past or would expect to see."

The majority states that "Clifton argues that . . . the Commonwealth was required to prove that he knew the intercourse was accomplished without the victim's consent." I believe that the majority misperceives Clifton's argument.

In his brief, Clifton argues that the jury could have found that he "actually and reasonably believed that she did [consent]." Clifton does not contend that the Commonwealth must affirmatively prove that he had an awareness that the complainant did not consent. Indeed, in Clifton's brief he acknowledges the principle that "[a] person who proceeds to accomplish intercourse, in the face of [the awareness that the consent of the other person is vital] . . . is a rapist unless he/she reasonably believed that his/her partner was truly consenting." Roger D. Groot, *Criminal Offenses and Defenses in Virginia* 380 (3d ed.1994).

The majority also states that Clifton's proposed instruction was erroneous because, although "[t]he accused's perception may be evidence bearing on the sufficiency of proof, . . . it is not itself an element of the crime." Whether the complainant ever actually gave verbal consent obviously may be an important consideration in a rape prosecution; however, if the jury believed Clifton's testimony, it was required to assess a circumstance in which the complainant made no verbal statement bearing on consent. The jury should have been instructed on the question of how to determine whether the victim consented in the absence of a verbal expression. Without a clear verbal manifestation of consent or lack thereof, the jury must consider the victim's conduct. I believe that question should be determined by the standard of a reasonable person. Thus, the ultimate issue posed by Clifton's evidence is whether a reasonable person in Clifton's position would have known, based upon the victim's *conduct*, that the complainant did not consent. Under the majority's reasoning, rape must be classified as a strict liability crime because only "the fact" of consent can be proven. The logical extension of that reasoning is that neither the conduct of a complainant, no matter how inviting, nor the intent of an accused, no matter how reasonable, is relevant in determining the manner in which to instruct the jury concerning the sufficiency of the evidence to prove consent.

In Virginia, rape is statutorily defined in pertinent part as follows:

> If any person has sexual intercourse with a complaining witness who is not his or her spouse . . . and such act is accomplished . . . against the complaining witness's will, by force, threat or intimidation of or against the complaining witness or another person, . . . he or she shall be guilty of rape.

Code § 18.2–61(A). Because the offense requires that the act be committed "against the complaining witness's will," *id.*, rape, by definition, must occur without the consent of the complainant. *See* Groot, *supra*, at 380. Indeed, Virginia Model Jury Instruction No. 45.100 states that the act must be committed "against [the complainant's] will and without her consent."

The issue that Clifton's appeal raises is what intent is required to prove rape. As Professor Groot notes, "rape is not a strict liability crime." Groot, *supra*, at 380. The Commonwealth must prove an intent by the accused. *Id.* However, the Commonwealth is not required to prove that an accused actually knew that the complainant did not consent. *Id.* The Commonwealth is only required to prove that under the circumstances the accused knew or should have known that the complainant did not wish to have sexual intercourse. This objective standard allows the fact finder to consider all of the circumstances, including the victim's conduct.

Clifton argues that the instruction he tendered was based on this theory of the evidence and that his testimony was sufficient to support the instruction. He further argues that he was entitled to have the jury instructed that he must be acquitted if he actually and reasonably believed that the complainant had consented. *See* Groot, *supra*, at 394 n. 20.

Although no Virginia cases address in detail the issue of consent, cases from other states have done so. For example, the Supreme Court of Connecticut ruled as follows:

> A finding that a complainant had consented would implicitly negate a claim that the actor had compelled the complainant by force or threat to engage in sexual intercourse. Consent is not made an affirmative defense under our sex offense statutes, so, as in the case of the defense of alibi, the burden is upon the state to prove lack of consent beyond a reasonable doubt whenever the issue is raised.

While the word "consent" is commonly regarded as referring to the state of mind of the complainant in a sexual assault case, it cannot be viewed as a wholly subjective concept. Although the actual state of mind of the actor in a criminal case may in many instances be the issue upon which culpability depends, a defendant is not chargeable with knowledge of the internal workings of the minds of others except to the extent that he should reasonably have gained such knowledge from his observations of their conduct. The law of contract has come to recognize that a true "meeting of the minds" is no longer essential to the formation of a contract and that rights and obligations may arise from acts of the parties, usually their words, upon which a reasonable person would rely. Similarly, whether a complainant has consented to intercourse depends upon her manifestations of such consent as reasonably construed. If the conduct of the complainant under all the circumstances should reasonably be viewed as indicating consent to the act of intercourse, a defendant should not be found guilty because of some undisclosed mental reservation on the part of the complainant. Reasonable conduct ought not to be deemed criminal.

It is likely that juries in considering the defense of consent in sexual assault cases, though visualizing the issue in terms of actual consent by the complainant, have reached their verdicts on the basis of inferences that a reasonable person would draw from the conduct of the complainant and the defendant under the surrounding circumstances. It is doubtful that jurors would ever convict a defendant who had in their view acted in reasonable reliance upon words or conduct of the complainant indicating consent, even though there had been some concealed reluctance on her part. If a defendant were concerned about such a possibility, however, he would be entitled, once the issue is raised, to request a jury instruction that the state must prove beyond a reasonable doubt that the conduct of the complainant would not have justified a reasonable belief that she had consented. *State v. Smith*, 210 Conn. 132, 141, 554 A.2d 713, 717 (1989) (citation omitted).

In his defense, Clifton testified concerning the facts and circumstances that he contends occurred on the day of the incident. His testimony described the complainant's attire and her conduct after, as he alleged, she invited him into her residence. His theory of defense was that, although the complainant did not verbally affirm her intentions, her conduct constituted consent or, at a minimum, gave rise to a reasonable belief in his mind that she consented. He contends that he actually believed from her conduct and surrounding circumstances that she consented and that his belief was reasonable.

The instruction that Clifton tendered was a correct statement of the law. It stated the following:

> If you find that the defendant actually believed that [the complainant] was consenting to have sexual intercourse, and if his belief was reasonable, then you shall find him not guilty. The burden is on the Commonwealth to prove beyond a reasonable doubt that the defendant either knew that [the complainant] did not consent to sexual intercourse, or that a reasonable person in the position of the defendant would have known that [the complainant] did not consent to sexual intercourse.

The instruction gave meaning to consent and clearly informed the jury that Clifton's subjective belief was insufficient to find him not guilty. "When the accused claims mistake as to the fact of consent, he/she should at most obtain an instruction that he/she cannot be convicted if (1) he/she actually believed the victim was consenting, and (2) the belief was reasonable." Groot, *supra*, at 394 n. 20. The instruction informed the jury that it could convict only if the Commonwealth proved beyond a reasonable doubt that Clifton subjectively did not believe the victim had consented or that a reasonable person in Clifton's position could not have believed the victim had consented. Thus, the jury was required to consider all of the circumstances surrounding the case, including whether the victim actually consented.

The trial judge instructed the jury on consent as follows:

> Consent by [the victim] is an absolute bar to conviction of rape. If, after consideration of all the evidence, you have a reasonable doubt as to whether [the victim] consented to have intercourse with him, then you shall find him not guilty.

Under the circumstances of this case, this instruction, which is Instruction No. 45.700 from the Virginia Model Jury Instructions (Criminal), was inadequate because it leaves ambiguous whether consent may be manifested by conduct in the absence of verbal expression. If consent can be manifested by conduct and I believe it can be, the jury must be given guidance. The instruction should include the directive that conduct will suffice to establish consent but only if the defendant both sincerely and reasonably interprets it as consent. This instruction failed to inform the jury that if they found, as Clifton testified, that the complainant made no verbal expressions, they could nonetheless find from the facts and circumstances of complainant's conduct that Clifton sincerely and reasonably believed she consented.

For these reasons, I would reverse the conviction and remand for a new trial.

Notes and Questions

1. The majority in *Clifton* holds that the state must prove only the victim did not consent, not disprove the defendant's belief there was consent. Thus, consent hinges on the victim's state of mind, and not the perpetrator's state of mind. Consequently, consent in cases such as this ("he said, she said") can hinge entirely on the credible testimony of the victim, so that where the jury believes the victim's testimony beyond a reasonable doubt, the element of lack of consent is established. In *Clifton*, the court refused the defendant's requested jury instruction because it believed the requested instruction made the defendant's state of mind an element of the offense of rape for the state to overcome beyond a reasonable doubt. The court pointed out that the defendant can attempt to undermine the credibility of the evidence on the element of lack of consent, but that the defendant's state of mind is not an element. Is this an unfair burden to overcome for a defendant? Or does the difficulty of providing sufficient evidence to convict of rape validate this apparent double-standard?

2. For the dissent, it is the defendant's reasonable belief about the alleged victim's consent, not the victim's subjective and unstated desire not to have sex that controls. What sort of policy argument supports this interpretation?

----

c. Capacity to Consent

A victim may lack capacity to consent because of age or other circumstances. An unconscious person, for instance, may not consent to sex. In *Ireland*, the issue is not the victims' consent to have sex. There were actually four victims in *Ireland*, all of whom were old enough to consent, were sober enough to consent, and agreed to have sex with the defendant for money. The question in *Ireland* is whether they came to lack the capacity to withdraw consent. This is certainly not a typical case. The defendant's contention in this case borders on the absurd. *Ireland*, though, as you will see, presents a lot of issues that occur in many common rape cases.

i. Threats

People v. Ireland

California Court of Appeal
188 Cal.App.4th 328, 114 Cal.Rptr. 915 (2010)

[On four separate occasions, the defendant retained the services of prostitutes. After each agreed to have sex with him, the women entered his car or went with him to a hotel to perform the act. Before they began, however, in each case, he pulled a knife on each of them and told them that he would harm them if they did not cooperate. Eds.]

Appellant argues there is insufficient evidence to convict him of any of the forcible rapes. He specifically contends that each woman consented to engage in sex acts in return for money and, although each woman objected to the use of the knife, the use of that knife did not automatically terminate the consent. He claims there was insufficient evidence to establish that each woman withdrew her consent and communicated that withdrawal of consent to appellant. We disagree.

* * *

Appellant was convicted of four counts of forcible rape within the meaning of section 261, subdivision (a)(2), which defines rape as an act of sexual intercourse "[w]here it is accomplished against a person's will by means of force, violence, duress, menace, or fear of immediate and unlawful bodily injury on the person or another."

Lack of consent is an element of the crime of rape. Consent is defined in section 261.6 as "positive cooperation in act or attitude pursuant to an exercise of free will. The person must act freely and voluntarily and have knowledge of the nature of the act or transaction involved." CALCRIM No. 1000, as given here, instructed that "[t]o consent, a woman must act freely and voluntarily and know the nature of the act."

"Actual consent must be distinguished from submission. [A] victim's decision to submit to an attacker's sexual demands out of fear of bodily injury is not consent [citations] because the decision is not freely and voluntarily made (§ 261.6). A selection by the victim of the lesser of two evils—rape versus the violence threatened by the attacker if the victim resists—is hardly an exercise of free will. [Citation.]" (*People v. Giardino* (2000) 82 Cal.App.4th 454, 460, fn. 3, 98 Cal.Rptr.2d 315.)

Where the woman's lack of consent was uncommunicated and could not reasonably be detected, however, the accused may not be guilty of rape. It is a defense that the accused reasonably and in good faith believed the woman engaged in the act consensually. (*People v. Mayberry* (1975) 15 Cal.3d 143, 153–158, 125 Cal.Rptr. 745, 542 P.2d 1337.)

Here the jury was instructed: "Evidence that the woman requested [appellant] to use a condom or other birth control device is not enough by itself to constitute consent." (See CALCRIM No. 1000.) And: "[Appellant's] is not guilty of rape if he actually and reasonably believed that the woman consented to intercourse. The People have the burden of proving beyond a reasonable doubt that [appellant] did not actually and reasonably believe that the woman consented." (See *ibid.*)[2]

Withdrawal of consent can occur at any time. (*In re John Z.* (2003) 29 Cal.4th 756, 762, 128 Cal.Rptr.2d 783, 60 P.3d 183.) Here the trial court gave the standard instruction on withdrawal of consent:

> "A woman who initially consents to an act of intercourse may change her mind during the act. If she does so, under the law, the act of intercourse is then committed without her consent if: [¶] One, she communicated to [appellant] that she objected to the act of intercourse and attempted to stop the act; [¶] Two, she communicated her objection through words or acts

---

2   During a discussion of jury instructions, the prosecutor argued this portion of CALCRIM No. 1000 was inapplicable to the facts of the case. Defense counsel argued that this portion of the instruction was applicable because appellant thought the victims agreed to the use of the knife. The trial court opined that it might be "unusual for someone to believe that's the case" and that, although it was a "very, very remote" possibility, it would allow that portion of the instruction to be read.

that a reasonable person would have understood as showing her lack of consent; [¶] and Three, [appellant] forcibly continued the act of intercourse despite her objection." (See CALCRIM No. 1000.)

Appellant's argument is that each victim gave her consent to the sex act that was committed, that his use of the knife during the act did not automatically negate that consent, and that there was insufficient evidence that any of the victims communicated a withdrawal of consent to him. Respondent, on the other hand, contends the determinative question is not whether the victims communicated a withdrawal of consent. Instead, according to respondent, appellant's use of the knife, along with his express or implied threat to harm his victims if they did not cooperate, did automatically negate their previously given consent.

We agree with respondent's analysis. There is no doubt that, at the beginning of each encounter, each victim freely consented to intercourse. But as to each of the victims, appellant communicated the express or implied threat that, if they did not continue to cooperate even after he produced the knife and held it to their throats, he would do them harm. As to the victim V.B., the testimony was that appellant told her "just to cooperate" and she "won't get hurt." When the victim J.W. asked appellant what he was doing with the knife, he told her to "'shut up.'" She did, because she was afraid he would otherwise "slice [her] neck off." He told her not to scream or make any sudden movements and he would not use the knife. When the victim A.H. reacted to appellant putting the knife to her throat by saying "no," appellant responded by instructing her to put a condom on his penis, remove her pants, and get on her knees. She complied because she thought he would otherwise kill her. To the victim C.S., appellant said "do what I say and you won't get hurt." She cooperated out of fear.

It is not appellant's position that there is insufficient evidence to show a lack of consent, from each of the victims, after appellant displayed his knife and threatened them. There is more than substantial evidence that each victim's continued participation in the sexual encounter with appellant was in fact non-consensual after that point.

Instead, appellant's position is that because, as to each victim, consent had once been given, each victim was required not only to withdraw that consent but also to communicate that withdrawal to him—to communicate it, if not expressly, at least by implication. We disagree.

The essence of consent is that it is given out of free will. That is why it can be withdrawn. While there exists a defense to rape based on the defendant's actual and reasonable belief that the victim does consent (*People v. Dominguez* (2006) 39 Cal.4th 1141, 1148, 47 Cal.Rptr.3d 575, 140 P.3d 866; *People v. Mayberry, supra,* 15 Cal.3d at pp. 153–158, 125 Cal.Rptr. 745, 542 P.2d 1337), we do not require that victims communicate their lack of consent. (See *People v. Maury* (2003) 30

Cal.4th 342, 403, 133 Cal.Rptr.2d 561, 68 P.3d 1 [lack of consent need not be proven by direct testimony but may be inferred from use of force or duress].) We certainly do not require that victims resist. (*People v. Griffin* (2004) 33 Cal.4th 1015, 1024–1025, 16 Cal.Rptr.3d 891, 94 P.3d 1089.) Yet this is what appellant proposes here. At the time of the offenses, appellant told his victims to cooperate or be hurt. Now he contends they were required to express to him their lack of cooperation. That cannot be the law. When appellant used the knife and expressly or impliedly threatened his victims, and in the absence of any conduct by the victims indicating that they continued to consent,[3] the previously given consent no longer existed, either in fact or in law. (Cf. *People v. Washington* (1962) 203 Cal.App.2d 609, 610, 21 Cal.Rptr. 788 ["[c]onsent induced by fear is no consent at all"].)

Furthermore, even were we to say that these victims were required to communicate their lack of consent to appellant, we would still find substantial evidence to support the convictions. V.B. testified that she never agreed to have sex with appellant with a knife held to her neck. When appellant pressed the knife to her throat, she was afraid and began to cry. She told appellant "please don't hurt me, don't hurt me." J.W. testified that, when appellant put the knife to her neck, she asked him what he was doing and asked him to move the knife. Appellant told her to "shut up" and refused to put the knife down because he thought she might scream. A.H. testified that she said "no" when appellant put the knife to her throat. C.S. testified she was "shocked" and "scared" she might die, and that appellant told her to "do what I say and you won't get hurt." In his confession, appellant stated that C.S. told him she did not want him to use the knife.

From all of this evidence, it is clear that these victims did not continue to consent when appellant put the knife to their throats and that appellant knew they did not continue to consent. Thus, if they were required to communicate a withdrawal of consent, they adequately did so.

Substantial evidence supports each of the convictions of forcible rape, and we reject appellant's claim to the contrary.

Notes and Questions

1. Consent to sex, like an agreement to join a conspiracy, is not something that will be memorialized in a formal declaration. The court describes consent as "positive cooperation in act or attitude pursuant to an exercise of free will."

---

3   Appellant does not argue that the record includes any such evidence

What burden does the prosecution have to prove regarding the victim's consent? Must the victim have done something suggesting consent to prevent a rape prosecution or it is enough that the victim did not do anything expressing her unwillingness to have sex? The court's analysis is not exactly clear on this issue. The jury instruction approved in this case requires the former but recall this double-speak from the opinion:

> Where the woman's lack of consent was uncommunicated and could not reasonably be detected, however, the accused may not be guilty of rape. It is a defense that the accused reasonably and in good faith believed the woman engaged in the act consensually.

Which version makes more sense?

2. The important point in this case is that the victims did not *withdraw* consent, they lost the capacity to withdraw consent because of the defendant's actions and, once they did, any further sexual activity by the defendant was rape.

---

ii. Age (Statutory Rape)

Perhaps the most litigated issue in statutory rape cases in American appellate courts is the question of whether the defendant's state of mind is relevant. This case also offers a reprise of strict liability, which we considered in some depth in the introductory chapter.

State v. Jadowski

Wisconsin Supreme Court
680 N.W.2d 810 (2004)

SHIRLEY S. ABRAHAMSON, C.J.,

This is an appeal from an order of the Circuit Court for Sheboygan County, L. Edward Stengel, Judge. Todd M. Jadowski, the defendant, faces prosecution on one count of sexual intercourse with a person who has not yet attained the age of 16 years contrary to Wis. Stat. § 948.02 (1999–2000). The circuit court granted the defendant's motion to introduce evidence of the victim's intentional misrepresentation of her age.

* * *

I

For purposes of this appeal, the facts are not in dispute. On April 15, 2002, the State filed a complaint against the 35–year–old defendant, alleging that on April 3, 2002, he had sexual intercourse with a person below the age of 16 in violation of Wis. Stat. § 948.02(2). The victim was born on September 13, 1986, making her about five and a half months shy of her 16th birthday on the date of the alleged assault.

Prior to trial the defendant moved to admit evidence that the victim fraudulently induced him to believe she was an adult. The circuit court held an evidentiary hearing on the motion. The defendant made an offer of proof that the victim was a chronic runaway; that the victim used what appeared to be a state-issued identification card showing her to be 19 years old; that the victim told the defendant and others that she was 19 years old; that the victim appeared to be 19 years old; and that the victim maintained in the defendant's presence that she was old enough to work as an exotic dancer.

The circuit court ruled that evidence of the victim's fraud was admissible under Wis. Stat. § 904.04 as relevant to the "issue of intent on behalf of the alleged victim as well as the absence of mistake or accident."

* * *

. . . The defendant asserts that his reasonable belief about the victim's age based on the victim's fraud regarding her age should be a defense to a charge under § 948.02(2). We read Wis. Stat. § 948.02(2) with § 939.23 and § 939.43(2) to preclude a defense predicated on a child's intentional misrepresentation of her age.

Section 948.02(2) governs second-degree sexual assault of a child and provides that "[w]hoever has sexual contact or sexual intercourse with a person who has not attained the age of 16 years is guilty of a Class BC felony." The defendant and the State agree that the State must prove only two elements for a conviction: that the accused had sexual contact or intercourse with the victim, and that the victim was under the age of sixteen. The defendant asserts, however, that a victim's intentional misrepresentation of her age is an affirmative defense to the crime.

* * *

Wisconsin Stat. § 939.23, governing criminal intent as an element for crimes, provides guidance in determining whether an accused's reasonable belief about a victim's age based on the victim's intentional misrepresentation is a defense.

Section 939.23 addresses criminal intent as an element of all crimes in chapters 939 to 951. When criminal intent is an element of a crime, the statute uses one of several words or phrases, such as "intentionally," "know," or "believe." The sexual assault offense in the case at bar (§ 948.02(2)) does not contain any of the words or phrases denoting criminal intent.

Even if Wis. Stat. § 948.02(2) included a word of criminal intent like "intentionally" or "know," the State would not have to prove an accused's knowledge of the age of the minor. Section 939.23(6) expressly provides that criminal intent "does not require proof of knowledge of the age of a minor even though age is a material element in the crime in question."

Thus the sexual assault statute in the case at bar read in conjunction with Wis. Stat. § 939.23(6) does not require an actor to know the victim's age and does not set forth an actor's reasonable (but erroneous) belief about the victim's age as a defense.

An actor's ability to raise mistake regarding his belief about the age of a minor as a defense is explicitly negated in Wis. Stat. § 939.43(2). The general rule about mistake, set forth in § 939.43(1), is that "[a]n honest error, whether of fact or of law other than criminal law, is a defense if it negatives the existence of a state of mind essential to the crime." The exception to this general rule applies here: "A mistake as to the age of a minor . . . is not a defense."

The defendant acknowledges that Wis. Stat. §§ 948.02(2), 939.23, and 939.43(2) prohibit an actor from raising mistake about the age of the minor as a defense to the charge of sexual assault. The defendant reasons that although these statutes prohibit the defense of mistake, they do not prohibit an actor from raising the affirmative defense of a victim's intentional misrepresentation about her age. The defendant distinguishes the defense of mistake from the defense of fraud. He asserts that he, as a victim of fraud, is not in the same position as an accused who is mistaken about the victim's age or who commits an honest error. The defendant urges that he was not mistaken about the victim's age; he was defrauded by the victim.

The defendant's affirmative defense of fraud is premised in part upon Wis. Stat. § 939.45, governing privilege as a defense to prosecution for a crime. The defendant relies on § 939.45(6), the "catch-all" provision of the privilege statute. The catch-all provision states that the defense of privilege can be claimed "[w]hen for any other reason the actor's conduct is privileged by the statutory or common law of this state." The defendant does not explain, however, upon what statute or common law rule he is relying under the catch-all privilege statute.

The crux of the defendant's position is that this court should engraft an affirmative defense of fraud onto Wis. Stat. § 948.02(2) even though the text of the statutes renders an actor mistaken as to a child's age liable for the crime.[14] We are not persuaded that any reason exists for this court to perform such a task. We agree with the State that § 948.02(2) is a strict liability crime with regard to knowledge of the child's age. Numerous indicia point to the conclusion that no affirmative fraud defense is part of or should be read into § 948.02(2) and that the defendant's proposed affirmative defense is contrary to the policy adopted by the legislature.

In making this determination a court considers the following factors: (1) the language of the statute; (2) the legislative history of the statute; (3) the seriousness of the penalty; (4) the purpose of the statute; and (5) the practical requirements of effective law enforcement. *State v. Stoehr*, 134 Wis.2d 66, 76, 396 N.W.2d 177 (1986) (citing *Collova*, 79 Wis.2d at 478–80, 255 N.W.2d 581; *Stanfield*, 105 Wis.2d at 560–61, 314 N.W.2d 339).

First, an examination of Wis. Stat. § 948.02(2) in the broader context of chapter 948, Crimes Against Children, demonstrates that the legislature has, in certain statutes, created an affirmative defense of reasonable cause to believe that the child had attained the age of 18 years. See, for example, Wis. Stat. § 948.11(2)(c), pertaining to exhibition of harmful materials to a child, and § 948.05, pertaining to sexual exploitation of a child. Inclusion of this "reasonable cause to believe" affirmative defense in some child exploitation provisions in chapter 948 but not in others supports the conclusion that the legislature did not intend to include this affirmative defense in § 948.02(2). Because the legislature did not expressly create the "reasonable cause to believe" defense in § 948.02(2), this court should not read it into the statute.

Second, Legislative Council drafting documents of the 1950–1953 criminal code, since which time Wis. Stat. §§ 939.23 and 939.43(2) have remained essentially the same, are replete with evidence that the drafters intended to impose strict liability on an actor regardless of the actor's knowledge or belief about a child's age in child sexual assault cases.[17]

Third, the purpose of Wis. Stat. § 948.02(2) is furthered by not engrafting onto the statute the affirmative defense proposed by the defendant. The statute is based on a policy determination by the legislature that persons under the age

---

14   The defendant relies on *United States v. United States District Court*, 858 F.2d 534 (9th Cir.1988), to support his position. In this federal case, the Ninth Circuit Court of Appeals engrafted a reasonable mistake of age defense onto a statute proscribing the production of materials depicting a minor engaged in sexually explicit conduct, reasoning that the First Amendment required a reasonable mistake of age defense and that congressional intent was to uphold the statute. The present case is not a First Amendment case, and it is not necessary for the court to read any language into these statutes to preserve their constitutionality.

17   *See Judiciary Committee Report on Criminal Code, Wisconsin Legislative Council Report*, vol. V, Bill No. 100A at 20, 21, 35 (1953).

of sixteen are not competent to consent to sexual contact or sexual intercourse. The statute is intended to protect children. The state has a strong interest in the ethical and moral development of its children, and this state has a long tradition of honoring its obligation to protect its children from predators and from themselves. The statutes are designed to impose the risk of criminal penalty on the adult, when the adult engages in sexual behavior with a minor.

Fourth, engrafting the defendant's proposed defense onto the statute undermines the policy of protecting minors from sexual abuse and would raise practical law enforcement problems. Age is difficult to ascertain, and actors could often reasonably claim that they believed their victims were adults. The requirements of practical law enforcement support a conclusion that Wis. Stat. § 948.02(2) is a strict liability statute with regard to the age of the victim.

Fifth, the traditional approach, originally accepted in virtually every state and still accepted in many jurisdictions, is to impose strict liability regarding the age of the victim no matter how reasonable the defendant's belief that the victim was old enough to consent, and no matter that the belief is based on the victim's own representations. [20] The need for or desirability of providing a mistake or fraud defense regarding the age of the victim has been subject to debate. [21] Professor LaFave, to whom this court often turns for assistance, concludes that in more recent times the issue of such a defense has been recognized as "a policy matter that ought to be specifically addressed in the statutory definition of the crime." [22]

Several jurisdictions have, however, adopted a defense based on the reasonable belief of an accused about the age of the minor by judicial decision or statute. Campbell, 46 A.L.R. 5th at 518–20.

Historically, the penalty imposed under a statute has been a significant consideration in determining whether a statute should be construed as dispensing with mens rea. Criminal liability without criminal intent almost always has involved statutes that impose only fines or short jail sentences. Indeed, some courts have justified the imposition of criminal liability without requiring proof of scienter in part because the offenses did not bear the same punishments as

---

20 *See, e.g.,* 2 Wayne R. LaFave, *Substantive Criminal Law* § 17.4(c) at 650 (2d ed.2003); Colin Campbell, *Mistake or Lack of Information as to Victim's Age as Defense to Statutory Rape,* 46 A.L.R. 5th 499, 509–18 (1997 & Supp.2004).

21 *See, e.g.,* Larry W. Myers, *Reasonable Mistake as to Age: a Needed Defense to Statutory Rape,* 64 Mich. L.Rev. 105 (1965–66) (arguing that "the time has come for more liberal and realistic laws" that permit a reasonable mistake as to age defense to a charge of statutory rape); Catherine L. Carpenter, *On Statutory Rape, Strict Liability, and the Public Welfare Offense Model,* 53 Am. U.L. Rev 313 (2003) (urging reconsideration of the imposition of strict liability in statutory rape cases); Michelle Oberman, *Regulating Consensual Sex with Minors: Defining a Role for Statutory Rape,* 48 Buff. L.Rev. 703 (2000) (suggesting various revisions to statutory rape laws).

22 2 LaFave, *supra* note 20, § 17.4(c) at 650.

"infamous crimes" and questioned whether imprisonment was compatible with the reduced culpability required for such regulatory offenses.

The severe penalties for violation of Wis. Stat. § 948.02(2) stand in sharp contrast to the less severe penalties at issue in other strict liability offenses. The maximum penalty for a conviction under Wis. Stat. § 948.02(2) is a $10,000 fine or 30 years imprisonment or both.[27] In addition to these penalties, an individual convicted of violating § 948.02(2) is subject to registration as a sex offender, including annual registration requirements. The offender is subject to the provisions of Wis. Stat. ch. 980 governing commitments of sexually violent persons. As a felon, the individual would also lose his or her right to possess a firearm, to hold an office of public trust, and to vote.

The severe penalties for violation of Wis. Stat. § 948.02(2) support an inference that the legislature did not intend to impose strict liability regarding knowledge of the age of the victim. Yet this inference drawn from the severe penalties is outweighed by the other factors we have set forth.

On the basis of the text of Wis. Stat. § 948.02(2) read in conjunction with §§ 939.23 and 939.43(2), the history and purpose of the statutes, and the practical requirements of law enforcement, and despite the severe penalties imposed, we conclude that no intentional misrepresentation defense exists in a prosecution under Wis. Stat. § 948.02(2). We decline the defendant's invitation to engraft an affirmative defense for fraud onto § 948.02(2).

Accordingly, we further conclude that the circuit court erred in ruling to admit the evidence the defendant proffered. If an accused's reasonable belief about the victim's age, based on the victim's intentional misrepresentation, is not a defense, then neither evidence regarding the defendant's belief about the victim's age nor evidence regarding the cause of or reasonableness of that belief is relevant. Therefore, evidence of the defendant's belief about the victim's age or the victim's intentional misrepresentation of her age is inadmissible in the guilt-determination phase of a criminal proceeding to support the defendant's asserted affirmative fraud defense to the crime.

We turn to the second issue: If an accused is not allowed an affirmative defense that his reasonable belief about the victim's age was caused by her intentional misrepresentation of her age, do Wis. Stat. §§ 948.02(2), 939.23, and 939.43(2) deny an accused his constitutional rights under the Fourteenth Amendment to the United States Constitution? We conclude that the statutes do not violate the defendant's constitutional rights.

* * *

---

27 Effective February 1, 2003, the offense became a Class C felony with a penalty of a fine not to exceed $100,000 or imprisonment not to exceed 40 years or both. Wis. Stat. § 939.50(3)(c) (2001–02).

The crux of the defendant's constitutional argument is that he is being held criminally liable for a felony with severe penalties when, if given the opportunity, he could prove himself morally blameless. He is morally blameless, he asserts, because he was fraudulently induced by the minor to have a reasonable belief that she was of age.[37]

Substantive due process protects citizens against arbitrary or wrongful state actions, regardless of the fairness of the procedures used to implement them.

It is a fundamental principle of law that an actor should not be convicted of a crime if he had no reason to believe that the act he committed was a crime or that it was wrongful. An intent requirement was the general rule at common law. The absence of a mens rea requirement in a criminal statute is a significant departure from longstanding principles of criminal law.

Nevertheless, strict liability crimes, that is, crimes defined without any culpable state of mind, are known at law. In general, when strict liability is imposed, the actor is deemed to have had sufficient notice concerning the risk of penal sanction inherent in the proscribed activity that it is not unjust to impose criminal liability without the necessity of proving moral culpability.[40] "[T]he existence and content of the criminal prohibition in these cases are not hidden; the defendant is warned to steer well clear of the core of the offense (as in the statutory rape case)."[41] Adults are well aware of the strict liability aspect of statutory rape laws.[42]

The legislature has broad powers to promote the public welfare and to create criminal offenses and impose punishment. A state legislature is free to define a

---

37 Professor Packer commented on the inappropriateness of the criminal sanction in the absence of scienter as follows:

> [To] punish conduct without reference to the actor's state of mind is both inefficacious and unjust. It is inefficacious because conduct unaccompanied by an awareness of the factors making it criminal does not mark the actor as one who needs to be subjected to punishment in order to deter him or others from behaving similarly in the future, nor does it single him out as a socially dangerous individual who needs to be incapacitated or reformed. It is unjust because the actor is subjected to the stigma of a criminal conviction without being morally blameworthy. Consequently, on either a preventive or retributive theory of criminal punishment, the criminal sanction is inappropriate in the absence of *mens rea*.

Packer, *Mens Rea and the Supreme Court*, 1962 Sup.Ct. Rev. 107, 109. *See also Model Penal Code* § 2.05 comment (Official Draft & Revised Comments 1985).

40 For example, courts have held that if an accused knowingly possessed a hand grenade, it is no defense to argue that the accused was not aware that the device in question was subject to regulation, but if accused's owned firearms that are in technical violation of a regulation, they may avail themselves of a "mistake of fact" defense. *See Staples*, 511 U.S. at 610–11, 114 S.Ct. 1793; *United States v. Freed*, 401 U.S. 601, 609, 91 S.Ct. 1112, 28 L.Ed.2d 356 (1971).

41 *United States v. Wilson*, 159 F.3d 280, 296 (7th Cir.1998) (Posner, C.J., dissenting).

45 "Sixteen will get you twenty!" is a common exclamation expressing the widespread awareness of statutory rape laws and the strict liability aspect of the offense.

criminal offense and a state may bar consideration of a particular defense so long as the result does not offend "some principle of justice so rooted in the traditions and conscience of our people as to be ranked as fundamental."

The strict liability crime of statutory rape, in which the victim's apparent maturity is not a defense, is a recognized exception to the general rule requiring mens rea in criminal statutes. Traditionally, according to the weight of authority, "mistake as to age" has not been a defense against the charge of statutory rape. This rule is still followed in many jurisdictions.

Furthermore, strict liability regarding the age of the minor furthers the legitimate government interest in protecting children from sexual abuse by placing the risk of mistake on the adult actor.

The long history of statutory rape as a recognized exception to the requirement of criminal intent and the well accepted legislative purpose for omitting scienter undermine the defendant's argument that Wis. Stat. § 948.02(2) offends principles of justice deeply rooted in our traditions and conscience.

We acknowledge that there has been movement away from strict liability for statutory rape in recent years. Under the Model Penal Code, for example, the defense of mistaken belief should be available when the critical age is more than 10 years of age. The theory is that the policies underpinning strict liability seem less compelling as the age of the minor increases; an accused who mistakenly but reasonably believes such a partner is above the critical age should have a defense because he "evidences no abnormality, no willingness to take advantage of immaturity, no propensity to corruption of minors."

Because the legislature's forbidding a reasonable mistake of age defense in statutory rape cases (whether the mistake is induced by intentional misrepresentation or otherwise) has a significant historical derivation and is widespread, and because of judicial deference to the legislature's discretion in the exercise of its police powers, we conclude it is not violative of due process for the state legislature to forbid a defense of fraud or reasonable mistake about the age of the victim.

In sum, we conclude that the plain language of Wis. Stat. § 948.02(2), read in conjunction with Wis. Stat. §§ 939.23 and 939. 43, precludes a defense predicated on a child's intentional misrepresentation of her age. We also conclude that the statutes do not violate the defendant's rights under the Fourteenth Amendment to the United States Constitution. Accordingly, we reverse the order of the circuit court and remand the cause for further proceedings consistent with this decision.

Notes and Questions

1. As this opinion observes, there is a strong modern trend toward allowing a defense that the defendant believed that he was having sex with someone who was old enough to consent. The state courts that are part of this trend, however, have not faced legislation that speaks with the clarity of the Wisconsin statute. It is very rare for a legislature to announce that it is creating a strict liability crime. Far more common is the statute the Tennessee Court of Criminal Appeals faced in *State v. Ballinger*, 93 S.W.3d 881 (2001) containing no *mens rea* element, prompting Judge Jerry Smith to conclude that Tennessee's legislative presumption in favor of a mental state of at least recklessness required the prosecution to prove some level of culpability on the defendant's part.

2. Because of the clarity with which the Wisconsin Legislature spoke to this issue, the defendant was left to argue that the legislature was not constitutionally permitted to create such a severe penalty for an act for which the defendant bore no culpability. The court observed that "[i]t is a *fundamental principle of law* that an actor should not be convicted of a crime if he had no reason to believe that the act he committed was a crime or that it was wrongful." (Emphasis added.) Further, the court recognized that there were no strict liability crimes at common law. Should a court be willing to defer to the legislature to fashion a law, at odds with fundamental principles of law, for which the defendant could be sentenced to a maximum punishment of 30 years?

3. Notice that the court in footnote 14 observes that the Ninth Circuit held that there must be a reasonable mistake of age defense for distributing sexually explicit images of those who are underage. The court quite flippantly contrasts that case by noting that First Amendment issues were raised in that case but not this one. Is that distinction compelling. If the defense is constitutionally compelled in a prosecution for producing a sexually explicit image, why is it not compelled in a case involving an interaction with a live person? Is the right to private sexual conduct not also constitutionally protected? *See, e.g., Lawrence v. Texas*, 539 U.S. 558 (2003) (forbidding states to pass laws criminalizing private homosexual conduct between consenting adults).

C

PRACTICE EXERCISE

You are a new Tennessee prosecutor, fresh out of law school. Your supervising attorney has asked you to draft a Motion to Exclude Evidence for her case, *State v. Alvin*. The State of Tennessee has charged Alvin with statutory rape in violation of Tenn. Code Ann. § 39-13-506.

The defense attorney will likely seek to admit evidence that his client, Alvin, did not act recklessly according to *State v. Parker*, 887 S.W.2d 825 (Tenn. Crim. App. 1994). *Parker* interprets one of Tennessee's sexual crimes statutes, Tenn. Code Ann. § 39-13-504 (below), as neither imposing nor dispensing with the requisite mental state as to the age of the victim. *Id.* at 827. *Parker* itself imposes a *mens rea* requirement of at least recklessness as to knowledge of the victim's age, as required by Tenn. Code Ann. § 39-11-301(c) (below). *Id.* at 827-28. Thus, the defense in this case will likely cite *Parker* for the proposition that the relevant statute in this case, Tenn. Code Ann. § 39-13-506 (below), also has a *mens rea* requirement of recklessness. If the defense counsel successfully admits his evidence, the jury will consider that evidence (below) in evaluating Alvin's culpability.

Tips for drafting your Motion to Exclude Evidence: (1) Do not research *State v. Parker*; (2) Attempt to distinguish the statute discussed in *State v. Parker* (§ 39-13-504), from the statute at issue in this case (§ 39-13-506), based on the (a) the different elements; (b) the different punishments; and (c) Tennessee's policy of protecting children from sexual predators; (3) Use the facts; and (4) Anticipate the defense's counterarguments, and try to negate them using these tips

Remember your goal: exclude any evidence that Alvin reasonably believed the victim was over eighteen years of age.

Tenn. Code Ann. § 39-13-504 Aggravated Sexual Battery

(a) Aggravated sexual battery is unlawful sexual contact with a victim by the defendant or the defendant by a victim accompanied by any of the following circumstances:

(1) Force or coercion is used to accomplish the act and the defendant is armed with a weapon or any article used or fashioned in a manner to lead the victim reasonably to believe it to be a weapon;

(2) The defendant causes bodily injury to the victim;

(3) The defendant is aided or abetted by one (1) or more other persons; and

(A) Force or coercion is used to accomplish the act; or

(B) The defendant knows or has reason to know that the victim is mentally defective, mentally incapacitated or physically helpless; or

(4) The victim is less than thirteen (13) years of age.

(b) Aggravated sexual battery is a Class B felony.

Tenn. Code Ann. § 39-13-506 Mitigated Statutory Rape; Statutory Rape; Aggravated Statutory Rape; Penalties

(a) Mitigated statutory rape is the unlawful sexual penetration of a victim by the defendant, or of the defendant by the victim when the victim is at least fifteen (15) but less than eighteen (18) years of age and the defendant is at least four (4) but not more than five (5) years older than the victim.

(b) Statutory rape is the unlawful sexual penetration of a victim by the defendant or of the defendant by the victim when:

(1) The victim is at least thirteen (13) but less than fifteen (15) years of age and the defendant is at least four (4) years but less than ten (10) years older than the victim; or

(2) The victim is at least fifteen (15) but less than eighteen (18) years of age and the defendant is more than five (5) but less than ten (10) years older than the victim.

(c) Aggravated statutory rape is the unlawful sexual penetration of a victim by the defendant, or of the defendant by the victim when the victim is at least thirteen (13) but less than eighteen (18) years of age and the defendant is at least ten (10) years older than the victim.

(d)

(1) Mitigated statutory rape is a Class E felony.

(2) (A) Statutory rape is a Class E felony.

(B) In addition to the punishment provided for a person who commits statutory rape for the first time, the trial judge may order, after taking into account the facts and circumstances surrounding the offense, including the offense for which the person was originally charged and whether the conviction was the result of a plea bargain agreement, that the person be required to register as a sexual offender pursuant to title 40, chapter 39, part 2.

(3) Aggravated statutory rape is a Class D felony.

Tenn. Code Ann. § 39-11-301 Mental State

(a)

(1) A person commits an offense who acts intentionally, knowingly, recklessly or with criminal negligence, as the definition of the offense requires, with respect to each element of the offense.

(2) When the law provides that criminal negligence suffices to establish an element of an offense, that element is also established if a person acts intentionally, knowingly or recklessly. When recklessness suffices to establish an element, that element is also established if a person acts intentionally or knowingly. When acting knowingly suffices to establish an element, that element is also established if a person acts intentionally.

(b) A culpable mental state is required within this title unless the definition of an offense plainly dispenses with a mental element.

(c) If the definition of an offense within this title does not plainly dispense with a mental element, intent, knowledge or recklessness suffices to establish the culpable mental state.

Potential Evidence Detrimental to Your Supervisor's Case

(1) Alvin will testify he saw the victim drive up to the house party where the alleged statutory rape occurred. (Extra facts: the legal driving age in Tennessee is 18 years old, unless one is driving with a permit and guardian in the vehicle.)

(2) Alvin's phone has dozens of text messages from "Katnise," identified as the victim, one of which says, "Ur cute ye Im over it," in response to Alvin's message, "How old R U?"

(3) Alvin's friend will testify that he asked the victim's friend at the party, "How old is the [victim]?" The friend responded, "She's eighteen." The friend then told Alvin the victim's age. (Extra facts: Alvin was dancing during a loud song when his friend relayed the information to him by nodding vigorously and yelling at him from a distance of five feet: "She's cool!")

(4) Alvin will further testify that he saw the victim show identification to the bartender at the party to obtain alcoholic drinks. (Extra facts: the drinking age in Tennessee is eighteen at private residences. The bartender is the underage brother of the underage hostess. Alvin only saw identification being shown, not the face of the identification.)

(5) The victim is fourteen years old. Alvin is twenty-six years old.

---

iii. Fraud

The California statute we examined does permit a conviction for rape when the victim is defrauded into having sex. Many statutes, such as the one in Massachusetts, does not expressly provide for such a basis for liability. The New Jersey Supreme Court concluded that "physical force or coercion" was equivalent to sex without consent. *Suliveres* considers the question of whether fraudulently portraying yourself as a person with whom the alleged victim regularly has sex is the equivalent of "force" in the Massachusetts statute.

Suliveres v. Commonwealth

Massachusetts Supreme Judicial Court
865 N.E.2d 1086 (2007)

COWIN, J.

In *Commonwealth v. Goldenberg*, 338 Mass. 377, 155 N.E.2d 187, cert. denied, 359 U.S. 1001, 79 S.Ct. 1143, 3 L.Ed.2d 1032 (1959), we concluded that it is not rape when consent to sexual intercourse is obtained through fraud or deceit. In determining that G.L. c. 265, § 22, required this result by its definition of rape as sexual intercourse compelled "by force and against [the] will" of the victim, we stated that "[f]raud cannot be allowed to supply the place of the force which the statute makes mandatory." *Commonwealth v. Goldenberg, supra* at 384, 155 N.E.2d 187. In the present case, the Commonwealth asks us to overrule the *Goldenberg* decision and hold that misrepresentations can in fact substitute for the requisite force. Because the *Goldenberg* case has been the law for nearly one-half century, during which the Legislature has had ample opportunity to change the rape statute and has not done so, we decline to overrule our decision in *Goldenberg*.

The crime of rape is defined in G.L. c. 265, § 22(*b*): "Whoever has sexual intercourse or unnatural sexual intercourse with a person and compels such person to submit by force and against his will, or compels such person to submit by threat of bodily injury, shall be punished. . . ." This definition has changed over time, but the requirement that the act be "by force and against [the] will" of the victim has remained constant for two hundred years. Compare St. 1805, c. 97, § 1 (crime to "ravish and carnally know any woman *by force and against her will*" [emphasis added]). We have said that "by force" and "against [the] will" are "two separate elements each of which must independently be satisfied."[1] *Commonwealth v. Lopez*, 433 Mass. 722, 727, 745 N.E.2d 961 (2001).

In *Commonwealth v. Goldenberg, supra*, we considered, as a matter of first impression, whether rape could be committed by fraud. *Id.* at 383, 155 N.E.2d 187. The *Goldenberg* case involved a woman who had gone to the defendant, a physiotherapist, to procure an abortion. *Id.* at 379–380, 155 N.E.2d 187. The defendant told her that, as part of the procedure, he "had to have intercourse" with her and that it would "help it some way." *Id.* at 380, 155 N.E.2d 187. He then proceeded to have intercourse with her. *Id.* at 381, 155 N.E.2d 187. We noted that "it could not be found beyond a reasonable doubt that the intercourse was without her consent," and that the evidence "negatived the use of force." *Id.* at 383, 155 N.E.2d 187. Thus, the only way the defendant could have been convicted was if his fraudulent representation that the intercourse was medically necessary could both invalidate the consent and supply the requisite "force." We concluded, however, that "[f]raud cannot be allowed to supply the place of the force which the statute makes mandatory," *id.* at 384, 155 N.E.2d 187, and cited with approval a Michigan case, *Don Moran v. People*, 25 Mich. 356 (1872), which on "facts strikingly similar" had found no rape to have been committed. *Commonwealth v. Goldenberg, supra* at 384, 155 N.E.2d 187.

We turn now to the facts of the present case, viewed in the light most favorable to the Commonwealth. On the night in question, the defendant had sexual intercourse with the complainant by impersonating her longtime boy friend, his

---

1   Under the statute, rape may also be proved by evidence of intercourse compelled by "threat of bodily injury." G.L. c. 265, § 22(*b*). *See Commonwealth v. Caracciola*, 409 Mass. 648, 653, 569 N.E.2d 774 (1991).

brother. According to the complainant, while she was asleep alone in the bedroom she shared with her boy friend, the defendant entered the room, and she awoke. In the dark room, the complainant assumed that the defendant was her boy friend returning home from work, and addressed him by her boy friend's name. He got into the bed and had intercourse with her. The complainant was "not fully awake" at the time of penetration. During the intercourse, she believed that the man was her boy friend, and had she known it was the defendant, she "would have never consented."

The defendant was indicted for rape and tried before a jury in the Superior Court. At trial, the main issue was whether the complainant knew at the time the identity of the person with whom she was having sex. The defense was that the sex was fully consensual. The defendant told an investigating police officer that the complainant had come to him while he was asleep in another room and had invited him to her bedroom to have sex with her. The Commonwealth argued that the defendant had procured the complainant's consent to sex fraudulently by impersonating her boy friend.

* * *

Taking the evidence in the light most favorable to the Commonwealth, we assume that the defendant fraudulently induced the complainant to have intercourse. However, as noted above, the rule of *Commonwealth v. Goldenberg*, 338 Mass. 377, 384, 155 N.E.2d 187, cert. denied, 359 U.S. 1001, 79 S.Ct. 1143, 3 L.Ed.2d 1032 (1959), is that intercourse where consent is achieved by fraud does not constitute rape. That rule compels the conclusion that there was no evidence of rape in this case, and we decline to overrule the *Goldenberg* decision.

For all purposes relevant to this case, the crime of rape is defined by statute as nonconsensual intercourse achieved "by force."* * *   G.L. c. 265, § 22(*b*). The Commonwealth, advancing the same argument that was rejected in the *Goldenberg* decision, contends that the defendant's fraud should be allowed to satisfy the requirement of force. In requesting that we overrule the *Goldenberg* case, the Commonwealth asks us to read "force" out of the statute in cases involving misrepresentation as to identity. Yet we have never suggested that force is not an element of the crime, or that "by force" is synonymous with lack of consent. *See Commonwealth v. Lopez*, 433 Mass. 722, 727, 745 N.E.2d 961 (2001) (each element "must independently be satisfied"). Because "[n]o portion of the statutory language may be deemed superfluous," *Commonwealth v. Caracciola*, 409 Mass. 648, 654, 569 N.E.2d 774 (1991), quoting *Commonwealth v. Gove*, 366 Mass. 351, 354, 320 N.E.2d 900 (1974), we are not free, any more than we were in the *Goldenberg* case, to adopt the Commonwealth's proposed interpretation.

We assume that, when it enacts legislation, the Legislature is not only aware of existing statutes, but is also aware of the prior state of the law as explicated by the decisions of this court. *Commonwealth v. Callahan*, 440 Mass. 436, 440–441,

799 N.E.2d 113 (2003). Thus, we find it significant that the Legislature has not seen fit to overrule the *Goldenberg* decision in forty-eight years, during which the rape statute was amended three times, scholarship and attitudes regarding rape changed considerably, see *Commonwealth v. Keevan*, 400 Mass. 557, 571, 511 N.E.2d 534 (1987) (Abrams, J., concurring), and the *Goldenberg* decision received criticism from at least one member of this court. The Legislature is free to amend the rape statute or create a new substantive offense to encompass the conduct at issue, as many other States have done.[9] However, where the Legislature has chosen not to do so, "[i]t is not for this court . . . to rewrite the clear intention expressed by the statute." *Commonwealth v. Leno*, 415 Mass. 835, 841, 616 N.E.2d 453 (1993), quoting *Mellor v. Berman*, 390 Mass. 275, 283, 454 N.E.2d 907 (1983).

* * *

Fraudulently obtaining consent to sexual intercourse does not constitute rape as defined in our statute. Accordingly, the defendant's motion for a required finding of not guilty should have been granted. This case is remanded to the county court for entry of an appropriate order by the single justice barring a subsequent retrial on double jeopardy grounds.

Notes and Questions

1. Under tort law, force is an element of battery, which can be no more than an unwanted touching. *See United States v. Castleman*, 134 S.Ct. 1405, 1410 (2014). Would it have been that much of a stretch for the court to have concluded that a touching that the victim would not have desired if she had known the defendant's true identity, amounted to force? The Mississippi Supreme Court affirmed a rape conviction in a case in which the defendant had sex with a woman he knew falsely believed him to be her husband—and did so under a statute that required force for rape. *Pinson v. State*, 518 So.2d 1220 (Miss. 1988).

2. It seems that this would have been an act of rape under the California statute we examined in the beginning of this section. So far courts have only considered cases in which defendants have posed as men with whom their victims have a present relationship. What if a man convinced a woman in a bar that he

---

9   See, e.g., Ala.Code § 13A–6–65 (LexisNexis 2005) (man who has sexual intercourse with woman "where consent was obtained by the use of any fraud or artifice" guilty of sexual misconduct); Cal. Pen.Code § 261(5) (West Supp.2007) (sexual intercourse "[w]here a person submits under the belief that the person committing the act is the victim's spouse, and this belief is induced by any artifice, pretense, or concealment practiced by the accused, with intent to induce the belief" constitutes rape); Mich. Comp. Laws Ann. § 750.520b (West Supp.2007) (sexual penetration of another "through concealment" constitutes criminal sexual conduct); Tenn.Code Ann. § 39–13–503 (LexisNexis 2006) (unlawful sexual penetration "accomplished by fraud" constitutes rape).

was George Clooney's brother and on the basis of this lie, she agreed to have sex with him? Should there be a conviction under the Massachusetts statute of issue in *Suliveres*?

---

d. Group Criminal Liability

One may be subject to criminal liability for conspiracy, complicity or attempt to commit a sexual crime. As *Vecellio* demonstrates, some jurisdictions will find the elements of these inchoate crimes satisfied even if the victim or co-conspirator does not actually exist, and it is impossible for any results to occur. As you read *Vecellio*, also note the repeated discussion of the defense's failures at trial, and the different outcome for the client that may have resulted absent the defense attorney's omissions.

People v. Vecellio

Colorado Court of Appeals, Div. VI
292 P.3d 1004 (2012)

Opinion by Judge LOEB.

Defendant, Todd George Vecellio, appeals the judgment of conviction entered on jury verdicts finding him guilty of conspiracy to commit sexual assault on a child by one in a position of trust; solicitation to commit sexual assault on a child by one in a position of trust; criminal attempt to commit sexual assault on a child; and enticement of a child. We affirm.

I. BACKGROUND

On August 19, 2008, defendant contacted "Karina" in an Internet chat room through a website called "Adult Friend Finder," which allowed registered users to post profiles that contained their biographical information and sexual interests and contact other users through e-mail or by instant message. According to her profile, Karina was a thirty-one-year-old single mother with a thirteen-year-old daughter, "Shayla." In actuality, Karina was an undercover police officer conducting internet investigations as part of the Internet Crimes Against Children (ICAC) task force. Shayla did not exist.

During an initial instant message conversation, defendant learned from Karina that she and her thirteen-year-old daughter were engaged in an incestuous relationship and that she was looking for a male to "teach" her daughter about sex by having three-way intercourse with them. Defendant responded that he was interested in having sex with both Karina and Shayla, and he asked Karina several questions about her and Shayla's sexual experiences together, often remarking that Karina's answers made him sexually excited. However, defendant also regularly expressed concerns that Karina was a "cop" and sought assurances from her that she was not.

Defendant and Karina had many instant message conversations over several weeks. During these conversations, defendant routinely asked Karina about her and Shayla's sexual activities together and expressed interest in meeting them in person. Defendant also asked Karina whether she was interested in his taking pictures of their future sexual encounter and whether he should wear a condom. They also exchanged photos. Karina sent defendant a photo of herself (in actuality, a photo of the undercover police officer) and Shayla (in actuality, a school-age photo of a different female police officer). Defendant sent Karina a photo of his erect penis. Eventually, they exchanged phone numbers, and the undercover police officer researched defendant's phone number and discovered that it belonged to Todd Vecellio of Colorado Springs. The officer also learned that Vecellio was a police officer for the University of Colorado at Colorado Springs (UCCS).

Eventually, defendant and Karina had several phone conversations over a few days. During these conversations, they made plans to meet at a convenience store in Penrose. They agreed that once they met and got "comfortable" with each other, they would go to Karina's house and have three-way sex with Shayla. They also agreed that defendant would purchase condoms before making the trip.

On September 24, 2008, defendant drove from Colorado Springs to the convenience store in Penrose. Once defendant arrived there, Karina called defendant and asked him to buy beer from the nearby liquor store. Defendant agreed to buy beer. Upon exiting the liquor store, however, defendant was arrested by police officers from the Cañon City Police Department and Fremont County Sheriff's Office. When he was arrested, officers found a box of condoms in defendant's pocket.

In connection with these events, defendant was charged with four counts:

(1) conspiracy to commit sexual assault on a child by one in a position of trust;

(2) solicitation to commit sexual assault on a child by one in a position of trust;

(3) criminal attempt to commit sexual assault on a child; and

(4) enticement of a child.

Defendant's theory of defense was that he was conducting his own secret undercover investigation into Karina and the possible abuse of her daughter, and defendant testified consistently with that theory at trial. According to defendant's testimony, he had been passed over for promotion several times while working as a police officer at UCCS and felt that conducting the investigation would give him a "chance to shine." As such, defendant stated that he did not drive to Penrose to have sex with Karina and Shayla; rather, he claimed he drove to Penrose to gather information about Karina so he could notify the authorities, save Shayla, and "be a hero." However, defendant also testified that he had never conducted an ICAC investigation, had never been trained in conducting an ICAC investigation, did not save the instant message conversations with Karina, did not record the telephone calls with Karina, and did not inform anyone, including his supervisor, of his secret undercover operation, nor did he obtain authorization to conduct the operation. The jury convicted defendant on all counts.

This appeal followed.

II. CONSPIRACY

Defendant contends that the evidence was insufficient to convict him of conspiracy to commit sexual assault on a child by one in a position of trust. Specifically, he contends that, in Colorado, the crime of conspiracy requires a real agreement between two true co-conspirators. Accordingly, because Karina was in actuality an undercover police officer who never intended to engage in any criminal activity, defendant contends that he never entered into an agreement with a true co-conspirator, and, thus, the evidence was insufficient to convict him of conspiracy.

On this issue of first impression, we conclude that Colorado's conspiracy statute reflects the "unilateral" approach to conspiracy, under which a defendant may be convicted of conspiracy by agreeing with another party to commit a crime, regardless of whether the other party is an undercover police officer who feigns agreement. Therefore, because the fact that defendant agreed to commit a crime with an undercover police officer does not preclude his conviction, and because the evidence was sufficient to support his conviction, we reject defendant's contention.

A. Standard of Review

When reviewing a sufficiency of the evidence contention, a court must determine whether any rational trier of fact might accept the evidence, taken as a whole and in the light most favorable to the prosecution, as sufficient to support a finding of guilt beyond a reasonable doubt. *People v. Sprouse*, 983 P.2d 771, 777 (Colo.1999); *People v. McIntier*, 134 P.3d 467, 471 (Colo.App.2005). The prosecution must be given the benefit of every reasonable inference that might be fairly drawn from the evidence. *McIntier*,134 P.3d at 471.

Here, defendant's sufficiency of the evidence contention turns on a question of statutory interpretation. Statutory interpretation is a question of law that we review de novo. *Bostelman v. People*, 162 P.3d 686, 689 (Colo.2007).

When interpreting a statute, we must give effect to the intent of the General Assembly, which is vested with the power to define criminal conduct and to establish the legal components of criminal liability. *People v. Hoskay*, 87 P.3d 194, 197–98 (Colo.App.2003). To determine the General Assembly's intent, we look first to the language of the statute itself, giving words and phrases their plain and ordinary meaning. *People v. Rice*, 198 P.3d 1241, 1244 (Colo.App.2008). We read words and phrases in context and construe them according to their common usage. *Id.* "[W]e must read and consider the statutory scheme as a whole to give consistent, harmonious and sensible effect to all its parts." *People v. Luther*, 58 P.3d 1013, 1015 (Colo.2002) (quoting *Charnes v. Boom*, 766 P.2d 665, 667 (Colo.1988)). If the statutory language is clear and unambiguous, we do not engage in further statutory analysis and apply the statute as written. *Bostelman*, 162 P.3d at 690; *People v. Witek*, 97 P.3d 240, 243 (Colo.App.2004).

B. Analysis

Defendant's argument raises an issue of first impression in Colorado, namely, whether Colorado's conspiracy statute adopts the bilateral or unilateral approach to conspiracy. *See Marquiz v. People*, 726 P.2d 1105, 1108 n. 6 (Colo.1986) (declining to decide as unnecessary to the resolution of the case whether the conspiracy statute adopts the unilateral approach and noting that the issue had never been presented to the court directly).

On appeal, defendant asks us to adopt the "bilateral" approach to conspiracy applied in the federal courts, as enunciated in *United States v. Barboa*, 777 F.2d 1420 (10th Cir.1985).[1] Under the bilateral approach, the crime of conspiracy is committed when at least two true co-conspirators agree to proceed in a prohibited manner. *See State v. Rambousek*, 479 N.W.2d 832, 833–34 (N.D.1992).

---

1   We note that the federal conspiracy statute, 18 U.S.C. § 371 (2006), under which Barboa was decided, beginning with the words, "If two or more persons conspire . . .," is clearly a bilateral approach, as discussed more fully below.

Accordingly, under the bilateral approach, a defendant cannot be convicted of conspiracy when the other party feigns agreement, such as in cases involving undercover government agents, because two true co-conspirators have not agreed to commit a crime. *See Barboa*, 777 F.2d at 1422 ("[T]here can be no indictable conspiracy involving only the defendant and government agents. . . .").

However, as defendant concedes on appeal, state courts have rejected the bilateral approach in favor of a "unilateral" approach. *See, e.g., State v. John*, 213 Neb. 76, 328 N.W.2d 181, 191 (1982); *Rambousek*, 479 N.W.2d at 835–36; *Miller v. State*, 955 P.2d 892, 897 (Wyo.1998) (the modern trend in state courts is to rule that a conspiracy count is viable even when one of the participants is a government agent or is feigning agreement). Under the unilateral approach, the crime of conspiracy is committed when the defendant agrees with another person to act in a prohibited manner; the second party can feign agreement. *State v. Heitman*, 262 Neb. 185, 629 N.W.2d 542, 553 (2001). Accordingly, because the unilateral approach requires only that the defendant agree to proceed in a prohibited manner, the fact that the other party is an undercover police officer is irrelevant. *Id.* For the reasons that follow, we conclude that Colorado's conspiracy statute adopts the unilateral approach.

The text of Colorado's conspiracy statute suggests that the General Assembly intended to adopt the unilateral approach. Colorado's conspiracy statute provides, in pertinent part:

> *A person commits conspiracy to commit a crime if,* with the intent to promote or facilitate its commission, *he agrees* with another person or persons that they, or one or more of them, will engage in conduct which constitutes a crime or an attempt to commit a crime, or he agrees to aid the other person or persons in the planning or commission of a crime or of an attempt to commit such crime.

§ 18–2–201(1), C.R.S.2011 (emphasis added). By its plain terms, the statute defines conspiracy as the actions of a single actor agreeing with another, rather than as an agreement between two or more persons. *Id.*; Wayne R. LaFave, *Substantive Criminal Law* § 12.2(a), at 268 n. 30 (2003) (stating that Colorado's statute, along with most states' modern criminal codes, defines conspiracy in terms of a single actor agreeing with another). Accordingly, the plain language of the statute suggests that a defendant can be guilty of conspiracy if "he [or she] agrees" with another person to commit a crime, regardless of whether the other person feigns agreement with the defendant. *See* § 18–2–201(1); *Rice*, 198 P.3d at 1244. Thus, by its plain terms, the conspiracy statute's focus on a single actor, rather than on two or more actors coming to an agreement, evinces a legislative intent to adopt the unilateral approach.

Moreover, a comparison of Colorado's previous and current conspiracy statutes, as well as the conspiracy provision found in the Model Penal Code (MPC), demonstrates that the General Assembly intended to adopt the MPC's unilateral approach to conspiracy when it revised the conspiracy statute in 1971. Before its revision in 1971, the conspiracy statute read:

> *If any two or more persons* shall conspire or agree, falsely and maliciously, to charge or indict, or be informed against, or cause to procure to be charged or indicted or informed against any person for any criminal offense, or shall agree, conspire or cooperate to, or to aid in doing any other unlawful act, each of the persons so offending shall on conviction, in case of a conspiracy to commit a felony, be confined in the penitentiary for a period of not less than one year, nor more than ten years. . . .

§ 40–7–35, C.R.S.1963 (emphasis added). This statute was "unequivocally of the bilateral variety" because it required that "two or more persons . . . agree, conspire or cooperate." Marianne Wesson, *Mens Rea and the Colorado Criminal Code*, 52 U. Colo. L.Rev. 167, 206 (1981); *see also Archuleta v. People*, 149 Colo. 206, 212, 368 P.2d 422, 425 (1962) ("In order to be convicted of a conspiracy there must be evidence that two or more conspired to do an unlawful act. . . . [Defendant] could not conspire with himself.").

In 1971, the General Assembly enacted a complete revision of the Colorado Criminal Code (the Code), which drew heavily from the recently drafted MPC. *People v. Vigil*, 127 P.3d 916, 931 (Colo.2006). The MPC, like the later version of the Colorado statute, defines conspiracy in the context of a single actor agreeing with another. *See* Model Penal Code § 5.03(1)(a) ("A person is guilty of conspiracy with another person or persons to commit a crime if with the purpose of promoting or facilitating its commission he. . . agrees with such other person . . . ."); *see also Wesson*, at 206. Moreover, the commentaries to the MPC expressly state that the MPC's conspiracy provision reflects the unilateral approach: Subsection (1) departs from the traditional view of conspiracy as an entirely bilateral or multilateral relationship, the view inherent in the standard formulation cast in terms of "two or more persons" agreeing or combining to commit a crime. Attention is directed instead to each individual's culpability by framing the definition in terms of the conduct that suffices to establish the liability of any given actor, rather than the conduct of a group of which he is charged to be a part. This approach has been designated "unilateral," and it has apparently been followed in all but a few of the recently revised codes. . . .

Model Penal Code and Commentaries § 5.03 cmt. 2(b), at 398–99 (1985). The General Assembly's adoption of the MPC's definition of conspiracy further demonstrates that Colorado's definition of conspiracy reflects the unilateral approach.

Other state courts, interpreting nearly identical statutory language, have come to the same conclusion we reach here. In *Miller v. State*, the Wyoming Supreme Court concluded that Wyoming's conspiracy statute adopted the unilateral approach, noting that it was adopted in part from the MPC. *Miller*, 955 P.2d at 897. Further, the court also stated that its "research discloses that most states that have adopted this second definition of the crime of conspiracy [with the focus on a single actor agreeing with another] have embraced a unilateral approach to conspiracy." *Id.*

Similarly, in *State v. John*, the Nebraska Supreme Court concluded that Nebraska's conspiracy statute reflected the unilateral approach because it contained similar language to the MPC, with a focus on a single actor agreeing with another rather than on two or more persons agreeing. *John*, 328 N.W.2d at 190–91. The Nebraska Supreme Court later applied the rule in *John* to uphold a defendant's conviction for conspiracy where he, like defendant in this case, agreed over the internet to have sex with an undercover police officer posing as an underage girl. *Heitman*, 629 N.W.2d at 553.

We are persuaded by the reasoning in these cases and find it applicable here. A person who believes he or she is conspiring with another to commit a crime is a danger to the public regardless of whether the other person has in fact agreed to commit the crime. *See Miller*, 955 P.2d at 897. The unilateral approach is justified, in part, because a person plotting a crime with a feigning accomplice has a guilty mind. *Id.*

Thus, we conclude that Colorado's conspiracy statute reflects the unilateral approach to conspiracy. Accordingly, the fact that defendant's agreement was made with an undercover police officer does not, as a matter of law, preclude his conviction for conspiracy.

C. Application

Given our interpretation of the conspiracy statute above, we now turn to whether the evidence was sufficient to support defendant's conviction for conspiracy to commit sexual assault on a child by one in a position of trust. We conclude that it was.

"The crime of conspiracy is the illegal agreement to commit a crime coupled with at least one overt act in furtherance of that agreement." *People v. Phong Le*, 74 P.3d 431, 435–36 (Colo.App.2003); *see also* § 18–2–201(1)–(2), C.R.S.2011.

The evidence at trial, when taken as a whole and viewed in the light most favorable to the prosecution, was sufficient to support defendant's conviction of conspiracy to commit sexual assault on a child by one in a position of trust.

The record is clear and shows that, during several conversations conducted via instant message and over the phone, defendant explicitly agreed with Karina to commit sexual assault on her thirteen-year-old daughter. The record also shows that defendant committed overt acts in furtherance of the conspiracy, specifically, his driving to Penrose to meet Karina and Shayla and his purchase of condoms and beer. *See* § 18–2–201(2).

Accordingly, we conclude that the evidence was sufficient to support a finding of guilt beyond a reasonable doubt on the conspiracy charge. *See Sprouse*, 983 P.2d at 777.

III. JURY INSTRUCTION ON COMPLICITY

Defendant next contends that the trial court reversibly erred by instructing the jury on the legal theory of complicity because the prosecutor did not allege or prove that another individual, besides defendant, committed any crime. We perceive no plain error requiring reversal of the conviction.

A. Standard of Review and Applicable Law

We review jury instructions de novo to determine whether the instructions as a whole accurately informed the jury of the governing law. *People v. Lucas*, 232 P.3d 155, 162 (Colo.App.2009). However, the trial court has substantial discretion in formulating the jury instructions so long as they are correct statements of the law and fairly and adequately cover the issues presented. *People v. Pahl*, 169 P.3d 169, 183 (Colo.App.2006).

At the outset, we reject defendant's contention that he objected to the jury instruction at issue. Rather, defense counsel affirmatively stated that he had no objections to any of the instructions. At trial, defendant objected to the trial court's response to a juror question regarding the elemental instruction on the enticement charge on the ground that the court's response unduly emphasized the complicity instruction. However, on appeal, defendant does not contend that the court's response to the juror question constituted error; rather, he contends that the court's giving the complicity instruction in the first instance was error. We do not view defendant's objection to the court's response to the jury's question as preserving an objection to the complicity instruction itself. Further, we reject defendant's contention that the alleged instructional error here constituted structural error warranting a new trial. *See Griego v. People*, 19 P.3d 1, 8 (Colo.2001) (instructional error not subject to structural error analysis). Therefore, because defendant did not object to the jury instructions at trial, we review his contention on appeal for plain error. *See People v. Boykins*, 140 P.3d 87, 95 (Colo.App.2005).

Plain error is error that is both "obvious and substantial." *People v. Miller*, 113 P.3d 743, 750 (Colo.2005). It is an error that "so undermined the fundamental fairness of the proceeding as to cast serious doubt on the reliability of the judgment." *People v. Sepulveda*, 65 P.3d 1002, 1006 (Colo.2003). To warrant reversal under a plain error standard in the context of jury instructions, the defendant must "demonstrate not only that the instruction affected a substantial right, but also that the record reveals a reasonable possibility that the error contributed to his conviction." *People v. Garcia*, 28 P.3d 340, 344 (Colo.2001) (quoting *Bogdanov v. People*, 941 P.2d 247, 255–56 (Colo.1997)). An erroneous jury instruction does not normally constitute plain error where the issue is not contested at trial or the record contains overwhelming evidence of the defendant's guilt. *People v. Zamarripa–Diaz*,187 P.3d 1120, 1122 (Colo.App.2008).

Complicity is not a separate and distinct crime or offense. *Grissom v. People*, 115 P.3d 1280, 1283 (Colo.2005). Rather, it is "a theory by which a defendant becomes accountable for a criminal offense committed by another." *Id.* (quoting *People v. Thompson*, 655 P.2d 416, 418 (Colo.1982)). Colorado's complicity statute provides: A person is legally accountable as principal for the behavior of another constituting a criminal offense if, with the intent to promote or facilitate the commission of the offense, he or she aids, abets, advises, or encourages the other person in planning or committing the offense. § 18–1–603, C.R.S.2011.

B. Analysis

Here, the trial court gave the following instruction to the jury regarding complicity:

A person is guilty of an offense committed by another person if he is a complicitor. To be guilty as a complicitor, the following must be established beyond a reasonable doubt:

1. A crime must have been committed.

2. Another person must have committed all or part of the crime.

3. The defendant must have had knowledge that the other person intended to commit all or part of the crime.

4. The defendant did intentionally aid, abet, advise, or encourage the other person in the commission or planning of the crime.

As noted above, defendant did not object to this instruction at trial, nor is there any dispute that the language of the instruction was a correct statement of the law. On appeal, however, defendant contends that the court erred in giving the instruction in the first instance because Karina was an undercover police officer who did not commit any crime. That is, defendant contends that it was improper for the trial court to give the complicity instruction because "[t]here was no principal actor responsible for an actual crime for which [defendant] could be complicit."

For purposes of our analysis, assuming, without deciding, that the court erred in giving the complicity instruction, we conclude that any such error did not constitute plain error.

In reaching that conclusion, we first consider how, if at all, each of the four offenses for which defendant was found guilty is pertinent to defendant's contention regarding the complicity instruction, and whether the alleged error in instructing the jury on complicity constituted plain error requiring reversal of the convictions on any of those offenses.

At oral argument, and to a lesser extent in his briefs on appeal, defendant contended generally that the alleged error in giving the complicity instruction required reversal of his convictions on all four offenses. However, the substance of his argument appears to be focused most specifically on his conviction for enticement. The offense of enticement of a child is defined in relevant part as follows: A person commits the crime of enticement of a child if he or she invites or persuades, or attempts to invite or persuade, a child under the age of fifteen years to enter any vehicle, building, room, or secluded place with the intent to commit sexual assault or unlawful sexual contact upon said child. § 18–3–305(1), C.R.S.2011.

During closing argument, the prosecutor argued that the jury could find defendant guilty of enticement under two theories, neither of which required the jury to find defendant guilty as a complicitor. First, the prosecutor argued that the jury could convict defendant of enticement because, during a phone conversation with Karina, he attempted to invite or persuade Karina and Shayla to enter his car. *See* § 18–3–305(1) ("It is not necessary to a prosecution for attempt under this subsection (1) that the child have perceived the defendant's act of enticement."). Second, the prosecutor argued that the jury could convict defendant of enticement because he was using Karina as his agent to invite or persuade Shayla to enter a secluded place. Accordingly, under either theory, the prosecutor argued that the jury could find defendant guilty of enticement as a principal actor without relying on a theory of complicity. Moreover, as discussed in further detail in Section IV below, there was sufficient evidence to convict defendant under either of these theories as a principal or under a complicitor theory of liability. Therefore, to the extent there was error here with respect to the charge of enticement, we conclude that any such error did not "so undermine[ ] the fundamental fairness of the proceeding as to cast serious doubt on the reliability of the judgment." *Sepulveda*, 65 P.3d at 1006.

Nor do we perceive any plain error with respect to defendant's convictions on the other three substantive offenses. Conspiracy, unlike complicity, is a substantive criminal offense, *see Palmer v. People*, 964 P.2d 524, 527–28 (Colo.1998), and, as discussed above, there was sufficient evidence to support defendant's conviction for conspiracy as a principal, without reliance on a complicity theory. *See People v. Dunaway*, 88 P.3d 619, 631 (Colo.2004); *People v. Sharp*, 104 P.3d 252, 257 (Colo.App.2004); *see also Trujillo v. Hartley*, 2010 WL 2692173, at *9 (D.Colo. No. 07–cv–02337–MSK, July 6, 2010) (unpublished opinion and order) (a defendant's convictions are constitutional if the evidence was sufficient to establish his guilt either as a principal or as a complicitor), *appeal dismissed*, 406 Fed.Appx. 280 (10th Cir.2010). Similarly, because defendant has not challenged the sufficiency of the evidence to support his convictions for solicitation to commit sexual assault on a child and criminal attempt to commit sexual assault on a child as a principal, we perceive no prejudice and thus, no plain error, with respect to his convictions on those two counts. *See Dunaway*, 88 P.3d at 631; *Trujillo*, 2010 WL 2692173, at *9.

As further support for our plain error analysis, we note that the trial court also instructed the jury as follows: "The prosecution is not required to prove that an actual child or an actual mother was involved in order to prove the crimes charged in this case." Defendant did not object to this instruction at trial, nor does he challenge it on appeal. Under these circumstances, we fail to see how defendant could have been prejudiced, where his only argument on appeal is that the court erred in giving the complicity instruction because the undercover officer was not "an actual mother" who could be a principal actor responsible for an actual crime.

IV. ENTICEMENT

Defendant also contends that the evidence was insufficient to convict him of enticement of a child because no child was actually involved in this case and because he never communicated with anyone pretending to be a child. We disagree.

When reviewing a sufficiency of the evidence contention, a court must determine whether any rational trier of fact might accept the evidence, taken as a whole and in the light most favorable to the prosecution, as sufficient to support a finding of guilt beyond a reasonable doubt. *Sprouse*, 983 P.2d at 777; *McIntier*, 134 P.3d at 471. The prosecution must be given the benefit of every reasonable inference that might be fairly drawn from the evidence. *McIntier*, 134 P.3d at 471.

A person commits the crime of enticement of a child if he or she invites or persuades, or *attempts to invite or persuade*, a child under the age of fifteen years to enter any vehicle, building, room, or secluded place with the intent to commit sexual assault or unlawful sexual contact upon said child. *It is not necessary to a prosecution for attempt under this subsection (1) that the child have perceived the defendant's act of enticement.* § 18–3–305(1) (emphasis added). Accordingly, a defendant may be convicted of enticement if he or she "attempts to invite or persuade" a child under fifteen years of age to enter any secluded place, regardless of whether the child perceives the defendant's act of enticement. *Id.*

In *People v. Grizzle*, the defendant had been convicted of enticement by engaging in several sexually explicit internet and phone conversations with an undercover police officer posing as a thirteen-year-old girl. *Grizzle*, 140 P.3d at 225. In discussing whether the defendant could raise an entrapment defense, the division analyzed the enticement statute's "attempt" language in conjunction with the criminal attempt statute, noting that neither factual nor legal impossibility is a defense to attempt "if the offense could have been committed had the attendant circumstances been as the actor believed them to be." *Id.* at 226 (quoting § 18–2–101(1), C.R.S.2011). Accordingly, the division concluded that where no "real" victim is involved, a defendant could commit enticement provided he or she believed that the person with whom a sexual encounter had been arranged was under the age of fifteen. *Id.; see also United States v. Sims*, 428 F.3d 945, 959–60 (10th Cir.2005).

We find *Grizzle* persuasive and applicable here. Based on the statutory language found in both the enticement and criminal attempt statutes, we conclude, as did the division in *Grizzle*, that a defendant may be convicted of enticement regardless of whether the victim is "real," provided the defendant believed the victim was under fifteen years of age and the other statutory elements are met. *See Grizzle*, 140 P.3d at 226; *see also* § 18–3–305(1) ("[a] person commits the crime of enticement" if he or she "*attempts to invite or persuade*, a child under the age of fifteen years to enter any . . . secluded place") (emphasis added); § 18–2–101(1) ("Factual or legal impossibility of committing the offense is not a defense if the offense could have been committed had the attendant circumstances been as the actor believed them to be. . . ."). Further, under the terms of the enticement statute, the prosecution need not show that the child perceived the defendant's act of enticement. § 18–3–305(1). Accordingly, the fact that Shayla did not exist and that defendant never communicated with her directly does not preclude his conviction for enticement.

Given our interpretation of the enticement statute above, we now turn to whether the evidence was sufficient to uphold defendant's conviction for enticement. We conclude that the evidence was sufficient to uphold defendant's conviction under both of the prosecutor's theories of liability: either directly as a principal actor, or as a complicitor.

First, the evidence at trial, when taken as a whole and viewed in the light most favorable to the prosecution, was sufficient to support defendant's conviction of enticement as a principal actor. The record shows that, during a recorded phone conversation, defendant attempted to invite or persuade Shayla to enter a secluded place with him (either his car or Karina's house) to commit sexual assault on her. The record also shows that defendant attempted to use Karina as his agent to invite or persuade Shayla on his behalf. Moreover, it was undisputed that defendant believed Shayla was thirteen years old while engaging in these conversations.

Second, the evidence was sufficient to uphold defendant's conviction as a complicitor. The record shows that defendant aided, advised, or encouraged Karina in planning the offense of enticement. Specifically, evidence at trial established that defendant aided Karina in committing the offense in several ways, including by purchasing condoms to help facilitate the sexual encounter; advising Karina in planning the offense, including by helping to plan the meeting at the convenience store in Penrose and the subsequent sexual liaison at Karina's house; and encouraging Karina in planning and committing the offense.

Accordingly, when reviewing the evidence as a whole and in the light most favorable to the prosecution, we conclude that the evidence was sufficient to support a finding of guilt beyond a reasonable doubt on the enticement charge under either of the prosecution's theories. *See Sprouse*, 983 P.2d at 777; *Dunaway*, 88 P.3d at 631; *Trujillo*, 2010 WL 2692173 at *9.

* * *

Judge BERNARD and Judge LICHTENSTEIN concur.

Notes and Questions

1. The *Vecellio* court adopts the unilateral theory of conspiracy because it interpreted the Colorado legislature as adopting such an approach. As the court noted, the unilateral approach does not hinge on whether there were multiple actors actually conspiring, but on the culpability of the individual. Do you find the unilateral or bilateral approach more just?

2. Is conspiracy a lesser included offense of complicity in Colorado? Should the defendant in *Vecellio* have been convicted of both conspiracy and complicity?

The following are the statutes for conspiracy and complicity as *Vecellio* cites them:

> Complicity, § 18–1–603, C.R.S.2011: A person is legally accountable as principal for the behavior of another constituting a criminal offense if, with the intent to promote or facilitate the commission of the offense, he

or she aids, abets, advises, or encourages the other person in planning or committing the offense.

Conspiracy, § 18–2–201(1), C.R.S.2011: A person commits conspiracy to commit a crime if, with the intent to promote or facilitate its commission, he agrees with another person or persons that they, or one or more of them, will engage in conduct which constitutes a crime or an attempt to commit a crime, or he agrees to aid the other person or persons in the planning or commission of a crime or of an attempt to commit such crime.

CHAPTER SIX

Property Crimes

THIS CHAPTER will consider crimes involving property, though the crimes do not just deal with property. Theft is a taking of property; arson is the destruction of property. Burglary requires an entry into a building with the intent to commit a felony therein. Most often, as you would expect, burglary charges involve those entering buildings to steal something. In fact, as you will see, there is a presumption that a person who unlawfully enters a building is doing so for the purpose of stealing something in the building. It will probably come as a surprise to many students that a person who enters a building intending to assault, rape, or kill the occupant has also committed the crime of burglary. Burglary committed in this way is better characterized as a crime against a person than it is a crime against property—the real property entered plays only a supporting role in this story. We consider it along with the property crimes because its most frequently known version is certainly a crime against property. Robbery, which we consider in this chapter, is also very much a hybrid crime, it is essentially larceny accompanied by force.

Thus, while the crimes in this chapter all necessarily involve property, they do not necessarily exclusively involve property. We begin with theft, which serves as the building block of most of the remainder of the crimes in the chapter.

A. Theft

The common law recognized four types of theft crimes: larceny, embezzlement, false pretenses, and larceny by trick. A larceny involves an unlawful taking of property with the intent to permanently deprive the owner of the property.

Embezzlement involves converting property entrusted to the defendant for his own purposes. The crime of false pretenses involves convincing someone to surrender title to property to the defendant through false statements. Finally, in larceny by trick, the defendant through falsehood wrongfully convinced the defendant to surrender possession but not title.

At one point—and still in some jurisdictions—these distinctions mattered a great deal. A store clerk who kept money given him by a customer could have his conviction overturned if the prosecutor wrongly charged embezzlement rather than larceny. If, however, the clerk first placed the money in a cash register, then embezzlement would have been the correct charge. *See State v. Ward*, 562 A.2d 1040 (Vt. 1989). In such jurisdictions, a prosecutor could lose a case by charging the wrong type of taking.

Talking the lead from the drafters of the Model Penal Code, many jurisdictions have adopted statutes that require less precision in the charging. New statutes prohibiting theft would cover both the situation where the store clerk has accepted the money from the customer as well as when he takes it from the cash register, to use the example above. The common law framework is nevertheless useful as it demonstrates what the prosecution must prove for each type of unlawful taking regardless of the label.

1. Larceny

Larceny generally requires the prosecution to demonstrate that the defendant committed a:

> (1) trespassory

> (2) taking

> (3) with the intent to permanently deprive the owner of his property.

We consider each of these elements below.

a. Trespassory

To commit a trespass to property, the defendant must not be entitled to use the property. The right of an individual to take and keep it from another party is ambiguous in two types of situations—marriages and business partnerships. The *Llamas* case considers whether it is a trespass to attempt to permanently deprive a co-owner of the use and enjoyment of jointly held property. Before you think this question is easy, consider a common case—every time one spouse writes a check on a joint checking account, he or she is permanently depriving the other of the use and enjoyment of the money in that account. Could every purchase of a sail boat, or a dress, not previously discussed by the couple, amount to larceny? If not, when does permanent deprivation of jointly held property become larceny?

People v. Llamas

Court of Appeal of California
51 Cal.App.4th 1729 (1997)

BENKE, Acting P. J.

Appellant Frankie Llamas was found guilty of [among other things] vehicle taking. . . . He appeals, arguing [there is] insufficient evidence of auto taking. . . .

FACTS

A. Prosecution Case

In late January 1995, Irma Llamas and her husband, appellant, argued over his taking her 1994 gray Nissan. Appellant took the car without permission and Irma filed a stolen vehicle report.

In the early morning hours of February 1, 1995, Officer Michael Walden drove to Tamarindo Way in Chula Vista in response to the report of a possible auto theft in progress. At the location, Walden stopped, got out of his vehicle and approached a gray Nissan parked on the street. As he did so, he noticed appellant get out of the car, walk to the front of the vehicle, open the hood and then almost immediately close it again. The officer saw no one else next to the car.

Unaware the officer was present, appellant walked toward him. The officer announced his presence and told appellant to stop and put up his hands. Appellant put his hands in his front pockets and continued walking toward the officer. When the officer again ordered him to raise his hands, appellant removed them from his pockets and made a tossing motion with his left hand. Although the officer saw nothing being tossed, he heard the sound of metal "jangling." Appellant put his hands in the air, continued walking toward the officer and challenged the officer to shoot him. He then made a turning motion, removed a backpack and threw it at the officer's feet. As this occurred, the officer saw a second man, later identified as Greg Rhea, in the bushes next to the sidewalk near the vehicle.

Appellant was detained. A check run on the gray Nissan indicated it was the vehicle appellant's wife had reported stolen. Appellant was placed under arrest. Rhea was detained but later released.

Officer Walden searched the backpack appellant had thrown at his feet and found a plastic baggie containing a substance later determined to be methamphetamine. The gray Nissan was searched, and under the hood, in the open next to the battery, the officer found a loaded .22-caliber revolver. The gun was not in a bag.

A search was conducted in the area where appellant made the tossing motion, and keys to the gray Nissan were found in bushes nearby.

Questioned by officers after appellant's arrest, Irma stated she did not own a gun and did not know if appellant did.

B. Defense Case

At trial, Irma testified the gun found in the engine compartment of the Nissan was hers and that she had placed it there in a bag about three weeks before appellant took the vehicle. She explained the gun was her mother's and she got it after her mother's death. It was her intention to give the gun to her father; but until she was able to do so, she wanted to keep it out of the house and away from her three sons. Irma admitted denying to the police any knowledge of the gun and stated she did so because she did not want to get into trouble.

Appellant testified that at the time his wife reported her car stolen, he was living with her on the weekends but was working in Las Vegas during the week. The Nissan was his wife's car, but he used it frequently. He admitted taking the vehicle on January 28, 1995. He stated he had permission to use the car but not to keep it for three days.

Appellant stated the incident resulting in his arrest occurred outside the condominium where he and his wife lived. He explained he came to the residence in the Nissan with Greg Rhea. Rhea was driving since appellant had no driver's license. It was appellant's plan to talk with his wife. Appellant left Rhea in the car and tried to awaken his wife so she would come down and talk with him. Unable to make contact with his wife, he went to the residence of a neighbor, Lorena Tweedle, where he believed he might find his wife. His wife was not there and appellant and Tweedle returned to the Nissan. Appellant awakened Rhea, who came out of the car. As the two men stood by the car, the police approached. Appellant stated it was Rhea and not he who tossed the keys into the bushes. Appellant stated he was confronted by an officer who told him to get on the ground. Appellant testified he fully cooperated, doing all the officer asked. Appellant denied throwing the backpack at the officer's feet and stated it was on the hood of the car when the officer approached. He stated he had never seen the gun before, he denied raising the hood of the car and stated he had merely banged on it to awaken Rhea. Appellant stated the backpack, while containing some of his property, was not his and he did not know it contained methamphetamine.

DISCUSSION

A. Sufficiency of Evidence

Appellant argues the evidence was insufficient to convict him of auto taking [as well as other crimes of which he was charged].

In determining whether evidence is sufficient to support a verdict, we examine the entire record, viewing the evidence in the light most favorable to the judgment and presuming in support of the verdict the existence of every fact the jury could reasonably deduce from the evidence. The issue is whether the record so viewed discloses evidence that is reasonable, credible and of solid value such that a rational trier of fact could find the elements of the crime beyond a reasonable doubt. (*People v. Brown* (1995) 35 Cal.App.4th 1585, 1598 [42 Cal.Rptr.2d 155].)

1. Auto Taking

Appellant makes several arguments related to the sufficiency of the evidence of auto taking. An auto taking within the meaning of Vehicle Code section 10851, subdivision (a), occurs when a person "drives or takes a vehicle not his or her own, without the consent of the owner thereof, and with intent either to permanently or temporarily deprive the owner thereof of his or her title to or possession of the vehicle, whether with or without the intent to steal the vehicle."

a. Consent and Intent

Appellant argues the evidence was insufficient to prove a lack of consent or an intent to permanently or temporarily deprive the owner of possession of the car.

Appellant's wife testified that in late January 1994, she owned the vehicle that appellant, her husband of three years, was charged with taking. She testified they argued and she did not want him to take the car; and when he took it, she filed a stolen vehicle report.

Irma testified she reported the car stolen because she had placed a gun under the vehicle's hood three weeks prior to its taking and was afraid if appellant opened the hood he would discover the weapon. Irma also stated appellant used the car from time to time to drive to his job in Las Vegas.

Appellant testified that while the Nissan belonged to his wife, he used it frequently. He admitted that on or about January 28, 1995, he took the car. Appellant stated that while he knew the car belonged to his wife, he had permission to drive it but not to keep it for three days.

Appellant suggests Irma, by her testimony that she reported the car stolen because it contained the gun, was recanting the claim appellant had taken the vehicle without permission. First, Irma's reason for reporting the crime has no necessary relationship to whether there was a crime. In our view, Irma never retreated from the position the car was taken without her permission. She merely claimed she decided to report the crime because of her concern about the gun. Second, Irma had before trial reported her car stolen and stated she believed her husband took it. Even if Irma recanted that claim at trial the jury was free to reject her trial testimony and accept the initial claim.

Likewise, there was sufficient evidence to support the conclusion appellant intended to either temporarily or permanently deprive his wife of possession of her car. Irma testified they argued about whether he could take the car. Appellant took it. At trial appellant admitted taking the car and keeping it for three days. When confronted by the police, he threw the keys to the car into the bushes. The jury could reasonably conclude appellant took the car intending to temporarily deprive Irma of possession of the vehicle. When appellant arrived back at his wife's residence, he came with a friend. Before going inside, he placed a gun under the vehicle's hood. The jury could reasonably believe appellant did not come to return the car but intended to leave with it and keep it permanently. (See *People v. Green* (1995) 34 Cal.App.4th 165, 180-181 [40 Cal.Rptr.2d 239].)

b. *Community Property and Vehicle Code Section 10851*

Appellant notes there was uncontradicted evidence at trial that the vehicle taken was purchased during his marriage to the victim. Appellant, citing the presumption that property acquired during marriage is community property (Fam. Code, § 760; *In re Marriage of Haines* (1995) 33 Cal.App.4th 277, 289-290 [39 Cal. Rptr.2d 673]), argues the only possible conclusion is that the vehicle taken was his community property. Appellant notes one element of the crime of auto taking is that the vehicle taken be the property of another. He argues since the vehicle was his own, he could not be guilty of taking it and therefore, the evidence was insufficient to support his conviction.

1. *Theft of Community Property*

The problem of whether an owner can be criminally liable for stealing property coheld with others is not a new one. (See 2 Lafave & Scott, *Substantive Criminal Law* (1986) § 8.2, pp. 335-336.) In California, theft occurs when a co-owner takes jointly held property with the intent to permanently deprive other owners of their interest in that property. (*Oakdale Village Group v. Fong* (1996) 43 Cal.App.4th 539, 545-546 [50 Cal.Rptr.2d 810]; *People v. Sobiek* (1973) 30 Cal. App.3d 458, 463-469 [106 Cal.Rptr. 519, 82 A.L.R.3d 804] (*Sobiek*); *see also People v. Kahanic* (1987) 196 Cal.App.3d 461, 463-467 [241 Cal.Rptr. 722] (*Kahanic*).)

The seminal California case is *Sobiek*. There, a partner was charged with grand theft based on the embezzlement of partnership funds. Rejecting prior authority, the court concluded the defendant could be criminally liable for embezzling such property. While relying on several bases, for example, the wording of the particular statute did not require the property embezzled be that of another, and that a partnership can be characterized as a legal entity separate from the partners, the court also importantly noted that the element of theft that the property be that of another did not require it be "wholly" that of another. The court concluded the fact a partner has an undivided half-interest in partnership property is meaningless to his liability for theft since stealing that portion of the partner's share that does not belong to the thief is no different than stealing any other property. (*Sobiek, supra*, 30 Cal.App.3d at pp. 463-469.)

Sobiek's reasoning was applied to community property in *Kahanic*. In *Kahanic* a wife, angry at finding the community property Mercedes Benz used by her husband parked in front of his girlfriend's apartment, threw a beer bottle through the vehicle's rear window and was charged with vandalism. Vandalism occurs when a person maliciously damages real or personal property "not his own." (Pen. Code, § 594, subd. (a).) The wife argued that since the automobile was community property, and thus hers, she could not be guilty of vandalizing it. (*Kahanic, supra*, 196 Cal.App.3d at pp. 462-463.)

The court, citing Civil Code section 5105 (now Fam. Code, § 751), noted that during the continuance of a marriage the interest of the spouses in their community property is "present, existing and equal." Citing *Sobiek*, however, the court concluded the requirement in criminal statutes that property be that of another or not the defendant's own "excludes criminality only when the actor-defendant is involved with property wholly his or her own." (*Kahanic, supra*, 196 Cal.App.3d at p. 466.) The court explained: "The essence of the crime is in the physical acts against the ownership interest of another, even though that ownership is less than exclusive. [Citation.] Spousal community property interests are no longer 'mere expectancies,' as they were for a married woman many years ago. [Citation.] Each community property owner has an equal ownership interest and, although undivided, one which the criminal law protects from unilateral non-consensual damage or destruction by the other marital partner." (*Id.* at p. 466.)[3]

We conclude a spouse may be criminally liable for the theft of community property.

---

3   There is language in *People v. Green* (1980) 27 Cal.3d 1, 50, footnote 37 [164 Cal.Rptr. 1, 609 P.2d 468], which seems to suggest by negative implication that a spouse cannot steal community property. The case, however, does not so hold.

2. *Taking of a Community Property Automobile*

The conclusion a spouse may be liable for the theft or criminal damage to a community property asset does not, however, resolve the issue in this case. The jury was instructed an auto taking within the meaning of Vehicle Code section 10851 occurs when the defendant drives or takes a vehicle not his or her own, without consent, with the intent either to permanently or temporarily deprive the owner of his or her title to or possession of the vehicle with or without the intent to steal the vehicle. It is possible, therefore, appellant was convicted based on his intent to temporarily and not permanently deprive his wife of the car. Is such an act criminal when the car is community property?

The theft of or the vandalizing of community property are acts which both exceed the defendant's rights to the property and offend the ownership and possessory interest of his or her spouse. However, when the auto taking is accompanied only by the intent to temporarily deprive, the act, while offending the spouse's possessory interest, does not exceed the taking spouse's right to the property. The vehicle is indivisible and its use by one spouse necessarily denies its use to the other. The decision to temporarily take sole possession of a community property vehicle may be based on agreement, misunderstanding or a peevish desire to deny temporarily, for whatever reason, use of the vehicle to the other. Still, in taking the vehicle, even with the intent to temporarily deprive a spouse of its use, the actor does not exceed his or her property right and the problem is properly viewed as a domestic and not a criminal one.

We conclude based on the legal analysis above, and on social policy, that when a spouse takes a community property vehicle with the intent to temporarily deprive the other spouse of its use, no violation of Vehicle Code section 10851 occurs since in legal effect that spouse has not taken a vehicle not his or her own. It is, therefore, not a crime for a spouse to take a community property vehicle with the intent to temporarily deprive the other spouse of his or her title to or possession of that vehicle.

It apparently occurred to no one at trial that appellant's presumptive community property interest in the car could negate any finding of guilt based on his intent to temporarily deprive his wife of that vehicle. When, however, the prosecution rested without rebutting that presumption, the evidence was insufficient to support a conviction of Vehicle Code section 10851 based on the theory appellant intended to temporarily deprive his wife of the vehicle.

3. *Prejudice*

The question remains whether the error was prejudicial. Vehicle Code section 10851 describes a single crime that can be committed in a variety of ways depending on the intent of the actor. Here, the prosecution's failure to rebut the presumption the vehicle taken was community property affected one of the theories on which the jury could have based its verdict of guilt but not the other. Under such circumstances the appropriate mode of prejudice review is that defined in *People v. Guiton* (1993) 4 Cal.4th 1116 [17 Cal.Rptr.2d 365, 847 P.2d 45] (*Guiton*).

Guiton teaches that if a jury is presented with multiple theories supporting conviction on a single charge and on review one theory is found unsupported by sufficient evidence, reversal is not required if sufficient evidence supports the alternate theory and there is no affirmative basis for concluding the jury relied on the factually unsupported theory because it is presumed jurors would not rely on a factually deficient theory. (4 Cal.4th at pp. 1128-1129.)

Guiton also instructs that if a jury is presented with multiple theories supporting conviction on a single charge and on review one theory is found legally defective, that is, the theory does not present a legally sufficient basis for conviction, reversal is required unless substantial reasons exist to find that the verdict was based on a legally valid theory. This is so since it is not presumed a jury will perceive the legal inadequacy of a theory and reject it as a basis for conviction. (*Guiton, supra*, 4 Cal.4th at pp. 1128-1129.)

In this case the jury was instructed conviction was possible either because appellant took the car intending to permanently deprive his wife of it or because he intended to temporarily deprive her of the car. Instruction on the second theory was defective since the jury was not informed the vehicle was presumptively community property and of that presumption's affect on the requirement in Vehicle Code section 10851 that the car not be appellant's own. While that omission technically resulted in insufficient evidence to support one of the two theories of guilt, it must be treated for *Guiton* purposes as legally deficient since, in effect, the jury was misinstructed concerning an element of the offense. We cannot presume the jury would have perceived this legal defect and based its verdict solely on the remaining theory of guilt.

We find nothing in the record suggesting the jury relied on the theory appellant intended to permanently, rather than temporarily, deprive his wife of the car, and the Vehicle Code section 10851 conviction must be reversed.

DISPOSITION

Appellant's convictions for auto taking . . . are reversed. . . and the matter is remanded to the trial court.

Notes and Questions

1. If the defendant can steal jointly owned property, why exactly does the court reverse this conviction?

2. Think back to the example we offered before we looked at this case. What protects a husband from prosecution when he makes a purchase of a fishing boat that he does not tell his wife about ahead of time? Is he protected? Should he be?

3. Isn't co-ownership necessarily allowing another to use the item jointly owned? Who would break a tie as to who should have the car? Notice that the court concludes that it is announcing a modern rule—and one that is more protective of women. The court concluded, "The essence of the crime is in the physical acts against the ownership interest of another, even though that ownership is less than exclusive. Spousal community property are no longer 'mere expectations' as they were for a married woman many years ago." Of course, for the spouse convicted of vandalizing her joint property upon finding out that her husband had an affair, this new conception of property is not necessarily an improved state of affairs.

4. Notice the upshot of this case. One spouse can *temporarily* deprive the other of jointly held property without consent but not permanently. This makes practical sense, of course, but if a co-owner of property has the right not to have his or property permanent deprived, does such an interest not extend to a temporary deprivation as well? And if the distinction between temporary and permanent deprivation is driven by an interest in not involving the courts in disputes within the household, would this concern not also extend to the permanent conversion of money in a checking account into a highly contentious purchase of a sail boat?

5. We will take up later the distinction between permanent and temporary deprivations of property. The most common example of temporary deprivation of property is most commonly referred to as joyriding, which is punished much less seriously than grand theft auto.

b. Taking and Carrying Away

This element of larceny is frequently described as asportation. In a number of settings, once the prosecution has demonstrated the defendant's intent to steal, proof of asportation is not difficult to show. Even minor movement is enough. There are times, however, when the defendant is entitled to move another's property. *Khoury* illustrates the best example—a store. When asportation occurs within a store, to prove larceny, the prosecution must prove, in addition to the defendant's larcenous intent, that he moved the property in a way in which the store did not consent. *Alamo* presents the same question in the context of auto theft. Attempt is different in this context because there is no sphere in which one person is permitted to have access to another's car (except for a valet). At what point has control ripened into asportation to make an attempted auto theft an auto theft? That is the question taken up in *Alamo*.

People v. Khoury

Superior Court, Appellate Division Los Angeles County, California
665 A.2d 264 (1980)

FAINER, Judge.

Defendant appeals his conviction, by jury trial, for violation of Penal Code section 487, subdivision 1 (grand theft). The pertinent facts of this case were that defendant, after being observed for several hours pushing a shopping cart around a Fed Mart Store, was seen pushing a cart, with a large cardboard chandelier box on it, up to a check stand in the store. An alert cashier at the check stand, noticing that the box was loosely taped, stated that he would have to open and check the contents of the box before he would allow defendant to pay the price marked and remove the box from the store. Defendant then walked back through the check stand and into the store, leaving the box with the cashier. Defendant was arrested by store security after the box was opened, disclosing in excess of $900.00 worth of store items, consisting of batteries, tools, and chain saws, but no chandelier.

Defendant contends that these facts were insufficient evidence to convict him of grand theft. More specifically, defendant contends that the evidence was insufficient to show an asportation or carrying away of the personal property of the Fed Mart Store and therefore was, at most, an attempt to commit grand theft.

Our function on appeal in this case is to determine first the applicable law of theft by larceny, which is the theft for which defendant was specifically charged, and then to examine the record to ascertain whether there was substantial evidence of the disputed element of the crime to support the judgment of conviction. (*People v. Farris* (1977) 66 Cal.App.3d 376, 383, 136 Cal.Rptr. 45; *People v. Roberts* (1975) 51 Cal.App.3d 125, 138, 123 Cal.Rptr. 893.)

The crime of larceny is the stealing or taking of the property of another. (Pen. Code, § 484.) "The completed crime of larceny as distinguished from attempted larceny requires asportation or carrying away, in addition to the taking. (citations omitted)." (1 Witkin, Cal. Crimes, Crimes Against Property, § 378.)

"The element of asportation is not satisfied unless it is shown that 'the goods were severed from the possession or custody of the owner, and in the possession of the thief, though it be but for a moment.'" (*Ibid.*)

The other element of theft by larceny is the specific intent in the mind of the perpetrator ". . . to deprive the owner permanently of his property . . . ." (CALJIC No. 14.03; 1 Witkin, Cal. Crimes, Crimes Against Property, ss 383, 384, 385, 386.)

The sufficiency of the evidence to support a finding of intent is not a claim of error on this appeal but is important in reviewing the jury's determination of the existence of the element of asportation or carrying away, a question of fact. The jury was instructed that "(I)n order to constitute a carrying away, the property need not be . . . actually removed from the premises of the owner. Any removal of the property from the place where it was kept or placed by the owner, done with the specific intent to deprive the owner permanently of his property . . ., whereby the perpetrator obtains possession and control of the property for any period of time, is sufficient to constitute the element of carrying away." (CALJIC No. 14.03.)

The cases make a distinction between fact patterns in which the defendant takes possession of the owner's property and moves it with the intent to carry it away, so that it is not attached to any other property of the owner (*People v. Tijerina* (1969) 1 Cal.3d 41, 47, 81 Cal.Rptr. 264, 459 P.2d 680; *People v. Thompson* (1958) 158 Cal.App.2d 320, 322, 323, 322 P.2d 489; *People v. Brown* (1963) 214 Cal. App.2d 128, 29 Cal.Rptr. 267) and those cases in which a thief is frustrated in his attempt to carry the property away (*People v. Meyer* (1888) 75 Cal. 383, 385, 17 P. 431). All of the cases cited above make it clear that the property does not have to be actually removed from the premises of the owner. The jury was properly instructed as to the necessary elements of the crime of theft by larceny. They were not told that there could be no taking or carrying away or asportation unless defendant was able to get the chandelier box containing other store property past the cashier. This was a factor to be considered by the jury, as the trier of fact, in determining whether there was or was not an asportation.

The defendant was seen pushing a shopping cart carrying a carton or container for packaging a chandelier; the chandelier had been removed from the carton and the items already described, of a value of $900, were in the carton. The carton was taped. It was the recent taping of the carton that prompted the cashier not to permit the defendant to go through the check stand until the contents of the carton were checked. The defendant, on being informed of this, walked back into the store, leaving the carton behind. These facts, and the reasonable inferences which can be drawn therefrom support the jury's finding of asportation by substantial evidence.

The intent to permanently deprive the store of its merchandise was clear. The defendant in this appeal does not even attempt to negate the element of intent by proof of innocent though careless mistake. (See 1 Witkin, Cal. Crimes, *supra*, § 385.)

The judgment of conviction is affirmed.

IBANEZ, P. J., concurs.

BIGELOW, Judge.

I respectfully dissent.

In my opinion, as a matter of law, the facts fail to show sufficient asportation of the items to constitute a completed theft. The defendant is only guilty of attempted grand theft in violation of Penal Code sections 664, 484, and 487, subdivision (1).

In *People v. Thompson* (1958) 158 Cal.App.2d 320, 322 P.2d 489, the defendant entered a Thrifty Drug Store, concealed several records under his coat and went through the check stand without paying for the records. He was arrested 10 feet beyond the check stand, but before he left the store.

The physical layout of the store in our case at bench was similar to that of the store in the Thompson case, *supra*. In each case there was a check stand where the items selected for purchase are to be paid for by the customer. The Thompson case, *supra*, at page 323, 322 P.2d at page 490, stated, "The carrying of the records through the check stand constituted an asportation of the goods, as the act effectively removed them from the store's possession and control, even if only for a moment. (*People v. Quiel* (1945) 68 Cal.App.2d 674, 679, 157 P.2d 446)."

In this case, an alert clerk at the check stand prevented defendant from removing the items from the store's possession and control, even for a moment. All the other facts of placing the items in a box, taping it, etc., are proof of his intent to permanently deprive the owner-store of its property without paying the proper marked prices for them. Defendant's attempted theft was frustrated and he did not asportate the goods past the check stand.

I would modify the verdict and judgment to provide that the defendant is guilty of the offense of attempted grand theft (Pen. Code, §§ 664, 484, 487, subd. 1), affirm the judgment as modified and remand the matter to the trial court for resentencing of the defendant.

Notes and Questions

1. Who do you think has the better part of this argument? Your view of the answer to this question likely turns on two issues: how much difference exists between the punishment for attempted larceny and larceny *and* how much you accepted David Lewis' argument (p. 48) about the problem of punishing attempts and completed crimes differently.

2. Based strictly on precedent as described, however, does the dissent not seem to have the better view of this? There are two important lessons from this. First, majorities can be "wrong," even if their view wins the days and is precedent for future cases. Their poor reasoning makes their decisions subject to distinction, if not outright overruling. The other lesson from the case is the importance of the *facts* of cases. The dissent in this case is far more compelling because it offers sufficient *facts* from the precedent it offers. The majority offers merely the rules it extracts from precedent. The dissent, in other words, allows the reader to check its math.

People v. Alamo

Court of Appeals of New York
315 N.E.2d 446 (1974)

GABRIELLI, Judge.

The Westchester County Grand Jury charged defendant with grand larceny, second degree for theft of an automobile, and with criminal possession of burglary tools and a hypodermic instrument which were found with defendant in the automobile. Defendant was found guilty after a jury trial on all charges except that the larceny count was reduced to the third degree by the jury pursuant, evidently, to the charge concerning the monetary worth of the vehicle. The Appellate Division has unanimously affirmed the convictions. The point raised on this appeal with which we are chiefly concerned is whether it was error for the Judge to charge the jury that they might find a completed larceny even though they found defendant to have started the car, but not to have moved it. A subsidiary and related issue is whether this Judge erred in refusing to charge attempted larceny.

The People's case insofar as it relates to the larcenous act was proved through the two police officers who made the arrest. Officer Davis testified that at approximately 1:00 a.m. on December 14, 1971 in the Town of Greenburgh he and fellow Officer Downey were cruising and spotted defendant in an automobile near the curb; that they felt the situation warranted a routine check whereupon the police cruiser was parked alongside the subject car to block its exit from the curb. Defendant, who was behind the wheel, was unable to produce a proper registration. Upon ascertainment that the true owner of the car was Stephen Solomon, a nearby resident, defendant was placed under arrest. The burglar tools and hypodermic needle were found in the car with defendant.

Officer Davis testified that 'we noticed a vehicle on the right-hand side, in a curb lane, with its headlights on, the motor running, and a person operating this vehicle. The wheels were cut to the left and the vehicle was inching out into the roadway.' Officer Downey rendered approximately the same account of these events and stated: 'As we approached the intersection of Hillside Avenue and Virginia Road, we noticed a vehicle to our right parked facing north with the engine running with the lights on just starting to pull out of a parking space.' There was additional evidence that the side vent window of the car had been forced. The only inroad which was made on the evidence that the car was in motion was Officer Davis' Grand Jury testimony that when he saw the car it was 'parked' at the curb. The defense produced no witnesses and introduced no proof.

The Judge instructed the jury on the larceny count reading to them subdivision 1 of section 155.05 of the Penal Law, Consol.Laws, c. 40, i.e., that larceny consists of the wrongful taking, obtaining or withholding of property. He also told them that if they found that defendant had forced the window, removed the ignition switch, started the automobile and exercised control over the automobile by any act, then they could find him guilty of larceny. After some deliberation the jury returned for further instruction on the meaning of control and whether movement of the vehicle was required to effectuate control. The Judge answered as follows:

> 'control would be a proprietary act, any act which constituted appropriating the automobile to the defendant's own use, exercising some degree of jurisdiction over the automobile, taking an affirmative act. In this case, the

entering of the car, the closing of the door, turning the lights on, and starting the vehicle may be considered acts of control.

'You have asked further the question: 'Does control require movement
of the vehicle? I would say to you that control in the sense as creating a larceny and as I included in my original charge would not require movement
of the vehicle.'

Although defendant argues that it was error for the Judge not to allow the
jury to find an attempt this is welded to the argument that there can be no completed larceny until the vehicle is moved by the would-be thief. The argument
has to be that not only was it error not to charge attempt, but that it was error to
tell the jury they could find a completed larceny even though they might find the
vehicle not to have been moved.

All the testimonial evidence on the point was that the car was beginning
to move out from the curb after the officers spotted it. There is no affirmative
proof that the car was not moving. Officer Davis' prior statement that the car
was 'parked' may to some small degree have affected his credibility on the question of the movement of the car, however. It may be argued that the jury may
have doubted the officers' testimony on this matter and this theory is supported
by the fact they asked for more specific instructions as to what they should do
depending on whether the car was moved. We have only recently and exhaus-
tively reviewed the rules concerning when the charge of attempt is appropriate
and concluded that despite the language in the definition of attempt in the new
Penal Law (s 110.00) which no longer requires a failure to effect the commission
of the crime, the attempt charge is inappropriate where no view of the evidence
would support the charge or where, citing *People v. Mussenden*, 308 N.Y. 558, 563,
127 N.E.2d 551, 554, "the evidence essential to support a verdict of guilt of (the
lesser crime) necessarily proves the guilt of the greater crime as well." (*People
v. Richette*, 33 N.Y.2d 42, 47, 349 N.Y.S.2d 65, 68, 303 N.E.2d 857, 859). If it be
assumed for the sake of argument on this point that a trespass short of moving
the car could only amount to an attempted larceny, then the Judge erred in refusing to charge attempt because the jury might have taken a view of the evidence
to the effect the car was not moved.

We cannot, however, stop on that observation and modify or remand. The
Judge not only refused to charge attempt; he told the jury that there could be a
completed larceny without movement of the car. We must, therefore, also deal
with the question whether that was a correct instruction.

It is woven into the fabric of the common law that asportation is an element
of a completed larceny. (*Commonwealth v. Sanders*, 225 Pa.Super. 432, 311 A.2d
706; *People v. White*, 71 Cal.App.2d 524, 162 P.2d 862; *State v. Maddaus*, 137

Minn. 249, 163 N.W. 507.) Indeed, these cases involve automobiles, the courts searching for the asportation element in all three. There does not appear to be, however, any authority including those cases just cited and including the two cases advanced by defendant (*Matter of Slattery* (Domestic Relations Ct.), 14 A.D.2d 805, 220 N.Y.S.2d 596; *Matter of Meyers*, 43 Misc.2d 170, 250 N.Y.S.2d 652), which approximates the facts in the instant case, i.e., where an automobile is entered, where the culprit positions himself behind the wheel, starts the engine, turns on the lights and starts to move the car or is about to do so. (*See, also, Commonwealth v. Kozlowsky*, 238 Mass. 379, 131 N.E. 207; *State v. Olson*, 59 Utah 549, 205 P. 337.)

The authoritative case in this jurisdiction on the essential elements of larceny is *Harrison v. People*, 50 N.Y. 518. There a pickpocket grasped the victim's wallet and lifted it no more than several inches and not all the way out of the pocket when the victim, having become aware, grabbed at the wallet and thrust it back down to the bottom of the pocket. The court held that a completed larceny had been committed. The temporary possession by the thief, even though for a moment, was sufficient as was the slight movement accompanying the possession. While it is to be conceded that the element of movement was a consideration in the court's reasoning, critical analysis of that reasoning discloses that the elements of possession and control were the paramount elements sought and that the fact of movement merely tended to support the idea of control. Thus, it was stated (p. 523): 'To constitute the offence of larceny, there must be a taking Or severance of the goods from the possession of the owner. * * * But possession, so far as this offence is concerned, is the having or holding or detention of property in one's power or command.' (Emphasis added.) There ensued discussion concerning instances where the object of the theft was connected to the owner by a string or chain and where, therefore, there could be no completed larceny because of the continued connection to the owner even though there was limited asportation. It was then stated (p. 524) concerning the wallet: 'It was in his possession. He directed, and, for the instant of time, controlled its movements.'

The actions needed to gain possession and control over a wallet, including movement of the wallet which, in itself, is merely an element tending to show possession and control, are not necessarily the actions needed to gain possession and control of any automobile. A wallet, or a diamond ring, or a safe are totally inert objects susceptible of movement only by physical lifting or shoving by the thief. An automobile, however, is itself an instrument of transportation and when activated comes within the total possession and control of the operator. In this situation movement or motion is not essential to control. Absent any evidence that the vehicle is somehow fastened or immovable because of a mechanical defect, the thief has taken command of the object of the larceny. He has, in the words of subdivision 1 of section 155.05 of the Penal Law, wrongfully 'taken' the property from its owner surely as much so as had the thief in Harrison.

Consistency is always desirable in the application of the various laws and such would not be achieved were we to hold that on these facts defendant and not gained possession and control of the car. An established line of authority in New York and elsewhere holds that for purposes of offenses for driving while intoxicated under the Vehicle and Traffic Law, Consol.Laws, c. 71, operation of the vehicle is established on proof that the defendant was merely behind the wheel with the engine running without need for proof that defendant was observed driving the car, i.e., operating it so as to put it in motion. (*People v. Marriott*, 37 A.D.2d 868, 325 N.Y.S.2d 177; *Matter of Tomasello v. Tofany*, 32 A.D.2d 962, 303 N.Y.S.2d 22, stay den. 25 N.Y.2d 647, mot. for lv. to app. den. 25 N.Y.2d 742, 305 N.Y.S.2d 1026, 252 N.E.2d 863; *Matter of Prudhomme v. Hults*, 27 A.D.2d 234, 278 N.Y.S.2d 67 and cases cited therein; *People v. Ceschini*, 63 Misc.2d 15, 310 N.Y.S.2d 581; Ann., 47 A.L.R.2d 570, *Driving While Drunk*, and suppl.) Quoted with approval in *Prudhomme* was the language from *People v. Domagala* (123 Misc. 757, 758, 206 N.Y.S. 288) that an individual 'began to violate the law (against operating while intoxicated) the instant he began to manipulate the machinery of the motor for the purpose of putting the automobile into motion', even though he did not succeed in moving it. (27 A.D.2d, at p. 236, 278 N.Y.S.2d, at p. 69) Also quoted approvingly was this language from *Commonwealth v. Uski*, 263 Mass. 22, 24, 160 N.E. 305: 'A person operates a motor vehicle within the meaning of (the statute) when, in the vehicle, he intentionally does any act or makes use of any mechanical or electrical agency which alone or in sequence will set in motion the motive power of that vehicle.' (27 A.D.2d, at p. 237, 278 N.Y.S.2d, at p. 70.)

It would be difficult to understand how a person who is operating a car, as defendant was under the authority just discussed, could be said nevertheless not to be in possession and control of that car. It is further to be noted that where the Legislature has specifically addressed itself solely to automobile taking, a person is guilty of unauthorized use where he 'takes, Operates, exercises control over, rides in or otherwise uses a vehicle.' (Penal Law, § 165.05, subd. 1; emphasis added.) Although it might be argued that the unauthorized use statute is not a larceny statute and thus utilizes lesser criteria, the distinction meant by the Legislature between the two kinds of offenses lies in the intent of the taker, not in the means used to effect the taking. Thus, the unauthorized use statute contemplates only a borrowing and not a complete appropriation. (Denzer and McQuillan, Commentary, McKinney's Consol.Laws of N.Y., Book 39, Penal Law, § 165.05.) If operation of the automobile can effect a taking under the unauthorized use statute then operation ought also to suffice under the larceny statute.

Finally, we do not, as stated in the dissent, 'disregard' the relative constancy of the statute under which defendant was convicted. It is to be noted that not since 1942 have we in this jurisdiction been strictly bound to the ancient common-law concepts of larceny. (Denzer and McQuillan, Commentary, McKinney's Consol.Laws of N.Y., Book 39, Penal Law, § 155.05.) At that time the first unnumbered paragraph of former section 1290 was enacted. That was the forerunner of current subdivision 1 of section 155.05 of the Penal Law which was charged to the jury in the instant case and which in very broad terms prohibits wrongful appropriation, taking, obtaining or withholding of another's property with the requisite intent. There is nothing in the definitions section which states that asportation is in all cases an essential element of such taking or obtaining (s 155.00). Subdivision 2 of section 155.00 defines 'Obtain' as follows: "'Obtain' includes, but is not limited to, the bringing about of a transfer or purported transfer of property or of a legal interest therein, whether to the obtainer or another.' Surely a person transfers an instrument of transportation to himself when he commences to operate the instrument for its intended purpose. At that point it comes under his sole dominion and control and, assuming requisite intent, amounts to the completed taking as envisioned under our broadened statutory concepts. To require that the vehicle be moved by the operator is to slavishly adhere to the auxiliary common-law element of asportation which is simply not necessary to the finding of the primary elements of dominion and control where an activated automobile is concerned.

Defendant's other points are too insubstantial to require discussion. The order appealed from should be affirmed.

BREITEL, Chief Judge (dissenting).

I dissent and vote to reverse and order a new trial because defendant was entitled to his requested charge that on the evidence the jury could conclude that only an attempt rather than a consummated larceny had been committed.

There is no significant disagreement in the court whether the jury was properly instructed on the issue of a completed larceny, if there had been a movement of the vehicle for which there was available evidence. There was, indeed, ample evidence to establish movement of the vehicle by defendant. The only issue which divides the court is whether the jury could be instructed, as it was, that no movement was required to establish a completed larceny.

Disregarded by the majority is that the 1967 statute under which defendant was tried and convicted is in its operative language substantively identical with the predecessor statute (compare Penal Law, § 155.05, subd. 1 with former Penal Law, § 1290). Moreover, the law of this State has always been, and indeed, the unanimous Anglo-American view insofar as discoverable is, that some movement, albeit slight, is required before a conviction for a completed larceny may be had (*Harrison v. People*, 50 N.Y. 518, 523—524; see Ann., Larceny—Asportation, 19 A.L.R. 724, supplemented in 144 A.L.R. 1383; *see, also, Rex v. Coslet,* 1 Leach 236 and Cherry's case cited in the Coslet case, at n. 1).

A person may be guilty of operating a motor vehicle while intoxicated although the vehicle was observed only as stationary (*compare People v. Blake*, 5 N.Y.2d 118, 120, 180 N.Y.S.2d 775, 776, 154 N.E.2d 818, 819 with *People v. Marriott*, 37 A.D.2d 868, 325 N.Y.S.2d 177, and *Matter of Prudhomme v. Hults*, 27 A.D.2d 234, 236, 278 N.Y.S.2d 67, 69; *see, also,* Ann., Driving While Drunk, 47 A.L.R.2d 570, and cases cited). Even if that principle be legally sound, it has no application to a larceny prosecution. The statutory proscription against persons operating a motor vehicle while intoxicated is directed at a different evil involving a lesser degree of turpitude and a special problem of proof hardly applicable to larceny. Moreover, an attempt to commit the crime of operating a motor vehicle while intoxicated most often would be inconceivable (*cf. People v. Brown*, 21 A.D.2d 738, 249 N.Y.S.2d 922).

Indeed, the majority helpfully cites automobile larceny cases, every one of which holds that movement of the automobile is necessary, and that possession with control, but without movement, constitutes only the attempt rather than the completed larceny (cf. Hale, *Pleas of the Crown*, 60–61, 64 (1678); LaFave and Scott, *Criminal Law*, p. 632 (1972)). Hence, these authorities demonstrate that on the evidence in this case the jury could have found either an attempt or the completed crime. Consequently, defendant was entitled to the requested charge on attempt.

The evidence was equivocal whether the automobile had been moved at all from its parking place. Merely sitting in the driver's seat, motor running, and with the lights on was not a taking of possession and control by defendant. This is not to say that the jury was not entitled to find on the other evidence of movement, if believed, that the completed larceny had occurred (*see, generally, People v. Richette*, 33 N.Y.2d 42, 46–48, 349 N.Y.S.2d 65, 67–69, 303 N.E.2d 857, 858–859).

In the concrete instance of automobile larceny it is particularly important to distinguish between seating one's self in the driver's seat, as children often do, and some child-like adults do, 'controlling' the vehicle, and, whether when the acts extend no further than that, there has been a taking. It is not a close legal question as the majority analysis would show, but is an inescapable issue of fact for any fact-finder, when considering the tinkering and dallying habits of human beings. A trespass or even an attempt there may be, on any view, but a larceny is another matter. As with the wallet in the Harrison case (*supra*), discussed in the majority opinion, control and possession to the exclusion of the owner is not shown without some movement, any more than it could be shown in the shoplifter case if the alleged larcenist did no more than put his fist around a bauble. In short, asportation under the applicable statute is, inevitably because definitionally, an element of larceny, and it may not be analyzed away (in contrast see American Law Institute, Model Penal Code, art. 223, especially § 223.2; American Law Institute, Tentative Draft No. 1 (1953), Comment D, at pp. 65–66, including examples).

Notes and Questions

1. The crucial question in this case is whether the trial judge incorrectly instructed the jury that no movement of the car was necessary to show that the defendant's act had moved from an attempt to a completed crime. The debate between the majority and the dissent demonstrates an issue of how to interpret precedent that plays itself out in a number of contexts. In the *Harrison* case, discussed by both the majority and the dissent, the pickpocket had obtained control over his victim's wallet and had slightly moved it. The court in *Harrison* did not indicate both control and movement of the wallet was required or whether having control over the wallet was itself sufficient. The movement can be read to be merely incidental to the control, or the movement can be viewed as the key act separating an attempt from a completed larceny. In your career, you will often find that precedent lends itself to different interpretation in a similar manner—facts can always be distinguished and it is only for subsequent courts to say which of the facts are pivotal to the decision.

2. The majority and dissent disagree on how the rules relating to drunk driving ought to apply to this offense. When we considered strict liability offenses, we observed that the state should be permitted to dispense with *mens rea* requirements when a crime carrying a relatively small penalty has the potential to create great harm to society. Driving while intoxicated is one of those crimes. Does it therefore make sense to require less in the ways of *actus reus* for crimes like DUI than for crimes like auto theft, that carry substantial penalties and do not, by themselves, threaten society? (Of course, if the auto thief engages in evasive maneuvers to avoid the police, then this is another matter entirely—but a separate crime.)

3. In some sense, is every prosecuted larceny not an attempted larceny? If the defendant has been discovered in possession of goods (and the goods have not

been destroyed) then the defendant has failed to achieve his goal of permanently depriving the victim of his goods. The line between an attempted and completed larceny is therefore, in some sense, necessarily an artificial one.

---

c. With Intent to Steal

Very often questions about a defendant's intent to steal arises in the context of automobile cases. Joyriding is punished differently than is a taking with the intent to permanently deprive the owner of his property, as you will discover in the *Bell* case. But what about an unlawful temporary taking of property that is rented? Is this theft or joyriding?

People v. Bell

Court of Appeal of California
197 Cal.App. 4th 822 (2011)

MALLANO, P.J.

Monique Bell used another person's name and personal identifying information to convince a lessor of an apartment that Bell was creditworthy. She leased the apartment and soon was delinquent in paying rent until she was evicted. A jury convicted Bell of identity theft and related charges, including grand theft. Bell challenges the grand theft conviction, claiming that it is not supported by substantial evidence that she had the intent to permanently deprive the lessor of its property. We disagree and affirm because Bell intended to permanently deprive the lessor of a leasehold interest, at least to the extent that Bell failed to pay rent during her occupancy.

BACKGROUND

The information charged Bell with one count of identity theft in violation of subdivision (a) of Penal Code section 530.5 (count 1), one count of false personation in violation of section 529 (count 2), one count of making a false financial statement in violation of subdivision (1) of section 532a (count 3), and grand theft of personal property in violation of subdivision (a) of section 487 (count 4).[1]

The charges were tried to a jury, which found Bell guilty on all counts. The court sentenced Bell to 2 years 8 months in state prison. Bell appealed.

---

2 All subsequent statutory references are to the Penal Code.

The evidence introduced at trial showed that Bell signed a one-year apartment lease in April 2007 under the name of Leah Taylor, using Taylor's social security number and other personal identifying information in order to obtain approval of Bell's rental application. Bell then resided in the apartment with another woman and a little girl. The director of operations of Healstone Property Management, which managed the apartment complex, described the rental history as follows: "There were collection issues, there were partial payments, late payments, and then the final was the returned check." "In June the late payments started." ". . . [H]aving the delinquent payments right off the bat was a red flag. . . ." After June, the problems persisted with "[l]ate payments July, August, partial payments through August, September, October. At which point in November there was a returned check along with a delinquency in which we had sent first the notice requesting that they surrender the property, pay the rent in full. And upon no response to that, we filed [an] unlawful detainer."

Pursuant to an unlawful detainer judgment, Healstone garnished $3,000 from the bank account of the real Leah Taylor for the unpaid rent. When Taylor sought to get her money back, claiming truthfully that she had never lived in or even applied to rent the apartment in question, the identity theft finally came to light. Taylor did get her $3,000 back but, as of the time of trial, was still trying to restore her credit rating to its previous status.

We appointed counsel to represent Bell on appeal. After examination of the record, counsel filed an opening brief raising no issues and asking us independently to review the record pursuant to *People v. Wende* (1979) 25 Cal.3d 436, 158 Cal.Rptr. 839, 600 P.2d 1071. On October 25, 2010, we advised Bell that she had 30 days within which she could personally submit any contentions or issues that she wished us to consider. We received no response.

After reviewing the record, we sent a letter to the parties requesting supplemental briefing on the issue of whether the conviction for grand theft is supported by substantial evidence. In response to our letter, the issue was briefed.

DISCUSSION

Bell challenges the grand theft conviction on the basis that it is not supported by substantial evidence that she had the intent to permanently deprive the lessor of its property. We disagree and affirm because Bell intended to permanently deprive the lessor of a leasehold interest, at least to the extent that Bell failed to pay rent during her occupancy.

As to the grand theft count, the information alleged that Bell "did unlawfully take money and personal property of a value exceeding Four Hundred Dollars ($400), to wit rent money and U.S. currency $3045.41 the property of

Leah Tomel Taylor, Healstone Property Management." According to the evidence, the rental arrearages exceeded that amount.

The court instructed the jury on only one legal theory with respect to the grand theft count, namely, theft by false pretenses. The instructions informed the jury that the defendant could be found guilty on that count only if the prosecution proved beyond a reasonable doubt that (1) the defendant made either a promise without intent to perform it or a false pretense or representation, (2) the defendant did so with the specific intent to defraud, (3) the victim believed and relied upon the promise or representation, which "was material in inducing [the victim] to part with [its] money or property even though the false pretense, representation or promise was not the sole cause," and (4) "[t]he theft was accomplished in that the alleged victim parted with [its] money or property intending to transfer ownership thereof."

The prosecutor argued to the jury that "the theft is, it is not the property itself, obviously the apartment is still there, they don't . . . walk away with the apartment, it is the value of the service, it is the value of the apartment during the months that they lived there without paying rent. That is a theft under false pretense because they get the apartment through false pretense, then they stop paying rent, and then the owner is out the benefit of those months' rent. That is the theft in this case."

On appeal, Bell contends that "[t]he facts that [she] paid the security deposit upon renting the apartment and then paid four [months'] rent, indicate that her intent was to use the false identification to effect the rental, but not to permanently deprive either the owner of the property or of the identity of possession of the apartment or the rent money." Respondent argues that Bell's false representations induced Healstone to allow Bell to take "possession and title to property that belonged to Healstone, namely the right to the apartment for one year pursuant to the lease which was worth around $12,000. The transfer of that property to [Bell] (e.g., the rights under the lease), based upon [Bell]'s fraudulent representations to Healstone (that she was Leah Taylor), cost Healstone approximately $4,700, based on the breach of contract, plus attorney and court costs of approximately $1,500. . . ." Respondent further argues that "Healstone transferred legal 'ownership' of the right to live in the apartment for one year pursuant to 'Leah Taylor,' based on [Bell]'s false personation."

Our Supreme Court has admonished that California's intent-to-deprive-permanently requirement for the crime of theft is flexible and not to be taken literally. "[T]he general rule is that the intent to steal required for conviction of larceny is an intent to deprive the owner *permanently* of possession of the property. [Citations.]" (*People v. Davis* (1998) 19 Cal.4th 301, 307, 79 Cal. Rptr.2d 295, 965 P.2d 1165; *see also People v. Turner* (1968) 267 Cal.App.2d

440, 443, 73 Cal.Rptr. 263.) The rule is not "inflexible," however, and in certain cases "the requisite intent to steal may be found even though the defendant's primary purpose in taking the property is not to deprive the owner permanently of possession," such as "(1) when the defendant intends to 'sell' the property back to its owner, (2) when the defendant intends to claim a reward for 'finding' the property, and (3) when . . . the defendant intends to return the property to its owner for a 'refund.'" (*People v. Davis, supra*, 19 Cal.4th at p. 307, 79 Cal.Rptr.2d 295, 965 P.2d 1165.) In each of those exceptions, although the defendant does not intend to deprive the owner permanently of possession of the property, the defendant does intend to appropriate the value of permanent possession of the property.

In *People v. Avery* (2002) 27 Cal.4th 49, 115 Cal.Rptr.2d 403, 38 P.3d 1, our Supreme Court expanded on the flexibility of the rule: "We now conclude that an intent to take the property for so extended a period as to deprive the owner of a major portion of its value or enjoyment satisfies the common law, and therefore California, intent requirement." (*Id.* at p. 55, 115 Cal.Rptr.2d 403, 38 P.3d 1.)

"The case generally cited (see, e.g., *People v. Kunkin* (1973) 9 Cal.3d 245, 251 [107 Cal.Rptr. 184, 507 P.2d 1392]) as establishing California's intent-to-deprive-permanently requirement itself implies that the requirement is not to be taken literally. In *People v. Brown* [(1894)] 105 Cal. 66 [38 P. 518], the defendant defended against a charge of stealing a bicycle by testifying that he intended to return it. We held that the testimony, if believed, would make him not guilty of larceny. 'While the felonious intent of the party taking need not necessarily be an intention to convert the property to his own use, still it must in all cases be an intent to wholly and permanently deprive the owner thereof.' (*Id.* at p. 69 [38 P. 518].) Despite the seemingly absolute language used here, the authority we cited 'as directly and fully sustaining this principle' (*ibid.*) shows we did not mean it absolutely. One of the cases we cited was *State v. Davis* [(1875)] 38 N.J.L. 176, which, as we explained in [*People v.*] *Davis, supra*, 19 Cal.4th at page 307 and footnote 4 [79 Cal.Rptr.2d 295, 965 P.2d 1165], helped establish that the intent to steal is satisfied when 'the defendant takes property with intent to use it temporarily and then to *abandon* it in circumstances making it unlikely the owner will recover it.' We also cited *State v. South* (1859) 28 N.J.L. 28, which, as noted in 2 LaFave and Scott, [Substantial Criminal Law (1986) Crimes Relating to Property], section 8.5(b), page 361, footnote 22, . . . applied 'common sense' and concluded that an intent to take temporarily but for an unreasonable length of time was 'ample evidence' of an intent to deprive permanently.

"For these reasons, we agree with the Court of Appeal in *People v. Zangari* [(2001)] 89 Cal.App.4th [1436,] 1443 [108 Cal.Rptr.2d 250], . . . that 'the intent to deprive an owner of the main value of his property is equivalent to the intent to permanently deprive an owner of property.'" (*People v. Avery, supra*, 27 Cal.4th at pp. 56–57, 115 Cal.Rptr.2d 403, 38 P.3d 1.)

Following *Avery*, we conclude that the grand theft conviction is supported by substantial evidence because Bell intended to permanently deprive Healstone of a leasehold interest in real property, at least to the extent that Bell failed to pay rent during her occupancy. Bell took possession of the apartment by false pretenses and was delinquent in rent payments "right off the bat." She made partial payments, late payments, and a payment with a bad check. The jury could reasonably have concluded that she intended to deprive the owner of months of rent when she moved into the apartment under false pretenses. Using another's identity not only permitted her to lease the apartment, but also to have that person's bank account garnished instead of Bell's. And because nothing in the record suggests that she intended to pay all the rent at a later time, it is evident that she intended to permanently deprive Healstone of its leasehold interest, at least to the extent of the unpaid rent.

Bell's reliance on *People v. Turner, supra*, 267 Cal.App.2d 440, 73 Cal.Rptr. 263, is misplaced. There, the defendant rented a car for two days at $7 per day and 7 cents per mile and made a $40 cash deposit, using "a false name and identification." (*Id.* at p. 441, 73 Cal.Rptr. 263.) He was arrested 13 hours later 20 blocks from the rental place. The defendant testified that he intended to return the car when due and had cash to pay whatever the deposit did not cover. The *Turner* court held there was insufficient evidence of intent given the facts before it. But unlike *Turner*, Bell offered no evidence as to her intent. And unlike *Turner*, she was not arrested 13 hours after entering the lease, having paid a deposit which covered the lease payments up to then.

Because a leasehold interest is by its very nature "temporary," in that the lessor will get the property back at the end of the lease, Bell argues that she did not commit theft because she never intended to keep the apartment. This ignores the obvious fact that she intended to permanently deprive Healstone of the unpaid rent.

Car theft cases are not analogous. If a car is taken for a "joy ride" with no intent to permanently deprive its owner of the car, there is no theft. (*People v. Turner, supra*, 267 Cal.App.2d at p. 444, 73 Cal.Rptr. 263.) But here a leasehold interest in a property was taken with the intent to permanently deprive the owner of rent; hence, there is a theft.

To say that a defendant's intent to deprive the owner permanently of a leasehold interest is the same as an intent to deprive the owner of property temporarily, and, thus, cannot support a theft conviction, confuses what is temporary and what is permanent and fails to adhere to the Supreme Court's stricture not to take literally the "intent-to-deprive-permanently requirement." The leasehold is temporary in that it is for a fixed term and not permanent in that sense, but its value in terms of rent, when taken by a thief, is permanent when the thief does not intend to pay rent.

DISPOSITION

The judgment is affirmed.

ROTHSCHILD, J., Concurring and Dissenting.

The majority opinion works a major change in California's law of theft. Under California law, a defendant is guilty of theft only if the defendant acted with "an intent to deprive the owner *permanently* of possession of the property. [Citations.]" (*People v. Davis* (1998) 19 Cal.4th 301, 307, 79 Cal.Rptr.2d 295, 965 P.2d 1165.) The majority holds that an intent to deprive the owner *permanently* of a *temporary interest* in possession of property constitutes an intent to deprive the owner permanently of possession of property. That holding eliminates the intent-to-deprive-permanently requirement— *every* intent to deprive the owner *temporarily* of possession is an intent to deprive the owner permanently of a temporary interest in possession, which in turn, under the majority's holding, is an intent to deprive the owner *permanently* of possession. Thus, under the majority opinion, every intent to deprive the owner temporarily of possession will satisfy the intent element for theft. Perceiving no basis or authority for such a rewriting of the law of theft, I respectfully dissent from the affirmance of Bell's theft conviction.

Bell's conduct, as proven at trial, was wrongful and criminal, and she has been convicted and is being punished. Her conduct constituted identity theft (count 1), false personation (count 2), and making a false financial statement (count 3). The only remaining question is whether, in addition to committing those three offenses, she also committed grand theft (count 4). The record contains no evidence that she did.

In order to determine whether Bell committed theft, we must first identify the property she allegedly took. The information alleged that Bell "did unlawfully take money and personal property of a value exceeding [f]our [h]undred [d]ollars ($400), to wit rent money and U.S. currency $3045.41 the property of Leah Tomel Taylor, Healstone Property Management." (Block capitals omitted.) The record, however, contains no evidence that Bell took any rent money or currency from anyone. The prosecution has never argued to the contrary, either in the trial court or on appeal. At trial, the prosecution likewise correctly conceded that Bell did not take the apartment ("obviously the apartment is still there, they don't . . . walk away with the apartment").

Instead, the prosecution took the position, variously phrased, that the property Bell took was a leasehold interest (or perhaps a portion of a leasehold interest) in the apartment. Respondent continues to advocate that position on appeal. The majority agrees and accepts the theory that the taking of (a portion of) a 12–month leasehold interest in an apartment can constitute a theft.

That theory is mistaken. For the reasons already explained, a temporary interest in possession of property cannot itself constitute stolen property for purposes of a theft charge. If it could, then so-called joyriding (the temporary taking of an automobile) would constitute theft—the joyrider intends to and does permanently deprive the owner of a temporary interest in the possession of the vehicle. But it is firmly established that joyriding does *not* constitute theft. (*See* 2 Witkin & Epstein, *Cal. Criminal Law* (3d ed. 2000) *Crimes Against Property*, §§ 23, 66, pp. 43, 95.) Indeed, joyriding was separately criminalized precisely because joyriders failed to satisfy the intend-to-deprive-permanently requirement that would be necessary for a theft conviction. (See *Id.* § 23, p. 43 ["The difficulty of convicting a 'joyrider' of larceny of an automobile under this rule led to the enactment of statutes imposing less serious punishment for temporary taking"].)

In effect, what Bell did was joyride in an apartment instead of a car. To the extent that her conduct carries an aura of theft, the reason is that the apartment's owner was in the business of selling temporary possessory interests—leasehold interests—in the apartment. Bell took (a portion of) such an interest, the owner can never get those lost months back, and the rent specified in the lease makes it easy to put a dollar value on the owner's loss. On reflection, however, none of those circumstances suffices to convert a temporary taking into a theft. A joyride in a rental car—taken directly from the owner's lot and with the intention never to pay—is still a joyride and not a theft.

The majority offers no persuasive argument to the contrary. It is true that the intent-to-deprive-permanently requirement is not absolutely "inflexible": If the defendant intends to sell the property back to the owner or claim a reward for "'finding'" it or return it for a refund, then the requirement is satisfied. (*People v. Davis, supra,* 19 Cal.4th 301, 307, 79 Cal.Rptr.2d 295, 965 P.2d 1165.) As the majority correctly notes, each of those exceptions involves an intent to appropriate the value of permanent possession of the property—there is, for example, no material difference between an intent to sell the stolen property back to the owner and an intent to sell it to someone else. Nothing of the kind is present here, just as nothing of the kind is present in an ordinary case of joyriding. The record contains no evidence that Bell ever intended to appropriate the value of permanent possession of the apartment.

Likewise, if the defendant intended to retain the property "for so extended a period as to deprive the owner of a major portion of its value or enjoyment," then the requirement is satisfied. (*People v. Avery* (2002) 27 Cal.4th 49, 55, 115

Cal.Rptr.2d 403, 38 P.3d 1.) Again, nothing of the kind is present here. Bell signed a 12–month lease, not a 100–year lease, and the record contains no evidence that she intended to retain the apartment for so extended a period as to deprive the owner of a major portion of its value.

Finally, the majority asserts that my position "confuses what is temporary and what is permanent" because the value of a leasehold interest "in terms of rent, when taken by a thief, is permanent when the thief does not intend to pay rent." (Maj. opn. *ante*, at p. 593.) The same can be said, however, for *any* temporary taking—the putative thief intends to and does deprive the owner permanently of a temporary interest in possession, and that temporary interest has value. (Cf. 2 Witkin & Epstein, *Cal. Criminal Law, supra*, § 16, p. 36 [the crime of theft "is committed if the thing taken has any value, however slight"].) The majority's argument thus confirms that, under the majority's holding, every intent to deprive the owner temporarily of possession satisfies the intent element for theft.

For all of the foregoing reasons, I conclude that Bell's theft conviction is not supported by substantial evidence. I therefore respectfully dissent from the affirmance of that conviction, but I concur in the affirmance of the remainder of the superior court's judgment.

Notes and Questions

1. Does the majority or the dissent have the better end of this argument? Analogies certainly work in each direction. Fraudulently obtaining access to another's concert seat involves a temporary taking, but the only use the concert seat has exists during the concert.

2. If you were a member of the California Legislature and were asked to re-write this statute, how would you do so? For unlawful takings of hotel rooms and concert tickets, would you describe different crimes for temporary takings versus permanent deprivations of property?

----

2. Embezzlement

Embezzlement requires the prosecution to prove that the defendant converted for his own purposes property that had been entrusted to him. A traditional embezzlement case involves an employee, or investor, who is given money or property for a specific purpose and the employee or investor uses the money for some other purpose. A person, entrusted with property for one purpose, who uses the property for another, is guilty of embezzlement. The *Archie* case lays out the traditional requirement of embezzlement and responds to the defendant's rather interesting argument that as a felon, the state could not have been entrusting him with the electronic monitoring device he was required to wear.

State v. Archie

Court of Appeals of New Mexico
943 P.2d 537 (1997)

BOSSON, Judge.

Defendant appeals his conviction for embezzlement after a trial to the court without a jury. Defendant was on probation, confined by the conditions of his probation to stay within 150 feet of his telephone. As part of his probation, Defendant agreed to wear an electronic monitoring device (EMD) around his ankle which would communicate electronically with a computer connected to his telephone and thereby verify his presence as long as he continued to wear the EMD. Contrary to the conditions of probation, Defendant removed the EMD, damaging it, and threw it into a field. The value of the EMD was placed at over $250 and under $2500, thereby making this a fourth degree felony. On appeal, Defendant does not dispute that he violated his probation or that he may have committed the lesser crime of criminal damage to property. Defendant contends that his actions do not constitute the specific crime of embezzlement. We analyze Defendant's actions in light of the specific statutory elements of embezzlement and affirm.

DISCUSSION

The embezzlement statute, NMSA 1978, Section 30-16-8 (Cum.Supp.1996), states: "Embezzlement consists of the embezzling or converting to his own use of anything of value, with which he has been entrusted, with fraudulent intent to deprive the owner thereof." The Uniform Jury Instruction 14-1641, further defines the elements of embezzlement:

For you to find the defendant guilty of embezzlement . . ., the state must prove to your satisfaction beyond a reasonable doubt each of the following elements of the crime:

1. The defendant was entrusted with _____ . . . . ;

2. The defendant converted this _____ (property or money) to the defendant's own use. "Converting something to one's own use" means keeping another's property rather than returning it, or using another's property for one's own purpose [rather than] [even though the property is eventually used] for the purpose authorized by the owner;

3. At the time the defendant converted _____ (property or money), the defendant fraudulently intended to deprive the owner of the owner's property. "Fraudulently intended" means intended to deceive or cheat;

Defendant first argues that there was no showing of a traditional fiduciary relationship, without which he maintains an embezzlement conviction cannot stand. We disagree. Our earlier case of *State v. Moss*, 83 N.M. 42, 44, 487 P.2d 1347, 1349 (Ct.App.1971), stands for the proposition that a specific or technical fiduciary relationship is not necessary to sustain an embezzlement conviction under New Mexico law. While some jurisdictions may require a special fiduciary relationship, such as employment or agency, as an element of the crime, New Mexico does not. *See State v. Green*, 116 N.M. 273, 275, 861 P.2d 954, 956 (1993); *Moss*, 83 N.M. at 44, 487 P.2d at 1349, 2 Wayne R. LaFave & Austin W. Scott, Jr., *Substantive Criminal Law* § 8.6, at 368-69 (1986).

Defendant maintains there was no such evidence because Defendant, a convicted felon, was not holding the EMD under any assumption of trust or confidence on his part. We disagree. "Entrustment" occurs when property is committed or surrendered to another with a certain confidence regarding the care, use, or disposal of that property. *See State v. Stahl*, 93 N.M. 62, 63, 596 P.2d 275, 276 (Ct.App.1979); *Moss*, 83 N.M. at 44, 487 P.2d at 1349. As *Moss* states, the usual and ordinary meaning of "entrustment" is applicable unless an expression of legislative intent requires otherwise. 83 N.M. at 44, 487 P.2d at 1349. In determining what is required by the element of entrustment, we are guided by legislative intent in enacting the embezzlement statute.

The crime of embezzlement did not exist at common law. 2 LaFave, *supra*, § 8.1(b), at 331; 3 Charles E. Torcia, *Wharton's Criminal Law* § 383, at 464-65 (1995). Larceny, a common law crime, required that the thief take property from the victim's possession and that there be a "trespass in the taking." 2 LaFave, *supra*, § 8.1(a), at 328; *see Green*, 116 N.M. at 275, 861 P.2d at 956. When the defendant is in lawful possession of the owner's property, which the defendant then fraudulently converts to his or her own use, the defendant cannot be convicted of larceny because there is no trespassory taking. 3 Torcia, *supra*, § 383, at 463-64; *see also* 2 LaFave, *supra*, § 8.1(b), at 331 (discussing 1799 case in which bank clerk who immediately pocketed money given him by depositor, rather than putting money in cash drawer, held not guilty of larceny).

Statutes establishing embezzlement as an offense were passed to eliminate this loophole in the common law. *Green*, 116 N.M. at 275, 861 P.2d at 956, 2 LaFave, *supra*, § 8.6(a), at 368; 3 Torcia, *supra*, § 383, at 464-65. We construe the term "entrusted" in New Mexico's embezzlement statute in accordance with this objective and in a manner to accomplish the legislative intent.

It is clear from the evidence that when the State turned over the EMD to Defendant, the State was relying on Defendant to act in a manner consistent with, and not adverse to, the State's interests with respect to the EMD. Defendant was after all on probation; he was free from incarceration on the strength of just such assurances that he would do what he was told and live up to his promises. Defendant even signed a written agreement with his probation officer by which he created these assurances with respect to his continued care and possession of the EMD. The agreement states:

EMD WEARER'S AGREEMENT

1. I Andre Archie, understand that the electronic monitoring device (EMD) and all of its accessories are the property of the Adult Probation Parole Division of the Corrections Department with the State of New Mexico.

2. I accept full responsibility for the care of and return of the electronic monitoring device.

3. I understand that it is my responsibility to immediately notify the Adult Probation Parole Office if the monitor is damaged in any way or if the bracelet is purposely/accidentally removed from my leg.

4. I understand that if any part of the electronic monitoring device is damaged or lost while it is in my possession, I will be charged with Embezzlement, Theft, or Criminal Damage. The cost of the device is $1,950.00.

In addition, although Defendant argues that the transfer of possession was only for the State's benefit, Defendant received the benefit of being placed on probation, rather than being incarcerated. Therefore, assuming that Defendant is correct in arguing that he must receive a benefit, we are satisfied from the record that there was an entrustment of property sufficient to meet the requirements of the statute.

Defendant argues there was no evidence that he "converted" the EMD "to his own use"; instead, he disposed of the EMD or abandoned it but did not put it to "use" within the meaning of the statute. Again, we do not agree. When a person having possession of another's property treats the property as his own, whether he uses it, sells it, or discards it, he is using the property for his own purpose. *See* UJI 14-1641 (conversion means "using another's property for one's own purpose [rather than] . . . for the purpose authorized by the owner"); *see also Newman v. Basin Motor Co.*, 98 N.M. 39, 42, 644 P.2d 553, 556 (Ct.App.1982) (conversion is, among other things, the unconsented exercise of dominion over a chattel to the exclusion or in defiance of the owner's right thereto); Black's Law Dictionary 1236 (6th ed. 1990) (defining "purpose" as "an end, intention, or aim, object, plan, project"). Because Defendant threw away the EMD in an effort to end the State's ability to monitor his movements, there was evidence in this case that Defendant was using the EMD for his own purpose.

According to Professor LaFave, the gravamen of conversion is interfering with the rights of the owner, either to the property itself or to the benefit from the manner in which the property was supposed to have been used. LaFave, *supra*, § 8.6(b), at 369. The details of the interference are less important than the interference itself. Professor LaFave describes the manner of the interference in broad terms: "using it up, selling it, pledging it, giving it away, delivering it to one not entitled to it, inflicting serious damage to it, claiming it against the owner . . . each of these acts seriously interferes with the owner's rights and so constitutes a conversion" within the meaning of embezzlement. *Id.* (footnote omitted). The statutory reference that the wrongdoer's conversion must be "to his own use" is more a reference to a "use" other than that authorized by the owner; or as LaFave states: "These words are not to be taken literally, however, for it is not a requirement for a conversion that the converter gain a personal benefit from his dealing with the property." *Id.* at 370.

Defendant also claims there was no evidence of the kind of specific fraudulent intent that is necessary to support a conviction for embezzlement. *See Green*, 116 N.M. at 277, 861 P.2d at 958 (fraudulent intent is a necessary element of embezzlement). Defendant protests that the district court had to infer intent, since it had not been specifically shown by the State. We do not see this as a basis for reversal. Defendant threw away the EMD after removing it, contrary to his promises in the EMD Wearer's Agreement. This gives rise to a reasonable inference that Defendant fraudulently intended to deprive the State of its property and the intended use thereof. Defendant knew that the EMD belonged to the State and not to him. Defendant also knew that he was not free to dispose of the EMD by throwing it away. Intent involves a defendant's state of mind and is seldom, if ever, susceptible to direct proof. *State v. Manus*, 93 N.M. 95, 98, 597 P.2d 280, 283 (1979). Therefore, intent may be proved by circumstantial evidence. *Id.* Under the circumstances of this case, it was reasonable for the fact finder to infer that Defendant threw away the State's property with the specific fraudulent intent "to deprive the owner thereof." Fraudulent intent is defined as an intent "to deceive or cheat." UJI 14-1641. In light of Defendant's surreptitious actions, the evidence supports a reasonable inference to that effect.

Defendant points to the district court's observation that the charges in this case might have been covered by another lesser criminal statute, such as criminal damage to property. There was sufficient evidence to support a conviction for embezzlement, including evidence of entrustment of property and conversion of property. Entrustment and conversion are not elements of criminal damage to property. *See* NMSA 1978, § 30-15-1 (Repl.Pamp.1994). Nor is damage an element of embezzlement. *See* § 30-16-8. Therefore, this is not the kind of situation discussed in *State v. Higgins*, 107 N.M. 617, 621, 762 P.2d 904, 908 (Ct.App.1988), where a general statute and a specific statute both cover the same subject matter, making the specific statute an exception to the general rule and requiring, in a criminal case, that the prosecution proceed under the specific statute. The two statutes prohibit different offenses, and therefore the prosecutor is free to select the statute and the charges to be brought against Defendant.

CONCLUSION

The conviction is affirmed.

IT IS SO ORDERED.

Notes and Questions

1. Think back to the *Llamas* case and the precedent cited therein of the angry spouse who was convicted of vandalizing her husband's Mercedes when she found it parked in her husband's lover's driveway (p. 953). Suppose that she had so completely injured the car that the cost of repairing it exceeded the value—that it was totaled in the language of insurance adjusters. Would she be guilty of the crime of larceny or embezzlement? Would it matter if she waited until the next day when the couple had agreed that she would go get groceries in the car?

2. Consider the facts of a very interesting case in which New York prosecutors claimed embezzlement. A courier service was given money by a bank with instructions to count it and deliver it to the Federal Reserve within 72 hours. The courier service was able to count the money in 24 hours and deposited

the money in a bank and obtain 48 hours-worth of interest off of the money. The New York Court of Appeals held that this was not a larcenous act because there was no intent to permanently deprive the bank of its money. The court also rejected the state's argument that the courier service had effectively gone "joyriding" with the money because the statute criminalizing misapplication of property requires a risk that the property will be injured or destroyed. The court noted that while there were likely civil actions for this unethical conduct, which deprived the bank of its opportunity to the interest during the 48 hours the courier service essentially lied about needing to count the money, there was no criminal action. *People v. Jennings*, 504 N.E.2d 1079 (N.Y. 1986).

---

3. Larceny by Trick/False Pretenses

Larceny by trick involves obtaining custody but not title over property by deceit, while obtaining property by false pretenses involves obtaining title to the property.

People v. Traster

California Court of Appeal
111 Cal.App.4th, 4 Cal.Rptr.3d 680 (2003)

JOHNSON, J.

Appellant, Kevin D. Traster, represented himself at trial. A jury found him guilty of two counts of grand theft by false pretenses. We will modify the judgment of conviction to reflect instead one count of grand theft by trick and one count of attempted grand theft by trick. Finding no other prejudicial error, we affirm as modified and remand for resentencing.

* * *

[A law firm provided the defendant, an employee of the firm, access to their credit card to obtain Microsoft licenses. He used the card to transfer money to himself and provided the law firm false documents that he purported were licenses.]

Appellant Was Convicted On The Wrong Theory Of Grand Theft.

To establish the crime of theft by false pretenses the prosecution was required to prove:

"1. A person made or caused to be made to the alleged victim by word or conduct, either (a) a promise without intent to perform it, or (b) a false pretense or representation of an existing or past fact known to the person to be false or made recklessly and without information which would justify a reasonable belief in its truth;

"2. The person made the pretense, representation or promise with the specific intent to defraud;

"3. The pretense, representation or promise was believed and relied upon by the alleged victim[s] and was material in inducing [them] to part with [their] money or property even though the false pretense, representation or promise was not the sole cause; and

"4. *The theft was accomplished in that the alleged victim[s] parted with [their] money or property intending to transfer ownership thereof.*"

The presence or absence of evidence of the fourth element of transferring "ownership" or "title" distinguishes the crime of theft by false pretenses from the crime of theft by trick and device. As our Supreme Court has explained, "Although the crimes of larceny by trick and device and obtaining property by false pretenses are much alike, they are aimed at different criminal acquisitive techniques. Larceny by trick and device is the appropriation of property, the possession of which was fraudulently acquired; obtaining property by false pretenses is the fraudulent or deceitful acquisition of both title and possession. [Citations.] In this state, these two offenses, with other larcenous crimes, have been consolidated into the single crime of theft (Pen.Code, § 484), but their elements have not been changed thereby. [Citations.]"

Because these crimes share so many similar characteristics, "[t]he distinction between larceny and false pretenses sometimes depends on a close analysis of facts and legal principles." If "title still remains in the owner, larceny is established: while the crime is false pretenses, if the title, as well as the possession, is absolutely parted with." Stated differently, if the defendant obtains possession of property for a specific or special purpose, the owner does not relinquish title and the crime committed is larceny by trick. On the other hand, it is theft by false pretenses if the owner of the property gives the property to the defendant or another he controls intending the defendant or this other entity to become the unconditional and unrestricted owner.

A noted treatise writer explains the difference between the two crimes when the property at issue, as in this case, is cash. "In most cases one who hands over money to another never expects to get that very money back; and so it might be thought that in most cases of money obtained by fraud the wrongdoer obtains title, making his crime false pretenses rather than larceny by trick. It is, of course, possible to pledge money as security, or to bail money for safekeeping, to the wrongdoer, in which case title does not pass, so that the crime, if any, falls into the larceny-by-trick category. What if the money is not pledged as security or bailed for safekeeping, but handed over to [ ] the wrongdoer to do something particular with it, something which when performed precludes any chance of the return of the identical money? It is generally held that where the victim hands money to the wrongdoer with the understanding that the latter is to spend it only for a particular purpose (thus creating an agency or trust, it would seem) title does not pass to the wrongdoer; he has only a power to pass title by spending it for the specified purpose. Thus where the victim hands money to the wrongdoer to be invested on the stock marker, or to purchase specified property, or to bribe a particular official, and the wrongdoer, instead of thus dealing with the money, absconds with it, the crime is larceny by trick rather than false pretenses, the wrongdoer never having acquired title."[30]

The law is the same in California. "It is essential in such cases [larceny by trick] that the owner shall intend to part with the possession only, and not to pass the title as well. If he intends to pass both the possession and the title, the transaction, though it may amount to the crime of obtaining property by false pretenses, will not constitute larceny. But the owner does not part with the title to the alleged thief where the thing which is the subject of the theft is delivered by the owner to the accused to be applied by the latter to a particular purpose, and the recipient of the property, having obtained the possession fraudulently with the preconceived intention to appropriate the property to his own use, does subsequently convert it to his own use instead of applying it to the purpose contemplated by the owner. . . ."

The evidence in the present case established the victims provided appellant funds, or access to funds, to purchase specified property. Specifically, both victims intended to acquire Microsoft licenses and provided appellant funds for the express purpose of purchasing Microsoft licenses, and for no other reason. Representatives from both the law firm and the company consistently testified the only reason they provided appellant funds was because he promised to use the funds to acquire Microsoft licenses on their behalf. No representative from either firm even suggested appellant received the funds unconditionally to use as he wished. Thus, the record evidence establishes beyond dispute the firms did not intend to pass title to the money until or unless it was spent for the specified

---

30 2 LaFave & Scott, Substantive Criminal Law (1986) Crimes Relating to Property, section 8.7, page 396.

purpose of purchasing Microsoft licenses, and then only to the ultimate vendor or supplier of the Microsoft licenses.

Because the evidence established appellant never acquired title to the money, the crimes in this case are more appropriately characterized as larceny by trick than as theft by false pretenses. Accordingly, appellant was convicted of theft crimes under an erroneous theory. The question of proper remedy remains.

"In this state, these two offenses, with other larcenous crimes, have been consolidated into the single crime of theft (Pen.Code, § 484), but their elements have not been changed thereby. [Citations.] The purpose of the consolidation was to remove the technicalities that existed in the pleading and proof of these crimes at common law. Indictments and informations charging the crime of 'theft' can now simply allege an 'unlawful taking.' (Pen.Code, §§ 951, 952.) Juries need no longer be concerned with the technical differences between the several types of theft, and can return a general verdict of guilty if they find that an 'unlawful taking' has been proved. [Citations.] The elements of the several types of theft included within section 484 have not been changed, however, and a judgment of conviction of theft, based on a general verdict of guilty, can be sustained only if the evidence discloses the elements of one of the consolidated offenses. (*People v. Nor Woods*, [(1951)], 37 Cal.2d 584, 586, 233 P.2d 897.)"

Thus the error in this case is merely a technical one in which the jury was instructed on a particular theory of theft which turned out to be the wrong one. In these circumstances, the instructional error is harmless. This is particularly so in this case where the instructional error "caused the People to carry the unnecessary burden of proving [the additional element] of corroboration in order to establish false pretenses."

The elements of theft by trick and device are: "(1) the obtaining of the possession of the property of another by some trick or device; (2) the intent by the person so obtaining possession to convert it to his own use and to permanently deprive the owner of it; and (3) that the owner, although parting with possession to such person, does not intend to transfer his title to that person."

DISPOSITION

The judgment of conviction is modified to reflect a conviction of grand theft by trick and device * * *. The cause is remanded for the trial court to exercise its discretion in resentencing appellant in accordance with the modified judgment of conviction.

Notes and Questions

As the court notes, in most jurisdictions, charging the defendant with the wrong type of theft is not fatal to the prosecution and the error can be corrected on appeal. This case does, however, lay out the distinction between the two crimes, though it does not provide a great deal of detail on larceny by false pretenses. A person commits larceny by false pretenses if he fraudulently convinces another to transfer title—so if the defendant convinced his victim to transfer title to a car based on counterfeit money, he would commit the crime of larceny by false pretenses. In this case, if the defendant had claimed to own Microsoft licenses which he purported to sell to the company, but the licenses were not real, then he would have committed larceny by false pretenses. In this case, by contrast, the defendant was not given money that he was supposed to keep, but money he was supposed to use to purchase the licenses.

PRACTICE EXERCISE

Albert wants to go on road trip to Palm Desert, but his car is too old and unreliable to take further than 50 miles or so. So, Anton calls up his friend, Brice, and relates his elaborate plan: "The age to rent cars is 21, but I'm still 20, but I can use my brother's driver's license because we look similar. Then, we can rent a car and not have to worry about mileage or anything. Plus, there's this great place that rents super cheap because they have some sort of rent-to-buy option." Brice is excited, and consents to chip in for the cost of the rental car and gas for the trip.

Albert fills in his brother's information online for "Valued Rentals," borrows his brother's license under the pretext he is going to buy alcohol with it, and then hitches a ride to the local rental store. At checkout, the clerk asks for Albert's name, which he gives as "Christoph" and hands Christoph's driver's license to the clerk, who glances at it and makes a copy. The clerk says, "You must return the car in one week, any time longer will be construed as exercising your option to buy, and the remaining amount will become due." The clerk then asks, "Are you the sole driver, Christoph?" Albert responds, "Yes, I am," knowing that he and Brice agreed they would share driving duties. Nonetheless, Albert pays in cash, takes the keys, and drives off a satisfied customer, intending to return the car in one week after putting the car "through its paces" and to avoid having to buy the car.

On the first leg of their journey, Alfonse and Brice enjoy the "new wheels," taking it for a spin on the desert highway at over 120 miles per hour. They have no other goal than to drive "where the road leads." Three days into their aimless wanderings, Brice asks Albert for the car for a couple of hours, "just to take some time to myself." Albert agrees. Brice drives away. Albert never sees Brice again, because Brice had planned all along to steal the vehicle by using Albert's foolish, but innocent plan to rent the car for the road trip.

When Albert realizes he has been duped, and is stranded without means to return home, he calls Christoph. Completely livid, Christoph calls the police. They arrest Albert and eventually find Brice five hundred miles away at an auto shop known for overhauling vehicles, to give them it new identification numbers and license plates. The one week rental period had expired under the "rent to buy" agreement, so that "Christoph" had obtained title in the vehicle.

Instructions:

California has indicted Brice for the following offenses: Larceny, Attempted Larceny, Embezzlement, and Larceny by Trick.

You are Albert's and Brice's defense attorney. Using the following California statutes as a basis, construct jury instructions for each client, for each indictment, using the facts.

Statutes:

- *Larceny*

Every person who shall feloniously steal, take, carry, lead, or drive away the personal property of another, or who shall fraudulently appropriate property which has been entrusted to him or her, or who shall knowingly and designedly, by any false or fraudulent representation or pretense, defraud any other person of money, labor or real or personal property, or who causes or procures others to report falsely of his or her wealth or mercantile character and by thus imposing upon any person, obtains credit and thereby fraudulently gets or obtains possession of money, or property or obtains the labor or service of another, is guilty of larceny.

- *Attempted Larceny*

A person is guilty of an attempt to commit a crime when, with intent to commit a crime, he engages in conduct which tends to effect the commission of such crime.

■ *Embezzlement*

Embezzlement consists of the embezzling or converting to his own use of anything of value, with which he has been entrusted, with fraudulent intent to deprive the owner thereof.

■ *Larceny by False Pretenses*

The larceny was accomplished in that the alleged victim[s] parted with [their] money or property intending to transfer ownership thereof.

■ *Larceny by Trick*

The larceny was accomplished in that the alleged victim[s] parted with [their] money or property intending to transfer possession but not ownership thereof.

---

4. Attempted Larceny

In other contexts, we have considered whether an act, with a clear intent to achieve an unlawful end, has come close enough to achieving the goal that the defendant may be charged with an attempt. As discussed earlier, there are a variety of standards used to determine whether preparation has ripened into an attempt, but context is everything. Courts do frequently observe, however, that the Model Penal Code's formulation for defining an attempt is the easiest to satisfy. New York, as you will learn in this case, has not adopted the MPC standard, but instead uses the standard it established in the *Rizzo* case.

People v. Mahboubian

Court of Appeals of New York
543 N.E.2d 34 (1989)

KAYE, Judge.

In a case involving a staged theft of Persian antiquities, with the objective of recovering $18.5 million in insurance proceeds, the central issues on appeal are whether joint trial of the two defendants was proper, and whether the acts charged amounted to attempted grand larceny and burglary.

I.

Viewing the evidence in the light most favorable to the People, the proof was sufficient to show that the defendants entered into a conspiracy to stage a burglary of defendant Houshang Mahboubian's collection of gold and silver Persian antiquities. Three art experts testified for the People that several pieces in the collection were of dubious authenticity, and indeed almost certainly modern forgeries. From the testimony of other witnesses, the jury could have concluded that Mahboubian became aware of this before the burglaries, and had been unsuccessful in his efforts to sell the collection.

In the summer of 1985, Mahboubian insured the collection with Lloyd's of London for $18.5 million, covering it while in transit for a 12–month period. The stated purpose for the insurance was to allow Mahboubian to ship the collection to the United States, where it would be offered for sale. In October, Mahboubian traveled to New York where he rented a vault at Morgan Brothers Manhattan Storage, a long-term storage facility. According to the assistant warehouse manager, codefendant Nedjatollah Sakhai accompanied him to Morgan Brothers. A month later, the day after he returned from a trip to London, Sakhai too rented a vault at Morgan Brothers, attempting unsuccessfully to get space on the same floor as Mahboubian's vault.

In early December 1985, Sakhai contacted Abe Garabedian, who in turn spoke to several men experienced in robberies and burglaries of art storage facilities. Garabedian told them that Sakhai had "an insurance job" for them. Unbeknownst to the others, one of the men—Daniel Cardebat—had agreed to act as a police informant, and secretly recorded all of their conversations with Sakhai.

When Cardebat and the others first arrived at Sakhai's New York City antiques store to discuss the job, Sakhai was speaking in Farsi on the telephone to someone in London named Houshang about a "job" that "they will do." Telephone company records established that Sakhai placed a call to Mahboubian's London gallery at that time. After hanging up, Sakhai explained to them that the job involved stealing a number of crates that would be flown from Switzerland to New York City and that he was leaving that night to "finalize everything with the guy." They accepted his offer of $100,000 for the theft. Three days later, Sakhai flew to England.

A few weeks later, Mahboubian came to New York City and made arrangements for his collection to be handled upon arrival by W.R. Keating Company—a customs brokerage firm—and then stored at Regency Worldwide Packing, a secure art packing and customs warehouse, where customs inspection and clearance would be conducted. Mahboubian was given a full tour of the Regency, during which he was told that his shipment would not be stored in the open warehouse, but would be placed inside a special steel-vaulted room.

While Mahboubian was in New York, telephone calls were made between his number and Sakhai's. In addition, right before Mahboubian's tour of the Regency warehouse, Sakhai met with Cardebat and Daniel Kohl, another of the hired thieves, and informed them that the shipment would be taken from Swissair to Regency for customs clearance, and then to Morgan Manhattan. During the meeting, Cardebat recorded another telephone conversation in Farsi in which Sakhai requested "the specifications from there." After hanging up, Sakhai told the others that the caller was "him" and that "he" was "going right now" to "find out where they're gonna be at the Regency."

Mahboubian then flew to Switzerland and visited the warehouse where his collection was stored. While there, in an unusual procedure, he marked his initials in red on the shipping crates in which it was packed; Sakhai had earlier told Cardebat and the others that that would be done. The crates were shipped to New York on December 24, 1985 and transferred to Regency the next day. Within 24 hours, two more telephone calls were made from Sakhai's house to Mahboubian's number, and Sakhai had met with Cardebat and the others to inform them that the marked boxes were at the Regency. There was an unresolved discussion concerning whether the theft would take place at the Regency or later at Morgan Manhattan. Sakhai drew the others a diagram showing where the collection would be stored at Morgan Manhattan in Mahboubian's seventh floor vault, and told them he had a key but preferred not to use it. The goods were cleared by customs the next day.

Sakhai met with the thieves again at the beginning of January. This time, he insisted that the burglary take place at the Regency, immediately. He also told them that it would ruin the entire plan even if one item went on the market, and that he had given his "word of honor that the whole thing is going to be returned to him." Sakhai showed the men a diagram of the Regency's warehouse floor, indicating that Mahboubian's crates were stored in the inner steel-vaulted room where Mahboubian had been told they would be placed when he toured the facility.

Two nights later, the burglary took place. Cardebat and his accomplice knocked down a retaining wall to gain entry. Inside, Cardebat found the room Sakhai had pointed out on his diagram and broke down its steel doors, but could not locate the boxes. He found them a few seconds later right outside the vault; Regency personnel had never in fact put the boxes inside the vault. Cardebat passed the boxes out of the warehouse to his colleagues, and the men began to remove the pieces from them. At that point, they were arrested by members of the Manhattan Robbery Task Force, who had been alerted by Cardebat and had observed the theft from the beginning. Cardebat telephoned Sakhai from the precinct on the pretext of arranging for delivery of the stolen goods, and agreed to meet him at La Guardia Airport. Sakhai was arrested on his way there.

Mahboubian was not charged with participation in the crime until several months later, after he had been interviewed by an Assistant District Attorney and allegedly made a number of significant misrepresentations about his arrangements to ship and store his collection.

This evidence in our view was sufficient for the jury to find that both defendants had conspired, as charged, to stage a burglary and fraudulent theft in order to collect the insurance proceeds covering Mahboubian's collection. We therefore reject defendants' claims that their convictions for burglary, attempted grand larceny and conspiracy must be reversed for insufficiency and the indictment dismissed.

* * *

[B]oth defendants contend that even if the People proved all of the allegations of the indictment, the acts they were charged with committing did not amount to an attempt to commit grand larceny or to a burglary. Contrary to the People's argument, those contentions were preserved by defendants' pretrial motions to dismiss on that precise ground, even though defendants did not specifically seek dismissal on that basis at the close of the People's evidence.

With respect to the attempted grand larceny charge, defendants claim that the scheme to steal the proceeds of Mahboubian's insurance policy from Lloyd's not only was aborted short of fruition but also had not yet advanced to the point where, legally, their actions constituted an attempt. We disagree.

The substantive crime of attempt is a relatively recent development of the common law. The modern doctrine is said to date from Lord Mansfield's decision in the case of *Rex v. Scofield* (Cald 397) in 1784, and to have fully emerged in *Rex v. Higgins* (2 East 5), where, citing *Scofield*, the court said "[A]ll such acts or attempts as tend to the prejudice of the community, are indictable." (*Id.*, at 21.) (*See generally*, Sayre, *Criminal Attempts*, 41 Harv.L.Rev. 821, 822–837 [1928].) As many commentators have noted, imposition of punishment for an attempt poses difficult questions for a criminal jurisprudence in which a basic premise is that bad thoughts alone do not constitute a crime. What justification, then, is there for punishing an attempt, when by definition the contemplated crime is not consummated? (*See generally*, Ryu, *Contemporary Problems of Criminal Attempts*, 32 NYU L.Rev. 1170 [1957].)

Commonly given answers are that persons who engage in attempts to commit a crime are as dangerous as those who succeed, and it would be unjust to punish only the latter; that law enforcement agencies should be encouraged to act before a crime is actually committed; and that criminal attempts are in and of themselves substantively harmful to society. Nonetheless, the right to think bad thoughts undeterred or unpunished by the criminal law has been protected by the requirement that in order to be punishable as an attempt, conduct must have passed the stage of mere intent or mere preparation to commit a crime.

Defendants contend that under the law of New York demarcating the boundary where preparation ripens into punishable attempt, their conduct had not gone far enough to subject them to liability for an attempt to commit grand larceny, for they had not yet reported any loss to Lloyd's or filed an insurance claim when police intervention put an abrupt end to their scheme. According to defendants, their acts, including the forced entry into Regency and the removal of Mahboubian's collection, must be characterized as mere preparation for the larceny, and while perhaps punishable in themselves, may not be punished as an attempt to commit a crime that would not be complete until they had taken additional steps. In essence, the argument made by defendants is that their actions failed to reach the level of an attempt in two related respects, either compelling reversal: (1) several steps, requiring time, remained to be taken; and (2) defendants could still have changed their minds and abandoned the scheme after the warehouse break-in. The cases do not support defendants' contention.

The definition of a criminal attempt is found in Penal Law § 110.00: "A person is guilty of an attempt to commit a crime when, with intent to commit a crime, he engages in conduct which tends to effect the commission of such crime." On its face, the statute would appear applicable to defendants' conduct, but in *People v. Di Stefano*, 38 N.Y.2d 640, 652, 382 N.Y.S.2d 5, 345 N.E.2d 548, we made clear that the revised Penal Law definition was not intended to eliminate the preexisting requirement that an attempt come "'very near to the accomplishment of the intended crime'" before liability could be imposed. Thus, the precise issue presented is whether defendants' conduct came "very near" or "dangerously near" completion of the larceny, as that requirement has been interpreted (*People v. Rizzo*, 246 N.Y. 334, 338, 158 N.E. 888). As is apparent, the boundary where preparation ripens into punishable conduct depends greatly on the facts of the particular case.

To be sure, the strictest possible approach to defining an attempt would be to require that the defendants have engaged in the last proximate act necessary to accomplish the intended crime. It is settled, however, that the defendants' act "need not be 'the final one towards the completion of the offense'". (*People v. Bracey*, 41 N.Y.2d 296, 300, 392 N.Y.S.2d 412, 360 N.E.2d 1094, citing *People v. Sullivan*, 173 N.Y. 122, 133, 65 N.E. 989.)[2] Thus, the fact that defendants had not yet taken the final step necessary to obtain the insurance money does not mean

2 The dissent is entirely correct when it notes that defendants' acts had not set in motion a chain of events that would "inevitably" have led to their fraudulent acquisition of the insurance proceeds (dissenting opn., at 199, at 783 of 544 N.Y.S.2d, at 48 of 543 N.E.2d). Although the defendants most surely had set a chain of events in motion, only the final act—according to the dissent, avoidance of detection—would have "inevitably" led to consummation of the crime if defendants were not interrupted. It is settled beyond peradventure, however, that the law does not require that the defendant's act be the final step in order for conduct to constitute a punishable attempt.

that the steps they had taken could not constitute an attempt to do so. Similarly, the theoretical possibility that defendants might yet have renounced the criminal venture does not obviate their liability for an attempt, for that is true of any attempt interrupted by the police. *People v. Sullivan* (*supra*) and *People v. Collins*, 234 N.Y. 355, 137 N.E. 753 stand for the very different proposition that a defendant who has in fact abandoned the criminal plan may not be liable for an attempt (*see also*, Penal Law § 40.10). Here, however, there was no evidence that defendants had or would have voluntarily abandoned their scheme.

The necessity of further steps for completion of the crime and the possibility of abandonment or renunciation are factors to be considered in evaluating whether conduct has come "dangerously close" to success, but are not dispositive. Those factors do not call for reversal in this case.

Where the boundary line between preparation and attempt should be placed differs with different crimes (*People v. Werblow*, 241 N.Y. 55, 61, 148 N.E. 786). Here, it is significant that defendants' conduct went far beyond mere discussion of a crime (*People v. Di Stefano*, 38 N.Y.2d 640, 382 N.Y.S.2d 5, 345 N.E.2d 548, *supra*), and beyond agreement to commit a crime (*People v. Warren*, 66 N.Y.2d 831, 498 N.Y.S.2d 353, 489 N.E.2d 240), and even beyond arming themselves in preparation for a crime (*People v. Rizzo*, 246 N.Y. 334, 158 N.E. 888, *supra*). Defendants hired professional burglars, provided them with tools, and caused them to break into a warehouse and steal property in the dead of night. These acts encompassed the most hazardous and difficult portion of their criminal scheme. What remained to be done was reporting of the supposed theft to the insurer.

Defendants' conduct had plainly "pass[ed] that point where most men, holding such an intention as defendant holds, would think better of their conduct and desist." (Skilton, *The Requisite Act in a Criminal Attempt*, 3 U.Pitt.L.Rev. 308, 309–310 [1937].) Defendants' actions in causing the nighttime break-in were potentially and immediately dangerous—a factor we weigh in considering whether they were "dangerously close" to the completed crime. Their activities had reached the point where police intervention was called for, lest the burglars escape or the collection disappear. Most important, defendants' acts "had gone to the extent of placing it in their power to commit the offense unless interrupted". (*People v. Sobieskoda*, 235 N.Y. 411, 419, 139 N.E. 558.)

We need not (and do not) adopt the Model Penal Code's definition of an attempt as a "substantial step" toward completion of the crime (*see*, ALI Model Penal Code § 5.01) in order to conclude that some acts—even if preparatory in a dictionary sense—go sufficiently beyond "mere preparation" as to be properly characterized as an attempt for which criminal liability may be imposed. Thus, for instance, in *People v. Sobieskoda* (*supra*) the defendants shot their intended victim's brother, but fled before even firing at the target himself who remained some distance away. We held that the jury could find that their actions constituted an attempted murder of the target, because they had put it in the defendants' power to commit the intended murder, if not interrupted. Under the analysis proposed by the dissent, on those facts there would be no attempt because (1) several contingencies remained before effectuation of the crime; (2) the defendants could have changed their minds before doing any of those things; and (3) firing at the target's brother was not an act that would have "naturally effect[ed] th[e intended] result" (*see*, dissenting opn., at 198 at 782 of 544 N.Y.S.2d, at 47 of 543 N.E.2d). Indeed, we have explicitly recognized that there comes a point where it is "too late in the *stage of preparation* for the law to conclude that no attempt occurred." (*People v. Mirenda*, 23 N.Y.2d 439, 446, 297 N.Y.S.2d 532, 245 N.E.2d 194 [emphasis added].)

Perhaps the real source of our disagreement with the dissent lies in the fact that defendants had planned a complex crime that necessarily had to proceed in several stages removed in time and space from one another. Thus, the fact pattern here is rather different from more typical attempts, where the would-be robber or burglar is apprehended on the premises, tools of the trade in hand. Simpler crimes proceed directly from preparation to completion, but defendants' scheme by its very nature involved a longer route.

Nevertheless, the principle remains the same: had defendants' acts reached the stage where they were very near or dangerously near completion of the larceny? Unlike a burglar or robber on the premises, defendants may not have been physically within striking distance of success, yet in all but the most literal sense, they were. The steps they had already taken were more than substantial: they had secured insurance, arranged for shipment of the goods from Europe and storage in a particular New York City warehouse, and hired thieves who actually broke in and removed the goods. These steps took defendants to the point where only a few comparatively minor acts—all wholly within defendants' own power—remained to be accomplished.

In the circumstances of this crime and this case, we therefore conclude that defendants' conduct went sufficiently beyond mere preparation and, as the jury found, constituted attempted grand larceny.

* * *

TITONE, Judge (concurring in part and dissenting in part).

I agree with my colleagues that the trial court's refusal to grant a severance constituted an abuse of discretion requiring reversal and a new trial. However, I would go further and hold that the facts presented were not legally sufficient to establish the crime of attempted grand larceny. In my view, upholding an attempt prosecution on these facts requires a drastic departure from our prior case law and, in effect, makes our State's law virtually indistinguishable from the law of those jurisdictions that have adopted the Model Penal Code. Such a dilution in our State's requirements for establishing an attempt cannot be justified in light of our strong recent statements in *People v. Di Stefano*, 38 N.Y.2d 640, 382 N.Y.S.2d 5, 345 N.E.2d 548 and *People v. Warren*, 66 N.Y.2d 831, 498 N.Y.S.2d 353, 489 N.E.2d 240 that the drafters of our Penal Law intended to adhere to the more demanding test established in *People v. Rizzo*, 246 N.Y. 334, 158 N.E. 888. Accordingly, I dissent from the majority's ruling to the extent that it permits a retrial on the attempted grand larceny counts.[1]

I. THE LEGAL STANDARD

To establish an attempt, the prosecution must prove both the requisite intent to commit a specific object crime and an act "which tends to effect the commission of such crime" (Penal Law § 110.00). The standard for determining whether a particular act rose to the level of an attempt is well settled. "The act need not be 'the final one towards the completion of the offense' * * * but it must 'carry the project forward within dangerous proximity to the criminal end to be attained'" (*People v. Bracey*, 41 N.Y.2d 296, 300, 392 N.Y.S.2d 412, 360 N.E.2d 1094; *see, e.g., People v. Sobieskoda*, 235 N.Y. 411, 139 N.E. 558; *People v. Werblow*, 241 N.Y. 55, 148 N.E. 786; *People v. Collins*, 234 N.Y. 355, 137 N.E. 753). The requirement of "dangerous proximity" means that "[t]he act or acts must come or advance *very near* to the accomplishment of the intended crime" (*People v. Rizzo*, 246 N.Y. 334, 337, 158 N.E. 888, *supra* [emphasis supplied]).

In contrast, the drafters of the Model Penal Code have formulated the standard for attempts in terms of taking a "substantial step" toward the completion of the crime. Their purpose in doing so was to "shift the emphasis from what remains to be done—the chief concern of the proximity tests—to what the actor *has already done*" (ALI Model Penal Code § 5.01, Tent Draft No. 10, comments, at 47 [emphasis in original]). The underlying goal was to "broaden the scope of attempt liability" by permitting prosecution where "the steps already undertaken are substantial", notwithstanding that "major steps must be taken before the crime can be completed" (*id.*). However, as we have very recently reaffirmed, New York has not adopted the Model Penal Code drafters' approach, but has instead elected to adhere to the proximity analysis articulated in (*People v. Rizzo*, 246 N.Y. 334, 337, 158 N.E. 888, *supra*) and its predecessors (*People v. Warren*,

---

1 I also disagree with the majority's analysis in relation to the burglary counts, since I agree with defendant Mahboubian that he should not be held accountable for an intent to facilitate his own future crime. However, I do not dissent on the majority's decision to uphold the burglary counts because I conclude that the evidence was sufficient to support the inference that both Mahboubian and Sakhai intended that the premises of the Regency warehouse be damaged in the course of the staged theft, thereby establishing an intent to commit the crime of criminal mischief.

66 N.Y.2d 831, 833, 498 N.Y.S.2d 353, 489 N.E.2d 240, *supra; accord, People v. Di Stefano*, 38 N.Y.2d 640, 652, 382 N.Y.S.2d 5, 345 N.E.2d 548, *supra*). Thus, the focus on the actor's proximity to the completion of the object crime is not merely archaic verbiage. To the contrary, it represents the current state of the law in New York.

Although, as the majority notes, the proper application of the proximity analysis is very much dependent on the facts of the particular case and the manner in which the intended crime is to be carried out, some general principles may be discerned. The cases have repeatedly stated, for example, that "dangerous proximity to the criminal end" exists when the defendant's acts have set in motion a chain of events that are likely to lead to the completion of the crime unless some external force intervenes. Thus, the court stated in *Rizzo* that "[t]he law * * * considers those acts only as tending to the commission of the crime which are so near to its accomplishment that in all reasonable probability the crime itself would have been committed but for timely interference" (246 N.Y. at 337, 498 N.Y.S.2d 353, 489 N.E.2d 240). In another formulation, the court indicated that an attempt could not be found where "[t]he force set in motion is neither continuous nor mechanical, and its operation may be broken before the stage of attempt has been attained by the withdrawal or repentance of the guilty intermediary" (*People v. Werblow*, 241 N.Y. 55, 65, 148 N.E. 746, *supra*). To the same effect are *People v. Mills*, 178 N.Y. 274, 285, 70 N.E. 786 [act "must be such as would naturally effect that (criminal) result, unless prevented by some extraneous cause"], *People v. Collins*, 234 N.Y. 355, 359–360, 137 N.E. 753, *supra* [same], *People v. Sullivan*, 173 N.Y. 122, 135, 65 N.E. 989 [attempt may be found where defendants' acts would have effected object crime "had their design not been frustrated by the presence or interference of (a third party)"], and *People v. Sobieskoda*, 235 N.Y. 411, 419, 139 N.E. 558, *supra* [act constituted attempt if it had "gone to the extent of placing it in (defendants') power to commit offense unless interrupted, and nothing but such interruption prevented the present commission of the offense"]; *see generally*, Annotation, *Attempts to Commit Offenses of Larceny by Trick, Confidence Game, False Pretenses, and the Like*, 6 A.L.R.3d 241, 246, § 2 [a]). Other factors that have been considered are the temporal and geographic proximity between the act and the object crime, the existence of "several contingencies" standing between the act and the object crime (*see, e.g., People v. Warren, supra*, 66 N.Y.2d at 833, 498 N.Y.S.2d 353, 489 N.E.2d 240) and the remoteness or immediacy of the act in relation to that crime (*People v. Rizzo, supra*, 246 N.Y. at 337, 158 N.E. 888). Finally, the courts have often relied on the distinction between acts of "mere preparation" and those tending to effect commission of the crime (*see, e.g., People v. Bracey, supra*, 41 N.Y.2d at 300, 392 N.Y.S.2d 412, 360 N.E.2d 1094; *People v. Collins, supra*, 234 N.Y. at 359–361, 137

N.E. 753). The concept of "mere preparation" has been persuasively defined by other courts as "the devising or arranging the means or measures necessary for the commission of the offense" (*e.g., People v. Von Hecht*, 133 Cal.App.2d 25, 38, 283 P.2d 764, 773; *People v. Murray*, 14 Cal. 159; *State v. Pollard*, 215 La. 655, 41 So.2d 465; *State v. Block*, 333 Mo. 127, 62 S.W.2d 428; *see*, Annotation, *op. cit.*, 6 A.L.R.3d, at 246). Moreover, our own court has indicated that to be guilty of an attempt, the accused must have both acquired the wherewithal to commit the object crime and made some direct movement toward the ultimate object (*People v. Collins, supra*, 234 N.Y. at 360, 137 N.E. 753; *People v. Sullivan, supra*, 173 N.Y. at 135–136, 65 N.E. 989). Absent the latter step, the accused is guilty of no more than "mere preparation."

The application of these standards to the fact patterns in prior cases is instructive. In *People v. Sullivan*, 173 N.Y. 122, 65 N.E. 989, *supra*, for example, the court upheld a conviction for murder committed in the course of an attempted burglary, but noted that an attempt might not be found where defendants had merely procured tools for the break-in. Further, the court declined to find an attempted larceny in *People v. Werblow*, 241 N.Y. 55, 148 N.E. 786, *supra*, where the defendants had only planned the crime and sent and received cablegrams in furtherance of the scheme. In *People v. Rizzo*, 246 N.Y. 334, 158 N.E. 888, *supra*, the defendants had armed themselves, set out in car looking for individual who they knew was carrying payroll money, and stopped at sites where the messenger was expected, but were intercepted by police before they actually encountered the messenger. Despite all of these concrete steps toward the commission of the crime, this court held them insufficient to constitute the crime of attempted robbery because the defendants never came dangerously close to the completion of the object crime (*see also, People v. Di Stefano*, 38 N.Y.2d 640, 382 N.Y.S.2d 5, 345 N.E.2d 548, *modfg* 45 A.D.2d 56, 356 N.Y.S.2d 316, *supra* [same result on similar facts]). Finally, in a very recent decision, (*People v. Warren*, 66 N.Y.2d 831, 498 N.Y.S.2d 353, 489 N.E.2d 240, *supra*), we held that an attempted drug-possession prosecution did not lie where the defendants had held two meetings with the police informant, had reached agreement regarding the terms of the sale, and had set up a third meeting for a later time "in a distant parking lot" before they were intercepted by officers who had been secretly watching. In reversing the conviction, we held that the defendants had not come "very near to the accomplishment of the intended crime" (66 N.Y.2d at 833, 498 N.Y.S.2d 353, 489 N.E.2d 240), since the planned purchase was to take place several hours later at a distant location and several additional steps needed to be taken before the transaction could be consummated.

II. ANALYSIS

As is evident from the foregoing, the set of facts presented here is unlike any other in which a conviction for attempt has been upheld.[2] Defendants Mahboubian and Sakhai were charged with attempting to commit larceny by obtaining insurance proceeds under false pretenses. The act which formed the basis for this charge was the abortive staged theft of Mahboubian's collection from the Regency warehouse. However, this act constituted no more than "mere preparation" analogous to the gathering of equipment for a burglary or the obtaining of weapons for the effectuation of a planned robbery. In other words, by staging the warehouse break-in and theft, defendants were, in effect, merely laying the foundation for the crime they planned ultimately to commit: defrauding Lloyd's of London. They had not yet taken "a step in the *direct* movement towards th[at] crime", as the case law requires (*People v. Collins, supra*, 234 N.Y. at 360, 137 N.E. 753 [emphasis supplied]; *see, People v. Sullivan, supra*). Further, the "dangerous proximity" test outlined in *People v. Rizzo (supra)* is unsatisfied because (1) the act on which the People relied, the warehouse break-in, was remote, both in time and place, from the ultimate goal (*see, People v. Warren, supra; People v. Rizzo, supra*, 246 N.Y. at 337, 158 N.E. 888); (2) there remained "several contingencies" standing between the act and the effectuation of the crime (*see, People v. Warren, supra*); (3) even after the break-in, defendants still had complete freedom of action and could therefore have easily changed their minds before taking the next step toward their goal; and (4) the act was simply not "such as would naturally effect th[e intended] result [i.e., the wrongful obtaining of insurance money], unless prevented by some extraneous cause" (*People v. Mills, supra*, 178 N.Y. at 285, 70 N.E. 786; *see, e.g., People v. Rizzo, supra*, 246 N.Y. at 337, 158 N.E. 888).

The majority's contrary conclusion seems to ignore these factors, particularly the last. Although the majority stresses, quite correctly, that the last act before interruption need not be the final step toward completion of the

---

2 The only New York case that I have found which seems to be directly on point is *People v. Rappaport*, 207 Misc. 604, 142 N.Y.S.2d 125, in which a staged theft was discovered before the defendant had the opportunity to make a false insurance claim and obtain the insurance proceeds. In that case, the court held that the crime of attempted larceny had not been established because, at the time he was caught, the defendant's acts had not "so irrevocably committed him to the scheme of defrauding his insurance company that his purpose would have been accomplished save for his arrest" (*id.*, at 605, 142 N.Y.S.2d 125; *see also, People v. Trepanier*, 84 A.D.2d 374, 446 N.Y.S.2d 829). Other jurisdictions which have considered similar fact patterns have rejected liability for attempt (*see, e.g., In re Schurman*, 40 Kan. 533, 20 P. 277; *Commonwealth v. Prius*, 75 Mass. 127; *State v. Block*, 333 Mo. 127, 62 S.W.2d 428; *State v. Fraker*, 148 Mo. 143, 49 S.W. 1017; *Nemecek v. State*, 72 Okla.Crim. 195, 114 P.2d 492; *Rex v. Robinson*, [1915] 2 KB 342). Finally, the cases on which the People rely (*People v. Vastano*, 117 A.D.2d 637, 498 N.Y.S.2d 87; *Steiner v. Commissioner of Correction*, 490 F.Supp. 204), as well as cases from other jurisdictions in which liability has been upheld for attempted larceny by insurance fraud (*Galbraith v. State*, 468 N.E.2d 575 [Ind App]; *State v. Grubbs*, 657 S.W.2d 380 [Mo.Ct.App.]), involved circumstances in which some step had been taken toward actually filing a loss claim with the insurer.

crime, the majority fails to address that the last act before interruption here, the break-in, did not even begin to set in motion the chain of events that would inevitably have led to defendants' fraudulent acquisition of the insurance proceeds if law enforcement authorities had not intervened. To the contrary, far more was required, including the safe disposition of the purportedly stolen goods, the collection of documents to establish the ownership and value of those goods, the filing of a loss claim with the insurance company and, finally, the successful avoidance of detection through the investigation that the insurer would unquestionably have undertaken. Hence, notwithstanding the majority's assertion to the contrary (majority opn., at 191, at 778 of 544 N.Y.S.2d, at 43 of 543 N.E.2d, quoting *People v. Sobieskoda*, 235 N.Y. 411, 419, 139 N.E. 558, *supra*), defendants' acts had not "'gone to the extent of placing it in their power to commit the offense unless interrupted,'" except in the sense that *any* step taken in the direction of their goal would have increased the likelihood of its accomplishment.[3]

Further, the facts on which the majority relies—that defendants' completed acts "encompassed the most hazardous and difficult portion of their criminal scheme" and that the nighttime break-in was itself "potentially and immediately dangerous" (majority opn., at 191, at 778 of 544 N.Y.S.2d, at 43 of 543 N.E.2d)— are, in fact, irrelevant in establishing "dangerous proximity" to the object crime. At best, these circumstances support the premise that the steps taken toward the completion of the crime were indeed "substantial." However, as noted above, the New York view of attempt, in contrast to the Model Penal Code view, does not accept the substantiality of the steps actually taken as the dispositive criterion. Instead, the analysis must focus on the relationship between the already completed acts and the object crime.

Finally, the weight that the majority places on the fact that defendants' "activities had reached the point where police intervention was called for, lest the burglars escape or the collection disappear" (*id.*, at 191 at 778 of 544 N.Y.S.2d, at 43 of 543 N.E.2d) is puzzling. While that observation would undoubtedly be

---

3   Contrary to the majority's view (majority opn., at 190, n. 2, at 777, n. 2 of 544 N.Y.S.2d, at 42, n. 2 of 543 N.E.2d), the language in some of the cases requiring forces which are "continuous" and "mechanical" does not, if applied literally, lead to the conclusion that the final step before completion must be accomplished. Rather, the point of this language is to provide a useful framework for analyzing cases where there remained several important steps between the defendants and their criminal goal. Thus, in *People v. Trepanier*, 84 A.D.2d 374, 377, 446 N.Y.S.2d 829, *People v. Vastano*, 117 A.D.2d 637, 498 N.Y.S.2d 87 and *Steiner v. Commissioner of Correction*, 490 F.Supp. 204, three attempted insurance fraud cases on which the People have placed heavy reliance, the defendants were held to have committed the crime of attempt even though no false claim had been filed because they had done everything within their power toward the accomplishment of their goal by placing the means to complete this final step in the hands of their confederates. It is in this context, where the defendants were not "very near to the accomplishment of the intended crime" (*People v. Rizzo, supra*, 246 N.Y. at 347, 158 N.E. 888), that the notion of setting a "continuous" and "mechanical" force in motion comes into play. Of course, no such circumstance is present here.

helpful if the defendants had been charged with attempted theft of the art collection, its relevance in this context, where the ultimate object of the charged attempt crime was the theft of insurance proceeds through fraud, is difficult to discern.

In sum, by upholding an attempt prosecution in these circumstances, the court has significantly diluted the well-established requirements for proving an act rising to the level of an attempt. Moreover, by blurring the important distinction between a "substantial step" toward the completion of the object crime and an act "tend[ing] to effect commission of such crime" (Penal Law § 110.00), the court has brought the law of New York a giant step closer to the less stringent analysis adopted in the Model Penal Code, an analysis which our Legislature has deliberately rejected.

For all of these reasons, I cannot join in the majority's decision to permit a retrial on the attempted grand larceny counts. Accordingly, I dissent on this aspect of the majority's holding.

Notes and Questions

1. The dissent refers to the New York state's standard for attempt, as stated in *Rizzo*, as requiring more of the prosecution than the Model Penal Code's standard. Produced below is the relatively brief *Rizzo* opinion, 246 N.Y. 334 (1927):

CRANE, J.

The police of the city of New York did excellent work in this case by preventing the commission of a serious crime. It is a great satisfaction to realize that we have such wide-awake guardians of our peace. Whether or not the steps which the defendant had taken up to the time of his arrest amounted to the commission of a crime, as defined by our law, is, however, another matter. He has been convicted of an attempt to commit the crime of robbery in the first degree and sentenced to State's prison. There is no doubt that he had the intention to commit robbery if he got the chance. An examination, however, of the facts is necessary to determine whether his acts were in preparation to commit the crime if the opportunity offered, or constituted a crime in itself, known to our law as an attempt to commit robbery in the first degree. Charles Rizzo, the defendant, appellant, with three others, Anthony J. Dorio, Thomas Milo and John Thomasello, on January 14th planned to rob one Charles Rao of a payroll valued at about $1,200 which he was to carry from the bank for the United Lathing Company.

These defendants, two of whom had firearms, started out in an automobile, looking for Rao or the man who had the payroll on that day. Rizzo claimed to be able to identify the man and was to point him out to the others who were to do the actual holding up. The four rode about in their car looking for Rao. They went to the bank from which he was supposed to get the money and to various buildings being constructed by the United Lathing Company. At last they came to One Hundred and Eightieth street and Morris Park avenue. By this time they were watched and followed by two police officers. As Rizzo jumped out of the car and ran into the building all four were arrested. The defendant was taken out from the building in which he was hiding. Neither Rao nor a man named Previti, who was also supposed to carry a payroll, were at the place at the time of the arrest. The defendants had not found or seen the man they intended to rob; no person with a payroll was at any of the places where they had stopped and no one had been pointed out or identified by Rizzo. The four men intended to rob the payroll man, whoever he was; they were looking for him, but they had not seen or discovered him up to the time they were arrested.

Does this constitute the crime of an attempt to commit robbery in the first degree? The Penal Law, section 2, prescribes, "An act, done with intent to commit a crime, and tending but failing to effect its commission, is 'an attempt to commit that crime."D' The word *tending* is very indefinite. It is perfectly evident that there will arise differences of opinion as to whether an act in a given case is one *tending* to commit a crime. "Tending" means to exert activity in a particular direction. Any act in preparation to commit a crime may be said to have a tendency towards its accomplishment. The procuring of the automobile, searching the streets looking for the desired victim, were in reality acts tending toward the commission of the proposed crime. The law, however, has recognized that many acts in the way of preparation are too remote to constitute the crime of attempt. The line has been drawn between those acts which are remote and those which are proximate and near to the consummation. The law must be practical, and, therefore, considers those acts only as tending to the commission of the crime which are so near to its accomplishment that in all reasonable probability the crime itself would have been committed but for timely interference. The cases which have been before the courts express this idea in different language, but the idea remains the same. The act or acts must come or advance very near to the accomplishment of the intended crime. In *People v. Mills* (178 N. Y. 274, 284) it was said: "Felonious intent alone is not enough, but there must be an overt act shown in order to establish even an attempt. An overt act is one done to carry out the intention, and it must be such as would naturally effect that result, unless prevented by some extraneous cause." In *Hyde v. U.S.* (225 U. S. 347) it was stated that the act amounts to an attempt when it is so near to the result that the danger of success is very great. "There must be dangerous proximity to success." Halsbury in his "Laws of England" (Vol. IX, p. 259) says: "An act, in order to be a criminal attempt, must be immediately, and not remotely, connected with and directly tending to the commission of an offence." *Commonwealth v. Peaslee* (177 Mass. 267) refers to the acts constituting an attempt as coming *very near* to the accomplishment of the crime.

The method of committing or attempting crime varies in each case so that the difficulty, if any, is not with this rule of law regarding an attempt, which is well understood, but with its application to the facts. As I have said before, minds differ over proximity and the nearness of the approach. (*People v. Collins*, 234 N. Y. 355; *People v. Sobieskoda*, 235 N. Y. 411; *People v. Werblow*, 241 N. Y. 55.)

How shall we apply this rule of immediate nearness to this case? The defendants were looking for the payroll man to rob him of his money. This is the charge in the indictment. Robbery is defined in section 2120 of the Penal Law as "the unlawful taking of personal property, from the person or in the presence of another, against his will, by means of force, or violence, or fear of injury, immediate or future, to his person;" and it is made robbery in the first degree by section 2124 when committed by a person aided by accomplices actually present. To constitute the crime of robbery the money must have been taken from Rao by means of force or violence, or through fear. The crime of attempt to commit robbery was committed if these defendants did an act tending to the commission of this robbery. Did the acts above describe come dangerously near to the taking of Rao's property? Did the acts come so near the commission of robbery that there was reasonable likelihood of its accomplishment but for the interference? Rao was not found; the defendants were still looking for him; no attempt to rob him could be made, at least until he came in sight; he was not in the building at One Hundred and Eightieth street and Morris Park avenue. There was no man there with the payroll for the United Lathing Company whom these defendants could rob. Apparently no money had been drawn from the bank for the payroll by anybody at the time of the arrest. In a word, these defendants had planned to commit a crime and were looking around the city for an opportunity to commit it, but the opportunity fortunately never came. Men would not be guilty of an attempt at burglary if they had planned to break into a building and were arrested while they were hunting about the streets for the building not knowing where it was. Neither would a man be guilty of an attempt to commit murder if he armed himself and started out to find the person whom he had planned to kill but could not find him. So here these defendants were not guilty of an attempt to commit robbery in the first degree when they had not found or reached the presence of the person they intended to rob. (*People v. Sullivan*, 173 N. Y. 122, 135.)

Does *Rizzo* definitively answer the question as the dissent claims? Since the dissent does not address the facts—or even the standard—in *Rizzo*, fill in the gaps for the dissent. How does *Rizzo* suggest that the prosecution failed to demonstrate sufficient evidence of an attempt?

2. The dissent finds great significance in the fact that this is an attempted larceny by false pretenses case, which required a false report to be made to the insurance company. Certainly nothing had been done toward falsely reporting a loss, which is the only way the theft could have been accomplished. Isn't the majority's opinion about something other than proximity? In some ways, the majority seems to be adding a momentum theory to proximity. A Smart car can stop in less distance than a freight train. Because the conspiracy involved a number of professional art thieves, the court held that result was more certainly foreordained than if it had been conducted by amateurs. The majority does not directly address the defendants in *Rizzo*, but an obvious contrast can be made. Do you accept the majority's conclusion that the complexity of the orchestration of events, and sophistication of the actors, that preceded a false claim is sufficient to show *proximity*? Recall that the majority claims not to be embracing the Model Penal Code's more lax proximity requirement. But is proximity really the basis of this decision at all?

B. Robbery

Robbery is quite often defined as larceny plus assault. Four elements are traditionally associated with this crime:

1) Trespassory Taking and Carrying Away the Property of Another;

2) Intent to Steal;

3) From the Person or Presence of the Victim;

4) By Means of Violence or Intimidation.

1. Trespassory Taking and Carrying Away the Property of Another

This first element contains two components that must be considered. First, what does it mean to trespass, or unlawfully take the property of another? Second, what is required to show that the defendant carried the property away? All jurisdictions require an unlawful taking to satisfy the elements of robbery, but not all jurisdictions require that the property to be carried away. In some jurisdictions, most of them in jurisdictions adopting the Model Penal Code's definition of robbery, it is enough that the defendant *attempted* to carry off the property. In those jurisdictions that do require a carrying-off of the property, frequently called asportation, courts have had to consider what conduct satisfies this element.

The first case presented in this section considers whether a defendant, who conspires with the owner of the property to steal from his employees in order to collect insurance money, has unlawfully taken the property. In other words, does the owner's consent vitiate the trespass, or unlawfulness, requirement of the taking? The second set of cases address the proof required to show asportation.

A trespassory taking is obviously required for a larceny (or theft, depending on the term chosen by the jurisdiction) but consider how the *Smith* case may present a different issue because it is a robbery rather than a larceny prosecution.

a. Trespass

People v. Smith

Court of Appeal, First District, Division Four, California
177 Cal. App.4th 1478, 100 Cal. Rptr.3d 24 (2009)

RUVOLO, P.J.

It was reported to be the largest jewelry heist in San Francisco history. Intruders entered a Union Square jewelry store while it was closed for the weekend, at a time when the store's safe room was being remodeled, and the store's security camera had exhausted its videotape and was not recording. A vacant restaurant space was located on the other side of the safe room's interior wall. The restaurant's exterior door had been rigged, by persons unknown, in a way that enabled the intruders to gain entry even though it was ostensibly locked. From the vacant restaurant, the intruders gained access to the jewelry store by cutting a hole through the common interior wall, in a location formerly occupied by a door. The hole led directly into the jewelry store's safe room. Ordinarily, the safes would have been located flush against the common wall, preventing the robbers from entering. But, on this particular weekend the safes had been moved temporarily into the middle of the room due to the remodeling.

Once inside the jewelry store, the intruders briefly set off a motion detector alarm in the safe room, but when the alarm company called the store owner, he took no action. The intruders were able to prevent further alarms by covering the motion detector with a cardboard box, using a ladder left in the safe room to reach it. They then concealed themselves until some employees arrived to open the premises on Monday. The intruders forced the employees to open the store's safes, and made off with almost $4.5 million worth of jewelry. Shortly after the robbery, the store's owner applied for and received a $4 million dollar insurance payment for the loss.

At appellant's robbery trial, the prosecution's theory of the case was that the robbery was an "inside job," set up by the store's owner in order to collect on the insurance. Based on this theory, appellant contends that if indeed the store owner conspired with the robbers and gave them his permission to rob the jewelry store, the elements of the crime of robbery have not been established.

In a case of first impression in this state, we reject appellant's claim, holding that even if the owner of a retail store consents to the taking of the store's property by third persons, those persons still commit a robbery if they take store property, by means of force or fear, from the custody of store employees who are unaware of the consent given to the robbers by their employer.

* * *

At appellant's trial, the prosecution advanced the theory that the crime was an "inside job" staged by Zimmelman in order to collect the insurance money on the stolen jewelry. On appeal, appellant contends that based on this theory of the case, his convictions for robbery must be reversed because, as a matter of law, one who takes property with the owner's consent does not commit a theft crime.

* * *

Appellant argues that in order for a crime to constitute robbery or larceny, the perpetrator must intend to deprive the owner of the property permanently, *without the owner's consent.* . . . Because the theory of the prosecution's case was that the owner was a participant in the crime, and thus gave his consent to the taking, appellant argues that the "felonious taking" element of robbery was not proved.

* * *

[B]ecause this situation presents a question of first impression under California law, we begin with the language of the statute defining the crime of robbery. Section 211 provides: "Robbery is the felonious taking of personal property in the possession of another, from his person or immediate presence, and against his will, accomplished by means of force or fear." Case law has elaborated this definition further. "Robbery is essentially larceny aggravated by use of force or fear to facilitate the taking of property from the person or presence of the possessor. [Citation.] Robbery requires the specific intent to deprive the victim of his or her property permanently. [Citations.] The taking of the property of another is not theft absent this intent. [Citation.] . . . [¶] . . . "'[A] bona fide belief of a right or claim to the property taken, even if mistaken, negates the element of felonious intent.""" (*In re Albert A.* (1996) 47 Cal.App.4th 1004, 1007–1008, 55 Cal.Rptr.2d 217.)

As noted, appellant's argument is, essentially, that the property owner's consent in the "inside job" scenario negates one of the elements of robbery by rendering the taking non-felonious. For guidance on this issue, we look to the California Supreme Court's examination of the meaning of the term "felonious taking." "[B]y use of the . . . term 'felonious taking' in section 211, the Legislature was . . . incorporating into the . . . statute the affirmative requirement, derived from the common law rule applicable to larceny and robbery, that the thief or robber has to intend to take property *belonging to someone other than himself* in order to be guilty of theft or robbery, that is to say, the common law recognition of the defense of claim of right." (*Tufunga, supra*, 21 Cal.4th at p. 946, 90 Cal.Rptr.2d 143, 987 P.2d 168, italics added.) *Tufunga* held, on the basis of this reasoning, that a good faith claim of right to the ownership of specific property can negate the element of felonious taking that is necessary to establish theft or robbery.

This holding does not, however, necessarily imply that the taking involved in an "inside job" robbery is *not* felonious, and may in fact, imply the opposite because it requires only that the property belong to someone other than the taker. The common law understanding of the "felonious taking" element of larceny and robbery, on which *Tufunga* relied, also includes the concept that "[a] person may be a victim of larceny even though he is not the owner [of the property taken]; he need only have a special property right, as in the case of a bailee or pledgee. It is enough that he has possession and that it is lawful as to the defendant, or that because of a legally recognized interest in the property he is entitled to possession as against the defendant. Moreover, the person from whom the property is taken qualifies as a victim of larceny even though he does not have the right of possession as against the true owner." (Wharton's Criminal Law, (15th ed.1995) § 381, pp. 454–456, fns. omitted.)[6]

California has long followed the common law in this regard. For example, in *People v. Shuler* (1865) 28 Cal. 490, a defendant was charged with robbery. The indictment stated that the defendant had robbed a man named Wyckoff by forcibly taking from him some property that belonged to another man named Whiting. On appeal, the defendant argued that the indictment was defective in failing to plead that the property was taken from Whiting without the latter's consent. The California Supreme Court rejected this argument, reasoning as follows. "The indictment does state that from the person and control of Wyckoff, and against his will, the defendants did feloniously, forcibly and violently steal, take and carry away the money and property described. It thus appears that Wyckoff had possession of the property when it was taken, for it was taken from his person and control. Having possession of it, the law deems that possession rightful, and therefore the right of Wyckoff to the possession need not be stated in the indictment." (*Id.* at p. 493.) The court went on to explain that "an indictment for robbery must contain an allegation as to the ownership of the property of which the party named was robbed, or that it did not belong to the defendant[, but] '[i]t is not necessary that the property should belong to the party from whose possession it was forcibly taken.'" (*Id.* at p. 494.)

Similarly, in a case in which a man found some money on the street, and another man then stole it from him, the court rejected the thief's argument that he could not be convicted of grand theft because the finder of the money was not its owner. The court reasoned that "the finder of the lost money . . . had the right of possession, and was entitled to retain it as against all the world except the true owner. . . . Any legally recognizable interest is sufficient to sustain an averment of ownership in a charge of grand theft." (*People v. Beach* (1944) 62 Cal.App.2d 803, 806–807, 145 P.2d 685.)

In short, "'[c]onsidered as an element of larceny, "ownership" and "possession" may be regarded as synonymous terms; for one who has the right of possession as against the thief is, so far as the latter is concerned, the owner.' [Citation.] It is, after all, a matter of no concern to a thief that legal title to the stolen property is not in the complainant. [Citation.] . . . 'Possession alone, as against the wrongdoer, is a sufficient interest to justify an allegation and proof

---

6 *See also* 18A Cal. Jur.3d Criminal Law: Crimes Against Property § 127, which states: "The law proscribes as larceny a taking from ownership or right of possession of any kind whatsoever, so long as it is in one other than the thief. . . . [¶] Considered as an element of larceny, 'ownership' and 'possession' may ordinarily be regarded as synonymous, for one who has the right of possession as against a thief is, so far as the thief is concerned, the owner. Any legally recognizable interest is sufficient to sustain an averment of ownership in a charge of theft by larceny." (Footnotes omitted.)

of ownership in a prosecution for larceny.'" (*People v. Price* (1941) 46 Cal.App.2d 59, 61–62, 115 P.2d 225.)

This result comports with the gravamen of the crime of robbery. "Although classified in the Penal Code as a crime against the person, robbery is actually a crime against both the person and property. [Citation.] 'Robbery violates the social interest in the safety and security of the person as well as the social interest in the protection of property rights.'" (*People v. Gomez* (2008) 43 Cal.4th 249, 264, 74 Cal.Rptr.3d 123, 179 P.3d 917.) "[T]he central element of the crime of robbery [is] the force or fear applied to the individual victim in order to deprive him of his property. Accordingly, if force or fear is applied to two victims in joint possession of property, two convictions of robbery are proper." (*People v. Ramos* (1982) 30 Cal.3d 553, 589, 180 Cal.Rptr. 266, 639 P.2d 908, fn. omitted, reversed on other grounds by *California v. Ramos* (1983) 463 U.S. 992, 103 S.Ct. 3446, 77 L.Ed.2d 1171.)

Reaffirming this rule, the California Supreme Court recently noted that "neither ownership nor physical possession is required to establish the element of possession for the purposes of the robbery statute. [Citations.] '[T]he theory of constructive possession has been used to expand the concept of possession to include employees and others as robbery victims.' [Citation.] Two or more persons may be in joint constructive possession of a single item of personal property, and multiple convictions of robbery are proper if force or fear is applied to multiple victims in joint possession of the property taken." (*People v. Scott* (2009) 45 Cal.4th 743, 749–750, 89 Cal.Rptr.3d 213, 200 P.3d 837.) As this discussion implies, it is the possession of property, not its ownership, which is the determining factor regarding whether a robbery has occurred. This principle makes sense, because the risk of injury or death resulting from confrontations between robbers and victims is not significantly reduced merely because the victims lack legal title to the property in their possession.

For all of the foregoing reasons, we hold that when the owner of a store consents to an "inside job" robbery that occurs while the store is under the control of employees who are unaware of the owner's plan, the owner's consent does not vitiate the "felonious taking" element of robbery. If the property that is taken was in the possession of the owner's innocent employees or agents, that is sufficient to make the taking felonious, even if the owner himself or herself is secretly in league with the perpetrators.[7]

---

7 This case does not present the question whether a robbery staged with the property owner's connivance is a "felonious taking" if the property owner is the only one present when it is committed, or if the purported victims are aware that the apparent robbery is feigned. Accordingly, we do not decide that question.

Notes and Questions

1. Would the rule in this case apply to an inside larceny, rather than an inside robbery? Suppose the owner of the jewelry store conspired with others to shoplift items of the store—so that the taking is from the possession of the employees, but with the permission of the owner. Would the owner's consent have any effect on a prosecution for larceny? Imagine, for instance, that the plan in *Mahboubian* had involved a shoplifting by the owners of a store to file a false insurance claim. Would this constitute a larceny against the employees of the store?

2. Notice that the court says that "[r]obbery is essentially larceny aggravated by use of force or fear. . ." Is the court's reasoning loyal to that definition?

----

b. Asportation

The question of whether a defendant actually has to carry away property in order to be convicted of robbery has enormous consequences for the definition of the law of robbery. If he does not, then attempted robbery is punished the same as robbery. *People v. Williams* addresses the question of whether the Michigan legislature's amendment of its robbery laws eliminated the asportation requirement of robbery that had existed at common law, and had certainly existed by statute in Michigan prior to the 2004 amendment to Michigan's robbery law. The case references a case we will consider later, *People v. Randolph*, which considers when force, or attempted force, must be used for a defendant to be guilty of robbery. *Randolph* appears at p. 48.

Most of the cases we have examined so far have looked at either jury instructions or sufficiency of the evidence. These are the two most common procedural mechanisms by which appellate courts interpret substantive criminal law. Occasionally, appellate courts will decide that evidence is, or is not, admissible based on its interpretation of a criminal statute. This case is quite unusual in that it involves an appellate court's interpretation of substantive criminal law to interpret the validity of a guilty plea.

People v. Williams

Supreme Court of Michigan
814 N.W.2d 270 (2011)

YOUNG, C.J.

Defendant appeals here his conviction of armed robbery. In particular, defendant argues that because he was unsuccessful in feloniously taking or removing any actual property from the intended target of his robbery, there was not a sufficient factual basis to support his guilty plea to the charge of armed robbery. We disagree. When the Legislature revised the robbery statute, MCL 750.530, to encompass a "course of conduct" theory of robbery, it specifically included "an attempt to commit the larceny" as sufficient to sustain a conviction for robbery itself. We conclude that this amendment effectuated a substantive change in the law governing robbery in Michigan such that a completed larceny is no longer necessary to sustain a conviction for the crime of robbery or armed robbery.

I. FACTS AND PROCEDURAL HISTORY

On July 13, 2006, defendant entered a gas station, declared that he had a gun, and ordered the attendant to give him all the money in the cash register. After the attendant complied, defendant forced the attendant into a back room and fled the scene with approximately $160 in stolen cash. The next day, defendant entered a tobacco shop, approached the clerk with his hand in his jacket, and stated, "You know what this is, just give me what I want." The clerk did not give defendant any money or property, and defendant fled from the store without having stolen anything. Defendant was apprehended later that day by the police.

The prosecutor charged defendant with armed robbery of the gas station and, in a separate information, charged defendant alternatively with assault with intent to rob while armed and armed robbery for the events related to the tobacco shop. Defendant elected to plead guilty in both cases. At defendant's plea hearing, the prosecutor advised that he would dismiss the charge of assault with intent to rob while armed in the tobacco shop case in return for defendant's guilty plea to armed robbery.

After advising defendant of his options and constitutional rights, the circuit court established a factual basis for the plea relating to the incident that occurred at the tobacco shop. Under questioning by the prosecutor, defendant admitted that he had entered the tobacco shop with the intent to steal money, had his hand "up under" his coat, and told the clerk, "You know what this is, just give me what I want." Defendant further admitted that "it was [his] intent, at that time, for [the clerk] to give [him] the money out of the cash register." The court accepted defendant's guilty plea On February 9, 2007, the court sentenced defendant pursuant to a plea entered in accordance with *People v. Cobbs*[4] to concurrent prison terms of 24 to 40 years for the tobacco shop and gas station robberies.

Defendant subsequently moved to withdraw his pleas, contending that an adequate factual basis did not exist to support either conviction. Pertinent here, defendant argued that there was no evidence that he had taken or removed any property from the tobacco shop and that, absent a completed larceny, he could not be found guilty of armed robbery. The circuit court denied defendant's motions. The court ruled that the language of the armed robbery statute as amended in 2004 allows for a conviction based on an attempted larceny, a basis that the plea discussions substantiated.[5] The Court of Appeals granted defendant's delayed application for leave to appeal, limited to the issue whether a factual basis existed for his conviction of the tobacco store robbery.

In a split decision, the Court of Appeals affirmed. The majority acknowledged that while at common law a robbery required a completed larceny, the crimes of robbery and armed robbery now encompass attempts to commit those offenses following the 2004 statutory amendments. The dissenting judge argued that when the 2004 revisions are viewed through the "lens of common-law definitions," there is inadequate support for the conclusion that the armed robbery statute would permit a conviction without an accomplished larceny.

We granted defendant's application for leave to appeal to determine "whether a larceny needs to be completed before a defendant may be convicted of armed robbery."

II. STANDARD OF REVIEW

In this appeal concerns the proper interpretation of MCL 750.529 and MCL 750.530 and, in particular, whether the Legislature intended to remove the completed larceny requirement from the crime of robbery when it amended those

---

4   *People v. Cobbs*, 443 Mich. 276, 505 N.W.2d 208 (1993). [Editor's Note: Cobbs provides that a defendant may enter a guilty plea, without conceding his guilt, if he recognizes that such a plea is in his best interest. *See also North Carolina v. Alford*, 400 U.S. 25 (1970).]

5   The circuit court also denied defendant's motion to withdraw his *nolo contendere* plea with regard to the gas station robbery, holding that the plea proceeding and the police report established a sufficient factual basis for the plea.

statutes in 2004. Matters of statutory interpretation raise questions of law, which this Court reviews de novo.

III. THE CRIME OF ROBBERY IN MICHIGAN

In this appeal, we are concerned with the statutes pertaining to robbery, MCL 750.530, and armed robbery, MCL 750.529. At common law, the offense of robbery was defined as "the felonious taking of money or goods of value from the person of another or in his presence, against his will, by violence or putting him in fear." "To constitute robbery, it [was] essential that there be a 'taking from the person.'" Thus, common law robbery required a completed larceny. Armed robbery required the same showing with the additional element that the robber was armed with a dangerous weapon.

The crimes of robbery and armed robbery have been codified by Michigan statute since 1838. All subsequent iterations of the robbery statutes required a completed larceny, consistent with the common law. Before the 2004 amendments, MCL 750.529, defining armed robbery, provided:

> Any person who shall assault another, and shall feloniously rob, steal and take from his person, or in his presence, any money or other property, which may be the subject of larceny, such robber being armed with a dangerous weapon, or any article used or fashioned in a manner to lead the person so assaulted to reasonably believe it to be a dangerous weapon, shall be guilty of a felony. . . .

[T]he Legislature amended the robbery statutes. MCL 750.529, as amended by 2004 P.A. 128, now provides:

> A person who engages in conduct proscribed under [MCL 750.530, the robbery statute] and who in the course of engaging in that conduct, possesses a dangerous weapon or an article used or fashioned in a manner to lead any person present to reasonably believe the article is a dangerous weapon, or who represents orally or otherwise that he or she is in possession of a dangerous weapon, is guilty of a felony punishable by imprisonment for life or for any term of years. If an aggravated assault or serious injury is inflicted by any person while violating this section, the person shall be sentenced to a minimum term of imprisonment of not less than 2 years.

Robbery is defined within MCL 750.530; as amended by 2004 P.A. 128, it states, in relevant part:

> (1) A person who, *in the course of committing a larceny* of any money or other property that may be the subject of larceny, uses force or violence against any person who is present, or who assaults or puts the person in

fear, is guilty of a felony punishable by imprisonment for not more than 15 years.

(2) As used in this section, "*in the course of committing a larceny" includes acts that occur in an attempt to commit the larceny, or* during commission of the larceny, *or* in flight or attempted flight after the commission of the larceny, or in an attempt to retain possession of the property.[20]

IV. ANALYSIS

The question before this Court is whether the Legislature intended to remove the element of a *completed* larceny from the crime of robbery when it amended the statutes in 2004. We hold that the Legislature demonstrated a clear intent to remove the element of a *completed* larceny, signaling a departure from Michigan's historical requirement and its common law underpinnings. Accordingly, an attempted robbery or attempted armed robbery with an incomplete larceny is now sufficient to sustain a conviction under the robbery or armed robbery statutes, respectively.

Our analysis begins, as it must, with the language of the robbery statutes themselves. "The cardinal rule of statutory construction is to discern and give effect to the intent of the Legislature." This Court may best discern that intent by reviewing the words of a statute as they have been used by the Legislature. When a statute's language is clear and unambiguous, this Court will enforce that statute as written.

The Legislature revised the robbery statute at issue here by removing the prior requirement that a robber feloniously "rob, steal or take" property from another, and it replaced this language with a new statutory phrase: "in the course of committing a larceny." Key to solving the interpretative puzzle presented in this case, the Legislature specifically defined that phrase to include acts that "occur in an attempt to commit the larceny, or during commission of the larceny, or in flight or attempted flight after the commission of the larceny, or in an attempt to retain possession of the property.

In revising the robbery statutes, the Legislature replaced the "familiar words" of the common law crime of robbery—"rob, steal and take"—with the phrase "in the course of committing a larceny," which the Legislature specifically defined to include "acts that occur in *an attempt* to commit the larceny." The word "attempt" has a well-known common and legal meaning.

---

20 Emphasis added.

1. The act or an instance of making an effort to accomplish something, [especially] without success. 2. *Criminal law.* An overt act that is done with the intent to commit a crime but that falls short of completing the crime.[28]

Particularly in the realm of the criminal law, the word "attempt" is widely used with regard to any type of crime in which a person intends to commit a crime and acts toward its commission but is unsuccessful in its completion.

Indeed, it is inherent in the word "attempt" that the illegal act intended is not accomplished. Accordingly, the plainest understanding of the phrase "in an attempt to commit the larceny" applies to situations in which a criminal defendant makes "an effort" or undertakes an "overt act" with an intent to deprive another person of his property, but does not achieve the deprivation of property. The language of this phrase is clear on its face and not ambiguous in the least, and therefore it must be enforced as written, free of any "contrary judicial gloss."

. . .The 2004 revisions *deleted* the words denoting *actual* deprivation of property—"rob, steal and take"—and replaced them with a broader phrase: "in the course of committing a larceny." The deletion and replacement of what this Court long ago called the "familiar words" of robbery is perhaps the best and most compelling indication that the Legislature intended an extensive deviation from the common law rule.

* * *

We further note that the Legislature's particular policy decision in amending the robbery and armed robbery statutes is consistent with the Model Penal Code (MPC), which provides:

(1) *Robbery Defined.* A person is guilty of robbery if, *in the course of committing a theft,* he:

    (a) Inflicts serious bodily injury upon another; or

    (b) Threatens another with or purposely puts him in fear of immediate serious bodily injury; or

    (c) Commits or threatens immediately to commit any felony of the first or second degree.

---

28 Black's Law Dictionary (8th ed.).

> An act shall be deemed "in the course of committing a theft" if it occurs *in an attempt to commit theft* or in flight after *the attempt* or commission.[41]

It is noteworthy that the MPC's definition of robbery is strikingly similar to that of Michigan's amended robbery statute. The almost identical usage of "in the course of committing a larceny/theft" in the MPC and MCL 750.530 indicates a more expansive conception of robbery than previously existed in Michigan law. In particular, like that of MCL 750.530, the MPC's definition for "in the course of committing a theft" *explicitly includes the attempt form of robbery* in an almost identical fashion. With regard to this change to subsume attempted robbery under the robbery provision itself, the official comment to MPC § 222.1 provides a useful and telling discussion:

> Since common-law larceny and robbery required asportation, the severe penalties for robbery were avoided if the victim had no property to hand over or if the theft were interrupted before the accused laid hold of the goods. Moreover, the penalties for attempted robbery were considerably milder than those authorized for the completed crime. The perception that one who attempts a robbery poses essentially the same dangers as the successful robber led legislatures to develop more serious sanctions for various forms of attempt. The offense of assault with intent to rob was one response and redefining robbery to include an assault with intent to rob was another. Often some distinctions in penalty were preserved.

> There is, however, no penological justification for distinctions on this basis. The same dangers are posed by the actor who is interrupted or who is foiled by an empty pocket as by the actor who succeeds in effecting the theft. The same correctional dispositions are justified as well. The primary concern is with the physical danger or threat of danger to the citizen rather than with the property aspects of the crime. By including attempted thefts within the time span during which robbery can occur, Section 222.1 therefore makes it immaterial whether property is obtained.[43]

---

41 2 American Law Institute (ALI), Model Penal Code and Commentaries (1980), § 222. 1, p. 96 (italics added).

43 2 ALI, Model Penal Code, comment 2(a) to § 222. 1, pp. 99–100.

At least 23 states in addition to Michigan have instituted changes including attempts to rob as sufficient to prove robbery itself, often adopting a "course of conduct" theory of when robbery occurs.[44]

The desire to punish attempted robberies the same as a robbery itself corresponds with the understanding, long recognized in Michigan, that the greater social harm perpetrated in a robbery is the use of force rather than the actual taking of another's property. As this Court has explained:

> Robbery, while containing elements of theft of property, is primarily an assaultive crime. "Robbery violates the social interest in the safety and security of the person as well as the social interest in the protection of property rights. In fact, as a matter of abstract classification, it probably should be grouped with offenses against the person. . . ." Classification as an offense against a person is particularly appropriate where the robbery is committed with the aggravating element of the perpetrator being armed. In this situation, the safety and security of the person is most severely threatened, and the larcenous taking is of secondary importance.

In accordance, the plain language of the 2004 statutory revisions of MCL 750.529 and MCL 750.530 establishes the Legislature's clear intent to include attempts to rob within the scope of the robbery statutes. Accordingly, when an intended robber is in possession of, appears to be in possession of, or represents that he is in possession of a dangerous weapon as stated in MCL 750.529, that person may be guilty of armed robbery even if the larcenous taking is not completed.

V. APPLICATION

Aside from the question whether a completed larceny is necessary to support a conviction for robbery, the parties in this case do not dispute that defendant's plea was sufficient to sustain a conviction for armed robbery of the tobacco shop. Having held that an attempted larceny may satisfy the requirements of MCL 750.529 and MCL 750.530, as amended, we affirm defendant's conviction.

At his plea allocution, defendant admitted that he assaulted, or otherwise used the threat of force or violence against, the clerk in "the course of

---

44 See *Alabama*—Ala. Code § 13A–8–40; *Alaska*—Alas Stat. § 11.41.510; *Arkansas*—Ark. Code Ann. § 5–12–102; *Delaware*—Del. Code tit. 11, § 831; *Florida*—Fla. Stat. § 812.13; *Hawaii*—Hawaii Rev. Stat. § 708–842; *Iowa*—Iowa Code § 711.1; *Kentucky*—Ky. Rev. Stat. Ann. § 515.030; *Maine*—Me. Rev. Stat. tit. 17–A, § 651; *Maryland*—Md. Code Ann., Crim. Law § 3–402; *Montana*—Mont. Code Ann. § 45–5–401; *New Hampshire*—N.H. Rev. Stat. Ann. § 636:1; *New Jersey*—N.J. Stat. Ann. § 2C:15–1; *North Carolina*—N.C. Gen. Stat. § 14–87; *North Dakota*—N.D. Cent. Code § 12.1–22–01; *Ohio*—Ohio Rev. Code Ann. § 2911.02; *Oregon*—Or. Rev. Stat. § 164.395; *Pennsylvania*—18 Pa. Cons. Stat. § 3701; *Texas*—Tex. Penal Code Ann. § 29.01; *Utah*—Utah Code Ann. § 76–6–301; *Vermont*—Vt. Stat. Ann. tit. 13, § 608; *West Virginia*—W. Va. Code. § 61–2–12; *Wyoming*—Wyo. Stat. Ann. § 6–2–401.

committing a larceny" of the tobacco shop. Defendant admitted that it was his intent to rob the clerk of the tobacco shop's money. It also was established at defendant's plea hearing that at the time of the robbery defendant intimated that he had a dangerous weapon, both by verbally alluding to this fact and by placing his hand under his clothing so as to represent that he was armed with a weapon. Even though defendant was unsuccessful in obtaining money, his attempt to complete a larceny while representing that he was armed with a dangerous weapon satisfied MCL 750.529. Accordingly, the facts elicited at the plea allocution were sufficient to sustain defendant's conviction for armed robbery, and the circuit court did not err by denying defendant's motion to withdraw that plea.

VI. CONCLUSION

In 2004, the Legislature considerably broadened the scope of the robbery statute, MCL 750.530, to encompass a "course of conduct" theory of robbery, which specifically includes "an attempt to commit the larceny." We conclude that this amendment effectuated a substantive change in the law governing robbery in Michigan such that a completed larceny is no longer necessary to sustain a conviction for the crime of robbery or armed robbery. The judgment of the Court of Appeals is affirmed.

MARKMAN, MARY BETH KELLY, and ZAHRA, JJ., concur.

MARILYN J. KELLY, J. (dissenting).

At issue in this case is whether a larceny must be completed before a criminal defendant may be convicted of armed robbery. The majority concludes that a completed larceny is not necessary to sustain a conviction for that crime. Because I disagree with its conclusion, I respectfully dissent.

* * *

Standard Of Review And Legal Background

Matters of statutory interpretation present questions of law, which we review de novo.

The common law underlies Michigan's criminal statutes. Indeed, this Court has long held that the common law definition of a crime binds Michigan courts unless and until the Legislature modifies the elements of a crime. Likewise, we recognized in *People v. Covelesky* that "when words are adopted having a settled, definite and well known meaning at common law it is to be assumed they are used with the sense and meaning which they had at common law unless a contrary intent is plainly shown."

Historically, Michigan's robbery statutes are derived from the common law crime of robbery. An essential element of the crime included the commission of a larceny. We observed as much in *Covelesky*, noting that

> [r]obbery at common law is defined as the felonious *taking of money or goods of value* from the person of another or in his presence, against his will, by violence or putting him in fear. This definition has been followed by most of the statutes, and even where the language has been varied sufficiently to sustain, by a literal interpretation, a narrower definition of the offense, it has usually been held that it could not be presumed that the legislature intended to change the nature of the crime as understood at common law.

Thus, at common law, robbery included three elements: (1) a larceny of money or goods of value from a person, (2) against the person's will, (3) by violence or putting the person in fear. Our Court of Appeals has also long observed that a completed larceny is an essential element of armed robbery.

In *People v. Randolph*,[14] we examined the original version of MCL 750.530 in the Michigan Penal Code, which provided, in relevant part:

> Any person who shall, by force or violence, or by assault or putting in fear, feloniously rob, steal and take from the person of another, or in his presence, any money or other property which may be the subject of larceny, such robber not being armed with a dangerous weapon, shall be guilty of a felony....[15]

The issue in *Randolph* was whether the crime of robbery set forth in MCL 750.530 was properly viewed by means of a "transactional approach." Under this approach, an offender is not viewed as having completed a robbery until he or she has escaped with stolen merchandise. *Randolph* rejected the transactional approach, holding that if force is used to *re*tain, rather than *ob*tain, property, the crime is outside the scope of MCL 750.530.[16] We further held that, under the common law, the force or violence element of robbery "had to be applied before or during the taking."[17] We explicitly noted that, after the initial larcenous act has been completed, the use of force against a victim to retain stolen property

---

14   *People v. Randolph*, 466 Mich. 532, 648 N.W.2d 164 (2002).

15   As enacted by 1931 P.A. 328.

16   *Randolph*, 466 Mich. at 541–543, 648 N.W.2d 164.

17   *Id.* at 538, 648 N.W.2d 164.

does not transform the offense into armed robbery.[18] Rather, the force or violence must be used before or contemporaneously with the larceny to elevate the offense to robbery.

In response to our decision in *Randolph*, the Legislature amended our robbery statutes in 2004.[19] MCL 750.529, the armed robbery provision, now reads in relevant part as follows:

> A person who engages in conduct proscribed under [MCL 750.530] and who in the course of engaging in that conduct, possesses a dangerous weapon or an article used or fashioned in a manner to lead any person present to reasonably believe the article is a dangerous weapon, or who represents orally or otherwise that he or she is in possession of a dangerous weapon, is guilty of a felony punishable by imprisonment for life or for any term of years.

At the same time, the Legislature also revised the statutory definition of unarmed robbery in MCL 750.530. It did so to clarify the scope of the unlawful conduct proscribed by MCL 750.529, which refers to MCL 750.530. MCL 750.530 now provides:

> (1) A person who, in the course of committing a larceny of any money or other property that may be the subject of larceny, uses force or violence against any person who is present, or who assaults or puts the person in fear, is guilty of a felony punishable by imprisonment for not more than 15 years.
>
> (2) As used in this section, "in the course of committing a larceny" includes acts that occur in an attempt to commit the larceny, or during commission of the larceny, or in flight or attempted flight after the commission of the larceny, or in an attempt to retain possession of the property.

Central to the resolution of this case is the definition of "in the course of committing a larceny" in MCL 750.529(2). Specifically, we must consider whether the addition of the phrase "acts that occur in an attempt to commit the larceny" in that definition eliminated the common law requirement of a completed larceny as a prerequisite for an armed robbery conviction.

---

18   *Id.* at 543, 648 N.W.2d 164.

19   2004 P.A. 128.

ANALYSIS

Against this backdrop, the starting point in any statutory interpretation dispute is the language of the relevant statutes. When considering the correct statutory interpretation, statutory language must be read as a whole. "Individual words and phrases, while important, should be read in the context of the entire legislative scheme." Furthermore, "'the Legislature is presumed to be aware of, and thus to have considered the effect on, all existing statutes when enacting new laws.'"

As Judge GLEICHER noted in her Court of Appeals dissent, the language of MCL 750.530 refutes the proposition that our robbery statutes allow for conviction without proof of a completed larceny.[24] Under MCL 750.530, a person who "in the course of committing a larceny" uses force or violence, puts in fear, or assaults another is guilty of a felony. The statutory phrase "in the course of committing a larceny" includes "acts that occur in an attempt to commit the larceny, or during the commission of the larceny, or in flight or attempted flight after the commission or the larceny, or in an attempt to retain possession of the property."

Through this language, the Legislature explicitly indicated that the use of force or violence at any time during the commission of a larceny subjects offenders to prosecution for armed robbery. Hence, "the Legislature intended to expand the temporal scope of the crime. . . ."[25] The language it chose merely reflects its rejection of *Randolph*. It does not eliminate the requirement of an actual larceny.

The House legislative analysis of H.B. 5015, which became 2004 P.A. 128, also supports my conclusion that the Legislature did not intend to abrogate the common law requirement of a completed larceny to sustain a robbery conviction. That analysis described our decision in *Randolph* as the problem that H.B. 5105 would rectify. It indicated that the bill would eliminate *Randolph*'s holding that applied only to those acts in which force was used to accomplish a larceny.[26] The section describing the contents of the bill indicated that it would expand the crime of armed robbery. The crime would include a person who, in the course of engaging in the proscribed conduct, "represented orally or otherwise that he or she was in possession of a dangerous weapon."[27]

The arguments for H.B. 5015 summarized in the House legislative analysis further illustrate the bill's purpose. For example, one such argument for the bill stated:

---

24 *Williams*, 288 Mich.App. at 96–97, 792 N.W.2d 384 (GLEICHER, J., dissenting).

25 *Id.* at 97, 792 N.W.2d 384.

26 House Legislative Analysis, H.B. 5015, February 12, 2004, p. 1.

27 *Id.*

Currently, a charge of robbery can only be made if force or violence were used to *commit the larceny*. Revising the statutes will allow prosecutors more latitude to prosecute similar crimes in similar ways. For example, under the recent court interpretation of the robbery laws, it would be a crime of armed robbery if a gun were brandished immediately before or while property *was being taken*. However, it would not be a crime of armed robbery if the gun was not brandished until the suspect was trying to evade capture by a security guard or passerby. The bill would revise the state's robbery statutes to include any *crime of larceny* that involved the use of force or violence, or fear, *at any time during the commission of the crime*. Therefore, if force or violence were used *to take property, to retain property*, or to evade apprehension *after taking property*, the act could constitute robbery. [28]

A second argument in support of the bill stated:

Before the 2002 state supreme court decision interpreted the robbery statutes as applying only in those cases in which force or violence were used *in the taking of property*, the state's appellate courts were moving towards what is known as the "transactional approach" . . . . Even though this approach included as robbery some acts that would not be considered robbery under the *Randolph* decision, it still is problematic. For example, say property *is taken* from a convenience store without force, but force is used to keep possession of the stolen property or in an attempt to flee from a security guard or police officer. Under the transactional approach, the crime would be elevated to robbery if the suspect escaped apprehension and attained temporary safety but would not be robbery if the suspect were apprehended by the security guard or police officer because that means he or she had never attained temporary safety. Moreover, the current law reflects the mindset of the early 1830s, whereas the bill is similar to revisions other states have made that include not only *the actual taking or larceny* as the crime of robbery, but also those acts committed in trying to keep possession of the property and acts committed in trying to escape apprehension. [29]

These arguments make clear that the revisions of the robbery statutes were intended to elevate to robbery any completed larceny that included force before, during, or after the taking. They explicitly indicate that a completed larceny remains part of a robbery. The Legislature was merely displeased with *Randolph* and enacted legislation to allow for an enhanced charge of robbery when a larcenist employs force.

---

28 *Id.* at 2 (emphasis added).

29 *Id.* at 2–3 (emphasis added).

While the language of the House legislative analysis provides an understanding of the Legislature's intentions, equally telling is what is lacking from that analysis. Nowhere in the public act or the House legislative analysis is there any indication that the Legislature intended to abrogate the common law requirement that a robbery include a completed larceny. Although the Legislature has the authority to set aside the common law, it has long been recognized that "[w]hen it does so, it should speak in no uncertain terms." In 2004 P.A. 128, there are no "terms," let alone "uncertain" ones, that support the conclusion that a completed larceny is no longer an element of robbery.

The Majority Obliterates the Distinction Between Armed Robbery and Assault With Intent to Rob and Steal While Armed

A further indication that the majority's statutory interpretation is incorrect is that it effectively writes out of existence the crime of assault with intent to rob and steal while armed. In this regard, MCL 750.89 provides:

Assault with intent to rob and steal being armed—Any person, being armed with a dangerous weapon, or any article used or fashioned in a manner to lead a person so assaulted reasonably to believe it to be a dangerous weapon, who shall assault another with intent to rob and steal shall be guilty of a felony, punishable by imprisonment in the state prison for life, or for any term of years.

Thus, a person violates MCL 750.89 if he or she intends to rob another while in possession of a weapon but fails and a completed larceny does not occur.

Under the majority's flawed analysis, the armed robbery statute, MCL 750.529, is now nearly identical to assault with intent to rob and steal while armed, MCL 750.89. Indeed, a defendant may now be convicted of armed robbery if (1) while armed with a dangerous weapon or any article used or fashioned in a manner to lead a person to believe it to be a dangerous weapon, (2) he or she assaults another with intent to rob and steal. There is no longer a distinction between armed robbery and assault with intent to rob and steal while armed. Yet the Legislature saw fit to draw a distinction between the two crimes by requiring a *completed* larceny for armed robbery, not merely an *intended* one. Otherwise, there would be no purpose to having two discrete statutes on the books.

The key distinction between armed robbery and assault with intent to rob and steal while armed . . . is whether a larceny is completed. To obtain a conviction, the prosecution must prove in both instances that an offender committed an assault. Likewise, both crimes require proof of the use of a weapon or an object fashioned as a weapon. But assault with intent to rob and steal while armed requires only the *intent* to commit a robbery; no completed larceny is required under CJI 2d 18.3(4). By contrast, armed robbery requires a *completed* larceny. In fact, CJI 2d 18.1(3) explicitly indicates that the prosecution must prove that a defendant "was in the course of committing a larceny" and defines "larceny" as "the taking and movement of someone else's property. . . ."

As discussed earlier, the Legislature is "'presumed to be aware of, and thus to have considered the effect on, all existing statutes when enacting new laws.'" Yet under today's decision, the majority has usurped the Legislature's statutory distinction between armed robbery and assault with intent to rob while armed. In essence, it has merged the two offenses into one. Had the Legislature intended to eliminate the crime of assault with intent to rob while armed when it enacted 2004 P.A. 128, it could have explicitly done so. It did not. The majority offers no response when confronted with this significant analytical flaw.

Applying my analysis to this case, I believe that the trial court abused its discretion by denying defendant's motion to withdraw his plea. There is no evidence that defendant committed a larceny at the tobacco store, and therefore there is an inadequate factual basis to support a finding that defendant is guilty of armed robbery. Therefore, I would reverse the judgment of the Court of Appeals.

CONCLUSION

I dissent from the majority's holding that a completed larceny is no longer necessary to sustain a conviction for armed robbery. The Legislature did not provide a clear indication that it wished to depart from the common law. Accordingly, I would reverse the judgment of the Court of Appeals and remand this case to the trial court for further proceedings.

MICHAEL F. CAVANAGH and HATHAWAY, JJ., concur.

Notes and Questions

1. This case involves perhaps all the tools courts use to interpret criminal statutes: plain reading of the text, legislative history, presumptions of consistency with the common law, consistency of interpretation with other jurisdictions, and policy.

2. Notice what the legislative history says that it is trying to achieve: increase flexibility for prosecutors. Academics have long argued that legislatures are not passing codes they expect to be enforced absolutely but are giving prosecutors a menu from which to select charges, giving them enormous power in plea bargaining. *See* William J. Stuntz, *The Pathological Politics of Criminal Law*, 100 Mich. L. Rev. 505 (2001). Rarely, however, is a legislature as candid

as it was in amendment of this robbery statute. The dissent, however, offered this aspect of the legislative history to show that the legislature intended to give prosecutors more power so that they could treat similar cases similarly—by charging a defendant the same regardless of whether he brandished a weapon before, during, or after the taking, *not* to treat defendants the same regardless of whether the defendant was successful in taking property. The legislature also may have had a very sanguine view of the way prosecutors use their power. As an opinion by Judge Easterbrook demonstrates, prosecutors are often more concerned about using their discretion in charging to obtain cooperation than they are to ensure equal treatment of similarly situated defendants. *See United States v. Brigham*, 977 F.2d 317 (1992).

3. The debate between the majority and the dissent is essentially one of context. For the dissent, the Legislature was simply trying to reverse the *Randolph* opinion and permit a robbery conviction whenever the force occurred—before, during, or after the taking. For the majority, the statute that the legislature drafted is itself the only relevant context and the plain language of the statute, which is nearly identical to the language used by the Model Penal Code, suggests a much broader reading—that robbery amounts to force in the effort to commit a larceny. But of course the Model Penal Code contains an express provision eliminating the distinction between attempted robbery and robbery, a provision not in the Michigan statute. What should one make of that omission?

4. In case you thought reading David Lewis' article was merely an academic exercise, this case proves you wrong. Notice the majority's policy justification for embracing an interpretation of the statute that makes no distinction between an attempted and completed robbery. The majority observes that there is "no penological justification" for a distinction in punishment between an attempted and completed robbery. Futher the court observed that "[t]he desire to punish attempted robberies the same as a robbery itself corresponds with the understanding, long recognized in Michigan, that the greater social harm perpetuated in a robbery is the use of force rather than the actual taking of property." It is not that the opinion is punishing harms the same as it is punishing completed crimes, the court is simply focusing on a *different* harm, the threat to the victim rather than the taking of his or her property. In deciding whether the statute in question ought to be interpreted to eliminate the distinction between attempted and completed robbery do you find it significant that "at least 23" states in addition to Michigan have

embraced a view of robbery that makes no distinction between attempted and completed robbery?

5. The dissent, by contrast, makes a point that you have seen elsewhere. There is a presumption that laws are consistent with the common law rules—and under the common law, robbery required asportation.

6. Is the dissent compelling when it observes that the legislature history reveals that the new law was only intending to reverse the *Randolph* decision and permit force before, during, or after a taking to be sufficient for a robbery conviction? Do we not assume that the legislature understands the words it is enacting?

7. The dissent objects that the majority has essentially eliminated the crime of assault with the intent to rob. Courts sometimes find the problem of one crime being covered by statutes with very different penalties problematic and at other times have not been concerned at all about the issue. Compare *Batchelder* (p. 102) and *Salamon* (p. 854).

---

2. Intent to Steal

See Larceny, at p. 950.

3. From the Person or Presence of the Victim

As you read the *Lake* case, you should see another example of a theme that has been developing in these property cases, indeed in many cases in which courts are called upon to interpret criminal statutes, at least in close cases. In these hard cases, there's often a tension between the literal words of a statute and the purpose of the statute. As you read *Lake*, consider which type of view then-Judge Alito and Judge Becker are taking of the federal carjacking statute, which is simply a special case of armed robbery. (And in case you haven't noticed, all of the cases in this book present close cases. That will not be true in much of your practice. Close cases, however, define legal boundaries and are therefore more prevalent in casebooks than they are on the call of an average criminal docket.)

United States v. Lake

United States Court of Appeals for the Third Circuit
150 F.3d 269 (1998)

ALITO, Circuit Judge

This is an appeal from a judgment in a criminal case. After a jury trial, the defendant, Hilton A. Lake, was convicted under 18 U.S.C. § 924(c)(1) of using or carrying a firearm during and in relation to a crime of violence, namely, a carjacking (see 18 U.S.C. § 2119). Lake challenges his conviction on numerous grounds, the most substantial of which is that he did not violate the carjacking statute because, he argues, he did not take the motor vehicle in question "from the person or presence" of the victim. We reject this and Lake's other arguments, and we therefore affirm.

I.

The events that led to Lake's prosecution occurred at Little Magen's Bay in St. Thomas, United States Virgin Islands. The road to the beach at Little Magen's Bay ends at the top of a hill. There is a steep path bordered by vegetation and rocks that leads from the road down to the beach, and the road cannot be seen from the beach.

On the day in question, Lake hitchhiked to Little Magen's Bay and encountered Milton Clarke, who was sitting on the beach reading a newspaper. Lake asked whether Clarke owned a white car parked up on the road. Clarke said that he did, and Lake initially walked away. However, Lake returned a few moments later and asked to borrow the car. When Clarke refused, Lake stated that it was an emergency. Clarke again refused, and Lake walked off. When Lake returned yet again, Clarke said:

> [L]isten, think about it. If I walked up to you and asked you, can I borrow your car[,] [a]re you going to lend it to me? Of course not. So why don't you leave me the hell alone. I'm here to have a nice time. Just chill. Go someplace else.

App. 140A.

Lake walked off and sat on a rock, while Clarke anxiously watched him out of the corner of his eye, but Lake soon returned with the same request. When Clarke swore again, Lake asked if he could have a drink from Clarke's cooler. Clarke said: "[D]on't you get it? Leave me alone." App. 141A. Lake then lifted up his shirt, showed Clarke the handle of a gun, and said: "[Y]ou know what that is?" App. 141A. Clarke stood up and started backing away, but Lake pulled the gun from his waist band, put it against Clarke's face, and demanded the car keys. App. 142A. Clarke said that he did not have the keys and started walking toward the water with Lake following. Clarke waded into waist-deep water, and Lake walked out onto a promontory overlooking the water. App. 143A-48A.

While Clarke was in the water, his friend, Pamela Croaker, appeared on the beach. Clarke shouted a warning, prompting Lake to approach Croaker. Lake demanded that Croaker surrender her car keys, and Croaker said:"I don't even know you. Why would I give you the keys to the car?" App. 183A. Lake then grabbed the keys, and the two wrestled for possession of the keys. When Croaker saw the gun, she surrendered the keys but asked to keep her house keys. App. 184A-86A. Lake went up the steep path to the parking area where Croaker had parked her car out of sight of the beach. Lake then drove away in Croaker's car after leaving her house keys on the hood of Clarke's car. App. 192A. As we will discuss later in more detail, both Croaker and Clarke followed him up the path, but when they arrived, he was driving away.

Later that day, the police apprehended Lake in the stolen car at a McDonald's restaurant. When questioned by the police and an FBI agent, Lake stated that he had used a toy gun and that he had thrown it in a swamp. He refused to take the officers to the site where he had allegedly disposed of the gun, and when asked to tell the truth about whether the gun was really a toy, he responded that he "would think about it." The gun was never recovered.

Lake was indicted for carjacking, in violation of 18 U.S.C. § 2119, and for using and carrying a firearm during and in relation to a crime of violence (the carjacking), in violation of 18 U.S.C. § 924(c)(1). At the close of the evidence in his jury trial, Lake moved unsuccessfully for a judgment of acquittal. The jury subsequently returned a verdict of not guilty of the carjacking charge but guilty of the firearms offense. Lake was sentenced to imprisonment for 60 months plus a three-year term of supervised release. He then took this appeal.

* * *

III.

Lake next argues that the evidence was insufficient to show that he violated the carjacking statute, 18 U.S.C. § 2119, and thus that he committed the predicate offense needed to support his 18 U.S.C. § 924(c)(1) conviction. Under the carjacking statute, 18 U.S.C. § 2119, the prosecution must prove that the defendant (1) "with intent to cause death or serious bodily harm" (2) took a motor vehicle (3) that had been "transported, shipped, or received in interstate or foreign commerce" (4) "from the person or presence of another" (5) "by force and violence or by intimidation." Lake contends that the evidence in this case was insufficient to prove elements one, three, and four. In reviewing the sufficiency of the evidence, we must decide whether the jury could have rationally found that each of the challenged elements had been established beyond a reasonable doubt. *United States v. Carr*, 25 F.3d 1194, 1201 (3d Cir.1994).

* * *

Lake maintains that the evidence did not show that he took Croaker's car "from [her] person or presence," as 18 U.S.C. § 2119 demands. Lake argues that he took her keys, not her car, from her person or presence and that the car was not in Croaker's presence when he took it because she could not see or touch the car at that moment.

The carjacking statute's requirement that the vehicle be taken "from the person or presence of the victim" "tracks the language used in other federal robbery statutes," H.R.Rep. No. 102-851(I), at 5 (1992), *reprinted in* 1992 U.S.C.C.A.N. 2829, 2834, such as 18 U.S.C. §§ 2111, 2113, and 2118. *See United States v. Perez-Garcia*, 56 F.3d 1, 3 (1st Cir.1995). Under these statutes, "property is in the presence of a person if it is 'so within his reach, observation or control, that he could if not overcome by violence or prevented by fear, retain his possession of it.'" *United States v. Burns*, 701 F.2d 840, 843 (9th Cir.1983). *See also United States v. W.T.T.*, 800 F.2d 780, 782 (8th Cir.1986); LaFave and Scott, *Substantive Criminal Law* § 8.11 at 443 (1986) ("'Presence' in this connection is not so much a matter of eyesight as it is one of proximity and control: the property taken in the robbery must be close enough to the victim and sufficiently under his control that, had the latter not been subjected to violence or intimidation by the robber, he could have prevented the taking").

Here, as previously described, Lake took Croaker's car keys at gunpoint on the beach and then ran up the path and drove away in her car. Croaker pursued Lake but did not reach the parking area in time to stop him. Applying the definition of "presence" noted above, we conclude that a rational jury could have found that Croaker could have prevented the taking of her car if she had not been fearful that Lake would shoot or otherwise harm her. Croaker testified that the sight of Lake's gun caused her great fear. She stated that when she first saw the gun she "felt like [she] was going to let go of [her] bowels [and] faint." App. 184A. Although Croaker did not say in so many words that she hesitated for some time before pursuing Lake up the path, the sequence of events laid out in her testimony supports the inference that this is what occurred. Croaker stated that at the point when she surrendered the keys, Clarke "was struggling back through the water to come back," App. 185A, but that she did not start to run up the path until Clarke emerged from the water. App. 186A. Clarke testified that, when Lake ran up the path, Croaker was "pulling herself together kind of." App.

150A. Clarke related that he "caught up to [Croaker] at the bottom of the paved driveway" and that the two of them proceeded up the path together. App. 150A. They reached the parking area in time for Croaker to see Lake driving away in her car but not in time to stop him. App. 186A. Both Croaker and Clarke stated that at this point they were very scared. App. 151A, 186A. Based on this testimony, a rational jury could infer that Croaker hesitated before pursuing Lake due to fear and that if she had not hesitated she could have reached the parking area in time to prevent Lake from taking her car without employing further force, violence, or intimidation. We do not suggest this inference was compelled, but because such an inference was rational, we hold that the evidence was sufficient.

* * *

BECKER, Chief Judge, dissenting.

When the defendant took the car keys from his victim, Pamela Croaker, Ms. Croaker's car was, in city terms, a block away, up the hill, out of sight. Under these circumstances, I would join an opinion upholding Lake's conviction for "keyjacking," or for both key robbery and grand larceny. I cannot, however, agree that he is guilty of carjacking. The majority draws upon federal robbery statutes to explicate how the vehicle (as opposed to its keys) may be considered to have been taken from the "person or presence of the victim." Disciples of the jurisprudence of pure reason may, in analytic terms, find this approach convincing. As I will explain below, I do not. At all events, my polestar is the plain meaning of words, and in my lexicon, Ms. Croaker's car cannot fairly be said to have been taken from her person or presence, hence I respectfully dissent.

The robbery statutes upon which the carjacking statute is based do not themselves define the phrase "from the person or presence of the victim." Webster's New International Dictionary defines presence as "the vicinity of, or area immediately near one." However, rather than relying on the plain meaning, the majority turns to a construction of the phrase "person or presence" adopted by the Ninth Circuit in *United States v. Burns*, 701 F.2d 840 (9th Cir.1983), where, in construing a federal robbery statute, that court reasoned that "property is in the presence of a person if it is 'so within his reach, inspection, observation or control, that he could if not overcome by violence or prevented by fear, retain his possession of it.'" *Id.* at 843. Based on this definition, the majority concludes that a rational jury "could infer that Croaker hesitated before pursuing Lake due to fear and that if she had not hesitated she could have reached the parking area in time to prevent Lake from taking her car without employing further force, violence, or intimidation." Maj. Op. at 273. This proves too much. If it is true that had Croaker not hesitated out of fear she could have followed Lake up the steep path leading from the secluded beach to the road, then it is equally true (barring physical limitations) that she could have followed him up that path and then halfway across St. Thomas. The fact that Croaker's car was nearby is thus not relevant; if she could have followed Lake up the hill, she could have followed him anywhere. I am aware, of course, that the craft of judging requires line-drawing, but I simply do not see how that endeavor can be principled when it is predicated on open-ended definitions of key statutory terms, especially where those terms admit of plain meaning.

The majority's reliance on a car robbery case to show that the evidence was sufficient to convict Lake of carjacking is of particular interest to me since, coupled with the typical fact pattern in federal carjacking cases, it strengthens my view that my dissent in *United States v. Bishop*, 66 F.3d 569 (3d. Cir.1995), was correct when it reasoned that the federal carjacking statute should be declared unconstitutional under the authority of *United States v. Lopez*, 514 U.S. 549, 115 S.Ct. 1624, 131 L.Ed.2d 626 (1995). The principal basis on which the *Bishop* majority found the carjacking statute to be a valid exercise of the interstate commerce power was the belief that carjacking is an adjunct of the interstate business of auto theft, in which the stolen vehicle is destined for a "chop shop." The majority adverted to references in the legislative history labeling carjacking as part of an economic enterprise in which profit is derived from the resale of stolen vehicles or their parts. In contrast, almost every carjacking case that I have seen or read about in the last several years-and there have been many-is a violent robbery in which the perpetrator has not even the remotest connection to a car theft ring or a chop shop.[2] The "effect on interstate commerce" underpinning of the carjacking statute is thus a chimera, and I hope that the Supreme Court will take up this issue before too long.[3]

Notes and Questions

This is not a course in Constitutional Law. You will learn about *Lopez* in another course. Judge Becker's concerns about the scope of federal authority is, however,

---

2 Indeed, the facts of the instant case are amongst the least egregious that I have seen where carjacking is alleged. That is probably because, as I have explained, this case does not involve a carjacking nor, for that matter, a car robbery.

3 In my view, carjacking cases are local crimes which belong in state courts not federal courts. *See Judicial Conference of the United States, Long Range Plan for the Federal Courts* 24 (Dec.1995) (Congress should be encouraged to allocate criminal jurisdiction to the federal courts only in limited situations; such a situation is not present where criminal activity has "some minor connection with and effect on interstate commerce".).

as much a comment about the *appropriate* use of federal power as it is the *constitutional* use of federal power. Note that in his second footnote, Judge Becker says that this is the least egregious carjacking case he has seen. Even though he clearly objects to the federal government prosecuting any of these cases, this case is itself an outlier for Judge Becker. Notice that Judge Becker does not, however, observe what consequences would flow, if he were in the majority, from his determination that this is the least egregious case he has seen. What do you think was his purpose in writing footnote 2.

---

4. By Means of Violence or Intimidation

a. When Must the Violence Occur

People v. Randolph

Supreme Court of Michigan
648 N.W.2d 164 (2002)

MARILYN J. KELLY, J.

On appeal from defendant's conviction for unarmed robbery, the Court of Appeals reversed the judgment for insufficient evidence and remanded for entry of a conviction of larceny in a building. 242 Mich.App. 417, 619 N.W.2d 168 (2000). It provided that the prosecutor could retry defendant on the original unarmed robbery charge if it had additional evidence. Both the prosecution and defendant appeal from that decision.

We conclude that defendant could not be convicted of unarmed robbery under the facts of this case. We also reassert that a defendant cannot be retried on a charge not previously supported by sufficient evidence where additional evidence is discovered to support it. Therefore, we affirm the Court of Appeals decision in part, reverse it in part, and remand for entry of a judgment of conviction of larceny in a building and for resentencing.

I. FACTUAL AND PROCEDURAL HISTORY

Defendant took merchandise valued at approximately $120 from a Meijer store. After purchasing other items, he left the store with a rotary tool, a battery, a battery charger, and a thermostat without paying for them. The store's loss-prevention staff observed the theft and acted to apprehend defendant when he emerged from the store.

There are several versions of what happened next. Taking the evidence in the light most favorable to the prosecution, when the plain-clothed security guards identified themselves, defendant lunged forward to run. At least one guard seized him, putting him in an "escort hold." Defendant broke free and swung his arm at the guards, physically assaulting at least one of them. In his efforts to escape, defendant lost possession of the merchandise. The prosecutor charged him with unarmed robbery, and a jury convicted him as charged. MCL 750.530.

When it reviewed defendant's unarmed robbery conviction, the Court of Appeals applied the "transactional approach," which it adopted explicitly in *People v. LeFlore*, 96 Mich.App. 557, 561-562, 293 N.W.2d 628 (1980). Under this approach, a defendant has not completed a robbery until he has escaped with stolen merchandise. Thus, a completed larceny may be elevated to a robbery if the defendant uses force after the taking and before reaching temporary safety. *See People v. Newcomb*, 190 Mich.App. 424, 430-431, 476 N.W.2d 749 (1991); *People v. Turner*, 120 Mich.App. 23, 28, 328 N.W.2d 5 (1982); *People v. Tinsley*, 176 Mich. App. 119, 120, 439 N.W.2d 313 (1989).

Applying that test, the Court of Appeals reasoned "there was insufficient evidence to support defendant's conviction of unarmed robbery because defendant was unsuccessful in escaping and thus he never completed the larcenous transaction." 242 Mich.App at 421, 619 N.W.2d 168. Therefore, it reversed the unarmed robbery conviction and remanded for entry of a conviction of larceny in a building, "unless the prosecutor opts to retry defendant on the original charge based on additional evidence." *Id.* at 423, 619 N.W.2d 168. We granted both parties' applications for leave to appeal. 465 Mich. 885, 636 N.W.2d 139 (2001).

II. UNARMED ROBBERY

Michigan's unarmed robbery statute, M.C.L. § 750.530, provides:

Any person who shall, *by force or violence, or by assault or putting in fear, feloniously rob, steal and take from the person of another, or in his presence,* any money or other property which may be the subject of larceny, such robber not being armed with a dangerous weapon, shall be guilty of a felony, punishable by imprisonment in the state.prison not more than 15 years. [Emphasis added.]

Robbery is a crime against a person. *People v. Hendricks*, 446 Mich. 435, 451, 521 N.W.2d 546 (1994). As the Court of Appeals acknowledged in *LeFlore*,[a] "Both the armed and unarmed robbery statutes are clear that the forceful act must be used to accomplish the taking."

We base our holding on the language of the unarmed robbery statute and the common-law history of unarmed robbery. From that we conclude that the force used to accomplish the taking underlying a charge of unarmed robbery must be contemporaneous with the taking. The force used later to retain stolen property is not included. Those Court of Appeals cases that have held otherwise, applying a "transactional approach" to unarmed robbery, are herein overruled.

A. Robbery at Common Law

Michigan's unarmed robbery statute is derived from the common law. The first robbery statutes, enacted in 1838, adopted the common-law definition of robbery, but divided the offense by levels of severity, depending on whether a perpetrator was armed. *People v. Calvin*, 60 Mich. 113, 120, 26 N.W. 851 (1886). The 1838 codification of unarmed robbery is nearly identical to our current statute.[5]

Other than stylistic changes, the only substantive modification since the first statute is the addition of the phrase "or in his presence." This modification is itself consistent with the common-law definition of robbery. *See* 4 Blackstone, *Commentaries, Public Wrongs*, ch. 17, p. 242 ("But if the taking be not either directly from his person, or in his presence, it is no robbery").

At common law the elements of the offense of robbery were "the felonious and forcible taking, from the person of another, of goods or money to any value by violence or putting him in fear." 4 Blackstone, Commentaries, Public Wrongs, ch. 17, p. 241; *see also, People v. Covelesky*, 217 Mich. 90, 96, 185 N.W. 770 (1921). The force or violence had to be applied before or during the taking. See *Id.* at 242. ("[T]he taking must be by force, or a *previous* putting in fear. . . .") (Emphasis added.) Accordingly, the common law concerning robbery that was received by the drafters and ratifiers of our constitution required (1) a taking from the person, (2) accomplished by an earlier or contemporaneous application of force or violence, or the threat of it. If force was used later to retain the property, the crime committed did not constitute robbery.

* * *

---

a　*Supra* at 562, 293 N.W.2d 628.

5　1838 RS, tit. 1, ch. 3, § 12 provided, with regard to unarmed robbery:

If any person shall, *by force and violence, or by assault or putting in fear, feloniously rob, steal and take from the person of another* any money or property, which may be the subject of larceny, (such robber not being armed with a dangerous weapon,) he shall be punished by imprisonment in the state prison not more than life, or for any term of years. [Emphasis added.]

The dissent offers the views of several other common-law commentators. However, read carefully, these commentators support the definition of robbery under the common law that we have related above. For example, Odgers states that common-law robbery consisted of "the unlawful taking possession of the goods of another by means of violence or threats of violence" and that the violence must occur "at the time of or *immediately before or immediately after* such robbery. . . ." 1 Odgers, *The Common Law of England* (2d ed.), ch. 8, p. 331. This definition acknowledges that the taking must be *by* violence or the threat of violence. In this case, the taking occurred without violence.

Contrary to the dissent's assertion, the use of the phrase "immediately before or immediately after" is consistent with our view that the use of force must be contemporaneous with the taking. Possibly, the dissent mis-apprehends the immediacy of the term "immediately." Odgers illustrated the point with the following: "[W]here the prisoner seized the prosecutor's watch and, on finding that it was secured by a chain around his neck, violently pulled and jerked until it broke, and then ran away with the watch, this was held to amount to robbery." *Id.* at 332, quoting *Rex v. Harman* (Harman's Case), 1 Hale, PC 534. Thus, force applied immediately after the taking is sufficiently contemporaneous. In this case, defendant did not use force until after he had completed the taking and left the store. Therefore, the use of force did not occur immediately after the taking.

* * *

It is useful to recall that at common law simple larceny was defined as "the felonious taking, and carrying away, of the personal goods of another." Blackstone, *supra*, p. 229; *see also, People v. Johnson*, 81 Mich. 573, 576, 45 N.W. 1119 (1890). Larceny was contrasted with robbery in that common-law larceny was a robbery minus the use of force to accomplish the taking and absent the requirement that the taking be "from the person." Blackstone stated this cogently when he summarized: "This previous violence or putting in fear, is the criterion that distinguishes robberies from other larcenies." *Id.* at 242.

We emphasize that a larceny is complete when the taking occurs. The offense does not continue. This fact is illustrated in *People v. Bradovich*,[11] in which two defendants in a store concealed two suits under their own clothing and attempted to leave. Realizing that store personnel were following them and that they would be apprehended, they abandoned the stolen clothing and departed. When later charged with larceny, they claimed to have abandoned the property before leaving the store, and therefore, not to have completed the

---

11   305 Mich. 329, 9 N.W.2d 560 (1943).

offense. This Court disagreed, holding that the larceny was complete when the thieves concealed the store's clothing under their own. *Id.* at 332, 9 N.W.2d 560.

The dissent acknowledges that larceny and robbery are distinct crimes. That the two crimes are distinct offenses indicates nothing more than that they have different elements: robbery is a larceny aggravated by the fact that the taking is from the person, or in his presence, accomplished with force or the threat of force. *People v. Wakeford*, 418 Mich. 95, 127-128, 341 N.W.2d 68 (1983) (opinion of Levin, J.).

However, the dissent asserts without supporting authority that "for the purpose of the crime of robbery, the relevant act encompasses a broader spectrum of time, and includes not simply an initial larcenous taking, 'by force and violence' or 'by assault,' but a robbing of the victim 'by assault' when the property remains in the victim's presence." Op. at 563, 648 N.W.2d at 181. Neither the common law nor contemporary authority supports the view that the taking that establishes the larceny element of robbery continues until the robber reaches a place of temporary safety.

* * *

We are also persuaded by *Tennessee v. Owens*,[12] where the Tennessee Supreme Court was faced with the question, "[H]ow closely connected in time must the taking and the violence be?" By way of response, the court compared the language of Tennessee's robbery statute with the language of other states' robbery statutes. The court noted that many jurisdictions have rejected the common-law rule in favor of the "continuous offense theory." *Id.* at 638-639, 639, n. 7.

However, most of those states have statutes that specifically define robbery to include the use of force to retain property or to escape. *Id.* at 639. Many of the statutes provide that a person commits robbery if he uses force "in the course of committing" a theft or larceny. See Ala. Code 1975, § 13A-8-43; Ariz. Rev. Stat., §§ 13-1901-1904; Conn. Gen. Stat., § 53a-133; Del. Code. Ann., tit. 11, § 831; Fla. Stat., § 812.13; Haw. Rev. Stat., § 708-841; Minn. Stat., § 609.24; Mont. Code Ann., § 45-5-401; N.J. Stat. Ann., § 2C:15-1; N.Y. Penal Laws, § 160.00; ND Cent. Code, § 12.1-22-01; Or. Rev. Stat., § 164.395; Tex. Penal Code Ann., § 29.02; Utah Code Ann., § 76-6-301.

All the statutes define "in the course of" to include either "escape," "flight," "retention," or "subsequent to the taking." In other jurisdictions that follow this approach, the statutes specifically include the expressions "resisting

---

12 20 S.W.3d 634 (Tenn., 2000).

apprehension,"[13] "facilitate escape,"[14] "fleeing immediately after,"[15] or used to "retain possession."[16]

By contrast, other jurisdictions have statutes that follow the common-law rule requiring that the force, violence, or putting in fear occur before or contemporaneous with the larcenous taking. These states have statutes substantially similar to Michigan's. *See* Ga. Code Ann., § 16-8-40; Ind. Code, § 35-42-5-1; Kan. Stat. Ann., § 21-3426; Miss. Code Ann., § 97-3-73; N.M. Stat. Ann., § 30-16-2; Tenn. Code Ann., § 39-13-401; *see also* 93 A.L.R.3d 647-649.

In summary, at common law, a robbery required that the force, violence, or putting in fear occur before or contemporaneous with the larcenous taking. If the violence, force, or putting in fear occurred after the taking, the crime was not robbery, but rather larceny and perhaps assault. Hence, the "transactional approach" espoused by the Court of Appeals is without pedigree in our law and must be abandoned. . . .

III. ANALYSIS OF THE CASE ON APPEAL

Turning to the facts of this case, the prosecution seeks to extend the transaction that began with the in-store taking to include the struggle in the parking lot. We point out that defendant not only failed to escape, but, more importantly, did not accomplish his taking by the use of force, violence, assault, or putting in fear.

While store security personnel observed him, defendant removed several items from the display shelves of the Meijer store and concealed them beneath his coat. He continued to retain possession of this property as he picked up two quarts of oil, went to a checkout lane, paid for the oil and walked from the store. The first use of force or violence was in the parking lot when a security guard attempted to restrain him. Hence, his use of force or violence was not to take the property, but to retain it and escape apprehension. It follows that defendant did not commit the offense of unarmed robbery.

The dissent makes much of the fact that the unarmed robbery statute applies to a taking from "the person of another, *or in his presence,*" but overlooks the context of that language. The dissent relies heavily on the notion of constructive possession and the intent to permanently deprive. However, we are left without a satisfactory explanation of why the use of force that does not accomplish a taking would escalate the offense of larceny to unarmed robbery.

---

13   Ark. Code Ann., § 5-12-102.

14   Nev. Rev. Stat., § 200.380.

15   Ohio Rev. Code Ann, § 2911.01.

16   Wash. Rev. Code, § 9A.56.190.

The dissent asserts that force used after a taking, while the victim has constructive possession of stolen property or while it is in the victim's presence, supports a charge of robbery. Notably, however, in each of the dissent's examples, the force used was to accomplish the ultimate taking. That did not occur in this case. The dissent attempts to merge a subsequent force not used to accomplish a taking with the completed taking that preceded the force.[18]

We think it significant that the statute identifies unarmed robbery as the taking of another's property in the other's presence "*by* force and violence, or *by* assault or putting in fear." MCL 750.530 (emphasis added). If the physical taking were accomplished without force, assault, or fear, the statute does not permit treating the larcenous crime as a robbery because of a subsequent forceful act. Such force used to retain stolen property is simply outside the scope of M.C.L. § 750.530. That defendant cannot be convicted of unarmed robbery is particularly clear here, because his force by no means accomplished a severing of the store's constructive possession of the merchandise.

We note that defendant's taking of the merchandise in this case is indistinguishable from the taking in *Bradovich*. Therefore, when defendant placed the merchandise under his clothing, he committed a taking without force, and his conduct constituted a completed larceny. The concealment evidences that, at the time he took the merchandise, defendant intended to permanently deprive the owner, Meijer, of it. Defendant's later acts, whether viewed as an unsuccessful attempt to retain the property or as an attempt to escape, are too removed from the completed taking to be considered contemporaneous.

* * *

V. CONCLUSION

In conclusion, the Court of Appeals correctly determined that there was insufficient evidence to support defendant's conviction for unarmed robbery. Because the defendant completed a taking without using force, violence, assault, or putting in fear, he could not be convicted of unarmed robbery.

We remand to the trial court for entry of a conviction for larceny in a building and for resentencing. Defendant cannot be retried for unarmed robbery. The opinion of the Court of Appeals is affirmed in part and reversed in part.

MICHAEL F. CAVANAGH, TAYLOR, and YOUNG, JJ., concurred with MARILYN J. KELLY, J.

---

18 Certainly, as the dissent asserts, it may be wise to wait to apprehend a thief who has not used force or violence until after he has left a populated store. In so doing, however, one would be apprehending a thief who committed larceny, not a robber.

MARKMAN, J. (dissenting).

I respectfully dissent. In affirming the Court of Appeals, the majority concludes that this Court has never adopted the "transactional approach" to robbery. Op. at 542, 648 N.W.2d at 170. The majority then proceeds to overrule more than thirty years of precedent in the Court of Appeals applying this view. In doing so, the majority states that "the force used to accomplish the taking underlying a charge of unarmed robbery must be contemporaneous with the taking." Op. at 536, 648 N.W.2d at 167. The majority concludes that defendant in this case "did not accomplish his taking by use of force, violence, assault, or putting in fear." Op. at 547, 648 N.W.2d at 172. Therefore, the majority concludes that defendant cannot be convicted of unarmed robbery. I strongly disagree with this analysis.

In my judgment, a person is guilty of the crime of robbery if, before reaching a place of temporary safety, the person uses force either to effect his initial taking of the property, or to retain possession of the property or to escape with the property, as long as the property remains "in [the] presence" of the victim. MCL 750.530. The language of the robbery statute, Michigan case law, and the common-law understanding of robbery each support the view that a person can be convicted of robbery even if the required element of force occurs after the perpetrator's initial seizure of the property, but before he has reached a place of temporary safety. Therefore, I would reverse the judgment of the Court of Appeals.

* * *

Because the statute, and the case law interpreting the statute, provide that the property may be "in the presence" of the victim, "actual possession" of the property by the victim at the time that the force is used is not required. MCL 750.530, *see also People v. Newcomb*, 190 Mich.App. 424, 430-431, 476 N.W.2d 749 (1991). The property continues to be "in [the] presence" of the victim where the property remains under his personal protection and control. *Id.*, *see also People v. Covelesky*, 217 Mich. 90, 97, 185 N.W. 770 (1921). It follows that, as long as the victim exercises this protection and control over the property, the requisite force element of robbery may still be used against him, because the property is still "in his presence". MCL 750.530. Thus, where an assault occurs at any time during which the property can be said to be in the victim's presence, a robbery within the meaning of the statute occurs. In this case, although defendant had initially seized items from the shelf of the Meijer's store, the security guards continued to exercise protective custody and control over that property, because they continued to monitor defendant and they still had the right to take the property back. Therefore, the property was "in [their] presence" within the meaning of M.C.L.

§ 750.530 when defendant, by assault, attempted to unlawfully deprive the security guards of the property. This "transactional view" of robbery,[2] as it has been applied in Michigan, is consistent with both the common-law definition and the statute defining robbery, and supports defendant's conviction.

* * *

The majority, in my judgment, errs in its analysis of the crime of robbery by interpreting too narrowly the statute's requirements of the force element, the act element, and the concept of possession. As a consequence, the majority's conclusion that defendant "did not use force, violence, assault or putting in fear to accomplish his taking of property" is also in error. Op. at 550, 648 N.W.2d at 174.

The statute requires only that the force and violence *or* the assault occur at some point during which the property is "in the presence" of the victim. The statute does not limit the force element to the initial seizure of the property. A robbery may occur "by force and violence" *or* "by assault" as long as the property remains "in [the] presence" of the victim. The property is in the presence of the victim, although it is in the actual physical possession of the perpetrator, where the victim exercises protective custody and control over the property. This is in accord with the statute.

* * *

MCL 750.530 provides:

Any person who shall, by force and violence, or by assault or putting in fear, feloniously rob, steal and take from the person of another, or in his presence, any money or other property which may be the subject of larceny, such robber not being armed with a dangerous weapon, shall be guilty of a felony. . . .

It is a settled rule of statutory construction that, unless otherwise defined in a statute, this Court will ascribe every statutory word or phrase its plain and ordinary meaning. *See* M.C.L. § 8.3a. Further, this Court shall ensure that words in a statute are not ignored, treated as surplusage, or rendered nugatory. *Hoste v. Shanty Creek Mngt, Inc.*, 459 Mich. 561, 574, 592 N.W.2d 360 (1999).

Here, to describe the element of force, the Legislature used the words "by force and violence, or by assault or putting in fear". MCL 750.530. To describe the act that must be accomplished, the Legislature used the words "rob," "steal," and

---

2   The "transaction" designates the events occurring between the time of the initial seizure of the property and the eventual removal of such property from the victim's presence.

"take," and to describe the allowable possession of the property that is subject to the robbery, the Legislature used the words "in his presence."

The majority argues that a robbery occurs only when a person, by force and violence, or by assault or putting in fear, uses that force initially to seize the property from the person of another, or in his presence. But, the statute plainly allows for more. A robbery occurs under the statute where, by force and violence or by assault, the perpetrator takes property from the person or in his presence. That is, where the robber initially seizes the property by force and violence or by assault. However, the statute also allows for a conviction of robbery where, "by assault" the perpetrator "robs" property that is "in [the] presence" of the victim. The phrase "by assault" cannot mean the same thing as "by force and violence." Rather, "assault" is defined simply as "a sudden violent attack." *Random House Webster's College Dictionary* (1991). The term is also defined more broadly as "illegal force." Black's Law Dictionary (6th ed.).

Further, the word "rob" cannot encompass merely the taking of the property, because the term "take" is already used in the statute. The Legislature is not presumed to have used different terms to mean the same thing. Here, the Legislature used the words "rob," "steal," and "take." "Rob" means to "[u]nlawfully deprive (a person) of or of something, esp. by force or the threat of force." *The New Shorter Oxford English Dictionary* (1993).

Thus, the statute, summarized, provides: "Any person who shall . . . by assault . . . rob . . . [property] from the person of another or in his presence . . . shall be guilty . . ." That is, a person may be guilty of robbery if "by assault" he "robs" property that is "in [the] presence" of the victim. As the majority recognizes, the defendant in this case committed an assault upon the security guards. Because the security guards exercised protective custody and control over that property, it remained in their "presence". Viewing the evidence in a light most favorable to the prosecutor, the assault was committed so that the defendant could remove the property "from [the] presence" of the security guards. Defendant's violent act of assault evidenced his intent to unlawfully and permanently deprive the guards of the property.

The majority asserts that the dissent misapprehends the context of the statutory phrase "in his presence". The majority emphasizes the words "*by* force and violence, or *by* assault or putting in fear," op. at 548, 648 N.W.2d at 173, and assumes that these words apply *only* to the initial taking itself, and therefore, concludes: "the statute identifies unarmed robbery as taking another's property in the other's presence '*by* force and violence, or *by* assault or putting in fear,'" and "[i]f the physical taking was accomplished without force, assault, or fear, the statute does not permit treating the larcenous crime as a robbery because of a subsequent forceful act." *Id.*

However, as I have indicated, I believe that, although property may be in the actual and wrongful possession of the perpetrator, it may still be "in [the] presence" of the victim such that the perpetrator may still, "by assault," "rob" the victim. MCL 750.530. While the statute provides that the act must be accomplished "by force and violence, or by assault," the requisite act is more than a mere taking or initial larceny of the property as evidenced by the statute's employment of the word "rob." As we have already indicated, "rob" means more broadly an unlawful deprivation of property by force.[5]

Therefore, although a larceny may be complete when the perpetrator initially wrongfully takes and conceals the property, the statute encompasses not merely a larceny, but a "rob[bing], steal[ing], and tak[ing]" by force and violence, or by assault or putting in fear, of property, that is "in [the] presence" of the victim. MCL 750.530. Thus, while through an initial larceny the perpetrator may steal property, he may not yet have "rob[bed]" that same property. Thus, an assault to "rob" may occur after the initial seizure of the property.

* * *

Thus, as long as the property is in the presence of the victim, that is, before the perpetrator reaches a place of "temporary safety," a robbery can occur when the perpetrator with actual possession attempts to sever the property from the victim's presence "by force and violence, or by assault or putting in fear." MCL 750.530.[9]

* * *

To clarify, consider the perpetrator who is observed shoplifting and manages to escape from the store before being apprehended. In such a case, the only crime that occurs is a larceny. The larceny is complete upon the perpetrator's concealment of the item, for it is at that time that the intent to deprive the owner of the property merged with the actual taking.

---

5   The majority approaches the statute in a piecemeal fashion, restricting its application to the initial act of defendant's seizure of the property, and ignoring the significance of the terms "by assault", "rob" and "in his presence." Indeed, in *People v. Calvin*, 60 Mich. 113, 119, 26 N.W. 851 (1886), the offense of robbery was described by this Court as separating these two phrases. Describing the robbery statute, the Court stated, of unarmed robbery, that "the offense is perpetrated by force and violence ... and robbing, stealing, and taking from the person of another, the robber not being armed with a dangerous weapon." *Id.*, citing How. Stat. § 9091.

9 The concept of "temporary safety" describes the point beyond which the property is no longer in the presence of the victim. Practically, the perpetrator has escaped. At this point, the perpetrator has consummated his wrongful possession by fully converting the property to his own use and may, unless apprehended, do with the property as he sees fit. Upon reaching a place of temporary safety, the perpetrator finally exercises full "dominion and control" over the property. Wharton, note 7, *supra*. However, until that point, the victim is viewed as continuing to exercise protective custody and control over his property. *Covelesky, supra* at 97-98, 185 N.W. 770.

Next consider the perpetrator who is observed shoplifting and who is followed out into the parking lot. Before being confronted by the security guards, he drops the property onto the ground or he is apprehended. Again, the crime is larceny, for no further criminal intent may be inferred from his acts.

Finally, consider the perpetrator who uses force in the parking lot, as in this case, while he is still in actual possession of the property. The perpetrator is still viewed under the robbery statute as having robbed the victim because the property was still in the victim's presence when the assault occurred. The property was at the time of the thief's initial taking of it, and is still at the time of the assault, "in [the] presence" of the victim. MCL 750.530. The security guards continued to exercise "protective custody and control" over the property. *Covelesky, supra* at 97-98, 185 N.W. 770.

* * *

[A]n analysis of the common law supports the view that force used after an initial wrongful seizure of property, to prevent the victim's resistance or to escape with the property, is sufficient to satisfy the elements of the crime of robbery. The common-law crime of robbery was defined as "the unlawful taking possession of the goods of another by means of violence or threats of violence, used with the object of obtaining those goods from the owner, without his consent and with the intention of depriving him permanently of all the benefits of his ownership." 1 Odgers, The Common Law of England (2d ed.), ch. 8, p. 331. In this work, which is a compilation of "all important statutes and decisions," the authors declare that where a person "used any personal violence at the time of or immediately before or immediately after such robbery, he may be sentenced" as a robber was at that time, "to penal servitude for life." *Id.* The difference between larceny and robbery is further explained: "If the only violence used occurs accidentally and unintentionally in the prisoner's efforts to obtain possession of the property, the offence is larceny from the person and not robbery. But if violence is necessary to enable the prisoner to obtain possession of the property, and the prisoner on discovering this intentionally resorts to violence with that object, this is robbery." *Id.* at 332. In an example that follows, the author sets out the distinction between the successful escape and the violent altercation before the robber completes the escape:

Thus, the snatching of a purse from a prosecutor, who is unaware of what is happening until after the purse is gone from his possession, cannot amount to robbery; but it will be otherwise if the prisoner does something to put the prosecutor in bodily fear before snatching the purse, for here the fear precedes the taking.

So, if the prisoner obtains possession of the property without actual violence or threats of violence, the crime is only larceny from the person, unless the prisoner immediately after taking possession of the property uses personal violence. [*Id.*]

* * *

Finally, I would point out that the transactional approach to robbery has the added practical advantage of being defined by a fixed beginning and end. Where does the majority draw this line? Can one never be convicted of robbery if he uses force to retain property or to escape simply because such force occurs after he has initially taken the property? When does the majority believe that a taking is completed? If a perpetrator does not use force at the moment he physically removes property from the shelf of a market and conceals it, would it be sufficient if he uses force when he is prevented from leaving the proximity of that shelf; when attempting to leave the particular aisle or department; when passing through the checkout area; or when attempting to leave the store itself? Is the fact that one purports to conceal the property beneath his clothes sufficient to find that he could not thereafter commit a robbery? In contrast to the lack of the majority's definition of "contemporaneous", the transactional approach to robbery recognizes that the use of force that occurs at any time before the perpetrator of a larceny has reached a place of temporary safety transforms such larceny into a robbery.

CONCLUSION

In my judgment, the "transactional view" of robbery as it has been described in this opinion, is deeply rooted both in the common law, and in the Michigan statute and case law. Under the "transactional view", a person can be convicted of robbery if, before reaching a place of temporary safety, such person uses force to permanently deprive an owner of the actual or constructive possession of his property. Such force may either be employed in initially taking the property, in attempting to retain the property, or in attempting to escape with the property. Defendant here used force in an attempt either to retain the property or to escape with the property. Therefore, I would reverse the judgment of the Court of Appeals and reinstate defendant's unarmed robbery conviction.

CORRIGAN, C.J., and WEAVER, J., concurred with MARKMAN, J.

Notes and Questions

1. As you recall from the *Williams* case (p. 1011), at a minimum, the Michigan Legislature reversed the *Randolph* opinion and allowed a robbery conviction if the force was used or attempted "in the course" of committing a larceny.

2. An analysis done of the proposed bill to reverse the *Randolph* opinion, which passed a unanimous Michigan Legislature, laid out the pros and cons of the proposed law. It is interesting how evenly divided the Supreme Court of Michigan was on this issue—and that the states are divided on this issue—but the Michigan Legislature was unanimous.

   > *For:*
   >
   > Currently, a charge of robbery can only be made if force or violence were used to commit the larceny. Revising the statutes will allow prosecutors more latitude to prosecute similar crimes in similar ways. For example, under the recent court interpretation of the robbery laws, it would be a crime of armed robbery if a gun were brandished immediately before or while property was being taken. However, it would not be a crime of armed robbery if the gun was not brandished until the suspect was trying to evade capture by a security guard or passerby. The bill would revise the state's robbery statutes to include any crime of larceny that involved the use of force or violence, or fear, at any time during the commission of the crime. Therefore, if force or violence were used to take property, to retain property, or to evade apprehension after taking property, the act could constitute robbery. This would also apply to carjacking. Since armed and unarmed robbery convictions would result in stiffer sentences, prosecutors and judges would be given an important tool with which to protect the public and more appropriately punish wrongdoers.
   >
   > *For:*
   >
   > Before the 2002 state supreme court decision interpreted the robbery statutes as applying only in those cases in which force or violence were used in the taking of property, the state's appellate courts were moving towards what is known as the "transactional approach". Under the transactional approach, the crime was looked at as commencing at the point in time that the taking occurred and ending at the point in time when the suspect reached temporary safety. Even

though this approach included as robbery some acts that would not be considered robbery under the *Randolph* decision, it still is problematic. For example, say property is taken from a convenience store without force, but force is used to keep possession of the stolen property or in an attempt to flee from a security guard or police officer. Under the transactional approach, the crime would be elevated to robbery if the suspect escaped apprehension and attained temporary safety but would not be robbery if the suspect were apprehended by the security guard or police officer because that means he or she had never attained temporary safety. Moreover, the current law reflects the mindset of the early 1830s, whereas the bill is similar to revisions other states have made that include not only the actual taking or larceny as the crime of robbery, but also those acts committed in trying to keep possession of the property and acts committed in trying to escape apprehension. Unless the armed and unarmed robbery and carjacking statutes are revised legislatively, the *Randolph* decision will hold precedence and prosecutors will lose an important tool in appropriately charging potentially dangerous criminals.

Against:

The *Randolph* court interpreted the robbery statutes based on a strict reading of the current language and the common law view of robbery at the time the law was codified in the late 1830s. It could be argued that the law has served many prosecutors and protected the public well for a very long time. The required element of using force or violence to accomplish the taking is there for a reason, and so distinguishes this crime from general larceny crimes such as shoplifting or stealing from a home when no one is there. To broaden the scope of what constitutes robbery could blur this distinction. It is conceivable, therefore, that a person who shoplifts a candy bar from a convenience store, but then panics and punches or slaps the store owner who chases him or her in an attempt to flee, could face a felony robbery charge with its longer incarceration penalties rather than a misdemeanor larceny offense. If he or she brandished a gun or a knife to scare the store owner into releasing him or her, even if no harm were done to the store owner, he or she could face up to life in prison for armed robbery. Yet, even without the bill, if someone is harmed or threatened with harm by a suspect trying to escape or trying to keep possession of the stolen goods, prosecutors can add other charges such as aggravated assault, felony assault, and others as fit the particulars of a case. Therefore, the bill really is not needed, as prosecutors already have the tools needed to appropriately prosecute crimes on a case by case basis. It is true that some multiple charges result in the sentences being served concurrently, and that the bill could result in prosecutors putting some people away longer, but it seems that the distinction between the crime of robbery and other larceny crimes shouldn't be dissolved.

First Analysis, House Bill 5105, Feb. 12, 2004.

3. The majority objects to minor distinctions having significant effects on how a defendant is punished. But the majority's position is not free from such consequences. What would the majority position hold if the defendant had "fumbled" the property, so that in a struggle it temporarily went into the possession of the security guard, but the defendant reacquired possession?

---

b. Contact Required for Force

The Michigan Supreme Court observed in *People v. Williams* that force was the most important component of robbery. The *Butts* opinion reveals, however, that force is not a terribly difficult standard to satisfy.

Butts v. State

Court of Appeals of Alaska
53 P.3d 609 (2002)

COATS, Chief Judge.

A jury convicted Clynton D. Butts of robbery in the second degree for forcibly taking a woman's purse from her. He appeals his conviction, arguing that the trial court erred in refusing to dismiss the indictment against him and that his sentence is excessive. We affirm.

Butts was indicted on January 20, 1999, for robbery in the second degree. The grand jury and trial testimony described the basis of the charge as follows: Butts accosted Cheryl Joens in the parking lot of the Bentley Mall Safeway in Fairbanks at about 10:30 p.m. on January 14, 1999. Joens heard footsteps, saw Butts running toward her, and felt him grab her purse. She screamed and struggled with Butts over her purse. She ended up on the ground, still struggling with Butts over her purse. After it was clear Butts was not going to give up the purse, Joens allowed Butts to pull the purse from her grasp in fear he would attack her with a weapon. Butts took her purse and ran away.

Joseph Fields was in the parking lot during the incident. He heard Joens scream, turned, saw Butts tackle her, and ran to help Joens. He yelled at Butts to stop. When Butts took the purse and ran, Fields chased him-first on foot, then in his car.

Mark Herz, also in the parking lot during the incident, saw the others and chased Butts in his vehicle. He and Fields followed Butts, who dropped the purse while running through a number of neighboring parking lots to the Back Door Lounge.

Butts entered the Back Door Lounge and, after meeting with another man, ran through the parking lot to nearby woods. The Fairbanks Police Department and Alaska State Troopers responded. Trooper Scott Johnson used a police dog to track Butts to a snow berm where he was hiding. Butts surrendered, stating that he had taken the purse because he owed $200 on a drug debt and that the man he owed the debt had a gun. Butts later told Fairbanks Police Detective Aaron Ring that he had taken the purse because he needed drug money.

Butts's first trial ended in a hung jury. But in a second trial, conducted by Superior Court Judge pro tem Raymond M. Funk, a jury convicted Butts of robbery in the second degree.

* * *

Butts's Challenge To His Indictment: Did He Commit a Taking By "Force"?

After Butts was indicted for robbery, he asked the superior court to dismiss the indictment on the ground that the prosecutor failed to instruct the grand jurors on the statutory definition of "force." Alaska Statute 11.81.900(b)(26) defines "force" as

> any bodily impact, restraint, or confinement or the threat of imminent bodily impact, restraint, or confinement[.]

Butts asserted that the grand jurors needed special instruction on this issue because the statutory definition of "force" differs significantly from the normal, everyday definition and because, given the facts of his case, the grand jurors reasonably might have concluded that Butts did not use "force" when he took the purse from Joens.

As explained above, the state presented evidence that Butts ran up to Joens and took hold of her purse. When Joens refused to let go of her property, Butts engaged in a tugging match with her, attempting to wrest the purse from her grasp. During this struggle, Joens fell to the ground. Joens believed that Butts would injure her if she did not relinquish the purse, so she let go.

Butts concedes that, under the everyday meaning of "force," he took Joens's purse by force. Butts argues, however, that if the grand jurors had understood that Alaska law defines "force" in a specialized, limited way, they might have refused to indict him-because, under the above facts, one reasonably could conclude that Butts did not effect any bodily impact on Joens, nor did he threaten her with bodily impact.

Butts's argument runs contrary to the generally accepted law on this issue. The dividing line between "purse snatching" (*i.e.*, theft from the person) and robbery is described in *Substantive Criminal Law* by LaFave and Scott:

> The line between robbery and larceny from the person . . . is not always easy to draw. The "snatching" cases, for instance, have given rise to some dispute. The great weight of authority, however, supports the view that there is not sufficient force to constitute robbery [if] . . . the thief snatches property from the owner's grasp so suddenly that the owner cannot offer any resistance to the taking. On the other hand, when the owner, aware of an impending snatching, resists it, or when[ ] the thief's first attempt . . . to separate the owner from his property [is ineffective and] a struggle . . . is necessary before the thief can get possession [of the property], there is enough force to make the taking robbery.[4]

Under this general rule, the sudden snatching of a purse, briefcase, or satchel will be only a theft. But if "a struggle ensues, where the victim is knocked down, or where the victim is put in fear," the crime will be robbery.[5] It is the act of "wresting" or "wrenching" (as opposed to merely "grabbing" or "snatching") that makes the offense a robbery.[6] "[E]ven [a] slight tug on the arm by the purse

---

4   2 Wayne R. LaFave & Austin W. Scott, Jr., *Substantive Criminal Law*, § 8.11(d)(1), p. 445 (1986) (citation omitted); *see also* Peter G. Guthrie, Annotation, *Purse Snatching as Robbery or Theft*, 42 A.L.R.3d 1381, 1383 (1972).

5   *Winn v. Commonwealth*, 21 Va.App. 179, 462 S.E.2d 911, 913 (1995).

6   *See State v. Sein*, 124 N.J. 209, 590 A.2d 665, 669-70 (1991).

thief who must use force to wrench the purse from the arm of the victim" is enough to convert the theft to a robbery.[7]

Thus, in *State v. Williams*,[8] the Connecticut Supreme Court affirmed a robbery conviction arising from a purse-snatching in which the victim suffered bruises on her shoulder.[9] The court concluded that, based on these bruises, the jury reasonably could have inferred that the victim offered resistance to the force exerted by the thief in attempting to wrench the shoulder strap from her-a resistance that converted the purse-snatching into a robbery.[10] Other courts have ruled that the resistance needed to convert a theft to robbery can arise simply from the fact that the victim's property was "so attached to the victim's person or clothing as to create resistance to the taking."[11]

However, even though these cases reject Butts's argument that his conduct did not amount to robbery, they are not conclusive authority on this question. Many of these states have definitions of robbery and force that differ from Alaska's. In particular, very few jurisdictions have definitions of "force" that restrict this term to "bodily impact," "restraint," and "confinement."

Under Alaska law, the ultimate issue is whether Butts effected a "bodily impact" on Joens when he grabbed her purse and tried to wrest it from her while she held on and resisted his efforts. We therefore must decide whether the phrase "bodily impact" includes indirect contacts such as this-instances where the defendant does not actually touch the victim but, instead, exerts impact on property that is attached to the victim or that the victim is holding onto. For the reasons stated below, we conclude that "bodily impact" does include such indirect contacts.

We reach this conclusion, in part, by analogy to the civil tort of battery, which consists of the intentional unlawful touching of another. This tort can be committed through an indirect touching of the victim- *i.e.*, by touching the victim's clothing or articles of property connected to the victim's body. This concept is explained in *Restatement (Second) of Torts*:

---

7   *Mackbee v. State*, 575 So.2d 16, 36 (Miss.1990) (quoting *Commonwealth v. Brown*, 506 Pa. 169, 484 A.2d 738, 742 (1984)).

8   202 Conn. 349, 521 A.2d 150 (1987), *overruled on other grounds, Griffin v. United States*, 502 U.S. 46, 112 S.Ct. 466, 116 L.Ed.2d 371 (1991).

9   *Id.* at 155-56.

10   *Id.* at 155.

11   *People v. Brooks*, 202 Ill.App.3d 164, 147 Ill.Dec. 519, 559 N.E.2d 859, 862 (1990), *abrogated on other grounds, People v. Williams*, 149 Ill.2d 467, 174 Ill.Dec. 829, 599 N.E.2d 913, 917 (1992); *accord, Raiford v. State*, 52 Md.App. 163, 447 A.2d 496, 500 (1982), *aff'd in pertinent part*, 296 Md. 289, 462 A.2d 1192 (1983).

Since the essence of the plaintiff's grievance consists in the offense to the dignity involved in the unpermitted and intentional invasion of the inviolability of his [or her] person and not in any physical harm done to his [or her] body, it is not necessary that the plaintiff's actual body be disturbed. Unpermitted and intentional contacts with anything so connected with the body as to be customarily regarded as part of the other's person and therefore as partaking of its inviolability [are] actionable as an offensive contact with [the victim's] person. There are some things such as clothing or a cane or, indeed, anything directly grasped by the hand which are so intimately connected with one's body as to be universally regarded as part of the person.[12]

Thus, in *Fisher v. Carrousel Motor Hotel, Inc.*,[13] the defendant snatched a patron's dinner plate from his hands without touching the patron.[14] The Texas Supreme Court held that the intentional grabbing of the patron's plate constituted battery.[15] Also, in *Morgan v. Loyacomo*,[16] the Mississippi Supreme Court held that the defendant's act of forcibly seizing a package from under a customer's arm constituted battery.[7]

This same principle applies in prosecutions for criminal battery. Direct physical contact between the defendant and the victim is not required; the crime can be committed by the indirect application of unlawful force.[18]

For example, in *State v. Gammil*,[19] the New Mexico Court of Appeals held that the defendant committed the crime of aggravated battery in circumstances much like Butts's case: the defendant grabbed the victim's purse and then, attempting to wrest control of the purse, spun around-with the result that the victim was thrown to the ground.[20] In *State v. Ortega*,[21] the court held that a defendant could be convicted of battery upon a police officer even if the jury

---

12   *Restatement (Second) of Torts* § 18 Cmt. C (1965).

13   424 S.W.2d 627 (Tex.1967).

14   *Id.* at 629.

15   *Id.* at 629-30.

16   190 Miss. 656, 1 So.2d 510 (1941).

17   *Id.* at 511.

18   *See generally* LaFave & Scott, *supra* note 4, § 7.15(b), at 303.

19   108 N.M. 208, 769 P.2d 1299 (App.1989), *overruled on other grounds, State v. Fuentes*, 119 N.M. 104, 888 P.2d 986, 988 (App.1994).

20   *Id.* at 1301.

21   113 N.M. 437, 827 P.2d 152 (App.1992).

believed the defendant's testimony that he merely grabbed the officer's flashlight and knocked it from the officer's hand.[22] And in *Nash v. State*,[23] the Florida Court of Appeals held that a criminal battery is committed not only by the intentional unlawful touching of the victim's person but also the touching of "an object that has such an intimate connection to the person as to be regarded as a part or extension of the person, such as clothing or an object held by the person."[24] The court concluded that the defendant was properly convicted of battery when he "intentionally touched the victim's closely held purse against her will."[25]

Neither the legislative history of our robbery statute nor the legislative history of our statutory definition of "force" gives any indication that our legislature intended to depart from these established rules of criminal law. We therefore construe the term "bodily impact" in AS 11.81.900(b)(26) to include indirect bodily impacts such as the one presented in this case. Butts effected a "bodily impact" on Joens when he attempted to wrest Joens's purse from her grasp because she actively resisted his effort. He therefore took the purse by "force" as that term is defined in AS 11.81.900(b)(26).

Having construed AS 11.81.900(b)(26) in this way, we conclude that Butts suffered no prejudice from the failure of the prosecutor to give the grand jury a special instruction on the statutory definition of "force." The evidence clearly established that Butts used "force" as we now have defined it. Indeed, the grand jury might have been led astray by the statutory definition of "force" unless it received a supplemental instruction that "bodily impact" includes the type of indirect bodily impact presented here.

---

5. Degrees of Robbery

States divide robbery into two, or sometimes three degrees. First-degree robbery generally involves either the use of a firearm or the infliction of serious bodily harm. Some states identify an aggravated category of robbery identified as "armed robbery," an offense which would, somewhat obviously, be described as first-degree robbery in the states with this designation.

Armed robbery statutes fall into two categories, those that require that the defendant actually possess a weapon and those that merely require that the

---

22　*Id.* at 154-56.

23　766 So.2d 310 (Fla.Dist.Ct.App.2000).

24　*Id.* at 311.

25　*Id.; see also People v. Harris*, 65 Cal.App.3d 978, 135 Cal.Rptr. 668, 674 (1977) (holding that indirect use of force constituted robbery when defendant tried to push a jewelry case lid open while the victim tried to hold it shut).

defendant reasonably communicate to his victim that he had a weapon. As you read these cases, consider which of the two versions you prefer and why. In other words, what rationale underlies the legislature's decision to require actual possession or merely threatened possession and which rationale do you find more compelling? And, as you read the decisions, are the requirements for conviction under each as different as the statutes would make them initially appear?

State v. Lopez

Supreme Court of Connecticut
889 A.2d 254 (2006)

DRANGINIS, J.

These appeals concern claims raised by the defendants, Clifton E. Kennedy and Albert Lopez, who were codefendants at trial. The jury found each defendant guilty of robbery in the first degree in violation of General Statutes § 53a–134(a)(2), unlawful restraint in the second degree in violation of General Statutes § 53a–96(a), and larceny in the sixth degree in violation of General Statutes §§ 53a–119 and 53a–125b(a). On appeal, Kennedy claims that (1) there was insufficient evidence to support his conviction of robbery in the first degree and (2) the trial court improperly denied his motion for a mistrial. Lopez claims that (1) there was insufficient evidence to support his conviction of robbery in the first degree and unlawful restraint in the second degree, (2) his conviction of robbery in the first degree and unlawful restraint in the second degree violate the constitutional prohibition against double jeopardy and (3) the court improperly denied his motion for mistrial. We affirm the judgments of the trial court.

The jury reasonably could have found the following facts. At approximately 10 p.m. on December 9, 2003, the victim, Cecile Lawrence, a University of Bridgeport security officer, was walking to her place of employment via Park Avenue. The weather was cold, and the victim wore a winter coat over her uniform. As she crossed Atlantic Street, she heard someone approaching from behind. She turned and saw two men, whom she subsequently identified as Kennedy and Lopez. Kennedy ordered the victim to give him her money or he would "do [her]." The victim described Kennedy as being very upset. He repeatedly threatened her by stating, "[G]ive me your money or I'll do you right here." The victim told Kennedy that she had no money, but he persisted, stating that he knew that she had money. The victim was afraid that she would be shot. She perceived an odor of alcohol on Kennedy and Lopez and believed that both men had been drinking.

The victim was wearing a backpack. Kennedy pulled on the backpack forcing the shoulder straps to draw the victim's arms behind her. This permitted

Lopez to unzip the victim's coat, rummage through her outer and inner coat pockets and the pocket of her shirt. Lopez removed the victim's keys, reading glasses and identification. Kennedy continued to threaten the victim by stating that he would "do [her]" then if she did not give them her money. Lopez informed him, however, that the victim did not have any money and told Kennedy not to "do her." Kennedy and Lopez took the victim's backpack with its contents and told the victim to walk away and not to look back. As the victim walked away, Kennedy again threatened her, stating, "Do not turn around or I'll do you."

The victim walked to the campus security office, which was about one and one-half blocks away. She met her supervisor, Jermaine Alston, who was operating a campus security vehicle, and informed him that she had been mugged. Alston told the victim to get into the vehicle, and they drove around the area looking for the perpetrators of the robbery. The victim described the perpetrators as a black man and a Hispanic man. Alston and the victim saw two men going through a backpack on Atlantic Street. The victim recognized them as the men who had robbed her. Alston stopped the vehicle and got out. Kennedy ran away. Lopez began to walk away, refusing to answer Alston's question about where he had gotten the backpack. Alston scuffled with Lopez and subdued him until the police arrived and took Lopez into custody. Kennedy was apprehended by the police a few blocks from the scene.

Most of the victim's belongings were recovered, except her cellular telephone, which was valued at approximately $200. After Kennedy and Lopez were taken into custody, the victim identified them as the men who had robbed her. She also identified them in court. Alston identified Lopez in court, as well, but he could not identify Kennedy.

Both defendants were charged with robbery in the first degree, unlawful restraint in the second degree and larceny in the sixth degree. Their cases were consolidated for trial on June 16, 2004. The jury returned verdicts of guilty on October 6, 2004. Each of the defendants received a total effective sentence of eleven years in the custody of the commissioner of correction and three years of probation. These appeals followed.

I

Kennedy and Lopez both claim that there was insufficient evidence to support the jury's respective verdicts of guilty of robbery in the first degree in violation of § 53a–134(a)(4). Lopez also claims that there was insufficient evidence to support the jury's verdict of guilty of unlawful restraint in the second degree as an accessory. We do not agree with these claims.

"The standard of review employed in a sufficiency of the evidence claim is well settled. [W]e apply a two part test. First, we construe the evidence in the light most favorable to sustaining the verdict. Second, we determine whether upon the facts so construed and the inferences reasonably drawn therefrom the [finder of fact] reasonably could have concluded that the cumulative force of the evidence established guilt beyond a reasonable doubt. . . . This court cannot substitute its own judgment for that of the jury if there is sufficient evidence to support the jury's verdict." (Internal quotation marks omitted.) *State v. Colon*, 272 Conn. 106, 270, 864 A.2d 666 (2004), cert. denied, 546 U.S. 848, 126 S.Ct. 102, 163 L.Ed.2d 116 (2005). "In conducting our review, we are mindful that the finding of facts, the gauging of witness credibility and the choosing among competing inferences are functions within the exclusive province of the jury, and, therefore, we must afford those determinations great deference." *State v. Conde*, 67 Conn.App. 474, 490, 787 A.2d 571 (2001), cert. denied, 259 Conn. 927, 793 A.2d 251 (2002).

* * *

A

Both Kennedy and Lopez claim that there was insufficient evidence to support their convictions of robbery in the first degree in violation of § 53a–134(a)(4) because the jury reasonably could not have concluded that Kennedy represented by his words or conduct the threatened use of a firearm. More specifically, Kennedy and Lopez argue that the jury's verdicts were based on speculation and surmise because the meaning of the words "do you" is too vague to be construed as a threat to shoot the victim, particularly when there was no evidence that either of the defendants had a firearm.[2] Kennedy and Lopez contend, therefore, that the state failed to prove beyond a reasonable doubt the firearm element of the statute. We are not convinced.

The state charged, in the respective amended informations, that "at the City of Bridgeport . . . on or about the 9th day of December, 2003, at approximately 10:35 p.m., at 296 Park Avenue within said City, the said [defendant] stole certain property from one CECILE LAWRENCE, and in the course of the commission of the crime he threatened the use of what he represented by his words or conduct to be a firearm, to wit: a handgun, in violation of Section 53a–134(a)(4) of the Connecticut General Statutes."

"Pursuant to § 53a–134(a)(4), a person is guilty of robbery in the first degree when, in the commission of the crime of robbery, that person displays

---

2 The police did not recover a firearm.

or threatens the use of what he represents by his words or actions to be a pistol, revolver, rifle, shotgun, machine gun or other firearm. This portion of the statute is satisfied when the state has proven beyond a reasonable doubt that the defendant represented by his words or conduct that he has a firearm; *the state need not prove that the defendant actually had a gun.*" (Emphasis added; internal quotation marks omitted.) *State v. Hansen*, 39 Conn.App. 384, 401, 666 A.2d 421, cert. denied, 235 Conn. 928, 667 A.2d 554 (1995).

"Robbery occurs when a person, in the course of committing a larceny, uses or threatens the immediate use of physical force upon the victim. General Statutes § 53a–133." *State v. Littles*, 31 Conn.App. 47, 54, 623 A.2d 500, cert. denied, 227 Conn. 902, 630 A.2d 72 (1993). "While there is no definition of the word threaten in the statutes, General Statutes § 1–1(a) provides that the commonly approved usage of the language should control. . . . A threat is 1. an indication of something impending and usually undesirable or unpleasant . . . 2. something that by its very nature or relation to another threatens the welfare of the latter. . . . A threat has also been defined as any menace of such a nature and extent as to unsettle the mind of the person on whom it operates, and to take away from his acts that free and voluntary action alone constitutes consent." (Citations omitted; internal quotation marks omitted.) *State v. Littles, supra*, at 54, 623 A.2d 500, citing *Hadley v. State*, 575 So.2d 145, 156, aff'd, 588 So.2d 938 (Ala.Crim.App.1991). "*This definition does not require that a threat be explicitly uttered.* . . . An implied threat is as effective as a stated threat, especially when the apparent ability to carry out the threat is overwhelming." (Emphasis added.) *State v. Littles, supra*, at 54, 623 A.2d 500.

In this case, Kennedy repeatedly told the victim to give him her money or that he would "do [her]." In support of their claim that the meaning of the expression "do you" is vague, Kennedy and Lopez rely on *State v. Aleksiewicz*, 20 Conn.App. 643, 569 A.2d 567 (1990). In *Aleksiewicz*, the defendant approached the victim after he had withdrawn $400 from an automatic teller machine. *Id.*, at 645, 569 A.2d 567. The defendant told the victim to give him his money or "'you're dead.'" *Id.* The victim reported to the police that "the defendant was holding his hand inside a 't-shirt' when he demanded the money. At trial, [the victim] testified that the defendant held his hand flat against his abdomen in a 'coat like or jacket.'" *Id.*, at 646, 569 A.2d 567. This court reversed the conviction, concluding that the victim's testimony had not established definitely the firearm element of the crime because no gun was shown, and the defendant did not give any specific indication, by words or action, that he had a gun. *Id.*, at 647, 569 A.2d 567. The victim had not testified that the defendant had a weapon, and the trial court would not permit him to testify as to whether he believed that the defendant had a gun. *Id.*, at 649, 569 A.2d 567. This court found the trial court's view of the evidence to be significant. To reach its verdict, the jury had to speculate that the defendant had a gun. *Id.*, at 650, 569 A.2d 567.

The state argues that the facts of *Aleksiewicz* are distinguishable and that the facts here are more consistent with those of *State v. St. Pierre*, 58 Conn.App. 284, 288, 752 A.2d 86 (victim testified defendant had weapon, but had no idea what weapon could have been), cert. denied, 254 Conn. 916, 759 A.2d 508 (2000). Here the victim, a security guard, testified that she was scared because she thought that she was going to be shot.[3] Furthermore, after Lopez had ransacked the victim's pockets, he told Kennedy not to "do her" because she had no money. Kennedy then told the victim to walk away and not to look back or he would "do [her]."[4] The state concedes that although Kennedy and Lopez were standing in close proximity to the victim, the term "do you" is susceptible of several meanings. It points out, however, that if Kennedy was going to "do" the victim *from a distance*, as she was walking away, the jury reasonably could have inferred that Kennedy had threatened to shoot the victim. We agree that the jury reasonably could have inferred that "to do" the victim from a distance, Kennedy had threatened to shoot her if she turned around while she was walking away from him and Lopez.

"Jurors do not live in a fishbowl. . . . In considering the evidence . . . [j]uries are not required to leave common sense at the courtroom door . . . . A threat need not be explicitly uttered." (Citations omitted; internal quotation marks omitted.) *State v. Glasper, supra*, 81 Conn.App. at 375, 840 A.2d 48. Viewing

---

3   The victim testified as follows on direct examination:

"[The Prosecutor]: . . . [A]fter the black man told you to give him your money or he'd do you, did he say anything else?

"[The Witness]: Yeah. He was very upset. He was, like . . . I was scared. He was, like, give me your money or I'll do you. Give me your money. I told him I didn't have any money. He says I know you got money. I know you got money. He says give me your money or I'll do you right here. I'll do you right here. And I was scared.

"[The Prosecutor]: What were you scared of?

"[The Witness]: I was scared that he was going to shoot me.

"[The Prosecutor]: Did you see a gun?

"[The Witness]: No, I didn't see a gun."

4   The victim also testified as follows:

"[The Prosecutor]: . . . Did there come a point in time when you were released?

"[The Witness]: Yes.

"[The Prosecutor]: And would you describe for the jurors how that—what happened at that point in time . . . ?

"[The Witness]: Well, they had [taken] my book bag, and they told me to walk. Walk straight, go straight ahead, don't look back or I'll do you, he says. *Do not turn around or I'll do you.*" (Emphasis added.)

the evidence in the light most favorable to sustaining the verdicts, we conclude, on the basis of the cumulative evidence presented, including the reasonable inferences to be drawn therefrom, that there was sufficient evidence for the jury to find Kennedy and Lopez guilty of robbery in the first degree in violation of § 53a–134(a)(4).

* * *

LAVERY, C.J., dissenting in part.

I concur with parts I B, II and III of the majority opinion, affirming the judgments of the trial court. Because, in my view, the present case is indistinguishable from this court's decision in *State v. Aleksiewicz*, 20 Conn.App. 643, 569 A.2d 567 (1990), I respectfully dissent from the conclusion in part I A that the evidence was sufficient to find the defendants, Clifton E. Kennedy and Albert Lopez, guilty of robbery in the first degree.

To be guilty of robbery in the first degree under General Statutes § 53a–134(a)(4), a defendant must either display or threaten the use of what he represents by his words or conduct to be a firearm.[1] As that requirement is an objective one; *State v. Aleksiewicz, supra*, 20 Conn.App. at 648, 569 A.2d 567; this court's focus properly is on the representation made by the defendants, rather than the victim's perception thereof.

I believe the present case falls squarely within this court's holding in *Aleksiewicz*. In that case, we observed that "[t]he only evidence . . . that the defendant threatened the use of what he represented by word or conduct to be a firearm was the testimony of one of the victims that the assailant held one hand flat against his body, inside his shirt, vest or jacket, and that he said, 'Give me that money or you're dead.' This testimony does not definitely establish the firearm element of this crime because no gun was shown and no specific indication was given, by either the defendant's words or actions, that he had in his possession or would use *specifically a gun* to accomplish his threat." (Emphasis in original.) *Id.*, at 647, 569 A.2d 567. In the present case, the only evidence the defendants threatened the use of what was represented by word or conduct to be a firearm was the testimony of the victim that Kennedy ordered her to "give me your money or I'll do you," and, "Do not turn around or I'll do you." That testimony is likewise deficient to establish the firearm element.

The majority reasons that the present factual scenario more closely resembles *State v. St. Pierre*, 58 Conn.App. 284, 752 A.2d 86, cert. denied, 254 Conn. 916, 759 A.2d 508 (2000). I disagree. In *St. Pierre*, the defendant announced that "'[t]his is a holdup'" and then "gestured by raising his hand inside his jacket from

---

1 At trial, the victim testified that she never saw a firearm.

beneath the counter to counter level while at all times keeping his hand and wrist covered by his jacket." *Id.*, at 286, 752 A.2d 86. At trial, the victim testified that he presumed that the defendant was holding a weapon under his jacket *due to that gesture. Id.*, at 289, 752 A.2d 86. We therefore concluded that the combination of "the defendant's words and the upward motion of his arm in his jacket . . . may properly have been considered . . . consistent with the representation and threatened use of a firearm." (Internal quotation marks omitted.) *Id.*

Aleksiewicz, however, involved no such gesture. Indeed, we specifically distinguished two New York decisions relied on by the state by explaining that the case involved no testimony that the defendant either (1) held his hand in his pocket in a manner meant to convey the impression that he had a gun or (2) placed his hand inside his vest as if he had a gun. *State v. Aleksiewicz, supra*, 20 Conn.App. at 649, 569 A.2d 567. No such testimony was provided in the present case. Consequently, *St. Pierre* is inapposite.

In *Aleksiewicz*, the defendant stated, "'Give me that money or you're dead.'" *Id.*, at 647, 569 A.2d 567. That statement was accompanied by no gesture indicating that the defendant possessed a firearm. In the present case, Kennedy stated, "[G]ive me your money or I'll do you," and, "Do not turn around or I'll do you." He made no gesture indicating that he possessed a firearm. Accordingly, I would conclude that insufficient evidence was presented on a necessary element of the crime of robbery in the first degree. Because on the facts of this case, the jury necessarily would have found the defendants guilty of the lesser charge of robbery in the third degree in violation of General Statutes § 53a–136, had it considered that charge; see *State v. Nicholson*, 71 Conn.App. 585, 592, 803 A.2d 391, cert. denied, 261 Conn. 941, 808 A.2d 1134 (2002), cert. denied, 543 U.S. 1162, 125 S.Ct. 1327, 161 L.Ed.2d 134 (2005); I would remand the case with direction to render judgments of conviction of robbery in the third degree as to each defendant.

Gray v. State

Supreme Court of Indiana
903 N.E.2d 940 (2009)

BOEHM, Justice.

Tony Gray was found guilty by a jury of robbing two fast-food restaurants while armed with a deadly weapon. We find the evidence sufficient to sustain a finding Gray was armed during the first robbery, but insufficient to sustain a finding Gray was armed during the second.

FACTS AND PROCEDURAL HISTORY

On the evening of February 14, 2007, Gray entered a Clarksville Arby's fast-food restaurant and, keeping his right hand in his jacket pocket, ordered employee Stacy Dodge to get behind the counter. Dodge saw "what looked like could have been a weapon" in Gray's jacket and "figured it was a gun." Gray took Dodge to the back of the restaurant and instructed the other employees to lie down on the floor. Gray ordered manager Stacey Clark to open the restaurant's safe and cash registers. Clark testified that Gray "had something in his right pocket. I saw a black handle. . . . [H]e told me that to stay calm and no one would get hurt. . . . I assumed there was a weapon in his pocket. I assumed it was a gun. I have no idea if it was or not, but I was really scared for my life and my employees' lives." Gray took over $1,000 and fled through a side door.

Four days later, Gray entered a Clarksville Long John Silver's restaurant, grabbed manager Kathleen Doss by the arm, and told her that he was robbing the restaurant. According to Doss, Gray "had something in his pocket, you know, I thought it was a gun and it was in his pocket and he, you know, grabbed my arm and put it to my, you know, like, like right by my, he was standing like right behind me." Ella Henley, a customer sitting in a booth, testified that Gray "had something in his pocket, which I thought was a gun. . . . I was afraid that he might just, you know, reflex might pull the trigger and might shoot her." Gray proceeded with Doss to the back of the restaurant where he ordered the employees to stand against a wall and instructed general manager Thomas Jones to remove the cash from the restaurant's safe and registers. When Jones tried stalling to permit another employee to call the police, Gray told Jones, "You act like you want to die today," and "you're going to end up getting yourself shot."

An employee called 911 while Gray and Jones were in the front of the restaurant at the cash registers. Henley had left the restaurant unnoticed and also called the police shortly after the employee's call. Gray took approximately $2,600 and left through the back door as Clarksville police officer Carl Durbin responded to the calls and approached the Long John Silver's. Durbin saw Gray running from the restaurant toward the back of a neighboring Firestone Auto Care Center. Several people exited the Long John Silver's and pointed at Gray. Durbin turned into the driveway along the side of the Firestone store. Gray had started his car and was driving from the rear of the Firestone store toward the street. Durbin swung behind Gray's car and activated his lights, and Gray immediately stopped his car, got out, and put his hands in the air. Durbin placed Gray under arrest and handcuffed him. Durbin estimated that ten to twelve seconds elapsed between the time he saw Gray running from Long John Silver's and the time he stopped Gray in his car. He estimated that the Firestone was roughly 200 feet away from the Long John Silver's.

Durbin was soon joined by Captain Dale Hennessey, who assisted in arresting Gray and inventoried Gray's car. Hennessey found the money from Long John Silver's in the front seat. No firearm was found on Gray's person, inside his automobile, or in the vicinity. An electric shaver was found in Gray's right jacket pocket.

Gray was convicted by a jury of two counts of armed robbery, Class B felonies, and three counts of armed criminal confinement, also Class B felonies, for confinement of three of the restaurant employees. Gray was also convicted as a habitual offender and sentenced to an aggregate term of seventy years imprisonment.

Gray appealed, arguing that there was insufficient evidence that he was armed with a deadly weapon in the course of these offenses.[1] The Court of Appeals affirmed, finding sufficient evidence that Gray had a gun in his pocket in each incident. *Gray v. State*, No. 10A01–0708–CR–356, slip op. at 15–18, 2008 WL 2313145 (Ind.Ct.App. June 6, 2008). Judge Barnes dissented, expressing his view that the evidence Gray had been armed was premised solely on the witnesses' beliefs and fears—as opposed to actual proof that Gray had a gun at the time of the offenses. *Id.* at 22, 2008 WL 2313145. Judge Barnes would have reduced Gray's robbery convictions to Class C felonies and his criminal confinement convictions to Class D felonies. *Id.* at 25, 2008 WL 2313145. Gray petitioned for transfer, which this Court has granted.

STANDARD OF REVIEW

Our standard of review for sufficiency claims is well settled. We do not reweigh evidence or assess the credibility of witnesses. Rather, we look to the evidence and reasonable inferences drawn therefrom that support the verdict and will affirm the conviction if there is probative evidence from which a reasonable jury could have found the defendant guilty beyond a reasonable doubt. *O'Connell v. State*, 742 N.E.2d 943, 949 (Ind.2001).

---

1 Gray raised four other arguments on appeal: that the trial court erred by denying Gray's motion to sever the Arby's counts from the Long John Silver's counts, Gray's motion to suppress statements he made to law enforcement, and Gray's motion to suppress identification evidence, and that Gray's robbery and criminal confinement convictions violated the double jeopardy provisions of the Indiana Constitution. The Court of Appeals resolved all four claims in favor of the State. *Gray v. State*, No. 10A01–0708–CR–356, slip op. at 6–9, 9–11, 11–15, 19–20, 2008 WL 2313145 (Ind.Ct.App. June 6, 2008). We summarily affirm the decision of the Court of Appeals as to all four issues. Ind. Appellate Rule 58(A)(2).

SUFFICIENCY OF THE EVIDENCE

Robbery is a Class C felony but "is a Class B felony if it is committed while armed with a deadly weapon." Ind.Code § 35–42–5–1 (2004). Similarly, criminal confinement is a Class D felony but is a Class B felony if it is "committed while armed with a deadly weapon." *Id.* § 35–42–3–3(b)(2)(A). "Deadly weapon" is defined to include a number of things, *see Id.* § 35–41–1–8, but in this case the charging instrument alleged that Gray was armed with "a gun" when he committed the robberies. Therefore, in order to elevate Gray's convictions to Class B felonies, the State was required to prove that Gray committed the offenses using a firearm. *See Mitchem v. State*, 685 N.E.2d 671, 677–78 (Ind.1997).

A conviction for armed robbery may be sustained even if the deadly weapon was not revealed during the robbery. *Schumpert v. State*, 603 N.E.2d 1359, 1364 (Ind.Ct.App.1992). Nor is it necessary that the weapon be admitted into evidence at trial. *Brown v. State*, 266 Ind. 82, 86, 360 N.E.2d 830, 833 (1977). It is, however, necessary that there be evidence to support the finding that the defendant in fact was "armed with a deadly weapon," in this case a "gun." In this respect, Indiana's statute requires more than its counterparts in some other states which elevate robbery based not only on the fact of use of a weapon, but also, for example, on the perception of the victim that the defendant was armed even if there was in fact no weapon. [2]

As Judge Barnes pointed out, Class B felony armed robbery typically involves "an actual heightened risk of harm to the victim." *Gray*, at 23, 2008 WL 2313145. Academic commentary has also concluded that "intimidation by some means is a necessary ingredient of simple robbery without violence; something additional in the way of dangerousness is needed for aggravated robbery. . . ." 3 Wayne R. LaFave, *Substantive Criminal Law* § 20.3(f), at 195 (2d ed.2003). "[T]he greater punishment is awarded for armed robbery so as to deter the dangerous person who is actually capable of inflicting death or serious bodily harm." *Id.* at 195 n. 110. Under statutes such as Indiana's, an armed robbery conviction requires proof that the perpetrator actually—rather than apparently—possessed

---

2 *See* N.H.Rev.Stat. Ann. § 636:1 (LexisNexis 2007) (robbery conviction is enhanced if defendant "[w]as actually armed with a deadly weapon" or "[r]easonably appeared to the victim to be armed with a deadly weapon"); Wis. Stat. Ann. § 943.32 (West 2005) (robbery conviction is enhanced if committed "by use or threat of use of a dangerous weapon . . . or any article used or fashioned in a manner to lead the victim reasonably to believe that it is a dangerous weapon"); S.C.Code Ann. § 16–11–330 (2003) (anyone who "commits robbery while armed with a pistol . . . or other deadly weapon, or while alleging, either by action or words, he was armed while using a representation of a deadly weapon or any object which a person present during the commission of the robbery reasonably believed to be a deadly weapon" is guilty of armed robbery); Okla. Stat. Ann. tit. 21, § 801 (West 2002) (anyone who, "with the use of any firearms or any other dangerous weapons, whether the firearm is loaded or not, or who uses a blank or imitation firearm capable of raising in the mind of the one threatened with such device a fear that it is a real firearm" is guilty of armed robbery).

a deadly weapon. As the Massachusetts Supreme Judicial Court has explained in interpreting its statute which also requires that the defendant be armed:[3]

> The crime of armed robbery, an aggravated form of robbery, is based in part on the potential for injury that arises from the possession of a dangerous weapon. When there is no such weapon, the potential is absent. The victim's apprehension is, of course, likely to be the same whether the defendant had a gun or only said he had a gun, but did not. The nature of any threats and a victim's apprehension may be relevant factors in sentencing a defendant on his conviction of unarmed robbery, but, in the absence of evidence warranting an inference beyond a reasonable doubt that a defendant, in fact, had some instrumentality in his possession, there can be no conviction of robbery while "armed with a dangerous weapon."

Commonwealth v. Howard, 386 Mass. 607, 436 N.E.2d 1211, 1213 (1982). Indiana is more expansive than Massachusetts, however, because our statute has broadly defined "deadly weapon" to include unloaded firearms, and convictions for armed robberies with blank or plugged guns have been upheld. *Barber v. State*, 418 N.E.2d 563, 568 (Ind.Ct.App.1981); *Rogers v. State*, 537 N.E.2d 481, 484–85 (Ind.1989). There is therefore no requirement under Indiana law that the victim be actually in danger of being shot. Presumably this reflects the view that use of a firearm as a club is possible, and the mere display of a firearm can provoke reaction in others that risk severe injury either by panic or attempted retaliation. Despite the broadened definition of "deadly weapon," Indiana's statute, like Massachusetts's, requires that the person actually possess the weapon at the time of the crime. And in Gray's case the information required the weapon to be a "gun."

We turn now to the question whether the evidence is sufficient to establish that Gray possessed a gun in either or both of these incidents. Stacey Dodge testified with respect to the object in Gray's pocket in the Arby's robbery that she "figured it was gun," "thought it was a gun," and saw "something that could have been a gun." But she also testified that she never saw a firearm. Stacey Clark saw a black handle in Gray's pocket and "assumed it was a gun." She said that Gray instructed her to stay calm and "no one would get hurt." But Clark also testified that she did not see a firearm and "did not know if [Gray] had a gun." In short, none of the Arby's witnesses testified that they saw a gun in Gray's jacket. *Cf. Harvey v. State*, 542 N.E.2d 198, 200 (Ind.1989) (evidence was sufficient to

---

3 The Massachusetts armed robbery statute provides that "[w]hoever, being armed with a dangerous weapon, assaults another and robs, steals or takes from his person money or other property which may be the subject of larceny shall be" subject to an enhanced robbery conviction and sentence. Mass. Gen. Laws Ann. ch. 265, § 17 (West 2008).

sustain armed robbery conviction where, among other things, victim testified, "I saw it was a gun.").

The Long John Silver's witnesses testified similarly to the Arby's witnesses. Ella Henley never saw a gun but thought Gray had one in his pocket. Henley "was afraid that he might just, you know, reflex might pull the trigger. . . ." Kathleen Doss testified that Gray "made it to look like" he had a firearm. And Thomas Jones testified that he never saw a firearm during the robbery but that Gray "made us believe that [he] had a gun."

The defendant's statement or implication that he had a weapon is itself evidence that he was in fact armed. *White v. State*, 455 N.E.2d 329, 332 (Ind.1983); *see also Munsey v. State*, 421 N.E.2d 1115, 1117 (Ind.1981) (finding sufficient evidence defendant was armed where victim did not see weapon but felt sharp instrument on her neck and defendant told victim "if [she] moved they'd cut [her] head off"); *Lyda v. State*, 272 Ind. 15, 17, 395 N.E.2d 776, 778 (1979) (defendant, inter alia, told victim he had a gun); *Owens v. State*, 497 N.E.2d 230, 231–32 (Ind.1986) (defendant, inter alia, gave note to victim stating he had a gun).

Although no one testified to seeing a gun, in both cases Gray communicated that he was armed. Gray's statement at Long John Silver's that Jones would end up getting himself shot is substantive, if not conclusive, evidence that Gray had a gun in his pocket when he robbed Long John Silver's.[4] Gray's conduct and statements in the Arby's robbery were less clear but nonetheless permitted the jury to infer that Gray had communicated to the victim that he had a gun. His keeping his hand in his pocket and statements that "no one would get hurt" if the employees cooperated clearly implied that he could and would injure those who resisted, and the cooperation of the employees who outnumbered Gray four-to-one is

---

4 On this note, we should briefly revisit the Arby's robbery to clarify one point. Gray, who told the court he was within one semester of completing his criminal justice degree, represented himself at trial. The transcript is somewhat confusing, and at some points reads as if authored by Joseph Heller. At trial Gray asked Arby's employee Stacey Clark about testimony she had provided in a prior deposition:

[Gray:] Ma'am, did the suspect ever tell you verbally he had a gun?

[Clark:] No, you did not say you had a gun.

. . . .

[Gray:] I think starting on page, starting on line 9, did you say, "I don't know if he said if he had a gun. But he said no one will get shot. That no one will get hurt", is that true, ma'am?

[Clark:] And it says something to that, something like that. . . .

. . . .

. . . [I]t says in here, from straight from line 9, I know if he said but he said no one would get shot. Something like that.

[Gray:] Right.

[Clark:] That no one would get hurt, something like that. That's what I said.

evidence that they believed he was armed. Their belief is not sufficient to establish armed robbery, but it is evidence that Gray communicated that he was armed.

Clark's deposition was not entered into evidence and it is unclear whether her live testimony confirmed either that Gray said he was armed or that he was in fact armed.

Without more, Gray's statements and conduct at both stores would be sufficient to permit the jury to find that he was in fact armed at the time of both offenses. The chain of events following Gray's flight from the Long John Silver's demonstrates otherwise as to that robbery. Gray was arrested almost immediately after leaving the Long John Silver's, and police found no firearm on Gray's person, in his car, or at the scene of the crime. Under these circumstances, it is impossible to conclude beyond a reasonable doubt that Gray was in fact armed at the time of the Long John Silver's robbery. *Compare Commonwealth v. Delgado*, 367 Mass. 432, 326 N.E.2d 716, 717–19 (1975) (defendant's statements are sufficient to prove that he was armed) *with Commonwealth v. Howard*, 386 Mass. 607, 436 N.E.2d 1211, 1211–13 (1982) (despite defendant's threats to shoot victim in street robbery, evidence was insufficient when defendant was arrested immediately without opportunity to dispose of a weapon and none was found).

In sum, Gray was spotted by Officer Durbin as he was exiting the Long John Silver's, and was arrested approximately ten to twelve seconds later only 200 feet away from the restaurant. Gray and his automobile were searched at the time of his arrest, and money was found but no weapon. No gun was found in the surrounding area, but an electric shaver in the pocket in which restaurant employees assumed Gray was concealing a weapon. We believe that the limited timeframe, the proximity of the arrest, the police's failure to recover a gun in the area, and the discovery of the shaver in Gray's jacket together preclude any finding beyond a reasonable doubt that Gray was in fact armed with a gun at Long John Silver's. We agree with Judge Barnes that "all of the evidence and all of the reasonable inferences therefrom lead to just one conclusion," "namely that Gray used an electric shaver, not a gun, to rob the Long John Silver's." *Gray*, at 24, 2008 WL 2313145. We thus hold the evidence insufficient as a matter of law to sustain Gray's enhanced convictions on the counts charging robbery and confinement at Long John Silver's.

CONCLUSION

This cause is remanded to the trial court with instructions to reduce Gray's convictions on the Long John Silver's crimes (Counts I and II) to Class C felony robbery and Class D felony criminal confinement. In all other respects, the judgment of the trial court is affirmed.

Notes and Questions

1. *Lopez* deals with the question of whether the words spoken were sufficient to create an inference that the defendant possessed a weapon. As the dissent points out, it was far from obvious that they were. Would *Lopez*, though, have been decided differently under Indiana law?

2. To ask the previous question a different way, can a person be convicted of armed robbery in Indiana who falsely represents that he has a weapon? If so, then why was Gray not convicted of armed robbery?

PRACTICE EXERCISE

Read the following set of facts, then read the instructions that follow.

Anfirney's old friend Billy used to work at the CVC Pharmacy. Before he quit, Billy used to complain constantly to Anfirney about the low-level of staff. "I can never 'take five,' man. In the evenings, there's usually only two people in the store, me and the assistant manager. Somebody could hold that place up easy, and get away with it because the store policy is to just to give up the money."

Anfirney meanders into CVC Pharmacy one evening, looking for cheap beer. Disgusted with his low-budget options, it occurs to him that it is 8:00 pm, and that the store is very quiet. He decides to make some money. Over the next half hour, Anfirney patrols the aisles putting every expensive product he can find in his cart. Then he decides to force the cashier to return all items to a gift card, so that he can walk away with a card as good as cash, or simply resell the gift card. His plan: pretend to wield a gun in his jacket pocket, and use the "Wild West Revolver" app on his phone to scare the cashier into surrendering to his demands.

Spurred on by the brilliance of his plan, Anfirney walks up to the cashier, who is reading a magazine: "I have something in my pocket you won't like. Return all these items onto a gift card, or things will get messy." Anfirney dumps his items on the counter, and holds his phone at an angle in his pocket to duplicate the barrel of a gun. Terrified and undercompensated for such a scenario, the cashier shrieks, but stutters that he does not have the authorization for so many returns. Anfirney knows better. He keeps his jacket pocket below the level of the counter, and "pulls the trigger" twice, swiping the simulated trigger on the phone twice, which produces two loud "pops." It suffices. The cashier breaks the returns into three transactions to stay below the return limit without manager authorization. Anfirney instructs the cashier to hand over the gift cards. The cashier complies. Anfirney takes the cards and walks out the door, pleased with the sheer genius of his plan.

The cashier calls the police immediately. CVC immediately voids the gift cards remotely from its accounting office. Anfirney does not have a car. The police watch the surveillance tape, and later identify Anfirney walking down the street two miles from the store, without the cards or any weapon. They walk the route Anfirney likely took from the CVC to the location of his arrest, but even the police canines cannot find anything that resembles a gift card, or weapon that Anfirney could keep in his jacket pocket. (Anfirney put the cards in a friend's mailbox during his walk.)

Instructions:

Gray is an authority in your jurisdiction. You may use it as a basis for your arguments.

Motion to Exclude Evidence

First, you are a prosecutor attempting to exclude evidence that no weapon was found on Anfirney. Draft a short argument, using the facts, that excludes evidence that no weapon can be attached to Anfirney's robbery.

Second, take the position of Anfirney's defense attorney: (A) Argue that the absence of a weapon is directly relevant as evidence to be presented to the jury: that Anfirney did not commit first-degree robbery (or robbery at all) because he had no weapon; (B) Argue that (i) there is insufficient evidence of actually taking property, because your jurisdiction has not settled the question of whether "Robbery" includes the "course of conduct" theory of robbery as stated in *Williams* (p. 1011); and (ii) give policy reasons for rejecting *William's* approach.

C. Burglary

The common law definition of burglary has very little to do with modern statutes defining the crime. Lord Coke defined the crime in 1641 as follows:

> A Burglar (or the person that committeth burglary) is by the common law a felon, that in the night breaketh and entereth into a mansion house of another, of intent to kill some reasonable creature, or the commit some other felony within the same, whether his felonious intent be executed or not.

Sir Edward Coke, *The Third Part of the Institutes of the Law of England* 63 (London, W. Clarke & Co. 1809) (1644).

1. Night Time

No state limits burglary to offenses that occur during the night. In most states, the hour of the day is not even relevant to the degree of burglary committed. In Massachusetts and Virginia, however, a night-time burglary is an aggravated form of burglary.

Massachusetts' has defined night time, for the purpose of its burglary statute, to be less broad that sundown and sunrise.

> If a crime is alleged to have been committed in the night time, night time shall be deemed the time between one hour after sunset on one day and one hour before sunrise on the next day; and the time of sunset and sunrise shall be ascertained according to mean time in the place where the crime was committed.

Mass. Gen. L. Ann. 278 § 10

2. Breaking

Only twelve jurisdictions require breaking, and for most of those jurisdictions breaking can occur constructively, through artifice, trick, fraud, or threat, or through the application of any force, such that involved in opening a door.

3. Unlawful Entry

Most jurisdictions have dispensed with the common law "breaking" requirement, but how does this change affect the requirement of an unlawful entry? The Clark case from Virginia presents this question: Is entry into a building with the intent to commit a crime in that building sufficient for burglary even where the defendant has been invited, expressly or implicitly, to enter?

Clark v. Commonwealth

Court of Appeals of Virginia
472 S.E.2d 663 (1996)

MOON, Chief Judge.

Timothy Lamont Clark appeals his conviction for statutory burglary. He contends that he could not be convicted of a violation of Code § 18.2-90 because he lawfully entered the store when it was open to the public. We hold that under Code § 18.2-90, a person who enters a store intending to commit robbery therein, enters the store unlawfully. Therefore, we affirm the conviction.

Clark was indicted on charges of robbery, statutory burglary, and use of a firearm in the commission of robbery. The statutory burglary indictment charged that Clark "unlawfully and feloniously, while armed with a deadly weapon, enter[ed] in the nighttime the storehouse of Kentuck Grocery, with the intent to commit robbery therein," in violation of Code § 18.2-90. Clark pled guilty to robbery, not guilty to statutory burglary, and not guilty to use of a firearm in the commission of a robbery.

The parties stipulated that on February 21, 1994, at 8:00 p.m., Clark entered the Kentuck Grocery during regular business hours and asked an employee where the bathroom was located. When Clark returned to the counter, he pulled an object from his pocket that appeared to be the butt of a gun. Clark stated, "open it up and I mean now," followed by, "let me have it all." The employee gave Clark all the money in the cash drawer. Later, after the employee identified Clark from an array of photographs, Clark was interviewed by the police and confessed to the robbery. He denied that he had a gun.

In addition to this stipulated evidence, Clark testified that he did not possess a gun during the robbery. He testified that he put his hand under his sweater and intended to give the appearance of possessing a gun. The trial judge found Clark guilty of statutory burglary and not guilty of use of a firearm in the commission of robbery.

Clark contends that he cannot be found guilty of statutory burglary because he entered the store during its regular business hours pursuant to the owner's general invitation to the public to enter the business establishment. He argues that Code § 18.2-90 has not eliminated the common law requirement that the Commonwealth must prove an unlawful entry in order to obtain a burglary conviction. He further argues that the legislature intended to eliminate the "force" aspect of breaking as required by the common law but did not intend to eliminate the defense of consent to enter or lack of trespassory conduct. We disagree.

Clark was indicted and convicted under the following statute:

> If any person in the nighttime enters without breaking or in the daytime breaks and enters or enters and conceals himself in a dwelling house or an adjoining, occupied outhouse or in the nighttime enters without breaking or at any time breaks and enters or enters and conceals himself in any office, shop, manufactured home, storehouse, warehouse, banking house, or other house, or any ship, vessel or river craft or any railroad car, or any automobile, truck or trailer, if such automobile, truck or trailer is used as a dwelling or place of human habitation, with intent to commit murder, rape or robbery, he shall be deemed guilty of statutory burglary, which offense shall be a Class 3 felony. However, if such person was armed with a deadly weapon at the time of such entry, he shall be guilty of a Class 2 felony.

Code § 18.2-90. Our reading of the statute is governed by the following well established principles:

> If [a statute's] language is clear and unambiguous, there is no need for construction by the court; the plain meaning and intent of the enactment will be given it. When an enactment is clear and unequivocal, general rules for construction of statutes of doubtful meaning do not apply. Therefore, when the language of an enactment is free from ambiguity, resort to legislative history and extrinsic facts is not permitted because we take the words as written to determine their meaning.

Brown v. Lukhard, 229 Va. 316, 321, 330 S.E.2d 84, 87 (1985) (citations omitted).
"When the sufficiency of the evidence is attacked, the judgment of the trial court sitting without a jury is entitled to the same weight as a jury verdict and will not be disturbed [on appeal] unless plainly wrong or without evidence to support it." *Evans v. Commonwealth*, 215 Va. 609, 613, 212 S.E.2d 268, 271 (1975). Although breaking is an essential element of common law burglary, the statute's language, "enter[ ] without breaking," specifically excludes breaking as an element. *Brown v. Lukhard*, 229 Va. at 321, 330 S.E.2d at 87 (1985) (courts must apply the plain meaning of a statute if its language is clear and unambiguous); *see Johns v. Commonwealth*, 10 Va.App. 283, 289, 392 S.E.2d 487, 490 (1990) (under Code § 18.2-93, breaking during entry is not necessary to impose liability). Furthermore, because other offenses under the same statute require proof of breaking, the General Assembly must have intended to require only proof of entry into the building.

In *Jones v. Commonwealth*, 3 Va.App. 295, 349 S.E.2d 414 (1986), we considered whether a burglary conviction under Code § 18.2-91 could be upheld where the defendant entered the store during normal business hours, concealed himself within the store and committed larceny once the store closed. In upholding the conviction, we stated:

> Where a store owner invites the public to enter his premises he consents for the entrant to view his merchandise for the limited purpose of purchase, or to otherwise engage in a lawful activity thereon. It is not the will of the owner that entrance be made to defraud or steal from him.

Id. at 300, 349 S.E.2d at 417. *See also Davis v. Commonwealth*, 132 Va. 521, 524, 110 S.E. 356, 357 (1922) (citing with approval cases holding that if a person who is "fully authorized to enter for purposes within the scope of the employment or trust, actually enters . . . to commit [robbery], he will be guilty of burglary").

Although this Court reversed the burglary conviction in *Johns*, because Johns did not commit a breaking, "[w]e agree[d] . . . that the bank . . . did not authorize, invite or consent to Johns' entry for the purpose of committing robbery." 10 Va.App. at 287, 392 S.E.2d at 489. Indeed, the opinion intimated that we would have upheld the conviction if Johns had been prosecuted under Code § 18.2-93, which only requires proof of entering and not breaking. *Id.* at 285 n. 1, 392 S.E.2d at 488 n. 1. We reiterate our holding in *Johns* that "'[i]t would be an impeachment of the common sense of mankind to say that . . . a thief who enters the store with intent to steal does so with the owner's consent and upon his invitation.'" *Id.* at 287, 392 S.E.2d at 489 (citation omitted).

The evidence was sufficient for the trial court to find beyond a reasonable doubt that Clark entered the store in the nighttime with the intent to commit robbery. The proof of those elements satisfied the provisions of Code § 18.2-90. Therefore, we affirm the conviction.

Affirmed.

BENTON, Judge, dissenting.

"At common law, burglary was defined as 'the breaking and entering of the dwelling house of another in the nighttime with the intent to commit a felony.'" *Rash v. Commonwealth*, 9 Va.App. 22, 24 n. 1, 383 S.E.2d 749, 750 n. 1 (1989) (quoting 3 Charles E. Torcia, *Wharton's Criminal Law* § 326 (14th ed. 1980)). Common law burglary required that the "entrance [be] contrary to the will of the occupier of the house." *Davis v. Commonwealth*, 132 Va. 521, 523, 110 S.E. 356, 357 (1922). A conviction could not be had at common law when the accused was invited onto the premises.

The [common] law was not ready to punish one who had been "invited" in any way to enter the dwelling. The law sought only to keep out intruders, and thus anyone given authority to come into the house could not be committing a breaking when he so entered.

Wayne R. LaFave & Austin W. Scott, Jr., *Criminal Law* § 96, at 708 (1972)(footnote omitted).

In 1874, the Supreme Court of Virginia overturned a conviction for common law burglary, citing the following well established view:

We have seen no case, and think there has been none, in which the entry was by the voluntary act and consent of the owner or occupier of the house, which has been held to be burglary. And were we to affirm the judgment in this case, we would establish a doctrine of constructive burglary which would not only be new, but contrary to the well known definition of that offence. While the legislature might make such a change, we think it would be judicial legislation in us to do so.

Clarke v. Commonwealth, 66 Va. (25 *Gratt.*) 908, 919-20 (1874). Thus, at common law, consent to enter was a defense to a burglary prosecution.

"The General Assembly [of Virginia] has declared that '[t]he common law of England, insofar as it is not repugnant to the principles of the Bill of Rights and Constitution of this Commonwealth, shall continue in full force within the same, and be the rule of decision, except as altered by the General Assembly.'" *Wackwitz v. Roy,* 244 Va. 60, 65, 418 S.E.2d 861, 864 (1992)(quoting Code § 1-10). To abrogate the common law, the General Assembly must plainly manifest its intent to do so. *Id.*

In Virginia, the General Assembly has enacted numerous statutory burglary offenses. One of those statutes, "Code § 18.2-89[,] describes an offense identical to common law burglary, save that the element of intent is expanded to include intent to commit a larceny." *Rash*, 9 Va.App. at 24, 383 S.E.2d at 750. In pertinent part, Code § 18.2-89 states as follows:

If any person break and enter the dwelling house of another in the nighttime with intent to commit a felony ... he shall be guilty of burglary, punishable as a Class 3 felony.

In addition, by enacting numerous offenses of "statutory burglary," the General Assembly also has proscribed conduct beyond the common law crime of burglary. Code §§ 18.2-89 to 18.2-93. These statutes create several offenses of statutory burglary, most of which would not constitute burglary at common law. For example, these statutes prohibit the following offenses against property:

1. Dwelling houses:

    (A) Break and enter in nighttime with intent to commit
        (i) a felony. Code § 18.2-89 (the common law definition of burglary).
        (ii) larceny. Code § 18.2-89.

    (B) Enter without breaking in the nighttime
        (i) with intent to commit murder, rape, or robbery. Code § 18.2-90.
        (ii) with intent to commit larceny or any felony other than murder, rape, or robbery. Code § 18.2-91.

    (C) Break and enter in the daytime
        (i) with intent to commit murder, rape, or robbery. Code § 18.2-90.
        (ii) with intent to commit larceny or any felony other than murder, rape, or robbery. Code § 18.2-91.

    (D) Enter and conceal [at anytime]
        (i) with intent to commit murder, rape, or robbery. Code § 18.2-90.
        (ii) with intent to commit larceny or any felony other than murder, rape, or robbery. Code § 18.2-91.

2. Occupied dwelling house:

    Break and enter day or night with intent to commit any misdemeanor except assault or trespass. Code § 18.2-92.

3. Office, shop, manufactured home, storehouse, warehouse, banking house, or other house, or vehicle of habitation:

    (A) Enter without breaking in nighttime
        (i) with intent to commit murder, rape, or robbery. Code § 18.2-90.
        (ii) with intent to commit larceny or any felony other than murder, rape, or robbery. Code § 18.2-91.

    (B) Break and enter at anytime
        (i) with intent to commit murder, rape, or robbery. Code § 18.2-90.
        (ii) with intent to commit larceny or any felony other than murder, rape, or robbery. Code § 18.2-91.

    (C) Enter and conceal at anytime
        (i) with intent to commit murder, rape, or robbery. Code § 18.2-90.
        (ii) with intent to commit larceny or any felony other than murder, rape, or robbery. Code § 18.2-91.

4. Banking house:

> Enter in day or night armed with deadly weapon with intent to commit larceny of money, bonds, notes or other evidence of debt. Code § 18.2-93.

In none of these various burglary statutes has the legislature explicitly stated or remotely implied that the statutory enactments were intended by implication to supplant the well established principle that anyone licensed or given authority to enter the premises could not be convicted of burglary.

Clark entered through its public entrance a retail establishment that was open for business. The burglary indictment charged Clark with an offense under the following statute:

> If any person in the nighttime enters without breaking or in the daytime breaks and enters or enters and conceals himself in a dwelling house or an adjoining, occupied outhouse or in the nighttime enters without breaking or at any time breaks and enters or enters and conceals himself in any office, shop, manufactured home, storehouse, warehouse, banking house, or other house, or any ship, vessel or river craft or any railroad car, or any automobile, truck or trailer, if such automobile, truck or trailer is used as a dwelling or place of human habitation, with intent to commit murder, rape or robbery, he shall be deemed guilty of statutory burglary, which offense shall be a Class 3 felony. However, if such person was armed with a deadly weapon at the time of such entry, he shall be guilty of a Class 2 felony.

Code § 18.2-90.

"Although the General Assembly can abrogate the common law, its intent to do so must be '"plainly manifested."'" *Wackwitz*, 244 Va. at 65, 418 S.E.2d at 864 (citations omitted). Thus, when a claim is made that a statutory enactment abrogates the common law, courts must decide the meaning of the statutory offense.

Two important rules of construction come into play where a statute is in derogation of the common law. First, "[t]he common law is not to be considered as altered or changed by statute unless the legislative intent be plainly manifested." Second, "[s]tatutes in derogation of the common law are to be strictly construed and not to be enlarged in their operation by construction beyond their express terms."

Hyman v. Glover, 232 Va. 140, 143, 348 S.E.2d 269, 271 (1986) (citations omitted). Furthermore, because this is a criminal appeal, other important rules of construction apply.

Penal statutes are to be strictly construed against the Commonwealth and in favor of the citizen's liberty. Such statutes may not be extended by implication; they must be applied to cases clearly described by the language used. And the accused is entitled to the benefit of any reasonable doubt about the construction of a penal statute.

Martin v. Commonwealth, 224 Va. 298, 300-01, 295 S.E.2d 890, 892 (1982) (citations omitted). In making these determinations, courts "must . . . presume[ ] that the [General Assembly] acted with full knowledge of the strict interpretation that must be placed upon a statute of this nature." *Hannabass v. Ryan*, 164 Va. 519, 525, 180 S.E. 416, 418 (1935).

The common law of burglary required proof of a "breaking [which] involve[d] the application of some force, slight though it may be, whereby the entrance is effected." *Davis*, 132 Va. at 523, 110 S.E. at 357. Thus, under the common law, if the accused entered a private dwelling through an open door or window, no "breaking" occurred because no force was used. LaFave & Scott, *supra*, 396 at 708. Clearly, the various statutory enactments convey the legislature's intent to eliminate the force aspect of "breaking" necessary for a conviction under common law burglary. That conclusion is manifest because in many of the statutes the legislature explicitly proscribed in certain instances "enters without breaking." *See, e.g.*, Code § 18.2-90. Thus, a person who entered a building through a door inadvertently left open and who was not an invitee would violate the prohibition of the statute.

No clear language in the statutes manifests the conclusion, however, that the legislature intended to eliminate the principle that an invitee could not be guilty of burglary. Obviously, if a phrase such as "whether or not invited" or "whether authorized or not" had been inserted in the statute to qualify the element, "enters," the General Assembly would have manifested an intent to eliminate the consent defense so well established as a bar against a burglary conviction. If the statutes had contained such language, this Court would have been able to infer that the General Assembly intended that the owner's consent to entry would not bar a conviction as stated in *Clarke*.

Furthermore, the explicit language in Code § 18.2-90 strongly suggests that the General Assembly did not intend for the statute to apply when an entry was made by a person invited, authorized, or licensed to enter. Code § 18.2-90 prohibits a person from "enter[ing] and conceal[ing] himself in any office, shop, manufactured home, storehouse, warehouse, banking house, or other house." The prohibition against entering and concealing clearly encompasses persons who initially enter with authority or by invitation and conceal themselves on the premises. Obviously, if this Court construes "enters without breaking" to apply to an invitee, then the phrase "enters and conceals," also contained in Code § 18.2-90, is rendered redundant.

It would be absurd to conclude that the legislature would say the same thing twice in one statutory provision. Yet, if we were to adopt the argument advanced by [the Commonwealth], this absurd result would obtain. The rules of statutory interpretation argue against reading any legislative enactment in a manner that will make a portion of it useless, repetitious, or absurd. On the contrary, it is well established that every act of the legislature should be read so as to give reasonable effect to every word and to promote the ability of the enactment to remedy the mischief at which it is directed.

Jones v. Conwell, 227 Va. 176, 180-81, 314 S.E.2d 61, 64 (1984).

The necessary consequence of the majority's decision is to extend the offense of burglary beyond any rational contemplation of the statute. Indeed, if the statutes are now to be construed as the majority mandates, they would encompass (1) any person who enters with consent in the nighttime in a friend's residence or any building to use a telephone, even if the person intends to commit a prohibited act at some other place, (2) any person who enters a retail establishment in the nighttime and is convicted of shoplifting a magazine, and (3) any person who enters retail establishments open for business along a route of travel, even if the person intends to commit the prohibited act some other place. Nothing in the statutes indicates a legislative intent to so broadly define burglary.

For these reasons, I would hold that Code § 18.2-90 has not eliminated the common law principle that an unlawful entry is required for a burglary conviction. The statutory enactments clearly manifest a legislative intent to eliminate the "force" aspect of breaking as required by the common law but not the defense of consent to enter or lack of trespassory conduct. Thus, I would hold that the burglary conviction must be reversed.

Notes and Questions

1. The tools used to interpret the statute in this case should be becoming very familiar to you. What does the context of the operative language suggest about its meaning? Has the legislature demonstrated its intent to abrogate the common law?

2. For the majority, the language is clear. As no breaking is required, the defendant entered a building for an unlawful purpose.

3. The dissent observes, however, that this creates a redundancy of language—in order to be convicted, the defendant must enter *and conceal* with the intent to commit one of the identified crimes. Entry is insufficient, according to the dissent, or the legislature has used redundant words. This is an argument we have seen divide judges before. Look back at the dissent in *People v. Randolph* (p. 1039) where a robbery statute made it a crime to use force "to feloniously rob, steal, or take from the person of another. . . ." The dissent in *Randolph* concluded that the legislature must have meant something different by the terms "rob" and "take," a distinction the majority did not accept.

---

4. Dwelling

A few states retain the requirement that the defendant enter the *dwelling* of another in order to be convicted of the crime of burglary. Most states permit a burglary conviction if entry was made into a "building" or "structure" for the purpose of committing a crime therein, though many states identify the entry into a dwelling as an aggravated form of burglary. This raises the question, of course, of what is a dwelling—and specifically, does a dwelling have to be occupied. *Johnson* addresses this last part of the question—does a building have to be occupied at the time of the prohibited entry for the defendant to have unlawfully entered a dwelling.

Johnson v. Commonwealth

Court of Appeals of Virginia
444 S.E.2d 663 (1994)

KOONTZ, Judge.

Lacy Hughes Johnson (Johnson) appeals his conviction in a bench trial on a charge of breaking and entering with the intent to commit a misdemeanor, Code § 18.2-92. Johnson asserts that Code § 18.2-92 requires that at the time of entry by an accused, the dwelling must be physically occupied. Johnson further asserts that the evidence was insufficient to show that he broke and entered the home or that he did so with the requisite intent to commit a misdemeanor. For the reasons that follow, we affirm Johnson's conviction.

I.

Factual Background

Johnson was indicted on a charge of burglary, Code § 18.2-89, and petit larceny, Code § 18.2-96, by the grand jury of the City of Danville. At the trial of those charges, the judge sitting without a jury found Johnson guilty of the lesser included burglary offense of breaking and entering with the intent to commit a misdemeanor, Code § 18.2-92, and not guilty of petit larceny.

The evidence at trial showed that on September 29, 1991, Brenda Broadnax (Broadnax) was at her apartment in Danville between 8:30 and 9:00 p.m. Johnson and several other men arrived at the apartment and knocked on the door. When Broadnax answered the door, one of the men asked, "Does Carlos live here?" Broadnax, whose son is Carlos Brooks, replied, "Yes, that's my son."

George Johnson (George), whom Broadnax knew as "Little Bee" claimed that Carlos had assaulted his aunt. Broadnax believed that the group intended to fight her son. Broadnax testified that she was nervous and scared because the group was so large. After one of the men said they should "[d]rag [Carlos's] a__ out of there . . . ain't gotta do all this talking," Broadnax asked George to come in alone and discuss the matter. When he refused, she closed the door.

Broadnax testified that the door was immediately kicked open by someone in the group. Broadnax closed the door again and locked it. Broadnax, her husband, and son escaped by another exit. As they drove away, several men from the group chased their car, and one threw a brick which hit the vehicle's rear windshield.

After calling the police and attempting to locate her brothers, who lived nearby, Broadnax returned to her apartment to find the front door broken in and considerable damage done to the home and its contents. A number of personal possessions were missing from the apartment.

Allen Lipscomb (Lipscomb) and Brian Terry (Terry) testified for the Commonwealth. Both men admitted being present at the Broadnax apartment on September 29. Lipscomb testified that Johnson told him that George was going to fight Broadnax's son and invited him to come watch. After Broadnax closed and locked the door, Lipscomb and several others decided to leave. Just as they stepped off the apartment house porch, Lipscomb "heard somthin[g] boom, and the door [to the Broadnax apartment] was open. . . ." The group returned to the hall outside the apartment. At that time, Johnson, George, and Terry had already entered the Broadnax apartment. Although Lipscomb saw the others "tearing up stuff," he only saw Johnson stand in the middle of the front room for about thirty seconds to a minute. Lipscomb said that Terry knocked over a television set.

Terry denied that he had entered the home. He testified that "Monty Boo" was the third person to enter the apartment with Johnson and George. Terry was unsure, but thought that "Monty Boo's" real name was Alan Lipscomb. Terry further testified that it was "Monty Boo" who knocked over and broke the television set. Although Terry confirmed that items were taken from the apartment, he did not testify that Johnson performed any acts of vandalism or took anything from the apartment.

After his motion to strike was denied, Johnson called Corey Payne (Payne) as a witness. Payne testified that after "Monty Boo" kicked in the door of the Broadnax apartment, Payne left the area. He testified that Johnson and George immediately left the area, following "behind" him. On cross-examination, Payne admitted that he failed to tell the investigating officer that Johnson and George had not entered the home, stating that the officer never asked specific questions about Johnson.

George "Little Bee" Johnson testified that he did not see who broke in the door of the Broadnax apartment. He further testified that Terry was the only person he saw enter the apartment. When he heard things being broken inside the apartment, George left and Johnson was "[r]ight behind" him and "gave [me] a little push." On cross-examination, George denied that he was the leader of the group and denied that he intended to fight Carlos Brooks. George testified that he and Johnson were on their way to his aunt's house when they encountered the group of men heading to the Broadnax apartment and joined them. He did not recall talking to Broadnax that night.

The Commonwealth called two rebuttal witnesses. Sandra Featherstone testified that she had seen Johnson in front of the Broadnax apartment, pushing against the front door. It is unclear from the testimony whether she was referring to the door to the apartment or the main entrance of the building. Detective W.I. Holley testified that he asked Payne about Johnson's actions and that Payne did not say Johnson left the area without entering the apartment.

II.

Burglary and Related Crimes

In this Commonwealth, there are four statutory forms of burglary and related breaking and entering crimes. Code § 18.2-89 defines traditional burglary (the breaking and entering of a dwelling house of another in the nighttime with the intent to commit a felony or any larceny therein). Code §§ 18.2-90 and 18.2-91 expand traditional common law burglary to include entry without breaking in the nighttime or breaking and entering in the daytime of any dwelling house and various other structures with the intent to commit murder, rape or robbery, Code § 18.2-90, or with the intent to commit larceny, assault and battery or any felony other than rape, murder, or robbery. Code § 18.2-91. Code § 18.2-92 further expands traditional common law burglary and provides that: "If any person break and enter a dwelling house *while said dwelling is occupied*, either in the day or nighttime, with the intent to commit any misdemeanor except assault and battery or trespass, he shall be guilty of a Class 6 felony." (Emphasis added.)[1]

A violation of any of the four burglary crimes while armed with a deadly weapon is a class 2 felony. Violation of Code §§ 18.2-89, if unarmed, is a class 3 felony. Violation of Code § 18.2-92 while unarmed is a class 6 felony. Thus, Code § 18.2-92 is a lesser included offense of Code § 18.2-89, the principal distinction being that under Code § 18.2-92 the crime intended upon entry is a non-theft misdemeanor rather than a felony. Other than by judicial extension in some jurisdictions, there was no common law equivalent to Code § 18.2-92.[2] *See* 12A C.J.S. *Burglary* § 2 (1980).

III.

Necessity of Physical Occupation of the Dwelling

Johnson asserts that the phrase "while said dwelling is occupied" in Code § 18.2-92 creates an additional element for the offense, namely that at least one occupant must be physically present in the dwelling house at the time of the breaking and entering. We disagree.

We begin our analysis by noting that in a minority of jurisdictions, the necessity of physical presence of an occupant in the dwelling is an element in determining the degree of the crime charged. *See* Annotation, *Burglary of Dwelling-No Occupants*, 20 A.L.R.4th 349, 355-56 (1983). In North Carolina, for example, "[i]f the burglarized dwelling is occupied, the crime is burglary in the first degree; but if it is unoccupied, however momentarily, and whether known to the intruder or not, the crime is burglary in the second degree." *State v. Simons*, 65 N.C.App. 164, 308 S.E.2d 502, 503 (1983). In other states, knowledge of actual occupation must be shown. *See, e.g., State v. Stewart*, 123 Or.App. 147, 859 P.2d 545, 546 (1993) (burglary in the first degree requires that the accused break and enter with the knowledge that the house is physically occupied at the time); *State v. Ponds*, 18 Kan.App.2d 231, 850 P.2d 280, 282 (1993). In each instance, however, physical presence of an occupant is an element for distinguishing the degree of burglary committed, not for determining commission of the crime.

In this Commonwealth, there is no distinction between burglary of a dwelling whose occupants are present and one whose occupants are temporarily

---

1　At the time of the indictment and trial that are the subject of this appeal, Code § 18.2-92 read, in pertinent part, "with the intent to commit assault or any other misdemeanor except trespass. . . ." This statute was amended to its current form in 1992.

2　Breaking and entering a dwelling with the intent to commit a non-theft misdemeanor was punishable as a trespass under the common law. Accordingly, Code § 18.2-92 exempts those merely committing trespass from its application.

absent. *See Rash v. Commonwealth*, 9 Va.App. 22, 383 S.E.2d 749 (1989) (holding that Code § 18.2-89 is applicable to dwelling houses even though the occupants are temporarily absent at the time of the unlawful entry). Our decision in *Rash* also aides our interpretation of Code § 18.2-92. There, we held that the term "dwelling house" means "a place which human beings regularly use for sleeping" and that a "house remains a dwelling house so long as the occupant intends to return [to it for that purpose]." Thus, we concluded that Code § 18.2-89 is applicable to dwelling houses even though the occupants are temporarily absent at the time of the unlawful entry. *Rash*, 9 Va.App. at 26-27, 383 S.E.2d at 751. This analysis is equally applicable to the provisions of Code § 18.2-92. Accordingly, we hold that the phrase "while said dwelling is occupied" in Code § 18.2-92 is not an element of the crime requiring the physical presence of the occupant at the time of the unlawful entry. Rather, it is language intended by the legislature to emphasize the character of the use of the dwelling as a place of current habitation rather than a dwelling that is temporarily vacant.

In so construing the statute, we recognize that "[t]he plain, obvious, and rational meaning of a statute is always preferred to any curious, narrow or strained construction." *Branch v. Commonwealth*, 14 Va.App. 836, 839, 419 S.E.2d 422, 424 (1992). Nonetheless, "[a]lthough penal laws are to be construed strictly [against the Commonwealth], they 'ought not to be construed so strictly as to defeat the obvious intention of the legislature.'" *Willis v. Commonwealth*, 10 Va.App. 430, 441, 393 S.E.2d 405, 411 (1990) (quoting *Huddleston v. United States*, 415 U.S. 814, 831, 94 S.Ct. 1262, 1271-72, 39 L.Ed.2d 782 (1974)). Nor should a statute be construed so that it leads to absurd results. *Branch*, 14 Va.App. at 839, 419 S.E.2d at 424.

To accept Johnson's interpretation of the statute, we would reach the absurd result that where, as in this case, occupants are forced to flee their home by terroristic threats immediately prior to a break-in, no criminal act of burglary occurs in the subsequent breaking and entering of the dwelling to commit acts of vandalism. This interpretation would clearly "defeat the obvious intention of the legislature" in extending the common law protection of habitation against unlawful entry for felonious and larcenous purposes to include instances where the criminal intent was to commit a non-theft misdemeanor.

We further note that where our legislature has desired to create as an element of a crime the contemporaneous physical occupation of a dwelling, it has done so expressly and without reservation. *See* Code § 18.2-279 (using the phrase "dwelling house or other building *when occupied by one or more persons*" in criminalizing the firing of a firearm or missile within or at a building or dwelling house) (emphasis added). Accordingly, we do not believe that our holding, a view in accord with the majority of other state jurisdictions, *see* Annotation, *Burglary of a Dwelling-No Occupants*, 20 A.L.R.4th at 357-60, renders a curious, narrow or strained construction of Code § 18.2-92.

IV.

Sufficiency of the Evidence

Johnson further asserts that the evidence presented at trial was insufficient to show that he broke and entered the Broadnax apartment, or that if he did so, he had the requisite intent to commit a misdemeanor as required by Code § 18.2-92. We disagree. "On appeal, we review the evidence in the light most favorable to the Commonwealth, granting to it all reasonable inferences fairly deducible therefrom. The judgment of a trial court sitting without a jury is entitled to the same weight as a jury verdict and will not be set aside unless it appears from the evidence that the judgment is plainly wrong or without evidence to support it." *Martin v. Commonwealth*, 4 Va.App. 438, 443, 358 S.E.2d 415, 418 (1987) (citing Code § 8.01-680). "'[T]he finding of the judge, upon the credibility of the witnesses and the weight to be given their evidence, stands on the same footing as the verdict of a jury, and unless that finding is plainly wrong, or without evidence to support it, it cannot be disturbed.'" *Speight v. Commonwealth*, 4 Va.App. 83, 88, 354 S.E.2d 95, 98 (1987) (*en banc*) (quoting *Lane v. Commonwealth*, 184 Va. 603, 611, 35 S.E.2d 749, 752 (1945)).

Here, the evidence proved that Johnson was present at the scene of the break-in and that he was inside the Broadnax apartment immediately following the break-in. Although Featherstone's testimony was not conclusive as to what door-the main door of the apartment building or the interior apartment door-she saw Johnson push against, the trier of fact was privileged to weigh this evidence and determine whether or not Johnson committed an act of breaking.

Moreover, the Commonwealth was not required to show that Johnson was the principal housebreaker. The evidence was sufficient to show that he acted as a principal in the second degree. *Rollston v. Commonwealth*, 11 Va.App. 535, 538, 399 S.E.2d 823, 825 (1991). Johnson's mere presence does not establish participation in the break-in; however, other circumstances surrounding his presence and his subsequent entry into the dwelling are sufficient to establish that he shared the criminal intent to break into the apartment. *See Id.* Accordingly, the trial judge could have determined either that Jonson was the housebreaker or that by his presence and actions he aided and abetted the housebreaker. In either case, the necessary elements of breaking and entering were established by the Commonwealth's evidence, and we cannot say that the trial court's finding that those elements were present was plainly wrong.

Similarly, the required intent to commit some misdemeanor could be inferred by Johnson's participation either as the principal housebreaker or as a principal in the second degree to the breaking and his subsequent entry into the home. The Supreme Court has held that presence during the commission of a crime in connection with other circumstances showing intent to aid and abet the commission of that crime supports a fact finder's determination that a criminal intent existed. *See Foster v. Commonwealth*, 179 Va. 96, 100, 18 S.E.2d 314, 316 (1942). Johnson's presence in the midst of various acts of vandalism and larceny is consistent with the trial court's finding that he possessed a guilty intent upon entry into the home. We cannot say that the trial court's finding that Johnson possessed the necessary intent was clearly wrong.

For these reasons, the judgment appealed from is affirmed.

Affirmed.

BENTON, Judge, dissenting.

This is a case that requires construction of a criminal statute. The statute reads as follows:

> If any person break and enter a dwelling house *while said dwelling is occupied,* either in the day or nighttime, with the intent to commit assault or any other misdemeanor except trespass, he shall be guilty of a Class 6 felony; provided, however, that if such person was armed with a deadly weapon at the time of such entry, he shall be guilty of a Class 2 felony.

Code § 18.2-92 (emphasis added).

"[B]ecause the statute in question is penal in nature, it must be strictly construed against the state and limited in application to cases falling clearly within the language of the statute." *Turner v. Commonwealth*, 226 Va. 456, 459, 309 S.E.2d 337, 338 (1983). Furthermore, rules of statutory construction also suggest as follows:

> Where possible, a statute should be construed with a view toward harmonizing it with other statutes. Because the Code of Virginia is one body of law, other Code sections using the same phraseology may be consulted in determining the meaning of a statute.

Branch v. Commonwealth, 14 Va.App. 836, 839, 419 S.E.2d 422, 425 (1992) (citations omitted). Moreover, the rule is well established that "statutes relating to the same subject should be read and construed together." *Turner*, 226 Va. at 461, 309 S.E.2d at 339.

In *Rash v. Commonwealth*, 9 Va.App. 22, 383 S.E.2d 749 (1989), this Court defined the term "dwelling house" as it is used in the common law and in Code

§ 18.2-89.[3] The Court held "that the term 'dwelling house' in Code § 18.2-89 means a place which human beings regularly use for sleeping." *Id.* at 26, 383 S.E.2d at 751. Thus, the Court reasoned that a "house remains a dwelling house so long as the occupant intends to return." *Id.* Because all dwelling houses must have an "occupant" in order to satisfy the definition of "dwelling house," all dwelling houses are necessarily "occupied" in the sense that they are regular residences.

Logic and the rules of statutory construction dictate that the term "dwelling house," as defined for purposes of Code § 18.2-89, has the same meaning when used in Code § 18.2-92, a related statutory burglary offense. Code § 18.2-92 prohibits any person from "break[ing] and enter[ing] a dwelling house while said dwelling is occupied." The word "occupied" is a modifier which, in the context of the statute, can only connote either an actual physical presence in the dwelling or regular and usual use of the dwelling by persons as a residence. *See Webster's Third New International Dictionary*, Unabridged (1981). If in interpreting the statute, we use the term "dwelling house" in the manner consistent with the holding in *Rash* (i.e., a residence that regularly and usually has an occupant), the word "occupied" in Code § 18.2-92 must be limited to actual physical presence. To do otherwise is to create a redundancy or to read out of the statute the word "occupied." When interpreting Code § 18.2-92, we may not do either because we "have a duty to give full force and effect to every word [of the statutes]." *Foote v. Commonwealth*, 11 Va.App. 61, 65, 396 S.E.2d 851, 854 (1990).

The evidence did not prove that Johnson entered the dwelling house "while said dwelling [was] occupied." No evidence proved that anyone was present within the dwelling. Indeed, the evidence proved that the three people who were in the apartment locked the door, got into an automobile, and drove away. After they left the apartment, Johnson and his companions entered the apartment. Accordingly, I would hold that the dwelling was not occupied and reverse the conviction.

---

3   Code § 18.2-89 reads as follows:

If any person break and enter the dwelling house of another in the nighttime with intent to commit a felony or any larceny therein, he shall be guilty of burglary, punishable as a Class 3 felony; provided, however, that if such person was armed with a deadly weapon at the time of such entry, he shall be guilty of a Class 2 felony.

Notes and Questions

Assuming Judge Benton has the better end of the textual interpretation (and it is not clear that he does), is there not a *very* strong policy reason for not allowing the defendants the benefit of an interpretation of the statute finding that this dwelling to be "unoccupied"? Were the acts of the defendants somehow mitigated because the occupants found it necessary to flee their home for their personal safety?

---

5. With the Intent to Commit a Crime

All states have retained the requirement that the defendant enter a dwelling with the intent to commit a crime. Most states require that the entry be for the purpose of a felony, though in some jurisdictions, entry for the purpose of committing any crime is sufficient. Some jurisdictions create a lesser included offense to burglary when the intended crime is not a felony—Virginia, for instance, has a crime of breaking and entering with the intent to commit a misdemeanor.

While criminal codes are filled with felonies, theft is the most common criminal motive for an unlawful entry that leads to a burglary conviction. As mental states go, one would think that proving intent would be more difficult than proving the other mental states, for instance, knowledge, recklessness or negligence. But, as with everything else, context is everything. Where the prosecution seeks to prove that the defendant sought to steal from a building, the proof of the other elements of burglary suffice to demonstrate the *mens rea*. Read the *Hall* decision and ask yourself whether the *mens rea* requirement for burglary places any real burden on the prosecution.

Hall v. State

Supreme Court of Tennessee
490 S.W.2d 495 (1973)

HUMPHREYS, Justice.

The plaintiff-in-error, Herman Hall, was indicted for first degree burglary with intent to commit larceny. He was tried and found guilty of an attempt to commit a felony, with punishment fixed at not more than four (4) years in the penitentiary.

The Court of Criminal Appeals affirmed the judgment of the trial court. This Court granted certiorari for the purpose of stating, definitively, the effect of certain fact situations in burglary cases.

The facts pertinent to our purpose are that Hall was apprehended by a neighbor of George Williams, who saw him breaking into the Williams' residence at 1:15 A.M., September 25, 1971. The neighbor held Hall with a shotgun until the police arrived. Hall had cut the screen in the back storm door in order to open the inner wooden door. The inner wooden door, although partly open, was still held by a night latch. The neighbor testified that he saw Hall's hand and arm inside the wooden door. Hall told the neighbor that he was lost.

After a standard Miranda warning, the defendant told the arresting officer he chose that house because he saw no car and assumed no one was at home. When arrested, Hall had in his possession a brake tool, pliers, a screwdriver, and a flashlight. Further, there was evidence of tool marks on the inner door.

The defendant contends that the State's evidence was insufficient to show the necessary intent to commit a specific crime. *Gervin v. State*, 212 Tenn. 653, 371 S.W.2d 449 (1963). The question, then, is whether the intent to commit a specific crime, such as entry with intent to commit larceny, can be inferred from the circumstantial evidence in this case. There is no specific statement in our case law on this particular subject.

An attempt to commit a crime requires three elements: (1) the intent to commit a specific crime; (2) an overt act; and (3) failure to consummate the intended crime. 1 Wharton, *Criminal Law and Procedure*, § 71 at 151–152 (1957). It is a general proposition of the criminal law, however, that 'circumstantial evidence may determine . . . such facts or elements as the existence of an intent . . . .' 3 Wharton, *Criminal Evidence* § 980 at 467—468 (1955). In fact, intent can rarely be shown by direct proof and must, necessarily, be shown by circumstantial evidence. While our cases say that all elements of a crime can be proved by circumstantial evidence, *McClary v. State*, 211 Tenn. 46, 362 S.W.2d 450 (1962); *Smith v. State*, 205 Tenn. 502, 327 S.W.2d 308 (1959); *Marable v. State*, 203 Tenn. 440, 313 S.W.2d 451 (1958), we have no case directly on the effect of such facts as were proved in this case.

In *State v. Morelock*, 164 N.W.2d 819 (Iowa 1969), the defendants were charged with attempt to break and enter a business establishment with intent to commit larceny. The evidence showed that when apprehended the defendants were attempting to gain illegal entry into a closed business establishment, they had damaged the door and lock by employing force, and they were apprehended at a time when entry was almost effected. They had in their possession gloves, a flashlight, a screwdriver, and a crowbar. The court held that the intent to steal could be inferred from the actual breaking and entering of a building which contains things of value or from an attempt to do so. A sample of other cases so holding is as follows: *People v. Nelson*, 89 Ill.App.2d 84, 233 N.E.2d 64 (1967); *State v. McClelland*, 164 N.W.2d 189 (Iowa 1969); *State v. Jones*, 143 Mont. 155, 387 P.2d 913 (1963); *State v. Smith*, 8 Ohio Misc. 148, 221 N.E.2d 627 (1966); *Hutchinson v. State*, 481 S.W.2d 881 (Tex.Cr.App. 1972).

These and other authorities warrant us in stating as a general proposition that where one is apprehended, attempting forcibly, or with present means of force, to gain illegal entry into a residence or a building in which there is property which is the subject of larceny, a jury would be warranted in inferring, in the absence of an acceptable excuse, that the entry was made, or attempted, with intent to commit larceny.

A review of the evidence in the case sub judice reveals that it comes within this proposition. The defendant was attempting to gain illegal entry into a residence, the attempt was being carried on through the use of force and with the use of several tools, the outside screen door had been cut and the inner door partially opened, and the defendant was apprehended still attempting to effect entrance. We hold that the intent to steal may be inferred from the breaking and entering of a building which contains things of value or from the attempt to do so. Here, there was sufficient circumstantial evidence from which the jury could infer that intent.

The judgment of the trial court and the Court of Criminal Appeals is affirmed.

Notes and Questions

1. Many state statutes have similar presumptions, that an unlawful entry is done for an unlawful purpose. *See* Wash. Stat. Ann. § 9A.52.040 ("In any prosecution for burglary, any person who enters or remains unlawfully in a building may be inferred to have acted with intent to commit a crime against a person or property therein, unless such entering or remaining shall be explained by evidence satisfactory to the trier of fact to have been made without such criminal intent.")

2. Professor Helen Anderson has persuasively argued that burglary should not be a crime at all. She observes that burglary is a compound crime—it punishes trespass, or breaking and entering, done as part of an attempt to commit larceny, assault, rape, or any felony. Punishment for each aspect of burglary is therefore already provided. Anderson argues that the common law elements of burglary have become so relaxed that a host of conduct now qualifies as

burglary—conduct already punishable under other provisions of criminal codes. Thus, burglary does nothing more than provide a means for prosecutors to seek additional punishment for crimes already defined and punished. Helen A. Anderson, *From the Thief in the Night to the Guest Who Stayed Too Long: The Evolution of Burglary in the Shadow of the Common Law*, 45 Ind. L. Rev. 629 (2012). After reading the *Hall* case, do you find her argument compelling? Burglary also relaxes the attempt requirement, especially where the burglar's intent is larceny because of the presumption that the intent is to commit larceny.

6. Attempted Burglary and Possession of Burglar's Tools

The ultimate conclusion of the *Hines* case should seem troubling to you. The court is willing to draw quite an inference from the fact that the defendant went to a front door and left when a light was turned on.

Hines v. State

Court of Criminal Appeals of Texas
458 S.W.2d 666 (1977)

MORRISON, Judge.

The offense is attempted burglary with two prior non capital convictions alleged for enhancement; the punishment, life.

The sufficiency of the evidence is challenged. The allegedly injured party testified that after midnight on Halloween night he was in his garage and observed a man, whom he later identified as appellant, at a door of his house with a hand on the door. At this time, he turned on the light, and the appellant fled. We need not pass upon the one man lineup identification of appellant, because we find the evidence insufficient to support the jury finding that appellant attempted to break and enter the injured party's house.

The writer has examined all previous holdings of this Court and finds that the facts in *Jackson v. State*, 145 Tex.Cr.R. 46, 165 S.W.2d 740, more nearly correspond to those before us here. In that case, the accused was seen on a 'ledge of a window in the Stevenson's house.' Judge Hawkins, with his usual dry wit, observed that 'appellant was certainly apprehended in a most embarrassing and suspicious position. He may have intended to enter the house for the purpose of stealing * * *. It may be fortunate for appellant that the vigilance of the officers brought them to the scene in time to save him from effecting his designs.'

This case, as well as Jackson, *supra*, is to be distinguished from all other cases brought under this article in that no physical injury to the building was shown which would evidence an actual intent to break and enter. Appellant was not shown to have any tools or equipment as commonly appears in cases of this nature. For all this record shows, he might have been a window peeper. See the cases annotated in 12 C.J.S. Burglary § 63.

Because the evidence is insufficient to support the conviction, the judgment is reversed and the cause remanded.

OPINION ON STATE'S MOTION FOR REHEARING

DOUGLAS, Judge.

In the original opinion, the Court held the evidence insufficient to support the conviction. The evidence, considered in the light most favorable to the State, will be reviewed again.

E. L. Flynt was in his garage in his yard between midnight and one o'clock in the morning checking a water heater when he heard the gate between his driveway and the yard close. He waited for someone to enter the garage, but when no one appeared, he went to the garage door and saw a man standing by the back door of his house. He then turned on the back yard light and saw appellant, who had one hand on the door handle and one hand on the wall of the house, looking through the screen door into the house.

Appellant jumped off the back step and ran and attempted to leave through another gate, but when he could not open it he jumped over the fence and fled.

On the night in question, the curtains at a large picture window in the front of the house were open. One passing the house could have seen a lady's purse on a couch in the room. The door from which appellant fled opened into the room where the purse was located.

Article 1402, Vernon's Ann.P.C., 'Attempt at Burglary,' provides:

> 'An 'attempt' is an endeavor to accomplish the crime of burglary carried beyond mere preparation, but falling short of the ultimate design in any part of it. * * *'

Here, appellant was within the enclosed back yard of a man who did not know him, after midnight, with a hand on the door. When the light was turned on, he attempted to open the gate and then jumped the fence and fled.

The jury had before it sufficient evidence to conclude that appellant was attempting to enter the house.

To show an attempt to commit burglary, the intent of the defendant must be established.

The act of breaking and entering a house at nighttime raises a presumption that it is done with intent to steal. *Green v. State*, Tex.Cr.App., 435 S.W.2d 513;

Sikes v. State, 166 Tex.Cr.R. 257, 312 S.W.2d 524; *Bonner v. State*, Tex.Cr.App., 375 S.W.2d 723; *Briones v. State*, Tex.Cr.App., 363 S.W.2d 466; *Rodgers v. State*, 164 Tex.Cr.R. 375, 298 S.W.2d 827.

We hold that the same presumption of intent to steal applies where there has been an attempted entry at nighttime.

Flight may be considered by the jury as evidence of guilt. *Churchill v. State*, 167 Tex.Cr.R. 26, 317 S.W.2d 541; 1 Branch's Ann. P.C.2d, Secs. 158, 161.

The evidence showing an attempt to enter the house at nighttime, without consent of the owner, plus the presumption that such attempted entry was with the intent to commit theft, is sufficient to support the conviction.

It is not necessary for one to be in possession of tools to show an attempted burglary. Article 1394, V.A.P.C., provides:

'By 'breaking,' as used in this chapter, is meant that the entry must be made with actual force. The slightest force, however, is sufficient to constitute breaking; it may be by lifting the latch of a door that is shut, or by raising a window, the entry at a chimney, or other unusual place, the introduction of the hand or any instrument to draw out the property through an aperture made by the offender for that purpose.'

* * *

The motion for rehearing is granted; the judgment of reversal is set aside. The judgment is affirmed.

MORRISON, Judge (dissenting).

I am convinced of the soundness of the original opinion and dissent to the affirmance of this conviction.

Consider how the crime of possession of burglary tools can be used to avoid the proximity requirements that Judge Morrison saw in the last case involving attempted burglary.

Henley v. State

Mississippi Supreme Court
136 So.2d 413 (2014)

WALLER, Chief Justice, for the Court:

Derrick Montrell Henley appeals the verdict of a Neshoba County Circuit Court jury finding him guilty of possession of burglary tools. We find that the State failed to present sufficient evidence that Rice intended to use the tools in question to aid in the commission of a burglary. Accordingly, we reverse and render Henley's conviction and sentence.

FACTS

The events of this case occurred at Central Mississippi Recycling in Philadelphia, Mississippi, just after midnight on June 20, 2011. Central Mississippi Recycling consists of a main office building and four other buildings. The property has one main entrance and four secondary entrances. When the business is closed, the main entrance is secured by a "gate" consisting of a metal cable hanging across the driveway. When property manager Gene Luke left the property on June 19, 2011, he made sure that the gate to the main entrance was locked.

Due to several previous burglaries at Central Mississippi Recycling, the Philadelphia Police Department had increased its patrol of the area. Sometime after midnight on June 20, 2011, Officer Jonathan Dearing was patrolling near Central Mississippi Recycling when he noticed that the gate to the main entrance of the property had been laid on the ground. He pulled onto the property, exited his vehicle, and checked the gate. The cable appeared to have cut marks on it, and the cable clamps for the gate had been loosened, which had caused the cable to fall to the ground. Dearing returned to his vehicle, drove over the cable, and began to investigate the rest of the property. After driving around the property for some time, Dearing observed a vehicle driving with its headlights off around the side of one of the buildings. Upon noticing Dearing, the vehicle turned around, turned its lights on, and started to leave the property. Dearing then initiated his blue lights and stopped the vehicle approximately three hundred yards from the main entrance of the property.

Dearing approached the vehicle and asked the driver what he was doing on the property. The driver responded that he was looking for a place to turn around. Dearing asked the driver for identification, but the driver had none, explaining that his license had been suspended. The driver then told Dearing that his name was Derrick Henley and gave Dearing his social security number. At that point, Dearing noticed pliers and bolt cutters on the floor of Henley's vehicle. Screwdrivers, wrenches, and a socket set also were found in Henley's car. Dearing asked Henley to exit the vehicle and searched him, finding a flashlight in Henley's pocket.

Henley was taken into custody and questioned by Lieutenant Dan Refre of the Philadelphia Police Department. Henley denied any involvement in any criminal activity and explained that he was merely turning around in the Central Mississippi Recycling parking lot when he was pulled over.

PROCEDURAL HISTORY

Henley was indicted for possession of burglary tools in violation of Section 97–17–35 of the Mississippi Code. *See* Miss.Code Ann. § 97–17–35 (Rev.2006). His indictment alleged that he "did willfully, unlawfully and feloniously possess tools designed to aid in the commission of a burglary, to-wit: bolt cutters, pliers and a flashlight[.]" A jury trial was held on November 7, 2012, in the Neshoba County Circuit Court. Luke, Dearing, and Refre testified for the State. The bolt cutters and pliers found in Henley's vehicle and the flashlight found on his person were admitted into evidence during the State's case-in-chief. At the conclusion of the State's case-in-chief, Henley moved for a directed verdict, arguing that the State had failed to prove that he had possessed the tools with the intent to commit a burglary. The trial court overruled Henley's motion, and Henley declined to offer any evidence in defense. During closing arguments, Henley's attorney argued that Henley had the tools in his vehicle because he worked as a mechanic and asserted that the bolt cutters showed no signs of use. Henley also requested that the Court give a peremptory instruction, which instructed the jury to find Henley not guilty, but this request was denied.

The jury returned a unanimous verdict finding Henley guilty of possession of burglary tools, and the court sentenced him to five years' imprisonment. Henley moved for a new trial, but the trial court denied his motion. Henley now appeals to this Court, arguing that the trial court erred in denying Henley's motion for a directed verdict, his request for a peremptory instruction, and his request for a new trial. Because we find that the State's evidence in this case was legally insufficient to secure a guilty verdict, we will discuss only Henley's argument regarding the trial court's denial of his motion for directed verdict and request for peremptory instruction.

STANDARD OF REVIEW

Both a motion for a directed verdict and a request for a peremptory instruction challenge the legal sufficiency of the evidence; thus, the standard of review for peremptory instructions and directed verdicts is the same. *Wall v. State*, 718 So.2d 1107, 1111 (Miss.1998). This Court reviews a challenge to the sufficiency of the evidence in the light most favorable to the State, giving the State the benefit of all favorable inferences reasonably drawn from the evidence. *Graham v. State*, 120 So.3d 382, 386–87 (Miss.2013) (citations omitted). "If the facts and inferences so considered point in favor of the defendant on *any* element of the offense with sufficient force that reasonable men could not have found beyond a reasonable doubt that the defendant was guilty," this Court must reverse and render. *Edwards v. State*, 469 So.2d 68, 70 (Miss.1985) (citing *May v. State*, 460 So.2d 778, 781 (Miss.1984)) (emphasis in original). We review a challenge to the sufficiency of the evidence on the last occasion that the trial court ruled on the sufficiency of the evidence. *McClain v. State*, 625 So.2d 774, 778 (Miss.1993). In this case, the last occasion on which the trial court ruled on the sufficiency of the evidence was in its denial of Henley's request for a peremptory instruction.

DISCUSSION

I. Whether the Trial Court Erred In Denying Henley's Request For a Peremptory Instruction.

Henley argues that he was entitled to a peremptory instruction because the evidence presented by the State was legally insufficient to prove that he intended to use the tools in question to aid in the commission of a burglary.

Section 97–17–35 of the Mississippi Code makes it unlawful "for any person to have in his possession implements, tools, or instruments designed to aid in the commission of burglary, larceny or robbery [.]" Miss.Code Ann. § 97–17–35 (Rev.2006). This Court has interpreted the statute to include the following elements: "(1) adaptation and design of the tool or implement for breaking and entering; (2) possession of such tools by one with knowledge of their character, and (3) a general intent to use or employ them in breaking and entering." *Pamphlet v. State*, 271 So.2d 403, 405 (Miss.1972) (citing *Johnson v. State*, 246 Miss. 182, 145 So.2d 156 (1962)). The elements of the design of the tool and the intent to use the tool are interrelated. Regarding the adaptation and design of the tool, this Court has held that "[I]t is not necessary that the tool or article be designed and made solely for use as a burglar's tool." *Fuqua v. State*, 246 Miss. 191, 199, 145 So.2d 152, 154 (1962). Whether the tools described in the indictment were intended to be used as burglary tools is a question for the jury. *Salisbury v. State*, 293 So.2d 434, 437 (Miss.1974). However, "[t]he carrying concealed about one's person, or in one's baggage, implements, tools, or instruments *peculiarly adapted* to aid in the commission of burglary, larceny or robbery, shall be prima facie evidence of intention to use them for such purpose." Miss.Code Ann. § 97–17–35 (Rev.2006) (emphasis added). As for the defendant's intent, this Court has held that "[a]lthough it is not necessary to show a specific intent to use the tools in a burglary, there must be evidence either that the tools have probably been recently used for the purpose of unlawfully breaking and entering or that they are about to be used for such purpose." *Pamphlet*, 271 So.2d at 405 (citing *McCollum v. State*, 197 So.2d 252 (Miss.1967)).

While this Court has held that possession of ordinary tools can be punishable under Section 97–17–35, we also have recognized an "underlying harmony in our opinions as to adaptation of *ordinary* articles and tools used to burglarize." *Salisbury*, 293 So.2d at 436 (emphasis added). "The outstanding evidence in each case [involving the possession of otherwise ordinary tools] points to at least one of the tools readily recognized as a burglary tool." *Id.* For example, in *Fuqua*, the defendant had in his possession spotlights, a box of socket wrenches, a pair of black gloves, a large flashlight, a keyhole flashlight, and two large magnets, all of which are susceptible to innocent use. *Fuqua*, 246 Miss. at 197, 145 So.2d 152. However, the defendant also possessed a box of 150 skeleton keys, recognized as tools peculiarly adapted to aid in the commission of a burglary, along with a police badge and a stolen firearm. *Id.* at 198, 145 So.2d 152. This Court affirmed the defendant's conviction for possession of burglary tools, finding that his unexplained possession of the numerous skeleton keys was "strong evidence that they were possessed for a felonious purpose."[1] *Id.* at 200, 145 So.2d 152. The other articles found in the defendant's possession were described by this Court as "useful adjuncts to burglar's tools," and the defendant's possession of them became unlawful when the evidence showed that the defendant intended to use them in combination with the skeleton keys and firearms for an unlawful purpose. *Id.* at 199, 145 So.2d 152. *See also McCollum*, 197 So.2d at 256 (possession of crowbars, hammers, and a bolt cutter, along with a "burglar alarm jumper," a device used to circumvent the "setting off" of a burglar alarm); *Corn v. State*, 250 Miss. 157, 159, 164 So.2d 777, 778 (1964) (possession of sledgehammer to which a chisel had been welded, a tool commonly used by burglars to break open safes).

In each of the cases cited above, the defendant's concealed possession of a tool peculiarly designed to aid in the commission of a burglary—skeleton keys, a burglar alarm jumper, a modified sledgehammer—served as prima facie evidence of the defendant's intent to use that tool in the commission of a burglary. However, this Court has never affirmed a defendant's conviction for possessing burglary tools in a case where the evidence did not point to at least one tool peculiarly designed as a burglary tool. The Court of Appeals has affirmed a defendant's conviction in such a case, but only upon proof that the defendant actually had committed a burglary. *Peters v. State*, 920 So.2d 1050, 1053 (Miss. Ct.App.2006). In *Peters*, the defendant was charged with possession of burglary tools, and with the burglary of two county-owned mechanic shops. *Id.* Police

---

1 This Court noted that cases from other jurisdictions reveal that possession of skeleton keys probably has resulted in more convictions for possession of burglary tools than any other implement. *Fuqua*, 246 Miss. at 200, 145 So.2d 152.

officers recovered a small crowbar, wire cutters, vice grips, two screwdrivers, and a pair of sunglasses from the defendant's vehicle. *Id.* At the defendant's trial, a shop employee testified that the sunglasses belonged to him and had gone missing after the burglary. *Id.* He also recognized the wire cutters and screwdrivers as tools used in the shop, but he did not recognize the crowbar. *Id.* The State also presented an expert witness who testified that shoeprints found at the crime scenes possessed "all the class characteristics" of the shoes the defendant was wearing when he was arrested. *Id.* On appeal, the defendant argued that the crowbar he possessed was an ordinary tool, and that the State had failed to prove that he intended to use the crowbar for an unlawful purpose. *Id.* at 1054. The Court of Appeals rejected this argument, finding that the State's evidence was sufficient "to show beyond a reasonable doubt that Peters possessed the crowbar knowing of its character, and that he intended to use, or had in fact used the crowbar to burglarize the county property." *Id.* at 1055.

This Court has reversed a defendant's conviction based on the State's failure to prove the element of felonious intent where the defendant possessed only ordinary tools. *Pamphlet v. State*, 271 So.2d 403 (Miss.1972). In *Pamphlet*, a tow-truck operator was towing the defendant's car out of a ditch when he noticed various tools inside the vehicle. *Id.* at 403–404. The truck operator informed a police officer of what he had seen in the vehicle. *Id.* at 404. The officer arrived at the scene, observed the tools inside the vehicle, and placed the defendant under arrest. *Id.* The officer then searched the car and found a pistol and some ammunition in the trunk. *Id.* The defendant was convicted of possession of burglary tools, but this Court reversed the conviction, finding that the State had presented no evidence showing that the defendant had intended to use the tools to commit a burglary. *Id.* The officer was not investigating a burglary, there was no evidence of an attempted burglary, and there was no proof that the defendant had used the tools found in his vehicle for any unlawful purpose or that he had intended to do so. *Id.* The evidence presented to the jury proved only that the defendant had unconcealed, ordinary tools lying on the back seat and floorboard of his car. *Id.* at 405. Because the State had presented insufficient evidence of felonious intent, this Court held that the trial court had erred in refusing to give the defendant's peremptory instruction. *Id.* at 404.

Viewing the evidence in the light most favorable to the prosecution, we find that the evidence in this case is more akin to *Pamphlet* than *Peters*. Henley does not contest his possession of the tools in question, but none of the tools he possessed was peculiarly adapted to be used as a burglary tool. Therefore, the State was required to present more specific evidence "either that the tools have probably been recently used for the purpose of unlawfully breaking and entering or that they are about to be used for such purpose." *Pamphlet*, 271 So.2d at 404.

We find that the State presented no such proof. Dearing was not investigating a burglary, nor was there any evidence of an attempted burglary, when Henley was discovered on the property. The State presented evidence that the gate to the property's front entrance had cut marks on it, but there was no proof that Henley's bolt cutters, or any bolt cutters for that matter, had produced the cut marks. Henley's presence on the property after business hours may raise suspicion, but this evidence alone fails to prove that he intended to use the tools in question to aid in the commission of a burglary. Unlike the defendant in *Peters*, who was found in possession of stolen property and whose shoes matched prints at the scene of a burglary, Henley was simply found in his vehicle with unconcealed tools that any mechanic or handyman would likely possess. The jury could only speculate regarding Henley's intent for possessing those tools. After reviewing the record in this case, we find that the State failed to present sufficient evidence "reveal[ing] circumstances from which it may be inferred *beyond a reasonable doubt* that [Henley] intended that he . . . use the article or articles in aid of [a] burglary or other similar crime." *Fuqua*, 246 Miss. at 199, 145 So.2d 152. Accordingly, we find that the trial court should have granted Henley's request for a peremptory instruction.

II. Whether the Trial Court Erred In Denying Henley's Motion For New Trial.

Because we are reversing the trial court's judgment based on the sufficiency of the evidence, it is unnecessary to discuss the weight of the evidence in this case.

CONCLUSION

Because the State failed to present evidence sufficient to prove Henley's felonious intent beyond a reasonable doubt, we reverse and render Henley's conviction and sentence.

REVERSED AND RENDERED.

KITCHENS, CHANDLER, KING and COLEMAN, JJ., Concur. DICKINSON, P.J., Dissents with separate written opinion joined by RANDOLPH, P.J., LAMAR and PIERCE, JJ. RANDOLPH, P.J., Dissents with separate written opinion joined by DICKINSON, P.J., LAMAR and PIERCE, JJ.

DICKINSON, Presiding Justice, dissenting:

Because the State presented sufficient evidence to sustain a conviction for possession of burglary tools, I respectfully dissent.

When we review the sufficiency of the evidence to support a criminal conviction, we must view the evidence in the light most favorable to the State, giving the State the benefit of all reasonable inferences which may be drawn from the evidence.[2] Because this case involves the possession of ordinary tools—as opposed to tools specifically designed to effectuate burglaries—the majority concludes that the State failed to prove felonious intent by showing "either that the tools have probably been recently used for the purpose of unlawfully breaking and entering or that they are about to be used for such purpose."[3]

But the majority errs by ignoring the considerable circumstantial evidence of felonious intent presented by the State. Dearing located Derrick Henley trespassing on the property of Central Mississippi Recycling in the middle of the night. Henley was driving around the property with his headlights off, and the property's main entrance gate—a gate that ordinarily is closed at the end of the work day—had been loosened to allow entry. When Henley saw Dearing, Henley attempted to leave the property, coming to a stop three hundred yards from the entrance, where Dearing found Henley in possession of pliers, bolt cutters, screwdrivers, wrenches, and a socket set.

Henley attempted to explain his presence on the property by claiming that he needed a place to turn around. But a reasonable jury could find that the State refuted Henley's story with the circumstantial evidence stated above. And while the majority is correct to state that a mechanic may very well have all of the tools Henley possessed in his car, a reasonable jury could find an innocent explanation unreasonable because Henley possessed those tools while trespassing in the middle of the night. Further, the jury was justified in finding criminal intent from the fact that Henley attempted to leave the property upon seeing law enforcement personnel.

This Court repeatedly has held that the State may prove the intent to distribute a controlled substance through nothing more than the amount possessed.[4] Certainly, the plethora of incriminating circumstantial evidence in this case is sufficient.

RANDOLPH, P.J., LAMAR AND PIERCE, JJ., Join this opinion.

RANDOLPH, Presiding Justice, dissenting:

Our standard of review for a challenge to the sufficiency of evidence has been repeated so often that supporting citations serve little value-we review the evidence in the light most favorable to the State. Today's majority fails to follow this established rule. I respectfully dissent.

---

2 *Bateman v. State*, 125 So.3d 616, 623, 624 (Miss.2013).

3 Maj. Op. ¶ 10 (quoting *Pamphlet v. State*, 271 So.2d 403, 405 (Miss.1972)) (citing *McCollum v. State*, 197 So.2d 252 (Miss.1967)).

4 *Keys v. State*, 478 So.2d 266, 268 (Miss.1985) (citing *Bryant v. State*, 427 So.2d 131, 132 (Miss.1983)).

Henley was indicted under Mississippi Code Section 97–17–35 for "willfully, unlawfully and feloniously possess[ing] tools designed to aid in the commission of a burglary, to-wit: bolt cutters, pliers and a flashlight. . . ." *See* Miss. Code Ann. § 97–17–35 (Rev.2006). Those tools are designed for a lawful use, but a tool "may be designed for a lawful use and still be a burglar's tool." *Fuqua v. State*, 246 Miss. 191, 145 So.2d 152, 154 (1962). Thus, Henley's possession of bolt cutters, pliers, and a flashlight "may or may not be unlawful . . . depending on whether the evidence reveals *circumstances from which it may be inferred* beyond a reasonable doubt that [Henley] intended" to use those tools "in aid of burglary or some other similar crime." *Id.* at 155 (emphasis added). The evidence is "sufficient if the circumstances justify the inference that the [tools] were possessed for such criminal purpose." *Id.* After the trial court rejected Henley's motion for a directed verdict, a jury found him guilty of the crime charged based on the circumstances surrounding his possession of the tools. Subsequently, the trial court denied Henley's motion for a new trial which challenged his conviction on the same grounds.

The circumstances surrounding Henley's apprehension in the middle of the night at Central Mississippi Recycling in Philadelphia, Mississippi, were sufficiently established at trial. The facility manager testified that, at the close of business prior to Henley's arrest, he secured the entrance to the facility with a cable and lock. After midnight that same evening, Philadelphia police officer Jonathan Dearing was patrolling the area and noticed that the cable was down. Upon closer investigation, Dearing observed that the "cable . . . appeared to [have] fresh cut marks on it" and "the cable clamps had been loosened." Dearing entered the facility and "observed a vehicle . . . coming around the side of [a] building with its headlights off [,]" more than 300 yards from the entrance. Upon spotting Dearing's patrol car, Henley turned his headlights on and attempted to exit.

Dearing testified that, after stopping the vehicle more than 300 yards from the gate, he approached the defendant's vehicle and saw "a pair of pliers on the center floorboard . . . and, on the passenger's side floorboard, [he] noticed a pair of bolt cutters." He testified that both were within Henley's reach. Dearing further testified that, upon searching Henley, he "found . . . a small flashlight in his front left pocket." Henley's only explanation for his presence at that location and time was that he was lost and looking for a place to turn around—an explanation reasonable jurors and the trial court obviously rejected, perhaps based on Henley's driving without his headlights on after midnight at a distance of more than 300 yards from the front gate and testimony that there was "plenty of room" to turn around at the gate without entering the property.

Viewing the evidence in the light most favorable to the State, sufficient evidence established that Henley entered the property with bolt cutters, pliers, and flashlight for a criminal purpose. Henley was found after midnight on property where he had no lawful right to be—property which earlier had been secured by a cable that was subsequently found on the ground with "fresh cut marks" and the "cable clamps loosened." He was found riding around the facility in the middle of the night with his headlights off, and, upon seeing Dearing's patrol car, he attempted to exit. The bolt cutters and pliers were on the front floorboard of Henley's car, and the flashlight was found in his pants pocket, all within accessible reach. Thus, I would affirm the trial court's conviction and sentence.

Notes and Questions

1. You should notice how this opinion very much feels like the type of analysis done in other types of attempt cases, where circumstantial evidence is crucial to the conviction. The difference here is that there is no proximity requirement, because the possession of the means to carry out the burglary provides all the necessary proximity. Nonetheless, the dissenting opinions rely heavily on the proximity of the defendant to the building and presence within the broken gate as circumstantial evidence that the otherwise normal tools were to be used for burglarizing the recycling plant. For the dissenting justices, this proximity was sufficient evidence that the burglary tools were to be used for an illegal purpose.

2. Does the majority substitute its opinion for the jury's? Note the majority cites *Salisbury v. State*, 293 So.2d 434, 437 (Miss.1974) for the proposition that the question of whether the tools described in the indictment were intended to be used as burglary tools is a question for the jury. If judges on a single court disagree on the sufficiency of the evidence, does that disagreement itself indicate that there is evidence sufficient to convict?

3. The majority relies on *Fuqua* for the proposition that particularized tools are strong evidence of possession of tools to be used to burglarize, and cites *Peters* and *Pamphlet* to demonstrate that tools which have not been particularized do not themselves provide sufficient evidence of possession of burglary tools. But are *Peters* and *Pamphlet* distinguishable? If you were a prosecutor handling this case, and read the defense counsel's brief citing these cases, how would you handle them?

PRACTICE EXERCISE

Read the following facts, statutes, and instructions.

Facts

  Akua was obsessed with Bethesda—everything about their "blossoming relationship" was wonderful. The two had been dating consistently—for two weeks. Akua saw great potential in their relationship, hoping it would "last forever," and was excited about joining Bethesda's family on their annual boating trip on Lake Champagne. Bethesda's parents were very wealthy, and enjoyed spending one week per year on the houseboat they owned, patrolling the blue waters on the lake, enjoying sunsets, and eating nice meals together.

  During the third day out on the lake, Akua noticed Bethesda's mother kept her very expensive diamond bracelet, Timerex watch, and prized ruby studded earrings in a small safe under the master bathroom sink. There were two bathrooms on the boat, but Akua noticed the safe, about the size of a large shoebox, because he was chatting with Bethesda's mother who wanted to "discuss plans for the day," while doing her makeup.

  On day five, Bethesda's father asked Akua to pilot the boat to the dock on the other side of the lake so that the three could have "just a few minutes of family time together." Akua was ready for this request, because it was discussed earlier in the week. After the three family members disembarked, and as the sun was setting, Akua shut off the boat, went to the tool locker at the rear of the boat, took the hand-truck (used for loading the boat with cargo for the week), opened the glass door to enter the hall, walked down the hall, opened the master bathroom door, and pulled the hand-truck up to the sink. After a good deal of effort and sweat, Akua succeeded in maneuvering the hundred pound safe onto the hand-truck. He immediately proceeded to the rear of the boat, with the safe, and pushed both the hand-truck and safe into the water ("splash!").

  Akua knew the water was only about fifteen feet deep at the docks where he had piloted the houseboat: "It'll be there to pick up later," he thought. Both the safe and hand-truck sank quickly to the bottom of the lake. When Bethesda and her family returned to the boat, Akua piloted the houseboat away from the dock, and all was well that night. At the end of the trip, Bethesda's mother opened the sink doors and shrieked—the safe was gone.

During the police investigation, the police found a snorkeling mask and 10-foot air tube in the trunk of Akua's vehicle, a weighted belt for diving, fins, and an underwater torch. The safe was discovered one month later, when another (better) houseboat "pinged" on the metal safe when it came into dock, because of its super-high-tech instruments. The hand-truck and safe were found directly below where Akua had docked the boat. The torch is capable of opening this particular type of safe, according to experts, but would require at least three straight minutes of cutting.

The police also discovered that Akua had two prior felony convictions: one for attempted robbery of a grocery store, and one for larceny; and that Akua is scuba-certified, meaning he passed a series of tests establishing his competency to safely dive with scuba gear.

Statutes

- *Burglary*

If any person in the daytime breaks and enters or enters and conceals himself in a dwelling house or an adjoining, occupied outhouse or in the nighttime enters without breaking or at any time breaks and enters or enters and conceals himself in any office, shop, manufactured home, storehouse, warehouse, banking house, or other house, or other place of human habitation, with intent to commit a crime, he shall be deemed guilty of statutory burglary.

- *Attempted Burglary*

If any person possesses tools which are likely to be used for carrying out a burglary, that person is guilty of attempted burglary.

Instructions: The Lake Champagne prosecutor has filed indictments against Akua for burglary and attempted burglary using all of the facts above. You are Akua's defense attorney. Draft a motion to dismiss for insufficient evidence, using the facts and the statutes. Assume Lake Champagne has not firmly decided any of the fundamental issues discussed in the readings. You may support your motion with a statutory analysis and policy arguments.

Consider: could Akua be convicted of larceny, larceny by trick, attempted larceny, embezzlement, or robbery?

D. Arson

The crime of arson involves the burning of either another's property without permission or the surreptitious burning of one's own property for the purpose of collecting on an insurance policy, or setting a fire or creating an explosion that places others in danger. Two primary questions arise in arson prosecutions: what *mens rea* is required for the initial fire or explosion and what *mens rea* applies to either the threatened harm or the harm that actually occurs from the fire or explosion. New Jersey's decision in *State v. M.N.*, reproduced in relevant part below, applies the *mens rea* element to the result of danger to persons or property as well as the act of lighting a fire, coinciding with the Model Penal Code approach. The Colorado Supreme Court's decision in *Copeland*, noted below, cites New Jersey's approach but arrives at a different conclusion under a legislative intent analysis. Colorado applies the *mens rea* element only to starting or maintaining a fire, not to the resulting danger to persons.

State v. M.N.

Superior Court of New Jersey, Appellate Division
267 N.J. Super. 482 (1993)

The opinion of the court was delivered by

SHEBELL, P.J.A.D.

On January 30, 1992, the juvenile, M.N., was charged in a delinquency complaint with acts which if committed by an adult would constitute third-degree arson (*N.J.S.A.* 2C:17-1b) and third-degree criminal mischief (*N.J.S.A.* 2C:17-3a(1)). The property damaged by M.N. was separated in the complaint into two counts:

1. Count One, charging third-degree arson of a garage.

2. Count Two, charging third-degree criminal mischief of a boat.

In April 1992, following a bench trial, the Family Part judge concluded that M.N. did not purposely set the boat or garage on fire, but that, beyond a reasonable doubt, M.N. "purposely lit a fire" by striking a match. Therefore, the judge found M.N. guilty of third-degree arson of the garage as alleged in count one of the complaint. The judge made no findings on the charge of third-degree criminal mischief involving the boat as contained in count two of the complaint. M.N. was sentenced on June 4, 1992, to two years of probation and was ordered to complete one hundred hours of community service and to attend individual counselling.

* * *

On December 10, 1991, at about 8:00 a.m., twelve-year-old M.N., a seventh grader, was walking to the school bus stop. As was his usual habit, he took a short-cut through three owners' properties. According to M.N., while walking, he found a book of matches near his house. He picked up the matches, lit one, and threw it onto the road. He continued on to the bus stop "throwing the matches around and cutting through the people's yards." When he got to a tree by the yard of the victim, M.N. lit a match, blew it out, threw it, and then threw the entire book of matches away and walked on to catch his bus.

An unknown man knocked on the door of a nearby house, shouted "fire," and ran away. The neighbor saw flames across the street, called the police, and attempted to put out the fire with a garden hose. He observed that the fire was actually coming from a boat parked next to a detached garage which was at the rear of the property. The owner of the property was summoned from work. When he arrived home, he saw his boat and garage on fire. The fire destroyed the boat, a substantial portion of the detached garage, one antique car, sporting equipment, and other personal items. The owner estimated the damage to the boat and the garage and its contents to be approximately $100,000.

A Franklin Township detective, assigned to the Police Arson Squad, investigated the fire. He arrived on the scene at 9:30 a.m. He observed that it had rained overnight and that the ground was very wet. He noted that the garage had burned from the outside in and that there were no "heat sources" (i.e. extension cords, batteries) in or near the boat.

After finding a piece of paper with "Franklin School" written on it and learning that the school bus picked up students at around the time the fire began, the detective asked a patrolman to go to the school and ask the principal and students if anyone had knowledge of the fire. M.N. became a suspect when the detective was informed by the property owner's daughter that M.N. had been observed on previous occasions taking a short cut through the yard on his way to the bus stop. The detective spoke to the principal at M.N.'s school and expressed his desire to talk with the student about the fire. M.N.'s mother came to school and in the presence of the principal, the detective questioned the young man. M.N., however, lied about the route that he had taken to the bus stop. At trial, M.N. explained that he had not told the truth because he knew he was playing with matches on the property and was afraid.

The following morning, the principal called the detective to say that M.N. and his mother wanted to speak with him again. They met at police headquarters shortly after the phone call. According to the detective, M.N. admitted that he had cut through the victim's property. M.N. also allegedly stated that he lit a match, blew it out, and threw it on leaves at the rear of the boat. M.N. was said to have further stated that he lit the entire book of matches and threw that away.

After this meeting, the detective returned to the property to look for a burned book of matches. He was directed by the owner's daughter to a burned matchbook she had discovered in a neighbor's backyard, began at approximately seventy feet away. M.N. testified that he was not near the boat that day. Although he was playing with matches on the property, he claimed it was by the street. M.N. asserted that he cut through the yard in front of the garage and did not see the boat at all.

The detective also testified as an arson expert at trial. He expressed his belief that the fire was a result of arson. He felt that the fire could have been started with only paper or matches and estimated that it began approximately 8:15 a.m.

I.

We first consider whether the judge misconceived the applicable law or mis-applied it to the facts. See *Kavanaugh v. Quigley, 63N.J.Super.* 153, 158, 164 A.2d 179 (App.Div.1960).

On the issue of whether M.N. purposely started a fire, the trial judge interpreted the statute to mean that merely lighting a match constitutes the purposeful starting of a fire, because the lighting of a match "starts a fire, albeit a small fire." The judge concluded that, in these circumstances, "[t]he purposeful act that the statute proscribes is the act of lighting the match." The trial judge, however, found that M.N. did not intend to set the boat or garage on fire. He found that M.N. only intended to light the match. Although the detective testified that M.N. had told him that after he lit the match he also lit the book of matches, the judge made no finding regarding the lighting of the book of matches.

N.J.S.A. 2C:17-1b provides:

> A person is guilty of arson, a crime of the third degree, if he *purposely* starts a fire or causes an explosion, whether on his own property or another's:
>
> > (1) Thereby *recklessly* placing another person in danger of death or bodily injury; or
> >
> > (2) Thereby *recklessly* placing a building or structure of another in danger of damage or destruction. . . . (Emphasis added).

In order for M.N. to be guilty of third-degree arson, two elements of culpability-"purposely start[ing]" and "recklessly placing"-must be proved. Therefore, the youth must have "purposely" started a fire and, in so doing, he must have "recklessly" placed the life or structure of another in danger.

"Purposely" is the highest standard of culpability in the Code of Criminal Justice. *N.J.S.A.* 2C:2-2b(1). According to this provision:

> A person acts purposely with respect to the nature of his conduct or a result thereof if it is his conscious object to engage in conduct of that nature or to cause such a result. A person acts purposely with respect to attendant circumstances if he is aware of the existence of such circumstances or he believes or hopes that they exist. . . . [*Ibid.*]

"Crimes entailing purposive conduct by definition focus on the subjective attitude of the accused: they require not only that he engage consciously in the proscribed conduct, but that he desire the prohibited result." *State v. Harmon*, 104 *N.J.* 189, 201, 516 A.2d 1047 (1986).

The State argues that M.N.'s act of striking a match "started" a fire and that is the only purposeful act necessary. The State adds that it need not prove that M.N. "set" the fire because "starting" and "setting" are two different things. M.N. submits "that the court's finding that he purposely started a fire by merely lighting a match is erroneous." M.N. further submits "that while his lighting a match may prove he literally started a fire *on a matchhead*, it fails to prove beyond a reasonable doubt that he 'purposely start[ed] a fire,' as within the statutory meaning of the term."

New Jersey's pre-Code arson statute provided that "any person who willfully or maliciously burns" another's dwelling house or its adjacent structures is guilty of arson. *N.J.S.A.* 2A:89-1; *see State v. Lucas*, 30 N.J. 37, 152 A.2d 50 (1959); *State v. Schenk*, 100 *N.J.Super.* 122, 241 A.2d 267 (App.Div.1968). This language was changed to "[a] person is guilty of arson, . . . if he purposely starts a fire or causes an explosion. . . ." N.J.S.A. 2C:17-1b. The definition of purposely provided in *N.J.S.A.* 2C:2-2b(1) means that "[defendant] acted purposely if it was his 'conscious object to engage in conduct of that nature or to cause such a result.'" *State v. Williams, 263 N.J.Super.* 620, 630-31, 623 A.2d 800 (App.Div.1993). Facial application of the statutory language to these facts can be seen to support the position of both the State and the defense. Therefore, we must determine the meaning which most comports with legislative intent, common sense, and legal precedent.

The Code Commentary to aggravated arson (*N.J.S.A.* 2C:17-1a) is instructive. That provision uses the same language-"starts a fire or causes an explosion," notes that the language employed was meant to include culpability "even though the fire is extinguished before any significant damage is done." *New Jersey Penal Code, Vol. II: Commentary, Final Report of the New Jersey Criminal Law Revision Commission*, § 2C:17-16 at 205 (1971). It is significant, however, that *N.J.S.A.* 2C:17-1b differs from Subsection a in that it does not require that the actor have the purpose of placing persons or property in danger so long as the fire or explosion is purposely started. The Commentary specifically gives the following example:

The requirement of purpose to destroy or damage, in clause (1) of Subsection a, makes it clear that the mere employment of fire with more limited purposes, *e.g.*, use of an acetylene torch to detach metal fixtures from a structure, or to gain entry to a building or safe, does not fall within the crime of Aggravated Arson defined by Subsection a. *See State v. Schenk, supra. It may, however, lead to liability for Arson under Subsection b.*

(*Commentary, supra* (emphasis added))

It is against this background that we look to the case law for some assistance on the question of whether in these circumstances merely lighting a match constitutes "purposely start[ing] a fire" under Subsection b.

In *State v. Krieger*, 96 N.J. 256, 475 A.2d 563 (1984), reversed for reasons expressed in the Appellate Division's dissent, 193N.J.Super. 568, 475 A.2d 608 (App.Div.1983), *cert. denied*, 469 U.S. 1017, 105 S.Ct. 431, 83 *L.Ed.*2d 358 (1984), two fires of incendiary origins occurred within two weeks of each other at a mattress factory. *Krieger, supra*, 193 N.J.Super. at 570, 475 A.2d 608. The defendant was a company employee who had applied to be a city fireman. He confessed to having a cigarette and playing with matches in the room where the fire took place. *Id.* at 572, 475 A.2d 608. He stated that he dropped the matches on the floor in order "to start paper on fire and burn the mats." *Ibid.* He claimed he had planned to start the fire the day before it happened because he wanted to gain the recognition that would come when he extinguished the fire. *Id.* at 573, 475 A.2d 608. He gave this same reason for starting the second fire. *Ibid.* In his confession regarding the second fire, defendant described how he lit a cigarette and put it near the book of matches with the intent of starting a small fire. *Id.* at 574, 475 A.2d 608.

At trial, defendant denied the truth of his confession. Ibid. The Appellate Division majority reversed the conviction based on the requirement of *State v. Lucas*, 30 *N.J.* 37, 152 A.2d 50 (1959), that when a confession is offered for the truth of its contents, "the State must introduce independent proof of facts and circumstances which strengthen or bolster the confession and tend to generate a belief in its trustworthiness, plus independent proof of loss or injury. . . ." *Krieger, supra*, 193 N.J.Super. at 575, 475 A.2d 608 (quoting *Lucas, supra*, 30 N.J. at 56, 152 A.2d 50). In his dissent, adopted by the New Jersey Supreme Court majority, Judge Michels held that the State's case was sufficient because it established that the defendant was on the premises at the time of the fire, the defendant's job duties entailed frequent trips through the area of the plant where the fire occurred, the defendant expressed a motive, and the fire investigators concluded that the fire had been intentionally set. *Id.* 193 *N.J.Super.* at 580-82, 475 A.2d 608. Even though the issue in *Krieger* was different than the case at bar, it is informative as to the proofs generally regarded as necessary to demonstrate arson.

Here, the judge concluded only that M.N. purposely lit a match. There was no finding that M.N. had a purpose to start any other fire, even the leaves, at that time. The judge did not conclude that M.N. purposely lit anything except the match. This is not enough reasonably to constitute an element of the crime of third-degree arson. In *Krieger*, the plaintiff planned and intended to start a small fire when he dropped the book of lit matches. M.N. had no such plan or purpose under the findings of the trial judge. We are convinced that "purposely" lighting a match does not, in these circumstances, satisfy the requirements of "purposely starts a fire" as proscribed in *N.J.S.A.* 2C:17-1(b). Moreover, purposely lighting the match, in the absence of an additional act or omission by the accused, could not in these circumstances have "*[t]hereby* recklessly plac[ed]" the structures of another in danger. *N.J.S.A.* 2C:17-1(b)(2) (emphasis added).

In view of the above, M.N.'s conviction for third-degree arson on Count One cannot stand. We need not consider his argument that his conviction was also deficient because of the failure of the judge to make a finding as to whether M.N.'s conduct was reckless. We do, however, remand to the Family Part for a determination as to whether the juvenile is guilty of criminal mischief, a lesser included offense of Count One. *See State v. LaPierre*, 39 *N.J.* 156, 166, 188 A.2d 10 (1963).

[The court acquitted on the criminal mischief charge.]

Notes and Questions

1. The New Jersey court holds that because the fire which caused the property damage was not started "purposely" within the meaning of the statute, there is no need to discuss whether the defendant "recklessly" caused the result of damage to the property, because the first element of "purposely" is not satisfied. The inference from the court's decision is that a "recklessly" caused result is not arson if the fire was started only by lighting a match without "purposely" intending to light a fire. Do you agree with the court's interpretation of the statute that "purposely" starting a fire requires more than lighting a match? What if one lights a cigarette with a match, discards the match in a trash can, and causes property damage? Does that arise to the level of "purposely" start-

ing a fire, so the question of "recklessly" endangering persons or property may be considered?

2. In *Copeland v. State*, 2 P.3d 1283 (2000), the Supreme Court of Colorado noted New Jersey's approach of applying the *mens rea* element to both starting a fire and endangering persons or property, but held that its *mens rea* element applied only to the element of starting or maintaining a fire, and not endangering persons. Colorado revised Statutes § 18-4-105 provides that "[a] person who knowingly or recklessly starts or maintains a fire or causes an explosion on his property or that of another, and by doing so places another in danger of death or serious bodily injury or places any building or occupied structure in danger of damage commits fourth degree arson." The Court cited the Colorado legislature's amendment to the arson statute to include a *mens rea* element for starting or maintaining a fire, without expressly applying the *mens rea* element to endangering persons. The Colorado Supreme Court interpreted this amendment as legislative intent to limit the *mens rea* element to the element of starting or maintaining a fire. Thus, the state in Colorado need only prove the fire was started knowingly or recklessly to satisfy the *mens rea* element. A primary difference between New Jersey and Colorado is the amount of emphasis placed on the results. Under *State v. M.N.*, New Jersey holds that after the state proves a fire has purposely been started, the state must also prove a *reckless* endangerment of persons or property. Under *Copeland*, the state must prove only that a fire has been knowingly or recklessly started, so if there is endangerment of persons resulting from that fire, criminal liability attaches. Which approach do you think is more just? Can you think of situations where either the New Jersey or Colorado approach would cause unfair results? Note that both the New Jersey and the Colorado courts under their respective statutory schemes could come to the same conclusion in *State v. M.N.*, because the Colorado court could agree that lighting a match alone is not knowingly or recklessly starting a fire.

PRACTICE EXERCISE

Read the following facts, statute, and instructions.

Facts

Zenith has been an avid dirt-bike rider for many years. Growing up in San Fuego, the nearby deserts offered the perfect location to "ride till the sun don't shine." Unfortunately, San Fuego has suffered from a number of devastating fires over the last five years. Zenith's parents almost lost their home to one of them. The drought and low, dry brush that covers the hills is perfect tinder for a fire, and many homes abut expanses of this Mediterranean landscape.

During one summer evening, while the sun still shone, Zenith decided to go for a ride, "just to keep the bike in shape." He fired up his dirt-bike and headed up his street to a dirt road that leads to government held property, about 10 acres in size. Zenith has ridden there for many years, riding the trails and catching air off a jump he built there. "I consider it my second backyard," Zenith has said to friends. The land-scape is dry and the brush is all but dead because of the lack of rain.

Fifteen minutes into his ride, Zenith smells smoke: not the type of smoke from a burnt-out engine, but firewood-smoke. Zenith stops and looks behind him, realizing to his complete horror that three whole sage-bushes are entirely alight. He rushes over and tries to stomp on the flames, but to no avail. The fire spreads. Zenith jumps on his bike and rides home. He calls the police and the fire department is sent out, but too late. The fire has spread and the hillside is alight, endangering homes and property. The fire ultimately burns four homes and kills four dogs who were locked in their yards.

When the police investigate, they find Zenith's bike is hot, a type of heat only produced from riding the dirt bike. Zenith denies going riding: "I only revved it for a few minutes in the garage here, to test it out." After asking around, the investigators are informed by neighbors that Zenith rode up the street that day before the fire, and was "dressed like he always is when he goes up to the hills to ride—been doing it for years." The San Fuego prosecutor decides to indict Zenith, and has produced the following facts to support her argument: (1) Zenith's bike does not have a spark arrestor, commonly used for trail riding to prevent sparks from exiting the exhaust and starting fires, and (2) there were three signs on Zenith's street that Zenith had to pass to enter the wilderness area; those signs read, "Motor vehicle use strictly prohibited off roadways. Fire danger!"

Statutes

- First Degree Arson

A person is guilty of first degree arson when that person recklessly starts a fire which damages property in excess of $10,000, or causes death.

- *Second Degree Arson*

A person is guilty of second degree arson when damages are less than $10,000.

Instructions

You are the prosecution. Draft a motion to admit evidence from the facts above, having successfully indicted Zenith for starting the fire. Assume San Fuego has not adopted a *M.N.* or *Copeland* standard for purposeful results. You may argue using policy and conduct a statutory analysis for either the *M.N.* or *Copeland* standard in your motion.

Plea Bargaining Practice Exercise

Instructions

You will be paired with another student. You will both read the statement of the case. Your instructor will provide each side with confidential facts. One will be a defense attorney, accessing only the defense attorney's confidential facts. The other will be a prosecutor, accessing only the prosecutor's confidential facts. You will have 10 minutes for this negotiation, after reading the facts and taking a few minutes to outline your negotiation plan. Based on your confidential facts, you will attempt to come to an agreement with the other side.

Statement of the Case

The prosecutor has indicted Amanda and Brett for arson.

The indictment specifies that witnesses saw Amanda drive with Brett to a gas station, purchase five gallons worth of gas, fill a gas canister, and drive to a rural wooded area outside of town. The theory is that Brett soaked an old redwood tree with gasoline, struck a match, and lit the tree on fire, because police found a five gallon gas canister in the car matching that driven earlier by Amanda, along with a book of matches—with one match missing. The fire completely decimated the tree and spread through the tree tops. Because of the potency of the burn and the height of the fire, firefighters were unable to stop its spread through the forest. The fire ultimately destroyed five homes, killed numerous pets, and destroyed five large pieces of foresting equipment, causing estimated damages in the amount of $4.45 million.

Amanda and Brett have retained counsel. The prosecutor is preparing to move ahead with the case, when defense counsel calls the prosecutor to meet to "work something out."

CHAPTER SEVEN

Defenses

A. Governmental Inducement Defenses

IN THE NINETEENTH century, the maxim "ignorance of the law is no excuse" was applied with a vengeance. If a government official mistakenly advised that conduct was permissible, a defendant who reasonably relied on that advice could nevertheless be prosecuted for it. With the rise of widespread government regulation, and a dramatic increase in the number of police and regulators, this came to be seen as unfair. There were (at least) three responses to the growth of the criminal law, and infrastructure to enforce it. First, as has previously been discussed, courts came to recognize that criminal laws cannot be unduly vague or overbroad, and may not be applied prospectively in unforeseeable ways. Second, courts and legislatures determined that certain offenses required "wilfulness" as a mental state, in the sense of intentional violation of a known legal duty. [The *Cheek* case is an example.] This chapter discusses the third response, the recognition of a set of defenses based on government misconduct or inducement.

1. Mistake of Law/Entrapment by Estoppel

United States v. Pennsylvania Industrial Chemical Corporation

Supreme Court of the United States
411 U.S. 655 (1973)

Mr. Justice BRENNAN delivered the opinion of the Court.

We review here the reversal by the Court of Appeals for the Third Circuit of respondent's conviction for violation of § 13 of the Rivers and Harbors Act of 1899, 30 Stat. 1152, 33 U.S.C. § 407. Two questions are presented. The first is whether the Government may prosecute an alleged polluter under § 13 in the absence of the promulgation of a formal regulatory-permit program by the Secretary of the Army. The second is whether, if the prosecution is maintainable despite the nonexistence of a formal regulatory-permit program, this respondent was entitled to assert as a defense its alleged reliance on the Army Corps of Engineers' longstanding administrative construction of § 13 as limited to water deposits that impede or obstruct navigation.

On April 6, 1971, the United States filed a criminal information against the respondent, Pennsylvania Industrial Chemical Corp. (PICCO), alleging that on four separate occasions in August 1970 the corporation had discharged industrial refuse matters into the Monongahela River in violation of § 13 of the 1899 Act. By its terms, § 13 prohibits the discharge or deposit into navigable waters of 'any refuse matter of any kind or description whatever other than that flowing from streets and sewers and passing therefrom in a liquid state.' The second proviso to § 13 provides, however, that 'the Secretary of the Army . . . may permit the deposit' of refuse matter deemed by the Army Corps of Engineers not to be injurious to navigation, 'provided application is made to (the Secretary) prior to depositing such material . . . .' At trial, it was stipulated that PICCO operated a manufacturing plant on the bank of the Monongahela River, that PICCO-owned concrete and iron pipes discharged the refuse mater into the river, and that PICCO had not obtained a permit from the Secretary of the Army prior to the discharges in question. PICCO argued, however, that the discharges did not violate § 13 because (1) the liquid solution flowing from tis pipes was 'sewage' exempt from the statutory proscription; (2) the discharge did not constitute 'refuse matter' within the meaning of § 13 because it was not matter that would 'impede nevigation'; and (3) the term 'refuse' as used in § 13 must be defined in light of the water quality standards established pursuant to the Water Pollution

Control Act of 1948 and its amendments. In addition, PICCO sought to introduce evidence to show that its failure to obtain a § 13 permit was excusable in
this instance because prior to December 1970 the Army Corps of Engineers had
not established a formal program for issuing permits under § 13 and, moreover,
because the Corps consistently construed § 13 as limited to those deposits that
would impede or obstruct navigation, thereby affirmatively misleading PICCO
into believing that a § 13 permit was not required as a condition to discharges of
matter involved in this case. The District Court rejected each of PICCO's arguments as to the scope and meaning of § 13, disallowed PICCO's offers of proof
on the ground that they were not relevant to the issue of guilt under § 13, and
intstructed in jury accordingly. PICCO was convicted on all four counts and
assessed the maximum fine of $2,500 on each count. 329 F.Supp. 1118 (W.D.
Pa.1971).

On appeal, the Court of Appeals for the Third Circuit affirmed the District
Court's holdings as to the application of § 13 to the matter discharged by PICCO
into the river, but rejected the District Court's conclusion that the § 13 prohibition was operative in the absence of formalized permit procedures. 461 F.2d 468
(CA3 1972). The Court of Appeals reasoned that this interpretation was tantamount to reading § 13 to be an absolute prohibition against the deposit of any
'foreign substance' into the navigable waters of the country and this would have
had such a 'drastic impact . . . on the nation's economy even in 1899,' *Id.*, at 473,
that this interpretation could not reasonably be imputed to Congress. Instead,
the Court of Appeals concluded that Congress intended to condition enforcement of § 13 on the creation and operation of an administrative permit program.
The Court of Appeals stated:

> 'Congress contemplated a regulatory program pursuant to which persons
> in PICCO's position would be able to discharge industrial refuse at the
> discretion of the Secretary of the Army. It intended criminal penalties for
> those who failed to comply with this regulatory program. Congress did
> not, however, intend criminal penalties for people who failed to comply
> with a non-existent regulatory program.' *Id.*, at 475.

The Court of Appeals seems to have found support for this interpretation
of § 13 in 'Congress' subsequent enactments in the water quality field.' *Id.*, at
473. * * * Accordingly, the Court of Appeals held that it was error for the District
Court to have refused PICCO the opportunity to prove the nonexistence of a
formal permit program at the time of the alleged offenses.

As an alternative ground for reversal, a majority of the Court of Appeals
held that the District Court erred in disallowing PICCO's offer of proof that it
had bene affirmatively misled by the Corps of Engineers into believing that it

was not necessary to obtain a § 13 permit for the discharge of industrial effluents such as those involved in this case. If such facts were true, the Court of Appeals stated, it would be fundamentally unfair to allow PICCO's conviction to stand.

Thus, the Court of Appeals set aside PICCO's conviction and remanded the case to the District Court to give PICCO an opportunity to present the proffered proofs that had been disallowed by the District Court.

We granted the Government's petition for certiorari. 409 U.S. 1074, 93 S.Ct. 689, 34 L.Ed.2d 662 (1972). We agree with the Court of Appeals that the District Court's judgment of conviction must be reversed, but we cannot agree with the Court of Appeals' interpretation of § 13 as foreclosing prosecution in the absence of the existence of a formal regulatory-permit program.

I

Section 13 creates two separate offenses: the discharge or deposit of 'any refuse matter' into navigable waters (with the streets-and-sewers exception); and the deposit of 'material of any kind' on the bank of any navigable waterway or tributary where it might be washed into the water and thereby impede or obstruct navigation. * * * The second proviso to § 13 authorizes the Secretary of the Army to exempt certain water deposits from the prohibitions of § 13, 'provided application is made to him prior to depositing such material.' In exercising that authority, the proviso requires the Secretary to rely on the judgment of the Chief of Engineers that anchorage and navigation will not be injured by such deposits. But, even in a situation where the Chief of Engineers concedes that a certain deposit will not injure anchorage and navigation, the Secretary need not necessarily permit the deposit, for the proviso makes the Secretary's authority discretionary—i.e., the proviso provides that the Secretary 'may permit' the deposit. The proviso further requires that permits issued by the Secretary are to prescribe limits and conditions, any violation of which is unlawful. It is crucial to our inquiry, however, that neither the proviso nor any other provision of the statute requires that the Secretary prescribe general regulations or set criteria governing issuance of permits.

Thus, while nothing in § 13 precludes the establishment of a formal regulatory program by the Secretary, it is equally clear that nothing in the section requires the establishment of such a program as a condition to rendering § 13 operative. * * *

II

We turn, therefore, to the Court of Appeals' alternative ground for reversing PICCO's conviction, namely, that in light of the longstanding, official administrative construction of § 13 as limited to those water deposits that tend to impede or obstruct navigation, PICCO may have been 'affirmatively misled' into believing that its conduct was not criminal. We agree with the Court of Appeals that PICCO should have been permitted to present relevant evidence to establish this defense.

At the outset, we observe that the issue here is not whether § 13 in fact applies to water deposits that have no tendency to affect navigation. For, although there was much dispute on this question in the past,[23] in *United States v. Standard Oil Co., supra*, we held that 'the 'serious injury' to our watercourses . . . sought to be remedied (by the 1899 Act) was caused in part by obstacles that impeded navigation and in part by pollution,' and that the term 'refuse' as used in § 13 'includes all foreign substances and pollutants . . . .' 384 U.S., at 228—229, 230, 86 S.Ct. at 1429, 1430.[24] * * *.

Nevertheless, it is undisputed that prior to December 1970 the Army Corps of Engineers consistently construed § 13 as limited to water deposits that affected navigation. Thus, at the time of our decision in *Standard Oil*, the published regulation pertaining to § 13 read as follows:

'§ 209.395. Deposit of refuse. Section 13 of the River and Harbor Act of March 3, 1899 (30 Stat. 1152; 33 U.S.C. 407), prohibits the deposit in navigable waters generally of 'refuse matter of any kind or description whatever other than that flowing from streets and sewers and passing therefrom in a liquid state.' The jurisdiction of the Department of the Army, derived from the Federal laws enacted for the protection and preservation of the navigable waters of the United States, is limited and directed to such control as may be necessary to protect the public right of navigation. Action under section 13 has therefore been directed by the Department principally against the discharge of those materials that are obstructive or injurious to navigation.' 33 CFR § 209.395 (1967).

In December 1968, the Corps of Engineers published a complete revision of the regulations pertaining to navigable waters. The new regulations pertaining to §§ 9 and 10 of the Rivers and Harbors Act of 1899, 33 U.S.C. §§ 401 and 403, dealing with construction and excavation in navigable waters, stated for the first time that the Corps would consider pollution and other conservation and environmental factors in passing on applications under those sections for permits to 'work in navigable waters.' 33 CFR § 209.120(d) (1969). But notwithstanding this reference to environmental factors and in spite of our intervening decision

---

23 The seeming ambiguity of the language of § 13 and the sparse legislative history of that provision caused the lower courts to disagree over the years as to the proper scope of § 13. * * *

24 *Standard Oil* involved an accidental discharge of aviation gasoline into navigable waters. The District Court had made the finding that the gasoline 'was not such as to impede navigation.' *United States v. Standard Oil Co.*, No. 291, O.T.1965, App. 8–11.

in *Standard Oil*, the new regulation pertaining to § 13 of the 1899 Act continued to construe that provision as limited to water deposits that affected navigation:

> 'Section 13 of the River and Harbor Act of March 3, 1899 (30 Stat. 1152; 33 U.S.C. § 407) authorizes the Secretary of the Army to permit the deposit of refuse matter in navigable waters, whenever in the judgment of the Chief of Engineers anchorage and navigation will not be injured thereby, within limits to be defined and under conditions to be prescribed by him. Although the Department has exercised this authority from time to time, it is considered preferable to act under Section 4 of the River and Harbor Act of March 3, 1905 (33 Stat. 1147; 33 U.S.C. § 419). * * *

At trial, PICCO offered to prove that, in reliance on the consistent, long-standing administrative construction of § 13, the deposits in question were made in good-faith belief that they were permissible under law. PICCO does not contend, therefore, that it was ignorant of the law or that the statute is impermissibly vague, see *Connally v. General Construction Co.*, 269 U.S. 385, 46 S.Ct. 126, 70 L.Ed. 322 (1926); *Bouie v. City of Columbia*, 378 U.S. 347, 84 S.Ct. 1697, 12 L.Ed.2d 894 (1964), but rather that it was affirmatively misled by the responsible administrative agency into believing that the law did not apply in this situation. Cf. *Raley v. Ohio*, 360 U.S. 423, 79 S.Ct. 1257, 3 L.Ed.2d 1344 (1959); *Cox v. Louisiana*, 379 U.S. 559, 85 S.Ct. 476, 13 L.Ed.2d 487 (1965).

Of course, there can be no question that PICCO had a right to look to the Corps of Engineers' regulations for guidance. The Corps is the responsible administrative agency under the 1899 Act, and 'the rulings, interpretations and opinions of the (responsible agency) . . ., while not controlling upon the courts by reason of their authority, do constitute a body of experience and informed judgment to which . . . litigants may properly resort for guidance.' *Skidmore v. Swift & Co.*, 323 U.S. 134, 140, 65 S.Ct. 161, 164, 89 L.Ed. 124 (1944); *Federal Maritime Board v. Isbrandtsen Co.*, 356 U.S. 481, 499, 78 S.Ct. 851, 862, 2 L.Ed.2d 926 (1958). Moreover, although the regulations did not of themselves purport to create or define the statutory offense in question, see *United States v. Mersky*, 361 U.S. 431, 80 S.Ct. 459, 4 L.Ed.2d 423 (1960), it is certainly true that their designed purpose was to guide persons as to the meaning and requirements of the statute. Thus, to the extent that the regulations deprived PICCO of fair warning as to what conduct the Government intended to make criminal, we think there can be no doubt that traditional notions of fairness inherent in our system of criminal justice prevent the Government from proceeding with the prosecution. *See* Newman, *Should Official Advice Be Reliable?—Proposals as to Estoppel and Related Doctrines in Administrative Law*, 53 Col.L.Rev. 374 (1953); Note, *Applying Estoppel Principles in Criminal Cases*, 78 Yale L.J. 1046 (1969).

The Government argues, however, that our pronouncement in *Standard Oil* precludes PICCO from asserting reliance on the Corps of Engineers' regulations and that, in any event, the revised regulation issued in 1968, when considered in light of other pertinent factors, was not misleading to persons in PICCO's position. But we need not respond to the Government's arguments here, for the substance of those arguments pertains, not to the issue of the availability of reliance as a defense, but rather to the issues whether there was in fact reliance and, if so, whether that reliance was reasonable under the circumstances—issues that must be decided in the first instance by the trial court. At this stage, it is sufficient that we hold that it was error for the District Court to refuse to permit PICCO to present evidence in support of its claim that it had been affirmatively misled into believing that the discharges in question were not a violation of the statute.

Accordingly, the judgment of the Court of Appeals is modified to remand the case to the District Court for further proceedings consistent with this opinion. *It is so ordered.*

THE CHIEF JUSTICE, Mr. Justice STEWART, and Mr. Justice POWELL dissent in part, because they agree with the Court of Appeals that the respondent on remand should also be given the opportunity to prove the non-existence of a permit program at the time of the alleged offenses.

Mr. Justice BLACKMUN and Mr. Justice REHNQUIST agree with Part I, but believing that the Court's opinion and judgment in *United States v. Standard Oil Co.*, 384 U.S. 224, 86 S.Ct. 1427, 16 L.Ed.2d 492 (1966), make absolutely clear the meaning and reach of § 13 with respect to PICCO's industrial discharge into the Monongahela River; that subsequent reliance upon any contrary administrative attitude on the part of the Corps of Engineers, express or by implication, is unwarranted; and that the District Court was correct in rejecting PICCO's offer of proof of reliance as irrelevant, would reverse the Court of Appeals with directions to reinstate the judgment of conviction.

Notes and Questions

1. Is it plausible that PICCO, a large corporation with access to many lawyers, was unaware of the *Standard Oil* case that the Court said clearly answered the legal question which PICCO claimed to misunderstand?

2. What result if a defendant is misled by an officer of a jurisdiction other than the one which is prosecuting her? For example, if state regulators had advised that it was permissible to deposit waste in the river, would PICCO have had a defense to federal prosecution? *Miller v. Commonwealth*, 492 S.E.2d 482 (Va. App. 1997).

3. What result if a defendant is misled by a private lawyer, or by someone she mistakenly believes is a government officer but is in fact not?

---

2. Apparent Authority Defense

United States v. Anderson

United States Court of Appeals, Eleventh Circuit
872 F.2d 1508 (1989)

MORGAN, Senior Circuit Judge:

Appellants Keith Anderson and Byron Carlisle were convicted on three separate conspiracies and eight substantive charges arising from an unauthorized removal from Fort Bragg, North Carolina and unlicensed transfer of a variety of military armaments and explosive devices. On appeal, appellants challenge these convictions on numerous grounds. The principal issues raised by appellants concern the exclusion of classified information in their defense that their actions were taken in reasonable good faith reliance on the apparent authority of a purported agent of the Central Intelligence Agency ("CIA"), and the imposition of consecutive sentences upon multiplicitous conspiracy counts. We vacate the sentence imposed and remand for resentencing, and otherwise affirm. We address only those issues that merit discussion.

I. BACKGROUND

In an eleven-count superseding indictment filed in the Southern District of Florida on October 16, 1985, appellants were charged with various federal violations involving firearms and explosives. In summary, appellants were each charged in ten counts as follows: I, II, and III, conspiracies to possess unregistered firearms, to transfer unregistered firearms, and to sell property of the United States, respectively, in violation of 18 U.S.C. Sec. 371; IV and V, possession and transfer, respectively, of firearms on August 24, 1984, and VII and VIII, possession and transfer, respectively, of firearms on October 6, 1984, all in violation of 26 U.S.C. Sec. 5861(d), (e); VI, unauthorized sale of government property on August 24, 1984, and IX, unauthorized sale of unregistered firearms on October 6, 1984, all in violation of 18 U.S.C. Sec. 641; and XI, knowingly engaging in the business of dealing in explosive materials without a license, in violation of 18 U.S.C. Sec. 842(a)(1). Additionally, appellant Anderson was charged in Count X with carrying a concealed unregistered weapon during the commission of a felony on October 6, 1984, in violation of 18 U.S.C. Sec. 924(c)(2).

Appellants filed a pretrial motion to dismiss Counts I, II and III. Each count charged conspiracies concerning the same time frame, alleging the same overt acts in furtherance thereof, but claiming that each had a separate criminal object. This motion was denied.

The government requested by motion that a pretrial conference be set in order to consider matters relating to the possible disclosure of classified information at trial. The government also filed a motion *in limine* to preclude assertion of an "apparent authority" or "CIA" defense, to which the appellants responded. * * *

On July 22, 1985, a one-week jury trial began before a visiting district judge. Thereafter, the case was submitted to the jury, and verdicts of guilty to all charges were returned as to each defendant. Appellants were each sentenced to incarceration for 40 years and were each ordered to pay $13,076.13 restitution to the United States Army. This appeal followed.

A. Government's Evidence at Trial

The government's case was presented almost entirely through the testimony of Special Agent Fredrick L. Gleffe of the Bureau of Alcohol, Tobacco and Firearms ("ATF"), and the videotapes and audiotapes introduced during that testimony. The government's evidence at trial established that the appellants, Sergeant First Class Keith Anderson and Sergeant First Class Byron Carlisle, both of whom were members of the Special Forces of the United States Army stationed at Fort Bragg, North Carolina, conspired with other unknown military personnel to steal high explosives and other military supplies from Fort Bragg and to sell this material to undercover government agents and an informant posing as narcotics distributors and dealers in stolen property. Pursuant to this conspiracy, the appellants made multiple transfers to the agents of large quantities of items such as Claymore anti-personnel mines, M-67 hand grenades, C-4 plastic explosives, T.N.T., dynamite, 35 mm. practice L.A.W.S. rockets, detonation devices, and tons of ammunition and other military supplies, including large shells such as 106 mm. and 90 mm. canisters. The government also presented evidence that appellants provided and offered to provide assistance to undercover agents in their purported activity as drug distributors.

In November 1982, following an arrest for attempting to sell two silencers to undercover ATF agents, Richard Flaherty agreed to cooperate with the government. Flaherty had once been with the Special Forces and, at the time of his arrest, was a captain in the Army Reserves. Flaherty later told ATF agents that during his last two-week period of active duty in July 1982, he had met appellant Anderson who offered to supply him with munitions from Fort Bragg. In July 1984, Agent Gleffe decided to pursue this lead and instructed Flaherty to reinitiate contact with Anderson. Agent Gleffe adopted the undercover name "Griff," and assumed the role of a narcotics smuggler and distributor of stolen property.

On August 14, 1984, Flaherty introduced "Griff" to Anderson at a motel in Fayetteville, North Carolina. Later the same day, Anderson delivered to them 196 pounds of military high explosives and accessories, together with a written inventory, in return for $3,200 cash. Both then and at subsequent meetings, Anderson described his unnamed "partner," but the agents did not actually meet Byron Carlisle until September 11, 1984.

At the August 14, 1984 meeting, Agent Gleffe expressed a special interest in acquiring Claymore mines and fragmentation grenades. At a later meeting, Anderson agreed to deliver thirty grenades and thirty Claymore mines when he was in Key West, Florida, on military business. On August 24, 1984, Anderson delivered thirty M-67 grenades and six Claymore mines from Fort Bragg to Gleffe in a Key West hotel room in exchange for $27,000 in cash; the other twenty-four Claymore mines were left behind in Fayetteville. The delivery and payment were recorded on videotape.

Following several further recorded telephone conversations, Agent Gleffe and Flaherty again met with Anderson at a Fayetteville motel on September 10, 1984. Anderson had the twenty-four remaining Claymore mines and a case of ammunition in his vehicle, but Gleffe arranged instead for a later delivery in Jacksonville, Florida. Thereafter, Anderson showed the agents the warehouse which he and his partner had rented in the name of their corporation, C-MAC, to store the military supplies.

On September 11, 1984, at the motel in Fayetteville, Anderson for the first time introduced the undercover agents to his partner, appellant Byron Carlisle.

The parties planned to make a large exchange in the future of one kilogram of cocaine for $27,000 in military ordnance. The appellants explained, however, that cash also was needed so that necessary payments could be made to other military personnel for their connivance in procuring munitions. Carlisle acknowledged that Anderson had advised him of his previous transactions with the agents. The meeting ended with an agreement to transfer the Claymore mines and ammunition in Jacksonville.

On September 15, 1984, in a Jacksonville motel, Anderson delivered to Agent Gleffe the twenty-four Claymore mines and a case of tracer ammunition in return for $6,000 cash. The transaction was recorded on videotape. At this time, Anderson said that a drug distribution network was almost in place at Fort Bragg, and plans were made to exchange drugs for munitions in early October.

Agent Gleffe and another agent met with Anderson and Carlisle in Fayetteville on September 26, 1984, to make preparation to trade a large quantity of high explosives and office supplies for one kilogram of cocaine and approximately $27,000 cash. The appellants again explained that cash was needed to pay military personnel to procure additional explosives from Fort Bragg. The agents were taken to the warehouse a second time, which on the previous visit had been almost empty, but now held a large quantity of office supplies, as well as crates of blank ammunition and military goods.

On October 6, 1984, Anderson drove a rented truck to Vero Beach, Florida, carrying over two tons of military ammunition and explosives. Anderson gave Gleffe an accurate written inventory itemizing an approximate value of almost $50,000. In exchange, Anderson received one kilogram of fake cocaine and $27,000 cash. After the transaction was completed, Anderson was placed under arrest. A loaded .380 pistol was seized from Anderson's shoulder bag. Carlisle was contemporaneously arrested in Fayetteville, where he had remained.

B. The Appellants' Testimony at Trial

Appellant Keith Anderson testified at trial that, as a member of the Special Forces, he had been trained in guerilla warfare, covert operations, demolitions, communications, and the use of American and foreign weapons. Anderson explained that Special Forces personnel also train foreign armies in such tactics and may work with both civilian and military intelligence agencies.

In July 1982, Anderson met Flaherty, a Captain in the Special Forces Reserves, during Flaherty's two-week period of active duty. Anderson averred that Flaherty described himself as an "international arms merchant." Flaherty also told him that he worked with the CIA and was involved in clandestine and covert operations within Central America. According to Anderson, Flaherty called him eight to ten times in the ensuing two years. In August 1984, Flaherty told him that arms were needed "for covert operation, especially in El Salvador and Honduras," and because of political sensitivity, such arms could not be traced back to that agency.

Anderson testified that Flaherty advised him that an individual whom he identified as "Griff," an entrepreneur and "drug merchant," would be providing the funding for this venture, and did not know and would not be advised of the true purpose of this operation. Instead, he would be advised that these munitions were for "drug operations." Thus, if detected, all those involved in this venture would appear to have engaged in criminal activity involving drugs, rather than an illegal CIA-orchestrated covert operation. Accordingly, Anderson testified that all discussions about narcotics in which Anderson engaged were a "lie" and "cover story" induced by Flaherty's deception.

Anderson also testified that he initially did not advise Carlisle of this matter, but did so later because "Flaherty told me I would need somebody trustworthy and competent who had extensive intelligence background for covert operations." Anderson contended that the money he received for transferring munitions was used entirely to purchase explosives and related supplies and expenses.

On cross-examination, Anderson acknowledged that he did not advise the military chain of command of this approach, did not check whether this was a government operation, and sought no approval for his participation except from Flaherty. He maintained that as a member of the Special Forces trained to work with government agencies, one follows instructions by other U.S. intelligence agents not to report contacts to his superiors, and Flaherty furnished such directions.[7]

Byron Carlisle testified that he had received special training in weapons, intelligence and medical care, and taught clandestine communications, guerrilla warfare, and other topics. From December 1982 until early 1984, when he was officially removed from the project, Carlisle traveled back and forth to Honduras on a covert operation, the subject matter of which is largely classified. In the summer of 1984, Carlisle described himself as being in a "state of suspended animation" between projects under Anderson's command. Carlisle claimed that he had been interviewed in a hotel and accepted for a covert project under similar conditions, so he had not questioned it. Carlisle averred that he did not ask

---

7   In rebuttal, the government produced two witnesses, Major Eugene E. Makowski, Chief of Operations for the Army First Operation Command at Fort Bragg, and James V. West, an Army Special Forces Officer at Fort Bragg. They testified that, as all personnel are instructed, every contact by a civilian or military U.S. intelligence agency must be reported to the chain of command, and participation in covert operations may only be authorized by and through normal channels. Anderson also asserted that Flaherty told him that the CIA does not show identification. West and Makowski, however, testified that such identification is required before a Special Forces Officer may even speak with a purported intelligence agent. Additionally, Major Makowski testified that only a superior officer within the chain of command can give orders, and that Flaherty was not within either appellant's chain of command. Moreover, he testified that an officer in the Reserves has no authority except when he is on active duty.

Flaherty for identification because, in his prior hotel interview with the CIA, he had been instructed not to do so.

Carlisle acknowledged signing for the removal of ammunition at Fort Bragg, but maintained that he did not intentionally participate in a theft. Based on the subsequent conversations with Anderson, Carlisle testified that he believed that a shipment had been approved through proper channels to Flaherty at a Special Forces unit of the National Guard. According to Carlisle, his extensive discussions of illegal activity were role playing pursuant to the cover story maintained by Anderson. He denied that he would ever participate in taking ammunition illegally, but conceded that he had offered other military personnel money for the munitions. Carlisle denied that he had any contact with the munitions after he delivered it to Anderson inside Fort Bragg.

II. APPARENT AUTHORITY DEFENSE

The most serious challenges on appeal revolve around the district court's rulings at the CIPA hearing and the trial relating to the so-called "apparent authority" or "CIA" defense. The thrust of appellants' defense was that they reasonably relied upon the apparent authority of Flaherty acting as a CIA agent to engage them in a covert activity. Appellants * * * contend that the district court erred in instructing the jury that "apparent authority" was not a defense to these charges.

Specifically, appellants argue * * * that the district court's instruction to the jury-that appellants' good faith reliance upon the apparent authority of another was no defense to these charges-effectively directed a verdict in favor of the government on the element of specific intent. Appellants submit that the district court's errors deprived them of their constitutional right to adduce facts and present a complete defense. * * *

B. Discussion

* * *

Recently, this court considered the validity of the so-called "CIA" or "apparent authority" defense in *United States v. Rosenthal*, 793 F.2d 1214, 1235-37 (11th Cir.1986), *cert. denied*, 480 U.S. 919, 107 S.Ct. 1377, 94 L.Ed.2d 692 (1987). The defendants there were led to believe by someone whom they allegedly thought was a CIA agent, "that their drug smuggling activities were part of an intelligence operation undertaken in pursuit of national security objectives." *Id.* at 1235. They contended that the district court erred in limiting their proposed evidence regarding the "CIA defense" and in rejecting a proposed instruction which set forth this defense. This court followed *United States v. Duggan*, 743 F.2d 59, 83-84 (2d Cir.1984), in holding that since "ignorance of the law or mistake as to the law's requirements is not a defense to criminal conduct," a "defendant may only be exonerated on the basis of his reliance on real and not merely apparent authority." 793 F.2d at 1235 (citing *Duggan*, 743 F.2d at 83). Because the CIA had no real authority to authorize such violations of law, the defendant's theory "that they were acting on apparent authority of a CIA agent is not a viable defense." *Id.* at 1236. Accordingly, the court found that the trial court did not err in limiting the evidence or in refusing to instruct the jury on this defense. *Id.*

In *Duggan*, the defendants were convicted of unlicensed exportation of munitions and of various firearm offenses. The defendants contended that their actions were taken in reasonable good faith reliance on the apparent authority of a government informant to act as an agent of the CIA. The trial court refused to give the requested instruction of apparent authority. In upholding the district court's refusal to give the instruction, the court found that the mistake advanced by defendants as an excuse for their criminal activities-their reliance on the informant's purported authority-"is an error based on a mistaken view of legal requirements and therefore constitutes a mistake of law." 743 F.2d at 83 (citing *United States v. Barker*, 546 F.2d 940, 946 (D.C.Cir.1976)).

In this case, there is no serious contention advanced by the appellants that a CIA agent possessed actual authority to approve exceptions to the laws regulating possession, registration and transfer of high explosives and other munitions, or to legally authorize theft of military property for the use of foreign factions. Officials of the CIA or any other intelligence agency of the United States do not have the authority to sanction conduct which would violate the Constitution or statutes of the United States, including the laws under which appellants are charged here. *See Rosenthal*, 793 F.2d at 1236 (citing Exec. Order No. 12333, 3 C.F.R. 200 (1982)). Because the CIA had no real authority to violate the statutes of the United States, appellants' theory that they were acting on apparent authority of an alleged CIA agent is not a viable defense. In light of *Rosenthal*, we conclude that the district court properly exercised its discretion in excluding evidence offered by the defense which, if believed, fails to establish a legally cognizable defense.

Appellants argue that when a defendant based his actions upon a mistake of fact, as opposed to a mistake of law, this circuit has recognized that such a defense is val7d. According to this view, a "mistake of fact" defense is really but another way of stating that a defendant lacks criminal intent, and thus must be permitted. *See United States v. Juan*, 776 F.2d 256 (11th Cir.1985) (where this court held that defendant made sufficient showing of materiality with respect to request under CIPA for documents which would show that he had at one time had a relationship with the government, thus making his belief that he was cooperating with the government at the time of the offense reasonable).

In this case, appellants contend that they believed, albeit mistakenly, that their unauthorized removal and unlicensed transfer of a variety of military armaments and explosives was for and to an agent of the CIA as part of a classified operation in which one of them recently participated. As such, appellants submit that their mistake was factual in nature which served to negate criminal intent. If the appellants' mistake of fact had been true, according to appellants, this transfer, and their concomitant possession, of the munitions would be exempt under 18 U.S.C. Sec. 925(a)(1):

> The provisions of this chapter shall not apply with respect to the transportation, shipment, receipt, or importation of any firearm or ammunition imported for, sold or shipped to, or issued for the use of, the United States or any department, agency, or political subdivision thereof.

We initially note that appellants' reliance on Section 925(a)(1), which provides that the "provisions of this chapter" do not apply to sales or transfers to any agency of the United States, is misplaced. Assuming for the moment that the purported CIA-orchestrated diversion of arms to the "contras" would qualify as an exemption under Section 925(a)(1), appellants were not charged with any violation under that chapter (Chapter 44-Firearms), with the exception of Count X charging Anderson with carrying a firearm during the commission of a felony. Instead, appellants were charged with violations of 26 U.S.C. Sec. 5861(d), (e), 18 U.S.C. Sec. 842(a)(1), and 18 U.S.C. Sec. 641. Appellants do not cite any authority which supports their proposition that Section 925(a)(1) should be broadly interpreted. Accordingly, we find the exemption under that section inapplicable to the charges in this case.

Regardless of whether we characterize appellants' mistake as one of law or fact, we find no merit in appellants' contention that the trial court's * * * jury instruction on apparent authority effectively directed a verdict in favor of the government on the element of criminal intent. Appellants' claim of innocent intent was adequately raised without the classified material. We note that * * * appellants remained free to claim that they thought Flaherty was a CIA operative and that their actions were part of a government-sanctioned operation. At trial, the defense presented testimony that Carlisle had been engaged in a covert and classified operation in Honduras involving the training of armed forces. The jury learned that both appellants held security clearances, and they had received training and experience in sensitive matters, including matters involving relationships with civilian and military intelligence agencies. Appellants were permitted to testify that they had been trained to conceal contacts with intelligence agencies from their superiors when so instructed, although prosecution witnesses refuted this claim. Carlisle was also allowed to testify to his "similar" experiences in being recruited in a hotel room for the mission in Honduras. The prosecution at trial never challenged the fact that these Special Forces sergeants had been trained and had participated in matters involving national security and covert operations. * * *

The question of intent was put squarely to the jury and resolved against appellants. *See United States v. Durrani*, 835 F.2d 410 (2d Cir.1987). The district court properly instructed the jury that government intelligence agents could not authorize violations of the law, so that it was not a defense that the defendants relied upon apparent authority of an agent to violate the law. On the other hand, the jury was charged that it should acquit unless it was satisfied beyond a reasonable doubt that the defendants acted with specific intent to violate the law, and that the defendants should be exonerated if the jury entertained a reasonable doubt whether the defendants acted in good faith under the sincere belief that their activity was exempt from the law.[14] We find that these instructions were not in error, "plain" or otherwise. *See* Fed.R.Crim.P. 30.

------

14   The court specifically instructed the jury, in part, as follows:

If you find that the Defendant was under a reasonable belief that he had legal authority to act with respect to any count charged in the Indictment, or that he had no predisposition to act as charged and would not have done so but for the active encouragement and enticement of Government Agents, then under either such circumstances, you would be required to return a verdict of not guilty. * * *

The word "willfully" as that term has been used from time to time in these instructions, means that the act was committed voluntarily and purposely, with the specific intent to do something the law forbids; that is, with bad purpose either to disobey or disregard the law.

* * *

So, if you find beyond a reasonable doubt that the acts constituting the crime charged were committed by the defendant voluntarily as an intentional violation of a known legal duty-that is, with specific intent to do something the law forbids-then the element of "willfulness," as defined in these instructions, has been satisfied even though the Defendant may have believed that his conduct was required, or that ultimate good would result from such conduct.

In this respect, it would be no defense to the commission of an unlawful act for a Defendant to rely on what such Defendant perceived to be the apparent authority of Flaherty.

I instruct you that all Agents of the United States intelligence agencies are prohibited by law from violating any statute of the United States. No one may lawfully assert as a valid defense to the violation of a law that he was authorized by an agent of an intelligence agency of the United States to violate the law.

On the other hand, if you have a reasonable doubt as to whether the Defendant acted in good faith, sincerely believing himself to be exempt by the law, then he did not intentionally violate a known legal duty; that is, he did not act "willfully," and that essential part of the offense would not be established.

Notes and Questions

1. Why did the defendants not pursue this as a mistake of law, instead of the official authority defense?

2. Did the instructions in Note 14 give the defendants a fair chance to persuade the jury that their conduct was not willful?

3. What is the difference between mistake of law and official authority? One commentator described it as follows: "The distinction between [entrapment by estoppel] EBE and the public authority defense is a subtle one. The defendant in EBE cases believed, due to erroneous official assurances, that his conduct constituted no offense. By contrast, the defendant in public authority cases knew his conduct to be otherwise illegal, but engaged in the conduct at the request of an official. The mistake of law involved not the substance of the official interpretation itself, but a misperception of the legal prerogatives attached to the official's status." *The Immunity-Conferring Power of the Office of Legal Counsel*, 121 Harv. L. Rev. 2086, 2096-97 (2008).

---

3. Entrapment

United States v. Poehlman

United States Court of Appeals, Ninth Circuit
217 F.3d 692 (2000)

KOZINSKI, Circuit Judge.

Mark Poehlman, a cross-dresser and foot-fetishist, sought the company of like-minded adults on the Internet. What he found, instead, were federal agents looking to catch child molesters. We consider whether the government's actions amount to entrapment.

I

After graduating from high school, Mark Poehlman joined the Air Force, where he remained for nearly 17 years. Eventually, he got married and had two children. When Poehlman admitted to his wife that he couldn't control his compulsion to cross-dress, she divorced him. So did the Air Force, which forced him into early retirement, albeit with an honorable discharge.

These events left Poehlman lonely and depressed. He began trawling Internet "alternative lifestyle" discussion groups in an effort to find a suitable companion. Unfortunately, the women who frequented these groups were less accepting than he had hoped. After they learned of Poehlman's proclivities, several retorted with strong rebukes. One even recommended that Poehlman kill himself. Evidently, life in the HOV lane of the information superhighway is not as fast as one might have suspected.

Eventually, Poehlman got a positive reaction from a woman named Sharon. Poehlman started his correspondence with Sharon when he responded to an ad in which she indicated that she was looking for someone who understood her family's "unique needs" and preferred servicemen. Poehlman answered the ad and indicated that he "was looking for a long-term relationship leading to marriage," "didn't mind children," and "had unique needs too." * * *

Sharon responded positively to Poehlman's e-mail. She said she had three children and was "looking for someone who understands us and does not let society's views stand in the way." She confessed that there were "some things I'm just not equipped to teach [the children]" and indicated that she wanted "someone to help with their special education." The full text of her first responsive e-mail is set out in the margin.[3]

In his next e-mail, also set out in the margin,[4] Poehlman disclosed the specifics of his "unique needs." He also explained that he has strong family values

---

3   Thanks for answering my posting. I got a lot of responses, but for some reason yours caught my eye.

I'll tell you a little about myself. I'm 30, divorced and have 3 children. We are a very close family. I'm looking for someone who understands us and does not let society's views stand in the way. I've had to be both mother and father to my sweethearts, but there are some things I'm just not equipped to teach them. I'm looking for someone to help with their special education.

If you have an interest, I'd love to hear your ideas, desires and experiences. If this doesn't interest you, I understand.

Appellant's Excerpts of Record at Tab 5 (July 27, 1995).

4   Hi There, talk about a pleasant surprise to see a answer from you, I too am divorced and have two boys not living with me they are 9 and 6. they live with their mother in upper N.Y. I don't get to see them very often matter of fact its been almost two years since last I saw them, I am planning a trip to see them now.

I am retired Air Force after 16.8 years I took the early retirement, decided it was time to get out and work for a living again..(g) I am extremely honest and straight forward type of guy I don't play head games and don't like to have them played against me. I tell you straight out and open that I am a in house tv, meaning I rather enjoy wearing hose and heels inside the house, not around small children of course but when mine are old enough to understand I will tell them that and the big foot fetish I have are about my only two major problems that need a open minded easy going woman, so as they say in the movies if you don't mind me wearing your hose and licking your toes then I am open for anything..(g),, I also have a sense of humor. as far as your children are concerned I will treat them as my own (as I would treat my boys if I had them with me) I have huge family values and like kids and they seem to like me alright too. well now you know all about me, if you are still interested then please write

and would treat Sharon's children as his own. Sharon's next e-mail focused on the children, explaining to Poehlman that she was looking for a "special man teacher" for them but not for herself. She closed her e-mail with the valediction, "If you understand and are interested, please write back. If you don't share my views I understand. Thanks again for your last letter." Appellant's Excerpts of Record at Tab 5 (Aug. 1, 1995).

Poehlman replied by expressing uncertainty as to what Sharon meant by special man teacher. He noted that he would teach the children "proper morals and give support to them where it is needed," *id.* (Aug. 2, 1995), and he reiterated his interest in Sharon.[5]

Sharon again rebuffed Poehlman's interest in her: "One thing I should make really clear though, is that there can't be anything between me and my sweethearts special teacher." *Id.* (Aug. 2, 1995). She then asked Poehlman for a description of what he would teach her children as a first lesson, promising "not to get mad or upset at anything written. If I disagree with something I'll just say so. I do like to watch, though. I hope you don't think I'm too weird." *Id.*

Poehlman finally got the hint and expressed his willingness to play sex instructor to Sharon's children.[6] In later e-mails, Poehlman graphically detailed his ideas to Sharon, usually at her prompting. Among these ideas were oral sex,

---

back, if not and I would understand why you didn't then I wish you all the best in finding the person you are look- ing for. if you wish to call my number is 904–581–5442, I am not home a lot due to work and school but there is an answering machine that only I listen to, (I you didn't th live alone) have a nice day.

Mark

Appellant's Excerpt of Record at Tab 5 (July 31, 1995).

5   Hi Sharon,

so happy to finnally learn your name, I am interested in being this special teasher, but in all honesty I really don't know exactly what you expect me to teach them other than proper morals and give support to them where it is needed.

Can I ask how old your sweethearts are and if you don't mind telling me what kind of teachings do you expect me to give them? But I will tell you that I am interested in their mom too, you would be part of the picture with them right? this is why I tell you all about myself and what I like, cause I ahve to be honest and tell you I would hope you would support and enjoy me sexually as well as in company and hopefully love and the sexual relations that go with it.

Hope you are well and your sweethearts are well too, I truly hope to hear from you and hopefully some more information about what you are looking for.. till then Have a very nice day.

Mark

Appellant's Excerpts of Record at Tab 5 (Aug. 2, 1995).

6   I am very open minded and willing to teach them everything you wish taught.

If they are all girls then I would help them to learn how to protect themselves by taking control over men I can be very submissive to the right women, though they will learn the right way to dress least in the house, you would be expected to dress as them also and prove to be a good example for them or face punishment.

Appellant's Excerpts of Record at Tab 5 (Aug. 3, 1995).

anal sex and various acts too tasteless to mention. The correspondence blossomed to include a phone call from Sharon and hand written notes from one of her children. Poehlman made decorative belts for all the girls and shipped the gifts to them for Christmas.

Poehlman and Sharon eventually made plans for him to travel to California from his Florida home. After arriving in California, Poehlman proceeded to a hotel room where he met Sharon in person. She offered him some pornographic magazines featuring children, which he accepted and examined. He commented that he had always looked at little girls. Sharon also showed Poehlman photos of her children: Karen, aged 7, Bonnie, aged 10, and Abby, aged 12. She then directed Poehlman to the adjoining room, where he was to meet the children, presumably to give them their first lesson under their mother's protective supervision. Upon entering the room however, Poehlman was greeted by Naval Criminal Investigation Special Agents, FBI agents and Los Angeles County Sheriff's Deputies.

Poehlman was arrested and charged with attempted lewd acts with a minor in violation of California law. He was tried, convicted and sentenced to a year in state prison. Two years after his release, Poehlman was again arrested and charged with federal crimes arising from the same incident. A jury convicted him of crossing state lines for the purpose of engaging in sex acts with a minor in violation of 18 U.S.C. § 2423(b). He was sentenced to 121 months. Poehlman challenges the conviction on the grounds that it violates double jeopardy and that he was entrapped. Because we find there was entrapment, we need not address double jeopardy.

II

"In their zeal to enforce the law . . . Government agents may not originate a criminal design, implant in an innocent person's mind the disposition to commit a criminal act, and then induce commission of the crime so that the Government may prosecute." *Jacobson v. United States*, 503 U.S. 540, 548, 112 S.Ct. 1535, 118 L.Ed.2d 174 (1992). On the other hand, "the fact that officers or employees of the Government merely afford opportunity or facilities for the commission of the offense does not defeat the prosecution. Artifice and stratagem may be employed to catch those engaged in criminal enterprises." *Sorrells v. United States*, 287 U.S. 435, 441, 53 S.Ct. 210, 77 L.Ed. 413 (1932). The defense of entrapment seeks to reconcile these two, somewhat contradictory, principles.

When entrapment is properly raised, the trier of fact must answer two related questions: First, did government agents induce the defendant to commit the crime? And, second, was the defendant predisposed? We discuss inducement at greater length below, *see* page 698 *infra*, but at bottom the government induces a crime when it creates a special incentive for the defendant to commit the crime. This incentive can consist of anything that materially alters the balance of risks and rewards bearing on defendant's decision whether to commit the offense, so as to increase the likelihood that he will engage in the particular criminal conduct. Even if the government induces the crime, however, defendant can still be convicted if the trier of fact determines that he was predisposed to commit the offense. Predisposition, which we also discuss at length below, *see* page 703 *infra*, is the defendant's willingness to commit the offense *prior* to being contacted by government agents, coupled with the wherewithal to do so. *See United States v. Hollingsworth*, 27 F.3d 1196, 1200 (7th Cir.1994) (en banc). While our cases treat inducement and predisposition as separate inquiries, *see, e.g., United States v. McClelland*, 72 F.3d 717, 722 (9th Cir.1995), the two are obviously related: If a defendant is predisposed to commit the offense, he will require little or no inducement to do so; conversely, if the government must work hard to induce a defendant to commit the offense, it is far less likely that he was predisposed. *See Hollingsworth*, 27 F.3d at 1200.

To raise entrapment, defendant need only point to evidence from which a rational jury could find that he was induced to commit the crime but was not otherwise predisposed to do so. *See United States v. Staufer*, 38 F.3d 1103, 1108 (9th Cir.1994). Defendant need not present the evidence himself; he can point to such evidence in the government's case-in-chief, or extract it from cross-examination of the government's witnesses. The burden then shifts to the government to prove beyond a reasonable doubt that defendant was *not* entrapped. *See Jacobson*, 503 U.S. at 549, 112 S.Ct. 1535.

The district court properly determined that the government was required to prove that Poehlman was not entrapped and gave an appropriate instruction. The jury nonetheless convicted Poehlman, which means that either it did not find that the government induced him, or did find that Poehlman was predisposed to commit the crime.[7] Poehlman argues that he was entrapped as a matter of law. To succeed, he must persuade us that, viewing the evidence in the light most favorable to the government, no reasonable jury could have found in favor of the government as to inducement or lack of predisposition. *See United States v. Thickstun*, 110 F.3d 1394, 1396 (9th Cir.1997).

---

7   Without a special verdict, we don't know which is the case. Because the determination of whether a defendant is entrapped is often confusing and difficult, we encourage district courts to use special verdict forms that query jurors as to the elements of the entrapment defense. Not only does this ease the process of appellate review, it encourages juries to focus their deliberations on the elements of the defense.

Inducement

"Inducement can be any government conduct creating a substantial risk that an otherwise law-abiding citizen would commit an offense, including persuasion, fraudulent representations, threats, coercive tactics, harassment, promises of reward, or pleas based on need, sympathy or friendship." *United States v. Davis*, 36 F.3d 1424, 1430 (9th Cir.1994). Poehlman argues that he was induced by government agents who used friendship, sympathy and psychological pressure to "beguile[ ] him into committing crimes which he otherwise would not have attempted." *Sherman v. United States*, 356 U.S. 369, 376, 78 S.Ct. 819, 2 L.Ed.2d 848 (1958).

According to Poehlman, before he started corresponding with Sharon, he was harmlessly cruising the Internet looking for an adult relationship; the idea of sex with children had not entered his mind. When he answered Sharon's ad, he clearly expressed an interest in "a long-term relationship leading to marriage." Testimony of Mark Poehlman, page 695 *supra*. His only reference to children was that he "didn't mind" them. *Id*. Even after Sharon gave him an opening by hinting about "not let[ting] society's views stand in the way," Poehlman continued to focus his sexual attentions on the mother and not the daughters: "[I]f you don't mind me wearing your hose and licking your toes then I am open for anything." Appellant's Excerpts of Record at Tab 5 (July 31, 1995).

It was Sharon who first suggested that Poehlman develop a relationship with her daughters: "I've had to be both mother and father to my sweethearts, but there are some things I'm just not equipped to teach them. I'm looking for someone to help with their special education." *Id*. (July 27, 1995). Poehlman's response to this ambiguous invitation was perfectly appropriate: "[A]s far as your children are concerned I will treat them as my own (as I would treat my boys if I had them with me) I have huge family values and like kids and they seem to like me alright too." *Id*. (July 31, 1995). Even when Sharon, in her next e-mail, became more insistent about having Poehlman be a special man teacher to her daughters, he betrayed no interest in a sexual relationship with them: "I am interested in being this special teasher, but in all honesty I really don't know exactly what you expect me to teach them other than proper morals and give support to them where it is needed." *Id*. (Aug. 2, 1995).

In the same e-mail, Poehlman expressed a continued interest in an adult relationship with Sharon: "I have to be honest and tell you I would hope you would support and enjoy me sexually as well as in company and hopefully love and the sexual relations that go with it." *Id*. It was only after Sharon made it clear that agreeing to serve as sexual mentor to her daughters was a condition to any further communications between her and Poehlman that he agreed to play the role Sharon had in mind for him.

The government argues that it did not induce Poehlman because Sharon did not, in so many words, suggest he have sex with her daughters. But this is far too narrow a view of the matter. The clear implication of Sharon's messages is that this is precisely what she had in mind. Contributing to this impression is repeated use of the phrases "special teacher" and "man teacher," and her categorical rejection of Poehlman's suggestion that he would treat her daughters as his own children and teach them proper morals with a curt, "I don't think you understand." *Id.*

In case the references to a special man teacher were insufficient to convey the idea that she was looking for a sexual mentor for her daughters, Sharon also salted her correspondence with details that clearly carried sexual innuendo. In her second e-mail to Poehlman, she explained that she had "discussed finding a special man teacher with my sweethearts and you should see the look of joy and excitement on their faces. They are very excited about the prospect of finding such a teacher." *Id.* (Aug. 1, 1995). To round out the point, Sharon further explained that "I want my sweethearts to have the same special memories I have . . . . I've told them about my special teacher and the memories I have. I still get goosebumps thinking about it." *Id.* From Sharon's account, one does not get the impression that her own special teacher had given her lessons in basket weaving or croquet. Finally, Sharon's third e-mail to Poehlman clearly adds to the suggestion of a sexual encounter between him and her daughters when she states: "I do like to watch, though. I hope you don't think I'm too weird." *Id.* In light of Sharon's earlier statements, it's hard to escape the voyeuristic implications of this statement. After all, there would be nothing weird about having Sharon watch Poehlman engaged in normal father-daughter activities.

Sharon did not merely invite Poehlman to have a sexual relationship with her minor daughters, she made it a condition of her own continued interest in him.[8] Sharon, moreover, pressured Poehlman to be explicit about his plans for teaching the girls: "Tell me more about how their first lesson will go. This will help me make my decision as to who their teacher will be." *Id.* (Sept. 19, 1995). The implication is that unless Poehlman came up with lesson plans that were

---

8   Sharon repeatedly held her own relationship with Poehlman hostage to his fulfilling the role of special man teacher. "I'm looking for someone to help with their special education. . . . If this doesn't interest you, I understand." Appellant's Excerpts of Record at Tab 5 (July 27, 1995). "If you understand and are interested, please write back. If you don't share my views I understand." *Id.* (Aug. 1, 1995). "I'd love to hear your ideas on lessons. . . . If you are still interested I'm looking forward to your next letter." *Id.* (Aug. 9, 1995). "If this is ok to you, please tell me so. If not, I wish you well and I'll continue my search." *Id.* (Sept. 18, 1995). "[I]f being their teacher is something you don't want to do[,] I will try to find another person like you to be their teacher." *Id.* (Dec. 13, 1995). Anytime Poehlman strays from the discussion of the daughters into a discussion of himself and Sharon, she refocuses him on the children. "[Y]our statement about wanting to be 'your friend and lover' . . . was this directed at me or the girls? If it was to the girls, that's fine, but not for me. I hate to keep making a thing about this but I just want you to know that there will be nothing sexual between us." *Id.* (Nov. 10, 1995).

sufficiently creative, Sharon would discard Poehlman and select a different mentor for her daughters.

Sharon eventually drew Poehlman into a protracted e-mail exchange which became increasingly intimate and sexually explicit. Approximately three weeks into the correspondence, Poehlman started signing off as Nancy, the name he adopts when dressing in women's clothes. Sharon promptly started using that name, offering an important symbol of acceptance and friendship. In the same e-mail, Sharon complained that Poehlman had neglected to discuss the education of her two younger girls. "I thought it curious that you did not mention Bonnie or Karen. Are they too young to start their educations? I don't want them to feel left out, but at the same time If you aren't comfortable with them please say so." *Id.* (Aug. 30, 1995).

Sharon also pushed Poehlman to be more explicit about his plans for the oldest daughter: "Abby is very curious (but excited) about what you expect her to do and I haven't been able to answer all her questions. Hope to hear from you soon." *Id.* Poehlman responded to Sharon's goading: "Bonnie and Karen being younger need to learn how to please, before they can be taught how to be pleased. they will start be exploring each others body together as well as mine and yours, they will learn how to please both men and women and they will be pleasein Abby as well." *Id.* (Aug. 31, 1995).

Over six months and scores of e-mails, Sharon persistently urged Poehlman to articulate his fantasies concerning the girls. Meanwhile Poehlman continued his efforts to establish a relationship with Sharon. For example, Poehlman twice proposed marriage, but this drew a sharp rebuke from Sharon:

> Nancy, I'm not interested in marriage or any type of relationship with my darlings' teacher. My quest as their mother is to find them the right teacher so that they get the same education I was fortunate enough to get at their ages. You need to understand this. This is not for me, but for them. I don't mean to sound harsh, but you can't imagine the number of people just looking for a wife or girlfriend online. I have to look past all this and concentrate on finding my darlings' special man teacher.

Id. (Sept. 18, 1995). Poehlman nevertheless continued to seek a familial relationship with Sharon and her daughters, expressing himself ready to quit his job and move across the country to be with them.

As Justice Frankfurter noted in his concurrence in *Sherman,*

> Of course in every case of this kind the intention that the particular crime be committed originates with the police, and without their inducement the crime would not have occurred. But it is perfectly clear [that] . . . where the

police in effect simply furnished the opportunity for the commission of the crime, that this is not enough to enable the defendant to escape conviction.

Sherman v. United States, 356 U.S. 369, 382, 78 S.Ct. 819, 2 L.Ed.2d 848 (1958) (Frankfurter, J., concurring). Whether the police did more than provide an opportunity—whether they actually induced the crime, as that term is used in our entrapment jurisprudence—depends on whether they employed some form of suasion that materially affected what Justice Frankfurter called the "self-struggle [to] resist ordinary temptations." *Id.* at 384, 78 S.Ct. 819 (Frankfurter, J., concurring).

Where government agents merely make themselves available to participate in a criminal transaction, such as standing ready to buy or sell illegal drugs, they do not induce commission of the crime. "An improper 'inducement' . . . goes beyond providing an ordinary 'opportunity to commit a crime.' An 'inducement' consists of an 'opportunity' *plus* something else—typically, excessive pressure by the government upon the defendant or the government's taking advantage of an alternative, non-criminal type of motive." *United States v. Gendron*, 18 F.3d 955, 961 (1st Cir.1994) (quoting *Jacobson*, 503 U.S. at 550, 112 S.Ct. 1535).

In *Jacobson*, the government conceded inducement based on the fact that the defendant there committed the offense after numerous contacts from the government spanning over two years, during the course of which government agents "wav[ed] the banner of individual rights and disparag[ed] the legitimacy and constitutionality of efforts to restrict the availability of sexually explicit materials." *Jacobson*, 503 U.S. at 552, 112 S.Ct. 1535. In doing so, "the Government not only excited petitioner's interest in sexually explicit materials banned by law but also exerted substantial pressure on petitioner to obtain and read such material as part of a fight against censorship and infringement of individual rights." *Id.* *Jacobson* is consistent with prior cases such as *Sherman*, where the government played upon defendant's weakness as a drug user, and *Sorrells*, where the government agent called upon defendant's loyalty to a fellow war veteran to induce him to commit the offense.

Cases like *Jacobson, Sherman* and *Sorrells* demonstrate that even very subtle governmental pressure, if skillfully applied, can amount to inducement. In *Jacobson*, for example, the government merely advanced the view that the law in question was illegitimate and that, by ordering the prohibited materials, defendant would be joining in "a fight against censorship and the infringement of individual rights." *Id.* at 552, 112 S.Ct. 1535. In *Sorrells*, the inducement consisted of repeated requests, made in an atmosphere of comradery among veterans. *See Sorrells*, 287 U.S. at 439–41, 53 S.Ct. 210. In *Sherman*, the inducement consisted of establishing a friendly relationship with the defendant, and then playing on his sympathy for the supposed suffering of a fellow drug user. *See Sherman*, 356

U.S. at 371, 78 S.Ct. 819. In *Hollingsworth*, the inducement was nothing more than giving the defendant the idea of committing the crime, coupled with the means to do it. *See Hollingsworth*, 27 F.3d at 1200–02.

Measured against these precedents, there is no doubt that the government induced Poehlman to commit the crime here. Had Sharon merely responded enthusiastically to a hint from Poehlman that he wanted to serve as her daughters' sexual mentor, there certainly would have been no inducement. But Sharon did much more. Throughout the correspondence with Poehlman, Sharon made it clear that she had made a firm decision about her children's sexual education, and that she believed that having Poehlman serve as their sexual mentor would be in their best interest. She made repeated references to her own sexual mentor, explaining that he could have mentored her daughters, had he not died in a car crash in 1985. *See* Appellant's Excerpts of Record at Tab 5 (Oct. 30, 1995). While parental consent is not a defense to statutory rape, it nevertheless can have an effect on the "self-struggle [to] resist ordinary temptations." *Sherman*, 356 U.S. at 384, 78 S.Ct. 819 (Frankfurter, J., concurring). This is particularly so where the parent does not merely consent but casts the activity as an act of parental responsibility and the selection of a sexual mentor as an expression of friendship and confidence. Not only did this diminish the risk of detection, it also allayed fears defendant might have had that the activities would be harmful, distasteful or inappropriate, particularly since Sharon claimed to have herself benefitted from such experiences. *See United States v. Gamache*, 156 F.3d 1, 11 (1st Cir.1998) ("[T]he government agent provided justifications for the illicit activity (intergenerational sex) by describing 'herself' as glad that Gamache was 'liberal' like her, expressing that she, as the mother of the children, strongly approved of the illegal activity, and explaining that she had engaged in this conduct as a child and found it beneficial to her.").

It is clear, moreover, that Poehlman continued to long for an adult relationship with Sharon, as well as a father-like relationship with the girls. He offered marriage; talked about quitting his job and moving to California; discussed traveling with Sharon and the girls; even offered his military health insurance benefits as an inducement. While refusing to give Poehlman hope of a sexual relationship with her, Sharon encouraged these fantasies; she went so far as to check out Poehlman's job prospects in California. The government thus played on Poehlman's obvious need for an adult relationship, for acceptance of his sexual proclivities and for a family, to draw him ever deeper into a sexual fantasy world involving these imaginary girls.

As the First Circuit noted in a case with very similar facts, "[t]he record is clear that it was the Government's insistence and artful manipulation of appellant that finally drew him into the web skillfully spun by the detective." *Gamache*,

156 F.3d at 10. Through its aggressive intervention, the government materially affected the normal balance between risks and rewards from the commission of the crime, and thereby induced Poehlman to commit the offense.

Predisposition

The jury could, nevertheless, have found Poehlman guilty if it found that he was predisposed to commit the offense. Quite obviously, by the time a defendant actually commits the crime, he will have become disposed to do so. However, the relevant time frame for assessing a defendant's disposition comes before he has any contact with government agents, which is doubtless why it's called *pre*disposition. *See Jacobson*, 503 U.S. at 549, 112 S.Ct. 1535 ("'[T]he prosecution must prove beyond [a] reasonable doubt that the defendant was disposed to commit the criminal act prior to first being approached by Government agents.'") (quoting *United States v. Whoie*, 925 F.2d 1481, 1483–84 (D.C.Cir.1991)). In our case, the question is whether there is evidence to support a finding that Poehlman was disposed to have sex with minors prior to opening his correspondence with Sharon.

The government argues that Poehlman was predisposed because he jumped at the chance to cross state lines to sexually mentor Sharon's children at the first opportunity available to him. But if willingness alone were the test, *Jacobson* would have come out differently. The defendant there had been contacted by government agents posing as organizations espousing the view that child pornography should be made legal, and asked a variety of questions about his interest in young boys. Jacobson expressed such an interest and, in response to "surveys," expressed the view that such materials should be made legal. The correspondence lasted two years, at the end of which the government (posing as one of these organizations) offered to sell him some magazines containing pictures of nude boys. Jacobson immediately placed an order and was arrested after the materials were delivered. As the Seventh Circuit noted in *Hollingsworth*, Jacobson "*never* resisted" the government's offer. *Hollingsworth*, 27 F.3d at 1199.

Despite Jacobson's willingness to commit the offense at the first opportunity offered to him, the Supreme Court held that the government had failed to show predisposition because it had failed to show that he would have been disposed to buy the materials before the government started its correspondence with him. The fact that he was willing to order illegal materials after he'd been harangued by the government for over two years was not deemed sufficient to show predisposition. Jacobson's decision to order, the Court reasoned, could have been a consequence of the government's inducement.

By analogy, the fact that Poehlman willingly crossed state lines to have sex with minors after his prolonged and steamy correspondence with Sharon cannot, alone, support a finding of predisposition. It is possible, after all, that it was the government's inducement that brought Poehlman to the point where he became willing to break the law. As in *Jacobson*, we must consider what evidence there is as to Poehlman's state of mind *prior* to his contact with Sharon.

On this score, the record is sparse indeed; it is easier to say what the record does not contain than what it does. The government produced no e-mails or chat room postings where Poehlman expressed an interest in sex with children, or even the view that sex with children should be legalized. Nor did the government produce any notes, tapes, magazines, photographs, letters or similar items which disclosed an interest in sex with children, despite a thorough search of Poehlman's home. There was no testimony from the playmates of Poehlman's children, his ex-wife or anyone else indicating that Poehlman had behaved inappropriately toward children or otherwise manifested a sexual interest in them. Sharon's ad, to which Poehlman responded, does not clearly suggest that sex with children was to be the object of the relationship: "Divorced mother of 3 looking for someone who understands my family's unique needs. Servicemen preferred. Please E-mail me at Darlings3@aol.com." Appellant's Excerpts of Record at Tab 5 (undated). While one might presume that one or more of the children are minors, the phrase "unique needs" could, just as easily, connote children with physical disabilities, or merely the plight of a single mother of three.

Poehlman does not appear to have responded to her ad because it mentions children or their special needs. During the crucial first few exchanges, *see* page 695–97 *supra*, when Sharon focused Poehlman's attention on those special needs, he expressed confusion as to what she had in mind. Instead of exploiting the ambiguity in Sharon's messages to suggest the possibility of sex with her daughters, Poehlman pushed the conversation in the opposite direction, offering to act as a father figure to the girls and teach them "proper morals." Appellant's Excerpts of Record at Tab 5 (Aug. 2, 1995). While Poehlman's reluctance might have been borne of caution—the way a drug dealer might demur when he is unsure whether a prospective buyer is a government agent—the fact remains that Poehlman's earliest messages (which would be most indicative of his pre-existing state of mind) provide no support for the government's case on predisposition. To the contrary, Poehlman's reluctance forced Sharon to become more aggressive in her suggestions, augmenting the defendant's case for inducement. *See* page 698–99 *supra*.

Poehlman's enthusiastic, protracted and extreme descriptions of the sexual acts he would perform with Sharon's daughters are, according to the government, its strongest evidence of Poehlman's predisposition. Indeed, once he got the idea of what Sharon had in mind, Poehlman expressed few concerns about the morality, legality or appropriateness of serving as the girls' sexual mentor. But Poehlman was not convicted of writing smutty e-mails; he was convicted of crossing state lines, some six months later, to have sex with minors. The problem with using Poehlman's e-mails as evidence of predisposition is that they were all in response to specific, pointed suggestions by Sharon. The e-mails thus tell us what Poehlman's disposition was once the government had implanted in his mind the idea of sex with Sharon's children, but not whether Poehlman would have engaged in such conduct had he not been pushed in that direction by the government. In short, Poehlman's erotic e-mails cannot provide proof of predisposition because nothing he says in them helps differentiate his state of mind prior to the government's intervention from that afterwards.

It is entirely plausible to infer that, as in *Jacobson*, it was the government's graduated response—including e-mail correspondence, handwritten letters from the girls and Sharon, the use of intimate names, a photograph of Poehlman sent to Sharon, Poehlman handcrafting gifts for the girls and Sharon's willingness to help Poehlman look for a job in Southern California—that brought Poehlman to the point where he was willing to cross state lines for the purpose of having sex with the three young girls. Since the government has the burden of proof as to predisposition, materials like these e-mails, which do not demonstrate any preexisting propensity to engage in the criminal conduct at issue, simply cannot carry that burden.

This is not to say that statements made after the government's inducement can never be evidence of predisposition. If, after the government begins inducing a defendant, he makes it clear that he would have committed the offense even without the inducement, that would be evidence of predisposition. But only those statements that indicate a state of mind untainted by the inducement are relevant to show predisposition. Poehlman's protracted correspondence with Sharon, in fact, undermines the view that he was predisposed to commit the offense. Even as his e-mails became more intimate and explicit—usually in response to Sharon's constant hectoring for more details about Poehlman's lesson plans—he never gave any indication that being a sexual mentor to the girls in any way fulfilled his preexisting fantasies. To the contrary, Poehlman repeatedly tried to integrate Sharon's expectations of him into his own fantasies by insisting that the girls (and Sharon) parade around the house in nylons and high-heeled pumps ("as high of a heel as they can handle," Appellant's Excerpts of Record at Tab 5 (Nov. 7, 1995))—as Poehlman himself apparently does.

The only indication in the record of any preexisting interest in children is Poehlman's statement in the hotel room that he has "always looked at little girls." Testimony of Mark Poehlman, page 695 *supra*. But this is hardly an indication that he was prone to engage in sexual relations with minors. *See Jacobson*, 503 U.S. at 545, 112 S.Ct. 1535 (while defendant expressed interest in "good looking young guys (in their late teens and early 20's) doing their thing together," the Court noted that he "made no reference to child pornography"); *see also Hollingsworth*,

27 F.3d at 1202 ("Whatever it takes to become an international money launderer, they did not have it."). Having carefully combed the record for any evidence that Poehlman was predisposed to commit the offense of which he was convicted, we find none. To the extent the jury might have found that Poehlman was predisposed to commit the offense, that finding cannot be sustained.

CONCLUSION

"When the Government's quest for convictions leads to the apprehension of an otherwise law-abiding citizen who, if left to his own devices, likely would have never run afoul of the law, the courts should intervene." *Jacobson*, 503 U.S. at 553–54, 112 S.Ct. 1535. So far as this record discloses, Poehlman is such a citizen. Prior to his unfortunate encounter with Sharon, he was on a quest for an adult relationship with a woman who would understand and accept his proclivities, which did not include sex with children. There is surely enough real crime in our society that it is unnecessary for our law enforcement officials to spend months luring an obviously lonely and confused individual to cross the line between fantasy and criminality. The judgment of conviction is REVERSED on grounds of insufficiency of the evidence and the case is REMANDED with instructions that defendant be released forthwith.

The mandate shall issue at once. Fed. R.App. P. 2.

THOMPSON, Circuit Judge, dissenting:

I respectfully dissent. Our task as an appellate court is not to reweigh the evidence but to uphold the jury's verdict so long as substantial evidence supports it. The fact that we would have decided the case differently is irrelevant.

Viewing the evidence in the light most favorable to the government, we may reverse the jury's verdict only if no reasonable jury could have concluded that Mark Poehlman was not legally entrapped. *See United States v. Citro*, 842 F.2d 1149, 1151 (9th Cir.1988). Because there was sufficient evidence for a reasonable jury to find that the government did not induce Poehlman to commit the crime, the jury's verdict should be upheld.

Entrapment as a matter of law was not established in this case. Entrapment as a matter of law requires undisputed evidence establishing that the government induced the defendant to commit the crime and that the defendant was not predisposed to commit the crime. *See United States v. Lorenzo*, 43 F.3d 1303, 1305 (9th Cir.1995).

Poehlman failed to present "'undisputed evidence making it patently clear that an otherwise innocent person was induced to commit the illegal act.'" *United States v. Skarie*, 971 F.2d 317, 320 (9th Cir.1992) (citation omitted); *see United States v. Manarite*, 44 F.3d 1407, 1418 (9th Cir.1995) (defining inducement as "government conduct that creates a substantial risk that an otherwise law-abiding person will commit a crime"). Even though during the first two weeks of Poehlman's e-mail communications with the government agent posing as "Sharon" Poehlman revealed no sexual interest in children, Poehlman soon began to interpret purposely vague e-mails from Sharon as containing sexual undertones. *But cf. United States v. Gamache*, 156 F.3d 1, 4 (1st Cir.1998) (holding that the district court should have given an entrapment instruction based in part on the government's improper inducement and the government's first mentioning of children as sex objects). While the government sent Poehlman messages, it did not first suggest sexual relations with children nor propose any specific sexual acts. Moreover, the government's e-mails never forced Poehlman to respond and, in fact, offered Poehlman many opportunities to end the communications if he were interested in a relationship with Sharon and not the kids or if he were at all uncomfortable. The majority contends that the "clear implication of Sharon's messages" suggested that Poehlman have sex with the children, but, so long as ambiguous evidence requires inferences to be made, it is the role of the jury to draw such inferences. *See United States v. Goode*, 814 F.2d 1353, 1355 (9th Cir.1987).

A reasonable jury could also have found that Poehlman was predisposed to commit the crime. We generally rely upon five factors in determining predisposition: (1) the defendant's character or reputation; (2) whether the government first suggested the criminal activity; (3) whether the defendant profited from the activity; (4) whether the defendant demonstrated reluctance; and (5) the nature of the government's inducement. *See Citro*, 842 F.2d at 1152. The defendant's reluctance generally receives the greatest weight. *See United States v. Thickstun*, 110 F.3d 1394, 1397 (9th Cir.1997).

Poehlman's character and the absence of a profit motive are two factors that weigh heavily in Poehlman's favor. Poehlman does not have a history of a sexual interest in children, and his e-mail communications with Sharon never revealed an interest in profiting from any sexual relationship. The other predisposition factors, however, tip in favor of the government. During the undercover operation, the government constructed purposely vague e-mail messages. While Poehlman claims that the government initiated the sexual conversation when Sharon wrote about the lessons for her children from a "special man teacher" and her desire to watch the lessons, Poehlman conceded at trial that Sharon "never came out and said that [he] have sex with the kids." Poehlman first introduced sexual remarks in his reply to the government's message stating Sharon's interest in finding a "special man teacher" for her children.

Although Poehlman's e-mail messages during the first two weeks of his communication with Sharon appeared free of sexual allusions directed toward her children, his communications for the next roughly 5–½ months detailed sexual acts that he would perform with Sharon's three children, even asking Sharon to put the two older girls on birth control. Moreover, just prior to Poehlman's arrest, a female undercover agent, posing as Sharon, presented Poehlman with a child pornography magazine and pointed to a particular picture depicting a child in a sexual act. When the officer asked Poehlman whether he thought the children "will be ready for this," Poehlman responded, "God, I hope so." Poehlman also remarked that he has "always looked at little girls." Although Poehlman at trial stated that he meant women over the age of eighteen, a reasonable jury could have concluded that he revealed a predisposition toward having sexual relations with young children.

At trial, the government established that Poehlman first mentioned having sex with the children, and each proposed sexual act originated from him. Even though this case is not as clear cut as a case in which a defendant, for example, exemplifies predisposition by owning a library of explicit materials before the commencement of a sting operation, the jury heard enough evidence for it to reasonably conclude that Poehlman in fact had a predisposition to commit the crime.

As the majority acknowledges, the district court properly instructed the jury,[1] and Poehlman does not contend otherwise. What we are left with is a case in which the jury followed the court's correct instructions, considered the evidence, and simply rejected the defense. I would affirm the conviction.

Notes and Questions

1. Why was the case not remanded for another trial? What is the meaning of the last clause of the majority opinion?

2. Is it really plausible that a person who was not predisposed could be persuaded—by email—to have sex with young children?

----

1   The district court followed the Ninth Circuit Manuel of Model Jury Instructions 6.2.1 (1997) in instructing the jury that the government must prove the following:

  1. The defendant was predisposed to commit the crime before being contacted by government agents, or

  2. The defendant was not induced by the government agents to commit the crime.

  Where a person, independent of and before government contact, is predisposed to commit the crime, it is not entrapment if the government agents merely provide an opportunity to commit the crime.

3. Does the entrapment defense apply to those to buy or sell drugs on the street, and unknowingly deal with government agents?

4. The entrapment defense was created as a matter of statutory interpretation, rather than constitutional law. The Supreme Court reasoned that in passing the prohibition laws, Congress could not have intended that people who were induced by the government to commit offenses could then be prosecuted. Nevertheless, every jurisdiction has it.

5. There are two main approaches to entrapment. Most jurisdictions, including the United States, apply the "subjective" test, which focuses on whether a defendant was "predisposed" to committing the offense. Other jurisdictions apply the "objective" test which examines the persuasiveness and intensity of government inducement.

6. In the first Supreme Court case recognizing entrapment, the Court stated: "We have no occasion to consider hypothetical cases of crimes so heinous or revolting that the applicable law would admit of no exceptions. No such situation is presented here. The question in each case must be determined by the scope of the law considered in the light of what may fairly be deemed to be its object." *Sorrells v. United States*, 287 U.S. 435 (1932). Should that exception have been applied here? How about government efforts to efforts to induce people to commit acts of "terrorism"?

7. Did you notice who investigated this case, and where it was prosecuted? It is common now for state and federal agencies to create task forces comprised of officers from various federal, state and local agencies and specialized agencies as well. It is also common for arrests by federal officers to be prosecuted as state crimes in state court, and vice versa. Often, state officers are given federal law enforcement powers, and vice versa. Does that affect your answer to the question of whether a state officer should be allowed to give advice which will estop a federal prosecution, or vice versa?

4. Outrageous Government Conduct Defense

United States v. Wiley

United States Court of Appeals, Ninth Circuit
794 F.2d 514 (1986)

KENNEDY, Circuit Judge:

Appellant Richard Lee Wiley appeals his conviction for conspiracy to possess and distribute marijuana in violation of 21 U.S.C. § 846. He argues that the district court erred in denying his motion to dismiss his indictment on the ground of outrageous government conduct. We affirm.

The essence of appellant's outrageous conduct claim is that the government was too active in suggesting a marijuana transaction and providing both an undercover courier and the contraband itself. We find nothing improper in the government's activation of the smuggling scheme. Given the difficulties of penetrating contraband networks in prisons, we cannot with confidence say the government's conduct here warrants dismissal of the indictment.

In the fall of 1982, an inmate informant at the Federal Correctional Institute at Lompoc gave prison authorities information on escapes, weapons, and drug trafficking. In early 1983, an associate warden asked the informant to find out about drug use at the prison. By telling inmates that he had access to a pound of marijuana and needed someone to smuggle the contraband inside the prison, the informant learned that Wiley could arrange the delivery. The informant met with Wiley various times to engage his participation in the drug transaction and further offered to finance the deal. After sampling some of the marijuana, Wiley agreed to help bring it into the prison in exchange for being allowed to keep one ounce himself.

As originally conceived, the plan was to deliver the marijuana to a courier who would transfer it in turn to Wiley's long-time contact, Garbiso, the prison cook. Garbiso would be responsible for smuggling the marijuana into the prison itself. Wiley suggested to the informant that Garbiso knew Wiley had a girlfriend called Lee who could be trusted as the courier. The problem was that Lee and Wiley were not on good terms, so the informant suggested someone simply pose as Lee in arranging delivery of the marijuana to Garbiso. Wiley agreed and, unknown to him, the informant used the government to choose an FBI agent for Lee's impersonator. The transaction went forward, with the agent and Garbiso speaking by telephone at various times. In the course of these conversations, Garbiso talked of "doing the deal for Rico Wiley" and explained that the arrangement was for Garbiso to keep half the marijuana for himself and deliver the other half to Wiley. Garbiso said Wiley would not deceive him.

Some two months after these conversations began, the agent delivered the marijuana to Garbiso. An embarrassment arises, for at this point the government lost control over the contraband. Based on subsequent statements of Garbiso and others, it appears the marijuana, or at least Wiley's half of it, was smuggled into the prison and smoked by members of the prison population at the Sunday night movie. A tawdry ending to an investigation, however, does not mean that the courts are required, or indeed authorized, to overlook the serious criminal enterprise that preceded it.

We may dismiss a criminal indictment when government conduct is so outrageous that it violates due process. *United States v. Bogart*, 783 F.2d 1428, 1433 (9th Cir.1986); *see United States v. Russell*, 411 U.S. 423, 431-32, 93 S.Ct. 1637, 1642-43, 36 L.Ed.2d 366 (1973). Because the conduct must shock the conscience, however, outrageous government conduct is not to be equated with negligence or poor judgment. Even such lesser charges are not established on this record; and even assuming we were to accept the dissent's criticisms of the government, the government's conduct can be described in no harsher terms.

The two principal cases in the courts of appeals that dismiss indictments for outrageous conduct have only limited application. In *Greene v. United States*, 454 F.2d 783, 786-87 (9th Cir.1971), we found that a number of factors, acting in combination, constituted outrageous government conduct. There, a special investigator initiated contact with the defendants for the purpose of running an illegal bootlegging operation. For two-and-one-half years, the investigator supplied the equipment needed for the still, urged the defendants to produce the liquor, and was their only customer. The *Greene* case, moreover, was decided prior to the Supreme Court's decision in *Russell*, which held that entrapment is not of constitutional dimension, leaving only the most shocking and extreme conduct, of undefined specificity, open to constitutional inquiry. In *United States v. Twigg*, 588 F.2d 373 (3d Cir.1978), an informant set up a speed laboratory, which he financed and operated, and convinced the defendants, who had no background in chemistry, to provide minimal assistance.

The government's steps to activate the smuggling plan in the case before us do not present a case of misconduct at all, much less conduct that is outrageous. The drug distribution scheme between defendant and Garbiso was in existence before the government became involved; the government merely activated it. *See United States v. O'Connor*, 737 F.2d 814, 817-18 (9th Cir.1984), *cert. denied*, 469 U.S. 1218, 105 S.Ct. 1198, 84 L.Ed.2d 343 (1985) (government approached persons already involved in criminal activity); *United States v. McQuin*, 612 F.2d 1193, 1195-96 (9th Cir.) (per curiam) (government infiltrated criminal organization), *cert. denied*, 445 U.S. 955, 100 S.Ct. 1608, 63 L.Ed.2d 791 (1980). When the investigation commenced, the associate warden learned from the informant that Garbiso may have been involved in smuggling drugs into the prison; the informant also confirmed that Garbiso was Wiley's courier. The established relation between Wiley and Garbiso is further illustrated by the latter's conversations with the undercover FBI agent. Garbiso spoke of "doing the deal for Rico Wiley" and made it clear that he trusted Wiley in drug transactions. By using the informant and the FBI agent posing as a courier, the government merely provided an impetus to Wiley and Garbiso to attempt once again to smuggle drugs into the prison. *See United States v. Marcello*, 731 F.2d 1354, 1359 (9th Cir.1984) (informant merely "tempted" defendants to "[take] the bait").

Under these circumstances, providing the drugs for the transaction did not constitute government misconduct either. *United States v. Lomas*, 706 F.2d 886, 890 (9th Cir.1983), *cert. denied*, 464 U.S. 1047, 104 S.Ct. 720, 79 L.Ed.2d 182 (1984); *see United States v. So*, 755 F.2d 1350, 1354 (9th Cir.1985) (providing funds and opportunity to launder money). That the smuggling was successful leads equally as well to the argument that a highly efficient scheme had to be broken as it does to the argument that the government blundered its investigation. The law is not displaced simply because some enforcement attempts go awry.

The result we reach is fully consistent with our earlier rejection of similar claims by Garbiso. *See United States v. Garbiso*, 782 F.2d 1054 (9th Cir.1986). Defendant's conviction is AFFIRMED.

FERGUSON, Circuit Judge, dissenting:

When the government's involvement in a criminal endeavor is excessive, the government's conduct violates a defendant's Fifth Amendment due process rights and any resulting indictment must be dismissed. *United States v. Bogart*, 783 F.2d 1428, 1432-33 (9th Cir.1986); *United States v. Wylie*, 625 F.2d 1371, 1377 (9th Cir.1980) *cert. denied*, 449 U.S. 1080, 101 S.Ct. 863, 66 L.Ed.2d 804 (1981). "Law enforcement conduct . . . becomes constitutionally unacceptable where 'government agents engineer and direct the criminal enterprise from start to finish.'" *Bogart*, 783 F.2d at 1436 (quoting *United States v. Ramirez*, 710 F.2d 535, 539 (9th Cir.1983)). The government's conduct here was sufficiently pervasive to require dismissal of Wiley's indictment.

I.

This is a case where the government itself planned and directed a scheme to smuggle drugs into a federal prison. The plan was so successful that marijuana was smuggled into the prison yet no evidence of the contraband was ever discovered.

In early 1983, due to an increase in drug trafficking within the Lompoc Federal Correctional Institution, an associate warden asked a prisoner informant to investigate the transmission of drugs into the prison. To start the investigation, the informant told another inmate that he had a pound of marijuana he wanted to bring into the prison. The inmate later told him that Wiley had "a mule" (a courier) willing to bring marijuana into the prison. The courier was co-defendant Garbiso, a cook at the prison.

The informant sought out Wiley to discuss smuggling the marijuana. Wiley did not agree to the proposition. The informant approached Wiley several more times, offering and providing Wiley with samples of marijuana; each time Wiley refused to agree to the deal. Wiley finally agreed to help the informant in exchange for one ounce of the marijuana.

When it became apparent that Wiley could not finance the purchase of marijuana or provide a courier to get the marijuana to Garbiso, the informant offered to do both so that the transaction would go through. The informant said that he would finance the deal, although the FBI, through the DEA, actually provided the marijuana. Wiley and the informant also discussed how to deliver the marijuana to Garbiso. The FBI rejected their idea of mailing the marijuana to Garbiso and decided that an FBI agent would personally deliver the marijuana to Garbiso. When the informant presented the personal delivery plan to Wiley, Wiley said he thought that Garbiso would prefer the courier to be someone he knew. Wiley mentioned that Garbiso had seen a picture of his girlfriend, Lee, and would not be suspicious of her. However, since he had not talked to Lee in "a couple of years," the informant agreed to find someone to pose as Lee. An FBI agent played the role of Lee.

Once the arrangements were made, the government set the drug smuggling plan in motion. At the informant's request, Wiley wrote out instructions for Lee to contact Garbiso. Initially, Lee had difficulty contacting Garbiso, so, at the informant's suggestion, Wiley obtained Garbiso's home telephone number. Lee then made and recorded several telephone conversations to Garbiso to arrange the delivery.

In February 1984, when the marijuana still had not been delivered, the informant became nervous. He was afraid that the transaction would not occur, and that his informant status would be discovered. In order to ensure completion of the deal, he told Wiley that he was going to be transferred to another prison "any day" because of a court date. Although the informant did not have a scheduled court date, as part of his cover, he was transferred from Lompoc on February 21, 1984.

Lee delivered the marijuana to Garbiso in late February 1984. There is evidence, from subsequent telephone conversations between Lee and Garbiso, that Garbiso delivered one half of the marijuana to Wiley. Prison authorities never found evidence of the marijuana in the prison.

II.

Wiley's conviction should be reversed and the indictment dismissed because the government's involvement in smuggling marijuana into the prison was excessive. The outrageous government conduct defense depends on the level of the government's involvement in the crime. *United States v. So*, 755 F.2d 1350, 1353 (9th Cir.1985). Outrageous government conduct exists when "the Government permits itself to become enmeshed in criminal activity from beginning to end." *Greene v. United States*, 454 F.2d 783, 787 (9th Cir.1971). However, isolated conduct such as infiltrating an existing criminal enterprise, *United States v. O'Connor*, 737 F.2d 814, 817-18 (9th Cir.1984), supplying part of the contraband, *United States v. Russell*, 411 U.S. 423, 432, 93 S.Ct. 1637, 1643, 36 L.Ed.2d 366 (1973), or providing a person to assist in committing the crime, *United States v. McQuin*, 612 F.2d 1193, 1196 (9th Cir.), *cert. denied*, 445 U.S. 955, 100 S.Ct. 1608, 63 L.Ed.2d 791 (1980), is not shocking and outrageous and thus does not violate a defendant's due process rights. *See United States v. Bogart*, 783 F.2d 1428, 1437-38 (9th Cir.1986) (collecting cases).

We should not countenance the government's conduct here, because it engaged in all of these activities, not just one. The government initiated the transaction through an informant who claimed to have access to marijuana outside the prison; the informant approached Wiley several times to convince him to agree to help smuggle the marijuana into the prison; the informant offered to finance the purchase; the FBI supplied the marijuana; the FBI supplied the courier to deliver the marijuana; and the informant fabricated a reason to speed up, and thus ensure consummation of, the transaction.

The government's orchestration of the drug smuggling scheme compares to the level of government activity that this court, and others, have found so excessive as to constitute outrageous conduct. In *Greene*, 454 F.2d at 786-87, this court reversed a conviction because a government informant helped to reestablish and sustain a bootlegging operation over the course of two years. Not only did the government agent initiate the operation with the defendants, from whom he previously had purchased illegal alcohol, but he also offered to provide the equipment, the site, and an operator, and did provide the sugar. Additionally, he applied pressure to the defendants to begin production and was the operation's only customer.[4] *Id.*

---

4   The government attempts to distinguish *Greene* by emphasizing the two-year duration of the scheme as compared to the three months here. Duration, however, was only one of the factors the *Greene* court relied on-that alone did not change the essential character of the government's involvement as being "from beginning to end." 454 F.2d at 787. In fact, "duration" cuts the other way here-it was the informant's conduct that accelerated the transaction to ensure the commission of a crime in the short time period.

Similarly, in *United States v. Twigg*, 588 F.2d 373, 380 (3d Cir.1978), the court reversed the conviction because the government's involvement in conceiving and contriving the crime reached "a demonstrable level of outrageousness." There, at the request of the DEA, an informant contacted the defendants about setting up a methamphetamine hydrochloride ("speed") laboratory. Although it was unclear whether the defendants had the money to purchase the chemicals or equipment, the government provided the supplies. When the defendants ran into difficulties finding an acceptable site, the government provided an isolated farmhouse. The court concluded that the government generated new crimes merely to press criminal charges against the defendant: "fundamental fairness does not permit us to countenance such actions by law enforcement officials and prosecution for a crime so fomented by them will be barred." *Id.* at 381.

As in *Greene* and *Twigg*, the crime here would not have occurred without the government's initiation and completion of the illegal transaction. The district court found:

> In sum, the government supplied three critical elements of the transaction upon which the indictment was based: the money, the drugs, and the courier. However, the mule, or Garbiso, was equally indispensable to completion of the smuggling. There was no government contact with Garbiso at all;[5] and there is substantial evidence that Wiley and Garbiso had been engaged in trafficking apart from [the informant's] involvement. There is no evidence of coercion or undue pressure applied by [the informant], or that Garbiso was not predisposed. Clearly he was. Despite testimony by Wiley that he did not want to get involved with [the informant], it is not credible.

Wiley's predisposition, however, is irrelevant to the outrageous government conduct defense. *See Greene v. United States*, 454 F.2d 783, 786 (9th Cir.1971). The record does not support a finding, and the district court did not find, that Wiley was part of an ongoing drug smuggling enterprise. In fact, the evidence suggests the absence of an established drug-smuggling operation. In a recorded conversation Garbiso indicated he had not seen or talked to Wiley in at least four months. When Lee could not contact Garbiso according to Wiley's original directions, Wiley did not have an immediate alternate plan: the informant had to suggest that Wiley obtain Garbiso's home telephone number. *Compare United States v. Batres-Santolino*, 521 F.Supp. 744, 752 (N.D.Cal.1981) (outrageous government conduct found when defendants, although somewhat culpable, were not embarked or about to embark on criminal activity until government set operation in motion), *with Russell*, 411 U.S. at 432, 93 S.Ct. at 1643

---

5   This statement is not accurate because Lee, the FBI courier, contacted Garbiso several times.

(no outrageous government conduct when informant contributed propanone to illegal manufacturing of drugs already in progress), *and O'Connor*, 737 F.2d at 817-18 (no outrageous government conduct when defendants called former partner, now informant, to complete a drug deal and she agreed to trade cocaine for stolen jewelry).

If there had been an ongoing drug smuggling enterprise between Wiley and Garbiso, which the government merely activated, I would vote with the majority. But the record does not show such an enterprise, and the statement of the majority that there was one, does not make it so. Because the existence of an ongoing enterprise would be dispositive of the defense, it is certain that the district court judge would have found one if the evidence supported that conclusion. As an appellate court our responsibility is to base our decision only on the evidence in the record.

The fact remains that the informant approached Wiley with a plan to smuggle in one pound of government-financed and government-provided marijuana. Wiley's participation was to provide the name of a "mule" and instructions for Lee, the FBI courier. Without the government's supplying the marijuana, which Wiley could not afford, and the courier, which Wiley could not provide, Wiley's participation alone would not have resulted in this crime. *See Twigg*, 588 F.2d at 381; *Greene*, 454 F.2d at 787. Because the government engineered, directed, and manufactured this crime from start to finish, I would reverse the conviction and dismiss the indictment.

Notes and Questions

1. Did the majority successfully distinguish *Greene*, or just decline to follow it? This case is typical to the extent that victories are exceedingly rare. *United States v. Dyke*, 718 F.3d 1282 (10th Cir. 2013) (noting that some circuits no longer recognize the defense, and others rarely allow it).

2. Why did Wiley not rest on an entrapment defense?

3. Would it be outrageous government conduct for an officer to lie to a physician about his symptoms and identity, and present false identification, in order to obtain a medical marijuana card for use in investigations of dispensaries? *State v. Fitzpatrick*, 291 P.3d 1106 (Mont. 2012).

C

PRACTICE EXERCISE

Read the following statutes, then the case. The scenario is taken from *United States v. McDavid*, 2:06-CR-00035-MCE, 2008 WL 850307 (E.D. Cal. Mar. 28, 2008). You are a judge. Should you grant the defendant's motion for an acquittal, or in the alternative, a new trial? Cite the cases above as grounds for your decision. If more facts are necessary for your decision, state what facts are necessary.

18 U.S.C.A. § 844 (West):

(f)(1) Whoever maliciously damages or destroys, or attempts to damage or destroy, by means of fire or an explosive, any building, vehicle, or other personal or real property in whole or in part owned or possessed by, or leased to, the United States, or any department or agency thereof, or any institution or organization receiving Federal financial assistance, shall be imprisoned for not less than 5 years and not more than 20 years, fined under this title, or both. (2) Whoever engages in conduct prohibited by this subsection, and as a result of such conduct, directly or proximately causes personal injury or creates a substantial risk of injury to any person, including any public safety officer performing duties, shall be imprisoned for not less than 7 years and not more than 40 years, fined under this title, or both. (3) Whoever engages in conduct prohibited by this subsection, and as a result of such conduct directly or proximately causes the death of any person, including any public safety officer performing duties, shall be subject to the death penalty, or imprisoned for not less than 20 years or for life, fined under this title, or both.

* * *

(i) Whoever maliciously damages or destroys, or attempts to damage or destroy, by means of fire or an explosive, any building, vehicle, or other real or personal property used in interstate or foreign commerce or in any activity affecting interstate or foreign commerce shall be imprisoned for not less than 5 years and not more than 20 years, fined under this title, or both; and if personal injury results to any person, including any public safety officer performing duties as a direct or proximate result of conduct prohibited by this subsection, shall be imprisoned for not less than

7 years and not more than 40 years, fined under this title, or both; and if death results to any person, including any public safety officer performing duties as a direct or proximate result of conduct prohibited by this subsection, shall also be subject to imprisonment for any term of years, or to the death penalty or to life imprisonment.

* * *

(n) Except as otherwise provided in this section, a person who conspires to commit any offense defined in this chapter shall be subject to the same penalties (other than the penalty of death) as the penalties prescribed for the offense the commission of which was the object of the conspiracy.

The matter was tried by a jury beginning September 10, 2007. During the course of the trial, the Government put on evidence regarding the Earth Liberation Front ("ELF"), the Animal Liberation Front ("ALF"), and various anarchist groups. The Government also introduced the testimony of "Anna," an undercover agent working closely with the Federal Bureau of Investigation. Anna began working with the FBI as a college student. As part of her work with the FBI, she attended protests in an undercover capacity. Anna first met Defendant at the Crimethink Convergence in 2004. She determined at that time that Defendant was interested in various forms of illegal protest activity, but otherwise appeared to be of little interest. In 2005, Anna met with Defendant at a BioTech conference in Philadelphia. At that point, Defendant told her he was planning something "big" in California. At this meeting, Anna believed Defendant to be much more radical in his thinking and he began talking to her about a bombing campaign.

Anna traveled to California, where she met with Defendant and the other co-conspirators charged in the indictment, Lauren Weiner and Zachary Jenson. At that point, Defendant and the co-conspirators began plotting a bombing campaign at various locations in Northern California as a part of their anarchist philosophy.

Anna agreed to obtain a cabin for the group to use and the FBI wired the cabin with surveillance equipment. During their time in the cabin, the group planned to bomb gas stations, the Nimbus Dam, the Institute of Forest Genetics ("IFG"), power stations and cell phone towers. In addition to the testimony from Anna, the Government also introduced recorded conversations, e-mails, books, and notes that corroborated her testimony. Defendant's co-conspirators, Weiner and Jensen, also testified and corroborated Anna's testimony.

Defendant put on several character witnesses who testified that Defendant was a peaceful person. At the close of the evidence, the Court instructed the jury as to the crime charged and the defense of entrapment. On September 27, 2007, after several questions from the jury and several supplemental instructions, the jury returned a guilty verdict. In a special verdict, the jury found that Defendant conspired with Weiner and Jensen.

* * *

Defendant argues there was insufficient evidence that he actually conspired with the two co-defendants. The parties stipulated the IFG, Nimbus Dam, and cell phone towers either received government funding or were used in interstate commerce. Defendant argues the government did not prove any other target of the conspiracy and the co-defendants, Weiner and Jensen, testified there was no agreement as to the stipulated targets. Therefore, the evidence was insufficient to convict Defendant under 844(n) of conspiring to commit 844(f)(1) or (i).

In response, the Government points to recorded conversations where the co-defendants and the government informant discussed gas stations, cell phone towers, and the IFG. The Government also points to recorded conversations where Weiner states she is "down for the Forestry Service" and where the parties discuss the IFG, getting schematics for the building, and determining the locations of the security cameras. Further, the "Burn Book" addressed cell phone towers and Nimbus Dam, among other targets. The Government also points to evidence that the group took scouting trips to the Nimbus Dam and to the IFG.

* * *

Defendant argues the jury was not presented with any evidence of an "explosive device" or "fire" as defined in 18 U.S.C. section 844. Although the jury was not instructed on this definition, Defendant contends there was insufficient evidence in the record to meet this definition.

In response, the Government argues because Defendant was charged with conspiracy to commit arson, and not with arson itself, the Government did not need to prove Defendant was in possession of an incendiary device.

* * *

It is clear from the recorded conversations the conspirators intended to cause explosions and they were concerned regarding the loss of life that might accompany those explosions. It is also clear they wanted to make a bomb.

* * *

Defendant argues there was no agreement for the purposes of a conspiracy because the co-conspirators testified they were "acting" when they interacted with McDavid at the times of importance. Defendant argues since the act of agreeing is a group act, when one person pretends to agree there is no actual agreement and therefore no conspiracy. . .

In response, the Government contends an agreement may be inferred from circumstantial evidence and to the extent the co-conspirators testified they were "acting" the jury did not find that testimony credible or it would not have convicted Defendant.

***

Defendant argues the government witness, Officer Naliboff, was not qualified as an expert, and therefore should not have been allowed to testify. Naliboff's testimony addressed ELF, ALF, and anarchist groups, explaining what the groups believe, and what activities group members have been known to partake in to support their causes.

The Government argues this was admissible testimony that was linked to subsequent evidence regarding Defendants' plans to follow ELF/ALF guidelines. In addition to denying this was expert testimony, the Government does not concede this was even lay opinion testimony. Naliboff was never asked, and never gave, an opinion as to whether the conspirators were members of any group. The testimony was used to assist the jury in understanding Defendant's motive for targeting the particular locations.

B. Self-Defense

Universally, self-defense is a defense to homicide and assault charges. The principle is that people have the right to protect themselves from unlawful force. Indeed, in recent cases on the Second Amendment, the Court suggested that the right was of constitutional dimension, although it is not clear what effect, if any, that will have on legal doctrine. *McDonald v. City of Chicago*, 561 U.S. 742, 130 S. Ct. 3020, 3036, 177 L. Ed. 2d 894 (2010) (noting that "Self-defense is a basic right, recognized by many legal systems from ancient times to the present day, and in [*District of Columbia v. Heller*, 554 U.S. 570, 599, 128 S.Ct. 2783, 2801–02

(2008)], we held that individual self-defense is 'the central component' of the Second Amendment right.").

Nevertheless, with regard to self defense, jurisdictions can and do vary in the details.

1. The Basic Principles

a. *California Criminal Jury Instructions*

505. Justifiable Homicide: Self-Defense or Defense of Another

The defendant is not guilty of (murder/ [or] manslaughter/ attempted murder/ [or] attempted voluntary manslaughter) if (he/she) was justified in (killing/attempting to kill) someone in (self-defense/ [or] defense of another). The defendant acted in lawful (self-defense/ [or] defense of another) if:

1. The defendant reasonably believed that (he/she/ [or] someone else/ [or] *<insert name or description of third party>*) was in imminent danger of being killed or suffering great bodily injury [or was in imminent danger of being (raped/maimed/robbed/ *<insert other forcible and atrocious crime>*)];

2. The defendant reasonably believed that the immediate use of deadly force was necessary to defend against that danger;

AND

3. The defendant used no more force than was reasonably necessary to defend against that danger.

   Belief in future harm is not sufficient, no matter how great or how likely the harm is believed to be. The defendant must have believed there was imminent danger of death or great bodily injury to (himself/ herself/ [or] someone else). Defendant's belief must have been reasonable and (he/she) must have acted only because of that belief. The defendant is only entitled to use that amount of force that a reasonable person would believe is necessary in the same situation. If the defendant used more force than was reasonable, the [attempted] killing was not justified.

   When deciding whether the defendant's beliefs were reasonable, consider all the circumstances as they were known to and appeared to the defendant and consider what a reasonable person in a similar situation with similar knowledge would have believed. If the defendant's beliefs were reasonable, the danger does not need to have actually existed.

[The defendant's belief that (he/she/ [or] someone else) was threatened may be reasonable even if (he/she) relied on information that was not true. However, the defendant must actually and reasonably have believed that the information was true.]

[If you find that <insert name of decedent/victim> threatened or harmed the defendant [or others] in the past, you may consider that information in deciding whether the defendant's conduct and beliefs were reasonable.]

[If you find that the defendant knew that <insert name of decedent/victim> had threatened or harmed others in the past, you may consider that information in deciding whether the defendant's conduct and beliefs were reasonable.]

[Someone who has been threatened or harmed by a person in the past, is justified in acting more quickly or taking greater self-defense measures against that person.]

[If you find that the defendant received a threat from someone else that (he/she) reasonably associated with <insert name of decedent/victim>, you may consider that threat in deciding whether the defendant was justified in acting in (self-defense/ [or] defense of another).]

[A defendant is not required to retreat. He or she is entitled to stand his or her ground and defend himself or herself and, if reasonably necessary, to pursue an assailant until the danger of (death/great bodily injury/ <insert forcible and atrocious crime>) has passed. This is so even if safety could have been achieved by retreating.]

[Great bodily injury means significant or substantial physical injury. It is an injury that is greater than minor or moderate harm.]

The People have the burden of proving beyond a reasonable doubt that the [attempted] killing was not justified. If the People have not met this burden, you must find the defendant not guilty of (murder/ [or] man-slaughter/ attempted murder/ [or] attempted voluntary manslaughter).

Notes and Questions

Assume you are a defense attorney. Might you argue that the first bracketed instruction in paragraph 3 is in the wrong place?

---

2. The Basic Principles Applied

State v. Harden

Supreme Court of Appeals of West Virginia
679 S.E.2d 638 (2009)

SYLLABUS BY THE COURT

1. "A reviewing court should not reverse a criminal case on the facts which have been passed upon by the jury, unless the court can say that there is reasonable doubt of guilt and that the verdict must have been the result of misapprehension, or passion and prejudice." Syllabus Point 3, *State v. Sprigg*, 103 W.Va. 404, 137 S.E. 746 (1927).

2. "The function of an appellate court when reviewing the sufficiency of the evidence to support a criminal conviction is to examine the evidence admitted at trial to determine whether such evidence, if believed, is sufficient to convince a reasonable person of the defendant's guilt beyond a reasonable doubt. Thus, the relevant inquiry is whether, after viewing the evidence in the light most favorable to the prosecution, any rational trier of fact could have found the essential elements of the crime proved beyond a reasonable doubt." Syllabus Point 1, *State v. Guthrie*, 194 W.Va. 657, 461 S.E.2d 163 (1995).

3. Where a defendant has asserted a plea of self-defense, evidence showing that the decedent had previously abused or threatened the life of the defendant is relevant evidence of the defendant's state of mind at the time deadly force was used. In determining whether the circumstances formed a reasonable basis for

the defendant to believe that he or she was at imminent risk of serious bodily injury or death at the hands of the decedent, the inquiry is two-fold. First, the defendant's belief must be subjectively reasonable, which is to say that the defendant actually believed, based upon all the circumstances perceived by him or her at the time deadly force was used, that such force was necessary to prevent death or serious bodily injury. Second, the defendant's belief must be objectively reasonable when considering all of the circumstances surrounding the defendant's use of deadly force, which is to say that another person, similarly situated, could have reasonably formed the same belief. Our holding in Syllabus Point 6 of *State v. McMillion*, 104 W.Va. 1, 138 S.E. 732 (1927), is expressly overruled.

4. Where it is determined that the defendant's actions were not reasonably made in self-defense, evidence that the decedent had abused or threatened the life of the defendant is nonetheless relevant and may negate or tend to negate a necessary element of the offense(s) charged, such as malice or intent.

5. An occupant who is, without provocation, attacked in his or her home, dwelling or place of temporary abode, by a co-occupant who also has a lawful right to be upon the premises, may invoke the law of self-defense and in such circumstances use deadly force, without retreating, where the occupant reasonably believes, and does believe, that he or she is at imminent risk of death or serious bodily injury. In determining whether the circumstances formed a reasonable basis for the occupant to believe that he or she was at imminent risk of death or serious bodily injury at the hands of the co-occupant, the inquiry is two-fold. First, the occupant's belief must be subjectively reasonable, which is to say that the occupant actually believed, based upon all the circumstances perceived by him or her at the time deadly force was used, that such force was necessary to prevent death or serious bodily injury. Second, the occupant's belief must be objectively reasonable when considering all of the circumstances surrounding the occupant's use of deadly force, which is to say that another person, similarly situated, could have reasonably formed the same belief. Our decision in Syllabus Point 2, *State v. Crawford*, 66 W.Va. 114, 66 S.E. 110 (1909), is expressly overruled.

6. "Once there is sufficient evidence to create a reasonable doubt that the killing resulted from the defendant acting in self-defense, the prosecution must prove beyond a reasonable doubt that the defendant did not act in self-defense." Syllabus Point 4, *State v. Kirtley*, 162 W.Va. 249, 252 S.E.2d 374 (1978).

KETCHUM, J.:

This case is before the Court upon the appeal of Tanya A. Harden (defendant) from the final order of the Circuit Court of Cabell County sentencing the defendant to a term of life imprisonment with the possibility of parole following defendant's conviction for first degree murder.

The defendant, who asserted a claim of self-defense at trial, has submitted several assignments of error in support of her appeal. After careful consideration of the parties' arguments, the record, and relevant authorities, we find one of those assigned errors to be dispositive. Specifically, we find that the State failed to prove beyond a reasonable doubt that the defendant's actions were not made in self-defense. Accordingly, for the reasons set forth in this opinion, we vacate the defendant's conviction and remand this matter to the circuit court with directions to enter a judgment of acquittal.

I. BACKGROUND

On September 5, 2004, the defendant was arrested upon her admission to having shot and killed her husband, Danuel Harden. At trial, the defendant asserted a claim of self-defense, arguing that her actions precipitously followed a "night of domestic terror" that ended only when the defendant shot and killed the decedent. The evidence adduced at the defendant's trial showed that the decedent, while drinking heavily (with a blood alcohol count ultimately reaching 0.22% at the time of his death) subjected the defendant to a several-hour-long period of physical and emotional violence. This violence included the decedent brutally beating the defendant with the butt and barrel of a shotgun, brutally beating the defendant with his fists, and sexually assaulting the defendant. An emergency room physician at Cabell Huntington Hospital, who examined the defendant on the morning of the shooting, testified that the defendant "had contusions of both orbital areas, the right upper arm, a puncture wound with a foreign body of the right forearm, contusions of her chest, left facial cheek, the left upper lip" and that "X-rays done at the time demonstrated a nasal fracture."

In addition to the physical violence summarized above, the evidence adduced at trial also showed that the decedent repeatedly threatened to kill the defendant and the defendant's nine-year-old son B.H., ten-year-old daughter A.H., and ten-year-old B.K. (a friend of A.H.'s who had been invited for a "sleep over"). This evidence included testimony from two of the children. B.H. testified to seeing and hearing the decedent say to the defendant "I am going to go get the gun and shoot you" and that the decedent did, in fact, go to a back room in the defendant's home and get a shotgun, and returned to the room with the gun where the decedent subsequently struck the defendant with the butt of the gun in the shoulders and arms while she was seated in a recliner. In addition to B.H.'s testimony, B.K. also testified that she was frightened by what she could hear from her bedroom and had difficulty falling asleep, and that after finally falling asleep, she was awakened by more sounds of fighting, at one point over-hearing the defendant say to the decedent that "she didn't want to get killed with her two kids."

It is conceded by the State that the defendant suffered a "night of domestic terror." During its opening statement the State described the evening's violence as a "knock-down-drag-out" fight. By the time of the State's closing argument, the State conceded to the jury that "Yes, she had a night of terror." In its brief to this Court, the State concedes that the decedent's death followed an "evening of physical and sexual abuse."

Notwithstanding the fact that it does not dispute that the defendant endured a night of extreme violence at the hands of the decedent, the State nonetheless argues that the defendant's claim of self-defense is "untenable." In its closing argument, the State argued to the jury that "the law . . . on self-defense says that in order to use deadly force in self-defense you must find that the apprehension existed at the time the defendant attacked, or in this case shot, the [decedent]." In addition, the State maintained that the defendant did not have a reasonable basis to apprehend any danger from the decedent at the time she used deadly force against the decedent because there had been a "cooling off" period, and the evidence showed that the decedent was lying down on a couch possibly "asleep" or, alternately, possibly "passed out drunk" when the defendant shot him.[3] The State further argued to the jury that the defendant's use of deadly force was not reasonable because the defendant could have retreated from any danger posed by the decedent, evidenced by the fact that the decedent "is on that couch with a BAC of .22 and she has got control of that shotgun, she . . . could have called the law, and she could have walked out of that trailer. Period. But she didn't."

II. STANDARD OF REVIEW

On appeal the defendant argues that the State failed to submit sufficient evidence to prove beyond a reasonable doubt that her actions were not made in self-defense. We have previously held that "[a] reviewing court should not reverse a criminal case on the facts which have been passed upon by the jury, unless the court can say that there is reasonable doubt of guilt and that the verdict must have been the result of misapprehension, or passion and prejudice." Syllabus Point 3, *State v. Sprigg*, 103 W.Va. 404, 137 S.E. 746 (1927). *Accord* Syllabus Point 1, *State v. Easton*, 203 W.Va. 631, 510 S.E.2d 465 (1998).

---

3   In our discussion, *infra*, of the State's duty to have proven beyond a reasonable doubt that the defendant did not act in self-defense, the fact that the State resorts to "suspicion and conjecture" when describing the decedent's disposition at the time he was shot has not escaped us.

We have further held that:

> The function of an appellate court when reviewing the sufficiency of the
> evidence to support a criminal conviction is to examine the evidence
> admitted at trial to determine whether such evidence, if believed, is suf-
> ficient to convince a reasonable person of the defendant's guilt beyond a
> reasonable doubt. Thus, the relevant inquiry is whether, after viewing the
> evidence in the light most favorable to the prosecution, any rational trier of
> fact could have found the essential elements of the crime proved beyond a
> reasonable doubt.

Syllabus Point 1, *State v. Guthrie*, 194 W.Va. 657, 461 S.E.2d 163 (1995).

With these standards in mind, we turn to the issues presented.

III. DISCUSSION

Given the complexity of the issues raised in our analysis of whether the
State submitted sufficient evidence to prove, beyond a reasonable doubt, that the
defendant's actions were not made in self-defense, we will divide our discussion
into three sections. In Section III.1., we address the State's argument that the
defendant's use of lethal force was unreasonable because our law precludes an
"apprehension of danger previously entertained," *i.e.*, prior threats of violence
or acts of violence, as justifying the use of deadly force. In Section III.2., we
address the State's argument that the defendant's actions were unreasonable
because the defendant had a duty to retreat from her home in lieu of using
deadly force against the decedent. In Section III.3., we address the sufficiency
of the State's evidence.

III.1. Apprehension of Danger

A long-standing tenet of our self-defense doctrine is that a defendant's use
of deadly force must be based upon a reasonable apprehension by the defendant
that he or she was at imminent peril of death or serious bodily injury. In Syllabus
Point 8 of *State v. Cain*, 20 W.Va. 679 (1882), we held that:

> In such a case as to the imminency of the danger, which threatened the
> prisoner, and the necessity of the killing in the first instance the prisoner
> is the judge; but he acts at his peril, as the jury must pass upon his action
> in the premises, viewing said actions from the prisoner's stand-point at the
> time of the killing; and if the jury believe from all the facts and circum-
> stances in the case, that the prisoner had reasonable grounds to believe,
> and did believe, the danger imminent, and that the killing was necessary

to preserve his own life or to protect him from great bodily harm, he is excusable for using a deadly weapon in his defense, otherwise he is not.

In the case before us, it is clear that the State does not believe that the defendant had a reasonable basis to believe that she was in imminent danger of death or serious bodily injury at the time she used deadly force against the decedent. The State acknowledges that the decedent's death followed an "evening of physical and sexual abuse" inflicted upon the defendant by the decedent, but argues notwithstanding this "night of terror" a reasonable juror could have found that the defendant's use of lethal force was not reasonable under our law.

The State's argument on this point is straightforward. Our law, the State argues, requires that deadly force be employed only to repel an apprehension of death or serious bodily injury existing at the time deadly force is used, and specifically excludes any apprehension of danger *previously entertained* as justifying the use of deadly force. Under the circumstances of the defendant's case, the State argues, the defendant did not have a reasonable basis to apprehend *any* imminent danger from the decedent at the time she used deadly force because the facts suggested that there had been a "cooling off" period after the decedent's violent acts. Therefore, the State argues, because the decedent's violent acts had ended, those violent acts constituted "an apprehension of danger previously entertained" and could not justify the defendant's use of deadly force.

It is clear from the record that the State bases its arguments largely on Syllabus Point 6 of our decision in *State v. McMillion*, 104 W.Va. 1, 138 S.E. 732 (1927)(emphasis added), where we held that:

> Under his plea of self-defense, the burden of showing the imminency of the danger rests upon the defendant. *No apprehension of danger previously entertained will justify the commission of the homicide; it must be an apprehension existing at the time the defendant fired the fatal shot.*

It is also clear that the State bases its argument on the trial court's self-defense instruction. This self-defense instruction, which was offered by the State, contained the following language relevant to the issue of the reasonableness of the defendant's belief that death or serious bodily injury was imminent:

> In order for the Defendant to have been justified in the use of deadly force in self-defense, she must not have provoked the assault on her or have been the aggressor. Mere words, without more, do not constitute provocation or aggression. Furthermore, *you must find that the apprehension existed at the time that the defendant attacked the victim. No apprehension of danger previously entertained will justify the commission of homicide.* (Emphasis added).

It is obvious that the referenced portion of the trial court's self-defense instruction was based entirely on Syllabus Point 6 of *State v. McMillion, supra*. The question our review thus presents is whether Syllabus Point 6 of *McMillion*, and the State's argument based thereon, conflicts with our more recent precedent holding that *prior* physical and mental abuse by a decedent *is* relevant evidence on the issue of the reasonableness of a defendant's belief that death or serious bodily injury were imminent. We find that it does.

We begin our analysis by noting that our precedent establishes that the "reasonableness" of a defendant's belief that he or she was at "imminent" risk of death or serious bodily injury is a two-part inquiry, with a subjective component and an objective component. In Syllabus Point 8 of *State v. Cain, supra*, we described this inquiry as requiring that "the jury must pass upon [the defendant's] action in the premises, viewing said actions from the [defendant's] stand-point at the time of the killing[.]" We further held in Syllabus Point 8 of *State v. Cain* that the jury must believe from "all the facts and circumstances in the case, that the [defendant] had reasonable grounds to believe, and did believe, the danger imminent."

More recently, we addressed the reasonableness inquiry in *State v. Cook*, 204 W.Va. 591, 515 S.E.2d 127 (1999), where we concluded that the two-part inquiry required a finding that a defendant "actually believe that [she] is in danger and that belief must be a reasonable one." *State v. Cook*, 204 W.Va. 591, 601, 515 S.E.2d 127, 137, *citing State v. Elam*, 328 N.W.2d 314, 317 (Iowa 1982) ("[T]he test of justification is both subjective and objective. The actor must actually believe that he is in danger and that belief must be a reasonable one.").

Plainly stated, the reasonableness inquiry is as follows. First, a defendant's belief that death or serious bodily injury was imminent must be shown to have been subjectively reasonable, which is to say that a defendant actually believed, based upon all the circumstances perceived by him or her at the time deadly force was used, that such force was necessary to prevent death or serious bodily injury. Second, that the defendant's belief must be objectively reasonable when considering all of the circumstances surrounding the defendant's use of deadly force, which is to say that another person, similarly situated, could have reasonably formed the same belief.

Having thus briefly summarized the standard by which the reasonableness of the defendant's actions are measured, we turn to the issue of *McMillion's* absolute prohibition that no "apprehension of danger previously entertained" may be used to justify a homicide as having been committed in self-defense.

Our precedent since *McMillion* clearly establishes that a defendant, who has been the victim of domestic violence that tragically ends with the defendant's killing the battering spouse, is entitled "to elicit testimony about the prior physical beatings she received in order that the jury may fully evaluate and consider the defendant's mental state at the time of the commission of the offense." *State v. Dozier*, 163 W.Va. 192, 197–198, 255 S.E.2d 552, 555 (1979), *citing State v. Hardin*, 91 W.Va. 149, 112 S.E. 401 (1922) (defendant entitled to introduce evidence that decedent was a quarrelsome man who had previously attacked defendant and threatened defendant's life).

We have similarly held that evidence of prior threats and violence is relevant to "negate criminal intent." *State v. Lambert*, 173 W.Va. 60, 63–64, 312 S.E.2d 31, 35 (1984). In *State v. Wyatt*, 198 W.Va. 530, 542, 482 S.E.2d 147, 159 (1996), we explained that a defendant's domestic abuse was relevant "to establish either the lack of malice, intention, or awareness, and thus negate or tend to negate a necessary element of one or the other offenses charged." * * *

It is clear to us that our precedent since *McMillion* provides that the decedent's violent criminal acts and threats of death are relevant to the determination of the subjective reasonableness of the defendant's belief that she was at imminent risk of death or serious bodily injury. This is to say, under the facts of this case, the defendant's subjective belief that death or serious bodily injury was imminent, and that deadly force was necessary to repel that threat, necessarily included the fact that the decedent had, precipitously preceding his death, physically and sexually assaulted the defendant and repeatedly threatened the life of the defendant and the lives of the children.

We therefore hold that where a defendant has asserted a plea of self-defense, evidence showing that the decedent had previously abused or threatened the life of the defendant is relevant evidence of the defendant's state of mind at the time deadly force was used. In determining whether the circumstances formed a reasonable basis for the defendant to believe that he or she was at imminent risk of serious bodily injury or death at the hands of the decedent, the inquiry is twofold. First, the defendant's belief must be subjectively reasonable, which is to say that the defendant actually believed, based upon all the circumstances perceived by him or her at the time deadly force was used, that such force was necessary to prevent death or serious bodily injury. Second, the defendant's belief must be objectively reasonable when considering all of the circumstances surrounding the defendant's use of deadly force, which is to say that another person, similarly situated, could have reasonably formed the same belief. Our holding in Syllabus Point 6 of *State v. McMillion*, 104 W.Va. 1, 138 S.E. 732 (1927), is expressly overruled.

We further hold that where it is determined that the defendant's actions were not reasonably made in self-defense, evidence that the decedent had abused or threatened the life of the defendant is nonetheless relevant and may negate or tend to negate a necessary element of the offense(s) charged, such as malice or intent.

Having thus concluded, we find the State's arguments above-described unpersuasive.

III.2. Duty to Retreat

In addition to its argument that the defendant's use of deadly force was unreasonable because there had been a "cooling off" period, the State further argues that the same "cooling off" period provided the defendant the opportunity to retreat from her home so as to avoid further attacks. Our review of the record shows that during closing arguments the State advanced this argument, telling the jury that the defendant "could have walked out of that trailer. Period. But she didn't." Implicit in this argument is that the defendant had a duty to retreat from her home.

As a general proposition, our precedent in self-defense cases clearly state that where an unlawful intrusion has occurred in the sanctity of one's home, an occupant of the home has no duty to retreat. Generally described as the "castle" doctrine, "castle" rule or "home" rule, our precedent succinctly states that "[a] man attacked in his own home by an intruder may invoke the law of self-defense without retreating." Syllabus Point 4, *State v. Preece*, 116 W.Va. 176, 179 S.E. 524 (1935). *Accord* Syllabus Point 1, *State v. W.J.B.*, 166 W.Va. 602, 276 S.E.2d 550 (1981).

The distinction of the present issue is that the decedent was not an intruder, but instead a lawful co-occupant having equal entitlement with the defendant to be present therein. In Syllabus Point 2, *State v. Crawford*, 66 W.Va. 114, 66 S.E. 110 (1909)(emphasis added), we held that:

> On a trial for murder, *instructions to the jury asserting defendant's right to stand his ground and not retreat,* based on the theory of a deadly attack by deceased on, and on defendant in his dwelling, or castle, *are inapplicable where the evidence shows defendant and deceased were at the time of the homicide jointly occupying the house where the killing occurred*; the ordinary rules as to self-defense, propounded in other instructions given at the request of defendant, alone being applicable.

Similarly, in *State v. Boggs*, 129 W.Va. 603, 615–616, 42 S.E.2d 1, 8 (1946), we held that a defendant, who was a co-habitant of a house where the decedent and decedent's wife also lived, was not entitled to an instruction on "defendant's right to stand his ground and not retreat" on the grounds that the decedent was a co-occupant of the same dwelling.

The question that our decisions in *Crawford*, *Boggs* and other similar cases present is whether we should continue to follow the proposition that an occupant of a home has a duty to retreat when a co-occupant of the same home has attacked or otherwise placed the occupant in danger of serious bodily injury or death. We conclude that we should not.

In reaching our conclusion, we have considered the decisions of other supreme courts that have addressed a similar issue. Initially we note that West Virginia is in the apparent minority of jurisdictions who impose upon an occupant of a home the duty to retreat from an attack by a co-occupant. In *Weiand v. State*, 732 So.2d 1044 (Fla.1999), the Florida Supreme Court was asked to reconsider its earlier decision in *State v. Bobbitt*, 415 So.2d 724 (Fla. 1982). In *Bobbitt*, the court made findings similar to those we made in *Crawford*, which is to say that both our decision in *Crawford* and the Florida court's decision in *Bobbitt* held that an occupant of a home had a duty to retreat when attacked by a co-occupant. In concluding that its decision in *Bobbitt* should be vacated, the Florida Supreme Court initially noted that its decision in *Bobbitt* reflected a minority view on the duty of an occupant's duty to retreat, and specifically noted that West Virginia was one of the jurisdictions holding the minority view * * *

After noting that its earlier decision in *Bobbitt* reflected a minority position, the *Weiand* court went on to conclude that *Bobbitt* should be vacated, holding that:

> There are two distinct reasons for our conclusion. First, we can no longer agree with *Bobbitt's* minority view that relies on concepts of property law and possessory rights to impose a duty to retreat from the residence. 415 So.2d at 726. Second, based on our increased understanding of the plight of victims of domestic violence in the years since our decision in *Bobbitt*, we find that there are sound policy reasons for not imposing a duty to retreat from the residence when a defendant resorts to deadly force in self-defense against a co-occupant. The more recent decisions of state supreme courts confronting this issue have recognized that imposing a duty to retreat from the residence has a potentially damaging effect on victims of domestic violence claiming self-defense.

   . . .

It is now widely recognized that domestic violence "attacks are often repeated over time, and escape from the home is rarely possible without the threat of great personal violence or death." [*State v.*] *Thomas*, 77 Ohio St.3d 323, 673 N.E.2d [1339,]1343 [(1997)]. As quoted by the New Jersey Supreme Court:

> Imposition of the duty to retreat on a battered woman who finds herself the target of a unilateral, unprovoked attack in her own home is inherently unfair. During repeated instances of past abuse, she has "retreated," only to be caught, dragged back inside, and severely beaten again. If she manages to escape, other hurdles confront her. Where will she go if she has no money, no transportation, and if her children are left behind in the "care" of an enraged man?

. . . .

What [the duty to retreat] exception means for a battered woman is that as long as it is a stranger who attacks her in her home, she has a right to fight back and labors under no duty to retreat. If the attacker is her husband or live-in partner, however, she must retreat. The threat of death or serious bodily injury may be just as real (and, statistically, is more real) when her husband or partner attacks her in home, but still she must retreat. *Gartland*, 694 A.2d at 570–71 (quoting Maryanne E. Kampmann, "*The Legal Victimization of Battered Women*," 15 Women's Rts. L. Rep. 101, 112–113 (1993)).

Weiand, 732 So.2d at 1051–1053.

* * *

Based on our review, we see no rational legal basis for imposing upon an occupant of a home the duty to retreat from his or her home and to abandon it to a co-occupant who, by his or her conduct, is engaged in such improper behavior as to place the occupant in danger of death or serious bodily injury. In such circumstances the occupant may use, without retreating, deadly force if the occupant reasonably believes such force to be necessary to prevent his or her death or serious bodily injury presented by the co-occupant's criminal behavior.

Accordingly, we hold that an occupant who is, without provocation, attacked in his or her home, dwelling or place of temporary abode, by a co-occupant who also has a lawful right to be upon the premises, may invoke the law of self-defense and in such circumstances use deadly force, without retreating, where the occupant reasonably believes, and does believe, that he or she is at imminent risk of death or serious bodily injury.[9] In determining whether the

---

9   While we have today set out certain standards under which an occupant of a home, dwelling or place of temporary abode does not have a duty to retreat when attacked by a co-occupant of the same home, dwelling or place of temporary abode, we wish to clarify that this standard is not equal to the standards that have been established for using deadly force against an intruder into a dwelling. Indeed, we do not believe that the use of deadly force by one occupant against a co-occupant presents the same nature of circumstances posed by an intruder into a home. For example, under the law in West Virginia, the occupant of a dwelling may respond with deadly force to an intruder who merely threatens physical violence or the commission of a felony where the occupant reasonably believes that deadly force is necessary. Given that heated exchanges may be commonplace between household occupants, we believe that the greater threat of imminent death or serious bodily injury is necessary to justify the use of deadly force between co-occupants. Therefore, we expressly decline to extend to self-defense cases involving co-occupants our holding in Syllabus Point 2, *State v. W.J.B.*, 166 W.Va. 602, 276 S.E.2d 550 (1981), which provides that:

> The occupant of a dwelling is not limited in using deadly force against an unlawful intruder to the situation where the occupant is threatened with serious bodily injury or death, but he may use deadly force if the unlawful intruder threatens imminent physical violence or the commission of a felony and the occupant reasonably believes deadly force is necessary.

circumstances formed a reasonable basis for the occupant to believe that he or she was at imminent risk of serious bodily injury or death at the hands of the co-occupant, the inquiry is two-fold. First, the occupant's belief must be subjectively reasonable, which is to say that the occupant actually believed, based upon all the circumstances perceived by him or her at the time deadly force was used, that such force was necessary to prevent death or serious bodily injury. Second, the occupant's belief must be objectively reasonable when considering all of the circumstances surrounding the occupant's use of deadly force, which is to say that another person, similarly situated, could have reasonably formed the same belief. Our decision in Syllabus Point 2, *State v. Crawford*, 66 W.Va. 114, 66 S.E. 110 (1909), is expressly overruled.

III.3. Sufficiency of the Evidence

We begin our analysis of the sufficiency of the State's evidence by briefly reviewing the required elements of our self-defense doctrine as it pertains to circumstances where one occupant of a home has killed a co-occupant of the same home.

III.3.A. Elements of Self–Defense

More than a century ago, this Court set forth the required elements of our self-defense doctrine in Syllabus Point 7 of *State v. Cain,* 20 W.Va. 679 (1882), where we held that:

> When one without fault himself is attacked by another in such a manner or under such circumstances as to furnish reasonable grounds for apprehending a design to take away his life, or to do him some great bodily harm, and there is reasonable grounds for believing the danger imminent, that such design will be accomplished, and the person assaulted has reasonable ground to believe, and does believe, such danger is imminent, he may act upon such appearances and without retreating, kill his assailant, if he has reasonable grounds to believe, and does believe, that such killing is necessary in order to avoid the apparent danger; and the killing under such circumstances is excusable, although it may afterwards turn out, that the appearances were false, and that there was in fact neither design to do him some serious injury nor danger, that it would be done. But of all this the jury must judge from all the evidence and circumstances of the case.

In *State v. Hughes,* 197 W.Va. 518, 524, 476 S.E.2d 189, 195 (1996) (citations omitted), we more succinctly stated the elements of our self-defense doctrine as follows:

> [A] defendant who is not the aggressor and has reasonable grounds to believe, and actually does believe, that he is in imminent danger of death or serious bodily harm from which he could save himself only by using

deadly force against his assailant has the right to employ deadly force in order to defend himself.

Our holding in Syllabus Point 7 of *State v. Cain*, and the numerous cases that we have decided under its tenets, makes clear the specific elements and circumstances that must exist before a person's use of deadly force is excusable under our law. The first required element is that a defendant show that he or she was not the "aggressor" and did not provoke the attack. This requirement reflects the common law rule that "one who is at fault or who is the physical aggressor can not rely on self-defense." *State v. Smith*, 170 W.Va. 654, 656, 295 S.E.2d 820, 822 (1982). *See, e.g., State v. Brooks*, 214 W.Va. 562, 591 S.E.2d 120 (2003)(defendant who forced her way into another person's home, then struck resident of the dwelling, was aggressor and therefore not entitled to self-defense instruction even though resident used force to repel defendant).

The second and third required elements are that a defendant show that the circumstances of the attack formed a "reasonable" basis to believe, and that the defendant did believe, that he or she was at "imminent" risk of death or serious bodily injury. As we have held in Section III.1., of this Opinion, the "reasonableness" of a defendant's belief that death or serious bodily injury was "imminent" is both a subjective and an objective inquiry.

The fourth required element is that a defendant must show that his or her actions were "proportionate" to the danger. In *State v. W.J.B.*, 166 W.Va. at 608, 276 S.E.2d at 554, (citations omitted), we noted that:

> the amount of force that can be used in self-defense is that normally one can return deadly force only if he reasonably believes that the assailant is about to inflict death or serious bodily harm; otherwise, where he is threatened only with non-deadly force, he may use only non-deadly force in return.

An example of when the use of deadly force was not reasonable is that set forth in *State v. Wykle*, 208 W.Va. 369, 540 S.E.2d 586 (2000), where we held that the defendant's stabbing of an unarmed victim nine times with a knife was not self-defense, where the only provocation was that the victim slapped the defendant's face during an argument.

The final element of our self-defense doctrine requires a defendant to present "sufficient evidence" on all of the above elements before being entitled to a self-defense instruction and shifting the burden of proof to the State. We have previously defined sufficient evidence as being that which creates a reasonable doubt as to whether the defendant acted in self-defense. "Once there is sufficient evidence to create a reasonable doubt that the killing resulted from the defendant acting in self-defense, the prosecution must prove beyond a reasonable doubt that the defendant did not act in self-defense." Syllabus Point 4, *State v. Kirtley*, 162 W.Va. 249, 252 S.E.2d 374 (1978).

III.3.B. Application of Facts to the Law

Having thus briefly reviewed the elements of our self-defense doctrine, we apply them to the facts of the defendant's case to determine, first, whether the evidence was sufficient to create a reasonable doubt on the issue of self-defense, and second, whether the State met its burden to prove beyond a reasonable doubt that the defendant's actions were not self-defense.

III.3.C. Whether the Defendant Submitted Sufficient Evidence of her Claim of Self-defense

Provocation. There is no evidence in the record that the defendant did any deed or act that provoked the attack upon her by the decedent. Accordingly, not only has the defendant established sufficient evidence that she did not provoke the attack, but this element is proven beyond a reasonable doubt as an uncontested issue.

Reasonableness. We next turn to the issue of whether the defendant submitted sufficient evidence that she actually believed and had a reasonable basis to believe that she was at risk of death or serious bodily injury as a result of the decedent's conduct. The record is clear that the decedent brutally attacked the defendant during the hours immediately preceding the decedent's death. The State concedes this point, acknowledging that the defendant suffered "an evening of physical and sexual abuse" and "night of terror" at the hands of the decedent. Evidence introduced at the defendant's trial regarding the "evening of physical and sexual abuse" and "night of terror" is summarized as follows.

At trial the State called K.B. to testify as to her recollections of the evening of her sleep over. K.B. testified that she recalled overhearing the defendant and decedent arguing and that the argument appeared to be about the decedent's drinking. At some point during the evening, K.B. testified that the defendant came to their room and told them to go to bed. When asked if there was anything unusual about the defendant when she came to the bedroom doorway, K.B. testified that "She had, like, bruises on her eyes." Following the defendant's instructions, K.B. and A.H. laid down to go to sleep, although K.B. could still hear the defendant and decedent arguing and testified that she was frightened. Finally falling asleep, K.B. testified that she was awakened by sounds of more arguing and, again becoming frightened, woke A.H. to ask her about what was going on. A.H. told K.B. that her parents were probably just "tumbling around" and not to worry about it. K.B., however, testified that she had difficulty trying to get back to sleep, and at one point overheard the defendant say to the decedent that "she didn't want to get killed with her two kids."

After K.B.'s testimony was concluded, A.H. was called to testify as to her recollections of the evening. A.H. testified that she also recalled being awakened by K.B. and that K.B. asked her "Are your parents fighting?" and that "I just figured they were wrestling like we normally do. We used to wrestle all the time, so I told her not to worry about it." A.H. also testified she could hear the defendant and decedent in the other room—"I just heard thumping. I heard thumping." When asked to describe the thumping sounds, A.H. testified that it "[j]ust sounded like they were stomping their feet or fell on the ground or something. I just figured they were wrestling like we would normally do." After telling K.B. not to worry, A.H. said she fell back to sleep only to be again awakened by K.B., who informed her that B.H. was in the room. Upon seeing B.H. in the room, A.H. testified that she "hollered for mom or one of them to come and get him, and he went back to the living room."

The defendant's youngest child, B.H., was also called to testify. A portion of B.H.'s testimony is as follows:

Q. Did you see Dad hurt Mom that night?

A. I seen him hit her with a back end of a gun.

Q. . . . And when did you—what else happened?

A. They just kept arguing and stuff.

Q. Where was Mom when that happened?

A. When what happened?

Q. When you saw—when you saw Mom get hit with the gun—

A. She was in a recliner.

Q. What kind of gun was it?

A. All I know is it was a black shotgun of some kind.

Q. Where did that gun come from?

A. Out of my dad's back room where he usually kept all of his guns and computer and stuff.

. . .

Q. How did the gun get into the living room?

A. He [Dad] carried it.

Q. . . . Did you see him go get it?

A. Uh-huh.

Q. . . . Why did he go get it?

A. I heard him—I heard them fighting and he said "I am going to go get the gun and shoot you," and that's really the reason I think he got it.

Q. Did you think he was going to shoot Mom?

A. Yeah. But I didn't really think he would have.

Q. Why didn't you think he would?

A. Well, because they—they would fight before and they just get over it and it would be fine the next morning.

When asked to further explain about what he saw and did when the decedent went to get the shotgun, B.H. testified that "I got on mom's lap and asked her, 'What's the matter, Mommie? Is everything going to be okay?' And she said, 'Yeah, it's okay, Bubby. Go back to sleep.'" When asked about seeing the decedent hit the defendant with the gun, B.H. testified that the decedent hit her with the gun in the arms and shoulders. B.H. was also asked, "Do you remember [saying] that you saw [the decedent] take the gun and point it to [the defendant's] belly and asked her if she wanted to die?" B.H. responded "I might remember that."

Dr. Lori Bennet, an Emergency Room physician at Cabell Huntington Hospital, was also called to testify. Dr. Bennet testified that she examined the defendant on the morning of the shooting, and that the defendant informed her she "was assaulted by her husband" and that the circumstances of the assault included that the decedent had "struck her about the head and back with the butt of a gun and threatened her with the gun" and that "she was struck with a fist and gun during the altercation." When asked about what injuries the defendant sustained, Dr. Bennet testified that "she had contusions of both orbital areas, the right upper arm, a puncture wound with a foreign body of the right forearm, contusions of her chest, left facial cheek, the left upper lip" and that "X-rays done at the time demonstrated a nasal fracture."

Photographic evidence of the defendant's injuries described by Dr. Bennet were also introduced during the trial. These photographs depict the defendant with two very large "black eyes," a battered and swollen nose, bruised lips, multiple bruising on her breasts, arms, legs, thighs and other parts of her body. A photograph of the shirt worn by the defendant at the time of the decedent's brutal attack was also introduced, which depicted copious amounts of blood on it.

The State Medical Examiner was also called to testify as to his findings. This testimony included serology tests showing that the decedent had a blood alcohol level of 0.22%, which the Medical Examiner testified was nearly three times the 0.08% level where a person would be presumed intoxicated in West Virginia. Also, the autopsy revealed that the decedent had a small gash on his hand that could be consistent with the decedent having struck the defendant in the face.

The defendant also testified on her own behalf. The defendant testified that the decedent started drinking early in the evening and that the decedent started "getting very, very angry" and as the evening wore on, the decedent became increasingly verbally abusive and started making threats that he was going to kill her. When asked what she thought when the decedent said he was going to kill her, the defendant testified "[i]t was a change in him, and I knew it was going to happen." At one point during the ordeal, the defendant testified that her youngest child, B.H., ran over to her and climbed on her lap and asked her what was going on. The defendant testified she told her son that everything would be okay and to go back to sleep "so he couldn't see nothing else."

The defendant further testified that the "beating went on for hours, and it was just a continuous beating and verbal abuse" during which the decedent told the defendant he was going to kill her, that she "wasn't going to live to see the next day" and that "the children wouldn't live." The defendant explained that "I was so scared and I was scared for my life, and not only mine but the three kids that was in my home" and that the decedent even "put the shotgun to my son's head and said he was going to kill him."

When asked what happened after the decedent put the gun to their son's head, the defendant said "I started talking to him so that he would leave B.H. alone and he went back to beating me." The defendant testified that she knew at this point that "none of us was going to walk out of the house."

As the evening wore on, the defendant testified that the decedent "made me have sex with him. (Crying). After he beat me. (Crying)." Photographic evidence and trial testimony from the State's blood spatter expert established that the decedent, at the time of his death, was lying naked from the waist down on the living room couch (notwithstanding that the three children were nearby) with one leg bent upwards and resting against the back of the couch and the other leg sprawled alongside the edge of the couch.

Following the sexual assault, the defendant testified that the defendant continued to be verbally and physically aggressive, and that the decedent started taunting her, daring her to shoot him or that he would shoot her, and that it was at this point that she got the decedent's shotgun and shot him. The defendant explained that "I thought I was going to die. I knew I was," and that the decedent "would have killed them [the children], too" because the decedent "said that nobody was going to walk out of the house that night."

It is clear to this Court that the evidence adduced at the defendant's trial, only a portion of which we have briefly summarized above, was sufficient evidence that the defendant did believe, and had a reasonable basis to believe, that her life was at risk of death or serious bodily injury.

Imminency. We next consider whether the defendant submitted sufficient evidence that she had reasonable grounds to believe, and did believe, that the danger of death or serious bodily injury was "imminent." The defendant's testimony established that precipitously preceding the defendant's shooting the decedent, that the decedent sexually assaulted the defendant and thereafter continued to threaten the defendant's life and the lives of the children, as well as physically assault the defendant. Considered in context with the evidence discussed above, and that the violence and threats had been ongoing for several hours, it is clear that the defendant submitted sufficient evidence upon which she could have reasonably believed, and did believe, that death or serious bodily injury were imminent.

Proportionality. The next element considered is whether the evidence showed the defendant's actions to be "proportionate" to the danger. As we discussed above, the evidence submitted sufficiently established that the decedent had threatened to kill the defendant and the children. Further, the evidence sufficiently shows that the decedent beat the defendant with a deadly weapon—the shotgun—as witnessed by B.H., and testified to by the decedent, and as was further evidenced from the photographs depicting multiple bruises on the defendant's body. In addition, the decedent had placed the shotgun against B.H.'s head and threatened to shoot him. Further, the decedent had sexually assaulted the defendant. Finally, the defendant testified that immediately preceding her shooting the decedent, the decedent had again threatened her life, the lives of the children, and physically assaulted her. This evidence, in the context of all the other evidence, would sufficiently warrant the use of deadly force.

Sufficiency. The final element considered is whether the defendant met her burden of proof. Our review of the record, discussed above, convinces us that the trial court was correct in its decision to give a self-defense instruction based upon the evidence in this case-the evidence was clearly sufficient to create a reasonable doubt that the killing resulted from the defendant acting in self-defense. Therefore, as we have previously stated, the burden shifted to the State to prove beyond a reasonable doubt that the defendant did not act in self defense. *See* Syllabus Point 4, *State v. Kirtley, supra.*

III.3.D. Whether the State Met its Burden of Proof

Having determined that the defendant submitted sufficient evidence to create a reasonable doubt as to the issue of whether her actions were made in self-defense, and that the trial judge was correct that the defendant was entitled to a self-defense instruction, we turn to the issue of whether the State met its burden to prove beyond a reasonable doubt that the defendant's actions were not made in self-defense. * * *

As we previously noted, but repeat herein for context, where the defendant has challenged on appeal the sufficiency of the State's evidence, we view that evidence in the light most favorable to the State. Syllabus Point 1, *State v. Guthrie*, 194 W.Va. 657, 461 S.E.2d 163 (1995). We are further mindful of our holding in *Guthrie* that:

> A criminal defendant challenging the sufficiency of the evidence to support a conviction takes on a heavy burden. An appellate court must review all the evidence, whether direct or circumstantial, in the light most favorable to the prosecution and must credit all inferences and credibility assessments that the jury might have drawn in favor of the prosecution. The evidence need not be inconsistent with every conclusion save that of guilt so long as the jury can find guilt beyond a reasonable doubt. Credibility determinations are for a jury and not an appellate court. Finally, a jury verdict should be set aside only when the record contains no evidence, regardless of how it is weighed, from which the jury could find guilt beyond a reasonable doubt. To the extent our prior cases are inconsistent, they are expressly overruled.

Syllabus Point 3, *State v. Guthrie, supra.*

While we clearly must, according to our precedent, construe the evidence in the light most favorable to the State where a defendant challenges the sufficiency of the evidence, this is not to say that we must abandon sound reasoning in so doing. Instead, we construe the evidence in the light most favorable to the State, and then apply it to the relevant legal standard. In this appeal, the relevant legal standard is proof beyond a reasonable doubt that the defendant did not kill the decedent in self-defense. In *State v. Goff*, 166 W.Va. 47, 272 S.E.2d 457 (1980), we offered a standard jury instruction on the presumption of innocence and burden of proof. This instruction, in part, defined "proof beyond a reasonable doubt" to mean:

> A reasonable doubt is a doubt based upon reason and common sense—the kind of doubt that would make a reasonable person hesitate to act. Proof beyond a reasonable doubt, therefore, must be proof of such a convincing character that a reasonable person would not hesitate to rely and act upon it.

> The jury will remember that a defendant is never to be convicted on mere suspicion or conjecture.

State v. Goff, 166 W.Va. at 54 n. 9, 272 S.E.2d at 463 n. 9.

Applying these standards, we consider the sufficiency of the State's evidence. Initially, we note that the State candidly acknowledges that the defendant suffered an "evening of physical and sexual abuse" and "night of terror" at the hands of the decedent and thereby concedes many of the facts of consequence in our analysis. However, the State nonetheless maintains that notwithstanding the evening of physical and sexual abuse, "the evidence viewed in a light most favorable to the State suggests that the [decedent] was sleeping when the [defendant] shot him" and, therefore, that the defendant "shot her unarmed husband while he was lying on his couch" from behind.

As we have noted in this Opinion, the State's argument is premised, in part, upon the incorrect assumption that the decedent's conduct in the hours immediately preceding his death were not relevant to the reasonableness of the defendant's use of deadly force. The State's argument is also premised, in part, upon the incorrect assumption that the defendant had a duty to retreat from her home before using deadly force. With these points made, we examine the sufficiency of the State's evidence.

Having fully considered the record in this appeal, and construing the evidence in the light most favorable to the State, we find that the State's evidence failed to prove beyond a reasonable doubt that the defendant did not have a reasonable basis to believe, and did not believe, that she was in imminent danger of death or serious bodily injury at the time deadly force was used against the decedent. The mere fact that the decedent was found on the couch after being shot creates only a "suspicion or conjecture," *State v. Goff, supra,* that the decedent might *possibly* have been "asleep" or *possibly* have been "passed out drunk," and that the brutal beatings, sexual assault, and threats to kill the defendant and the children had ended.

The fact that even the State cannot say with any certainty the decedent's disposition at the time of his death is compelling evidence of reasonable doubt on this issue. Evidence that the decedent had sexually assaulted the defendant, and thereafter lay sprawled naked from the waist down on the living room couch does not amount to proof beyond a reasonable doubt that the defendant was asleep or passed out drunk; instead, it is equally plausible that the decedent could have been doing exactly what the defendant testified he was doing, which was renewing his threats to kill her and the children and again becoming physically aggressive.

Reviewing the record, there is just no evidence, only conjecture, that the defendant's "night of terror" had ended or that the defendant and the children in her care were safe from death or serious bodily injury. As we have found in Section III.2., of this Opinion, the defendant did not have a duty to retreat from her home before using deadly force against her attacker. Our law entitled the defendant under the circumstances of this case to her subjective belief that she was in imminent danger of death or serious bodily injury and to abate that threat, without retreating, with the use of deadly force.[12] Under the circumstances shown by the evidence in this case, the defendant's use of deadly force to protect herself, without retreating, is subjectively reasonable.

Additionally, the overwhelming evidence demonstrates that any reasonable person similarly situated would have believed that death or serious bodily injury were imminent. Uncontested evidence from multiple witnesses and sources (e.g., the photographs depicting the defendant's numerous injuries and that the decedent was naked from the waist down), as discussed *supra*, established that the decedent's death precipitously followed the decedent's having physically and sexually assaulted the defendant, as well as having threatened—on numerous occasions—the life of the defendant and the lives of the children. Uncontested evidence also established that the decedent was drinking heavily and had a blood alcohol level of 0.22%—nearly three times that where a person would be presumed intoxicated in West Virginia. In this intoxicated state of mind, the uncontested evidence is that the decedent's behavior immediately preceding his death was violent, unpredictable, criminal and placed the defendant at risk of death or serious bodily injury. Under such circumstances the defendant's use of deadly force to protect herself, without retreating, is objectively reasonable. The State's evidence failed to prove otherwise. Supposition and conjecture are not evidence.

---

12 In *State v. Mechling*, 219 W.Va. 366, 379–380, 633 S.E.2d 311, 324–325 (2006), we recognized that "[b] attered women are at an extremely heightened risk of violence—and even death—at the moment they seek to separate from their abusers." It is clear from the record that the defendant was a battered spouse. In addition to the physical and emotional violence we have discussed in detail in this Opinion, the record also shows that the defendant married the decedent when she was sixteen years old, and during her marriage was not permitted to work outside of the home or family Flea Market booth, have a driver's license, have friends or family to the marital home without the decedent's permission and supervision, and was often unjustly accused by the decedent of seeing other men.

In *State v. Cook*, Justice Davis, writing for the Court, properly noted that while we must be "[m]indful of the jury's province over the evidence presented on the issue of [self-defense], this Court will not permit an injustice to occur because a jury failed to adequately understand the evidence presented at trial." We agree with that principle, and conclude that "[t]his is such a case." *State v. Cook*, 204 W.Va. at 602, 515 S.E.2d at 138. Accordingly, we hold that the State failed to prove beyond a reasonable doubt that the defendant's actions were not made in self-defense and, therefore, the defendant's conviction and sentence must be vacated and this matter remanded for immediate entry of a judgment of acquittal.

IV. CONCLUSION

For the reasons set forth herein, we vacate the defendant's conviction and sentence and remand this matter to the circuit court for entry of a judgment of acquittal on the indictment returned against her in this action. The defendant is ordered released. The Clerk of the Court shall issue our mandate forthwith, which shall direct the circuit court to enter a judgement of acquittal immediately upon receipt of the mandate.

Vacated and Remanded for Judgment of Acquittal.

BENJAMIN, Chief Justice, dissenting:

I dissent because I believe the majority opinion's conclusion that the State failed to prove beyond a reasonable doubt that the defendant's actions were not in self-defense is erroneous. Here, the defendant resorted to a type of self-help that previously has not been permitted by our law, but that the majority has now vindicated. While there is no doubt that the defendant was brutalized by the decedent, as the jury heard, and that the decedent should have been criminally prosecuted for his actions, I question the wisdom of a self-defense standard in our jurisprudence which sanctions the use of deadly force to defend one's self from a person who is unconscious or incapacitated, and who poses no threat of imminent harm.

I also question how such a lessened self-defense standard, which may be seen by some as condoning or even tacitly encouraging the use of self-help violence or vigilantism in a domestic setting, can be seen as a positive advancement in our efforts to reduce domestic violence. Our focus should be on the reduction of violence, where appropriate, in the domestic setting. Retaining an "imminent harm" requirement for self-defense in the domestic setting achieves this goal while permitting victims the opportunity to meet domestic violence with more domestic violence only when needed to actually defend one's self. In the emotionally charged environment which surrounds domestic violence, I further worry that the rational, objective definition which we may accord to this new standard of "self-defense" in the vacuum of an academic or legal setting will yield to an irrational, self-serving, and narcissistic justification to a troubled mind to, in the spur of the moment, "right" some perceived domestic wrong and thereby defend one's honor as much as one's self. In other words, in the real world, the line between a legitimate and a non-legitimate defense of one's self in a highly charged emotional environment may get blurred—a situation which I fear may work against victims of domestic violence as much as for them.

The evidence presented at trial does not support the defendant's claim of self-defense. The defendant's alleged belief that at the time she used deadly force, that force was necessary to prevent serious bodily injury or death to the defendant is not objectively reasonable under new Syllabus Point 3. In other words, another person, similarly situated, could not have formed the belief that it was necessary to shoot the decedent in the head to prevent serious bodily injury or death to himself or herself. The State presented evidence at trial through the testimony of Dr. Hamada Mahmoud, Chief Deputy Medical Examiner for the State and a forensic pathologist, that the decedent was shot above his right ear with a left and downward trajectory. Dr. Mahmoud also testified that the stippling found around the entrance wound as well as the 25 shotgun pellets and the shell's wadding found in the decedent's brain cavity indicate that the shotgun blast came from close range, specifically one to five feet away. Sergeant David Castle, a Huntington Police Officer, testified that both high and low velocity blood spatter and blood pooling present on the carpet indicated that the decedent was lying flat on his back when he was shot from behind. He further testified from the blood stain evidence that the decedent's left hand was lying just above his head and resting on a pillow, and the decedent's right hand was clutching a blanket. Sergeant Castle concluded from this that the decedent could not have been holding a weapon at the time the defendant shot him.[1] From this evidence, a reasonable trier of fact could conclude that the defendant, while standing behind the decedent, fired a shotgun blast from close range into the right temple of the decedent as he lay flat on the sofa. A rational trier of fact could also infer that because the decedent made no effort to prevent the defendant from walking up to him and firing a shotgun blast into his right temple, the decedent must have been unconscious. Finally, a rational trier of fact could additionally infer that

---

[1]   The jury had reason to doubt the veracity of the defendant's testimony at trial. In a recorded statement the defendant gave to Sergeant James M. McCallister of the Cabell County Sheriff's Department on the day of the shooting, which was played for the jury, the defendant did not indicate that the decedent had threatened their son with the shotgun or that the defendant was sexually assaulted by the decedent prior to the shooting. However, in her testimony at trial the defendant claimed that the decedent had put the shotgun to their son's head and threatened to shoot him, and that the decedent had forced the defendant to have sex with him.

because the decedent was unconscious, he could not pose an imminent risk of serious bodily injury or death to the defendant. These reasonable conclusions drawn from the evidence negate the defendant's theory of self-defense.

While I do not disagree with new Syllabus Point 5, it has no application to the facts of this case. Simply because a co-occupant of a residence has no legal obligation to retreat from the residence in the face of the imminent threat of serious bodily injury or death, it does not follow that the co-occupant has the right to shoot an incapacitated person in the head at close range. Because the facts of this case do not support a self-defense claim, Syllabus Point 5 is wholly irrelevant to the decision of this case.

Further, new Syllabus Point 4 was created by the majority from whole cloth and has absolutely no support in the precedent of this Court. Under this Court's precedent, evidence that the decedent had abused or threatened the life of the defendant is admissible to support a self-defense claim but is not admissible to negate a necessary element of the offense charged in the absence of self-defense or other specific defenses enumerated by this Court. In addition, the cases cited by the majority opinion in support of Syllabus Point 4 simply do not stand for the proposition for which they are cited. Specifically, *State v. Dozier*, 163 W.Va. 192, 255 S.E.2d 552 (1979), permitted evidence of physical beatings the defendant had received at the hands of the decedent *where the defendant's primary theory of defense was self-defense*. The same is true of *State v. Hardin*, 91 W.Va. 149, 112 S.E. 401 (1922) in which this Court stated that "where self defense is relied upon to excuse a homicide, and there is evidence tending to establish that defense, it is competent to show the character of the deceased party for violence[.]" 91 W.Va. at 153, 112 S.E. at 402–403. The case of *State v. Lambert*, 173 W.Va. 60, 312 S.E.2d 31 (1984) concerns the effect of the defenses of compulsion, coercion, and duress upon criminal intent and provides that "[t]he compulsion or coercion that will excuse an otherwise criminal act must be present, imminent, and impending, and such as would induce a well-grounded apprehension of death or serious bodily harm if the criminal act is not done[.]" 173 W.Va. at 62, 312 S.E.2d at 33, *citing* Syllabus Point 1, *State v. Tanner*, 171 W.Va. 529, 301 S.E.2d 160 (W.Va.1982). In the instant case, the defendant did not raise the defenses of coercion, compulsion, or duress. The majority also cites *State v. Wyatt*, 198 W.Va. 530, 482 S.E.2d 147 (1996). However, *Wyatt* concerned the Battered Spouse Syndrome which was not raised by the defendant at trial and was not supported by the evidence. Finally, *State v. Plumley*, 184 W.Va. 536, 401 S.E.2d 469 (1990), and *State v. Summers*, 118 W.Va. 118, 188 S.E. 873 (1936) were both in regard to self-defense or defense of another. In sum, none of the cases cited in the majority opinion stands for the proposition that in the absence of evidence supporting a claim of self-defense, evidence that the decedent had abused or threatened the life of the defendant is nonetheless relevant and may negate a necessary element of the offense charged.

Moreover, beside having no support in our law, new Syllabus Point 4 may well have the unintended consequence of promoting vigilantism, an attempt to affect justice by one's own hand according to one's own understanding of right and wrong. The law properly recognizes as a defense to murder that the defendant acted to defend himself or herself from the threat of imminent serious bodily injury or death. Significantly, the threat of serious bodily injury or death must be imminent. An imminent threat of serious bodily injury or death separates a killing in self-defense from a retaliatory killing or a preemptive killing. In other words, the requirement that the threat is imminent distinguishes a killing in self-defense from a killing to redress a previous wrong or to prevent a non-imminent threat. Thus, the law is based on the proper understanding that the recognition of defense of self absent the element of an imminent threat would be to countenance violence and lawlessness. By placing absolutely no limit on the use of evidence of prior abusive conduct to negate an element of the crime charged, the majority unwittingly permits a defendant to claim that the most senseless murder is justified by an allegation that the decedent had wronged the defendant or posed a threat to the defendant. Until the creation of new Syllabus Point 4, such a notion was totally foreign to our jurisprudence.

Sadly, the majority opinion disregards the progress that this State has made in recent years in the prevention, treatment, and remediation of domestic violence. Thanks to the diligence efforts of our legislature and courts, our society now works to educate, treat, aid, and prevent the scourge of violence among family members. Spouses who find themselves in abusive or threatening situations now have resources that previous generations of abused spouses did not. In the instant case, no reasonable person believes that the appellant should have quietly endured the abusive actions of the decedent. But once the decedent fell asleep or passed out on the sofa, the threat of imminent harm was over and the appellant had several options available short of resorting to homicide.

Finally, in ignoring the evidence presented by the State at trial, the majority of this Court abandons our standard of review and usurps the fact-finding role of the jury. As quoted in the majority opinion, "the relevant inquiry is whether, after viewing the evidence in the light most favorable to the prosecution, any rational trier of fact could have found the essential elements of the crime proved beyond a reasonable doubt." Syllabus Point 1, in part, *State v. Guthrie*, 194 W.Va. 657, 461 S.E.2d 163 (1995). First-degree murder is defined, in part, as any "willful, deliberate and premeditated killing." W. Va.Code § 61–2–1 (1991). The State presented evidence that the defendant took a shotgun, walked up behind her unconscious husband lying on the sofa, and fired the shotgun at close range into his right temple. From this evidence, the jury clearly could find that the defendant committed a willful, deliberate and premeditated killing. Further, as noted above, the State presented evidence from which a rational trier of fact could find beyond a reasonable doubt that the defendant's actions were not made in self-defense. This is because a person lying unconscious on a sofa with one hand raised above his head and the other hand clutching a blanket cannot pose an imminent threat of serious bodily injury or death. Therefore, if the majority had properly adhered to the standard of review, it would have been compelled to find that the State presented sufficient evidence to find the defendant guilty of first-degree murder.

In the instant case, the State presented evidence that the defendant shot the decedent from behind at close range in the right temple while the decedent was lying unconscious on the sofa. Because the decedent was unconscious, there was no imminent threat to the defendant when she shot the decedent. The defendant's only real defense was that the decedent had abused and threatened her earlier that evening. Under our law, however, this is not a defense to murder. Therefore, the jury properly found the defendant guilty. Unfortunately, the majority improperly has replaced the sound verdict of the jury with its own idea of justice and created bad law in the process.

While there may be legal error herein on other grounds that merits the reversal of the defendant's conviction and the granting of a new trial, the majority's decision to vacate the defendant's conviction and bar retrial is contrary to the evidence at trial and without support under our law. Accordingly, I dissent.

Notes and Questions

1. Is the majority holding that West Virginia law allows a person to kill a sleeping abuser, assuming a deadly threat existed at some point or is likely to exist in the future?

2. How could prior attacks by the decedent affect malice or intent for homicide?

3. Note the discussion of procedure in the opinion. In general, the defendant has the "burden of going forward," also called the "burden of production." That is, the issue is not in the case until there is some evidence before the factfinder that suggests self defense. If the sole question at trial, for example, is alibi, whether the defendant is the person who committed the act, there will be no jury instruction on self-defense. However, if, through prosecution evidence or defense evidence, a reasonable jury could find self-defense, then a self-

defense instruction is warranted. Once the burden of production has been met, the question becomes the burden of proof. Most states now require the prosecution to disprove self-defense beyond a reasonable doubt. However, the Supreme Court has upheld placing the burden on the defendant to a preponderance of the evidence.

4. No state, to our knowledge, allows self-defense on a purely subjective basis, where killing is non-criminal if the defendant honestly believed it was necessary, even if that belief was entirely unreasonable on an objective basis. In addition, every state, to our knowledge, has a subjective component; a defendant must honestly believe that force is necessary. Thus, if a reasonable person might have thought that force was necessary, but the defendant did not (because of special expertise, for example, enabling her to determine that the assailant's pistol was not real), deadly force may not be employed. Thus, generally self defense requires both an honest belief that force is necessary, and that belief must be objectively reasonable.

The Model Penal Code handles the problem by making the defense purely subjective; the defense applies "when the actor believes" that force is necessary. MPC 3.04(1). However, if that subjective belief is reckless or negligent, the defendant can be convicted of reckless or negligent crimes. MPC 3.09(2). Thus, under the traditional common-law approach, a close but failed defense would impose liability for murder. The MPC is more nuanced. If the belief was based on simple negligence, there would be no liability. If based on MPC negligence, the defendant could be convicted of negligent homicide. If the belief was reckless, the defendant could be convicted of manslaughter.

Some common law jurisdictions recognize imperfect imperfect self-defense. This defense mitigates murder to manslaughter if the defendant's belief that force is necessary is honest but unreasonable.

5. Imminence. Traditionally, using deadly force in self-defense required an immediate threat. That is, the threat of death or serious bodily harm has to be happening now, or in the next few seconds. As a matter of policy, why might an imminent attack be required? The Model Penal Code rejected the imminence requirement, holding that the defensive force had to be "immediately necessary." MPC § 3.04(1). This was designed to relax the requirement.

6. Retreat. Historically, people were required to retreat "to the wall" before using deadly force in self-defense. Now, most jurisdictions do not require retreat.

A person is free to "stand her ground." Jurisdictions requiring retreat often recognize the "castle doctrine," not requiring retreat where the defendant is confronted in their home or office. As with most criminal law doctrines, the details vary by jurisdiction.

Nevertheless, even in a jurisdiction not requiring retreat, the deadly force must be necessary. Imagine that Dennis sees Victor 50 feet away, running towards him with a knife, shouting "I'm going to kill you, Dennis!" Dennis could easily run away. He could also close and lock a secure metal door and keep Victor out. If Dennis instead leaves the door open, and shoots Victor when he is in range, is he liable?

7. Proportionality. In addition to being necessary to respond to an imminent deadly threat, many jurisdictions require that the force be proportional. It is not clear what independent analytical work is done by this element. For example, the West Virginia Supreme Court explained that it would be disproportionate to respond to non-deadly force with deadly force. But there would be no defense in such a case anyway, because the other elements would not have been met.

8. Other Exceptions. Other jurisdictions have other, specific exceptions. For example, the Model Penal Code denies the right to use deadly force if "the actor knows that he can avoid the necessity for using such force with complete safety . . . by surrendering possession of a thing to a person asserting a claim of right thereto or by complying with a demand that he abstain from taking any action that he has no duty to take." MOC 3.04(2)(b)(ii). What circumstances do these exceptions contemplate?

9. Question. Debbie and Veronica are sitting on bar stools in the Dew Drop Inn out near the county line. They hate each other. Debbie has a knife only. Assume state law requires an imminent threat to use deadly force. Can Debbie kill Veronica in the following circumstances? Assume in each case that Veronica's threat is credible and that Debbie reasonably believes it. Veronica says:

A. "Now, I will reach on my pocket for a gun to shoot you," but no gun is visible and she does not say where she will shoot.

B. "I'm going to order a brandy Alexander, and after I finish it, I will reach into my pocket for a gun to shoot you."

C. "I'm going to my car in the lot to get my gun to kill you." Assume other people are in the bar, there are multiple exits, and that Debbie has a cell phone.

D. Same as C, except that, for some reason, no one else is in the bar, and there is only one way out.

PRACTICE EXERCISE

You are a criminal defense attorney consulted by Dave for the following legal problem. Dave, a store clerk, was a witness to an armed robbery committed by Vince, a member of a criminal crew. Vince has threatened to severely beat or kill Dave unless Dave agrees not to testify. Dave reasonably believes that the threat is legitimate based on prior criminal conduct of Vince. Dave wants to know if preemptively kills Vince, will he have a self-defense claim. What other facts might be relevant to this question? Apply West Virginia law, and the Model Penal Code.

C. Provocation

A person who uses force in response to a threat will not have a defense, in some circumstances, if she is at fault for the altercation. Various cases use a range of standards for what constitutes fault; in some circumstances, words alone or mere presence could be provocative. It is important to remember what is at stake: If the law concludes that a person has lost the right to self-defense because of provocation (also sometimes stated as being an "aggressor"), she is required by law to allow herself to be killed. Accordingly, there must be a balance between avoiding unnecessary force on the one hand, and avoiding a requirement of unreasonable precautionary measures on the other. For example, even if one could avoid the necessity for using force by not living, working or visiting high crime areas, few would argue that those things, in and of themselves, constitute aggression.

Thompson v. United States

Supreme Court of the United States
155 U.S. 271 (1894)

Mr. Justice SHIRAS * * * delivered the opinion of the court.

The evidence in the case substantially disclosed the following facts:
The defendant, Thompson, was an Indian boy about 17 years of age, and lived
with Sam Haynes, a Creek Indian, who had a farm near Okmulgee, in the Creek
Nation. The deceased, Charles Hermes, lived with his father on land rented from
Haynes, and distant about half a mile from the house of the latter. There was testimony tending to show ill feeling on the part of Hermes and his sons towards this
Indian boy, and that they had threatened to injure him if he came about where
they were. Thompson could not speak or understand the English language, but he
had been told by Haynes and another witness that old man Hermes had claimed
that he, Thompson, had been abusing and killing his hogs, and that if he 'came
acting the monkey around him any more he would chop his head open.'
In the afternoon of June 8, 1893, Mrs. Haynes directed the boy to take a
bundle to Mrs. Checotale's, who lived two or three miles away. The boy caught
a horse, got on it without a saddle, took the bundle that Mrs. Haynes gave him,
and went off on his errand. Mrs. Haynes testified that he had no arms of any
kind when he left her house, and that he appeared in a good humor with everybody at that time. The road to Checotale's ran by a field where the deceased,
his father, and brother were working, plowing corn. There was testimony on
the part of Thompson tending to show that as he rode along past the field the
old man and the deceased began quarreling with him; that Thompson saw that
they were angry with him, but could not understand much that was said to him,
although he could tell that they were talking about hogs. Thompson says that he
remembered the threats against him they had made to Haynes and Checotale,
and thought they were going to hurt him. He further states that he rode on to
Checotale's, where he left the bundle; that he got to thinking about what Sam
Haynes had told him as to the threats that Hermes had made, and as there was
no other road for him to return home by except the one alongside of the field,
he thought it was best for him to arm himself, so that he could make a defense
in case he was attacked; that he went by Amos Gray's house, and there armed
himself with a Winchester rifle belonging to Gray. The defendant further testified that after he got the gun he went back by the road, and as he got opposite
where the men were plowing the boys were near the fence, and the old man was
behind; that the boys called at him, and said something about a gun, and the
deceased started towards a gun that was standing in the corner of the fence,

and that, thinking they intended to kill him, he drew his gun, and fired at the deceased, and then ran away on his horse, pursued by the old man, who afterwards shot at him. These particulars of the transaction were principally testified to by Thompson himself, but he was corroborated to some extent by William Baxter and James Gregory, who testified that they visited the field where was the body of the deceased, and that Hermes, the father, described the affair to them, and, as so told, the facts differed but little from Thompson's version.

In this state of facts, or, at all events, with evidence tending to show such, the court instructed the jury at great length in respect to the law of the case. Exception was taken to the charge of the court as a whole, because it was 'prolix, confusing, abstract, argumentative, and misleading,' and this exception is the subject of one of the assignments of error. But we do not need to consider this aspect of the case, as the record discloses errors in vital portions of the charge, and specifically excepted to, which constrain us to reverse the judgment, and direct a new trial.

In instructing the jury as to the right of self-defense, the learned judge said: 'It is for you to say whether at the time of the killing of Charles Hermes by this defendant this defendant was doing what he had a right to do. If he was not, notwithstanding Charles Hermes might have made a violent demonstration that was then and there imminent, then and there impending, then and there hanging over his head, and that he could not avoid it except by killing him; if his conduct wrongfully, illegally, and improperly brought into existence that condition,-then he was not in an attitude where, in the language of the law, he was in the lawful pursuit of his business.' And again: 'Now, in this connection, we have a maxim of the law which says to us that, notwithstanding the deceased at the time of the killing may be doing that which indicates an actual, real, and deadly design, if he by his action who seeks to invoke the right of self-defense brought into existence that act upon the part of the deceased at that time by his wrongful act,—his wrongful action did it,—he is cut off from the law of self-defense, no matter what may have been the conduct of the deceased at that time.'

It is not easy to understand what the learned judge meant by those portions of these instructions in which he leaves it to the jury to say whether the defendant was 'doing what he had a right to do,' and whether the defendant brought into existence the act of the deceased, in threatening to attack the defendant, 'by his, defendant's, wrongful act.' Probably what was here adverted to was the conduct of the deceased in returning home by the same route in which he had passed the accused when going to Checotale's, and the implication seems to be that the accused was doing wrong, and was guilty of a wrongful act, in so doing. The only evidence on that subject was that of the defendant himself that he had no other mode of returning home except by that road, because of swamps on the other side of the road, and there was no evidence to the contrary.

The learned judge, in these and subsequent instructions, seems to confuse the conduct of the defendant in returning home by the only convenient road with a supposed return to the scene of a previous quarrel for the purpose of renewing it. Thus he further instructed the jury that 'if it be true that Charles Hermes, at the time of the killing, was actually and really or apparently in the act of executing a deadly design, or so near in the execution of it that the defendant could not avoid it, and that it was brought into existence by his going to that place where Charles Hermes was with the purpose of provoking a difficulty, or with the intention of having an affray, he is cut off from the law of self-defense.' And again: 'You are to look to the evidence to see whether the defendant brought that state of case into existence, to see whether or not, in consequence of a conception on his part of a state of grudge or ill will or any hard feelings that existed between the parties, that he went off and armed himself for the purpose of making an attack on Hermes, or any of the party whom the government offered as witnesses, this law of self-defense cannot avail him. Of course, the law of self-defense gives him the right to arm himself for the purpose of defending himself so long as he is in the right, but if he has a conception that deadly danger may come upon him, but he is away from it, so he can avoid it, his duty is to stay away from it and avoid it, because he has no right to go to the place where the slain person is, with a deadly weapon, for the purpose of provoking a difficulty, or with the intent of having an affray.'

These instructions could, and naturally would, be understood by the jury as directing them that the accused lost his right of self-defense by returning home by the road that passed by the place where the deceased was, and that they should find that the fact that he had armed himself and returned by that road was evidence from which they should infer that he had gone off and armed himself and returned for the purpose of provoking a difficulty. Certainly the mere fact that the accused used the same road in returning that he had used in going from home would not warrant the inference that his return was with the purpose of provoking an affray, particularly as there was evidence that this road was the proper and convenient one. Nor did the fact that the defendant, in view of the threats that had been made against him, armed himself, justify the jury in inferring that this was with the purpose of attacking the deceased, and not of defending himself, especially in view of the testimony that the purpose of the defendant in arming himself was for self-defense.

We had occasion to correct a similar error in the recent case of *Gourko v. U. S.*, 153 U. S. 183, 14 Sup. Ct. 806. That was a case where the deceased had previously uttered threats against the defendant, and there had been a recent rencontre at the post office. The parties then separated, and the defendant armed himself, and subsequently, when the parties again encountered each other, the defendant shot and killed the deceased. The court instructed the jury that in those circumstances there was no right of self-defense, and that there was nothing to reduce the offense from that of murder to manslaughter.

In discussing the question, this court, by Mr. Justice Harlan, said:

'If he armed himself for the purpose of pursuing his adversary, or with the intention of putting himself in the way of his adversary, so as to obtain an opportunity to kill him, then he was guilty of murder. But if, in view of what had occurred near the post office, the defendant had reasonable grounds to believe, and in fact believed, that the deceased intended to take his life, or to inflict upon him great bodily harm, and, so believing, armed himself solely for necessary self-defense in the event of his being pursued and attacked, and if the circumstances on the occasion of the meeting at or near the saloon were such as by themselves made a case of manslaughter, then the defendant arming himself, after the difficulty near the post office, did not, in itself, have the effect to convert his crime into that of murder. * * *'

We think there was also error in that portion of the charge wherein the court instructed the jury as to the effect which they should give to the evidence on the subject of previous threats uttered against the defendant by Hermes and his sons. The learned judge seems to have regarded such evidence not merely as not extenuating or excusing the act of the defendant, but as evidence from which the jury might infer special spite, special ill will, on the part of the defendant. The language of the learned judge was as follows:

'Previous threats fill a certain place in every case where they are brought out in the evidence. If at the time of the killing the party is doing nothing which indicates a deadly design, or a design to do great bodily mischief,-if he is doing nothing, I say, of that kind,-then previous threats cannot be considered by the jury. If they are satisfied from the law and the testimony that the deceased was not doing anything that amounted to a deadly attack, or there is no question in their minds as to what the attitude of the deceased was, previous threats cannot be considered by them; they cannot enter into their consideration of the case by the way of justifying any act that resulted in the death of Charles Hermes from the act of defendant; they cannot be considered, I say, because you cannot kill a man because of previous threats. You cannot weigh in the balance a human life against a threat. There is no right of that kind in law. Threats are only admitted as illustrative of another condition that exists in the case. If the party, at the time of killing, who is killed, is doing that which indicates a purpose to do great bodily harm, to kill, or is about to do it, so near doing it, and goes so far, that it can be seen from the nature of the act what his purpose is, then, for the purpose of enabling you to more clearly see the situation of the parties, you can take into consideration the threats made by him. But if there is an absence in the case of that which indicates a deadly design, a design to do great bodily harm, really or apparently, threats cannot be considered in connection with the asserted right of a defendant that he can avail himself of the right of self-defense. You cannot do that. But if threats are made, and there is an absence from the case of the conditions I have given you where you can use them as evidence, you can only use them and consider them for the purpose of showing the existence of special spite or ill will or animosity on the part of the defendant.'

And again:

'If this defendant killed this party, Charles Hermes, because the old man, the father of Charles Hermes, had threatened him with violence, or threatened to have something done to him because of his belief that he had done something with his hogs, or killed them, and made threats, that is no defense, that is no mitigation, but that is evidence of malice aforethought; it is evidence of premeditation; it is evidence of deliberation of a deliberately formed design to kill, because of special spite, because of a grudge, because of ill will, because of animosity that existed upon the part of this defendant towards these people in the field.'

While it is no doubt true that previous threats will not, in all circumstances, justify, or perhaps even extenuate, the act of the party threatened in killing the person who uttered the threats, yet it by no means follows that such threats, signifying ill will and hostility on the part of the deceased, can be used by the jury as indicating a similar state of feeling on the part of the defendant. Such an instruction was not only misleading in itself, but it was erroneous in the present case, for the further reason that it omitted all reference to the alleged conduct of the deceased at the time of the killing, which went to show an intention then and there to carry out the previous threats.

The instructions which have thus far been the subject of our criticism were mainly applicable to the contention that the defendant acted in self-defense, but they also must have been understood by the jury as extending to the other proposition that the defendant's act constituted the crime of manslaughter, and not of murder. The charge shows that the instructions of the learned judge on these two distinct defenses were so blended as to warrant the jury in believing that such instructions were applicable to both grounds of defense.

Whether this be a just view or not, there were distinct instructions given as to the contention that the act of killing in this case was manslaughter, and not murder, which we think cannot be sustained. A portion of such instructions was as follows:

> ' * * *The law says that the previous selection, preparation, and subsequent use of a deadly weapon shows that there was a purpose to kill contemplated before that affray existed; and whenever that exists, when it is done unlawfully and improperly, so that there is no law of self-defense in it, the fact that they may have been in an actual affray with hands or fists would not reduce the grade of the crime to manslaughter.'

The error here is in the assumption that the act of the defendant in arming himself showed a purpose to kill formed before the actual affray. This was the same error that we found in the instructions regarding the right of self-defense, and brings the case within the case of *Gourko v. U. S.*, previously cited, and the language of which we need not repeat.

These views call for a reversal of the judgment, and it is therefore unnecessary to consider the assignments that allege errors in the selection of the jury.

The judgment is reversed, and the cause remanded for a new trial.

Notes and Questions

1. What, precisely, was the conduct of the defendant that the trial judge seemed to find provocative? How did the trial judge and the Supreme Court differ in their understanding of the import of the victim's prior threats against the defendant? Is the Supreme Court saying that arming one's self is irrelevant per se in a self-defense case?

2. There are two ways to become a provoker or aggressor and lose the right to self-defense. Some assaultative conduct, regardless of intent, justifies a response. Thus, if Dennis hits Chris on the head with a bat, Dennis is an aggressor, and cannot use force in self-defense, even if Dennis hoped and expected that Chris would not respond.

   In addition, some statements or actions which would not justify self-defense might nevertheless constitute provocation if they are made or done with the intent to generate an excuse to use force. Imagine that Sonia insults Sandra's religion, hoping and expecting that Sandra will retaliate, giving Sonia the legal right to assault or kill Sandra. Imagine that Sandra responds with deadly force. Words alone (except credible threats) are insufficient to warrant physical response, so if Sandra assaults or kills Sonia, she is criminally responsible for that conduct. But, if, as she planned, Sonia successfully uses force in response, Sonia would be criminally liable because she intended to create a situation where force could be used. *See, e.g.,* Cal. Crim. Jury Inst. § 3472 ("Right to Self-Defense: May Not Be Contrived. A person does not have the right to self-defense if he or she provokes a fight or quarrel with the intent to create an excuse to use force."); MPC § 3.05(2)(b)(i) (denying defense if "the actor, with the purpose of causing death or serious bodily injury, provoked the use of force against himself in the same encounter.")

3. If someone is an aggressor, they may regain right to use self-defense by withdrawing. As *California Criminal Jury Instruction* § 3471 states:

> A person who (engages in mutual combat/ [or who] starts a fight) has a right to self-defense only if:
>
> 1. (He/She) actually and in good faith tried to stop fighting;
>
> [AND]
>
> 2. (He/She) indicated, by word or by conduct, to (his/her) opponent, in a way that a reasonable person would understand, that (he/she) wanted to stop fighting and that (he/she) had stopped fighting(;/.)
>
> <Give element 3 in cases of mutual combat.>
>
> [AND
>
> 3. (He/She) gave (his/her) opponent a chance to stop fighting.]
>
> If the defendant meets these requirements, (he/she) then had a right to self-defense if the opponent continued to fight. * * *
>
> [A fight is mutual combat when it began or continued by mutual consent or agreement. That agreement may be expressly stated or implied and must occur before the claim to self-defense arose.]

4. Non-Deadly Aggressor. States vary in the treatment of non-deadly aggressors who are met with deadly force. If Sonia slaps Sandra, and Sandra responds by

trying to shoot Sonia, there are three possible outcomes. A jurisdiction might say that Sonia remains an aggressor and cannot regain her right to use deadly force unless she withdraws. Another alternative is that if Sonia manages to kill Sandra without withdrawing she is guilty of manslaughter. Finally, a jurisdiction might provide that even if she is guilty of some offense for the initial slap, she can freely use deadly force without homicide liability. What are the possible outcomes if, instead, Sandra kills Sonia?

Gibbs v. Florida

District Court of Appeal of Florida, Fourth District
789 So.2d 443 (2001)

TAYLOR, J.

Joelle Gibbs appeals her conviction of culpable negligence with injury. We reverse because the trial court gave an inadequate jury instruction on self-defense.

The facts of this case are a sad and disturbing reminder of the tragic consequences that racial conflict can lead to. Appellant, a 40–year old black woman, saw an elderly white man and woman sitting on a bench outside an apartment building and said to them, "Good morning. How are you?" When the couple did not respond, she asked why they did not return her greeting. The woman, Julia Osmun, said to appellant, "Get away from here you dirty nigger, you don't belong here." Appellant responded with a racial slur and an obscene "mooning" gesture and the two women wound up in a physical altercation. According to appellant and her witness, Sheldon Solomon, Osmun got up from the bench, approached appellant, and started swinging at her. In response, appellant stepped back and pushed Osmun. Osmun staggered back and then fell down on some shrubbery. Solomon and the man who had been sitting next to Osmun helped her back up on the bench, where she remained for a few minutes until a friend drove up and carried her to Manor Care. Within a half hour, Osmun died of heart failure.

The medical examiner ruled the death a homicide caused by cardiac arrhythmia due to stress after an altercation. The deceased was sixty-five years old with a history of heart disease, obesity, and other chronic ailments. She had undergone cardiac surgery several years before the altercation. The state charged appellant with murder in the second degree. After a jury trial, appellant was found guilty of culpable negligence with injury, a lesser included offense.

Witnesses at trial gave different accounts as to who initiated the physical confrontation between the two women and the amount of force used by appellant. Appellant's theory of defense was that she pushed the victim in self-defense. At the jury charge conference, appellant requested an instruction on justifiable use of non-deadly force, but asked that the standard instruction be modified to clarify what "provocation" means. The standard instruction read:

> The use of force not likely to cause death or great bodily harm is not justifiable if you find Joelle Gibbs initially provoked the use of force against herself.

Appellant sought addition of the words "by force or threat of force" to the standard instruction, so that it would read:

> The use of force not likely to cause death or great bodily harm is not justified if you find Joelle Gibbs initially provoked the use of force against herself, *by force or the threat of force.* (Emphasis added).

Defense counsel wanted the jury to understand that any provocation by appellant had to be "by force or the threat of force." He was concerned that the jury might be confused and think that "merely provoking someone by complaining that they didn't say good morning" justified the victim's attack on appellant and did not justify appellant in defending herself against that attack.

The court denied the request for clarification and gave the standard instruction on justifiable use of non-deadly force. Appellant adequately preserved the issue for our review. *See Avila v. State*, 781 So.2d 413, 415 (Fla. 4th DCA 2001); *Layman v. State*, 728 So.2d 814, 817 (Fla. 5th DCA 1999).

We agree with appellant that the jury instruction given by the trial court was inadequate to properly charge the jury in this case. The instruction stated that appellant could not defend herself with non-deadly force if she "initially provoked" the victim. By not limiting provocation to the use or threat of force, the court failed to make the jury aware that the word "provoked," as used in the instruction, did not refer to mere words or conduct without force. Stated another way, the instruction given by the court eliminated the use of non-deadly force in self-defense if there was any provocation by the defendant—no matter how slight or subjective the provocation. By that standard, a mere insult could be deemed sufficient to prohibit defending oneself from an attacker.

In this case, appellant's self-defense was based on testimony that the victim verbally attacked her and then aggressively approached and swung at her. According to the defense, it was only then that appellant pushed the victim and used some force against her. Because the instruction did not limit provocation to some force or threat of force, the instruction could have misled the jury to believe that appellant's pointedly asking the victim why she failed to acknowledge her greeting and/or appellant's racial retorts and obscene gestures were sufficient provocation to preclude appellant from defending herself from an attack by the victim.

The state argues that the trial court did not err because it gave the standard jury instruction. However, the Florida Supreme Court's approval of the standard instructions cannot relieve the trial judge of responsibility under the law to charge the jury properly and correctly in each case as it comes before that judge. *Matter of Use By Trial Courts of Standard Jury Instructions*, 431 So.2d 594, 598 (Fla.1981). The clarification that the defense sought here was peculiarly applicable to the facts of the case and should have been given. *See Outlaw v. State*, 82 Fla. 68, 89 So. 342, 343 (1921) (where there is the potential for the jury to be misled as to who was the provocateur or aggressor it is reversible error not to give a clarifying instruction on the issue). *See also Chandler v. State*, 744 So.2d 1058, 1061 (Fla. 4th DCA 1999)(reversing conviction of disorderly conduct where trial court failed to give a requested jury instruction when there was a reasonable possibility that the jury would be misled or confused by failure to give that instruction).

For the above reasons, we reverse appellant's conviction and sentence. Our reversal on the jury instruction issue renders the remaining issues on appeal moot. REVERSED.

WARNER, C.J., and POLEN, JJ., concur.

Notes and Questions

1. This is one of hundreds of examples of cases finding error by giving the standard pattern instruction. General rules must often be tailored to account for the particular facts of the case.

2. Did Gibbs "start a fight" within the meaning of the California jury instruction cited above?

3. A widely cited but loosely reasoned case provides: "The right of homicidal self-defense is granted only to those free from fault in the difficulty; it is denied to slayers who incite the fatal attack, encourage the fatal quarrel or otherwise promote the necessitous occasion for taking life." *United States v. Peterson*, 483 F.2d 1222, 1231 (D.C. Cir. 1973). Under that standard, is Gibbs an aggressor?

D. Unknown Information About a Defendant

Generally, the defendant's knowledge about the victim is relevant and admissible in a self-defense case, including threats, a defendant's past criminality and other misconduct, and her general reputation for violence. This information goes to the defendant's state of mind, and, therefore, whether she acted reasonably.

Information about a victim's reputation and history might be meaningful even if the defendant did not know it. Leaving aside the rules of evidence for the moment, as a lawyer or judge evaluating a situation where there was only on surviving witness, would you want to know that the decedent had convictions for assault, robbery or domestic violence, while the victim's record was clean—or vice-versa?

Burgeon v. State

Supreme Court of Nevada
714 P.2d 576 (1986)

PER CURIAM:

This is an appeal from a judgment of conviction upon jury verdict of one count of second degree murder with the use of a deadly weapon. For the reasons expressed below, we affirm.

At appellant Burgeon's jury trial, the state presented testimony by Jesus Salas, the state's only eyewitness to the events which led to the death of the victim, Luis Badillo. Salas testified that he and the victim had driven to a local convenience store on the evening in question. The victim went into the store and Salas remained in the car in the parking lot. Appellant approached the vehicle and asked Salas if he wanted to buy a revolver. Salas told appellant that he did not have the money to purchase the revolver. At this point, the victim returned to the car and entered the passenger's side of the vehicle.

Appellant was standing outside the car when another individual, Eddie Bustamante, approached the car, spoke to the victim, and hit the victim in the face. Salas testified that appellant attempted to stop the altercation between the victim and Bustamante and that Salas simultaneously put the car in reverse and began to back away. As Salas was backing up the car, Eddie Bustamante threw a beer can at the car, hitting the windshield. Finally, Salas testified that appellant then drew a gun and fired approximately three shots, one of which hit the victim in the head and killed him.

Appellant testified on his own behalf at trial. His testimony was consistent with Salas' with one major exception. Appellant stated that as the car was backing away, the victim had pointed a gun at appellant and Eddie Bustamante. Appellant, believing that his life was in danger, then drew his gun and fired.

Eddie Bustamante also testified at trial, and his testimony corroborated appellant's version of the events. In particular, Bustamante also stated that he and the victim disliked each other and had previously fought.

Appellant also presented the testimony of Luis Talavera, who had been standing in the parking lot of the convenience store during the altercation. Talavera testified that he saw the victim point a gun at appellant before appellant drew a gun.

Appellant's theory at trial was that he acted in self-defense. Before closing his case-in-chief, appellant's counsel moved to introduce evidence of specific acts of violence previously committed by the deceased victim for the purpose of showing that the victim was the likely aggressor. A detailed offer of proof was presented in support of the motion. Appellant's counsel also sought to call the victim's father to testify regarding his son's character and reputation for violent behavior. The state opposed both motions. The district court denied appellant's motions and refused to allow the testimony of the father relating to his son's reputation or the testimony of other witnesses concerning specific acts of violence attributable to the victim, for the purpose of proving the issue of self-defense. The court's ruling was apparently based on the fact that appellant did not have any knowledge of the victim's reputation or specific acts of violence. Appellant contends that this ruling was in error.

When it is necessary to show the state of mind of the accused at the time of the commission of the offense for the purpose of establishing self-defense, specific acts which tend to show that the deceased was a violent and dangerous person may be admitted, provided that the specific acts of violence of the deceased were known to the accused or had been communicated to him. *See State v. Sella*, 41 Nev. 113, 138, 168 P. 278, 286 (1917). In the present case, appellant concedes that the specific acts of violence of the victim were not previously known to him. Since appellant did not have knowledge of the acts, evidence of the victim's specific acts of violence were therefore not admissible to establish the reasonableness of appellant's fear or his state of mind.

Appellant also admits that he did not have any knowledge of the deceased's general character. NRS 48.045(1)(b), however, permits the admission of evidence of the character of the victim of the crime when it is offered by the accused, whether or not the accused had knowledge of the victim's character. Appellant's lack of knowledge of the victim's character was irrelevant to the issue of the admissibility of evidence of general reputation tending to prove that the victim was the likely aggressor. *See State v. Jacoby*, 260 N.W.2d 828 (Iowa 1977). Under NRS 48.055(1), proof of character may be established by testimony as to reputation or in the form of an opinion.[2] The character of the victim cannot be established by proof of specific acts. *See also Government of Virgin Islands v. Carino*, 631 F.2d 226 (3rd Cir.1980) (interpreting similar federal statutes). Thus, although the district court correctly excluded evidence of the deceased's prior acts of violence, we conclude that evidence of the victim's general reputation would have been admissible. *See State v. Helm*, 66 Nev. 286, 300–01, 209 P.2d 187, 193–94 (1949); *State v. Sella*, 41 Nev. at 136–37, 168 P. at 285–86.

In determining whether the trial court erred in refusing to allow the deceased's father to testify concerning his son's reputation for violence, it is necessary to consider both the motion and the offer of proof made by the appellant in connection with such testimony. Appellant's counsel sought to call the victim's father to the stand with the following statement to the court: "And, lastly, I intend to call the father of the alleged victim in this case, Mr. Pedro Badillo, to inquire of him, not specific acts of the prior conduct, but general character and reputation of his son for violent behavior." The state has conceded that the father's testimony concerning his son's general reputation for violence, if indeed the father has such knowledge, is admissible. We are simply unable to conclude from the record what, if anything, the father may have known on the subject. Appellant's counsel merely indicated he wished to inquire of the father about the victim's general reputation for violence. For all we may surmise, the father may have denied that his son had a reputation for violence. Since Appellant's counsel made no offer of proof as to the father's testimony we, like the trial court, can only speculate as to what the father may have said.

If the trial court sustains an objection to testimony sought for the consideration of the jury, it is the responsibility of the party against whom the objection is sustained to make an offer of proof that specifies what the party expects to prove by the proffered testimony. We have consistently held that this Court will not speculate as to the nature and substance of excluded testimony. *Van Valkenberg v. State*, 95 Nev. 317, 594 P.2d 707 (1979). If appellant desired to preserve for our review the testimony that he reasonably expected the jury to hear, absent the adverse ruling of the trial court, a detailed offer of proof was essential. *See Foreman v. Ver Brugghen*, 81. Nev. 86, 398 P.2d 993 (1965); *McCall v. State*, 97 Nev. 514, 634 P.2d 1210 (1981). As noted previously, no such offer of proof was provided to the district court. Appellant's failure to make an offer of proof as to what the father would have presented by way of testimony not only prevented this Court from reviewing the trial court's adverse ruling, it also deprived the

---

2   NRS 48.055(1) provides:

    In all cases in which evidence of character or a trait of character of a person is admissible, proof may be made by testimony as to reputation or in the form of an opinion. On cross-examination, inquiry may be made into specific instances of conduct.

trial judge of the opportunity to change or modify his ruling because of added enlightenment that frequently results from such an offer. We are therefore unable to conclude that the district court erred in refusing to allow the victim's father to testify.[3]

Moreover, it is clear from the record that the jury heard substantial testimony from both state and defense witnesses concerning the victim's gang-related activities of a violent nature. We cannot conclude, therefore, that appellant was prejudiced by the court's ruling on the testimony of the victim's father.

* * * Accordingly, we hereby affirm appellant's judgment of conviction.

Notes and Questions

1. *Bergeron* states the general rule: Evidence of a victim's alleged violent reputation is admissible whether the defendant knew about it or not, but specific instances are not admissible unless the defendant knew about it. However, some jurisdictions hold that "for the evidence of the victim's reputation for violence to be admissible, the defendant's knowledge of the victim's reputation must be proved." *State v. White*, 909 S.W.2d 391, 394 (Mo. Ct. App. 1995). By the same token, some courts allow evidence of specific acts of violence or misconduct, even if the defendant did not know about them. *See, e.g., Commonwealth v. Adjutant*, 664, 824 N.E.2d 1, 13 (Mass. 2005) ("[W]here the identity of the first aggressor is in dispute and the victim has a history of violence . . . the trial judge has the discretion to admit evidence of specific acts of prior violent conduct that the victim is reasonably alleged to have initiated, to support the defendant's claim of self-defense.").

2. Was defense counsel in *Burgeon* ineffective for not making a proper offer of proof? *Johnson v. State*, 266 Ga. 380, 382, 467 S.E.2d 542, 545 (1996) (finding counsel ineffective for not seeking to introduce evidence of reputation based on misunderstanding of the law). What other reasons might have led the attorney not to lay a proper foundation for the evidence?

---

3 Obviously, we may not infer that the testimony of the father would have been favorable to appellant merely because of appellant's intent to have the father testify. To do so would effectively negate both the purpose and necessity of making an offer of proof since it could always be presumed that counsel would not intentionally call a witness who would provide testimony detrimental to the client.

C

PRACTICE EXERCISE

The following is taken from *People v. Garvin*, 110 Cal. App. 4th 484, 486-88, 1 Cal. Rptr. 3d 774, 776-77 (2003). You are an appellate judge. First, answer the following based on Part 1: is there sufficient evidence to give a jury instruction on self-defense? Second, read the court's conclusion in Part 2, concerning the defense counsel's tactical move.

[Part 1]

On December 20, 2001, defendant and five other inmates were escorted inside the visitation room of the Kings County main jail by Sergeant Arnett and Deputy Leonardi. The deputies remained outside the room. Instead of sitting down and beginning his visit, defendant remained standing and began to pace back and forth in the room. Sergeant Arnett opened the door and told defendant to sit down and begin his visit. Defendant walked to the door and cursed at the sergeant. The sergeant repeated his command; defendant continued his abuse. Sergeant Arnett told defendant that his visit was terminated and to exit the room. Defendant became more agitated and challenged the sergeant to come in and get him. Sergeant Arnett entered the room with Deputy Leonardi behind him. Defendant backed into a corner and took a combative position. As Sergeant Arnett attempted to grab defendant by his left arm, defendant yanked his arm away, struck the officer on the right jaw and put the sergeant in a chokehold. The sergeant could not breathe and thought he was going to die. Deputy Leonardi grabbed defendant by the hair. All three men fell to the floor. Defendant continued to maintain his chokehold on the sergeant. He yelled, "I got you, mother-fucker, you're going to die." Defendant finally released the sergeant after Deputy Leonardi struck him three times in the face and Sergeant Arnett grabbed and squeezed his testicles. Defendant was restrained with the help of additional deputies. While being escorted back to his cell, he attempted to kick a deputy and to head-butt Sergeant Arnett.

Two days later, Sergeant Angela Hunter served a disciplinary action report on defendant for an unrelated matter. He became angry and said, "I choked the shit out of a deputy. I tried to kill him and break his fucking neck. The D.A. ain't done fucking shit about it because you see I'm still here with no other charges, and I tried to kill that motherfucker. So you see I don't care shit about no fucking write-up."

Defendant testified that Sergeant Arnett attacked him. He said that the sergeant grabbed his arm. Defendant pulled away and faced him. The sergeant punched him in the chest and defendant pushed him away. The sergeant was going to tackle him so defendant put him in a chokehold. Deputy Leonardi grabbed defendant's hair and punched him. Defendant was dazed and lost his grip on Sergeant Arnett when they hit the ground. Sergeant Arnett kept hold of defendant's testicles even after defendant let go of his neck. Defendant does not remember if he said anything to the sergeant. Sergeant Arnett later tried to bang defendant's head against a wall in an unprovoked attack in the hallway. At no point did he intend to kill Sergeant Arnett. He was trying to protect himself from Sergeant Arnett's aggression. He did not tell Sergeant Hunter that he had choked a deputy and tried to kill him.

During cross-examination, defendant testified that he always tells deputies to get away from his cell door. The prosecutor attempted to find out why, querying whether this was because he did not like deputies. Defendant replied, "No, it's not because I don't like them[;] it's because the way they do me." Upon further questioning, defendant testified that he had been beaten for no reason on four or five prior occasions by an unspecified number of deputies. Apparently, Sergeant Arnett was one of his tormentors. He had written the district attorney's office about the beatings four or five times. This is why he was laughing when he was choking Sergeant Arnett. It relieved "all my stress. Many times as they beat me up before, your department knew about it." Now, "I finally got him back for jumping on me all those times." Defendant "felt good about [this]." He said, "I love it, I love it" at the end of the altercation, "[b]ecause they all got caught. They finally got caught beating me, they had to take me to the hospital. Just like they did the other times."

***

[Part 2]

We believe that defense counsel's avoidance of this topic and her failure to request instruction on the antecedent assaults was an objectively reasonable tactical decision. If she had elected to pursue this issue, it would have forced her to vilify not only the actual victim, but also the staff at the jail and the district attorney's office. Obviously, this would have been a dangerous tactical move. It could have destroyed defendant's credibility and could have turned the jury against him if counsel did not provide evidence substantiating his uncorroborated testimony that he had been repeatedly beaten for no apparent reason and that the district attorney's office had ignored his numerous letters of complaint. Furthermore, even if defense counsel had proved that the beatings occurred as alleged by defendant, a wily prosecutor could have used the beatings against defendant because they provided defendant with a strong motive to attempt to murder Sergeant Arnett—revenge. Defendant finally had obtained vengeance for the prior unjustified beatings. This could have decimated defense counsel's closing argument that defendant did not have the intent to kill and that, at the very most, he was guilty of assault. It must be remembered that the jury did not find defendant guilty of attempted murder, which requires proof of intent to kill . . . The Judgment is affirmed.

Index